ENCYCLOPEDIA
OF
FRONTIER
BIOGRAPHY

ENCYCLOPEDIA

OF

FRONTIER BIOGRAPHY

VOLUME 4
SUPPLEMENTAL VOLUME

by
DAN L. THRAPP

THE ARTHUR H. CLARK COMPANY
Spokane, Washington
1994

Copyright, 1994, by
Dan L. Thrapp

LIBRARY OF CONGRESS CATALOG CARD NUMBER 92-75560
ISBN 0-87062-222-6

SUPPLEMENTAL FOURTH VOLUME

The Arthur H. Clark Company
P.O. Box 14707, Spokane, WA 99214-0707

Introduction

The purposes, format, and something of the philosophy behind the *Encyclopedia of Frontier Biography* were explained at length in the Introduction to the original set. Those three volumes included around 4,500 subject articles. The Supplement now adds about 1,030 entries for an overall total of some 5,530 biographies.

Reviewers and users of the compendium took up with alacrity my invitation to report gaps in the original coverage. They suggested many persons whom they believed should have been included. I hope they will feel that their thoughtfulness is compensated for in this latest work.

Several mentioned a paucity of coverage of Alaskan frontier personalities. In the present volume the Russians of Alaska (as well as the Russian-Aleuts), and the explorers (including American Army explorers), along with the navigators of various nations who probed the coasts, discovered the islands, named geographical features and contributed significantly to knowledge of that northernmost state, are now represented, to the number of a couple of hundred, or more. So are the sea otter hunters, the administrators, writers, artists, scientists and those others who devoted their energies and years to making known all manner of fascinating aspects of that enormous region.

A somewhat spartan California coverage also was protested. In this volume, added to those described earlier, there appear virtually all those who explored that region for Spain or Mexico or Russia, for purposes of religion, trade, understanding, administration, profit, or out of curiosity—or for predation.

In addition fresh attention has been paid to the southeastern portions of what is now the United States: to South Carolina, Georgia and Florida. Added Texas research has resulted in entries on the earliest cattle drovers, from 1782 through 1846 and onward, until the Civil War put a temporary halt to such movements.

There is much more detailed coverage of personalities of the frontier of the Old Northwest, principally Ohio and Indiana, as well as in Kentucky and Tennessee during the turbulent period of the late 18th century. And, of course, there are many others from various regions across the 48 contiguous states.

Only a very few of those who made valuable suggestions can be paid tribute to here, for space reasons. But some simply cannot be omitted.

E.F. (Ted) Mains of Cottonwood, Arizona, sent in scores of suggestions, each with dates of birth and death and references to further sources of information. Virtually all of his offerings resulted in entries, each being greatly appreciated. John Sugden of Coventry, England, mailed scores of invaluable ideas for Indian entries from his inexhaustible knowledge of the subject. Not only that, but he also supplied generous copies of his own copious, meticulous and invaluable notes about otherwise shadowy individuals. My gratitude to him is unbounded. Frederick W. Nolan, renowned historian of Billy the Kid and his times, also resolved knotty problems in welcome letters sent all the way from his Buckinghamshire home. And Allan Radbourne of Taunton, Somerset, than whom there exists no more thorough—and genial—researcher on Apache matters, found solutions to what had appeared insoluble problems.

Richard A. Pierce of Fairbanks, Alaska, author of unparalleled biographical works on Russians in Alaska, was most generous in helping round out this volume. His research corrected numerous dates and clarified countless matters with respect to early Alaskan figures about whom he is beyond question the most knowledgeable authority.

Colonel E.W. Giesecke, Midlothian, Virginia, introduced me to the Winships and launched me in pursuit about facts on the Northwest Coast sea otter trade. Cultural anthropologist Bernard Fontana was of invaluable and cordial help. So were Bill Secrest of Fresno, California; Ed Sweeney of St. Charles, Missouri, the expert on Cochise and his times and associates; Phil Nickell of Mesilla, New Mexico, whose expertise covers a good part of the West; and Dale L. Walker, retired editor-in-chief of Texas Western Press, whose vast knowledge blankets everything from Jack London to Alan Seeger to the French Foreign Legion to Teddy Roosevelt's Rough Riders.

And there were so many more than it would require still another additional volume to give them the recognition and appreciation they deserve!

DAN L. THRAPP
Tucson, Arizona

Abbreviations used in the bibliographical citations

Adams, *Six Guns and Saddle Leather*   Ramon F. Adams, *Six-Guns and Saddle Leather: A Bibliography of Books and Pamphlets on Western Outlaws and Gunmen.* Norman, University of Oklahoma Press, 1969.

Bancroft (plus title)   Hubert Howe Bancroft, *Works,* 39+1 vols. San Francisco, The History Co., 1874-1890.

Bancroft, Index   *The Zamorano Index to History of California by Hubert Howe Bancroft,* 2 vols., comp. by Members of the Zamorano Club, ed. by Everett Gordon Hager, Anna Marie Hager. Los Angeles, University of Southern California, 1985.

Bancroft, *Pioneer Register*   *Register of Pioneer Inhabitants of California 1542 to 1848 and Index to Information Concerning Them in Bancroft's History of California Vols. I-V.* By Hubert Howe Bancroft. Los Angeles, Dawson's Book Shop, 1964.

Barry, *Beginning of the West*   Louise Barry, *The Beginning of the West.* Topeka, Kansas Historical Society, 1972.

BDAC   *Biographical Directory of the American Congress 1774-1971.* Washington, Government Printing Office, 1971.

BHB   Kenneth Hammer, *Little Big Horn Biographies.* Crow Agency, Montana, Custer Battlefield Historical and Museum Assn., 1965.

Black Hawk War   *The Black Hawk War 1831-1832,* 4 vols., comp. and ed. by Ellen M. Whitney. Springfield, Ill., Collections of the Illinois State Historical Library, vols. XXXV-XXXVIII, 1970-78.

Bourke, *On Border*   John G. Bourke, *On the Border With Crook.* N.Y., Charles Scribner's Sons, 1891 (Edition with Index, Glorieta, N.M., Rio Grande Press, 1969).

CE   *The Columbia Encyclopedia,* 3rd edn.

Chittenden   Hiram M. Chittenden, *The American Fur Trade of the Far West,* 2 vols. Stanford, Calif., Academic Reprints, 1954.

Clarke, *Lewis and Clark*   Charles G. Clarke, *The Men of the Lewis and Clark Expedition.* Glendale, Calif., Arthur H. Clark Co., 1970.

Coleman, *Captives*   Emma Lewis Coleman, *New England Captives Carried to Canada between 1677 and 1760,* 2 vols., Portland, Me., Southworth Press, 1925.

Contemporary Authors   *Contemporary Authors: A Bio-Biographical Guide to Current Authors and Their Works,* eds. James M. Ethridge, Barbara Kopala. Detroit, Gale Research Co., 1965 to present.

Cullum   George Washington Cullum, *Biographical Register of the Officers and Graduates of the U.S. Military Academy at West Point, N.Y.,* 11 vols. Boston, Houghton, Mifflin Co., 1891-1930.

DAB   *Dictionary of American Biography,* 22 vols., plus supplements. N.Y., Charles Scribner's Sons, 1958.

DCB   *Dictionary of Canadian Biography,* vols. I-V. University of Toronto Press, 1966-1979.

DNB   *Dictionary of National Biography,* 21 vols. London, Oxford University Press, 1973.

EA   *Encyclopedia Americana.*

EB   *Encyclopaedia Britannica.*

EHI   *Records of Engagements with Hostile Indians within the Military Division of the Missouri, from 1868 to 1882,* comp. from official records, Washington, Government Printing Office, 1882.

Farish   Thomas Edwin Farish, *History of Arizona,* 8 vols. San Francisco, Filmer Brothers Electrotype Co., 1915-18.

Griswold   Gillett M. Griswold, "The Fort Sill Apaches; Their Vital Statistics, Tribal Origins, Antecedents." Unpublished manuscript courtesy of Field Artillery Museum, Fort Sill, Okla., 1970.

Headquarters Heliogram   *Headquarters Heliogram,* Council on America's Military Past, U.S.A., P.O. Box 1151, Ft. Myer, VA., 22211.

Heitman   Francis Bernard Heitman, *Historical Register and Dictionary of the United States Army, from 1789 to 1903,* 2 vols. Washington, Government Printing Office, 1903 (repr. Urbana, University of Illinois Press, 1965).

Historical Times... Encyclopedia of the Civil War   *Historical Times... Encyclopedia of the Civil War,* ed. by Patricia L. Faust. N.Y., Harper & Row, 1986.

HNAI   *Handbook of North American Indians,* 20 vols., William C. Sturtevant, general editor, Washington, Smithsonian Institution, 1978 to present.

Hodge, HAI   *Handbook of American Indians North of Mexico,* 2 vols., ed. by Frederick Webb Hodge. Washington, Smithsonian Institution (BAE Bulletin 30), Government Printing Office, 1907, 1910.

HT   *The Handbook of Texas,* 3 vols., ed. by Walter Prescott Webb, H. Bailey Carroll; Eldon Stephen Branda. Austin, Texas State Historical Assn., 1952, 1976.

Hunter TDT   *The Trail Drivers of Texas,* 2 vols., comp. and ed. by J. Marvin Hunter. Nashville, Cokesbury Press, 1925 (reprint, N.Y., Argosy-Antiquarian, 1963).

McWhorter, *Hear Me*   Lucullus V. McWhorter, *Hear Me, My Chiefs! Nez Perce Legend & History,* ed. by Ruth Bordin. Caldwell, Ida., Caxton Printers, 1952.

MM   *The Mountain Men and the Fur Trade of the Far West: Biographical Sketches of the Participants,* 10 vols., ed. by Le Roy R. Hafen. Glendale, Calif., Arthur H. Clark Co., 1965-72.

NCAB   *National Cyclopedia of American Biography,* 60 vols. N.Y., Clifton, N.J., James T. White & Co., 1898-Present.

Narratives of Explorations in Alaska   *Compilation of Narratives of Explorations in Alaska.* 56th Congress, 1st Sess., Senate Report No. 1023, Washington, Government Printing Office, 1900.

Ogden   Adele Ogden, *The California Sea Otter Trade 1784-1848.* Berkeley, University of California Press, 1941 (Kraus Reprint Co., Millwood, N.Y., 1974).

O'Neal, *Gunfighters*   Bill O'Neal, *Encyclopedia of Western Gunfighters.* Norman, University of Oklahoma Press, 1979.

Orth   Donald J. Orth, *Dictionary of Alaskan Place Names: Geological Survey Professional Paper 567.* Washington, Government Printing Office, 1967.

Oscar Williams   *The Personal Narrative of O(scar) W(aldo) Williams 1877-1902: Pioneer Surveyor—Frontier Lawyer,* ed. by S.D. Myers, El Paso, Texas Western Press, University of Texas at El Paso, 1968.

Orton   Richard H. Orton, *Records of California Men in the War of the Rebellion, 1861-67.* Sacramento, State Office, 1890 (Index: J. Carlyle Parker, *A Personal Name Index to Orton,* Vol. 5, Gale Genealogy and Local History Series, Detroit, Gale Research Co., 1978).

Parkman   Francis Parkman, *Works—Frontenac Edition,* 16 vols. Boston, Little Brown and Co., 1899.

PCA   Roscoe G. Willson, *Pioneer and Well Known Cattlemen of Arizona,* 2 vols. Phoenix, McGrew Commercial Printery (for Valley National Bank), 1951, 1956.

Pierce, *Russian America: A Biographical Dictionary* Richard A. Pierce, *Russian America: A Biographical Dictionary*. Kingston, Ontario, Fairbanks, Alaska, The Limestone Press, 1990.

Porrua *Diccionario Porrua de Historia, Biografía y Geografía de Mexico,* 2nd ed. Mexico, D.F., Editorial Porrua, S.A. 1965.

Powell William H. Powell, *Powell's Records of Living Officers of the United States Army.* Philadelphia, L.R. Hammersley Co., 1890.

REAW *Reader's Encyclopedia of the American West,* ed. by Howard R. Lamar. N.Y., Thomas Y. Crowell Co., 1977.

Robert N. Mullin Notes Research notes compiled by Robert N. Mullin, now held by the Nita Stewart Haley Memorial Library, Midland, Tex.

Russian American Colonies *The Russian American Colonies: A Documentary Record 1798-1867,* ed. and trans. by Basil Dmytryshyn, E.A.P. Crownhart-Vaughan, Thomas Vaughan. Portland, Oregon Historical Society Press, 1989.

Russian Penetration of the North Pacific Ocean *Russian Penetration of the North Pacific Ocean: A Documentary Record 1700-1797,* ed. and trans. by Basil Dmytryshyn, E.A.P. Crownhart-Vaughan, Thomas Vaughan. Portland, Oregon Historical Society Press, 1988.

Swanton, *Tribes* John R. Swanton, *The Indian Tribes of North America.* Washington, Smithsonian Institution (BAE Bulletin 145), Government Printing Office, 1953.

Sylvester Herbert Milton Sylvester, *Indian Wars of New England,* 3 vols. Boston, W.B. Clarke Co., 1910.

Thwaites, *Dunmore* *Documentary History of Dunmore's War 1774,* ed. by Reuben Gold Thwaites, Louise Phelps Kellogg. Madison, Wisconsin Historical Society, 1905.

Thwaites, EWT *Early Western Travels, 1748-1846,* 32 vols., ed. by Reuben Gold Thwaites. Cleveland, Ohio, Arthur H. Clark Co., 1904-1907 (reprint: N.Y. AMS Press, 1966).

Thwaites/Kellogg, *Frontier Defense on the Upper Ohio, 1777-1778* Reuben Gold Thwaites, Louise Phelps Kellogg, *Frontier Defense on the Upper Ohio, 1777-1778: Compiled from the Draper Manuscripts.* Madison, Wisconsin Historical Society, 1912; Kraus Reprint Co., Millwood, New York, 1977.

Thwaites/Kellogg *The Revolution on the Upper Ohio, 1775-1777.* Reuben Gold Thwaites, Louise Phelps Kellogg, *The Revolution on the*

Upper Ohio, 1775-1777: Comp. from Draper Manuscripts. Madison, Wisconsin Historical Society, 1908.

Twitchell, *Leading Facts*   Ralph Emerson Twitchell, *The Leading Facts of New Mexican History,* 2 vols. Cedar Rapids, Ia., Torch Press, 1911, 1912 (reprint: Albuquerque, N.M., Horn & Wallace, Pubs., 1963).

Zagoskin   *Lieutenant Zagoskin's Travels in Russian America 1842-1844: The First Ethnographic and Geographic Investigations in the Yukon and Kuskokwim Valleys of Alaska,* ed. by Henry N. Michael. Toronto, Ont., University of Toronto Press, published for Arctic Institute of North America, 1967.

ENCYCLOPEDIA
OF
FRONTIER
BIOGRAPHY

A

Abbey, Edward, writer, conservationist (January 29, 1927-March 14, 1989). B. at Home, ten miles north of Indiana, Pennsylvania, Abbey became in time a blazing literary lodestar for the radical conservationist movement and what amounted to a cult developed around his impassioned, humorous, deeply serious character and writings. His mother was a Women's Christian Temperance Union member and his father, Paul Revere Abbey, a registered Socialist "and old Wobbly [Industrial Workers of the World] organizer." At seventeen he hitchhiked to the Southwest for his initial view of the desert country he ultimately came to love, and which he made his future base. He was graduated from the University of New Mexico in 1951 and earned a master's degree there in 1956; he also attended the University of Edinburgh, Scotland, lived in Italy and visited Alaska. He later worked as a National Forest fire spotter on the Grand Canyon's North Rim, in Glacier National Park, on Aztec Peak in the Tonto National Forest, and for the National Park Service in such places as Arches National Monument, Utah, during which he developed a taste for river-running which merged into his glowing hatred of Glen Canyon Dam and its consequent drowning of some of Utah's most spectacular scenery. This may have inspired his famed *The Monkey Wrench Gang* (1975), a novel about radical environmentalists planning to blow up that dam; the book has sold more than 500,000 copies. An earlier volume was *Desert Solitaire* (1968), a collection of essays about his wanderings and which some believe incorporates his finest writings. Two of his books, *The Brave Cowboy* and *Fire on the Mountain* (1962) were made into movies; the former sold to Hollywood for the "munificent" sum of $7,500. Abbey said he never made much money from his products, however popular they became. His published books, in addition to those named, included: *Jonathan Troy* (1958); with photography by Eliot Porter, *Appalachia* (1970); *Black Sun* (1971); with photography by Philip Hyde, *Slickrock* (1971); *The Journey Home* (1977); *The Hidden Canyon* (1978); *Abbey's Road* (1979), and others. For several years he taught creative writing at the University of Arizona. A contradictory man, he was driven principally by his love for the desert and his hatred for the despoiling of it. One of his sayings, "Growth for the sake of growth is the ideology of the cancer cell," is often quoted, and he readily adopted as mottos Walt Whitman's "Resist much, obey little," and Thoreau's "If I repent of anything, it is very likely to be my good behavior." He had at least two wives and five children by the time of his death from a circulatory problem at 62 in his home at Tucson, survived by his widow, the former Clarke Cartwright and his children. He had instructed that there be no funeral service, that he be "transported in the bed of a pickup truck" into the desert and buried anonymously, wrapped in his sleeping bag where his grave would never be found, even by the coyotes and buzzards, both species of which he loved, as he did all desert creatures. His wishes were carried out. His legacy remains his vibrant writings, the Earth First radical environmental group he inspired, and a legion of ardent fans, who inherited dynamism from his literature and his life.

Edward Hoagland, "Edward Abbey: Standing Tough in the Desert," *New York Times Book Review,* May 7, 1989, 44-45; *Arizona Daily Star,* March 15, 1989, May 22, 1989; *Sierra,* Vol. 74, No. 3 (May/June 1989), 100-101; Arizona Chapter, Sierra Club *Canyon Echo,* May 1989, p. 5; *Contemporary Authors.*

Abbott, Edward, military officer (fl. c. 1764-1788). A British artillery officer, he was at Detroit soon after the close of the French and Indian War. In 1775 he was commissioned British Indian agent on the Ohio River. In the spring of 1777 he was sent to command at Vincennes "where he was the first and only British governor." While there he built Fort Sackville which was captured in 1779 by George Rogers Clark. Abbott was at Vincennes as a captain-lieutenant, and Thwaites/Kellogg reported that he "seems to have been a brave and humane officer," filing a protest with Haldimand against the employment of Indians in frontier conflicts with the settlers, although his protests were disregarded. In February 1778 he was recalled to Detroit and in July, Haldimand sent him to the West Indies where his name appeared on army lists until 1788. Nothing further is reported of him.

Thwaites/Kellogg, *Frontier Defense on the Upper Ohio, 1777-1778.*

Abercrombie, William Ralph, military officer (Aug. 16, 1857-Nov. 17, 1943). B. in Minnesota, he was commissioned from New York a second lieutenant in the 2nd Infantry March 1, 1877 and May 31, 1884 was ordered to command an Alaskan exploration supplementary to the Yukon expedition of Frederick Schwatka (see entry) of the year before. Little was positively known of the interior of Alaska at that date, and Abercrombie was to investigate the country drained by the Copper and Tanana rivers, learn what he could of the Indians of that section, their numbers, character and disposition, as well as their past attitudes concerning the Russians who had governed Alaska until 1867. Abercrombie also was to assess "the character of the country and the means of sustaining a military force, should one be needed" in that region. The officer arrived at Sitka by steamer June 14, 1884 and Nuchek, on Hinchinbrook Island two days later. June 21 the party reached Alaganick, on the westernmost branch of the Copper River delta, as what he believed the first American (white) group to reach that point. He found the Indians friendly, but unfamiliar with the Copper more than 10 miles inland, and afraid of the upriver Indians. Abercrombie and the expedition surgeon, Dr. (Captain) Samuel Quincy Robinson (see entry) attended an Indian ceremonial welcome to the expedition before heading upstream. They found the start of their journey arduous in the extreme. It was the wrong time of year to attempt to ascend a river such as the Copper, now burdened with ice water from numerous glaciers and the current so swift that boats must be cordelled by towline. This effort was more difficult by the impossibility of using the driftwood-and brush-laden banks for footing, but must be done by men wading in ice water and occasionally being wholly submerged by unseen depressions in the streambed. From June 24 until September 1 the expedition inched northward along the Copper, making very little progress despite heroic efforts. Abercrombie named glaciers on either side after Sheridan and Nelson Miles, George Washington Childs and W. E. Goodwin. Worthwhile progress up the river was impossible. July 21 was spent in "watching the

river and building a levee in front. On the left flank of the camp, the roar of the water forcing its way between the icebergs, some of which were from 300 to 500 feet long and half as broad and from 30 to 80 feet thick, was deafening. The trails cut in the river bottoms by these bergs are often excavated to a depth of 20 feet, and as they come scouring down the stream carrying a deck-load of passengers in the shape of bowlders [sic], some of which weigh tons, they shake the river banks for some distance back from its brink." Native helpers from the coast turned back. Some Indians who had gone down to Nuchek with furs to trade, returned with a white miner, John Bremner who had been as far upstream as Taral, a tiny native settlement to which he would guide Henry T. Allen (see entry) the following spring when traveling over the ice was easier than breasting the horrendous summer floods caused by melting ice. "I felt satisfied," wrote Abercrombie, "that the only course left was a winter journey." September 1 he started back downstream having made only negligible progress upstream. Port Etches was gained September 9. About the only valuable information the expedition returned with was that black bears were more succulent than grizzlies, and a lot safer to hunt. Abercrombie included extensive notes on the Indian tribes of this and neighboring regions, his writings covering varied subjects and being of value at the time he wrote. He became a first lieutenant March 20, 1885, and a captain August 27, 1896. Abercrombie took part in two additional expeditions to Alaska, in 1898 and 1899. Exploration of the northern territory was virtually complete by that time, and the renewed effort was to develop communications and military roads into secluded areas and across difficult terrain. Commanding the 1898 expedition he was to pick up reindeer for transportation at Haines Mission, near the Lynn Canal just below Skagway, but the animals proved unserviceable and pack mules were unavailable, so Abercrombie proceeded to Port Valdez on Prince William Sound, arriving April 18. From Valdez to the Copper River valley was about 50 miles, straight-line, and considerably farther by trail. Abercrombie still identified the Copper Valley as "that unknown region," but there were guides familiar with it by 1898, and prospectors anxious to work in it. Abercrombie's efforts to cross the coast range, opening a new route to the Copper River valley from Valdez without recourse to the harrowing ascent from the delta, proved almost equally frustrating. It was impossible to employ men to pack the necessary supplies over Corbin Pass, which he named, so he returned to Yakima, Washington, purchased pack horses and shipped them north. From the pick of these First Lieutenant Percival G. Lowe (see entry) selected eleven head and was directed to proceed if possible with a party over Mentasta Pass to Forty-Mile River and chart an "All-American" route from Valdez to the Yukon. Abercrombie's exploration of a route from Valdez overland to the Copper River was hazardous and the narrative of it, particularly the crossing of Valdez glacier in twenty-nine hours at a season when such a feat was thought impossible, makes a thrilling account. His expedition descended to the river at Copper Center, rounded Mount Sanford and gained the Slahna (Slana) Valley below Mentasta Pass; it returned to Valdez by October 6 after covering about 800 miles on horseback and by boat since August 5. His report of his 1898 expedition includes extensive notes on geographical aspects of the region, its zoology, geology and natural history, and an interesting addenda on the 1898 mining rush to Alaska, the numerous prospectors attracted to the region, how they traveled and worked. In 1899 Abercrombie was instructed to open a military road from Valdez to Copper Center, and from there by "the most direct and practicable route to Eagle City," on the Yukon just west of the Canadian line. He left Washington, D.C., March 22, 1899, and reached Valdez April 21. His expedition, under various able leaders with subsidiary missions, cut trails and mapped much of the Copper River valley and adjacent regions, but did not reach the Tanana and explored little new country. Abercrombie became a major of the 30th Infantry September 27, 1901, a lieutenant colonel December 23, 1907 and retired April 2, 1910. He died at Spokane, Washington.

Abercrombie, "A Supplementary Expedition into the Copper River Valley, 1884," "A Military Reconnaissance of the Copper River Valley, 1898," and "Survey and Opening Up of a Military Road from Valdez to Copper Center, 1899," all in *Narratives of Explorations in Alaska*; Heitman; information from the U.S. Army Military Hist. Inst., Carlisle Barracks, PA.

Adams, Alexander Buell, author, conservationist, banker (July 18, 1917-Feb. 19, 1984). B. at Bronxville, New York, he was graduated from Yale and went into banking. He was vice president of Mellon Bank and Trust Company from 1946-58, and vice president of Bankers Trust Company, 1958-63. He thereafter devoted himself to writing and conservation work. He was a board member of Nature Conservancy from 1960-72, president from 1960-62 and chairman of the board from 1966-69. Adams was "credited with first bringing together in the Conservancy the business and conservation techniques" which gained for it important resources and helped it become the power for conservation that it is today. "When the environmental movement gathered momentum in the sixties [Adams] was determined that the Conservancy keep step. He took on the task of designing a professional organization that could effectively handle the large resources that would be called for [and] the more difficult and painful task of getting the necessary changes accepted. That ... made him, in a real sense, the founder of the new Conservancy." Adams also devoted himself to writing on conservation and historical subjects. Among his nine books were: *Thoreau's Guide to Cape Cod; Geronimo; Sitting Bull; Sunlight and Storm: The Great American Plains; The Disputed Lands; John James Audubon; Eternal Quest: The Story of the Great Naturalists;* and *Eleventh Hour: A Hard Look at Conservation.* He was married. Adams died at Norwalk, Connecticut.

New York Times, Feb. 23, 1984; *Nature Conservancy News,* Vol. 34, No. 3 (May/June 1984), 30; *Contemporary Authors;* Adams death certificate.

Adams, Ansel, photographer (Feb. 20, 1902-Apr. 22, 1984). B. at San Francisco he early determined to become a concert pianist, but became interested in photography and on the eve of departing for New York to further his musical career, decided upon one with the camera instead. "I doubt if I would really have become a concert pianist," he later said. "The competition in virtuoso playing is something awful. Teaching and occasional recitals would probably have been my future." He made the career decision in 1930. Like other photographers he initially tried to imitate paintings with his camera, but quickly became dissatisfied with that approach. After seeing the work of photographer Paul Strand at Taos, New Mexico, in 1931, he decided he could be "as direct in photography as in music." He also became a strong voice for conservation and a weighty influence for it, a pursuit he followed all of his life. His fame as a photographer spread and he helped found the photography department of the Museum of Modern Art at New York, and another at the Art Institute of San Francisco. He became a "maestro of modern photography, a virtuoso in composition of scenes from his beloved Yosemite Valley in the Sierra Nevada, and other natural wonders of the West," including Death Valley, Taos, the Indian pueblos of New Mexico and in many other areas. For 34 years he was a board member of the Sierra Club, sometimes controversial for his adamant fundamentalism in conservation matters and unwillingness to compromise in what he saw as their present-day need. He was a founder of the University of Arizona's Center for Creative Photography, to which he conveyed about 1,500 master prints and his collections of other artists' works. "It is the pre-eminent Adams collection anywhere in the world," said the center's director, James Enyeart. "I think Ansel's works will explain the legacy that he has left the art world and western civilization." Adams also was an accomplished portrait photographer with a wide range of subjects. He published at least 30 books, most of them collections of his photographs which were largely scenic in nature, and almost entirely black-and-white which was his favorite medium, although he sometimes used a color instant camera, identical in size, setting it up alongside his black-and-white instrument in order to more meticulously decide upon the field in which he intended to make his finished negative. Adams died of a heart condition at 82 in the Monterey, California, hospital near his Carmel home. A 12,000-foot peak in Yosemite National Park was named Mount Ansel Adams in his honor; Adams had climbed the peak in 1921, and some of his most famous photographs were of Yosemite's natural wonders. He was survived by his widow, a son and a daughter.

Los Angeles Times, Jan. 15, 1975; *Arizona Daily Star,* Apr. 24, 1984.

Adams, Edward, physician, naturalist (Feb. 24, 1824-Nov. 12, 1856). B. at Great Barton, Suffolk, England, he participated as an assistant surgeon on a Franklin Relief Expedition in 1848-49, his collections of drawings and notes on Arctic ornithology and geology eliciting praise upon his return. In January 1850 he shipped as assistant surgeon aboard the *Enterprise,* Captain Richard Collinson, on a subsequent search for the lost Franklin expedition, this time by way of Bering Strait. In October 1850 Adams and John James Barnard (see entry) were put ashore at St. Michael on Norton Sound; Adams remained at the post while Barnard went inland to Nulato on

the middle Yukon seeking information on reports of whites in the interior of Alaska. In late February a native brought a note from Nulato saying that Koyukuk Indians had slain Deryabin (see entry) and mortally wounded Barnard. Adams hastened up the river, but arrived after Barnard had died. In four years in the Arctic Adams had completed a collection of bird drawings. In China he contracted an illness of the lungs and a subsequent attack of typhus in West Africa caused his death. His *Notes on the Birds of Mikhailovskii, Norton Sound,* was published posthumously.

Pierce, *Russian America: A Biographical Dictionary.*

Ainsworth, Ed(ward) Maddin, writer (June 7, 1902-June 15, 1968). B. at Waco, Texas, he was educated at Texas A & M and the University of California at Los Angeles and was a newspaperman all of his working life, beginning as sports reporter on the *Waco News Tribune,* 1919-21. He worked on the *Bakersfield Californian, Atlanta Constitution* and the *Los Angeles Times* for 44 years until his retirement in 1968, having been successively state editor, city editor, editorial page editor and columnist. He wrote a number of books, those of frontier relevance including *Painters of the Desert* (1960); *Golden Checkerboard* about the development of the Palm Springs region (1965); *The Cowboy in Art* (1968), and, with his wife, Katherine, *In the Shade of the Juniper Tree: A Life of Fray Junipero Serra* (1970), published posthumously. Ainsworth was also consultant and associate of playwright Meredith Willson on *1491,* a short-lived musical about the year before Columbus sailed for the New World. He produced several documentary films and won awards for his literary output. Ainsworth was survived by his widow and two daughters.

Contemporary Authors; personal acquaintance with author.

Akeley, Carl Ethan, taxidermist, sculptor (May 9, 1864-Nov. 17, 1926). B. at Clarendon, Orleans County, New York, he early became interested in natural history and, by extension, in taxidermy, at that time "merely a trade." Akeley, in the course of a remarkable career "raised it to the dignity of an art," completely revolutionizing it, inventing procedures now used in museums all over the world and that have brought enhanced enjoyment through his innovations and skills to countless millions of people. In his teens he began to study taxidermy, at 19 went to work for Ward's Natural Science Establishment at Rochester, New York, which then was the headquarters of taxidermy in the nation, since few museums did this work. At 23 he joined the Milwaukee Museum and established a studio of his own. The first habitat group he built was of a Lapp herder and a reindeer hauling a sled in the snow. Sir William Flower, director of the British Museum had invented habitat exhibits about that time, and William T. Hornaday, a friend of Akeley's, introduced them to this country while he was chief taxidermist at the U.S. National Museum. Akeley also created a habitat group of muskrats, so excellent that it remained on view for many years and may still be so. After eight years in Milwaukee, Akeley went to the Field Museum of Chicago where he spent considerable time creating a four-section habitat group showing Virginia whitetail deer in each of the annual seasons. His four years there "mark the period of greatest development in the Akeley method" which totally renovated the science of taxidermy. Before his time animal and bird skins were "simply stuffed" with straw or other substances; there was little attempt to recreate the animal or bird as it was in life. Akeley devised a method by which the skinless body of the subject was modeled in clay into its precise original proportions and in whatever position the sculptor/taxidermist had in mind. Then a plaster mold was coated over the clay figurine, and from its cast, a papier-mache exact copy of the sculpture was made of a nonperishable material. The prepared skin, treated with preserving material so it would never deteriorate, would be snugly fitted over the permanent model; the result, if the work was done carefully as Akeley always did it, would be a permanent lifelike replica virtually indistinguishable from a living creature. Animals of any size, however minute or gigantic, could be recreated in this manner. Akeley made the first of his several trips to Africa in 1896 and on his second, in 1905, he secured the materials for his notable recreation of "The Fighting [Elephant] Bulls" which remains today in the Stanley Field Hall of the Field Museum as that institution's most spectacular exhibit. In 1909 Akeley became affiliated with the American Museum of Natural History at New York City where he completed notable bronze sculptures of groupings of African mammals and one of Nandi (Masai) spearmen hunting lions. He was instrumental in designing and commencing the collecting for that museum's outstanding African Hall. Akeley also was quite inventive. To solve an immediate problem of refurbishing the exterior of a museum he created a "cement gun," with which a concrete structure could be resurfaced easily and permanently; this "gun" with modifications was found to be useful in the Federal World War I concrete ship program and in various other ways, such as cementing roofs of coal mine shafts to prevent collapse. There are thousands of cement guns now in use around the world, which evolved from his crude initial one. Another of his creations was a motion picture camera which was considered for many years the best naturalist's camera ever created to that time, and with this camera Akeley took the first motion pictures ever filmed of wild gorillas in their natural habitat. During the first World War he devoted his time to the government for mechanical research and investigation, contributing particularly to concrete construction and improving the functioning of large searchlights. Akeley, always a conservationist, inspired King Albert of Belgium to create the first wildlife sanctuary established in central Africa, although in Zaire (the former Belgian Congo) there are today several great parks, all generally modeled on the first. Akeley was married twice, each of his wives contributing substantially to the success of his field research and work; his first marriage ended in divorce after 21 years, and his second wife survived him. He died on his fifth expedition to Africa and was buried on the slopes of Mount Mikeno, just north of Lake Kivu on the eastern border of Zaire. Mikeno, with Mt. Karisimbi and Mt. Visoke form a triangle of volcanic peaks which outlined a region where many gorillas normally live, so that Akeley thought it should be made a national park and recommended that it be done. He also wrote an autobiography, *In Brightest Africa.*

Carl Ethan Akeley, *In Brightest Africa,* N.Y., Garden City Pub. Co., 1920, 1923; CE; DAB.

Akliaiuk (Oglayuk), Pavel, interpreter (d. 1851). Akliaiuk was b. probably in Alaska but was raised at Fort Ross, California and when that place was sold in 1841 he returned to Alaska. In 1842 he was assigned as a hunter to Zagoskin's (see entry) expedition, but was useless at that calling and quit the expedition at Nulato, on the middle Yukon River. In 1848 from St. Michael on Norton Sound he was hired as an interpreter for the British sloop *Herald,* but he was ignorant of English and had to communicate with Captain Collet in "pidgin" Spanish. Akliaiuk proved similarly inept in later employments. In 1850-51 he apparently accompanied John James Barnard (see entry) to Nulato and was involved as a victim in the Koyukuk uprising in February 1851 when Barnard and the Russian factor Deryabin (see entry) were killed and Akliaiuk seriously wounded. He managed to regain St. Michael with word of the attack, but died there of his wounds.

Pierce, *Russian America: A Biographical Dictionary.*

Albright, Horace Marden, National Park builder, conservationist, businessman (Jan. 6, 1890-Mar. 28, 1987). B. at Bishop, California, he was graduated from the University of California at Berkeley in 1912 having majored in economics and mining law, studied law at Georgetown University and was admitted to the bar in the District of Columbia and California in 1914. He became assistant attorney for the Department of the Interior, charged with National Park affairs from 1915-17, assistant national director for the National Park system, the first civilian superintendent of Yellowstone National Park from 1919-29, then, over his protests, director of the National Park Service from 1929-33. As assistant to Stephen T. Mather, first director of the NPS, and successor when Mather became ill, Albright through "improvising and stubborn persistence" within three years oversaw establishment of Mt. McKinley, Grand Canyon and Zion National Parks, and the first national park in the East, Lafayette in Maine, later renamed Acadia. Since Albright, Mather and one secretary were the entire staff of the Service in the beginning, it fell to Albright to find office quarters, hire personnel, handle the budget and move complex legislation before Congress, while promoting the principle of Park protection to the public. He conceded that much of what he did to create the Park system "that today is the envy of the world," was done with massive financial and other support from his close friend, John D. Rockefeller Jr. who for 35 years relied on Albright's judgment and advice in channeling millions of dollars to safeguard important lands for public use, being instrumental in creation of the Great Smoky Mountains National Park, the Grand Tetons and Jackson Hole Park, the Virgin Islands Park, and others. Albright also was a power in the American Planning and Civil Association which he headed for 20 years, and in the movement to restore important historic places, including George Washington's birthplace at Wakefield, Virginia, Colonial Williamsburg, Jamestown Island and many other sites, and the transfer of administration of military and battlefield parks from the War Department to Interior. In 1933, following his 20 years in government service, Albright resigned to become general manager and later president of the United States Potash Company, though his enthusiasm and energetic participation in conservation, natural history and public parks did not wane during that time, and he remained active in many directions. He collected a vast number of books reflecting his interests: Theodore Roosevelt, mining, forestry, wildlife, the National Parks, and California, and in his lifetime was associated with scores of causes ranging from the Hudson River Conservation Society, the American Scenic and Historic Preservation Society, the American Pioneer Trails Association, to the Museum of Navajo Ceremonial Art in New Mexico, Save-the-Redwoods League and others. He once said that the mission of conserving the best of America takes many forms of expression in different individuals and the real requirement is "wider support from more citizens who will take the trouble to inform themselves of new needs and weak spots in our conservation program." In 1981 he received the Medal of Freedom to cap his countless honors and awards. He authored or co-authored several books on the Park Service, including *Oh, Ranger!* (1928), and *The Birth of the National Park Service: The Founding Years, 1913-1933* (1986), co-written with Robert Cahn. Albright died at 97 at Los Angeles following a heart attack.

Michael Frome, "Portrait of a Conserver," *Westways,* Vol. 56, No. 10 (Oct. 1964), 26-28; *Who's Who in America;* Council on America's Military Past *Headquarters Heliogram* 184 (Apr. 1987).

Alden, Ichabod, military officer (Aug. 11, 1739-Nov. 11, 1778). B. in Duxbury, Massachusetts, he was the great grandson of John Alden (c. 1599-1687) whom Longfellow made fairly immortal with his fable about the courtship of Myles Standish. Appointed lieutenant colonel in 1775 he was assigned to the 25th Continental Infantry and on November 1 became colonel of the 7th Massachusetts Infantry. He was "a brave and honorable man," but knew nothing of Indian warfare when he came into command at Cherry

Valley, New York, a frontier community south of the Mohawk River. November 6, 1778, Alden was warned of the likelihood of an attack upon his post, but since the information came from a single Oneida Indian, Alden brushed it off as unreliable. He refused to allow the villagers to store their possessions inside the makeshift "fort" for greater safety, assuring them that he had good scouts out and would give them plenty of warning of any attack, allaying their fears as much as he could—and taking no measures whatever to assure their safety. "It was part of the tragedy of Cherry Valley to be at the mercy of a criminally incompetent commander." The attacking party, under the slightly experienced, yet haughty ranger captain Walter Butler and the Mohawk Joseph Brant (see entries), a far more able commander, approached the post after capturing a picket of nine men sleeping around a campfire. The British force launched an attack at dawn on November 11 and it soon turned into a massacre despite all that Butler and Brant could do to save the lives of noncombatants. Early in the attack Ichabod Alden, attempting to escape, was slain by a thrown tomahawk and scalped. "Thus, in the very outset of the battle, fell the commander, who, had he been as prudent as he was brave, might have averted the tragic scenes of that hapless day." In all 16 soldiers and 32 inhabitants were slain, most of the latter women and children, and upwards of 70 were carried away as prisoners, although about 40 of those eventually were sent back. It was one of the memorable frontier disasters of New York during the Revolution.

William L. Stone, *Life of Joseph Brant—Thayendanegea ...,* 2 vols., N.Y., George Dearborn and Co., 1838; Barbara Graymont, *The Iroquois in the American Revolution,* Syracuse (N.Y.) Univ. Press, 1972; DAB; information from E. F. (Ted) Mains.

Allee, Alfred: *see* Alfred Alonzo Lee.

Allen, Henry Tureman, military officer (Apr. 13, 1859-Aug. 30, 1930). B. at Sharpsburg, Kentucky, he went to West Point and was commissioned a second lieutenant, 2nd Cavalry June 13, 1882. He visited Nuchek, Hinchinbrook Island, Alaska, briefly in November 1884. In 1885 he was ordered by the Secretary of War through Brigadier General Nelson A. Miles, commanding the Department of the Columbia to lead a small but important expedition into the interior of Alaska, "the first of many such assignments which made his career notable." Essentially he was to explore the three largest Alaskan streams as yet virtually unknown—the Copper, Tanana and Koyukuk rivers. Two of them, the Copper and Koyukuk had been visited by whites for parts of their lengths, but Allen was to develop this knowledge more fully, and in addition to report on natives, wildlife, resources, geology and meterology, while making accurate astronomical fixes on important geographical sites associated with them. He was instructed to leave in February and commence his exploration of the Copper River at least by March when ice would make traveling easier. Allen's party included Sergeant Cady Robertson, Private Frederick W. Fickett, a meteorologist, and two civilians, Peder Johnson and John Bremner, a miner who had ascended the Copper as far as Taral (the present Chitina), and the necessary natives. The officer left Portland, Oregon, January 28, 1885, and reached Sitka, Alaska February 10 and Nuchek Harbor March 19. By the 27th the party was at Alganik at the mouth of the Copper and after great difficulties gained Taral, a two-house community with traces of a onetime Russian redoubt of scant importance and the remains of an Orthodox cross erected when the post was active. A side excursion explored the Chitina River for some distance; by reason of their starvation diet Allen celebrated his April 13 birthday by "eating rotten moose meat" from an animal killed by wolves in the winter just past. The expedition returned to Taral May 4 and moved on up the Copper, more often cordelling their boats than rowing or paddling them. The measured current was 7 to 9 miles per hour, and progress upstream was arduous. To their right the view of the Wrangell Mountain range was superb. Allen bestowed names upon the higher peaks: Mount Blackburn for Kentucky Senator Joseph C.S. Blackburn; Mount Tillman for Colonel Samuel E. Tillman of the West Point faculty; Mount Drum for Adjutant General Richard C. Drum; and Mount Sanford, Allen not defining for whom named. May 15 they reached the mouth of the Tazlina River and from here the Indian toyon Nikolai (see entry) was sent with photographic plates and several letters describing the trip, to Nuchek for delivery to superiors. However, enroute "curiosity" led the Indians to open the box, exposing the negatives to light and thus ruining most of them. All the month of May and into June the explorers, usually verging on outright starvation and weakened by their great and constant physical exertion, worked up the Copper, seeking a pass between the Alaska Range and Wrangell Mountains in order to cross to the Tanana River valley. June 3 they reached the village of Chief Batzulneta and from there followed a well-beaten path over a low mountain ridge to the Tanana, Allen considering the establishment of the Copper and Tanana valleys as so nearly joined, one of the significant discoveries of his expedition to this point. The Tanana was reached June 21 at a still existing place named Tetlin. Having there built a baidara, the expedition on June 14 started downstream and the next day reached Khiltat's (Kheeltat), the toyon and namesake of which had been reported very hostile and apt to slaughter all members of the expedition in order to maintain his primacy in the region—but he proved to be, if not cordial, at any rate cooperative. Below that settlement the explorers encountered rapids so vigorous as to cancel out Allen's hope that the Tanana would prove a navigable river. He named Robertson River after his sergeant and Johnson River for Pete Johnson of the party. To most of the tributaries of the Tanana Allen gave Anglo names, since he had no natives with him to identify them by their Indian names. June 19 he passed the Volkmar River, which he named and below that were three houses, deserted at this season and no doubt used only in wintertime, he thought. Reduced to consuming the tallow brought to fry the fish they could not catch, the party was spared more intense starvation by occasional natives who contributed, however reluctantly, what scant food supplies they possessed. June 24 they reached the Toclat River, being now tormented by clouds of mosquitoes. The next day they reached the Yukon, having been spared from even more severe hunger by a large community of Indians who supplied them for the first time with an abundance of salmon, now moving upstream to spawn. They went two and one-half miles down the Yukon before realizing they had come to it, since they had been seeking a place called Nuklukyet (Nuclucayette) which they supposed to be a village whereas it was only a wide river bottom at the confluence of Tanana and Yukon. The larger stream already had been thoroughly explored and Allen's party hurried downstream to Nulato, arriving July 14. Here he met steamers upbound and the party had their first good meals of the summer. It was here also that Peder Johnson and John Bremner chose to remain to prospect, and Sergeant Robertson was detached to proceed downstream to Fort Michael on Norton Sound, leaving only Fickett of the original party to accompany Allen up the Koyukuk. When the necessary Indians and dogs (as pack animals) were obtained the regenerated group left the Yukon July 28 from about the mouth of the Tanana, worked across country and August 4 reached the upper Koyukuk near the village of Konootena, below present Allakaket. By August 9 they had ascended the Koyukuk to the vicinity of Mount Lookout, which they climbed as a point for observation, finding that the Koyukuk fragmented above their camp at the present Bettles. Here the party turned about and started downstream, "bound for home." The entire Koyukuk was charted as accurately as possible along the 500 miles to Nulato. August 13 camp was made opposite a 14-mile-long island Allen named Huggins, after a 2nd Cavalry colleague, Captain Eli Lundy Huggins (see entry). Nulato was gained August 21, "several hours too late for the steamboat," and Allen started down the Yukon by canoe the following morning. August 23 he left the river, going up the Autokakat tributary, crossed to the principal tributary of the Unalakleet and down that stream to Norton Sound and thence to St. Michael, reached August 30. Allen left for San Francisco September 5 following a summer of unrivaled success in exploring the interior of Alaska, his feat, journals and scientific results being equalled by no previous explorer save the Russian, Zagoskin (see entry) who had explored another great segment of the interior 40 years earlier. Allen became a first lieutenant June 22, 1889; he was military attache in Russia from 1890-93 and in Germany from 1897-98. He was cited for gallantry at El Caney, Cuba, during the Spanish American War, became captain of the 6th Cavalry November 10, 1898, and as Brigadier General of Volunteers created the Philippine Constabulary, remaining as its chief until 1907. In 1916 he commanded his regiment in the Pancho Villa campaign in Mexico, becoming Brigadier General of the Army and as temporary Major General took abroad the 90th Division which he had trained, participating in hard actions during the St. Mihiel and Meuse-Argonne offensives. In July 1919 Allen commanded the American forces in Germany, "the most difficult of all his tasks, perhaps the most brilliantly executed of them all." Early in 1923 he returned to the United States "to the regret of all parties in the zone of occupation," including the defeated Germans, the vindictive French and the others, and "it seems simple truth to say that by no human possibility could the task have been better done than was done by Allen." He retired April 23, 1923, and died at Buena Vista Springs, Pennsylvania. He was married and fathered two daughters and a namesake son, an officer in the Army.

Heitman; Cullum; DAB; NCAB, Vol. 44, 302-303; Allen, "Report of a Military Reconnoisance in Alaska," *Narratives of Explorations in Alaska.*

Allen, Hugh, frontiersman (d. Oct. 10, 1774). B. probably in Virginia, he served on an expedition against the Shawnees in 1756 and that fall was sent by Governor Robert Dinwiddie with a message to the Cherokee chiefs. In 1773 Lord Dunmore, then Virginia governor, gave him a patent for 2,000 acres of land as a reward for his services. As a lieutenant in Captain George Matthews' Augusta County company he was killed in the battle of Point Pleasant, West Virginia, which effectively ended Lord Dunmore's War against the Shawnees. A family tradition had it that the tree behind which Allen was sheltered bore the marks of 60 to 70 bullets, and that he finally was killed from behind. His widow afterward married William Craig, who served as a sergeant in the Point Pleasant action. Allen also left three sons, Hugh Jr., John and William.

Thwaites, *Dunmore.*

Allyn, Joseph Pratt, justice (Mar. 9, 1833-May 24, 1869). B. at Hartford, Connecticut, he had little formal education and suffered ill health from 13; at 19 he spent a year at New Orleans and the following year in Florida seeking to cure a persistant ailment. His health was so far improved that he returned to Hartford, entered business and worked so assiduously that he again impaired his health, traveled abroad for a time, returned to Connecticut and studied law, went to Washington as an assistant clerk in the House of Representatives, returned to Hartford to campaign for Abraham Lincoln and when Arizona Territory was created March 11, 1863, Allyn was appointed by Lincoln an associate justice of the territorial court. By this time Allyn had become a frequent contributor to the *Hartford Evening Press* under the pseudonym, "Putnam." He was to continue this lengthy and interesting correspondence during his two years in the wilds of Arizona. The suitably escorted judicial party traveled to Santa Fe by wagon, meeting Indians and frontiersmen until they entered northern Arizona late in December 1863. The observant Allyn reported it all in letters published in the Hartford newspaper. He continued westward to Fort Whipple, making exploratory trips to the gold mines in the vicinity and as far south as the Pima villages in the Gila River valley. When Whipple was moved in May 1864 to near the newly-founded Prescott, Allyn located at that community before being assigned to the Second Judicial District, the region west of 114º Longitude with its headquarters at La Paz, a gold mining town (now disappeared) on the Colorado River. Allyn was directed by the chief justice to hold court for two weeks twice yearly, in June and November, the sessions at La Paz, but he found that the lack of court business made the schedule inappropriate and held court at times as the legal requirements dictated. Most of the cases were mining matters, and he was a careful, meticulous interpreter of the law, applying even-handed justice. He found plenty of time to become embroiled in political matters and was frequently at Prescott, the territorial capital. With respect to crime, he warned of the prospect of murders in a society where conditions made necessary citizens to be armed constantly. He noted in a letter that "universal talk of fraud and corruption...fills the air," and apparently it was not irresponsible gossip. He urged grand jury investigations, as well as the strongest vigilance against treason in the Civil War times then upon the nation and its territories. Allyn quickly became a political foe of territorial secretary Richard McCormick, an ambitious and intelligent man who owned the Prescott *Miner* and thus had a publicity advantage over the justice. Allyn visited Tucson and the Santa Cruz valley just north of Mexico, passed through the Papago region to Yuma, and in 1865 went by steamer up the Colorado River to the limit of navigation near present Hoover Dam. He ran unsuccessfully for the position of delegate to Congress, losing out to Governor John Goodwin, though receiving a respectable number of votes. He entertained hope of being governor succeeding Goodwin, but was passed over in favor of his political foe, McCormick. After a brief visit to California, he held one final session of court at La Paz and, after two years as a frontier judge, abandoned Arizona for the east. Allyn had a sharp sense of humor, evident from his first appearance in Arizona on a horse he named "Swindle," and an intense "interest in all aspects of the life around him." He was an excellent writer and "had he lived he might have become a great novelist." In his letters he presented the "most interesting and sensitive descriptions of the life and land of Arizona in the 1860s." Enroute home he went by a roundabout way to Yosemite, visited Portland, Oregon, reached Virginia City, Nevada, and the Comstock mining area, stopped by Salt Lake City briefly, and returned to Hartford suffering again from his old nemesis, tuberculosis, from which he succumbed on another trip to Europe and the Mediterranean countries. He died at Paris and was buried at Hartford.

John Nicholson, ed., *The Arizona of Joseph Pratt Allyn: Letters from a Pioneer Judge,*Tucson, Univ. of Arizona Press, 1974.

Alvarado, Juan Bautista, governor (Feb. 14, 1809-July 13, 1882). B. in Monterey, the capital of California, he was educated privately, held clerical positions with foreign traders and entered public life in 1827 as secretary of the territorial *Diputación,* or informal deputation to aid in governing California following Mexico's separation from Spanish rule. Alvarado was secretary until 1834 and in addition was territorial treasurer, was president of it in 1836 and with José Castro (see entry) unseated Governor Nicolas Gutiérrez and assumed the governorship himself December 7 of that year, on July 9, 1837, by submitting to Mexico became regular governor ad interim, and November 24, 1839, was made constitutional governor by Mexican appointment. Differences with Mariano Vallejo in the north and Pío Pico in the south (see entries) complicated his administration, as did his later estrangement from Vallejo over a petty quarrel while his forthright acts in the so-called Graham affair (see Isaac Graham entry), policy matters in connection with mission and Indian affairs, treatment of foreigners, relations with the Russians at Fort Ross and Alaska, all occupied his tenure fully. His governorship ended December 31, 1842 but from 1843 he held a commission of colonel in the Mexican army with pay, and from 1847 colonel of the Defenders of the Fatherland, as it was titled. He was a leading spirit in the revolution of 1844-45 that unseated Micheltorena and made Pico the last governor of Mexican California. He took only a slight part in the affairs of 1846 when California was lost to the United States, being arrested briefly and paroled and attending then to his several large properties, which he ultimately lost. "In the flush times and period of land litigation Alvarado saved no land

or money" but subsequently moved to the San Pablo estate inherited by his wife, Martina Castro, whom he had married in 1839. Though it was "always in litigation," he was enabled to live there in comfort until his death, his wife having died in 1875; they left several children and Don Juan "also had several natural daughters before his marriage." In physique he was of medium height, stout, fair complexion and light hair, genial in temperament, courtly in manner, and possessed "rare powers of winning friends." Bancroft added that "much will be found in him to praise, much to condemn," but the latter resulted principally from his environment which forced him to live by intrigue. He drank too much alcohol, but "he had more brains, energy, and executive ability than any three of his contemporaries combined," while in most of his many controversies "he was right as well as successful." Bancroft added that Alvarado was "honorable in his private dealings, true to his political friends, and never used his position to enrich himself."

Bancroft, *California,* II-IV, *Pioneer Register;* DAB.

Amherst, Jeffrey, military officer (Jan. 29, 1717-Aug. 3, 1797). B. near Sevenoaks, England, the record of his early military career is confused but he served in a good cavalry regiment in Ireland, becoming a lieutenant in 1740 under a fine officer, Major General John Ligonier. Amherst's early service was on the continent and by 1758 he was a colonel. Ligonier by then was commander-in-chief of British forces, determined to take the stout French fortress of Louisbourg on the tip of Cape Breton Island, and he selected Amherst to direct the assault. Amherst was made "Major General in America" for the task and subsidiary duties. In a well-managed operation, Louisbourg was taken by July 27 and Amherst spent the following winter at New York. In 1759 he was directed to follow the Lake Champlain Line into Canada and capture Montreal, while Wolfe went up the St. Lawrence to attack Quebec. Amherst made slow, ponderous progress, but it was not until September 8, 1760, that he took Montreal (Wolfe's command had seized Quebec a year earlier, it surrendering September 18, 1759). Amherst could now turn his attention to military affairs in the present United States, largely focused on frontier and Indian conflict. There "his dislike and contempt for the Indians are amply reflected in his journals and correspondence, though it may perhaps be doubted whether he was more bigoted than the average official of his time," according to Charles P. Stacey, writing in the *Dictionary of Canadian Biography,* IV. Once the troubles with France had subsided, Amherst commenced cutting back on presents to the tribes, including those potentially hostile, and this was a major factor in bringing about the Pontiac War (1763-64), a major frontier disaster for Britain. Amherst knew very little about Indians, and cared less, and he found it hard to believe that the rising storm on the frontier was anything but a minor eruption which good officers and trained British soldiery could readily handle. But as report followed report, each more serious than the former, he was goaded into action which unfortunately was piecemeal and too late. He still did not believe in "purchasing" good behavior of Indians or anyone else with largesse, and believed that when they misbehaved they "must be punished but not bribed" with gifts or lavish allowances. He sent his aide, James Dalyell (see entry), with 260 reinforcements to Detroit only to have them defeated by Pontiac and the commander slain. He sent to Henry Bouquet (see entry) what Parkman described as the "detestable suggestion" that "Could it not be contrived to send the small pox among the disaffected tribes of Indians? We must on this occasion use every strategem in our power to reduce them." Bouquet readily accepted the idea, replying that he would try to spread an epidemic with infected blankets, adding that he also wished to hunt "the vermin" with dogs as the Spanish did. Amherst replied July 16, 1763, to Bouquet: "You will do well to try to inoculate the Indians by means of blankets, as well as to try every other method that can serve to extirpate this execrable race. I should be very glad your scheme for hunting them down by dogs could take effect, but England is at too great a distance [to supply the necessary dogs] to think of that at present." Amherst's endorsement of the small pox weapon did more to assure his name to infamy than any other action he suggested or undertook during his military career in America. In November 1763 he embarked for England with "no thought of returning to America," and he never again crossed the Atlantic for that purpose. He declined a King's offer in January 1775 to take command in America, and again declined in 1778 a renewed invitation. He finally was promoted to field marshal July 30, 1796, a year before his death. He had married twice, both marriages being childless.

DCB, IV; Howard H. Peckham, *Pontiac and the Indian Uprising,* Univ. of Chicago Press, 1947, 1961; REAW, "Pontiac's Rebellion" entry, 948-49; Parkman, *Conspiracy of Pontiac,* I, II (the small pox interchange with Bouquet is reproduced textually, II, 44-45.

Anderson, William (Kikthewanund), Delaware chief (c. 1755-1831). The Delaware Indians respect his memory as a great leader who helped maintain the cultural identity of their people. Before 1795 he became chief of the Unami division, or Turtle people, who held precedence over the other Delawares. This important grouping traditionally occupied the Pennsylvania side of the Delaware River from the confluence of the Lehigh River south to about the Delaware line. Anderson expelled the Moravian missionaries from the White River, Indiana, in his determination to avoid white inroads into the Delaware culture, and he worked to keep his people from Tecumseh's confederacy, arguing that conflict would only facilitate the destruction of the Indians. Anderson's Turtle people were largely neutral during the War of 1812. In October 1817, then in his early sixties, he was described as the principal chief. On October 3, 1818, the Delawares, by the Treaty of St. Mary's, Ohio, which Anderson signed under the name of Kithteeleland "or Anderson," the Delawares agreed to "cede to the United States all their claims to land in the state of Indiana," and to remove west of the Mississippi. Apparently Anderson hoped to renovate Delaware society in the west, free from white interference. He moved with his people to Missouri in 1820 and endeavored to unite the fragmented Delaware nation, but ceded this new land in 1829 for territory in Kansas, where he died.

Information from John Sugden; R.T. Ferguson, *The White River, Indiana, Delawares,* a doctoral dissertaton available from University Microfilms, Ann Arbor, Michigan.

Anderson, William Marshall, traveler (June 24, 1807-Jan. 7, 1881). B. near Louisville, Kentucky, his mother was a first cousin of Chief Justice John Marshall and a relative of George Rogers Clark. Young Anderson studied at Transylvania University of Lexington, but did not graduate; he studied law and was licensed to practice in 1832, becoming active in business affairs. In 1834 it was suggested by another relative, Brigadier General Henry Atkinson that for his persistent health problems he accompany an expedition led by Colonel Henry Dodge of the 1st Dragoons to the Pawnee-picts (Wichitas); the General later recommended that instead he join a fur trading party headed by William Sublette for the Rocky Mountains. Anderson kept a journal of this expedition, noticing everything and writing of whatever came to his attention. The manuscript was purchased for $12,000 in 1954 by the Huntington Library; it had been in the collection of W.J. Holliday, an Indianapolis industrialist. Robert Glass Cleland, director of research for the Huntington said "We consider this journal of very great importance, not only because of its account of fur trading, but also because of its contribution to the whole history of the opening of the West." It was published in 1967. Anderson returned home in the fall, his health restored and weighing 50 pounds more than when he had departed St. Louis. He married, practiced law, became a Roman Catholic, and settled near Chillicothe, Ohio. He was deeply interested in archeology, explored the famous mounds of southern Ohio and assembled a collection of Indian artifacts. In 1853 he moved to Circleville, Ohio, becoming prosperous and prominent in the community and was active in cultural and intellectual pursuits. His first wife died and in 1857 he married a wealthy widow, fathering children by both of his spouses. During the Civil War raid of John Hunt Morgan into Ohio, Anderson served fleetingly as captain of the Pickaway County Home Guards but voluntarily relinquished the commission to serve as sergeant until the company was dissolved about a month later. He was intensely dissatisfied with Reconstruction policies and this may have spurred his "enigmatic trip to Mexico in 1865-1866." Ostensibly on an archeological expedition, he assisted in the establishment of a small Confederate colony near Vera Cruz, and in December 1865 received a commission from the Emperor Maximilian to survey lands in northeastern Mexico for possible colonization by defeated Confederate self-exiles. His royal commission made him an enemy of the Liberal forces of Benito Juarez, dominant in the region; he was captured, narrowly missed being shot (as he believed), ultimately escaped to the French lines and eventually sailed from Vera Cruz, suffering an attack of yellow fever the day after the vessel put to sea. He disembarked in Cuba and finally reached Circleville in the summer of 1866. In the winter of 1871 he visited the Lake George area of Mississippi to study a mound complex, discovering interesting

pottery, a calendar stone with feathered serpent figures and other other artifacts he thought indicated a close tie with the Toltec culture of Mexico. In 1878 he suffered injuries in a railroad accident and died of double pneumonia at Circleville.

Dale L. Morgan, Eleanor Towles Harris, eds., *The Rocky Mountain Journals of William Marshall Anderson: The West in 1834,* San Marino, Calif., The Huntington Library, 1967; *Los Angeles Times,* Apr. 25, 1954; information from E.F. (Ted) Mains.

Antelope Jack: *see* John Thompson Jones

Apache Bill: *see* William H. Young

Appleton, Samuel, military officer (1624-May 15, 1696). B. at Waldingfield, Suffolk, England, he was taken at 11 by his father to Ipswich, northeastern Massachusetts. Samuel Appleton became an outstanding officer in King Philip's War. He was married twice and fathered children by each of his wives. He became deputy under the title of lieutenant in 1668 by the General Court, serving intermittently until 1675 when the sanguinary conflict broke out, Appleton quickly being called for military service, initially as captain. Around September 1, 1675, he marched his command from the Bay to Hadley, near Northampton, making Hadley his headquarters. On October 5 Indians sacked and burned Springfield on the Connecticut River in southern Massachusetts and shortly Appleton succeeded John Pynchon as commander in chief in the western theater of operations, principally the Connecticut Valley. His mission was complicated by rivalries between Connecticut and Massachusetts which made a unified direction fragile at best. Appleton's command had an authorized strength of about 500, though its actual strength was considerably less. On October 19 the Indians heavily attacked Hatfield where the defenses had been augmented and the hostiles were defeated after heavy fighting. This battle virtually terminated hostile activities in the Connecticut valley for the year. On November 16 Appleton released the Connecticut forces under Major Robert Treat to withdraw for home, made provision for garrisoning the river towns, and returned east. Promoted to major he prepared to lead a Massachusetts contingent of around 1,000 men south to join in handling the Narragansetts adjacent to Narragansett Bay. His force operated in conjunction with other units from Connecticut and Rhode

Island, the whole under the overall command of Governor Josiah Winslow of Plymouth Colony. In the Great Swamp Fight of December 19, 1675, the Appleton contingent took part, suffered casualties and conducted themselves vigorously. Soon afterward Appleton "retired from his protracted and arduous service in the field." On October 19, 1676, he was appointed to command another military expedition, but apparently declined, since the order was rescinded four days later. Appleton held civil offices of significance until Edmund Andros became first governor of the Dominion of New England in 1686 when Appleton was considered "factious," suggesting that he refused to bow to the controversial new government. He consequently was arrested on the general complaint of being "evil disposed and seditious," that is, adamantly opposed to the new regime. October 19, 1687, refusing to submit and give bonds for his future "good behavior," he was committed to Boston jail where he was held for about five months until "his age and increasing infirmities forced a reluctant submission," and he was released March 7, 1688. At his death he left "an honored name. Of all the military commanders of [King Philip's War] I must consider Major Appleton the ablest; and the tide of warfare in the western towns [of Massachusetts] turned towards safe and successful methods from the time of his appointment to the command."

George Madison Bodge, *Soldiers in King Philip's War*, Leominster, Mass., p.p., 1896; Douglas Edward Leach, *Flintlock and Tomahawk: New England in King Philip's War*, N.Y., The Macmillan Co., 1958.

Aram, John, pioneer, (b.c. 1828). B. near Utica, New York, he was a brother of Joseph Aram (see entry). At 21, "imbued with the gold fever," he shipped from New York with about 600 others aboard the English steamer, *Sara Sands* for San Francisco. The ship lost its rudder and drifted aimlessly for six weeks until it finally grounded on Lower California in May. All food had run out except rice, and the captain, his vessel unseaworthy, offered to settle with the passengers for $30 apiece, which most accepted. Aram and 50 others took the money and hiked 600 miles to San Francisco, buying cattle enroute and drying the meat for provisions. After a few adventurous years, Aram in 1852 returned to Ohio where he married Sara Elizabeth Barr. In 1854 he headed west again, driving 3,000 sheep from Iowa, working for his food and transportation, supplied

by a dozen wagons; California was reached in six months. Mrs. Aram with her infant had taken ship for the Isthmus of Panama which she crossed afoot, boarding another vessel for San Francisco where she joined her husband upon his arrival. Aram entered the sheep business in California, but quickly wearied of it, did some mining in Calaveras County with little success, and went in December 1859 to Portland, Oregon. In 1865 the family moved to a place a mile south of Grangeville, Idaho, where they settled permanently. The date of his death is not reported.

Information from Mrs. Ruth Aram, Lewiston, Id.

Aram, Joseph, pioneer (Mar. 24, 1810-1896). B. near Utica, New York, his father was a farmer-horticulturist; the boy was graduated from Lima, Ohio, College and in 1840 moved with the family to Illinois. In 1846 he decided upon California, leaving St. Joseph, Missouri, with Charles Imus, a Black Hawk War veteran, as captain. Kit Carson was an initial guide. They had assorted contacts, all peaceful, with Indians, Aram finding the Sioux at Fort Laramie, "the best behaved Indians that we found on the whole journey." He added with respect to their music and dancing that, "there was some degree of refinement in it all, which was more than we expected to find amongst Indians." Leaving the South Platte the train was threatened by a buffalo stampede at which "we lost no time in unhitching our teams and getting them on the opposite side of the wagons. [The buffalo] rushed by us but generally between the wagons. One very large bull ran his head under [one] wagon and raised it off the ground, and when it fell it came down with such force as to break the hind axletree..." On the Green River the Imus/Aram train met that of the Donner party, and also Lansford Warren Hastings (see entry), coming east from California by way of Salt Lake. Hastings urged the Aram party to take his "cut-off" as the best way west, but luckily their guide, by then Caleb Greenwood, warned that rather than saving a month's travel, as Hastings promised, it would be safer to go by way of Fort Hall, though the Donner party fatally accepted Hastings' advice. In the Fort Hall vicinity the trail forked, one branch going to Oregon, the other to California; many of the emigrants went on to Oregon, but about 12 wagons and 50 people under Imus and Aram headed for California. On the Humboldt where they had expected to meet again with Donner, they found that party had not yet arrived, Indians informing them that it was far back to the east and had "lost many cattle." Greenwood left and Chief Truckee (see entry), a Northern Paiute, agreed to guide the train across the Sierra Nevada into California, an offer the emigrants were happy to accept. "Chief Truckee was of much service to us [since] he had been in California," Aram wrote. Crossing the great range was difficult and at times it was necessary to use five yoke of oxen to a wagon to pull the vehicles up steep grades, but by that means and other ingenuity the mountains were conquered. Aram, Imus and Dr. James C. Isbel, an Ohio physician, had a rousing experience with a mother grizzly and her two half-grown cubs, but came through unscathed and with enough bear meat for the company. On the Yuba River Mrs. Aram, while washing clothes, picked up a "piece of gold about the size of a ten cent piece of silver"; this was two years before Marshall's discovery that set off the Gold Rush. About October 3 Sutter's Fort was reached and "we received a very warm reception" from the captain. "We next found Fremont (see entry) camped on the American river," who informed Aram of conditions in California, a somewhat biased view emphasizing the supposed hostility of Mexicans toward Americans, an enmity which did not then exist to any appreciable extent. Fremont suggested that the emigrants "go to Santa Clara and take possession of the [abandoned] mission buildings..., organize a company for our own protection [and] elect officers to whom he would give commissions," Aram being chosen captain of the 33-man company. The mission buildings were in a dilapidated condition; they were cleaned up and the place made as defendable as possible. It was more or less besieged late in 1846 and early in 1847 by a Mexican force of semi-militia numbering 150, according to Aram; it was headed by "Captain" Francisco Sanchez. Around January 2 the Mexicans approached, there was some long-range and mostly ineffectual shooting, the Americans had two or three men wounded and the Californians none, and that was the "battle" of Santa Clara (see Bancroft, *California* V, 378-81 for details). Aram's men saw no other significant action, although Aram reported that all of Sanchez's men "surrendered" their arms. March 1, 1847, he disbanded his company and with his family moved to Monterey, by way of Santa Cruz. He remained at Monterey for two years, visited the mines in 1848 "with tolerably good success," based principally at Placerville, and on

the Tuolumne River. He then removed to San Jose, became a member of the 1849 California Constitutional Convention, and was a signer to the constitution itself. Later he was a member of the first legislature and for several years a member of the San Jose city council. His wife died March 1, 1873, and on a visit to the eastern states he married again in 1876 and visited the Philadelphia Sesquicentennial Exposition before returning to San Jose where he lived until his death.

Information from Mrs. Ruth Aram, Lewiston, Id.; information from Vernay S. Thrapp, Lewiston; Joseph Aram's "Narrative," a copy in author's collection; Bancroft, *California,* V, VI, *Pioneer Register;* information from E.F. (Ted) Mains.

Aram, Thomas, frontiersman (d. Aug. 1848). A brother of Joseph Aram (see entry), he was b. near Utica, New York, and in 1847, a year after Joseph had gone to California, he too joined a wagon train, this one headed for Oregon. He and his wagon, with nine young men riding in it, arrived at The Dalles, Oregon, about a week before the rest of the train and had a fight with Indians, escaping over the newly-cut Barlow Road across the south slopes of Mount Hood. One of Aram's companions in the scrap was a man named Leonard whose first name is not given, thought it might have been Dan. Leonard "pawned" his rifle to Aram. He subsequently went to retrieve it on the present Sauvies Island at the mouth of the Willamette River, apparently with no attempt to return the money loaned on it. A dispute arose and Aram "pursued him with hostile intent. Leonard ran until he came to a fallen tree too large for him to scale in haste, and finding Aram close upon him he turned, and in his excitement fired, killing Aram." Leonard was arrested and discharged, there being no witnesses to the affair. Aram, according to Bancroft or, more probably, Frances Fuller Victor who authored Bancroft's *Oregon* volumes, wrote that Aram was a bully, while Leonard was "a small and usually quiet man," who said the shooting was accidental since he didn't know the rifle was loaded. "Leonard left the country soon after for the gold-mines and never returned."

Information from Mrs. Ruth Aram, Lewiston, Id.; Bancroft, *Oregon,* II, 37n.

Arey, H.T. (Ned), prospector (fl. 1901-12). Arey went by dogsled from Point Barrow, Alaska to the Canning River west of the Alaskan-Canadian border and spent the following 11 years in that area, coming to know it thoroughly, and learning the Eskimo names for its features. In 1902-1903 he wintered with S.J. Marsh (see entry) and F.G. Carter in the mountains to the south. He gave Marsh the native names to the Kuparuk, Shagavanirktok and Shaviovik rivers, names incorporated in Geological Survey maps of 1903. Arey was first to explore the mouths of the Canning, Julahula, Jago and Okpilak rivers and to gain a detailed knowledge of the coastline of that region. Arey Island west of Barter Island commemorates him. Arey originally was from Cape Cod, Massachusetts. In 1907 he materially assisted Leffingwell (see entry) in his explorations, particularly of the Okpilak River.

Orth, 19, 86.

Arguello, Concepción, Spanish woman (c. Feb. 25, 1790-Dec. 1857). Concepción became famed for her tragic love affair with Russian Court Chamberlain Nikolai Petrovich Rezanov (see entry) in 1806 at San Francisco. Her father, José Arguello, was commandant of the presidio there and when the ship *Neva* arrived in 1806 the beauteous Concepción was charmed by the 42-year-old intellectual and sophisticated Russian. Their betrothal aided Rezanov in securing necessary supplies for the Alaskan post of Sitka. When the *Neva* sailed in May, Rezanov promised to solicit from Emperor Alexander I permission to marry a non-Orthodox girl, while her family would ask a similar dispensation from Pope Pius VII. But Rezanov died March 13, 1807, at Krasnoyarsk, Siberia, while enroute to Russia. "By legend Conception did not hear of his death for 35 years, but actually A.A. Baranov informed her father of it in 1808." She never married and in 1850 became a nun, dying at a convent in Benicia, California. Her brief romance has been often written about and Pierce reports that in 1982 it was the theme of a rock opera in the Soviet Union.

Pierce, *Russian America: A Biographical Dictionary;* Bancroft, *Alaska, California,* II.

Arguello, José Darío, military officer (c. 1763-1828). B. at Querétaro, Mexico he enlisted in the dragoons in 1773, served more than eight years as an enlisted man and in 1781 was commissioned alférez of the company of Rivera (see entry) planned for the projected presidio of Santa Barbara in Upper California. Although Rivera was killed by Yuma Indians, Arguello arrived at Santa Barbara in April 1782. In February 1787 he was promoted to lieutenant of the San Francisco company, serving as commandant at its presidio until March 1791, then commanded at Monterey until 1796 when he returned to San Francisco, commanding there until July 1806. In October 1797 he became a brevet captain. He was often praised for his intelligent and useful work at San Francisco, which included dealings with occasional Russian American Company vessels and officials, among them the noted Nikolai Rezanov (see entry), to whom his daughter, fifteen-year-old Concepción (see entry) became betrothed in 1806—unhappily for her, since her fiancé died before a wedding could take place. From the autumn of 1806 Arguello was stationed again at Santa Barbara. In 1807 he was commissioned captain. As the ranking officer in California, Arguello, following the death in July 1814 of Governor José Joaquin Arrillaga, became acting governor, remaining however as commandant at Santa Barbara until December 31, 1814, when he was named governor of Baja California, leaving for there in October 1815. His nine children had all been born in Upper California; his wife, Ignacia Moraga was a niece of José Joaquín Moraga (see entry), founder of San Francisco. Arguello's incumbency in Baja California was an unhappy, unprofitable and unsatisfactory one, and he resigned June 26, 1821, spending his final years in penury and ill health at Guadalajara. He died at 75, and his widow died April 12, 1829.

Bancroft, *California,* II, 358-60n.

Arkhimandritov, Illarion Ivanovich, sea captain (1820-c. 1872). B. on St. George Island, Pribylov group, in September 1831 he was a crew member on the sloop *Urup* on a voyage to California and November 20, 1832, left Sitka on a transport, the *Amerika,* for St. Petersburg where he enrolled in a merchant seafaring school, completing his course in 1837 when he returned to Sitka as an assistant navigator. He became navigator, junior grade, in 1841. On September 27, homeward bound from California his ship, the *Naslednik Aleksandr* was almost swamped in a sudden storm, the captain and first mate were swept overboard, and Arkhimandritov assumed command, saved the vessel and for this was honored with a gold medal and in other ways. March 4, 1843, he became a captain for Russian American Company shipping. In 1846 he mapped Cook Inlet, including today's Anchorage vicinity and other sites. Some of his results were used in an atlas compiled during Tebenkov's governorship of Alaska and copies of his manuscript maps and charts were used by the company. His survey of Port Graham in Cook Inlet was published as a harbor chart in 1869 by the U.S. Coast and Geodetic Survey. In 1849 Arkhimandritov commanded the steamer, *Nikolai,* was active in trading with the Kolosh (Tlingit) Indians, and also performed such functions as towing sailing ships into harbor and towing out barges and lumber rafts for disposal elsewhere by the company. In 1854 he commanded the brig *Velikii Kniaz Konstantin* taking goods and supplies from Sitka to Petropavlovsk, Kamchatka, returning to Sitka August 31. With the steamer *Imperator Aleksandr II* Arkhimandritov left Sitka for Unalaska Island, the Pribylov Islands of St. Paul and St. George, and the St. Michael and Kolmakov (on the Kuskokwim River) redoubts with supplies for each of them, bringing furs back to Sitka which was regained August 28, 1858. On March 29, 1859, he sailed to Pavlovsk Harbor on the Alaska Peninsula, and to English Bay, returning to Sitka April 23. During the Crimean War his vessel was given fictitious American registry to avoid capture as a British or French prize, and he served under the American flag and with an American captain. February 27, 1860, Arkhimandritov left Sitka with the bark *Kodiak* for Woody Island where he took on a cargo of ice for California but March 30 struck a subsurface rock off Spruce Island, the vessel being lost though all personnel were saved. He remained however in company service. In May 1864 he made fresh charts of coastal features on the Pribylov Islands, at St. Michael on Norton Sound and possibly near Unalaska Island. Following sale of Alaska to the United States in 1867, Arkhimandritov settled for a time at San Francisco, becoming president of the Russian Society, then returned to Alaska working for the firm of Hutchinson, Kohl and Company, bringing their ships occasionally into San Francisco, arriving the final time on September 22, 1872. Pierce believed that "he probably died soon after that voyage." He was married. Features named for him included the Archimandritof Shoals in Kachemak Bay on the Kenai Peninsula.

Pierce, *Russian America: A Biographical Dictionary; The Russian American Colonies;* Orth, 7.

Armstrong, John, military officer, legislator

(Oct. 13, 1717-Mar. 9, 1795). B. at Brookbor, County Fermanagh, Ireland, he studied civil engineering and emigrated to America, laid out the town of Carlisle, Pennsylvania, and settled there. Following Braddock's disaster in July of 1755, the whole frontier came under attack by hostile Indians; Armstrong was commissioned a captain in January 1756, a lieutenant colonel in May and was sent with 300 men to assail the Delaware town of Kittanning (called by the French Attiqué, its Iroquois name) on the upper Allegheny River, believed to be a base for the enemy Indians. The town was taken in a dawn attack on September 8, though Armstrong was shot in the shoulder in the affair. Thirty cabins were burned, food, supplies and a quantity of French ammunition were destroyed and during the engagement a Delaware leader, Captain Jacobs, his wife and a son were killed, among many others; the white loss was 17 killed and 13 wounded and Armstrong recovered 11 men, women and children of the supposed 100 white prisoners held in the village. The others either never existed or were spirited off to other Indian towns. "A medal was given to each officer, not by the Quaker-ridden [pacificist] Assembly, but by the city council of Philadelphia," and Armstrong assumed the lasting soubriquet of "the Hero of Kittanning." In 1758 he was senior Pennsylvania officer in the John Forbes expedition sent to occupy the abandoned and burned French Fort Duquesne (Pittsburgh) and had the honor of raising the flag over the ruins. He also served in Pontiac's War of 1763. The atrocities of 1755 and 1756 were repeated in 1764 and Armstrong in September led an expedition to Big (Great) Island, the present Lock Haven, Pennsylvania, then an Indian stronghold. The hostiles retreated before him, and he set fire to the emptied cabins, destroyed growing crops ready for harvest and otherwise devastated that location and another 30 miles distant. With the Revolution imminent, Armstrong was commissioned a Brigadier General and was sent to Charleston, South Carolina, then returned to the northern theatre. April 4, 1777, he was commissioned a Major General of the Pennsylvania militia although "it does not appear that his actual achievements measured up to his reputation gained in the Seven Years' War." He served in the Continental Congress in 1779-80, and again in 1787-88. He died at Carlisle and was buried in the Old Carlisle Cemetery. He was married and fathered children.

Parkman, *Montcalm and Wolfe,* II, *Conspiracy of*

Pontiac, II; BDAC; Clinton A. Weslager, *The Delaware Indians,* New Brunswick, N.J., Rutgers Univ. Press, 1972; DAB.

Armstrong, John, military officer, explorer (Apr. 20, 1755-Feb. 4, 1816). An officer with Pennsylvania regiments in the Revolution, he afterward sided with Pennsylvania in its land dispute with settlers from Connecticut in the region of Wyoming, Pennsylvania. On organization of a standing army, he was commissioned an ensign of the U.S. Infantry Regiment August 12, 1784, a lieutenant of the 1st Infantry September 29, 1789, a captain, September 26, 1790, a major September 27, 1792, and resigned from the army March 3, 1793. During his service he was engaged in arduous duties on the Ohio frontier, "becoming one of the best-known woodsmen, explorers and military characters of the early West." He commanded Fort Pitt (Pittsburgh) in 1785-86, then moved into Ohio where, among his other accomplishments won note by "planting fruit Trees of various kinds & making Gardens" wherever he went for "the real emolument of mankind." He commanded at the falls of the Ohio (Louisville) from 1786-90. In 1790 the government determined to secretly explore Spanish trans-Mississippi territory and the Missouri River, and Armstrong was entrusted with this delicate enterprise. In the spring of 1790 he "proceeded up the Missouri some distance above St. Louis, *not with an army to deter the savages, nor yet an escort, but alone.* It was his intention to examine the country of the upper Missouri, and cross the Rocky Mountains, but, meeting with some French traders, was persuaded to return in consequence of the hostility of the Missouri bands to each other, as they were then at war, that he could not safely pass from one nation to another." The foregoing is from a biographical sketch by Armstrong's son, William Goforth Armstrong (1844) published in Charles Cist's *Cincinnati Miscellany,* I, 40, and was confirmed by Secretary of War Henry Knox in a letter quoted by Nasatir in which Knox said he had "detached Lieutenant Armstrong to undertake the business recommended in [Harmar's] secret letters. No written orders have been given him upon that subject..." Upon his return Armstrong was detailed to explore the Wabash River of Indiana and its communications with Lake Erie. He did this accompanied only by two friendly Indians. He made other important military explorations. In October 1790 he accompanied Josiah

Harmar's ill-fated expedition against the Ohio Indians, the first federal effort to neutralize these hostile tribes. Armstrong reportedly commanded the only regulars engaged in the initial encounter of that campaign on October 19, and when militia deserted them the regulars stood their ground until only seven men remained alive and Armstrong's "escape from the field forms a remarkable chapter in the history of western adventure and woodsmanship." He served on Arthur St. Clair's disastrous campaign of 1791 when on November 4 occurred the worst catastrophe ever to befall United States arms when fighting Indians (see St. Clair entry). Armstrong built Fort Hamilton at Hamilton, Ohio and was commandant there, but resigned from the army in 1793, shortly after marriage to a daughter of William Goforth, an influential builder of the Ohio commonwealth. Armstrong became treasurer of the Northwest Territory, held local offices and in 1814 moved to Armstrong's Station, which he founded in Clark County, Indiana, in 1796. He died at that place.

Heitman; A.P. Nasatir, ed., *Before Lewis and Clark,* 2 vols., St. Louis Hist. Doc. Foundation, 1952; DAB; information from E.F. (Ted) Mains.

Asi-Yahola, Seminole chief: *see* Osceola

Astor, John Jacob, fur trader, businessman (July 17, 1763-Mar. 29, 1848). B. at Waldorf, near Heidelberg, Germany, the son of the village butcher, he left for London at 16, joining there a brother who manufactured musical instruments. In 1793, taking for sale a supply of flutes and little else as capital, he left for America. Enroute he fell in with a fur dealer who persuaded him to go to New York, sell his instruments and invest the proceeds in furs, which he could dispose of profitably at London. He followed this advice, learned all he could about the American and European ends of the fur trade, swiftly expanded his interests and "by the end of the century he had become the leading fur merchant of the United States and probably the leading authority in the world upon that business." He had worked hard, made trips to the frontiers, once it is reported going even to the Straits of Mackinac. His early transactions often were accomplished at Montreal, since tariff restrictions made that more profitable initially than dealing through New York. With Jay's Treaty (1794) however, and with the consequent British abandonment of many interior positions of the West, Astor could expand operations along the shores of the Great Lakes and "conduct it more readily from New York" as a primary base, that now being financially in his favor. The Louisiana Purchase "opened up an entirely new vista of almost illimitable scope." April 6, 1808, his American Fur Company was chartered in New York. It was to be an umbrella for his operations and in 1810 he founded the Pacific Fur Company as its initial subsidiary; a second was the South West Company to concentrate on the Great Lakes and in which Canadian interests had about a 50 percent holding. The AFC's chief rivals were always the Hudson's Bay Company and the vigorous North West Company run largely by French-Canadians and Scots. With return from the Pacific of the Lewis and Clark Expedition, Astor envisioned enormous possibilities for himself. China could become a market for Pacific coast fur, his ships could supply the Russian Alaskan enterprises which seemed usually to be bordering on starvation or at least severe deprivation; lines of trading posts would be established along the Columbia River from the ocean to its source and connecting by way of the Missouri waterways with St. Louis and thence via the Great Lakes to New York, and "Astor saw that his business would indeed be worldwide in scope and international in importance." The federal government apparently "applauded his views, but could lend him no other aid than tacit encouragement," which was all that Astor sought: applause and no regulation. The nucleus of his grand scheme for the Pacific coast was to be establishment of a center at the mouth of the Columbia River "from which trade was to be prosecuted in all directions." Supplies were to be sent out from New York with an annual ship, which would collect returns of that trade, dispose of the furs in China, and return to New York with goods for the domestic market. Astor caused to be organized an overland expedition in support of the maritime mission. The land party, following the general route of Lewis and Clark, was headed by Wilson Price Hunt (see entry); it was intended to reach the mouth of the Columbia about the same time the *Tonquin,* the company ship, arrived there. But the *Tonquin* anchored earlier, then was blown up and destroyed by an overwhelming Indian attack off Vancouver Island (see Jonathan Thorne entry) while on a brief trading mission. Hunt's party reached Astoria, the base already established at the Columbia's mouth, on February 15, 1812. On a second

ship, the *Beaver,* Hunt visited Baranov (see entry) at Sitka, Alaska, then picked up 75,000 sealskins at the Pribylov Islands and shipped them to Canton. Hunt remained in Hawaii meanwhile, where at length he chartered still another ship, the *Albatross,* to return to Astoria. The War of 1812 had been declared June 18, 1812, the Canadians bringing the first word of it to the coast by early 1813, and North West Company men, by duplicity as was supposed, purchased Astoria and its properties from the Astorians for $58,000, "a mere fraction of their value," before Hunt had arrived from Hawaii. He had no recourse but to approve the already completed sale, and leave for home. The twin disasters—the loss of the *Tonquin,* and sale of the Astoria properties—terminated Astor's grand plans for a Pacific fur empire. He had long since commenced turning his fur trade profits into New York real estate, and his general prosperity regularly enhanced, as did his political clout. Largely through his efforts Congress on April 29, 1816, passed an act which virtually excluded any but U.S. citizens from engaging in the fur trade (except as employes) on American soil and within a year Astor controlled all former Mississippi Valley posts of the North West Company, and was pushing his interests up the Missouri drainage. He succeeded in persuading Congress to abolish government trading posts (the factor system) in favor of private enterprise, meaning his own interests, and in 1822 established a Western Department of the American Fur Company; at the same time he gave the name of Northern Department to the firm's previous field of operations outside the area of the new Western Department. The latter was concerned with the Missouri and lower posts on the Mississippi and the Illinois rivers, and was directed by Samuel Abbott at St. Louis. The Northern Department embraced the region of the Great Lakes and the upper Mississippi, and was headed by Robert Stuart at Michilimackinac. In 1827 the Western Department absorbed its chief competitor, the Columbia Fur Company. Astor's firm met its match in the far west, however, from the Rocky Mountain Fur Company manned by such seasoned trappers as Fitzpatrick, Sublette and Bridger. The result was that Astor's returns were not particularly satisfactory, the fur trade itself had commenced its long decline, and in addition, Astor became convinced that silk hats inevitably would replace beaver hats for the fashionable—

an evil omen for the fur enterprise. June 1, 1834, therefore, he sold the Northern Department to a concern headed by Ramsay Crooks, former general manager of the AFC, and the Western Department to [Bernard] Pratte, [Pierre] Chouteau [Jr.] and Company of St. Louis. Astor thereafter turned his full attention to real estate and his other New York business interests, and his further career had little frontier interest. At his death he was regarded as the wealthiest man in America with an estate "conservatively" estimated at $20 million. He left $400,000 for the founding of a library, which became an element of the famed New York Public Library (see CE, p. 1395 for a brief history of that important institution), but bequests to his faithful, longtime employees reflected his acute parsimony which bordered on miserliness. He was described by the *New York Weekly Tribune* as stout and square built, 5 ft., 9 in., in height, with a high forehead and heavy features; he never lost his German accent and "wrote a wretched scrawl, setting spelling and grammar equally at defiance." Although there were those who praised what they detected as his good qualities, others were not so generous. James Gordon Bennett's *New York Herald* on April 5, 1848, said "He has exhibited at best but the ingenious powers of a self-invented money-making machine," while James Parton, author of an 1865 biography, found him selfish, grasping and ruthless, and his record assuredly confirms the latter characteristic. His employees, taking their key from the influence they knew their employer to wield in government quarters, grew arrogant and lawless in pursuit of their trade and, when interfered with by government agents, threatened to have them summarily dismissed. His traders, in company with most others, purveyed inordinate amounts of liquor to debauch the Indians and gain their furs at the cheapest possible price, while selling them their needs at the dearest. His fur trade machinations were not often particularly admirable. He died at New York City. In about 1785 he had married Sarah Todd, who aided him greatly as his fur interests expanded.

Literature abundant; CE; DAB; REAW; DCB; Cittenden, I; Paul Chrisler Phillips, *The Fur Trade,* II, Norman, Univ. of Okla. Press, 1961; Bernard DeVoto, *Across the Wide Missouri,* Boston, Houghton Mifflin Co., 1947; *Wall Street Journal,* June 5, 1979.

Aten, Ira, lawman (Sept. 3, 1863-Aug. 5, 1953). B. at Cairo, Illinois, the son of a Methodist minister, the Aten family moved to a farm near Round Rock, Texas, in 1876. As a teen-ager Aten was at Round Rock when Sam Bass was brought into town mortally wounded; he was ministered to by Ira's father, the Rev. Austin C. Aten. Ira became a crack shot and joined Company D of the Texas Rangers at 20, assigned to Border duty. In May, 1884 seven Rangers on the Rio Grande 80 miles below Laredo sighted two presumed cattle thieves and in a shootout Frank Sieker, a Ranger, was killed and another Ranger, Ben Reilly shot in the thigh, while Aten wounded both outlaws; the Rangers however were jailed by county Sheriff Dario Gonzalez on trumped-up charges, Ira spending 27 days in confinement. He was promoted to corporal and sent to west central Texas. In Williamson County in April 1887, Aten and Judd Roberts had a shootout, Roberts escaping with a wounded hand; in June Aten caught up with him again and once more shot him in the hand, Roberts escaping anew. In July in a third shootout Roberts was killed by Aten and Ranger John R. Hughes. In 1889 Aten was named sheriff of Fort Bend County during the noted Jaybirds-Woodpeckers feud and December 25 he and other lawmen, including Ira's brother, Cal, killed Alvin and Will Odle, rustlers and accused murderers in a moonlight gunbattle near Bull Head Mountain in Edwards County. Aten became sheriff of Castro County and then superintendent of the Escarbada Division of the XIT Ranch, remaining from 1895 to 1904. With his wife and five children he then moved to California where he lived until his death at Burlingame. His brothers, Cal Aten (1868-1939) and Edwin D. (Eddie) Aten (1870-1953) also joined Company D of the Texas Rangers and performed superior service.

O'Neal, *Gunfighters;* Robert W. Stephens, *Texas Ranger Sketches,* Dallas, p.p., 1972; Walter Prescott Webb, *The Texas Rangers,* Boston, Houghton Mifflin Co., 1935; information from E.F. (Ted) Mains.

Augooshaway, Ottawa chief: *see* Equeshawey

Aull, James, trader (1804-June 23, 1847). B. at Wilmington, Delaware, he went in 1836 to Lexington, Missouri, where an older brother, John Aull was established as a merchandiser; later a third brother, Robert, joined them. "The brothers were well known throughout the western country, and accumulated great fortunes." James Aull joined Samuel C. Owens in the Santa Fe trade, and both met violent deaths on their 1846 expedition. Aull was assassinated in his store at Chihuahua where he was working alone one evening when four Mexicans entered, stabbed him fatally and carried away most of his goods and money. A gold watch was overlooked and this, with his Bible, was "faithfully preserved and brought back to Missouri by his Negro servant, Andrew." "No man in western Missouri commanded [more] respect and and affection in those days, when Independence and Lexington were the starting points for Santa Fe and Oregon trails, than James Aull. He was an elder in the Lexington Presbyterian Church…an unassuming gentleman, of energy and judgment. He never married."

Susan Shelby Magoffin, *Down the Santa Fe Trail and Into Chihuahua*, Lincoln, Univ. of Neb. Press, 1982, pp. 24-25n. by Stella M. Drumm.

Austin, Tex, rodeo entrepreneur (Aug. 26, 1885-Oct. 26, 1938). The facts and date of death of flamboyant rodeo promoter Tex Austin are well established, but his origins seem permanently clouded. Even his true name is not known in this day, nor is there any definite information on his early life. An obituary article in the Santa Fe *New Mexican* restated a common belief that he was born in Victoria, East Texas, while the *New York Times* said he was born in South Carolina of Jewish parents. S. Omar Barker wrote that rodeoman Dee Bibbs told him Tex was born at St. Louis and his real name was Clarence Van Nostrand. Austin himself claimed on his marriage license application that he was born in El Paso County, Texas, the son of John Austin and Clara Crabb Austin. Other sources affirm he was born at Chicago, or on a ranch in West Texas. The legend that he went to Mexico "and threw in with Pancho Villa" sounds like a press agent's fantasy, but at any rate, following a stint in the earliest cowboy movies in California he developed an interest in "cowboy contests," as rodeos then were sometimes called, and saw for them a great future if properly promoted, which he was eager to do. At 6 ft., 4 in., in height and with a lithe build, he was a competent horseman and a man of intelligence and drive. In 1916 he was hired as arena director of the Cowboy's Reunion at Las Vegas, New Mexico. In 1917 as a full-time (though short on cash) promoter he organized a five-day rodeo at El Paso; he counted on heavy patronage from servicemen of nearby Fort Bliss, but the great influenza epidemic of that year was

just getting underway and the army base was quarantined, "attendance was poor and Tex lost his shirt." However he scratched together more funds and organized another major rodeo, this one at Wichita, Kansas, in 1918, the first on record to take place under a roof. It was a huge success, and Tex Austin was on his way. He organized rodeos of growing proportions around the country. In 1922 "he put on a granddaddy at New York's Madison Square Garden," with prizes reaching the until then unheard-of total of $25,000. Two years later he invaded London with an immense troupe, some of the cowboys arriving in London atop double-decker buses and enjoying themselves by roping top hats off of unsuspecting street strollers. At London Tex promptly ran into difficulty with the Royal Society for the Prevention of Cruelty to Animals until he assured authorities that calf-roping and some other program features would be eliminated. One legend had it that the British were cool to the show until a Cockney horseman put up a sizable bet that he could conquer one of the "trained" (as he believed) bucking horses, and after a pretty good ride was thrown for his trouble, and the crowd loved it. A Scottish animal breeder who was convinced the bulldogged steers also were trained to roll over offered a good wager that one of his wild and shaggy Highland steers would not prove so docile; when the animal was loosed in the arena and promptly downed by a bulldogger the crowd grew even more enthusiastic. The show overall proved a success. Austin went on to promote ever-growing rodeos at major American cities—Chicago, New York and elsewhere, and came to be called by some the "Daddy of Rodeo," or at least of its promotion. But as the years passed his popularity waned; a London rodeo in 1934 flopped, and Austin turned to dude ranching on his Forked Lightning Ranch east of Santa Fe. In 1936 he quit that occupation and rodeo promotion to operate a Santa Fe restaurant. This career too eventually palled and at 52 he committed suicide by inhaling automobile exhaust in his garage, after pleading in a note to his wife for "forgiveness." In addition to his widow he also left a son.

Information from Marc Simmons; Simmons, "Tex Austin, Cowboy Showman," *Santa Fe Reporter,* April 8, 1992; Jerry Armstrong, "Picked Up in the Rodeo Arena," *Western Horseman,* Vol. XLVIII, No. 5 (May 1975), 184-87; *New York Times,* Oct. 27, 1938; S. Omar Barker, "Git Fer Vegas, Cowboy!" *Frontier Times,* Vol. 42, No. 1 (Dec.-Jan. 1968), 20-21, 59, 62;

copy of marriage license, Lake Co., Ind., Oct. 27, 1923; information from National Cowboy Hall of Fame, Oklahoma City.

Avote, Southern Paiute Indian (d. c. 1897). Avote was a Southern Paiute who with his fellows lived from hand to mouth among the southern Nevada mining camps. He reportedly became incensed because of attentions miner Lars Frandsen paid to Avote's wife. At Huess Spring, a mile below El Dorado in the canyon of that name on May 12, 1897, Avote ambushed Frandsen and his helper. Frandsen was killed and the helper badly wounded. Later the Indian met Charlie Nelson for whom the present community of Nelson at the head of El Dorado Canyon was named, and killed him. Later he hid in the cabin of Charlie Monohan, partner in a mining operation, and shot and killed him, as well. The morning after the latter slaying, Avote surprised "Judge" Morton preparing a breakfast. Hoping to protect himself, Morton offered a plate of beans to the Paiute who ate the food, then killed Morton. Avote's band members became incensed at the difficulties the Paiute's slayings were causing them, arousing the antagonism of the whites. They tracked Avote to Cottonwood Island, 25 miles downriver from El Dorado, killed him and brought his head back to prove they had done so.

Don Ashbaugh, *Nevada's Turbulent Yesterday,* Los Angeles, Westernlore Press, 1963.

Ayres, George Washington, sea captain (fl. 1802-1820). In 1802-1803 he was navigator for the ship *Alexander* which left Boston July 10, 1802, under Captain John Brown to trade along the California coast. Ayres left the ship at Monterey August 17, 1803, and returned to Boston.

He joined the *Mercury* whose captain was William Heath Davis, leaving Boston in January 1806, for the Northwest Coast. After trading for furs as far north as Alaska, the vessel visited California. At Canton, China in 1808 Ayres became captain of the *Mercury,* returning to the western America coast to continue trading. From Sitka he obtained 50 Kodiak Aleut sea-otter hunters, whose catch he was obliged to share with the Russian American Fur Company. In 1809 he ransomed an Aleut held captive at the mouth of the Columbia River. After several years more of trading on the coast, Ayres and the *Mercury* were seized June 2, 1813, off Santa Barbara by the Spaniard, Nicolas Noé in the semi-privateer *Flora,* the captain and his crew held prisoner in the presidio during an investigation. José Darío Arguello, commandant, determined that Ayres was indeed engaged in clandestine trade. Noé took over the *Mercury* while the prisoners were taken to San Blas in October on another ship, the *Catalina.* Ayres had on his vessel at the time of its seizure, a Hawaiian woman, María Antonía de la Ascensión Stuart and their infant daughter, who were left in California and, according to Bancroft, "became good Catholics." Ayres' personal property was held and at his petition, the *Mercury* which was breaking up, was sold in 1815. Ayres at last was compensated for goods seized in the capture of his ship, and he either remained in California or in some manner reached Boston again. In 1820 he was reported interested with Abel Stearns (see entry) in obtaining Sacramento valley lands for a settlement, but Bancroft reported that he probably did not personally visit California again.

Pierce, *Russian America: A Biographical Dictionary;* Bancroft, California, II, *Pioneer Register.*

B

Babcock, Walter Crosby, military officer (Aug. 16, 1870-Aug. 9, 1937). B. in Massachusetts, he went to West Point and was commissioned a second lieutenant in the 8th Cavalry June 12, 1893, served at Dakota posts from 1893 to 1896 and became a first lieutenant March 2, 1899. He was assigned to Alaska and April 29, 1899, left Valdez with a pack train and necessary personnel and authority to begin construction on what was later called the "Trans-Alaskan Military Road," the route closely followed from Valdez to the Tanana River by the Richardson Highway No. 4. In this occupation Babcock was more a military engineer than cavalry officer; the initial mileage from Valdez to Copper Center on the Copper River being the most difficult to construct of the entire route. Babcock completed it in rudimentary form during his first season on the job. Rather than crossing the difficult Valdez Glacier by way of Bates Pass, he followed the Lowe River east, crossed Thompson Pass at 2,840 feet by July 27, thence worked down Ptarmagin Creek to the Chena River, continued northward by way of Tonsina valley where he also surveyed and mapped Tonsina Lake, the first time this had been done, and eventually reached the mouth of the Klutina on the Copper River at the present Copper Center. At the close of the season he returned to Valdez with his crews, arriving October 10. He had constructed or laid out 93 miles of road, built 26 bridges, one of them 121 feet long and the road excavation varied from 5 feet to 10 feet, with the right of way being grubbed out to as much as 35 feet and averaging 25 feet. This all was done at a cost of $25,000. His detailed summary of his season's work was published in *Narratives,* 670-80. Babcock became a captain of the 13th Cavalry February 2, 1901. He served in the Philippines and afterward in the United States, becoming a major of Cavalry July 1, 1916, lieutenant colonel June 28, 1917, and earned a Silver Star and Distinguished Service Medal with the American Expeditionary Force in France during World War I. He became a colonel July 1, 1920, and retired at his own request after thirty years' service November 1, 1921. He died at 67 at Washington.

Heitman; Cullum; *Narratives of Explorations in Alaska;* information from the U.S. Army Military History Inst., Carlisle Barracks, Pennsylvania; *Army Register,* Jan. 1, 1937.

Baby (often called **Duperon), Jacques,** fur trader (c. Jan. 1, 1731-c. Aug. 2, 1789). B. at Montreal, he belonged to a prominent family which had established itself in trade at Detroit before the English conquest of Canada. By 1753 he was a fur trader and Indian agent at Logstown, 18 miles below Fort Duquesne (Pittsburgh), on the Ohio River, two of his brothers also associated with the wilderness fur trade in Ohio. After the conquest of Canada, Baby refused to take the oath of allegiance to the British king but returned east; he was briefly jailed at Detroit on suspicion of plotting with Indians against the English, then went on to Montreal where he arrived in 1761. There he found that the fur business was good, profits were still to be made and another brother had moved the family headquarters from Paris to London so, according to Thwaites, "he became a loyal British subject, and during Pontiac's conspiracy furnished much assistance to the English garrison. His influence with the Indians was large, and during the Revolution and succeeding Indian wars the Detroit commandants utilized it for the British cause." In 1777 he was appointed a captain and interpreter in the Department of Indian Affairs. Although he came on hard times, in a business sense, late in the Revolution and for a time afterward, he recovered enough so that in 1785 his profits were the largest of his career. He received grants of land from various Indian tribes, some in the United States and others in Canada. He became lieutenant colonel of the Detroit militia in 1787. At some point he had lost one of his eyes, but it did not affect his business activities. He was, wrote Dale Miquelon in the *Dictionary of Canadian Biography,* "straightforward, impulsive and marked by the stubborn tenacity of the self-made man," and possessed "the warmth and humour of a generous personality." Married, he fathered 22 children, 11 of whom survived to maturity.

Reuben Gold Thwaites, Louise Phelps Kellogg, *The Revolution on the Upper Ohio, 1775-1777,* Madison, Wis. Hist. Soc., 1908; DCB IV.

Bacon, Nathaniel, colonial rebel (Jan. 2, 1647-Oct. 26, 1676). B. at Friston Hall, Suffolk, England, Bacon was a graduate of Cambridge, was related to eminent individuals, traveled on the continent, married and emigrated to Virginia, settling at Curl's Neck, on the James River. He quickly obtained a seat on the colonial council of state. Indian hostilities, or purported hostilities rose along the Potomac by the fall of 1675, ignited by the theft of a few hogs, over-reaction and murders of peace-seeking chiefs, Indian retribution to the point of killing some thirty-six whites to apparently equalize the slaying of Indians by whites, and, according to report, there were some 300 white deaths in all. The immediate result was to bring the colony into uproar. In March 1676 the Assembly ordered forts erected and rangers enrolled, but the hot-blooded Bacon (he was then twenty-nine and had been in the colony less than two years) was wildly dissatisfied with such actions of Governor Sir William Berkeley and the legislative body. The latter had sought to distinguish between hostile and friendly Indians, but Bacon would have none of it. He "urged a punitive and aggressive policy" toward *all* Indians, and when the governor refused to implement such ideas, Bacon joined a mob of frontier planters who also wanted to fight Indians—all Indians. They marched to the Roanoke River island fortress of the Occaneechi Indians near the border of Virginia and North Carolina; the natives received them as friends. Bacon told the Occaneechis that he intended to attack the Susquehannocks, formerly friends of the English but now hostile. The Occaneechis offered to assail a nearby colony of Susquehannocks for him "as a token of their friendship for the English." They returned with prisoners and furs, desiring to turn the prisoners over but to keep as booty the furs they had seized. Bacon wanted it all. His men cut down a number of Indians, seized what furs they could, and withdrew. Governor Berkeley condemned their action, as did the Council, but Bacon and his men besieged the Assembly, demanded a formal commission to hunt any Indians; under duress, the legislative body acceded to the demand, as did the governor who, however, quickly withdrew his approval and commenced to raise troops to operate against the Bacon insurgents. Bacon reacted swiftly. The governor fled across Chesapeake Bay whereupon Bacon jubilantly drew up a "Declaration of the People," on July 30, 1676, denouncing the

Berkeley administration and set off on the trail of further glory while Berkeley slipped back into Jamestown only to be forced once more to flee by Bacon's return. The young insurgent recaptured Jamestown, burned it to the ground, attempted to set up a government of his own, drafted an oath of fidelity to himself and sought to compel every citizen to sign it. But he became ill of dysentery and other ailments (the "bloody flux" and the "Lousey disease") and died some six months after he had commenced his uprising. With his passing the movement fell apart while "the Indian war subsided with cessation of expeditions against them." Berkeley once more returned, was reproved by a royal commission for severity toward the defeated rebels and was succeeded as governor by Colonel Herbert Jeffreys. Berkeley returned to England in May 1677 to plead his case before the Crown but died on July 9, "a broken man, before seeing the king." There is a distinct lack of consensus in the assessment of Bacon's Rebellion, students differing as to whether he was a distinguished "torchbearer of the Revolution" a century later, or "a ne'er-do-well rabble-rouser who sought to vent his anger and frustration on defenceless Indians." These poles are represented best by the Wertenbaker and Washburn studies.

DAB; REAW; Thomas J. Wertenbaker, *Torchbearer of the Revolution: The Story of Bacon's Rebellion and Its Leader,* Princeton (N.J.) Univ. Press, 1940; Wilcomb E. Washburn, *The Governor and the Rebel: A History of Bacon's Rebellion in Virginia,* Chapel Hill, Univ. of N.C. Press, 1957; Douglas Edward Leach, *Arms for Empire,* N.Y., The Macmillan Co., 1973; info. from E.F. (Ted) Mains.

Bagley, James Warren, topographer (1881-1947). A topographer for the Geological Survey, he began work in the Yukon-Tanana rivers region of Alaska in 1907, continuing it until 1911 when he commenced five years' work on topographic surveys in south-central Alaska. Orth said that during the latter period he "experimented with the use of panoramic cameras for mapping."

Orth, 7.

Bagot, Charles, diplomat (Sept. 23, 1781-May 19, 1843). B. at Staffordshire, England, he was named on July 31, 1815 minister plenipotentiary to the United States where he helped settle differences resulting from the War of 1812 and secured neutrality of the Great Lakes. The (Richard) Rush-Bagot Convention of 1817, as ratified by the U.S. Senate provided for virtual disarmament of the U.S.-Canadian frontier and "it is important because it set a precedent for the pacific settlement of the Anglo-American difficulties and because it inaugurated a policy of strict peace between the United States and Canada" which has largely endured to the present time. May 23, 1820, Bagot was named ambassador to St. Petersburg where he not only worked to modify a Russian edict of 1821 which purported to make the North Pacific a Russian sea, but also labored on negotiations to define the boundary between Russian and British possessions on the northwestern continent. Besides urging an east-west southern limit to Russian territory, he worked for a north-south eastern limit to it. "This eventually was adopted, in spite of efforts by the Russian American Company representative, N.S. Mordvinov to establish the Rocky Mountains as the eastern boundary." Bagot's efforts were largely responsible for establishment of the present Alaskan-Canadian boundary northward to the Arctic Ocean. Charles Bagot's subsequent career was noteworthy, although with little impact on the American frontier. He became governor-general of Canada in 1841, but died two years later at Kingston, Ontario. Mount Bagot, a 7,155-ft. peak 13 miles southeast of Skagway on the border with Canada, was named for him in 1923.

Pierce, *Russian America: A Biographical Dictionary;* CE; Orth, 99.

Bailey, John, military officer (May 4, 1748-July 3, 1816). B. in Northumberland County, Virginia, he moved to Kentucky around 1776, living at Harrodsburg. In 1778 he was commissioned a lieutenant and joined George Rogers Clark's Kaskaskia expedition; in August Clark sent him to the aid of Captain Leonard Helm at Vincennes. He then returned to Kaskaskia and became part of an expedition to recapture Vincennes and was sent with a detachment of fourteen men to initiate an attack on Fort Sackville, the first post built at Vincennes. When Clark left the community, Bailey was left in charge of part of the garrison. In November 1779 he attended a council of war at Louisville, where he was promoted to captain. In 1780 he was with Colonel John Montgomery on a campaign to Rock River, and early in 1781 commanded Fort Jefferson, on the Mississippi.

In January 1781 he was named to command at Vincennes, subsequently served at other posts. At the close of the Revolution he became a Baptist minister, influential in spreading the faith. He died at his home in Lincoln County, Kentucky.

Thwaites/Kellogg, *Frontier Defense on the Upper Ohio, 1777-1778.*

Baker, George, pioneer (d. 1802). Of German birth, Baker arrived in America in 1750 and married an English girl; they had five children. About 1772 they moved west and settled about four miles below Logstown on the divide between the Ohio River and Raccoon Creek. In late July 1777 a raiding party of Indians captured the family, destroyed what possessions they had in their cabin, and took the prisoners to Detroit, treating them well enroute and at the post upon arrival. Eventually the family was released unharmed, lived for a time on the south branch of the Potomac River and finally returned to their home on Raccoon Creek where Baker died in 1802.

Thwaites/Kellogg, *Frontier Defense on the Upper Ohio, 1777-1778.*

Baker, Henry, captive (fl. c. 1781). A youth of 18, he was captured about 1781 by a party of hostile Indians, probably Shawnees, at the Narrows of Wheeling Creek, presently West Virginia. Brought to Upper Sandusky, Ohio, he joined nine Kentucky prisoners. All ten were required to run the gantlet, Baker being first and very active, did so without receiving a blow, which so enraged one young Indian that he knocked Baker down with a club before he reached the council house. The nine Kentuckians were burned, one each day until all had "miserably perished." Baker was forced to witness each execution before his turn came. Ordered to be tied to a stake, he parleyed with the Indians, for he sighted a white man on horseback approaching. When the man arrived Baker ran to him, imploring him to save his life and learning that the white was the notorious Simon Girty (see entry). Girty questioned Baker as to who he was and where he was from, and interceded in his behalf, his efforts successful. The Indians relented and let Baker go free. Girty interviewed him at length, questioning him closely about Wheeling and its environs, leading Baker to believe that Girty intended to make him a guide for a war party to that place. Instead, Girty arranged for him to be sent to Detroit, where Major Arent Schuyler DePeyster (1736-1822) set him free. Baker went to work with a trader to the Indians, then with two other captives escaped and the three made their way to their homes safely.

C.W. Butterfield, *History of the Girtys*, Cincinnati, Robert Clarke & Co., 1890 (1950), 127, with ref..

Baker, Joseph, naval officer (1767-1817). He joined the British navy at an early age becoming a lieutenant in 1790 and joined Vancouver's *Discovery* for the exploration of the Northwest Coast. April 30, 1792, during an extensive examination of Puget Sound, Baker, as third lieutenant, discovered the mountain named for him, a 10,750-ft. peak in the North Cascades range (see Vancouver entry). Later that year at Nootka Sound Baker was named second lieutenant of the *Discovery* and within a year its first lieutenant. "The principal charts made of the exploration of the Northwest Coast were drawn by Baker...and were models of drafting skill." Point Baker, the northwesternmost tip of Prince of Wales Island, was named for him September 8, 1793, by Vancouver. In 1795 when the expedition had returned to England, Vancouver turned over command of the ship to Baker. His subsequent naval career was creditable. Baker was married and fathered sons of noteworthy records.

Pierce, *Russian America: A Biographical Dictionary;* Orth, 100.

Baker, Marcus, cartographer (Sept. 23, 1849-1903). B. at Kalamazoo, Michigan, Baker was graduated from the University of Michigan in 1870 (and earned a doctorate from Columbia University in 1896). He worked for the Coast and Geodetic Survey from 1873 to 1886, and from 1886 to 1903 for the Geological Survey. He surveyed the Aleutian Islands and the Alaskan coast from Dixon Entrance, at the lower extremity of the Alaskan Panhandle, to Point Belcher, northeast of Wainwright on the Arctic coast, accomplishing this vast task in 1873, 1874 and 1880, this in the party of William Healey Dall. Baker and Dall compiled an *Alaskan Coast Pilot* published in 1883, incorporating the names bestowed by himself, additional C&GS personnel and others on Alaskan features. Baker also prepared the first listing of Alaskan names which was published by the Geological Survey in 1900 and led to a 1902 publication of a *Geographic Dictionary of Alaska.* He commenced preparation of a second edition, but died before the work

was completed; it was carried on by James McCormick of the Survey, and published in 1906. Baker also was cartographer for the Venezuela Boundary Commission, and authored *Northwest Boundary of Texas; Survey of Northwestern Boundary of the United States,* and other bulletins, geological and mathematic papers.

Orth, 7; *Who Was Who.*

Baldwin, Evelyn Briggs, polar explorer (July 22, 1862-Oct. 25, 1933). B. at Springfield, Missouri, he was graduated in 1885 from North Central College, Naperville, Illinois, traveled in Europe, taught school and was an observer for the federal Weather Bureau from 1892 until 1900. In 1893 he joined Peary as meteorologist and fifth in rank on an expedition to north Greenland, his "Meteorological and Auroral Notes" being published in Peary's *Northward Over the 'Great Ice'* in 1898. Baldwin published *The Search for the North Pole or Life in the Great White World* (1896) and the following year went to Spitsbergen to join Salomon August Andrée's balloon expedition toward the Pole, fortunately arriving after the doomed expedition had departed. In 1898 he was second in command of William Wellman's polar expedition, serving principally as meteorologist. He explored Franz Josef Land, north of Siberia in late 1898 and in 1899 explored Graham Bell Land, the northeasternmost island of the Franz Josef archipelago. In 1901 he published *Meteorological Observations of the Second Wellman Expedition* and other papers. In April 1901 he was appointed inspector for the Signal Corps, but found patronage for his polar work with William Ziegler (see entry), who financed the Baldwin-Ziegler polar expedition which left Norway in three vessels July 27, 1901, with the avowed intention of reaching the North Pole. It had a complement of 42 men, with vast stores, 15 Siberian ponies and 400 dogs. Three supply depots were established on Franz Josef Land and three reserve stations on the Greenland coast for the return trip. But the expedition floundered during the winter when half the dogs died, equipment was wrecked, supplies were depleted and the failure of a supply ship to reach the base occurred. July 1, 1902, the return voyage was commenced. Baldwin was unable to get financing for another expedition, and the Cook and Peary explorations claiming to have reached the Pole disheartened him and he "relapsed into obscurity." He worked for a variety of government agencies and died in an automobile acci-

dent at Washington, D.C., "an inglorious ending of an adventurous career." He never married.
Who's Who in America, 1901-1933; DAB.

Baldwin, Gordon C., archeologist, anthropologist (June 5, 1908-Dec. 20, 1983). B. at Portland, Oregon, he was graduated and received his master's degree from the University of Arizona and a doctorate in archeology and anthropology in 1941 from the University of Southern California. From 1934-36 he specialized in tree-ring dating matters at the Arizona State Museum under auspices of the Carnegie Institution of Washington, D.C. Baldwin was an archeologist with the National Park Service from 1940-53, and instructor in archeology at the University of Omaha, 1953-54. He participated in archeological expeditions to sites in Arizona, New Mexico, Nevada, Utah and Colorado. During his career he wrote twenty-five books, fiction and non-fiction, on Indians and archeology. Among them were *America's Buried Past* (1962); *The Ancient Ones* (1963); *The World of Prehistory* (1963); *Stone Age Peoples Today* (1964); *The Riddle of the Past* (1965); *The Warrior Apaches: A Story of the Chiricahua and Western Apache* (1965); *Race Against Time* (1966); *Strange People and Stranger Customs* (1967); *Calendars to the Past* (1967), and *How the Indians Really Lived* (1967). Baldwin died at Mountain View, California, survived by his widow and two daughters.
Tucson, *Arizona Daily Star*, Jan. 10, 1984; Bernard Klein, Daniel Icolari, *Reference Encyclopedia of the American Indian*, N.Y., B. Klein and Co., 1967.

Bancroft, John, sea captain (d. Nov. 1838). An American captain and fur trader, in 1835 he took the brig *Convoy*, a Honolulu vessel owned by Eliab Grimes from Hawaii to Kaigani, southeastern Dall Island on the north side of the Dixon Entrance of the Alexander Archipelago. Here he picked up twenty-seven Haida Indian hunters, taking them to the California coast for sea otter hunting. "From California the brig seems to have gone to Honolulu before returning the Haida hunters to their homes." August 6, 1837, Bancroft, now captain of the brig *Lama* left Hawaii and picked up twenty-five Haidas at Kaigani, reached California January 1, 1838, and made two round trips from those waters to Hawaii; Bancroft's wife joined him at least for the second voyage. She was described by Ogden as "a Kanaka lady," that is, of Hawaiian birth. Bancroft's heavy drinking, his wife's "strong racial antago-

nisms toward the wild Kaiganies," added to the "quarrelsome nature" of the Indian hunters themselves, who became incensed over the slim rations given them when hunting was poor, all contributed to dangerous friction. Off Santa Cruz of the Channel Islands, Bancroft and the Haidas came to a shouting match, the Indians brought guns aboard from their baidarkas and possibly under prodding by Yeltenow, one of the Indian leaders, firing commenced and Bancroft was mortally shot; his wife, trying to protect him being "terribly wounded." The Indians then demanded that the mate, a Mr. Robinson, take the ship back to Kaigani. There on December 26, 1838, they disembarked, taking most of the valuable otter pelts but "leaving 5 skins and 21 tails as a present for Mr. Robinson." Mrs. Bancroft returned her husband's body to Hawaii for burial. The Bancroft affair had far-reaching ramifications for controlling illegal otter hunting along the California coast.
Pierce, *Russian America: A Biographical Dictionary;* Ogden; Orth, 485.

Banner, Ivan Ivanovich, Russian administrator (d. 1816). A Dane, he is first reported as a provincial inspector in Zasheiversk, province of Irkutsk, Siberia. He left to establish a colony of agriculturists at Bering Bay, but the ship was damaged and Banner forced to remain about a year on one of the Kurile Islands. At Unalaska Island, Banner found that a planned agricultural endeavor had been shelved, so in 1804 he was ordered to Kodiak Island. Here upon the departure of Baranov (see entry) for Sitka, Banner assumed charge of the first permanent white settlement in the Alaskan region, and remained there for the rest of his life. When the shipwrecked Archibald Campbell (see entry) arrived there in 1808, and both feet were amputated because of frostbite, Banner hired Campbell to teach the native children English so that they could serve as interpreters and Campbell have an immediate source of income. Banner was favorably mentioned by Langsdorff, Rezanov and others during his twelve years on the island. March 22, 1817 the administration of the Russian American Company noted in a communication to Baranov that it had learned of the death of "the elderly Banner," who had left in charge of the Kodiak station one Grigorii Potorochin, of whom little more is known. Banner Bay on Atka Island, Banner Lake on Baranof Island and Banner Point on Banner Bay were named for Ivan Banner.

Bancroft, *Alaska; The Russian American Colonies;*
Zagoskin; Orth, 104.

Baraga, Frederic, Roman Catholic missionary
(June 29, 1797-Jan. 19, 1868). B. in Slovenia,
then part of Austria but today of Yugoslavia, his
parents were Slovenians of good family, though
not of the aristocracy. When he was 9 he was sent
to be privately educated at Laibach (today's
Ljubljana), later took a law course at the University of Vienna, but determined in 1821 to enter
the church. He returned to Laibach for seminary
and was ordained September 21, 1823. For seven
years he did parish work but in 1830 offered himself for missionary service in America, in his
application stating he was familiar with German,
Illyrian (an ancient language of the Balkans),
French, Latin, Italian and English. He was
accepted, reached Cincinnati in 1831 and at once
commenced learning Ottawa; in May he was sent
as a missionary to the Ottawa village of Arbre
Croche (now Harbor Springs, Michigan). He set
to work enthusiastically, visiting other villages
of the tribe, islands in Lake Michigan and in 1833
established a mission at Grand River, the site of
Grand Rapids, Michigan. He soon incurred the
enmity of traders however, who objected to his
scathing denunciation of their liquor traffic and
in 1835 Baraga was transferred to distant Lake
Superior. July 27, 1835, he arrived at La Pointe,
the American Fur Company's post of Madeline
Island, near Bayfield, Wisconsin. Here he found
himself among Chippewa Indians and set about
learning their language for it was the *lingua fran-
ca* of the North Woods. He wrote several religious works in that language, and also wrote
*Theoretical and Practical Grammar of the
Otchipwe Language* (the Chippewas also being
known as Ojibways), published in 1850, and the
Dictionary of the Otchipwe Language (1853),
still useful to scholars of those Indians. He served
an 80,000 square mile area, sometimes referred
to today as "Baragaland." He made constant
journeys by canoe in summer and snowshoe in
winter, visiting among other places Grand
Portage, Fond du Lac and L'Anse at Keweenaw
Bay which is now the seat of Baraga County,
Upper Michigan. There he began a mission in
1843, soon removing his residence to there,
where he built log houses for his Indian converts
and taught them some of the ways of civilization.
November 1, 1853, he was consecrated bishop of
Upper Michigan, based at Sault Ste. Marie. In
1865 he built a cathedral at Marquette, a new

community, and there Baraga moved his residence, and there he was buried following his
death. He had become known in life as the
"Apostle of the Chippewas," the foremost
Catholic leader in Michigan, Wisconsin and Minnesota during the first half of the 19th century.
New York Times, July 1, 1984; DAB.

Baranov, Aleksandr Andreevich, Russian
administrator-trader (1746-Apr. 16, 1819 O.S.).
B. into a middle-class family at Kargopol, 300
miles northeast of St. Petersburg, Baranov at 15
became a clerk in a Moscow store and commenced a program of self-education. In 1780 he
settled at Irkutsk, near Lake Baikal, Siberia
where he managed a glass factory and distillery,
then moved to the Anadyr River in northeastern
Siberia and became a fur trader, successful until
the Chukchi natives plundered his business,
bankrupting him. At Okhotsk, on the
Khabarovsk coast he met Grigori Shelikhov who
with Ivan Golikov had formed a fur company
headquartered on Kodiak Island, Alaska. Shelikhov was impressed with Baranov and named
him organizing manager for the Kodiak firm
under an initial five-year contract, the terms at
the outset clearing him of his debts for the
Anadyr debacle. Baranov had left a wife and
children at his Kargopol home, and never saw
them again during the remaining thirty years of
his life, although he provided "amply" for them.
In Alaska he would take a Kenai native, probably
an Aleut, for a more conveniently located "wife,"
continuing the alliance during his years as head
of an ever-expanding trading concern. August
10, 1790, Baranov sailed from Okhotsk aboard
the *Trekh Sviatiteli* for Kodiak Island, but the
ship stopped over at Unalaska Island for water. A
storm thrust her upon the shore, the wreck broke
up, an effort to secure succor from Kodiak failed
and Baranov was forced to winter with his 52-
man company under straightened circumstances,
though through his energy and ingenuity all but
three survived. He reached Three Saints (the present port of Kodiak) June 27, 1791. He immediately assumed charge of all establishments of the
Shelikhov-Golikov concern; several other private trading companies were rivals, but he out-
managed and outlasted them when in 1799 the
Russian American Company was chartered and
granted a monopoly for colonization and trade in
Alaska with Baranov (who did not hear about
this development or his allotment of shares worth
25,000 rubles until 1802) as virtual monarch over

all. He would not be bothered by directives or advice from the company directors or imperial agencies so long as generous dividends arrived regularly, and he saw that they did. Baranov, wrote Bancroft, "was no ordinary man. [He was] of broad experience, liberal-minded and energetic, politic enough to please at once the government and the company, not sufficiently just or humane to interfere with the interests of the company, yet having care enough...to avoid bringing discredit on himself or his office...That he was not burdened with religion, was loose in morals, sometimes drunk and would lie officially without scruple, there is no doubt; yet...his indulgences were periodical rather than continuous." He was subject to melancholy and occasional passionate rages, invariably followed by "contrite generosity" to smooth over ruffled feelings. He was open-handed to the poor, shrewd if uncultured and "among all those who came from Russia, he alone was able to stem the tide of encroachment by roving traders from the United States or Britain." The natives, so cruelly oppressed by more ruthless Russians, respected Baranov despite his unprepossessing appearance. He was short, thin, clean-shaven, balding with a red fringe around his pate and, in later years, wearing a grotesque black wig bound to his overlarge head with a black handkerchief. He must have presented a novel appearance but, so far as company affairs went, he was all business. He dispatched exploring expeditions into the wilderness. Fur-bearing creatures were abundant in Alaska, but the traders were primarily interested in the sea otters that thrived among the island-bound waterways and along the coast as far south as Spanish California. Their luxuriant fur was so highly prized in Europe and China and profits from the trade so enormous as to bring the animals to virtual extinction within a century. During the first twenty years alone of the Russian American Company furs valued at 35 million rubles ($17.5 million) were sent out of Alaska. Baranov organized huge fleets of baidarkas, or Aleut kayaks and sent them on massive hunts among the archipelagos to the south as far as they could safely go, though many of the tiny craft still were lost to accidents or the hazards of their perilous specialty. Elsewhere Baranov was endlessly occupied: pacifying hostile natives when possible and fighting them when not, settling vexing problems with Orthodox missionaries who often "had neither the training nor the temperament for life in a hard country," trying to win

cooperation from aloof Russian naval officers who brought in an occasional vessel and the notion that they were superior to "the mere trader" Baranov in social position and therefore in judgment, trading with canny merchantmen from New England or elsewhere for supplies for his empire, building ships for the company's use, writing reports and letters describing the complexities of the business or seeking material support. In 1802 Tlingit Indians, an Athapascan people, captured and destroyed Baranov's post at Sitka, slaughtering many people; he retook the site in 1804 and built a stronger station called Novo Arkhangelsk. His contracts with the company were routinely renewed for five-year terms until he was finally relieved in 1818 after 28 years of service in Russian America. In 1803 he made the first of many agreements with Yankee captains to loan them Aleuts and their baidarkas by which sea otter hunting could be pursued down the coast as far as Lower California, with half of the number of pelts turned over to Baranov in payment; this was profitable for both parties, and extended the lucrative trade to Canton and beyond. Fort Ross in California north of San Francisco was built by Baranov's protege Ivan Kuskov in 1812 as the southernmost Russian colony, but an attempt to extend the company's influence to the Sandwich Islands (Hawaii) failed. Vagrant rumors and whispers of irregularities in his accounts, and possible profiteering at company expense had reached Russia from time to time, as it would about any employee so long maintained in so isolated and profitable a see. Over the years Baranov had repeatedly asked to be relieved; on two occasions the requests were accepted but his relief had died before reaching Alaska. When at length a successor arrived, Leontii Andreianovich Hegemeister (Gagemeyster), all the company's books and records were peremptorily ordered turned over to its commissioner, Kyrill T. Khlebnikov who in the most minute examination failed to find a single discrepancy—everything was in perfect order and every ruble accounted for. Baranov had been "ill requited for his long and faithful service," wrote Bancroft. "To him was due, more than to all others, the success of the Russian colonies in America...Here, amid these wintry solitudes, he had raised towns and villages, built a fleet of sea-going ships, and laid the basis of trade with American and Asiatic ports. All this he had accomplished while paying regular dividends to shareholders; and now [he was] called to render an account as an unfaithful steward," a test which he passed triumphantly. Upon the advice of Captain Vassili M. Golovnin he determined to return to Russia where, his old friend urged, he could "still be of great service to the company by giving advice to the managers on colonial affairs." November 27, 1818, he sailed on the *Kutusof,* arrived at Batavia March 7 and on April 16, 1819, he died at 73 aboard ship in the strait of Sunda, his body committed to the sea. Khlebnikov wrote of him, "He never knew what avarice was, and never hoarded riches. He...gave freely to all who had any claims upon him...He always lived on his means, and never drew his balance from the company...There are not a few now living in the colonies whom he helped out of difficulty, and many a remittance he sent to Russia to the relatives of persons who had died, or were by misfortune prevented from supporting those dependent upon them." While diminutive in stature, Baranov was an empire-building giant as in his relationships with others, in the basic integrity of his dealings with the varied peoples who came his way, and in the truly great impact he left upon northwestern America and Russian expansionism.

Literature abundant; Bancroft, *Alaska;* Khlebnikov, *Colonial Russian America,* trans. by Basil Dmytryshyn, E.A.P. Crownhart-Vaughan, Portland, Or. Hist. Soc., 1976; REAW; DAB.

Barber, Henry, sea captain (d. c. 1807). B. at Hamburg, he became a sea captain in England and was active on the Alaskan coast, once described as a "pirate," which if overstated did nothing to obscure the fact that he was something of a freebooter. In 1794 he took the brig *Arthur* from Bengal to Australia and from there to the Northwest Coast, arriving at Chichagov Island July 15 and leaving for Bengal on the 23rd. Barber made a second trading voyage to the Northwest Coast in 1795-96. A Kolosh (Tlingit) chief complained that around that time Barber invited him aboard, shackled and would not release him until the Kolosh had delivered over sea otter pelts, but this may be a confusion with a second incident of this kind several years later, or perhaps it was simply Barber's manner of doing business. Enroute to Canton, Barber's ship struck a shoal near Pearl Harbor, Oahu, the vessel being lost, six crewmen drowned, but the cargo salvaged. Commanding the *Cheerful,* Barber visited the Northwest Coast in 1801, according to report, taking a cargo to China the

following year. As captain of the *Unicorn,* Barber once more reached the Alaskan coast June 28, 1802, two days after the Kolosh had destroyed the RAC post near present Sitka, slaying Russians they found there and confiscating a wealth in otter pelts. The assault was led by a chief named Sheatka, for whom Sitka was named. Barber was quoted by Pierce as having reported in his journal, part of which was published in the *Sydney* (Australia) *Gazette* November 18, 1804, that he had found the scene "utterly destroyed by fire, and the mangled bodies of about twenty men lying scattered among the ruins, a prey to the ravens and wild beasts of the forests, a sight as horrid and shocking as human beings could witness." He rescued what survivors he could find. Ivan Petrov (see entry), in *Narratives of Exploration in Alaska* (p. 186) wrote that Barber "succeeded in enticing two of the most prominent chiefs on board of his craft and into his cabin. After feasting them at his table and plying them with drink he placed them in irons, and, having quite a battery of guns, was able to make his own terms for the release of [the] prisoners," including 18 women who had been washing clothes when captured by the Indians. "His terms were the surrender of the captive women and of 2,000 sea-otter skins...The conditions were accepted, and Barber sailed at once for Kadiak. Here the captain demanded of Baranov (see entry) for his men and women a payment of 50,000 rubles for the time spent in rescuing them. With this demand Baranov could not or would not comply, and after many days an agreement was arrived at on the basis of the payment of 10,000 rubles." The Boston sea captain John Ebbets apparently accompanied Barber to Kodiak from Sitka and according to Khlebnikov (see entry) the RAC interests on the island purchased an additional 70,000 rubles worth of goods from the two vessels. Pierce reports that according to a Rezanov letter of 1805, Barber, when he reached Hawaii, learned that Russia and England were then at war and was incensed because he had not been aware of it while at Kodiak when he might have plundered the company whose warehouse bulged with furs and other potential booty. According to one report, Barber late in 1802 took the *Unicorn* to London, but c. October 1804 he arrived at Sydney, Australia, where he acknowledged that he had hanged one of the Indian hostages at Sitka, asserting it had been done in concert with Ebbets and Captain William Cunningham, also from Boston, the execution an example to recalcitrant tribesmen who were reluctant to bring forth the captives sought, "after which the rest of the captives…were delivered." In 1805 Barber was said to have gone to Kodiak, again reportedly with designs upon the settlement there, but was dissuaded by the presence of an armed Russian ship in the harbor. Whether true or not, the incident had a peaceful conclusion and in the spring of 1807 he once more arrived at Kodiak Island, selling the ship and its cargo to the RAC for 42,000 Spanish piasters. In June he sailed from Kodiak with the RAC brig *Sitkha* for Okhotsk with a cargo of furs. After a rough passage the ship arrived at Petropavlovsk September 7 and Barber left there as a passenger September 27, the vessel laden with about 100,000 rubles worth of Cantonese goods, bound for Okhotsk. October 2 the ship struck a shoal at the mouth of the Kamchatka River, rolled over on her side, then was blown helplessly to sea and although the crew and passengers were all saved, the cargo and personal belongings were lost. Barber was left without funds or resources and "later, probably in the same year, he committed suicide."

Pierce, *Russian America: A Biographical Dictionary; Narratives of Explorations in Alaska;* Bancroft, *Alaska; Colonial Russian America: Kyrill T. Khlebnikov's Reports, 1817-1832,* trans. by Basil Dmytryshyn, E.A.P. Crownhart-Vaughan, Portland, Or. Hist. Society, 1976.

Barcelo, Gertrudes (La[s] Tules), gambler, madame (d. c. 1851). B. at Taos, New Mexico, she removed around 1830 to Santa Fe where opportunities appeared more lucrative for one of "very loose habits," such as she. She became an habitué of gambling establishments where monte was the favored game; although luck proved elusive for several years and "she spent her days in lowliness and misery," finally good fortune came her way and she collected enough funds to open a bank of her own. She was a woman of obvious intelligence, considerable presence, her profession(s) supplied her with not only a wide clientele but also influence, until "she found herself in possession of a very handsome fortune." In 1843 she sent to the United States around $10,000 to be invested in goods, no doubt for resale in New Mexico to add to her competence. During all this time she continued her infatuation with monte and came to be considered "the most expert 'monte dealer' in all Santa Fe." In 1846 Susan Magoffin found her "a stately dame of a certain age, the possessor of a portion of that shrewd sense and fascinating manner necessary to allure the wayward, inexperienced youth to the hall of final ruin." Stella M. Drumm, editor of Magoffin's narrative, continued that Gertrudes "of fascinating manners and distinctly Spanish type of beauty,…became a great favorite in official circles. In her long sala balls were given, where the officers attached to the Mexican garrison disported themselves as inclination demanded…The card rooms were patronized by the *elite*, and hundreds of thousands of dollars were won and lost in this 'sporting emporium.'" She was a favorite among American officers during the invasion of 1846 and afterward, particularly after she had learned from a mulatto servant of the conspiracy which culminated in the Taos Uprising of January 19, 1847; La Tules communicated to military authorities the facts of the pending revolt, and the names of important figures connected with it. It was reported that Gertrudes loaned to the United States government $1,000 to enable Lieutenant Colonel David D. Mitchell to fulfill his instructions to open communications between Brigadier General John Ellis Wool., supposed to be in Chihuahua, and the Army of the North during the Mexican War. Gertrudes was unenthusiastic about loaning the money, legend says, until Mitchell won her good graces by escorting her to a ball, walking into the room "with this notorious woman on his arm, which so flattered her that she consented to make the loan." She died, probably at Santa Fe, but the exact date and circumstances of her demise are not reported.

Josiah Gregg, *Commerce of the Prairies,* ed. by Max L. Moorhead, Norman, Univ. of Okla. Press, 1954; Susan Magoffin, *Down the Santa Fe Trail and Into Mexico,* Lincoln, Univ. of Neb. Press, 1982; Twitchell, *Leading Facts,* II, 233n, 168.

Barnard, Edward Chester, topographer (Nov. 13, 1863-Feb. 6, 1921). B. at New York City, he was graduated from Columbia University in 1884 and immediately went to work as a topographer for the Geological Survey. He mapped sections of Kentucky, Tennessee, Virginia and New York State in the east, and California, Idaho, Montana, Oregon and Washington in the west. In 1898 he had charge of a Geological Survey party sent to Alaska to map the Fortymile River mining area near the Canadian border northwest of Dawson. His work was published the next year by Congress under the title, *Maps and Descriptions* *of Routes of Exploration in Alaska in 1898.* In 1900 he made surveys of the Nome district of the Seward Peninsula, his work published as an atlas sheet in the Geological Survey's *Reconnaissance of the Cape Nome and Norton Bay Regions,* in 1900. Barnard was chief topographer for the United States and Canadian Boundary Survey from 1903-15, surveying and relocating the boundary line along the 49th Parallel from the Pacific Coast, through Lake of the Woods, along the Rainy River and through Rainy Lake. He was appointed commissioner on the part of the United States for defining and marking the boundary except through the Great Lakes and St. Lawrence River, and surveying and marking the boundary between Alaska and Canada from 1915-21. His home was at Washington, D.C.

Orth, 8-9; *Who Was Who..*

Barnard, John James, British naval officer (July 29, 1826-Feb. 16, 1851). B. at Tothill, near Plymouth, the son of Admiral Edward Barnard, he entered the Royal Navy October 28, 1841. In November 1847 he took his examination for a lieutenancy and in that rank served aboard HMS *Enterprise,* engaged in the widespread search for the lost Sir John Franklin and his polar expedition. While Barnard's vessel was anchored at St. Michael on Norton Sound, Alaska, he was sent inland to investigate rumors that a Franklin party had been murdered near Lake Mintokh, 300 miles east of Nulato near the present Minto, 40 miles northwest of Fairbanks. He reached Nulato, on the middle Yukon River, where he was guest of the fur company commandant, Vassili Deryabin (see entry). In furtherance of his mission Barnard wished to interrogate Larion, a shaman and great chief of the militant Koyukon, an Athapascan Indian people, but the peremptory manner in which he summoned the chief was so abusive it enhanced the Indian's ire, already stirred by white advances to his two daughters. An attack was organized against the trading post and Barnard and Deryabin were among those killed. The officer, who had been reading in bed, aimlessly fired two pistol shots as the assailants burst in upon him, but was stabbed mortally in the stomach by Larion himself, as the chief later boasted, the Indian adding that he had slain Deryabin as well. Details of the affair, in which many of the post personnel and hangers-on were slain, were learned by Bancroft from Ivan Konnygen who had accompanied Larion on the adventure, although taking no hostile part, as he

insisted. Pierce, who has done the most complete research of the incident and described it most fully, considered a fiction the Ivan Konnygen version as given by Bancroft.

Bancroft, *Alaska;* info. from William Foote, British Pub. Rec. Svc, Kew, Richmond, Surrey; Orth; Pierce, *Russian America: A Biographical Dictionary.*

Barney, James Mitchell, historian, pioneer (Oct. 22, 1874-June 15, 1965). B. in Arizona, he was educated in private schools in California and, at length, was graduated from Stanford University in 1895 with a degree in engineering. One of his classmates was Herbert Hoover, later President of the United States. Barney worked as a surveyor in Arizona, then became a licensed land surveyor in California and returned finally to Arizona in 1902, becoming a topographical draftsman with the U.S. Surveyor's Office. He performed federal work until 1932, becoming a draftsman for the State Land Department in 1938 and later was assistant office engineer in the U.S. Grazing Service, District of Arizona. He had meanwhile pursued his interest in territorial history, writing columns for the *Phoenix Gazette* and other journals, while the maps he created were occasionally used to illustrate the books of others. He knew many of the pioneers of the Territory, including such figures as Wyatt Earp and Charles Poston. His historical articles were distinguished by careful and accurate research, often from original and primary sources. His best-known work of frontier interest was a 45-page pamphlet, *Tales of Apache Warfare* which remains today, more than half a century later, as historically sound and as useful as the day it was printed. He also published a pamphlet-history of Yuma and studies of the noted Arizona pioneers, King S. Woolsey and Jack Swilling. Barney assembled a considerable collection of photographs of historical Phoenix and the pioneers of Arizona, most of the collection given to the State Library at Phoenix and to Arizona State University at Tempe. He was a 10th generation descendant of Benjamin Franklin. Barney died at Phoenix.

Patricia Bowe, "James Mitchell Barney: Historian of Historians," *Arizoniana,* Vol. IV, No. 2 (Summer, 1963), 28-34; Barney, *Tales of Apache Warfare,* Phoenix, p.p., 1933; *Phoenix Gazette,* June 15, 1965; info. from Dee Riegel of the *Arizona Republic.*

Barr, Alexander, frontiersman (d. c. 1785). One of a group of Scot-Irish who in 1769 removed from the Cumberland Valley to Derry Township, Westmoreland County, Pennsylvania, of which Barr eventually became county lieutenant. The Barr settlement was about a mile from New Derry, northeast of Greensburg; the settlement included a blockhouse known as Fort Barr. During a 1778 attack on the fort, one of the Barrs was shot and killed. Alexander Barr went down the Ohio River about 1785 with Richard Wallace (see entry), and was killed by Indians, reportedly for "trespassing" on their lands while he and Wallace were engaged in locating lands for their own. Wallace also was killed.

Thwaites/Kellogg, *Frontier Defense on the Upper Ohio, 1777-1778.*

Barrera, José, lariat artist (May 10, 1876-Nov. 16, 1949). B. at San Antonio, Texas, he became a cowboy in the Rio Grande brush country and an expert roper. In 1897 he helped deliver show stock to Major Gordon W. (Pawnee Bill) Lillie (see entry) for his traveling Wild West show. Lillie was impressed with Barrera's abilities as roper and horseman and signed him on as "Mexican Joe," to become "chief" of his vaqueros. In Barrera's first season with Lillie the show toured the east, going from one success to another. In his many years with that show and others, he toured every state in the union, several Canadian provinces, Mexico and Europe. Mexican Joe won national publicity at Washington, D.C., when for a local zoo he roped a runaway elephant; at Albany, New York, a heavy circus wagon careened out of control down a steep grade and Joe roped the two lead horses. The weight of the wagon upset his riding horse and Joe's leg was broken though the vehicle was stopped and spectator casualties avoided. At Chicago a woman bronc rider was thrown and dragged across an arena when her boot caught in the stirrup; Joe's ready rope stopped the bucking horse and saved the rider from certain injury. He was master of the show's rough string and an able rider of bucking horses himself. Joe also was placed in charge of Pawnee Bill's show buffaloes. But he had time for still other activities and February 23, 1905, he married Effie May Cole at Beverly, Ohio. She too became an expert trick roper and a star of the show. Joe had developed a number of outstanding lariat maneuvers, one of which was throwing a figure eight which under his expertise would result in startling catches. He met Will Rogers (see entry) and they practiced their skilled rope tricks together, each admiring

the other's artistry. From 1908 until 1913 the Pawnee Bill organization and that of Buffalo Bill Cody joined in combined performances, with Mexican Joe always a star. In 1914 Joe and Effie put together a show for Ringling Brothers Circus. Joe at Madison Square Garden roped an African lion which had escaped its cage, again winning national publicity for his quick solution to what otherwise might have been a tragic situation. In 1919 Joe quit Ringling to join the Miller Brothers 101 Ranch Wild West Show, later worked with other outfits and finally became foreman on Lillie's Blue Hawk Peak Oklahoma ranch, taking part in rodeos and helped oversee historical recreations organized by Pawnee Bill. Lillie died in 1942 and Effie died in 1945. Joe's final performance with the Blue Hawk Ranch Memorial Rodeo was on July 4, 1949. He died four months later following a major operation.

Glenn Shirley, "Mexican Joe—Lasso Genius," *True West,* Vol. 36, No. 12 (Dec. 1989), 16-23.

Bartlett, John (Yank), mule packer (Nov. 2, 1827-May 15, 1905). B. at Newbury, New Hampshire, he became a famous mule packer on the West Coast and in Arizona, he and his partner, James H. (Hank) Hewitt (see entry) forming the pack train company known everywhere as "Hank and Yank." In 1861 Bartlett in northern California bought the pack train of Hewitt and a man named Smith, the next year going into partnership with Hewitt, the company packing in the northwest for several years and going to Arizona from Oregon in 1869. While in the Northwest they apparently had come to Crook's favorable attention, and when Crook went in 1871 to Arizona to launch his operation against Yavapais and Apache Indians, he engaged the packers with their 145-mule train at $1.25 per animal a day to furnish transportation for his military and other supplies. "The two men's names were in the early seventies household words in all homes of Arizona." When Crook left Arizona in 1875 Hank and Yank retired from the government service "with a snug fortune," of which Yank Bartlett invested his portion in horses, cattle and mining enterprises near the southwest Santa Cruz County community of Oro Blanco. In late April 1886 during Geronimo's final raid into southern Arizona, the Apaches had killed three people in and near the Peck Ranch and now descended upon Bartlett's place not far from Oro Blanco; they already had wounded a neighbor, James Shanahan, fatally, as it turned out. Bartlett told his 10-year-old son, Johnny, to ride to Oro Blanco for help. The Indians fired on the house after the boy left, wounding Yank in the shoulder; the injury was not serious. The hostiles, presumably led by Geronimo himself, quitted the scene with darkness and relief came from Oro Blanco with morning to find them gone, though they took with them some fifty of Bartlett's fine mares and colts. Yank continued his mining and ranching activities afterward and provided hospitably for Hank Hewitt's last days which he spent with Yank, dying at Oro Blanco July 30, 1896, being buried there. Bartlett himself died in a common ranch accident of the day: he was driving a team which, startled at something, ran away, upsetting the wagon which rolled over on Bartlett, injuring him so that he died a few hours afterward; it was 10 a.m. Monday, May 15. Bartlett was 77 and left his widow, two daughters, and his son.

Info. from the Ariz. Hist. Soc.; Allan Radbourne, "Geronimo's Last Raid Into Arizona," English Westerners' *Tally Sheet,* Vol. 37, No. 2 (Spring, 1991), 29-33.

Bashmakov, Petr, explorer, fur trader (fl. 1753-1764). From Archangelsk, he early went to sea and became captain of vessels in exploration and trade among the Aleutian Islands. In July 1753 he left Kamchatka with the *St. Ieremiia,* assigned to seek new islands and the coast of the "great land," or North America. East of the Near Islands he sighted eight supposedly undiscovered islands, but was prevented by wind from landing on any of them. September 2 his vessel was wrecked on a previously unknown island which Pierce suspects may have been Adak; out of the wreckage was built the smaller *Sv. Petr i Pavel,* and Bashmakov returned to Kamchatka in 1755 after wintering on the northern coast of the peninsula. In 1756-58 he discovered thirteen new islands and for a time the Russians called the western islands of the Andreianov group (the present Rat Islands) the Bashmakov Islands. On a third voyage from 1759-63 Bashmakov again explored and traded for furs in the Aleutians, but on the return wrecked the *Sv. Petr i Pavel* on Shemya Island, easternmost of the Semichi Islands of the Aleutians; baidaras were built of the wreckage and the company eventually regained the Siberian coast. Bashmakov may have made another voyage in 1761-64, but his fate is described by Pierce as unknown.

Pierce, *Russian America: A Biographical Dictionary.*

Basov (Bassof), Emilian Sofronovich, Russian fur trader (c. 1705-1765). A peasant from Tobolsk and a sergeant in the Okhotsk Port Command, he was the first to engage in hunting sea otters and other fur-bearers on the islands east of Kamchatka. In 1743 he "led the Russian drive of private entrepreneurs across the North Pacific," hunting in the Commander Islands and, according to one source, as far as the Aleutians. He early formed a partnership with Andrei Serebrennikov, a merchant from Moscow and built a small *shitika,* or vessel made with minimum iron fastenings, the planks sewn together with leather or sealskin thongs. It was named the *Kapiton* and with it Basov made a voyage to Bering Island in the Commanders, returning to Kamchatka in 1744 with a fur cargo. Basov made a second voyage in 1745 and a third in 1747 with Trapeznikov (see entry), the locale of the hunting or trading not reported, but bringing back a cargo worth 121,200 rubles. He made a fourth voyage in 1749, spending most of this time on Copper Island. It appears that almost all of his fur gathering on each of his voyages took place on Copper or Bering islands, but the significance of his career, for Alaskan history, is that he led the way for the many who followed and gradually created the fur trading enterprise for which Russian Alaska became widely known. Basov himself accumulated much wealth and spent it all in trying to develop what he thought was a rich ore deposit on Copper Island, but he never could gain support for his project. At length he tried to "raise funds by making counterfeit coins, but was caught." February 11, 1756, he was sent to Irkutsk where he was convicted and sentenced to life, being dispatched to Nerchinsk to do his time. Pierce said he was reported to have died in 1765. He left a daughter.

Zagoskin; Bancroft, *Alaska; The Russian American Colonies;* Pierce, *Russian America: a Biographical Dictionary.*

Batts, Thomas, explorer: *see,* Robert Fallam entry

Bazhenov, trader, explorer (fl. 1803-1844). It is possible that there were two men of this name, or reports might indicate the same man. In 1803 Baranov sent an individual named Bazhenov up the Copper River, Alaska, the mouth of which is east of present Cordova; it is one of the major streams of Alaska, and Bazhenov was first to explore a significant length of it, ascending 300 versts, or to near the confluence of the Copper and Chistochina rivers. He returned with specimens of copper ore, a report that the river was navigable by ships for some distance, and its upper reaches were through a region plentifully supplied with game. In 1805 he visited the river again, reaching it by way of Cook Inlet. According to Pierce he set out on a third expedition into the Copper River country, "only to die at the hands of savages." Zagoskin signed on as a hunter a man named Bazhenov for the 1842-44 expedition into the Alaskan interior; he early proved his durability and faithfulness in severe winter traveling. In mid-January 1843 he took over the work of Glazunov who had become incapacitated from frostbite. Bazhenov accompanied Zagoskin on his exploratory journey up the Koyukuk River toward Kotzebue Sound, although the expedition did not gain that feature. Nothing further is reported of Bazhenov who, Zagoskin reported, was a onetime coachman from Ryazan, 130 miles southeast of Moscow.

Pierce, *Russian America: A Biographical Dictionary;* Zagoskin.

Bear Hunter (Wirasuap, Bear Spirit), Shoshoni chief (d. Jan. 29, 1863). A powerful Shoshoni leader, his career was abruptly terminated in the Connor massacre of hundreds of Shoshoni on the Bear River, Idaho, and Bear Hunter therefore "has never received the historical recognition he deserves," according to Madsen. The chief was said to be "an older contemporary" of Chief Pocatello (c. 1815-1884) and was leader of the Northwestern Shoshoni living along the Logan River and Bear River in Cache Valley in southern Idaho and northern Utah. His people numbered almost 2,000 before the tragic massacre, and Bear Hunter was regarded as the equal in power and influence of the famed Washakie (see entry) to the east. When Mormon farmers and settlers gradually inched northward, rivalry and conflict between whites and Shoshonis was inevitable, and intensified, while depredations grew more frequent. As emigrant travel to the west increased, Bear Hunter became one of the major figures in hostilities along the principal trails. In March 1861 Bear Hunter and about 20 of his followers journeyed to Salt Lake City to request of Indian Superintendent Benjamin Davies food and other supplies. They were granted some part of their requirements, Bear Hunter promising to take his people into the mountains to hunt, and away from the settlers for several months. On their return to Cache Valley in September Indi-

ans stole 60 horses, but Bear Hunter decried the deed, returned 21 head himself and saw to recovery of most of the others. By 1862, however, the Shoshonis bordering white settlements had been reduced to destitution, leading to more active plundering of stage stations and other centers where food and plunder seemed available. Depredations grew more common, the military were prepared to act strongly, and Colonel Patrick Connor (see entry) in mid-January organized his infamous offensive. He recruited noted Mormon Agent Orrin Porter Rockwell (see entry) as scout for $5 a day. Reports circulated that the Shoshonis had expressed no animosity toward the settlers, but were irate against the harshness and prisoner executions of Major Edward McGarry (see entry) and were preparing to battle any troops sent against them. Company K of the 3rd California Infantry and four companies of the 2nd Cavalry marched under Connor into Franklin, Idaho, January 28, 1863. Soldiers reached the bluffs overlooking the Indian encampment on the Bear River at 6 a.m. the 29th and the battle commenced almost immediately. Connor listed the result as 224 Indians killed, among them Bear Hunter; other estimates put the Indian loss at around 250 which Madsen accepts as a probable figure, although one apparently reliable estimate is 368 and others run as high as 400. The white loss was more than a score killed and many wounded, and incapacitated by frostbite.

Brigham D. Madsen, *The Shoshoni Frontier and the Bear River Massacre,* Salt Lake City, Univ. of Utah Press, 1985; Newell Hart, *The Bear River Massacre,* Preston, Id., Cache Valley Newsletter Pub. Co., 1892; HNAI, 11, p. 530.

Beardslee, Lester Anthony, navy officer (Feb. 1, 1836-1903). B. at Little Falls, New York, he was graduated from the Naval Academy in 1856, as executive officer aboard the monitor *Nantucket* participated in the attack on Charleston in April 1863 and in October 1864 had a role in the capture of the Confederate steam sloop *Florida* at Bahia, Brazil, as prize master bringing her to the United States. In command of the *Jamestown* in 1879 he was sent to Sitka, Alaska, because of a feared Indian uprising which however did not materialize. He helped organize the local government, negotiated with Indians to open Chilkoot Pass (to become important in the later Gold Rush), attempted to halt the illegal manufacture of liquor and believed he had discovered Glacier Bay, but this was not the case since the estuary had been entered by Second Lieutenant Charles Erskine Scott Wood (see entry) in 1877 and was explored by John Muir (see entry) in 1879. Among Beardslee's officers were Lieutenant (and later Rear Admiral) Frederick Martin Symonds (1846-1926) and Lieutenant (and later Commander) Gustavus C. Hanus (1848-1931), both of whom had worked for the Coast and Geodetic Survey and "were enthusiastic surveyors." Beardslee and his officers examined in detail the Alexander Archipelago at the lower end of the Alaskan Panhandle and "their work increased the geographic knowledge of that area and including the reporting of many new geographic names." A map of Sitka harbor was made and a report of the *Jamestown* work was published in 1882. Geographic features were named for Beardslee, Symonds and Hanus. Beardslee became a Rear Admiral in 1895, was Commander-in-Chief of Pacific naval forces from 1894-97. He retired February 1, 1898, and lived in retirement at Beaufort, South Carolina. He had served in the Navy before being appointed to the Naval Academy and during that period had taken part in Commodore Matthew Perry's memorable opening of Japan.

Orth, 8, 368; *Who Was Who.*

Becharof: *see,* Dmitry Bocharov

Becker, George Ferdinand, geologist (1847-1919). Accompanied by William H. Dall and C.W. Purington, Becker visited Alaska in 1895 to geologically examine gold and coal resources. The examination was confined to the south coast of the territory, from Sitka to Unalaska Island. It also included localities in the Alexander Archipelago, in the Kodiak Island and Cook Inlet areas and along the Alaska Peninsula and Bogoslof Island in the Bering Sea, north of Umnak Island.

Orth, 8.

Beechey, Frederick William, British sea explorer (Feb. 17, 1796-Nov. 29, 1856). He entered the British Navy in 1806, served off Portugal, in East India and in a Madagascar action of 1811, and was on the lower Mississippi River January 8, 1815, during the British defeat by Andrew Jackson. In 1818 Beechey was aboard the *Trent* under Captain John Franklin on an Arctic expedition of which he wrote *Voyage of Discovery Towards the North Pole.* In 1819 Beechey was an officer under William Edward Parry in an unsuccessful search for the Northwest Passage, though in the course of the expedition several

islands of the Canadian Arctic archipelago were discovered. After a period of surveying the north coast of Africa, he was appointed commander of the sloop, *Blossom* for its important 1825-28 voyage into the upper Pacific Ocean. Beechey left Spithead May 25, 1825, reached Cape Horn August 16, sighted Easter Island November 16 and Pitcairn Island December 4, remaining there until the 21st. After touching other island groups in the South Pacific, Beechey on April 26, 1826, reached the Sandwich Islands (Hawaii), Petropavlovsk on Kamchatka, and Bering Island July 10, 1826, went on to St. Lawrence Island and Bering Strait and arrived at Kotzebue Sound, Alaska, July 22, having made thorough and careful geographical, zoological and ethnographical notes as the expedition progressed, and continued compiling them during the several years' voyage. In the Sound, Beechey discovered and named for Henry Hotham, a lord of the Admiralty, Hotham Inlet, which had escaped the observation of Kotzebue; because the water was too shoal for the ship, he sent in a boat under Master Thomas Elson to determine the extent of the waterway. Meanwhile Beechey made his temporary base at Chamisso Island, at the mouth of Eschscholtz Bay, for according to Admiralty instructions and a memorandum with Captain Franklin, who was to survey the Arctic coast westward from the Mackenzie River delta, it was at Kotzebue Sound that the two parties were most likely to meet. This was not to be however; they were never able to contact each other. Beechey wished to take no chances, and in order that Franklin "should not want provision in the event of his missing" the *Blossom,* directed that a tight barrel of flour be buried on Chamisso Island with instructions nearby to direct Franklin to it. Twenty-three years later three English vessels devoted to the prolonged hunt for Franklin, then missing after a subsequent search for the Northwest Passage, anchored off the Island, located the buried flour, found it in such perfect condition that cakes and pastry made from it were served at an impromptu dinner party. July 30, 1826, the *Blossom* left the Sound with her accompanying "barge" (this vessel was not a barge by modern definition and could be carried on the deck of a ship; pictures sketched by Admiralty Mate William Smyth show her to have been a small craft, rigged as a two-masted topsail schooner of broad beam and shallow draft, suitable for working in coastal waters too shoal for the *Blossom*). They proceeded along the northwestern Alaskan coast. Eskimos Beechey encountered were adept at trading apparently because of exchanges with Chukchi natives of Siberia, or otherwise. August 3 Point Hope was sighted and named for Vice Admiral William Johnstone Hope. The *Blossom* touched Cape Lisburne and on August 9 discovered and named Cape Beaufort for another admiral, Sir Francis Beaufort. Beechey found the Eskimos this far north possessed of iron kettles and other trade items and exhibiting no surprise at the appearance of his ship, judging therefore that Russian promyshlenniki, often illiterate and unable to leave a written record of their transactions, were accustomed to visit this part of Alaska. He located and named Point Franklin and the bay east of it after his able 1st Lieutenant George Peard. Fearing the hazard of offshore ice Beechey then sent the barge, under Elson to pursue a course along the narrow channel between ice and shore as far to the northeast as he could safely go, charting the coast and keeping watch for any sign of Franklin's party. Beechey and the *Blossom* came about and returned to Kotzebue Sound, anchoring at Chamisso Island August 28. The barge under Elson meanwhile continued its most hazardous exploration, encountering grave risks and great difficulties with the restless ice pack which occasionally reached the shore itself. On August 22 Point Barrow, the most northerly point of the North American continent was discovered, ultimately named for Sir John Barrow, second secretary of the Admiralty and promoter of Arctic expeditions. A feature immediately to the east was named Elson Bay (Lagoon) in honor of the master of the barge. With his feat the configuration of the Alaskan coastline was essentially clarified. By September 10 the barge had rejoined the *Blossom* off Chamisso Island. Nearby Beechey had named Elephant Point on the south coast of Eschscholtz Bay for the mastadon tusks and bones found there, and a major river emptying into the bay from the south for William Buckland, geology professor at Oxford University. October 13 Beechey quit the Sound, threaded Bering Strait, passed within view of the Pribylov Islands, cleared the Aleutian chain by Unimak Strait and by early November reached San Francisco Bay. He spent weeks traveling, studying and writing about California culture, the military, missions and native peoples. His comments are cogent, interesting and valuable as a learned Englishman's assessment of the region at this stage of its existence; Beechey's talent as writer comes into full view in these passages. In January 1827 the *Blossom* left Monterey for Hawaii, China and Kamchatka (Beechey was promoted

to captain May 8 but of course did not learn of it until much later). He left Petropavlovsk July 18, visited Bering Island again, sighted St. Lawrence Island August 1, threaded Bering Strait and re-entered Kotzebue Sound August 5, anchoring at Chamisso Island. The purpose of his return was to try once again to contact Franklin. Having refitted his barge, now under command of Lieutenant Edward Belcher, the *Blossom* and its escort bore once more along the coast but floes prevented it from proceeding much farther than Icy Cape (which was the northern limit for Cook on his 1778 journey). Belcher, with the barge, advanced but a short distance farther. No indications of Franklin were found, since he had never reached this coast, and Beechey returned to Chamisso August 26. He then conducted a brief mission of exploration around Cape Prince of Wales, investigating features discovered earlier by Elson, giving names to Port Clarence, Grantley Harbor, Cape York and others, all for prominent Englishmen of the time. He left September 5 for Chamisso Island again, losing a man overboard enroute and arriving September 10 only to find that the barge had been wrecked on Choris Peninsula with the loss of three more men. Subsequently the commander and his crew weathered violent clashes with increasingly hostile Eskimos, taking casualties and dealing out some although making every effort to minimize them in keeping with Admiralty instructions. On October 6, with all hope of contacting Franklin evaporated, the *Blossom* left the Sound, passed through the Aleutian chain and anchored at Monterey October 29. Beechey arrived at Spithead October 12, 1828 after a 73,000-mile voyage of three and one-half years. He was married in December and in September 1835 commenced surveying a portion of the eastern coast of South America. From 1850 until his death he was superintendent of the marine department of the Board of Trade, in 1854 became a rear admiral and in 1855 was elected president of the Royal Geographic Society. He wrote an extended narrative of his Pacific tour and other important works, including a number of papers for various scientific societies.

Beechey, *Narrative of a Voyage to the Pacific and Beering's Strait*, 2 vols., London, Henry Colburn, Richard Bentley, 1831 (repr., Da Capo Press, N.Y., 1968); DNB; Zagoskin.

Belaev, Illarion (Beliaief, Larion or Alexei), promyshlenniki killer (fl. 1745-1756). Sailing from Kamchatka September 19, 1745 with Nevodchikof (see entry), the party of promyshlenniki and Cossacks reached the outer Aleutian Islands within a few days, anchoring at Agattu. Composed of violent, unruly men as well as prospective fur traders the whites quickly ran into difficulties with the natives, wounding one "and the long era of bloodshed, violence, and rapine for the poor Aleuts was begun." Various contacts, some friendly, others hostile, ensued. The ship subsequently anchored at Attu where Belaev and ten men were sent to explore the island. They found inoffensive natives, picked a fight and killed fifteen of them. Even the tough Cossack Shekhurdin was appalled and told his chief, Yakov Chuprov, "who said nothing, but merely sent the butchering party more powder and lead." Such outrages were not known in Russia for years but "if they had been it would have made little difference." Belaev won ill fame as among the most villainous of the lawless elements of the promyshlenniki.

Bancroft, *Alaska; Russian Penetration of the North Pacific Ocean.*

Belcher, Edward, British naval officer (1799-Mar. 18, 1877). He entered the British Navy in 1812, served on several ships in Newfoundland and on the English Channel and in 1816 was a midshipman aboard the *Superb* at the bombardment of Algiers. He became a lieutenant July 2, 1818, and in 1825 was appointed assistant surveyor and supernumerary aboard the *Blossom,* Frederick William Beechey, captain, on a several years' voyage to the North Pacific (see Beechey entry). Belcher, whose avocations were geology and natural sciences, was considered "the most [physically] active among the officers on board," and he figured in many adventures which befell the expedition. At Oeno islet, about 90 miles northward of Pitcairn Island, Belcher twice narrowly escaped drowning in December 1825 while trying to investigate the unpopulated speck of land; one man was lost in this endeavor. An island of the Gambier group was named for Belcher, with others for additional officers of the *Blossom* and the lieutenant made interesting ethnological observations about the islanders who had not previously been visited by Europeans. On one occasion his intrepidity helped rescue a fellow officer, Lieutenant John Wainwright, from natives suddenly hostile. "Lieutenant Belcher, whose scientific attainments enabled him to appreciate what fell under his observation [collected] specimens of zealite, carbonate of lime," chalcedony and other rocks and had "his

other duties admitted" he might have made an informed geologic assessment of the Gambier Islands. He made significant discoveries as well at Tahiti. In Alaska, above Kotzebue Sound, Belcher conducted studies of various Eskimo groups, carefully noting matters of interest to European explorers, and occasionally collected plant specimens. In 1827 Belcher was sent in the *Blossom's* tender to sail as far as possible up the northwest coast of Alaska seeking traces of the John Franklin expedition which Beechey was assigned to contact if possible. He got not much farther than Icy Cape where floes prevented further progress, and after stubbornly persisting in futile attempts to advance returned to Kotzebue Sound and Chamisso Island, the tender being wrecked on Choris Peninsula with the loss of three men. After investigation and hearing the story of their adventures, Beechey wrote that "I must exonerate Lieutenant Belcher from any blame...[His] strenuous exertions...to save the crew, and his resolute conduct toward the natives, after he was thrown amongst them unprovided with arms, a brace of pistols excepted, show him to be an officer both of humanity and courage...Mr. Belcher was a great loser by this unfortunate accident, as he was well provided with instruments, books, papers, &c., and had some expensive fowling-pieces and pistols, all of which was lost or spoiled," although the government after the return in 1828 to England "made him a compensation." Belcher was with Beechey at San Francisco in November 1826 where some surveys of the Bay were undertaken with the assent, or at least non-interference of Mexican officials. He became a commander March 16, 1829, and captained the *Aetna* for several years surveying African coasts, then was employed on the home survey, principally in the Irish Sea. Beechey, in command of a two-ship Pacific expedition, had fallen ill at Panama and Belcher took command in February 1837 aboard the *Sulphur,* a 380-ton man-of-war. The principal object of the expedition was to complete a hydrographic survey of the western coasts and islands of America. Belcher visited Sitka, Alaska, spent a week at Nootka Sound and anchored at Yerba Buena (San Francisco) October 19, 1837, later writing that the straggling Mexican settlements presented a discouraging aspect. "Harassed on all sides by Indians, pestered by a set of renegade deserters from whalers and merchant ships, who start by dozens and will eventually form themselves into a bandit gang and domineer over them, unable from want of spirit to protect themselves, they will soon dwindle into insignificance," his dire prediction of trouble ahead for Mexican California a forecast of the 1840 Isaac Graham affair. "Belcher's own crew," as Bancroft noted, "contributed some half-dozen men to this army of deserters." The principal object of Belcher's second visit to San Francisco Bay was to complete the survey begun by the Beechey party in 1826-27. Surveys were conducted of the Carquines Strait and the Sacramento River, reaching the highest point October 30, 150 miles upstream where the water became too shoal for the ship. The work was completed by November 24 when Belcher sailed for Monterey, arriving December 2, leaving on the 6th for southern points. In 1839 Belcher again visited Sitka briefly, then dropped down to the mouth of the Columbia River where he remained from July to September. He wrote "in condescending terms of the establishment on the Columbia (Fort Vancouver), and...expresses his surprise that pilots are not kept in waiting to guide vessels in" over the dangerous bar at the mouth of the great river. September 20, 1839, Belcher with his two vessels arrived at Bodega Bay, on the northern California coast, then made a 48-hour trip to San Francisco and back. He did not visit Fort Ross, formerly a Russian outpost in California, but continued down the coast, visiting San Francisco briefly once more, Monterey on October 5, Santa Barbara on the 9th and San Pedro, near Los Angeles, on the 11th. One of the ships visited Santa Catalina Island and the vessels arrived at San Diego on the 17th, leaving five days later for southern coasts. Belcher received post rank (that of full captain) May 8, 1841, and arrived back in England after a seven years' absence in July 1842. In January 1843 he received a knighthood and that year published his two-volume *Narrative of a Voyage round the World...1836-42.* His further service was performed in far seas and foreign coast surveys and in 1852 he was named to command an expedition to the Canadian Arctic in search of the lost Sir John Franklin. "The appointment was an unfortunate one," said the *Dictionary of National Biography,* the author of the treatment being no admirer of Belcher who, he wrote, "though an able and experienced surveyor, had neither the temper nor the tact necessary for a commanding officer under circumstances of peculiar difficulty. Perhaps no officer of equal ability has ever succeeded in inspiring so much personal dislike, and the customary exercise of his authority did not make Arctic service less trying." The article went on, "His expedition is distinguished from all other Arctic expeditions as the one in which the commanding officer showed an undue haste to abandon his ships when in difficulties, and in which one of the ships so abandoned rescued herself from the ice, and was picked up floating freely in the open Altantic." While Belcher received no later commands, "in due course of seniority he attained his flag 11 Feb. 1861, became vice-admiral 2 April 1866, and admiral 20 Oct. 1872." He passed the remainder of his life "in literary and scientific amusements," some of his book-length writings of a useful nature.

DNB; Frederick W. Beechey, *Narrative of a Voyage to the Pacific and Bering's Strait,* 2 vols., London, Henry Colburn, Richard Bentley, 1831 (1968); Bancroft, *Northwest Coast* I, II; *Oregon,* I; *California,* III, IV.

Bell, Edwin, military officer (Feb. 25, 1870-Apr. 30, 1951). B. at Washington, D.C., he entered West Point from New York and was commissioned a second lieutenant of the 8th Infantry June 12, 1894. He served at Forts McKinney and D.A. Russell, Wyoming, from September 1894 and was in the field in Idaho during Indian troubles at Jackson Hole from July 27 to October 26, 1895. Bell became a first lieutenant April 26, 1898, and was assigned to Fort St. Michael on Norton Sound, Alaska, September 9, 1898, then commanded the post at Rampart City on the middle Yukon to August 1899. Bell found the place consisting of 450 cabins, 10 stores, 12 saloons, 6 restaurants and a brewery with gold fever at its height and the government falling into his hands by default since the civilian rule was forced out by public discontent with practically every political move it made. Captain Wilds Richardson (see entry) said in his report that "Too much praise cannot be given to Lieutenant Bell for the patience and good judgment shown by him in preserving the peace in the Rampart district, and in settling amicably the many disputes submitted to him." Bell himself reported only that "During the year the camp has been most orderly and law abiding. In cases involving property I simply acted as arbitrator and had the parties agree to a settlement before me." Since the established hospital went broke and closed, Bell rented a building and "started a hospital for the destitute. Much suffering was relieved." He thought gold in the region was plentiful, but "it requires capital to get it out," adding that "it will be several years before capitalists can be induced to invest here." He left Alaska in August 1899, served in the Philippines and China and at Fort Snelling, Minnesota, for a time. He became a captain February 2, 1901, major July 1, 1916, a lieutenant colonel January 19, 1918, taking part in the Meuse-Argonne offensive in France, and became a colonel December 3, 1922 on the day he retired. He died at Washington, D.C.

Heitman; Cullum; *Narratives of Explorations in Alaska;* information from the U.S. Army Military Hist. Inst., Carlisle Barracks, Penn.

Benijovski, "Count," Mauritius, Augustine, adventurer (c. 1741-May 23, 1786). B. either 1741 or 1746 at Verbowa, Slovakia, of a wealthy Polish family, Benijovski was among the numerous individuals in the early 1770s exiled by Russia to Siberia as "political castaways, prisoners of war, or victims of too deep diplomacy" or even as common criminals. Banijovski (Benyovsky, Benyowsky), according to Bancroft had "played somewhat too recklessly at conspiracy. Nor was Siberia to deprive him of this pastime." He quickly organized a secret society of exiles whose primary aim was escape from that land. By skillfully forging a document on stolen official paper and dispatching it ahead of his party to Okhotsk, on the Siberian coast, Benijovski and his band were welcomed there by the commandant, Colonel Frederick C. Plenisner, a veteran of Bering's famous voyage which discovered northwestern America. The officer, "of little education and dissipated habits" on the basis of the forged document greeted them as unfortunate gentlemen rather than criminals, supplying all their necessities including arms. Benijovski and his conspirators were sent on to Kamchatka, which had been mentioned in the forged document as their official destination, the count believing escape would be easier from there than from Okhotsk. In October 1770, exiles, including the conspirators were sent there, Benijovski writing that their passage aboard the *Sv Petr i Sv Paul* was a stormy one and that he alone had managed to save the ship and its personnel, his "heroism" deeply impressing the Bolsheretsk commandant, a Captain Nilof, one "given to drink, and easily deceived." The exiles were treated liberally and their restraint was nominal while the count was busy ingratiating himself with Nilof's family. He forged further documentary support, strengthening the commandant's perception of his "loyalty." Meanwhile Benijovski's secret society

expanded rapidly, drawing in many who were in no way exiles or of shady background but were attracted by the expansive prospectus which the count advanced. Among these was probably Gerrasim Izmailov (see entry). Benijovski's own narration of his exploits on Kamchatka, commented Bancroft, "for unblushing impudence in the telling, borders on the sublime," but by early 1771 his elaborate scheme commenced to unravel. His ultimate plan, much of which was withheld from his more-criminal adherents called for overcoming the Bolsheretsk garrison, imprisoning the commander, plundering the public treasury and storehouses, and sailing for Japan or some Pacific island with as many as would accompany him. April 26, 1771, Nilof having been informed of the more sinister elements of the plot, abruptly summoned Benijovsky to the chancellery. The count realized that it was now or never. He mustered his conspirators, Nilof was killed, the murder premeditated as the best means of committing his followers irrevocably, and other elements of the plan were swiftly put into effect. Benijovski had already brought to his standard the commander of the *Sv Petr i Sv Pavel* and with the plot's momentary success his followers hastened to ready the ship for sea. On May 12 the vessel left the harbor "midst the firing of salvos, the ringing of bells, and the solemn te deum on the quarterdeck" and made for Bering Island, arriving May 19. Benijovski's narration of the voyage subsequently is most confused and much of it improbable, to put it kindly. He wrote that by June 4 the ship had reached latitude 64° off the Chukotski Peninsula of Siberia and on June 10, he landed on "Kadiak" Island, a thousand miles away; he must have meant St. Lawrence Island rather than Kodiak, but then, he was no geographer. On June 21 the ship reached Amchitka Island of the Andreanof Islands in the Aleutian chain and later was off Ourumusir, one of the Kurile Islands north of Japan. Here Izmailov and Fedor Paranchin were cast ashore since Benijovski had learned they planned to seize the ship and return her to Kamchatka; he had killed men for less. Heavily discounting the adventurer's narration, Bancroft concluded that "the only part of this journey susceptible of proof is the [eventual] arrival of the survivors in the harbor of Macao." near Canton, China. From Macao Benijovski somehow reached Madagascar. He went on to Paris to seek French government aid in "subjugating the natives" of Madascagar, but his success was only partial. On April 14, 1774, he embarked on the *Robert and*

Anne for Baltimore, Maryland, arriving July 8 with a cargo valued at 4,000 pounds sterling, intended for Madagascar. The American Revolution intervened, but eventually he persuaded American merchants to charter the 20-gun ship *Intrepid.* October 25, 1784, he finally left Baltimore, the last letter from him dated off the Brazilian coast. Within months he reached Madagascar again, where he busied himself with a fresh conspiracy to establish an independent filibuster government. However in an action with French colonial troops he was killed.

Bancroft, *Alaska; The Russian American Colonies;* Maurice A. Benyovski, *Memoirs and Travels,* London, 1790; Pierce, *Russian America: A Biographical Dictionary.*

Bennett, Andrew S., military officer (d. Sep. 4 1878). B. in New York State, he was commissioned a second lieutenant in the 5th Wisconsin Infantry July 12, 1861, and was mustered out a first lieutenant August 2, 1864. He was commissioned a first lieutenant in the 15th U.S. Infantry March 7, 1867, and a captain February 28, 1869. He was assigned to the 5th Infantry January 1, 1871. On April 6, 1875, at the Cheyenne Agency, Indian Territory, Cheyennes who had surrendered following the Red River War were being shackled and a young chief, Black Horse, broke loose and tried to escape. Bennett and the 5th Infantry guard pursued and killed Black Horse which led to an important exodus of many of the Cheyennes who had previously come in. During the Bannock hostilities of 1878, Nelson Miles on September 4 struck a camp of Bannocks, killed 11 Indians and captured 31, together with 200 horses and mules, but Bennett, the interpreter who was a man named Rock, and a Crow scout were killed and one enlisted man wounded. In his *Personal Recollections,* pp. 299-300, Miles wrote that Bennett was "a most accomplished, meritorious and valuable officer. It was a sad sight as his friends gazed upon his dead body...placed against a tree...The bullet hole was in the center of his breast, and had evidently caused instant death. It seemed hard and strange that this good soldier, who had risked his life on many a hard-fought battlefield...must meet his death at last in that wild and rugged region...His body was...sent to his relatives in Wisconsin." A portrait of Bennett is on p. 299 of Miles' book.

Heitman, EHI, 46, 78; Miles, *Personal Recollections,* Chicago, Riverside Pub. Co., 1897.

Benton, Thomas Hart, statesman (Mar. 14, 1782-Apr. 10, 1858). B. at Hart's Mill, near Hillsboro, North Carolina, Benton experienced episodic and occasionally violent youthful years, attended Chapel Hill College (now the University of North Carolina) and studied law at William and Mary College, but his fiery temper and immature excesses led to his departure from institutions of higher learning. The family moved to the Cumberland Valley of Tennessee in 1801. Here Thomas helped to farm, taught school, completed his law studies, and was licensed in 1806 to practice. He became a state senator in 1809. During the War of 1812 he was a colonel of Tennessee militia and aide to Andrew Jackson until 1813 when their close association ended with a brawl at Nashville following Jackson's role as second for his friend, William Carroll, in a duel with Benton's brother, Jesse. In the fracas Benton shot Jackson and was stabbed five times by Jackson's supporters. He finished out the war as lieutenant colonel of the 39th U.S. Infantry, being honorably discharged June 15, 1815. Because of his rancorous differences with Jackson, Benton saw that a political future in Tennessee was bleak and he moved to Missouri, establishing a lucrative law practice, becoming acquainted with St. Louis leadership and major fur dealers and others. In 1817 the short-fused Benton engaged in a fresh "affair of honor" in which he dueled twice with the same man, on the second occasion killing him, which "caused Benton so much anguish that, despite many insults and challenges" of the future he refused ever again to engage in a duel. In 1818 he became editor of the St. Louis *Enquirer,* remaining its nominal editor until 1826. The paper helped him advance his political career, and he was elected a U.S. senator in 1820 when Missouri became a state; he entered the Senate August 10, 1821 and served there continuously until March 3, 1851, the first senator to serve thirty consecutive years, which he made memorable for himself and for the nation. He became recognized as the spokesman for the West, for the frontier and for the explorers, small land-owners, settlers, developers and builders of the almost limitless area between Missouri and the Pacific. He early threw his support to popular democracy and in doing so in 1825 he healed his rift with Jackson and became one of his staunchest and most outspoken supporters. For one thing he authored a resolution to expunge from the Senate Journal a resolution of censure upon Jackson; he supported Jackson in his presidential campaign against John Quincy Adams, and became the Missouri spokesman for two principles on which Jackson's strength was largely based: greater popular democracy and equality of social and economic opportunity. He was instrumental in defeating the effort to recharter the Bank of the United States and supported a program to separate the government from banking activities except for their regulation. Benton championed cheap land in every possible way, believing in the benefits for the common good in rapid settlement at low cost of vacant land, his efforts ultimately culminating, posthumously, in the Homestead Act of 1862. In 1832 he supported abolition of the government factory system in the western fur trade, a development which Astor and other entrepreneurs fervently desired for their own benefit; Benton was aware that elimination of that system and turning the fur trade completely over to civilian interests meant an economic windfall for the fur men, but in his view it also meant expansion of an aggressive business into the west and toward the Pacific, which he felt ultimately was good for the nation. Benton's fascination with the Far West was boosted after his daughter, Jessie, over her father's strenuous objections, eloped with John Charles Fremont (see entry) October 19, 1841; once the marriage had taken place, however, Benton readily accepted Fremont into his family and just as the willful Jessie became Fremont's loyal supporter, so Thomas Hart Benton became his most powerful booster at Washington, remaining so through all the vicissitudes of the volatile "explorer's" career so long as Benton lived. Although he believed in a form of manifest destiny, popular at the time, he was never an imperialist. He opposed unilateral annexation of Mexican territory, supported a compromise to the Oregon problem with Britain as opposed to the Democrats' "54-40 or Fight" bombast. The problem of Texas also concerned him for several years. In 1830 he had tentatively urged the peaceful acquisition of Texas from Mexico, but in 1836, following Texas's successful revolt Benton opposed annexation because of the slavery controversy involved, and in 1843 once more opposed it, which he then believed might incur war with Mexico. As chairman of the Senate Committee on Indian Affairs he was instrumental in securing Creek withdrawal from Georgia and in "inaugurating the removal of Indian tribes" to the west, one of the least-admirable episodes in United States-Indian relations. Benton was an early advocate of a transcontinental railroad and a government-sponsored, constructed and defended public road to Oregon, but his conviction that slavery would not be beneficial in new western states and positions on peripheral matters led to alienation from him of significant slavery interests and states and his influence in the Senate rapidly dwindled. In 1851 he was defeated for re-election, but subsequently served a term in the House of Representatives from March 4, 1853, to March 5, 1855. He was not re-elected and also lost a bid for the governorship of Missouri in 1856. During the final period of his life he wrote *Thirty Years' View,* a two-volume autobiographical overview of the national government from 1820-50 from his perspective, edited a 16-volume abridgment of congressional debates, and wrote *Historical and Legal Examination,* a refutation of the Dred Scott decision of the Supreme Court. Benton died at Washington, D.C., survived by four daughters and having been predeceased by his wife and three sons. He was buried in Bellefontaine Cemetery, St. Louis.

Literature abundant; BDAC; REAW; EA; DAB.

Berger, Jacob (Jacques), trader (fl. 1809-1847). B. in Canada and probably a French-Canadian since he was fluent in French, Berger around 1809 became associated with the Hudson's Bay Company, assigned initially to Fort des Prairies, below the junction of the North and South branches of the Saskatchewan River near the present Prince Albert, Saskatchewan. He learned the fur business under John Rowand, factor. He may also have served under Rowand, later chief factor for the HBC, at Fort Augustus, at the present Edmonton, Alberta. In the course of his work he became proficient in the Blackfoot language, knew famous chiefs and other noted men and had friends among them. By 1830 he had left the HBC and moved south to Fort Union, an American Fur Company post at the confluence of the Missouri and Yellowstone rivers. Here the famous Kenneth McKenzie (see entry) was in charge, eager to extend trade to the Blackfeet, but uncertain how to do it since they were implacable enemies of American trappers. McKenzie requested Berger to make a tentative approach to those Indians and Berger, a "very conciliatory character," agreed to undertake the perilous mission. With four other Canadians he set out on foot in the winter of 1830-31 and for forty days sought some Blackfoot encampment. He finally came across a 17-man Piegan war party. The five whites were about to be overrun when Berger called out his name in Blackfoot, and what appeared likely to become a bloodbath turned instead into a warm and enthusiastic reception for this old friend of the tribe. The Piegans took the whites to a larger Blackfoot camp where they arrived March 5. Berger persuaded the Indians to accompany him to Fort Union, which none of them had yet seen. The band of 92 men and 32 women arrived at the post in late May—after Berger and his tiny party had been given up for lost. So successful was the trade that developed that McKenzie sought Piegan consent to build a post in their country, and Fort Piegan (Fort McKenzie) was constructed at the mouth of the Marias River in the autumn of 1831. Berger was retained by McKenzie as Blackfoot interpreter at a salary of $800 a year. He was of much assistance as a source on Blackfoot language and customs for Maximilian (see entry) on his journey to the upper river in 1833-34. Berger remained in the Indian country. In February 1844 he apparently had some sort of undefined role, although it could not have been major, in Alexander Harvey's (see entry) "cannon-massacre" of a few Blackfeet at Fort Union. In 1845 Berger, Malcolm Clarke and James Lee had an altercation of sorts with Harvey, an able trader handicapped by an explosive temper and violent impulses. Following an accidental meeting aboard a steamboat on the Missouri, a fight broke out and as was not unusual among such men, it turned murderous. Clarke struck Harvey in the head with a tomahawk, Berger knocked him down with a rifle butt, and Lee incapacitated him with a blow which damaged his pistol arm. Accounts leave uncertainty about the whole thing, but it is improbable that any "assassination" attempt was involved (although many on the river would have been happy with such a result, for Harvey had as numerous enemies as friends). The incident on the whole seems to have been no more than an impromptu fight and in no way an "ambush," as it has been called. But Harvey, as was his nature, nursed a deep grudge, convinced himself that it was the result of a plot to kill him concocted by the noted trader (and Harvey enemy) Francois Chardon (see entry). Still seething, Harvey made his way to St. Louis where he persuaded Indian Affairs Commissioner T.H. Harvey to order the trio out of the Indian country as a form of reprisal. The order was issued, but postponements followed and the matter finally was dropped. Berger was of assistance to the Rev. Nicolas Point, S.J., when the priest visited Blackfoot country in 1846 and 1847. Point, an enthusiastic amateur painter, made a side-view portrait of Berger, showing him with white hair due to his advanced age, his face beardless and the trader dressed as befit one of his status; the picture is reproduced on page 222 of Point's book. Nothing further has been located about Berger.

Annie Heloise Abel, ed., *Chardon's Journal at Fort Clark 1834-1839,* Pierre, S.D., State Dept. of Hist., 1932; Thwaites, EWT, 23, 24; Charles Larpenteur, *Forty Years a Fur Trader on the Upper Missouri,* Lincoln, Univ. of Neb. Press, 1989; John S. Galbraith, *The Hudson's Bay Company as an Imperial Factor, 1821-1869,* Berkeley, Univ. of Calif. Press, 1957; John C. Ewers, *The Blackfeet: Raiders of the Northwestern Plains,* Norman, Univ. of Okla. Press, 1967; Paul Chrisler Phillips, *The Fur Trade,* II, Norman, 1961; Nicolas Point, S.J., *Wilderness Kingdom: Indian Life in the Rocky Mountains, 1840-1847,* N.Y., Holt, Rinehart and Winston, 1967.

Bering, Vitus Johanssen, sea explorer (1681-Dec. 8, 1741. B. at Horsens, Jutland, Denmark, Bering entered the Russian navy in 1704, fought in the war against Sweden and was an accomplished seaman with experience in both East and West Indies. He was sent by Peter the Great's directive, signed a month before the Tsar's death, across Siberia to Kamchatka to build vessels for a voyage of exploration. He sailed north July 13, 1728, aboard the *Sv. Gavril* with 44 men, including Lieutenant Aleksey Ilich Chirikov and Lieutenant Martin Spanberg, like himself a Dane. St. Lawrence Island was discovered August 11 and by the 16th Bering had reached Latitude 67° 18´ and put about; he had sailed through Bering Strait without realizing it. (Dezhnev [see entry] had already demonstrated that Siberia and America were separated by water). Bering on August 17 raised and named the island of St. Diomede, but fog or low clouds concealed the American shore and it was not sighted. Kamchatka was regained September 7. Bering returned to St. Petersburg March 1, 1730. He then conceived of a more extensive expedition, the plan modified in part by Chirikov's suggestions and the project then endorsed by the government. In 1739-40 on Avatcha Bay on the eastern coast of the Kamchatka Peninsula Bering founded the seaport of Petropavlovsk, named for his two ships, the *St. Peter* and *St. Paul.* June 4, 1741, with himself in command of the *St. Peter* and Chirikov of the other the expedition set out under definite instructions to seek the American coast which was known from Spanish discoveries to lie somewhere beyond Siberia. They followed a predetermined course but by the 20th the vessels had drifted apart and did not meet again. By July 11 Chirikov's journal showed that his ship, on a generally northeast course had come upon signs of land: driftwood, wild ducks and other evidences, and at 2 a.m. on July 16 land was sighted in Latitude 56° 15′. A boat was put close inshore, but a sighted bay proved unsatisfactory for a landing. The ship proceeded northwest until it reached what apparently was Lituya Bay, midway between Sitka and Yakutat and adjacent to today's Glacier Bay National Monument. Here two armed parties were successively sent ashore, disappeared and were never heard from again, more likely victims of violent seas than native hostility, as Golder believed. Chirikov from this point returned to Kamchatka. Bering, meanwhile had spent much time sailing about in the Gulf of Alaska. Bearing north-northeast and crossing the 52nd Parallel the *St. Peter* at last came upon signs of land. Georg Wilhelm Steller, the surgeon-naturalist aboard whose journal is the principle surviving record of the cruise (Bering's original journals' whereabouts are unknown, although a copy by Sofron Khitrov [Chytref] is held at Leningrad) wrote that on July 15 he glimpsed land ahead, but his report was not believed. The following day high, snow-capped peaks were raised in Latitude 58° 18′; this was July 16 by the boat's reckoning, but actually the 17th, making the sighting one day after Chirikov observed the land. Bering now was suffering from scurvy with consequent mental depression and even an indifference to his notable accomplishment. He had raised what probably was Mt. St. Elias, at 18,000 feet a major peak, and virtually discovered Alaska, so far as he was aware (see Gwosdef entry). Although some cursory exploration was attempted, Bering himself did not set foot on land, being impatient to depart, so irritable and restless that he would not permit Steller, the most competent scientist of the company, to conduct any but a superficial survey of their landfall. As quickly as possible the commander weighed anchor and put to sea, bearing southwest until July 31 when a course was set to north by west, to contact again the land suspected to lie in that direction. On August 2 the ship passed close by Ukamak Island (Chirikof Island), southwest of Kodiak Island. The *St. Peter,* hampered by adverse winds, continued more or less paralleling the unseen Alaska Peninsula until August 30 when a seaman named

Shumagin died of scurvy and was buried on a small bit of land named for him, the name later extended to the entire group of islands below the Peninsula's southwestern tip. Bering by now was too ill to often leave his cabin and Lieutenant Sven Waxel had taken command of the ship. Contacts, in the main friendly although there was no interpreter, were made with natives of the Shumagin Islands where contrary winds held the *St. Peter* for some days. The Atka group of islands at Latitude 52°, Longitude 175° were contacted but contrary gales then blew the ship easterly with headway toward Kamchatka impossible for many days. Amchitka, Kiska and the Semichi Islands at length were sighted. By now half the crew was down with scurvy, twenty-four seriously ill and Bering was offering prayers to all celestial powers, Catholic or Protestant, Greek or German, for fair weather and a following wind. Foul conditions persisted. With crew so weakened as to be virtually useless, the ship so storm-battered as to become almost unmanageable, its rigging rotted and sails all but shredded, the *St. Peter* at last was wrecked upon a barren island scarcely 351 miles from the nearest cape of the Kamchatka Peninsula the company had so long sought. Bering was carried ashore November 9. His scurvy-ridden crewmen died off in numbers. Bering himself died a month later at 60 years of age, the island being given his name. He was married and fathered two sons. Survivors, recruited from scurvy by fresh meat from stranded whales and other sources, managed in succeeding months to construct a new vessel from the wreckage of the old and eventually sailed her to Avatcha Bay, arriving August 26, 1742.

Bancroft, *Alaska;* F.A. Golder, *Russian Expansion on the Pacific 1641-1850,* N.Y., Paragon Book Reprint Corp., 1971; CE; EA.

Berkh, Vasily Nikolayevich, historian (May 18, 1781-Dec. 21, 1834). B. at Moscow. A specialist on geographical discoveries, he was author of works on the history of travels in the Pacific and polar regions. Among these was his *Chronological History of the Discovery of the Aleutian Islands,* published at St. Petersburg in 1820. Berkh was a naval officer and a member of Lisyanskiy's complement on the *Neva* during its 1803-1806 circumnavigation of the world. During it he visited Kodiak Island, Alaska, in 1804-1805, where he became interested in Alaskan history and interviewed many veterans of service with fur-gathering companies. He retired from the navy because of poor health, but continued his researches and writing. His works "have become classics," in good part because of his considerable use of previously unpublished and original material.

Zagoskin; *Russian Penetration of the North Pacific Ocean.*

Bierstadt, Albert, painter (Jan. 7, 1830-Feb. 18, 1902). B. at Solingen, near Dusseldorf on the Rhine River in Germany, he was brought at age one by his parents to New Bedford, Massachusetts. From 1853 to 1857 he studied painting at Dusseldorf under landscape artists of the romantic school, visited Rome and returned to the United States. In 1858 he joined an Army surveying expedition under Frederick Lander (see entry), charting a new wagon route through the West. He made scores of sketches on his travels which continued as far as California and the Yosemite Valley, from them later creating huge paintings of unduplicatable scenes he had witnessed from a vanishing period. Current "fashion" sometimes finds them dull, "without dramatic vigor or imagination," which seems singularly obtuse. No painter of record, except perhaps Bodmer, recorded more accurately the West of that early day, in all its detailed exquisiteness and raw vigor than Bierstadt. No one can ever do it again, not even with photography. Among his major western paintings were "Laramie Peak," "Lander's Peak, Rocky Mountains," "North Fork of the Platte," "Looking Down Yosemite Valley," "Great Trees of California," "Estes Park, Colorado" and "Mountain Lake, Sierra Nevada." Two of his works, "The Discovery of the Hudson River" and "The Settlement of California" are in the National Capitol. His large studio at Irvington-on-the-Hudson was burned in 1882 and he opened another at New York City. He revisited Europe three times, one notable result being his "Storm on the Matterhorn," done in 1884 following a stay in Switzerland. In 1885 he commenced painting wild animals and concentrated on historical themes. Although he fell into some disfavor among certain elements, there has been a revival of interest in his work, dating from the mid-twentieth century. Bierstadt was married twice, his first wife predeceasing him. He died at New York City.

Literature abundant; DAB; *Webster's American Biographies,* Springfield, Mass., G. & C. Merriam Co., 1974; EA.

Big Head (Mahk-si-ah), Cheyenne chief (fl. 1856-1878). A Cheyenne Dog Soldier, he was the uncle of George Bent, and became a very prominent war leader, being involved in celebrated Plains incidents of the middle 19th century. In late August 1856 Big Head, Good Bear and Black Hairy Dog were arrested and taken to new Fort Kearny (near present Kearney, Nebraska), but escaped, Big Head being shot "in several places" as he broke loose. He recovered. In late summer 1863 Big Head was reported by Bent to have been killed in a fight on Solomon's Fork, Kansas, but this was in error, for he reported him alive on several occasions afterward. Big Head was in the Chivington fight on Sand Creek, eastern Colorado, in November 1864 and again Bent reported he had been killed, but once more this is mistaken for he was noted in later incidents. February 25, 1866, Major Edward Wynkoop (see entry) and Indian Agent J.C. Taylor met with Big Head and Medicine Arrows, referred to as important band chiefs, on Bluff Creek, Kansas, and suggested they accept the Treaty of the Little Arkansas. The chiefs at first refused, Big Head objecting that the treaty permitted white travel over the Smoky Hill road, which ran through the Cheyennes' best hunting ground; travel and emigrants would drive away the buffalo, and he and his people did not want to live south of the Arkansas River in the country of other tribes. Wynkoop prevailed, however, and the Cheyenne leaders signed a paper accepting the treaty. Big Head was with a hunting party of Cheyennes and Sioux when it surprised Lieutenant Lyman Kidder (see entry) with a detachment of nine men and a Sioux guide, and killed them all; no Cheyennes were lost in this fight, but two Sioux were slain. In Custer's South Plains campaign of 1868 which concluded with the confrontation at a Cheyenne village in present west Texas, Big Head and Dull Knife, chiefs, were held by the white officer as hostages until two German sisters (see entry) were freed by the Indians, when the chiefs were released. Whether Big Head was in the Custer fights of 1876 is not reported, but he was in the Cheyenne village attacked in November by Ranald Mackenzie, apparently escaping unhurt. He was sent south with the captured Cheyennes, but fled the Oklahoma exile with Dull Knife in 1878; he was one of six Cheyennes later tried at Lawrence, Kansas for killings of whites during the northward hegira, but all were released for lack of evidence. Nothing has been learned of the date or circumstances of his demise.

George E. Hyde, *Life of George Bent,* Norman,

Univ. of Okla. Press, 1968; George Bird Grinnell, *The Fighting Cheyennes,* Norman, 1956; Donald J. Berthrong, *The Southern Cheyennes,* Norman, 1963; Thomas B. Marquis, *The Cheyennes of Montana,* Algonac, Mich., Reference Pubs., Inc., 1978; Alan W. Farley, ed., "Reminiscences of Allison J. Pliley, Indian Fighter," Kansas City Posse of Westerners *Trail Guide,* Vol. 2, No. 2 (June 1957), 10-11; information from E.F. (Ted) Mains.

Big Mouth, Mescalero Apache scout (c. 1857-1958). Big Mouth's tombstone at the cemetery on the Mescalero Reservation, New Mexico, states the year of his birth as 1863, but Big Mouth had clear recollections of the forced move of his people to the Fort Sumner, Bosque Redondo Reservation in 1863 and said that at the time he was "six or seven years old," although he did not know the exact date of his birth. He was born on the Rio Bonito above Fort Stanton, and detailed, largely from stories told by the People, the miserable journey to Bosque Redondo, several unhappy years there and eventually the Mescaleros' slipping away at night to escape back to their homeland. He told his interviewer how the Mescaleros were mistreated when they got home again, how most of their ancestral land was stolen from them by whites and white officialdom, and of the years of hardship, neglect and cruelty they faced before they were secure on their reservation. When Big Mouth matured he enlisted as a scout and served against Victorio and Geronimo for a considerable period. Eventually he received a small pension and a "medal" of some sort in recognition of his services. He became, before his death, "the last living scout of the Apache wars," he believed. He died at around 100 years of age.

Eve Ball, "Big Mouth — Apache Scout," *Frontier Times,* Vol. 32, No. 2 (Spring, 1958), 14-16, 35-36; this story is repeated in Eve Ball, *Indeh: An Apache Odyssey,* with Nora Henn, Lynda Sanchez, Provo, Brigham Young Univ. Press, 1980, 200-203; information from Phillip G. Nickell.

Big Spotted Horse (Uh-sah-wuck-oo-led-ee-hoor), Pawnee raid leader (c. 1837-c. 1875). A member of the Kitkehahki people, one of the four Pawnee tribes, he was a noted horse thief, warrior and, at one time, a Pawnee scout for the army. Big Spotted Horse at 15 or 16 killed the noted Cheyenne war leader Alights-on-the-Clouds. It happened on a misty morning. Alights-on-the-Clouds was trying to count coup

on Big Spotted Horse, riding up from in back on his right side to do so, since a bowman cannot easily shoot behind and to his right; Big Spotted Horse however was left-handed. He like most of the Pawnees was terrified of Alights-on-the-Clouds who seemed spirit-protected from arrows and bullets. As the Cheyenne moved in to strike, Big Spotted Horse who later conceded he was so frightened he didn't see where he was shooting, loosed an arrow and darted off until he heard a "great shout from the Pawnees, and looking around beheld the terrible Cheyenne stretched on the ground with an arrow sticking in his [right] eye," the wound fatal. The Pawnees discovered that Alights-on-the-Clouds wore under his robe a suit of Spanish chain armor protecting him from neck to knee from arrows or even smooth-bore bullets; they cut his chain mail to pieces, carrying them off as trophies. From that moment, Big Spotted Horse was a man of note. He grew to six feet, two inches in height, according to Luther North, and was "a big, good-natured fellow, always laughing and joking, when not fighting. As a 'progressive,' he disapproved violently of Quakers [Indian agents] and all white men who preached against fighting and horse-lifting. In both these arts he was an adept; but being an inveterate gambler, he lost in Pawnee games and white man's poker most of the horses and other valuables he gained by risking his life on the warpath." He was very fond of his wife and child, and unlike other Pawnees he helped his spouse with her fieldwork and "openly and shamelessly carried the baby," no Pawnee daring to jeer at him for doing so. Big Spotted Horse around 1870 serve briefly in the Pawnee Scouts under Captain Sylvanus E. Cushing (see entry), and in 1874 served with Indian scouts under Captain Richard H. Pratt, fighting Kiowas and other hostiles on the South Plains. In 1867 he joined Lone Chief and others in a "most dangerous" attempt to steal Osage horses, bringing back thirty head. The next year they raided southward again, all the way to the Red River, on this trip rediscovering the Wichitas, southern cousins of the Pawnees. In October 1869 Big Spotted Horse gathered a party of adventurous Pawnees who went south of the Arkansas River, found a 75-lodge camp of Cheyennes, stole into it in darkness and cut loose all the fine horses tied next to lodges, then rounded up the general herd and dashed north with 600 head of enemy horses. They crossed the Arkansas River safely and pushed on by obscure trails, through a savage early winter snowstorm and regained the Pawnee villages in Nebraska. Quaker Indian agent Jacob M. Troth ordered Big Spotted Horse to take the animals back to the Cheyennes, unaware or uncaring that only murder would await them there, and the Indian raider refused to cancel out his honorable and daring feat in such a suicidal way. Troth ordered Big Spotted Horse and five of his "fellow criminals" turned over to the military and they were jailed at Fort Omaha. They enjoyed their stay in the guard house where poker games were customary, the rations good, the quarters warm and comfortable and late in the spring a judge decided there was no law against Indians stealing horses from Indians and they were taken back to the reservation aboard a Union Pacific train. Here Spotted Horse discovered that by ruse his 600 stolen Cheyenne horses had vanished and he angrily bolted the reservation and its Quaker agent and went to the land of the Wichitas, where he was welcomed and there were no such agents. In July 1873 a large number of Pawnees, hunting buffalo along the Republican River, were surprised by a larger party of Sioux and upwards of 100 were killed in one of the worst massacres of Pawnee history. Partly as a result, Big Spotted Horse and Lone Chief who had returned north for a visit, persuaded many Pawnees to steal away from the reservation and join the Wichitas. The death of Big Spotted Horse is variously told. By one account he was shot by Texas cowboys who caught him rustling horses, Hyde commenting that he "did not have it in him to become a good reservation Indian; he had always desired such a death, and to be left on the prairie for his brothers, the wolves." Luther North wrote that "my general impression is that he made off with a large number of Cheyenne horses, and was either killed or murdered by officers of the United States, who probably did not appreciate what a skilled performer he was in that line."

George E. Hyde, *The Pawnee Indians,* Norman, Univ. of Okla. Press, 1974; Donald F. Danker, ed., *Man of the Plains: Recollections of Luther North 1856-1882,* Lincoln, Univ. of Neb. Press, 1961; Thomas W. Dunlay, *Wolves for the Blue Soldiers,* Lincoln, 1982.

Billings, Joseph (Osip Osipovich), naval officer (1761-1806). B. at Turnham Green, Chiswick, west London, he sailed as an able-bodied seaman on the *Discovery* on Cook's third voyage and following Cook's death was transferred in the same rating to the *Resolution.* After return of the expedition to England Billings entered the merchant marine, became a mate and in that capacity reached St. Petersburg where he joined the Russian navy as a lieutenant. In 1784 the Tsarina Catherine II determined to send an expedition to the North Pacific to accomplish certain ends and Billings, by then known as a "companion" of Cook was selected as the man to lead it. Instructions August 8, 1785, from the tsarina and the Admiralty College to Billings were to establish precisely the latitude and longitude of the Kolyma River delta in eastern Siberia, survey the Chukotski Peninsula as far as East Cape and to "prepare an accurate chart of the islands in the Pacific Ocean extending to the coast of America," conducting also studies of ethnological matters, linguistics and geographical, zoological and various natural history subjects. He was to commence his task as a captain lieutenant and to promote himself step by step as his work progressed to captain of the fleet first rank. His payment and that of his officers and men were to be generous. The purposes of the expedition, and Billings' many-sided mission, were covert, in keeping with the traditional Russian obsession with secrecy. The directive was minutely detailed even to instructing the commander how much weight to put on each packhorse and how he must greet and conduct relations with native peoples, whether friendly or hostile, although a great deal also was left to his discretion and judgment. Lieutenant Gavriil A. Sarychev (see entry) was named second in command and was to captain the second vessel of the two-ship flotilla. In September 1785 Sarychev was sent to Okhotsk, on the Siberian coast, to begin construction of the ships. Billings left later, accompanied by Martin Sauer, secretary and journalist of the endeavor which also had as lieutenants Robert Hall and Christian Bering, a nephew of Vitus Bering, the discoverer. In 1786, while awaiting construction of the vessels Billings decided to visit northeastern Siberia. He wintered at Nizhne Kolymsk and left May 25, 1787 for the Arctic Ocean, bearing east along the coast until July 25, perhaps reaching the present Mys (Cape) Billings, where the captain decided to turn back although Sarychev, Sauer and others believed the route ahead was open into the Pacific. Trouble meanwhile was encountered assembling supplies at Irkutsk and it was September 1788 before the expedition could be readied at Okhotsk. It was not until July 1789 that the larger of the two bottoms could be launched; she was named the *Slava Rossie (Glory of Russia).* The second ship, launched in

August, was wrecked trying to clear the harbor of Okhotsk. The *Slava Rossie* alone therefore sailed September 19, reaching Petropavlovsk on the east coast of Kamchatka October 1. Here the expedition wintered, clearing the port May 1, 1790, sighting Amchitka Island of the Aleutians May 22 and arriving at Unalaska June 1, sailed on past the Sanak and Shumagin islands and arrived at Three Saints Harbor, Kodiak Island, June 29 where Delarov (see entry) was in charge. Everywhere he went Billings took astronomical readings and fulfilled as well as possible the assignments given him by the empress. In his report of Kodiak he mentions a possible water route across the Alaska Peninsula by way of Iliamna Lake, the Eskimo natives stating they could pass by canoe from Shelikhov Strait across the lake and to Bristol Bay without important portaging. Billings sailed to Montague Island, at the entrance to Prince William Sound July 19, sending boat parties on exploration missions into the Sound and to nearby islands. The expedition determined that Kayak Island was the "Cape St. Elias" discovered by Bering in 1741. On August 1 a council of officers determined that it would be best, in view of the lateness of the season and shortage of supplies, to return to Kamchatka for the winter. The *Slava Rossie,* buffeted by gales and heavy seas, entered the Bay of Avatcha October 14 and anchored once more at Petropavlovsk. To replace a navigator who had died Billings hired Gerassim Pribylof (see entry), and a second ship having been built, the first part of the expedition left May 19, 1791, for Bering Island. The second vessel, the *Chernui Orel (Black Eagle),* under Lieutenant Hall, was to meet with the flagship at Bering Island, or if that was not possible, at Unalaska Island. Bad weather prevented a reunion at Bering and the *Slava Rossie* went on to Tanaga Island in the Aleutians and June 25 reached Illiuliuk Harbor (Dutch Harbor) at Unalaska. Here Billings decided to abandon his former intention to thoroughly chart Cook Inlet and instead to make for St. Lawrence Bay (Zaliv Lavrentiya) on the Chukotski Peninsula to complete his earlier work in that area. The *Slava Rossie* passed by Pribylov and St. Matthew Islands, investigated St. Lawrence Island, on July 27 sighted Cape Rodney on the Alaskan coast, on August 2 attained its highest latitude, 65°23'50", the next day anchoring in St. Lawrence Bay. From this point Billings determined to set out overland for the Kolyma River delta while the *Slava Rossie,* under Sarychev

returned to Unalaska Island. There it made a delayed contact with Hall and after passing a harsh and uncomfortable winter, returned to Petropavlovsk in mid-June, having lost many men from scurvy or otherwise. Billings had finally reached the Kolyma after a difficult overland journey, frustrated by belligerent and uncooperative Chukchi natives upon whom he must depend for guides. Upon his return to Yakutsk the expedition came to an end. It was "inaugurated on a truly magnificent scale after long years of preparation" but its "geographical results may be set down at next to nothing," concluded Bancroft, although he conceded that "an important feature, however was the preliminary experience gained by Sarychef, who subsequently published the most complete and reliable charts" of the Aleutians, their accuracy "acknowledged to the present day." He thought Sauer's acidulous estimate of his commander "was nearly correct," although others differed. The *Dictionary of National Biography* concluded that "Mr. Sauer did not love his captain, and implies that he was greedy, selfish, ignorant, and tyrannical, but makes no definite charge." The most recent scholarly study of the endeavor and assessment of its result, concluded that while the expedition accomplished only some of its objectives, "its failure in others was not due to Billings' ineptitude, as some patriotic Russian and Soviet writers have suggested, nor [were] its success[es] due to Sarychev's abilities." The expedition had "overly ambitious" assignments, needed to combat hostile natural conditions, but it did provide materials for the preparation of the first thoroughly accurate maps of the North Pacific, and gathered valuable ethnographic and linguistic materials. Bancroft wrote that "the principal benefit derived from this costly undertaking was the ventilation of abuses practised by unscrupulous traders upon helpless natives. The authorities in Siberia and St. Petersburg became at last convinced that an end must be put to the barbarous rule of the promyshlenniki," and the best way to do that would be to grant monopoly to a single strong company which might be held accountable to the government for its conduct. It seems possible that the otherwise unattributed report of complaints by natives of Unalaska about treatment of them by promyshlenniki and seamen *(Russian Penetration of the North Pacific Ocean,* 368-72) may have originated with members of the Billings expedition which was at Unalaska from June 1-13, 1790. No other "government inspectors" were reported to be present at the time, and Martin Sauer made extended references to like abuses in his book although, as Bancroft points out, it was published too late to have been an influence upon the Russian government in the matter. Billings' later movements are not known with certainty, but he must have remained in Russian service for the British encyclopedia had no record of his death though the Russians provided its date for the compilers of the most recent edition of Zagoskin's work. Pierce has the best summary of his explorations.

Russian Penetration of the North Pacific Ocean; Bancroft, *Alaska;* DNB; Zagoskin; Pierce, *Russian America: A Biographical Dictionary.*

Bird (Byrd), Henry, British military officer (d. 1800). Reportedly of American (possibly Virginian) ancestry, he probably was b. before the middle of the 18th century, although this is conjecture. He was commissioned in the British army as a lieutenant in 1764 and entered the 8th, or King's, Regiment which in 1768 was ordered to Canada. Under leadership of a Captain For[r]ster, Bird had a part May 19, 1776, in the affair at The Cedars (Les Cedres), near the confluence of the St. Lawrence and Ottawa rivers, the action an offshoot of the Benedict Arnold campaign into eastern Canada. At The Cedars an American force under Colonel Bedel[1], although directly commanded by a Major Butterfield, surrendered under threat of Indian barbarities if they resisted. The American unit numbered 390 effectives, the British had 100 whites and 300 Indians; on the following day a detachment of 120 Americans coming from Montreal, 42 miles downstream, to the relief of The Cedars surrendered to a force of 80 Indians and 18 whites. Washington, who heard of the twin affairs only after an unconscionable delay, described the disaster as due to the "base and cowardly" conduct of the officers concerned. Lieutenant Bird also was with British Colonel Barry St. Leger on the 1777 Mohawk Valley campaign and took part in its most notable engagement. Sir John Johnson and Seneca chiefs had laid an ambush near Oriskany Creek, about six miles from Fort Stanwix (Schuyler) at the present Rome, New York. Bird had commanded an advance party, the main army reaching the fort August 2 prepared to invest it, although St. Leger was dismayed to find it better defended and much stronger than he had been led to believe. The siege failed, but the principal action was the Oriskany engagement where a Patriot column under General Nicholas Herkimer was ambushed and in proportionately one of the "bloodiest battles" of the Revolution the relief force was all but wiped out with some 500 Americans killed, wounded or captured. On the British side losses were light: the Indians had 33 killed and 29 wounded, and the whites half a dozen killed and a few wounded. Bird, by now a captain, reached Detroit with reinforcements in October 1778 and, as an engineer officer, helped build there a new fort. He became second in command at Detroit under Captain Richard Berrenger Lernoult. In February 1779 Lachlan McIntosh (see entry), commandant of the West at Fort Pitt, sent a provisioning party under Major Richard Taylor, father of the later President Zachary Taylor to Fort Laurens, on the Tuscarawas River near present Bolivar, Ohio. Detroit authorities sought to capture "this handful of Americans defiantly planted in the heart" of the Indian-British dominated territory, and Bird was sent with a few British regulars and many Indians into the region. From his post at (Upper) Sandusky Bird was to "stimulate successive attacks on the offending garrison." He organized a largely Indian party to lay siege to Fort Laurens, although whether he took part himself is uncertain; if he did, it would have been in the early stages. The siege lasted for about six weeks and rendered desperate the position of the garrison under John Gibson (see entry), with starvation imminent. A member of the complement slipped past besieging parties and reached Fort McIntosh, 29 miles from Pittsburgh; a relief under McIntosh hastened to Laurens, reaching it in three days only to find that the investment had been lifted, not due to the advancing Americans, but because of news of George Rogers Clark's capture of Vincennes and the seizure of Hamilton, thus turning the tide in the Old Northwest. Bird for about six months remained at Upper Sandusky from where he directed the activities of British-inclined Indians and watched to prevent an anticipated American march on Detroit. He returned to Detroit in June. The officer was satirically described by Big Cat of the Wyandots in a communication to Daniel Brodhead: "Capt Bird is much like a duck. He has a big mouth and makes a great Noise but like other Birds he will be ready to fly as soon as the hunters come near him...Captn Bird is flying over to Detroit again with his Men and Cannon. He said he found that nobody had a mind to go to War with him, and therefore his Buissness [at Upper Sandusky] was over." The Moravian missionary John Heck-ewelder of Coshocton, Ohio, wrote more calmly that Bird was "not without humanity." "When among the Wyandot at Sandusky they tortured a prisoner. Bird interceded in vain and cursed them for cowards and rascals. Thus [he] brought ill will of Indians upon him. Had determined if he took Fort Laurens to protect the garrison and allow them to march under arms to Detroit." This estimate of his character is born out by his actions in Kentucky the following year. In the spring of 1780 Captain Bird "was ordered by Major A.S. De Peyster, then British comman-dant, from Detroit with a force of [British] Regu-lars, a contingent of artillery, Simon, James and George Girty, Alexander McKee and a thousand Indian warriors" (other reports say about 600 or 700) to attack Kentucky settlements, largely to divert attention from a planned British expedi-tion against St. Louis and upper Mississippi posts. At the Falls of the Ohio (Louisville) "news of Bird's approach was brought by Lieutenant Abraham Chapline," who had just escaped from the Shawnees and now warned Kentucky of its danger. Bird found the Louisville area too strongly garrisoned for a profitable attack, his Indians reluctant to assail the region. So the com-mand moved up the Ohio to the present Coving-ton, Kentucky, and then proceeded up the Licking River to its forks and there attacked Isaac Ruddle's Station occupied by several fami-lies and "many adventurers." The place was reached June 22. Cannon fire persuaded Ruddle to surrender "provided the inhabitants should be considered prisoners to the British, and not to the Indians," to which Bird assented. When the gates were opened, however, the Indians rushed in and commenced an indiscriminate slaughter, Isaac Ruddle being among the first tomahawked and scalped. Bird said he was unable to control the warriors which apparently was true. "That he had the inclination to stop them, cannot be doubted—his subsequent conduct furnished the most con-vincing evidence, that the power to effect it, was alone wanting in him." Some 300 surviving whites were made prisoner. The Indians then clamored to be led against Martin's Station, five miles distant. Bird, "affected with the barbarities which he had just witnessed,... peremptorily refused, unless the chiefs would guarantee that the prisoners...should be entirely at his dispos-al." The chiefs finally consented and Martin's Station, too, was easily taken with 50 or more

prisoners added to the total. The Indians crossed the Ohio at the mouth of the Licking and went to their separate villages; the Canadian troops with the prisoners ascended the Great Miami River of Ohio, thence continued overland to Detroit. Upon the close of the Revolution, Bird settled on a land grant at the present Amberstburgh, Ontario. In 1784 he was summoned to England on legal business, and never returned to America. He settled near Usk, midway between Mon-mouth and Newport, Wales, for a time, but during the Napoleonic wars re-entered the army as a lieutenant-colonel of the 54th Infantry. He died during an expedition to Egypt. It is not reported whether he ever married or fathered children.

Info. from the State Hist. Soc. of Wis.; Louise Phelps Kellogg, *Frontier Advance on the Upper Ohio 1778-1779,* Madison, State Hist. Soc. of Wis., 1916; Kellogg, *Frontier Retreat on the Upper Ohio 1779-1781,* Madison, 1917; Barbara Graymont, *The Iroquois in the American Revolution,* Syracuse, N.Y., Univ. Press, 1972; Justin Winsor, *The American Revolution: A Narrative, Critical and Bibliographical History,* N.Y., Sons of Liberty Pub., 1972; Reuben Gold Thwait-es, ed., Alexander Scott Withers, *Chronicles of Border Warfare,* Cincinnati, Robert Clarke Co., 1895 (1970).

Bird, Junius Bouton, archeologist (Sep. 21, 1907-Apr. 2, 1982). B. at Rye, New York, he studied at Columbia University until in 1927 at 19 he joined an expedition to Baffin Island head-ed by Robert (Bob) Bartlett (see entry). He also accompanied Bartlett on four other expeditions, to Siberia in 1928, Labrador in 1929, and to the northeast corner of Greenland in 1930 and again in 1931. On these explorations he developed into "an excellent sailor, mechanic and outdoors-man." During this Arctic work he became affili-ated with the American Museum of Natural History, remaining with that institution for fifty-four years. He was best known for his subsequent field work in Tierra del Fuego and Peru, but earli-er in his career he also was active in Alaska, sev-eral parts of the contiguous United States, the Yucatan, Central America and Bolivia, bringing "great physical strength and energy to his arche-ological work." From 1934-37 he and his wife in a nineteen-foot sailboat explored and studied human and other remains at Fell's and Palli Aike caves north of the Strait of Magellan in Chile's southernmost extremity. He found human remains until then the earliest discovered in South America, dating to 11,000 years ago and associated with fossils of extinct horses and giant sloths. These indicated that man had reached the southern tip of South America at approximately the date of the earliest human remains known from North America at the time. Another sensational discovery resulted from his work in 1946-47 at Huaca Prieta in northern Peru. Until then the site had been considered a primitive Indian fishing and farming community of 5,000 years ago, but Bird's team found there thousands of textile fragments. He and his assistant, Milica Dimitrijevic Skinner discovered designs embedded in the structure of the fabrics from which all original colors had disappeared. "When the warp patterns of nondescript gray fragments" were charted by microscope, however, "elaborate designs and complex images of snakes, condors, and felines emerged," revealing that, so early in Andean prehistory, "textiles were a major medium of cultural expression and a source of designs that were carried on for thousands of years, influencing other art forms as well." In his many years of textile analysis he developed a "comprehensive code for the study of prehistoric fabrics," using computers to analyze his field discoveries. One study of Bird's was of the characteristics of primitive Peruvian cotton in an effort to determine whether it may have been of Asian provenance or influence, as some had suspected; he is not known to have published anything on this question. Most of his publications were scientific in nature. As a result of his work he became "the world's leading authority on pre-Columbian textiles." He was curator and, after his nominal retirement, curator emeritus of South American archeology at the museum. A meticulous scientist, holding others to his precision in investigative procedures and knowledge, but cautious about expressing his views in public when at variance with others, he remained genial and cooperative with specialists or with laymen, noted for his "sense of fair play and decency." For a time he was president of the Society of American Archaeologists, and held other important positions. He was survived by his widow, Margaret McKelvy (Peggy) Bird, who had shared in his field work, and three sons; he was a brother of Roland T. Bird, a paleontologist.

Natural History, Feb. 1989, 84-89; *New York Times,* Apr. 4, 1982.

Bird, Roland Thaxter (R.T.), paleontologist (Dec. 29, 1899-Jan 24, 1978). B. at Rye, New York, a brother of Junius B. Bird (see entry), poor health caused him at 15 to leave school to live on a Catskills farm where he developed an interest in cattle and husbandry which remained all his life. As a young adult he moved to Florida, caring for registered Jersey cattle and showing them at exhibitions around the country; he invested his limited capital in real estate, and went broke when the Florida boom collapsed in the 1920s. He then built a camper fitted like a sidecar to his motorcycle and wandered around the nation, visiting all 48 states. In November 1932 in the desert near the Petrified Forest of Arizona, by chance he located a natural stone mold of the palate of an amphibian, though search as he might he could not find more of the specimen. He expressed the weighty rock to his father at Rye, an ardent amateur scientist, and the parent showed a life-size sketch of the stone to Barnum Brown, curator of fossil reptiles at the American Museum of National History of New York City. Brown instantly recognized it as probably a new genus and asked, "Where is the rest of it?" The father wrote of Brown's enthusiasm to his son, by then wintering at Mazatlan, Mexico, and with spring Bird returned to the site and at last located the other half of the palate, which presumably had been uncovered by winter storms. The palate was shipped to Brown, whom Bird had not yet met; eventually the fossil was named *Stanocephalosaurus birdi,* a new genus of *Stegocephalia* from the Triassic age, and was scientifically described. Meanwhile Bird learned of dinosaur tracks in northern Arizona, and hunted for them east of Cameron. It was a tough search, but he located them and was thrilled to find the carved name of Brown on a nearby sandstone wall, the scientist having visited the site some years earlier (the find was again lost after Bird departed and was not relocated until 1986 by Scott Madsen of the Museum of Northern Arizona, and Keith Becker; the location was then charted but not publicized to avoid damage by vandals to the 300 distinct tracks). Bird went north to Shell, in the Big Horn Basin of Wyoming where he understood Brown had located a possible dinosaur quarry, leaving detailed work however for the following year. In 1934 at the invitation of Brown, whom Bird had come to idolize, he joined the excavation crew for a season of uncovering and removing enormous quantities of fossil bones. His great contribution was compilation of a sketch map of the tangled remains of creatures which perished in an undefinable disaster 100 million years ago. The chart depicted some 4,000 bones representing at least 20 different animals as they were uncovered, and according to Brown was "surpassed in value only by the bones themselves." The map has often been reproduced. Bird, now placed on the permanent staff of the museum, became Brown's understudy and chief assistant. Over the years the two of them explored, dug out bones, and inspected sites across the nation and at one point, in Canada. Bird's most publicized feat commenced in the autumn of 1938 when he discovered in the bed of the Paluxy River (or Creek), near Glen Rose southwest of Fort Worth, Texas, an elaborate network of dinosaurian tracks (there are many places in central and south Texas where dinosaur tracks are known). With difficulty he extracted and shipped to the New York Museum a double set of them suggesting (although "this is but a guess," he said) that a smaller, more active carnivore may well have been *Acrocanthosaurus,* a relative of *Tyrannosaurus,* and the larger animal possibly a *Pleurocoelus,* a type of *Brontosaur.* Bird's work at the museum continued eventfully and productively, with numerous field trips and many discoveries to enliven it, until World War II when he was employed by the government to search out deposits of vanadium (used for hardening steel) and uranium for the secret Manhattan Project. Illness caused him to cease active employment following the war; he married Hazel Russell June 4, 1946, and they moved to Florida, settling at Homestead. In 1952 the museum planned to redo its so-called Brontosaur Hall, the new arrangement overseen by Edwin H. (Ned) Colbert, Brown's successor as curator of fossil reptiles. Colbert decided to install Bird's Paluxy sauropod footprints behind and leading to the brontosaurus skeleton; only Bird could do this since the specimens shipped to New York were heaped in deteriorating crates in outside weather. Bird, despite his failing health, agreed to return to New York and oversee the job, which in the course of time will be viewed by millions of visitors. The spectacular exhibit is his permanent monument, and a vivid one it is, suggesting how the mighty brontosaurus was dramatically pursued and perhaps attacked and slain by its ferocious smaller assailant on that distant day. Bird died at 79 in Florida and was buried with a gastrolith (a dinosaur stomach stone) in his pocket at Grahamsville, New York, among the Catskill Mountains. His headstone is carved with a representation of a brontosaur and bears the legend: "Discoverer of Sauropod Dinosaur Footprints."

Roland T. Bird, *Bones for Barnum Brown: Adventures of a Dinosaur Hunter,* ed. by V. Theodore Schreiber, intr. and enlightening and useful notes by James O. Farlow, Fort Worth, Tex. Christian Univ. Press, 1985; Tucson, *Tucson Daily Star,* Apr. 18, 1986; Edwin H. Colbert, *A Fossil-Hunter's Notebook,* N.Y., E.P. Dutton, 1980, personal acquaintance of author with Bird and Brown.

Black, Arthur, mountain man (fl. c. 1823-1832). Arthur Black, described by Harrison Rogers as a "Scotchman," may according to one unverified report have saved Jedediah Smith from a grizzly in the Black Hills in late summer of 1823. At any rate he accompanied Smith on many adventures, and seems to have been a man depended upon, and a tried companion of the noted leader and explorer. Black probably was with Smith in 1824 on the spring hunt when Black's Fork of the Green River was named, suggesting either that he was its discoverer, or was a well-regarded member of the small party. In August 1826 he was of the company of eighteen selected by Smith for his initial exploration of the Southwest. Black took part, though with no noteworthy role in events involving Smith and Mexican authorities and clergy in southern California, and remained at the 1826-27 Stanislaus River camp while the leader and two men returned to Bear Lake where Smith recruited eighteen more men, retraced his earlier course in 1827 to the Mohave villages on the Colorado River where he lost ten men in an Indian fight, then rejoined his reduced original party on the Stanislaus. After fresh difficulties with Mexican authorities in mid-California, the Smith expedition, including Black, went north, toward the Columbia River. The coast was attained with difficulty, the explorers continuing on to the Umpqua River of southern Oregon. Here on July 14, 1828, fourteen men and a native boy were killed in a fight with Kalawatset (Umpqua) Indians. Smith and two others, being away from camp at the time, escaped and only Arthur Black, sorely wounded, survived the massacre. He made his solitary way northward to the Hudson's Bay Company post of Fort Vancouver, run by a fellow Scotsman, John McLoughlin. He generously cooperated with Smith, Black and the other two survivors in retrieving from the Indians whatever was possible of their belongings. Black in 1829 was Smith's sole companion on the journey back to the Rocky Mountains. The final documentary evidence of him was a directive of June 30, 1832, by Kenneth Mackenzie at Fort Union on the Missouri River to Pierre Chouteau Jr. at St. Louis to pay to Arthur Black's order $1,501 "for value received in beaver." Miles Goodyear, a mountain man, told Heinrich Lienhard at Fort Bridger, Wyoming, in 1846 that "at this spot, over there in the willow thicket, 14 years ago, a man named Black had been killed by a band of fifty Blackfoot Indians. For some time he had courageously defended himself and killed or wounded several of them before they succeeded in doing away with him." If the tale is true, as Dale Morgan pointed out, Goodyear must have gotten it by hearsay, for he did not come to the mountains until 1836, four years after the presumed fight. Morgan quotes another story, more likely apocryphal, that Black had been severely wounded by Blackfeet and died later at a tavern at St. Louis; this tale, however unlikely, at least would confirm in part that it was Blackfeet who accounted for Black in some manner. In any event he is not reported after 1832.

Dale L. Morgan, *Jedediah Smith and the Opening of the West,* Indianapolis, N.Y., Bobbs-Merrill Co., 1953; Morgan, *The West of William H. Ashley...1822-1838,* Denver, Old West Pub. Co., 1964; George R. Brooks, *The Southwest Expedition of Jedediah S. Smith...1826-1827,* Glendale, Calif., Arthur H. Clark Co., 1977; Harvey L. Carter, "Jedediah Smith," MM VIII; information from E.F. (Ted) Mains.

Black Bear (Wah-tah-nah), Northern Arapaho chief (fl. 1865-1911). Black Bear, the Arapaho is not to be confused with Black Bear, the Cheyenne who was killed July 29, 1857, in Edwin Vose Sumner's saber charge on Solomon's Fork of the Kansas River. The Arapaho was a principal chief and achieved fame for his harassment of James A. Sawyer's expedition and as a result of a hard fight with Connor's force of soldiers and Pawnee scouts. This occurred August 31, 1865, with an attack on Black Bear's village at the mouth of the Tongue River where seven of Connor's men were wounded or killed, including his aide, Lieutenant Oscar Jewett, and an estimated thirty-five Arapahoes slain. Connor's force captured about 500 horses. A son of Black Bear was among the Indians killed. On May 10, 1868, Black Bear was among thirteen Northern Arapahoes and Northern Cheyennes who signed a treaty at Fort Laramie; by it the Indians agreed to accept reservations to be designated. Signing for the whites were Generals Sherman, Harney, Terry and Augur, among oth-

ers. Black Bear on July 18, 1911, told Walter Camp that he had witnessed the approach of Custer June 25, 1876, on the Sioux villages on the Little Bighorn River of Montana, his account supported by He Dog in an interview of July 13, 1910, and by Standing Bear in an interview of July 12, 1910. Black Bear said that he was on the Red Cloud reservation and had lost some horses. Following their trail he thought they had been stolen by Indians planning to join the Crazy Horse-Sitting Bull hostiles. He went to the hostile camp on Greasy Grass Creek (the Little Bighorn River), found his horses and left with them. "While crossing the divide early on the morning of 6/25/76 we discovered soldiers marching toward the village. We ran into the high hills and watched them...We did not go to warn the village. As we were not hostiles we continued on toward the agency." His party consisted of six men and one woman, the spouse of Knife, who was of the group. Black Bear apparently was with Two Moon's band in 1877 when they surrendered to Miles on April 22, on the Tongue River. Of the 300 Indians, most were Cheyennes, but not all, and there were some Arapahoes. Whether Black Bear was with the Dull Knife people on their 1878 hegira northward from Oklahoma toward their old country is not clear but his wife was with that people and was imprisoned at Fort Robinson with the band. At the January 9-10 breakout, Black Bear's wife, who had a carbine "hanging down my back," as one of the secreted weapons of the prisoners, "was one of the first to get out" when the prisoners broke loose. Apparently she escaped the ensuing massacre and if Black Bear was in the emeute he also escaped. Nothing has been learned of the date and circumstances of Black Bear's death, but it must have occurred well into the 20th century.

George E. Hyde, *Life of George Bent,* Norman, Univ. of Okla. Press, 1968; George Bird Grinnell, *The Fighting Cheyennes,* Norman, 1956; LeRoy R., Ann W., Hafen, *Powder River Campaigns and Sawyers Expedition of 1865,* Glendale, Calif., Arthur H. Clark Co., 1961; Charles J. Kappler, *Indian Treaties 1778-1883,* N.Y., Interland Pub. Inc., 1972; Kenneth Hammer, ed., *Custer in '76: Walter Camp's Notes on the Custer Fight,* Provo, Utah, Brigham Young Univ. Press, 1976.

Black Fish (Ma'kahday-wah-may-quah), Shawnee chief (d. c. June 1779, or 1788). Nothing is reported of his birth, and little of his early life, but he became an aggressive war leader and must have come to prominence among his own people at an early age. Puckeshinwa, father of the great Tecumseh, was killed by whites in 1774 near Old Piqua, six miles southwest of the present Springfield, Ohio, and the boy at six was adopted by Black Fish who then was chief of Old Chillicothe, near the Miami River south of Old Piqua. Black Fish ws idolized by the youngster, according to Tucker. He was "a big, hearty, companionable Indian who laughed often, ruled his village with a code as inflexible as the flint of his arrowheads, formed quick attachments, angrily inflicted corporal punishment with his own hands." While he never took part in truly major Indian-white battles, "none was more active in harassing the Kentucky settlements, besieging the stations and spreading terror through the land across the Ohio." When Cornstalk was murdered in 1777 by lawless whites, Black Fish succeeded him as principal chief of his faction of the Shawnees; one source says that under Black Fish was Black Hoof (see entry), another prominent chief. Even before Cornstalk's demise Black Fish had led a large war party against Harrodsburg, Kentucky, on March 7, 1777, surprising a group four miles from the fort, killing William Ray and slaying four others closer to the place. April 24 Black Fish and an estimated one hundred men struck Boonesborough where Daniel Boone and Simon Kenton (see entries) were among the defenders. At one point Kenton saved the wounded Boone from capture or worse. May 23 Black Fish and his warriors returned to Boonesborough for a "siege" but it lasted only a scant two days. At some point Black Fish lost a son to Boone's rifle in Kentucky, making it ironic that through his agency Tecumseh and Boone would become adoptive brothers, since Black Fish eventually extended a fatherly shield over both. January 1, 1778, Boone and thirty others left Boonesborough for the Blue Licks (near Lexington) to make salt. Boone was bringing in buffalo meat on February 7 when he was accosted by four Shawnees who captured and brought him to Black Fish; the Shawnees managed to take most of the other salt makers as well. In the Shawnee camp were James and George Girty, brothers of the notorious Simon, all of whom knew Boone well. The prisoners were conducted to Little Chillicothe, three miles north of present Xenia, Ohio, arriving February 18. Ten were distributed among the Shawnees for adoption while others, including Boone, were taken by Black

Fish to Detroit to be sold to the English governor, Henry Hamilton. Black Fish, having taken a strong liking to Boone, declined to turn him in, however, despite the considerable reward Hamilton offered for him because Boone had convinced the governor, on the basis of a King's commission he had received during Lord Dunmore's War, that he was loyal to British interests. Returning to Chillicothe with Black Fish, Boone noted preparations for a fresh invasion of Kentucky. He escaped the camp and in four days covered 160 miles to reach Boonesborough with news of the impending assault. It occurred September 7, 1778, but the attack by several hundred Indians and a few Frenchmen failed to reduce the place. Kentuckians, having learned from Boone and probably others where the Shawnee towns were located, determined to carry the war to them. In preparation Chillicothe was scouted by George Clark (whose relationship, if any, to George Rogers Clark is not stated), and Alexander Montgomery. Bowman (see entry) commanded the expedition which reached the town in late May 1779 (the often-stated date of late July is in error). By the first of two versions of Black Fish's death, he received a wound, the bullet entering his leg at the knee and traveling upward. Believed at first superficial, a subsequent illness proved mortal. A second version of Black Fish's demise was presented by Tucker: "The manner of Blackfish's death was shameful from an Indian viewpoint, and the true story had to be suppressed...It happened when he was on an invasion of Kentucky in 1788" in company with Tecumseh and others. "Blackfish had grown old and rheumatic and had lost his alertness. He entered the house of Joseph Stinson and was about to dispatch the owner when Polly, one of the Stinson girls, suddenly drove a butcher knife into his back. He fell dead. The chief was buried secretly. Of course it had to be hushed up that a woman had killed him. It was given out that he had lost his life manfully, in different circumstances...that he had died years earlier from the wound taken during the Bowman attack... Polly's fate may be conjectured."

Reuben Gold Thwaites, *Daniel Boone,* N.Y., D. Appleton & Co., 1902; Alexander Scott Withers, *Chronicles of Border Warfare,* ed. by Thwaites, Cincinnati, Robert Clarke Co., 1895 (1961); Glenn Tucker, *Tecumseh: Vision of Glory,* N.Y., Bobbs-Merrill Co., 1956; Patricia Jahns, *The Violent Years,* N.Y., Hastings House, 1962; information from E.F. (Ted) Mains, Cottonwood, AZ.

Black Hoof (Catahecassa, Ma'ka-tawikasha), Shawnee principal chief (c. 1740-1831). Black Hoof was one of the greatest and most famous leaders of the militant Shawnees when "they were dreaded as inveterate and merciless foes of the whites." He was present at the defeat of Braddock (see entry) in 1755 and in the hard fight against Virginia militia under Andrew Lewis (see entry) at Point Pleasant during Lord Dunmore's War of 1774. As an active leader he had a significant role in the battles against Harmar in 1790 and St. Clair in 1791 (see entries), but his fighting days ended with the victory of Wayne in 1794 and Black Hoof was a signer of the important Treaty of Greenville, Ohio, on August 3, 1795. Thereafter his career continued as orator and counselor and "when finally convinced of the hopelessness of struggling against encroachment of the whites, he used his influence to preserve peace." As head chief of the Shawnees he kept most of the tribe in restraint when British agents sought to incite them into rebellion against the American government, and "succeeded in seducing Tecumseh and some of the younger warriors." He signed (or X'd) treaties in 1803 and 1805. Black Hoof tried to lead his people along a new way of life. He visited Washington, D. C., in the winter of 1802-1803, urging federal officials to provide his Shawnees with farming tools and instruction in agriculture and construction of log houses like those the whites lived in. He requested of War Secretary Henry Dearborn a specific deed to Shawnee lands in western Ohio as a guarantee "that nobody" would take away their lands. Dearborn was wary of legalizing the Shawnee claim to the Auglaize River valley, and put Black Hoof off. Agricultural assistance in any major way was not forthcoming either, and Black Hoof made a second trip to Washington in February 1807; federal officials authorized Quaker missionary William Kirk to establish a mission at Wapakoneta for the Shawnees. Through him was commenced the instruction that Black Hoof had requested and the start of agriculture on a modest scale. Tension increased between the Shawnees under Black Hoof and those under the prophet, Tenskwatawa, but major bloodshed was avoided. Although Tecumseh tried, he was unable to wean Black Hoof's people from their allegiance to the white Americans. During the War of 1812 he led a contingent of Shawnees with the white American forces, though his presence was of little significance. Lewis Cass, governor of Michigan Territory, sought to persuade Black Hoof and other Shawnee leaders to remove from Ohio to the west, but was unable to do so, and treaty provisions upheld their right to remain in Ohio. In his advanced age Black Hoof lived on an annuity or pension. He died at about the age of 91 at his town of Wapakoneta, a community still in existence southwest of the present Lima, Ohio.

Hodge, HAI; Glenn Tucker, *Tecumseh: Vision of Glory,* N.Y., Bobbs-Merrill Co., 1956; R. David Edmunds, *The Shawnee Prophet,* Lincoln, Univ. of Neb. Press, 1983; Henry Harvey, *History of the Shawnee Indians,* Cincinatti, Ephraim Morgan & Sons, 1855 (1977); information from E.F. (Ted) Mains, Cottonwood, AZ.

Black Kettle (Chaudiére Noire), Onondaga chief (d. c. 1697). This chief first became important in King Williams War (1688-97) when a French force of some 300 was sent to attack the Iroquois at Fort Niagara, New York, and Black Kettle with 80 warriors gave them a running fight and severe casualties, though the Onondaga force in the end was eliminated. The next season he laid waste French settlements in western Canada. In 1691 the Iroquois planned to destroy French settlements and trading posts west of Montreal, but their plans were revealed to the French commander by Indian women prisoners; the French destroyed the maurauding parties. Black Kettle retaliated by killing Indians who traded with Montreal and the French escort sent to guard them. July 15, 1692, he attacked Montreal and carried off prisoners who were recaptured by a pursuing party. Also in 1692 he attacked a party led by a French commander, de Lusignan, who was killed. In 1697 Black Kettle arranged a peace with the French. But before it was concluded he was killed by Algonquin Indians while hunting near Cattaraugus, southeast of Buffalo, New York.

Hodge, HAI; information from John Sugden.

Black Moon, Hunkpapa Sioux chief (d. June 25, 1876). Some assert that "Black Moon" actually means "Black Sun," and referred to a total eclipse of the sun which occurred during a war party's outing; it turned back. But this is based upon Grinnell's *The Fighting Cheyennes,* and concerns a Cheyenne dog soldier chief, Black Moon, who took part in the famed battle of Beecher Island and was killed in Carr's victory over the Cheyennes at Summit Springs, Colorado, on July 11, 1869. This does not preclude the Hunkpapa chief's being named for a similar event, but there is no recorded basis for that explanation, or any other. Black Moon, a very powerful chief of the hostile Hunkpapas first comes into view in 1862 when the Hunkpapas associated with the Minnesota Mdewakanton Sioux who had been forced into Dakota and with them, "became bitterly hostile." Four Horns and Sitting Bull were also of this faction. They fought Sully in the July 28, 1864, battle of Killdeer Mountain in which Sully lost five killed and ten wounded to an admitted Indian loss of thirty-one killed. Black Moon with other powerful chiefs met De Smet (see entry) in 1868 at the Sioux camp on Powder River, but the meeting, designed to seek a general peace, was inconclusive. Neither Black Moon, Crazy Horse nor Gall signed the 1868 Fort Laramie Treaty which other less hostile Sioux chiefs were cajoled into approving. On August 14, 1872, near Pryor's Fork in southern Montana a 2nd Cavalry column under Major E.M. Baker consisting of four troops each of the 2nd and 7th cavalries, was attacked by several hundred Sioux and Cheyenne warriors, led by Black Moon. One soldier was killed, four of the white column wounded and two Indians killed outright, ten wounded, some mortally. Black Moon was in charge of the noted Sun Dance ending June 14, 1876, at which Sitting Bull purportedly received a vision which told him that the soldiers were coming to attack, but that the Indians would be victorious. Black Moon was in the counter-attack on the Reno forces on June 25 and once the soldiers had retreated to the hills and were besieged, he and the great chiefs, Crazy Horse, Gall "and many other famous men" hastened to attack the main Custer column as it crested the hills beyond the Little Big Horn River. Just after crossing the ford, and before he could become fully engaged, Black Moon was killed, and Gall took over as leader of that faction of the Hunkpapas.

George E. Hyde, *Red Cloud's Folk*, Norman, Univ. of Okla. Press, 1957; Doane Robinson, *A History of the Dakota or Sioux Indians*, Minneapolis, Ross & Haines, Inc., 1956; Edgar I. Stewart, *Custer's Luck*, Norman, 1955; George Bird Grinnell, *The Fighting Cheyennes*, Norman, 1956; Stanley Vestal, *Sitting Bull: Champion of the Sioux*, Norman, 1969; information from E.F. (Ted) Mains.

Black Shield, Miniconjou Sioux chief (fl. 1858-1876). Nothing is reported of Black Shield's birth or young manhood. In 1859 or perhaps 1858 he led a "huge" war party that wiped out a small camp of Crows. The Crows, either in this action or an earlier one, killed Big Crow, a son of Black Shield which may have precipitated a retaliatory affair. By 1866 he had become one of six hereditary chiefs or "Scalp-Shirt Men" of the Miniconjou Sioux. The Miniconjou were a division of the Teton Sioux, closely related to the Oglala, Brulé and Hunkpapa Tetons. The first report by whites of the Miniconjous was in 1804 by Lewis and Clark who found them living on both sides of the Missouri above the Cheyenne River; they were considered by later whites unruly and troublesome. The Miniconjou were signers of the peace treaty of Fort Sully, South Dakota, on October 10, 1865, and Fort Laramie, April 29, 1868, but Black Shield did not sign either, at least by that name, and his Dakota name is unreported. Vestal wrote that Black Shield was "the principal chief leading the Minniconjou" in the Fetterman fight of December 21, 1866, near Fort Phil Kearny, Wyoming, an engagement from which no white survived and more than eighty perished. Many believe Red Cloud led the Oglalas in this engagement, but Vestal insisted it was Crazy Horse. Black Shield was reported in 1868 at a great camp of various bands of Sioux at which Sitting Bull came into tribal prominence, and in 1873 he came into Fort Peck with Frank Grouard and others. In 1876 Black Shield was reported by Vestal at the Custer battle on the Little Bighorn, but says nothing of his actual participation or fate. He is not mentioned in literature examined for the period after that date.

George E. Hyde, *Red Cloud's Folk*, Norman, Univ. of Okla. Press, 1957; Stanley Vestal, *Warpath*, Lincoln, Univ. of Neb. Press, 1984; Vestal, *Sitting Bull, Champion of the Sioux*, Norman, 1969; Edgar I. Stewart, *Custer's Luck*, Norman, 1965; Joe DeBarthe, *Life and Adventures of Frank Grouard*, Norman, 1958; Charles J. Kappler, Indian Treaties 1778-1883, N.Y., Interland Pub., 1972.

Blake, Amanda, actress (Feb. 20, 1929-Aug. 16, 1989). B. Beverly Neill at Buffalo, New York, she became best known for her starring role for nineteen years in the television series, *Gunsmoke.* During that famed program she played opposite James Arness (Matt Dillon), portraying the kind-hearted Kitty Russell, owner of the Longbranch saloon, and once conceded that saloon-keeping was not supposed to be her only profession, adding that "I didn't take in laundry for a living, either!" She lived in retirement at

Scottsdale, Arizona, was actively supportive of animal rights, and also backed women's rights and was elected in 1978 to the board of directors of the Arizona-Sonora Desert Museum of Tucson. In 1977 she underwent surgery for throat cancer and thereafter made appearances throughout the country for the American Cancer Society.

Tucson, *Arizona Daily Star,* Aug. 17, 1989, Nov. 7, 1989.

Blasingame, Ernest (Ike), cowboy (1884-1962). B. at Italy, between Dallas and Waco, Texas, he came up the trail with cattle at 14 in 1898, with other hands delivering the herd in South Dakota. In 1904 he accompanied another herd to Dakota delivered by train, for the Matador Land and Cattle Company under the direction of Murdo MacKenzie and with Con McMurry, "one of the best cowmen I ever knew," his immediate boss. The Matador established ranches on the Cheyenne River Reservation. Eventually Blasingame set up his own spread on the Little Moreau River near Timber Lake, married Clara Condon (1896-1968) May 11, 1914, and became one of the best-known cowboys and cattlemen of the region during the formative years of its livestock industry. His autobiographical book, *Dakota Cowboy,* written by Clara largely from Ike's dictation and recollections, gives a vivid description of cowboy life in the 20th century transition between the earlier open range days and the more controlled stock raising environment of tightly fenced, thoroughly managed enterprises. Blasingame was a rough-string rider and at one point, in a typical exploit, was sent from Dakota into Montana to try to recover Matador horses that had been rustled. It took him some time to locate them all, but he did it and drove them back to the home ranch. His book, while short on dates and some details, gives a vivid picture of range work of that period, how it was done, what it entailed and the adventure and satisfaction in performing it that abundantly corrects the sometimes-heard view that a cowboy of that day was "little more than a hired laborer." The work was highly specialized, required abundant initiative, brains, dedication and willingness to undergo unlimited hardships as part of the day's work, and Ike described it well. He and his wife and their two sons and daughter moved to Wyoming in the 1930s, and later to California, settling at Avenal, southeast of Coalinga in Kings County. Both Ike and Clara died in California.

Info. from the S.D. State Hist. Soc.: *Timber Lake and Area 1910-1985,* ed. by Ginny Cudmore, Jim Nelson, Timber Lake and Area Hist. Soc., 1984; Blasingame, *Dakota Cowboy: My Life in the Old Days,* Lincoln, Univ. of Neb. Press, 1958.

Bledsoe, Anthony, military officer (1739-1788). B. in Culpeper County, Virginia, he early left home and made for the frontier, being a merchant at Fort Chiswell as early as 1766; Chiswell had been built in 1758 at the lead mines in the present Wythe County, Virginia. In 1774 he removed to live near the Shelbys on the Holston River. Being magistrate of Botetourt, Fincastle and Washington counties, he was active in many public affairs. In 1774 he was a major and acting commissary, or quartermaster, for the Point Pleasant, West Virginia, campaign which virtually terminated Lord Dunmore's War. In 1776, holding high rank under William Christian (see entry), he commmanded forces at Long Island, Tennessee, during Cherokee disturbances. He took part in the operation against the Chickamaugas, a Tennessee band of Cherokees, in 1779 and "only remained home from King's Mountain [a battle of the Revolution] upon the representation that it was his duty to defend the frontier." He removed to Cumberland County, North Carolina, in 1784, representing it in the North Carolina Assembly until killed, either by Indians or by white enemies. "A prominent, able officer and representative, his death was a great loss to the young community of which he made part."

Thwaites, *Dunmore.*

Blegen, Theodore Christian, historian (July 16, 1891-July 18, 1969). B. at Minneapolis, he was graduated from Augsberg College in 1910 and earned a second bachelor's degree at the University of Minnesota in 1912, became a high school teacher, spent considerable time with the Minnesota and Wisconsin historical societies and in 1920 became assistant professor of history at Hamline University, St. Paul. He also served as assistant superintendent of the Minnesota Historical Society; he received a master's degree in 1915 and his doctorate in 1925, both from the University of Minnesota. He joined the history department of that university in 1927, becoming a full professor in 1937 and also became superintendent of the Minnesota Historical Society, serving it for many years. He taught an American history survey course and others on the history of immigration, the history of the West and promoted courses in American Civilization. He "pioneered the study of Norwegian immigration in the United States," helped found the Norwegian-American Historical Association and became managing editor of its publications. His *Norwegian Migration to America 1825-1860* (1931) was the first of his major publications on the subject, a second volume appearing in 1940. He died at St. Paul. His published book-length works included: *Grass Roots History* (1947); *The Land Lies Open* (1949); *Land of Their Choice; The Immigrants Write Home* (1955); *Minnesota: A History of the State* (1963); *The Kensington Rune Stone: New Light on an Old Riddle* (1968), and an autobiography, posthumously, *The Saga of Saga Hill* (1970). He was married and fathered a son and a daughter.

John T. Flanagan, "A Dedication to the Memory of Theodore C. Blegen, 1891-1969," *Arizona and the West,* Vol. 26, No. 3 (Autumn 1984), 204-208.

Blocker, Ab (Albert Pickins Blocker), trail boss (1856-Aug. 9, 1943). B. at Austin, Texas, Blocker became generally known, among cowmen and others, as the foremost trail driver of Texas history, and he himself claimed, in his non-boastful way, that he had "looked down the back of more cows and...drunk more water out of more cow tracks than any other man who ever pointed a herd toward the North Star." He grew to be 6 ft., 4 , every inch a cowman all his life. He was one of four sons, in 1876 left his parents' home and went to work for his brother, John Rufus Blocker (1851-1927) on a Blanco County ranch, gathering and roping Longhorns from the brush country where they ran wild as deer. In 1877 Ab and his brother with fifteen cowboys drove a herd in eighty-two days to Cheyenne, Wyoming. The cattle "seemed to feel it was part of their daily routine to stampede...and they tried it most every night." Beyond Dodge City a freezing norther blew in, the riders worked their horses unmercifully, attempting to hold the herd together after it had strung out for three miles, though it eventually split in two; the horses were unsaddled wet with sweat and by morning "we found every one of them stretched out dead, simply chilled to death, that's all." Ab went up the trail twice as a hand, nine times as a trail boss, making his first drive in 1877 and his final one in 1893, the last year Texas cattle were trailed to markets. His drives ended sometimes in Wyoming, or the Dakotas, Montana and once just short of the Canadian line. He said he never

could count the numbers of Longhorns he had pushed north, but overall they were high in the thousands, and his herds suffered all the hardships and dangers attendant upon that arduous and frequently heroic business. In 1886 alone the Blockers, John and Will, had 57,000 head of their own cattle on the trail. In 1885 John Blocker sold 2,500 cows and heifers to a syndicate which had obtained 3 million acres of the Staked Plains for a range, managed at the outset by B.H. Campbell who from an earlier brand of his, Bar B Q, had acquired the nickname of Barbecue. The herd was turned over to Ab for delivery and after crossing the plains the herd one night was within a few miles of the ranch headquarters. The moon came up full, the night was gentle, Ab was aware that rival boss Joe Collins was driving a herd nearby for the same ranch and a competitive spirit arose. He turned to his crew and said, "Boys, Joe Collins is out ahead of us. He is due to reach the ranch first. There will be no night herding tonight. We are going to drive," and by morning they arrived at the headquarters, the boss telling Barbecue, "I'm Ab Blocker. Here's your cows." Blocker recalled that Campbell was in a quandry for a brand for the new ranch. "He wanted, for some reason, a brand with three letters and one that couldn't be blotted." Blocker began drawing letters in the dirt with his boot heel. "For no reason at all I drew an XIT. 'How's this?' I asked, and Barbecue said, 'Get to branding them cows,'" and that was how the most famous brand in Texas originated. As a young man, in order to help his mother out, he quit the trail and farmed for a year and nearly broke his back picking cotton. After it was ginned he recalled, "I got down on my knees and promised God Almighty that if I ever planted another cotton seed I would first boil it for three days to make sure it would never come up." He married once and although he and his wife had a baby girl, the marriage did not succeed. "He belonged only to cattle, grass, trails, cow camps," and a bottle of whiskey occasionally. Until he died at 87 "he had never put his hands on the steering wheel of a car. He ignored all machinery of the machine age. The first airplane he ever saw stampeded a bunch of cattle he was driving through the brush," and that was all he wanted to see of a flying machine. The only vegetable he ate was potatoes, but "he had to have meat." He never had any cattle of his own, most of his life bossing trail herds for "Brother Johnnie," and happy to do so. Even after he quit riding in his eighties he continued to wear his spurs, for he felt undressed without them. "He wanted to die with his boots on. He was buried with them on, the spurs strapped to them...and a fresh, white handkerchief was around his neck." His death occurred at San Antonio; he was buried at Dignowitty Cemetery.

Cora Melton Cross, "Ab Blocker Tells About Trail Driving Days," *Frontier Times,* Vol. 5, No. 1 (Oct. 1927), 20-22; Lewis T. Nordyke, "The Last of the Old Drovers," *Frontier Times,* Vol. 16, No. 6 (Mar. 1939), 272-74; J. Frank Dobie, "Ab Blocker: Trail Boss," *Arizona and the West,* Vol. 6, No. 2 (Summer, 1964), 97-103; HT.

Bloody Knife, Arikara scout (c. 1837-June 25, 1876). B. of a Hunkpapa Sioux father and an Arikara mother in a Hunkpapa town in present Norh Dakota, he chose while young to follow his mother as she returned to live with her people, and Bloody Knife grew up as virtually one of that nation. Mail for the Missouri River military posts was carried overland from Fort Totten, west of Grand Forks. It was a risky undertaking because of Indian hostility, particularly after the defeated Sioux migrated west from Minnesota in the mid-1860s. Many mail riders were killed and few volunteers would take their places, but Bloody Knife, half Sioux and fluent in the language, took up the task and "almost always got the mail through on time." At some point he and the famed Hunkpapa chief, Gall, came into a feuding relationship, almost a vendetta, which endured as long as Bloody Knife lived; there was no hint however that Gall had engineered the scout's death. When Fort Abraham Lincoln was established three miles below Bismarck on June 14, 1872, Bloody Knife became a leader among Arikara scouts attached to it. Already having become Custer's favorite scout, he accompanied the 1873 David Stanley exploration up the Yellowstone River, with Custer commanding the escort. He pointed out fresh Indian sign to Custer in early August and on the 4th Sioux attacked the advance but were beaten off. Four days later Bloody Knife discovered the site of the Indian village, estimating it at 400 to 500 lodges, probably a major portion of Sitting Bull's followers. Bloody Knife knew little or no English and communicated most often through interpreter Frederick F. Gerard (see entry), a veteran Indian trader married to an Arikara who doubtless perfected his knowledge of her language; he also learned Sioux. May 30, 1874, Bloody Knife enlisted for six months with duty as scout on the Black Hills

Expedition. He was reported to be "commander" of some 100 Indians on that memorable tour, although the figure may be much exaggerated. William Elroy Curtis (see entry) of the Chicago *Inter-Ocean* described Bloody Knife as one who "especially deserves credit of honesty, faithfulness and frankness...His authority among his braves is that of a dictator" and who in an emergency communicated with Custer by pantomime and signs, which the officer usually understood. In appearance, Curtis wrote, Bloody Knife was "a slender man, below the usual size, and has a decided stoop to his shoulders...but a glance at his face shows that he is no ordinary man...His mouth and nose are small, the latter a smooth aquiline, and his lips are superbly cut...He wears no ornaments—no rings in his ears, no beads braided in his heavy, long hair, no bracelets on his arms, or feathers in his scalp-lock—nothing but a small steel horse-shoe hanging to his cartridge belt—the significance of which I have never been able to discover." The Indian also had a sense of humor, a taste for whiskey and the ability to turn aside a "fool question" with a sarcastic retort. An account of a curious incident on this 1874 undertaking was related by Young Hawk, then a 15-year-old Arikara who accompanied the expedition. Charley Reynolds (see entry) and Bloody Knife were scouting the trail ahead when the wagons got mired and useless. Custer rode up, demanded whose faulty advice led the vehicles into that predicament and Reynolds said it was Bloody Knife's mistake. "Then Custer drew a revolver and shot at them several times, and they saved themselves by dodging behind trees." Young Hawk's narrative continued: "When Custer put up his pistol, Bloody Knife came to where he sat on his horse and said, 'It is not a good thing you have done to me; if I had been possessed of madness [been angry] too you would not see another day.' Custer replied, 'My brother, it was the madness of a moment that made me do this, but it is gone now. Let us shake hands and be friends again.' So Bloody Knife agreed and they shook hands." One wonders who translated the interchange, unless Reynolds knew enough Arikara to do it, or perhaps Young Hawk understood English. In any event, Custer obviously did not try to kill either of his opponents, but merely expressed outrage at their carelessness in getting some of his wagons into trouble. There were no residual hard feelings between Bloody Knife and Custer, and they continued to get on well. The scout was discharged

November 30, 1874, as a private of excellent and reliable character. He re-enlisted March 13, 1876, for duty with Custer's Sioux expedition, leaving Fort Lincoln with the command May 17, again as Custer's favorite scout. Early on June 25 he accompanied the party with Custer to the "Crow's Nest," or observation point near the hostile camp; enroute Custer directed Fred Gerard to have the scouts pursue any side trails, for he wanted no Sioux camp, however small, to escape him. Bloody Knife grumbled to Gerard that "he needn't be so particular about the small camps; we'll get enough when we strike the big camp." Later Bloody Knife told Custer "we would find enough Sioux to keep us fighting two or three days. The General remarked laughingly that he thought we could get through in one day." At another point Bloody Knife urged Custer to use extreme caution because there were more Sioux ahead than the soldiers had bullets. The scout was assigned to the Reno element that was to attack Gall's village from its lower point, Custer apparently deciding Reno needed all the strength and wisdom he could muster, and Bloody Knife being the most reliable scout. The Indian was standing next to Reno during the valley fight before the withdrawal to the bluffs. He was struck in the head by a bullet, his brains and blood splashing Reno's face, understandably unnerving that officer. Of course no one knew who had killed him. His remains were probably buried in the valley in a day or two by Colonel John Gibbon's men. One of the colonel's soldiers found later, in a deserted Sioux lodge, a scalp identified by the Arikaras as Bloody Knife's for it exhibited the gray streaks only Bloody Knife's hair possessed. The soldier kept the scalp because his father had known and had been a friend of Bloody Knife.

Hodge, HAI, I, 155; BHB; O.G. Libby, *The Arikara Narrative of the Campaign Against the Hostile Dakotas June, 1876,* N.Y., Sol Lewis, 1973; Herbert Krause, Gary D. Olson, *Prelude to Glory: A Newspaper Accounting of Custer's 1874 Expedition to the Black Hills,* Sioux Falls, S.D., Augustana College, 1974; Edgar I. Stewart, *Custer's Luck,* Norman, Univ. of Okla. Press, 1955; Robert M. Utley, *Cavalier in Buckskin,* Norman, 1988; John S. Gray, *Custer's Last Campaign,* Lincoln, Univ. of Neb. Press, 1991; Ben Innis, *Bloody Knife! Custer's Favorite Scout,* Fort Collins, Col., Old Army Press, 1973.

Bocharov, Dmitry Ivanovich, naval officer, explorer (fl. 1771-1798). By Shelikhov's instructions dated May 4, 1786, Bocharov was directed to conduct a "minute survey" of Kuiktak (Kodiak) Island, the coast from Kenai Bay to Chugachuik (Prince William Sound) and "if possible" around Kayak Island, all in the Alaska region. As a naval master and accomplished navigator, Bocharov and Izmailov (see entry) were directed to take the ship *Trekh Sviatiteli* on a trading and exploration voyage eastward from Kodiak, the expedition supplied with painted posts and copper plates to "mark the extent of Russia's domain" in light of aggressive Spanish, English, and other explorers pushing up the Alaskan coast. May 3, 1788, the ship arrived off Cape Cleare of Montague Island and the 10th anchored at a harbor on Hinchinbrook Island, returning to Montague Island May 27. The explorers proceeded to Achakoo (Middleton) Island well out in the gulf and after a skirmish with natives reached Kayak Island June 1 and Yakutat Bay June 11 where two copper plates were buried. They continued down the coast to Lituya Bay (Port des Francais) where a monument left by La Perouse (see entry) may have been destroyed by the Russians who, after leaving identifying marks of their own, returned to Kodiak. Bocharov may have developed a drinking habit by this time, for on August 30, 1789, Shelikhov by letter warned Delarov, his deputy in charge at Kodiak, that "Bacharov has been drinking ever since he came [with us] and I do not expect any improvement in the future. I have not been at all successful in sobering him up." Yet the problem seems not to have been longlasting, since he soon was placed in sole command of the *Trekh Sviatiteli* which returned to Okhotsk on the Siberian coast. From there August 10, 1790, the ship, with Bocharov in command and Alexandr Baranov in its complement, left for Alaska. Leaking water casks made it necessary for the ship to put in at a bay on the northwestern coast of Unalaska Island for fresh water. A storm September 30 threw the ship on the rocky coast where she broke up. A messenger sent to Kodiak to report the loss never arrived. The party, under Baranov's leadership, survived a very difficult winter. With spring, three large umiaks were constructed, Bocharov directed to take two of them and to explore and hunt along the northern coast of the Alaska Peninsula, until then not certainly known to the Russians. With twenty-six men he set out late in April 1791, while Baranov with most of the rest of the complement took the remaining craft along the southern coast, making for the Kodiak base of the Shelikhov company where they arrived June 27. Bocharov explored and hunted for five months along the north coast of the Peninsula, then decided to cross it. From either Ugashik or Egegik Bay he accomplished the feat in three days, the first Russian to do so, and enroute discovered Becharof Lake, mispelled though named for him, as well as Lake Ruth and emerging at Portage Bay and Kanatak, a still existing community, where he repaired his boats which had become water-logged. The party crossed Shelikhov Strait to Kodiak Island, reaching Three Saints (the present Kodiak) September 12, 1791, after a notable voyage of exploration which had revealed what Shelikhov conceded as late as 1794 was "the shortest overland route" across the Peninsula. In 1792 Bocharov was navigator of the *Sv Mikhail* which took Delarov (see entry), heading into retirement, to Okhotsk. An important dividend of Bocharov's earlier exploration was the later arrival of an important chief from the north coast of the Peninsula; he met with Baranov and offered assistance to the Russians if they wished to expand their fur collecting operations to his country and on into western Alaska, which they assuredly did. In 1798 Bocharov commanded the "large brigantine" *Elizaveta* to Three Saints from Okhotsk, having wintered in the western Aleutians but bringing a welcome cargo of food, laborers and needed supplies to succor the struggling Russian trading company. Little more is heard of Bocharov in authorities consulted.

Bancroft, *Russia; Russian Penetration of the North Pacific Ocean;* James W. VanStone, *Russian Exploration in Southwest Alaska: The Travel Journals of Petr Korsakovskiy (1818) and Ivan Ya. Vasilev (1829),* Fairbanks, Univ. of Ak. Press, 1988; Orth, 120.

Boggs, John, militia officer (1736-Feb. 1824). B. on the Susquehanna River of Pennsylvania he was taken as a child to Berkeley County, present West Virginia, and in 1768 moved to the Youghiogheny River of Pennsylvania. In 1771 he was at Beeson's Fort, the present Uniontown, Pennsylvania, and three years later moved to Chartier's Camp, three miles west of Catfish Camp, near Wheeling, West Virginia. He was there when the first siege of Wheeling's Fort Henry occurred on September 1, 1777. In 1781 while living on Buffalo Creek, Pennsylvania, his oldest son was captured by Indians. In August that year he built a cabin near Wheeling and the

following spring removed his family to Fort Henry for safety. At the siege of 1782 he was sent out to secure reinforcements, for he then was a militia captain, but returned after the Indians-British abandoned the attack and departed. He had visited Kentucky in 1776, but with the Revolution he was occupied on the Ohio frontier. In 1778 he was out with Lachlan McIntosh (see entry) from Pittsburgh in command of a company. His final removal was to Pickaway County, Ohio, where he lived the rest of his life.

Thwaites/Kellogg, *Frontier Defense on the Upper Ohio, 1777-1778.*

Boggs, Lydia, pioneer (Feb. 26, 1766-Sept. 1867). B. in Berkeley County, present West Virginia, in 1768 the family moved to the Youghiogheny River, Pennsylvania, and in 1771 to Beeson's Fort (now Uniontown, Pennsylvania). In 1777 they lived on Buffalo Creek where Captain John Boggs commanded a militia company. In August 1781 the family moved to West Virginia, to a site three miles below Wheeling, but the next year withdrew to Fort Henry at Wheeling and were there during the second siege of the place in 1782. She was convinced that Betty Zane did *not* run a desperately needed supply of powder to the fort through a hail of enemy fire, but that the heroine was Molly Scott and stated that Betty Zane was not even present, being at the home of her father, near Washington, Pennsylvania, at the time. As an eye-witness version of the events, her testimony naturally carries weight. She affirmed she was a close friend of both Betty Zane and Molly Scott. Shortly afterward Lydia married Moses, son of David Shepherd, living at his homestead until his death in 1832 when she married General Daniel Cruger, but kept her home at the stone mansion on Wheeling Creek until her death. Thwaites wrote that "she was a woman of extraordinary memory, and great intellectual power. Her reminiscences are entitled to much credit, except where warped by personal prejudice."

Thwaites/Kellogg, *Frontier Defense on the Upper Ohio, 1777-1778;* Wills De Hass, *History of the Early Settlement and Indian Wars of Western Virginia,* Phila., H. Hoblitzell, 1851, 1960, pp. 280-281.

Bolton, Mason, British military officer (d. Oct. 31, 1780). Mason Bolton had seen much service in America. He had campaigned in Florida and in the West Indies, and at one time had been at Mackinac and on the Illinois River. As a lieutenant colonel of the 34th Royal Artillery Regiment, he commanded at Fort Niagara from c. 1775 (Thwaites said 1777) until 1780, making it an effective headquarters for New York Loyalists, and a fount for Indian and ranger parties which harried the frontier settlements throughout the Revolution. The Iroquois, particularly the Senecas, made Niagara their major base. It was the point of origin from which many Tory-Indian expeditions laid waste Cherry Valley, Wyoming Valley and other targets. Major John Butler (see entry) brought one hundred Mohawks to Fort Niagara on July 26, 1775, readying that people for frontier forays in the event of a Revolution, which soon developed. The extent of his activities between the time of his arrival and May 1776 was reported by Bolton, commandant at that time. He wrote he had drafted a bill of 14,176 pounds sterling for Indian supplies and Butler's activities. Although he disapproved of atrocities such as almost invariably accompanied frontier raids, Bolton felt unable to wholly prevent them. "I am really of opinion that to keep the Indians in good Temper (as it's called) has cost Old England much more than all the Posts are worth, and as to their scalping women Children and Prisoners I find it not possible to prevent them, [though] such cruelties must make an Expedition very disagreeable to the King's Troops when order'd on service with them," he wrote in February 1779 to his superior, General Frederick Haldimand. During the succeeding summer Bolton was much concerned about the expedition into Iroquois country of Major General John Sullivan, presuming that Fort Niagara was the ultimate objective. That may have been true, but following the victory of the Americans over Indians and their British support at Newtown, New York, on August 29, 1779, the expedition was directed to conclude its campaign and return to base, which it did. This relieved Bolton of the military problem, but one almost equally grave arose in the fall when more than 5,000 Indians pressed into the area around the post and Bolton had to provide for them, adding substantially to his expenses in operating the place. Ailing for many months, Bolton late in 1780 applied for leave to go to Montreal for treatment. The request was granted and October 31 he boarded the *Ontario* and embarked on Lake Ontario for Canada. That same evening a violent storm came up, broke the ship to pieces and all on board were lost. In addition to Bolton there were on the ship a lieutenant and twenty-five men of his 34th Artillery. "It was a sad ending for a gallant and conscientious offi-

cer who had served so capably in a difficult and trying post," concluded Graymont. He was succeeded at Niagara by Brigadier General H. Watson Powell.

Thwaites/Kellogg, *Frontier Defense on the Upper Ohio, 1777-1778;* DCB V; Robert B. Roberts, *New York's Forts in the Revolution,* Cranbury, N.J., Assoc. Univ. Presses, 1980; Barbara Graymont, *The Iroquois in the American Revolution,* Syracuse (N.Y.) Univ. Press, 1972.

Bonga, George, interpreter, trader (c. 1802-post 1837). Bonga, his brother Stephen and possibly other siblings were no doubt the offspring of Jean Bonga, who, with his wife Marie-Jeanne were black slaves of British military officer Daniel Robertson (c. 1733-1810). They were freed when Robertson left Mackinac Island in 1787 and "became prominent tavern keepers on the island, and their sons important fur traders." George was reported to be the son of Jean Bonga and a Chippewa (Ojibwa) woman, and was raised in a trinational atmosphere, speaking English, French and Chippewa, thus becoming a useful interpreter. He was a voyageur for the American Fur Company, and was an interpreter for Lewis Cass in 1820 at an Indian council at Fond du Lac, Minnesota. Russell W. Fridley wrote that he also was interpreter for government agents when a Chippewa land treaty was signed at Fort Snelling in 1837, but the treaty shows this to have been Stephen Bonga, not George. Bonga became a fairly prominent trader operating posts for the AFC at Lac Platte, Otter Tail Lake and Leech Lake, Minnesota and "later became an independent trader with his own establishment." The date of his death is not reported.

REAW; DCB V; info. from E.F. (Ted) Mains; Charles J. Kappler, *Indian Treaties 1778-1823,* N.Y., Interland Pub. Inc., 1972.

Booth, James, pioneer (d. June 16, 1778). Captain Booth and Nathaniel Cochran, working in a field on Booth's Creek near Morgantown, were surprised by Indians who killed Booth and captured Cochran. The loss of Booth was felt severely by inhabitants of the West Virginia region, he being active, enterprising and endowed with "superior talents and a better education than most pioneers." Cochran was taken to Detroit, attempted to escape but fell again into the hands of the enemy and was returned to Detroit, eventually being exchanged and reaching home "after having to endure much suffering and many hardships."

Alexander Scott Withers, *Chronicles of Border Warfare,* Cincinnati, Robert Clarke Co., 1895, 1970.

Bowen, William (Billy), frontiersman (1744-c. 1777). B. in Maryland, when he was very young he emigrated to Augusta County, Virginia, and in 1759 joined William Christian in pursuit of an Indian war party. He was on many frontier expeditions and operations, sometimes as a scout, again as a militia officer up to lieutenant. At the significant battle of Point Pleasant, which effectively terminated Lord Dunmore's War against the Shawnees, Bowen had "a terrific hand-to-hand struggle with an Indian antagonist, whom he finally overpowered." Thwaites said that in 1784 he removed to what is now Sumner County, Tennessee where he lived the rest of his life, the information coming from his daughter in 1844. However Arnow wrote that in the Cumberland area a man named William Bowen around 1777 shot into a buffalo herd, wounding an animal which charged, but "the cane being thick Bowen could not get out of the way; he was trodden down so that he could not move, nor could his companions find him; he lay there seven days; when found, the bruised parts had mortified [gangrene had set in] and he died on the 18th day." This may possibly have been another William Bowen from the one born in 1744.

Thwaites, *Dunmore;* Harriette Simpson Arnow, *Seedtime on the Cumberland,* N.Y., The Macmillan Co., 1960.

Bowman, John, frontiersman (1738-May 4, 1784). B. in Frederick County, Virginia, he was a son of George Bowman whose wife was a daughter of the earliest white settler of the region, Joist Hite. John Bowman visited Kentucky in 1775 and the following summer was at Harrodsburg where he was named to the committee on safety. In the fall of 1776 he was commissioned colonel of Kentucky militia. Bowman became best known for commanding a 1779 expedition against the Shawnee village of Old Chillicothe on the Little Miami River about four miles north of the present Xenia, Ohio. Black Fish was chief of that region, having succeeded Cornstalk (see entry) who was murdered in 1777; subordinate to Black Fish were Black Hoof and Black Beard. Bowman and Colonel Benjamin Logan, together commanding 263 Kentucky frontiersmen, approached the village at dusk May 29 (the date of July 29 which frequently appears in narratives of the expedition is in error). Bowman's right wing and Logan's command were to encircle the unsuspecting village and by dawn this had nearly succeeded when one of Bowman's men inadvertently fired a rifle, alarming the camp. Logan then advanced into the village, sweeping away token forces before him, when an unexpected order from Bowman to withdraw reached him; he had no choice but to do so. What had inspired the directive was a mistaken rumor reaching Bowman that Simon Girty with one hundred Shawnees from the Piqua village were hastening to the support of Black Fish. At any rate a full retreat to the Ohio commenced, the whites having lost seven killed and one wounded, and the Indians perhaps five killed, others wounded. But unknown to the whites, Black Fish, their principal enemy, was reported among the casualties and from his wound, believed slight at first, he later died, as is generally believed, although there is some dissent. Withers called this an "illy conducted expedition," but added that Bowman undoubtedly believed his decision was wise and "the gallantry and intrepidity displayed by him on many occasions, forbid [the judgment of] any unmilitary feeling [and] his motives were certainly pure." In 1781 Bowman became sheriff and county-lieutenant of the new Lincoln County, Kentucky. He died at his home in that county.

Reuben Gold Thwaites, Louise Phelps Kellogg, *Revolution on the Upper Ohio 1775-1777,* Madison, Wis. Hist. Soc., 1908; Alexander Scott Withers, *Chronicles of Border Warfare...,* ed by Thwaites, Cincinnati, Robert Clarke Co., 1895 (1961).

Bowman, Mason T. (Mace), lawman (1847-June 6, 1881). B. in Kentucky, he became prominent on the New Mexico frontier and in 1879 ran a livery stable at Otero, head-of-the-rail town in Colfax County near the foot of Raton Pass. He was reported to have been a friend, and perhaps a rival, of Clay Allison (see entry), but the legend of a stand-off between them appears without foundation and is probably mythical. Parsons reprints an obituary on Allison from the *Raton Range* reporting that Mace and Clay met at a dance at an unstated date: "Each one envyed the other his reputation for nerve and...before morning were having a little dance together with nothing but their underclothes and pistols on. Those who witnessed this little war dance momentarily expected to see one or both killed, but it ended without tragedy." If the report is true, it may be the genesis for the legend of a confrontation. When in early 1879 Deputy Sheriff Harry Bassett, brother of Dodge City's Charlie Bassett (see entry) was killed, Bowman took his place as the only deputy in Colfax County. At one point Bowman and Allison rode down a fleeing gunman, captured and brought him back to Otero to a fate unreported. Bowman must have been respected as a deputy, for in November 1880 he was elected sheriff of Colfax County. He died half a year later in a Trinidad, Colorado, hospital.

Ed Bartholomew, *Wyatt Earp: The Man and the Myth,* Toyahvale, Tex., Frontier Book Co., 1964, 26; Chuck Parsons, "Mace Bowman vs. Clay Allison," *True West,* Vol. 38, No. 3 (March 1991), 12 (including a photo of Bowman); Parsons, *True West,* Vol. 38, No. 5 (May 1991), 13, info. from Chuck Hornung.

Bracken, Matthew, surveyor (d. Oct. 10, 1774). In 1773 Bracken surveyed in Kentucky with Hancock Taylor (see entry), and Bracken Creek and Bracken County in that state were named for him. Bracken, as either an ensign or a lieutenant (both ranks are given him by authorities) of militia was killed in the battle of Point Pleasant, West Virginia, an action which virtually terminated the Lord Dunmore War.

Thwaites, *Dunmore.*

Bradstreet, John, military officer (Dec. 21, 1714-Sept. 25, 1774). B. at Annapolis Royal, Nova Scotia, he commenced his long military career as a volunteer in the 40th Foot in 1735, shortly becoming an ensign. He had carried on a lucrative commercial business with the French at Louisbourg fortress, initiated a plan for capture of the place by 1745 which may or may not have been instrumental in its reduction, but with a commission as lieutenant colonel of the 1st Massachusetts he contributed notably to the victory there. Bradstreet became lieutenant governor of Newfoundland in 1747 but in 1751 went to England and with the assistance of powerful friends, returned to America in 1753 with Braddock's expedition, although he was not on the disastrous foray against Fort Duquesne. In the spring of 1755 he became commandant at Fort Oswego on Lake Ontario, assigned to prepare an attack on Fort Niagara. That did not materialize so he was ordered to prepare one against Fort Frontenac (the present Kingston, Ontario). Bradstreet's most noted success was the swift conquest of Frontenac in 1758 and "with this one brilliant stroke the lifeline of the French Great Lakes empire had been severed. More directly, the capture of French provisions at the post, the destruction of the French naval flotilla on Lake Ontario, and the resultant blow to French pres-

tige among the Indians all contributed to the final defeat of New France." Bradstreet consequently was promoted to colonel in America. In 1760, during preparations for the final offensive against the French, Bradstreet's health failed. After a very serious illness, he recovered sufficiently by 1763 when the Pontiac War broke out to be offered by Amherst command of an expedition to Detroit to relieve that place and carry the offensive to the Indians. He reached Detroit in August 1764 with a force of 1,200 men and sent a command of 300 under Captain John Howard to reoccupy Michilimackinac and western posts, which was accomplished. Thwaites said that he became a Major General in 1772, dying two years later at Detroit; the *Dictionary of Canadian Biography* reported that he died at New York City and makes no mention of his becoming a general officer. Bradstreet was ever convinced of the failure of superiors and the British government itself to recognize his obviously great contributions to colonial defense and military matters, and his many applications to be named governor of one colony or another also went unrequited. He was often as much concerned with his persistent financial undertakings and moonlighting as with military duties, and his spectacular career was somewhat blighted by many shadows and a few dark omissions, but he was a brilliant soldier and his accomplishments were considerable. He was married and fathered children.

Reuben Gold Thwaites, Louise Phelps Kellogg, *The Revolution on the Upper Ohio, 1775-1777,* Madison, Wis. Hist. Soc., 1908; DCB, IV.

Brashears, Richard, military officer (d. May 1822). A lieutenant in Captain William Harrod's company in Kentucky, he accompanied George Rogers Clark on his expedition to Kaskaskia and Vincennes and was in charge of the latter garrison from April to August 1779. He then returned to Kaskaskia and early in 1780 was of the garrison at Fort Jefferson, five miles south of Greenville, Ohio. He went back to Kaskaskia in the fall of 1780, married Ann Brocus (Brooks) and with her family emigrated to Natchez, Mississippi, becoming an army captain before resigning from the service. He lived in Mississippi and died in the southern part of the state, leaving one daughter by whom there were other descendants.

Thwaites/Kellogg, *Frontier Defense on the Upper Ohio, 1777-1778.*

Bremner, John, prospector, explorer (d. 1887). Bremner, who was an early Alaskan sourdough made the first recorded Anglo ascent of the Copper River in 1884 as far as Taral, and wintered there, although it is possible that Russian fur men preceded him by some years, since relics attributed to them were found in the vicinity. Henry T. Allen (see entry) gave the name of Bremner River for the prospector, its nominal discoverer, to a tributary of the Copper, flowing in from the east, north of the mouth of the river which is east of Cordova. Bremner Glacier in the Chugach Mountains is named for the river. Allen added Bremner and another prospector, Peder (Pete) Johnson, as civilian members of his expedition (see Allen entry for its history). Bremner rendered good service until June when Allen "noticed that the severe hardships to which Bremner had so long been exposed were affecting both his mental and physical condition," and his earlier sprained ankle having swollen to unusual size, this due to scurvy as it later developed. July 26, on reaching the confluence of the Tanana and Yukon rivers, Allen found to his surprise that Bremner was "in critical condition from scurvy," and here both Bremner and Johnson "chose to remain on the Yukon to continue prospecting during the remainder of the summer," not desiring to make the arduous further exploration of the Koyukuk River at this time. Bremner in 1886 and 1887 prospected the Fickett River, so named by Allen for his meteorological observer who alone had accompanied him up the Koyukuk in 1885; Bremner was killed by the Koyukan Indians near Dolmikaket in 1887, and the stream subsequently became known to prospectors as "Old Johns River," or "Johns River" for him, and the Fickett name unfortunately was lost. The stream is a tributary of the Koyukuk River.

Henry T. Allen, *Narratives of Explorations in Alaska;* Orth, 159-60, 475.

Brenton (Brinton), James, military officer (d.c. 1788). Brenton had served with Angus McDonald (see entry) in his 1774 expedition against the Ohio Indians. He also was involved with Indian operations in 1777, and served under General Edward Hand (see entry) in early 1778; later he commanded a company on Lachlan McIntosh's expedition and was a major on William Crawford's Sandusky expedition of 1782, being slightly wounded in that operation. Butterfield wrote that Brenton was "a man of much spirit—a soldier, brave and active...He unquestionably commanded the esteem as well as the confidence of the volunteers. His coolness and bravery in the face of imminent danger, were long after alluded to by his surviving comrades, in terms of the highest commendation." He moved to Kentucky after the Revolution and lived in Mercer County where he was killed by Indians about 1788.

Reuben Gold Thwaites, Louise Phelps Kellogg, *The Revolution on the Upper Ohio, 1775-1777,* Madison, Wis. Hist. Soc., 1908; Consul W. Butterfield, *An Historical Account of the Expedition Against Sandusky under Col. William Crawford in 1782,* Cincinnati, Robert Clarke Co., 1873.

Brims, Creek chief, or "emperor" (d. c. 1732). Brims was an important chief of Coweta, one of four traditionally prestigious towns of the Creek confederacy, Coweta and Cussita being of the Lower Creeks, and Coosa (Okchai) and Tuckabatchee of the Upper Creeks. Each had a "mico," or king, or emperor who achieved his rank by heredity or achievement and, if able, might have a voice "of considerable dimension" in regional or national affairs for the Creeks; if he also were a great war chief, this added to his influence and power. Brims was reportedly the founder of the Creek system of neutrality in the early 18th century. The influential Mary Bosomworth (see entry) was his niece. Although plural marriages were sanctioned by the Creeks, they were rare, but Brims had "at least two wives and probably more." During Queen Anne's War (1701-1713) a festering feud between Choctaws and Chickasaws was reopened, supposedly at British instigation, and the South Carolina Assembly, to forestall French intervention, planned an expedition intended to wipe out the Choctaw nation "and so destroy the bulwark of Louisiana" for the French. It commissioned Captain Theophilus Hastings (see entry) to lead the Creeks, and commissioned Brims as co-leader with Hastings. Thomas Welch was named a captain to lead a supporting element of Chicasaws. The 1711 expedition included about 1,300 Creeks, 300 of them bowmen. With Brims and Hastings leading, it ravaged Choctaw towns, burning out 400 hundred plantations, but killed only 80 of the enemy and took some 130 prisoners; the rest of the Indians, forewarned, escaped and resistance was feeble. In 1715 the devastating Yamasee war broke out in South Carolina, the Creeks siding with the Yamasees and Brims charged by French and English alike with having sparked the uprising. The Creeks were allies of the Yamasees in this conflict which seems to have been directed mainly against English traders across the southeast. Following this affair, Brims sought neutrality for his people with relation to the white powers. A description of the "emperor" at this time, which apparently refers to Brims, says, in part: "The nation of Caouita [Coweta] is governed by an emperor who in [1715] caused to be killed all the English there were, not only in his nation, but also [in neighboring tribes]. Not content with that he went to commit depredations as far as the gates of Carolina. The English...made very great presents to the emperor to regain his friendship and that of his nation. The French do the same thing, and also the Spaniards, which makes him very rich...He is a man of a good appearance and good character. He has numbers of slaves who are busy night and day cooking food for those going and coming to visit him. He seldom goes on foot, always [riding on] well harnessed horses, and followed by many of his village. He is absolute in his nation. He has a quantity of cattle...No one has ever been able to make him take sides with one of the three European nations [as against the others], he alleging that he wishes to see everyone, to be neutral, and not to espouse any of the quarrels which the French, English, and Spaniards have with one another." Brims sent a mission headed by his elder son, Sepeycoffee, to St. Augustine to smooth over differences with the Spanish; he allowed the French to build Fort Toulouse, on the Coosa River four miles above the Tallapoosa, in 1716 or 1717, and became reconciled with the English in 1717, signing at Charles Town (Charleston) in the fall the first treaty between the Creeks and English whose details are known. Governor Robert Johnson (1676-1735) ordered trade to be reopened but now under a state monopoly, since private enterprise had been guilty of the excesses which caused the Yamasee War. Brims felt strongly that true Creek policy was to remain friendly with the English, French and Spanish. He accepted a French invitation to Mobile for a ceremonial visit, and concluded an agreeable understanding with the Spanish. When difficulties again arose between the English and the Yamasee, now under Spanish protection in Florida, efforts were made to bring Brims in on the side of the English, but he was indecisive until the Yamasees killed his son Ouletta and committed other offenses which swung him to the English side for the 1727-28 war. Sepeycof-

fee was killed in a drunken dispute, and Brims bequeathed his policy of neutrality to his remaining twin sons: Essabo and Malatchi, who would become his successors upon their attaining maturity. Brims died between 1730 and 1733, and in the interim his brother, Chigelley, as head warrior, served following a brief internship by Youhowlakee, who died in 1733-34.

Info. from John Sugden; David H. Corkran, *The Creek Frontier, 1540-1783,* Norman Univ. of Okla. Press, 1967; Verner W. Crane, *The Southern Frontier 1670-1732,* Ann Arbor, Univ. of Mich. Press, 1929; John R. Swanton, *Early History of the Creek Indians and Their Neighbors,* 67th Cong., 1st Sess., HR Doc. 97, Gov. Pr. Off., 1922, pp. 225-26.

Brookfield, Robert Morris, military officer (Mar. 13, 1873-Dec. 20, 1940). B. at Philadelphia he went to West Point and June 12, 1896, was commissioned a second lieutenant of the 2nd Infantry, becoming a first lieutenant of the 23rd Infantry September 28, 1898. He was a member of the Abercrombie (see entry) expedition of 1898 to Alaska, serving as topographical assistant on various explorations. Leaving Valdez at the head of Prince William Sound, Brookfield was directed to explore a route across a glacier between Valdez and the Copper River valley and left May 2 for a route north of the port, Brookfield to sketch in the glacier and Pass through which he was to proceed. Two days later he was found on the glacier suffering from snowblindness, and had to be led back to camp for the painful and incapacitating ailment to be cured, which was done within four days. May 21 with two enlisted men and several packers he again attempted to cross the glacier, but "I was abandoned by all but three of the civilian packers" because of the unsafe snow conditions which became so severe he was forced to return once more to base. By May 26, with the weather clearing and snow conditions favorable he started out again, this time with four enlisted men. "My instructions now were to survey the trail as far as the summit of the glacier, and if possible to find out and report upon the character of the country on the other side of the divide," he wrote in his report. With difficulty he reached the summit of the pass at 6,450 feet. He descended into a wooded valley and made camp, his men having been forty-three hours without sleep. Further exploration revealed that the Copper River could not be reached directly from his location, but an effort in another direction brought the party to a stream he named the Kotsena River, where a raft was built and the party embarked for downstream. Rough water and a narrowing canyon eventually shipwrecked the raft and it was with difficulty that the men extracted themselves and their gear from a most unpromising situation. By June 4 Valdez was once again gained after a strenuous exploration with minimum results. Brookfield had found the country swarming with prospectors, although he was the first Army officer to explore Bates Pass, which he named for Colonel John Coalter Bates, 2nd Infantry, and he also charted a route through it in the direction of the Copper River, which was his goal. By the end of June, Brookfield's health had become "so much impaired from exposure and overwork that it was deemed best to send him south," Abercrombie reported. He did not return to Alaska for further duty, and resigned from the Army October 15, 1900. He resided at Philadelphia, studied law, was admitted to the Bar June 16, 1904, and continued active in civilian and National Guard pursuits. He rose steadily in rank in the Guard, rejoined the Regulars at the outset of World War I and as a lieutenant colonel of the 110th Infantry in September 1917 went to France. He took part in the Marne offensive, the Argonne action and other affairs. He became a Brigadier General May 17, 1926. Brookfield died at Philadelphia, aged 67 years.

Heitman; Cullum; *Narratives of Explorations in Alaska,* 564-65; Brookfield, "Across Valdez Glacier," *Ibid,* 593-99.

Brooks, Alfred Hulse, geologist (July 18, 1871-Nov. 22, 1924). B. at Ann Arbor, Michigan, he was taken as an infant by his parents to Germany, remaining there five years; the family returned to the United States and after residing at Newburgh, New York, and in Georgia, again went to Germany for two years. Upon the return once more to this country Brooks went to Harvard, graduating in 1894 with a major in geology. He worked briefly in the Southern Appalachians, attending a Russian geological congress in 1897, took advanced studies at Paris and joined the U.S. Geological Survey. He was assigned in 1898 to Alaska where except for a time during World War I he worked until his death. He traveled widely within the Territory, perhaps knew it as well as or better than anyone else, and many Alaskan features were named for him, most notably the immense Brooks Range which divides the Yukon Valley from the Arctic littoral, extends east and west the width of Alaska, and includes within it many distinct ranges: De Long, Baird, Schwatka, Endicott, Philip Smith, Romanzof, Shubelik, Davison and British uplifts. Although interested in geology generally, Brooks was a specialist in metallurgy and wrote many papers on that subject. His 1903 publicaton, *Geography and Geology of Alaska,* is still considered a definitive work; his *The Mount McKinley Region* (1911) won awards from the American Geographical Society and a Paris society and Brooks steadily achieved international attention for his Alaskan work. A good narrative of one of his early field trips describes his party's journey from Tyonek on Cook Inlet on the southern Alaska coast, along the western slope of the Alaska Range, which is capped by Mt. McKinley, thus by way of the Nenana and Tanana rivers to the Yukon at Rampart. It was an 800 mile survey conducted from June 2 to September 15, 1902, and the natural hazards and difficulties were immense, but the task was done. The article includes a photograph of the geologist in field attire. When Charles Willard Hayes resigned in 1911 as chief of the Geological Survey the position was offered to Brooks who declined, preferring to remain in Alaska. During the World War he was, by his own devising, Chief Geologist of the American force in France and became a lieutenant colonel; at war's end he returned once more to Alaska. He was a "likeable, companionable man and thoroughly loyal to his calling and to his friends...He was of medium height, rather stoutly built with an unusually large head, and with sandy hair and beard." He was married and fathered two children. He wrote and published widely.

Mel Griffiths, "Brooks of Alaska," *True West,* Vol. 36, No. 8 (Aug., 1989), 16-23; DAB; CE.

Brooks, Juanita Leavitt, historian (Jan. 15, 1898-Aug. 26, 1989). B. at Bunkerville, Nevada into a devout Mormon family, she taught school and married, though her husband of a year died of cancer in 1920 and she moved to St. George, Utah to attend Dixie Junior College. She was graduated from Brigham Young University, Provo, Utah, in 1925, returned to Dixie College to teach and in 1933 married William Brooks, sheriff of Washington County, Utah. By then she had become interested in history, in 1942 publishing her first book, *Dudley Leavitt: Pioneer to Southern Utah,* a biography of her grandfather. From 1944 until 1951 she was a field fellow of the Huntington Library at San Marino, California and in 1950 published *The Mountain Meadows Massacre* (Stanford University Press; a new edition in 1962 was published by the University of Oklahoma Press). In 1955 Mrs. Brooks co-authored with Robert Glass Cleland, *A Mormon Chronicle: The Diaries of John D. Lee, 1848-1876,* and in 1961 she alone brought out *John Doyle Lee, Zealot, Pioneer Builder, Scapegoat.* Among her fifteen books, those of frontier interest also included: *On the Mormon Frontier: The Diary of Hosea Stout* (1963); *Journal of the Southern Indian Mission: Diary of Thomas D. Brown* (1972); *Frontier Tales: True Stories of Real People* (1972); *History of the Jews in Utah and Idaho* (1973); *Jacob Hamblin: Mormon Apostle to the Indians* (1980), and her autobiography, *Quicksand and Cactus* (1982). She died at 91 at St. George, Utah.

Brooks, *Quicksand and Cactus: A Memoir of the Southern Mormon Frontier,* intr. by Charles Peterson, including a review of Brooks' works, Chicago and Salt Lake City, Howe Bros., 1982.

Brown, Barnum, paleontologist (Feb. 12, 1873-Feb. 5, 1963). B. at Carbondale, Kansas and receiving his first name, by report, because circus magnate P.T. Barnum was in the region at the time of his birth, Brown himself "was endowed with a healthy dose of a showman's flamboyance," and as a world-ranking paleontologist he was the "last" discoverer of sensational reptile fossils of the so-called Big Three of early fossil-collecting history. In the view of his associate Roland T. Bird (see entry) and not a few others, he was the greatest collector of the triad, the other two being Othniel Marsh and Edward Cope (see entries). Brown's father made a prosperous living farming, selling coal and hauling freight for the Army's western outposts. While attending the University of Kansas, Barnum Brown studied paleontology under Samuel W. Williston, who had collected fossils under Marsh, and later worked with Jacob Wortman, who had been with Cope. Brown accompanied Williston on collecting expeditions to Nebraska, Wyoming and South Dakota; on one of their trips he worked with a party from the American Museum of Natural History of New York, led by Wortman. He left the university before graduation and was promptly hired by the Museum. In 1897 Brown, with Wortman and Walter Granger (see entry), who eventually became curator of fossil mammals at the Museum, went to Como Bluff, about nine miles east of Medicine Bow, Wyoming

where Marsh had located rich deposits of Jurassic era dinosaur bones; the American Museum wished to replicate that success, and did so, for the site remained fossil-rich. American Museum collectors gathered 483 dinosaur specimens in the Como Bluff vicinity between 1898 and 1903, among them the huge *Brontosaurus* skeleton that today dominates exhibits in the Museum's fossil halls; it was discovered by Granger. Brown in 1902 commenced working in eastern Montana, exhibiting clearly his knack for always locating at least one spectacular find wherever he prospected. From Montana he brought back the greatest of carnivorous dinosaurs, *Tyrannosaurus,* now sharing with brontosaurus the stellar role in the museum's dinosaur exhibit. In 1910 he explored for fossils along the Red Deer River in Alberta, alarming some Canadians by the wealth in fossils he was removing from their country, but Brown's work nevertheless proceeded amicably until 1915 after which he hunted successfully for specimens in Mexico, Cuba, India and the Mediterranean region. He became so successful he was named the Museum's curator of vertebrate paleontology in 1927. In 1926 a sensational find of early atlatl flint points in association with bones of an extinct form of Pleistocene bison at Folsom, northeastern New Mexico was later dated at about 9000 B.C. Brown was not in on that discovery but, according to Bird, in the early 1900s had found a stone point lodged in the bones of such a bison, the missile of the same design as the Folsom points. He was one of the first nationally-known scientists to visit the Folsom site, which was first worked by researchers from the Denver Natural History Museum; he supported their conclusions about it. In 1934 he led a party which uncovered and shipped to the Museum some 4,000 bones from a Wyoming quarry ten miles north of Shell; they represented twenty or more animals which perished in a tangled mass from some undefined catastrophe and included both plant-eating and carnivorous creatures. This expedition was widely publicized, although its specimens have yet to be thoroughly described. Brown's many discoveries and the unique finds which seemed almost invariably to accompany his field work, made him a renowned collector. He was not so prolific in describing his discoveries, nor in producing numerous scientific papers about them, and that perhaps prevented his name from being enshrined among the top echelon of paleontologists, but as a *collector* he was without a peer. He worked for the Museum for more than fifty years overall, and retired in 1942 having reached the mandatory age limit. He was a consultant on petroleum exploration for the federal government during World War II, pursuing this specialty as occasional consultant for petroleum companies until his death, which occurred at New York City. He had been married twice, his first wife predeceasing him and the second, who wrote of her adventures in the field with him in such books as *I Married a Dinosaur,* surviving him. The showman in Brown would have been dismayed to learn that the *New York Times* gave his death only a scant paragraph under an 8-pt. heading on an inside page, for he obviously was one of the great paleontologists of American history.

James O. Farlow's Introduction to Roland T. Bird's *Bones for Barnum Brown,* Ft. Worth, Tex. Christian Univ. Press, 1985; *New York Times,* Feb. 6, 1963; personal acquaintance with author.

Brown, George W. (Hoodoo Brown), frontiersman (1847-post 1902). B. in Newton County, Missouri, he is not to be confused with Hyman G. Neill, also called Hoodoo Brown (see entry), a disreputable frontier character. The family moved shortly to Barry County in southwestern Missouri and then, because the father was a Union man, to Illinois. In 1863 George, at 17, joined Company F, 3rd Illinois Cavalry, saw considerable action, spent time in an army hospital and later fought Indians in Dakota, possibly in the Sully operation. He was mustered out at Fort Snelling, Minnesota, on October 18, 1865. In 1868 he drifted west, worked for Joseph G. McCoy (see entry) at Abilene, was a bullwhacker, drove cattle into Colorado, served as an army scout on occasion and traded in buffalo hides, following which he hunted buffalo, first for meat for army posts, and later for hides. He married Sallie Lemon in 1867, operated a saloon at Granada, Colorado, and another at Dodge City where, he said, the nearby Arkansas River made it as handy to cut his whiskey as it was for Texas men to water cattle before selling them by weight. Brown thought the first killing in a Dodge City saloon was at his place. About 1879 he built two soddies in Meade County, making of them the first road ranch in that region, on a main trail southward from Dodge City to Texas. His store was well-stocked, liquor was plentiful, there were corrals for oxen, horses and mules, and his customers were mail contractors,

freighters and occasional cattlemen driving a herd or traveling to Dodge City on business. When the Dull Knife Northern Cheyenne exodus passed through Meade County, Brown lodged his family at Dodge City but then returned to his road ranch. Brown killed a man there shortly before he left southern Kansas. He was tried for it at Kingfisher, Oklahoma in 1890 but was cleared. Meade City had a brief boom in population and fancied prospects and Brown apparently lost much of his money when the boom collapsed in a few years. He moved to Oklahoma and spent his declining years there. His wife died in 1902 and Brown died at the National Home for Disabled Soldiers, Leavenworth, Kansas, the date unreported.

C. Robert Haywood, *Trails South: The Wagon-Road Economy in the Dodge City-Panhandle Region,* Norman, Univ. of Okla. Press, 1986.

Brown, Hoodoo: *see,* Hyman G. Neill; George W. Brown entries

Brush, Daniel Harmon, Jr., military officer (May 9, 1848-Mar. 8, 1920). The son of Volunteers brevet Brigadier General Daniel Harmon Brush, young Brush went to West Point from Illinois where he was born and following brief enlisted service with the 145th Illinois Infantry during the Civil War. He was commissioned a second lieutenant of the 17th U.S. Infantry June 12, 1871, and commanded Indian scouts under Custer on the May to October 1873 Yellowstone expedition of David Sloane Stanley. In August the Custer command had several skirmishes with Sioux, both sides suffering minor casualties. Brush accompanied Custer in a pursuit along an 80-lodge trail. It was followed for several days, but appeared to have been lost when the Sioux crossed the Yellowstone to gain its south side and the river was deemed "too swift and fierce for our heavy cavalry." A force of Indians Custer estimated at 800 to 1,000 warriors under Sitting Bull however attacked the bivouac of white troopers at dawn August 11 on the north side of the Yellowstone. The fight raged until Stanley came up with his command and fired several artillery shells at the hostiles who then withdrew. Losses to the Indians were estimated by Custer at 40, while the whites lost Second Lieutenant Charles Braden, heavily wounded, four enlisted men killed and three others wounded. Brush became a first lieutenant August 4, 1876, captain May 2, 1892 and major of the 25th Infantry January 17, 1901. He fought in the Philippines after 1900. He commanded the Departments of the Columbia in 1908-1909; Colorado in 1911, and California in 1911-12. He was a lieutenant colonel with the 11th Infantry August 15, 1903, colonel of the 24th Infantry May 4, 1907, became a Brigadier General February 17, 1908, and retired May 9, 1912. He died at Baltimore.

Heitman; Cullum; Mark H. Brown, *The Plainsmen of the Yellowstone,* N.Y., G.P. Putnam's Sons, 1961.

Bryant, Edwin, journalist, adventurer (c. 1805-Dec. 16, 1869). B. in Massachusetts, he settled as a newsman at Louisville, Kentucky, and from there in 1846 went overland to California, keeping an extensive diary enroute and eventually writing *What I Saw in California,* which quickly became a standard reference work on the events of 1846 and 1847. His observations during his crossing of the Plains were reliable and more accurate than most, and the record of his months in California were also thorough-going and acceptable as authoritative for the events he witnessed or learned about. He took a prominent part in enlisting men for the California Battalion in which he served as first lieutenant of Company H, composed mainly of Walla Walla and California Indians and, with other companies, serving under Fremont. Under the military rule of California and Stephen Watts Kearny, Bryant was alcalde of San Francisco from February to May of 1847. In June 1847 he returned to the States with Kearny. Enroute the party buried what remains they could discover of the ill-fated Donner party (see entries) which had been trapped by deep snow in 1846 and many of whom perished of famine during a particularly severe Sierra Nevada winter. Bryant had travelled with part of the Donner group for some distance while on the way to California in 1846, but had left it to proceed over the mountains safely before winter fell. He testified at the Fremont court-martial for the prosecution. Bryant returned to the coast across the Plains in 1849, and for four or five years was a prominent citizen, a property owner, and a politician. He then went east again, but visited California several more times in later life. He died at Louisville, Kentucky, in 1869 at the age of 64.

Bancroft, *Pioneer Register,* with refs.; Parkman, *The Oregon Trail,* ed. by E.N. Feltskog, Madison, Univ. of Wis. Press, 1969; Bernard DeVoto, *The Year of Decision 1846,* Boston, Little Brown & Co., 1943;

Bryant, *What I Saw in California;* information from E.F. (Ted) Mains.

Buchanan, William, frontiersman (d. 1782). Buchanan was a frontier rover and sometimes militia officer, about whom not too much is known. A tree in Warren County, Kentucky, bore his carved name with the inscription, "1775," the year after Harrodsburg, first permanent settlement in Kentucky, was founded. In 1778 he was at Boonesborough and was one of nine selected to treat with the Indians, from whom he had a narrow escape. In between he was captain of a militia company from Montgomery County, Kentucky. He was killed in August 1782 by Indians in what Thwaites' *Dunmore* called "Holder's Defeat," but in the historian's earlier volume, *Daniel Boone,* was cited an incident in which "Captain Holden, chasing a band of scalpers, was defeated with a loss of four killed and one wounded," the slain, if it is the same incident in both reports, undoubtedly including Buchanan. He was married and left no descendants.

Thwaites, *Dunmore; Daniel Boone,* N.Y., Appleton & Co., 1902.

Buck, Rufus, desperado (d. July 1, 1896). The five-man Rufus Buck gang were minor outlaws in Oklahoma who carried out a 13-day spree of murder, rape, robberies and associated deviltry in 1895 and were hanged together after a brief trial in Judge Isaac C. Parker's court at Fort Smith, Arkansas. Buck was a Yuchi (Euchees) Indian and leader of the band which also included Sam Sampson and Maoma July, Creeks, and Lewis and Lucky Davis, Creek freedmen, a mixture of Creek and black strains. All had been before Judge Parker before and served time for minor offenses. Now, on July 28, 1895, they shot and killed John Garrett, a black deputy marshal near Okmulgee, Oklahoma. They then embarked upon their spree: assaulting a woman captive; robbing a man for trifling possessions; shooting up a home while attempting to steal horses; robbing a stockman; assulting Rosetta, the wife of Henry Hassan while holding him at gunpoint, and robbing a store. A huge posse arrested them after a seven-hour gunfight in which no one appears to have been injured; a mob bent upon vigilante action was molified when told the five would be tried in Judge Parker's court. They were taken to Fort Smith August 11, arraigned August 20, tried September 20, sentenced on

September 25 and after a brief, abortive attempt to win a stay from the Supreme Court, Parker resentenced the gang to be hanged on July 1, 1896, which was done.

Glenn Shirley, *Law West of Fort Smith,* Lincoln, Univ. of Neb. Press, 1968; info. from E.F. (Ted) Mains.

Buford, John, military officer (Mar. 4, 1826-Dec. 16, 1863). B. in Woodford County, Kentucky, he went to West Point from Illinois, became a brevet second lieutenant in the 1st Dragoons July 1, 1848, and a second lieutenant of the 2nd Dragoons February 17, 1849. He became a first lieutenant July 9, 1853. Buford saw frontier service in Texas, New Mexico and Kansas. He was a member of the William Harney (see entry) command of 1855 to punish Sioux believed responsible for the Grattan defeat. In the action against Little Thunder's band near Ash Hollow, Nebraska, on September 3 Buford won the approval of Lieutenant Colonel Philip St. George Cooke, commanding the 2nd Dragoons. Buford served briefly in Kansas before the 2nd Dragoons were assigned to the Utah campaign in 1857. A difficult 1,100-mile winter march toward the Salt Lake Valley saw Buford, as regimental quartermaster, become "the hardest-worked man in the command" and won Cooke's praise anew as a "most efficient officer." During the Civil War Buford served at Washington from October 1861 as captain, then major and July 27, 1862 as a Brigadier General of Volunteers and a cavalry commander. His service was distinctly creditable; he was wounded severely, recovered to become chief of cavalry for the Army of the Potomac, a nominal position, and eventually commanded a division. He continued effective service through major battles of the war until failing health led him to return to Washington for treatment, which was unavailing. His commission as a Major General of Volunteers reached him a few days before his death from typhoid fever. He was married.

Heitman; *Historical Times Illustrated Encyclopedia of the Civil War;* DAB; info. from E.F. (Ted) Mains.

Bulkley, Charles Seymour, engineer, army officer (1825-Apr. 1, 1894). B. probably at Port Chester, New York, he engaged in private telegraph construction, including a line down the Atlantic seaboard and on to New Orleans. He was commissioned a captain January 15, 1863, and became a brevet colonel before his resignation September 7, 1864, after service as assistant superintendent of military telegraphs in the Department of the Gulf. He and his men, according to Pierce, "built many miles of telegraph line in the Southwest, often under enemy fire, including the first military telegraph line in Texas." He left the army to become chief engineer of the Collins Overland Telegraph, commonly known as the Western Union Telegraph Expedition, which sought to construct a line from the United States across Canada and Alaska, hoping to push it on across Siberia to European Russia. In early 1865 he visited Sitka, then returned to San Francisco where he organized his expedition along military lines. A steamer, three barks and a schooner were used as transport and work progressed through British Columbia, Alaska and Siberia until 1866 when success of the Atlantic Cable made abortive the endeavor to link the United States and Europe across Siberia. Nothing is known of Bulkley's further career until February 12, 1892, when in Guatemala he concluded a will at the American consulate-general; he died in Guatemala. Pierce added that reports Bulkley forwarded to Secretary of State William Seward "may have been a determining factor in the [American] decision to purchase Alaska from the Russian government in 1867."

Pierce, *Russian America: A Biographical Dictionary.*

Bullitt, Thomas, military officer (1730-1778). B. in Fauquier County, Virginia, he became an ensign in Washington's 1st Virginia Regiment July 20, 1754, and a lieutenant October 30. Reports that he was at Braddock's 1755 defeat are not supported by the records, but he may have been on detached service. In May 1756 he was stationed at Winchester, in July commanded Fort Frederick on Jackson's (New) River and in November commanded Fort Cumberland. By 1758 he was a captain, distinguished himself in checking the French and Indians in the September 14 rout of James Grant's command (see entry), and shared in John Forbes' (see entry) successful campaign to occupy Fort Duquesne, Pennsylvania. In May 1759 Bullitt with 100 men and 15 supply wagons was defeated by a strong party of French and Indians, losing 35 men killed or captured and all his wagons. Bullitt was a prominent surveyor and explorer of Kentucky for some years. In September 1775 he became adjutant general of all Virginia forces, and in March 1776 became deputy adjutant general of the Southern Department as a lieutenant colonel, becoming a colonel in May. He died in Fauquier County. It is possible that Bullitt County, Kentucky was named for him.

Alexander Scott Withers, *Chronicles of Border Warfare,* Cincinnati, Robert Clarke Co., 1895, 1970.

Bulygin, Nikolai Isakovich, Russian navigator (1784-Feb. 14, 1810). Joining the Russian navy he took part in actions against the Swedes but in 1801 left government service at Okhotsk, Siberia to serve on Russian American Company ships in Alaskan waters. In 1807 he arrived from Kodiak Island at Sitka which had been retaken after a Kolosh (Tlingit) Indian reduction of the place, the Kolosh still holding Aleuts and children seized when the post was destroyed. Baranov sent Bulygin to Yakutat Bay, below Sitka to capture Kolosh in order to swap them for the prisoners the tribe held. September 13 Bulygin returned to Kodiak with the widow of the slain manager, Stepan Larionov, and three of their sons, along with two other wives and their children. In 1808 Bulygin was assigned to the southward movement of RAC influence, instructed to reconnoiter the coast and choose locations for future posts. Bulygin was directed to open trade with natives near the mouth of the Columbia River, then join Kuskov (see entry) for a major thrust southward and establishment of a settlement. He was unable to take his vessel into the mouth of the Columbia, however, and on November 1 the ship was wrecked on Destruction Island, off the northern Washington coast south of the present community of Quillayute. Local Indians of the small Quillayute tribe killed a sailor and wounded almost all the other whites, finally seizing four women prisoners including Bulygin's wife, Anna Petrovna. The rest of the party wandered in the dense rain forest for months and in the spring made a small boat with which they hoped to reach Gray's Harbor to the south, but they were so weakened by illness and starvation that they were easily captured by the Makah tribe living about Cape Flattery on the Strait of San Juan de Fuca. Held as slaves, they were bartered or sold to other Indian tribes. In August 1809 Anna Petrovna died, and when Bulygin heard of it he abandoned hope and himself died. One member of the party was sold to a distant people and never was recovered; 12 others were freed by Captain Thomas Brown, an American of the brig *Lydia* and taken to Sitka,

and seven others had died, while still another had been ransomed in 1809 by Captain George Washington Ayres (see entry) of the brig *Mercury.*

Pierce, *Russian America: A Biographical Dictionary.*

Bush, George Washington, black frontiersman (1790-Apr. 5, 1863). Bush was b. in Louisiana, according to the REAW, although Bancroft said in Pennsylvania; in either event he moved in early life to Missouri from whence he went to the Rocky Mountains as a free trapper "as a youth" and from 1814 to 1829 was a fur trader with the Robidoux brothers in the southwest. In the Columbia River valley of the northwest he worked for the Hudson's Bay Company. As a free black he farmed in Missouri from 1830 until 1843, then guided a party of 32 white Americans to The Dalles, Oregon. Because local regulations prohibited blacks from remaining in Oregon, the Bush party moved on to Puget Sound, becoming what was said to be the first permanent American settlers in the later Washington Territory. Despite the HBC policy to discourage American residence in "its" territory, Bush was permitted to remain because of his former service to the company. He farmed land south of the present Olympia on what is still called Bush Prairie; his wheat was high quality and he became moderately wealthy. "Bush's success with farming and the high regard his neighbors had for him and his family contributed to pioneer 'respect for color' in the Northwest." Bancroft wrote that "he was respected and honored by the pioneers for his generous and charitable traits and manliness of character," adding that he died suddenly of a hemorrhage caused by the bursting of a blood-vessel. His son George became an esteemed citizen, was president of the Washington Industrial Association and his wheat, raised on Bush Prairie, was awarded the first premium at the Centennial Exposition at Philadelphia in 1876. The son also was a member of the state legislature of 1889. Keith Murray wrote in REAW that Bush Sr. died in 1867.

Bancroft, *Washington, Idaho and Montana;* REAW; info. from E.F. (Ted) Mains.

Butcher, Solomon Devo(r)e, photographer, local historian (Jan. 24, 1856-May 18, 1927). B. at Burton, Wetzel County, present West Virginia he was raised from age four in LaSalle County, Illinois, learning at an early age something of the photography business. He went to military school, to medical school in Minnesota, and tried teaching school, had a turn as justice of the peace, sold irrigated land in Texas, was a traveling salesman for a grain and flour mill, invented an "electro-magnetic oil detector," that was never reported to have detected any oil, and patented "an alcohol-laced medicine called Butcher's Wonder of the Age," which failed to generate any wonderful sales (or perhaps cures). Eventually he joined his parents who in 1880 had filed a land claim in Custer County, northeast of North Platte, Nebraska. Butcher and his wife, whom he had met while at medical school, established a photography "gallery" in a sod structure, built like scores of others in that portion of the Plains. Later he moved to Walworth, then a community (now virtually vanished) on the Middle Loup River in northeastern Custer County. Still interested in photography about 1886 he formed the concept of an illustrated photo book of Custer County, then a relic of the Old West swiftly evolving into a new society which would leave the early days in limbo, to shortly become oblivion. He advertised in the local press for photographs to be taken, and for articles "of 3,000 words or less, of the early settlement and up to date." In seven years he had taken 1,500 farm and ranch views and collected as many biographies written by the pioneer settlers. Then on March 12, 1899, his home and studio burned to the ground and with it all his writings and photographs, although his glass negatives were in the main saved. Butcher was nothing if not stubborn, and he set about recreating the material for his "history book." George B. Mair, editor of the newspaper at Callaway where Butcher now lived, helped edit the flood of manuscript material coming in from all over the county. He finally found an established cowman, Ephraim S. Finch, who would finance publication of the book, although there was little profit for anyone in it. The book was published in 1901 though overall probably fewer than 2,000 copies appeared; it has recently been republished without alteration. The book is liberally illustrated with Butcher's pioneering photographs, principally of ranch scenes and people who lived in Custer County before the turn of the century. There also are "re-enactments," never labeled as such, of stirring events earlier in the county, such as the lynching and burning of Ami (Whit) Ketchum and Luther Mitchell (see Isom Prentice Olive entry for details); the lynching of Kid Wade in 1884; the activities of monumental horse thief Doc Mid-

dleton (prudently called Dick Milton by Butcher), and similar incidents of which in early Custer County there was no shortage. The re-enactments are crudely done, with Butcher's painted-in weapons and the stiffly-posed "actors," who were mainly farm boys, but they illustrated the stories. The pioneer recollections and tales are often interesting, as in the narrative of buffalo hunter Alfred S. Burger (see entry), whose name Butcher spells as Burgher, with details on his techniques as a hide hunter. Even today Custer County, of 2,571 square miles has a total population of scarcely 12,000, and in Butcher's time there were fewer people there, so his photographic collection is probably a good cross-secton of its inhabitants in his day, and his determination to photograph many phases of their lives, dwellings, churches and activities is as complete as anything on record anywhere on the Plains. A discouraged Butcher died at Greeley, Colorado, considering himself something of a failure. He was buried May 22, 1927 at Gates Cemetery, Broken Bow, the county seat of Custer County.

Butcher, *Pioneer History of Custer County, Nebraska,* intr. by Harry E. Chrisman, Sage Books, Denver, Co., 1965 (Chrisman is the authority on I.P. Olive and his faction); Alex Harris, review of Pam Conrad, *The Life and Times of Solomon Butcher,* in the *New York Times* Book Review Section, September 1, 1991.

Butler, Zebulon, military officer (Jan. 23, 1731-July 28, 1795). B. at Ipswich, Massachusetts, he grew up at Lyme, Connecticut, from 1736. He came to own ocean-going sloops and engaged in the West Indies trade, but entered military service in the French and Indian War. He was commissioned an ensign in 1757, a lieutenant and quartermaster in 1759 and a captain in 1760. Ordered to Cuba, he was shipwrecked enroute but arrived in time to take part in the siege of Havana. As a civilian he led a group of Connecticut settlers to the Wyoming Valley in today's Luzerne County, Pennsylvania, settling in 1769 on disputed lands along the Susquehanna River, the situation soon coming to armed conflict. In July 1771 Butler besieged Fort Wyoming and its Pennsylvania garrison, captured it and then repulsed invaders of the valley in a 1775 action at Nanticoke Gap. With the Revolution, Butler became colonel of Connecticut militia, later lieutenant colonel and then colonel of the Continental forces. In March 1778 when the Wyoming residents were away with the Army and before reinforcements could arrive, the valley was invaded by the New York Loyalist Major John Butler whose force included rangers, part of the King's Royal Regiment of New York, and several hundred Iroquois under the Seneca chief Old King (Sayenqueraghta) (see entry). Zebulon Butler, home on leave, found that his "command" at Forty Fort in the valley consisted of some 60 regulars and about 300 militia, largely the undisciplined, the youthful and the aged. He wanted to wait within the Fort for reinforcements but was overruled by the council of war and it was decided to quit the Fort and initiate an engagement with a clearly superior enemy. On June 3 the force of something under 400 marched out and were sighted about 2 p.m. by the enemy Indians; around 4:30 the Americans were within a mile of them. The British and Indian force established an ambush in an open wood. As they neared the wood the Americans formed battle lines, Butler proclaiming, "Stand firm the first shock, and the Indians will give way!" The Americans advanced steadily and when 200 yards distant fired their first volley, firing two more at the prone enemy before closing to within 100 yards. At that point the enemy opened fire from virtually point-blank range, causing very heavy casualties. As the Iroquois closed around the flanks, the Americans left gave way for a more advantageous position, but the move was mistaken by the untrained militia for a full retreat and "the result was a rout." A few reached Forty Fort, but many were tomahawked or were cut down in half an hour of furious firing. Colonel Butler fled the field and Colonel Nathan Dennison, the second in command, the next day surrendered the fort, stating he had lost 300 men, though John Butler claimed 376 Americans had been killed. The British losses were slight: one Indian killed, two Rangers and eight Indians wounded of whom two war chiefs, Soskawek and Sohnage, died of their wounds. In the sweep of the valley John Butler also claimed eight forts destroyed, one thousand dwellings burned, and much livestock stolen although he stated that not a single unarmed citizen had been slain. Zebulon Butler returned to W, 'ming as commandant, remaining during th' Jullivan campaign against the New York Iroquois. December 29, 1780, Washington recalled him from Wyoming at the request of Congress to ease the friction over the territory between Connecticut and Pennsylvania. He was stationed at West Point for the rest of the Revolution. He was married three times, his first two spouses predeceasing him, and died at Wilkes-barre, Pennsylvania, at 64, leaving children by each of his wives.

DAB1 Barbara Graymont, *The Iroquois in the American Revolution,* Syracuse (N.Y.) Univ. Press, 1972; info. from E.F. (Ted) Mains.

Byrd, William, pioneer (1652-Dec. 4, 1704). B. probably at London he came to America as a youth. In 1671 he was bequeathed by his uncle, Thomas Stegg, 15,000 acres of land lying on both sides of the James River of Virginia, including the site of the future Richmond, laid out by his son and namesake (see entry). Five years later he "courted ruin" by accompanying Nathaniel Bacon (see entry) on his aggressive southern Indian expedition, but later made his peace with Virginia Governor Sir William Berkeley. Byrd was intelligent, possessed business acumen and a considerable station in life with plenty of resources and was active politically as well as commercially, being a successful Indian trader and merchant in addition to carrying on enterprises such as raising tobacco, and the importation of large numbers of black slaves, some for his own use and others for sale to his neighbors. His trade interests spread to Barbados, England and the frontier where he became engaged in a profitable fur trade. He lived near The Falls, discovered by Christopher Newport in 1607 at the site of Richmond. The estate was at the head of a 400-mile trail leading southwest to the Catawba Indians of Carolina and Tennessee. Along this wilderness road Byrd sent packhorse expeditions managed by woods rangers and bearing cloth, guns, powder, kettles and other items to exchange for deerskins and beaver. "It was a dangerous business for in 1684 five traders were killed by the Indians, and in 1686 two more lost their lives." Byrd sometimes was selected by the Virginia colony to treat with Indians, and in 1685 went north with Virginia Indians to conclude a treaty with the far-ranging Iroquois at Albany. Byrd, sometimes known by the title of captain, headed Henrico County militia with the duty of protecting the upper James River country from Indian raids. In his numerous undertakings and leadership roles "he typified the spirit of the seventeenth-century Virginia aristocracy." In 1691 William Byrd established a new headquarters at Westover at The Falls, later naming his estate for the site and "for generations the seat of the Byrd family." He had been a member of the Virginia House of Burgesses from 1677 to 1682 when he entered the Council of State or what amounted to the House of Lords of the colony. He became president of the Council in 1703, the year before his death. He was the father of William Byrd (1674-1744).

DAB; George F. Willison, *Behold Virginia: The Fifth Crown,* N.Y., Harcourt, Brace and Co., 1952.

Byrd, William, colonial leader (Mar. 28, 1674-Aug. 26, 1744). The son of William Byrd (see entry), he was sent to England for his education, visited Holland in 1690 and in 1692 returned to Virginia, assuming an important position in the colony based upon his wealth, social position and native ability. In 1697 he returned to England to defend Virginia governor (1692-97) Edmund Andros, an overbearing individual who had been charged, among other things, with hostility toward the Anglican Church. In 1698 Byrd became agent for Virginia in London, remaining there until the death of his father in 1704, returning to the colony in 1705, soon to be married and then, as an influential member of the Council of State becoming embroiled in a lengthy, bitter feud with Lieutenant Governor Alexander Spotswood (see entry), which has little frontier relevance. In 1728 he was one of several commissioners charged with surveying the border between Virginia and North Carolina. In pursuit of this objective, Byrd in 1728 named Great Dismal Swamp, a region of 750 square miles in southeastern Virginia. As an extensive landowner on the frontier, he was interested in western expansion. Many years before the French had established themselves upon the Ohio River, Byrd warned of danger from that source, writing that "they may build forts to command the passes, to secure their own traffic and settlements westward [and] to invade the British colonies from thence." He ultimately came to own 179,000 acres; on one of his estates he laid out the city of Richmond. His writings included *A History of the Dividing Line,* based upon his diary entries of the border survey; *A Journey to the Land of Eden,* and *A Progress to the Mines,* which were extracted from his diaries and published in 1841 from the collection called the Westover Manuscripts. Since then "admiration for [his] limpid prose, the crisp wit, and the almost incongruously urbane tone he displays have won more and more admirers. He is generally considered one of the foremost colonial authors." Byrd possessed a library of more than 4,000 volumes and a collection of paintings. He was married twice, his first wife predeceasing him.

DAB; CE.

C

Caamaño, Jacinto, Spanish navigator (fl. 1789-1804). In 1789 Caamaño was one of six naval officers assigned to accompany the explorer Bodega y Quadra (see entry) to San Blas on the west coast of Mexico in order to bolster the Spanish presence on the northwest coast in the face of Russian expansion southward from Alaska. Caamaño with the corvette *Aranzazu* brought supplies to Nootka Sound on the western coast of Vancouver Island, arriving May 13, 1792. June 12 Caamaño left in accordance with instructions from Mexico's Viceroy, the Conde de Revillagigedo, to chart the coast southward from Bucareli Sound, between Baker and Suemez islands of the Alexander Archipelago of the Alaskan Panhandle. Caamaño took formal possession for Spain of various islands and even points on the mainland. Despite the fearsome reputation among traders of the Haida Indians, Caamaño found them invariably cordial and hospitable to him, and he even brought with him an Indian youth who desired to accompany the expedition southward (the Indian died in November at Monterey "after a short & severe illness"). "Caamaño was determined to explore every single fjord, for each winding channel held the enticement of being the gateway" to a Northwest Passage, a principal object of discovery, and investigation if it existed. Caamaño had one harrowing brush with natives which was resolved by an aged Indian leader whom he had previously befriended. The explorer determined that the lands he investigated were largely an archipelago, and he traced Clarence Strait, hoping it might prove to be the fabled Passage, but could not explore its ultimate dimensions due to lateness of the season. He rejoined Bodega at Nootka Sound September 8 and arrived at San Blas February 6, 1793. He had met Vancouver (see entry) on his expedition, Vancouver obtaining copies of certain of Caamaño's maps, their features incorporated in some of the Englishman's maps.

Warren L. Cook, *Flood Tide of Empire: Spain and the Pacific Northwest, 1543-1819,* New Haven, Yale Univ. Press, 1973; Orth, 9, 172.

Caldwell, John, frontiersman (Jan. 22, 1753-1840). B. in Ireland, he was brought to America by his parents who settled at Baltimore. In 1773 Caldwell removed to a place near Wheeling, West Virginia, and for several years was active in the Indian wars. As a member of Dunmore's division he took part in the October 10, 1774 climactic battle of Point Pleasant which in effect terminated Lord Dunmore's War. Two years later, under command of William Harrod, Caldwell was of a party that went down the Ohio River to rescue the wounded and bury the dead of Robert Patterson's (see entry) Kentucky party. In 1777 Caldwell was a volunteer under Captain Samuel Mason (see entry), stationed first at Shepherd's Fort, then at Fort Henry, six miles distant where he was at the start of its 1777 siege. Caldwell, at the outset of the attack, ran up a hill toward the fort, tripped and fell, wedged between two trees. He wrenched himself loose by great effort just as an Indian assailant threw a tomahawk at him; it missed. Caldwell escaped to Shepherd's Fort. He was a volunteer guard at Wheeling in 1778-1779, and the latter year attended Daniel Brodhead's campaign up the Allegheny River of Pennsylvania. He served briefly at Rail's Fort on Buffalo Creek, Pennsylvania, then established a place 14 miles up from the mouth of Wheeling Creek in West Virginia where he lived until his death.

Thwaites/Kellogg, *Frontier Defense on the Upper Ohio, 1777-1778.*

Caldwell, William, partisan (c. 1747-1822). Caldwell, who became "one of the most noted border partisans of the West," was probably b. in Ireland and migrated to Pennsylvania before the Revolution. He served in Dunmore's division at the climactic battle of Point Pleasant, West Virginia, October 10, 1774. After Dunmore's War and the outbreak of the Revolution he was hired by Dunmore to carry dispatches. He evaded American forces and reached Niagara where he raised a company of partisans for Butler's Rangers which was sent in 1776 to Detroit. In 1777 he was sent back to Niagara as a lieutenant, participating in the siege of Fort Stanwix, New York, and the raids against Wyoming, Pennsylvania, and Cherry Valley, New York. In 1781 he returned to Detroit and in 1782 commanded the force that defeated Colonel William Crawford at Sandusky; in that significant action Caldwell was wounded. Recovering, he went as captain with the military force that penetrated Kentucky, besieged Bryant's Station and on August 19 defeated Kentuckians in the savage battle of Blue Licks, northeast of Lexington. Following the Revolution Caldwell was retained in the British Indian Department and was reported to have been with the Indians who were defeated by Wayne in 1794 at Fallen Timbers, although no British force as such was involved. When the Americans occupied Detroit in 1796 Caldwell removed to Ontario and laid out a town near the mouth of the Malden River where he became a justice of the peace and a militia colonel. In 1812 as quartermaster general he was involved in the capture of Detroit. When Matthew Elliott (see entry) retired in 1814 as superintendent of the British Indian Department, Caldwell took over the post, but two years later, after a disagreement with the military commandant, he resigned. Thwaites/Kellogg wrote that "Caldwell was popular with the Indians, and his half-breed son, Billy Caldwell, became a Potawatomi chief." Three other sons, William, James, and Thomas served with the British in the War of 1812, two of them still living in 1863. Caldwell Sr. died at his Canadian home at 75 years of age.

Thwaites/Kellogg, *Frontier Defense on the Upper Ohio, 1777-1778.*

Cameron, Alexander, British Indian agent (d. Dec. 27, 1781). Whether there was any relationship between Allen and Alexander Cameron is not reported, but they wore the same tartan. Alexander Cameron was Southern Indian Superintendent John Stuart's deputy commissioner for the Cherokees. Stuart had been appointed c. 1760, and Cameron was named around 1766, as was David Tait(t) to the Creeks, Charles Stuart, a brother of John, to the Choctaws and Farquhar Bethune to the Chickasaws. Cameron promptly took a Cherokee wife and fathered a son, settling in today's Abbeville County, South Carolina, on land given him by the tribe, the chief Oconostota (see entry) informing Stuart that the Cherokees all loved Cameron because he told them the truth and did justice to them. "We desire that he may educate [his halfbreed son] like the white people, and cause them to be able to read and write, that he may resemble both white and red, and live among us when his father is dead," the chief said.

The Cherokees fondly called Cameron "Scotchie," and he returned their affection. He found them involved in difficulties posed by unscrupulous traders. "No nation was ever infested with such a set of villains and horse thieves," he wrote Stuart. "A trader...will invent and tell a thousand lies; and he is indefatigable in stirring up trouble against all other white persons that he judges his rivals in trade." The effectiveness of Cameron with the Cherokees may be inferred by an attempt of Creek assassins to murder him in 1774; fortunately it failed, as did subsequent like attempts, as in 1777, this time by American-influenced Cherokees. Under directives from Stuart, Cameron sought early to keep his charges clear of burgeoning troubles between King and colonials, but by 1775 this course was modified. Now Cameron was directed to enlist Cherokees in support of English arms, if that became necessary, although Stuart was still opposed to general or indiscriminate attacks upon the frontier. This policy was welcomed by many Cherokees, already disturbed by colonial intrusions into their lands, belligerence and hostility, but it came to little, initially. Cameron was not present at the council between Cherokees and Henderson's Transylvania Company at Sycamore Shoals on the upper Tennessee, the company purchasing a huge tract between the Tennessee and Kentucky rivers. Many Cherokees, led by Dragging Canoe, violently opposed the sale, but the document was signed by Chief Oconostota and others. Cameron urged Stuart to have the pact nullified, but this was not done. Cherokees were particularly upset by white settlement along the Watauga and Nolichucky rivers near the North Carolina-Tennessee line, and this heightened tension. At a spring 1776 council at Chota, the favored town or "capital" of the Cherokees, Cameron "raged and fumed" against the Sycamore Shoals treaty, even though he sought to prevent open hostilities, since the settlements included Loyalists as well as Patriots who might be equally damaged by war. Cameron and Henry Stuart, another brother of John's, sent the Watauga-Nolichucky frontiersmen by trader Isaac Thomas, a letter with a copy of a talk by Cherokee chiefs, demanding the area be cleared within 20 days. But the Cameron-Stuart letter was altered in transmission and when delivered it "was very different from the original." Believing that the Indians had passed beyond arbitration and that war obviously was at hand, the settlers might strengthen their appeal for assistance if they could convince "easterners" that British agents were inciting the Cherokees toward hostility. The altered version of the letter outlined a plan by which the Indians and Loyalists would attack the frontier where the houses of the King's friends would be marked to give them immunity. The forged letter was widely accepted and published, and the alteration served its purpose. Cameron and Henry Stuart penned a second letter, but by mid-June admitted failure and "despite all their exertions to the contrary, they could no longer restrain the Cherokee." One hundred pack-horse loads of ammunition, sent by the British to Chota for use in the event of organized American attacks on the Cherokees had been appropriated by Dragging Canoe and his belligerent followers and Stuart, now in Creek country, was delivered a message from Cameron that "all our rhetoric could no longer dissuade them from taking up the hatchet." This war faction attacked white establishments but lost 13 men to 18 whites slain and, defeated, withdrew momentarily. "More vengeful than ever," the warriors renewed guerilla activities which spread all along the southern border. Cameron's "handsome estate" near the ruins of Fort Prince George on the Savannah River, South Carolina, was burned by American forces pushing into Cherokee country on punitive operations which also struck supposed English advisers and inciters. As the Revolutionary War intensified, Dragging Canoe and his faction withdrew from the main body of Cherokees and, becoming known as Chickamaugas, settled in the region of today's Chattanooga; here Stuart and Cameron kept them "supplied with food and ammunition, hoping to weld them into an effective British fighting force" with other like-minded Indian peoples. The expedition of Evan Shelby (see entry) against the Chickamaugas effectively neutralized them for a time, and dramatically reduced their power. When John Stuart died March 21, 1779, at Pensacola, Cameron took his place temporarily as Commissioner of Southern Indian Affairs. However the area as such was seen as too large for a single administrator to handle, and Cameron in 1779 was named by Lord George Germain of London, secretary of state for the colonies, to be superintendent for the Mississippi District, having oversight of Choctaws and Chickasaws, while Lieutenant Colonel Thomas Brown was named head of the Atlantic District, including Cherokees and Creeks. Each man was subordinate to the ranking military officer in his

district and for the balance of the war they were to supply auxiliaries only, when requested. Cameron was dismayed. He had worked closely with John Stuart, believed he should promptly have been named his successor, was shocked by his new assignment when he felt he should have remained in his familiar territory with Indians he knew so well, and he was concerned that tight financial controls would prevent his properly fulfilling his responsibilities. He must also contend with increasing Spanish intrigues for the favor of his charges, and that would cost money—now in dimished supply. He quickly became distressed with the bumbling of General John Campbell's incoherent Indian policy, demands for large numbers of auxiliaries whom he haughtily dismissed when the supposed need passed, and being overly penurious where Indians were concerned. The Spanish captured Mobile, which Cameron thought an unnecessary loss, and he complained with increasing fervor about General Campbell's obtuse Indian policies, "but still the general remained myopic." Now stationed at Pensacola, Cameron supposed the Spanish had placed a high price on his head because of his Indian position and the mounting Choctaw hostility and harassment of the Mobile garrison. Strong Spanish forces assailed Pensacola in 1781, and on May 8 Campbell surrendered the place which "signaled the end of effective functioning of the Southern Indian Department." John Stuart had established his headquarters at Pensacola after the fall of Charleston, and Cameron had maintained his headquarters there, but with its fall, he took refuge in the Creek country, rested briefly intending to move on to Georgia, perhaps to Loyalist Augusta, but that too soon fell to the Americans and Cameron died at Savannah as the era of strong British control and influence over the southern Indians verged on becoming extinguished.

Grace Steele Woodward, *The Cherokees,* Norman, Univ. of Okla. Press, 1963; James H. O'Donnell, III, *Southern Indians in the American Revolution,* Knoxville, Univ. of Tenn. Press, 1973; R.S. Cotterill, *The Southern Indians,* Norman, 1954; David H. Corkran, *The Creek Frontier, 1540-1783,* Norman , 1967; Thwaites, *Dunmore.*

Cameron, Allen, Loyalist, Indian agent (fl. c. 1775-1778). B. in Scotland, he may have been related to British Indian agent John Stuart (see entry); according to John Connolly he was Indian agent under Stuart and "had suffered much for his principles, and had refused offers of military rank from South Carolinian patriots." He had come up to Virginia with dispatches from the governors of East Florida and South Carolina, and "knowing the Indian character was considered by Lord Dunmore a proper person to join [Connolly's] expedition" of 1775 designed to sever the northern from southern colonies by use of Irish troops and Indian partisans. Cameron was arrested and in December 1776 tried to escape from a Philadephia prison, but a rope broke and he fell 50 feet, "being found in an apparently dying condition." He partially recovered, however, and was released from custody in 1778 when he returned to England, "his physical condition debarring him from further military service."

Thwaites/Kellogg, *The Revolution on the Upper Ohio, 1775-1777,* Madison, Wis. Hist. Soc., 1908.

Campbell, Archibald, seaman (July 19, 1787-post 1821). B. at Wynford, near Glasgow his father, a 45th Regiment soldier, died on St. Lucia in the West Indies when the boy was 4. He was apprenticed to a weaver at 10 but in 1800 went to sea as an apprentice aboard the *Isabella* out of Glasgow, Hugh Peterson, master; he made three voyages to the West Indies, served a year on a coaster and made another West Indies trip aboard the *Robina.* At Madeira he was impressed for service on a frigate, the *Diana,* but escaped at Portsmouth in 1806. He signed on to serve the *Thames,* an Indiaman; he deserted at Canton and was persuaded by Captain Joseph O'Cain (see entry) of the American trader *Eclipse* to sign on with him, which he did under the name of Archibald Macbride to disguise the unauthorized parting from his former berth. May 8, 1807, the *Eclipse* left Canton, traded in Japan, then at Kamchatka, leaving the latter August 8, and on September 10 struck a reef south of Sanak Island of the Aleutians and was fatally damaged, the crew getting off in the long boat the following morning. O'Cain was determined to build a new, smaller vessel out of the wreckage of the 343-ton *Eclipse* but Campbell and some others left to seek aid from whatever Aleuts or Russians they might encounter. After great hardships, during which Campbell froze both of his feet, he was rescued and taken to the Russian base on Kodiak Island where there was a hospital of sorts. An inept operation amputated both of his feet but "unfortunately for me...cut them off below the ankle joint, from a wish to take as little away as

possible; the sores extended above the place, and [they] have never healed. By the month of August [1808] I could creep about on my hands and knees." His case aroused compassion. A subscription launched by Governor Baranov among officers of ships in the harbor, raised for him 180 rubles ($90). Campbell learned then that O'Cain had indeed completed his rebuilt brig, put to sea and was lost when the ship when down. Ivan Ivanovich Banner, being left in charge at Kodiak when Baranov went to his primary base at Sitka, hired Campbell to teach native children English, in order that they might become interpreters for American ships arriving on fur-trading missions; by this time Campbell had acquired a smattering of Russian. At length he secured passage on a Russian ship to Hawaii where he spent two years, from 1809-10, became friendly with King Kamehameha I, and started the initial sail-making loom on the Islands. He returned home by way of Cape Horn in 1811-12, and enroute, at Rio de Janeiro, chanced to meet a Scotsman named Lawrie who supplied him with a letter to Lawrie's father in Edinburgh; upon arrival there in April 1812 Lawrie senior had him admitted to the city's infirmary to see if something could be done about his lower legs, for the wounds from the unskillful operation were still troublesome. After four months, Campbell was dismissed as "incurable." Lawrie then presented him with a barrel organ, a sort of primitive piano accordion. With this Campbell "contrived to earn a miserable pittance, by crawling about the streets of Edinburgh and Leith, grinding out music" for passers-by. He eventually learned to play the violin, a more portable instrument and found "employment on board the steam-boats that ply upon the river Clyde, by playing for the amusement of the steerage passengers." While so doing he came to the attention of James Smith who took down his narrative, edited and had it published. Campbell was still living in 1821.

Campbell, *A Voyage Around the World, from 1806 to 1812...,* Edinburgh, 1816 (Honolulu, Univ. of Hawaii Press, 1967).

Campbell, Arthur, frontiersman (1743-1811). B. in Augusta County, Virginia, he was a son of David Campbell, one of the earliest Scot-Irish settlers of the region. In 1751 he was captured by northwestern Indians near Dickenson's Fort, established by Colonel John Dickenson in what is now Bath County, Virginia. He was taken to their towns on Lake Erie and held for three years, then escaped to the British army. His return to Virginia was "hailed with great joy." The state eventually awarded him, for his subsequent services as scout or guide, 1,000 acres on Beargrass Creek, near Louisville, Kentucky, then part of Virginia. Campbell built a mill on his father's estate in Smyth County and when Fincastle County was established in 1772 became a justice of the peace and soon was appointed major of militia. "As one of the most prominent men of southwest Virginia, he took part in all stirring border events." In 1776 he was chosen county lieutenant for the new Washington County, an office he held for 30 years. In 1780 he conducted "a brilliant campaign against the Cherokee," but turned over leadership of the King's Mountain expedition later that year to his cousin, General William Campbell. The following year he became involved in attempts to found the new state of Franklin and was removed from office by Governor Patrick Henry, but reinstated by the legislature. Although a man of much ability, "his imperious and hasty temper made him many enemies." In late life he joined his sons in Kentucky, and died near Middlesborough.

Thwaites, *Dunmore.*

Campbell, Charles, militia officer, judge (d. c. 1837). Campbell was a descendant of the Argyle family, one of whom fled to America after the battle of Culloden Moor, Scotland, April 16, 1746, in which the Highlander followers of Bonnie Prince Charlie (Charles Edward Stuart) were bested by English forces. Campbell built a mill on Blacklick Creek in the present Indiana County, Pennsylvania, then part of Westmoreland County. He and four friends, Randall Laughlin, John Gibson, a Gibson brother and a man named Dickson were preparing a meal in Laughlin's cabin in August 1777 when they were surprised by Indians who captured them. Campbell was allowed to leave a note telling of their being seized "& used well," and then the group was taken to Detroit and later to Canada where the surviving three were exchanged, two, the Gibson brother and Dickson, having died in captivity. At the time of his capture Campbell was lieutenant colonel of the county. Later he became county lieutenant and was prominent in Westmoreland defense during the Indian wars of 1789-1795. In 1827 he was an associate judge of the county, a position he held until his death in Indiana County. His brother, Richard Campbell, was on Lochry's expedition (see entry) and was

killed August 24, 1781, in the disastrous Iroquois ambush that destroyed the American party.

Thwaites/Kellogg, *Frontier Defense on the Upper Ohio, 1777-1778.*

Campbell, Donald, military officer (d. July 4, 1763). Campbell was a Scot officer who came to America with the 62nd Regiment in 1756, and became captain of the Royal Americans (60th Regiment) in 1759. Late in 1760 he accompanied Major Robert Rogers (see entry) on an expedition to Detroit where he became commander of the post. He was not overly fond of Indians and gradually lost some of the affection he originally had for the French residents of Detroit, except for the women, who, he wrote "surpasses our expectations." He was called "fat and unweildy" and was near-sighted, but "he was an alert and competent commander." He was respected and trusted by Pontiac and "unfortunately for his own safety, Campbell trusted Pontiac as well." May 1, 1763, Detroit came under siege by Pontiac and his Indian allies from several tribes. Pontiac invited the British to a council May 10 and Campbell and Lieutenant George McDougall volunteered to meet with the chief, left the fortified base and were immediately made hostage. On July 3 or 4 a nephew of Wasson, a noted Chippewa chief, was killed in a skirmish near the fort; an irate Wasson demanded of Pontiac the person of Campbell for his revenge. The officer was turned over, taken to Wasson's camp, stripped and tomahawked by Wasson himself, the body thrown into the river, from which it was retrieved and buried by whites of the post.

Thwaites, EWT, I, 101-102; Howard H. Peckham, *Pontiac and the Indian Uprising,* Chicago, Univ. of Chicago Press, 1961; *Journal of Pontiac's Conspiracy 1763,* Detroit, Mich. Society of the Colonial Wars, 1912; DCB, III.

Campbell, John, military officer (d. 1799). B. in Ireland, he came to America while young and entered the Indian trade in the west. In 1764 he laid out a town on the present site of Pittsburgh and a decade later purchased a large tract adjoining Dr. John Connolly's at the present Louisville, Kentucky. Early in the Revolutionary War he was commissary at Fort Pitt. In the summer of 1779, while on a visit to the Falls of the Ohio (Louisville), he took passage with the Colonel David Ro(d)gers party from New Orleans on their return up the river. Near Cincinnati Rogers was defeated by a large party of Indians with whom Simon Girty was operating; Rogers was killed and Campbell captured, taken to Detroit and then to Quebec where "because of his open defiance" the British refused to exchange him until the end of the Revolution. He later resided in Kentucky, was sent as a delegate to the Virginia legislature, was a member of the Kentucky constitutional convention in 1792 and speaker of the Kentucky Senate in 1798, dying the following year.

Thwaites/Kellogg, *The Revolution on the Upper Ohio, 1775-1777*, Madison, Wis. Hist. Soc., 1908.

Campbell, Joseph Boyd, military officer (Nov. 26, 1837-Aug. 28, 1891). B. in Pennsylvania he went to West Point from New Hampshire and was commissioned a second and a first lieutenant June 24, 1861, emerging from the Civil War a captain. He became a captain with the 4th Artillery February 5, 1867. After serving at a variety of domestic posts Campbell was assigned August 16, 1874, to be Indian agent for Alaska, and to command the Sitka post which in effect made him commandant of Alaska, since Sitka was the dominant post there at the time. Brigadier General Oliver Otis Howard then commanded the Department of the Columbia, which included Alaska, and visited Sitka in July 1875. In his narrative of that tour he included an interesting passage in Campbell's report of July 17, 1875, which said: "With what are known as Hudson Bay muskets the Indians are comparatively harmless...It will be a very different thing, however, if they succeed in arming themselves with modern arms of precision and power. They are much more intelligent than the Indians of the plains; good marksmen, and throughout the coast are united by a class or caste of warriors called Koch-won-tons. This will enable them to concentrate in vast numbers." He added that "arms are shipped to Kadiak and Unalaska, of any kind and in any quantity, and from there distributed among the various trading posts of the Alaska Commercial Company, to be disposed of as they see fit." In a supporting letter Campbell wrote that ships of the Alaska Commercial Company land regularly "vast quantities of superior arms of all kinds at Unalaska" from where they are "distributed throughout Upper Alaska by means of the company's agents, agencies and ports." Campbell was relieved of his Sitka command June 17, 1876. He was on frontier duty at Fort Robinson, Nebraska, from August to November 1876, and commanded a battalion on the Powder River Expedition in December. The remainder of his active duty was at domestic posts and assignments. He became a major of the 2nd Artillery July 1, 1891, two months before his death, which occurred at age 55 at Montreal, Canada.

Heitman; Powell; Cullum; O.O. Howard, "A Visit to Alaska in June, 1875," 45, 50-51, *Narratives of Explorations in Alaska;* info. from the U.S. Army Mil. Hist. Inst., Carlisle Barracks, Penn.

Cantwell, John C., Coast Guard officer (fl. 1884-1902). Cantwell, of the U.S. Revenue-Cutter Service, was taken to Cape Krusenstern at the north entrance of Kotzebue Sound, Alaska, in 1884 by Navy Captain Michael A. Healy, who commanded the cutter *Corwin.* Cantwell explored the Kobuk River, whose mouth is on Hotham Inlet of the sound, for about 185 miles, preceding the expedition of Navy Lieutenant George Morse Stoney (see entry) by a few days. On his return Cantwell explored Selawic Lake, at the head of Kotzebue Sound. In 1885 Cantwell again explored the Kobuk River, this time going all the way to Walker Lake, which he named. During the summers from 1899-1901 Cantwell commanded the revenue steamer *Nunivak* on the Yukon River, wintering at the mouth of the Dall River during these years; his reports of the cruises of the steamer were published in 1902.

Orth, 9.

Captain Jacobs, Delaware chief (d. Sept. 8, 1756). A militant Delaware war leader and chief, Captain Jacobs participated in the ambush of Braddock and his command in July 1755 in Pennsylvania and was an associate of Shingas (see entry) in raids and massacres that followed the British disaster. Like Shingas, he had a price put on his head. With Francois de Villiers and a small party of his own warriors and French he captured Fort Granville on the Juniata River near present Lewistown, Pennsylvania, August 2, 1756. Captain Jacobs' base was at Kittanning. Colonel John Armstrong (see entry) attacked this place on September 8, 1756, and Captain Jacobs, his wife and a son were among those killed.

Info. from John Sugden; Hodge, HAI, I, 627; C.A. Weslager, *The Delaware Indians: A History,* Brunswick, N.J., Rutgers Univ. Press, 1972.

Captain Johnny (Kekewepelethy: Great or Tame Hawk), Shawnee chief (fl. 1776-1808). Captain Johnny, as he was known to the whites, was a war chief of the Mekoche division of the Shawnee Indians of Ohio, and from 1787 he was the principal chief of the Shawnees. He was significant primarily for his contribution to militant pan-tribalism in the 1780s and 1790s. With other chiefs he visited Pittsburgh in 1776 and conferred with the new American authorities there, and in 1778 moved to the Delaware town of Coshocton, Ohio, in order to sit out the Revolutionary War. The Delawares, too, were neutral until about 1780. The Mekoche Shawnee, or some at least, moved in with them while other Shawnee divisions: Pekowi, Chillicote, and Kispoko, joined the British in 1777. About 1780-81 the Coshocton Indians, too, drifted to the British side, and probably moved to Mackachack, on a tributary of the Mad River in present Logan County, Ohio, from where they aided the English during the rest of the Revolutionary conflict. Following it, Captain Johnny in 1784 opened negotiations with the United States, but was turned off by their claim to have defeated the Indians, and demands for land north of the Ohio River. He embraced the notion of pan-tribalism to defend the Old Northwest; the idea had circulated among the Shawnees since 1740 and was revived in 1783 by the Mohawk Joseph Brant (see entry). In 1785 speaking for the Shawnees, Delawares and Mingoes, Captain Johnny said, "the people of one color are united so that we make but one man, that has but one heart and one mind." He repudiated the "conquest" treaties thrust upon the Iroquois by the United States at Fort Stanwix, New York, October 22, 1784, and at Fort McIntosh, Pennsylvania, January 21, 1785, upon the Wyandot, Delaware, Chippewa and Ottawa tribes. Captain Johnny insisted that only the whites who wished to trade should be allowed north of the Ohio—no settlers. The United States next sought to impose a treaty of cession upon the Shawnees at Fort Finney, at the mouth of the Great Miami River of Ohio. Reluctant to attend, the Shawnees listened to Captain Johnny as he tried to form a concerted opposition to the endeavor, but unity within the tribe was weak, and the Shawnees eventually assembled for the treaty January 31, 1786. Captain Johnny refused to cede land or give hostages, but white commissioners cowed the Indians and the Shawnees were coerced into signing. While the pact did cede land north of the Ohio River and east of the Great Miami, Johnny and other chiefs refused to accept the treaty as valid. Fighting broke out. In October 1786 Kentuckians destroyed several Shawnee villages, the tribe withdrawing to less accessible areas, closer to British support, Johnny building a new town on the Upper Maumee River. In the destruction of Mackachack by the Kentuckians, Molunthe, the principal chief, was murdered and Captain Johnny appears to have succeeded him. In that capacity he negotiated an exchange of prisoners at Limestone, on the Ohio River, in 1787. At the two treaties of Fort Harmar, near Marietta, Ohio, signed on January 9, 1789, some of the assembled Indians accepted American land claims and Brant's "confederacy" was fatally fractured. Captain Johnny, from his base at the head of the Maumee, and other Shawnees sought to reconstitute it and canvassed the Iroquois with that view. The chief planned an inter-tribal council in the winter of 1789-90, but the only tribal bodies much interested were local Delawares and Miamis. This confederacy, however, terminated the disastrous campaigns of Generals Harmar and St. Clair (see entries) in 1790-91. These great Indian victories, plus the influence of such British agents as Alexander McKee (see entry), reduced any tendency toward compromise on the part of the tribes, but Captain Johnny's hopes for his confederacy were dashed anew by the Indian defeat at the Battle of Fallen Timbers in August 1794. The reverse and Britain's poor support of the confederacy, sapped confidence among many Indians, even though the lieutenant governor of Upper Canada, John Graves Simcoe and Brant visited the confederacy leaders late in 1794 and urged them on. In February 1795 Blue Jacket, representing some of the Shawnees, Delawares and Miamis, made his peace with General Anthony Wayne at Greenville, Ohio, signing the important treaty August 3, 1795, though Captain Johnny refused to treat and aided by McKee kept most of the Shawnees from the council. Johnny even tried to reinvigorate the war, calling upon the Indians to again raise the hatchet, but without success. He and his Shawnees withdrew toward Detroit in 1796. When Detroit was surrendered to the United States, the Shawnees moved to Canada, settling on Bois Blanc Island in the Detroit River. Eventually they moved again to the Maumee River, reaching there by 1801. Captain Johnny remained a close ally of Britain and was a reliable source of information for British agents as late as 1808, when he fades from view. A younger Captain Johnny, whose relationship, if any, to the older man is unknown, served the United States during the War of 1812.

Information from John Sugden.

Captain Pipe (Hopacan, Konieschguanokee), Delaware war chief (d. 1794). The Pipe, or Captain Pipe as he was known to white Americans, first appears in history attending a 1759 conference with George Croghan at newly erected Fort Pitt. By 1764 he was "the principal captain of the Wolf tribe [or division] of the Delawares, becoming afterward its tribal chief," according to Butterfield. The Wolf people, or Munceys (Monsey, Minsi) were the northerly and most warlike of the three divisions of the Delawares. They were displaced by the Walking Purchase (see Teedyuscung entry) from their lands on the Delaware River and many moved west, taking their resentment at the treatment given them to new homes on the Allegheny River of western Pennsylvania or to the Muskingum River of Ohio; Captain Pipe was of the latter faction. His original Delaware name was Hopacan ("Tobacco Pipe"), but after removal he was called Konieschguanokee ("Maker of Daylight") by his people; he was known to frontier whites as Captain Pipe. During Henry Bouquet's operations against the Ohio Delawares as part of the so-called Pontiac War, Bouquet arrived at Fort Pitt. While there ten Indians appeared on the north bank of the Ohio River, asking a conference. Three of them, including Captain Pipe, were lured into the fort and detained as spies, Bouquet charging they planned to take the fort by ruse. The chief remained a prisoner until Bouquet returned from his expedition to the Muskingum where he had dictated a peace to gathered Indians. Upon regaining the fort, his mission accomplished, he ordered Pipe and his companions released. In May 1765 Bouquet held another meeting with Delaware chiefs and leading men, probably at Pitt. Among those listed as present were Simon Girty and "Capn. Pipe." At some point Pipe succeeded his uncle, Custaloga, as full chief of the Wolf division. He had "a reputation for wisdom and a remarkable gift of oratory," and proved to be a strong and able leader in either peace or war. His people remained largely at peace until around 1780, although the Wolf division "came near being drawn into hostilities" during the 1774 Lord Dunmore's War. In February 1778 Brigadier General Edward Hand led an expedition against Upper Sandusky, three miles below the Upper Sandusky of today, where the British were reported to have a major supply base. The 500-man command did not reach that place because of "an open winter, with heavy rains," the troops instead attacking a peaceful Delaware village at Salt Spring on Mahoning Creek near the present Warren, Ohio and on a well-trodden trading route. Killed was Captain

Pipe's brother, the chief's mother was wounded and a number of women and children were casualties. One member of Hand's expedition was Colonel William Crawford (see entry) who would suffer grievously four years later for his suspected role in the unfortunate affair. Because there were no further actions on the winter operation it was derisively known to frontiersmen as "the Squaw Campaign," and as such became part of border legend. September 17, 1778, at Fort Pitt was signed the first treaty between the United States (though not yet so named) and any Indian nation, in this case the Delawares. Andrew and Thomas Lewis (see entries), veteran frontiersmen, were negotiators and signers as commissioners; signers on the Delaware side were Captain Pipe of the Wolf Division; Captain White Eyes of the Turtle Division, and Captain John Killbuck Jr. of the Turkey Division. Colonel Crawford attended this conference and signing, so renewing his acquaintance with Pipe. By this time the chief had "a reputation for wisdom" in addition to his oratorical talent. Under his guidance the Wolf people, initially neutral in Revolutionary hostilities, gradually edged toward support of the British while the other two divisions favored the American side. The Pipe held his people aloof from the guerilla conflicts of the Border until around 1780. During this period he lived on the Walhonding River, about 15 miles above Coshocton; in 1780 he moved with other increasingly hostile Delawares to the camp of the Wyandot (Huron) Half King near Upper Sandusky. "Pipe had become a notable figure on the frontier and [that a large number of Delawares] in 1780 took up the hatchet against the Americans, forming a close alliance with the British Indian, was almost wholly due to his machinations." Although he had opposed the Moravian missionaries strongly on political grounds, he did not dislike them personally, and staunchly defended them at Detroit where they had been accused of treason against the Crown. Eventually Pipe "accepted British pay and fought the Americans and the friendly [to American interests] Indians, but told the British commander at Detroit that he would not act savagely toward the whites, having no interest in the [Revolutionary] quarrel...and expecting that when the English made peace with the colonists the Indians would be punished for any excesses that they committed." Yet this restraint was not in evidence in June 1782 when Crawford, commander of a military expedition against the Ohio Indians fell as a prisoner into the hands of Captain Pipe near Upper Sandusky. The chief and Wingenund (d. c. 1791) staged the torture-execution of Crawford and would have done so with others captured with him, had they not escaped. The excruciating ordeal of the colonel and events surrounding it became a frontier black legend, and has remained so for two centuries. It was certain that Pipe knew of Crawford's presence in the Squaw Campaign and suspected his complicity in the Delaware losses, and he may have considered him responsible for the murder of nearly 100 Delaware Christians not long before at Gnadenhutten on the Muskingum though it was Crawford's second in command of the 1782 expedition, David Williamson (see entry), who had commanded the earlier militia force that perpetrated the Gnadenhutten atrocity, and Crawford had nothing to do with it. Pipe and Wingenund accomplished the execution by strategem, for neither Half King nor the British Rangers from Detroit would have countenanced it had they been aware of Pipe's intentions. With those moderating influences departed, Captain Pipe personally painted black the faces of those chosen for the stake, and by that they were forewarned of the gruesome fate planned for them. Simon Girty, whom Crawford considered a friend, was present and promised to do what he could for the officer, but if he did, it accomplished little and the execution was carried out. Pipe and Wingenund X'd the January 21, 1785, Treaty at Fort McIntosh, Ohio, and the January 9, 1789, Treaty of Fort Harmar on the Muskingum. Although he continued to push publicly for peace with white Americans, Captain Pipe fought against them in the campaign of Josiah Harmar (see entry) in October 1790, while at the great disaster of St. Clair (see entry) Pipe again "distinguished himself, slaughtering white men until his arm was weary with the dreadful work." The place and circumstances of his death have not been learned.

Hodge, HAI; C.W. Butterfield, *An Historical Account of the Expedition Against Sandusky Under Col. William Crawford in 1782,* Cincinnati, Robert Clarke Co., 1873; Paul A.W. Wallace, *Thirty Thousand Miles With John Heckewelder,* Univ. of Pitts. Press, 1958; Clinton A. Weslager, *The Delaware Indians. A History,* New Brunswick, N.J., Rutgers Univ. Press, 1972; Charles J. Kappler, *Indian Treaties 1778-1883,* N.Y., Interland Pub. Inc., 1972.

Carmack, George Washington, prospector (Sept. 24, 1860-June 5, 1922). B. in Contra Costa County, California, the son of a Forty-niner, he early became an adventurer-prospector, following the latter pursuit fruitlessly through the northwest starting with the Juneau, Alaska, strike of 1881, and eventually reaching Yukon Territory of northwest Canada. He had taken for a wife a woman of the Tagish, a small tribe living about Tagish and Marsh lakes of southern Yukon Territory and probably an Athabascan people. Rather than intensifying his search for gold, Carmack, according to Morgan, "liked Indians, and wished only to be accepted as one," devoting much of his time to wandering with Tagish rovers of his choice. Carmack had other interests, too, far removed from prospecting. In his cabin at Carmack's Landing (now Carmacks on the upper Yukon between Dawson and Whitehorse) he had an organ, it was stated on good authority, and a library including such periodicals as *Scientific American* and *Review of Reviews.* He enjoyed conversations on scientific topics and on occasion "wrote sad, sentimental poetry." In the summer of 1896 Carmack was catching salmon at the confluence of the Klondike and Yukon rivers, drying the fish for winter dog food, and thinking about cutting timber on Rabbit Creek, a tributary to the Klondike from the south, just east of the Klondike-Yukon juncture. With Carmack were two Indian friends, Tagish Charlie and Skookum Jim who was considered "a giant of a man, supremely handsome with his high cheekbones, his eagle's nose, and his fiery black eyes—straight as a gun barrel, powerfully built, and known as the best hunter and trapper on the river." Carmack and the two Indians ventured up Rabbit Creek, panning a little, finding color but not much of it. After one wearisome day they camped half a mile below the forks of the creek. Here, according to Carmack, he found a thumb-sized gold nugget in a rim of bedrock. Skookum Jim and Tagish Charlie claimed that Carmack was napping under a birch tree when Jim, cleaning a dishpan in the creek, made the find. Whoever made it, there was gold "lying thick between the flaky slabs of rock like cheese in a sandwich." The great northwestern Gold Strike was made on August 17, and "that night a change came over George Carmack. He ceased to...think of himself as an Indian." He now was a thorough-going prospector, staking claims like everyone else in the region, and intending to get rich, which by all accounts he did. One report stated Carmack "salted away a cool million in gold" by the time he returned to the States in 1898. The nuggets used in 1909 to make the Golden (telegraph) Key with which President Taft opened the Alaska-

Yukon-Pacific Exposition on June 1 were taken from Carmack's gold. Carmack died at Vancouver, British Columbia, "wealthy and honored as a real benefactor." He married October 30, 1900, Marguerite Saftig, daughter of Joseph Saftig, a mining operator, with no mention of what had become of his Tagish wife of his younger days.

NCAB, Vol. 19, 437; *True West,* Vol. 8, No. 1 (Sept.-Oct. 1960), 37; Dale L. Morgan, intr. to Jeremiah Lynch, *Three Years in the Klondike,* Chicago, Lakeside Press, R.R. Donnelley & Sons, 1967, xviii-xxiv, 309-10; Murray Morgan, "Off to the Klondike!" *American Heritage,* Vol. XVIII, No. 5 (Aug. 1967), 109-10; Hodge, HAI, II, 669; Orth, 187.

Carmichael, Lawrence, mountain man (d. 1846). A Scottish trapper, he was in New Mexico as early as 1830, and may have been associated with Isaac Graham (see entry) at that time. He reached California in 1833 and accompanied Ewing Young and Hall J. Kelley (see entries) to Oregon in 1834. Young, for some undefined reason, came under Dr. John McLoughlin's disfavor, but resolved to stay on in Oregon anyway. He and Carmichael decided to construct a distillery which aroused opposition, not only of McLoughlin but also of Methodist missionaries, to the point where the project was abandoned. Instead, Young assented to William A. Slacum's (see entry) suggestion that cattle be purchased in California for the Oregon settlers, and driven overland to Oregon by Young, Carmichael and others. Slacum transported the 11 men to San Francisco aboard his chartered brig, the *Loriot,* they reaching the Bay at the end of February 1837. Young and presumably Carmichael continued south to Santa Barbara where Young persuaded the somewhat reluctant Mexican officials to permit the purchase of 700 cattle at $3 each to be delivered to San Francisco and San José missions. A wild bunch of cattle they were, difficult to handle. The herd forded the San Joaquin and Sacramento rivers, reached the Shasta Valley October 14, 1837, and continued north, the "journey one of extraordinary hardships." There was much dissension among the drovers; an Indian was murdered in vengeance for previous outrages and several riders were wounded by arrows in consequence. The drivers reached the Willamette River in Oregon before the end of October with 600 of the cattle, Bancroft reporting that "this was the first instance clearly recorded in which cattle were obtained in California for the north," although the Hudson's Bay

Company may have driven a few from Fort Ross by the coast route earlier. In May 1838 Carmichael returned to California by way of Honolulu as the only passenger aboard the English ship *Nereid.* He settled at San Jose, south of San Francisco. Carmichael became involved in the so-called Isaac Graham affair and with others was exiled to Mexico for a time, and on his return in 1841 put in a claim for $7,000 damages for interrupted business; while he was in Mexico his correspondence with Thomas Larkin (see entry) shows him to have been an intelligent man who was quite literate and doubtlessly of good education. His name occurs frequently in documents between 1841 and 1845. Early in 1845 he was of a party of four Anglos who captured the prefect, Manuel Castro (see entry), but the extent of his involvement otherwise in California political and military turbulence is not recorded. In 1846 he was shot "by a party of Mexicans for the alleged reason that he was bearer of dispatches for the Americans, but very little is known of this affair," and Bancroft could find no contemporary record of it.

MM, II, 393; MM, III, 145; Kenneth L. Holmes, *Ewing Young: Master Trapper,* Portland, Or., Binford & Mort, 1967; Bancroft, *California,* III, IV, V, *Pioneer Register.*

Carroll, John Melvin, Custer historian, writer (Mar. 4, 1928-July 14, 1990). B. at Bryan, Texas, he was the son of Lester N. Carroll, an Army officer and was graduated from the University of Texas in 1951. Although he lived most of his life at Bryan, he also resided for a time in the 1970s at New Brunswick, New Jersey. Carroll was a Custer enthusiast and wrote and published extraordinarily prolifically on that officer and other frontier subjects; the exhaustive list of titles would be a very extended one. He wrote or edited more than 60 books, in addition to his other writings. A recent Upton and Sons book catalogue lists 107 Carroll works, and that by no means encompasses his total output. Besides his own writings, Carroll edited a wide variety of frontier-type works, ranging from Charles J. Kappler's *Indian Treaties 1778-1883* (1972) to *The Sand Creek Massacre: A Documentary History* (1973). In addition to his enormous output every item of which reflects meticulous craftsmanship and historical integrity, Carroll was always generously helpful to others engaged in the various fields in which he possessed expertise, and freely shared an unrivaled store of information and knowledge with a wide range of serious scholars and writers, embryo or accomplished. Among his most significant output were: *Buffalo Soldiers West* (1971); ed., *The Black Military Experience in the American West* (1971); ed., *Grand Duke Alexis in the U.S.A.* (1972); *Harold Von Schmidt, the Complete Illustrator* (1973); with Byron Price, *Roll Call on the Little Big Horn, 28 June 1876* (1974); *Custer in Periodicals: A Bibliographic Checklist* (1974); *The Benteen-Goldin Letters on Custer and His Last Battle* (1974); *The Two Battles of the Little Big Horn* (1974); *Eggenhcffer: The Pulp Years* (1975); *Custer in Texas* (1975); ed. *Custer in the Civil War: His Unfinished Memoirs* (1978); ed., *General Custer and the Battle of the Little Big Horn: The Federal View* (1978); *The Papers of the Order of Indian Wars* (1975); Carroll also edited *The Life and Death of Crazy Horse: The Hinman Interviews; The Indian Removals,* 5 vols.; *Annual Reports of the Bureau of Indian Affairs 1824-1848,* 12 vols.; and *The Red Man Magazine,* 8 vols. He was engaged in editing several works by Robert G. Carter, compiling Custer genealogies, and preparing other works for publication at his death. He was to be buried at Custer Battlefield National Cemetery.

Contemporary Authors; writer's file on Carroll; info. from *The Early West,* College Station, Texas.

Carter, F.G., prospector (fl. 1901-1903). Carter was a prospecting partner of S.J. Marsh (see entry), coming down the Arctic Ocean coast with him from Point Barrow to Camden Bay where they wintered in 1901-1902. They explored some of the inland streams, including one called by the Eskimos Ekalnukliurak ("the place where fish are caught early"); this stream was named Carter Creek for the prospector by Leffingwell (see entry). In 1902 Carter, with Marsh and H.Y. (Ned) Arey (see entry) wintered in mountains to the south, a segment of the Brooks Range. In the spring of 1903 Carter moved farther south, by way of a pass through the Philip Smith Mountains, and this pass was named for Carter by Marsh, who said the other preceded him through it by two months.

Orth, 19, 189.

Carter, John, Indian trader, militiaman (1737-1781). B. in Virginia, he became a prominent settler of east Tennessee and at his death was one of the largest landholders west of the Appalachian Mountains. With a good education he quickly rose to prominence. In 1772 he began trading with Indians west of the Holston Valley, settling in what became known as Carter's Valley. By the Treaty of Sycamore Shoals of March 1775 (by which the Cherokees sold much of Kentucky to Richard Henderson and his colleagues) Carter received indemnification for losses suffered to Indian hostility. About this time he moved to the Watauga River where he became colonel of militia, commanded Fort Caswell, and was prominent in civic affairs. Carter was a mover in the state of Franklin endeavor, and when it failed continued his land acquisitions. Carter County, Tennessee, was named for him.

Thwaites, *Dunmore;* DAB.

Case, Leland Davidson, Westerners founder (May 8, 1900-Dec. 16, 1986). B. at Wesley, Iowa, he was raised in western South Dakota, served in the army in World War I and was graduated from Macalester College, St. Paul, Minnesota, in 1922. He became city editor of the *Lead* (South Dakota) *Call* 1923-25, was on the staff of the Paris *Herald-Tribune* from 1926-27 and during this period was one of the first American newsmen to interview Charles A. Lindbergh following his flight across the Atlantic in 1927. During his long news and magazine career he also interviewed such subjects as Herbert Hoover, Albert Einstein and Will Durant. In 1928 with his brother, Case became co-publisher of the *Hot Springs (South Dakota) Star;* in 1930 he became editor of *Rotarian* magazine for Rotary International, holding the post for 20 years. Meanwhile in 1939 he helped organize the "Friends of the Middle Border," a group determined to gather, study and preserve historical resources of the upper Plains and Prairies. Most significant for frontier history however was the founding of The Westerners by Case and Elmo Scott Watson (see entry) at Chicago. These two with others, including Don Russell, met for the first time February 25, 1944, at Chicago; since then the organization has grown to well over 100 "corrals," or chapters across the nation and, beginning in 1954 with the English Westerners' Society, has extended its work and interests overseas. So vigorous did the organization overall become that Case organized a "Westerners International" body to help found new corrals, assist those in trouble and form an umbrella establishment for corrals desiring to join with it. First permanently stationed at Tucson, the Westerners International headquarters is now located at the

National Cowboy Hall of Fame at Oklahoma City. Case, after leaving the *Rotarian,* became in 1955 founder-editor of *Together Magazine,* a popular publication sponsored by the Methodist denomination, Case himself being of that faith. In 1963 he moved to Stockton, California, became editor of the *Pacific Historian* and helped create the Holt-Atherton Center for Western Studies and the Jedediah Smith Society, Smith's career being one of Case's enthusiasms. In 1968 Case retired to Tucson, from where he continued his work for Westerners International and to promote its development in this country and abroad. He died at Tucson, leaving his widow whom he had married 55 years earlier, and two sisters. His brother, Francis Higbee Case (1896-1962) had been a U.S. Representative and Senator from South Dakota.

David B. Miller, "Leland D. Case: His Legacy to Wetern History," *Black Hills Historian,* Black Hills State Coll., Spearfish, S.D., Vol. 10, No. 1 (Summer 1987); *Arizona Daily Star,* Dec. 21, 1986; Joseph G. Rosa, "Leland D. Case—A Tribute," English Westerners' *Tally Sheet,* Vol. 33, No. 2 (Spring 1987), 26-27; *Who's Who in America;* REAW: long acquaintance of author with Case.

Castner, Joseph Compton, military officer (Nov. 18, 1869-July 8, 1946). B. in New Jersey, he graduated Phi Beta Kappa from Rutgers College in 1891 and was commissioned a second lieutenant of the 4th Infantry August 1 of that year. He became a first lieutenant April 26, 1898. He was a member of the Alaskan expedition of Edwin Glenn (see entry) in 1898 and reached Valdez April 18, the next day being directed by Glenn to establish a base camp at Portage Bay on the west side of Prince William Sound, since Glenn was instructed to commence his work at the head of Cook Inlet. May 10 Castner left the Portage Bay camp for Turnagain Arm and the Cook Inlet to secure guides and sketch the head of the inlet for future mapping use. He visited Sunrise, then a city of some 800, mainly prospectors waiting to go inland, conferred with some who had been to the head of the Susitna River and one who had explored the length of the Matanuska River. On June 7 Castner and his expedition party including seven enlisted men and several civilians with pack stock, were landed by steamer on Knick Arm of the inlet, instructed to make for the Yukon River. Proceeding north, on June 23 the expedition reached the Matanuska River, 90 miles from Knick Arm, and

arrived at Chickaloon Creek the 29th. August 6 the party passed Lake Louise and a couple of days later was forced to abandon those mules which had given out. They reached the Gakona River, flowing south out of the Alaska Range on August 11, followed the trail up and through a pass in the Range, probably where Richardson Highway today crosses the mountains, and August 16 entered the Tanana River valley. About August 18 they reached the Delta River, tributary to the Tanana. Captain Glenn, who had been following Castner's trail for several days, arrived at the Castner camp August 25 (see Glenn entry). Glenn turned over to Castner two fresh pack animals to speed his movements, and instructed him to make for Circle City on the Yukon and from thence go to Vancouver Barracks, Washington. August 30 Castner, with his party now reduced to two enlisted men and himself, reached the Tanana at the mouth of the Delta, followed down the river and September 5 reached the Volkmar River, following up it toward the northeast. The last mule gave out, was shot and butchered since the expedition needed the meat. "We were so weak we could not go far," wrote Castner. "The covering on our feet was nearly gone. We were now making bread once in three days. One loaf was made to last for six meals." During the advance September 10 "we were compelled to abandon our blankets and many other articles. I realized we must reach Birch Creek and white men or Indians, or else we would be in desperate straits. It rained and snowed every day to add to our discomfort." September 14 they camped at the forks of the Volkmar River. "Whether we looked north, east, south, or west, all we could see were mountains...very steep and rugged...We continued north of east all day over rugged mountains, hoping to see a way out, but in vain. With strength all but gone, we stood at sunset on the summit of a high mountain...With powerful glasses I could see nothing but mountains as far as my eye could reach." He continued, "I knew we could not climb out of these mountains in a week, even if we possessed good health and strength and had plenty of food. In our present condition, without food, or strength, or shoes, our feet torn and bleeding, and no chance to find game...our only way was to turn back..." His maps were "all erroneous." Going down the river they killed a wolf and found its meat "good eating; tasted much like mutton." They built a raft of fire-trimmed logs tied together with strips of blankets recovered from where they had cached them. For six days they continued down the Volkmar "living on cranberries and rose apples. For breakfast we gathered around a rosebush; for lunch we rested near a cranberry patch; dined at 4 p.m. off another rosebush." He went on that "it would be impossible to make others understand what we suffered those days. No tongue or pen could do the case justice." Then on September 25 near the mouth of the Volkmar "we heard the sound of an ax." An Indian woman fixing a birchbark canoe saw them and aroused her village, the men greeting the wanderers "in the most friendly manner." "We ate caribou, moose, and salmon, and drank plenty of tea. Two hours afterward we ate again," and again. Castner hired three of the Indians to take them down the Tanana in birchbark canoes. "We had to keep moving, as the Arctic winter was closing around us." September 30 they reached the mouth of the Chena River, up which the Indians told them were white men and a steamboat. Going 100 miles up the Chena Castner found at the forks of the river "the steamboats and 18 white men," who were much surprised to see him. Castner obtained a boat, rifle and ammunition, cooking utensils, clothing, a month's provisions and "salve for our sore feet." The whites could spare no more food lest they themselves come upon hard times during the winter, and Castner's Indians became "very angry with me" as he had promised them supplies when they reached white men, and "they could see... with their own eyes" that the whites had good stocks of groceries and could not understand why these could not be obtained. Castner ran down the river in his boat and October 6 rejoined his two companions, the three starting down the Tanana. They reached the Yukon October 11, finding plenty of ice floating on it. Castner and his men were royally treated by trading agents at the settlement of Weare (named for Ely E. Weare, vice president of the North American Trading and Transportation Company) at the confluence of the rivers. November 5 they arrived at Rampart, 75 miles upstream, traveling on the river ice to get there. Castner had written most of his report at Weare, and platted his trail on wrapping paper at Rampart City, turned his two companions over to Lieutenant Edwin Bell, commanding a 60-man detachment there, while Castner himself determined to proceed up the Yukon on a midwinter 1,300-mile ice and snow journey to Skagway, Alaska. "If I remained until the ice broke up, it would be

August before I would be able to reach the States, and the knowledge I had gained would be useless to another party going in the following season," he wrote. He obtained seven dogs, two sledges and the experienced services of a civilian, W.J. Cram and departed December 9, encountered temperatures of 60° below zero and December 28 reached Fort Yukon, January 5 arriving at Circle City and January 22 reached Dawson, 330 miles from Circle City. Leaving February 1 he reached Fort Selkirk on the 7th and finally Skagway on February 25, left aboard the steamer *City of Seattle,* and arrived at Vancouver Barracks, Washington, March 1. His expedition had been outstanding on several counts, not least for the dogged persistence with which he fulfilled his mission. For sheer pluck, endurance, single-minded devotion to his instructions and to duty, as well as for the very real hardships he surmounted in finding his way through a virtually unexplored wilderness, Castner's expediton ranks among the very finest endeavors of frontier exploration. He became captain of a squadron of Philippine cavalry April 3, 1900; captain in the U.S. Army February 2, 1901, served as Brigadier General with the American Expeditionary Force in World War I, retired as a Brigadier General November 30, 1933, and later was promoted to Major General. He had received three Silver Star citations, two for gallantry against Filipino insurgents and one for gallantry in action during the World War, also being awarded the Distinguished Service Medal for his efforts in that conflict. Castner lived at Oakland, California in retirement.

Heitman; *Narratives of Explorations in Alaska; Who Was Who.*

Castro, José, military officer (c. 1810-1860). He attended school at Monterey, California, from 1815-20 and his first public position was as secretary to the municipal government in 1828. He was arrested occasionally by rebel factions or others and from 1831-34 engaged in hunting sea otters along the California coast and islands. He became acting governor of California from September 1835 until January 1836 and held other offices. In October and November 1836 he was chief supporter of Juan Bautista Alvarado as military commander in the overthrow of Governor Nicolas Gutiérrez, who fled on November 5, 1836; Castro held important positions and when Mariano Vallejo took command in the north, Castro went south to take charge of Alvarado's cause in the "complicated campaigns" of that region. In 1839 he was commissioned by the Mexican government as captain of the Monterey complement, holding also political positions. He figured prominently in the volatile political affairs of California preceding the United States occupation; in 1844 as a lieutenant colonel he was sent to establish a frontier garrison in the San Joaquin Valley. Castro was a leader in the revolt against Governor Manuel Micheltorena in 1844-45 and after Micheltorena's overthrow became commanding General of California. He was a controversial man in many respects, engaged in differences with Governor Pío Pico and his treatment of immigrants from the United States was sometimes questioned. He also had troubles with Fremont and the Bears of the Bear Flag Revolt, negotiated with Larkin (see entry) and at length withdrew to the south where he handled final operations, which were futile, against the Americans, negotiated with Robert Stockton and eventually fled to Mexico, returning to California from Sinaloa in 1848. He lived as a private citizen at Monterey and San Juan until 1853 when he went to Mexico again, being appointed political and military chief along the Baja California-California border from about 1856. While holding this office he was killed in a drunken brawl ("some say assassinated"), by a man named Manuel Marquez. He was married. Bancroft wrote that "No Californian has been so thoroughly abused as he in what has passed for history...Of his conduct in the sectional quarrels of '45-'46, there is not much to be said in his favor, except that it was somewhat less discreditable than that of his opponent, Pico; but of his acts in contest with the settlers and the U.S. little fault can be justly found...His conduct was far more honorable, dignified and consistent than that of Fremont...In the southern negotiations of August he bore a much more honorable part than did Stockton...His record as a public man in Upper California was, on the whole, not a bad one. He had much energy, was popular with most classes, was true to his friends, and as a public officer fairly honest. About his private character...he must have had some good qualities, yet it is clear he had some very bad ones. He was addicted to many vices, and when drunk...was rough to the verge of brutality; yet a kind-hearted man when sober." He was therefore, and remains, a complex but not unimportant man in the history of California in the middle 19th century.

Bancroft, *California,* II-V; *Pioneer Register.*

Cather, Willa, writer (Dec. 7, 1873-Apr. 24, 1947). B. near Winchester, Virginia, her family moved in 1883 to Webster County, southern Nebraska near the Republican River. She was schooled at the county seat, Red Cloud, "raw, bleak, and jerry-built," though distinguished by its "cultivated people who introduced her to French and German culture, classical languages, and music," all integral to her notably catholic lifetime works. During her college years at the University of Nebraska she acquired a local reputation for dramatic criticism and lively newspaper columns which foreshadowed to a marked degree her future career. Following graduation she went to Pittsburgh, editing a small magazine and becoming wire editor and reviewer on the *Daily Ledger,* then briefly becoming a high school teacher while publishing fiction and poetry on the side. She also brought out several books. She became for several years editor of New York's *McClure's,* which had by then become "probably the best general magazine ever to be published anywhere," with a circulation of around 300,000. In it appeared many of the great writers of the day and just as the publication was lavishly profitable, so it spent lavishly to supply its readers with a constant stream of superb investigative reporting in all areas of commerce, society and science. Cather joined *McClure's* in 1906 and within two years had become its managing editor. She was an excellent editor, but basically she was a writer and with her, authorship was bound to take precedence. Her initial success, an outgrowth of her Nebraska heritage, was *O Pioneers!* (1913) which won virtually unanimous praise from critics and public alike, and established Cather as a major American author. The second of Cather's important novels with a frontier premise was *My Ántonia* (1918) which also was a considerable commercial success, although in the beginning it received small praise from literary critics and it took them two years to discover the book, as Cather sardonically remarked. In 1923 she produced the third of her Nebraska frontier works, *A Lost Lady,* portraying the end of the pioneering era. Her most famous volume of the frontier, however, was *Death Comes for the Archbishop,* a novel based upon the careers of two French priests in the American southwest, one of whom became Archbishop Jean Baptiste Lamy and who appears in the novel as Father Latour. With this book Cather "reached the pinnacle of success...Not only was the book a great critical triumph, but it also brought joy to the publisher's business office and to booksellers everywhere." Willa Cather "knew she had written an important book...and came to believe before she died that it was her best novel." Someone presented Supreme Court Justice Oliver Wendell Holmes with a copy of *My Ántonia* a dozen years after it appeared and, a year later, with a copy of *Death Comes for the Archbishop,* upon which Holmes, then 89, wrote her: "I think you have the gift of the transforming touch. What to another would be prose, under your hand becomes poetry without ceasing to be truth. Among the changes of old age, one is that novels are apt to bore me, and I owe you a debt for two exceptions, both of which gave me delight." The foregoing are merely a few of the many volumes she authored; her oeuvre deals with subjects as diverse as France in World War I, French-Canadian Quebec, grand opera, biography, poetry and other themes. Willa Cather always retained her ties to Red Cloud while extending them to New York and New England. She never married. She died at New York City and by her request was buried at Jaffrey, in southern New Hampshire, where she had annually spent the autumn months.

Literature abundant: James Woodress, *Willa Cather: A Literary Life,* Lincoln, Univ. of Neb. Press, 1987; DAB.

Cautivo, Chiricahua Apache: *see,* El Cautivo

Chambers, James, frontiersman (May 1749-post 1846). B. in Ireland, he emigrated to America about 1768 and settled in the fall of 1773 on Kiskiminitas Creek, Westmoreland County, Pennsylvania. Chambers reported that in August 1777 he and half a dozen others were reaping oats near Adam Carnahan's blockhouse, a mile south of the creek when they received word of skulking Indians who plundered several cabins and then attacked the blockhouse itself. On stepping to the door John Carnahan was shot dead; the attackers were driven off. Carnahan's son James joined the Continental service and became "an officer of repute." The blockhouse was the rendezvous for the 1781 expedition of Archibald Lochry (see entry). In 1781 Chambers was captured by British-influenced Indians while on a scout near Sewickley Creek. He was taken to Detroit and later shipped to Prison Island, near Montreal. In 1782 he escaped and made his way back to Pennsylvania. When Lyman Draper interviewed him in 1846 he found Chambers' memory "very retentive" and "he gave Dr. Draper many facts about Indian warfare." This was at his Westmoreland County home where he continued to live.

Thwaites/Kellogg, *Frontier Defense on the Upper Ohio, 1777-1778.*

Chamisso, Ludovik, naturalist (1781-1838). B. in Champaign, France, he was raised in Germany, entered the Prussian army briefly, at Geneva studied science and languages, and at Berlin medicine, botany and zoology. In 1815 he became naturalist on the global circumnavigation of the ship *Ryurik,* commanded by Otto von Kotzebue (see entry), keeping a detailed journal during the voyage. Pierce wrote that Chamisso's research on the journey "encompassed languages, ethnography, geology, botany, zoology and climate." On Unalaska Island, where the expedition visited three times, he gave "special attention to flora, and in the Bering Sea to whales and other animal life. He was interested in origins, culture and language of the Eskimos and Aleuts," sympathizing with them for their lot under Russian American Company control and predicted that the race would soon become extinct under conditions as he found them. His journal was published in full in 1836 as part of his collected works. In 1819 he became head of the Berlin Royal Botanical Garden, leaving that position in 1837 following the death of his wife. He died the following year.

Pierce, *Russian America: A Biographical Dictionary.*

Chapel, Charles Edward, gun specialist (May 26, 1904-Feb. 20, 1967). B. at Manchester, Iowa, Chapel was graduated from the University of Missouri in 1926, commissioned in the Marine Corps and served in Nicaragua and China before being mustered out a first lieutenant the following year for service-connected injuries. He became an aeronautical engineer, working for major aircraft firms and served at least six terms as a representative of the 46th California Assembly as a Republican; he lived at Palos Verdes Estates. A specialist in firearms and gun collecting, he wrote around 4,000 articles on subjects relating to that and other fields, as well as a number of books. Among them were: *Guns of the Old West* (1961); *U.S. Martial and Semi-Martial Single-Shot Pistols* (1962); *Complete Guide to Gunsmithing* (1943; 1962), and *The Complete Book of Gun Collecting.* He died at Sacramento, California.

Whittier (California) *Daily News,* Feb. 20, 1967; information from Charles Edward Chapel.

Chapin, Gurden, military officer (1831-Aug. 22, 1875). B. in the District of Columbia he was graduated from West Point and commissioned a brevet second lieutenant of the 7th Infantry July 1, 1851, becoming a second lieutenant August 24 and a first lieutenant March 3, 1855. Serving at Fort Brown at Brownsville, Texas, he seemed involved in marital difficulties, securing a divorce "under peculiarly atrocious circumstances," according to Heintzelman (see entry), then re-marrying only to find his new wife involved with another officer of the regiment by which "everybody says he is served right." Chapin arrived in Arizona with Pitcairn Morrison's command in 1860 and when Morrison left Chapin commanded Fort Buchanan until the post was abandoned in July. May 18, 1861, he confirmed in a communication to the AAG, Department of New Mexico that the Chiricahuas, Mimbres and other Apaches had been at war with the whites since the Bascom affair at Apache Pass the previous February, his communication thus refuting modern assertions that *no* contemporary account confirmed that the ill-managed confrontation between Bascom and Cochise had ignited an Apache war. After satisfactory service as a regimental adjutant Chapin became a captain April 22, 1861. He was dismissed August 26 but reinstated November 16 and earned a brevet for "gallant and meritorious service" in the battle of Peralta, New Mexico April 15, 1862. Chapin became a major of the 14th Infantry May 18, 1864, winning brevets to colonel for Civil War service. He transferred to the 32nd Infantry September 21, 1866, and commanded Fort Goodwin, Arizona, during which "irregularities" were found in his administration, though nothing came of them. He retired January 27, 1869, presumably because of ill health, and returned to his home at Culpeper, Virginia where he died at 44.

Heitman; Cullum; Constance Wynn Altshuler, *Cavalry Yellow & Infantry Blue: Army Officers in Arizona Between 1851 and 1886,* Tucson, Az., Arizona Hist. Soc., 1991; Edwin R. Sweeney, *Cochise: Chiricahua Apache Chief,* Norman, Univ. Of Okla. Press, 1991.

Chapman, Huston Ingraham, attorney (Apr. 28, 1847-Feb. 18, 1879). B. in Burlington, Iowa, he was taken as an infant with the family to Oregon, arriving at Marysville (Corvallis) November 13, 1847. His father was a self-educated lawyer, a successful California prospector, an Indian campaigner and a noted pioneer of Port-

land, and Huston was the brother of Arthur I. Chapman (see entry). May 19, 1860, Huston accidentally wounded himself with a shotgun, the result being that his left arm was amputated near the shoulder. He probably graduated from the Portland Academy, qualified as an engineer and lawyer, in 1874. He practiced law at Steilacoom, Puget Sound, until 1877 when he went east and became associated briefly with the Atchison, Topeka and Santa Fe Railroad. In 1878 he formed a legal firm at Las Vegas, New Mexico, where Susan McSween became one of his first clients. As her attorney he developed into a bitter antagonist of Dudley and the Dolan faction in the Lincoln County War. He was shot standing before the Post Office at Lincoln about noon, according to Keleher, or at 10:30 p.m., as Utley wrote. His slayers, Keleher believed, were William Campbell and Jesse Evans (see entries); according to Mullin were Campbell, Evans, Billy Matthews and Jim Dolan, but Utley wrote that the killing was done by Campbell alone after Dolan had sparked the incident by firing a wild shot into the air. The event was witnessed at close range by Billy the Kid who offered to testify as to the killer(s), testimony for which Governor Lew. Wallace fervently wished, in return for a pardon for Billy for any past misdeeds. He did testify before a grand jury which indicted Campbell and Dolan, with Evans as accessory, but no one was convicted, and the Kid received no pardon.

Information from Frederick W. Nolan; Robert N. Mullin notes; Robert M. Utley, *Billy the Kid,* Lincoln, Univ. of Neb. Press, 1989; William A. Keleher, *Violence in Lincoln County 1769-1881,* Albuquerque, Univ. of N.M. Press, 1957.

Chapman, William Williams, pioneer (Aug. 11, 1808-Oct. 18, 1892). B. at Clarksburg, present West Virginia, he studied law while serving as a court clerk, was admitted to the bar, practiced and became one of the first settlers of Burlington, Iowa, which then was in Michigan Territory. He held public positions in successively, Michigan, Wisconsin and Iowa territories as they became organized, and served as a Representative in Congress from 1838-40. He married Margaret Ingraham and they became parents of seven children, including Arthur and Huston I. Chapman (see entries). In 1847 the Chapmans with two ox-wagons joined about 100 emigrants for Oregon, arriving at Marysville (Corvallis) November 13, and settled at Salem. Chapman joined a party for California in 1848 and worked the goldfields "successfully" but returned to Oregon within a year, purchasing land in newly founded Portland and built a house where the present courthouse stands, becoming "unquestionably one of the leading founding fathers" of the community. He was Oregon's surveyor-general and served in some capacity in the 1855 Rogue River War in southern Oregon, although if he had any combat service it is not reported; Nolan says he was "commander of the Southern Battalion" in that operation, although Bancroft says he served as lieutenant of volunteers (Bancroft's *Oregon* histories were largely written by Frances Fuller Victor (see entry), who was an authority on the territory's Indian wars). With Stephen Coffin as partner Chapman built the *Gold Hunter,* the first ocean steamer owned in Oregon which "through the bad faith of her officers, ruined her owners," at least temporarily. Chapman chartered a route for a prospective railway via the Columbia and Snake rivers to Salt Lake City, one free of much winter snow and which would greatly aid development of eastern Oregon and Washington and Idaho's mining regions, but the project was negated by the powerful Central Pacific Railroad of California which opposed any road connecting Oregon to the east unless a tributary to it. Another company finally did construct a railroad over the route surveyed by Chapman. He meanwhile had founded and named the *Oregonian,* a famed Portland newspaper existing to this day. His wife predeceased him. An obituary for him commented that "no man probably ever was so inherently opposed to trickery, machinations, and frauds in politics as he," though if his accomplishments were many, reverses also occasionally occurred, but he was a public figure important in the development of Oregon.

Information from Frederick W. Nolan; Bancroft, *Oregon,* I, II.

Chartier, Martin, adventurer (d. 1718). Described as a French-Canadian by Thwaites/Kellogg, he was one of La Salle's party of 1680-83, although never a close follower or confidante of the French explorer. Afterward he resided at Fort St. Louis in the Illinois country. He married a Shawnee woman and migrated south and east with a band of that tribe, finally appearing in 1692 in Maryland. Later this company settled on the Susquehanna River of present Pennsylvania where Chartier died. He had one son, Peter, who grew to maturity. Peter Chartier had great influence with the tribe and moved his

people to the Ohio River, where his village was known as Chartier's Town. This was placed by Hodge about 60 miles upriver from Logstown, which was 14 miles below Pittsburgh; Chartier's Town was near the present Kittanning in Armstrong County, Pennsylvania. He was persuaded to embrace the French interest and in 1745 moved his band down the Ohio River and his further history is not reported. Two places in western Pennsylvania are named for him: Chartier's Run and Station in Westmoreland County, and Chartier's Creek.

Thwaites/Kellogg, *Frontier Defense on the Upper Ohio, 1777-1778;* Parkman, *LaSalle and the Discovery of the Great West;* Hodge, HAI.

Cheek, James, mountain man (d. Apr. 12, 1810). B. in Tennessee he was six feet tall, tough and leathery, a buoyant man who "seemed to prefer fighting to most any other occupation," loyal to his friends and generally a good man to be out with—if he liked you. Cheek joined the 1809 Manuel Lisa expedition up the Missouri to the Three Forks as a trapper and potential mountain man. The "main trading party" left St. Louis June 17, some 190 men in all, half of whom were Americans, the remainder French and Creole hunters and boatmen. Rations were a problem. Lisa had brought plenty of corn, and expected to augment that spartan supply with game when he got far enough up the river. Thomas James (see entry) was in command of one of the keel boats, and Cheek was in his party. Above the mouth of the Platte the crewmen had become desperate for food, and envious of the French for whom was supplied their traditional pork, freighted in barrels. The men of James's boat finally seized a cask and "Cheek, astride it with a tomahawk," for breaking it open, called out "Give the word, Captain." James told him to wait a bit, informed an agent of Lisa that his men "should and would have some" of the meat, and Lisa himself, armed with pistols, ran out shouting, "What the devil is the matter with you and your men?" "We are starving," said James, "and we must have something better than boiled corn." Cheek was chanting, "Shall I break it open, Captain? Speak the word!" while the rest of the crew lined up, rifles in hand, to back whatever decision was made. Lisa relented before this mutinous show of force "and gave us a large supply of pork; that is, as much as we pleased to take," and the "uprising" was over. Cheek, wrote James, "who figured as ring-leader on this occasion...was well proportioned. His courage was equal to any enterprise," although his rashness and headlong obstinacy at last would cost him his life. In the company was "a very impertinent Irishman." One day James berated him for not doing his share of the work. "The Irishman took my treatment in very ill humor and swore he would have satisfaction for the insult." When the boat tied up to load firewood, Cheek and the Irishman disappeared into the underbrush. Cheek returned without him and told James "he had whipped him 'for saucing the Captain.' I said: 'Cheek I can attend to my own fighting...'" but Cheek retorted, "No, by G—d! My Captain shan't fight while I am about!" The Irishman returned so badly bruised he was "unable to work for several days." Pierre Chouteau (see entry), a partner in the Lisa enterprise, "conceived a prejudice" against Cheek and "on one occasion ordered him to leave the boats." James protested against the "cruelty of sending a man adrift in a wilderness, 1400 miles from home," but the trader insisted. Cheek picked up his rifle and made to depart when he was ordered to leave the weapon behind, which he refused to do. James was directed to take the rifle away from Cheek, and retorted that Chouteau could take it away himself, if he thought he could. The men of the boat once more seized arms and "avowed their determination of defending Cheek and sharing his fate. The order was not pursued any further." Cheek for a time was at Lisa's Fort Raymond at the confluence of the Yellowstone and Big Horn rivers, then late in 1809 at a Lisa fort on the Missouri. The Chouteau name was mentioned and Cheek "coolly remarked that if he caught Chouteau a hundred yards from camp he would shoot him." "Cheek! Cheek!" exclaimed Lisa, "mind what you say." "I do that," said Cheek, "and Lisa, I have heard some of our boys say that if they ever caught you two hundred yards from camp they would shoot you, and if they don't I will. You ought not to expect anything better from the Americans after having treated them with so much meanness, treachery, and cruelty as you have. Now Lisa," he continued, "you are going to the Forks of the Missouri. Mark my words, you wil never come back alive." According to James, "Lisa's cheeks blanched at this bold and reckless speech from a man who always performed his promises, whether good or evil..." Cheek himself accompanied a trapping party to the Three Forks of the Missouri, where a post of sorts was to be erected in Blackfoot country where John Colter (see entry) had had his

great adventure with the Indians and where danger lurked everywhere. Even Cheek eventually became despondent; "his mind was uneasy, restless and fearful. 'I am afraid,' said he, 'and I acknowledge it. I never felt fear before but now I feel it.'" His forebodings were justified. On April 12 Cheek, men named Hull and Ayers and several others were setting up camp when the place was overrun by more than 30 Gros Ventre Blackfeet. A witness reported that "The sharp reports of Cheek's rifle and pistols were soon heard...and then a volley of [Indian] musketry sent the poor fellow to his long home." Michael Immell (see entry), a former army lieutenant and now an associate of Lisa's, and another came in from hunting about dusk and found the camp site deserted, went down to the river bank and through the willows saw a new Indian camp and a white man, no doubt Hull, bound to a tree. Returning to the camp Immell found Cheek's body "without the scalp, lying where he bravely met his end." An Indian was found dead with two bullets in his body, "supposed to be from Cheek's pistol." A large party from the downstream fort buried the dead.

Thomas James, *Three Years Among the Indians and Mexicans,* ed. by Milo Milton Quaife, N.Y., Citadel Press, 1966; Burton Harris, *John Colter,* N.Y., Charles Scribner's Sons, 1952; Richard Edward Ogelsby, *Manuel Lisa and the Opening of the Missouri Fur Trade,* Norman, Univ. of Okla. Press, 1963; M.O. Skarsten, MM, IV, 77-79; information from E.F. (Ted) Mains.

Cherepanov, Stepan, Russian fur trader (fl. 1759-1773). A trader from Totma, Siberia, he became a ship's captain and in 1759 left Okhotsk, Siberia, for a hunt on Attu Island of the Aleutians, returning July 24, 1762, with 1,750 sea otters and 530 blue foxes, a rich cargo. In 1768 he hunted at Atkha Island and in the Andreanov group, part of the time with Dmitrii Pankov, returning to Petropavlovska, Kamchatka, in 1773 again with a good fur cargo. Cherepanov and Panov, unlike some of the ruthless traders of the time, got on rather well with the Aleuts who reported to government inspectors in 1789-90 that Cherepanov and Nagaiev (see entry) "do not indulge in such tyranny and murder as [do others] although they send us against our will to procure food and do domestic work without pay. From Cherepanov's company we get for each sea otter either a kettle, a shirt, a knife, a kerchief or a plane for making arrows, or ten strings of coral beads or five, six to ten leaves of tobacco with the addition of a handful of beads to each of these things…"

Pierce, *Russian America: A Biographical Dictionary.*

Chernov, Ivan, Creole seaman (d. 1877). As a boy he was given as hostage by the Kolosh (Tlingit) Indians to Baranov to assure that the natives would abide by a peace arrangement. Chernov is termed a "creole" by Bancroft and Zagoskin, but there are reasons to doubt that status (see Andre Klimovsky entry for discussion). Chernov received his Russian name when accepted and was sent with other hostages to a naval pilot school at Kronstadt, from where he returned qualified as navigator and ship's officer. While a navigator he drafted maps and charts of the Aleutian islands and many parts of the Alaskan coast. He captained various ships for the Russian American Company. In 1838 he commanded the brig *Poliphemus* which carried the explorer Aleksandr Kashevarov (see entry) to Cape Lisburne, northwest of Kotzebue Sound. Because of ice conditions at sea and shoal waters near the coast, Kashevarov continued the exploration along the Arctic shore of Alaska in skin boats, native hostility eventually causing him to turn back, but not until he had reached Point Barrow, discovered in 1826 by a Beechey party and had gone considerably beyond. Chernov lived a decade after transfer of Alaska from Russia to the United States, and two of his sons, according to Bancroft, were engaged in shipbuilding and shipping from Afognak Island, north of Kodiak, as late as 1886.

Bancroft, *Alaska;* Zagoskin.

Chernykh, Egor, agronomist (c. 1813–July 30, 1843). B. in Kamchatka, he was sent by Moscow to enter a new agricultural school of the Imperial Moscow Agricultural Society, and returned in 1827 to further agriculture on the Kamchatka Peninsula of Siberia. In 1833 he was called to Sitka, Alaska, for assignment to the Russian colony of Fort Ross, California, where he arrived January 14, 1836, after an overland trip through Spanish California from Monterey. He worked at the Ross settlement north of San Francisco for several years, doing much to develop its agriculture; Rancho Chernykh, at Russian Gulch south of Ross, was named for him. In 1841 he accompanied A.G. Rotchev, manager of Ross, and I.G. Voznesenskii in what may have been the first ascent of Mount St. Helena, south of the present Middletown, California. A plaque was placed on the 4,343-ft. summit. Shortly afterward John Sutter (see entry) purchased the Ross settlement and the Russian inhabitants left for Sitka. There Chernykh served as chief inspector until his death of "nerve fever," leaving his common law widow and a son.

Pierce, *Russian America: A Biographical Dictionary.*

Cherum (Scherum), Hualapai (Walapai) chief (d. c. 1903). B. in the Hualapai country of northwestern Arizona before the arrival of significant emigrant parties around 1851, Cherum was not a "chief" through birth, although his grandfather had been one; his father had not. He became subtribal chief of the Middle Mountain region (about a third of Hualapai territory) upon the death of a chief, and in the lack of a successor, and because of his considerable intelligence, talents and forcefulness. Until late in life Cherum knew no English, although his influential half-brother (same father, different mothers) Walapai Charley (Sudjikwo'dime, or Susquatama) had learned English during a lengthy imprisonment for one cause or another. Charley often acted as a Cherum interpreter. The chief had become a successful war leader, acquiring the honorary title of 'Tokoomhet, sometimes used as his name. He clearly foresaw impending hostilities between his people and Anglos, either of the army or as prospectors, and armed his followers through an elaborate trade network. He secured woven materials from Pueblo Indians, traded these to the Mohave for horses, and drove them to the Southern Paiutes to swap for firearms they secured from Utah Mormons. Another version, or perhaps a variant, has him trading tanned deerskins to Hopis for New Mexico horses, and the animals to the Paiutes for munitions. In either case the arrangements were efficacious. During subsequent hostilities he was said to have mustered around 70 arms and a fighting force of some 250. He also "married well," and possibly often. "Coming from the smallest of the Walapai subtribes, he necessarily extended his marriage ties outside the Middle Mountain people [and gained] political influence throughout the tribe." Eventually he "won recognition as the head chief of all the Walapai," a position supported by the Army as leverage for control over the tribe. Cherum's notably warlike followers were ready with outbreak of the so-called Walapais War of

1866-68. It was precipitated by the wanton murder by freighter Samuel Miller of Wauba Yuma (see entry), until that time the best known and most influential Hualapai leader. Ensuing hostilities saw approximately 25 whites slain, principally isolated prospectors and miners, and after the army moved into the theater, it, along with civilian whites, claimed to have killed 300 to 400 Indians, or about twice the number Cherum had at the start. There were several small skirmishes in which the Hualapai scored as many "wins" as the army, but the major clash occurred January 15, 1868, when a white contingent under Captain Samuel Baldwin Marks Young and guided by the noted Dan O'Leary (see entry) struck a rancheria in Scherum's Canyon in the Cerbat Mountains. "The Indians were armed with Henry, Spencer, and Sharp's rifles and fought with great bravery" until a shortage of ammunition forced the soldiers to give way. O'Leary had severely wounded Cherum in the thigh, causing him to "drop his Henry, but he picked it up again," and gained protection among the rocks. Shortly afterward a second element of Young's command under First Lieutenant Jonathan D. Stevenson attacked Cherum, but was forced to withdraw after the officer had been seriously wounded. His command thought they had killed five hostiles and Young claimed another 16, but Cherum held the field. Eventually the whites proved too many for the Hualapai, however, and in August 1868 Cherum agreed to a peace. He and his people were assigned a reservation with the Mohaves on the Colorado River, but it was low, hot and malarious. Officials would not correct the situation, and in 1875 Cherum led his people in exodus to their higher, cooler country where they were permitted to remain. Peaceful relations continued as did the respect for the leader. Arizona Governor Anson P.K. Safford noted in 1876 that Cherum "was their great war chief, and is presently chief of the tribe. He is a man of firmness and courage, and is respected by both Indians and whites. It may be truly said of him that he was first in war, and is now first in peace." He got on well with the redoubtable Captain Thomas Byrne (see entry) who was assigned to oversee Hualapai-white relations, and together they managed to maintain tranquility for a decade, barring a minor eruption now and then. Cherum quickly caught on to white ways. He once supplied Hualapai laborers for a construction project, insisting that their pay be made to him when he would dole out what he thought each worker had

earned. When the contractor objected, Cherum called a kind of primordial strike, pulled his workers off the job, not permitting them to return until his payment scheme was reinstated. He retained influence over his people for a generation after the Walapai War. About 1903 he became ill and was moved to Kingman, Arizona. "All the neighboring Indians were notified. In six weeks Serum [Cherum] died. The funeral was large. All the Walapais Indians were there as well as the Mohave from Fort Mohave. Clothes..., silks, feathers, etc., were burned, and the body was buried." He might have been aged 75 or 80 at his demise, although this is conjecture. About six months later Walapai Charley also died, "and all the Indians had a big cry, just as they had done for Serum. The body was buried at the same place, about one and one-half miles from Canyon Station." Cherum had fathered at least three sons, two surviving him.

HNAI, 10; *Walapai Ethnography,* Fred Kniffen et al., ed. by A.L. Kroeber, *Memoirs of the American Anthropological Association,* No. 42, Menasha, Wis., 1935, various references, including p. 219; Henry F. Dobyns, Robert C. Euler, *Wauba Yuma's People,* Prescott [Az.] College Press, 1970; Dennis G. Casebier, *Camp Beale's Springs and the Hualapai Indians,* Norco, Ca., Tales of the Mohave Road Pub. Co., No. 7, 1980, reproducing, p. 67, an indistinct photograph of Cherum, together with Walapai Charley and Leve Leve, another famed tribal leader; Richard J. Hinton, *Handbook to Arizona,* Tucscon, Az. Silhouettes, 1954, 355-56; Prescott, *Arizona Miner,* Feb. 20, 1868.

Chew, Colby, frontiersman (fl. 1750-1756). Chew was an older son of Thomas Chew, probably b. at Orange in the then Spottsylvania County, Virginia, and he became an early explorer of Kentucky. He entered that region with Dr. Thomas Walker (see entry) in 1750. Walker and Chew, with four other Virginians, left the settlements about March 24, following the "Great War Path" of the Indians through Cumberland Gap. In Kentucky, Chew was injured when his horse fell with him but Walker wrote in his journal that "I bled and gave him volatile drops & he soon recovered." Chew was a member of Andrew Lewis's expedition of February and March 1756 against the Shawnees in retaliation for the Indian raid that destroyed the Roanoke settlement earlier. The expedition was unsuccessful. Chew was an older brother of Major James Chew, for a time surveyor of Monongalia County and who was special agent and commissary for the Ohio forts. James Chew died "before January 27, 1783," but the date of death of Colby Chew is not reported.

Thwaites/Kellogg, *The Revolution on the Upper Ohio, 1775-1777*, Madison, Wis. Hist. Soc., 1908; Harriette Simpson Arnow, *Seedtime on the Cumberland*, N.Y., The Macmillan Co., 1960, 109; Alexander Scott Withers, *Chronicles of Border Warfare*, Cincinatti, Robert Clarke Co., 1895, 1970.

Chie, Chiricahua Apache (c. 1851-c. 1877). Chie was probably the son of Coyuntura (see entry), Cochise's younger brother, and his wife, Yones. Following the execution of his father at Apache Pass February 19, 1861, as a result of the Bascom confrontation (see Cochise entry), Chie was raised by Cochise and became his trusted follower. He spent much time in New Mexico. In the late 1860s he married a Chihenne (Mimbres) woman, "probably into Mangas Coloradas's family, and went to live with her people." In 1872 he was at the new Apache reservation at Tularosa, the present Aragon, when Howard arrived, determined to visit Cochise in the Dragoon Mountains of Arizona in an effort to conclude a peace treaty with him. Learning of Chie's relationship with Cochise, Howard hired him as guide for his party, giving him a horse and an incentive. Chie agreed to go, providing another Cochise favorite, Ponce, would also be hired. The conference between Howard and Cochise commenced in the Dragoons October 1, 1872, and continued intermittently for nearly two weeks. When Chie and Howard were at nearby Apache Pass, Chie became "distressed because this was where his father had been slain," according to Sweeney. Even after the Chiricahua Reservation was established in southeastern Arizona Chie remained at Cañada Alamosa, New Mexico, with his wife's people. He was killed in 1876 or 1877 by Apaches in an incident possibly sparked by alcohol. Sweeney noted that "it is ironic that the death of his father [Coyuntura] ignited the Cochise war and the efforts of his son helped bring peace to Arizona," through his guiding Howard to his momentous conference with the aging chief.

Edwin R. Sweeney, *Cochise: Chiricahua Apache Chief*, Norman, Univ. of Okla. Press, 1991.

Chigelley (Chekilli), Creek chief (fl. 1733-1752). He was considered the principal chief of the Kasihta of the Creek confederacy during the settlement of Georgia in 1733, having succeeded his brother, the Emperor Brims (Bream) who died c. 1732 (see entry). Chigelley remained emperor until 1746; he was related to the famous Mary Bosomworth. Kasihta was one of two great tribes constituting most of the pure Muskogee element among the Lower Creeks. Chigelley may have been one of the Creeks who visited England in 1733 with Tomochichi. In 1735, as "emperor of the Upper and Lower Creeks," he led a delegation to a council with the English at Savannah. On this occasion he recited the national legend of the Creeks (including their migration) as recorded in pictographs upon a buffalo hide "which was delivered to the commissioners and afterward hung up in the London office of the colony. It is now lost, but the translation has been preserved...." Chigelley was reluctant to bring his Creeks in on the side of the English in their 1739-48 war with the Spanish, listening rather to the French importunities, but finding they demanded that he sever relations entirely with the English, he instead broke with the French and finally aided the English sporadically though not very enthusiastically. In 1752 Chigelley was residing at Coweta, his headquarters town, and although still considered the principal ruler of the confederacy, actual authority was delegated to the younger Malatchi, a son of Brims. Little more is reported of Chigelley.

Hodge, HAI, I, 241-42; David H. Corkran, *The Creek Frontier, 1540-1783*, Norman, Univ. of Okla. Press, 1967; Larry E. Ivers, *British Drums on the Southern Frontier: The Military Colonization of Georgia, 1733-1749*, Chapel Hill, Univ. of N.C. Press, 1974.

Chiles, Joseph Ballinger, pioneer (July 16, 1810-June 25, 1885). B. in Clark County, Kentucky, his wife had left him a widower by 1837 and in 1841, leaving his four small children with family members he emigrated to California with the Bartleson-Bidwell wagon train, first to make the transit. The company reached California around November 1 after an uneventful passage but a difficult crossing of the Sierra Nevada. Chiles visited Monterey, Sonoma and other places and received from Mariano Vallejo (see entry) "the promise of a mill site." He returned to the States in 1842 to obtain a grain mill, traveling with Charles Hopper from Los Angeles to New Mexico and reaching Independence September 9. The mill obtained, Chiles in 1843 led the only overland company that year to California. It left Independence in May. In the vicinity of Fort

Laramie Joe Walker (see entry) was engaged as guide, the company henceforth known as the Chiles-Walker party. From Fort Hall, because of scarcity of provisions, Chiles and about eight or nine men made their way to Fort Boise and reached California by a new route crossing the mountains by the Malheur and Pit rivers, while the other group, after considerable hardships and under guidance of Walker reached California by a southerly route, but had to abandon the mill to make it. In 1844 Chiles became owner of the Catacula rancho in the Napa Valley. Bancroft wrote that no definite record was found that "he joined either the Bears or the California Battalion" in the pre-independence unrest of 1846, although he may have done so and "certainly aided Fremont with supplies and information." Chiles went east again in 1847, "probably as guide and hunter in Stockton's party," and apparently testified at the Fremont court-martial. In 1848, bringing his four children with him, a son and three daughters, Chiles led a train of 48 wagons to California. He settled permanently in Napa and Lake counties, operated a ferry for a time, became familiarly known as "colonel," and, Bancroft wrote, was "I think, a famous hunter notwithstanding his years, and a good citizen." A final round trip was made to Missouri in 1853-54, on which he married a second wife on Christmas Day 1853, and by her he raised a second family. In later years Chiles suffered financial reverses "mainly because he trusted others." In 1872 he built a house at St. Helena, northeast of Santa Rosa, where he died.

Doyce B. Nunis Jr., *The Bidwell-Bartleson Party: 1841 California Emigrant Adventure...,* Santa Cruz, Ca., Western Tanager Press, 1991; Bancroft, *California,* IV, V, VI, *Pioneer Register;* Helen Giffen, *Trail-Blazing Pioneer, Colonel Joseph Ballinger Chiles,* San Francisco, John Howell, pub., 1969.

Chirikov, Aleksey Ilich, sea explorer (1703-1748). Russian-born and a navy man all his life, Chirikov was said to be "one of the best officers of his day, the pride and hope of the fleet." He was considered by peers well educated, courageous, kind, straightforward and intellectual. He was graduated from the St. Petersburg naval academy in 1721, commissioned a sub-lieutenant, skipping the rank of midshipman and after brief fleet service became a naval academy instructor. He was presented to Peter the Great upon being selected to serve under Vitus Bering on the Dane's initial arctic expedition and was promoted to lieutenant in 1725. Under Bering's direction a ship, the *St. Gabriel,* was built at the mouth of the Kamchatka River. July 13, 1728, the expedition got under way with Bering in command and Chirikov and Martin Petrovich Spanberg, another Dane, as lieutenants; the primary mission was to learn definitely whether Siberia and North America were separated by a strait or connected by an isthmus, although the forgotten Dezhnev (see entry) had solved this problem a century earlier. August 11 St. Lawrence Island was discovered. On the 13th the *St. Gabriel* reached 65° 30' of latitude. Bering polled his officers for views on what further course to follow. Spanberg, senior among them, urged continuing on a northerly bearing only until August 16, trying to reach 66°; then "in God's name" come about and head back to Kamchatka where they could winter comfortably. Chirikov however urged that "as we have no positive information [how far] Europeans have ever reached in the Arctic Ocean..., we cannot know with certainty whether America is really separated from Asia unless we touch at the mouth of the Koluima," a river to the west, or at least contact the permanent ice pack to the north. If the Kolyma River were reached, it would prove there was no isthmus, while if permanent ice were found the ship might locate a wintering place in a high latitude. Bering listened closely to Spanberg rather than to Chirikov and after attaining 67° 18' came about and returned to Kamchatka, enroute discovering and naming the Diomede Islands, although the American coast was not sighted; he had navigated Bering Strait without realizing it. Back in Russia Chirikov assisted Bering in finalizing a prospectus for a second and more elaborate expedition, this one to discover the northern extension of North America. It provided that two brigs be built on the Pacific coast. Bering was to be captain-commander and Chirikov captain-lieutenant, becoming a full captain two years later. Initial elements left St. Petersburg early in 1733, but the ships were not quickly completed and embarkation from Avatcha Bay, Kamchatka was delayed until June 4, 1741, Bering commanding the *St. Peter* and Chirikov the *St. Paul.* June 20, while approaching the Gulf of Alaska, the vessels became separated and never afterward rejoined. Chirikov hunted for the *St. Peter* until June 23 when the search was abandoned, the *St. Paul* continuing upon the primary mission. July 11 signs of land were noted, the coast itself being raised at 2 a.m. July 15, 1741,

Chirikov thus becoming the discoverer of Alaska (see Bering entry). The ship hove to close inshore at Latitude 56° 15' and on the 16th a boat was lowered but reported that a sighted bay was unsuitable for an anchorage; on the 17th another inlet was approached, this probably Lituya Bay, midway between Sitka and Yakutat. A boat was sent in to investigate and although it passed beyond sight preconcerted signals were received, according to Chirikov's journal; it was assumed the boat had been landed safely. As the party failed for several days to return, the ship's other boat was dispatched on the 23rd to support the first. It was observed to land, but it too failed to return. On the 24th two Indian craft loaded with savages approached the ship but would not close with it, the natives paddling off and Chirikov cursing his failure to lure them aboard when hostages might have been seized for an exchange of prisoners. "His heart was very sore, for he was a humane man and warmly attached to his comrades," but with no more boats there was no way in which he now could contact the shore parties, even if any of the men still lived. Juan José Perez Hernandez (see entry), a Spanish explorer, in 1774 found in possession of native Alaskans on this coast an old bayonet and iron implements which apparently could only have come from the Chirikov or Bering parties (Bancroft, *Alaska*, 196), although the fate of the seamen was not revealed. A council of Chirikov's officers agreed that they should now make for Kamchatka before winter. The want of boats prevented replenishing their scant water supply; they caught rainwater and attempted to distill sea water, and somehow survived. July 31 they sighted snow-covered mountains. They quitted the coast then, bore southwest and September 4 glimpsed what probably was Unalaska Island. September 9 they came upon Adak Island where natives were seen but who refused to come aboard. September 21 Attu Island, outermost of the Aleutians was raised; Chirikov supposed all his sightings were of the continental coast. By now he himself was down with scurvy as were a number of his men, some of whom perished. By October 8 the Kamchatka coast was sighted and on the 10th the *St. Paul* dropped anchor in Avatcha Bay where Chirikov, very ill, was carried ashore. Even before recovering fully he sailed May 25, 1742, in the *St. Paul* to seek and if possible rescue Bering who still had not returned. He visited Attu and Atka but foul weather forced him to return to Avatcha Bay by July 1. In August, before the

Bering survivors arrived, he sailed for Okhotsk and the Siberian mainland. He lived in Yeniseisk, north of Krasnoyarsk in central Siberia, suffering from tuberculosis until 1746 when he was ordered to St. Petersburg and appointed once more to the naval academy. Later in 1746 he was called to Moscow to attend to naval affairs of importance and there made proposals for further explorations. He died with the rank of captain-commander, leaving a widow and daughter.

Bancroft, *Alaska*; F.A. Golder, *Russian Expansion on the Pacific 1641-1850*, N.Y., Paragon Reprint Corp., 1871; Zagoskin.

Chistiakov, Petr Egorovich, administrator (1790-Jan. 21, 1862). Chistiakov entered the Russian naval cadet corps August 11, 1802, and saw much combat duty in his early years, taking part in three actions against the Turks in the Mediterranean, in the blockade of the French fleet at Flessingen and its landings on the Dutch coast. In 1819-21 he made a round-the-world voyage on which he touched at Sitka, Alaska. June 31, 1824 he left Kronstadt in command of the *Elena* and arrived at Sitka June 29, 1825, finding the chief manager of the Russian American Company ill and took over his duties. Muravyev departed November 4, 1825, aboard the *Elena* for Russia and Chistiakov remained as chief manager of the company. He was made Captain-Lieutenant January 7, 1826; Captain, Second Rank December 21, 1826, and Captain, First Rank January 1, 1829, all while serving in Alaska. In 1826 he established a trading post on Atkha Island of the Aleutians, organized a successful sea otter fur post in the Kuriles and in 1829 sent Ensign Ivan Vasilev (see entry) to the Nushagak and later to the Kuskokwim rivers and in 1830 sent Etolin (see entry) on an exploration to Norton Sound and islands in and near Bering Strait. Chistiakov was troubled by supply problems for Alaska and the almost insuperable difficulties in obtaining grain and other necessities, at one time sending a ship as far as Chile to obtain foodstuffs. Baron Wrangel reached Sitka to succeed Chistiakov September 26, 1830, the captain departing for Russia April 28, 1831, leaving behind his Creole mistress and their two sons, Peter and Paul. Arrangements were made for her to marry another Creole and financial help tendered for the raising of the boys. Chistiakov became an Admiral August 25, 1856, and died in Russia.

Richard A. Pierce, *Builders of Alaska: The Russian*

Governors 1818-1867, Kingston, Ont. Limestone Press, 1986; Bancroft, *Alaska;* Zagoskin.

Choris, Ludwig, artist (1795-Mar. 22, 1828). B. of a German family, he was educated at Kharkov, Russia, and in 1831 as an artist was a member of the Friedrich von Biberstein expedition to the Caucasus. The following year he enrolled in the St. Petersburg Academy of Arts. In 1815-18 he participated in the global circumnavigation voyage of Otto von Kotzebue (see entry). Enroute he "made hundreds of drawings and paintings depicting the life of the indigenous peoples and the natural history of America, Asia, Africa and Polynesia. His drawings were original and realistic, unlike those...who idealized primitive peoples and their lives." He lived at Paris from 1819-27 during which he published two volumes of his art work, the first with text by Ludovic Chamisso (see entry). Choris visited Mexico early in 1828 and in central Mexico he was killed by bandits.

Pierce, *Russian America: A Biographical Dictionary.*

Christian, Gilbert, frontiersman (c. 1734-Nov. 1793). A relative of William Christian (see entry), Gilbert settled in the Holston Valley between Tennessee and Virginia and became a frontier militia officer. He commanded a company on the 1776 Cherokee campaign and also was on the Chickamauga campaign of 1779 against the Tennessee Cherokees. He fought at King's Mountain in the frontiersmen's victory over the British in 1780. He was active in affairs of the abortive state of Franklin, and was colonel in the Cherokee War of 1788. He died at Knoxville, Tennessee.

Thwaites, *Dunmore.*

Christie, Ned, gunman (Dec. 14, 1852-Nov. 3, 1892). B. near Tahlequah, Oklahoma, he was a gunsmith-blacksmith by profession and a reported whiskey runner and horse thief by avocation. As a young man he served on the Cherokee tribal council. On May 5, 1885, a deputy U.S. marshal, Dan Maples, was killed near Tahlequah and Christie was accused of the slaying, although he always maintained his innocence and, according to O'Neal, "decades later evidence surfaced which seemed to support his claims." Christie lived in a cabin about 15 miles southeast of Tahlequah aided by some who were sympathetic with him, and he fought off several attempts to seize him under a "dead or alive" proclamation.

Soon after the Maples shooting Deputy Joe Bowers tried to serve a warrant on Christie and was wounded in the leg. Later that month Deputy John Fields tried to talk Christie into surrendering and was shot in the neck, but not seriously. Around 1886 a posse approached the cabin and Christie wounded three deputies, when the lawmen abandoned their mission. In 1889 Deputy Marshal Heck Thomas (see entry) and others assaulted the retreat. Christie was shot in the face, blinded in one eye and his son seriously wounded but although the cabin was burned to the ground Christie was not taken and the deputies withdrew. Christie built what was called Fort Mountain, a structure fortified as much as possible, about a mile from the ruins of his earlier cabin. In 1891 Deputy Marshal Dave Rusk and a posse of Indians attacked the place; four were wounded and the posse withdrew. October 11, 1892, lawmen assaulted the fort ineffectually, two officers were wounded, and the assailants again withdrew. It will be seen from the foregoing that Ned Christie did not run, nor did he hide. Every gunfight was the result of aggression toward him. Christie never took the initiative. Everyone knew where he lived. All attempts against him were for the purpose of taking him to answer for a crime he insisted he did not commit. The climactic action came on November 2-3, 1892, when a 16-man posse headed by Deputy Marshal Paden Tolbert assailed Fort Mountain bringing along a "three-pounder cannon" and six sticks of dynamite. The cannon was ineffective; the dynamite, placed against the rear wall in darkness, exploded and set the fort on fire. Christie and a companion, an Indian fugitive named Dave Wolf, ran for the timber and Christie was killed by Wess Bowman, while Wolf escaped only to be arrested later and sentenced to prison for an earlier offense. After Christie fell, young Sam Maples, son of the slain deputy, emptied his revolver into Ned's body.

Bill O'Neal, "Ned Christie vs. Posse of 25," *True West,* Vol. 37, No. 1 (Jan. 1990), 60-61; O'Neal, *Gunfighters;* Chuck Parsons, "Ned Christie's Death," *True West,* Vol. 34, No. 8 (Aug. 1987), 10-11, featuring a collective photo of nine heavily armed men who were in on the final battle.

Chytref, Sofron: *see* Sofron Khitrov

Clark, Georgie Helen (Georgie White), Colorado River rafter (Nov. 13, 1910-May 12, 1992). B. in Oklahoma as Georgie Helen De Ross, she was raised at Chicago and spent about

45 years of her life running whitewater rivers from Alaska to South America. She at length became the best-known and probably most successful tourist-rafter down the Colorado River, ferrying visitors by the thousands on memorable journeys on the rough-water stream. She lost track of how many trips and how many people she had transported, usually from Lees Ferry southward, but she claimed to have run the river more times than anyone else, "living or dead." In her second year of high school she married Harold Clark and moved to New York City of which she was not enthralled after learning it was "nothing but more of Chicago." She and her husband set out on bicycles for California in 1936; they arrived at Los Angeles without important incident, but she soon divorced Clark; a later marriage to a man named White also ended in divorce. Her first marriage produced a daughter who was killed at 15 by a hit-and-run driver when the girl was on a weekend bicycle trip. In 1944 Georgie discovered the Colorado River, and it was "love at first sight." She and the man who introduced her to the canyon country, Harry Aleson, in 1945 agreed to Georgie's bizarre idea of swimming the river in life jackets. That year they swam 60 miles to the mouth of Lake Mead. The next year they swam twice as far, which was enough for Aleson, who swore he would never do it again, but Georgie said that in 1947 she swam by herself from Phantom Ranch, where the Kaibab Trail crosses the river, to Mead Lake downstream. The swims led to trips in 10-man rubber rafts, and the woman's career as a river runner was launched. She had found the trip through the canyon something of a religious experience, and she wanted to make it available to others. In the mid-1950s she commenced lashing three rubber pontoons together into one huge craft that could safely shoot the worst of rapids without capsizing; with these rafts she took people aged 5 to 86 through the canyon, and with never an untoward incident, her veterans ever afterward known as Georgie's Royal River Rats. She also had run the Green River in Utah, and the San Juan and Escalante tributaries to the Colorado. She was a vegetarian, not from principle but from taste, and she lived on vegetables and Coors beer, which she loved. Her headquarters was at Las Vegas, Nevada, where she lived late in life. Georgie Clark was a vocal supporter of Jim White (see entry) and his purported feat of running the Grand Canyon on a three-log raft in 1867, two years before John Wesley Powell (see entry) made the first "official" trip down the river. Georgie said, "I positively think White made the trip," adding that it would be "very possible, even in high water," to do so, although others, such as Dellenbaugh and Stanton (see entries) were unconvinced. Georgie Clark died of cancer at 81 at Las Vegas and was buried at Henderson, Nevada. She had no known survivors.

Tom Foust, "As Her River, Clark Keeps Rolling On," *Arizona Daily Star,* Aug. 21, 1987; Georgie Helen Clark death cert.

Clark, Meriwether Lewis, military officer (Jan. 10, 1809-Oct. 28, 1881). B. at St. Louis, he was the oldest reported son of William Clark of the Lewis and Clark Expedition and his wife, the former Julia Hancock. He went to West Point and was commissioned a brevet second lieutenant of the 6th Infantry July 1, 1830. He was sent to Jefferson Barracks, Missouri, upon commissioning and in 1831 became aide-de-camp to Brigadier General Edmund P. Gaines. In 1832 he served during the Black Hawk War as a volunteer officer on the staff of Colonel Henry Atkinson, holding at the same time the rank of colonel on the staff of the Illinois Volunteers from May 9 to October 11, 1832, and by one report was wounded in action, but which action is not stated, nor are the circumstances. He resigned his army commission in 1833 and entered civilian life as a civil engineer, also being qualified as an architect. He was a member of the Missouri House of Representatives from 1836-38, a recorder for St. Louis in 1843 and during the Mexican War was commissioned a major with a Missouri artillery battalion. He took part in the battle of Sacramento, just north of Chihuahua City and during occupation of the latter place was quartered in the Palace Library; there he found the books "not properly classified" and directed a detail to do the job thoroughly. He was mustered out June 24, 1847, and was U.S. surveyor general for Missouri from 1848-53. With the Civil War, Clark served with the Confederate army as a colonel. He married twice. He died at Frankfort, Kentucky.

Heitman; Susan Shelby Magoffin, *Down the Santa Fe Trail and Into Chihuahua,* Lincoln, Univ. of Neb. Press, 1982, pp. 143-44 note by Stella M. Drumm; *Black Hawk War,* Vol. II, Pt. I, 80n.

Clark, Walter Van Tilburg, writer (Aug. 3, 1909-Nov. 11, 1971). B. at East Orland, Maine he was the son of Walter Ernest Van Tilburg, later president of the University of Nevada. The writer was graduated from the University of Nevada in 1932 and had master's degrees from that school and from the University of Vermont. He devoted his professional career to teaching and writing, authoring fiction for the most part, including novels and short stories, and contributing to many periodicals. He is best known for two of his western novels: *The Ox-Box Incident* (1940), and *The Track of the Cat* (1949). He also edited the three-volume, 2,381-page *Journals of Alfred Doten 1849-1903* (1973), a memorable collection of diaries and other writings of a Nevada pioneer-journalist, and at his death Clark was working on a biography of Doten. He was a conservationist, fond of out-of-doors activities and once said "my favorite diversion, by long odds, is socializing..., talking to all kinds of people about all kinds of things." He was married and fathered three children.

Contemporary Authors; REAW.

Claus, Christian Daniel, Indian official (Sept. 13, 1727-Nov. 9, 1787). Born near Heilbronn, Germany, he reached Philadelphia in 1749 where he met Johann Conrad Weiser (see entry), Indian agent for Pennsylvania and in 1750 accompanied him to the Six Nations (Iroquois) where Claus commenced gathering a vocabulary of Onondaga words. On his return he met the governor of Pennsylvania, who in order to develop further Claus's linguistic interests arranged for him to live among the Mohawks. There Claus resided for a time with King Hendrick (see entry) who instructed him in the language and history of the Iroquois. During the French and Indian War Claus was commissioned a lieutenant of the 60th Regiment and deputy Indian agent under Sir William Johnson with whom he had become friendly during his period of Iroquois instruction. He married Ann, or Nancy, the daughter of Johnson and Catherine Weissenberg in 1762. At the close of the war he became superintendent for the Canadian Indians, holding office until 1775, when he was summarily dismissed following the death of Johnson, Claus in November leaving for England. He returned in June 1777 with an appointment as superintendent of the Iroquois who were to accompany the St. Leger expedition into New York State; he was present at the unsuccessful siege of Fort Stanwix at Rome, New York. With St. Leger's failure and Burgoyne's defeat, British efforts to recover control of New York were doomed and the Claus family removed to Canada. In 1778 he was named deputy agent for the Six Nations in Canada, under Guy Johnson (see entry). Seeking compensation for his considerable losses in the Revolution, he went to England and while there died at Cardiff, Wales.

Thwaites/Kellogg, *The Revolution on the Upper Ohio, 1775-1777,* Madison, Wis. Hist. Soc., 1908; DCB, IV.

Clay, John Jr., cattleman, writer (Apr. 24, 1851-Mar. 17, 1934). B. at Winfield, Berwickshire, Scotland, he was educated at St. Andrews and Edinburgh universities and came to the United States in 1874, becoming naturalized in 1888. He had commenced farming in Scotland, and was a manager of a farm near Brantford, Ontario from 1879-82 after which he became a cattle rancher in Wyoming. According to Helena Huntington Smith, the "bullet-headed Scottish businessman...came out to Wyoming...as a promoter of cattle companies," becoming president from 1890-95 of the Wyoming Stock Growers Association, which controlled the Board of Livestock Commissioners during a turbulent time in the state's ranch history. Smith called him "the historian *par excellence* of that superb folly, the great beef bonanza on the western plains...He was in the thick of it from start to finish and was one of the few who came out still wearing his shirt." She noted that Clay "writes freely on the financial excesses of the time, [but] is silent on the errors of policy committed by the [association, though] not surprisingly, since he himself was one of the chief authors of the policy and the errors." Clay apparently had nothing to do with the lynching, July 20, 1889, of James Averell and Ella Watson (see entries), but George Henderson (see entry), manager of Clay's 71 Quarter Circle Ranch on the Sweetwater River was not so absolved. Clay wrote that Henderson "was not a party directly to this business [the lynchings] but he was indirectly connected with it." When Henderson was killed in the summer of 1890 Clay said it was by a "rustler" which was not true, and he knew it: the killing was done by John Tregoning, another of his employees who had been fired. Clay had no direct, personal involvement in the so-called Johnson County War of 1892, but that he knew of its development and inevitability there is no doubt: he wrote in his famous *My Life on the Range* that on July 4, 1891, Frank Wolcott (see entry) proposed to him "a lynching bee," a plan "so bold and open" that Clay considered it "impossible," and asked to be left out of it. He left immediately for England and wrote that he first heard of the "war" after it was concluded. Larson wrote that "hard feelings persisted [over it] for years." Clay told the Stock Growers Association convention in April 1893 that "technically, legally they [the Invaders, or big ranchmen-hired gunmen] did wrong, but...I count every one of them a friend." The major ranch holders for the most part finally lost out, Clay writing that "the settlers were too much for them. You can fight armies or disease or trespass, but the settler never. He advances slowly, surely, silently...pushing everything before him," and the settlers' conquest would have been complete had it not been for nature—the aridity of Wyoming was too much for most of them. Clay became chairman of the board of the Stock Growers National Bank of Cheyenne, and later in life lived at Chicago. He wrote his *My Life on the Range* (1924) which has been accepted as one of three or four best cattlemen's books. Ramon Adams said that Clay was "one of the better-known ranch owners of the Northwest and a well-educated Scotchman. His picture of ranch life is interesting and authentic." Clay also wrote *Old Days Recalled* (1915), largely about his youth, several works on livestock matters and *The Tragedy of Squaw Mountain,* which bears no date and according to Adams, "contains a story about Tom Horn," but is a rarity. Clay married his first wife in 1881, who predeceased him, a second in 1925, and fathered a son, also named John Clay.

Who Was Who, Clay's writings; Helena Huntington Smith, *The War on Powder River,* N.Y., McGraw-Hill Book Co., 1966; T.A. Larson, *History of Wyoming,* Lincoln, Univ. of Neb. Press, 1965; Adams, *Six-Guns and Saddle Leather,* Norman, Univ. of Okla. Press, 1969; Adams, *The Rampaging Herd,* Norman, 1959.

Clover, Richardson, naval officer (July 11, 1846-Oct. 14, 1919). B. at Hagerstown, Maryland, he was graduated from the Naval Academy in 1867 and was commissioned an ensign December 18, 1868; master, March 21, 1870, and lieutenant March 21, 1871. As acting lieutenant commander he commanded the Coast and Geodetic Survey steamer *Patterson* and was in charge of a survey of southeastern Alaska in 1885-86, surveys being made of the south end of the Alexander Archipelago of the Alaskan Panhandle. An island and other features were named for him, his reports published in the Survey's annual publication for 1886. Clover served as hydrographer for the Bureau of Navigation from 1889-93, became a commander in 1897 and was chief of the Office of Naval Intelligence in 1897-98. He became a captain April 11, 1902, and a Rear Admiral October 9, 1907. He retired in 1908 and made his home at Washington, D.C.

Orth, 11, 225; *Who Was Who.*

Coat[e]s, James, trapper, guide, pioneer (fl. 1830-1848). An experienced Rocky Mountain beaver trapper, Coats met a war party of Crows in August 1834 who "well knew" him as he was enroute from his spring hunt to the American Fur Company fort at the mouth of the Marias River, Montana. He "had been several years living and trapping with the Crow Indians, spoke their language tolerably well, and had some friends among them." It was said that Coats "was in league with them," the Crows, for the purpose of pillaging the fort, Denig adding that "as his usual character was of that description of renegades it may have been so, 'tho...his conduct does not merit this reproach." The Crows besieged the fort and on the second or third day Coats "came to the fort and told [Alexander] Culbertson (see entry) for the first time the real purpose of the Crows, advising him by no means to admit any of them. This certainly showed well on the part of Coats, but he also was particular in his enquiries regarding the amount of provisions on hand. It is thought he was sent by the Indians to ascertain this point. If so, he failed either in getting admission or information." The Crow siege failed. Nothing more of James Coats has been uncovered until 1842 when a James Coates, as Barry spells it, or Coats as Bancroft has it (in *Oregon,* I, 256n., 259) was hired as "pilot" or guide for the famed Lansford Warren Hastings (see entry) wagon party for Oregon. This may well be the same man as the James Coats who was earlier with the Crows. The makeup of the considerable wagon train is given in Bancroft, *ibid.,* and Barry, 447-48. The Elijah White party joined Hastings at the outset, but later split off. The train left Independence, Missouri, May 16, reached the Blue River May 31, the Platte June 9 and Fort Laramie in late June. Since Coat's knowledge of the Trail went no farther than Laramie, Thomas Fitzpatrick (see entry) was hired to guide the train on to Fort Hall, which was reached in mid-August when Fitzpatrick left, and Willamette Falls, Oregon, was attained in October, the journey in effect terminating there. In May 1843

Hastings gathered a party of 53, including 25 armed men and left Oregon for California; near the Rogue River they encountered cattle drovers with whom many of the Hastings party determined to return to Oregon, but 16 armed men, including James Coates (as Bancroft now spells the name) pushed on to California. In a night attack by Indians on the Shasta River, George W. Bellamy was seriously wounded in the back by an arrow, and on the Sacramento River a more serious altercation occurred in which 20 hostiles were killed. Bancroft remarked that "there is reason to suppose that [the Indians] were not altogether the parties at fault" for the affrays. The party arrived at Sutter's Fort about July 10, 1843. Coates, whom Bancroft described as a shoemaker, tanner and farmer and, as we have seen, earlier a Rocky Mountain trapper and familiar with the Overland Trail from Independence to Fort Laramie, settled in 1844 at Monterey, California, where he was "naturalized," presumably in order to marry. He became a lieutenant in Sutter's force in 1845 during the Micheltorena troubles and, commanding 15 men of John Gantt's company was captured with his party by Californians, probably under Manuel Castro; they were well treated and released under parole with the pledge to take no further part in hostilities. In 1847 Coates was living at San Francisco and was a tanner later at New Helvetia (Sutter's Fort, the later Sacramento). At length he moved to a house on the American River. In March 1848 he was injured seriously in a fall from a horse, "being also robbed of $300," according to Bancroft. Nothing further has been located on Coates. There were half a dozen men named Coates or Coats who served with California troops during the Civil War, including a James Coates, who may have been a son of the pioneer. Young James Coates was a corporal in Company A, 4th California Infantry, and later a sergeant in Company E.

Edwin Thompson Denig, *Five Indian Tribes of the Upper Missouri,* Norman, Univ. of Okla. Press, 1973; Barry, *Beginning of the West;* Bancroft, *Oregon,* I, *California,* IV, *Pioneer Register;* Orton.

Cobell, Joe, frontiersman (fl. 1870). Joe Cobell, b. in Italy, came to America accompanied by an uncle. He reached New Orleans, worked his way up the Mississippi River to St. Louis and hired out to the American Fur Company, becoming a herder and, eventually, a hunter. When the concern changed ownership he took his savings and purchased a ranch near Rock Creek, Montana, but as settlers began to crowd him, sold out and

moved to a site east of Cascade, Montana; settlers again forced him to move and he took up a fine ranch property on Shonkin Creek where, when settlers once more nudged him, he sold out for $5,000 and moved onto the Blackfeet Reservation. His first wife, who died in 1865, was a sister of Little Dog, famed Blackfoot warrior and chief; his second wife, whom he named Mary, was a younger sister of Mountain Chief. Through his wives, Joe became fluent in Blackfoot and thus was chosen, with Joe Kipp (see entry) by Philip De Trobriand, district commander, as scout for Eugene Baker's Marias River, Montana, operation in January 1870. Two villages were known to be within range, one headed by Heavy Runner, a chief considered friendly and peaceable, and the other by Mountain Chief, an inveterate hostile. Baker's force first approached the village later determined to be Heavy Runner's, and when the chief ran out of his tepee waving a paper to affirm his peaceful character, Joe Cobell shot him (as he later conceded) to initiate the fight and save his brother-in-law Mountain Chief's village from attack. His ruse succeeded, and the infamous Baker massacre ensued. Cobell was paid for 12 days' service "at a rate not to exceed $5 per day." At some point before the close of the 19th century Cobell told his close friend Joe Connelly that it was his shot which, by murdering Heavy Runner, had diverted the military from attacking Mountain Chief's village. Following the engagement, Cobell returned to his latest ranch, on Prickly Pear Creek. Connelly, interviewed in 1931, at that date revealed for the first time publicly, the information of how the Marias engagement commenced; both Cobell and Connelly were considered "truthful men."

Robert J. Ege, *Tell Baker to Strike Them Hard!",* Bellevue, Neb., Old Army Press, 1970; Paul Andrew Hutton, *Phil Sheridan and His Army,* Lincoln, Univ. of Neb. Press, 1985.

Coburn, Walt, writer (Oct. 23, 1889-May 24, 1971). B. at White Sulphur Springs, Montana, he was raised on a cattle ranch and spent most of his life on ranches or writing about the cowboy West. He served in the Army Air Service from 1917-19 becoming a sergeant first class. Coburn started writing western short stories in 1922 "and after two years of rejection slips I sold around 900 novelettes to 37 different pulp paper magazines," and had the cover story in each of them at one time or another. When the pulp westerns rode into the sunset around 1950 Coburn turned to writing novels and several autobiographical works, including *Pioneer Cattleman: The Story of the Circle C Ranch,* published by the University of Oklahoma Press in 1968. He said late in life that he was "born and raised in the cattle business, both in Montana and Arizona [and] am still interested in the cattle industry." He added that he did "little research...I have never read another Western author's work in my lifetime of writing." He worked steadily, taking a day or two off between stories, and rode horseback for relaxation. As another well-known western writer, Fred Gipson put it: "This shy little sawed-off ex-Montana cowhand knows which end of a cow gets up first—which end of a horse gets up first—and the color of burnt-hair smoke...from under a hot branding iron..." Coburn was married and died near Prescott, Arizona.

Contemporary Authors; Matt Dodge, "Remembering Walt," *True West,* Vol. 24, No. 6 (July-Aug. 1977), 4-7, 34; REAW; information from E.F. (Ted) Mains.

Coghlan, Joseph Bullock, naval officer (Dec. 9, 1844-1908). B. at Frankfort, Kentucky, he was graduated from the Naval Academy in 1863, becoming an ensign May 28 and was promoted through grades. As a commander he commanded the *Adams* in 1884 in southeast Alaska, surveying interior passages north and east from Sitka Sound, through Peril Strait to Chatham Strait and in the vicinity of Barlow Cove toward the south end of Lynn Canal. An island in the Alexander Archipelago was named for him in 1885. He advanced to captain and commanded the *Raleigh* with the Asiatic Fleet during the Spanish American War, taking part in the battle of Manila Bay May 1, 1898, being cited for eminent and conspicuous conduct during that action. Coghlan became a Rear Admiral April 11, 1902, and retired December 9, 1906.

Orth, 11, 229; *Who Was Who.*

Colbert, Levi, Chickasaw leader (d. 1834). The son of James Colbert, a white, and his Chickasaw wife, he encouraged establishment of schools among his people as early as 1820 and economic development on the white model. He was considered by some to have become the "soul" of the Chickasaw people and wrested control of tribal affairs from the full-bloods while retaining such traditional customs as polygamy. He was invited to Washington in 1824 but refused to sell more tribal land despite pressure from Mississippi to do so. He repudiated the federal removal commission in 1826. The tribe was encouraged to remove across the Mississippi in 1827, and Colbert in 1828 agreed to assess the country chosen for them, heading an exploration party. He decided that the new land was inadequate for his people, and supported a tribal resolution against removal. But the federal Indian Removal Act and the extension of Mississippi and Alabama state laws to apply to the Chickasaws compelled him to accept removal, though much against his will. He explored Arkansas and Texas in 1830 and 1831, choosing the Sabine River in Mexican territory as a new home for the Chickasaw nation, but this selection was ruled improper and since the removal agreement was contingent upon a satisfactory location being found this nullified it. Under coercion, however, the Chickasaws nonetheless eventually were forced to comply, but Colbert was too ill to attend later discussions and died in the summer of 1834.

Info. from John Sugden; Arrell M. Gibson, *The Chickasaws,* Norman, Univ. of Okla. Press, 1971; G.B. Braden, "The Colberts and the Chickasaw Nation," *Tennessee Historical Quarterly,* Vol. 17 (1958).

Colcord, William Clay, cattleman (Jan. 14, 1867-May 16, 1961). Considered by Forrest and others as "the last man" of Arizona's sanguinary Pleasant Valley War, he was b. in Jefferson Parish, Louisiana, and reached Arizona in 1886 with his mother and younger brother, Harvey. Early in the year he started to work for the Babbitt Brothers cattle interest near Flagstaff, his other brother, Charles, already had come in charge of the well-known A 1 Ranch in the vicinity. Bill and Harvey later located several ranches, one in Pleasant Valley. In 1887 rustlers stole "most" of the horses owned by Colcord and his neighbor, famed gunman and peace officer Jim Roberts (see entry). In the ensuing feud, Bill favored the Tewksburys, although he ever asserted he had remained neutral, a hard thing to do in the times and circumstances. Others reportedly have said that Colcord killed a sheepherder in February 1887, an act that some believe ignited the war, and one participant said that Colcord "was involved in the killings" that ensued. When afterward Tom Graham and Charley Duchet returned to Pleasant Valley in 1892 for Graham's share of the cattle he had left there "it was Colcord who met them to ask, '...is it peace or war?'" When Graham assured him it was peace, they shook hands and as Graham drove his cattle out of the valley, "Colcord saw to it that they were not molested." During ensuing years Colcord operated various ranches, "gathered wild horses with John Rhodes, the Tewksburys and the famous Tom Horn." He was married in 1894, served as Gila County Supervisor for six years and continued his ranching operations on various spreads until 1928 when he settled down as a storekeeper for a decade. Late in life he lived with his "lion-hunting son, Frank," who also was active in ranching near Phoenix. Bill Colcord died at 94 at Globe, Arizona, having "long outlived every man in any way connected with the feud."

Earle R. Forrest, *Arizona's Dark and Bloody Ground,* Caldwell, Id., Caxton Pntrs., 1964, p. 371; Clara T. Woody, *Globe, Arizona* (with photos of Colcord), Tucson, Az. Hist. Soc., 1977; Roscoe G. Willson, *Pioneer and Well Known Cattlemen of Arizona,* II, Phoenix, Valley Natl. Bank, 1956, p. 40; Charles G. Heath, "The Real Last Man," English Westerners' *Tally Sheet,* Vol. 33, No. 1 (Winter 1986), 4-5.

Colden, Cadwallader, government official, scientist (Feb. 7, 1688 n.s.-Sept. 28, 1776). B. in Ireland of Scot ancestry, he was graduated from the University of Edinburgh in 1705, studied medicine at London and arrived at Philadelphia in 1710, practicing his profession and also operating a mercantile business. In 1718 he moved to New York where he became surveyor-general, in 1721 was appointed to the Governor's Council and in 1761 became lieutenant-governor of New York colony. Frontier interest in his career centers upon his formulation of an Indian policy, and publication in 1727 of his *The History of the Five Indian Nations Depending upon the Province of New-York in America,* Part I of a work, Part II being published in 1747. The book was reprinted in 1866 and, most recently, in 1958 and 1964 and is considered "still an authority on the subject." It included a map of the Indian country with which it was concerned. The *Dictionary of American Biography* complained that "though Colden was closely associated with the Indian tribes of New York, the book was based on French sources and is both dull and confused," although an informed reading of it today fails to support such criticism, at least so far as "dull" is concerned, and the confusion seems minimal. Colden probably based the work largely on French sources because by that time only the French missionaries, military and political writers alike, had produced any considerable oeuvre on the subject. In one interesting passage Colden wrote that French prisoners of the Iroquois "had full liberty from the Indians [and despite entreaties from their countrymen

and officials] few of them could be persuaded to return [to white civilization, and] the English had as much Difficulty to persuade the People, that had been taken Prisoners by the French Indians, to leave the Indian Manner of living...No arguments, no Intreaties, nor Tears of their Friends and Relations, could persuade many of them to leave their new Indian Friends and Acquaintance; several of them that were by the Caressing of their Relations persuaded to come Home, in a little Time greatly tired of our Manner of living, and run away again to the Indians, and ended their Days with them. On the other Hand, Indian Children Have been carefully educated among the English, cloathed and taught, yet, I think, there is not one Instance, that any of these, after they had Liberty to go among their own People, and were come to Age, would remain with the English, but returned to their own Nations, and became as fond of the Indian Manner of Life as those that knew nothing of a civilized Manner of living." In addition to delving into many fields of intellectual endeavor (he was a veritable Benjamin Franklin in the scope of his interests) he became deeply engrossed with botanical classification as developed by the Swedish scientist Linnaeus (Karl von Linné, 1707-78), founder of modern systematic botanical and zoological classification. Following Linnaeus's system, Colden classified the flora of the region around his estate of Colden(g)ham (just west of Newburgh, New York). He sent his results to Linnaeus, who issued them in connection with his own work. Colden also published widely on medical subjects, philosophy, on mathematics, gravitation and astronomical matters. He became on several occasions acting governor of New York, was a staunch Loyalist in principle, and with the Battle of Lexington and rise of Revolutionary forces retired to his other estate on Long Island, where he shortly died. He had fathered at least three children who survived him.

DAB; Colden's writings; CE.

Collier, Arthur James, geologist (1866-1939). A scientist with the Geological Survey, Collier was an assistant to Alfred Brooks doing work in the Cape Nome region of the Seward Peninsula in Alaska in 1900. He wrote the notes on climate and vegetation in the Survey's special report, *Reconnaissance of the Cape Nome and Norton Bay Regions,* published in 1900. Collier returned to the Seward Peninsula in 1901 as a geologist with the Thomas Golding Gerdine party. In 1902

Collier examined coal deposits along the Yukon River from Dawson to its mouth. In 1903 he returned to the Seward Peninsula to continue mineral resource investigations, visiting nearly all of the placer mining camps of the region and examining tin deposits in the York area, about 40 miles northwest of Teller. In 1904 he again visited Seward Peninsula studying gold and tin deposits, investigated coal deposits in the Cape Lisburne region of the northwest Alaskan coast, and made a geologic and topographic survey for 140 miles of the coast between Cape Beaufort and Cape Thompson. His observations were published in the Survey's 26th Annual Report of 1905.

Orth, 11.

Collins, Perry McDonough (1813-1900). B. at Hyde Park, New York, he was the originator of the Collins Overland Telegraph project, best known in Alaska as the Western Union Telegraph operation. Collins studied law, went to New Orleans and in 1849 sailed to San Francisco, settling at Sonora, California, where he became active in many pursuits, gradually becoming interested in North Pacific shipping routes and the expansion of the Russian empire eastward, aware that in the Pacific it and the North American interests burgeoning westward would meet. In 1853 he became associated with the American-Russian Commercial Company and with the 1855 arrival at San Francisco of Navy Captain John Rodgers (see entry), returned from an exploring expedition to western Alaska, learned of Russian Governor Matvei Muravyet's interest in the Amur River as a gateway into eastern Asia and Siberia. In 1856 Collins went to Washington, D.C., seeking authorization for an American mission to the Amur, which he would head. With American approval, Collins went to St. Petersburg, spent two years in Russia and Siberia, developing grandiose plans for the development of eastern Siberia and the Amur as a commercial gateway for relations between the two continents. He was particularly intrigued by possible telegraphic communications between the Amur waterway and Europe. Collins returned to Washington in 1858, urging a "telegraph communication...uniting Europe and America." It would run north of the Western Union's planned transcontinental system and cross British Columbia, Alaska, pass beneath Bering Strait by cable, and continue down the eastern coast of Siberia to a point on the Amur where it would connect with the Amur line being constructed eastward by the Russians. William Sibley of Western Union favored the plan, since it might head off the projected trans-Atlantic cable projected by Cyrus Field and his American Telegraph Company. Collins eventually received authorization from Russia to cross Alaska, and from London to cross British Columbia. Sibley then bought Collins' rights to the project for $100,000 and other benefits. Western Union planned eventually to bring China and Japan into the network and beyond that considered a linkage with all of Latin America. After temporary setbacks, construction work commenced in the summer of 1865, but completion of the Atlantic cable July 27, 1866, doomed the enterprise, although the Alaska work was not cancelled until the spring of 1867. "The main result of Collins' projects was the part they played in the purchase of Alaska," wrote Pierce. "The telegraph project stimulated interest in the Russian territories during the Civil War years [and] knowledge of the territory accumulated by the expedition's scientific corps helped to include public and Congressional opinion toward acquisition of the region." Collins, who had won and lost several fortunes during his adventurous life, profited from payments from Western Union, invested successfully in western railroads and died well off at 87 at New York City.

Pierce, *Russian America: A Biographical Dictionary*.

Colton, Harold Sellers, archeologist, zoologist (Aug. 29, 1881-Dec. 29, 1970). B. at Philadelphia he was graduated from the University of Pennsylvania in 1904 and received his doctorate there in 1908, meanwhile having joined its faculty. He became a full professor in 1926 and was professor emeritus from 1954 until his death. He served in military intelligence in 1918-19. From 1928 onward he also was associated with the Museum of Northern Arizona at Flagstaff, its director from 1928-58 and director emeritus for the rest of his life, becoming a recognized authority on the pre-history of northern Arizona and wrote widely on subjects related to that field. But his interests were broad: he was director of the San Francisco Mountain Zoological Station at Flagstaff from 1929-54, a member of the Archeological Commission of Arizona, and was associated with the Santa Fe Laboratory of Anthropology from 1934-53, was president of the southwest division of the American Association for the Advancement of Science, belonged to the American Geographic Society, American Society of Naturalists, American Anthropological Association, Ecological Society of America, American Microscopic Society. American Genetic Society and other organizations, Among his publications were *Hopi Kachina Dolls* (1949, 1959); *Potsherds: An Introduction to the Study of Prehistoric Southwestern Ceramics and Their Use in Historic Reconstruction* (1953); *Black Sand: Prehistory in Northern Arizona* (1960); *Hopi History and Ethnobotany* (1974), and wrote many bulletins and other works. He was married and fathered two sons, one of whom survived him.

Who Was Who; Contemporary Authors; info. from E.F. (Ted) Mains.

Compton, Charles Elmer, military officer (Jan. 24, 1836-July 20, 1909). B. at Morristown, New Jersey, he enlisted as first sergeant and sergeant major of the 1st Iowa Infantry May 7, 1861, became a captain of the 11th Iowa Infantry October 19 and emerged from the Civil War a lieutenant colonel of the 53rd U.S. colored Infantry. He became a major of the 40th Infantry July 28, 1866 and joined the 6th Cavalry December 15, 1870. Compton commanded a 6th Cavalry battalion in Nelson Miles's Red River campaign of 1874. On August 30 he led a "gallant and successful" charge against hostile Indians on the Salt Fork of the Red River; it was a minor skirmish otherwise, but Compton won a brevet for it. At the removal of the Chiricahua Indians in 1876 from their southeastern Arizona reservation to San Carlos Reservation, Compton had a major military role and apparently performed it incompetently. He, with Ebin Stanley as chief of his White Mountain Apache scouts, was directed to patrol the region east of the Chiricahua Mountains, while Brayton and Sieber covered the western slopes, the commands to assure no Indians escaped the removal operation which itself was handled by Agent John P. Clum. Brayton and Sieber performed their mission diligently and successfully, while Compton and Stanley (who was a competent and reliable chief of scouts) permitted Juh, Geronimo and 208 largely Nedhni Apaches to escape into Mexico. Stanley later told Arizona Governor Anson P.K. Safford that Compton's command had discovered and followed a broad trail made by the escaping Indians for a few miles "when further pursuit was abandoned," the column returning to its post,

Camp Grant. When the operation was cancelled, Stanley reported, Compton's men were "close behind the Indians," and that by energetic effort "they could not have escaped." Stanley said he told Compton this, and that he was "politely informed by [Compton] that when his advice was desired it would be asked." The result was a disaster. The escaped Indians found haven in Mexico from where they raided into Arizona and New Mexico at will for many months. Compton became lieutenant colonel of the 5th Cavalry April 29, 1879. Posted to Fort D.A. Russell at Cheyenne, Wyoming he took part in the autumn relief of the troops beseiged by Ute Indians at Milk Creek, Colorado, and participated in raising the siege and the skirmish there October 5. He commanded cavalry at the Ute Agency on White River until November, when he returned to Fort Russell. Compton was made colonel of the 4th Cavalry October 19, 1887, stationed for a time at Fort Huachuca, Arizona. In the summer of 1891 at Walla Walla, Washington, he was charged with neglect of duty in failing to suppress what was reported as a seditious demonstration. He was suspended from rank and command on half pay for three years but in January 1893 the unexpired portion of his sentence was remitted, it being apparent that his punishment was unjust for the fault had lain largely with civic officials. He became a Brigadier General of Volunteers May 4, 1898 and was honorably discharged from the Volunteers December 6, retiring June 6, 1899. In 1904 he became a Brigadier General, retired, of the army. He died at Hollywood, California, leaving a widow and a daughter.

Heitman; Powell; Tucson, Arizona *Citizen,* Feb. 17, 1877; Constance Wynn Altshuler, *Cavalry Yellow & Infantry Blue,* Tucson, Az. Hist. Soc., 1991.

Connelly, Henry, physician, trader (1800-Aug. 12, 1866). B. in Virginia, he was taken at 4 to the present Spencer County, Kentucky. He graduated in medicine in 1828 from Transylvania University at Lexington, Kentucky, opened an office at Liberty, Missouri, but within a year abandoned his practice to join a trading party to Chihuahua, reaching that city after great hardships. He established a mercantile business there and for many years traveled between Chihuahua City and Independence, Missouri, first with pack mules, later with wagon trains. In 1839 he attempted to chart a new and shorter route between Chihuahua City and Independence, by crossing Texas directly. He led a caravan of 100 men who succesfully made the trip to Missouri and return, taking a year to accomplish it, but the journey was never repeated. In 1843 he entered a partnership with Edward J. Glasgow of St. Louis for business pursuits. He served as an emissary between Manuel Armijo, governor of New Mexico, and Stephen Watts Kearny before Kearny had advanced to Santa Fe in 1846, and may have been responsible for the bloodless occupation of New Mexico. Connelly later was arrested at El Paso and taken to Chihuahua, but the charges, if any, were dropped. After the Mexican War he moved from Chihuahua to New Mexico where he lived until his death from an accidental poisoning; the funeral rites were conducted by Bishop Jean B. Lamy in the cathedral of Santa Fe. By then he had established the largest mercantile business in New Mexico with branches in major centers. He was appointed governor of New Mexico by Lincoln in 1861 and reappointed in 1864, and his influence was said to have been a major factor in keeping New Mexico out of the Confederacy. Connelly was married twice, by his first wife fathering three sons; after she died he married the widow of Mariano Chavez.

Susan Shelby Magoffin, *Down the Santa Fe Trail and Into Chihuahua,* Lincoln, Univ. of Neb. Press, 1982, pp. 104-105n. by Stella M. Drumm; Calvin Horn, *New Mexico's Troubled Years: The Story of the Early Territorial Governors,* Albuquerque, Horn & Wallace, 1963.

Conner, Richard, frontiersman (d. 1808). B. in Maryland, he went west as a hunter and trapper. Among the Shawnees he met a white captive, Mary Myers, whom he bought from the Indians for $200 and married, the Shawnee agreement being that their first child should reside with the tribe. After Lord Dunsmore's War, the Conners were released from captivity by the Shawnees and settled near Pittsburgh. In 1775 they returned to the Indians to ransom their son, James, and enroute visited the Moravian missionaries in eastern Ohio, became faithful members of the missionary church, were removed to Michigan with the mission Indians in 1781 and settled three years later near the present Mount Clemens. They became the first white settlers of St. Clair County, Michigan, where Richard Conner died. Their sons became noted "interpreters and scouts" in the War of 1812.

Louis Phelps Kellogg, *Frontier Advance on the Upper Ohio 1778-1779,* Madison, State Hist. Soc. of Wis., 1916.

Connolly, John, adventurer (c. 1743-Jan. 30, 1813). B. at Wright's Ferry, York County, Pennsylvania, he was a nephew of George Croghan (d. 1782), a noted frontiersman who was conversant in Iroquois and Delaware and active in Indian matters. Connolly was apprenticed to a Philadelphia physician and though he did not complete medical studies he practiced as a physician and thereafter used the title of doctor. He was a medical officer on Indian campaigns from 1762 to 1764, after which he became associated with the frontier-wise Croghan. Connolly resided from 1767-70 at Kaskaskia, Illinois, where he learned something of Indian languages and failed in business, then withdrew to Pittsburgh where he practiced medicine and speculated in land. He became associated in some manner with Lord Dunmore, governor of Virginia and became Dunmore's agent at Pittsburgh, which offered opportunities for his fertile, active mind. Of strong Loyalist tendencies, Connolly appeared somewhat sinister to American frontiersmen, although in his own mind he may have believed he was only about the King's business, and his own. He supported Dunmore in claiming the land around Fort Pitt for Virginia; it also was claimed by Pennsylvania. Dunmore commissioned him militia captain and commandant of Fort Pitt, but in January 1774 when he tried to collect settlers into a Virginia militia unit he was arrested by Pennsylvania authorities; ordered to appear in court, he did so, accompanied by 200 of his militiamen, and arrested three Pennsylvania justices. Connolly's "halting of the Pennsylvania trade, which supplied the Indians, and his imposition of the Virginia fur tax in Pittsburgh almost precipitated civil war there between Pennsylvania traders and Virginia speculators; meanwhile the rival courts engaged in an *opera bouffe* of arrests and jail deliveries." When Lord Dunmore's War broke out in 1774, Connolly sent his militia to Wheeling, present West Virginia, to build Fort Fincastle, named for one of Dunmore's titles, but later by Patriots called Fort Henry for Patrick Henry, who followed Dunmore as governor of Virginia. The doctor had no combat role in Dunmore's War, but as the Revolution loomed he saw the necessity of winning Indian support for England. In July 1775 he arranged a treaty, or understanding, with Iroquois and Delaware elements. He left Pittsburgh and in August 1775 joined Dunmore aboard a ship off Yorktown, bringing with him an elaborate scheme for an offensive against the American colonies from the Ohio frontier. The proposal was that Connolly would go by way of Canada to Detroit to meet Captain Hugh Lord who had been assigned to the 18th Royal Irish Regiment in the Illinois country. With two companies of Lord's command along with field pieces and stores as the backbone of the offensive force, Connolly was to raise a regiment, or as many Indians and partisans as he could, and with the combined force destroy Fort Pitt and Fort Fincastle (Henry) if the Americans should offer resistance and march overland to meet Dunmore, April 20, 1776 at Alexandria on the Potomac. Dunmore would have landed, under shelter of ships' guns, "an army" which would be joined to Connolly's force, which would have effectively cut the colonies in two. Dunmore believed Connolly's proposal was worthy, sent the doctor to Boston where he presented it to General Thomas Gage, commander-in-chief of British forces in America and governor of Massachusetts. Gage formally approved the scheme. Connolly went north in an effort to implement operations, but the capture of Montreal and Benedict Arnold's expedition against Quebec thwarted him, and he returned to Lord Dunmore, in Virginia, and sought to reach the frontier by way of Maryland and Pennsylvania, being commissioned a lieutenant colonel in preparation for the movement. Suspicion about his "diabolical scheme" had surfaced, however, and Connolly was arrested in November at Hagerstown, Maryland; in January 1776 he was sent to Philadelphia for imprisonment; he remained there, with an occasional parole, until 1780 when he sought once more to revive his visionary undertaking but though this worried Washington and George Rogers Clark to some extent, it failed, as did his health. He was captured with Cornwallis at Yorktown, released in 1782 to go to England, the next year publishing his *Narrative of the Transactions, Imprisonment, and Sufferings of John Connolly, an Am. Loyalist...* He went to Quebec in 1787 and the next year to Detroit as lieutenant governor. While there he plotted to initiate an independence movement for Kentucky. He went to Louisville supplied with funds by Lord Dorchester, governor of Canada and the offer of British troops and equipment in order to open the Mississippi "at the price of Kentucky's allegiance to Britain." He was unsuccessful. He returned to Canada and died at Montreal. Washington had once found Connolly "a very intelligent, sensible man," and Patrick Henry also commended him.

"Although he was devious and sometimes self-seeking, he was consistantly loyal to his convictions," and to his own interests.

Thwaites/Kellogg, *The Revolution on the Upper Ohio, 1775-1777,* Madison, Wis. Hist. Soc., 1908; Thwaites, *Dunmore;* DAB.

Cook, James, navigator, explorer (Oct. 27, 1728-Feb. 14, 1779). B. in Marton-in-Cleveland, North Yorkshire, England, at 18 he signed a three-year agreement with a Whitby ship owner and served an apprenticeship on coastal vessels. June 17, 1755 he enlisted in the Royal Navy, shortly becoming a master's mate and within two years secured his master's papers. As master of the *Pembroke* he was present at the surrender of Louisbourg to Amherst in July 1758 and for several years was occupied with navigating, charting and surveying the coasts of eastern Canada and Newfoundland. As a lieutenant in August 1768 he commanded the *Endeavor* on a three-year cruise to the South Pacific on which he explored the coasts of Australia and New Zealand and at length completed a circumnavigation of the globe. From 1772-75 he commanded the *Resolution* and *Adventure* on a voyage which disproved the hypothesis of a vast southern continent (although it did not demonstrate the existence of Antarctica), and made certain South Sea discoveries, but his major contribution to long-term seafaring was his demonstration that citrus juice and other fresh foodstuffs could prevent scurvy, the millenia-old nemesis of long months on sea rations; during this trip no man was lost to the dread affliction. At his return Cook was given navy post rank— that is, of a full captain qualified to command a vessel of more than 20 guns. He was highly honored, admitted as a fellow of the Royal Society and was described as "the first navigator of Europe" by Lord Sandwich, First Lord of the Admiralty. Desiring to seek out a possible Northwest Passage which, if it existed, must lie in high latitudes as recent explorations had indicated, Cook left Plymouth on his third extended voyage in command of the *Resolution* July 12, 1776, reached the Cape of Good Hope where the *Discovery,* his second ship, joined him on November 10, and on his northerly course through Pacific waters became the discoverer of record (although possibly not the actual European discoverer) of Hawaii, which he named the Sandwich Islands. He made the Oregon coast about at the site of the present Newport March 7, 1778, and touched the Washington coast at Cape Flattery, which he named, but missed the Strait of Juan de Fuca because of bad weather, expressing the mistaken conviction that such a waterway never even existed. He touched Vancouver Island, British Columbia, remaining at Nootka Sound for a month, observing among the natives articles which suggested previous contact with whites, probably Spaniards. April 26 the expedition left the sound, being driven by gales from sight of land until they contacted it once again May 1 in Latitude 55° 20' near Bucareli Bay on Prince of Wales Island, the inlet named by Bodega y Quadra in 1775. May 2 and 3 Cook sighted and named Mt. Edgecumbe, also first seen by Bodega y Quadra in 1775, and named the Bay of Islands, northeasterly of Edgecumbe. May 3 a wide inlet was labeled Cross Sound and Mount Fairweather to the north received its current title. May 5 from a distance of 120 miles Mt. St. Elias was sighted, although the Bering expedition had seen it nearly four decades earlier, and the next day Yakutat Bay, or Bering Bay, as Cook called it, was come across. May 10 Cook named Suckling Bay and after two days of thick weather Kayak Island was discovered, and Controller Bay named. Locating Cape Hinchinbrook at the southern tip of Nuchek (Hinchinbrook) Island on May 12, Cook anchored at a cove to the north the following day, later met natives who were unacquainted with firearms but experienced in thievery and possessed a few blue glass beads, probably from Russians. After exploring further into the great inlet and finding it held no passage north, Cook came about, discovered Montague Island, and named the whole waterway he had investigated Prince William Sound after the third son of King George III, and later King William IV. May 21, 1778, Cook reached a headland he called Cape Elizabeth on the southeastern entrance to what is now Cook Inlet. A gale blew the ships southward to Marmot Island and within sight of Afognak and Kodiak islands which, with Cape Douglas beyond he thought all part of the western coast of the inlet. Cook bore north into it but by May 27 he saw the shorelines closing in, because of the strong ebb tides believed he was at the mouth of a river and eventually came about and sailed away, still holding his misapprehension. June 4 Iliamna Volcano was sighted although it was not named by Cook. Shuyak, Afognak and Kodiak islands were coasted and on June 16 Foggy Island, which Bering had called Tumannoi, was raised. On the

19th Cook's vessels passed through the Shumagin group. Natives, working for the Russians as hunters, were met with occasionally, but Cook pressed on by way of the Sanak Islands, passing Unimak with its volcanoes and failing to investigate the pass between Unimak and Akun islands, the best route to the Bering Sea. He managed to cross the Aleutian chain by way of the worst passage of all, between Unalga and Unalaska islands. July 2 the ships stood to sea toward the northeast, following the north shore of the Peninsula until the navigators observed the northern coast of Bristol Bay which Cook named. July 16 they sighted Cape Newenham, southernmost point of the Kuskokwim estuary. After pursuing first a westerly, then a northerly course Cook on August 3 made a landfall at an island he called Sledge (Aziak) from a wooden sledge with bone runners found there, the island west of today's Nome. King Island to the northwest was observed August 7 and the westernmost point of the continent, Cape Prince of Wales rounded August 9, with the coast then bearing to the northeast. After touching briefly on Siberia, the ships ran up the American coast to Icy Cape, midway between Points Hope and Barrow, where floes prevented further progress and confirmed Cook's impression that no ice-free Northwest Passage existed. September 6 he penetrated Norton Sound and named Capes Darby and Denbigh. September 17 the expedition left the sound intending to survey the coast to the south, but shallow water forced it far to sea and consequently sighting of the mouth of the Yukon River and Nunivak Island was missed; he arrived at Unalaska October 2 and the next day dropped anchor for a brief overhaul of the two ships. While there a Russian messenger contacted the Cook party but language difficulties precluded exchange of much information. Cook sent John Ledyard (see entry), a corporal of marines and an adventurous man, with the returning messenger to locate the Russians, obtain what information he could, and invite them to visit the anchorage. Ledyard spent a few days at the Russian settlement at Illiuliuk about where Dutch Harbor is today, and brought back three hunters who conveyed such information as could be transmitted by signs and numerals. On October 14 the Russian commander of the area arrived and a friendly, though limited, interchange resulted. October 26 Cook's two ships left to winter in Hawaii; at Kealakekua Bay in the district of Kona on the west coast of the island of Hawaii Cook was killed by a native, a white monument marking the site today. Cook was married and fathered six children.

Literature abundant; Bancroft, *Alaska;* DCB; DNB; CE.

Cook, Sherburne Friend, demographer (Dec. 31, 1896-Nov. 7, 1974). B. at Springfield, Massachusetts, he was raised in New England, studied for a year in Germany and then at Harvard, interrupting his education with military service in France until 1919 when he returned to Harvard. He had commenced college work as a history major, but switched to biology, earning a master's degree in 1923 and a doctorate in 1925. In 1928 he joined the University of California at Berkeley, retiring as a full professor of physiology in 1964, though recalled for two more years of professorship. Until 1935 his major interest was physiology, including a study of high altitude effects upon human beings and the fossilization of bone. He wrote in 1935 about "Diseases of the Indians of Lower California in the Eighteenth Century" (published in *California and Western Medicine,* Vol. 43, No. 6), and followed that with historical studies of disease and its treatment in California and Mexico; his prolific writing and extensive researches into California pre-Conquest demographics developed thereafter. The *Handbook of North American Indians,* Vol. 8, *California,* lists 22 entries of Cook's published works as references. He became a "distinguished and frequent contributor to the university's Ibero-Americana series," beginning with *Population Trends Among the California Mission Indians* (17; 1940), and continuing with, among other titles, *The Conflict Between the California Indians and White Civilization* (I, "The Indian Versus the Spanish Mission"; II, "The Physical and Demographic Reaction of the Nonmission Indians in Colonial and Provincial California"; III, "The American Invasion 1848-1870," and IV, "Trends in Marriage and Divorce Since 1850," all published in 1943; these were collected in book form in 1976 by the University of California Press, published under the original overall title; *The Aboriginal Population of the San Joaquin Valley, California* (1955); *The Epidemic of 1830-1833 in California and Oregon* (1955); *The Aboriginal Population of the North Coast of California* (1956); *Colonial Expeditions to the Interior of California: Central Valley, 1800-1820* (1960); *Expeditions to the Interior of California: Central Valley, 1820-1840* (1962), and *The Population of the Califor-*

nia Indians 1769-1970 (1976), published posthumously with a foreword by Robert F. Heizer and Woodrow Borah. Cook became a foremost student of the demography of California Indians, arriving at a probable pre-Conquest population total of more than 300,000, as compared with Kroeber's low estimate in 1925 of 125,000, and Cook's figure is largely accepted today. Cook "brought to his studies a most unusual breadth and competence in many different areas of science, anthropology, and history...His ingenuity in finding ways around barriers of apparent lack of direct evidence continually impressed colleagues. Many of his conclusions...have been verified by other scholars using techniques developed later." Heizer and Borah believed that his final volume "will stand for a long time to come as the most authoritative analysis of native California demography in the period since discovery to the present decade." Cook died near Monterey, California, at 77, still "reaching out in new directions" with his meticulous, innovative research.

Robert F. Heizer, Woodrow Borah, in *The Population of the California Indians 1769-1970,* xi-xiii; HNAI, 8, 728.

Coolidge, Dane, naturalist, writer (Mar. 24, 1873-Aug. 8, 1940). B. at Natick, Massachusetts, he was graduated from Stanford University in 1898 and studied at Harvard through 1899. A trained naturalist he collected mammals in Nevada for Stanford in the summer of 1895, for the British Museum in Lower California in the summer of 1896; for the U.S. Biological Survey in Southern California in the summer of 1897; was a field collector of live animals, birds and reptiles in California for the National Zoological Park in 1898; in 1899 in Arizona and California for the New York Zoological Park, and was a field collector of live mammals in Italy and France in 1900 for the U.S. National Museum. Coolidge also was a photographer. He authored books beginning in 1915 with *The Desert Trail,* following with about a novel a year. In 1930 with his wife, the former Mary E.B. Roberts, he wrote *The Navajo Indians.* He also wrote *Fighting Men of the West* (1932), a work supposedly of nonfiction which Ramon Adams found almost the reverse; *Texas Cowboys* (1937); *Arizona Cowboys* (1938), which has a chapter on the Pleasant Valley War; *Old California Cowboys* (1939), and *Death Valley Prospectors* (1939). He and Mary Coolidge also wrote *The Last of the Seris,* about the Mexico Indians of that name on Tiburon Island and the adjacent shore of Sonora (1939). Coolidge wrote *Gringo Gold: A Story of Joaquin Murieta, the Bandit* (1939), a novel on Murieta's life, Adams finding that "as history it is unreliable." Coolidge lived at Berkeley, California.

Who Was Who; Ramon F. Adams, *Six-Guns and Saddle Leather*, Norman, Univ. of Okla. Press, 1969; info. from E.F. (Ted) Mains.

Cordero y Bustamente, Antonio, military officer (1753-Mar. 1823). B. at Cádiz, Spain, he entered as a cadet of 14 the Zamora Regiment and three years later accompanied it to Mexico, probably as a *subteniente,* or second lieutenant. Promotion was swift and by 1773, already a captain he commanded the presidios of Janos and San Benaventura in the north of Mexico. As a lieutenant colonel he was commandant inspector of troops in the Interior Provinces under Brigadier General Pedro de Nava who was deeply concerned with controlling the Apache menace to the north, and encouraged his officers to foster Apache friendship and learn all they could of these Indians, including the difficult language, from those who elected to settle peacefully near the presidios. Cordero "fought the savages for the space of many years [and] knew their language, and had dealings and contacts with them." In 1785 he led an expedition in pursuit of hostiles as far as the Santa Rita copper country of southern New Mexico. He commanded other operations, including one to reopen the road from Arizpe, Sonora, to Santa Fe, New Mexico. In 1796 he completed an important paper on the Apaches, which as the most knowledgeable and possibly intelligent frontier officer of the time he was directed by Nava to draft. "No other [officer] could speak like him [on the subject] with such aptitude and exactness." His work is thorough and so far as his knowledge permitted, accurate, going into all aspects of Apache culture known to him or to his informants. Following the valuable ethnological first portion, the manuscript includes what was then known to the Spanish of the various bands and divisions of the people [footnoting by Matson and Schroeder supplies much additional information]. Cordero conceded that the Apaches were not entirely to blame for the "cruel and bloody war" which then engaged them with the Spanish, adding that current Spanish efforts did not "aspire to the destruction or slavery of

these savages, but...their happiness by the most efficacious means," policies unfortunately not to be long-lived. In 1796 Cordero was named interim governor of Texas, but did not immediately assume that post because he also was named governor of Coahuila; it was probably his impending move that led Nava to request that "most expert of all his officers" to assemble the paper as a guide to those charged with dealing with the several Indian groups, and assistance to "authorities who wrestled with issues of policy" involving them. Cordero was interim governor of Coahuila from March 26, 1797, to December 1798 when he became governor, a position he held periodically until 1817. He was appointed acting governor of Texas from October 1805 until 1809, retaining meanwhile the titular governorship of Coahuila, returning to that province in 1810. In Texas he dealt with troublesome boundary questions, encouraged friendly relations with powerful Indian tribes and supported Spanish immigration into that territory. He was heavily involved, initially as a royalist, in the insurrection turmoil of 1811 and after, became a Brigadier General in 1813, commanding at times in Sonora and Sinaloa. Eventually he assumed command of the Internal Provinces of the West. He at first refused to accept Iturbide's Plan of Iguala, but in Chihuahua City "circumstances" forced him to change his mind, accept it, and later to recognize Iturbide as emperor of Mexico. He went to Mexico City, was honored and commissioned a Field Marshal in December 1822, but resigned March 6, 1823, possibly for reasons of health, and a few days later died in Durango. He left a manuscript on the Comanche Indians which probably has not been translated into English for publication.

Porrua; José Cortés, *Views from the Apache Frontier: Report on the Northern Provinces of New Spain,* Norman, Univ. of Okla. Press, 1989; Daniel S. Matson, Albert H. Schroeder, eds., "Cordero's Description of the Apache—1796," *New Mexico Historical Review,* Vol. XXXII, No. 4 (Oct. 1957), 335-56; HT.

Corkran, David Hudson Jr., historian (May 11, 1902-Dec. 1991). The son of a Protestant minister, Corkran was graduated from Wesleyan University, Middletown, Connecticut, in 1923, earned a master's degree at Harvard in 1926 and spent most of his professional life as a high school and university teacher of English and history. He was a demonstration teacher in 1938 at the U.S. Indian Bureau summer school at Chilocco, Oklahoma, held a Newberry Library fellowship in 1962 and received American Philosophical Society grants in 1964 and 1966. Corkran published two superior books on Indian history: *The Cherokee Frontier, 1740-1762* (1962), and *The Creek Frontier, 1540-1783* (1967). Late in life he was working on a manuscript entitled, *American Indian in the Colonial Period.* He was married and fathered a daughter and three sons. The place of his death is not reported.

Contemporary Authors; info. from Harvard Univ., Alumni Rec. Off., Mar. 20, 1992.

Cortés y de Olarte, José María, military officer (c. 1770-Jan. 4, 1811). B. at Tarifa, southern Spain, he enlisted in the Regiment of Toledo at 15 and was commissioned a second lieutenant in the Royal Corps of Engineers in January 1789. In May 1794 he became a first lieutenant, posted to Mexico's Interior Provinces where he served three and one-half years, part of the time at Janos Presidio, "one of the liveliest hubs of interaction with Apaches." Cortés, who throughout his New World service had apparently made good use of archives he was stationed near, also plumbed oral resources he came across. At Janos, for exmple, the chaplain was the Franciscan Francisco Atanasio Domínguez who had been the actual leader of the so-called Escalante Expedition of 1776 and who had much to tell Cortés of peoples beyond the northern frontier. Cortés's "immediate fascination," however, was with the Apaches, many of whom settled from time to time near Janos. Commandant General of the Interior Provinces, Pedro de Nava, encouraged his officers to learn all they could of the militant tribe, and Cortés apparently made the most of his opportunities. By May 3, 1799, Cortés had completed his remarkable *Memorias sobre las provincias del norte de Nueva España,* a manuscript of 142 folios, or pages. Although parts have been used by an occasional scholar writing of the Borderlands frontier, it was not published in its entirety until Elizabeth A.H. John came across a copy in the British Museum Spanish collection, realized its value and traced down the various surviving manuscript copies. The earliest of these and thus presumably the most reliable, was translated by John Wheat, official translator of the Bexar Archives, University of Texas, and the result published in 1989 in a work edited by John. The first part, a description of the Interior Provinces, includes a section on the presidios and the quality of troops. In a section on "Indians at War" he

insists that the Apaches desired peace more than war, adding that "it is no inconstancy to break the peace when agreements have been breached," and that Spanish failure to abide by agreements had sometimes been the cause of hostilities. "If the Indians had a defender who could represent their rights on the basis of natural law, an impartial judge could soon see that every charge we might make against them would be offset by as many crimes committed by our side," which reflected a novel attitude for an officer of Spain at that time. His comments on general strategy for the protection of Spain's northernmost American territories are those of an eager, intelligent, but relatively inexperienced junior officer, but his analysis of the ultimate threat to Spain as he saw it, by a growing and expanding United States reveals prescience of a high order and, in many cases, his forebodings eventually were confirmed. Most interesting, from a frontier viewpoint, is the second section of Cortés's report, on the Apache Indians with whom he had had some contact and acquired rather mature understandings. In these passages he followed closely the 1796 report of Lieutenant Colonel Antonio Cordero y Bustamente (see entry), inspector general of the Interior Provinces. His discussion of an elaborate funeral he attended had new and somewhat controversial observations, ethnologists and historians offering varied possible interpretations of them. Yet they remain virtually unique in the literature. The concluding third portion of the report summarizes Spanish understanding of the many tribes beyond the perimeters of their holdings. In 1802 Cortés became a captain and, at his request, was posted to Cádiz, in Spain. In March 1805 he became a lieutenant colonel and in November 1807 was named sergeant major of brigade and one of the five-member Superior Council of Royal Engineers, charged with evaluating military construction in Europe and the Indies. In June 1809 he married Catalina Ximénez Bretón y Landa. He was injured in a fall, and following a long period of recuperation he and his wife gained permission to seek treatment at Cartagena, but pirates captured them enroute there by sea and landed them destitute on the North African coast. Eventually they reached Murcía, near Cartagena, where treatment proved ineffective and where Cortés died. No record has been found of the fate of his wife and child.

José Cortés, *Views from the Apache Frontier: Report on the Northern Provinces of New Spain,* ed. by Elizabeth A.H. John, trans. by John Wheat, Norman,

Univ. of Okla. Press, 1989; Janet R. Fireman, *The Spanish Royal Corps of Engineers in the Western Borderlands: Instrument of Bourbon Reform 1764 to 1815,* Glendale, Ca., Arthur H. Clark Co., 1977.

Cortina(s), Juan Nepomuceno (Cheno), irregular (May 16, 1824-Oct. 30. 1894). B. at Camargo, Tamaulipas, Mexico, of good family he was unlettered because he refused to go to school, but became a "freebooter...the champion and idol of the humble Mexicans as well as the high born living on both sides of the Rio Grande." He served under Mariano Arista in the Mexican War in the opening minor engagements of Palo Alto and Resaca de la Palma. Following the war he became noted as a rustler, dealer in stolen stock on both sides of the border and while often indicted, was never tried, let alone convicted. He inspired the so-called Cortina Wars which in effect opened when Cortina forcibly extracted Mexican prisoners from American jails and became a "defender" of Mexican rights. September 28, 1859, he and half a hundred of his men captured Brownsville, Texas, was persuaded to withdraw by influential Mexicans, but from his mother's ranch at Santa Rita, eight miles upriver from Brownsville, two days later issued a sweeping proclamation, declaring he was a Texas citizen, defending rights and property of Mexicans, that he hoped Anglos threatening those rights would be properly punished by Texans, making it unnecessary for him to punish them. He crossed the river then into Mexico until his lieutenant, Tomás Cabrera, was jailed at Brownsville. After a threat failed to free the prisoner, Cortina collected a force at Santa Rita again, easily repulsed a combined attack by Anglos and militia from Matamoros, and seized control of the region around Brownsville. November 10, 1859, Captain W.C. Tobin and a force of Texas Rangers "who were no credit to the service," reached Brownsville, hanged Cabrera, and launched an attack on Cortina, being routed as completely as the earlier element had been, Cortina's prestige soaring anew. Brigadier General David Twiggs (see entry), commanding the Department of Texas, sent troops to the area, Fort Brown at Brownsville was reoccupied by the military, and Major Samuel Heintzelman (see entry), as commanding officer acted swiftly. December 14 with 165 regulars and 120 Texas Rangers he advanced against Cortina's force of some 350 men; a December 27 battle at Rio Grande City routed Cortina, his men abandoning

their equipment and crossing the river into Mexico, their losses said to be about 60 men killed for no American losses. Cortina, at a river pocket called La Bolsa, attempted to capture the steamboat *Ranchero,* belonging to Richard King and Mifflin Kenedy, prominent ranchers, but February 4, 1860, John S. Ford (see entry) and a Ranger force routed Cortina anew. Colonel Robert E. Lee, now commanding the Department, was instructed to demand that Mexico break up Cortina's bands, and if that were not done, to pursue marauders into Mexico. Lee moved into the lower Rio Grande Valley and peace was hastily restored, the Cortina "Wars" concluded. Cortina, however, made one additional sally into Texas, but was defeated and returned once more to Mexico. During the American Civil War Cortina alternately favored Confederate and Union forces, though in a minor way. He became governor of Tamaulipas, favoring Juarez, later the Emperor, then Juarez again, being recognized as leader of the region by Benito Juarez since it was a rich commercial area and Juarez needed the income from it. Cortina apparently continued cattle rustling on the side, however, and Mexico caused him to be taken into custody in July 1875. He never regained power and was paroled to the vicinity of Mexico City for the rest of his life. He was buried with full military honors at the Panteón de Dolores, in Mexico City.

HT; Clarence C. Clendenen, *Blood on the Border: The United States Army and the Mexican Irregulars,* N.Y., The Macmillan Co., 1969; M.L. Crimmins, "The Cortina Trouble in 1859 and 1860," *Frontier Times,* Vol. 17, No. 3 (Dec. 1939), 99-101.

Courville, Cyril Brian, physician, researcher (Feb. 19, 1900-Mar. 22, 1968). B. in Michigan, he became a medical doctor, held responsible positions on various fronts at Los Angeles, was a managing editor of the *Bulletin of the Los Angeles Neurological Society,* and devoted much research time to study of cranial injuries among North American and early California Indians. This led him to seriously collect Indian weaponry designed for skull-assaulting purposes, and skulls and photographs of skulls exhibiting effects of flint weaponry, as well as impact results of war club, tomahawk, and bludgeoning implements of all kinds. Some of his conclusions were very interesting. He wrote that a "feature of arrow wounds of the skull which has had considerable misinterpretation in the past is the possible lethality of such wounds. Observers are usually over-impressed with the size of the arrowhead and the possible depth of its penetration," concluding that the wound must have been fatal. "Actually it is very doubtful that such wounds in and of themselves were often fatal, unless a large intracranial or extracranial blood vessel was interrupted and the patient bled to death. Meningitis or other intracranial infections may have caused the death of some of those who survived the immediate impact. But it is also possible that other victims may have survived such a wound for some time." His publications included photographs of many skulls with flint points—arrowheads, spear points or atlatl projectiles—deeply buried in a skull whose bone has grown about the incision, plainly indicating that the victim long survived such an impact. North American Indians made little consistent effort to protect the head from injury, the exceptions being some of the Mexican peoples; the Tlingit and Haida Indians of the northwest coast who, according to Cook, wore "helmets [of wood] with peculiarly shaped visors," probably adapted from the Japanese who may have visited that coast; the Mohawks of the northeast and possibly some of the Pueblos. Weaponry designed for cranial effect included the tomahawk which, although developed crudely by early Indians was supplied in manufactured form in abundance by British and French fur-seekers; war clubs, the most primitive and durable of such weapons, used very widely; stone-headed warclubs, or maces, used by the Sioux and many other tribes and retained to the very end of the Indian wars, and native copper celts and axes. Also, as Courville pointed out, it is evident from Indian legends and tales that "in addition to formal weapons, anything they could lay their hands on was utilized to crack skulls and spill brains when the occasion demanded." The whites naturally adopted the Indian cranial weaponry, particularly the tomahawk, and stone weaponry was used by the native side to the very end of the Indian wars. Captain George Daniel Wallace (see entry) was killed at Wounded Knee December 29, 1890. He had entered a tepee searching for arms when firing began and his body was found at its entrance, his revolver with every chamber discharged and his head crushed in front and back by stone battle-axes, this at the virtual conclusion of the centuries-old conflict for the continent. The worst injury Dr. Courville ever came across, he said, was a New Mexico

skull with a great hole and an axe head still imbedded in it. Recovery was possible in certain cases from what would seem to have been fatal wounds. "It is true that medical science was not then so far advanced," he said, "nor were first aid facilities so available as now. But, on the other hand, neither were weapons so powerful and deadly, and it is surprising what wounds a victim could survive. Arrow penetrations into the skull were not always fatal nor, for that matter, were even bullet wounds." He had a skull with a bit of flattened lead in a depression in the rear of it. It was caused by a spent lead bullet that inflicted an actual dent in the skull but did not penetrate it, and the condition of the surrounding bone indicated that the wound healed and the victim long survived it. Courville died at Glendale, California, and was buried there. He was marrried and was survived by his widow.

Author interview with Courville, 1957; Courville, "Cranial Injuries Among the Indians of North America: A Preliminary Report," *Bulletin of the Los Angeles Neurological Society,* Vol. 13, No. 4 (Dec. 1948), 181-219; Courville, "Cranial Injuries Among the Early Indians of California," *Bulletin of the Los Angeles Neurological Society,* Vol. 17, No. 4 (Dec. 1952), 137-62; Courville death cert.

Couts, Cave Johnson, military officer, pioneer (Nov. 11, 1821-June 10, 1874). B. at Springfield, Tennessee, he was a nephew of Cave Johnson who served seven terms as Congressman and was postmaster general under Polk; through his influence Couts received an appointment to West Point. He was commissioned a brevet second lieutenant of the Regiment of Riflemen July 1, 1843; when the Riflemen reverted to the 2nd Dragoons Couts became a brevet second lieutenant of that organization April 4, 1844, a second lieutenant of the 1st Dragoons March 31, 1845 and a first lieutenant February 16, 1845. He served in the Mexican War and in July 1848, in command of Company A participated in a march to California under Captain (brevet major) Lawrence Pike Graham. The column included about 500 men, 275 of them military personnel. It departed from Monterrey, Chihuahua, early in September, went by way of Janos, Sonora; Tubac, and reached Tucson, Arizona, late in October and the Colorado River November 22, according to Couts's diary, the best summary of the march. He not only was a writer of vivid prose but "an idealist of strong character." In his journal he was critical of his commanding officer whose liquor-lubricated daily demeanor depended upon whether he was "drunk or very drunk." The command reached Warner's Ranch December 29 and went on to Los Angeles. Couts and a detachment left San Diego September 14, 1849 as escort to the Bartlett Boundary Commission and to Second Lieutenant Amiel Whipple, engaged in surveying the region of the confluence of the Gila and Colorado rivers. Here Couts established the short-lived Camp Calhoun October 2, 1849, the forerunner of Fort Yuma which came into being February 29, 1852. During his time on the river he "greatly aided the worn-out and hungry gold seekers" enroute to the mining camps. Couts, wrote Bancroft, "does not mention the purchase of any [Yuma] ferry, but many pioneers remember crossing the river on his ferry," the historian giving details of the craft, its construction and charges for transporting men and animals across the Colorado. Couts left Yuma around December 1 and returned to the coast. While still an army officer he became friendly with San Diego Mayor Joshua H. Bean (see entry), and with Bean came into legal difficulties over an unsuccessful attempt to seize the town hall. In late January 1851 he was tried by General Court-Martial at San Francisco, charged with gambling and with "conduct prejudicial to good order and military discipline" for allegedly authoring an unsigned letter in the *Alta California* accusing another West Point officer, Captain Justus McKinstry of attempting to fix a court which was trying a swindling charge; Couts was freed on both through insufficient evidence. Back in San Diego he wed Ysidora Bandini April 5, 1851. She was a daughter of Juan Bandini, another of whose daughters, Arcadia, married Abel Stearns (see entry); thus Couts and the noted Stearns became brothers-in-law. As a wedding gift Stearns had presented Ysidora the square-league Rancho Guajome near Mission San Luis Rey, five miles east of Oceanside, and Couts made a successful ranch out of what had been a wasteland. He resigned from the army October 9, 1851. The next year he drove 800 cattle and 100 horses north, selling the herd July 24 for $20 a head a San Joaquin City, a now-vanished community at the confluence of the San Joaquin and Stanislaus rivers near the present Modesto. When Bean became a major general of the state militia he bestowed upon Couts the rank of colonel. Bean presided over the trial in January 1852 of a Cupeño Indian, Juan Antonio Garra, charged with organizing an uprising in

which there had been casualties on both sides. Bean named Couts judge advocate (or prosecutor), while McKinstry defended Garra. The Indian was found guilty and executed. In the following summer Couts was jury foreman for the trial of three desperadoes from the mining camps who had wandered south to San Diego; he recommended death for the leader, "Yankee Jim" Robinson, who was hanged while the other two served brief prison terms. Couts held various public positions: judge for San Diego County, probate court service, justice of the peace at San Luis Rey and sub-agent for the San Luis Rey Indians. From 1856 he also periodically held the office of "judge of the plains," regulating and overseeing livestock matters. In 1855 Couts was tried—and acquitted on a technicality—for manslaughter after beating to death an Indian with a rawhide reata. February 6, 1865, he shot one, Juan Mendoza, who had threatened to kill Couts as he allegedly had slain others before. October 10, 1866, Couts was tried, and acquitted the following day. He was involved in a further shooting affair in 1870. Although he wounded his opponent the results were not fatal and the charges were dropped. Couts died at 53 at the Horton House, San Diego, of an aneurism. Ysidora Couts "quite successfully" managed the ranch at San Luis Rey thereafter.

Heitman; Cullum; Henry F. Dobyns, ed., *Hepah California! The Journal of Cave Johnson Couts...1848-1849,* Tucson, Az. Pioneers Hist. Soc., 1961; Bancroft, *California* V, 522-23, VII, 458-59n., *Arizona and New Mexico,* 486-87 and n.; HNAI, 8, 110, 589; Ray Brandes, *Frontier Military Posts of Arizona,* Globe, Dale Stuart King, Pub., 1960; James M. Jensen, "Cattle Drives from the Ranchos to the Gold Fields of Arizona," *Arizona and the West,* Vol. 2, No. 4 (Winter 1960), 345-50, Vol. 4, No. 4 (Winter 1964), 393-94; Richard J. Coyer, "On Both Sides of the Law," *True West,* Vol. 36, No. 12 (Dec. 1989), 40-43; *History of San Bernardino County, California...,* San Francisco, Wallace W. Elliott & Co., 1883, 196-97; info. from Thomas W. Patterson, Riverside, Ca.

Cox, Breezy, rodeo star (Apr. 29, 1900-Jan. 21, 1960). B. as Lionel Bert Cox at Sonora, Texas, his father, George W. Cox, took the family to Eddy County, New Mexico, when Breezy was 2. The boy grew up on a horse and cattle ranch and as a young man drifted into rodeo work. Bronc riding was one of his best events. In 1925 he won the North American Bucking Horse championship at the Calgary (Alberta) Stampede; the next year at the same rodeo he won the North American Calf Roping title, "thus proving his dexterity in a pair of events that many purists feel should be the criteria in determining a positive all-around cowboy." He also was a bulldogger of competence. The author saw Breezy make a fine ride at a Chicago rodeo c. 1926. In 1931 at Lordsburg, New Mexico he made what seemed then a sensational performance: every rodeo devotee knows that when riding a bucking horse the thing is to keep one's eyes on the animal's ears, for its head-movements signal which way it is going to jump; on this occasion Breezy came out of the chute with his own face turned so that he was looking back over his right shoulder and completed the entire ride in this manner, showing his disdain for what turned out to be a very good bucking horse. "Breezy was fun to travel with. He told a good story, played...practical jokes...and would take a drink now and then." His brother-in-law, Carl Arnold, once remarked that Breezy would "tell you what he was going to do and sound like he was bragging. Then he'd go out and do it...and more." Like some of his rollicking fellows, Breezy on occasion came to cross-purposes with the law, but never to any particular disadvantage. In his later life he became a trainer of thoroughbred race horses and once was lightly fined by racing stewards for interfering with a race on his lead mule. He suddenly collapsed and died at the Rillito Track at Tucson, Arizona. At the time of his death his home was at Pinetop, Arizona. He was accepted into the National Cowboy Hall of Fame at Oklahom City in 1982. Cox was married and fathered a son.

Info. from the Natl. Cowboy Hall of Fame; Ed Gallardo, Tucson, *Arizona Daily Star*, Jan. 22, 1960; personal recollections of the author.

Coxe, William, historian (1747-1828) Described by Pierce as a "British traveller, historian and cleric," he became an authority on Russian explorations in the North Pacific. He was the son of a physician to the Royal household, and was educated at Eton and Cambridge. In 1771 he took holy orders and traveled in Europe as tutor and companion to the wealthy, then accepted church posts in England, becoming in 1804 archdeacon of Wiltshire. He wrote memoirs of statesmen and other noted Britons and a journey to Russia in 1778 and another in 1785-86 led to his *Account of the Russian Discoveries between Asia and America* (1780) and *A Comparitive View of the Russian Discoveries with those made*

by Captain Cook and Clerke (1787), among other books not related to Pacific discoveries. His Russian works were based partly on Russian sources, and largely on German translations; in Russia Coxe consulted with G.F. Muller, famed historian, and others, and endeavored to check his findings with Russian primary sources where possible. He secured some previously unpublished material. A fourth edition of his *Russian Discoveries* in 1803 brought the voyages up to 1792 and "added translations of Steller's (see entry) narrative of Bering's expedition, and the accounts of Shelikhov and several other voyagers," Coxe presenting them in English for the first time, with charts and maps. In 1818 Coxe became blind, but his "remarkable memory" enabled him to continue scholarly work for the last decade of his life.

Pierce, *Russian America: A Biographical Dictionary*.

Coyuntura (Kin-o-tera), Chiricahua Apache (d. Feb. 19, 1861). A younger brother of Cochise (1810-1874), Coyuntura first comes into view when he drew rations in the fall of 1843 at Janos, Chihuahua, with other Chokonen, a band of the central Chiricahuas. He may have taken part in a truce talk with Sonoran (Mexican) officials the following March, and again March 9, 1857, at Fronteras, Sonora, when he was accompanied by his wife, Yones, who was fluent in Spanish. By that time Coyuntura's reputation was "high among the Chiricahuas," noted Sweeney, quoting a student of the times that the subchief was "never known to go out on an expedition...without bringing back stock...He was more dreaded in Sonora than the captain of any other band of Apaches." February 4, 1861, Coyuntura accompanied Cochise to the fateful Apache Pass meeting with Second Lieutenant George N. Bascom, the chief bringing his wife, two of his children, his brother, Coyuntura, and two or three other warriors believed to have been Cochise's nephews; obviously he was anticipating no trouble (see Cochise entry for details of the meeting). When a blowup came, Cochise with his knife slit the front of the tent and escaped, while Coyuntura dove through the rear of the shelter but tripped and fell and was captured by soldiers. One warrior was killed and the other Indians captured. On February 18 the Apache-mutilated bodies of four captured whites were found and Bascom's three male captives and three White Mountain Apaches seized earlier by Bernard

John Dowling Irwin (see entry) all were executed in reprisal by hanging. One of Bascom's three was Coyuntura and was probably he who "went to the gallows dancing and singing, saying that he was satisfied as he had killed two Mexicans in the last month." His death in such a manner deeply distressed Cochise who, in partial revenge, launched his years-long war against Americans as a result. One of Coyuntura's sons apparently was Chie (see entry) who had a major role in bringing peace many years later.

Edwin R. Sweeney, *Cochise: Chiricahua Apache Chief,* Norman, Univ. of Okla. Press, 1991.

Crabtree, Isaac, Indian killer (fl. 1774). Crabtree was a sort of desperado, typical of many frontiersmen of the time, for whom killing Indians was an avocation bordering upon obsession. Major Arthur Campbell, in a letter to Colonel William Preston of about June 20, 1774, reported on the "rash killing of a Cherokee on Wattaugo," a branch of the Holston River, the incident greatly alarming the settlers. "One Crabtree is generally suspected to be the Principal, in the late dispatching of Cherokee Billey," who was a relative of a powerful Chief, Oconastota (see entry). Campbell added, however, that "it would be easier to find 200 men to screen [Crabtree] from the Law, than ten to bring him to Justice." Crabtree, he added, also was guilty of various robberies. In a second letter in a day or two Campbell reported that in spite of all that decent folks could do to "prevent a calamity," that is, an Indian strike of revenge, "it appears that Crabtree and a few mislead followers, will frustrate all we can do." Over on the Nolichucky River, an eastern affluent of the Holston, he heard of two or three Indians and took out after them, but found to his dismay they numbered 37 warriors and "upon this intelligence, he departed the place, with great precipitation." Campbell added, "Yet still restless he went down the River a few days ago to make another attempt." Campbell believed most of the people disapproved of Crabtree's activities, however inconsistent they had been "in avowing they would screen him from Justice." Colonel William Christian wrote Preston June 22 that he had thought to hire Crabtree to seek out wilderness surveyors, warn them of imminent Indian hostility, "and if he did that business well, it might serve to atone for his guilt in killing the Cherokee." Too many disreputable men were eager for an Indian war, he thought. Campbell in another letter to Preston expressed the belief that

"the Cherokees would willingly avoid a War with us, except some repeated affront from Crabtree, provokes them to it." In July Campbell wrote that "Crabtree is become a very insolent person; but I believe his timidity, on dangerous attempts, will mostly get the better of his ferocity." Apparently there were various attempts made to arrest Crabtree, but by one ruse or another he eluded them. Lord Dunmore, governor of Virginia, in December 1774 said he had issued by proclamation a 100-pound reward for Crabtree's apprehension, added to 50 pounds offered by a magistrate in the case, "but both have been fruitless." Thwaites concluded that Crabtree's "conduct illustrates the darker passions of border life, and the brutality of a certain class of backwoodsmen."

Thwaites, *Dunmore.*

Cracroft, Charles, military officer (d. 1824). B. near Frederick, Maryland, he lived near Harper's Ferry until he moved west in 1774, settling near Van Buren, Washington County, Pennsylvania. In 1779 he served as major under Daniel Brodhead. In 1781 he volunteered to serve under George Rogers Clark, again as major. He was captured August 24, 1781, with Lochry's doomed detachment, and was imprisoned at Quebec until the end of the Revolutionary War. He died on his farm in Pennsylvania.

Thwaites/Kellogg, *The Revolution on the Upper Ohio, 1775-1777,* Madison, Wis. Hist. Soc., 1908, 75-77; Consul W. Butterfield, *History of the Girtys,* Cincinnati, Robert Clarke Co., 1890, 1950.

Crocker, Captain, fur trader (fl. 1798-1803). On August 25, 1798, he cleared Boston for the Northwest Coast with the *Hancock* and by mid-April 1799 was trading in Prince William Sound, Alaska. June 1 while at Sitka Sound there was a mutiny aboard and 13 men by their own request were put ashore, though six later returned to the ship. The remainder may have lived with the Kolosh (Tlingit) Indians, an Athapascan people inhabiting that part of the coast. In 1801 Crocker left Boston with the *Jenny,* by 1802 was at Sitka Sound again and according to a Russian source, Fedor Shemelin writing in 1816, six men fled Crocker's ship and disappeared among the natives. Crocker reached Boston again after visiting Canton and London, on September 16, 1803. Deserters from the *Hancock* or perhaps those from the *Jenny,* or possibly from both vessels were probable participants in the destruction of the Russian fort near Sitka in June 1802. When Henry Barber (see entry) arrived at Sitka June 28, shortly after the massacre of the Russian personnel and others there, three Americans who said they had deserted from the *Jenny,* and later three others came aboard which, Barber reported, "vexed me a good deal, knowing nothing of the characters of the above men, and their having deserted from their ship and residing with the Indians had a very bad appearance." Pierce believed the six were of the *Hancock,* not the *Jenny,* but Shemelin's statement leaves the matter in some doubt. There is no report on what happened to the six who joined Barber.

Pierce, *Russian America: A Biographical Dictionary.*

Crosby, Robert Anderson (Bob), rodeo cowboy (Feb. 27, 1897-Oct. 20, 1947). From the Cross B Ranch near Kenna, midway between Roswell and Clovis, New Mexico, Crosby, a cowboy from childhood, became one of the premier rodeo stars of the 1920s and 1930s. He was adept at most cowboy sports, but shone at steer and calf roping, and was competent as a bulldogger and bronc rider. He was the only rider of his era who won the Roosevelt Trophy three times (in 1925, 1927 and 1928) and therefore got to keep it. The trophy was awarded by the Roosevelt Hotel of New York City to the cowboy who won the highest total points at the two greatest American rodeos: the Cheyenne Frontier Days and the Pendleton (Oregon) Round-Up. Crosby was "a rough, tough man who was either well liked or thoroughly disliked," who, in a period of very slender purses, won overall $150,000, and had a high-spirited, exuberant time doing it despite frequently competing with injuries that would have hospitalized anyone else. One famous legend is that in an arena accident he broke his leg, gangrene developed, the doctors wanted to amputate but he wouldn't let them, packed cow manure around the limb which apparently drew out the poison. He again broke the leg at a Prescott Rodeo, refused to let doctors pin the bone, went to the Mayo Clinic at Rochester, Minnesota, where amputation was advised and Crosby hobbled out and continued to have trouble with the leg, despite his cowboy cures, until a doctor at Omaha operated and eventually cured him. In a Salt Lake rodeo while bulldogging, a steer ran its horn up Crosby's nostril and loosened the eyeball, but as it did not sever the optic

nerve, he did not lose the eye, showing up bandaged the next day and continuing to compete, becoming the top money winner at the show. "Those who disliked Crosby based their criticisms on his 'fighting' tendencies and on his harsh treatment of animals," on which he was tough as on himself. His horses were well trained but his rough handling of them irritated many. Crosby's finest arena love and most noted accomplishments were in roping, he and other top ropers sometimes staging memorable multi-animal match contests, which Crosby generally won. Crosby was an abstemious man who did not use alcohol, tobacco or profanity. He was married once, to Thelma Jones. They met when Thelma doused Crosby with a bucket of water to halt a series of pranks and he doused her in a spring to retaliate. "I guess there were times when he wished he had drowned me, and there were times when I could have killed him," Thelma conceded, "but it was a very happy marrige!" Crosby was killed when the jeep he was driving missed a bridge (since named for him) over a deep arroyo called Acme Draw in eastern New Mexico. He was aged 50. He was elected an honoree of the National Rodeo Hall of Fame where are exhibited the Roosevelt Trophy he won to keep and his battered old black hat that he always wore for luck after winning his first Roosevelt Trophy with it on his head. He was survived by his wife, a daughter and a son.

Thelma Crosby, Eve Ball, *Bob Crosby: World Champion Cowboy,* Clarendon (Tex.) Press, 1966; REAW, pp. 1029-30; info. from the Natl. Cowboy Hall of Fame.

Croxen, Fred W., pioneer (Oct. 17, 1887-Sept. 25, 1977). B. at Atalissa, Iowa, he migrated to Nevada and in 1910 to Arizona where he was employed out of Flagstaff for 19 years as a forest ranger in the Tonto and Coconino National Forests. In 1921 he was the ranger on the Bly District of the Coconino Forest. Charles Quayle, an ex-convict on parole "had made trouble" for the ranger and threats against him, Croxen informing his superintendent and the sheriff of the situation. While performing his duties, Croxen and Quayle got into a shooting match and Croxen killed Quayle; a coroner's jury brought in a verdict of justifiable homicide. The case was dismissed and Mrs. Quayle put her arm around Croxen's wife and said, "I'm glad he got it instead of your husband." After 1929 Croxen worked for the Border Patrol from Nogales to Hereford, Arizona, for six years. He then became chief law enforcement officer on the Navaho Reservation for another six years, in 1942 becoming a mounted guard at the Navajo Ordnance Depot on the reservation. He remained there four years before removing to Tucson where he lived the remainder of his life. He was much interested in Arizona frontier history. Croxen said he had supplied Will C. Barnes with information on the Pleasant Valley War (accumulated while he was a forest ranger in the Pleasant Valley vicinity), gave the Arizona Historical Society information on pioneer packer Sam Hill, and was knowledgeable in other areas of early Arizona. He died at Flagstaff. His widow, Edith L. Croxen, died at Flagstaff July 8, 1987 at the age of 94. They left two sons.

Arizona Daily Star, Sept. 29, 1977, July 10, 1987; Edwin A. Tucker, George Fitzpatrick, *Men Who Matched the Mountains: The Forest Service in the Southwest,* U.S. Dept. of Ag., Forest Svc., Southwestern Region, 1972; info. from the Az. Hist. Soc.

Croy, Homer, writer (Mar. 11, 1883-May 24, 1965). B. near Maryville, Missouri, he attended the University of Missouri, was the first student of the first journalism school in the United States but did not graduate because he failed senior English. He was a reporter for several small newspapers, went to New York City and became assistant to Theodore Dreiser, editor of periodicals for Butterick Publications. He commenced writing books with one published in 1914, following it up with others including, of frontier interest, *Corn Country* (1947) which had a brief account of Lame Johny (Cornelius Donahue, John A. Hurley); *Jesse James Was My Neighbor* (1949); *He Hanged Them High: An Authentic Account of the Fanatical Judge Who Hanged Eight-Eight Men,* the story of Judge Isaac Parker (1952); *Our Will Rogers* (1953); *Wheels West* (1953); *Last of the Great Outlaws* (1956, a biography of Cole Younger); and *Trigger Marshal: The Story of Chris Madsen* (1958). Many of Croy's novels, reportedly more than those of any other writer, were made into movies for Will Rogers. Croy also wrote for the screen and for radio, and he became known as a humorist, Ramon Adams commenting that "one of the first things I do with a new book by Mr. Croy is read the index, which is invariably full of humor."

Adams, *Six-Guns and Saddle Leather,* Norman,

Univ. of Okla. Press, 1969; *Contemporary Authors;* REAW; info. from E.F. (Ted) Mains.

Cruger, Mrs. Lydia Boggs: *see,* Lydia Boggs

Cruzat, Francisco, administrator (1738-1790). B. in Navarre, Spain, he went to Louisiana with Alexander O'Reilly (see entry), and became lieutenant governor of Illinois in 1775. He was, as Thwaites reported, a popular and efficient administrator, and in sympathy with the Americans, but he incurred the displeasure of Bernardo de Galvez (see entry). In 1778 he was succeeded by Fernando de Leyba, who died in office when Cruzat in 1780 resumed his role as lieutenant governor. His wife died in 1786 and two daughters died in epidemics. Cruzat on November 27, 1787, was succeeded by Manuel Perez. Cruzat died in 1790 at Pensacola, Florida, at the age of 51.

Abraham P. Nasatir, Noel M. Loomis, *Pedro Vial and the Roads to Santa Fe,* Norman, Univ. of Okla. Press, 1967; Nasatir, ed., *Before Lewis and Clark,* 2 vols., St. Louis Hist. Docs. Found., 1952; Thwaites/Kellogg, *Frontier Defense on the Upper Ohio, 1777-1778.*

Cullins, John, frontiersman (b. c. 1758). As a resident of Hampshire County, Virginia, he volunteered at 19 in August 1777 to serve on the frontier under Captain William Foreman, a militia officer. The company was marched to Pittsburgh, then moved on to Wheeling, West Virginia, to be placed under command of Colonel David Shepherd, commanding Fort Henry. Cullins was a member of the 46-man scouting party of Foreman that was ambushed by Indians September 27, 1777, near Grave Creek, above Wheeling, with many killed and others wounded, Cullins among them. His thigh was broken by a musket ball, and he threw himself over a large log and lay there until rescued by Captain William Linn (see entry). The small Linn party could not evacuate Cullins to Fort Henry at the time, but secreted him under a fallen tree-top, Linn leaving him with food and the promise to return for him after dark. He kept his promise, carried on his back 11 miles to Shepherd's Fort, six miles from Fort Henry. A doctor wished to amputate Cullins' leg, but the wounded man resisted and in time was able to walk again, although with a limp. In later life Cullins wished to hunt up Linn to thank him for saving his life, but found instead the wrong man, and learned that the William Linn he sought had moved to Kentucky and there been killed by Indians. In 1834, then living in Muskingum County, Ohio, Cullins petitioned Congress for a pension, citing the facts of his case, and the 23rd Congress, 1st session, granted the request. The date of his demise is not reported.

Thwaites/Kellogg, *Frontier Defense on the Upper Ohio, 1777-1778.*

Cummings, Charles, Presbyterian clergyman (d. 1812). B. in Pennsylvania of Scot-Irish parentage, he first preached at North Mountain Presbyterian Church in Augusta County, Virginia, from 1766-1772 when he received a call to the Holston Valley where he became pastor of the Wolf Hills Sinking Spring Church at Abingdon in extreme southwestern Virginia. He was a strong supporter of the Revolutionary cause, is supposed to have drafted the Fincastle Resolutions of 1775 and also was a "fighting parson." He accompanied William Christian (see entry) on the 1776 Cherokee expedition and organized a company for relief of Fort Watauga at Elizabethtown, Tennessee, when it was beseiged by Indians, also in 1776. Cummings served his Abingdon church until his death.

Thwaites, *Dunmore.*

[The following is a replacement for the entry which appears in Vol. I, pp. 358-59]

Curry (Currie), James, gunman (fl. 1867-1891). B. in County Clare, Ireland, he was brought as a child to America by his parents, moving eventually from New York City to Cincinnati. He served with a Union cavalry outfit during the Civil War, reportedly as a scout, afterward settling for a time in Iowa. He worked for the Kansas Pacific Railroad, eventually becoming a locomotive engineer. For some reason he abandoned railroading and reached Hays City, Kansas, meanwhile was rumored to have killed several men. Shlesinger, who claimed to know him well, said Curry was a scout with Forsyth at the Battle of Beecher Island in September 1868. He was listed among the 50 plainsmen hired by Major Henry Inman, quartermaster at Fort Harker, Kansas, to serve from August 28 to December 31, 1868, at a salary of $50 a month. Surviving veterans of the Beecher Island affair said that Curry's name "should be" on the monument at the site, commemorating whites who fought there, but it was omitted. Curry may also

have scouted for Custer. Burkey said Curry killed one Ed Estes, possibly a soldier, in Hays City in 1869. Curry was wounded in a Hays City melee between black soldiers of the 38th Infantry and citizenry. Jim came into a feuding relationship with Hickok, apparently over a prostitute, Ida May, who supposedly helped Curry in a restaurant operation. At any rate, Curry in a celebrated incident came across Hickok playing cards at Uncle Tommy Drum's saloon in Hays City, held a pistol to the back of his head and threatened to kill him but Hickok's coolness and Drum's resourcefulness ended the affair without bloodshed, and with Hickok and Curry shaking hands. In 1878 Curry surfaced at Marshall, Texas as a Texas & Pacific Railroad detective seeking to stop thefts from freight cars. If the Jim Curry of Kansas is identical with Jim Currie of Marshall, as seems probable, he continued his escapades with slight letup. In 1876 a young actor named Maurice Barrymore (1847-1905) came to America from England. He had been born Herbert Blythe at Fort Agra, India, where his father was surveyor for a British firm. Blythe graduated from Cambridge and studied law but found the stage more attractive; meanwhile for recreation he had taken up boxing in an amateur way, with some success. Coming to America in 1875 he married Georgiana Drew, daughter of John and Louisa Drew, well known on the stage. Barrymore in 1878 fathered Lionel Barrymore (d. 1954) and would also father Ethel (1879-1959) and John Barrymore (1882-1942), thus founding something of a thespian dynasty. In 1878 Maurice Barrymore and Frederick Warde purchased road rights to *Diplomacy,* organized a traveling company which included Barrymore, his brother-in-law John Drew, Ellen Cummins and Benjamin C. Porter. On March 19, 1879, the troupe played at Marshall, Texas. Following the performance and before leaving for Hot Springs, Arkansas, for the next one, Barrymore, Porter and Miss Cummins entered the White House, a restaurant-saloon for a late supper. They were alone in the cafe, save for proprietor Sam Harvey, but Jim Currie was at the adjacent bar, loading up on whiskey. He felt somewhat insulted because he could not buy the seat he wanted at the opera house earlier, commenced to cast aspersions on Miss Cummins, and Barrymore and Porter came to her defense. Barrymore, expecting a fist fight, removed his monocle when Currie, despite his earlier claim not to be armed, produced a pistol and commenced firing. He killed Porter and wounded Barrymore in the shoulder. Currie was arrested by Deputy Sheriff Arch Hall, armed with a double-barreled shotgun he knew well how to use. Railroad surgeons successfully treated Barrymore. The actor remained three weeks at Marshall, recuperating under care of his wife (pregnant with Ethel) and the railroad furnished a casket and transportation east for the body of Porter. Currie's trial was set for May 28, and Barrymore and Miss Cummins returned for it, but the case was postponed and they did not come back for its later unfolding; Currie was acquitted, in part due to the excellent attorneys hired by his older brother, Andrew Currie, mayor of Shreveport, Louisiana. Jim Currie married a Marshall girl and left Texas for New Mexico where he became a saloon keeper and prospector. In 1888 he was sentenced to the territorial prison for killing his mining partner, and as convict 271 was incarcerated from September 10, 1888, to March 27, 1891, when he was pardoned by Governor Edmund G. Ross on condition he leave New Mexico forever. Eventually he died at Portland, Oregon, but the date of his demise and the circumstances have not been learned.

The Battle of Beecher Island, Beecher Is. Battle Mem. Assoc., Wray, Col., 1960, 31-33, 49; Joseph G. Rosa, *They Called Him Wild Bill,* Norman, Univ. of Okla. Press, 1974; Blaine Burkey, *Custer, Come At Once!,* Hays, Ks., Thomas More Prep, 1976; Burkey, *Wild Bill Hickok: The Law in Hays City.* Thomas More Prep, 1975; Ed Bartholomew, *Wyatt Earp: The Untold Story,* Toyahvale, Tx., Frontier Book Co , 1963, 117; Bill O'Neal, "Big Jim Currie vs. Maurice Barrymore and Company," *True West,* Vol. 17, No. 9 (Sept. 1990), 55-57; Clifton Seymour, "The Shooting of Maurice Barrymore," *Frontier Times,* Vol. 4, No. 7 (Apr. 1927), 1-4 (repr. in *True West,* Vol. 9, No. 4 (Mar.-Apr. 1962), 24-25, 56-57; O'Neal to author, Aug. 20, 1990.

Curtis, Ken (Festus Haggin), actor, singer (July 12, 1916-Apr. 28, 1991). B. as Curtis Gates at Lamar, Colorado, he was the son of a sheriff and worked on the jail farm as a boy. He made his Hollywood debut as a singer, succeeding Frank Sinatra with Tommy Dorsey's band, Curtis going on to Shep Field's orchestra. He served with the army during World War II, then joined Johnny Mercer's radio show and recorded the hit, "Tumbling Tumbleweeds," which caused Columbia Pictures to sign him on as a singing cowboy. He joined the popular group, Sons of the Pioneers when director John Ford hired them for a western film, *Wagon Master,* which launched Curtis on a lucrative motion picture and television career. He won his greatest popularity for his 1963-75 role as deputy Festus Haggin, Marshal Matt Dillon's sidekick on the TV show, *Gunsmoke.* He also acted with John Wayne in such films as *The Searchers, The Quiet Man* and *The Alamo,* besides appearing in *How the West Was Won, Cheyenne Autumn* and popular TV westerns. He died at his Fresno, California, home at 74, survived by his widow and two children.

Tucson, *Arizona Daily Star,* Apr. 30, 1991.

Custaloga, Delaware chief (fl. 1760-1775). The uncle of Captain Pipe (see entry), who succeeded him as chief of the Wolf element of the Delaware tribe, Custaloga dwelt in a town named for him in 1760. It was on French Creek, opposite the present Franklin, Pennsylvania. He removed from that village probably around 1763 to the Walhonding River, Coshocton County, Ohio, and established around 1766 another village named for him. Here he was called by Mooney chief of the Unalachtigo (Turkey) Delawares, but this may be in error. Nothing is reported of his birth or death.

Hodge, HAI; Clinton A. Weslager, *The Delaware Indians,* New Brunswick, N.J., Rutgers Univ. Press, 1972.

D

Daggett, Mike: *see,* Shoshone Mike

Dall, William Healey, naturalist, Alaskan expert (Aug. 21, 1845-Mar. 27, 1927). B. at Boston, the son of a Unitarian minister, he studied at Harvard although he did not graduate. He early became interested in natural history and became acquainted with Louis Agassiz under whom he studied zoology, taking courses also in anatomy and other medical subjects. He found employment with the Illinois Central Railroad at Chicago and continued his studies at night with the Chicago Academy of Sciences, in part under direction of Robert Kennicott, who became his close friend. At 19 he joined Kennicott's scientific staff with the Western Union International Telegraph Expedition to Alaska, the operation intended to construct a telegraph line from North America across Bering Strait to Siberia where it was to be connected with Europe. When Kennicott died May 13, 1866, at Nulato on the middle Yukon River, Dall took over as head of the scientific staff. In 1866 the successful establishment of a trans-Atlantic cable service caused cancellation of the Western Union plans for a Siberian connection with Europe, but Dall remained in Alaska. He mapped the Yukon from Fort Yukon at the confluence of the Porcupine and Yukon rivers to its mouth. He also made valuable collections in natural history, particularly of mollusks in which he commenced to specialize, devoting much of his life to their study. In 1868 he left Alaska and joined the staff of the Smithsonian Institution where in 1880 he was made honorary curator of mollusks. In 1870 he published his famous *Alaska and Its Resources,* of which there have been several editions, and for many years it was the accepted authority on the Territory. In 1871 Dall was appointed to the United States Coast Survey, continuing with it until 1884. During this time he spent part of each year in Alaska. He was in charge of a scientific survey of the Aleutians and adjacent coasts. publishing *Pacific Coast Pilot: Coast and Islands of Alaska; App. I, Meteorology* (1879) and *Pacific Coast Pilot* (1883). In 1884 he joined the Geological Survey with the title of paleontologist. He wrote hundreds of papers and monographs on mollusks. He taught invertebrate paleontology at the Wagner Institute of Science at Philadelphia and from 1899-1915 was an honorary curator of the Bishop Museum of Honolulu. In 1915 he also published *Spencer Fullerton Baird: A Biography* of the famed zoologist who, among other notable undertakings, was the first head of the U.S. Commission of Fish and Fisheries and helped establish the Wood's Hole, Massachusetts, marine laboratory. Dall was much honored for his own accomplishments and authors of works in botany and zoology have conferred his name on various organisms. He was married and fathered four children of whom three, with his widow, survived him. He died at Washington, D.C. In Alaska his name was bestowed, among other things, on Mount Dall, northwest of Talkeetna; Dall Island in the Alexander Archipelago; Dall Lake southwest of Bethel; Dall Mountain and Dall River, west of Yukon Flats; Dall Point, on the Bering Sea and, best known of all, to the white Dall mountain sheep of the Alaskan highlands.

DAB; NCAB, Vol. 27, 342-43; Orth, 255; Pierce, *Russian America: A Biographical Dictionary.*

Dalyell (Dalzell), James, military officer (d. July 31 or Aug. 1, 1763). Termed by Peckham "an ambitious young officer [and the] younger son of a baronet," he had obtained a lieutenancy in 1756 in the Royal Americans, a regiment raised for participation in the French and Indian War, and Parkman wrote that he was "the companion of Israel Putnam in some of the most adventurous passages of that rough veteran's life," suggesting he may have seen action against Montreal in 1760 and come to know Robert Rogers (see entry) who served under Putnam for a time. Dalyell was promoted to captain and served under Lieutenant Colonel Thomas Gage in the 80th Light Infantry regiment Gage had raised, "the first in the British army to be trained in both regular and irregular tactics," based on lessons learned from Braddock's defeat in which Gage had shared. In September of 1760 Dalyell was transferred to the 1st Regiment and "was taken into General Amherst's official family as an aide-de-camp," family connections having no doubt played a role in securing this coveted position. Dalyell was named by Amherst to command a force of around 260 men to relieve Detroit, then under heavy siege by Pontiac (see entry) and his mixed assemblage of Indians. On the march westward Dalyell at Albany had picked up Rogers, who had received the surrender of Detroit from the French in 1760, and 21 of his rangers, several companies of the 55th and 60th regiments, and 40 men from Fort Niagara. The command proceeded along the south shore of Lake Erie in bateaux to Presqu'Isle (at the site of today's Erie) where he inspected the charred ruins of the post that hostile Indians had reduced, proceeded to Sandusky Bay, near where he demolished the Huron village of Junundat from which the Indians had fled, entered the Detroit River and after a brush with Hurons in which 14 of his men were wounded, reached the beleaguered fort. He reported to Major Henry Gladwin (see entry), rested his men for two days, and pronounced to his superior that he was ready for a surprise attack on Pontiac's village, an operation he was certain would prove a disaster for the enemy and quickly terminate the war. Gladwin, well-seasoned in Indian warfare and aware of Pontiac's proven capabilities and the great number of warriors at his disposal, was reluctant to approve the perilous mission, but Dalyell persisted, possibly throwing in Amherst's name as wishing the Pontiac matter promptly quashed, and at last Gladwin, "against his better judgment" gave permission for the attempt. It was set for the night of July 31, 1763, and Dalyell had 247 men to work with, including Rogers, "who should have led the whole force," and his small complement of rangers. Pontiac of course had been aware of the arrival of the Dalyell force, and had been tipped off by a French Canadian of the impending attack, and so laid a skillful ambush for his enemy. Dalyell had two Frenchmen for guides, Jacques Duperon Baby and Jacques St. Martin, though unlike a Rogers operation he had no scouts out, and ordered no reconnaissance to probe the enemy defenses and locate any ambuscades. Instead he marched his column from the fort as though on parade at 2:30 a.m. and Pontiac was awaiting them. At two miles from the fort they came to Parent's Creek, to be known hereafter as Bloody Run. Pontiac had divided his more than 400 warriors into two parties, one of about 160 at the creek to await the British, and a force of 250 at a place about two-thirds of a mile from the fort, to cut off a British retreat. The attack began as the English tried to cross a bridge over the creek, the Indians opening fire and causing casualties. As the fight developed, Dalyell was wounded in the thigh, not seriously. Firing opened also upon the rear of the column under Captain James Grant of the 80th Regiment who returned the fusillade briskly although virtually blindly in the darkness. At the opening of the fight Rogers looked for cover, swiftly occupied a farmhouse of which he made a blockhouse and was able to prevent the Indians from closing in on that flank of the white command. With dawn Dalyell ordered a retreat which succeeded in part, thanks to Rogers' protective fire. Pontiac's forces still held a strong position nearer the fort and Dalyell ordered a charge to open the route, bravely leading it. However imperfect his judgment, there was nothing wrong with his courage, but in the course of the assault he was shot dead, reportedly by an Indian named Geyette, supposed to have been Pontiac's brother-in-law. By 8 a.m. the expedition, or what remained of it, was back in the fort. Dalyell and 19 of his men were killed outright and three others wounded mortally; there were 39 other wounded, including three officers while the hostiles also took prisoners. The troops had received a "damn'd drubbing," in the words of a militia officer and Detroit trader, James Sterling, while the Indian loss "certainly did not exceed 15 or 20," according to Parkman. Dalyell's body was recovered by the hostiles, the head cut off, his heart snatched out and the Indians "wiped it on the faces of the prisoners." Jacques Campau recovered the remains of Dalyell's body next day and took them to the fort for burial.

Howard H. Peckham, *Pontiac and the Indian Uprising,* Univ. of Chicago Press, 1947, 1961; Parkman, *The Conspiracy of Pontiac,* I; Mich. Soc. of the Colonial Wars, *Journal of Pontiac's Conspiracy 1763,* author unknown, n.d., c. 1912.

Dana, Richard Henry Jr., writer, attorney (Aug. 1, 1815-Jan. 6, 1882). B. at Cambridge, Massachusetts, of good family he entered Harvard in 1831 but two years later was forced to temporarily give up his education because measles had left him with eye trouble. He cast about for some alternative to restore his health. Boston was a major port and Dana wrote later that "there is a witchery in the sea" and the mere sight of a ship and sailor's togs "has done more to [crew ships] than all the press gangs of Europe." August 14, 1834, he shipped out of Boston on the brig *Pilgrim,* bound round Cape Horn for Mexican California and two years of collecting raw cattle hides, casks of otter skins and beaver furs before he could leave what he had come to consider "that hated coast." He returned to Boston aboard the *Alert,* a fine ship which reached port September 19, 1836. His famous narrative of that sometimes exhilarating, often monotonous, occasionally exciting and always educational voyage was published in 1840 as *Two Years Before the Mast.* It is a true classic of the sea, an informative and priceless narrative of an important American business of that era, and an imperishable addition to the nation's literature. January 3, 1835, the *Pilgrim* raised Point Conception and the following day anchored off Santa Barbara, then a miserable collection of adobe huts with the gleaming white mission a short distance off. At Monterey, to the north, it was necessary to get clearance from Customs in order to trade along the coast, although the inspection was haphazard and ships' captains well knew how to manage easier permission and more than legal profit for the owners. For a year the *Pilgrim* cruised up and down the coast: Monterey, Santa Barbara, San Pedro, what is now called Dana Point, San Diego and once as far north as San Francisco where Dana predicted that "if California ever becomes a prosperous country, this bay will be the center of its prosperity," little realizing that within a mere dozen years his prediction would come vividly to life—thanks to the Rush for Gold. Though Dana, scarcely emerging from his teens, was professedly unimpressed by what he observed of the places and populace of a somnolent and dreary territory, he was so acute mentally, so observant and, despite himself, so interested in it all that he brings to his descriptions and his before-the-mast experiences a vigor and life that reveals a deep fascination underlying his outward deprecation of it all. He almost instantly learned Spanish well enough to communicate in that tongue, became a favorite of the Hawaiian *Kanakas* who manned many of the ships and thronged parts of the coast, learned something of their language and became admiring friends of them, as he did with as fascinating a collection of sometimes weird acquaintances as any writer ever made permanent fixtures through his published journal. Even for a landsman his descriptions of working a ship under all sorts of weather and unforeseen crises are intelligible and thrilling. His is a well-rounded book and a permanent addition to maritime literature. Upon his return to Boston he joined the Harvard senior

class in December 1836, was graduated in June at the head of his class and became a lecturer in the university's law school, being admitted to the bar the year he published his book which was based upon a journal he kept throughout the voyage. He set about seeking legal justice and corrections for the often brutal, always arbitrary and frequently reprehensible treatment by ships' officers of forecastle hands. He specialized in admiralty cases. His manual, *The Seaman's Friend,* published in 1841 became a standard work on maritime law in this country and England. He became interested in the problems of slavery; and "although he did not become an Abolitionist, his political and legal activities involved him deeply in the anti-slavery movement." While he was an important figure in many prominent legal and political matters, he would not descend to machine politics, which perhaps kept him from high office. In his later life his principle interest was international law. His 1866 edition of Henry Wheaton's *Elements of International Law* was accepted as authoritative. He was an avid traveler, visiting England twice, journeying around the world in 1859-60, and in 1878 he went to Europe again; while in Rome he died suddenly of pneumonia and was buried in the Protestant cemetery where also lie the remains of Keats and Shelley. He had married in 1841 and fathered six children who, with his widow, survived him. "He was a man of distinguished and dignified manner, with a certain formality that did not encourage intimacy" in his mature life, which was quite distinct from the outgoing forecastle personality of his career as a seaman.

Dana, *Two Years Before the Mast,* the best edition of which is the two-volume work edited by John Kemble (see entry), Los Angeles, Ward-Ritchie Press, 1964; DAB.

Dandridge, Alexander Spottswood, pioneer (Aug. 1, 1753-1785). The grandson of Alexander Spotswood, a Virginia governor who first crossed the Blue Ridge in 1714, and closely related to Martha Dandridge Custis who married George Washington, Alexander Dandridge was b. in Hanover County, Virginia, and well educated for the time. He was a popular young man, considered to be of "great promise." He went to Kentucky with Richard Henderson (see entry) in 1775 when Henderson's Transylvania Company established Boonesborough. At the outbreak of the Revolution he joined the colonial army and became an aide to Washington. About 1780 he married the daughter of Colonel Adam Stephan in Jefferson County, Virginia, where he died, aged 32.

Thwaites, *Dunmore.*

Daniels, James, gunman: *see,* Jim Talbot(t)

Daniels, William A. (Billy), lawman (d. June 10, 1885). Born in Ohio, Daniels was a deputy sheriff assigned to Bisbee, Arizona, in 1883 and as such did heroic work in arresting and bringing in gunmen who perpetrated the Bisbee Massacre of December 8, 1883. He had fired five shots at the fleeing gunmen, and Red Sample (see entry) was slightly wounded, whether by Daniels was undetermined. The deputy accompanied posses scouring the countryside, and when they ran out of clues, continued the search alone. He learned the identities of the desperadoes from ranchers who had encountered them. Billy picked up Daniel Kelly (see entry) at Deming, New Mexico. A Mexican informant led him to Big Dan Dowd's (see entry) hideout at Sabinal, near Corralitos, Chihuahua, and he brought Dowd back to Arizona. On new information Daniels went back across the border to Minas Prietas, Sonora, and picked up William Delaney (see entry). Other officers had arrested Red Sample and Tex Howard (see entry) near Clifton, Arizona, and John Heath (see entry) also was charged; the Bisbee desperadoes at length were all taken, and Billy Daniels had caught three of them. March 22, 1884, John Hiles planned to rob a safe in a saloon Daniels was operating. Learning of the impending theft, Daniels lay in wait for Hiles, who forced entry at 2 a.m. When Hiles attacked the safe with a crowbar, Daniels spoke to him, but got no answer and fired his shotgun, killing the burglar; a coroner's jury exonerated him, since he was protecting his personal property. That year Daniels ran for sheriff of Cochise County, but was beaten out by Bob Hatch. He thereafter was appointed a mounted Inspector of Customs. Early on June 10, 1885, Daniels with Dave Malcolm and a boy followed an Apache trail in Dixie Canyon of the Mule Mountains ten miles east of Bisbee. Daniels, in advance, rode into an ambush; Indians killed his horse, the animal falling and pinning Daniels to the ground. In spite of his skill with a rifle, and boundless courage, he was helpless. The Indians killed him, cut his throat and mutilated the corpse, while his companions escaped. A posse next day had no success in following the Indians. Traywick prints a portrait of Daniels on Page 12.

Ben T. Traywick, *The Hangings in Tombstone,* Tombstone, Red Marie's Bookstore, 1991; Dan L. Thrapp, *Conquest of Apacheria,* Norman, Univ. of Okla. Press, 1967; A.D. LeBaron, "Black Ghosts of Bisbee," *True West,* Vol. 7, No. 6 (July-Aug 1960), 12-14, 56-57.

Darragh, John, scouts commander, builder (1830-post 1884). B. at Enfield, New York, he reached Oregon in 1851 and worked in various civilian capacities near The Dalles on the Columbia River in the 1850s and 1860s. He was a miller at the Warm Springs Indian Agency between Bend and The Dalles in 1861, was a packer on the operation, or extended reconnaissance led by Captain John M. Drake, who commanded the Oregon Volunteers camp at Salem, one diarist complaining that Drake "is like a shotgun, he scatters," though he must have been a competent officer. Darragh may have picked up something of Indian languages, for in 1866 he and William C. McKay (see entry) were commissioned "interpreters," with the pay of lieutenants and were expected to lead scout companies in a year-long operation against the hostile Paiute Indians in eastern Oregon. However the official appointment as "interpreter" was purely nominal in order to obtain their services as scouts commanders, and it may be that a competent interpreter was assigned to Darragh. His command included 36 or more Wasco Indians, the Wascos being a Chinookian tribe from the neighborhood of The Dalles. McKay commanded as many Des Chutes scouts. The Des Chutes, living on the Deschutes River of Oregon, were a people combining remnants of several tribes; the Des Chutes and Wascos did not mix well. Darragh was in the field with his scouts from December 30, 1866, until November 13, 1867, under the distasteful instructions (as was McKay) "to kill and destroy without regard to age, sex, or condition." The directive originated with vengeance-minded Oregon Governor George L. Woods, and although protested by more reasonable army officers, and by scouts who believed the Paiutes would only retaliate in kind against their own families when they had the opportunity, it was incorporated in verbal if not written orders. The result of the long operation was a series of minor clashes when more women and children were killed than men and, despite the detestable directive, some prisoners, mainly a few surviving children, were taken. Considered a "versatile man," Darragh later served a term as superintendent of schools for Wasco (Oregon) County. He was described by one who knew him as "a morose, backward, unsocial man, never mingling in any social affairs whatever," though he was "esteemed highly by those who knew him best, but they were very few, for he encouraged but few to come near enough to know him." In 1884 he removed to New York City to engage in construction work with his brother, probably the noted contractor and builder Robert Leach Darragh (May 26, 1825-June 19, 1894) who had amassed a considerable fortune in putting up some of Manhattan's foremost edifices. The date, place and circumstance of John Darragh's demise have not been ascertained, and there were others of the identical name residing in New York simultaneously.

Keith, Donna, Clark, "William McKay's Journal, 1866-67, Indian Scouts" parts I, II, *Oregon Historical Quarterly,* Vol. LXXIX, Nos. 2, 3 (Summer/Fall 1978), 120-71, 268-333; Bancroft, *Oregon,* II; *A Webfoot Volunteer: The Diary of William M. Hilleary 1864-1866,* ed. by Herbert B. Nelson, Preston E. Onstad, Corvallis, Or. State Univ. Press, 1965; info. from Mariam Touba, ref. librarian, N.Y. Hist. Soc.; for Robert L. Darragh: *New York Times,* May 18, June 20, July 7, 1894; Robert Darragh death cert.

Daurkin, Nikolai, Chukchi cossak, explorer (c. 1730-1792). A Chukchi native, he was b. near Cape Serdtse-Kamen, Siberia, under the name of Tamgetana. In 1744 he was taken captive and transported to Iakutsk, Siberia, being baptized under the name of Nikolai Daurkin, learned to speak and read Russian and eventually the governor of Siberia, seeking an instrument for better relations with the Chukchi, ordered him freed, accepted as a cossack, and sent to Anadyrsk Fort. In 1764 the commandant, Fedor Plenisner sent Daurkin to collect specific information about the Chukotchi Peninsula, and the cossack went as far as his birthplace, Cape Serdtse-Kamen, the peninsula's northernmost point. In April 1765 he went by baidarka to St. Lawrence Island, midway between the peninsula and Alaska. Daurkin then returned to Anadyrsk, with Plenisner's assistance drafted maps of where he had been or places of which he had heard reports. Based upon Chukchi information, since those people had visited Alaska since earliest times, he depicted islands in Bering Strait, and a large river on the American mainland which he called the Kheuveren, which Pierce believes probably was the Kuzitrin, a river emptying into the sea through several lakes east of Teller on the Seward Penin-

sula. In 1787 Daurkin joined the expedition of Joseph Billings (see entry) as an interpreter. Around 1790 with Ivan Kovelev he visited the coast of Alaska (with the aid of the Chukchi), as confirmed by a "letter" written on a walrus tusk now in the Historical Museum at Moscow. The party found what they believed was the mouth of the Kuzitrin River, but did not penetrate inland. Martin Sauer, private secretary to Billings on the latter's expedition, wrote of Daurkin as of a "sullen, jealous and revengeful disposition," but there is no confirmation of this description elsewhere.

Pierce, *Russian America: A Biographical Dictionary.*

Davidson, George, geodesist, astronomer (May 9, 1825-Dec. 1, 1911). B. in Nottingham, England, he was brought to the United States in 1832 and went to school at Philadelphia, eventually earning a doctorate and receiving other honorary degrees. He worked for the Coast and Geodetic Survey from 1845 to 1895, as a geodesist and astronomer in the eastern states from 1845 to 1850 and coast survey work in California, Oregon, Washington and Alaska from 1850 to 1895. In 1867 he went to Alaska aboard the revenue cutter *Lincoln* before the territory was purchased by the United States from Russia and while negotiations were underway. He made observations at Sitka, Chilkat, Kodiak and Unalaska islands, his report published in the C&GS annual report for 1867. He returned to Alaska in 1869 and did further reconnaissance work in the Alexander Archipelago of the panhandle. While in the Chilkat Valley to observe a total solar eclipse on August 7 he ignored a warning that the Chilkat Indians had been provoked into hostility. The observation was made near a populous village and when the eclipse took place the Indians fled into the woods "in silent dismay." Bancroft added that "They had not believed Davidson's prediction the day before, and its fulfillment probably caused the safety of the party." Davidson contributed natural history and ethnological collections to the Smithsonian Institution. He separated from the Survey in 1895. Several geographic features in Alaska were named for him. From 1870 to 1911 he was professor of astronomy, geodesy and geography at the University of California at Berkeley. Davidson received many honors and awards, some from foreign governments, for his scientific work.

Orth, 12, 258; Bancroft, *Alaska.*

Davy, Peter B., wagon train entrepreneur (1830-1889). B. in Canada, he attended the Toronto Normal Academy and taught school for several years before moving to the United States, settling in 1857 at Blue Earth, a new village south of Mankato, Minnesota. He bought a sawmill and for some time was a patent medicine salesman. At the 1862 outbreak of the Great Sioux Uprising, Davy was commissioned December 10 a first lieutenant in Company K, 1st Regiment of Mounted Rangers, and as a captain commanded H Company, 2nd Minnesota Cavalry from December 3, 1863 to April 8, 1866. He served under Sibley and Sully in their campaigns and was active in the rescue in 1864 of the James L. Fisk (see entry) wagon train beleaguered by Hunkpapa Sioux west of Fort Rice. Shortly after his discharge from military service he announced he would lead a wagon expedition to the Montana gold fields by the northern route, his effort becoming the final major use of that route from Minnesota. Davy designated nine Minnesota towns as outfitting points for the expedition, with his headquarters at Mankato. The main body of emigrants, about 70 men and 22 wagons, left Minneapolis June 17, 1867, and at St. Cloud was joined by another, smaller group, reaching Fort Abercrombie, near today's Wahpeton, North Dakota, early in July. Other emigrants were met there so that the entire train included 60 to 75 wagons, and more than 220 persons, some of them a German group bound for Oregon. Davy's train, in three divisions, left Abercrombie July 13 accompanied by two other groups not aiming for Montana. The train reached the Sheyenne River in five days where the military was constructing Fort Ransom, south of Valley City. Dissension had broken out, largely over Davy's autocratic management of the expedition's affairs, and the train was believed under-supplied for so long a journey, many considering Davy an inefficient manager. But "somehow the situation was resolved, although details are lacking." Davy, deposed briefly as leader, was reinstated, fresh supplies were purchased and the expedition on July 25 broke camp and followed behind a military escort that had been bestowed upon it. August 8 the train reached the Missouri River. By their arrival at Fort Stevenson, a new post 15 miles below Fort Berthold, the train again was low on food but the difficulty was overcome, although some of the emigrants declined to go farther under Davy's leadership. The wagons around the end of August reached Fort Buford a

few miles below Fort Union at the mouth of the Yellowstone. The train crossed Montana Territory without military escort, since it was deemed safe to do so. On September 3, along the Milk River the party passed a camp of about 100 Indians, probably Crows, when warriors rushed down upon them and, according to recollections penned much later, Davy, "white as a sheet and trembling with fear," asked, "My God, what are we going to do?" An emigrant retorted, "Order out the brass band at once and don't act like a cur!" The band, which was an integral part of the company, rendered a rousing "Yankee Doodle" which so astonished the Indians that peace at once replaced seeming hostility, and all was well. On September 16, the train reached Fort Benton and later Helena, where an acrid dispute between the Germans and Davy ended up in court over payment for services and other things; Davy lost. In 1868 Davy planned a gold-seeking enterprise in the Black Hills, but the government set the area aside for a Sioux reservation which aborted the entrepreneur's project. He settled into a quiet life at Blue Earth, where he died at 59.

Helen McCann White, *Ho! For the Gold Fields: Northern Overland Wagon Trains of the 1860s,* St. Paul, Minn. Hist. Soc., 1966; *Minnesota in the Civil War and Indian Wars,* St. Paul, Pioneer Press Co., 1891.

Dease, Peter Warren, explorer, trader (1788-1863). He served with the North West Fur Company and from 1821 with the Hudson's Bay Company as a trader. In 1826 he was a member of Franklin's Arctic expedition which sought inconclusively to chart the unexplored segment of the continent's northern coast. From 1836 to 1839 Dease and Thomas Simpson together commanded an expedition to complete Franklin's work. June 1, 1837, they left by boat from Fort Good Hope, on the Mackenzie River just below the Arctic Circle, passing downstream to the sea. They coasted the shore westerly as far as Return Reef where Franklin in 1826 had been stopped by ice. Since ice likewise now prohibited further progress by boat, Simpson continued on foot and by Eskimo craft to Point Barrow. This completed exploration of the coastline since Beechey, Elson and others earlier had worked out the conformation of it from Bering Strait to Barrow. Dease Inlet, the former Prokofiyev Inlet as named by Kashevarov (see entry) was renamed by Simpson, either in ignorance of the earlier Russian appelation or in substitution for it, while Kupriyanov Bay at this time or possbly earlier was renamed Smith (Smyth) Bay, perhaps in honor of William Smyth(e) of the Beechey party. The Dease-Simpson expedition was concluded in August 1837.

Zagoskin; *Narratives of Explorations in Alaska,* 367; Bancroft, *Northwest Coast,* II; Orth, 32, 261.

Debo, Angie, historian (Jan. 30, 1890-Feb. 21, 1988). B. on a farm near Beattie, east of Marysville, Kansas, she was taken in 1895 by her parents to Manhattan, Kansas, and in 1899 by covered wagon to a farm near Marshall, between Enid and Guthrie, Oklahoma. She attended rural schools in Kansas and Oklahoma, managed a year of high school and at 16 took a territorial examination and became a rural school teacher; when Marshall finally established a four-year high school, she returned and was graduated from it at 23, entered the University of Oklahoma in 1915 and graduated in 1918 with a major in history, having come to the attention of Edward Everett Dale (see entry) who had earned his doctorate at Harvard under Frederick Jackson Turner. Debo in 1924 received a master's degree at the University of Chicago (her thesis was published, with J. Fred Rippy as co-author, as *The Historical Background of the American Policy of Isolation*); she had chosen Chicago because she felt she needed urban experience, having matured in a wholly rural atmosphere. She taught for a decade at West Texas State Teachers College (now West Texas State University) at Canyon, where she served briefly as curator of the Panhandle-Plains Historical Museum. Under Dale's supervision she earned her doctorate from the University of Oklahoma, publishing her dissertation as *The Rise and Fall of the Choctaw Republic* (1934), winning an award from the American Historical Association for it. She subsequently had connections with several universities, and in 1947 joined the library staff of Oklahoma State University, retiring in 1955, then settling in at Marshall where she lived and worked the rest of her life. Her second Indian book, and the one she esteemed most highly (and also the most difficult to have published) was *And Still the Waters Run: The Betrayal of the Five Civilized Tribes.* This invaluable volume, detailing from primary documents and other sources how Oklahoma whites had cheated, despoiled and stolen from proper Indian owners the lands bestowed upon them at the time of removal into what is now Okalhoma, was too hot for the University of Oklahoma Press to handle in the 1930s. Many of the wealthy disparagingly cited in the text were generous—and vigilant—supporters of the University and its fledgling press, although Rhodes scholar Joseph A. Brandt, the press director, ardently championed the manuscript and tried by every means to have it accepted. Eventually he left to take over Princeton University Press, which was hampered by no such obstacles as those at Norman, and the volume in 1940 was published by that house, although with certain names excised to avert possible libel suits, if that could be done. In a letter to this author April 9, 1977, Debo wrote that "If one were to put everything I have written on one side of the scales, and that book on the other side, it would outbalance them all." Every statement in that book, she wrote, "is proved; there is not a loose thread anywhere" (for an extended study of the difficulties she met publishing this important volume, the reader is referred to Schrems and Wolff, below). Others among the books she wrote included: *The Road to Disappearance: A History of the Creek Indians* (1941); *Tulsa: From Creek Town to Oil Capital* (1943); *The Five Civilized Tribes of Oklahoma* (1951); ed., by Oliver Nelson, *The Cowman's Southwest,* (1953); ed., by Horatio B. Cushman, *History of the Choctaw, Chickasaw, and Natchez Indians; A History of the Indians of the United States* (1970); and *Geronimo: The Man, His Time, His Place* (1976). She also contributed to a wide range of periodicals and with less extended works to a number of books and publications. In April 1985 Oklahoma placed her portrait in the rotunda of its capitol, describing her as "a treasure for the whole state," and "a treasured asset." She received many other honors. Debo died at 98 at Enid, Oklahoma. She never married.

Angie Debo: A Biographical Sketch and a Bibliography of Her Published Works, Stillwater, Okla. State Univ., 1980; Suzanne H. Schrems, Cynthia J. Wolff, "Politics and Libel: Angie Debo and the publication of *And Still the Waters Run," Western Historical Quarterly.,* Vol. XXII, No. 2 (May 1991), 184-203; years of correspondence with author.

De Grazia, Ettore (Ted), artist (June 14, 1909-Sept. 17, 1982). B. at Morenci, Arizona, of Italian immigrant parents, he was graduated from the University of Arizona in 1944 and earned a masters in arts in 1945, having worked his way through by painting murals and playing trumpet in local bands while cementing his friendships with the Pápago, Yaqui and Apache Indians. His early years as an artist were hard; he was ignored by critics and rejected by local galleries, so he went to Mexico for several years. He worked under "two of the world's great revolutionary painters, Diego Rivera and José Clemente Orozco, who once said that "De Grazia's painting has all the freshness, simplicity and power of youth. He is able to go from simple and graceful movement...to the understanding of human misery. He will be one of the best American painters some day." Orozco and Rivera were so impressed that they sponsored an exhibit of his paintings at the Palacio de Belles Artes of Mexico City. But when he returned to Arizona he still could not locate a gallery that would show his work, so he planned to build one himself. By about 1948 he had refined a style that stuck, "a simplistic, gently curving, repetitive stroke that left a 'cultural impression' rather than a detailed representation." He took no notebooks with him on his regular visits to Indian reservations for, he said, if he didn't remember it, it wasn't important. Success, however delayed, finally came to him all at once. He had a one-man show at a new gallery in Scottsdale, Arizona, and it proved a hit. A thousand people attended the opening and he sold $1,500 in paintings and found his distinctive work abruptly in great demand. The nationally-circulated *Arizona Highways* printed some of his pictures and brought them wide attention. In 1960 UNICEF used his "Los Ninos" of dancing Indian children on a Christmas card that resulted in international attention; it has been used by the United Nations organization for 30 years and some 7 million boxes of cards have been sold. In 1950 De Grazia bought 10 acres of mountain foothills near Tucson, a location for which his widow has since rejected bids of millions of dollars. De Grazia built there a small house and studio and in 1965 completed his Gallery in the Sun. It was constructed by the artist and his Yaqui friends wholly of adobes they made themselves, the building conforming to the land; no bulldozers were allowed on the place, and ground unevenness remained to dictate structure. The rooms follow the natural contours. The building includes theme galleries and other specialty spaces, resulting in "a gallery for people who don't like art galleries." De Grazia in his career produced a prodigious amount of work. He was sometimes criticized for "simplistic images, commercializing art and catering to uneducated

tastes," but he believed his output was true to the soul of the native and Mexican people he loved. He once said, "some people object to my art on the grounds that it is not photographic. They think I'm too abstract." He added that "Life is not precise. It is not 'frozen movement,' no matter how beautifully captured. We observe life around us as movement and color and sound; ever-changing and evasive of precise interpretation. Most of what we see around us is on the periphery of our vision—we feel it more than we see it. This is the essence I try to capture in my paintings." He worked successfully in oils, pastels, ceramics, sculpture, serigraphs, lithographs, drawings and pen-and-ink. He gave away and traded countless originals, donating images to churches, the American Cancer Society, the Peace Corps and Easter Seal Society. How much money he made is not known, but it was not inconsiderable. In the 1970s he learned to his dismay about inheritance taxes and in 1976 invited reporters and friends to witness the burning in the Superstition Mountain range of $1.5 million worth of originals to protest the tax, since the appraised value would be so high upon his death that his family would have been left bankrupt. Then he learned about foundations. In 1980 he created the De Grazia Art & Cultural Foundation to perpetuate his work and make it available to the public. The Foundation is well funded and its income continues. Each year it donates some $70,000 in grants to such beneficiaries as the noted Heard Museum of Phoenix, artist-in-residence programs in the schools, local public television stations and community organizations. An estimated 200,000 people a year visit his gallery. He illustrated many books, including a number of his own, among them *Ah-Ha-Toro* (1967); *Yaqui Easter* (1968); *The Rose and the Robe* (1968); *De Grazia and His Mountain, The Superstition* (1972); *De Grazia Paints Cabeza de Vaca...* (1973); *De Grazia Paints the Legends of the Papago Indians* (1975); *De Grazia Paints the Apache Indians* (1976); and *Christmas Fantasies* (1977). The artist died of cancer, survived by his widow. He was buried near his gallery, "close to his work and the people who come to see it."

Allyson Armstrong, "Gallery in the Sun," Tucson, *Desert Leaf,* Vol. 3, No. 2 (Feb. 1989), 1-3; George A. Miller, "De Grazia: The Legacy Endures," *Tucson Lifestyle,* Vol. 8, No. 10 (Oct. 1989), 66-67; William Reed, "De Grazia," *Troopers West,* Ray Brandes, ed., Illus. by De Grazia, San Diego, Frontier Heritage Press, 1970; *Who Was Who.*

Delaney, William, desperado (d. Mar. 28, 1884). Delaney was one of five gunmen who December 8, 1883, robbed the Joseph Goldwater-A.A. Casteñada general store at Bisbee, Arizona, seizing between $900 and $3,000 (reports differ), but missing the $7,000 payroll they were after because it had not yet arrived. The other four were Daniel Kelly, Omer W. Sample, James (Tex) Howard and Daniel Dowd (see entries). Bill Delaney reportedly was married, his wife and children living at Clifton, Arizona, where he was said to have owned "valuable mining interests" which he deeded to his wife before his execution. Bisbee Deputy Sheriff W.A. (Bill) Daniels (see entry) learned from Mexican informants that Delaney was hiding at Minas Prietas, Sonora; the deputy went there, arrested Delaney by ruse and brought him back to Arizona where with the other four they were tried for the robbery in which four by-standers were slain outright: Deputy Sheriff Tom Smith, J.C. Tapiner, Mrs. R.H. (Anna) Roberts and R.E. Duvall, while Albert Nolly was wounded mortally, and Dave Rousseau reportedly died in a related accident. All of the gunmen were convicted February 11 and executed simultaneously on a five-noose scaffold in the courtyard of the Tombstone county courthouse. John Heath, alleged mastermind of the robbery, was tried separately as he had taken no physical part in the crime; he was sentenced to life imprisonment, but was extracted February 22, 1884, from the Tombstone jail by a Bisbee crowd and hanged from a telegraph pole.

Ben T. Traywick, *The Hangings in Tombstone,* Tombstone, Red Maric's Bookstore, 1991; Robert E. Ladd, *Eight Ropes to Eternity,* pub. by *Tombstone Epitaph,* 1965; A.D. LeBaron, "Bisbee's Five Black Ghosts," *True West,* Vol. 7, No. 6 (July/Aug. 1960), 12-14-, 56-57.

Delarov, Evstrat Ivanovich, fur trader (c. 1740-1806). Said by Bancroft to be from the Peloponnesus and by Shelikhov to be a Macedonian, Delarov was chosen by the latter in 1787 to head up his fur trading colony on Kodiak Island, Alaska. He proved to be an able administrator and a humane man who got on smoothly with Aleuts, Russians and other peoples his position caused him to deal with. Bancroft wrote that "the contemplation of this amiable Greek's character affords a pleasant relief from the ordinary conduct of the Russians in America. Had there been more such men, I should have less to record of outrage, cruelty, and criminal neglect; had

Delarof been bad enough to please his directors [of the Russian fur company operating in Alaska] Baranof might have remained at home." Delarov had been a Moscow merchant, and later became partner in firms trading with the American natives. "He was in command of many vessels, stations, and expeditions," wrote Bancroft. "He finally became a director of the Russian American Company, and was honored by the government with the rank of commercial councilor." In 1780 Delarov commanded the *Alexandr Nevski* on a trading cruise to the Kuril Islands, then turned her over to Potap Zaikov (see entry) who took her to Unalaska Island. Here Delarov, now in command of the *Sv. Alexei,* joined Zaikov, who assumed overall command of three ships for a voyage to Prince William Sound (Chugach Bay) on an adventurous trading foray. They reached Kayak Island July 27, 1783, soon moving westward to an anchorage off Nuchek (Hinchinbrook) Island from where roving parties were dispatched to investigate the resources of the sound. Often they ran into trouble from the fiercely hostile Chugach Eskimos; one company from Delarov's ship lost nine men killed and 14 wounded in a single night attack by the Eskimauans. Delarov later told Captain Joseph Billings (see entry) about the expedition: "On arriving at Prince William Sound a number of canoes surrounded the vessel and on one of them they displayed some kind of flag. I hoisted ours, when the natives paddled three times around the ship, one man standing up waving his hands and chanting. They came on board and I obtained fourteen sea-otter skins in exchange for some glass beads; they would accept no shirts or any kind of clothing; they conducted themselves in a friendly manner, and we ate, drank, and slept together in the greatest harmony...Suddenly, on the 8th of September, the natives changed their attitude, made a furious attack on my people. I knew of no cause for this change until one of my boats returned, when I learned that there had been quarreling and fighting between the boat's crew and the natives. I have no doubt that my people were the aggressors." By the winter of 1785-86 Delarov was manager of the Shelikhov station on Unalaska Island, where in August he was host to Captain John Meares (see entry), treating him as graciously as possible though being dismissed superciliously in Meare's book, published in 1790. Delarov was named in 1787 administrator of the Shelikhov company headquarters colony on Kodiak Island, attaining with it widespread influence over other trading stations on the Alaskan bight. Shelikhov sent a comprehensive letter to Delarov August 30, 1789, on how to conduct his frontier station; it was printed textually in an English translation in *Russian Penetration of the North Pacific Ocean*. Baranov assumed command of all establishments of the Shelikhov-Golikov Company, relieving Delarov June 27, 1791, although he remained nominal manager until July. "The superficial pacification of the natives by Shelikhov had been completed by Delarof," and he did it in a kind-spirited, if disciplined, way. "As much system had been secured as lay in the power of one right-minded intelligent man, surrounded by an unruly band of individuals but little if any above the criminal class. [Delarov] was strict in his sense of justice and of fair administrative ability." He had sent expeditions to the mainland and established a permanent station named Alexandrovsk at the mouth of the Susitna River at the head of Cook Inlet. "Delarov's administration at Kadiak won him the good-will of all under his command, both Russians and natives, and he received well merited praise from all visitors, Spanish, English, and Russian. In all reports...prominence is given to his justice for all, and his kindness to the natives; but just and amiable men are not usually of the kind chosen to manage a monopoly. In this instance Delarof was too lenient to suit his avaricious and unscrupulous partners," so he was succeeded by Baranov. He must soon have returned to Moscow or St. Petersburg and by 1802 he was a director of the Russian American Company which held a monopoly for all trade in and with Alaska. He died at St. Petersburg.

Bancroft, *Alaska; Russian Penetration of the North Pacific Ocean;* Pierce, *Russian America: A Biographical Dictionary.*

Delaware George (Nenatcheehunt), Delaware chief (fl. 1754-1777). A chief of the Unami (Turtle) division of the Delawares by his own statement, George was, in Thwaites's view, the head chief of the whole nation, having been chosen and installed "with great ceremony and rejoicing." He took part in the French and Indian War at first on the side of the English. However, he was a close friend of Shingas and Beaver (see entries) and when they became hostile to the English and favored the French, Delaware George temporarily did also; when French supplies and largesse gave out, he returned to the English. In 1758, according to Parkman, Delaware George, Shingas and Beaver befriended the Moravian missionary, Christian Frederick Post (see entry) when he sought to estab-

lish peace in the Fort Duquesne (Pittsburgh) region of Pennsylvania (the post was burned and abandoned by the French and occupied by John Forbes that year). Earlier George had been a follower of Post's in his mission, and Post wrote in his journal for August 18, 1758, that "*Delaware George* [now] is very active in endeavoring to establish a peace. I believe he is in earnest..." At a formal council in early September at which English authorities were present George affirmed that "I now let you know that my heart never was parted from you. I am sorry that I should make friendship with the *French* against the *English*...and I now assure you that my heart sticks close to the English interest..." Apparently he was faithful to the English thereafter. This loyalty may have persisted during the American Revolution, for he probably was present at the first siege of Wheeling in September 1777 and possibly was killed or wounded in that or some peripheral event. Something of the sort seems suggested by an address by George Morgan (see entry) to the Delawares at Fort Pitt October 1, 1777, in which he said that "I am sorry for Delaware George & Buckangehela's Son, but they should not have gone with foolish People," i.e., the English and their allies. Thwaites/Kellogg added that the son mentioned was of Wingenund, not of Buckingehelas and "was wounded at the siege of Wheeling. No doubt it was to this affair that Morgan refers." No further report of Delaware George has been located.

Thwaites, EWT, I; Parkman, *Montcalm and Wolfe,* II; Clinton A. Weslager, *The Delaware Indians,* New Brunswick, N.J., Rutgers Univ. Press, 1972; Thwaites/Kellogg, *Frontier Defense on the Upper Ohio, 1777-1778.*

Delaware Prophet (Neolin), Indian mystic (c. 1740-post 1766). A key figure in promoting anti-English feeling among Pontiac's followers on the eve of the 1763 uprising, his origins and demise are unreported; the date of birth cited above is conjecture. The Prophet, or Neolin, appearing as a young man told a Presbyterian minister, Charles Beatty, that he had had his first vision six years before, i.e., 1760. His name meant "four," and Sugden considered him "the greatest of all the Delaware prophets," the first major nativist prophet, the predecessor of Handsome Lake and Tenskwatawa (see entries). His career commenced when, musing alone on the degeneration of the Indians, a figure appeared before him, confirming the religious aspect of the phenomenon and instructing him that those who followed evil ways would go to Hell when they perished, while those who did not would find eternal happiness. He was instructed to reveal to his people that message and others things by way of prophecy and religious instruction. John McCullough, who had been captured by the Delawares and was living at Mahoning on Beaver Creek in western Pennsylvania, referred to the Prophet in 1762 and told something of his teachings: that the Indians could purify themselves from sin through emetics and abstinence from sexual practices, abandonment of firearms, they must live by the old pre-white ways, avoid creating fire by flint and steel but use rubbing sticks instead and if they would do all these things—and others—they would eventually be able to drive the whites from their country. It was said that the Prophet, when giving his instructions, almost always wept, enhancing his visible sincerity and his authority from heaven. The Delaware Prophet, according to Peckham "was not a war chief...He decried the baneful influence of all white men because that influence had brought the Indians to their present unhappy plight. He was an evangelist, a revivalist, preaching a new religion," although it incorporated obvious precepts and understandings absorbed from his conception of Christianity, learned from the missionaries. The Prophet lived on the Cuyahoga River near Lake Erie, but traveled widely preaching his message which, Sugden wrote, was "acutely nativistic, and anti-white." Pontiac appeared impressed with the Prophet and his teachings. The chief "emphasized the military message for his own purposes, but it is clear in all accounts of the Delaware Prophet." He seemed to predict that within seven years the English would be overthrown. He recognized the need for French assistance, however, and taught that the French were to be exempted from attack, while apparently transmitting the message he believed he had received from the Master of Life that "if you suffer the English among you, you are dead men. Sickness, smallpox, and their poison will destroy you entirely." Thus, according to Sugden, "Neolin threw divine sanction behind a war against the British [and] taught that such conflict was not only desirable, but necessary if the Indians were to achieve salvation." The Prophet's message spread widely, in large part through Pontiac who sent it to the Ottawas (his people), the Potawatomis and Wyandots. "No previous nativist prophet had a comparable effect." With the Pontiac uprising defeated, Neolin may have moved to the Shawnee towns by 1764. He appears finally in 1766 when he seems to have cooled his anti-British fervor in favor of a greater emphasis on his clearer views of Christianity. He sought to perfect his knowledge of it and

learn more of the faith from Presbyterian missionaries such as Charles Beatty. The date and circumstances of Neolin's death are not reported.

Information from John Sugden, including illuminating notes he has drafted upon "Delaware Nativism in the Eighteenth Century"; Howard H. Peckham, *Pontiac and the Indian Uprising*, Univ. of Chicago Press, Phoenix Books, 1947/1961; John Heckewelder, *History, Manners, and Customs of the Indian Nations*, Philadelphia, Hist. Soc. of Penn., 1876, repr., Arno Press and *New York Times*, 1971, pp. 291-93; Parkman, *Conspiracy of Pontiac*, I, 212; II, 298-99; DCB, III, 527.

De León, Martín, impresario (1765-1833). B. at Burgos, Nuevo Santander (present Tamaulipas), Mexico, he early rejected his father's plans for his extensive education and instead commenced packing supplies to the mines, in 1790 joining a regiment to repel Tamaulipas Indians. Becoming a rancher, he made a visit to Texas in 1805 and established a ranch on the Aransas River, later moving to a site on the Nueces River near the now vanished San Patricio, in southwestern San Patricio County. When garrisons were withdrawn to counter a Mexico revolution, De León and his family moved to San Antonio. In 1823 De León learned of Mexico's newly adopted liberal colonization laws and applied for permission to establish a town with 41 families on the Guadalupe River southeast of San Antonio, the petition granted April 13, 1824. He named the settlement Guadalupe Victoria, located at what was thought to be the site where the river had been discovered by Alonzo de León (see entry) in 1689. By October 1824 the present city of Victoria (1980 population 50,000) was founded with not all of the colonists Mexicans, others being from Ireland, Louisiana and elsewhere in the United States. In 1829 De León received permission to add 150 families to his colony. His death in 1833 cancelled the colonial contract, but by that time the community was firmly established. The actual place of De León's burial is uncertain. Descendants believe Martín's remains were finally interred in Evergreen Cemetery, Victoria, and a state marker was placed there in 1936. De León County, Texas was named for him. His relationship, if any, to Alonzo De León is unreported.

HT; *Porrua*.

Dellenbaugh, Frederick Samuel, explorer, artist, author (Sept. 13, 1853-Jan. 29, 1935). B. at McConnelsville, Ohio, he became a "drawer" of some talent although he had no formal art training when he signed on at Chicago at 17 as artist and boatman for Major John Wesley Powell's second expedition down the Colorado River in 1871-72. The "flame-haired" Dellenbaugh was described by Bartlett as "spirited, literate, and agreeable, a lover of the outdoors and an inveterate romanticist," and he performed his assignments well on the expedition, which proved to be a high point of his long life. The expedition and its amateur scientists embarked in three rowboats, the *Emma Dean, Nellie Powell* and *Cañonita* at Green River, Wyoming May 22, 1871. Fred found time to keep a diary and occasionally to study a *Manual of Drawing* which helped him produce a number of sketches, later to become paintings of geological features and other points of interest on the adventurous journey. He was assigned in August to assist Almon Harris Thompson, topographer, in mapping the Grand Canyon region the expedition was passing through. He completed his map and his connection with the expedition February 28, 1873. It had been a time of excitement and prosaic work, the expedition hampered by lack of funds and many interruptions, but for Dellenbaugh it was an unforgettable experience. He studied oil painting under a private instructor at Buffalo, New York, and later at Munich and Paris, and traveled the West and abroad many times. In 1899 he was a member of the Harriman (see entry) Alaskan expedition. Dellenbaugh after the turn of the century commenced a successful writing career, his first book, *The North-Americans of Yesteryear*, appearing in 1901. He published the *Romance of the Colorado River* (1902) and *A Canyon Voyage* (1908). His other books included, of some frontier interest, *The Breaking of the Wilderness* (1905); *Fremont and '49* (1914) and *The Life of General George A. Custer* (1917). He was a member of the American Anthropological Society, a founder of the Explorers Club, for three years librarian of the American Geographical Society and belonged to other organizations. Dellenbaugh was a personable man, made many friends and held strong loyalties—over the years his respect and admiration for Powell grew into adulation. He had shortcomings as a researcher and was not overly careful of facts, but his best works were worthy and are respected today. He died at 81 of pneumonia and was buried at Ellenville, New York. His wife had predeceased him.

Martin J. Anderson, "Artist in the Wilderness: Frederick Dellenbaugh's Grand Canyon Adventure," and Robert C. Euler, "Frederick Dellenbaugh: Grand Canyon Artist" (with illus., many in color, of Dellenbaugh's work), both articles in *Journal of Arizona History*, Vol. 28, No. 1 (Spring 1987), 31-68; Richard A. Bartlett, *Great Surveys*

of the American West, Norman, Univ. of Okla. Press, 1962; DAB.

De Long, George Washington, polar explorer (Aug. 22, 1844-Oct. 30, 1881). B. at New York City, he was graduated from Annapolis in 1865, served for three years on the *Canandaigua* in European waters and those of Africa and in the Mediterranean. He became a lieutenant in 1869, and a lieutenant commander in 1879. In 1873 he was assigned to the *Juniata,* sent to the Arctic in search of the missing steamer *Polaris* of the C.F. Hall expedition; the adventure awakened in him a fascination with polar exploration. At New York he interested publisher James Gordon Bennett and they eventually acquired the steamer *Pandora,* rechristened her the *Jeanette,* and fitted her out for what was to be a transit of Bering Strait and a dash for the North Pole under the joint auspices of the U.S. Navy. July 8, 1879, the vessel cleared San Francisco with a complement of 33. September 5, about 25 miles east of Herald Reef, some 300 miles north of Bering Strait, the ship was frozen in. She drifted northwest for more than 21 months, attaining Latitude 77° 15′ N., Longitude 155° east by June 12, 1881, when the ice crushed her; she sank at 4 a.m. June 13. The ship was abandoned in orderly fashion with most of the provisions and equipment salvaged and for two months De Long and his men worked south over the floes toward Siberia. When open water was reached they embarked in their three boats for the Lena Delta on the Siberian coast. In a storm September 12 the craft became separated; one, under a Lieutenant Chipp, was never heard from again. De Long's boat reached the northern arm of the Lena River, an uninhabited area, and Engineer George Wallace Melville's boat landed at an eastern mouth of the river where his party was rescued by natives. De Long, with dwindling provisions, led his men southward, sending two of the strongest ahead to try to find relief; they survived. Toward the end of October, De Long's remaining party succumbed one by one to starvation and hardship, their bodies, journals and other relics discovered the following season by Melville who had led an expedition in search of them. Their remains were brought to New York to be buried with honors. De Long's journal was published by his widow, the former Emma J. Wotton, under the title, *The Voyage of the Jeanette* (1883). The expedition had determined that Wrangel Island was not the southern tip of a northern continent, and demonstrated the first leg of a circumpolar drift, which eventually was carried farther by Fritjof Nansen in the *Fram* and by later explorers, including Russian scientists who have made extended journeys on the floating ice pack. The De Long effort also discovered a small group of islands and reefs now named for the explorer and his vessel.

CE; DAB; Edward Ellsberg, *Hell on Ice* (1938), a fictionalized account of the De Long expedition.

Dementev, Avraam, seaman (d. 1741). Fleet master with Chirikov (see entry), off Lisianskii Strait on July 18, 1741, he took the longboat of the *Sv. Pavel* under orders, ashore with ten armed men; they were never seen again. July 24 boatswain Savelev led a party with the ship's remaining small boat in toward shore to search for the missing men, and the second boat's complement was never seen again, either. Both parties may have been ambushed by American Indian natives. Chirikov had actually discovered the Northwest Coast, although Bering is often given credit for having done so. Chirikov, having no other small boat, was unable to search for the missing seamen and cleared the coast following disappearance of the second group.

Pierce, *Russian America: A Biographical Dictionary.*

DeQuille, Dan (William Wright), journalist (May 9, 1829-Mar. 16, 1898). B. in Ohio of Quaker ancestry, at 18 he went to Iowa and soon commenced to write for local newspapers and for *Graham's Monthly Magazine* of Philadelphia. He married in Iowa and fathered a daughter who continued to reside in that state as long as DeQuille lived. In 1857 he went west as a prospector to California and reached Nevada in 1861. By then he had become a regular contributor to California's leading literary journal, the *Golden Era,* which described him as possessing "rare humor, and inexhaustible fund of anecdote and descriptive powers unsurpassed," and his reputation as an entertaining and responsible journalist had reached even the East coast where Charles Godfrey Leland of the New York *Knickerbocker* highly praised his output. He had also tried his hand at prospecting in central California without much success. When news arrived of rich silver strikes in southern Washoe County of Nevada, DeQuille happily joined the rush and settled in the boom town of Silver City which, with nearby Gold Hill and Virginia City, struggled for the title of "queen of the Comstock," to become the richest mining property of the region. DeQuille built a stone house where he settled with his mineral collection and his pets: several spotted

lizards, one with a forked tail, fat, hairy tarantulas, several horned toads and a scorpion. Here he was happy and remained busy, aside from his mining activities, at writing for the *Golden Era* and other publications. He rambled over the region on "prospecting" journeys that were more for adventure than profit but added to his geological expertise. He conceded in one article that "A majority of those who go on prospecting expeditions do not want to find a place where there is going to be much hard work to be done. They prefer rambling through the country and viewing new and curious sights to sinking shafts and running tunnels," and if they can't find surface wealth they "continue to travel." Unlike the vast majority of his fellows, DeQuille was fond of Indians, learned as much of the Paiute language as he could, fed Indians whenever they showed up, which was regularly, learned their customs and legends, and made many valued friends among them. DeQuille was a genial, gregarious man who was so much a master humorist that many of his admirers believed him more so than Mark Twain, who worked under him on the *Territorial Enterprise* of Virginia City and profited from the association. But in addition, DeQuille was a superb reporter, considerably better than Twain, and DeQuille was a serious student of mining and became a scientifically-accepted writer and authority on Nevada mines, lodes and similar matters, so much so that his first book, *History of the Big Bonanza* (1876) not only was accepted as the finest and most scientifically accurate history to that time of the Comstock mines, but is considered today as the foremost technical and encompassing study of that impressive discovery and its working. Whereas Twain never visited a mine because he "could not get past the brewery," DeQuille had an intimate knowledge of the important mines of his area and, in fact, was among those who suggested the site where the greatest Comstock discovery was made, this on the basis of his geological knowledge. He became a reporter for the *Enterprise* in 1862 and stayed with it (minus intervals when he was "discharged" in order to sober up) for 31 years, until its near-demise. He was an originator of the "hoax" stories that sometimes were so apparently factual they confused even the experts, and his other humorous works were widely reprinted. His *History of the Comstock Silver Lode Mines* (1889) was the only other book published in his lifetime; it was a reliable and worthy work, but he never made much from either of his volumes. When Virginia City dwindled to a ghost town and his newspaper temporarily ceased publication, De Quille was left without resources, while his health rapidly deteriorated. Millionaire John W. Mackay, who had made a fortune in the Comstock mines, arranged for DeQuille, his valued friend, to be taken to any place he wished to go and provided for during his lifetime. Alfred Doten, also a journalist and his longtime friend, saw Dan off when he returned to Iowa with his wife and daughter, Lou: "He never expects to come back, for he is so terribly broken down with rheumatism and used up generally that he cannot live long anyway." He added that though only 68 DeQuille "looks to be 90 yrs old." He died at the home of his daughter at West Liberty, Iowa. Many newspapers paid him tribute in obituary notices, and the *Mining and Scientific News* commented that "if every one whom this veteran writer delighted were to contribute a penny he would start on his trip a millionaire." In the summer of 1861 DeQuille had written a series of articles published in the *Golden Era* as "Washoe Rambles," for this was before the Comstock was developed. Sixty-five years later these were collected and published in book form, as they should have been much earlier. But as Richard E. Lingenfelter, foremost historian of Southwestern desert prospectors, mining and characters wrote in its introduction: "Dan intended during his lifetime to write several books which would doubtless have incorporated many of his writings from the *Enterprise* and earlier works," but he failed to do so, and "his best and most spontaneous writings are still entombed in the aging files of long dead journals and their resurrection…is coming only slowly." *The Fighting Horse of the Stanislaus,* a compilation of his stories and essays and edited by Lawrence I. Berkove, is a recent effort toward bringing to modern print the work of the author. It was published around 1990 by the University of Iowa Press of Iowa City 52242.

The Journals of Alfred Doten 1849-1903, ed. by Walter Van Tilburg Clark, 3 vols., Reno, Univ. of Nev. Press, 1973; Dan DeQuille, *Washoe Rambles,* intr. by Richard E. Lingenfelter, Los Angeles, Westernlore Press, 1963; DAB; info. from E.F. (Ted) Mains.

Deryabin (Deriabin, Dershabin), Vassili, explorer, fur trader (d. c. Feb. 15, 1851). Deryabin accompanied Andrei Glazunov (see entry) in 1833-34 on the initial organized penetration of the Alaskan interior, becoming possibly the first Russian to visit the Yukon River. They traveled from Fort St. Michael on Norton Sound to Unalakleet, thence overland to the Anvik River and its confluence with the Yukon, exploring the latter to its delta. They returned to the Kuskokwim River valley and after immense hardships regained the Yukon. Deryabin apparently remained in the employ of the Russian American Company. Malakhov (see entry) in 1838 had founded a post at Nulato, on the middle Yukon; it was burned by Indians in 1839, and Deryabin rebuilt it in 1841, managing it for a decade. It was a strategic post, in the heart of rich fur country, and it prospered. With the approaching Crimean War raising world tensions, Russian and English fur trading interests sponsored a convention of neutrality for the Northwest Coast region, so that the Russian American Company and the Hudson's Bay Company might peacefully continue relationships and their separate fur-gathering enterprises. The convention was approved by the potential belligerents. In 1851 Lieutenant John Barnard (see entry), a British naval officer of the *Enterprise,* a ship engaged in the search for the lost Franklin Arctic expedition, was sent overland from Norton Sound to investigate rumors of the murder of a party of Englishmen near Lake Mintokh, 40 miles northwest of the present Fairbanks. He arrived at Nulato and was hospitably received by Deryabin. Barnard however imperiously ordered Larion, a shaman and great chief of the Koyukons, to come in for questioning. His manner, according to Bancroft, incensed the Indian and, although there probably was more to it than that, the Koyukons attacked the post. They killed a Russian at the outskirts, destroyed three warehouses in which many Nulato families were housed, slaying all except one man who escaped and a few women "to serve as slaves." The attackers then descended upon the fort itself and stabbed Deryabin to death. Barnard, reading in bed, fired two aimless pistol shots but was stabbed mortally in the stomach. A report by one Ivan Konnygen of Unalakleet, who was present, said 100 warriors took part and that Larion boasted that he personally had killed both Deryabin and Barnard. Konnygen who at the time was suitor for one of Larion's daughters, had taken part in the affray, though by his account shooting no one. Pierce considers the Konnygen version, as reported by Bancroft, fiction. Russian sources report only three people killed including one Aleut and that the cause of the attack was protection given by the Russians to certain Nulatos who had offended the Koyukons. Bancroft commented that "Russian authorities appear to be ill informed on this matter or to have purposely misrepresented it."

Bancroft, *Alaska;* Johan Adrian Jacobsen, *Alaskan*

Voyage 1881-1883, Chicago, Univ. of Chicago Press, 1977, p. 240; Swanton, *Tribes;* Pierce, *Russian America: A Biographical Dictionary.*

De Trobriand, Philip Regis Denis de Keredern, military officer (June 4, 1816-July 15, 1897). B. near Tours, France, he was graduated in 1834 from the College of Tours and received a law degree from the University of Poitiers in 1837. He wrote poetry and a novel and had time to engage in an occasional duel, toured America in 1841, became engaged to an heiress, Mary Mason Jones, and married her at Paris in 1843; they settled in New York in 1847. De Trobriand became something of a literary figure. August 28, 1861, he was commissioned colonel of the 55th New York Infantry, transferring to the 38th New York Infantry December 21, 1862, and being mustered out November 21, 1863. He became a Brigadier General of Volunteers January 5, 1864, and a brevet Major General for "highly meritorious services" in the campaign concluding the Civil War at Appomatox. De Trobriand became colonel of the 31st U.S. Infantry July 28, 1866, transferring to the 13th Infantry March 15, 1869, serving in Dakota, Montana, Utah and Wyoming. He was an intelligent, reflective officer. Commenting on the hasty, sometimes unwise reduction of the Army following the Civil War he wrote that one "unavoidable result is that finally an excessive reduction of the Army becomes more expensive than would its maintenance to a normal strength, and...costs the people more to stop evils and repair damages than it would cost to prevent them." He also commented on surprise attacks on Indian villages, where the obvious goal was annihilation of the enemy: "The confessed aim is to exterminate everyone, for this is the only advantage of making the expedition; if extermination were not achieved, just another burden would be added—prisoners," although many officers sought to minimize killings and spare noncombatants. De Trobriand supported the arguments for fighting Indians by their own methods in order to defeat them. This might be done, he believed, first "by forming auxiliary squadrons composed of frontiersmen who knew the Indians and who are able to fight them in their own way" and secondly, "by enrolling in volunteer companies the Indians themselves...who are at war with the hostile tribes, the line officers being taken exclusively from among the men of the plains who are familiar with the habits, ideas, and languages of the tribes." Although his thoughts were not original, the few attempts to combat Indians with "hard-

ened frontiersmen" were fiascos, although the use of Indians to fight Indians scored major successes. In 1874 De Trobriand acquired the title of count upon the death of a cousin, but he remained in the Army until his retirement March 20, 1879, at the age of 62. He lived thereafter at New Orleans having been assigned in 1875 to uphold an "alien" government in Louisiana and by his tact "won the regard even of his opponents." He cultivated roses and between travels to France spent the summers with his daughter on Long Island, dying at Bayport. He had published in French in 1867-68 his reminiscences of the Civil War, the two volumes shortly translated into English as *Four Years Campaigning with the Army of the Potomac,* a highly praised work.

Heitman; DAB; Robert M. Utley, *Frontier Regulars: The United States Army and the Indian, 1866-1890,* N.Y., The Macmillan Co., 1973.

DeWitt, Green C., entrepreneur (Sept. 16, 1787-May 18, 1835). B. in Lincoln County, Kentucky, he moved to St. Louis, Missouri, at 32 and later to Ralls County southwest of Hannibal where he was elected sheriff. In the 1820s he went to Mexico City seeking a land grant as a Texas impresario, or promoter. April 15, 1825, he obtained a contract to introduce 400 families and settle them on the Guadalupe, San Marcos and Lavaca rivers, Mexico, agreeing to this sort of arrangement as security for its northern borders against Indians and other perceived threats to its territorial integrity. The present town of Gonzales, east of San Antonio, was laid out and to it DeWitt brought his wife and six children in 1828. On May 18, 1835, about a year short of Texas independence, DeWitt died at Monclova, capital of Coahuila, Mexico, while trying to obtain a land grant for an additional 80 families. DeWitt County, Texas was named for him.

HT.

Dezhnev, Semen Ivanov, Cossack explorer (c. 1605-c. 1673). Described by Bancroft as a "Cossack chieftain," Dezhnev was b. near Pinega or Ustiug, east of Archangel and the White Sea. He was in government service by 1638 and a decade later commenced the voyage that would make him famous, embarking from the community of Nizhne-Kolymsk near the mouth of the Kolyma River in eastern Siberia. June 20, 1648, seven *kochi,* or Siberian littoral sea-boats, set out eastward in an attempt to locate the Anadyr River of which reports had been heard but whose course was unknown.

Most of the boats were lost but Dezhnev reported that his and another rounded what became known as East Cape, the easternmost point of Siberia and after many adventures he and about a dozen survivors reached the mouth of the Anadyr, which empties into the Bering Sea. He had demonstrated, 80 years before Bering and more certainly than the Dane, that northeastern Siberia was bounded by sea and that it and North America were not linked by an isthmus. On the journey two islands, apparently Big and Little Diomede which lie between Siberia and Alaska, were sighted, and thus Dezhnev became discoverer of North America's northwesternmost extremity; in addition he heard tales from Chukchi natives about continental lands to the east, even if he did not sight them. The truth of Dezhnev's important, though long forgotten, voyage was affirmed by Gerhard F. Muller, a pioneer in Siberian historiography, in 1758. The full reality of the journey was disputed by an American historian, Frank A. Golder in 1914, but Golder's position in turn was rejected by Raymond H. Fisher in 1973, based in part upon the findings of B.P. Polevoi, a Soviet scholar who, supported by persuasive evidence, held that Dezhnev's key geographical discovery and around which he traveled was indeed East Cape and the entire Chukotsk Peninsula. East Cape in 1898 was renamed Cape Dezhnev and there is a monument there to the explorer. He died at Moscow in 1672 or 1673.

Bancroft, *Alaska;* F.A. Golder, *Russian Expansion on the Pacific 1641-1850,* N.Y., Paragon Book Reprint Corp., 1917 (1914); Raymond H. Fisher, "Dezhnev's Voyage of 1648 in the Light of Soviet Scholarship," *Terrae Incognitae,* Vol. 5 (1973), 7-26.

Dickinson, John, military officer (d. 1799). B. in the present Bath County, Virginia, he served actively in the French and Indian War and from his Fort Dickinson young Arthur Campbell was captured by northwestern Indians in either 1751 or 1758, as variant accounts have it. Dickinson led a retaliatory pursuit of Cornstalk's Shawnee war party after a raid on the Carr's Creek settlement during Pontiac's War of 1763; the Indians attacked settlers at a number of sites in Virginia and present West Virginia. It was Cornstalk's second raid on Carr's Creek, the first and most destructive occurring October 10, 1759. Later Dickinson, by now a militia colonel, planned a retaliatory raid (in 1777) on the Shawnee towns on the Scioto River of Ohio, but the slaying of Cornstalk that autumn at the Point Pleasant fort aborted the operation. Dickinson remained a distinguished citizen of Bath County until his death.

Thwaites, *Dunmore;* Alexander Scott Withers, *Chronicles of Border Warfare,* Cincinnati, Robert Clarke Co., 1895, 1970.

Di Peso, Charles Corradino, archeologist (Oct. 20, 1920-Nov. 20, 1982). B. at St. Louis he became as an archeologist best known for his years directing excavation of an important prehistoric complex at Casas Grandes, Chihuahua, his final report published in the 8-volume *Casas Grandes: A Fallen Trading Center of the Gran Chichimeca* (1974). He was graduated in 1942 with degrees in anthropology and geology from Beloit (Wisconsin) College, received a master's degree in 1950 and a doctorate, both in anthropology from the University of Arizona, and served in the Army Air Corps during World War II. As a student he had done field work at Ackmen, Colorado, and Pine Lawn (Pine Park) west of Reserve, New Mexico, both projects under supervision of Paul S. Martin. Di Peso in 1945 became Phoenix City Archeologist, a position he described as "mainly public relations." In 1948 he joined the Amerind Foundation near Dragoon, Arizona, as archeologist-in-charge, becoming director in 1952. In that year he became the first person to receive a doctorate in archeology from the University of Arizona. He was given the Alfred Vincent Kidder Award for achievement in American archeology in 1959 from the American Anthropological Association, was president of the Society for American Archeology in 1972-73 and belonged to other professional scientific organizations. His principal interest was always in field studies. In 1949 he worked on a Babocomari village in southeastern Arizona; studied the Sobaipuri village at the important site of Quiburi on the San Pedro River in 1951, the village of San Cayetano del Tumacacori in 1954-55, and at Casas Grandes principally from 1958-61. He published scientific reports on the results of his various field investigations. He died at Tucson at 62, leaving his widow and two sons.

Views on the Military History of the Indian-Spanish-American Southwest: A Seminar, ed. by Bruno J. Rolak, Ft. Huachuca, Az., 1976, 189-90; *Arizona Daily Star,* Nov. 22, 1982.

Doane, Aaron, partisan (fl. Sept. 1781-1815). The dates of birth and death of Aaron Doane are unreported, but he was a member of the Doane band of partisans who terrorized Bucks County, Pennsylvania, during and after the American Revolution. He was charged with taking part in the October 22, 1781, looting at Newtown, Pennsylvania, of the county treasury, but there was sworn testimony that he was under confinement at the time and did not participate in that affair (see Moses Doane entry for details). He was in on raids on the collectors of public moneys of 1783 at Buckingham, Makefield and other places, came under the Proclamation of Outlawry of 1783 as an outlaw and was arrested August 1784 in Baltimore County, Maryland, and extradited to Pennsylvania. He was tried at Philadelphia and sentenced in September 1784 to hang. He petitioned authorities for leniency on two occasions and the Supreme Council of Pennsylvania granted his petitions on condition that he "transport himself across the seas [and] not return to the United States." He went to Canada and settled in the township of Humberstone, Welland County, Ontario, attaining a good reputation for honesty and integrity. During the invasion of Canada by the Americans he was drafted and served in the British army. He married Rhoda Cook in Welland County and they had seven children who survived infancy. Aaron Doane died at Humberstone.

Info. from Mrs. Emma Barrows, natl. historian, The Doane Family Assn. of America, Inc., Vestal, N.Y.; the assn.'s *The Doane Family,* Vol. I, 238-40.

Doane, Abraham, partisan (c. 1765-Sept. 24, 1788). B. probably at Plumstead, Bucks County, Pennsylvania, he was of an age with his cousin, Levi Doane (see entry), engaged with him and other members of the Doane "gang" in outlawry or, it may be partisan activities since they all were Tory-Loyalists, at least when it suited them to be so, and occasionally were agents of British interests. Abraham was a son of Israel Doane and a brother of Mary Doane, who married Joseph Doane, and thus Abraham was a brother-in-law of that important member of the group. Abraham's name appeared with other Doanes on the Proclamation of Outlawry of July 26, 1783, placing a price of 100 pounds sterling in specie on the head of each. In June 1784 Abraham and several accomplices were arrested on their way to Detroit and jailed in Washington County, Pennsylvania; he probably escaped, but with Levi Doane was arrested in 1788 in Chester County, Pennsylvania, and held in June in the Philadelphia jail. Sentenced to hang, the two petitioned Benjamin Franklin, President of the Executive Council, for clemency, their request supported by pleas of numerous relatives and friends, but the petitions were denied and both men were hanged publicly on the commons at Philadelphia and buried at Plumstead. They "died with great firmness," and "it was commonly said of them, with special reference to Abraham, 'they have hanged the smartest two men in Pennsylvania.'"

Info. from Mrs. Emma Barrows, natl. historian, The

Doane Family Assn. of America, Inc., Vestal, N.Y.; the assn.'s *The Doane Family,* Vol. I, 242-44.

Doane, Joseph Jr., partisan (1752-1844). As were his four siblings and cousin Abraham Doane, Joseph was b. at Plumstead (Plumsteadville), Pennsylvania, north of Philadelphia, and became one of a Tory-Loyalist band of outlaws under leadership of his older brother, Moses Doane, during the Revolutionary War years. He married his cousin, Mary Doane, daughter of his uncle Israel and sister of Abraham. Joseph received a good education and taught school until he became involved in outlawry, or perhaps partisan activity against the larger and more powerful Whig element. Joseph's name appeared on a Proclamation of Outlawry of September 13, 1783, as of the band of "Tory Doanes" wanted, with a reward for each. Subsequently Squire Shaw, a Whig, was attacked, robbed and brutally beaten by the Doanes, including Joseph. For this offense a party of citizenry pursued the Doanes and overtook Joseph near Skipjack Creek in Montgomery County west of Plumstead, where they had a rendezvous point. Jumped at their refuge the boys hastily mounted horses but someone took Joseph's, leaving him an inferior mount. The fleeing outlaws raced through a cornfield, the pursuers firing at them. A bullet struck Joseph's jawbone and knocked out some teeth; his horse failed to clear a fence and fell with Doane, who was captured. The rest of the gang escaped. Joseph was taken to the Newtown county seat jail, ten miles west of Trenton, Pennsylvania; he was arraigned March 30, 1784, tried and sentenced to be hanged for his role in the county treasury robbery of October 22, 1781, and perhaps other offenses. Joseph subsequently wrote that "sometime after this my wife paid me a visit bringing an augur, rope, file and case knife in her clothes...With the file I converted the knife into a saw and with it sawed off my irons, then bored off the lock and got into the yard, where I attached a heavy stone to the end of a rope, and threw it over the wall and by this means I scaled the wall." He was injured in a tumble into a quarry, but managed to find his way to the house of a friend and secreted himself inside a straw stack in the barnyard where he burrowed out a hole and remained for two or three weeks, his friend supplying him each night with food. When he felt well enough Joseph left his retreat and made his way to New Jersey where he started a small school in order to raise funds, boarding at the village tavern. He chanced to glimpse a fellow townsman and while escaping observation "I felt this was no place for me." He pleaded indisposition, closed his school, collected what money he could and left to make his way to Canada where his brother, Aaron, had preceded him. Before leaving, however, Joseph revisited Bucks County on a farewell visit to his old home. He was recognized by a neighbor who seized and threw him to the ground, but Joseph managed to draw a penknife, opened it with his teeth and stabbed his assailant in the neck, "inflicting a wound which permanently affected the man's speech." Then Joseph, "like the good Samaritan" bound up his assailant's wound, "advised him to seek help at the nearest house" and made off. In Canada he with his wife settled about 1790 in Humberstone Township, Welland County, and resumed teaching, at which he prospered, acquiring an excellent reputation among his patrons. About 1815 he moved to Walpole township, some 40 miles distant, purchasing a 200-acre farm in a fine location. When the American Army occupied Fort Erie, Ontario, in the War of 1812, Joseph, who was said to possess "an inveterate hatred of all Americans," was seized as inimical to U.S. interests, although he was not in arms. He was made a prisoner of war and sent to Greenbush, New York, where he was confined in miserable conditions for 18 months before he was released. In 1823 he again visited relatives in Bucks County, Pennsylvania, called on Squire Shaw who as a Quaker was ready to forgive past injustices, and they held a warm conversation. Doane had said his purpose was to obtain the value of his father's confiscated farms but if he actually tried to do so, it was without effect. One who met him at that time recalled that he was "a portly, good looking, active, intelligent man of seventy-two years, straight as an Indian, very nearly six feet high," and even at that age of considerable athletic ability. Joseph returned to Canada and lived past 90, he and his wife becoming parents of seven children. He died at Walpole, Haldimand County, Ontario, his widow dying in 1850.

Info. from Mrs. Emma Barrows, natl. historian, The Doane Family Assn. of America, Inc., Vestal, N.Y.; the assn.'s *The Doane Family*, Vol. I, 233-38.

Doane, Levi, partisan (c. 1765-Sept. 24, 1788). B. at Plumstead, Bucks County, Pennsylvania, he was a member of the so-called Doane gang of outlaws or, perhaps, partisans who terrorized Bucks County and neighboring areas during the Revolutionary War, in which they occasionally served the British interest. Levi Doane was a particular friend of his cousin, Abraham Doane, another member of the group, and who was hanged at the same time as Levi. They were of the same age. Both appeared in the Proclamation of Outlawry of July 26, 1783,

with a reward of 100 pounds sterling on each of their heads. Both were arrested in Chester County, Pennsylvania, in 1788 and taken to Philadelphia where they were sentenced to hang for outlawry. They twice petitioned Benjamin Franklin, President of the Executive Council, for leniency on the basis of their extreme youth at the time of the alleged crimes, and their petitions were supported by numerous others forwarded by relatives and acquaintances, but all to no avail. Levi and Abraham were hanged on the commons of Philadelphia. The bodies were carted to Plumstead where the Society of Friends (Quakers) refused to permit them to be buried in their graveyard, so the bodies were interred at the edge of the woods opposite the Meeting House. Levi's mother "was in the habit of visiting his grave, over which with Bible in hand she would read and weep for hours at a time."

Info. from Mrs. Emma Barrows, natl. historian, The Doane Family Assn. of America, Inc., Vestal, N.Y.; the assn.'s *The Doane Family*, Vol. I, 238-40.

Doane, Mahlon, partisan (fl. 1781-1783). B. at Plumstead, Bucks County, Pennsylvania, he was one of the six-member Doane band of outlaws or, perhaps, partisans who terrorized Bucks County during and after the Revolution. With the others he was sometimes considered a Tory-Loyalist when it was convenient to be so. He was the smallest of the band, but wiry and active. "He was recognized by his long coal-black hair, and a peculiar habit he had of looking down, but more positively by a blemish in one eye, and a scar beneath it." By a confession of Jesse Vickers of August 9, 1782, Mahlon took part in the robbery of the Bucks County treasury on October 22, 1781, and "in the robberies of certain [other] collectors of taxes and military fines." His name therefore appeared on the Proclamations of Outlawry of June 30 and July 26, 1783, by which merely being identified in court as the person listed was tantamount to a sentence of death by hanging. Following issuance of the proclamations Mahlon Doane fled to western Pennsylvania where he was captured September 27, 1783, and lodged in the Bedford County jail. With the aid of confederates he soon escaped, but before departing he released all the other prisoners from the jail except a man who had been guilty of robbing a woman. What became of Mahlon is conjecture. There is a tradition that in freeing himself from his irons, he mutilated his feet and died in the woods from loss of blood. Another tradition is that he drowned himself in Chesapeake Bay to avoid further persecutions. His nephew, Levi Doane, the Canadian son of Aaron

Doane, about 1880 said of Mahlon that "He escaped from prison and went on board a ship at New York on which were four hundred Loyalists. I believe they sailed for England. We never heard any more of Mahlon."

Info. from Mrs. Emma Barrows, natl. historian, The Doane Family Assn. of America, Inc., Vestal, N.Y., the assn.'s *The Doane Family*, Vol. I, 244-45.

Doane, Moses, partisan (c. 1752-Sept. 1, 1783). Probably the oldest of the children of Joseph and Hester Doane, he apparently was the leader of the notorious outlaw band of Tory-Loyalists which included his four siblings, Joseph, Aaron, Levi and Mahlon and their cousin, Abraham Doane. Moses was "a leader by nature, and probably possessing greater natural abilities than any of the others [he was] the master spirit of them all, and always appeared as captain of the band." Horan/Sann judged the Doanes the "most important of the outlaw gangs [of Revolutionary years], famous in legend and story, and possibly America's first outlaw brotherhood." All were born at Plumstead (Plumsteadville) in Bucks County, Pennsylvania, about 28 miles north of Philadelphia and half a dozen miles west of the Delaware River. Moses married Rachel Tomlinson and fathered a son, Moses, born in 1781. Activities of the Doanes terrorized Bucks County and ultimately generated citizen reprisals. They became "the terror of their day." They became quite as famous in their county and Philadelphia "as any hero of the Revolution." Of good family, they eased into outlawry gradually. They tried to remain neutral when war broke out, but refused to accept militia drafts or to pay fines for non-service, and their property as a result was sold piecemeal and themselves harassed, and at length they "set out to live in highways and hedges and wage a predatory and retaliatory war" upon those they considered their persecutors. "They were men of fine figures and address, elegant horsemen, great runners and leapers and excellent at stratagem and escapes. [They] did no injury to the weak, the poor or the peaceful. They were in league with the British while in Philadelphia, and acted as occasional spies. They became of so much importance as to have 300 pounds sterling apiece set on their heads. They went generally on horseback, sometimes separate, sometimes together with accomplices ...Some of them were occasionally apprehended but as often broke jail." Their central act of outlawry was a raid on October 22, 1781, of the county treasury at Newtown, which became "one of the exciting events of the day." John Hart was treasur-

er. Early in the evening Moses Doane rode through the town to see if the way was clear for the robbery. At 10 p.m. the treasurer's house was surrounded by the Doane-led gang of about 25 men, and Hart was captured. The gang ransacked the house, obtained keys to the county treasury, "stole all the public money to be found," and got away with 735 pounds, 17 shillings and 19½ pence in coin and 1,307 pounds in paper. At the Wrightstown schoolhouse that night they divided the loot. The Doanes often made their headquarters in a cave on Tohickon Creek, north of Plumstead, and retreated there when prices on their heads had risen to amounts threatening to interfere with their depredations. Forced at last by hunger to emerge from the cave, Moses, with his brother Levi and cousin Abraham ventured to the cabin of a confederate named Halsey at Gallows Run, Plumstead. Word of their presence seeped out and 14 citizens volunteered under leadership of a Colonel Hart (perhaps John Hart) and a Major Kennedy to try for their capture. They surrounded the cabin, Hart pushed open the door and commanded those inside to surrender. The Doanes swept up their weapons and fired, a bullet ripping a splinter from a gun which struck Kennedy in the back, giving him a mortal wound. Hart wrestled Moses Doane to the floor and bound him when Robert Gibson rushed up and shot and killed the helpless man. It was rumored that Gibson had participated in some of the Doane outlawry and "it is supposed he shot Moses to close his mouth against the utterance of testimony against himself." Levi and Abraham Doane escaped through a window at the rear of the cabin, Abraham effecting his escape by capturing Halsey's wife and using her as a shield while he got away.

Info. from Mrs. Emma Barrows, natl. historian, The Doane Family Assn., Vestal, N.Y.; the assn.'s *The Doane Family*, Vol. I, 231-33; James D. Horan, Paul Sann, *Pictorial History of the Wild West*, N.Y., Crown Pub., 1954; Paul I Wellman, *Spawn of Evil*, Garden City, N.Y., Doubleday & Co., 1964; info. from E.F. (Ted) Mains.

Dodd, Charles, HBC factor (1808-June 2, 1860). B. at Norwich, England, he joined the Hudson's Bay Company and as second mate arrived aboard the *Beaver* on the Pacific Coast in 1835; he became first mate as the ship reached Fort Vancouver at the mouth of the Columbia River. In 1841 he joined the bark *Cowlitz* as the first mate and with Sir George Simpson (see entry) made a voyage to California, Hawaii and Sitka, Alaska. In April 1842 the *Cowlitz* was towed by steamer to Fort Stikine, the present Wrangell, at the north end of Wrangell Island in the Alexander Archipelago. It was learned that the factor there, John McLoughlin Jr., had been killed and Simpson placed Dodd in charge, a post he held for a year, when he was given command of his old ship, the *Beaver,* remaining with her for a decade. Dodd was named a chief factor for the HBC in 1860 and was put in charge of operations on the Northwest Coast. He was taken ill, however, and died at Victoria.

Pierce, *Russian America: A Biographical Dictionary.*

Doddridge, Joseph, historical writer (Oct. 14, 1769-Nov. 9, 1826). B. in Friend's Cove, south of Bedford, Pennsylvania, his father, having lost his property through an imperfect title, moved with the family in 1773 to western Washington County, then in the wilderness. He was educated in Maryland and for several years was an itinerant preacher for the Methodist Church. He was ordained in 1800 a priest in the Episcopal Church and also became a practicing physician. He preached and practiced medicine in Virginia and Ohio and helped start a number of parishes. Meanwhile Doddridge became interested in the settlement of the frontier and the Indian wars which accompanied that process. In 1824 he published *Notes on the Settlement and Indian Wars of the Western Parts of Virginia and Pennsylvania from 1763 to 1783...,* to be followed by two other posthumous editions. The second edition (1876) was edited by Alfred Williams of Circleville, Ohio; this included sketches of significant pioneers and military figures with an impact on the border. A third edition, published at Pittsburgh in 1912, was edited by John S. Ritenour and William T. Lindsey. They eliminated three of the earlier sketches but added "valuable and enlightening footnotes" by James Simpson of Cross Creek, Pennsylvania, and other material, including information on Cresap and Girty. Doddridge had conceded that his work was "imperfect [for] want of information," but as it now stands it is a valuable source on the American frontier. Doddridge died at 57 at his Wellsburg, West Virginia home, following a lengthy illness.

Joseph Doddridge, *Notes on the Settlement and Indian Wars,* repr. by McClain Printing Co., Parsons, W.Va., 1960.

Dodge, Henry Lafayette (Linn), military officer, Indian agent (Apr. 1, 1810-c. Nov. 19, 1856). The eldest surviving son of Henry Dodge (see entry) and brother of U.S. Senator Augustus Caesar Dodge (1812-1883), Henry L. Dodge always detested his middle name, preferring Linn for reasons unknown. He was b. probably at Ste. Genevieve, Missouri, was self educated though not

extensively, and had some slight training in law. Dodge served as a first lieutenant for eight months during the 1832 Black Hawk War in Captain James H. Gentry's company, part of a regiment commanded by Henry Dodge, Sr. Reportedly Henry L. Dodge with his company took part in the climactic battle of the war at Bad Axe River, Wisconsin, and observed the defeat of the Sauk and Fox leaders, Black Hawk and Keokuk. In 1836 he married at Ste. Genevieve, Adele Becquet; they lived for seven years at Dodgeville and Mineral Point, Wisconsin, where Dodge mined lead. He then went west, apparently alone. July 15, 1847, he enlisted in Battery A, Light Artillery of the Santa Fe Battalion of the Mounted Volunteers. His battery later was attached to the 1st Dragoons at Taos. At that time Dodge was 5 ft., 9 in., tall, had gray eyes, dark hair and a florid complexion, according to his enlistment papers. He was discharged at Las Vegas August 27, 1848. Hostilities breaking out with the Jicarilla Apaches, Colonel John M. Washington, military governor, ordered four companies of volunteers formed, Dodge becoming a captain of a company of 85 infantry stationed at Jemez, New Mexico. Later he was directed to become subsistence agent in the Quartermaster department at Cebolleta, west of Albuquerque, a thankless job, McNitt commenting that "perhaps no one else would have made such an utter botch of his [records], but perhaps no other man could have been more effective" in carrying out his unrewarding duties. Apparently he had commenced learning the difficult Navaho language, for he was given the duty of interpreter as well as forage master for Captain and brevet Lieutenant Colonel Daniel T. Chandler, commanding two companies at Cebolleta. Word was received at Santa Fe May 26, 1853, that Dodge had been appointed Indian agent, and June 26 it was learned his assignment was to the Navahos. His salary was $1,500 a year and he was directed to establish his agency at Fort Defiance; in addition to the Navahos he was to be responsible for the pueblos of Laguna, Acoma and Zuñi and for seven Hopi villages to the west. When David Meriwether (see entry) became governor of New Mexico in 1853, Dodge fully informed him on Navaho matters, estimating their total population at that time at around 10,000 and their livestock of all sorts at about 250,000 head. He brought leading men to meet the new white governor. It was about this time that Dodge married a niece of Zarcillos Largo (see entry), noted Navaho peace chief. Nothing was said then or later about his first wife, Adele Becquet, to whom he apparently was still wed; he reportedly fathered children by both wives. Dodge for a time was engaged recovering sheep stolen from the Mexicans by Navahos, remaining in the saddle for days on end while "his easy way of dealing with Indians, usually produced good results." His agency remained at Fort Defiance though in the spring of 1855 he established temporary headquarters in the Chusca Valley north of Defiance, at Laguna Negra, then at Washington Pass, and back again at the fort. Somehow he had developed an affinity for the color red, wearing a shirt of that hue enough that the Navahos referred to him as *Bi'ee lichii,* or Red Shirt. Dodge became a veteran frontiersman of the Navaho country. McNitt judged that "as well as any white man and better than most, perhaps...he knew the Navajo country. Better yet, he knew the Navajos as few [white] men ever did, and his liking for them was returned in kind." An Apache raid in October 1856 on the important pueblo of Zuñi in western New Mexico prompted Captain Henry Lane Kendrick of the 2nd Artillery to plan a scout in that direction, and he asked Dodge to accompany it along with Armijo, a Navaho friend of Dodge's and a few other tribesmen. The detachment left Fort Defiance November 16, 1856. From Cedar Springs, 30 miles south of Zuñi, Dodge and Armijo left before dawn on the 19th for a hunt. To the west rose Haashk'aan Silah Mesa; Dodge and Armijo reached the summit, jumped a deer which Dodge shot and, as it was still early, left Armijo with the slain animal while he went to find another. He never returned. Kendrick expressed no initial concern, saying that as Dodge was intelligent and "a good woodsman & during the march [we had] seen no signs of Indians other than the friendly Navajoes & Zuñis...his absence...gave...no other anxiety than the fear that he might suffer from the cold before finding us." Dodge's trail eventually was followed, finding where he had been accosted by five or six Indians who the Navaho trackers said were a mixed band of Mogollons and Coyoteros. It later was learned that Dodge had been shot to avenge the loss of a Coyotero in the October raid on Zuñi, and that he had been killed by a Coyotero who in turn was reported slain in Bonneville's (see entry) vengeance raid the following summer. Dodge's remains were found February 11, 1857, and buried at Fort Defiance. Certain of Dodge's Navaho offspring attained positions of tribal importance, including Henry (Chee) Dodge, first chairman of the Navaho Tribal Council.

Frank McNitt, *Navajo Wars: Military Campaigns, Slave Raids and Reprisals,* Albuquerque, Univ. of New Mex. Press, 1972; Dan L. Thrapp, *Victorio and the Mimbres Apaches,* Norman, Univ. of Okla. Press, 1974; David Meriwether, *My Life in the Mountains and on the Plains,* ed. by Robert A. Griffen, Norman, 1966; *Black Hawk War;* Thrapp, *Encyclopedia of Frontier Biography,* Glendale, Ca., Arthur H. Clark Co., 1988.

Dodge, John, trader (c. 1749-1794). B. in Connecticut, he entered the Indian trade around 1770, settling in the Wyandot villages on the Sandusky River of Ohio. He acquired considerable influence over the Indians. In July 1775 Captain James Wood (see entry) asked him to accompany Wood to various villages, inviting the natives to come to Fort Pitt in the autumn for a treaty meeting; they agreed to attend and Dodge was to be their interpreter. After Wood departed the Detroit commander told the Sandusky dwellers that those at Fort Pitt were bad people who sought only to massacre them all, and their only hope was to follow directives of the King's emissaries and remain loyal to the English monarch. "This talk so dismayed the Indians, that they came to me, and said they would not go to the treaty," wrote Dodge. He reassured them and promised that if they would attend the Fort Pitt council he would be their surety and pledge for their safe return. "This...induced some of them to go with me to the treaty," Dodge reported. Charged with leaning toward the colonists' side, Dodge was arrested by the English in January 1776, confined at Detroit, then sent as a prisoner to Quebec. He escaped in 1778 and reached Boston, being received cordially by Horatio Gates and George Washington, while the Continental Congress granted him a land compensation for his losses at Sandusky. He then visited Virginia where Thomas Jefferson appointed him Indian agent for the Illinois country. At Kaskaskia he became leader of the military party, and also was accused of peculation and arbitrary violence toward the inhabitants. "After 1782 he dominated the settlement, having seized and fortified a commanding site." In 1787 he removed to Ste. Genevieve in the present Missouri, where he died.

Thwaites/Kellogg, *The Revolution on the Upper Ohio, 1775-1777,* Madison, Wis. Hist. Soc., 1908.

Donelson, John, expansionist (c. 1726-Spring 1786). B. in Maryland, he somehow came by the title of colonel. He early removed to Pennsylvania County, Virginia, where he became a man of influence, owning iron mills and representing his county in the House of Burgesses. In 1771 he was employed to survey the Cherokee boundary line and became interested in western lands. He moved with his family in 1779-80 to central Tennessee. Descending the Tennessee River with a fleet of flatboats, he joined James Robertson (see entry) at Nashville and laid the foundation of that settlement. In 1781 he removed to Kentucky, returning to the Cumberland settlement in 1785, visited Virginia again and was employed by Georgia to lay out a town at the Tennessee bend, below Chattanooga. He was killed in the wilderness in the spring of 1786, the circumstances unreported. His daughter, Rachel, became the wife of Andrew Jackson.

Thwaites/Kellogg, *The Revolution on the Upper Ohio, 1775-1777,* Madison, Wis. Hist. Soc., 1908.

Donner, Tamsen, pioneer (Nov. 1801-c. Mar. 26, 1847). B. Tamsen Eustace in Massachusetts, she attended school there and at some point married a man named Dozier by whom she had children. She taught in a North Carolina academy during the 1820s, but lost her husband and children in a fever epidemic and moved to Sangamon County, Illinois. There she cared for the motherless children of her brother, William Eustace, who farmed near Sugar Creek 15 miles south of Springfield. As a teacher she had acquired a reputation for "her ability to muster effective classroom control without resort to violence," for which she was ill-equipped in any event by reason of of her "quiet face and diminutive form." She taught all subjects and won the wholesome affection of her students. On one botany field trip she met George Donner (see entry) whose second wife had died, and in 1839 Tamsen and George Donner married and settled on his farm 15 miles from Sugar Creek. They lived there until 1846 when George Donner, his relatives, friends and others decided to go to California, and left the Midwest for that purpose. Tamsen Donner perished, trapped in the winter snows of the Sierra Nevada, dying either of starvation or more sinister causes (see George Donner entry for details of the trip to California and fate of members of the party).

John Mack Faragher, *Sugar Creek: Life on the Illinois Prairie,* New Haven, Yale Univ. Press, 1986; Thrapp, *Encyclopedia of Frontier Biography,* Glendale, Ca., Arthur H. Clark Co., 1988.

Donoho, Mary Wyatt, frontierswoman (Nov. 24, 1807-Jan. 12, 1880). The first Anglo-American woman to reach New Mexico over the Santa Fe Trail, she was born in Tennessee as Mary Dodson, the family moving westward and at length settling in Camden County, Missouri, where her father, James Dodson, founded the now-vanished Glaize City. By 1831 she was at Columbia, Missouri

where on November 27 she married William Donoho (Sept. 19, 1798-Sept. 23, 1845). In 1833 the couple with an infant daughter joined a wagon train for Santa Fe, a party of 328 men, including 184 employees of trader Charles Bent, and a 144-man escort commanded by Captain William N. Wickliffe of the 6th Infantry. The train left Diamond Spring(s), 15 miles west of Council Grove, Kansas with Bent as their civilian captain June 20 and reached Santa Fe safely on August 4, 1833, (without the military escort which had turned back upon reaching Mexican territory on July 10). Susan Shelby Magoffin (see entry) had believed she was the first Anglo-American woman to reach Santa Fe, but Meyer shows that 16 others had preceded Magoffin, Mary Donoho being the first known to have completed the journey. She and her husband remained in the Mexican community for several years. A second daughter was born there in 1835 and a son in 1837. The Donohos operated a hotel at Santa Fe, sold the "large quantity of freight" they had brought from Missouri, and Donoho also ransomed from Comanches three white women captured in 1836 in Texas: Sarah (Mrs. John) Horn, a Mrs. Harris, and Rach(a)el Plummer, who later in a narrative of her ordeal, wrote that "I have no language to express my gratitude to Mrs. Donoho. I found in her a mother, a sister, to condole me in my misfortune..." An uprising in 1837 against Governor Albino Perez generated turmoil and the Donohos, with the children and the three rescued Texas women, abandoned Santa Fe for Missouri where they lodged briefly with Mary's mother-in-law, Lucy Donoho. William Donoho escorted Rachel Plummer back to her home in Texas (all three of the rescued women died within a year of reaching safety). William returned to New Mexico to wind up business matters and in October 1839 moved his family to Clarksville, Texas, where they founded the Donoho Hotel, a noted hostelry for half a century. William died in 1845 and Mary inherited the hotel, managing it well. She became a prominent citizen of the community. She outlived her five daughters and her son inherited the hotel, continuing its profitable history. Both Mary and William Donoho are buried at Clarksville.

Marian Meyer, "New First Lady of the Santa Fe Trail," *True West,* Vol. 39, No. 8 (Aug. 1992), 50-55, including a sidebar on Meyer's "Search for Mary Donoho"; Barry, *The Beginning of the West;* HT; Heitman.

Dorman, Timothy, renegade (fl. 1779-1782). B. in England, he had led there "a most abandoned life." At length he was transported to America, probably as an indentured servant, and became the servant of

William Gregg, who resided near Buckhannon Fort, West Virginia. Dorman, a quarrelsome individual "was so reckless of reputation and devoide of shame for his villainies, that he would often recount tales of theft and robbery in which he had been a conspicuous actor ." Yet he must have had some redeeming qualities for when Captain George Jackson in 1779 or 1780 raised a company of scouts, Jacob Drake, a former Indian captive, became lieutenant and Dorman was commissioned ensign; the company had several brushes with Indians. Dorman came to know well the territory around Buckhannon and apparently, being a vengeful man, developed intense hatreds for some of its citizens. At some time he seems to have come in touch with hostile Indians from the Ohio country, and it was suspected that he was a "spy" or informant for them on occasion. He had married, meanwhile, and lived with his wife half a mile from Buckhannon. At the fort resided William White (see entry), a noted scout and Indian killer who, on one expedition, had chased down and tomahawked a young Indian whose father thereby acquired a hatred for White and for "several years" according to McWhorter, lurked about the settlements, hoping to catch his son's slayer off guard. Details are sparse and contradictory, but it is likely that during this time the vengeful Indian made contact with Dorman. On March 8, 1782, Dorman and his wife were riding toward Buckhannon and probably pointed out White to the Indian, who succeeded in shooting "his man, within sight of the fort." The avenging Indian tried to get White's scalp, but "an attacking party from the fort were so close upon him that he fled before accomplishing his object." With him disappeared Dorman and his wife, supposedly "captured" by the Indians, but actually, as it appears, having willingly gone off with them, thereafter to reside, campaign and fight with the hostiles. With the supposed capture of Dorman it was resolved to abandon Fort Buckhannon and seek security elsewhere "from the greater ills which...would befall them if they remained." In no small part this was due to the general conviction that Dorman, "to gratify his enmity to particular individuals and from his knowledge of the country, would be enabled to conduct them the more securely to blood and plunder." Dorman had been known to boast that "if he caught [those] with whom he was at variance, in the woods alone, he would murder them and attribute it to the savages." It was believed that but for the flight of the inhabitants, "all would have fallen before the fury of savage warriors, with this abandoned miscreant at their head." Edward Tanner, a youth captured by the Indians, reported that as he was being taken to their Ohio towns he met between 20 and 30 Indians headed by Dorman, proceeding to attack Buckhannon Fort. Tanner told them that the post was being evacuated, and the Indians hastened foward at such a gait that Dorman could scarcely keep up. They found the place deserted, and burned it. When the former residents returned to recover items they had left behind, they found a paper signed by Dorman affixed to the ruins. It was dated at the Indian towns, containing information of those who had been taken prisoner in that region and transported to the Ohio communities. Operating against these Indians was Captain George Jackson, Dorman's erstwhile commanding officer. The raiders continued their foray, killing an occasional white, and attacking the house of Mrs. Gregg, wife of Dorman's onetime master who appeared to be away at the time. The only victim was Gregg's daughter, with whom Dorman was at odds. She refused to go with the hostiles and "Dorman sunk his tomahawk into her head and then scalped her. She, however, lived several days and related the circumstances" of the incident. Further information on Dorman has not been found; it is possible that being of English origin he willingly opted for the British side of the Revolutionary affair, but given his lifelong criminal record, and detestation for anything smacking of authority, that explanation for his alliance with the Ohio Indians seems unlikely.

Lucullus V. McWhorter, *The Border Settlers of Northwestern Virginia*, Hamilton, Ohio, Republican Pub. Co., 1915, Alexander Scott Withers, *Chronicles of Border Warfare*, Cincinnati, Robert Clarke Co., 1895, 1970.

Dorofeev, Iakov Dorofeevich, explorer (d. Sept. 21, 1832). B. in Olenets gubernia, he joined the Russian American Company as a promyshlennik in 1802. Around 1822 he accompanied Carl John Schmidt, the new manager, to the Ross Russian colony in California, north of San Francisco. With Schmidt and a party of Aleuts, Dorofeev explored by baidara up the Slavianka River (today's Russian River). The party went about 60 miles upstream, finding when past the coastal range "beautiful meadows and forests, where many Indians lived." Pierce believes that they reached the vicinity of the present town of Ukiah and "this appears to have been the maximum penetration of the interior made by the Russians from Fort Ross." Dorofeev in 1829 became manager of the RAC's Unalaska office, holding that position until his death.

Pierce, *Russian America: A Biographical Dictionary*.

Dorr, Levi Lewis, physician, contract surgeon

(1840-Sept. 10, 1934). B. in Massachusetts, Dorr in 1861 enlisted in a state Volunteers infantry company, and was seriously wounded at Antietam; during his lengthy recuperation he began taking courses at Georgetown Medical School. He was mustered out of his military service July 16, 1864, worked at Bellevue Hospital in New York City where he satisfied requirements for a medical degree. In 1866 Dr. Dorr went to California, the following year became an acting assistant surgeon with the Army at $125 a month and was assigned to Arizona, being stationed at Tubac and Camp Crittenden, near Patagonia, and briefly at Camp (later Fort) Bowie. He returned to San Francisco in August, renewed his Army contract November 20 and was re-assigned to Arizona, serving at Camp Wallen until July 1869, then at Camp Grant from where he served as field surgeon for Colonel John Green's expedition into the White Mountains. He was re-assigned to Crittenden where he arrived October 22. Two days later he accompanied a scout toward the Chiricahua Mountains. The operation, under Captain Harrison Moulton, followed Apache activity against travelers on the southern route toward Tucson and the Pacific coast. The scout of 35 men on October 30, 1869, joined Captain Reuben Bernard (see entry), who had been fighting the Chiricahuas, presumably under Cochise and probably others, for several weeks. The combined force launched a fresh attack on Indians south of Bowie, getting into position during a moonlit night, but unable with daylight to dislodge the Apaches. The command returned to Bowie where Bernard obtained reinforcements and renewed the operation a fourth time, but the Indians had decamped and he (and Dorr, as surgeon) returned to Bowie once more. Moulton's command with Dorr reached Crittenden again November 19. Dorr remained at Crittenden until February 22, 1870, went to San Francisco and March 31 had his Army contract annulled. He signed another two weeks later, however, and served at Camp Warner, Oregon, until June 1872. At Oakland, California, he married Jeanette Raymond and settled into private medical practice at San Francisco where he lived thereafter. He was buried at the National Cemetery at the Presidio there.

"The Fight at Chiricahua Pass in 1869 as described by L.L. Dorr, M.D.," ed. by Marian E. Valputic, Harold H. Longfellow, *Arizona and the West*, Vol. 13, No. 4 (Winter 1971), 369-78.

Dorsey, James Owen, ethnologist (Oct. 31, 1848-Feb. 4, 1895). B. at Baltimore, Maryland, he learned the Hebrew alphabet at 6 and was able to read that language at 10. He attended the Episcopal Theological Seminary at Alexandria, Virginia, and was ordained a deacon in 1871. His first missionary work was among the Ponca Indians of Dakota and he soon was able to speak their language. Illness caused him to return to Maryland where he engaged in parish work until the Bureau of American Ethnology sent him to study the Omaha Indians in Nebraska. He gathered linguistic and ethnographic information there until 1880. John Wesley Powell employed Dorsey as a permanent member of the BAE staff in 1879. He worked among various Siouan groups, also studied Athapascan languages, and became "one of America's leading linguists and the acknowledged authority on the Ponca, Osage, and Omaha tribes." He published much highly technical work and *Omaha Sociology,* BAE *Report* for 1881-82; *Osage Traditions,* BAE *Report* for 1884-85, and *Siouian Sociology,* BAE *Report,* 1893-94 are considered classics. But he wrote much more, on such disparate tribes as the Kansas, the Biloxi and the Ofo. In an obituary article in the *American Anthropologist,* J.N.B. Hewitt, himself a pre-eminent linguist-ethnologist, wrote that Dorsey "in the field of linguistics and sociology...collected many facts and much data, which are a permanent addition to our heritage of knowledge." Although of delicate constitution and ever engaged in absorbing, difficult work, he always found time to help others and "endeared himself to a large circle of fellow workers."

REAW; DAB; info. from E.F. (Ted) Mains.

Doubleday, Ralph Russell (Dub), rodeo photographer (July 4, 1881-June 30, 1958). B. at Canton, Ohio, he was the son of a physician. When the boy was 17 the family moved to the Black Hills where he became a range rider for the CY Ranch. In 1900 the family moved again, this time to Sycamore, Illinois, where Doubleday became interested in photography; his picture of a frozen standpipe during a hard winter found plentiful local sales and he decided to enter photography as a profession. He became attracted to rodeo and developed into unquestionably the first great rodeo photographer, his action pictures being everywhere reproduced and even today considered rarely equalled for grasping the excitement of arena rough riding. "I always rode the horse with the cowboy," he once said, "and just when I felt I was going to buck off, I snapped the shutter." He took most of his marvelous rodeo shots with a 7 by 7 in. plate Graphic, a camera which was wrecked by rampant animals many times but Doubleday would patch it up and use no other. In 1910 he took the first known picture of a cowboy suspended in the air over a bucking horse; the rider was Gus Nylen, the horse named Teddy Roosevelt and the event was at the Cheyenne Frontier Days. From then on he covered most of the great and many of the smaller rodeos around the country; his work was not only great in his day, but remains a virtually unrivaled mark for later-day cameramen to shoot at and for. Doubleday pioneered many of the procedures followed today, including picturing a bucking animal from a low angle shooting upward, which makes the result more dramatic—and riskier to shoot. He had bucking horses jump over him and irate bulls brush him away, but he continued to get his shots. He won endless praise from contestants as well as from the public. Foghorn Clancy, a rodeo announcer and statistician, called Doubleday the "world champion rodeo photographer," adding that he had followed the sport for 40 years, taken many thousands of pictures, and that his work "has been a big factor" in the development of rodeo. Will James used 15 of Doubleday's photographs as models in illustrating his book, *Flint Spears,* about an arena contestant, and Will Rogers said Doubleday "could put on his own rodeo any time he pulled out his pictures and started talking about them." The cameraman also won a reputation as an early photo-journalist. He befriended Florida Seminole Indians and took many pictures of them. He traveled with Mexico's Francisco Madero during the campaign against Villa and "probably his greatest single photo was the rare shot of all five World War I Allied Generals together." This photograph was reprinted around the world. But rodeo was his greatest interest and the arena the scene of his most spectacular work. He was the first cameraman to feature Tom Mix with three reels of motion pictures. Doubleday was a very good businessman. Late in life he commenced to lose his sight, and he died at Council Bluffs, Iowa. In the early 1980s Albert Conover of Xenia, Ohio, donated 4,000 Doubleday rodeo negatives to the Oklahoma Cowboy Hall of Fame, including 287 glass negatives of some of the earliest rodeos ever held, the whole a priceless collection.

Willard H. Porter, "Shooting the Rodeo: The Story of R.R. 'Dub' Doubleday," *True West,* Vol. 36, No. 4 (Apr. 1989), 40-43; info. from the Natl. Cowboy Hall of Fame.

Doublehead (Taltsuska, Chuquilatague), Cherokee chief (d. June 1807). A brother of Old Tassel (see entry), he also was an uncle of John Watts (see entry), noted Cherokee leaders. Doublehead became a notorious scourge of the Tennessee frontier

from around 1780. He was of the Chickamauga Cherokees who under the leadership of Dragging Canoe had quit the eastern bands and settled near the present Chattanooga from where they continued inveterately hostile to white intrusion. Doublehead, Tassel and others were considered Dragging Canoe's "hotbloods." They made their rendezvous at Lookout Town, on the east bank of Lookout Creek. In June 1788 Old Tassel was killed while under a flag of truce by "militia" of the abortive "state" of Franklin, this calling for revenge on the part of Doublehead and another brother, Pumpkin Boy, among others. Doublehead, under the name of Chuquilatague, signed the July 2, 1791, Holston Treaty, negotiated at White's Fort (Knoxville) where 1,200 Cherokees and 40 chiefs were gathered; Dragging Canoe also was there, it appears, although he evidently did not sign the pact, nor did the treaty "presage the immediate end of his reign of terror." In 1793 Doublehead and Pumpkin Boy with their nephew, Bench, slew from ambush Captain William Overall and a companion named Burnett, scalped them and ate some of their roasted flesh in order, as they said, that it might endow them with their victims' courage. By that time Dragging Canoe had died and though John Watts formally succeeded the old man, Doublehead aspired to follow him in warlike activity and lead the hostile Chickamaugas. He was elected to the tribal council and became its speaker in 1794. Doublehead and a Chickamauga deputation met with President Washington and Secretary of War Henry Knox and June 26 signed a treaty at Philadelphia designed to correct imperfections in the pact of 1791; it raised the Cherokees' annuity from $1,500 to $5,000 but it did not pacify the Chickamaugas, who eventually had to be "subdued by force." Brigadier General John Robertson and Major James Ore took care of that. By October both the peace and war parties of Cherokees were ready for peace, although Doublehead did not sign the treaty. But righteousness did not accompany the pact. Federal negotiators bribed Doublehead and others to assent to a large cession of Cherokee land between the Duck and Tennessee rivers, accomplished by a treaty signed January 7, 1806. Conservative Cherokees warned the Chickamaugas that willful violation of an ancient Cherokee law prohibiting land cessions without the National Council's consent would bring the death penalty. Doublehead's murder, or execution for treason by Major Ridge (The Ridge) came in June 1807 when he was wounded, sought shelter in a schoolhouse loft, and was followed there by The Ridge, who split his skull with a tomahawk.

Info. from John Sugden; Grace Steele Woodward, *The Cherokees,* Norman, Univ. of Okla. Press, 1963.

Douglas, James, frontiersman (d. 1793). Douglas, by profession a surveyor, in 1773 led an exploring party down the Ohio River and visited a place called Big Bone Lick because of a profusion of giant bones lying about, most of mammoth or mastodon origin. He used some of the longer bones for tent poles. The question arises as to how such an assemblage of bones came to accumulate. The site was heavily quarried, with specimens being sent to Thomas Jefferson, to Europe and elsewhere, and yet there remained numerous specimens when Thwaites visited the site in 1894. One wonders whether man had been an agent in the demise of so many megafauna specimens. But Dr. Paul S. Martin, an originator and foremost student of man as an agent in megafauna extinctions pointed out that a major difficulty in determining the manner of demise in such numbers as were found at Big Bone Lick is the present impossibility of establishing the *rate* of deposit. There is no way to tell whether it was a truly catastrophic phenomenon or an accumulation perhaps over centuries or millenia: "If only one mastodon (on average) were preserved per century [this] would in 10,000 years yield 100 individuals and many hundreds of bones," Dr. Martin said. No reports of Clovis or other 10,000-year-old weapons points have been located but, in Martin's words, "the presence or absence of Clovis points in such a deposit can mean little." The outbreak of hostilities with the Shawnees from north of the Ohio River caused the Douglas party to flee southward. They went down the rivers by pirogue to New Orleans, thence via Pensacola, Florida and Charleston, South Carolina, to Williamsburg, Virginia, where Douglas arrived in December 1774. In the spring of 1775 he went to Harrodsburg, Kentucky, finally settling in Bourbon County, where he died.

Thwaites, *Dunmore;* info. from Dr. Paul S. Martin, Dept. of Geosciences, Univ. of Arizona.

Dowd, Daniel (Big Dan), desperado (d. Mar. 28, 1884). Already wanted for a stage holdup near Benson, Arizona, Dowd was one of five gunmen who perpetrated the so-called "Bisbee Massacre" December 8, 1883, during a holdup at the Joseph Goldwater-A.A. Casteñada general store at the southern Arizona mining camp. The other four were Daniel Kelly, Omer W. Sample, James (Tex) Howard and William Delaney (see entries); four non-participants were killed outright: J.C. Tapiner,

Mrs. R.H. (Anna) Roberts, Deputy Sheriff Tom Smith and R.E. Duvall, while Albert Nolly was wounded mortally. Between $900 and $3,000 (reports differ) were taken. Detective Bob Paul (see entry), one of the sleuths tracking down the desperadoes, learned that ranchers of the area "all knew about Dan Dowd and his bunch of alleged cattle thieves." It was learned eventually from a Mexican informant that Dowd was hiding near Sabinal, north of Corralitos, Chihuahua. Deputy Sheriff W.A. (Billy) Daniels (see entry) of Bisbee visited Sabinal disguised as an ore buyer, seized Dowd by ruse and carted him back to Arizona for a Tombstone trial with the other four. Dowd muttered as the nooses of the five-man scaffold were being affixed that "this is a regular choking machine!" Alone among the four his drop appeared bungled and he choked to death rather than having his neck broken and death instantaneous.

Ben T. Traywick, *The Hangings in Tombstone,* Tombstone, Red Marie's Bookstore, 1991; Robert E. Ladd, *Eight Ropes to Eternity,* pub. by *Tombstone Epitaph,* 1965; A.B. LeBaron, "Bisbee's Five Black Ghosts," *True West,* Vol. 7, No. 6 (July-Aug. 1960), 12-14, 56-57.

Draper, John, pioneer (1730-1824). Draper was an early settler at a place called Draper's Meadow in present Montgomery County, Virginia, the site now occupied by the community of Blacksburg, midway between Roanoke and Bluefield. It first was settled by Colonel James Patton in 1745, but the original settlement was wiped out in a Shawnee raid in July 1755 when Draper saw his wife carried off as a captive. He searched for her six years, finally found her in Ohio, paid a ransom and brought her home again. The Drapers then resettled in the present Pulaski County about 1765, the present community named for the pioneer. In 1774 he was a lieutenant in one of the Fincastle companies raised for the Lord Dunmore War. Draper lived to the age of 94, dying at his home.

Thwaites, *Dunmore;* James Hagemann, *The Heritage of Virginia: The Story of Place Names in the Old Dominion,* Norfolk, Donning Co., Pubs.; info. from the Va. Hist. Soc.

Draper, Mary: *see,* Mary Draper Ingles

Drennon, Jacob, military officer (d. 1787). B. in Greenbriar County, Vriginia he was educated in England and commissioned in the English army. He returned to America with Lord Dunmore in 1770 and when Dunmore became governor of Virginia, followed him there. In 1773 Drennon was in Kentucky with the McAfee party, and visited the site thereafter known as Drennon's Lick. In 1774 he was back in the present West Virginia and served in Dunmore's division at the battle of Point Pleasant on the Ohio River. He generally made his home near Wheeling, although frequently was in Kentucky, settling eventually in Mason County. When descending the Ohio River in 1787, Drennon was mortally wounded by Indians and he jumped from his boat into the water so that the Indians would not secure his scalp. He was married and fathered children.

Thwaites/Kellogg, *Frontier Defense on the Upper Ohio, 1777-1778.*

Duffield, Will Ward, topographer (b. 1841). Duffield, of the Coast and Geodetic Survey was sent in April 1897 to the Pribylov Islands to make a topographical survey of the seal rookeries and the islands themselves. Complete surveys were made of St. Paul, St. George, Walrus and Otter islands. The results appeared on the C&GS charts in 1898. It is not known what relationship, if any, there was between Will Ward Duffield and William Ward Duffield (November 19, 1823-1907), who was superintendent of the Coast and Geodetic Survey from 1894 until 1898 following a distinguished military and political career. He was a civil engineer, born at Carlisle, Pennsylvania; his late residence was at Washington, D.C.

Orth, 12, 288; *Who Was Who.*

Duke, Francis, frontiersman (Feb. 11, 1751-Sept. 1, 1777). B. in Ireland, the family moved to the present Berkeley County, West Virginia, and there in 1773 Francis Duke married Sarah, the eldest daughter of Colonel David Shepherd, removing with the Shepherd family to Wheeling Creek. He was appointed by Shepherd deputy commissary (quartermaster) and as such was stationed at Beech Bottom Fort. On September 1, he approached Fort Henry at Wheeling in a desperate attempt to join its defenders already under Indian siege, sometime in the afternoon and was shot from his horse near the gate of the post. He fell about 75 yards from the fort, so near that the Indians "did not venture for his scalp, until after nightfall, when they dragged his body into one of the cabins and scalped and stripped him. The Indians shot down large numbers of cattle, hogs, geese, and took a good many horses." Duke left his widow, an infant son, John, and a posthumous son, Francis, who had numerous descendants. The widow married Levi Springer.

Thwaites/Kellogg, *Frontier Defense on the Upper Ohio, 1777-1778;* Alexander Scott Withers, *Chronicles of Border Warfare,* Cincinnati, Robert Clarke Co., 1895, 1970.

Duncan, William, Anglican missionary (1832-1918). A British lay missionary of the Anglican Church Missionary Society, his endeavors led to the founding among the numerous Tsimshian (Skeena) Indians of British Columbia in 1857 of Metlakatla, seven miles northwest of Prince Rupert, and, in 1887, of New Metlakatla on Annette Island, southernmost Alaska, 75 miles northwest of the original Metlakatla, and 20 miles south of Ketchikan. Duncan, Scottish born, reached Fort (now Port) Simpson, 17 miles north of Prince Rupert, and commenced radical cultural change among the Indians, his methods widely emulated by other missionaries among northwest coast people. Fort Simpson was protected by a high stockade and six brass cannons and Thomas Clark, the factor of the Hudson's Bay Company, allowed but two Indians at a time to enter the compound to trade, and they only between the hours of noon to 4 p.m. Duncan was greatly assisted at the outset by Klah, son of a Tsimshian chief; Klah had learned English and served as interpreter for Duncan, presenting his sermons in the colloquial and highly imaginative language he knew would influence the Indians, regardless of what the churchman had actually said. During the first winter Klah persuaded Duncan to seclude himself while Klah taught him the language. Meanwhile, he assured the Indians that the missionary had gone to heaven for the winter and would return in the spring, well versed in their own tongue. Duncan never made it to heaven, at that time, but he did emerge in the spring able to converse in the Tsimshian tongue, his reputation hugely enhanced by Klah's ploy. Shortly after his arrival Duncan was asked by colonial authorities to act as magistrate, Bancroft commenting that "it was an exceedingly strange mixture...Here was law and barbarism, divinity and demonism incoherently mingled until the poor fellow scarcely knew his own mind," but he somehow weathered the assignment. The liquor traffic, leading occasionally to excessive violence, greatly troubled him until he declined even to serve wine at Communion, bringing him into difficulties with Anglican officials in England, who failed to comprehend the problems Duncan faced. Eventually it led the missionary to break relations with the English church, and start Port Chester, called later New Metlakatla on the Alaskan island. It succeeded, starting with the 800 followers who accompanied Duncan there, its population remaining about the same until today. Duncan oversaw construction of a church and a salmon cannery at his new center, which soon boasted a town hall, sawmill and schoolhouse, "all with their promises of democracy, education, and economic industriousness." Yet his tight, even dictatorial control over his people led eventually to resentment on their part, and in 1915 they peacefully "rebelled," demanding authority over their work as well as a share in the cannery profits over which Duncan had until that point full control. In short they insisted upon economic and political rights, and in the end they won out. The circumstances of Duncan's death are not known.

HNAI, 4, p. 641; Francis Dickie, "Duncan Wintered in Heaven," with portrait, *Frontier Times,* Vol. 44, No. 1 (Dec./Jan., 1970), 15, 42-43; Orth, 636; Swanton, *Tribes,* 606-607; Bancroft, *British Columbia;* William H. Goetzmann, Kay Sloan, *Looking Far North: The Harriman Expedition to Alaska, 1899,* Princeton, N.J., Princeton Univ. Press, 1982.

Dunn, Jacob Piatt Jr., historical writer (Apr. 12, 1855-June 6, 1924). B. at Lawrenceburg, Indiana, he was a graduate of Earlham College of Richmond, Indiana, where he earned a master's degree in 1874 and from the University of Michigan a bachelor of laws degree in 1876. Although he wrote other books, he is best known for his impressive *Massacres of the Mountains: A History of the Indian Wars of the Far West 1815-1875* (1886, 1958), a valued standard in its field ever since its initial publication. Its remarkable accuracy, thoroughness of coverage, scope and the sound judgment displayed have enabled it to retain its place as a cornerstone in the history of Indian-white conflicts ever since its original appearance. Dunn was secretary of the Indiana Historical Society from 1886 to 1893 when he became state librarian of Indiana, holding that position until 1903. He was an editorial writer for the Indianapolis *Sentinel* in 1893-94, city comptroller of Indianapolis, 1904-06 and 1914-16 and in 1923 became private secretary to U.S. Senator Samuel Moffett Ralston (1857-1924), dying the following year. He was married. In addition to *Massacres of the Mountains,* he wrote *Indiana* (1888); *Indiana - A Redemption from Slavery* (1905); *True Indian Stories* (1909); *History of Indianapolis* (1910); *The Unknown God* (1914), and *Indiana and the Indianans* (1919). He lived at Indianapolis for most of his life.

Who Was Who; dust jacket info. from *Massacres of the Mountains,* 1958.

Dustin, Hannah, captive (b. 1657). B. Hannah Emerson, she married Thomas Dustin and by him had eight children, their ages in 1696 ranging from 2 to 17, the last being a new-born baby. The Dustins lived at Haverhill, Massachusetts. At 7 a.m. March 15, 1696/97, "some thirty Indians came upon the town like a whirlwind, killing twenty-seven persons—more than half being children—and capturing thirteen." Thomas, unable to save his wife from being carried off, seized his rifle and kept between the enemy and his escaping children, "firing and being fired upon until their slow steps took them to safety." Hannah and her baby, and Mrs. Mary (Corliss) Neff, the neighbor caring for her during the birth recovery, were captured, the infant brained. The Indians and their captives went northward; with them was a boy, Samuel Lenorson, seized two years earlier from near Worcester. After 150 miles the party reached an island, since called Dustin Island, at the confluence of the Merrimac and Contoocook rivers at the present Penacook, just north of Concord, New Hampshire. The two women became servants to an Indian family. April 29, angered by what had happened and terrified by further threats to them, the women with the help of Samuel somehow killed ten Indians of the family, six of them children; from the sanguinary incident only one sorely-wounded woman escaped, while the whites spared a native boy to take with them. The slain were scalped in order to secure the reward the Massachusetts government offered, of from 15 to 200 pounds for each scalp. As quickly as possible upon their return to Haverhill they packed the scalps to Boston, finding that the government had withdrawn its bounty offer. But Thomas Dustin, because of the "extraordinary Action of his wife (with one Mary Neff) and because of losing his Estate in the Calamity," asked "for what consideracon the publick Bounty shall judge proper." The Dustins received 25 pounds, and half that amount was given to each of her companions "as a reward for their service in slaying divers of those barbarous salvages." Hannah's feat became a famed incident of the border wars, and a monument has been erected to her at Penacook. Cotton Mather (1662-1727) repeated the story, having heard it from Hannah Dustin herself.

Coleman, *Captives,* I, 342-46; Parkman, *Frontenac,* 405-407; DAB.

Dykes, Jeff(erson) C(henworth), writer, bibliographer (July 20, 1900-Dec. 29, 1989). B. at Dallas, Texas, he graduated from Texas A & M in 1921, taught vocational agriculture at Stephensville, Texas, from 1921-26 and at Texas A & M was professor of agricultural education until 1935 when he joined the Federal Soil Conservation Service, becoming at length assistant administrator at Washington, D.C., until 1965. Meanwhile he had become a book collector, eventually accumulating some 16,000 volumes; book appraiser (he appraised the J. Frank Dobie collection for the University of Texas); book reviewer and bibliographer. He wrote *Billy the Kid: The Bibliography of a Legend* (1952) which Ramon Adams judged "more like a check list than a true bibliography, but each entry contains much information on the content of the book listed, and the author points out many false and inaccurate statements...It is the first complete list of materials on this young outlaw..." Dykes was working on a revised edition at his death. He also wrote *Flat Top Ranch* (1957), *My Dobie Collection* (1971), and edited *Great Western Indian Fights* (1960). Dykes died at College Station, Texas, after surgery for cancer. His wife, the former Martha Lewin Read, predeceased him by six months. They were parents of a daughter.

Contemporary Authors; Headquarters Heliogram 205, Jan.-Feb. 1990; Western Hist. Assoc. *Newsletter,* Winter 1990.

E

Eastman, Seth, military officer, artist (Jan 24, 1808-Aug. 31, 1875). B. at Brunswick, Maine, he went to West Point, was commissioned a second lieutenant in the 1st Infantry July 1, 1829, and was stationed at Fort Crawford, Wisconsin, and Fort Snelling, Minnesota, until 1831. He then joined the Topographical Corps, serving until he was assigned in 1833 to instruct in drawing at West Point, remaining there until 1840. He became a first lieutenant November 14, 1836, and a captain November 12, 1839. Eastman served in the Seminole War in Florida in 1840-41 and returned to Fort Snelling where he stayed until 1848. His competence as a draftsman and increasing repute as a painter of Indians and Indians scenes, following a Texas tour in 1848-49 led to an assignment to illustrate and paint maps for Schoolcrafts's six volume *History and Statistical Information Representing...the Indian Tribes of the United States* (1853-56), more than 300 of his works being reproduced in the set. He became major of the 5th Infantry October 31, 1856, having concluded another two-year tour in Texas, and was assigned to the office of the Quartermaster General from 1857-58. Eastman became a lieutenant colonel of the 1st Infantry September 9, 1861, and retired for disability December 3, 1863; he was breveted to Brigadier General for Civil War services following the conflict. Eastman was engaged in painting Indian scenes and professional views of western forts for the Capitol at Washington, D.C., from 1867 until his death in 1875. His Indian work was displayed in the rooms of the House Committee on Indian Affairs, and his western fort series by the Committee on Military Affairs. The latter works are now permanently displayed in the west corridor of the main floor of the central portion of the Capitol, and fourteen were reproduced in black-and-white and reduced size (the originals are 36 by 24 inches) in *Periodical*. Eastman died while completing a view from West Point of the Hudson River. Some of the officer's work was published in 1853 in the *American Aboriginal Portfolio* written by his wife, Mary, and some of his original works are held, in addition to those at the Capitol, by the Corcoran Gallery of Art at Washington, the Minneapolis Institute of Art and the Thomas Gilcrease Institute of American History and Art at Tulsa, Oklahoma. Steve Hall, in *Fort Snelling* reproduces (p. 8) in color Eastman's watercolor of Fort Crawford at Prairie du Chien, Wisconsin; also in color, "Dakota [Indians] playing lacrosse on the St. Peter's River," Minnesota, an oil, and in black-and-white an Eastman oil of the village of St. Paul done in 1858.

Heitman; *Who Was Who;* Henry R. Schoolcraft, *History of the Indian Tribes of the United States* (1857), and 6th vol., cond., Hist. Amer. Indian Press, n.p., n.d. (1951); Council on Abandoned Military Posts, *Periodical*, Vol. VIII, No. 1 (Whole No. 27) (Spring, 1976), 21-36; Steve Hall, *Fort Snelling: Colossus of the Wilderness*, St. Paul, Minn. Hist. Soc. Press, 1987; info. from E.E. (Ted) Mains.

Ebbets, John, sea captain (d.c. 1835). Ebbets was a fur trading captain of Boston, making several voyages to the Northwest Coast, as described in some detail by Pierce. In June 1802 at the site of Sitka he and Captain Henry Barber (see entry) rescued survivors of the Kolosh (Tlingit) massacre of Russians and their Aleut helpers when a fur trading post was destroyed. In 1835 or thereabouts Ebbets died at sea while enroute from Canton, China, to Hawaii with the brig *Diana.*

Pierce, *Russian America: A Biographical Dictionary.*

Edmiston (Edmondston), William, military officer (1734-1822). B. in Maryland, he emigrated while young to Virginia, settling at Augusta. He served as a private in the French and Indian War and in the Cherokee campaign of 1760; this experience led to his commission as ensign, and later a lieutenant (in 1763) of the Augusta County militia. He was one of the earliest settlers of the middle fork of the Holston River, as were the Campbells, his neighbors, and he served as second in command to William Campbell, when needed. Edmiston served in that capacity at the battle of King's Mountain October 7, 1780; eight members of his family were in that engagement, three being killed and one wounded. Upon the death of William Campbell in 1782 Edmiston became colonel of the Washington County militia. He was prominent in all the civic and political affairs of his time and died at his home in Washington County.

Thwaites, *Dunmore.*

Egan, Howard, frontiersman (June 15, 1815-Mar.

16, 1878). B. at Tullamore, King's County, Ireland, his family took him at 8 overseas, locating at Montreal. Egan became a seaman and at 23 was married. In 1842 he and his wife were converted to Mormonism by Elder Erastus Snow and went to Nauvoo, Illinois, where Egan joined the police force, was a major of the Nauvoo Legion and reportedly became a Danite (for formation and organization of the Danites, see Bancroft, *Utah,* 124-27 with notes). In 1846 the family located with other Mormons at Winter Quarters, across the Missouri from Council Bluffs, Iowa. Egan was forthright and of some temper. John D. Lee, in his diary of the 1846 trip across Iowa noted on June 8 a "little confab between Bro. J. Pack & Howard Egan, the former wishing to take his place in front of the latter in traveling the road contrary to [Egan's] wishes smote his team with a stick 3 times when Bro. H.E. with a blow of his fist brought him to the earth and then kicked him for falling. This however can alone be attributed to the weakness & depravity of mortal man for they are both good men..." Egan was directed to accompany Lee and First Lieutenant James Pace to Leavenworth and thence to Santa Fe to overtake the Mormon Battalion and bring back from the soldiers' pay funds for use by the faithful at Winter Quarters. The mission collected about $1,200 and Egan, "a frontiersman who was a stranger to fear," with Lee returned November 20, 1846. Lee "thought of Howard Egan with some affection careless as he was with his language at times and apt to drink too much if he were in a drinking crowd." In the spring of 1847 Egan was named captain of the ninth ten of the Brigham Young company for Salt Lake. A diary he kept "is of great value" and has been published by his son in a volume, *Pioneering the West.* On the trip, west of the Loup Fork of the Platte River, Egan and Thomas E. Hicks had a scrap with unidentified Indians of whom several were killed while both Egan and Hicks were wounded, Hicks seriously and Egan "shot in the right arm just above the wrist." Both recovered. Once the Mormons were established in the Salt Lake Valley, Egan accompanied Young back to Winter Quarters, returned to the valley in 1848 with his family, and settled there. He was of use to the leadership in various ways. At some point he was accused of the murder of a gentile, James Monroe, was defended by George A. Smith (see entry) as Smith's initial significant legal case, and was cleared. Egan became "one of the great trail blazers of Mormon history," most famed for his discovery of a more direct route to California than the historic Overland Trail. The latter, from the Great

Salt lake, struck northwest to follow the Humboldt River in a loop northward and then bore southwest again to reach the California border east of Sacramento. Egan believed a direct route westward would save around 200 miles, and so it proved once sufficient water was located to make a trail feasible for animal transport. The route he pioneered in 1855 became known as Egan's Trail. Ashbaugh wrote that Egan "had such faith that it was shorter and better than the Humboldt route that he wagered he could ride a mule from Salt Lake City to Sacramento [over it] in ten days. He won his bet, causing a national sensation at the time. As far as anybody knows, nobody ever has beaten that time horseback without relief or changes of mounts." The course became the route of the Pony Express in 1860, of the overland telegraph, the Overland Stage Line, and today is followed closely by U.S. Highway 50 (the Lincoln Highway); the distance by it between Salt Lake City and Sacramento is around 700 miles. The government, in order to properly establish the roadway "officially," in 1859 sent Captain James Hervey Simpson (see entry) of the Topographical Engineers to chart this mid-Nevada route, and he did so, following Egan's earlier effort; it is appropriate that Egan Canyon and the Egan Range, north of Ely, should have been named for the true discoverer. When the stage line was established during the Civil War, Egan became superintendent of the Salt Lake division and his two sons Pony Express riders and later stage drivers. Paiute recollections of Howard Egan as a stage driver across Nevada may confuse the elder Egan with one of his sons. Egan senior held many civil offices in Utah, and was "successful as a missionary and intermediary among the Indians." He died at Salt Lake City, "survived by a family trained as pioneer and colonizers."

Hist. Dept., Church of Jesus Christ of Latter-day Saints, Salt Lake City; Andrew Jenson, *Latter-day Saint Biographical Encyclopedia,* Vol. 4, SLC, Andrew Jenson Mem. Assn., 1936, 699-700; Juanita Brooks, *John Doyle Lee: Zealot-Pioneer Builder-Scapegoat,* Glendale, Arthur H. Clark Co., 1961; William Wise, *Massacre at Mountain Meadows,* N.Y., Thomas Y. Crowell Co., 1976; Bancroft, *Utah;* Don Ashbaugh, *Nevada's Turbulent Yesterday,* Los Angeles, Westernlore Press, 1963; Jack D. Forbes, *Nevada Indians Speak,* Reno, Univ. of Nev. Press, 1967; info. from E.F. (Ted) Mains.

Eggenhofer, Nick, illustrator, artist (Dec. 5, 1897-Mar. 7, 1985). B. at Gauting, Bavaria, near Munich, he early became interested in sketching, and in observing craftsmen fashioning animal-drawn vehicles, gear, and in learning how stock was handled. A neighbor was a wheelwright and wagon builder, and "I spent many happy hours watching the making of a wagon wheel and its subsequent ironing by a blacksmith," while down the road "there was the shoeing of horses and of oxen," activities he found equally absorbing. In 1913, the family emigrated to America. Young Nick, then 16, was imbued with Buffalo Bill-inspired legends of the West and Bronco Billy Anderson western flicks nurturing this interest. Nick clerked in a shoe store, a hardware business, worked on a production line and became an apprentice lithographer while taking evening art lessons at Cooper Union in New York City. Much of his practice art work was on western subjects (although he had then to make his initial trip to the West). In 1919 he sold his first illustrations to a pulp magazine. Their authenticity of detail and dramatic action caught on and Eggenhofer became a favored illustrator for Street and Smith's *Western Story,* while he appeared regularly in such other magazines as *Cowboy Stories* and *Ace-High.* It became "not at all unusual to tally twenty to twenty-four illustrations" by Eggenhofer in a single issue. He commenced making his many trips west of the Mississippi to sketch, observe and study the western landscape, people and artifacts. With his fine eye for detail he became not only a foremost illustrator of his day, but also an authoritative and relied-upon source for writers, historians and others. Ramon Adams wrote in 1961 "I feel I know something about the West [but] I learned much from him. Like all true artists, he is exact in getting the small details correct, and perhaps that is why he is still my favorite living Western artist." With the advent of television and consequent folding of most pulps, Eggenhofer turned to book illustration with equal success. Adams reported that Eggenhofer had illustrated Adams's own first book and "nearly all the reviews I received had as much praise for the illustrations as for the book itself," although the artist was not even mentioned on the title page. In a subsequent book the University of Oklahoma Press wanted a different illustrator, but Adams insisted upon Eggenhofer and also that his name be listed on the title page. "Since that time," he wrote, "he has illustrated many books for Oklahoma, and their wide circulation has created a demand for his art. I feel that I have played a small part in his success. If so, I am proud...He has a style all his own which is becoming more widely known and more popular every day." Eggenhofer illustrated books for a variety of publishers, his work present in more than 40 volumes by 1970, and his paintings, as distinct from his illustrations, appearing on numerous dust-wrappers of others. "A close estimate would put [his production over the years] at something in the neighborhood of twenty thousand paintings and pen-and-ink drawings since his first commission in 1919," according to Les Beitz. "Through perseverance, dedication, and sound management of his unique talents, he has drawn and painted with consummate distinction a West that's bold and rugged, dramatic and colorful. There is no Truer West than the West of Nick Eggenhofer." The only book he not only illustrated profusely but also wrote was his remarkable *Wagons, Mules and Men: How the Frontier Moved West,* which explains in words as well as pictures, in the most intricate detail-drawings the transportation apparatus used by freighters, travelers, military, prospectors, wagoneers, pack men, Indians, Mexicans, breeds, mountain men, cowboys and others in their peregrinations west of the Mississippi over more than a century. The book is a resource of inestimable value for all interested in the frontier. Eggenhofer was married and fathered a daughter. After living and working at New Milford, New Jersey, for much of his active career, he moved to Cody, Wyoming, where he died at 87.

Eggenhofer, *Wagons, Mules and Men,* N.Y., Hastings House, 1961; Les Beitz, "Nick Eggenhofer's West," *True West,* Vol. 15, No. 4 (Mar.-Apr. 1968), 28-29, 42; Chicago, The Westerners *Brand Book,* Vol. XXXXI, NO. 2 (Summer, 1986), 33; info. from the McCracken Research Lby., Cody, Wy.

Egorov, Prokhor, Russian fur man (d.c. June 1824). This intriguing figure had a somewhat checkered career in which little can be proved with certainty. Richard A. Pierce reports that in December 1820 he was sent from Sitka, Alaska, to the Ross settlement of the Russian American Company north of San Francisco; he went south on the brig *Golovnin,* Khristofor Martynovich Benzeman (1774-1842) captain. Pierce continued that "a few months later he deserted, and took refuge with Indians living independently of the Spanish missions. His motives are unknown, but K.T. Khlebnikov (see entry), quoting Governor Luis Arguello of California, states that an uprising began at Missions Purísima and Santa Inéz, with the Indians acting under Egorov's leadership...The rebellion spread to the Mission Santa Barbara, after which, evidently repulsed, the Indians went 'to an island on the large lake near Santa Barbara' [possibly Lake Casitas, 22 miles east, which has such an island, this possibility resting upon the supposition that Casitas is a natural, rather than a man-made lake]. Egorov was found dead on one of the trails, evidently murdered by his new-found friends. Twice the Spanish sent military detachments. Eight soldiers had been killed when finally the Padre Presidente went and got the Indians to listen and return on the promise of no punishment." Bancroft reports no significant Indian troubles at the California missions from 1820 through 1823, but an uprising broke out on Sunday, February 21, 1824, at Santa Inés, the trouble apparently ignited when an Indian neophyte was flogged for an unremembered offense. None of the whites was killed "but a large part of the mission buildings were burned," and when Sergeant Anastasio Carrillo arrived with a small force the next day the hostiles fled to Mission Purísima where the Chumash also revolted and seized the mission. Seven Indians and four whites were killed there. On Monday news of the revolt reached Santa Barbara where an insurrection also occurred, Indians losing two killed and three wounded, and the soldiers four wounded before retiring to the presidio. Some fighting continued thereafter and 12 whites were buried at the mission cemetery. Troop reinforcements meanwhile were sent to Purísima where the insurrectionists now numbered an estimated 400, having seized cannon, which they could not effectively fire, and other weapons. The Spanish lost three wounded, and the Indians 16 killed and "a large number wounded." Seven Indian prisoners were executed, and the four ring-leaders sentenced to 10 years imprisonment and perpetual exile, which Governor Arguello considered a punishment too lenient. However the Santa Barbara rebels had withdrawn to the tulares in the interior. March 21 Franciscan Father Blas Ordaz (1792-1850) of Mission Purísima wrote the governor that the situation was threatening with the rebels being "at San Emigdio rancho where a Russian was instructing them in the use of firearms," the Russian no doubt being Egorov. Arguello organized a fresh expedition to the tulares for late spring and a force of 130 men was sent, with Father Vicente Francisco de Sarría (1767-1835), the President of the California missions since the death on August 24, 1823, of Father José Francisco de Paula Señán. Arguello was persuaded to issue a general pardon for all those in insurrection and the command, with the late hostiles, returned to Santa Barbara June 21, the revolt at an end. It is most probable that it was on the return march to Santa Barbara in June that Egorov was found "dead on one of the trails." Beyond the single mention of the "Russian" at San Emigdio rancho, Bancroft makes no further reference to Egorov, but Arguello, in conversation with Khlebnikov apparently did so and Pierce's description of his death leaves the cause and circumstances unknown. "With the scanty information available no one can now say how a Russian fur hunter got involved in this disturbance in a distant land, what he sought and how he met his end," the historian concluded.

Pierce, *Russian America: A Biographical Dictionary;* Bancroft, *California,* II, 527-37; Maynard Geiger, O.F.M., *Franciscan Missionaries in Hispanic California,* San Marino, Ca., The Huntington Lby., 1969.

Egushwa, Ottawa chief: *see,* Equeshawey

El Cautivo, Chiricahua Apache war leader (fl. 1856-1872). He probably was the Chiricahua described by Sweeney as having been a Mexican captive (hence Cautivo) from childhood to maturity when he escaped and joined Cochise's people where he proved useful not only as a vigorous and determined warrior, but as an interpreter between Spanish and Apache. In 1856 he and his small band had slain Henry Linn Dodge, agent to the Navahos in revenge for the earlier loss of an Apache to a military expedition in the Mogollon Mountains of New Mexico. He also was an apparently inveterate raider into Mexico. In October 1872 General Howard's literate aide, Joseph Sladen, described El Cautivo (if the passage indeed refers to him) as "a short and stout man [and] a very important factor in the negotiations and the old chief often deferred to and referred important questions to him before deciding them." Sweeney reported this Indian to be "an obstreperous individual disliked by both Howard and Sladen." He was a band leader under Cochise. He had a significant role in deciding upon the boundaries the Apaches would accept for the proposed Chiricahua Reservation which Cochise would then approve. Not much is heard of El Cautivo after that meeting in the Dragoon Mountains.

Dan L. Thrapp, *Victorio and the Mimbres Apaches,* Norman, Univ. of Okla. Press, 1974; Edwin R. Sweeney, *Cochise: Chiricahua Apache Chief,* Norman, 1991.

Eldridge, George Homans, geologist (Dec. 25,

1854-1905). B. at Yarmouth, Massachusetts, he was graduated from Harvard in 1876 and engaged in geology and teaching until 1879. He was with the Geological Survey from 1884. In 1898 with Robert Muldrow (see entry) Eldridge made a reconnaissance of the Susitna River basin from the mouth of the river at the head of Cook Inlet, Alaska, to approximately the north boundary of the present Mount McKinley National Park. Eldridge is commemorated by Mount Eldridge in the McKinley (Denali) Peak region named for him in 1953 by (Henry Bradford Washburn Jr., and for Eldridge Glacier, named for him in 1913 by Alfred Brooks (see entry). His home was at Chevy Chase, Maryland.

Orth, 12, 308; *Who Was Who.*

Elliott, Henry Wood, naturalist (1846-1930). Wood was a member of the 1865-67 Western Union Telegraphic Expedition to Alaska, but served it solely in Canada. In 1872 he was assistant agent of the Treasury Department for the Pribylov Islands, remaining there through 1873. In 1874 he and Navy lieutenant Washburn Maynard again visited the Pribylov group and later the islands of Sitka, Kodiak, Unalaska, St. Matthew and St. Lawrence, his reports published in 1875 and 1876. Elliott strongly supported the leasing of the Pribylovs and the seal pelts taken from them to private interests, and believed wholly in the integrity and performance of the lessees in that business, as witnessed in his report of 1876. He also wrote a monograph on the Pribylovs, published in the 10th Census of 1880, and reprinted in 1881 and 1882. The monograph includes maps of the islands made in 1874 by Maynard and Elliott.

Orth, 12; Bancroft, *Alaska.*

Elliott, Matthew, trader, Indian man (c. 1739-May 7, 1814). B. in County Donegal, Ireland, he came to America in 1761 and settled in Path Valley, east of the Alleghenies in Pennsylvania. He was with Bouquet in 1763 during the Pontiac War in the relief of Fort Pitt, and in his 1764 expedition against the Ohio Indians. Later he engaged in Indian trading out of Fort Pitt (Pittsburgh), most notably with the Ohio Shawnees on the Scioto and Sandusky rivers. During the 1774 Lord Dunmore's War and its aftermath, Elliott remained in Shawnee country until after the Battle of Point Pleasant, October 10, 1774, and was sent by the Shawnees as emissary to Dunmore, then advancing toward the Ohio towns with a

military column. Elliott met Dunmore and may have been instrumental in bringing the English and Shawnee chiefs together eight miles east of Chillicothe, where peace was concluded. Following the Dunmore War Elliott resumed trading with the Ohio Indians until November 13, 1776, when he was accosted near the present Dresden, north of Zanesville by six Wyandots (or, as some say, Senecas) who confiscated his trade goods and "he would have been murdered but for the interposition of some [Moravian] Indians who had followed the warriors, purposely to intercede for him." Elliott with his servant, Michael Herbert, reached Detroit in March 1777 seeking recompense for the depredation, but Governor Hamilton (see entry) sent Elliott to Quebec under suspicion he was an American spy. He probably persuaded Canadian officials of his Loyalist sympathies and was returned to Pittsburgh by way of New York under parole, arriving early in 1778. He did not remain long. "Last Saturday night," said a March 30 letter from T. Ewing to Jasper Yeates, "Mr. McKee, Matt. Elliott, and Simon Girty (see entries)...ran off [from Pittsburgh]. It is conjectured that Elliott brought dispatches for McKee from Quebec. As he was reputed to be a gentleman of the strictest honor and probity, no body had the least idea of his being capable of acting in so base a manner. A man of his capacity, and so well acquainted with our affairs...will be no unwelcome guest at Detroit." Elliott was taken into the Indian service, if he had not been in British pay before, and was a scout on Hamilton's expedition to Vincennes, Indiana, in late 1778, leaving before George Rogers Clark recaptured the place in early 1779. The three, Elliott, Girty and McKee, were used persistently to stir up the Indians against Americans. They circulated among the Delawares, telling them that "the patriot armies were all cut to pieces, that General Washington was killed, that there was no more Congress, that the English had hung some of [them] and taken the remainder to England to hang them there," according to Moravian missionaries sent to assure the tribesmen of American sympathy and support. The Supreme Executive Council of Pennsylvania adjudged all three Loyalists "traitors" to the American cause. Elliott became a captain in the Indian Department with pay of 16 York shillings a day (a York shilling was valued at 12½ cents, New York currency, his pay the equivalent of $2 a day or $60 a month). He reportedly was at the October 4, 1779, ambush by a large party of Shawnees, Mingos, Wyandots and Delawares of the David Rogers party of about 70 men at a point on the Ohio River just above the mouth of the Licking. Rogers and 42 of his men were killed (Simon Girty shooting Rogers, as he later boasted), and immense loot fell into Indian hands. In 1780 Elliott reportedly accompanied Henry Bird's expedition against the Kentucky settlements, though he did not figure as prominently in it as Alexander McKee did. This expedition, on which Simon Girty took part, reduced Isaac Ruddle's station at the forks of the Licking River, where 300 prisoners were taken, and nearby Martin's station, taking another fifty—the operation the most successful against Kentucky of the Revolutionary period; it returned to Detroit August 4. In the spring of 1781 Elliott accompanied another war party to Kentucky, but the results were scant. In August and September Elliott was spokesman, and perhaps leader, for a strong force which descended upon the Moravian towns along the Muskingum River in Ohio and persuaded them to accept removal. This maneuver was forced (in the British view) because the towns were on the routes to the Ohio River and settlements south of it, and Moravians sometimes tipped off the commandant at Pittsburgh about war parties heading south, so that the target settlements could prepare to defend themselves. By weeks of orating, involving duplicity and circumlocution, the Indians and the Moravian missionaries were convinced they must go, and were removed to Upper Sandusky from where the missionary leaders went on to Detroit to argue their case before De Peyster, after which they were permitted to return to the Muskingum. In June 1782 Elliott, dressed as a British captain, was present and had a commanding role in the successful fight against American forces led by William Crawford near Upper Sandusky. Butterfield musters evidence that he also was present, or nearby, the site of the gruesome torture-execution of Crawford by Indians, although if actually present, he did not interfere. Elliott also took part in the August 19, 1782, battle of Blue Licks, northeast of Lexington where of 176 whites involved, 61 were killed and eight taken prisoner, with the Indian loss unknown. Following the Revolution Elliott turned to farming near Amherstburg, Ontario, on 4,000 acres he had accumulated, along with the slaves he had acquired to work the fields. He continued to influence Indians in opposition to American expansion into Ohio. In 1790 he

became assistant to Alexander McKee, now Indian superintendent at Detroit. "Much of his time was spent in distributing British supplies to the Indians...and it is likely that he went beyond official British policy...to strengthen their resistance." He was present at the massive defeat of St. Clair (see entry) in November 1791, the worst debacle ever suffered by Americans at the hands of Indians, although Elliott "kept himself at a respectable distance from danger." He was an observer, not a participant, in the August 1794 defeat of the Indians at the battle of Fallen Timbers, in which Anthony Wayne made amends for the St. Clair disaster. Elliott permitted Moravians who had once saved his life to settle first on his farm after their move to Canada, and then arranged for them to settle permanently at Thamesville, Ontario. In 1796 Elliott became superintendent of Indians and Indian affairs for Detroit, but was fired a year later for alleged financial irregularities and on other charges. "Elliott appears to have been about as honest as the average officer," though he had a sharp eye for profit and personal advantage. His efforts to be reinstated to his Indian position were for years unavailing. From 1800-1808 he was a member of the Ontario House of Assembly. In the latter year he was reappointed superintendent of Indian affairs, succeeding Thomas McKee, son of Alexander. Until the War of 1812 he tried to influence Indians to join the British in event of hostilities, and encouraged Tecumseh and his brother, Tenskwatawa (see entries) in their efforts to organize a united and militant Indian front. When the war commenced, he became lieutenant colonel of militia, was present at the August 1812 capture of Detroit from the Americans and in September accompanied an abortive campaign against Fort Wayne, Indiana. In 1813 he operated with Indians against posts in Ohio and continued his partisan efforts until his death on May 7 after half a century of frontier warfare. A Shawnee woman mothered two of his sons, and in 1810 he married Sarah Donovan and they had two sons. Elliott was black-haired, dark complexioned and according to one source "his look was haughty," and while he was "always willing, and often able, to turn any situation to his own advantage,...he was also effective in maintaining British influence among the Indians." Elliott was an uncle of U.S. Commodore Jesse Duncan Elliott (1782-1845) who won fame on Lake Erie by building the fleet Oliver Hazard Perry used to win command of the lake from the British.

Consul W. Butterfield, *History of the Girtys,* Cincinnati, Robert Clarke Co., 1890, 1950; Butterfield, *An Historical Account of the Expedition Against Sandusky under Col. William Crawford in 1782,* Robert Clarke, 1873; Alexander Scott Withers, *Chronicles of Border Warfare,* ed. by Reuben Gold Thwaites, Cincinnati, Clarke, 1895, 1970; Paul A.W. Wallace, *Thirty Thousand Miles with John Heckewelder,* Univ. of Pittsburgh Press, 1958; DCB V.

Elson, Thomas, discoverer (fl. May 25, 1825-Oct. 12, 1828). Elson was a "master" aboard the exploring ship *Blossom* on her 1825-28 voyage to the North Pacific Ocean. A master in the British Navy was a commissioned officer next below a lieutenant, performing the duties of the later "navigating officer," his rank corresponding to that of a lieutenant junior grade in the American navy. Elson was praised by the commander, Frederick Beechey for his "indefatigable attention to the minor branches of surveying," and he made several significant discoveries. Off Pitcairn Island he was given command of the "barge," a two-masted topsail schooner built at Woolwich, England, and carried ofttime on the deck of the *Blossom,* but now set afloat. Beechey considered Elson "well qualified" for the varied services demanded of the barge. Upon arriving at the atoll ringing the Gambier group of islands, a scuffle ensued with natives unaccustomed to dealing with Europeans and Elson fell, apparently wounded. His shipmates fired a musket, wounding a native; gunfire so startled the remaining Polynesians that they thereafter kept their distance from ship and barge. An island in the group was named Elson for the master, who apparently was not seriously injured in the encounter. On a later occasion the ship, as guided by the barge and "Mr. Elson's skillful pilotage" negotiated a dangerous reef to anchor in a lagoon at Bow Island, east of Tahiti. Elson truly came into his own during difficult and dangerous explorations of the northwest coast of Alaska. In Kotzebue Sound above Bering Strait he was sent with the schooner to explore the intricacies of newly discovered Hotham Inlet. July 28, 1826, he reported back, his findings essentially that the inlet was too shoal for large craft. July 31 Elson commenced what was to be his longest and most notable exploration. In command of the barge he was directed to accompany the *Blossom* as she charted the northwest coast of Alaska as far as ice permitted; the barge was to proceed between the ship and the coast in waters the *Blossom* could

not navigate, vigilantly watching for signs of John Franklin and his expedition assigned to explore the coast west of the Mackenzie River delta. In addition Elson was to explore the coast, rendezvous with the ship when indicated and contact and observe so far as time permitted those Eskimo people encountered. The *Blossom* proceeded some distance beyond Icy Cape, northernmost point reached by Cook in 1778, then returned to that point and made contact with Elson. Beechey had determined to withdraw to Kotzebue Sound, but directed Elson to continue northeastward along the unknown coast as far as possible, then return to the sound or, if the little craft should become hopelessly icebound, the men might try to return overland, no one realizing they would have the elevated and difficult Brooks Range to cross since that system had not yet been discovered. No sooner were Beechey's plans disclosed than he had "urgent applications for the command of the barge from the superior officers of the ship...but Mr. Elson...who had hitherto commanded the boat, had acquitted himself so much to my satisfaction, that I could not in justice remove him." He assigned Admiralty Mate William Smyth(e), an accomplished artist by avocation, to accompany Elson who also had at his command six seamen and two marines. Elson was given several significant matters to investigate and the vessels parted company. The master continued to the northeast as close to the coastline as possible, narowly escaping entrapment by the icepack whose movements depended upon a somewhat fickle wind. At his farthest north Elson came upon "a low narrow neck" of land ending in a point which was at 71°23'31" N. Lat., and 156°21'30" W. Long., the feature ultimately named Point Barrow for John Barrow, an Admiralty secretary and promoter of Arctic expeditions. This was the northernmost extension of the American continent, and although Elson failed by only 146 miles of reaching the most westernly position attained by Franklin, the configuration of the coastline was now clear and any possibility of a continental "Strait of Anian," or Northwest Passage was precluded. Finding himself beset by currents and ice, Elson was trapped for some days and contemplated sinking the barge secretly to avoid possibility of her falling into hostile Eskimo hands, then endeavoring to make his way by one means or another to Kotzebue Sound. An unexpected change in the wind however obviated that necessity; the barge broke free, and September 10 she arrived back at

Chamisso Island with her mission essentially accomplished. Smyth wrote an extended report on the voyage of discovery which Beechey published in his book. The captain named the bay east of Point Barrow, Elson Bay, "in compliment to the officer," adding the hope that a more impressive feature be named in the future after Elson. At Eschscholtz Bay in the sound Elson sought to explore the Buckland River, but native hostility prevented. Beechey withdrew from Kotzebue Sound for the winter, but returned in 1827. In August Elson, again in command of the barge, this time operating independently, was assigned to carefully inspect the southern coast of the Seward Peninsula and did so, but was unable because of weather to examine Shishmaref Inlet immediately to the north of Cape Prince of Wales. Beechey followed up Elson's reconnaissance, naming many of the prominent coastal features the master had located and finding others of some interest. Back in Kotzebue Sound the explorers encountered rising native hostility, largely caused by communications failure, and in one action Elson shot an Eskimo while four marines were wounded by arrows. Beechey regretted the incident "but it was unavoidable," he concluded, and "some consolation to reflect that [it involved] a party from whom we had received repeated insult" and occurred under intense provocation.

Frederick W. Beechey, *Narrative of a Voyage to the Pacific and Bering's Strait*, 2 vols., London, Henry Colburn, Richard Bentley, 1831 (1968).

Emmell, Michael: *see,* Michael E. Immell

Equeshawey (Egushwa, Augooshaway), Ottawa chief (c. 1730-post 1808). B. probably in the region of the Detroit River, he became war chief of the Ottawas in southeastern Michigan and successor to Pontiac after failure of the latter's 1763 uprising. Perhaps he was related to him. Although he early fought for the French, he became affiliated with the British after the Pontiac uprising and was faithful to them, attended all their councils, and accompanied Hamilton to Vincennes, Indiana, in 1778, being a principal adviser to him particularly as related to Indians of the various tribes contacted. He was at Vincennes when George Rogers Clark arrived, but escaped with Captain Isadore Chene of the English Indian Department who on September 7 of the same year attacked Boonesborough with a force of more than 400, almost all Indians; there is no notice as to whether Equeshawey was

among them. The attack failed. In 1780 the chief probably accompanied Captain Henry Bird on an expedition against Kentucky. His influence expanded through the 1780s and in 1790 he was a signatory to a Detroit treaty by which Indians of various tribes ceded land in Ontario to the British. The chief actively sought to muster support against the Americans in Ohio in the early 1790s, was wounded at Fort Recovery, Ohio, in 1794, but recovered in time to take part in the Battle of Fallen Timbers against Anthony Wayne. He spoke and signed the important Treaty of Greenville, Ohio, August 3, 1795, and Thwaites/Kellogg observe that "the last mention [of him] noted was in 1808, so that he probably died before the Battle of Tippecanoe." The *Dictionary of Candian Biography* gives his name as Egushwa, and on the Greenville Treaty it is written as Augooshaway; the DCB lists his year of death as c. 1800.

Thwaites/Kellogg, *Frontier Defense on the Upper Ohio, 1777-1778;* DCB IV; Charles J. Kappler, *Indian Treaties 1778-1883,* N.Y., Interland Pub. Inc., 1972.

Erickson, Hjalmar, military officer (May 25, 1873-Mar. 2, 1949). B. in Norway, Erickson enlisted in the 8th Cavalry February 6, 1893, and in five years was sergeant of B Troop. He reenlisted for a second hitch, but on April 5, 1899, was commissioned a second lieutenant of the 15th Infantry, transferring to the 7th Infantry March 29, 1900, and becoming a first lieutenant February 2, 1901. He was ordered to explore and locate the most feasible route for a military road from Rampart, Alaska, to Eagle "southward of the Yukon Flats." Erickson, accompanied by William Yanert (see entry), a former Army sergeant but now working as a civilian for the Army Signal Corps, left St. Michael on Norton Sound in August 1900. They spent several months in explorations of the region to which they had been directed, on the south side of the Yukon River. As a result of this survey Erickson recommended against construction of a road, and urged the building of a telegraph line, instead. Erickson Creek and perhaps other features were probably named for the lieutenant. Erickson in 1902 published a map of his explorations in Alaska. His rise in rank was steady thereafter. He became a captain October 23, 1907; a major May 15, 1917; a lieutenant colonel in the National Army August 5, 1917, and a colonel July 30, 1918. He held the Distinguished Service Medal and was a graduate of the Infantry-Cavalry School and the Army War College. Erickson died at 75, a retired Brigadier General, at Reno, Nevada.

Heitman; Orth, 12-13; info. from the Army Military Hist. Inst., Carlisle Barracks, Penn.

Erwin, Allen Alfred, adventurer, author (Nov. 20, 1911-May 9, 1979). B. in Canada, he came to this country and engaged in a wide variety of undertakings. Ramon F. Adams, in a foreword to Erwin's best-known book, *The Southwest of John Horton Slaughter,* wrote that he first met Erwin at Dallas where he "had a radio program...telling western stories and singing cowboy songs." In the early 1950s he met him again at Tucson where Erwin was doing "some roughriding for the movies." He discovered much of Erwin's background, learning that his father, Henry Ernewein, and his mother were of French-Canadian ancestry and Allen, the youngest of seven children, was born in Saskatchewan. He grew up as a cowboy and followed many other occupations, including rodeo riding, trapping and prospecting, as a wild horse hunter, motion picture cowboy and adviser, and worked on a number of ranches in Alberta, Oregon, Montana and Colorado, Adams listing some of them. Erwin became fascinated by the life story of Slaughter and spent years researching it by every avenue; the book he ended up with is considered authoritative and by many definitive. Erwin died at 67 at Riverside, California. He had lived at Palm Springs, California, his occupation for the 25 years previous to his death listed as "writer." He was buried at Desert Memorial Park, Palm Springs.

Erwin, *The Southwest of John Horton Slaughter,* Glendale, Ca., Arthur H. Clark Co., 1965; Erwin death cert.

Eschscholtz, Johann Friedrich, physician (Nov. 1, 1793-May 7, 1831). B. at Dorpat (Tartu) Esthonia he became a doctor of medicine and professor of anatomy at Tartu University, and took part in two of the voyages of exploration of Otto von Kotzebue (see entry) in the early 19th century. The *Ryurik* departed from Kronstadt July 30, 1815, and in the summer of 1816 left Petropavlovsk, Kamchatka, for Bering Strait. In early August Kotzebue Sound on the northwest coast of Alaska was discovered and Dr. Eschscholtz located there an "ice mountain," whose origin was unknown to him, but which Bancroft speculated was merely a large berg trapped in the inlet, although quantities of mammoth bones and tusks were imbedded in it. A

decade afterward Beechey and his geologists investigated the site and found it an ordinary cliff face over which water had flowed following the spring thaw and had frozen into a sheet of ice a few inches thick; Beechey also confirmed the finding of mammoth bones and named a nearby prominence Elephant Point for that reason. Eschscholtz Bay was named for the vigorous physician, the name by which it still is known. Eschscholtz also shipped on Kotzebue's third circumnavigation, 1823-26 on which the *Predpriatie (Enterprise)* twice put in at Novo Arkhangelsk. He died of "nerve fever" at St. Petersburg.

Bancroft, *Alaska;* Zagoskin; Pierce, *Russian America: A Biographical Dictionary.*

Eskinya, Apache militant (c. 1820-June 4, 1876). A brother, or half-brother of Pionsenay (see entry) he was reported near Janos, Chihuahua, in 1843-44 and became an important raider and persistently hostile group leader, a member of Elias's band and Taces' band by the early 1860s. Sweeney reported that he was said to have been Cochise's head medicine man, and an influential leader in the Chokonen grouping of the Chiricahua tribe. Late in September 1863 a Mexican scouting party under Captain Eraclio Escalante out of Fronteras attacked the Taces band in the Pitaicache Mountains of Sonora, Taces being killed, to be succeeded by Eskinya as leader. When Cochise died in 1874 Eskinya was among those spoken of as a possible successor, although that position devolved upon Taza, Cochise's son. Eskinya was with Pionsenay in the irruption of a stagecoach station in which Nicholas Rogers and A.O. Spence were killed (see Pionsenay entry), and later with Pionsenay attempted to persuade Taza not to consent to removal of the Chiricahuas from their southeastern Arizona reservation to San Carlos. In an ensuing fight, Eskinya was killed, shot by Naiche, according to Sweeney. Six others of his men were killed and two, including Pionsenay, were wounded.

Edwin R. Sweeney, *Cochise: Chiricahua Apache Chief,* Norman, Univ. of Okla. Press, 1991; Dan L. Thrapp, *Conquest of Apacheria,* Norman, 1967; Woodworth Clum, *Apache Agent: The Story of John P. Clum,* N.Y., Houghton Mifflin Co., 1936.

Etolin (Yetolin), Adolf Karlovich, explorer, Russian governor (Jan. 9, 1799-Mar. 17, 1876). B. at Helsingfors (Helsinki), Finland, the name was "Russianized" from his Finnish birth name of Arvid Adolph Etholen. Hodge says that Etolin was a Creole, that is, of mixed Russian-native parentage, but in view of his place of birth this seems unlikely and possibly a case of confused identity (Hodge, II, 400). He joined the Russian navy and as a midshipman sailed in 1818 with Vasilii M. Golovnin's expedition to Sitka, Alaska, where he met Baranov, legendary governor of the Russian American Company. After Baranov's retirement the company received a second 20-year charter, and following the brief interlude governorships of Leontii Andreianovich Hagemeistr and Semen Ivanovich Yanovsky, who had married Baranov's daughter, Matvei Ivanovich Muraviev on December 15, 1820, began a full five-year term as governor and chief manager of the comany. He was a navy officer, the new charter providing that no one beneath the navy rank of captain, second class could be governor; the assistant manager must also be a naval officer (Bancroft, 534). Muraviev, scion of an ancient Russian noble family, energetically set about bringing Alaskan garrisons, practices and economy up to what he considered suitable standards, modernizing its administration while also vigorously pushing exploration. Etolin became important in this latter work. He joined an 1821 expedition headed by Vassili Khromchenko and Mikhail N. Vasiliev, and frequently acted as mediator between the quarreling co-leaders before the party was split into several elements with separate missions, Etolin heading one of these. His name was given to a strait separating from the mainland the large island of Nunivak which he discovered independently of Khromchenko, who also "discovered" it. Remaining out two years the explorers surveyed the coast from Bristol Bay to the mouth of the Kuskokwim River, and coursing the shoreline to Norton Sound, exploring its eastern and northern coasts. Khromchenko and Etolin "made contacts with Eskimos all along the coast [providing] a foundation for trade relations that later proved extremely profitable for the company," and helped lay the groundwork for the opening up of southwestern Alaska to the fur trade (HNAI, V, 151). In 1830 Etolin was sent in the brig, *Chichagof* to Norton Sound again for further explorations. He was among other objectives to touch at St. Lawrence Island, Asiak (Sledge) Island near Cape Nome, and Ookivok (King) Island, south of Cape Prince of Wales, westernmost point of the Alaska mainland. Etolin found Ookivok (Ukivok) an island so barren "one wonders how people could ever settle upon it, but the countless number of walrus...soon solves the riddle," the natives easily gaining from trade in walrus products all their necessities. At St. Lawrence Island he found five native villages, whose inhabitants also survived by trading walrus products. Etolin urged establishment of a fort on or near Stuart Island to control entrance to Norton Sound. He thereafter commanded a series of Russian American Company ships, advancing steadily in rank. In 1840, by now a navy captain, he was named governor of Alaska and manager of the company, serving a full five-year term. Afterward he returned to naval service, eventually retiring a rear admiral in 1847. He died at 77. During his Alaska service he assembled an important collection of Tanaina ethnological objects, Tanaina meaning southwestern Alaska from Cook Inlet north and west of that bay, some of the natives being of Eskimo origin and others Athapascan Indians. The collection is held by the National Museum of Finland at Helsinki; parts of it are described and illustrated in *The Far North,* a catalogue of a 1973 exhibition at the National Gallery of Art, Washington, D.C.

Bancroft, *Alaska;* Kyrill T. Khlebnikov, *Colonial Russian America,* trans. by Basil Dmytryshyn, E.A.P. Crownhart-Vaughan, Portland, Ore. Hist. Soc., 1976; HNAI, V, 151, 210, VI, 50; Zagoskin.

Evans, John, pioneer (c. 1738-1834). Of Welsh descent, Evans was b. in Loudon County, Virginia, and was an early settler on Decker's Creek on the Monongahela River. He served with Lachlan McIntosh's expedition of 1778 out of Fort Pitt against the Ohio Indians; Evans was a colonel serving under Daniel Brodhead in 1779, and was "prominent in militia affairs throughout the Revolution." He died at 96 at his home in Monongalia County, present West Virginia. His son, Captain Jack Evans, was a noted scout in the Indian wars.

Thwaites/Kellogg, *The Revolution on the Upper Ohio, 1775-1777,* Madison, Wis. Hist. Soc., 1908.

Evans, Robert, mountain man (fl. 1826-1835). A Rocky Mountain beaver trapper, Evans was b. in Ireland at an unspecified date. He was chosen in the summer of 1826 to become a member of Jedediah Smith's exploration party which reached California from the Rendezvous in the Bear River Valley near the Utah-Idaho line. Evans seems not to have been especially prominent in the party, but was selected by Smith to accompany him and Silas Gobel in the return overland to the 1827 Rendezvous at the south end of Bear Lake. The trio left the camp on the Stanislaus (Appelamminy) River, made the first crossing of the Sierra Nevada by white Americans and the first crossing of the Great Basin as well, a trip during which grave hardships almost did the party in. Evans collapsed enroute and was saved only by the fortuitous discovery by Smith of a spring a few miles farther on, and his bringing back to Evans enough drinking water to revive him. It was a close call. The three reached the Rendezvous at 3 p.m. July 3, being joyously greeted by the assembled trappers by whom they had been given up for lost. Evans had had enough of exploration in the West and declined to accompany Smith on his second trip to California following the Rendezvous although Silas Gobel did so, perishing c. August 18, 1827, when Mohave Indians slew 10 of Smith's men at the crossing of the Colorado River. Evans was on Ashley's payroll out of the mountains in 1827 and did not return for several years. In the summer of 1833 he was a member of Bridger's trapping party in the Laramie Mountains of today's Wyoming. He was sent with three other men: Jefferson Smith, Philip Thomson and Charbonneau to hunt up Fitzpatrick, Nathaniel Wyeth and party. While doing this Thomson was wounded by a bullet in the head and an arrow in the back, their horses were swept off by Shoshones (Snakes) and the group was left afoot when Wyeth and Fitzpatrick encountered them. In July 1834 Evans was named by Wyeth to take charge of Fort Hall, Idaho, and did so for several months, being relieved January 10, 1835, by Abel Baker Jr., who explained that Evans "drank alcohol too freely and squandered a great part of the goods left in his charge." Little further has been located certainly about Evans; a Robert Evans, a "prospector" from California, was killed by Indians in 1858 in British Columbia (see entry).

Dale Morgan, *Jedediah Smith and the Opening of the West,* N.Y., Bobbs-Merrill Co., 1953; Maurice S. Sullivan, *Jedediah Smith: Trader & Trailbreaker,* N.Y., Press of the Pioneers, 1936; Harvey Carter, "Jedediah Smith," MM, VIII; Janet Lecompte, "Abel Baker Jr.," MM, I; George R. Brooks, *The Southwest Expedition of Jedediah S. Smith,* Glendale, Ca., Arthur H. Clark Co., 1977; Fred R. Gowans, *Rocky Mountain Rendezvous,* Provo, Utah, Brigham Young Univ. Press, 1975; info. from E.F. (Ted) Mains.

F

Fargo, William George, expressman (May 20, 1818-Aug. 3, 1881). B. at Pompey, New York, he became a horseback mail carrier at 13, failed in an attempt to operate a grocery store, was a freight agent for a railroad and entered the booming express business. In 1844 he became one of three partners, with Henry Wells and Daniel Dunning in Wells & Company, the first such firm operating into the nation's midlands. In 1850 the American Express Company was created with Wells as president and Fargo as secretary. Following the California gold rush and development of a need for rapid transportation and express service between the east and west coasts, Wells, Fargo and Company was organized in 1852, quickly becoming dominant in the express business and eventually having a monopoly in California, being agent for stages transporting passengers, gold, mail and packages across many routes, the company also entering the banking business. Fargo supervised its field operations. He was president of Wells, Fargo and Company from 1870 to 1872, and when Wells retired as head of the American Express Company in 1873, Fargo became its president. He was politically active, was Democratic mayor of Buffalo, New York, for two terms, "had a dynamic personality, a commanding presence, and was gregarious and popular." He was married.

Literature abundant: DAB; REAW; CE; info. from E.F. (Ted) Mains; Waddell F. Smith, *Pony Express versus Wells Fargo Express,* San Rafael, Ca., Pony Express History and Art Gallery, 1966; W. Turrentine Jackson, "Wells Fargo: Staging over the Sierra," *Calif. Hist. Soc. Qtly.,* Vol. LIX, No. 2 (June 1970), 99-133.

Faris, Robert Lee, civil engineer (Jan. 13, 1868-Oct. 5, 1932). B. at Caruthersville, Missouri, he was graduated as a civil engineer from the University of Missouri in 1890, taking a special course in mathematics at George Washington University in 1893. He joined the Coast and Geodetic Survey in 1898, making surveys of the Yukon delta in Alaska, the results incorporated in C&GS charts. In 1901 he took part in surveys of the Sannak Islands, south of the western tip of the Alaska Peninsula. He was chief of the Division of Terrestrial Magnetism from September 1906 until November 1914, and became assistant director of the Coast and Geodetic Survey in March 1915. He lived at Washington, D.C.

Orth, 13, 328; *Who Was Who.*

Far[e]well, Josiah, Indian fighter (d. c. May 19, 1725). A brother-in-law of John Lovewell (see entry), he may have been of approximately the same age. He was at Dunstable (present Nashua), New Hampshire, when Indians attacked in 1724 and carried off two men. With 10 others Farwell went in pursuit, but fell into an ambush and nearly all were killed, Farwell alone escaping according to one report, although another says eight were slain. Soon after this a petition signed by Lovewell, Farwell and Jonathan Robbins asked the Boston House of Representatives that "in order to kill and destroy their enemy Indians" the petitioners and 40 or 50 others were ready to spend a year hunting them "provided they can meet with Encouragement suitable." The legislators accepted the proposal, voting to give each hunter two and one-half shillings a day, plus a generous bounty for male Indian scalps. A company of 30 was raised with Lovewell captain, Farwell lieutenant and Robbins, ensign. They set out near the end of November and returned in January bringing one scalp and a boy prisoner. A second expedition on February 21 killed ten Indians, a war party from Canada enroute on an apparent foray against the border settlements. A bounty of 1,000 pounds sterling was paid for the scalps. April 15, 1725, Lovewell set out again with 46 men including Farwell and Robbins as lieutenants. At Lovewell's Pond, near the present Fryeburg, Maine, a heavy engagement ensued with Pequawket Indians; in it Lovewell, Farwell and Robbins were all wounded mortally. As the white survivors pulled out for Dunstable, Robbins asked someone to load his musket for him so that he might shoot one more Indian before he died, the gun was loaded. Lovewell already had died and Farwell struggled along with the survivors until he, too, was forced to lag behind. Farwell "held out on his return till the eleventh day; during which time he had nothing to eat but Water and a few Roots which he chewed; and by this time the Wounds thro' his

Body were so mortified, that the Worms had a thorow Passage. [Eleazer Davis, also badly wounded] caught a Fish which he broil'd, and was greatly refresh'd therewith; but the Lieut. was so much spent that he could not taste a bit," and died.

Parkman, *Half Century of Conflict*, I; Samuel Penhallow, *History of the Indian Wars*, 1726 (Williamstown, Mass., Corner House Pub., 1973); Sylvester, III.

Fedorov, Ivan, navigator (d. 1733). He, with Michael Gwosdef (Gvosdev) became the first Europeans known to have discovered the American coast in the Bering Strait region, although their achievement did not become established for a decade after they had accomplished it. In 1728 Fedorov was assigned to an expedition under A.F. Shestakov who was under orders to subdue the Chukchi and seek a "great land" to the east of the Chukchi Peninsula. In 1732 Fedorov took command of the *Sv. Gavriil* and with the geodesist Gwosdef sailed to Chukotskii Nos (or Cape), thence to Cape Dezhnev and from there to the Diomede Islands. From one of them they saw to the east the "great land," which was Seward Peninsula, Alaska, and sailed to Cape Prince of Wales, as it is known today, but were unable to land because of adverse winds. They followed the coast southeast, then southwest and discovered an island which may have been King Island. Fedorov drew a map showing Bering Strait and the intervening islands. Returning to Nizhne-Kamchatsk, the explorers sent to Anadyrsk a log and detailed report of their work, but superiors failed to forward the materials to the Admiralty; Fedorov died at Nizhne-Kamchatsk in February 1733.

Pierce, *Russian America: A Biographical Dictionary*.

Fellows, Dick (George Lyttle, Richard Perkins), outlaw (1846-post 1915). B. George Lyttle in Harlan County, Kentucky, he came from a good family, served in the Confederate forces under Brigadier General Humphrey Marshall, was captured in 1863 and remained in a northern prison camp until 1865 when he returned home. An alcohol problem interfered with his obtaining a legal license and he went to California, arriving in 1867. Low on funds he took to robbing stagecoaches near Los Angeles, adopted the name Dick Fellows and when law-

men closed in he hid out on Castaic Creek, off the trail leading to Fort Tejon, where he met Ed Clark. After listening to Fellows' recital of his adventures, Clark urged the outlaw to go into hog raising and "quit stealing." By mustering their resources the two bought 600 hogs, but accidental fire burned them out and Dick felt compelled to return to holdups for support. A sharp-minded Fellows, he could almost always turn disaster into some kind of gain although double-barreled calamities seemed to haunt him. His good luck ran out however and when escape was impossible from a home of a friend, he persuaded his host to fake his capture in order to obtain the reward for his arrest, since "you might as well get it" instead of the posse; he was taken to Los Angeles, tried and by January 22, 1870, sentenced to eight years, arriving at San Quentin January 31, being pardoned in April 1874 and soon returning to his old ways. He planned to hold up a coach bearing Wells Fargo's chief detective, James B. Hume; a man of such importance, Fellows reasoned, must be escorting a major money shipment. But the horse he had stolen threw him, knocking him cold, and he missed the opportunity to seize $240,000. Glumly he stole another horse and held up an alternative stage, getting the treasure box and then recalling he had no tools to open it; trying to raise it to the saddle he startled his mount and it, too, raced off without him. Lugging the box he set out during the darkness but inadvertently fell over a bluff he had not detected in the blackness and when he recovered consciousness he found he had broken his left leg and the box had crushed his left foot where it had fallen upon it. Fellows stole an axe from a Chinese construction gang's camp, fashioned crude crutches, broke open the box and found $1,800 within it. He stole a farmer's horse which had been newly shod so that its tracks were readily followed by the owner, who cornered Fellows with the aid of a deputy. Hume also had followed the bandit, who now called himself Richard Perkins and recovered all but $500 of the loot, a sum which Dick had paid the deputy to let him "escape," and then had betrayed him. Fellows explained this to Hume, a man he greatly respected; the money was recovered, the deputy fired and at Bakersfield, the county seat, Fellows was sentenced to eight years. But that night Dick escaped from the makeshift holding jail and was gone. Within a week however he was recaptured and was shipped off to San Quentin again, arriving January 16, 1876, being released May 16, 1881. At Santa Cruz he worked briefly for a newspaper and under an approximation of his real name of G. Brett Lytle he even taught Spanish for a time, but that was not very profitable and as a result the San Luis Obispo-Soledad stage was held up July 19, 1881, followed by a flurry of stage robberies by a lone bandit whom Jim Hume and others identified as the "troublesome Dick Fellows." December 27, 1881, Fellows tried to stop the San Luis Obispo coach again but failed when the horses ran off with the coach; he stopped the same stage January 8, 1882, broke open the treasure box and robbed the driver. Hume by now had had enough of Dick. He assigned his best detective, Captain Charles Aull, to settle the case. Aull flooded the region with wanted circulars, Fellows was taken by surprise at Mayfield, near Santa Clara, but escaped again enroute to San Jose. He was recaptured February 4, 1882, and lodged in the San Jose jail. Hume arrived to take Dick to Santa Barbara for trial, but they remained over the weekend at San Jose, during which time "not less than 700 citizens called to see Dick, who treated them all courteously, not in the least displeased at this evidence of his notoriety," according to Hume. In Santa Barbara Fellows was tried March 27, 1882, convicted and sentenced to life, escaped April 2, sprinted down the street, tried to steal a horse and was bucked off and recaptured, and on the 3rd finally was enroute to Folsom Prison. Here he devoted part of his time to teaching inmates courses in moral philosophy. He finally was pardoned in March 1908 and disappeared from California, probably returning to his early Kentucky home, for in 1915 he was in charge of the Kentucky state exhibit at the Panama-Pacific Exposition at San Francisco, and while on the coast reportedly visited some of his old haunts. Many writers have jeered at Fellows for his losing battles with errant horseflesh, but Secrest calls that a "bad rap," asserting that while he might have been "a lousy horseman [he was] not an ineffective outlaw," and Hume conceded that Fellows was the boldest stage robber of his time. "For daring he is the equal of any outlaws with whom I have ever had dealings. His nerve, morally and physically is superb, his resource in hours of peril is apparently inexhaustible and his ability, natural and acquired, would have made him great in any honest profession he might have chosen." The date of his death is not stated.

William B. Secrest, "Dick Fellows: Hard-Luck Outlaw," *True West,* Vol. 37, Nos. 10,11 (Oct., Nov. 1990), 14-18; 14-19.

Festus Haggin: *see,* Ken Curtis

Fickett, Fred Wildon, soldier, explorer (Aug. 29, 1857-Feb. 7, 1928). B. at Dixmont, Maine, he enlisted in the Army Signal Corps at Washington, D.C., on January 5, 1882, giving his former occupation as "college student." From December 31, 1882, until August 31, 1884, he was assigned to Sitka, Alaska, and in September 1884 to Portland, Oregon, headquarters of the Department of the Columbia. In March 1885 he was instructed to join an expedition headed by Lieutenant Henry T. Allen (see entry) into the little-known interior of Alaska; the other Army member of the party was Sergeant Cady Robertson (see entry). As private and meterologist, Fickett was the key scientific observer in the exploration of the virtually unknown Copper, Tanana and Koyukuk rivers and he alone continued with Allen during the entire rugged, and highly successful, journey. He kept a log and meterological notes throughout which are printed, with his account of the operation, in *Narratives of Explorations in Alaska* (1900). Fickett was hampered early in the undertaking by foul weather which made observations for a time impossible, and later by the fact that his hygrometer was stolen by Indians and the barometer "rendered useless by the natives who were curious to understand the nature of its interior construction." During the months in the interior the party suffered "indescribable hardships and privations which is a matter of record, and became afflicted with scurvy and other ailments," according to a Washington summary. Robertson was first to come down with scurvy, Lieutenant Allen subsequently was afflicted, and the hardy Fickett contracted scurvy last; it failed to incapacitate him entirely, and he kept up his scientific observations. Fickett concluded that some vegetables and perhaps buckwheat and barley could be raised "in favored localities" on the middle and upper Yukon and the Tanana because the growing season, though short, was made intense by continuous sunlight during the summer months. Allen named a major stream the Fickett River which as a tributary to the Koyukuk flows in from the north just east of Lookout Mountain; today it is known as the Johns River for John Bremner (see entry), who as a civilian accompanied part of the Allen expedition and who subsequently visited the stream. The ailing Fickett reached St. Michael on Norton Sound with the equally ill Allen August 30, 1885, and from there returned to the United States by steamboat. Fickett re-enlisted in the Signal Corps January 5, 1887, the day after his initial enlistment expired, and as a corporal was honorably discharged at his own request at Galveston, Texas, June 16, 1890, still suffering as he later testified, from ailments he had contracted in Alaska. At Galveston he became an "attorney at law." He moved to Tucson, Arizona, in 1917 where he listed his occupation as "taking care of mines" or perhaps, mining matters, and there he died. He was married and fathered one daughter and three sons; one, Fred W. Fickett Jr., was captain in the 354th Infantry during World War I, and another, Webster L. Fickett, became a sergeant of the 81st Division during the same conflict.

Fickett, "Meterology," *Narratives of Explorations in Alaska,* 488-94; Orth, 331; Fickett's Pension File, Veterans Admin., Phoenix, Az.

Fidalgo, Salvador, Spanish trader, explorer (fl. 1789-1794). Fidalgo arrived in Mexico from Spain in 1789 and with the *San Carlos* of Spanish registry on February 3, 1790, cleared San Blas for the Northwest coast; his pilot, Esteban Mondolfia, could converse in Russian. April 4 Fidalgo reached Nootka Sound on Vancouver Island, continuing north May 4 and on the 23rd reached Prince William Sound, by small boats exploring some of its bays and waterways and naming some. June 21 the ship went to Cook Inlet, meeting Russians at Port Graham; August 8 Fidalgo called at Three Saints Bay, Kodiak Island and reached Monterey, California, September 15. From 1791 until 1794 Fidalgo was again at Nootka Sound.

Pierce, *Russian America: A Biographical Dictionary.*

Field, Darby, explorer (d. 1649). Although termed an "Irishman" by Governor John Winthrop of Massachusetts, scholarship by Warren W. Hart in *Appalachia* suggests he probably was b. at Boston, Lincolnshire, England. He is generally credited with being the first European to have explored the White Mountains of New Hampshire, and the first to ascend Agiocochook, as it was called by the Indians but is today's

Mount Washington, at 6,288 feet the tallest peak north of the Great Smoky Mountains and east of the Mississippi. The White Mountains as early as 1628 were called "the Christall hill," but so far as is known had not been visited by whites. Field was living at Exeter, New Hampshire, on April 3, 1638, when he was a grantee of an Indian deed, and on April 10, 1639, witnessed the deed of confirmation of Watohantowet (Wehanownowitt), the sagamore of Pusscataquke (Pascataquack), the name of the region along the Piscataqua River. By this deed land was granted to John Wheelwright. In June of 1642 Field made two expeditions to the White Mountain region. Winthrop wrote that Field, "accompanied with two Indians, went to the top of the white hill. He made his journey in 18 days. His relation—at his return was, that it as about one hundred miles from Saco, that after 40 miles travel he did, for the most part, ascend, and within 10 miles of the top was neither tree nor grass, but low savins [junipers], which they went upon the top of sometimes, but a continual ascent upon rocks, on a ridge between two valleys filled with snow, out of which came two branches of the Saco River, which meet at the foot of the hill, where was an Indian town of some 200 people. Some of them accompanied him within 8 miles of the top, but durst go no further, telling him that no Indian ever dared go higher, and that he would die if he went. So they staid there till his return, but his two Indians took courage by his example and went with him. They went divers times through the thick clouds for a good space, and within 4 miles of the top they had no clouds, but very cold. By the way, among the rocks, there were two ponds, one of blackish water and the other reddish. The top of all was plain about 60 feet square. On the north side there was such a precipice, as they could scarcely discern to the bottom. They had neither cloud nor wind at the top, and moderate heat. All the country about him seemed a level, except here and there a hill rising above the rest, but far beneath them. He saw to the north a great water which he judged to be 100 miles broad [possibly the St. Lawrence where it flows from south to north], but could see no land beyond it. The sea by Saco [the Atlantic] seemed as if it had been within 20 miles. He saw some great waters in parts to the westward which he judged to be the great lake which the Canada River comes out of [Lake Ontario]...About a month after he went again, with five or six of his company, then they had some wind on the top, and some clouds above them which hid the sun. They brought some stones which they supposed had been diamonds, but they were most crystal." A bridle path to the summit was completed in 1840, an 8½ mile road in 1861, a cog railroad in 1869, and a hotel and meteorological station were completed at the summit in 1932. In 1645 Field was living at Oyster River, now Durham, New Hampshire, where he died, leaving children.

Charles H. Bell, *History of the Town of Exeter,* p.p., Exeter, 1888; info. from the New Hampshire Hist. Soc.; Sylvester, III, 257-58n.

Field, John, military officer (1720-Oct. 10, 1774). B. in Culpeper County, Virginia, he served in the French and Indian War, was on frontier duty in 1756, and was a captain under John Forbes in the 1758 expedition to occupy Fort Duchesne in western Pennsylvania. Field became a major by the time he joined the Henry Bouquet expedition of 1764 to the Ohio Indian towns, and was made colonel of militia in 1766. In 1774 while exploring up the Great Kanawha River of present West Virginia he had a narrow escape from hostile Indians; his son, Ephraim and a black woman were captured and in revenge Field enlisted a company of 40 men and joined Andrew Lewis's party at Camp Union (the present Lewisburg, West Virginia). It is said that Field felt he should outrank Lewis, but Lewis remained in command through the October 10, 1774, Battle of Point Pleasant against the Shawnees. In this action John Field was killed. Ephraim, seized earlier by Indians, was rescued from captivity, and was killed at the Battle of Blue Licks, Kentucky, August 19, 1782.

Thwaites, *Dunmore.*

Field, Matt(hew C.), journalist (1812-Nov. 15, 1844). B. at London of Irish parentage, he was brought to America at 4 and grew up in Baltimore and New York, following the trade of jeweler until 1834. He then moved to New Orleans, briefly joined his brother, Joseph, as a stage actor, playing with the Ludlow-Smith Company at Mobile, New Orleans and St. Louis until May 1839. Never in robust health he decided upon a trip to Santa Fe, traveling there from St. Louis. He wrote features, often in verse, for the New Orleans *Weekly Picayune* about his adventures. His caravan left Independence about July 1, in

1839, with 18 men and a few wagons. It reached Cottonwood Crossing (near present Durham, Kansas) and arrived at Walnut Creek (near present Great Bend) July 21, a week later sighting Pawnee Rock which Matt thought looked like "a huge wart" upon the prairie. He found 20 names carved into the stone of this "signpost of the Plains," some "as far as ten years back." Field continued on to Taos and Santa Fe. He left in late summer from San Miguel, between Santa Fe and Las Vegas, regained Council Grove October 24, and Independence October 30. He then joined the staff of the *Picayune,* contributing to it feature articles on his travels and establishing "something of a reputation as a newspaper poet." In 1841 he married Cornelia Ludlow, with whom he had two children and by 1843 was assistant editor of the *Picayune.* William Drummond Stewart (see entry) that year visited New Orleans, commencing to organize his final pleasure excursion to the Rocky Mountains. He was attracted by the "lively, intelligent" Field, finding him "versatile, adaptable, talented and with a wide streak of whimsical gaiety," and invited him to join the overland party. Field was reluctant to leave his wife for the season without support, but Stewart promised to provide her with funds and Matt then agreed to join the expedition. He believed he had tuberculosis (he had stomach ulcers, instead), and that mountain air and camp life would benefit his health. The rather uneventful foray left St. Louis, traveled a bit north of the Overland Trail to avoid the traffic, gained the upper Platte and Green River and reached Fremont Lake, near present Pinedale on the upper Green. On August 17, was commenced the return journey. Ash Hollow was gained September 23, and St. Louis October 30. Matt returned to New Orleans where he penned a series of vivid narratives and poetic works on the summer's adventure. He then joined Joseph and Charles Keemle in founding the St. Louis *Reveille* where some of his plains and mountains efforts were reprinted. Mae Reed Porter examined the *Picayune* originals, the reproduced works in the *Reveille,* and several of Field's notebooks held by the Missouri Historical Society, incorporating them, or elements from them, in her books touching on Field's journeys. Still suffering ill health, and believing that a sea voyage might prove beneficial, Matt Field on November 13, 1844, cleared Boston aboard the bark *Huma* bound for New Orleans, but two days out he died, being buried at sea.

Matthew C. Field, *Prairie and Mountain Sketches,* coll. by Clyde and Mae Reed Porter, ed. by Kate L. Gregg, Joseph Francis McDermott, Norman, Univ. of Okla. Press, 1957; Field, *Matt Field on the Santa Fe Trail,* coll. by Clyde, Mae Reed Porter, ed. by John E. Sunder, Norman, 1960; Barry, *Beginning of the West;* Mae Reed Porter, Odessa Davenport, *Scotsman in Buckskin: Sir William Drummond Stewart and the Rocky Mountain Fur Trade,* N.Y., Hastings House, 1963; info. from E.F. (Ted) Mains.

Findlay, John, Kentucky explorer: *see,* John Finley

Fisher, Vardis (Alvero), writer (Mar. 31, 1895-July 9, 1968). B. at Annis, Idaho, he grew up on the Snake River at the foot of the Big Hole Mountains. He served in the army during World War I. Fisher was graduated from the University of Utah in 1920, earned his master's degree and in 1925 a doctorate, magna cum laude from the University of Chicago. He taught English at the University of Utah and New York (N.Y.) University, was director of the Idaho Federal Writers Project from 1935-39, the last two years of which he was also general editor for the Rocky Mountain states. He wrote many books beginning in 1927 and they were of a wide variety in subject and treatment. His fiction works of frontier interest included: *Children of God,* the story of the Mormons (1939); *City of Illusion* (1941); *The Mothers* (1943); *Pemmican: A Novel of the Hudson's Bay Company* (1956), and *Tale of Valor: A Novel of the Lewis and Clark Expedition* (1958). His nonfiction books of frontier interest included: *Suicide or Murder? The Strange Death of Governor Meriwether Lewis* (1962); *Mountain Man* (1965), and with Opal Laurel Holmes, his wife, *Gold Rushes and Mining Camps of the Early American West* (1968). He was general editor and contributor to *Idaho: A Guide in Word and Picture* (1937); *Idaho Encyclopedia* (1938), and *Idaho Lore* (1939). Fisher's most famous novel was *Children of God* which won widespread praise, was financially successful and was probably the most widely-read of his books. He was a very complex individual, some of his works are deeply philosophical and one critic wrote, "Fisher is not every man's writer, and it is quite conceivable that readers will approve him in one kind of novel—or genre—and not in another, in itself a tribute to his range." He was married three times: his first wife ended her own life; his second marriage was unsuccessful, and his third endured, his widow surviving him. He

fathered three children. His final residence was in the Thousand Springs Valley of Idaho.

Contemporary Authors; REAW; info. from E.F. (Ted) Mains.

Fisher, William S., military officer (d. 1845). Fisher went to Texas from Virginia in 1834 and settled at Gonzales. March 10, 1836, he joined the Texas army, the 26th reinforced Sam Houston's army with a company he had raised, Company I, 1st Texas Volunteers and took part in the Battle of San Jacinto where Texas's independence was won. He served as Secretary of War for Texas from December 21, 1836, to November 13, 1837. Appointed lieutenant colonel of a frontier cavalry regiment, he commanded two or three companies at San Antonio at the March 19, 1840, Council House Fight, Texans against Comanches. He became attracted to the abortive Republic of Rio Grande, an effort by Mexicans of the states of Tamaulipas, Coahuila and Nuevo Leon to set up an independent nation and led 200 men to its support; they returned after a short period when it appeared the independence movement was doomed. In 1842 Fisher was named captain of the equally short-lived Somervell Expedition, and when Alexander Somervell quit the enterprise, Fisher was elected leader of an operation called the Mier Expedition. During an attack on the Mexican community of Mier, south of the Rio Grande and a short distance west of Carmargo, Fisher was wounded and captured by Mexican General Pedro Ampudia. He was imprisoned with Mier Expedition survivors at Perote Prison in Veracruz State, released in 1843 and returned to Texas where he died in Jackson County two years later.

HT.

Fisk, James Liberty, plainsman (Sept. 12, 1835-Nov. 2, 1902). B. at Royalton, New York, he was raised near Niagara Falls, learned the trade of wagonmaking and made several rafting journeys on the Allegheny and Ohio rivers. At Lafayette, Indiana, he worked for a newspaper, became interested in western expansion and in the spring of 1857 moved to Minnesota, settling near White Bear Lake hard by St. Paul. He farmed, wrote occasional pieces for a St. Paul newspaper and became associated with the Dakota Land Company, a firm of St. Paul speculators interested in properties in southern Minnesota and Dakota. During the summer of 1857 he joined a William Nobles expedition constructing a wagon road from Fort Ridgely, Min-

nesota, to South Pass. "In the West he became a
hardy sportsman, a fancier of good horses, and a
dead shot with rifle or pistol." October 26, 1861,
he enlisted in Company B, 3rd Minnesota
Infantry for Civil War service; following the Battle of Shiloh, he was appointed assistant quartermaster of volunteers from May 29, 1862, with
rank of captain. Meanwhile Minnesota Congressman Cyrus Aldrich (1808-1871) had prevailed upon Secretary of War Edwin Stanton to
assign funds for protection of a northern route
across the Plains toward the Idaho goldfields,
following the course of a projected railroad
route. On May 19, Fisk, then stationed near
Columbia, Tennessee, was summoned to Washington, D.C., where he was appointed superintendent of emigration between Fort Abercrombie
(about 15 miles north of present Wahpeton,
North Dakota) and Fort Walla Walla, Washington. Fisk later recalled that Aldrich, upon Fisk's
arrival at the capital, "took me by the shoulder,
had me appointed, confirmed, commissioned,
mustered out and mustered in, my bonds satisfactorily filed, the appropriation transferred, my
instructions furnished me, all in twenty-four
hours..." He was instructed to organize and outfit a corps of men for the protection of emigrants
"not only against hostile Indians but against all
dangers including starvation, losses, accidents,
and the like," hire guides, Indian interpreters,
physicians, wagon masters, teamsters and
arrange for wide advertising of his plans. His
responsibility was to terminate at Fort Benton,
Montana, after which the emigrants would be on
their own. Fisk was instructed himself to proceed
over the Mullan Road to Walla Walla, sell his
government property, and return home by way of
Panama. His appropriated funds never covered
the activities his instructions directed and it was
not until years after the War that he succeeded in
settling his expedition accounts. He reached St.
Paul June 3. He appointed Nathaniel Pitt Langford (see entry) as assistant in charge of commissary, and other acquaintances and friends to
various positions, including Pierre Bottineau
(see entry) as guide. Fisk and some of his staff
left St. Paul June 16, 1862, reaching Fort Abercrombie July 4 and three days later moved out,
the expedition including 53 wagons, 117 men
and 13 women, and a small howitzer on a later
occasion being used effectively by the Montana
vigilantes. It was only two months before the
Great Sioux Uprising would break out in southern Minnesota. The train made Fort Benton without serious mishap by mid-September. Fisk

arrived at Walla Walla in late October and eventually reached New York by ship from Panama
as instructed. "As a result of the journey Fisk
became convinced of the importance of the
northern route for Minnesota, the gold fields, and
the country as a whole. From this time he considered his duties as army officer and superintendent of emigration secondary to his role as
explorer and promoter." He actively promoted
his enthusiasms over the following four years.
Congress heartily approved the 1862 expedition
and Fisk in 1863 led the only wagon train that
year to reach Montana from Minnesota by the
northern route. Before his departure he also completed his book, *Idaho: Her Gold Fields and the
Routes to Them* which was published as a pocket-
sized guide in April 1863. With 60 men in camp,
36 of them on his payroll, Fisk left Fort Ripley,
Minnesota, June 25, reached Fort Abercrombie
July 13, well in the buffalo country, met only one
party of Sioux and that a small one—no threat—
had later meetings with Assiniboines and Gros
Ventres and arrived at Fort Benton September 7.
Although he had been instructed to go to Walla
Walla, he rather determined to visit the new gold
camps of Bannack and Virginia City, early
snows giving him an excuse not to proceed westward over the mountains to Washington Territory. With "a valise full of gold and a mind full of
equally golden prospects" he took a stage to Salt
Lake City and reached Minnesota in mid-
December. He received a rousing welcome and
at once began planning his third expedition, to go
west in 1864. A six-week lecture campaign,
which took him to New York and Chicago
among other places prepared the way and mustered support. He finally formed a wagon train of
some 170 emigrants. He planned a new, shorter
route to take his people to Virginia City and Bannack and his visionary plans for the future took
him to Washington, D.C., where on February 29
he met with President Lincoln, giving him sample nugglets. However, his congressional support had dwindled; he was directed to make his
1864 expedition along his original route to Fort
Benton, which he had no intention of doing. The
expedition got underway July 23, reached Dakota and turned southerly toward the headwaters of
the Little Missouri and mouth of the Bighorn on
the Yellowstone River. September 2 near the present Rhame, North Dakota, Hunkpapa Sioux
attacked the rear of the train, killing nine and
mortally wounding three others; a bad rainstorm
blew up and under continuous Indian attack the
wagons moved 12 miles in the following two

days and established a camp 15 miles east of the Montana line. Here the emigrants waited 16 days and Fisk tried unsuccessfully to ransom Fanny Kelly (see entry), a Sioux captive. Some of the emigrants left strychnine-laced hardtack along the way and 25 Indians were poisoned. A relief column of troops from Fort Rice, south of present Bismarck, arrived, informed Fisk that no military escort was available to take him farther west and the expedition withdrew to the fort and dissolved, Fisk returning to St. Paul where he found himself the center of much dissension and criticism about his conduct of the expedition and such matters as the poisoning of the Sioux, for which Fisk was not personally responsible. In 1866 Fisk "lobbied, planned, propagandized, and recruited for his fourth expedition, which was to be the largest and last he took over the northern Plains." The 1864 expedition's failure was among many factors hindering his efforts for this last effort. He was financially overextended: creditors were suing for $7,000 (he claimed he had lost $20,000 in promoting the northern route). This time he proposed a new route to the Montana mines but military support not forthcoming he became for the first time a private expedition leader. His train reached Fort Abercrombie June 22, 1866. His party of between 300 and 400 emigrants and 100 to 200 wagons left the fort June 25 and struck the Missouri River below Fort Berthold, reaching the Fort Benton area August 27 from where part of the company went to Helena, Montana, the rest prospecting first on the Sun River before they too wound up at Helena. Fisk had now completed his career as a pathfinder and emigrant leader. He became editor of the Helena *Herald* for some months of 1867, was appointed a colonel of the Montana militia, promoted a quartz mining project and then for years "moved restlessly between Montana, Dakota, Minnesota, and Washington, engaging in one ephemeral project after another." In the late 1890s he moved into the Minnesota Soldiers Home, Minneapolis, where he resided until his death.

Helen McCann White, *Ho! For the Gold Fields: Northern Overland Wagon Trains of the 1860s,* St. Paul, Minn. Hist. Soc., 1966; *Minnesota in the Civil and Indian Wars,* Vol. I, St. Paul, Pioneer Press Co., 1891, pp. 181, 549-51, "Rescue of Captain Fisk's Party" in 1864.

FitzGerald, Gerald, topographer (b. 1899). A Geological Survey topographer from 1917 to 1957, he did his initial work in Alaska on the Iniskin oil field on Cook Inlet. FitzGerald spent four seasons beginning in 1923 on topographical surveys of the Naval Petroleum Reserve 4 in northwestern Alaska; he also did topographic work in southwest Alaska. He was Chief Alaskan Topographer from 1938 to 1942 and Chief Topographic Engineer from 1947 to 1957 for the Geological Survey.

Orth, 13.

Flake, William, cattleman (July 3, 1839-1932). B. in North Carolina, he moved to Utah with his Mormon parents in 1849. The next year his father was killed while examining a San Bernardino California colony site, but his mother took the family to the new settlement in 1851 and when the colony became less viable returned to Utah in 1857. In 1858 William Flake married Lucy White and a year later started a cattle ranch at Beaver, Utah. It prospered for about 20 years, but in 1877 Flake with other Mormons left by wagon with their herds of cattle for the Little Colorado region of Arizona, where they arrived in January 1878. The colonists were forced to live in their wagons that winter. In the spring Flake traded cattle for James Stinson's ranch, which was under irrigation and growing corn and wheat. That summer Flake's family and their poverty-stricken neighbors lived largely on beef and roasting ears, but by fall had raised enough food for the coming winter. In the fall of 1848 Erastus Snow, an Apostle of the Mormon church, arrived and decided that Flake's ranch was a promising place for a settlement. He joined with Flake in creating the town of Snowflake, today a thriving community of some 2,000 in eastern Arizona. When Apache County was created in 1879 Snowflake temporarily was the county seat and the first term of court was held in Flake's home. Noted for his generosity, Flake provided thousands of meals for all comers, wealthy or broke. He established a Thanksgiving-time custom of distributing free wood and free beef to every widow or needy person around, a practice carried out today by his descendants. Flake remained healthy and rode the range until shortly before his death at 93. "He was a thorough cowman in every respect."

PCA, II; REAW, which is a rewrite of PCA by way of the Okla. City Cowboy Hall of Fame; info. from E.F. (Ted) Mains.

Flemer, John Adolph, topographer (fl. 1898-

1905). Flemer, of the Coast and Geodetic Survey, arrived in Alaska in 1898 to make a topographic reconnaissance of the Lynn Canal in the territory's panhandle, his reports appearing in the Survey's annual report for 1899. Flemer also took part in the boundary surveys in southeastern Alaska in 1903-1905 under the Alaska Boundary Tribunal.

Orth, 13, 342.

Flinn, John, frontiersman (d. 1786). Flinn and his family were the first settlers on Cabin Creek, West Virginia, an affluent of the Kanawha River. He was a sergeant, probably in the militia in 1777 and apparently saw duty against the Shawnees or other Indians, serving for a time under Captain Matthew Arbuckle. In 1786 the Flinn station was attacked by Indians; Flinn was killed, his wife, two daughters and a son captured, and another daughter escaped. Chloe, one of the captured daughters, was later redeemed by Daniel Boone.

Thwaites, *Dunmore:* Thwaites/Kellogg, *Frontier Defense on the Upper Ohio, 1777-1778.*

Ford, Henry Chapman, painter (1828-Feb. 27, 1894). B. at Livonia, New York, he studied abroad from 1857-60, principally at Paris and Florence. With the Civil War he enlisted in the army, but was discharged within a year for disability. Later in the war his sketches of battle scenes, reproduced in the illustrated press, brought him some public attention. He opened a studio at Chicago and became the first professional landscape painter known to have worked in that city, although much of his early work was destroyed by the Great Fire of 1871. He helped organize the Chicago Academy of Design and in 1873 was its president. Ford made occasional trips to Colorado, painting Rocky Mountain scenes, and in 1875 he moved to Santa Barbara, California, presumably for reasons of health, but spending the rest of his life there. Ford became intrigued by the old California missions and "painted them many times," the best known of his works being a portfolio of etchings of the missions published in 1883. He also compiled a history of the missions which however was not published during his lifetime, but portions of which, edited by Norman Neuerburg, a professor of art history at a branch of the California State University, were to be published by the Book Club of California about a century after Ford's death.

Robert Taft, *Artists and Illustrators of the Old West 1850-1900*, N.Y., Bonanza Books, 1953.

Ford, John, motion picture director (Feb. 1, 1895-Aug. 31, 1973). B. at Cape Elizabeth, Maine, as Sean Aloysius O'Feeney, he had a high school education, went to Hollywood in 1913, took on the name of John Ford and went to work for Universal Studios as a stagehand and eventually a bit actor. In 1919 he moved to Fox Studios and began directing short films and serials, including a few with Tom Mix (see entry), the Pennsylvania-born cowboy actor. Ford evolved into directing major pictures, making more than 80 in all, an early example of which was *The Iron Horse* based upon construction of the transcontinental railroad. He also worked for M-G-M, United Artists and RKO. Ford won his initial Academy Award with *The Informer,* but his second major western was *Stagecoach* (1939) and that year he also made *Drums Along the Mohawk* about the eastern frontier. Other films with some frontier relevance included *My Darling Clementine, Fort Apache, She Wore a Yellow Ribbon, Rio Grande, Wagonmaster, The Man Who Shot Liberty Valance, How the West Was Won,* and *Cheyenne Autumn.* Ford, a lieutenant commander in the Naval Reserve, was chief of the Field Photographic Branch of the Office of Strategic Services and shot award-winning documentaries on phases of the World War II effort. He was associated with John Wayne (see entry) in a number of films. In addition to his action pictures Ford also dealt at times with social themes in such works as *The Grapes of Wrath* and *How Green Was My Valley,* they, too, award-winners. He died at Palm Desert, California. He was married and fathered a son and a daughter.

Literature abundant: EB; *Webster's American Biographies,* Springfield, Mass., G & C Merriam Co., 1974; *Who's Who in America;* info. from Richard J. Coyer.

Foreman, William, military officer (d. Sept. 27, 1777). Foreman, as a militia captain, raised a volunteer company in Hampshire County, present West Virginia, and marched it to Wheeling in the fall of 1777, arriving in mid-September. The company was part of a force raised by Governor Patrick Henry to form an expedition against the Indian towns on the Scioto River of Ohio. Foreman, wrote De Hass, was "a gallant soldier, but wholly unfamiliar with Indian warfare [and] proved himself unfit for the service" by his initial essay into hostile territory. September 26, from Wheeling smoke was seen in the direction of

Grave Creek, which empties into the Ohio near Tomlinson (present Mound City). Foreman headed a scout made up of 24 of his own men, Sergeant Jacob Ogle with ten men,and Captain William Linn (see entry), a man of much Indian experience, with nine. They found Tomlinson sacked, burned and deserted and proceeded to Grave Creek, spending the night there, the next morning starting their return. When they reached the Grave Creek Narrows, Linn urged Foreman to abandon the trail in the defile and progress instead along high ground, but Foreman "hooted at the idea of so much caution and ordered the march continued," while Linn "whose great experience as a [scout], added to his sagacity and judgment should at least have rendered his opinions...entitled to weight," continued to object. According to Robert Harkness, a survivor, the "controversy" between Linn and Foreman "ran high," but the two commands separated, and Foreman's took the low ground. When it reached the upper end of the Narrows there was come upon "a display of Indian trinkets, beads, bands, &c., strewn in profusion along the path. With a natural curiosity, but a great lack of perception, the entire party gathered about...the decoy, and whilst thus standing in a compact group" the Indians, a war party under the Wyandot chief, Half King, opened "a most deadly and destructive fire." Foreman and his two sons, Hambleton and Nathan Foreman, were killed at the first fire. Jacob Ogle, who on the first of the month had escaped a massacre before Fort Henry at Wheeling, also was slain, as were almost 20 others. The story persists that when Linn and his small group heard the firing, they dashed down the slope toward the scene, firing their weapons and shouting so that the Indians, probably fearing that reinforcements had arrived, fled. Thwaites commented that the story of "Linn's gallant attack...is without foundation," but whether he meant without responsible support, or was a wholly false tale is not clear. Four days later Colonel David Shepherd from Fort Pitt arrived to bury the dead. In 1835 an inscribed stone was placed at the Narrows to commemorate the event.

Wills De Hass, *History of the Early Settlement and Indian Wars of Western Virginia,* Wheeling, H. Hoblitzell, Publ., 1851, 1960, 230-34; Alexander Scott Withers, *Chronicles of Border Warfare,* ed. by Reuben Gold Thwaites, Cincinnati, Robert Clarke Co., 1895, 1970.

Forrest, Earle Robert, writer (June 29, 1883-Aug. 25, 1969). B. at Washington, Pennsylvania, he was graduated from Washington and Jefferson College of his home town and took graduate work at the University of Michigan in 1908-1909. Forrest worked as a civil engineer from 1910-13 when he became a forest ranger in Montana for a year and then went into newspaper work successively for the *Daily News,* the *Reporter* and *The Observor,* all of Washington, Pennsylvania. His books included: *History of Washington County, Pennsylvania* (1926); *Missions and Pueblos of the Old Southwest* (1929); with Joe E. Milner, *California Joe, Noted Scout and Indian Fighter* (1935); *Arizona's Dark and Bloody Ground* (1936); with Edwin B. Hill, *The Lone War Trail of the Apache Kid* (1947); *Patrick Gass, Lewis and Clark's Last Man* (1950); *The Snake Dance of the Hopi Indians* (1961), and *The House of Romance* (1964). His final book was *With a Camera in Old Navaholand.* Forrest reported that he also had worked from time to time as a cowboy in Colorado, Arizona and Montana. He was married and fathered a daughter who survived him.

Contemporary Authors.

Fouts, William D., military officer (c. 1814-June 14, 1865). B. in Indiana, he had become a Methodist preacher before moving in 1857 to Albia, Iowa, where he opened a mercantile business. At the outbreak of the Civil War he helped raise a company and was mustered in April 28, 1863, as captain of Company D, 7th Iowa Cavalry which was assigned frontier duty in Nebraska and Wyoming. The regiment was commanded by Colonel Samuel W. Summers. Stationed initially at Fort Kearny, Fouts and his company later were assigned to Fort Laramie, Wyoming, arriving there July 27, 1864. February 4, 1865, hostiles attacked a stage station at Mud Springs, 105 miles southeast of Laramie and Captain Fouts commanded one element of the relief, arriving at the Springs early February 6, the Sioux quickly brushed aside, D Company having a man killed and two wounded before returning to Laramie. In June Fouts was ordered to take D and detachments from A and B companies and escort 185 lodges of Brulé and Oglala Sioux from Laramie to Fort Kearny. Two days out of Laramie the column bivouacked at the confluence of Horse Creek and the North Platte River, while Indian resentment at being moved, and apprehenson over being taken into Pawnee country, together with irritation at what they considered white injustices toward them, made for a dangerous situation. The Indians had been allowed to retain their arms, and Fouts issued no ammunition to his company, a fatal mistake. On July 14, the Indian camp refused to move out while much of the column's escort had gone ahead. Fouts and some of his men moved to the Sioux camp to hurry them up. Shots were fired and Fouts was killed with a bullet in the head, possibly fired by a Brulé subchief named White Thunder; three soldiers also were killed and others wounded while the Indians escaped to the north and were not recaptured.

Dean Knudsen, "Death on Horse Creek," *True West*, Vol. 36, No. 3 (Mar. 1989), 14-19.

Francisco, White Mountain Apache (d. Nov. 10, 1865). Probably an eastern White Mountain, or Coyotero, chief, he had been perhaps in his childhood a Mexican captive and thus inherited his Spanish name. Sweeney believed he may have been Na-ginit-a (He Scouts Ahead), whom Goodwin described as very friendly with the Chiricahuas, with whom Francisco was long associated. He was a particular friend of Cochise and during his lifetime took part in some important incidents in Cochise's career. In appearance he was, according to James H. Tevis, the peer in physique of Cochise, whom he considered "as fine a looking Indian as one ever saw. He was about six feet tall and as straight as an arrow, built...as perfect as any man could be." If he was the Indian called by whites Fresco (or Frisco?) he met the Indian agent Michael Steck December 30, 1858, at Apache Pass. April 24, 1859, Francisco and Cochise with their combined war party left Apache Pass for Mexico, attacking Mexicans near Fronteras three days later. Francisco continued the operation deeper into Mexico (he had once told Tevis he would fight Mexicans "as long as he lived and had a warrior to follow him"). Francisco had an important role as an ally of Cochise in the famed Bascom confrontation at Apache Pass in February 1861. When Cochise faded south into Sonora, Francisco headed toward the Gila with Mangas Coloradas. Later Francisco and Cochise may have cooperated in raiding in southern Arizona, their combined forces being successful in several events. Such incidents occurred sporadically through the Civil War years. May 5, 1862, Francisco and Cochise killed four men and ran off 55 mules and horses from a Confederate command at Dragoon Springs, Arizona, and Francisco may have participated with Cochise and Mangas Coloradas in the July Battle of Apache Pass with the California Column of Union troops. Francisco came to Fort Goodwin, Arizona, in the fall of 1865, probably to discuss peace, but was placed in the guardhouse, instead. There on November 10 soldiers shot him, ostensibly "trying to escape," the incident rekindling Apache hostilities that had been dwindling for some time.

Edwin R. Sweeney, *Cochise: Chiricahua Apache Chief,* Norman, Univ. of Okla. Press, 1991; Grenville Goodwin, *The Social Organization of the Western Apache,* Tucson, Univ. of Arizona Press, 1969.

French, Jim, frontiersman (fl. 1870s). Not to be confused with James Hansell French (see entry), this man, known at times as "Big Jim," or "Frenchy," was also active in the Lincoln County, New Mexico, troubles of the late 1870s, but details of his career are sparse. Captain George A. Purington on June 21, 1879, reported that he had been killed in a dispute over stolen cattle, but by that time he himself wrote that he was living at Keota, Indian Territory. A Jim French was killed during a store robbery at Catoosa, Oklahoma, 80 miles northwest of Keota in 1895, but no connection of French of Keota and the Catoosa incident has yet been made.

Information from Frederick W. Nolan.

French, William, cattleman (July 4, 1854-Oct. 6, 1928). B. at Dublin, Ireland, he was of English lineage and a British army officer from 1876 to 1882, attaining the rank of captain. On November 4, 1883, at 29 years of age, he took ship for New York. After an episodic journey by rail to California he was persuaded by English stockmen who had preceded him to locate in New Mexico. He settled near Alma, 80 miles northwest of Silver City. French stopped at the WS Ranch owned by Harold C. Wilson, an English friend and became acquainted with James H. Cook (see entry), finding him "a wonderful shot and the very best game hunter I have ever met," who also initiated French "into the mysteries of the lasso and...branding." On a wandering trip through New Mexico French reached Socorro November 6, 1883, while Joel Fowler (see entry) was on a mad drunk during which he knifed one of his several victims, for which he subsequently was jailed and then lynched, an event French witnessed to his disgust, since Fowler died a craven coward. At last he caught up with the English party he had been trailing, headed by Montague Stevens, partner of French's friend, Edward (Ned) Upcher in the fledgling SU Ranch, titled for their initials. The party was to receive a herd of cattle for which French had put up the capital, and drive it back to their spread, northerly from the WS where French made his headquarters. French appears to have been involved in virtually everything of excitement occurring in that part of New Mexico (and something of interest seemed always to be going on). He managed to become a key player in the renowned Baca's Battle (see Elfego Baca entry) at Frisco (the present Reserve, New Mexico), recounting it in detail and with his usual good humor in his *Recollections,* a very useful account of the engagement. He took a gleeful part in all ranch activities: hunting down feral or semi-wild cattle, breaking horses, branding livestock, treating wounded or ill individuals, foe or friend, visiting saloons, hosting army officers who stopped by on their Indian-hunting missions, and recounting these and many other things with lacings of droll British wit. He ran into occasional court matters involving his lands or livestock, learning that in such cases in a bi-racial community it was valueless to make friends with judge, prosecutor or rival attorneys. The thing to do if one wished to win was "to become a warm friend of the interpreter" who, he discovered, could make or break any case regardless of the testimony to be translated. During the 1885-86 Geronimo war Apaches raided the Alma region and French typically was involved, through acquaintance with Lieutenant Samuel Warren Fountain (see entry), with the worst incident of Army-Apache conflict during the months of campaigning. In the late 1890s, with a rise in stock prices, French's holdings were among those depredated upon. About that time his foreman left and he hired a "stoutly built [and] fair complected" man who said his name was Jim Lowe, and his companion, younger, taller and darker and of some education whose name was given as William McGinnis. New hands seemed to show up whenever Lowe wanted them and the employees possessed a wonderous pacifying effect, for all rustling immediately ceased, at least so far as the French holdings were concerned. "They brought a complete change all over the range," wrote French. "Their zeal for everything in connexion with the outfit was beyond all praise." If an animal showed up with a strange brand "they assumed without question that it belonged to the WS," and added it to the herd, there never being a question raised about previous ownership. The newcomers were excellent stockmen and McGinnis a wonder at breaking horses. French liked both men and all the employees they managed to find jobs for from time to time. It was much later that he learned that Jim Lowe was really Butch Cassidy, that McGinnis was Elza Lay and the other employees who appeared from time to time were linked with or members of the "Wild Bunch," a notorious band of desperadoes. So far as French was concerned they were remarkably competent workers he was sorry to lose, as he did when Pinkerton agents arrived to solve through his ranch hands certain train robberies or other misdeeds. French also had contacts with Thomas E. or Black Jack Ketchum and his brother, Sam, accomplished outlaws in their own right, and others of like bent. Not long after the Wild Bunch moved on, or around 1899 he shifted his ranching operations to near Cimarron, Colfax County, New Mexico. His enterprises had proven profitable and he settled at Oakland, California, for the remaining 25 years of his life. He was married and had fathered a daughter. He died at Oakland of pneumonia at 81 years of age. His *Some Recollections of a Western Ranchman* was warmly praised by Ramon Adams as "one of the really good, though obscure, books on the West," containing much previously unknown material on the Wild Bunch, Joel Fowler, and Black Jack Ketchum. It also is a most delightful narrative, and appears to be as accurate as it is entertaining. The second volume of his manuscript was published posthumously.

French, *Some Recollections of a Western Ranchman,* N.Y., Frederick A. Stokes, 1928, repr. Silver City, N. Mex., High-Lonesome Books, 1990; French, *Further Recollections of a Western Ranchman,* N.Y., Argosy-Antiquarian, 1965; William French death cert.; Adams, *Six-Guns and Saddle Leather,* new edition, 1969.

Frogg, John, sutler (d. Oct. 10, 1774). From Staunton, Virginia, he accompanied the militia army to Point Pleasant, West Virginia, as a sutler. Thwaites describes him as young, handsome, generous, gallant and "fond of display." The day of the battle which was the climax of the Lord Dunmore's War, Frogg wore a brilliant red jacket, which made him an excellent target. When he fell, an Indian ran to scalp him, but he and four others on the same mission were shot and killed, their bodies found in a heap above Frogg's body. A family tradition was that on October 10, his little daughter in Staunton awakened three times, crying to her mother that the Indians were killing her father—a fact that news from the battlefield did not reach the family until many days later. Frogg's widow married Captain John Stuart, a veteran of the Point Pleasant action.

Thwaites, *Dunmore.*

Frost, Lawrence A(ugust), historian (May 1, 1907-Aug. 14, 1990). B. at Ann Arbor, Michigan, he studied podiatric medicine at the University of Toledo and elsewhere, became a Doctor of Podriatic Medicine and followed that profession throughout his life. Frost settled at Monroe, Michigan, which had been George Armstrong Custer's home town and soon became interested in that officer and among the foremost students of Custer's life and career, writing prolifically on the subject and related matters. Among his works were: *The Custer Album* (1964); *The U.S. Grant Album* (1966); *The Phil Sheridan Album* (1968); *The Court-Martial of General George Armstrong Custer* (1968); *General Custer's Libbie* (1976); ed., with John M. Carroll, *Private Theodore Ewart's Diary of the Black Hills Expedition of 1874* (1976); *With Custer in '74* (1979); *Addressing the Custer Story* (1980); *Some Observations on the Yellowstone Expedition of 1873* (1981); *Custer Legends* (1981); *Boy General in Bronze: Custer, Michigan's Hero on Horseback* (1985); *General Custer's Thoroughbreds* (1986), and *Custer's 7th Cavalry and the Campaign of '73* (1986). Frost was mayor of Monroe from 1960-64, and held many professional and public service positions. He was honored for his achievements in his profession and for outstanding historical work. He once wrote, "I have always been a hero worshipper. George Washington, Thomas Jefferson, Abe Lincoln, Thomas Edison, Babe Ruth and Jack Dempsey are a few of our country's heroes that have made me proud I am an American. Here in Monroe I discovered a hero—as American as apple pie— who was being denigrated and besmirched by crepe hangers and followers of our national guilt corps. Americans usually support the side of the underdog. I choose to follow the same path." He was married and fathered a daughter.

Contemporary Authors; Upton and Sons, Pub./Booksellers, *Catalogue 37,* El Segundo, Ca., 1990.

Frye, Jonathan, frontiersman (c. 1704-c. May 11, 1725). From Andover, Massachusetts, he graduated from Harvard College in 1723 with the intent to become a minister, studying theology for that purpose. In April 1725 he enlisted as chaplain with John Lovewell's Indian hunting expedition (see Lovewell entry for narrative) and, "chaplain though he was, he carried a gun, knife, and hatchet [tomahawk] like the others, and not one of the party was more prompt to use them." Of the 46 men who signed on, two returned to Dunstable, New Hampshire (today's Nashua) because of illness, reducing the number to 44. When the west shore of Lake Ossipee was reached, Benjamin Kidder fell ill; his comrades built a small fort, or palisaded log cabin and left him in charge of the surgeon and eight men, leaving the hunting party at 34, Frye among them. In the battle which began at 10 a.m. on May 8 near Lovewell's Pond, southeast of Fryeburg, Maine, Frye received a mortal wound about mid-afternoon and "unable to fight longer, he lay in his blood, praying from time to time for his comrades in a faint but audible voice." The Indians broke off the engagement with darkness and the whites, those who survived, also left the scene on the back trail, but after a mile or two Frye and three other wounded men could go no farther and, "with their consent, the others left them, with a promise to send them help as soon as they should reach the [Ossipee] fort." However, they found the fort vacated and there was no help to be sent the wounded. Frye and the others at length "found strength to struggle forward again, till the chaplain stopped and lay down, begging the others to keep on their way [and saying] tell my father that I expect in a few hours to be in eternity, and am not afraid to die," which he did three days after the engagement. A contemporary narrative said, "he has not been heard of since." He had kept a journal of the expedition, which was lost with him. Fryeburg, Maine, was not named for him, but for another.

Parkman, *Half Century of Conflict,* I; Samuel Penhallow, *History of the Indian Wars,* 1726 (Williamstown, Mass., Corner House Pub., 1973).

Furnas, Robert Wilkinson, military officer, governor (May 5, 1824-June 1, 1905). B. near Troy, Ohio, he was left an orphan at 8, learned printing and in 1856 settled at Brownville, Nebraska, where he founded the *Nebraska Advertiser,* which came to "exercise great influence in the South Platte region." He served in the territorial legislature from 1856-59. With the Civil War, Furnas was commissioned in the militia, organized three regiments of Indians in Indian Territory and saw active service with them. He was instrumental in raising the 2nd Nebraska Cavalry. He commanded this regiment with Alfred Sully's 1863 operation against the Sioux, a reverberation of the Great Sioux Uprising of 1862 in Minnesota following which many Sioux had been driven into Dakota. Furnas's journal of the operations from June 16 to September 12, 1863, has been published. A principal action of the campaign was the battle of Whitestone Hill, about 20 miles northwest of the present Ellendale, North Dakota, the affair occurring September 3. "After going into camp," wrote Furnas, "news came that a camp of 600 [Indian] lodges had been discovered 8 miles distant. The Genl immediately ordered out all the forces. The 2d Neb being the first ready was given the right and we put out at a gallop. After marching about 4 miles the Genl ordered the 2d Neb forward. We then went at full speed. When we discovered the camp they were all in full retreat about 1500 in all. I flanked them on the right formed a line of Battle and made an attack completely routing and killing large numbers of Indians and horses. We commenced about dark and fought as long as we could see. We lost 2 men and 7 wounded and several horses. We held the ground until morning, in line." Another report said that the two regiments making up the entire command lost 19 killed and 32 wounded, one mortally, but a fuller account said there were 30 men killed and 38 wounded. In 1864 Lincoln appointed Furnas agent for the Omaha Indians, later combining some Winnebago with his Omahas; he remained agent until relieved by President Johnson for political reasons in 1866. Furnas returned to Brownville and pursued farming and nursery interests, became president of the State Board of Agriculture and secretary of the State Horticultural Society. He was elected Nebraska governor in 1872, did not seek re-election in 1874, but turned his attention back to horticultural interests. Always a promoter of tree planting, he is said by some to have originated the idea for national Arbor Day to further that cause (although others credit his friend, J. Sterling Morton with originating the observance). Furnas was a leader in organizing the Nebraska State Historical Society. He was married twice. By his first wife, who predeceased him, he fathered eight children. He died at Lincoln, Nebraska.

REAW; DAB; Richard D. Rowen, ed., "The Second Nebraska's Campaign Against the Sioux," *Nebraska History,* Vol. 44, No. 1 (Mar. 1863), 3-25; info. from E.F. (Ted) Mains.

Furuhjelm, Johan Hampus, naval officer, administrator (Mar. 11, 1821-Sept. 21, 1909). Born at Helsingfors (Helsinki), Finland, he entered the Russian navigation school March 24, 1836, and July 7, 1839, became a midshipman in the navy, having come to the attention of Etolin (see entry), another Finlander destined to become important in Alaskan affairs. On Etolin's recommendation Furuhjelm was promoted to lieutenant and placed in the St. Petersburg headquarters of the Russian American Company. June 30, 1850, he was assigned to Sitka, arriving there April 23, 1851. He reported in letters home caustically on the company personnel, the churchmen and others at Sitka. January 21, 1853, he commanded the *Kadiak* on a trading voyage to California and Hawaii, then was sent with the *Prince Menshikov* to join a Russian squadron visiting Japan following U.S. Commodore Matthew Perry's opening of that country to the west. During this voyage Furuhjelm was promoted to Captain-Lieutenant; by December 1854 he was Captain, First Rank and became Chief of Ports for Anian and Okhotsk, Siberia. In 1858 he returned to Russia and December 1 became chief manager of the Russian American Company, reaching Sitka again on June 22, 1859. Development of the Alaskan possessions continued steadily under his administration, shipping suffered losses though with some gains, and steamers continued to replace sailing vessels. In 1861 came news of a gold strike on the upper Stikine River in British territory, but Furuhjelm feared that a rush might spill over into the Russian American Company territory, although mining specialists he sent to investigate the discovery reported it of low yield and of little concern. During his administration Furuhjelm smoothed relations between Russians and the Tlingit Indians. He received chiefs in his residence, went among the Indians accompanied only by an interpreter, did not interfere with tribal feuds except to mediate when possible and once saved two elderly women from torture and death after they were accused of witchcraft. During his term as governor his Finnish wife bore three children who, educated in Europe, rose to prominence. The Furuhjelms were close friends of Prince Maksutov (see entry), assistant manager of the American colony, who reached Sitka in 1859. Maksutov, on a return to Russia was appointed acting governor and arrived back at Sitka May 26, 1864. The Furuhjelms left June 1 for home. One year later he was named military governor of the Maritime Province in eastern Siberia, remaining there until 1870; in 1874 he became a Vice Admiral. He died at 88 at the family estate at Homola, Finland.

Richard A Pierce, *Builders of Alaska: The Russian Governors 1818-1867,* Kingston, Ont., Limestone Press, 1986.

G

Gage, Charles, Jesuit missionary (fl. c. 1684-1689. Charles Gage was one of three English Jesuits brought to America by Governor Thomas Dongan of New York with a view to influencing the Iroquois away from French Jesuits. The other two were Thomas Harvey and Henry Harrison (see entries). The program called for them to establish a village of Catholic Indians under English sway, act as chaplains for the governor and maintain a Latin school which was to become a Jesuit college in New York City. However a revolution in England cancelled out these plans and when Jacob Leisler in December 1689 usurped the government of New York the Jesuits were driven from the colony.

Thwaites, JR LXIV, 280-81n33.

Gage, Thomas, military officer (c. 1719-Apr. 2, 1787). B. in Sussex, England, he entered military service early, was a captain by 1743 and held various posts, becoming a lieutenant colonel by purchase in 1750 and went to America in 1755 with Braddock (see entry). His role in Braddock's disaster near the forks of the Ohio on July 9, 1755, is controversial. It has been charged that as commander of the advance party, he should have stopped its rout which precipitated the disorganization of the main force, although he personally displayed marked bravery in the battle. Gage was convinced that Braddock would not have been defeated had he possessed regulars trained for forest war and in 1757 he suggested raising a light regiment to be trained in both regular and irregular tactics and with himself as colonel—it was the 80th Regiment which in 1758 served in the attack on Ticonderoga where Gage was slightly wounded. The regiment had been raised in New Jersey where Gage also found a wife by the time he became a Brigadier General; he and his wife over time became parents of six sons and five daughters. In July 1759 Amherst ordered him to capture the French post of La Galette (near Ogdensburg, New York) to support Wolfe's siege of Quebec, and to advance toward Montreal, but he temporized, imagined mountainous difficulties and did little, enraging Amherst. Yet the commander respected Gage's administrative skills and in September 1760 made him military governor of Montreal. There he was "regarded as honest, fair and conscientious." In October 1763 he left Montreal and "this cursed climate" for New York where following Amherst's departure he became acting commander-in-chief, remaining such until 1775 when he was recalled; from May 1774 he also served as governor of Massachusetts. Pushed to react more strongly to Massachusetts unrest, he ordered the seizure of "rebel" stores at Concord on April 19, 1775, and this opened the hostilities that evolved into the Revolutionary War. Gage has been held responsible for the British use of Indians against the white settlers. Some Stockbridge (Christian) Indians were identified among American forces besieging Boston and this gave him an excuse to push his idea, reporting "we need not be tender of calling the Savages, as the Rebels have shewn us the Example," neglecting to mention that these Indians were as civilized and opposed to barbarities as the whites they fought with and against. Because of his lack of military talents and usefulness for the rising crisis, Gage was recalled in August 1775 and did not return to America. He became a full General in 1782. He died at London.

Literature abundant in most reference works; DCB, IV; Howard H. Peckham, *Pontiac and the Indian Uprising,* Univ. of Chicago Press, 1947, 1961.

Gagemeister, Leontii Andreanovich: *see,* Hagemeister, Ludwig von

Garfias, Henry, lawman (1851-May 9, 1896). B. in California of Spanish descent, he became a constable at Phoenix at 23 in 1874, the Arizona town then having a population of around 1,500. He shortly killed one man and wounded another in a saloon shootout. Garfias tracked three stagecoach holdup men to Wickenburg, northwest of Phoenix, killed one, wounded another and brought him and the third bandit back to Phoenix. In May 1879 he trailed a Mexican who had wounded several Phoenicians into Mexico, captured him by ruse, jailed him at Phoenix, and killed him in an attempted jail break. Late in August vigilantes cleaned out the jail, hanged two men while another jailed inmate, named

Oviedo, escaped their net. In a subsequent shootout Oviedo missed Garfias with a shotgun blast and was himself killed. In the spring of 1881 Garfias, now the town marshal, had a shootout with four Texas cowboys hurrahing the place. Garfias was wounded, one cowboy killed outright, another wounded mortally, a third slightly wounded and the fourth captured. Legend has it that William O. (Buckey) O'Neill was deputized and took part in this scrap, but in fact Garfias refused to deputize O'Neill, then a newspaper reporter, as more hindrance than help, and took care of the situation himself. That year Garfias became deputy under Sheriff Lindley H. Orme and was retained as such by Orme's successors. In the late winter of 1882 Garfias solved a stagecoach repeat-robber, captured him and although the bandit, blacksmith Henry Seymour of Gillette north of Phoenix, was convicted in district court in April and sentenced to 10 years imprisonment, the $67,000 loot he had taken was never found, or reported if it was. The Francisco and Ynocente Valenzuela gang, noted outlaws from Yavapai County north of Phoenix's Maricopa County, in 1886 depredated within Garfias's county, killing Barney Martin, his wife and their two children. The family was moving to Phoenix and Barney was carrying $2,700, his total wealth, with him. A $1,000 reward was offered by Governor Conrad M. Zulick, but since even this did not lead to capture of the outlaws Garfias was assigned to the case by Noah M. Broadway, sheriff, and retained on it by his successor, Andrew J. Halbert. Garfias located the Valenzuelas at Stanton, a stage stop on the Prescott to Phoenix stage road. Garfias surmised that Charles B. Stanton for whom the place was named was the brains of the gang, and also learned that the Valenzuelas were wanted in San Luis Obispo County, California, where Ynocente Valenzuela had killed a sheriff and wounded a jailer in an escape earlier in his career. Garfias learned that Stanton had planned the Martin murders and received most of the $2,700 loot. A sheriff's posse struck the village at night, captured only Stanton, but he was released for lack of evidence. Garfias took this result hard, but bided his time. In March 1888 Cyrus Gribble, superintendent of the famous Vulture Mine south of Wickenburg, started for Phoenix in a buckboard with a $7,000 gold bar; he was guarded by John Johnson and Charley Doolittle, both heavily armed. That afternoon the three bodies were found in a wash beside the road. Garfias and two deputies located the scene of the ambush, and

signs that the three killers had headed south, probably for Mexico, with their booty. A posse next morning joined the Garfias party, as did two deputy U.S. marshals, Billy Breakenridge (see entry) and Will Smith. However they lost the bandit trail; one of the fugitives later was arrested at Phoenix and turned informer, saying he had been forced to accompany the two Valenzuelas. A posse with Garfias at last caught up with Ynocente and in a shootout, killed him, finding Gribble's watch in the victim's vest pocket. The gold bar was recovered. Garfias now learned that Francisco had reached Mexico, and came up with him at Altar on the Rio de la Concepción. Valenzuela was killed in a shootout. Garfias reported to the Phoenix sheriff what had taken place, but because of the risk of a Mexican protest or even a murder charge against Garfias for the shooting, details were not released. Garfias continued as a law officer until 1895 when illness and old wounds caused him to retire. On May 2, 1896, a horse fell with him and the lawman was badly injured. He lingered for a week before succumbing. In its obituary, the *Phoenix Herald* said, "He had many narrow escapes from violent death and had the reputation of never going after a man that he did not return with him dead or alive."

Maurice Kildare, "Fastest Gun in Phoenix," *Frontier Times,* Vol. 42, No. 1 (Dec.-Jan. 1968), 16-19, 57-59; info. from E.F. (Ted) Mains.

Garretson, Fannie, music hall actress (fl. 1876-1878). Fannie Garretson, who reportedly was generous with her favors, was in Deadwood, South Dakota, in 1876 performing with her partner, "Handsome Banjo Dick" Brown. In the midst of the act "a dim figure staggered to the footlights, muttered incoherently, and hurled an axe upon the stage." Brown drew a pistol and shot the attacker dead, he proving to be Ed Shaunessey of Laramie, Wyoming, who, it developed, was Miss Garretson's discarded lover. He had come to Deadwood hoping to regain her affections. Miss Garretson or "as she then styled herself, Mrs. Brown," wrote the newspapers to stifle a "malicious rumor" that she had once been Shaunessey's wife. She conceded that she had lived with Shaunessey for three years, but they never married so, she wrote, there was nothing "immoral" about running away with Brown. In October 1878, by then having discarded Brown, she was living at Dodge City, Kansas, with Dora Hand (see entry), the two apparently performing in variety shows. Dora Hand was shot and killed accidentally by an assassin who hoped to slay a male companion of Miss Garretson's (some believing this to be Mayor James H. [Dog] Kelley) who was absent the night of the shooting. Fannie Garretson described the incident in detail in a lengthy letter published in the St. Louis *Daily Journal* October 11, 1878, the missive addressed to J.E. Esher, producer of the variety shows in which she appeared. Fannie concluded her letter: "Well, I want to leave here now...I think I have had enough of Dodge City." No further word of her has been located.

Watson Parker, *Gold in the Black Hills,* Norman, Univ. of Okla. Press, 1966; Nyle H. Miller, Joseph W. Snell, *Why the West Was Wild,* Topeka, Kansas State Hist. Soc., 1963, pp. 361, 363, photo, 239.

Gass, David, pioneer (c. 1729-1806). B. in Pennsylvania he early moved to Albemarle County, Virginia, and about 1769 went on to Castlewood on the Clinch River in extreme southwestern Virginia. In 1773 he prepared to move his family to Kentucky with Daniel Boone's party, but Indian hostility deterred him and he resettled along the Clinch. Boone's people lived as neighbors to the Gass family there for several years. In 1774 during the Lord Dunmore War turbulence Gass was employed as a scout. He went to Kentucky with Boone in 1775, and eventually settled in Madison County, where he died.

Thwaites, *Dunmore.*

Gass, Octavius Decatur, pioneer (Feb. 29, 1828-Dec. 10, 1924). B. on a farm near Mansfield, Richland County, Ohio, he studied civil engineering and Spanish at Oberlin (Ohio) College, and in 1849 shipped around Cape Horn for California. Gass prospected in El Dorado County, accumulated some funds and moved south to Los Angeles where thanks to his facility in Spanish, he became water steward, an important post overseeing water canals and ditches and assuring fair distribution. Gass continued his interest in prospecting and for a time was involved in tin mines south of Corona. That enterprise not sufficiently profitable, he decided to try gold mining anew in El Dorado Canyon, south of today's Hoover Dam in present Nevada. By the end of 1864 he had filed 18 claims, though none profited him very much, and he moved north to a site near present Las Vegas. Gass explored up the Colorado River, further upstream than any white man was known to have gone, carved his name on the stone cliffs bordering the river and returned downstream. On the trip he located a salt deposit which he worked with some success.

Late in 1865 he established himself on a ranch near Las Vegas, the place founded 20 years earlier by Mormons who later abandoned it. Gass expanded his holdings, engaged profitably in farming and stock raising, and invested in the development of Callville, "Nevada's first seaport on the Colorado River" or at least the head of navigation. Callville turned out to be no seaport. Gass learned a bit of Paiute and was well-liked by those Indians. He also entered politics. The region at that time was part of Mohave County of Arizona and Gass served several terms, until 1869, in the Territorial Legislature. In 1872 he married Mary Virginia Simpson of a wealthy Missouri family, they becoming parents of six children. Indian unrest between Mohaves and Paiutes generated nervousness among whites, but it subsided without serious incidents. Hard times eventually befell the Las Vegas ranch; Gass fell heavily into debt and finally sold out in June 1881, moving to Pomona, California, and later to a site between San Bernardino and Colton. He became acquainted with Tom Cover (see entry), a wealthy landowner who had been co-discoverer of the great Alder Creek gold placer of Montana and now was settled at Riverside; Cover also had become entranced by the Pegleg Smith gold lode myth of the southern deserts. He, too, had been raised in Richland County, they were nearly of an age, and they joined in horticultural experiments, though without notable success. Gass had joined Cover in prospecting trips into eastern Riverside County and when Cover disappeared on a subsequent expedition, Gass joined the most important search party which succeeded in working out Cover's last trail, but he never was found and the nature of his fate became a complex—and not improbable—legend. Shortly after 1900 Gass moved to the Redlands area where he died after a fall at the age of 96. A street was named for him near Las Vegas, and 6,943-ft. Gass Peak, 14 miles north of that city also commemorates him, but "he deserves better. Politician, landowner, miner, farmer, entrepreneur, dreamer and indefatigable frontier booster, Gass made an indelible mark on the American Southwest."

Ralph J. Roske, Michael S. Green, "Octavius Decatur Gass, Pah-Ute County Pioneer," *Journal of Arizona History,* Vol. 29, No. 4 (Winter 1988), 371-90; Dan L. Thrapp, *Vengeance: The Saga of Poor Tom Cover,* El Segundo, Ca., Upton & Sons, 1989.

Gatewood, Charles Bhaer, military officer (Jan. 4, 1883-Nov. 13, 1953). The son of Charles

Bare (Baehr) Gatewood, notable hero of the Apache wars, there is confusion about the spelling of the middle name: His father's middle name is spelled Bare and Baehr, and the son's name is spelled as presented above on his Arlington Cemetery tombstone. The younger Gatewood was b. in Arizona and appointed at large to West Point from which he was graduated and commissioned a second lieutenant in the Artillery Corps June 12, 1906. He served at Fort Totten, New York, with the 54th (torpedo company) Coast Artillery until June 28, 1907, and as an instructor in the School for Submarine Defense until July 1, 1908; he had become a first lieutenant January 25, 1907. Gatewood was detailed to the Ordnance Department July 12, 1908, and became a captain July 2, 1909, remaining with Ordnance through World War I from which he emerged as a temporary colonel, reverting to captain August 31, 1919, and becoming a major, Coast Artillery July 1, 1920. He was retired December 15, 1922, for disability "incident to the service," and was promoted to colonel, retired, June 21, 1930, later stating that his "activities since retirement [have been] few; has included building construction engineering, historical research work in Arizona military records, and writing, all limited by poor health." His historical work was impressive. He painstakingly assembled a monumental collection of data and literature on the career of his famous father, including all orders and official papers he could track down, much peripheral material, an imposing photograph collection and almost a minute-by-minute data record on the career of the intrepid officer who did more than any other individual to bring the Geronimo activities to a close, as well as being, from 1878 to 1887, constantly in the field against Apaches, completing more of such service than any other officer in the army of his era. The material is held by the Arizona Historical Society at Tucson as the Gatewood Collection. He was buried at Arlington National Cemetery as was his wife, Lillian (April 14, 1897-December 17, 1977), his father and his mother, Georgia (October 6, 1854-November 13, 1946).

Cullum; Gatewood Collection; info. from Susan and Richard C. Platte.

Gatschet, Albert Samuel, ethnologist (Oct. 3, 1832-Mar. 16, 1907). B. at St. Beatenberg, Switzerland, he studied at the Universities of Bern and Berlin and became deeply interested in linguistics, emigrating to America in 1868. Intrigued by Indian languages, his writings on related subjects came to the attention of John Wesley Powell (see entry) who appointed Gatschet ethnologist of the still unformed U.S. Geological Survey and with the organization of the Bureau of American Ethnology in 1879 he joined that agency. Gatschet, one of the few highly-trained linguists in the country at the time, was largely responsible for much of the material in John Wesley Powell's enduring *Indian Linguistic Families of America North of Mexico* (1891, 1966), and Powell, in the conclusion of this work does pay tribute to Gatschet "for the preparation of many comparative lists necessary to my work," which seems modest enough. Gatschet's major technical publications numbered 72, and adding to his "many smaller articles published in the United States and abroad, and hundreds of linguistic, ethnographic and bibliographic notes and reviews...show that his life was a busy one." Among his publications was the two-volume *The Klamath Indians of Southwestern Oregon* (1890); another was *A Migration Legend of the Creek Indians* (1884, 1969). His colleague, James Mooney (see entry) concluded an obituary of Gatschet in the *American Anthropologist* for July 1907: "When philology shall take its proper place as the essential basis of anthropology, his name will stand...in the front rank of American science." Gatschet married late in life, and there were no children.

DAB; J.W. Powell, *Indian Linguistic Families of America North of Mexico,* Lincoln, Univ. of Nebraska Press, 1966; CE.

Gauss, Gottlieb (Godfrey, Gottfried G.), character (c. 1825-Mar. 1902). B. in Baden, Wurttemberg, his first name is often given as Godfrey and Nolan believed it was Gottfried, but Mullin found an affidavit filed by Gauss "and it is apparent that his first name was...Gottlieb," although his account of the Billy the Kid escape and some of his letters are signed simply G. Gauss. Gauss came to write excellent English and was regarded, apparently by both sides in the Lincoln County, New Mexico, "War" as little more than a fatherly, gentle old man. He emigrated at an early age to America and joined Company I, 3rd U. S. Infantry February 3, 1851, deserted in August but was apprehended and served out a five-year enlistment, being discharged at Fort Craig, New Mexico. He re-enlisted March 1, 1856, again in the 3rd Infantry and was discharged, still a private, March 1, 1861, at Fort Defiance, New Mexico. Gauss enlisted once more, this time in the 3rd New Mexico Mounted Infantry and served as a hospital steward until New Mexico Civil War hostilities ceased in 1862 when he was released at Albuquerque allegedly with failing eyesight, which may or may not have been a temporary condition. He worked for Murphy interests in Lincoln County for 18 months, by his own account being roundly cheated at every turn by Dolan and others. At length Gauss became a ranch cook for Tunstall, and a minor figure in the Lincoln County War except in one important instance: his presence at a high point of that conflict had his assistance to Billy the Kid in that key figure's escape after slaying his two guards April 27, 1881 at Lincoln. Gauss's account of that incident was drafted a decade afterward, but it is invaluable as an extended eye-witness version of the affair. Gauss wrote that Bell, one of the guards, had fallen dead in his arms, and that he and Bob Olinger, the other victim, were standing "not over a yard apart" when Olinger, too, was shot down. Gauss tossed a small prospector's pick to Billy to assist him in freeing himself of his leg shackles, then saddled "a small skittish pony belonging to Billy Burt," the county clerk, and eventually, so mounted, the Kid "went on his way rejoicing." Nolan wrote that, "although considerably short of definitive [the Gauss account] seems to be the only one that exists." Gauss never married, worked at odd jobs around Lincoln County into the 1890s, drifted east and died, perhaps in Kansas.

Robert N. Mullin notes; Mullin to author, July 25, 1977; Frederick Nolan, *The Lincoln County War: A Documentary History*, Norman, Univ. of Okla. Press, 1992; Robert M. Utley, *Billy the Kid: A Short and Violent Life*, Lincoln, Univ. of Neb. Press, 1989.

Gedeon (Gideon), Orthodox churchman (1770-1843). B. in Russia, he studied at Sevskaia Seminary and from 1790 at Belogradskaia Seminary, in 1799 becoming a monk at the Aleksandr-Nevskaia monastery at St. Petersburg. Intellectually-inclined, he taught a variety of courses and in 1803 became a hieromonk and was selected by the Metropolitan Amvrosii to travel to Kamchatka and Alaska as "the Metropolitan's eye." He sailed from Kronstadt July 16 on the *Neva*, commanded by Yuriy Lisianskii (see entry) who had little patience with religion or its advocates and gave the monk a hard time on the lengthy voyage to Sitka, Alaska. The *Neva* reached Kodiak Island July 2, 1804, where Gedeon found that he was to be thereafter opposed in his work by Ivan Banner (see entry), the assistant manager in charge. Baranov treated him no better, not being particulary anti-religion, but having no patience with those obstructing his sometimes oppressive policies. July 26 Gedeon and an interpreter set out in baidarkas to circumnavigate Kodiak and neighboring islands baptizing 503 individuals and performing marriages for 32 couples. He returned to Pavlovskaia Harbor August 24. He spent his spare time translating French theological works into Russian, started schools, instructed the natives in agricultural practices, and worked at linguistics interests. He organized a collection of vocabularies for a dictionary of native languages, and commenced the first attempt to provide a written grammar of the Aleutian language, assisted by a team of native students. Gedeon, continuing to have trouble with Russian American Company personnel, probably because he opposed some of their heavy-handed policies toward the natives, also managed to find difficulty with recalcitrant churchmen working in Alaska. At long last Captain Henry Barber (see entry), reached Kodiak with his brig *Sitkha* and on May 15, 1807, Gedeon informed Baranov he was leaving for Okhotsk on that vessel. It cleared Kodiak June 11, reaching Unalaska after a storm-lashed passage June 29, departed July 7 and after a further difficult passage reached Petropavlovsk, Kamchatka, September 21. Gedeon fulfilled his directive to examine the work of the church in Kamchatka, visiting by dogsled congregations in remote places, and arrived at Okhotsk July 19. He crossed Siberia and after six years absence returned to St. Petersburg in 1809. His tour had pleased the Metropolitan. Gedeon was appointed to high offices and died at the Andrusov retreat of St. Nicholas in Olonetsk diocese. In his extensive journal the monk described "competently and in detail the customs of the inhabitants of Kadiak, of great value to ethnography." Part of the journal was published in 1894 and "materials discovered since provide additional information on the voyage and his stay in the colonies."

Pierce, *Russian America: A Biographical Dictionary.*

Gelelemend: *see,* John Killbuck Jr.

Genung, Charles Baldwin, pioneer (July 22, 1839-Aug. 18, 1916). B. at Penn Yan, Yates

County, New York, when he was 11 his mother took him by way of Cape Horn to San Francisco, visiting Marysville and settling at Downieville, Sierra County. There she established a daguerrotype studio; before long Charlie worked for the *Sierra Citizen* at Downieville. His mother moved her studio to San Francisco, then took her son to Hong Kong for a year before returning to California where Charlie did some mining and was a cowboy in the Sacramento Valley. In 1863 to cure persistent health problems he went to Arizona where Charlie became a prominent pioneer on a perilous frontier, eventually settling near Prescott. He lived first at Weaver, some 15 miles north of Wickenburg and voted there in the first territorial election, July 18, 1864. Genung had helped Henry Wickenburg build and operate the first arrastra (an ore-grinding device) to extract gold at the famed Vulture Mine. Indian-white hostilities were on the rise and Genung aided Jack Swilling and King Woolsey (see entries) on several forays against Indians, although with little success. July 24, 1867, George W. Dent, brother-in-law of General Grant and superintendent of Indian affairs, made Genung agent at the Colorado River Indian Reservation. Although he became friendly with some Yavapai and Apache Mohaves, he did not remain long. His most notable Indian campaign was the lengthy Jack Townsend scout in the summer of 1871, Genung shooting four Indians to Townsend's eight. In July 1871, he commenced building a wagon road from Wickenburg to the Kirkland Valley, northwest of Prescott. To do this he hired Indian labor as well as Anglo and Mexican workers. While constructing this road, George Crook, newly arrived at Fort Whipple, contacted Genung and asked him to have as many Mohave Apaches and Yavapais as he could gather meet him at Date Creek, which was done, Genung informing them of his understanding that Crook wanted to enlist them to fight the Tonto Apaches, to the east. At the Date Creek meeting, however, the Indians suspected of perpetrating the Loring (see entry) Massacre were identified and in an ensuing embroglio eight Indians were killed. Crook explained to an irate Genung why he had done what was done, reporting that Iretaba (see entry) had informed him the dead Indians had committed the massacre. Genung "told Crook that it was a lie; that I knew it was Mexicans who had done the killing and robbing of the stage," and that what Genung called white "treachery" now risked Indian retaliation upon his family and oth-

ers whom the Indians would believe betrayed them. Crook, with Genung's help, eventually pacified the Indians who had escaped the slaughter, and the matter passed, but it was a close call. Genung knew most of the prominent Indians, soldiers and pioneers of early central Arizona, including Wauba Yuma (see entry), Pauline Weaver and Weaver's son, Ben. He was a justice of the peace, a postmaster, took out mining claims, was a constable and deputy sheriff, and pursued other pioneer vocations from time to time. He married Ida M. Smith at San Francisco in 1869, and they became parents of nine children. He died at the age of 77 and was buried at Prescott; Ida Genung died November 12, 1933.

Kenneth M. Calhoun, ed., Charles Baldwin Genung's "Yavapai County Memories, 1863-1894," Tucscon Westerners, *The Smoke Signal,* Nos. 43-44 (Spring & Fall, 1982), 33-72; Farish, IV, 27-92 (incorporating some of the material in *Smoke Signal*).

Geoghegan, Richard Henry, linguist (1866-1943). B. in Ireland, Geoghegan was a master of many languages, including Gaelic, Greek and Chinese. He studied at Oxford and went to Alaska as a court reporter for U.S. District Judge James Wickersham. Geoghegan became interested in Alaskan native languages. He is best known for his translations from Russian of Veniaminov's Aleut and Tlingit vocabularies. Richard and his brother, James T. Geoghegan, collected word lists of various Indian tribes. Most of his manuscript material is at the University of Alaska and at the State Historical Library of Juneau.

Orth, 14.

Gerdine, Thomas Golding, engineer (June 2, 1872-1930). B. at West Point, Mississippi, he was graduated with an engineering degree from the University of Georgia in 1891 and joined the Geological Survey as a topographical engineer in 1893. In 1899 Gerdine worked with Frank Charles Schrader (see entry) on a topographical survey of the Chandalar River, a Yukon tributary whose mouth is 20 miles northwest of Fort Yukon, and the Koyukuk River, a major Yukon tributary coming in 16 miles northeast of Nulato. Gerdine was in charge of all topographic surveys of Alaska under Alfred Brooks from 1902 until 1907. In 1908 he became Pacific Region Engineer for the Survey. He is commemorated in Alaska by Mount Gerdine in the Tordrillo Mountains, 55 miles northwest of Tyonek, a port on

Cook Inlet. Following his service as geographer in charge of the Pacific Division topographic survey, he moved to the Northwestern Division from 1912-16 and successively thereafter was in charge of geographic, topographic and mapping work in Texas and New Mexico, 1917; Northwestern and Rocky Mountain divisions, 1917-19; Rocky Mountain Division, 1920-21 and the Pacific Division from 1922.

Orth, 14, 365; *Who Was Who.*

German, monk and saint (c. 1757-c. Nov. 15, 1836). B. of the merchant class at Sepukhov, near Moscow, his family name is not reported, but at 16 he became a monk with "a burning desire to do good works," though without much education; he then took the name of German. He resided in monasteries or retreats and when eventually promised an archimandriteship and assignment to Peking "with typical humility he refused." In 1793 he became one of a famed spiritual mission sent to Russian America, arriving September 24, 1794, at St. Paul's Harbor, Kodiak Island. The mission was successful though often at odds with Baranov and other Russian American Company officials who resented the "reforms" urged upon those natives in RAC employ. In 1798 Ioasaf, one of the original group, enroute to be ordained a bishop, was lost when his ship went down with all hands while making for Okhotsk, Siberia, two others of those perishing being churchmen accompanying the archimandrite. This left only German and three co-workers of the faith in Alaska. German later "retired" to Spruce (Elovoi) Island, just north of Kodiak, where he "lived a life of prayer and contemplation." Baranov wrote that "we have a hermit here now by the name of German [who] is a great talker and likes to write," adding that "he keeps himself in his cell most of the time, not even going to church out of fear of worldly temptations." German gradually acquired a "reputation for sanctity." During an 1819 epidemic, Semyon Yanovskii (see entry), acting RAC manager, noted Father German's indefatigable labors on behalf of the afflicted and the next year petitioned for more funds for the use of the priest. Yanovskii, who confessed he had been a "free thinker" with not much concern for religion, found himself greatly moved and spiritually renewed through his acquaintance with the devout priest. German died in his 81st year and "with him ended the spiritual mission which in 1794 had established Orthodoxy in Alaska," for

he was the last to go of the original group. Although the date cited for his death is that which the then governor gave in a dispatch to the main office, Alaska Church Records list the date as December 13, 1836. Following his demise stories burgeoned about the sanctity of his life and "occurrences after his death." On August 9, 1970, German was canonized as the first saint of the Orthodox Church in America. A modern chapel now occupies the site where he lived on Spruce Island.

Pierce, *Russian America: A Biographical Dictionary.*

Gibson, Arrell Morgan, historian (Dec. 1, 1921-Nov. 30, 1987). B. at Pleasanton, Kansas, he was graduated from the University of Oklahoma in 1947 and earned his doctorate there in 1954. He had studied under Edward Everett Dale (see entry) and was Dale's final doctoral student. Gibson was professor of history at Phillips University, Enid, Oklahoma, from 1949-57, and professor of history at the University of Oklahoma thereafter until his death. He guided 35 doctoral candidates and 68 seeking master's degrees. He was chairman of the history department, curator of the Western History Collections and curator of history for the Stovall Museum which is now the Oklahoma Museum of Natural History. Gibson wrote or edited about 25 books as a historian of the Indian and the West. Among them were: *The Kickapoos: Lords of the Middle Border* (1963); *Life and Death of Colonel Albert Jennings Fountain* (1965); *Oklahoma: A History of Five Centuries* (1965); *Fort Smith: Little Gibraltar on the Arkansas* (1969); *The Chickasaws* (1971), and *Wilderness Bonanza: The Tri-State District of Missouri, Kansas, and Oklahoma* (1972). Gibson was vice-president of the Western History Association at the time of his death, and had served it in many other capacities. He was married and fathered three children. He was buried at Joplin, Missouri.

Council on America's Military Past *Heliogram* 190 (Jan.-Feb. 1988), 7; WHA *Newsletter* (Winter, 1988); *Who's Who in America.*

Gibson, George, military officer (Oct. 1747-Dec. 14, 1791). B. at Lancaster, Pennsylvania, he was a brother of John Gibson (see entry). He was well educated, entered a mercantile house at Philadelphia and made several voyages to the West Indies as supercargo, at length coming to speak French, Spanish, German and Delaware to some extent. He early became interested in western lands, went to Fort Pitt and in 1768 received a large tract on the Cumberland River of Kentucky-Tennessee. In 1774 he participated as a second lieutenant in Captain George Matthew's company in Lord Dunmore's War against the Shawnees. At the outbreak of the Revolutionary War he raised a company around Fort Pitt where his men were known as the "Gibson Lambs," perhaps because of their combative nature toward other colonials, for they rarely saw action against the British. In 1776 he was agent to purchase gunpowder from the Spanish at New Orleans for use by colonial troops. He left Fort Pitt July 19 with some 25 men disguised as traders, reaching New Orleans in August, purchased 10,000 pounds of powder, with the cooperation of Bernardo de Galvez (see entry), soon to become governor. Galvez obligingly placed Gibson under arrest to quiet suspicions of any British agents about, then assisted his escape with the powder, Gibson returning it to Pittsburgh in 1777. This feat brought him promotion, and he joined Washington as colonel, serving in the Jersey and New York campaigns. From 1783 onward he resided at his farm, becoming county lieutenant of Cumberland County. In that capacity and as a lieutenant colonel he joined Arthur St. Clair (see entry) for the campaign against the Ohio Indians. The doomed column was soundly whipped by British-backed Indians in the worst disaster United States arms ever suffered at the hands of Native Americans. The column on November 3, 1791, on the upper Wabash River in western Ohio met the enemy and suffered 918 casualties, including 647 dead, among them 35 officers. Gibson was twice wounded and after the battle was carried by litter to Fort Jefferson, 30 miles distant, where five weeks later he succumbed.

Thwaites/Kellogg, *The Revolution on the Upper Ohio, 1775-1777,* Madison, Wis. Hist. Soc., 1908; DAB.

Gilbert, John Jacob, surveyor (fl. 1900-1901). Commanding the Coast and Geodetic Survey steamer *Pathfinder,* he surveyed the shore of Norton Sound in western Alaska in 1900, covering the coastline from St. Michael to Golovnin Bay. In 1901 he surveyed the Fox Islands of the Aleutians and the passes between Unalaska and Unimak islands. Gilbert's reports were published by the C&GS in 1901 and 1902.

Orth, 14, 366.

Gillespie, Archibald H., Marine Corps officer (c. 1813-Aug. 14, 1873). B. in Pennsylvania, he joined the Navy's Marine Corps and as a lieutenant was sent on an important confidential mission to California in October 1845. He bore a duplicate of the secret instructions sent to Thomas Larkin (see entry), the U.S. agent to California, based at Monterey. He, and Fremont as well, were to cooperate with Larkin in carrying out the instructions. Before he crossed Mexico he had committed the contents of his official dispatch to memory and swallowed the original. At Mazatlan on the west coast he boarded the U.S. sloop of war *Cyane* for California by way of Honolulu, arriving at Monterey in April 1846, when he rewrote his memorized instructions, with copies for Larkin and Fremont. He delivered one set to Larkin, and left for the Oregon frontier to overtake Fremont. The explorer asserted he received a very different dispatch from that given to Larkin, and Bancroft conceded that there was "a bare possibility that Gillespie deceived him," although with no assurance he had done so. Fremont reported that the information he received through Gillespie had "absolved me from my duty as an explorer, and I was left to my duty as an officer of the American Army, with the further authoritative knowledge that the Government intended to take California." Bancroft wrote that "In the various events of May to July, Gillespie took an active part, being made adjutant of the California Battalion at its first organization." The marine went south in July and was left at Los Angeles in command of the garrison, but although a brave man, Gillespie was not a conciliatory administrator. According to Larkin all would have been well at Los Angeles and in California generally if "proper and prudent" persons had been in charge, but Gillespie, he indicated, was not such. Larkin wrote, "It appears even from the Americans [at Los Angeles] that Captain A.H.G. punished, fined and imprisoned who and when he pleased without any hearing," with the eventual result that the Californians by October revolted and drove Gillespie and his command out of Los Angeles. The marine officer, by now a brevet captain, went south to San Diego where he joined Commodore Robert Field Stockton (see entry), also of course a naval officer, who was in command there. He sent Gillespie and 39 men, dragging along a small brass four pounder, to support Kearny who had arrived at Warner's Ranch from Santa Fe with 100 dragoons; they joined in time for at least some of the combined command to take part against the Mexicans in the Battle of San Pasqual which, although minor, was the heaviest engagement of the Mexican War in California. San Pasqual was about ten miles east of the present Escondido. The action on December 6-7, 1846, in a confused and scattered manner commenced "before dawn of a dark and misty day" and involved less than half of Kearny's force and all of Gillespie's against around 70 or fewer Mexican lancers under Andrés Pico; twenty-two of Kearny's force were killed (only two by gunfire), and about 16 were wounded, including Kearny and Gillespie. "A number of Californians who had hated Gillespie in Los Angeles recognized him and set up a wild yell...A horde of them rushed upon the marine...Somehow he successfully parried the first four lance thrusts but as he tried to dodge the next, was struck on the back of his neck. The blow threw him from his horse, and he went down with his saber pinned beneath him. Another lance pierced him over the heart and penetrated his lungs. As he turned to face this latest assailant, another Mexican charged him at full speed, aiming at Gillespie's face. The weapon cut his upper lip, broke a front tooth [but] in some fashion Gillespie managed to rise and, recovering his saber, slashed his way out of the confused throng toward one of the howitzers." He ordered it or another to fire its load of grape and that, Gillespie later reported, "decided the action," although there are those, including the badly wounded Kearny, who believe no cannon had been fired at all; an analysis of the battle shows that this view is probably mistaken, and Gillespie believed two cannon shots had been touched off. Recovered, Gillespie was ranked as a major of Stockton's "army" and was involved in the action at San Gabriel January 8, 1847, when again he was wounded, this time slightly. The Californians were defeated in this action with only minor American casualties. Gillespie declined the offer to become "secretary of state" in Fremont's abortive government, was relieved from duty in California and in May reported to Commodore James Biddle of the Pacific Squadron. He then went east overland with Stockton and testified for Fremont at the explorer's court-martial and also testified on other matters concerning affairs in California. Bancroft added that Gillespie "seems to have returned to California in 1848 and to have spent much of his later life [there], though for some years previous to 1861 he was in Mexico, per-

haps as secretary of the legation. He was never prominent after 1849, having to a certain extent 'lost his grip' in the battle for life." He died at 60 at San Francisco.

Bancroft, *Pioneer Register;* Bancroft, *California,* V; Dwight L. Clarke, *Stephen Watts Kearny: Soldier of the West,* Norman, Univ. of Okla. Press, 1961; John Charles Fremont, *Narratives of Exploration and Adventure,* ed. by Allan Nevins, N.Y., Longmans, Green & Co., 1956, 495-99; info. from Andrew Rolle; info. from the Cal. State Lib.

Gilmore family, pioneers (fl. 1759-1781). On October 10, 1759, the Gilmore family with others on Carr's Creek in the present Rockbridge County, Virginia, were savagely attacked by Cornstalk, the great Shawnee chief (see entry) and "the 'Carr's Creek massacre' was long remembered on the border as one of the most daring and cruel on record." In it the Shawnees killed John Gilmore, his wife and son Thomas, the wife of William Gilmore and captured the wife and three children of Thomas, although these were recovered by close pursuers. The same settlement was raided again in 1763 when "some of the Gilmore connection [once more] suffered." In 1777 Cornstalk was held as a hostage at Fort Randolph at Point Pleasant, West Virginia, lest he "go with the stream," in his own words, joining his fellow tribesmen siding with the British during the Revolutionary operations. Cornstalk was well-liked and respected by officers and men of the garrison, and was congenial with them. His son, Ellinipsico, another chief, Redhawk and a one-eyed Shawnee chief, Petalla, also were held. Two men, Ensign Robert Gilmore and Hamilton, of Captain James (John) Halls' company of Rockbridge militiamen crossed the Great Kanawha River on a hunting excursion. Two Indians had concealed themselves on the banks of the stream and when the whites approached Gilmore was killed and scalped while Hamilton escaped, reporting the affair to Captains Matthew Arbuckle and John Stuart (see entries). Hall was related to Gilmore and on November 10 a party of his men brought in the bloody body and the cry arose,"Let's go kill the Indians at the fort!" This led to the murder by Captain Hall and his men of Cornstalk and his son, and the two other chiefs, none of whom had anything to do with the Gilmore slaying. The atrocity ignited a Shawnee war that endured for twenty years. There is no evidence that the Gilmores mentioned above were all related, but it is probable that they were. Still another of the family was Lieutenant James Gilmore who had served under Captain William McKee in Dunmore's War of 1774. In 1776, when the Revolution broke out, he became a lieutenant in McKee's company in the Continental Army; he resigned before 1781 and raised and commanded a militia company from Rockbridge County for relief of the Southern Army and participated in the famous engagement at Cowpens, South Carolina, February 17, 1781, under Daniel Morgan.

Alexander Scott Withers, *Chronicles of Border Warfare,* Cincinnati, Robert Clarke Co., 1895, 1970; Thwaites/Kellogg, *Frontier Defense on the Upper Ohio, 1777-1778.*

Gipson, Fred(erick) B., writer (Feb. 7, 1908-Aug. 14, 1973). B. at Mason, Texas, he studied journalism for three years at the University of Texas, was a newspaper reporter for two or three more years, published his first book in 1946: *Fabulous Empire: Colonel Zack Miller's Story* about the 101 Ranch figure, and from then on worked as a free-lance writer. He was best known for *Old Yeller* (1956) and *Savage Sam* (1962) for which he did the screenplays as well, and *Hound-Dog Man* (1950) for which he also worked on the movie script. Gipson did the teleplay for his short story, "Brush Roper." He wrote about ten books and contributed to periodicals. He was married (and divorced), and fathered two children.

Contemporary Authors; REAW; info. from E.F. (Ted) Mains.

Girty, Catharine Malott; *see,* Catharine Malott

Glassford, William Alexander, army officer (Apr. 11, 1856-Aug. 31, 1931). B. in Indiana he was a cadet at the Naval Academy from September 27, 1871, to June 13, 1873, but did not graduate. He enlisted in the Signal Corps November 20, 1874, became a sergeant and was commissioned a second lieutenant November 1, 1879. As a Signal Corps inspector he visited stations throughout the nation until January 1, 1881, when he became officer-in-charge of military telegraph lines at Santa Fe, then resumed duties as inspecting officer. He built an observatory and telegraph lines on Pike's Peak, Colorado, and in 1884 became an assistant to the Chief Signal Officer. Under Miles during the 1886 Geronimo campaign Glassford conducted reconnaissances and established sig-

nal and heliograph stations connecting military posts in Arizona and other points likely to become involved in military operations against hostile Indians. The network performed its function well, but it was of little use against enemy raiders. Glassford became a first lieutenant December 19, 1890, a captain November 14, 1893, a lieutenant colonel of volunteers in 1898 and major in the Army Signal Corps February 2, 1901. He retired as a colonel to his home at Phoenix, Arizona, and moved to California shortly before his death at San Francisco.

Heitman; Powell; *Arizona Historical Review,* Vol. IV, No. 3 (Oct. 1931), 81.

Glazunov, Andrei, explorer (fl. 1833-1842). Described as "probably the first Russian to see the Yukon River" of Alaska, Glazunov was a Creole, or of mixed Russian-native American parentage, his mother probably an Aleut since he was fluent in several Innuit (Eskimo) dialects. Bancroft said he had been instructed in the use of astronomical instruments (navigation). He was selected to head a small expedition in 1833-34 to pursue Wrangel's directives for inland exploration of Alaska following Tebenkov's founding of Mikhaielovsk (St. Michael) on Norton Sound. Accompanying him were four volunteers: Vassili Domskoi, who died of injuries during the journey; Vassili Deryabin (see entry), to be killed in a subsequent Indian uprising; Ivan Balachev and Jacob Knagge. Glazunov's original plan was to start up the Pastolik River west of Mikhaielovsk and make a short portage from it to the Yukon of which he had heard, but native hositility made it impossible to secure a guide. He decided therefore to go easterly to Kigikhtowik (Kliktarik) and left with two five-dog sledges on December 30, 1833. Farther east the party crossed several ranges of hills with difficulty, arriving at the Anvik River. After a brief and difficult excursion up that frozen stream they reversed course and followed it down to its mouth on the Yukon, at the present village of Anvik. Glazunov questioned Eskimos he found there about a portage to the Kuskokwim River, which comes within about 30 miles of the Yukon, although Glazunov did not realize that; he was told of a difficult portage between the two waterways rather than an easier two-day alternative route, so gave up for the time reaching the Kuskokwim which had been a principal objective. He went down the Yukon to its delta, "the remarkably accurate .At least one meticulous student of the regional development, has called Glazunov's serious work "one of the great accomplishments in the history of Alaskan exploration. He now determined to push back to the Kuskokwim since he had received from the natives fresh and more feasible directions; he arrived at that river February 19, 1834. Glazunov heard of a Kuskokwim tributary a short portage from which would take one to another stream which fell into Cook Inlet. He could find no guide to take him there because of continuing native hostility enroute, so he tried to find it himself. His party became confused in the mountains because he had lost his compass, and he and his companions were reduced to near starvation, they being forced to eat dog-harness, boots and sealskin provision bags to survive. On March 19 they finally regained the Kuskokwim River, secured food supplies from friendly natives and at last reached the Yukon once more and eventually Mickhaielovsk. In 104 days they had traveled 1,200 miles, explored much country unknown to the whites but had not located a feasible route from Norton Sound to Cook Inlet as had been their primary goal. On another expedition in 1837 Glazunov made the initial contact in their territory with the Koyukon, an Athabascan people, possibly near the present community of Koyukuk. From 1842 he was manager of the fur trading post at Ikogmyut (the present Russian Mission) on the lower Yukon. The Russians never expanded fur gathering operations into the interior of Alaska despite the conscientious work of their explorers. Only excerpts have been published of Glazunov's travel journal; the original is in the State Archive of the Perm (Molotov) Region in the Ural foothills of Russia.

Bancroft, *Alaska,* HNAI, VI; Zagoskin.

Glazunov, Timofey, hunter (fl. 1842-1844). A Creole, half native American, half Russian, he joined Zagoskin at Novo Arkhangelsk (Sitka) and went with him to Fort St. Michael, on Norton Sound, to begin an expedition into the interior of Alaska. Zagoskin considered him "one of the most modest and hard working of my companions," although the outset was unpropitious since Glazunov appeared in poor health, if faithful. At Khogoltlinde, an Eskimo village opposite the present Kaltag on the lower Yukon, Glazunov froze the toes and heels of both feet one January day, and was forced to return to the fort from Nulato despite Zagoskin's reluctance to see him leave. Bazhenov took his place. Nothing more is reported of Glazunov.

Zagoskin.

[The following is a replacement for the entry which appears in Vol. II, p. 565.]
Glenn, Edwin Forbes, military officer (Jan. 10, 1857-Aug. 5, 1926). B. near Greensboro, North Carolina, he went to West Point and was commissioned a second lieutenant of the 25th Infantry June 15, 1877. He became a first lieutenant December 4, 1884, and a captain July 5, 1895. In 1888 he instituted military training and taught mathematics at the University of Minnesota; he earned a law degree from that school in 1890 (and overall received honorary degrees from five other colleges). He was admitted to the Minnesota bar and became judge advocate of the Military Department of Dakota and of the Department of the Columbia from 1896-98. Given command of an Alaskan expedition he left Vancouver Barracks April 6, 1898, with instructions to begin his journey from Cook Inlet and explore northward seeking the most direct and practical route from tidewater to the crossings of the Tanana River, striking the Yukon between Forty-mile Creek and Circle City; enroute he was to discover any possible passes through the Alaska Mountains south of the Tanana. He was to explore as thoroughly as possible the region between the Yukon, Tanana, Copper and Susitna rivers, to report information likely to be of benefit in development of that country: topographical features, travel routes, feasible railroad construction routes, and to note the general resources of the country, including timber supplies, capability of the area for livestock maintenance, to make maps, take photographs and detach small parties to make side explorations, and he was authorized to enlist up to 50 Indians for duty with the expedition. Second in command was to be First Lieutenant Henry G. Learnard (see entry), and the party was to include three commissioned officers and such guides as Luther S. Kelly (see entry). For transport he was to have 50 reindeer with appropriate handlers, but on arrival near Skagway the reindeer were found totally unfit and Allen resorted to pack mules and horses. His expedition reached Portage Bay (near the present Whittier, Alaska) April 23, leaving shortly for Port Wells and on April 29 crossed Prince William Sound to Port Valdez and May 1 to

Orca, near Cordova. Glenn explored waterways near Port Wells, determining that there was no passage to Cook Inlet from them. Glenn with the main part of his expedition then went up Knik Arm and the Matanuska River by way of Moose Creek which he reached July 26. He divided his command—Sergeant Frederick Mathys, E Company, 14th Infantry, was to take a segment by way of Chickaloon Riveer to the Talkeetna River, while Glenn was to continue up the Matanuska toward the Copper River, which he did not reach. He continued northeast and north of today's Glenn Highway, named for him, and which termiantes at the Copper River town of Glennallen, named for Glenn and Lieutenant Henry T. Allen (see entry). August 12 the party sighted Lake Louise, at the head of a tributary of the Susitna River, "by far the most beautiful lake seen on our journey." The next day Glenn struck the trail of First Lieutenant Joseph Castner (see entry), whose expedition was exploring toward the Tanana River. Later he again crossed the trail and August 24 reached Castner's camp, giving the lieutenant two good pack mules that he might make Circle City on the Yukon. Glenn continued north, probably on the route of Richardson Highway of today (State Highway 4), and may have reached Isabel Pass through which he believed he had contacted a tributary of the north-flowing Delta River, which met the Tanana; he thus had accomplished that important part of his mission, and had learned that a railroad or other line of communication was feasible to the Tanana from Cook Inlet. Winter was now at hand and it became a race against the elements whether Glenn was to regain the Inlet before animals and men gave out, but the command successfully reached base camp September 22. "The total distance traveled into and returning [from] the interior was 672 miles, of which 347 miles were made in the advance," reported Glenn. September 28 he took his party to Tyonek and October 10 reached Homer at the base of the Kenai Peninsula. November 10, 1898, the command reached Vancouver Barracks, Washington. By his extended report and field work he had fulfilled his objectives so far as possible. In 1899 Glenn returned to Alaska with a second expedition, Captain Charles P. Elliott (see entry) second in command, the party to be based at Tyonek. His expedition was instructed by several sections to explore the interior by way of the Susitna, Kuskokwim and other streams, and this was done in part. There were no significant discoveries,

however, and Glenn returned to Seattle November 3, 1899. He became major of the 5th Infantry April 22, 1901. He retired in 1919 as a Brigadier General and died at Glendon, North Carolina. He authored *Glenn's International Law* (1895) and *Rules of Land Warfare* (1914).

Narratives of Explorations in Alaska; Heitman; Cullum; *Who Was Who.*

Glottof (Glotov), Stepan, discoverer (fl. 1758-1769). A merchant of Turinsk, in western Siberia, Glottof was first to carry on peaceful trade with natives of Umnak and Unalaska islands and later was discoverer of record of Kodiak Island where the initial Russian permanent base in Alaska was to be established. He commanded the small *Yulian,* built at Nizhne Kamchatsk, leaving September 2, 1758, on an exploratory voyage. Beset by gales the company was forced to winter on Bering Island. In August 1759, Glottof sailed eastward for 30 days, landing probably at Umnak, an island previously unknown to him. The natives were so friendly that the traders remained three years, meanwhile exploring further into the Aleutian chain of islands, to Unalaska and eight large islands northeast of there. An accurate map of the region thus far known was compiled by Glottof's Cossack colleague, Savas Ponomaref. On August 31, 1762, the *Yulian* arrived back at Bolsheretsk on the lower west coast of Kamchatka, its cargo including 1,465 sea otter pelts, 280 sea otter tails, 1,002 black (silver) foxes, the first to be received from Alaska, 22 walrus tusks and a number of other skins, the whole valued at 130,450 rubles ($65,225). October 1, 1762, Glottof left the Kamchatka River in the *Andreian i Natalia* on a four-year voyage that proved "by far the most important of the earlier expeditions to the [Aleutian] islands, and constitutes an epoch in the swarming [there] of the promyshlenniki," or trader-trappers and frontier entrepreneurs. He wintered at Copper Island, near Bering Island and on July 26, 1763, again put to sea, sighting Umnak Island August 24 and later Unalaska, but anchoring at neither. He pushed on past a multitude of other islands, many previously unseen by whites, until September 8 when he hove to off the coast of hitherto unknown Kodiak Island, the native name for which was Kikhtak. While most had never seen a Russian before, the inhabitants knew all about them by reputation, and of their sometimes brutal, merciless ways. A few natives approached the ship in kayaks or baidarkas, but the interpreter, Ivan Glottof, godchild of the commander, was from a more westerly island and could not understand them. Later other natives brought an Aleutian boy who had been captured by the Russians, learned their language, and acted as interpreter and intermediary. The natives, who refused to pay tribute and furnish hostages (which the Russians always demanded at initial contact) were of "fiercer aspect, more intelligent and manly, and of finer physique" than any the whites yet had encountered. The point where Glottof made his landfall was opposite the small island of Aiaktalik, at the southern tip of Kodiak. Repeated skirmishing with the Aleuts included a hard fight October 26 whereafter the natives withdrew from further contact until April, nine Russians dying of scurvy in the interval. The islanders at last consented to trade a bit. Bancroft (144-47) presents an interesting narrative by an Aleut describing this first Kodiak contact with Europeans, from the aborigine viewpoint. Glottof left Kodiak May 24, 1764, and landed on Umnak Island, littered now with bodies of the many Russians slain in a series of massacres their excesses had provoked and which all but wiped out most trading and fur gathering for the time being; among the important whites slain was Dennis Medvedev, commander of the last vessel to arrive at Umnak before Glottof. Veniaminov, the great Russian missionary-ethnologist, on the basis of his researches concluded of the Russian "reign of terror [that] there is no reason for concealing what was done by the first promyshlenniki, or for palliating or glorifying their cruel outrages upon the Aleuts." After weathering many adventures, wintering and collecting still more furs, Glottof sailed from Umnak July 3, 1765, and on August 13 arrived at the Kamchatka River "happily with a rich cargo." He died on Unimak Island in 1769. He was said to have been the first European to set foot on Kodiak Island, and Mount Glottof, at 4,505 feet its tallest mountain, was named for him.

Bancroft, *Alaska;* William Coxe, *Account of the Russian Discoveries,* N.Y., Argonaut Press, 1966 (which includes the ship's log of Glottof's major voyage); Zagoskin; Orth, 372.

Glover, Ridgway, photographer (d. Sept. 14, 1866). B. at Philadelphia, he became a photographer and in the summer of 1866 left home to make photographs "to illustrate the life and character of the wild men of the prairie," but he had persistent bad luck. He wrote a letter June 30 from Fort Laramie, saying he was forced to use water that "was so muddy." He had obtained, the letter said, a good photograph of the post and a group of eight Brule Sioux and another of six Oglala. By July 29 he was at Fort Phil Kearny, present Wyoming, arriving there with an army train which was attacked by Indians and First Lieutenant Napoleon H. Daniels (see entry), 18th Infantry, was killed. He wrote that "Our men with their rifles held the Indians at bay until we reached a better position on a hill, where we kept them off until night when Captain [Thomas Bredin Burrowes], coming up with a train, caused the redskins to retreat..." He said he had wanted to make "some instantaneous views of the Indian attack, but our commander ordered me not to." Anyway, other pictures he shot were flawed because "the collodion was too hot." In a letter of August 29, still at Phil Kearny, he complained he was doing no photography because certain necessary materials had run out, and he was awaiting arrival of a medical supply train with ether or alcohol to prepare the collodion. The supplies apparently were replenished for there followed a brief news notice saying he had been killed by Sioux near the fort with a companion, they intending to take some views, but "they were found scalped, killed, and horribly mutilated."

Clifford Krainik, "Photography and the Old West," Chicago Westerners *Brand Book,* Vol. XXVIII, No. 10 (Dec. 1991), 74.

Gobel, Silas, mountain man (d. c. Aug. 18, 1827). B. in Ohio, Silas Gobel was a durable mountain man and a blacksmith by profession. He attended the 1826 Rendezvous near the Bear River north of Salt Lake and in July was chosen by Jedediah Smith to join his southwestern exploration. In California Gobel practiced blacksmithing occasionally, making bear traps when iron could be had. In the spring of 1827 from the Stanlislaus River camp west of the Sierra Nevada, he and Robert Evans accompanied Smith on the first crossing by white Americans of the Sierra Nevada range from west to east, of the Great Basin, and to the 1827 Rendezvous on Bear Lake. Although Evans gave out on the fearful passage across the Basin, Gobel did not and after Evans recuperated the three arrived July 3 at the Rendezvous, being heartily greeted by the assembled mountain men who had believed them lost. Gobel was tough enough to sign on for Smith's second overland trip to California, but with nine others was killed by Mohave Indians at the Colorado River crossing, Smith and the remnants of his party continuing on into California.

Dale Morgan, *Jedediah Smith and the Opening of the West,* N.Y., Bobbs-Merrill, 1953; George R. Brooks, *The Southwest Expedition of Jedediah S. Smith,* Glendale, Ca., Arthur H. Clark Co., 1977; info. from E.F. (Ted) Mains.

Goddard, Pliny Earle, ethnologist (Nov. 24, 1869-July 12, 1928). B. at Lewiston, Maine, he was graduated from Earlham College, a Quaker school of Richmond, Indiana, in 1892 and received a master's degree there in 1896. After teaching for several years he became interested in the Indians and secured an appointment as a lay missionary to the Hupa Indians of California, becoming engrossed in studies of ethnology and linguistics. His work on those subjects enabled him to enter the University of California at Berkeley, partly through the personal interest of President Benjamin Ide Wheeler; he secured an instructorship of the newly created Department of Anthropology. The university awarded him a doctorate in 1904. He became an assistant professor, remaining as such until 1909 when he joined the American Museum of Natural History at New York City, by 1914 becoming curator of ethnology, a post he held until his death. He wrote specialized monographs and papers on the Hupa Indians, marking his ability in that Athapascan language. "His seventy publications, mostly intensive, uniformly valuable studies predominantly on Indian languages" appeared in university, museum and *American Anthropologist* outlets. He published *Indians of the Southwest* and *Indians of the Northwest Coast* for the museum. He also did important research among the Apaches. His publications on that field included *Myths and Tales of the White Mountain Apaches; Myths and Tales from the San Carlos Apaches,* and *Jicarilla Apache Texts.* Goddard was editor of the *American Anthropologist* from 1915 to 1920, and founder and co-editor with Boas of the *International Journal of American Linguistics.* Alfred Kroeber (see entry) "considered him one of the most vivid personalities in American anthropology." Goddard was married.

DAB; info. from E.F. (Ted) Mains.

Golder, Frank Alfred, historian (Aug. 11, 1877-Jan. 7, 1929). B. near Odessa, south Russia, he was brought to Bridgeton, New Jersey, as an infant. He was graduated in 1898 from Bucknell University, Lewisburg, Pennsylvania, and taught three years in a government school in Alaska where he became interested in the territory's history and particularly in that of the Aleut natives whose myths he collected and in part published. On his return to the States he "began investigations with a view of writing the story of Alaska as a part of American history," while sketching briefly related Asian topics of the North Pacific. However he found his sources inadequate and, greatly assisted by his fluency in the language he had to go to the originals in Russian and many other archives and repositories. It gradually became clear to him that "the discovery of Alaska, which I had regarded as the beginning chapter of American history, I found to be the closing chapter of a period of Russian expansion," and that the history of Alaska was bound tightly with the history of Siberia. His focus altered, he at length published *Russian Expansion on the Pacific 1641-1850* (1914), still an important work on its subject. In 1914 Golder studied Russian archives for source material on American history, from this effort coming his *Guide to Materials for American History in Russian Archives* (1917); he also secured letters of John Paul Jones's service, 1788-89, with Catherine the Great's navy as a rear admiral in operations against the Turks and from this came *John Paul Jones in Russia* (1927) which was blessed, according to Morison, with "a good introduction." He published *Bering's Voyages* in two volumes (1922, 1925) of documents relating to the Dane's explorations in Russian service. Golder went repeatedly to Russia for study purposes or on special missions, assisted with Herbert Hoover's American Relief Administration during the Ukraine famine and eventually became director of the Hoover War Library at Stanford University, where he was professor of history. Among the several other works he published was an edition of *The March of the Mormon Battalion* (1928), the diary of Henry Standage, Company E.

Golder, *Russian Expansion;* DAB.

Golovnin , Vasilii Mikhailovich, Russian naval officer (Apr. 8, 1776-June 30, 1831). A naval captain, Golovnin was sent in 1807 with the 18-gun sloop *Diana* to make a circumnavigation of the world. He left Kronstadt for Japan and Petropavlovsk, Kamchatka, where he arrived in

1809, wintering there and in June 1810 reaching Sitka (Novo Arkhangelsk). The arrival of his warship removed from Baranov "all anxiety as to further revolt among Russians or Kolosh (Tlingit)" Indians who a few years earlier had reduced the place. Golovnin, who "like other naval officers, was not predisposed in the [Russian American] company's favor," gives an interesting description of Sitka as it appeared in 1810, of Baranov's luxuriously furnished quarters, large library "in nearly all European languages," and fine paintings, "this in a country where probably only Baranof can appreciate a picture." Baranov explained that furnishings, library and art works had been sent out by the Company though "it would have been wiser to send out physicians, as there is not one in the colonies, nor even a surgeon or apothecary." He added that "we doctor ourselves a little, and if a man is wounded so as to require an operation, he must die." At Golovnin's arrival Baranov had received a lengthy and flattering letter from the American fur trader, John Jacob Astor, delivered by Captain John Ebbets of the *Enterprise,* a fur trade vessel. Golovnin promptly perceived a deep plot by Astor to intrude into the Russian American American Company's trade, bolstered by Ebbets's blunder in handing over private instructions he had received from Astor to guide his conduct in dealing with the Spanish American and Russian American officials. Golovnin courteously returned the instructions to Ebbets "without saying anything, but immediately wrote down the gist of the instructions and laid them before Baranov, who thought it best to forward them to the board of the managers [of the Company], who ...will no doubt...make the best use of this information for themselves." Golovnin took on board a cargo of furs and trading goods for Kamchatka and made ready for sea on August 2, departing after briefly showing Russian muscle in a slight interchange involving Ebbets and Captain Jonathan Winship (see entry) of the *O'Cain.* In 1811 Golovnin and seven of his crew were captured on Kunashiri Island off Hokkaido by a Japanese ruse, they nettled by a previous incident involving Russians. The prisoners were held two years, released only after Russian officials finally convinced the Japanese that earlier troubles had been caused by Russians acting without authorization. Golovnin's writings about his journeys and imprisonment were widely popular and went into many editions, the most

recent in 1949. August 13, 1817, he was instructed by the Admiralty to make a second circumnavigation with the sloop *Kamchatka.* He was to endeavor to make fresh discoveries in the Pacific, in northern seas to "locate more accurately on naval charts remote places, and if possible to discover new islands." He was instructed to enumerate Russian subjects on the Aleutians and the American mainland, to sail both north and south of the islands in his hunt for unexploited lands, and to survey the "hitherto unexplored...American coast from Bristol Bay to Norton Sound." The instructions noted that Cook had been unable to do this because of shoal water and "for this reason the coast should be surveyed from rowed boats, for which purpose you will need...a large hide-covered baidara." He was also directed to make a search for a reported mysterious colony of a "certain people not related to American natives," the so-called long-bearded white men who spoke Russian and whom other seafarers had sought in vain (see Ivan Kobelev entry). Among the ship's company was the Russian artist Mikhail Tikhanov whose "superb portraits of natives [encountered on the lengthy voyage] are considered ethnographic as well as artistic treasures." He was directed to investigate the affairs of the colonies and matters under control of the Russian American Company. His criticism of the Company and its founder, Shelikhov (see entry), was harsh. Clergy whom Shelikov petitioned for and exiled laborers and artisans he asked be sent to increase the resources of Russian America were equally abused and their basic needs neglected. They labored under overwhelming hardships and "for all this I am in possession of written proofs," reported Golovnin, as well as the frequency with which they "fell victims to his avarice and that of his successors." He recommended improvements in the assignment of duties to various Company officers and a "regular uniform" to impress foreigners with the existing settlements as indisputably and officially Russian. Partly as a result of his report, it was established that future managers of the Company must be naval officers of rank no lower than captain, while other strictures were placed upon officials and safeguards incorporated in the subsequent charter against the most flagrant abuses of employees. Golovnin returned to Krondstadt and St. Petersburg in 1819. He was inspector of the Naval Academy in 1821, and Quartermaster-General of the Navy from 1823 to

1830; during his career he trained many officers who became outstanding and were referred to as of the "Golovnin School." Golovnin died during a Russian cholera epidemic of 1831. He was an officer of extraordinary competence, decisive action, and great intelligence.

Bancroft, *Alaska; The Russian American Colonies;* Zagoskin.

Good, John H., cattleman (fl. 1877-1890). B. near Lockhart, Texas, he was of fighting stock and carried on the tradition. He fought Indians and white enemies in the Texas hill country, but when he killed one, Robinson, in Blanco City, although exonerated by a jury, he was forced to move westward. About 6 ft., 2 in. tall, full-bearded, he raised cows for a living, raced horses and played poker for amusement, "and bullied his neighbors from lifelong habit." By late 1877 he was living at Coleman and in 1880 at Colorado City, Texas. In 1881 he removed to La Luz, New Mexico, in the Tularosa Valley. By 1886 he was comparatively rich, had built a patriarchal home ranch, but he figured as a principal in the Lee-Good feud in the valley in which George McDonald and Walter Good, son of John, were among those killed and others suffered. As a result, Good was forced to sell out, lived at Las Cruces for about a year, then at Deming and in Arizona and last was heard from "working for somebody in Oklahoma, his glory departed and his purse flat."

C.L. Sonnichsen, *Tularosa: Last of the Frontier West,* Old Greenwich, Ct., Devin-Adair Co., 1972.

Goodwin, Millard Fillmore, army officer (May 25, 1852-July 19, 1888). B. in New York State he went to West Point, became a second lieutenant in the 9th Cavalry June 14, 1872, and saw south plains service in Texas before being ordered to Fort Stanton, New Mexico, serving under Henry Carroll much of the time. Goodwin became a first lieutenant April 4, 1879. He "played a very active role in [the] Lincoln County [War]," frequently commanding troops ordered out by N.A.M. Dudley whose adjutant he was, or others to assist law officers in their official duties. Goodwin, as Rasch suggests, might have had "but little use for the McSween faction," but that may have been because of Dudley's apparent partisanship and directives that Goodwin received. June 19, 1879, he led troops which surrounded Lincoln while Sheriff George Peppin searched the town. Goodwin also was active dur-

ing the five-day battle between the factions. After Chapman's murder Goodwin was sent to Lincoln to maintain order and his troops attempted unsuccessfully to arrest Billy the Kid. The Kid later warned Governor Wallace to watch Goodwin since "he would not hesitate to do anything." After the Lincoln County difficulties abated Goodwin was transferred to Fort Bayard, near Silver City, and took part in some Apache operations. Goodwin contracted tuberculosis and went on sick leave August 1, 1882, resigning from the army August 31, 1883. He died at Yonkers, New York.

Heitman; Cullum; Philip J. Rasch, *The Men at Fort Stanton,* English Westerners' Society *Brand Book,* Vol. 3 (April 1961), 4; Robert N. Mullin, ed., *Maurice G. Fulton's History of the Lincoln County War,* Tucson, Univ. of Ariz. Press, 1968; William A. Keleher, *Violence in Lincoln County,* Albuquerque, Univ. of New Mexico Press, 1957.

Gorby, Sarah, wildlife savior (May 7, 1916-Apr. 30, 1991). B. Sarah Pearce on a farm near Huntingdon, Pennsylvania, she worked in a sawmill at 12 and claimed she was among the first American women to drive big trucks, which she did at Philadelphia during World War II. She moved to Tucson, Arizona, in 1947 to marry Dan Gorby, a Marine Raider who had been badly wounded April 17, 1945, on Okinawa, lost sight in both of his eyes, but lived 30 more years to die April 17, 1975. Shortly after the Gorbys were married Sarah commenced caring for orphaned javelinas and skunks that she found near her rural home. "A game warden came out to cite me," she recalled, "but when he saw what I was doing, he said, 'You don't need to be cited, you need to be licensed.' That's how I became the first licensed caretaker for Arizona Game and Fish." She restored to health hundreds of birds and animals, enabling them to return to the wilds or to zoos around the country. She spent $500 a month on her unique work. An annual fund-raising dinner and private donations helped defray her expenses. She maintained a rigorous year-round schedule, starting at 4 a.m., and demonstrated creativity in utilizing a variety of sources to keep her ever-changing menagerie fed and healthy, from salvaging road kills to supply them with meat to purchasing stale bread and other unmarketable produce to supplement their varied diets. Javelinas had the run of her house, but her converted stable-home was always overrun with owls, mountain lion cubs, black bears, hawks, vultures, porcupines, skunks, raccoons, deer and coyotes along with many other creatures. Her friend, the late motion picture actor Lee Marvin, complained that "You have the only house I've ever been in where you wipe your feet when you *leave*." Sarah at one time maintained that "the more I see of people, the better I like my pigs," but admitted she had to modify that view because some "people will supply funds for the pigs, but the pigs can't supply money for people." She had serious health problems late in life, but kept up her grueling schedule. According to Tom Spalding, deputy director of Arizona Game and Fish, many people volunteer for Sarah Gorby's specialized type of work, but few are right for it. He said, "she was very realistic as well as hardworking. She knew how nature worked—some animals would make it and some wouldn't." She was blunt, though not unfriendly, in speech, and while she was caustic about people in general she had countless friends and admirers. Spalding said that "there is a whole lot of people in this department who worked with her and we're all going to miss her." She died in her sleep shortly before her 75th birthday.

Tucson, *Arizona Daily Star*, May 2, 1991.

Goycoechea, Felipe de, military officer, governor (1747-Sept. 7, 1814). B. probably at Alamos, Sonora, he was an alférez, or ensign in the presidial company of Buenavista in January 1783 when a lieutenant's commission was sent him with orders to take command of the presidial post at Santa Barbara, California, succeeding Lieutenant José Francisco Ortega (see entry). Goycoechea arrived at San Diego August 26 and reached Santa Barbara January 25, 1784 (a chart of the presidio drawn by Goycoechea is reproduced in Bancroft, *California* I, 464). The service there was largely routine and Governor Pedro Fages (see entry) "often reprimanded" Goycoechea for "carelessness, neglect of duty in minor matters, and arbitrary actions" and warned Fages's successor as governor, José Antonio Romeu, that the officer was one who "must be watched." But after Fages left, noted Bancroft, "we hear no further complaint, and it is evident that Goycoechea performed his duties as commandant and habilitado [paymaster] with zeal and ability." In 1795 Governor Diego de Borica determined to open communications between California and New Mexico and instructed Goycoechea to make inquiries about the eastern country and suggest some way to send a commu-

nication by natives to New Mexican Governor Fernando de la Concha, the Indians at the same time exploring the route. In January 1796 Goycoechea sent what information he could collect, admittedly vague and unreliable, respecting the eastern country with which the coastal natives were little familiar, telling Borica he had arranged with a native chief, Juan María, to carry the letter intended for New Mexico, but that the Franciscan missionary at Santa Barbara Estevan Tapis (1756-1825) forbade the departure, at least until he had received an order permitting it from Fermín Francisco de Lasuén, president of the California missions. Lasuén argued that it was dangerous to send Indians so far among foreign and perhaps hostile tribes since one side or the other was bound to commit excesses; in addition Juan María was very useful to the mission and any accident to him would lead to trouble with his people. There communications ceased. Bancroft judged that it was unlikely that the expedition actually was undertaken "and certain that communication was not opened with New Mexico." April 17, 1797, the Franciscan missionary Antonio de la Concepción Horra, aged about 30, arrived at San Francisco and was assigned with the experienced missionary Buenaventura Sitjar to found Mission San Miguel at San Luis Obispo. Within a month Horra was reported showing signs of insanity, Sitjar hastening to Santa Barbara where Lasuén was briefly staying to report confidentially on the matter. Lasuén sent an emissary to San Miguel to attempt to conduct Horra to Borica, which was done, Lasuén meanwhile informing the governor of specifics of the charge of mental illness or aberrations. Two surgeons at Monterey certified Horra insane and he was returned to Mexico, but the investigation into the matter covered four more years. From the College of Querétaro Horra addressed a memorial to the Viceroy, Miguel José de Azanza, complaining of treatment afforded him on an insanity assertion that he claimed was false, and leveling serious charges against Californian friars of cruelty toward neophytes and mismanagement of the missions. "There was nothing in the document to indicate that the writer was of unsound mind," commented Bancroft, except possibly his closing statement that his life would be in danger if it were known he had presented his charges to the Viceroy directly. August 31, 1798, the Viceroy sent Horra's communication to Borica and ordered him to investigate and report on the facts. Borica sent private instructions to the four presidio commandants to answer 15 questions about the friars' activities. "These replies," wrote Bancroft, "especially those of Goycoechea and [Hermenegildo] Sal [commandant at Monterey] went far to support some of the mad friar's accusations." Goycoechea's statements had been "more full than those of the others and slightly less favorable to the friars." Lasuén himself finally prepared a "comprehensive exposition of the whole subject...the most eloquent and complete defence and presentment of the mission system in many of its phases which is extant." Goycoechea's observations, where inimical to the missionaries and their practices, were refuted by the president. The entire matter, charges and rebuttals and explanations, made for a detailed and clear outline of mission practices and procedures. October 28, 1797, Goycoechea was commissioned a brevet captain by the Viceroy, receiving his papers January 26, 1798. In 1802 he was elected paymaster general for California with "no votes against him...except his own." The officer received his formal appointment as paymaster general from the Viceroy at Mexico City in the autumn, he continuing to hold his position as commandant at Santa Barbara. In 1805 he was appointed governor of Baja California, taking office July 5, 1806. In 1811 he was impeached for misconduct on such charges as speaking ill of the superior government, permitting illegal trade, neglect of duties, favoring private business, inattention to religion and defrauding the soldiers. The governor effectively refuted each charge, and he continued to hold office until his death, which occurred at Loreto, Baja California. He was described by a contemporary as tall and stout with a light ruddy complexion, affable to his men and presumably popular among them. The English navigator George Vancouver (see entry) spoke highly of him and named Point Felipe, south of Ventura, in his honor. Goycoechea was not married but, said Bancroft, "he was not a woman-hater so far as I can judge from [a record of] baptisms to the effect that a certain [Santa Barbara] widow had presented him with a son."

Bancroft, *California*, I, II, *Pioneer Register;* Maynard Geiger, O.F.M., *Franciscan Missionaries in Hispanic California 1769-1848,* San Marino, Ca., Huntington Lib., 1969; info. from Benard L. Fontana.

Graham, James, frontiersman (1741-Jan. 18, 1813). B. in Ireland, he established a fortified home on Greenbriar River, present West Virginia. It was attacked on the morning of September 11, 1777, by Shawnee Indians; Walter Caldwell, John Graham and a black, James Graham, were killed and Graham's daughter, Elizabeth was captured. Others were wounded. Elizabeth was taken to Cornstalk's camp where she was adopted into the chief's family. Her father, James Graham, ransomed her "with great difficulty" in 1785, and she married Joel Stodgill. She and her husband settled in Monroe County, West Virginia, where she died in 1858.

Thwaites/Kellogg, *Frontier Defense on the Upper Ohio, 1777-1778.*

Graham, Lawrence Pike, military officer, Shakespearian scholar (Jan. 8, 1815-Sept. 12, 1905). B. at The Wigwam, Amelia County, Virginia, he was commissioned from civilian life a second lieutenant of the 2nd Dragoons October 13, 1837, and sent to Florida for service in the Second Seminole War. He took part in the battle of Loche Hachee January 24, 1838, in which the Seminole loss was unknown, while the whites lost seven killed and 31 wounded, including the commander, Brigadier General Thomas Sidney Jesup, who was shot in the face. Graham became a first lieutenant January 1, 1839, and captain August 31, 1843. He took part in the Mexican War battles of Palo Alto and Resaca de la Palma in Texas and the heavy engagement at Monterrey, all in 1846, earning a brevet to major. In 1848, following the war, he commanded two squadrons of dragoons in a march from Monterrey to California, meanwhile apparently having acquired a taste for alcohol. He led the column to Los Angeles via Janos, Chihuahua; Tubac and Tucson, the Pima villages and the Gila River of Arizona, the trek "one of the least known of overland journeys by a large body of U.S. troops." The journey was devastatingly described by diarist Cave Couts (see entry) who wrote that Graham's daily demeanor depended upon whether he was "drunk or very drunk" and, rather than taking a previously defined route followed what Couts called "Major Graham's wagon route," whose course seemed unpredictable. The Mexican officer at one presidio planned a parade and a rousing reception for the Americans, but "Major Graham was in no condition to take advantage of this opportunity to promote better relations between his country and the Mexicans." Graham's command left Tucson October 27, 1848, reaching Warner's Ranch in southern California December 29 and continuing to Los Angeles. He left California in June 1849, served in New Mexico until August 1852, taking part in a

Navaho expedition under Edwin Vose Sumner which penetrated Canyon de Chelly for a few miles but located no hostile strength of any significance. Graham commanded the Abiquiu, New Mexico, garrison briefly. He served thereafter at Forts Leavenworth, Randall, in Dakota Territory and in the field in Kansas, taking part "in expeditions on the Plains," and in the 1857-58 Utah Expedition; he was promoted to major June 14, 1858. Graham became lieutenant colonel of the 5th Cavalry October 1, 1861, colonel of the 4th Cavalry May 9, 1864, and brevet Brigadier General of the army March 13, 1865, for his service with the Army of the Potomac. He was retired December 16, 1870, at his own request after completing 30 years' service. He resided at the capital thereafter, according to one biographer becoming "one of the most prominent Shakespearian scholars of Washington, D.C.," where he died.

Heitman; Powell; Jay J. Wagoner, *Early Arizona: Prehistory to Civil War,* Tucson, Univ. of Arizona Press, 1975; Frank McNitt, *Navajo Wars,* Albuquerque, Univ. of New Mexico Press, 1972; Ezra J. Warner, *Generals in Blue,* Baton Rouge, Louisiana State Univ. Press, 1964; *Who Was Who.*

Graham, William Alexander, military officer, historical writer (Jan. 23, 1875-Oct. 8, 1954). B. at Chicago, he studied at Beloit College and Stanford University and received a law degree from the University of Iowa in 1897. He practiced at Cedar Falls, Iowa, until 1902 and then at Des Moines until 1916. He had become captain of infantry in the Iowa National Guard, served on the Mexican Border in 1916-17, as a major became judge advocate for the 88th Division from 1917-18, served with the AEF in France until 1919 and became a lieutenant colonel in in the Judge Advocate's department for the army in 1920. He was promoted to colonel in 1931 and retired in 1939. Meanwhile he had become intensely interested in the Custer action in 1876 and in 1926 published *The Story of the Little Big Horn,* a brief, though superior narrative of that event which has been reprinted several times. Graham's greatest contribution was his monumental *The Custer Myth* (1953) which printed "important items of Custeriana," and Fred Dustin's comprehensive bibliography. The book includes a great number of valuable documents bearing on the action and peripheral fields of interest, and has been an essential resource for countless historical writers. Graham also published an *Abstract of the Reno Court of Inquiry*

(1954). Utley wrote that Graham approached the controversial Custer event "with an objectivity almost as passionate as the prejudice of the others. To Graham, objectivity meant not only a scrupulously open mind in the handling of evidence, but also the avoidance, in presentation, of all judgments and most interpretations. He was concerned almost exclusively with events, not motivations." His work was "nonetheless refreshing [and] undeniably the greatest contributions of his era to unravelling the events of the Little Bighorn campaign." Graham died at his Pacific Palisades, California, home and was buried at Arlington National Cemetery.

Who Was Who; Graham's works; Robert M. Utley, *Custer and the Great Controversy,* Los Angeles, Westernlore Press, 1962.

Granger, Walter Willis, paleontologist (Nov. 7, 1872-Sept. 6, 1941). B. in Middletown Springs, near Rutland, Vermont, he early discarded his middle name. Granger had only two years of high school education when through a family friend in 1890 he secured a position with the American Museum of Natural History of New York, with which he would remain for the rest of his life. He initially was assistant in taxidermy under supervision of ornithologist Frank M. Chapman, but in 1894 he accompanied a field expedition to the South Dakota Badlands and became fascinated by its abundant mammalian fossil remains; in 1896 he transferred to the museum's department of vertebrate paleontology. That year he accompanied Jacob L. Wortman who had worked with Cope (see entry) to collect fossil mammals in the San Juan basin of northern New Mexico. In 1897 he accompanied a museum party extracting fossil dinosaur bones from Como Bluff, near Medicine Bow, Wyoming. In 1898 he discovered and brought out the skeleton of the famed *Brontosaurus,* the most massive land creature discovered to that time and which, cleaned, assembled and mounted, is today the stellar attraction in the museum's Brontosaurus Hall. In 1903 Henry Fairfield Osborn, president of the museum, assigned Granger to take charge of fossil mammal collections and studies (he eventually became curator, equivalent of full professor) of fossil mammals, holding that position thereafter. Working with Canadian-born William D. Matthew, and Albert (Bill) Thomson as field technician, Granger "revolutionized knowledge of the Age of Mammals and laid the main basis for early Cenozoic faunal and stratigraphic studies in North America." His important studies during this period included expeditions into Wyoming, New Mexico, Colorado and South Dakota, although his "work on other continents became better known than his work in the United States, though it was of no greater importance." He accompanied Osborn in 1907 to the Fayum region of Egypt; from 1921-31 he made very important collections in Mongolia and China as second in command to Roy Chapman Andrews of the Central Asiatic Expeditions. As chief pale-ontologist came under his supervision the "stun-ning discovery of a long sequence of rich and bizarre faunas of fossil vertebrates, hitherto completely unknown, extending from dino-saurs...through a whole succession of faunas... up to our own time. The collections revealed lit-erally hundreds of animals new to science [including] a whole growth series of frilled dinosaurs, the earliest known mammal skulls, the largest known land mammal...and shovel-tusked mastodons." Granger and others pub-lished many preliminary description of some of these animals, but not all of them have yet been described although "a third generation of paleon-tologists" still carry out important research on Granger's discoveries. Granger published about 75 research papers along with other materials. He was married and, a jovial extrovert, he was a "highly social person, loved by his associates." He died near Lusk, Wyoming (see Colbert, 83-86, 98-99). His ashes were interred in Vermont.

Who Was Who; DAB, Supplement 3, article by George Gaylord Simpson; Edwin H. Colbert, *A Fossil-Hunter's Notebook,* N.Y., E.P. Dutton, 1980.

Gratiot, Charles, frontier trader (1752-Apr. 20, 1817). B. at Lausanne, Switzerland, he went to London at 17 and then to Montreal to join an uncle in the fur trade, remaining with him six years before making a rather disastrous trading campaign of his own in the west. In 1777, he joined in a partnership and in December opened a store at Cahokia, Illinois, his partners establish-ing themselves at Kaskaskia. When George Rogers Clark invaded Illinois in 1778, Gratiot formed a firm friendship with him and rendered Clark many services. In 1781 Gratiot moved to St. Louis where on June 25 he married a half-sis-ter of Auguste Chouteau (see entry), thus allying himself with the wealthiest and probably most powerful fur trading family on the frontier. Gra-tiot's affairs prospered and around 1793 or later he met and formed an association of sorts with John Jacob Astor (see entry), remaining in touch

with him as long as Gratiot lived. It was on Gra-tiot's front porch that the formal transfer of Upper Louisiana was finalized March 10, 1804, with Gratiot as interpreter. He became first pre-siding justice of the court of quarter sessions at St. Louis. The *Dictionary of American Biogra-phy* summed up his carrer reporting that "though not the wealthiest of the St. Louis traders, Gratiot was the most widely known, and he brought the frontier fur center to the attention of the world," through his trips to the east and abroad. It added that he was "a man of exceptional initiative, ener-gy, and persistence," and had a thorough knowl-edge of, and experience in, the practice of law. His son, Charles, went to West Point, eventually became a colonel, chief engineer of the army, and a brevet Brigadier General.

DAB; Heitman.

Gray, John Stephens, physician, historical writer (Aug. 11, 1910-Dec. 25, 1991). B. at Chicago, he was graduated from Knox College, Galesburg, Illinois, in 1932, earned a master's degree in 1934 and a doctorate in 1936 from Northwestern University at Evanston, Illinois, and an M.D. in 1946 from the university's School of Medicine. There he became an instruc-tor in 1934, rising to full professor of physiology by 1970, having been chairman of the depart-ment of physiology from 1946; he became pro-fessor emeritus in 1974 after which he resided at Fort Collins, Colorado. His faculty colleague at Northwestern, Ray Allen Billington (see entry) early introduced Gray to "the world of western history" and through Billington he joined the Chicago Corral of Westerners where he pub-lished numerous thoroughly-researched articles in its *Brand Book,* among the first of which was "On the Trail of 'Lonesome Charley' Reynolds," in October 1957. Billington privately expressed amusement that anyone would expend so much arduous physical and mental effort and archival study seeking to document the life of a character "so minor" to western history as Reynolds, but this was the manner in which Gray pursued his virtually unrivaled research on every life and every issue that attracted his attention, and is what made him great in the view of most students of the areas of Gray's concern. Gray explained in *Contemporary Authors:* "My passion is research and the communication of its results...[Upon my] retirement from the University, I was ready for full-time research and writing in history. My goal in both areas has always been to dig and dig for facts, analyzing them repeatedly in every way I can, discarding in the process whole series of unsatisfactory interpretations until I find one that holds up even as more facts come in. Should I ever end up with a picture remotely resembling my initial ignorant idea, I will know that I have neither researched nor learned." In addition to his medical writings, which included at least one book and many articles, Gray wrote the universally hailed *Centennial Campaign: The Sioux War of 1876* (1976), and *Custer's Last Campaign: Mitch Boyer and the Little Bighorn Reconstructed* (1991); Robert M. Utley, himself a pre-eminent authority on Custer and author of major works on that officer and his campaigns, wrote that he considered Gray's *Centennial Campaign* the best single volume on the 1876 Sioux War at its time of publication, and believed that the later *Custer's Last Campaign* was "the most important book ever written about the Battle of the Little Bighorn." He added that Gray's analysis "is brilliant, revolutionary, and all but unassailable," and his overall product and conclusions will probably resist major challenges. In addition to the foregoing, Gray was senior historical editor of Bruce E. Berends' *The Poudre River* (1976) and was reportedly working on *Fort Collins: Army Post on the Cache la Poudre.* He died at Fort Collins on Christmas Day, survived by his widow and two daughters.

Who's Who in America; Contemporary Authors; Western Hist. Assn. *Newsletter,* Spring 1992, p. 5; conversation, Billington with author; Utley's Foreword in *Custer's Last Campaign.*

Gray, Michael (Mike), rancher, frontiersman (Apr. 1, 1827-Sept. 8, 1906). B. "in the backwoods" of Tennessee, his parents took him to Texas in 1831 where they settled at the present site of Huntsville. At 14 young Mike enlisted in President Sam Houston's Texas army, and in the Mexican War he served under Jack Hays (see entry), rising to the rank of first lieutenant; it may have been during this time or earlier that he served in the Texas Rangers under Hays. In 1849 from St. Joseph, Missouri, Gray with his parents joined the wagon emigration to California. His father died of cholera along the Platte and Gray became captain of the train which arrived at the Feather River, California. He moved into Yuba County where at Marysville, the county seat, he married Sarah Ann Robinson who had accompanied his wagon trek from Missouri. Gray became acting sheriff of Yuba County from 1851-53, his

under-sheriff being Charles Newton Felton who succeeded Gray as sheriff and eventually became a U.S. Senator from California and a prominent financial figure. Felton termed Gray "the bravest man I ever knew," often reciting how Gray had killed with a single-shot derringer a pistol-armed man in a gunfight outside the sheriff's office. In the early 1860s Gray and his wife settled for a time in western Mexico where he engaged in mining. In 1862 his youngest son was born at Guaymas, Sonora, and was named Dixie Lee Gray, in commemoration of the South and Robert E. Lee; the boy was slain in a celebrated shooting affair August 13, 1881 (see Dixie Lee Gray entry, and also the Billy Lang entry), near Guadalupe Canyon on the Arizona-New Mexico border. The Gray family settled at Mazatlan on the Mexican Pacific coast while Mike Gray's mining endeavors prospered until the Maximilian-Juarez fighting broke out, when he found it impossible to continue operations and took his family by the old side-wheeler *Brother Jonathan* to San Francisco. Gray became intrigued by what became known later as the "Great Diamond Hoax," an elaborate plot by swindlers to profit from a salted "diamond field" in the southwest, but he reached the scene too late, which is just as well: it had already been uncovered as a faked source of diamonds. Almost immediately afterward, around 1872 or 1873, Gray wandered down to the Animas Valley of New Mexico where he found a beautiful site with only one major drawback: it was the constantly used funnel for smugglers and outlaws between Mexico and the United States. Nevertheless, there he established what has become famous in this day—and earlier—as the Gray Ranch. The 5,000-ft. high valley lies between the Peloncillo Mountains to the west, the Pyramid Range to the north, the Animas Mountains to the east and the Sierra San Luis to the south. The immense ranch covered 321,703 acres, or 502 square miles. After nearly a decade, however, and following his son's murder by unidentified assailants, along with New Mexico's smugglers and their guns getting the better of him, Gray sold out, "My father and I felt that conditions were too hard at that time to fight against," wrote John Pleasant Gray, another son, many years later. In November 1882, Mike turned over the Gray Ranch to mining-ranching baron George Hearst (1820-1891), father of publisher William Randolph Hearst and a month later bought a ranch in Arizona, became a justice of the peace, and entered politics. Hearst meanwhile had made the Gray Ranch the headquarters of his fabulous Diamond A which sprawled across southern New Mexico in county-sized grazing plots; the ranch and Hearst's operation was named the Victorio Land and Cattle Company. After Hearst's death, the Gray Ranch passed from one owner to another until 1982 when Pablo Brener, a wealthy Mexican businessman, came into possession of it. Nature Conservancy purchased it from him for around $18.2 million and implied it was determined to itself save its unrivaled kingdom of wildlife and scenic beauty for generations to come. "More separate species and subspecies of mammals are found on the Gray Ranch than on any existing national wildlife refuge or national park in the continental United States," said Bill Waldman, director of Nature Conservancy's New Mexico office. The ranch supports 718 species of plants, many of them rare, about 75 species and subspecies of mammals, and 52 kinds of reptiles and amphibians, including three on the Federal list of endangered species, while 150 species of birds nest on the land. There also are 13 significant pre-Columbian archeological sites. The acreage "is not pristine, but it has remained relatively unimpacted," said a spokesman. "All the ecosystems are still there and functioning. All the pieces are intact." However, in 1993 the Conservancy sold the ranch for only $13.2 million to an "Animas Foundation," described as a non-profit group founded by a neighboring rancher family, the rancher quoted as saying his interest was "to preserve the Gray Ranch as a working cattle ranch," among other things. Mike Gray and his family settled eventually at Tombstone, and later at Pearce, Arizona, both in the southeastern portion of the territory. He served in the 14th, 17th, 20th and 21st Arizona Legislative Assemblies, yet he never lost his frontier skills. His son, John, wrote of seeing his father helping out an apparently novice teamster whose 20-horse team hauling three wagons loaded with 20 tons of flour was stuck in a sandy wash because the young driver was unable to get the teams to pull together. Gray quieted the horses by talking softly and stroking each one, then grabbed the jerkline and with the help of the voluble profanity teamsters of the day ever believed necessary to get teams to work together in such an emergency, had them draw the wagons free and onto hard ground. Such teamster feats are "of the lost arts now," John Pleasant Gray wrote in

1940. Mike Gray eventually retired to San Francisco where he died at 79 in 1906. Earlier that year the great San Francisco Earthquake and Fire occurred on April 18-19.

Richard Benke, a researched article on Gray and the Gray Ranch written for the Associated Press Aug. 7, 1990; info. from Benke; John Pleasant Gray, "When All Roads Led to Tombstone," unpub. manuscript, Arizona Hist. Soc.; *New York Times Magazine*, "The Secrets of the Gray Ranch," June 3, 1990; Jay J. Wagoner, *Arizona Territory 1863-1912*, Tucson, Univ. of Arizona Press, 1970.

Gray Beard, Cheyenne chief: *see,* Grey Beard

Gray Lock (Wawenorrawot), Waranoke (Abenaki) chief (d. c. 1727). Probably a chief or sachem of the Waranoke tribe, an Abenaki people dwelling in the vicinity of present Westfield, Massachusetts, he appears over such a space of time that Day believed a father and son of the same name may have been involved. His name came from a streak of prematurely white hair. He was reported active in King Philip's War (see entry) in 1675-76 and to have escaped to Mohawk country after Philip and most of his followers were destroyed. At any rate he was fiercely hostile to the English during virtually all of his life. Following King Philip's War he seems to have settled with the Missisquoi (or Missiassik) on the Missisquois River in today's Franklin County, northern Vermont. In 1712 Gray Lock took part in an attack on Northampton, Massachusetts, in one of the last raids of Queen Anne's War (1701-13). Gray Lock achieved his greatest notoriety during Dummer's War (1722-25), so named for Massachusetts Bay and New Hampshire Lieutenant Governor William Dummer, acting governor since Samuel Shute had returned to England. Gray Lock conducted daring raids against Massachusetts and the upper Connecticut Valley settlements, and his wiliness and elusive tactics prevented the colonials from ever catching up with him, or preventing his depredations. Since New York was not involved in the war and had retained contacts with the Scaticook settlement on the east bank of the Hudson River from which Gray Lock drew many recruits, Albany tried to negotiate a truce, but failed to contact the chief. He fell upon Northfield and Rutland in 1723 and although pursued, was not taken. Again he attacked Northfield and escaped. In 1724 he once more raided western Massachusetts communities, was followed into Vermont but eluded his enemies and returned to the Connecticut Valley, then raided Deerfield, Northampton and Westfield. He continued his offensive operations through 1725, and hostilities until early in 1727, after most of the Abenakis had already made peace with the English, when he indicated that he, too, finally wished to come in. Thomas Ingersoll (see entry) of Westfield, reportedly shot and killed Gray Lock; the date is not given, but since English reports of the chief ceased in 1727 it may be assumed that his death occurred around that time. The slaying was done as Gray Lock supposedly was preparing to scalp Mrs. Ingersoll in retaliation for some earlier slight by her husband.

Gordon M. Day, "Gray Lock," DCB, III; Lillian Drake Avery, *A Genealogy of the Ingersoll Family in America*, N.Y., F.H. Hitchcock Pub. Co., 1926, p. 132; HNAI, 15, p. 151; Douglas Edward Leach, *Arms for Empire: A Military History of the British Colonies in North American 1607-1763*, N.Y., The Macmillan Co., 1973, pp. 181-86; info. from Atara Clark.

Greely, Adolphus Washington, military officer, explorer (Mar. 27, 1844-Oct. 20, 1935). B. at Newburyport, Massachusetts, he enlisted July 26, 1861, in B Company of the 19th Massachusetts infantry, rising to first sergeant by March 18, 1863, when he was commissioned a second lieutenant of the 81st U.S. Colored Infantry, emerging from the Civil War a captain and brevet major of Volunteers. He became a second lieutenant March 7, 1867, of the 36th Infantry and July 14, 1869, joined the 5th Cavalry. He was promoted to first lieutenant May 27, 1873. Greely served as acting chief signal officer for the Department of the Platte until March 1871, when he joined his company at Fort Laramie, Wyoming. He served as company commander until July when he was assigned to the office of the chief signal officer of the Army at Washington. He superintended construction of military telegraph lines in Texas, Dakota and Montana and in other capacities until 1881. Greely volunteered for polar duty and was chosen to head the Lady Franklin Bay expedition, assigned to establish a meteorological and supply station near the northern tip of today's Ellesmere Island and across Hall Basin from Greenland. The station was one of 13 circumpolar scientific posts designed principally to study weather and climate according to an 1879 plan devised by the International Polar Geographical Conference.

Greely was authorized to enlist two other officers and 21 soldiers and hire those Eskimo hunters needed from the Greenland coast. The 467-ton barkentine sealer *Proteus,* equipped with auxiliary engines was selected to transport the expedition, manned by experienced Newfoundland fishermen trained in ice navigation. The ship sailed from St. John's July 7, 1881, and arrived at Lady Franklin Bay August 11; the *Proteus* departed August 26 leaving the party of 25 including three officers, a doctor, 19 enlisted men and two Eskimos at a post they named Fort Conger. They recorded some 500 observations daily, kept weather and tidal reports, studied natural history and carried out explorations, one party attaining their farthest north at Latitude 83° 24' on May 13, 1882, and another crossing upper Ellesmere Island to what they named Greely Fjord, the extension inland of the present Nansen Sound. The summer of 1883 passed without arrival of the expected relief ship, the *Proteus,* which, sent for that purpose, had been caught in the ice and sunk when its consort, the *Yantic* was forced to turn back. The following winter was tragic, for supplies had run out, starvation was inevitable for inexperienced polar travelers, the party eating what leather clothing they possessed and what scant food the hunters brought in. In mid-January the first man died; six died in April, four in May, and seven in June. When hope was all but gone Captain Winfield Scott Schley in the *Thetis,* Lieutenant W.H. Emory in the *Bear* and two other vessels sent by the government forced their way through the ice and rescued what was left: Greely, six of his men and their records and papers, though one of the rescued died at Godhavn, Greenland, enroute home. There were rumors, later confirmed, that cannibalism had been resorted to by some to prolong their lives, although this hastened their deaths as Stefansson made clear, the flesh being so barren of fat that those who resorted to this practice (of which Greely was unaware) appeared briefly strengthened by it, but perished of protein poisoning, since fat must accompany lean meat for proper diet. Apparently none of the survivors had resorted to anthropophagy or they would also have succumbed. Schley had reached Greely on June 22, 1884. Greely initially was blamed by many for the tragic outcome of the expedition, which was in no way his fault, for he had conducted himself flawlessly. The soundness of his judgment and leadership skills gradually became apparent and due credit was his; Congress authorized for him the Medal of Honor, presented on his 91st birthday. Records of the expedition were published in two volumes in 1888 and Schley's account of the relief expedition appeared in 1884. Greely became a captain June 11, 1886, the chief Signal Corps officer with rank of Brigadier General March 3, 1887, remaining such until 1906 during which period he built or supervised construction of communication lines in Puerto Rico, Cuba, China, the Philippines and from 1900 to 1904 oversaw construction of 13,900 miles of telegraph line and ocean cable in Alaska and is said to have established the first successful long-distance wireless system from Nome to St. Michael. In 1906 he terminated a Rocky Mountain Ute threat of an uprising without bloodshed. February 10, 1906, he became Major General and retired in 1908. He was much honored in his later years. Greely died at Walter Reed Hospital, Washington, D.C., and was buried in·Arlington National Cemetery; he was survived by two sons and four daughters. He was a prolific writer; a list of his publications is carried in Supplement I of the *Dictionary of American Biography.* The most comprehensive and among the best narratives of Greely's Arctic expedition is by Todd.

A.L. Todd, *Abandoned: The Story of the Greely Arctic Expedition of 1881-1884,* intr. by Vilhjalmur Stefansson, N.Y., McGraw-Hill Book Co., 1961; Heitman; Powell; Price, *Fifth Cavalry,* 529-31; DAB.

Grenadier Squaw (Non-hel-e-ma, Katty or Katy), Shawnee (fl. 1774-1785). A sister of the famous Shawnee chief Cornstalk (see entry), she lived in Grenadier Squaw's Town on Scippo Creek, Pickaway County, Ohio. She acquired the name by which she was known to the whites by reason of her unusual height. She had been baptized Catherine, and often was called Katy, or Katty. She was a woman of note, was attached to the white Americans and "frequently brought them valuable information." Following the murder of Cornstalk she abandoned her own people and with 48 head of cattle, some horses and other property made her way to Fort Randolph at the mouth of the Great Kanawha River, West Virginia, and stayed with the garrison, being frequently employed as an interpreter. Later she moved to Pittsburgh where in 1785 she petitioned the Indian commissioners for relief and for a land grant on the Scioto River, Ohio, where her family had lived and her mother was buried. The petition was referred to Congress but seems never to have been acted upon. Her probable daughter was known as Fawny (Fanny); she had been at Fort Randolph with her mother.

Hodge, HAI; Thwaites/Kellogg, *Frontier Defense on the Upper Ohio, 1777-1778.*

Grey Beard, Cheyenne chief (d. c. May 21, 1875). Grey Beard, or Grey Head, who first became a Southern Cheyenne medicine man, was probably b. around 1840, although this is conjecture. He helped incite young Cheyennes to initiate the fight with Colonel E.V. Sumner in the spring of 1857, an action which became famous for a trooper sabre charge, the only such event in Plains history; as a result Sumner reported that he had lost two men killed, Lieutenant J.E.B. Stuart badly wounded along with eight other men wounded, and claimed nine Cheyennes killed, although Bent said there were only four Indians slain. By 1865 Grey Beard was a Dog Soldier chief of about 50 lodges, and took part in the intense hostile activity of 1864-65 on the central Plains. Grey Beard was present at the April 1867 confrontation between Hancock (see entry) and the Cheyennes, but it was Bull Bear rather than Grey Beard who dissuaded Roman Nose from assassinating Hancock, Bull Bear having "great influence" over Roman Nose. Grey Beard fought in the second Battle of Adobe Walls, Texas, June 27, 1874, but did not have an important role. Grey Beard had no part in the attack on the German family (see entry) September 11, 1874, but two of the captive girls were deposited in his tepee village afterward, and were freed by Lieutenant Frank D. Baldwin after an attack on the village November 8, 1874. On March 6, 1875, about 820 Cheyennes under Grey Beard and Stone Calf, whose band held the other two German girl captives, surrendered at Darlington, Indian Territory. Learning that many of the Cheyennes were to be ironed and shipped east, among them Grey Beard, Heap of Birds and Minimic, the Cheyennes bolted for the nearby sand hills, but most were recaptured. Grey Beard was among those sent under guard to Fort Sill and from there, in May 1875 entrained for Fort Marion, St. Augustine, Florida. None had had a trial, or even a hearing. Between Red Oak and Lake City, Florida, Grey Beard jumped from the train, then traveling around 25 miles per hour. The train was stopped, the guard hunted him down and shot him as he tried to escape. He died two hours later.

George E. Hyde, *Life of George Bent,* ed. by Savoie

Lottinville, Norman, Univ. of Okla. Press, 1968; Stan Hoig, *The Peace Chiefs of the Cheyennes,* Norman, 1980; Donald J. Berthrong, *The Southern Cheyennes,* Norman, 1963.

Grigorov, Spiridon, explorer (fl. 1843-1860). A Russian American Company employee he was directed by Governor Etolen in October 1843 to lead a small expedition up the Copper River and seek out Tazlina Lake which lies north of the Chugach Mountains and west of the Copper. The party reached the lake, but the season was too late to go farther. In 1860, Grigorov was manager of the Konstantinovskii Fort, the present Nuchek, on Hinchinbrook Island.

Pierce, *Russian America: A Biographical Dictionary.*

Guero, El Guero (Nac-cogé, Napé, Najoee), Mimbres Apache chief (c. 1776-post 1828). B. probably in the El Compá rancheria in the Mexico-United States borderlands, he was known to the Spanish as El Guero (the light-haired one) and in 1791-92, although only 15 was listed by the Mexicans as a chief. According to Griffen he matured into "an important Apache chieftain." He may have been a close relative of Compá's wife, or of Compá himself. He headed his own rancheria in 1793 and 50 or more people were residents of it "until sometime after 1800." He was generally a peace chief with respect to the Mexicans of the Janos-Bacoachi area, but in the late 1820s his people camped near the Santa Rita mines in southwestern New Mexico. There he may have associated closely with the sons of El Compá, Juan Diego and Juan José (see entries). Little or nothing is reported of El Guero following 1828; it is not known whether he was with his friends, the Compá brothers at the time of the Juan José massacre by the scalp hunter John J. Johnson April 22, 1837, but if so he must have escaped, for the slaying of so prominent an Apache would scarcely have gone unreported.

William B. Griffen, *Apaches at War & Peace,* Albuquerque, Univ. of New Mexico Press, 1989.

Guthrie, Alfred Bertram Jr., writer (Jan. 13, 1901-Apr. 26, 1991). B. at Bedford, Indiana, the son of an educator and newspaper editor, he was raised at Choteau, Montana, attended the University of Washington for two years and graduated from the University of Montana in 1923, receiving an honorary doctorate from that school in 1949. Guthrie's first important novel was The

Big Sky (1947), a classic depiction of the Mountain Men which deserved a Pulitzer Prize but did not get it; two years later he published *The Way West,* which scarcely deserved a Pulitzer, but won it, apparently by way of amends. Guthrie worked for the *Lexington* (Kentucky) *Leader* from 1926-47 as reporter, city editor, editorial writer and executive editor, and taught creative writing at the University of Kentucky from 1947-52, by which time he was established nationally as an outstanding author of historical fiction. He wrote the screenplays for the acclaimed motion picture *Shane* (1953) and *The Kentuckian* (1955). Among the 14 books he published were: his first, a mystery, *Murders at Moon Dance* (1943), which he later characterized as "a trashy piece of work"; *The Big Sky, The Way West* (1949), and *These Thousand Hills* (1956), the three forming a trilogy; *The Big It* (1960); *The Blue Hen's Chick* (1965); *Arfive* (1971); *Wild Pitch* (1973); *Fair Land, Fair Land* (1982), depicting in conclusion the Eugene M. Baker (see entry) directed massacre of Blackfeet in 1870, and *A Field Guide to Writing Fiction* (1991). Guthrie was drawn to nature studies and once said that "If I had to do it over, I would have been a naturalist." He was incensed at Eastern critics' labeling him "a regional writer" which was the "worst title I know." He said that "A good book is not 'regional.' It is a good book, set in a region," and insisted he was no more a "regional writer" than Faulkner, Welty, Thomas Wolfe or others who wrote superlative fiction using a "region" as a backdrop. He insisted that part of the problem was that "people in the East don't understand the West, and don't seem to want to," adding that "they think *we're* parochial. If any place in the world is *parochial* it's New York City." Guthrie was married twice, his first wife predeceasing him and the second surviving him. He also was survived by two children and two stepchildren. He died at 90 at his home at Choteau.

Tucson, *Arizona Daily Star,* Oct. 17, 1982; *New York Times* obituary, reprinted in *Arizona Star,* Apr. 27, 1991; *Who's Who in America.*

Guyasuta (Guyashusta, Kiasutha, Kayashuta), Iroquois chief (c. 1725-c. 1794). Sometimes considered a Mingo, he more likely was a western Seneca chief of that people who sided with the French while others of the New York confederacy were English allies. He was probably b. on the Genesee River of New York

State, but his family moved west when he was young. He thereafter resided on the Allegheny River of western Pennsylvania. In 1753 he accompanied Washington from Logstown, 18 miles below Pittsburgh, to French posts upstream. Washington considered him a young hunter, and Nathanial Gist as a "young warrior." In 1755 Guyasuta was with the French-Indian force that destroyed the Braddock column making for Fort Duquesne. In the autumn the Indian led a party of 20 Senecas who visited Montreal with Daniel Chabert de Joncaire as interpreter; they conferred with Governor Pierre de Rigaud de Vaudreuil. Guyasuta was with the Indians and French defeating Major James Grant (see entry) in 1758. In July 1759 Guyasuta with two other chiefs and 16 Iroquois, along with many Delawares, Shawnees and Wyandots, held a Fort Pitt conference with George Croghan, Johnson's deputy Indian agent, and a treaty was signed. The chief was a power in Indian preparations for the Pontiac War of 1763, and was among the first to urge force against the English. During that conflict he and his followers fought with Delawares in the siege of Fort Pitt, and against Bouquet and his relief force, and he may have taken part in capture of the British post at Venango (Franklin), Pennsylvania. At the end of October 1764 the chief, with delegates of the Delawares, Shawnees, and Mingos came to Fort Laurens (at the present Bolivar, Ohio) to meet with Bouquet for a peace conference. In 1765 Croghan met with Indians at Fort Pitt, and Guyasuta was named delegate to a conference in July with William Johnson at Johnstown, New York, where a final peace was negotiated. During the decade following he often was a British emissary to the Ohio Indians, Johnson considering him a "Chief of much Capacity and vast Influence." Largely neutral early in the Revolution, Guyasuta and others by 1777 began working actively for the British cause. He was in on the siege of Fort Stanwix at Rome, New York, and in a battle at Oriskany, New York. Unsuccessful in his appeal for 100 British soldiers to oppose Brodhead's sweep of the Allegheny Indian towns in 1779, he left the American commander virtually unopposed. Guyasuta may have commanded a Wyandot party raiding near Fort McIntosh, at Rochester, Pennsylvania, in July 1780, and in July 1782 he burned Hannastown, Pennsylvania, and attacked Wheeling, West Virginia. He met with Anthony Wayne in 1792 and 1793, possibly seeking to head off the military campaign being

prepared for Ohio which had its triumphant conclusion at Fallen Timbers in August 1794. By then Guyasuta had probably died at Cornplanter's Town, although the date and circumstances of his demise are not known.

Hodge, HAI; William M. Darlington, *Christopher Gist's Journals,* 1893, N.Y., Argonaut Press, Ltd., 1966; Thwaites/Kellogg, *The Revolution on the Upper Ohio, 1775-1777,* Madison, Wisconsin Hist. Soc., 1908; DCB, IV.

Gwosdef (Gvosdef), Michael Spiridovinich, geodicist, explorer (d. post-1754). His date of b. is unreported, but Gwosdef began his education in 1716 at the Russian school of navigation, and in 1719 attended the St. Petersburg naval academy, enrolling in the surveying class. In 1721 he was sent on government duty to Novgorod, remaining until 1725; two years later he obtained his degree as surveyor (and navigator) and was sent to Siberia to join Afanase Shestakof, a Cossack chief engaged in the conquest of northeastern Siberia. Shestakof was killed in action, and Gwosdef was assigned to an expedition aboard Bering's former ship, the *St. Gabriel,* to seek out the "Large Country" somewhere beyond the Chukchi Peninsula, reports of it having been heard from Chukchi natives. The expedition left the Kamchatka River July 23, 1732, worked up the coast and visited the Diomede Islands which Bering had discovered shortly before. By now Ivan Federof, nominal leader, was confined to his cabin by illness and Gwosdef was the effective commander. From the Diomedes they could see to the east a land toward which they sailed August 21, anchoring four versts (about two or three miles) offshore, not daring to approach closer because of shoal water. They met people in kayaks, saw timber and were told by natives that there were plenty of animals, large rivers and other continental elements on the land they had discovered. Unable to disembark, however, they returned to Kamchatka, arriving September 28. The officers were requested to send in a report on their voyage, but Federof died in February 1733, and five months later Gwosdef forwarded the log book and a brief account of the journey. Nobody formally notified the Admiralty of these accomplishments, but word came to it indirectly years later and in 1741 Gwosdef and another were asked to draw up fuller reports. In 1743 Captain Martin Petrovich Spanberg, a veteran of Bering's expeditions, was commissioned to investigate results of the Gwosdef voyage. Spanberg was satisfied that the initial report of the expedition was correct, with Gwosdef's assistance drew up a chart of the journey, which eventually reached the Admiralty, and along with it sent an expanded report based upon Fedorof's private journal. The several sources agreed that natives of the "continent" used skin kayaks unlike any in use on the Siberian coast and their general description of the land they found supported to Bancroft the coast of Norton Sound, Alaska, "the only point on all that coast where the timber approaches the shore. The shallow water found going to the southward, would also indicate that they approached the remarkable shoals lying off the mouths of the Yukon River." Thus it appears that the Gwosdef people were the true white discoverers of Alaska a decade before Chirikov and Bering made their heralded landfalls. Gwosdef remained in Siberia, exploring and charting little known lands, until 1754 when he was appointed instructor for the naval corps of cadets, presumably at St. Petersburg. The date of his death is not reported.

Bancroft, *Alaska;* F.A. Golder, *Russian Expansion on the Pacific 1641-1850,* N.Y., Paragon Book Reprint Corp., 1971.

Hagemeister (Gagemeister), Ludwig von, Russian naval officer, governor (June 16, 1780-Dec. 23, 1833). B. in Latvia of a German family, he volunteered at 15 for the Russian Baltic fleet and soon became a midshipman. In 1802 he was sent with other officers to England and served with the British fleet in the West Indies, Africa and in the Mediterranean. At one point he distinguished himself in a Horatio Nelson battle with Spanish warships. In 1806 he was given command of the *Neva* which he took to Sitka, Alaska, with supplies for the Russian American Company headquartered there, then wintered at Kodiak on the island of that name, returning in 1808 to Sitka. Aleksandr Baranov (see entry), head of the company, directed Hagemeister to sail to the Sandwich Islands (Hawaii) to obtain food supplies for the Russian fur company, and also to scout the archipelago for a site for a Russian colony. Hagemeister recommended the island of Molokai after wintering in Hawaii. In late spring, 1809 he took the *Neva* to Petropavlovsk, Kamchatka, then to Okhotsk where he received orders to return overland to St. Petersburg, arriving in 1811 to be decorated for his world-girdling cruise, promoted to Captain-Lieutenant and for several years served his country on missions to foreign capitals, and elsewhere. September 24, 1816, in command of the *Suvorov* and the *Kutuzov* he left Kronstadt for Sitka, arriving November 21, 1817. He bore secret orders to succeed the venerable Baranov as chief manager of the Russian American Company and to investigate allegations of misdeeds against his predecessor and to correct any management imperfections he might uncover. He directed Kirill Khlebnikov (see entry) to go over company accounts with Baranov, and this was done, finding them in perfect order and the allegations against the chief manager wholly unwarranted. Hagemeister's regime, however brief, was "more disciplined and businesslike" than Baranov's, if scarcely more effective. The new governor sailed to California on July 22, 1818, to lay in fresh food supplies, leaving in charge at Sitka Lieutenant Semen Ivanovich Yanovskii, who had married Baranov's daughter, Irina. The chief manager returned to Sitka October 3, 1818, but illness determined him to return to Russia. Sailing aboard the *Kutusov* with him was the aged Baranov, determined to spend his retirement in his native country, but he died at sea shortly after the vessel left Batavia. The *Kutusov* arrived at Kronstadt September 7, 1819. Hagemeister left the naval service in 1821 but in 1828 re-entered it and commenced a third circumnavigation of the world in the sloop *Krotkii*. In October he arrived at Sitka, enroute having discovered Kwajalein Atoll in the Pacific. He reached Kronstadt once more in September 1830, received more honors, was promoted to Captain, First Rank and named director of the merchant marine training school. In 1833 he was ordered to undertake his fourth circumnavigation, but died of a stroke before he could embark. "Hagemeister was an excellent navigator, mathematician, and astronomer." He kept voluminous diaries in Russian, German, English, Spanish, French and Portuguese. Several Alaskan geographical features were named for him.

Richard A. Pierce, *Builders of Alaska: The Russian Governors 1818-1867,* Kingston, Ont., Limestone Press, 1986; Zagoskin; Bancroft, *Alaska;* Orth, 400.

Haggin, John, frontiersman (1753-Mar. 1, 1825). B. near Winchester, Virginia, he moved in early life to western Pennsylvania where he married and served on the 1774 Lord Dunmore campaign. He was an early settler of Kentucky, going there in the spring of 1775 with his wife's uncle, Colonel John Hinkston or Hinkson (see entry). The next year Haggin brought out his family and built a cabin on Hinkston's Fork of the Licking River. Because of Indian hostilities, however, he removed that summer to McClelland's Station (the modern Georgetown). When George Rogers Clark arrived with gunpowder for the Kentucky settlements, Haggin and others transported it from Maysville to Harrodsburg where Haggin removed in early 1777. He had numerous adventures with Indians, was once pursued and disappeared, supposed for over two weeks to have been killed or captured, but later strolled into his cabin with a nonchalant greeting for his wife, and may never have explained what had happened to him. In May 1777 he went to Fort Pitt to take part in a proposed treaty, but it did not take place. In 1778 he participated in Clark's Kaskaskia campaign and the following year in Bowman's operation against the Ohio Indian towns (see John Bowman entry). In 1780 Haggin and his family settled Haggins' Station, near Harrodsburg, becoming a planter and landholder. His wife died June 15, 1821. He left descendants.

Thwaites/Kellogg, *Frontier Defense on the Upper Ohio, 1777-1778.*

Haldimand, Sir Frederick, military officer, administrator (Aug. 11, 1718-June 5, 1791). B. at Yverdon, Switzerland, he early was attracted to military life but there being little opportunity to follow it in his native country, he served as a soldier of fortune in several European armies, seeing considerable action. He joined the British army with rank of lieutenant colonel in 1756, commanding initially the second battalion of the Royal American Regiment, known as the 62nd and later the 60th Infantry. He reached New York in June and served in the French and Indian War, including the unsuccessful attack on Fort Crillon, near Ticonderoga, New York, and other operations within that colony, at times ordering out offensive patrols of Robert Rogers' Rangers. His frontier experience was episodic, but he performed well and came to be considered a very able, intelligent and worthy officer, being promoted to colonel January 8, 1758. In May 1762 he became acting military governor of Three Rivers, Quebec; he served in various capacities in Canada until mid-1765. When his friend, Henry Bouquet (see entry) died at Pensacola, Florida, Haldimand was promoted to Brigadier General to succeed him in command of the Southern Department, which included Florida and as far west as the Mississippi. He served at Pensacola from 1767 to 1773 and during Gage's absence was acting commander-in-chief of British forces in North America from 1773-74. He was recalled to England at the opening of the American Revolution because it was thought preferable to have an officer of English origin in chief command. In 1778 he was sent to Quebec to succeed Guy Carleton as governor and to command the important Northern Department for the British. He was innovative and successful as a governor, his native knowledge of French assisting him in retaining the loyalty of French Canadians when France was aiding the Americans in their revolt. Haldimand did his best to ease the difficulties that the British-American peace

made for the former's Indian allies, who found their ancestral lands cavalierly disposed of by the two principal combatants, despite the very real assistance the Indians had given the British during the conflict. But his efforts were to little avail. He returned to England in 1784. Two years later, still in Britain, he was succeeded as governor of Quebec by Carleton and never returned to America. He was comfortably well off when he died as a Lieutenant General at his birthplace at Yverdon. He never married.

Literature abundant; CE; DCB V, Appendix.

Half King (Scarouady), Oneida chief: *see,* Scarouady

Half King, Wyandot (Huron) chief (d. 1788). The Wyandot Half King should not be confused with the Seneca Half King (see entry). The former was an important chief and headed the element of his people at Upper Sandusky, Ohio. He was known to the Delawares as Pomoacan, but to his own followers as Petawontakas, Dunquad, or some variant of that name. Under British pay, Half King aided the Delawares in resisting the push of white settlements west from the Alleghenies. His intervention in 1777 was credited with saving from possible massacre the Moravians of Lichtenau, on the east side of the Muskingum two miles below Coshocton. According to Bishop George Henry Loskiel, Half King at the head of many Wyandots and other Indians, in addition to some French, the party doubtless enroute to raid settlements south of the Ohio, stopped at Lichtenau and guarded the Moravians against presumably border white ruffians. In September of that year Half King and 40 of his men set out from Ohio to harry the country about Wheeling, in present West Virginia. On the 26th Captain William Foreman with 24 men, Joseph Ogle with 10 and William Linn with 9, left Wheeling's Fort Henry on a scout. They intended crossing the Ohio River at Grave Creek, but they found the Tomlinson settlement (the present Mound City) sacked by Indians and abandoned, the next morning commencing their return to Wheeling. At a defile known as Mechen's (McMahon's) Narrows they were ambushed by Half King; Foreman and 20 men were killed. In May 1778 Half King with British support attacked Fort Randolph at Point Pleasant, West Virginia, but the several days' siege did not accomplish much. In 1781 another expedition was directed against Wheeling. It was headed by Matthew Elliott and included 250 Indians, mostly Wyandots with Half King their leader, but with Delaware Captain Pipe (see entry) and others along. The assemblage paused at Gnadenhutten on the Muskingum August 17 and David Zeisberger, learning of its plans, secretly sent a message to Fort Pitt which raised a frontier-wide alarm, caused the garrison at Wheeling's Fort Henry to prepare itself and the expedition came to nothing. It returned September 2 to Gnadenhutten, thirsting for revenge against the Moravians for alerting the enemy. The town was sacked, the missionaries held as prisoners and released September 6 on their promise to remove their converts from the line of warpaths to the south. September 11 the Moravians moved out, proceeded downriver to the Walhonding, up that stream to arrive at Upper Sandusky October 1. On the 15th they were summoned to Detroit to meet the British commandant De Peyster. They were charged with treason for having thwarted the British/Indian expedition against Wheeling, but were stoutly defended by Half King and Captain Pipe. De Peyster paroled them, they reached Upper Sandusky November 22 and returned to the Muskingum to glean what corn they could from the ravaged fields; while they were there a band of border rangers took them prisoners once more and conveyed them this time to Fort Pitt to be turned over to the American commander, Brigadier General William Irvine. He treated them kindly and released them, many returning to their old villages "to complete their dismal harvesting." Within months their towns were destroyed by David Williamson's ruffianly militia and nearly 100 Christian Indians slaughtered. Half King was a potent factor in the defeat of the Crawford command sent against Upper Sandusky in June 1782, but he knew nothing of the torture-execution of the captured colonel until after the event, being shielded from knowledge of it by the machinations of Captain Pipe and Wingenund lest he prevent it. Under the name of Daunghquat he signed the Treaty of Fort McIntosh, Ohio, January 21, 1785, but his son, Haroenyou, signed the next important treaties: Greenville (1795); Greenville again (1814), and Spring Wells (1815). The signature of "Duquad, or Half King" is attached to the Treaty of Miami Rapids, Ohio (1817), but this must be another Indian since the original Half King is believed to have died in 1788, and nothing is heard of him thereafter.

Alexander Scott Withers, *Chronicles of Border*

Warfare, Cincinnati, Robert Clarke Co., 1895, 1970; Hodge, HAI; Paul A.W. Wallace, *Thirty Thousand Miles With John Heckewelder,* Univ. of Pittsburgh Press, 1958; Charles J. Kappler, *Indian Treaties 1778-1883,* N.Y., Interland Pub. Inc., 1972.

Hall, James (John), militia officer (fl. 1777-1778). Hall, of Rockbridge County, Virginia, was a militia captain. In August 1777 he was a member of a court martial called by Colonel William Fleming (see entry) to decide on a military matter. He was at Fort Randolph at Point Pleasant, West Virginia, in October with his command. On November 10, 1777, Ensign Robert Gilmore, a relative of Hall's, while hunting with a man named Hamilton, was shot and scalped by Indians near the Great Kanawha River mouth, the bloodied body brought to the post by Hall and some of his men. At the post were held as hostages the great Shawnee chief Cornstalk, his son Ellinipsico, the chief Redhawk and still another Shawnee, Chief Petalla, known familiarly as Old Yie, because he had lost one eye. They had visited the post so Cornstalk could inform the soldiers that it was probable he would be forced to join the English in the war with the Americans, and the latter had determined to hold him to prevent that occurrence. Cornstalk was very popular with the American garrison, and was a noble and widely-respected chief of integrity and courage. Captain John Stuart (see entry) warned the commandant, Captain Matthew Arbuckle (see entry) that the unruly Hall militia might seek to take revenge on Cornstalk, but Arbuckle "supposed the[y] would not commit so great an outrage on the innocent who were not accessary to Gilmore's murder." But, continued Stuart in his narrative of the affair, the canoe with Gilmore's body was "scarsely landed...when the cry was raised let us kill the Indians in the fort and every man with his gun in his hand came up the bank pale as death with rage. Capt. Hall was at their head. Captain Arbuckle and myself met them endeavoring to dissuade them from so unjustifyable an action but they cocked their guns threatened us with instant death if we did not desist and rushed into the fort." According to the interpreter's wife who was present, Cornstalk's son "trembled exceedingly," but Cornstalk "told him not to be afraid, for the great Spirit above had sent him there to be killed. The men advanced to the door, the Corn Stalk arose and met them, seven or eight bullets were fired into him, and his son was shot dead as he sat upon a stool. Redhawk made an attempt to go up the chimney but was shot down. The other Indian was shamefully mangled." In a furious letter, Virginia Governor Patrick Henry wrote Colonel Fleming as county lieutenant that "I must tell you Sir that I really blush for the occasion of this War with the Shawanese [that the murders ignited]. I doubt not but you detest the vile assassins who have brought it on us at this critical Time when our whole Force was wanted in another Quarter. But why are they not brought to justice? Shall this Precedent establish the Right of involving Virginia in War whenever any one in the back Country shall please?...Some say the People of your County will not suffer the Apprehension of the Murderers. I desire it may be remembered, that if the frontier people will not submit to the Laws, but thus set them at Defiance, they will not be considered as entitled to the protection of the Government, and were it not for the miserable Condition of many with you, I should demand the Offenders previous to every other Step. For where is this wretched Business to end?" Henry's rage may have been responsible for formally charging the offenders, although the temper of the community was such that conviction for killing Indians was impossible. April 13, 1778, Captain Hall was brought to trial in the Rockbridge County court for the "murder of the Cornstalk Indian, his son and two other chiefs of the Indians on the 10th of November last." Hall denied the charge. The trial was adjourned until April 28 when, no witness appearing against him, he was acquitted. Three other militiamen: Hugh Galbraith, Malcolm McCown, and William Rowan, also were "tried" and acquitted because no witnesses testified against them. No further report has been located on Hall or his three colleagues.

Thwaites/Kellogg, *Frontier Defense on the Upper Ohio, 1777-1778.*

Hamilton, Henry, military officer, governor (c. 1734-Sept. 29, 1796). B. at Dublin it is believed, he was commissioned an ensign in the British 15th Infantry in 1755 and became a lieutenant in 1756. He saw service in the French and Indian War in Canada (being slightly wounded at Louisburg in 1758) and in the Caribbean. In 1766 as a captain he was in command at Crown Point, New York, but as a major in 1775 he sold his commission since, though able, he had no taste for military service. He was appointed lieutenant governor of Detroit in 1775, taking office

November 9, while Edward Abbott became governor of Vincennes, Indiana, and Matthew Johnson governor of Kaskaskia, Illinois. Hamilton was accused by Americans of cruelty in inciting Indians to war against them, and was referred to contemptuously as "the hair buyer," for alleged payments to Indians for white scalps, although proof that he did so is lacking. Historian Milo Milton Quaife believed Hamilton was "a brave and high-minded soldier." He did make payments to Indians for white prisoners brought from the frontier to Detroit, and once sought to purchase for a considerable sum Daniel Boone, captured in Kentucky by Black Fish (see entry) and his Shawnees, but the chief would not turn Boone over. Elizabeth Arthur in the *Dictionary of Canadian Biography* wrote that "as early as 1776 he had apparently proposed employing Indians against the Americans, and in March 1777 he was authorized to assemble as many Indians as possible and to use them in 'making a Diversion and exciting an alarm upon the frontiers of Virginia and Pennsylvania'." In October 1778 Hamilton moved his headquarters from Detroit to Vincennes; the organization of his forces there was faulty, however, and in the subsequent winter George Rogers Clark (see entry) with key assistance from Francis Vigo (see entry), a Spanish subject, took a force of 130 men in 18 days across flooded bottomlands and winter prairies to capture the post February 24, 1779, from Hamilton. Hamilton was ironed and sent off to Virginia. He was held for 18 months, "denied any consideration as a prisoner of war" and frequently treated as "a common criminal." George Washington finally secured his parole and eventual exchange, which Thomas Jefferson, governor of Virginia, had refused to grant. Hamilton returned to England by way of New York. In 1782 he succeeded Sir Frederick Haldiman as governor of Canada, holding office until 1785; he became governor of Bermuda in 1790 and in 1794 governor of Antigua, where he died. He was married and fathered at least one daughter.

Revolution on the Upper Ohio, 1775-1777, ed. by Thwaites/Kellogg, Madison, Wis. Hist. Soc., 1908; *Chronicles of Border Warfare,* by Alexander Scott Withers, Cincinnati, Robert Clarke Co., 1895 (1961); REAW; DCB.

Hamilton, John, frontiersman (d. 1822). He lived in Washington County, Pennsylvania, until the Revolution when he served in the eastern armies until 1777 when he was ordered to Fort

Pitt, serving in the west until his discharge on November 23, 1778. Ten years later he moved to Ohio with Benjamin Stites, or Stiles, and John C. Symmes who were settling in the Miami country. Hamilton became an Indian trader, and died in Ohio.

Thwaites/Kellogg, *Frontier Defense on the Upper Ohio, 1777-1778.*

Hamilton, William, whaler (c. 1643-1746). Hamilton was reported to have been the first citizen of the Cape Cod region to successfully engage in whale killing, but he became so expert "he was obliged to remove from that section of the country, as his fellow-citizens persecuted him for his skill, attributing his success to undue familiarity with evil spirits." He moved to Rhode Island, and from there to Connecticut where he died at an age of 103 years. Alexander Starbuck tended to disbelieve the legend, however, since he found no mention of Hamilton in genealogical records nor elsewhere, nor did he find any court records of the man as a criminal, adding that Cape Cod settlers were "too familiar with fishing to attribute success to aught but skill and natural causes," and noted that the Cape was "more an asylum for the persecuted than the source of persecution." Whaling, he added, "had certainly become a pursuit of much importance in other sections of the country long before [Hamilton] was old enough to handle a harpoon." Yet the tradition of William Hamilton persisted in the Cape Cod region for a long time.

Starbuck, *History of the American Whale Fishery,* Secaucus, N.J., Castle Books, 1989, 7-8.

Hammond, Nathan, military officer (fl. 1773-1779). Hammond first visited Kentucky in 1773, and two years later was a founder of the Boiling Springs settlement; he was a delegate to the Transylvania legislature at Boonesborough. He may have returned up the Ohio River in 1776. He was mentioned as a militia lieutenant in early 1777, later returned to Kentucky and was killed by Indians "before 1780," probably on Hammond Creek in Anderson County.

Thwaites/Kellogg, *The Revolution on the Upper Ohio, 1775-1777,* Madison, Wis. Hist. Soc., 1908.

Hammond, Philip, scout (fl. 1774-1778). Hammond, with John Pryor served well as a scout during the Lord Dunmore War against the Shawnees, indicating considerable previous experience in Indian country, the details unre-

ported, however. He was among the Botetourt County, Virginia, volunteers and may have descended from a prominent Maryland family of that name, among whom the patronymic Philip was common. Hammond and Pryor were sent in September 1774 to warn settlements of southeast Greenbrier County, West Virginia, of the presence of hostile Indians, and passed a camp of the Indians on Meadow River. In 1777 he and Pryor set out from Fort Randolph, at the mouth of the Kanawha River to warn residents again of the proximity of a large party of Indians. "His title to fame," wrote Thwaites, "is his notification to the inhabitants of Donnally's Fort," eight miles north of the present Lewisburg, West Virginia, of the approach of Indians and "his gallant defense of that fort." Little is reported of him thereafter.

Thwaites, *Dunmore;* Thwaites/Kellogg, *Frontier Defense on the Upper Ohio, 1777-1778.*

Hammond, Thomas Clark, military officer (Aug. 19, 1819-Dec. 6, 1846). B. at Fort McHenry, Maryland, he went to West Point and was commissioned July 1, 1842, a brevet second lieutenant of the 2nd Dragoons, transferring to Company K, 1st Dragoons March 6, 1843, and becoming a second lieutenant March 4, 1845. He eloped January 28, 1845, with Mary A. Hughes, daughter of a Platte County, Missouri, judge, and they were married on horseback; their son, Thomas C. Hammond Jr., became a prominent Platte County physician. Hammond senior was with Captain Benjamin Moore's Company K and accompanied Stephen Watts Kearny on the march to California. On the Warner Highlands of southern California it was reported that a large body of enemy was near. Kearny sent Hammond, with a sergeant and 10 men to reconnoiter the night of December 5-6. As they neared huts at San Pasqual they saw a light, two men pushed on to the settlement and saw "a number of men sleeping," and Hammond reported back to Kearny at 2 a.m., saying he had seen the enemy but was not pursued. Kearny immediately mounted his men, many on mules, moved toward the Mexican faction and the engagement of San Pasqual took place, Hammond being killed by a lancer while trying to save Moore who was mortally wounded, also by a lance thrust.

Heitman; Susan Shelby Magoffin, *Down the Santa Fe Trail and Into Chihuahua,* Lincoln, Univ. of Neb. Press, 1982; Bancroft, *California,* V.

Hand, Edward, military officer, politician (Dec.

31, 1744-Sept. 3, 1802). B. in Clyduff, County Kings (Offaly, Leinster) Ireland, he accompanied the 18th Royal Irish Regiment to America as surgeon's mate in July 1767. The regiment eventually was ordered to Fort Pitt, where Hand "made himself popular with all classes." In 1772 he purchased an ensign's commission but when his regiment was ordered east in 1774 he resigned, settling at Lancaster, Pennsylvania, to practice medicine. He married in 1775. On the outbreak of the Revolution he enlisted, then was appointed lieutenant colonel of the 1st Battalion, Pennsylvania riflemen, and became a colonel March 7, 1776. He joined Washington before Boston, was with the Continental Army at Long Island and in the New Jersey campaign. April 1, 1777, he became a Brigadier General and was sent to Fort Pitt as commander-in-chief of the West, remaining until 1778. Henry Hamilton from Detroit was engaged in stirring up the Indians to conduct raids in Pennsylvania and south of the Ohio River. Hand, whose command extended from Kittanning, north of Fort Pitt, to the Great Kanawha of present West Virginia, "determined on an aggressive policy" and in February 1778 commanded a force of 500 men against the Ohio Indians. An open winter with heavy rains prevented the expedition from going beyond Mahoning Creek, a tributary to the Muskingum, and it settled for an attack on a peaceful Delaware village near the present Warren, Ohio, in which one man, a brother of the Delaware chief, Captain Pipe, was killed and Pipe's mother wounded along with numerous other female and children casualties and prisoners. Because of this fiasco the affair became derisively known to Pennsylvania frontiersmen as "the Squaw Campaign." "Hand was a competent officer, but was much pestered at Fort Pitt, with the machinations of tories, who were numerous among the borderers," and later in 1778 he was succeeded in command by Brigadier General Lachlan McIntosh (see entry), Hand having become commander at Albany. In 1779 he had an active role in hostilities thereabout; had his advice been heeded the Walter Butler-Joseph Brant raid of November 11, 1778, on Cherry Valley might have been far less disastrous for the settlers. Hand was active in the affair against the Iroquois at Chemung in August 1779; on August 29 he again was prominent in an action at Newtown also against the Iroquois, and he commanded a brigade throughout Major General John Sullivan's inconclusive campaign against those Indians that summer. In

1780 he became adjutant general of the Continental Army and as such was present at the siege of Yorktown. Following the Revolution he resumed the medical practice at Lancaster. He was brevetted Major General September 30, 1783; was a member of the Continental Congress in 1784-85, became Major General of the Army June 19, 1798, in anticipation of a war with France, which did not materialize, and was honorably discharged June 15, 1800. He died at Rockford, Lancaster County, and was buried in an Episcopal cemetery.

BDAC; Alexander Scott Withers, *Chronicles of Border Warfare,* ed. by Reuben Gold Thwaites, Cincinnati, Robert Clarke Co., 1895, 1970; Thwaites/Kellogg, *Revolution on the Upper Ohio, 1775-1777,* Madison, Wis. Hist. Soc., 1908, p. 256; Barbara Graymont, *The Iroquois in the American Revolution,* Syracuse (N.Y.) Univ. Press, 1972; Paul A.W. Wallace, *Thirty Thousand Miles with John Heckewelder,* Univ. of Pitts. Press, 1958.

Hank and Yank, mule packers: *see* John (Yank) Bartlett; James H. (Hank) Hewitt entries

Hanley, William Danforth, cattleman (Feb. 8, 1861-Sept. 5, 1935). B. at Jacksonville in the Rogue River country of southwestern Oregon on the ranch of his father who specialized in raising quality mules, in 1878 he figured at 17 he was man enough to start out on his own, and with 200 cattle loaned by his father he drove 300 miles to Harney County in eastern Oregon. "Gradually, by dint of perseverance and native business acumen," he established near Burns the Bell A cattle ranch of 10,000 acres and the Double O ranch of 18,000 acres 35 miles southwest of the city; he considered the Bell A his home ranch, and until illness overtook him in 1933 actively managed both spreads. Six years before Hanley had arrived, Pete French, a "disputacious" cattleman, had established a ranch south of Burns and made it into a major kingdom. He was a "short, dark-complexioned autocrat of the range" whose "gunfire encounters with Indians and his even more bitter clashes with homesteaders...constitute dramatic chapters of rimrock lore." Finally homesteader Ed Oliver on December 26, 1897, put a bullet into Pete's brain, being acquitted by a "homesteader jury." With Pete's demise Hanley also came to manage French's P Ranch and temporarily took charge of 195,000 acres in the broad Harney Valley; it is reported that he annually shipped 30,000 to 50,000 head of cattle, after driving them 300 miles to a railhead, and he became known as the last of the great cattle barons in the Northwest. But Hanley also was appreciated for his broad vision and wisdom, for his hearty spirits and kindliness to everything that had life in it. He loved animals and allowed no hunting on his ranches; he was "a cattle king with a heart, a lover of humanity and the land," and he was known as much for his home-spun philosophy as for his friendship with the great. He became a much sought after speaker and raconteur. Hanley's utterances were widely quoted in the Oregon country: "At the end of the day comes night, but it's not night—it's only day resting"; "Maybe if we are all judged by the wrongs we do, knowing they are wrongs, but not for those we do in ignorance, it won't go quite so hard with the white man for what he did to the Indian"; "A bucking horse is like what is generally called a bad boy—has too much life and energy for the use he can make of it. He ain't bad naturally"; "Time is the big grinding machine through which granite is turned to soil, and ignorance to understanding"; "Brains are an awful responsibility. Man's been wobbling around with them ever since it happened"; "A great art of life is the art of giving. A good giver is the master of life." Many prominent people of his day visited at his Bell A ranch: Will Rogers, poet Edwin Markham, Tom Mix, Teddy Roosevelt, Zane Grey, Frederic Remington, Charlie Russell, and on his various trips east he met Woodrow Wilson, William Howard Taft and J. Pierpont Morgan; while on travels to Europe he also visited with the prominent, though never forgetting his Oregon cattleman's roots. Saturday, September 14, 1935, the last day of the Pendleton Round-Up, believed by many to be America's greatest annual rodeo, was "Bill Hanley Day." The full attendance gave him a standing ovation. Early that evening he suffered a stroke and at 3 a.m. Sunday he died, "the happiest man on earth," according to his wife of 43 years, the former Clara Cameron. Hanley also was survived by two sisters and a brother.

Gary Meier, "Bill Hanley, Cattleman Philosopher," *True West*, Vol. 36, No. 5 (May 1989), 50-55; Pendleton *East Oregonian*, Sept. 16, 1935; Portland *Journal*, Apr. 18, 1954; info. from the Oregon Hist. Soc.; Ralph Friedman, *Oregon for the Curious*, Caldwell, Id., Caxton Printers, 1972.

Hanna, Mrs. Robert, frontierwoman (fl. 1773-1783). The wife of Robert Hanna, proprietor, inn-keeper and probable founder of Hannastown, Pennsylvania, northeast of Greensburg a few miles, she was "a woman of ability and character, and much revered in her neighborhood." In July 1782 Indians, reportedly led by John Connolly (see entry), although it seems improbable that he was present in person, sacked the town and "on that occasion she saved the life of Captain Matthew Jack, by her resource and quickness in giving warning." She was captured, taken to Detroit where "she won favor with the Indians and British," was sent east as a prisoner to Montreal, and at the Peace of Paris of September 3, 1783, which formally ended the American Revolution, she was restored to her home. Hannastown was an important station on the road to Pittsburgh, 28 miles to the northwest, and in 1773 it became the seat of the new county of Westmoreland, and was the first seat of justice west of the Alleghenies. From 1774-78 it rivaled Pittsburgh in importance. Following the Indian sack of the place in 1782 it was partially rebuilt and remained the county seat until 1786 though "it never regained its earlier importance," and today is a town of under 500 population.

Thwaites/Kellogg, *Frontier Defense on the Upper Ohio, 1777-1778.*

Harpes, The Terrible, desperadoes (c. 1768-1804). (William) Micajah (Big) Harpe and his brother, Wiley (Little) Harpe were b. in North Carolina where their father was a Loyalist, Big Harpe in 1768 and Little Harpe in 1770. The brothers in 1795 made their way to Tennessee, living among the Cherokees for a time, then tried farming near Knoxville, and gradually veered into robbery and then wholesale murder. Some believed that "their tawny appearance and dark curly hair betrayed a tinge of African blood," though others did not accept this. Two sisters, Susan and Betsy Roberts, came west with them and at Knoxville Little Harpe added a third by wedding Betsy Rice, her preacher father performing the ceremony. "All three women seemed available to both men—and all seemed perpetually pregnant." The Harpes, who had been suspected of hog stealing and other petty crimes, now began to leave corpses behind them, when they did not dispose of the bodies by ripping out the entrails, loading the carcasses with stones or sand before dropping them into deep rivers. Once they lived in a cavern that might have been Mammoth Cave, Kentucky. Their murder toll grew steadily. Wellman adds up the score of Big Harpe (with plenty of help from Little Harpe) at 39, listing the names and other details, and those were only the ones "*of whom there was some record.* Nobody knows if even these were all. There probably were more, for the Harpes must have participated in murders while waylaying flatboats…and there almost certainly were others, slain in their various 'raids,' whose bodies were never found in that primitive country." The Harpes at length joined the gang of Samuel Mason (see entry) at Cave-in-the-Rock south of Shawneetown, Illinois, preying upon passing boatmen as notorious river pirates. But their savagery was too much even for other desperadoes, who ran them out after a particularly atrocious torture murder. Shortly afterward Big Harpe tomahawked a fellow lodger for snoring too loudly, then descended the loft ladder and for good measure killed the woman of the cabin and her baby. Little Harpe disappeared into the forest, but a posse ran down Big Harpe and the husband of the woman he had killed fired a bullet into his spine. He was "too slow" in dying, and the widower commenced sawing off his head with a dull butcher knife. It was a job that seemed to Harpe tedious and he reportedly snarled, "You're a God Damned rough butcher, but cut on and be damned!" The avenger at last cut around the neck to the bone, then twisted off the head "as he might have done in slaughtering a hog." Big Harpe's head was nailed to a fork in a tree near the present Henderson, Kentucky, where it was viewed over the years by travelers, reminded of the trail of blood Big Harpe and Little Harpe had sown. Wiley Harpe continued the course of horror he had forged with his older brother and worked his way down the Mississippi, perpetrating murders, mutilations and bloody crimes along the Natchez Trace and in continuing piracy on the lower river. He again operated with Mason and in January 1803 Mason and Harpe, with others, were arrested by Spanish authorities from the west bank of the river near New Madrid, Missouri. The Spanish concluded that the Mason/Harpe crimes had been committed on the other bank of the stream, not under Spanish jurisdiction, and the desperadoes were turned over to American authorities at Natchez. Enroute there, Mason on March 26 killed the Spanish commander of the boat, and with his outlaw party escaped. Rewards were offered for him, large enough that Little Harpe killed Mason and brought in his head. Rather than being paid, he and his companion were recognized for the out-

laws they were and hanged February 8, 1804, at Old Greenville, Mississippi. Harpe's head was put on a pole north of Greenville and the head of his companion in crime, James Mays, lofted atop another pole south of town to remain in view of passers-by for a long time to come.

Paul I. Wellman, *Spawn of Evil,* Garden City, N.Y., Doubleday & Co., 1964; Otto A. Rothert, *Outlaws of Cave-in Rock,* Cleveland, Arthur H. Clark Co., 1924; Jonathan Daniels, *The Devil's Backbone: The Story of the Natchez Trace,* N.Y., McGraw-Hill Book Co., 1962; James D. Horan and Paul Sann, *Pictorial History of the Wild West,* N.Y., Crown Pub., 1954; info. from E.F. (Ted) Mains.

Harriman, Edward Henry, railroad financier (Feb. 20, 1848-Sept. 9, 1909). B. at Hempstead, Long Island, he was the son of an Episcopal clergyman, commenced working on Wall Street at 14, at length married Mary Averell, daughter of a banker and railroad president, eventually entered railroad management and financing and became a foremost capitalist. His business career is covered in many reference works; he belongs in this collection because in the summer of 1899 he organized, headed and financed an "expedition" to Alaska, then in a gold rush frenzy, being converted from a remote frontier into a phase of "development" that would forever change its quality and culture. Harriman's expedition broke no new ground and for him was more an amusement cruise than otherwise, undertaken to satisfy a physician's advice that for his health he embark upon a lengthy vacation from his intense business activity. His 126-member party included 25 scientists or luminaries, among them C. Hart Merriam, head of the Biological Survey; George Bird Grinnell, Indian life student and conservationist; John Muir, conservationist and writer; Edward S. Curtis, photographer; Grove Karl Gilbert, geologist and glaciologist; William H. Dall, paleontologist and Alaska specialist; Albert K. Fisher and Louis Agassiz Fuertes, ornithologists; Frederick S. Dellenbaugh, explorer, artist and writer, and John Burroughs, nature writer. The expedition left Seattle aboard a chartered steamer, the *George W. Elder,* May 31, 1899, and returned July 30. It had traveled up the Alaskan panhandle, visiting Ketchikan, Wrangell, Juneau, Skagway, Sitka, Glacier Bay and Yakutat. It continued by way of Prince William Sound, Kodiak Island, where Harriman managed to kill a smallish Alaskan brown bear while Yellowstone Kelly, guide and one-time army scout, shot its cub lest it starve. The party journeyed on to the Shumagin Islands and Unalaska of the Aleutian chain, crossed the Bering Sea by way of Bogoslov Island to Plover Bay, Siberia, then across Bering Strait to Port Clarence (Harriman was rumored to be contemplating a possible tunnel under Bering Strait for a railroad to link up with the Trans Siberian and create eventually a line tying together the Old World and the New. Nothing came of this idea, which had been held by others before him as, for example, by John Healy). With stops at St. Lawrence Island, the Pribylovs and back along the Alaska underside, more or less retracing the outbound course, the expedition grandly returned to Seattle after, one report said, some 9,000 miles of leisurely travel, counting the various side trips for scientific or amusement purposes. A historian concluded that "the Harriman Expedition was more than a rich man's junket," but it was not much more. "All the scientists involved recognized that [it] was a reconnaissance rather than a comprehensive or definitive survey," although it had elements of a "serious scientific venture." Harriman gave the specialists every opportunity to carry on their researches, but the time was far too short, and their fieldwork too brief to result in novel discoveries or much major work. Thirteen volumes of the *Harriman Alaska Series* or scientific *Reports* were published at the financier's expense, some of them posthumously, although two additional planned volumes never appeared. The publications were the major scientific legacy of the adventure, varying in quality as in depth although never entirely without merit. Gilbert's Volume III, *Glaciers and Glaciation,* incorporating important theories backed or inspired by his Alaskan observations and studies, was perhaps of most permanent value. Many of the returned wildlife and other specimens found their way into museum collections with the results published eventually, so that on the whole it was not a scientifically unproductive two months.

William H. Goetzmann, Kay Sloan, *Looking Far North: The Harriman Expedition to Alaska, 1899,* Princeton, N.J., Princeton Univ. Press, 1982.

Harris, John, trader, frontiersman (1726-July 29, 1791). The founder of Harrisburg, Pennsylvania, Harris was b. at Harris Ferry near Paxtang and the Susquehanna River where his father had opened a trading post, acquired considerable land and established a ferry as an added business.

The father died in 1748 and young John Harris took over. He was for 30 years a trader, frontiersman and occasionally an officer in the militia. He frequently urged greater protection for the frontier against Indian raids, warning that sparse white settlements were endangered by lack of military protection. During the French and Indian War he stockaded his home, recruited men and held out, sometimes inviting conferences with Indians at his headquarters; at one on April 1, 1757, a large Iroquois delegation attended. He was firm with Indians, but held their respect and Indians trusted his business dealings with them. In 1766 Harris built a "fine residence" on his property and planned to lay out a town in 1775, but the Revolution intervened. In 1785 Dauphin County was organized with Harrisburg its county seat. Harris lived there the remainer of his life as an influential and progressive settler although he probably never envisioned its becoming the capital of the state which it did in 1812. "A lover of his gun, rod, and dog, he was very much a part of the back-country in which he lived." He was married.

DAB.

Harrison, Henry, Jesuit missionary (fl. c. 1684-1689). He, the Reverend Thomas Harvey and the Reverend Charles Gage were brought to America by New York governor Thomas Dongan with a view to extending English influence among the Iroquois as opposed to that of French Jesuits. The three were to establish a village of Catholic Indians, act as chaplains for the governor, and maintain a Latin school which was to become a Jesuit college in New York. A revolution in England and usurpation of the New York government by Jacob Leisler in December 1689 drove the Jesuits from the colony.

Thwaites, JR LXVI, 280-81 n33.

Harrod, James, frontiersman (1742-July 1793). B. at Big Cove in today's Bedford County, Pennsylvania, the family narrowly escaped the raid of the Delaware war chief Shingas (see entry) in Novemer 1755, by fleeing to Fort Littleton in Fulton County. At 16 James, with his older brother William, saw service as a private on Brigadier General John Forbes' 1758 operation in the French and Indian War and "very likely saw further service" during that conflict. Another brother, Samuel, in 1767 accompanied Michael Stoner on the noted expedition and hunting excursion down the Ohio River and into Kentucky. James and William in 1772 settled on Ten Mile Creek, a tributary of the Monongahela and the next year James and others explored into Kentucky, returning by way of the Greenbrier River. With 41 companions James in 1774 was surveying the site of Harrodsburg, southwest of the present Lexington, Kentucky, when Daniel Boone and Stoner warned them of rising Indian hostility, which would culminate later in the year in Lord Dunmore's War. Harrod prudently withdrew to the Holston River between Virginia and Tennessee; he joined the regiment of William Christian (see entry), but it arrived at Point Pleasant after the October 10 climactic engagement against the Shawnees concluded. Harrod revived his Harrodsburg settlement, March 18, 1775, a fortnight before Boonesborough was founded, thus becoming the initial permanent white settlement of Kentucky. In 1779 he commanded a company on John Bowman's (see entry) campaign against the Chillicothe, Ohio, Shawnee community, and that year he also was elected to the Virginia legislature, Kentucky being still a part of that state. Harrod was a captain with George Rogers Clark's 1,000-man Kentucky force which laid waste Ohio Shawnee communities in retaliation for Henry Bird's earlier raids on settlements below the Ohio. Offered a promotion to major, Harrod declined and served as a private on Clark's 1782 successful operation against Indians on the Great Miami River. By now one of the most prominent Kentucky frontiersmen, Harrod was chosen a member of the December 1784 political convention at Danville, ten miles south of Harrodsburg. Having recently made out his will, Harrod set out in February 1792 from Washington, Kentucky, with two men, purportedly seeking Swift's Silver Mine, a rumored and probably fictitious discovery supposed to exist near Three Forks, east of the present Bowling Green. Harrod was never heard from again. His widow, Ann, was convinced that a man named Bridges, one of Harrod's traveling companions and an individual with whom he was engaged in a lawsuit over a property matter, had murdered him. In addition to Ann, Harrod left a daughter and a considerable estate. "Though unlettered, [he] was a man of fine presence and many sterling qualities, and made a strong impression on his generation," wrote Thwaites. "He [was] remembered in Kentucky as one of the worthiest pioneers of that state."

Alexander Scott Withers, *Chronicles of Border Warfare*, ed. by Reuben Gold Thwaites, Cincinnati,

Robert Clarke Co., 1895, 1970; Thomas D. Clark article in REAW; DAB; Thwaites, *Dunmore;* info. from E.F. (Ted) Mains.

Harrod, William, frontiersman (1737-1801). B. at Big Cove, Bedford County, Pennsylvania, he was an older brother of James who founded Harrodsburg, Kentucky. William served under John Forbes in 1758 on the expedition to take over the ruins of the French Fort Duquesne which, after rebuilding, became Fort Pitt at Pittsburgh. About 1772 Harrod settled on Ten Mile Creek, a tributary of the Monongahela River. Commissioned a captain he was commissary (quartermaster) during the 1774 Lord Dunmore's War against the Shawnees. He joined his brother James at Harrodsburg in 1775 and in 1777, though retaining his home in Pennsylvania where a captain's commission again was granted him, he organized a company in 1778 for the Illinois expedition of George Rogers Clark, joined it at the Falls of the Ohio (Louisville), and served throughout the campaign. The next year he joined John Bowman's expedition against the Ohio Indians and in 1780 still served in that region.

Thwaites, *Dunmore.*

Hart, Pearl, bandit (1871-Dec. 30, 1955?). B. according to one source at Petersborough, Ontario, or by her own statement at Lindsay, 20 miles to the west, her parents took her to Toronto. She said she eloped at 16 but her husband abused her and the marriage did not last. She reportedly arrived at Phoenix, Arizona, in 1892 "with a dancehall musician and tin-horn gambler named [or called] Dan Bandman." When he went away to the Spanish American War, Pearl moved to Globe, an Arizona mining camp, where she took up with a self-styled German named Joe Boot. Needing money, she and Boot on May 29, 1899, held up a stagecoach driven by Henry Bacon on the run between Globe and Florence, taking $421 from the three passengers and giving back $1 to each for "something to eat." Sheriff W.E. Truman of Pinal County easily followed the bandit trail and arrested the pair June 4, 20 miles north of Benson. Boot was jailed at Florence and for lack of accommodations for a woman Pearl was housed at Tucson, from which jail she promptly escaped, with some male help. Noted lawman George Scarborough (see entry) recognized her at Deming, New Mexico, some time later, arrested and returned her to Tucson. She and Boot were tried at Florence, he getting 30 years and she five; Boot later was made a trusty, walked off and was never retaken. Pearl Hart, the only woman at the Yuma jail, became pregnant and to save the Territory embarrassment Governor Alexander O. Brodie pardoned her December 19, 1902. The prison gates closed behind her, she got on a train and rode into folklore. It was said she appeared briefly on the Orpheum vaudeville circuit but she wasn't much of an attraction and that employment didn't last; it also was reported that she toured briefly with Buffalo Bill's Wild West Show, though Don Russell's exhaustive *Lives and Legends of Buffalo Bill* makes no mention of her, nor do other sources consulted. The most probable theory of her later life, as expounded by Clara T. Woody, was that Pearl married Calvin Bywater of Dripping Springs Ranch at Cane Springs between Globe and Florence; Mrs. Woody in her courthouse duties signed the marriage certificate as a witness, reporting that the bride called herself Pearl Bywater initially, although later she always referred to herself simply as Mrs. Cal Bywater; Clara Woody called on her twice, in 1940 and 1949 in the course of census-taking duties. Jess G. Hayes, who also believed Mrs. Bywater may have been Pearl Hart, wrote that she died December 30, 1955, and described her as "soft-spoken, kind, and a good citizen in all respects." And historian Leland Sonnichsen, who wrote the Pearl Hart segment of Mrs. Woody's book (although anonymously) concluded that, "it will do you no harm to believe that she came back to the Globe vicinity and lived a good life, beloved by all who knew her." Historian Bert Fireman, however, who did much research on her life, was less generous: "There is *no* evidence," to round out her story factually, he concluded.

Clara T. Woody, Milton L. Schwartz, *Globe, Arizona*, Tucson, Ariz. Hist. Soc., 1977, 221-38; Jess G. Hayes, *Boots and Bullets: The Life and Times of John W. Wentworth*, Tucson, Univ. of Ariz. Press, 1967, p. 134; Konrad F. Schreier Jr., "Pearl Hart—More Sad Case Than Hard Case," *True West*, Vol. 30, No. 4 (Apr. 1983), 52-54.

Harvey, Thomas, Jesuit missionary (fl. 1683-c. 1695). He was one of three English Jesuits brought to America by New York governor Thomas Dongan (see entry) in 1683 and later. The intent was to counteract the work of the French Jesuits among the Iroquois, and to form a village of Catholic Indians under English influence. They also were chaplains to the governor and were to maintain a school intended to become a Jesuit college at New York City. The revolution in England canceled out these plans and the Jesuits were driven from the colony, though Harvey returned c. 1690, continued his mission for several years until his health failed, compelling him to retire to Catholic Maryland "where he soon afterward died."

Thwaites, JR, LXIV, 280-81n33.

Hassell, Benjamin, frontiersman (b. Aug. 9, 1701). Hassell, b. at Dunstable, New Hampshire (today's Nashua), was the son of Joseph Hassell, brother of Anna Hassell Lovewell, so that Benjamin was a cousin of John Lovewell of border fame. He was a member of the 46-man Indian-hunting party Lovewell took north from Dunstable April 16, 1725 (see Lovewell entry for narrative of expedition). When Lovewell built the rude fort at Lake Ossipee he left ten men to garrison it and took the remaining party, including Hassell, to the vicinity of today's Fryeburg, Maine, where on May 8 a fierce engagement with the Pequawket Indians ensued. At its outset Hassell in uncontrollable terror fled the scene, regained the Lake Ossipee fort "and to excuse his flight told so frightful a story of the fate of his comrades that his hearers [the fort's garrison] were seized with a panic, shamefully abandoned their post, and set out for the settlements, leaving a writing on a piece of birch-bark to the effect that all the rest were killed." The panic-driven band reached Dunstable on May 11. The Massachusetts governor, Samuel Shute, ordered a Colonel Tyng of the militia, then at Dunstable, to hurry to the scene of the fight, succor the wounded if there were any yet alive, and attack the Indians "if he could find them." Tyng called upon Hassell to go with him as guide, but Hassell had had enough of Indians and pleaded illness, while one who had been in the fight and returned from it agreed to guide Tyng back to the scene.

Parkman, *Half Century of Conflict*, I; Samuel Penhallow, *History of the Indian Wars,* 1726 (Williamstown, Mass., Corner House Pub., 1973); Sylvester, III.

Hastings, Theophilus, military officer, Indian agent (fl. 1711-1725). Although deeply involved in putting down Tuscarora unrest to the north, South Carolina in 1711 found itself greatly alarmed by reported French efforts to forge an alliance between Choctaws and Chickasaws in furtherance of its own expansionist desires. It determined upon prosecution of its Indian trade to the West and "a vigorous renewal of the partizan warfare which was the characteristic method of the Carolinian advance." Thus in May 1711 the traditional Choctaw-Chickasaw feuding was reinvigorated due to British instigation, as the French were convinced, and in June the Carolina assembly approved an expedition "intended to ruin the great Choctaw nation utterly, and so destroy the bulwark of Louisiana." Commissions to further this aim were issued to Militia Captain Theophilus Hastings, who was to lead the Creeks, and to Emperor Brims (see entry), the leader of the Lower Creeks with base at Coweta, present Alabama. Thomas Welch was to captain a supporting body of Chickasaws. By fall Hastings had mustered 1,300 Creeks, of whom 300 were bowmen, the rest bearing firearms. Led by Hastings and Brims this army ravaged Choctaw towns, burning, killing and taking prisoners. About 400 houses and plantations were torched, but the Choctaws had not been surprised, put up only a feeble resistance and most escaped the assailants. Hastings killed 80 and captured 130 prisoners, while Welch, with only 200 Chickasaws did about the same amount of damage. The expedition was successful from the English standpoint, but Bienville (see entry) managed to weather it and reinstitute the Indian bulwarks for Louisiana defense, so in the end nothing was gained for the British. South Carolina's attention now turned more sharply to the north where the Tuscaroras were in open hostility, and Hastings was among the officers of an expedition headed by James Moore, son of the combative former governor of South Carolina. Indians were recruited from the Creek, Cherokee and Catawba tribes. The expedition marched north along the traders' path, having to forage for supplies to the point they became "almost as dreaded as the Tuscaroras." March 20, 1713, the invaders stormed the Indian fort of Nooherooka (Necheroka or Nahucke) in the present Greene County near Snow Hill. The siege lasted from March 20 to 23. Moore reported that 392 prisoners were taken, 192 scalps secured, 200 Indians were killed or burned in the fort, and 166 killed or captured outside for a total hostile loss of 950. The South Carolinans lost 22 killed and 36 wounded, while their Indian allies had 35 killed and 58 wounded. The prisoners were taken to South Carolina and sold as slaves. In 1715 Hastings, by now a militia colonel, joined Maurice Moore, another veteran Indian fighter from South Carolina in the subju-

gation of the Cheraw (Saraw) and other piedmont hostiles; each white officer had a company of 50 men in addition to 60 North Carolina Indian auxiliaries. By 1716 the Yamasee War to the south had ended, hostility in North Carolina was abated and Hastings apparently commanded the last of the organized troops. He became a chief factor among the Cherokees until "his talents were requisitioned for the difficult business of negotiating peace and trade with the Creeks." Originally it had been planned for him to remain among the Cherokees "on a pretence of trade but actually in the capacity of intelligence officer and diplomat." For several years Hastings was involved in business matters concerning the Indian trade. In view of his services in 1717 in opening relations with the Creeks, Hastings was retained as chief factor among them. That position was soon abolished when, from 1721 to 1725, he continued to reside among the tribesmen "in the double character of a private trader and an Indian agent." When the positions of "trader-agents" were discontinued he was discharged, as were others of his specialities. No further word on Hastings has been discovered.

Verner W. Crane, *The Southern Frontier 1670-1732,* Ann Arbor, Univ. of Michigan Press, 1929/56; Douglas L. Rights, *The American Indian in North Carolina,* Winston-Salem, John F. Blair, 1957.

Hay, Jehu (John), military officer, Indian official (d. Aug. 2, 1785). B. at Chester, Pennsylvania, in 1758 he was commissioned an ensign in the 60th (Royal) American Regiment stationed at Fort Niagara, becoming adjutant, and in 1762 was promoted to lieutenant. He was sent to Detroit with Henry Gladwin, was active in defense of the fort against Pontiac in 1763 and "his diary is a major source for the history of this episode." He became fort major in 1764 and in 1766 was made Indian commissary; in 1776 he was appointed deputy Indian agent and a major of the Detroit militia. Hay and Hamilton (see entry) became close friends and Hay was important in Hamilton's expediton to retake Vincennes, Indiana, in late 1778, leading the advance party which occupied the post. When George Rogers Clark recaptured Vincennes in February 1779, Hay participated in negotiations for its surrender. With Hamilton, Hay was taken prisoner and sent to Virginia, Jefferson refusing to release them under parole until October 10, 1780, when the two returned to England by way of New York. In June 1782 Hay was again at

Quebec and was appointed lieutenant governor of Detroit, succeeding Arent De Peyster. He reached Detroit July 12, 1784; his administration was an unpopular one, Hay's health deteriorated and he died little more than a year later.

Thwaites/Kellogg, *The Revolution on the Upper Ohio, 1775-1777*, Madison, Wis. Hist. Soc., 1908; DCB, IV.

Haycox, Ernest, writer (Oct. 1, 1899-Oct. 13, 1950). B. at Portland, Oregon, he entered military service with the Oregon National Guard in 1915 and participated in the Pershing expedition into Mexico in pursuit of Pancho Villa; he served in France from 1917 to 1919. Returning to Portland he studied at Reed College and was graduated from the University of Oregon in 1923, receiving a doctor of letters degree from Lewis and Clark College of Portland in 1946. He had studied journalism in college and while a police reporter for the Portland *Oregonian* papered a wall of the editorial office with rejection slips. His writing finally caught on, he quit the paper, went to New York and "nearly starved out" before returning to Oregon. An editor of pulp magazines urged him to "master the technique of the western," which he did consummately, making his home at Portland from 1926 and "influencing a generation of popular writers." Among the authors in generous praise of his products were Bernard DeVoto, Luke Short (Frederick Glidden) and Frank Gruber. Haycox's first book was *Free Grass* (1929) and among his 20 other novels and important short stories were *Bugles in the Afternoon* (1944), a Custer story; "Trouble Shooter," in *Collier's* magazine (1936) from which came the motion picture, *Union Pacific;* "The Stage to Lordsburg," *Collier's,* from which came the memorable film, *Stagecoach,* and his ambitious and successful, *The Earthbreakers* (1952). In the latter "he used universal themes convincingly, treated the settlers' experience realistically, and developed protagonists that were complete human beings rather than stereotypes, [in it] producing not just another western but rather a novel of the West." He worked on the screen stories for several pictures in addition to those mentioned, including *Apache Trail, Abilene Town,* and *Canyon Passage.* Haycox was married and fathered a daughter and a son.

Who Was Who; REAW; info. from E.F. (Ted) Mains.

Hayes, Charles Willard, geologist (1859-1916). A Geological Survey scientist from 1887 to 1911, he accompanied an expedition of Lieutenant Frederick Schwatka, organized by a newspaper syndicate, to explore the region between Lynn Canal, in the Alaska Panhandle, and the Copper River. The route followed up Taku Inlet, down the Tetlin and Lewes rivers, up the White River and over Skolai Pass in the Wrangell Mountains, then down the Chitina and Copper rivers. Hayes made the first classification of Alaskan physiographic provinces.

Orth, 15, 411-12.

Hayes. Jess G., historical writer (Aug. 25, 1901-Aug. 6, 1968). B. at the mining camp of Globe, Arizona, he was a school teacher from 1928 until 1940 when he was elected Gila County school superintendent, a position he held until his death, which also occurred at Globe. Hayes became interested in records relating to the Apache Kid (see entry), and grew accustomed to rummaging through old files at the county courthouse, which he made his second home. His book *Apache Vengeance,* a biography of the Kid, was published in 1954 by the University of New Mexico Press, and was well received. Hayes also wrote, "*...And Then There Were None...,*" which he described as "a long-buried chapter in Apache history" and published privately in 1965; *Boots and Bullets: The Life and Times of John W. Wentworth* (1967), the biography of an attorney and Gila County Superior Court official, and *Sheriff Thompson's Day—Turbulence in the Arizona Territory* (published posthumously in 1968). The Wentworth and Thompson books were both brought out by the University of Arizona Press. Hayes was a friendly, cooperative man, generous with the results of his historical researches, and had a wide acquaintanceship among historians and writers interested in Gila County history; among these was Erle Stanley Gardner, famed mystery writer. Hayes collapsed and died minutes after addressing a Democratic rally at Globe, leaving his widow, two sons and two daughters.

Author's file on Hayes; *Phoenix Gazette,* Aug. 7, 1968.

Heath (Heith), John, outlaw (c. 1853-Feb. 22, 1884). B. in Texas, he lived at Bisbee for several days before the bloody "massacre" associated with a robbery December 8, 1883, of the Joseph Goldwater-A.A. Casteñeda general store; Heath apparently masterminded the attempt. He was rumored to have taken part in previous train robberies with James (Tex) Howard, one of the gunmen. But he was unknown to law officers who were organizing a pursuit, and volunteered to lead them on a horseback hunt for the desperadoes since, he explained, he was skilled at such endeavors and knew the country; instead he led the posse on a wild-goose chase until all traces of the fleeing robbers had been obscured by time and traffic. Nearby ranchers confirmed that Heath earlier had been with five gunmen when planning the operation. Heath was tried separately since he had taken no physical part in the crime, was found guilty of second degree murder and given life imprisonment, while the other five were executed. A Bisbee crowd, displeased with the verdict, stormed the Tombstone jail, extracted Heath and lynched him from a telegraph pole three blocks away. Dr. George E. Goodfellow (see entry) gave the opinion of the coroner's jury that Heath "came to his death from emphysema of the lungs which might have been and probably was caused by strangulation, self-inflicted or otherwise."

Ben T. Traywick, *The Hangings in Tombstone,* Tombstone, Red Marie's Bookstore, 1991; Robert E. Ladd, *Eight Ropes to Eternity,* pub. by *Tombstone Epitaph,* 1965; A.D. LeBaron, "Bisbee's Five Black Ghosts," *True West,* Vol. 7, No. 6 (July-Aug. 1960), 12-14, 56-57.

Hegg, Eric A., photographer (Sept. 17, 1867-Dec. 13, 1947). B. at Bollnas, Sweden, 150 miles north of Stockholm and 25 miles inland from the Gulf of Bothnia coast city of Soderhamm, Hegg became an expert photographer and during many years in the sub-Arctic took an estimated 4,000 pictures that survived largely by chance and today form the finest pictorial history of the great Alaska Gold Rush late in the 19th century. The stampede commenced when George Washington Carmack (see entry) or others discovered nugget-sized gold August 17, 1896, on Rabbit (later renamed Bonanza) Creek, a tributary of the Klondike River, Yukon Territory. By 1897 the flood was in full swing. Eric Hegg, then 29, had two photographic studios on Bellingham Bay, Washington, and he was entranced with the discovery in the Far North—not because of the gold itself, but for photographic possibilities. He turned control of his studios over to his brother, Peter, went to Seattle, joined others in chartering a boat, the *Skagit Chief.* Hegg photographed everything the turn of the paddle-wheel brought into view, from embarkation to landing at Dyea, three miles from Skagway. He photographed the

mountainous difficulties faced, and usually overcome, by hopeful prospectors getting ashore with their equipment, Hegg himself having tons of photographic essentials, including his countless glass negatives. Dyea, a year earlier a village of 250, by late 1897 was a boomtown of 3,000 to 10,000—nobody knew for sure. Hegg decided to spend the winter in Dyea because he knew he could not reach Dawson before the weather closed in. He set up a shop to make and develop pictures for sale to miners and other adventurers. He photographed the endless linkup of miners scaling Chilkoot pass, the picture reproduced around the world, and he also covered a rescue operation for scores trapped in a spring avalanche, at least 63 miners perishing. Hegg was soon joined at Dyea by his brother, Peter, and W.B. Anderson, also of Whatcom County, Washington; Anderson and Pete Hegg would cross the mountains early to Lake Bennett and build boats for the river run to the Yukon, while Eric Hegg remained behind to earn money taking and selling pictures. He joined the others in May; they already had constructed two sturdy boats. When the ice broke on the 29th the Hegg party started down the river heading north. They ran the rapids, and Hegg photographed others doing the same, some successfully, some not. They reached Dawson intact in July of 1898 where 40,000 men had discovered that the era of discovery was all but over, although rumors and rushes still occurred, and exploitation and development was the order of the day. Hegg continued to picture everything. He set up a studio in a cabin with log walls and a tent roof that he soon boarded over, and he remained in and out of Dawson for three years. "He pictured celebrations and fires; he photographed the official thermometer stuck at minus sixty-eight one January, and the townsfolk at work under the midnight sun in June; he aimed his camera at laundresses and society women, at dance-hall girls and the dreary whores in 'cribs' outside the town." He also made many trips to the goldfields; he undertook a few visits to Skagway and one "outside," during which he went to New York City, where he caused a carriage jam when he exhibited his pictures of the climb over Chilkoot Pass. In all he spent 20 years in the Yukon and in Alaska, having studios in Skagway, Dawson, Cordova, Nome and other centers. Hegg never turned prospector. He had come for pictures, not gold, and he made gold out of his art. "Lugging his bulky camera, improvising chemicals from herbs and egg whites to sensitize his unwieldy glass plates, working with a minimum of sunlight and often in ferocious temperatures, Hegg still managed to record with beauty and detail the whole astonishing spectacle of men searching for gold." His plates survived only by chance—or miracle. He had to cache his heavy negatives at various places. Many were stored in the walls of a Dawson house, to be found by a later resident who planned to use the glass for a greenhouse, the negatives saved only because no one could figure how to get the "grey stuff" off the glass. Gradually the prints and negatives known to exist were gathered by the University of Washington Special Collections Library, where they reside today. Hegg meanwhile had returned to Bellingham, reopening a studio where he worked until in his late 70s. About June 1946 he retired and moved to San Diego, California, to live near his son, Roy E. Hegg. He died there at the age of 80, never knowing what had become of his immense photographic legacy which forms an invaluable portraiture of one of the great gold stampedes of American history. He was married, his wife predeceasing him.

Info. from Richard H. Engeman, photographics and graphics librarian, Special Collections, Univ. of Wash. Lib.; *Bellingham* (Washington) *Herald*, Dec. 26, 1950; Murray Morgan (photos by Eric Hegg), "Off to the Klondike!" *American Heritage*, Vol. XVIII, No. 5 (Aug. 1967) 34-49, 107-11; Morgan, *One Man's Gold Rush: A Klondike Album*, Seattle, Univ. of Wash. Press, 1967; Hegg death cert.

Helm, John Turner Jr., pioneer (May 9, 1910-Aug. 28, 1988). Born in the Warner Highlands of southern California, he was the grandson of (Harmon) Turner Helm, a cousin of the notorious Boone Helm (see entries). John T. Helm was well versed in the history of the Helm clan, particularly their years spent in the Warner Highlands region where they had countless adventures in and out of the law. Helm was generous with his information, giving much help to various researchers, and he was regarded as an extraordinarily reliable source of information. He died at San Diego, mainly, according to his daughter, of moroseness over the death of his wife of 53 years, whose decease preceded his own by one year, one month and four days. Both he and his wife were cremated, their ashes mixed and buried in San Felipe Creek Canyon, under a huge oak tree with no headstone and only the tree and an adjacent granite boulder marking the spot.

Information from Johnna Theresa Helm, daughter, Nov. 2, 1989.

Henderson, Richard, expansionist (Apr. 20, 1735-Jan. 30, 1785). B. in Hanover County, Virginia, he was raised in North Carolina from 1745 and became a lawyer; in 1767 he became an associate justice of the Superior Court, serving for six years. He had heard repeatedly of the exploits of Daniel Boone, and of Boone's reports of the fertility and beauty of Kentucky. Late in 1774 Henderson and Nathaniel Hart visited the Cherokees, nominally claimants of the region of Kentucky, to see whether they would sell the area, which they agreed to do, probably since their right to it was imperfect at best. The agreement called for the two sides to meet at Sycamore Shoals on Watauga River. When the necessary trade goods were forwarded to the Watauga, Boone was sent to collect the Indians and the council opened March 14, 1775, with 1,200 Indians assembled. March 17 the "great grant" deed was signed, providing for sale of the land between the Kentucky and Cumberland rivers as far north as the Ohio. "The Indians were conscious that they had sold what did not belong to them; and Dragging Canoe and other chiefs were outspoken in their opinion that the whites would have difficulty in settling the tract." They also were dissatisfied with the amount of the 10,000 pounds sterling worth of goods for the sale; the total, when divided among so many, allotted trivial amounts to each. Governors Josiah Martin of North Carolina and Lord Dunmore of Virginia formally opposed the purchase as illegal by reason of royal proclamation, but those who had taken part in the treaty, including such noted borderers as Boone, James Robertson, John Sevier, Isaac Shelby and others, "were heedless of such proclamations, and eager to become settlers under the company's liberal offer made to them." Boone at once left for Kentucky, blazing a trail over Cumberland Gap and across the river to the banks of the Kentucky where "after a running fight with the Indians" they arrived April 1 and founded Boonesborough. Henderson, with 30 men bringing wagons and supplies, arrived April 20, Nathaniel Hart accompanying him. May 23 met there the new Legislature of Transylvania consisting of 18 deputies from four frontier posts, all established at about the same time: Boonesborough itself, Harrodsburg, Boiling Springs and Logan's Station (or St. Asaph's). It was the first legislative assembly held in the Mississippi Valley. Virginia and North Carolina did not approve an independent government in Kentucky, and annulled the title of the Henderson company, though Virginia in 1795 granted the proprietors in recompense 200,000 acres on Powell's and Clinch rivers. In 1779 Henderson was a North Carolina commissioner to extend the western boundary between that state and Virginia. Later he was at French Lick on the Cumberland, where he opened a land office. He died at his home in Granville County, North Carolina. Two of his sons became prominent attorneys.

Alexander Scott Withers, *Chronicles of Border Warfare,* Cincinnati, Robert Clarke Co., 1895, 1970.

Hennisee, Argalus Garey, military officer (Jan. 16, 1839-May 30, 1913). B. at Trappe, Talbot County, Maryland, he was commissioned a first lieutenant, 1st Eastern Shore Maryland Infantry September 30, 1861, became a captain July 24, 1862, fought at Gettysburg and was mustered out February 11, 1865. He became a second lieutenant of the 19th U.S. Infantry January 22, 1867, was assigned to a post at Madison, Arkansas, in May 1867, became a first lieutenant May 14, 1868, remaining in Arkansas until March 1869. Hennisee was named agent for the Mescalero and Southern Apache Indians of New Mexico in July 1869, ably handling that trying position until December 1870. He reached Fort Craig on the Rio Grande in June. He found that the militant Southern Apaches numbered around 360, could hunt little for fear of being killed by whites, and were being rationed for 30 days at a time, a system Hennisee did not approve because "all of the food is consumed or made into liquor within 10 days [giving them] an excellent chance to get hungry and insubordinate before the next issue." He found that Mexican bootleggers at Cañada Alamosa (the present Monticello) which came under his purview were peddling whiskey to the natives and "so long as these people trade with the Indians...just so long will the Indians be thieves and uncontrollable by the Agent." Investigation showed that José Trujillo, justice of the peace, and Juan N. Montoya, constable, were "the principal traders," and he resolved to prosecute only them because there were too many others to gather evidence against. He searched Montoya's house, found 28 gallons of whiskey which he destroyed, arrested Montoya and Trujillo, against whom he also had abundant evidence. But Montoya and Trujillo "summoned a Posse Comitatus of about 40 Mexicans...and disarmed my party of men," which included his interpreter, an officer and three enlisted men. Hennisee planned to kill if necessary any person who resisted, but it was just as well it turned out

as it did, for had a fight started "not one of my party would have escaped alive." He obtained a writ for the Mexicans to appear before a U.S. district court at Albuquerque, but doubted it would do any good since it was almost impossible to obtain a conviction "by an ordinary Mexican jury." Trujillo meanwhile brought an action against him for assault before a local justice of the peace and "I was tried, convicted and sentenced to...County Jail for three months." He appealed, of course, and evidently won out; Hennisee had had several years experience as a general court martial judge advocate and escaped the New Mexico legal embarrassment with no discernible scars. In December 1870 he was assigned to the 8th Cavalry, then being posted to Chicago until 1888, when he marched with his regiment to Dakota. He had become a captain March 16, 1881; a major of the 2nd Cavalry May 31, 1898; lieutenant colonel of the 11th Cavalry February 2, 1901, colonel of the 5th Cavalry September 13, 1902, retired by reason of age January 16, 1903, and was promoted to Brigadier General on the retired list April 23, 1904. Hennisee was described by Major General Elwell S. Otis as "a careful and painstaking officer," and by Colonel E.V. Sumner as possessing "good talents, character and soldierly requirements." He lived at Los Angeles in retirement, and died at San Francisco. Hennisee was married.

Heitman; Powell; *Who Was Who;* Hennisee's military file in Old Military Records Div., NARS; Dan L. Thrapp, *Victorio and the Mimbres Apaches,* Norman, Univ. of Okla. Press, 1974; info. from John J. Slonaker, U.S. Army Military Hist. Inst., Carlisle Barracks, Penn.

Henson, Ahnahkaq, Matt Henson's son (c. 1907-June 29, 1987). The half-Eskimo son of the black North Pole explorer Matt(hew) Henson (see entry), Ahnahkaq Henson was b. of an Eskimo woman as was Kale (Karree) Peary, son of Robert E. Peary in northwesternmost Greenland, although both Henson and Peary had wives awaiting them in the United States. The births occurred following the 1906 expedition, three years before Henson and Peary announced they had reached the North Pole on April 6, 1909. The two sons, both 80 years old, made their first trip outside Greenland in 1987 to visit relatives they had never seen, in the United States. Their journey was arranged by Dr. S. Allen Counter of Harvard, a neuroscientist and black historian to whom Ahnahkaq Henson had revealed it was "the dream of his life" to visit America and meet his relatives. While in the United States they visited Peary's grave at Arlington National Cemetery, and Henson's at Woodlawn Cemetery in New York. Subsequently Henson's remains were reburied adjacent to Peary's at Arlington; this was done on April 6, 1988, by Presidential order. However, the younger Henson did not live to see the final justice done to his father; he died of cancer three weeks after returning to Moriusaq, 60 miles south of Thule, Greenland. He was survived by five sons and 23 grandchildren.

Arizona Daily Star, Tucson, May 31, Oct. 8, 1987; *New York Times,* June 7, July 11, 1987; S. Allen Counter, "The Henson Family," *National Geographic,* Vol. 174, No. 3 (Sept. 1988), 422-29 (reburial at Arlington, 429).

Herron, Joseph Sutherland, military officer (July 27, 1869-May 4, 1964). B. in Ohio he went to West Point and joined the 1st Cavalry as a second lieutenant June 12, 1895. He served at Fort Sill and Fort Reno, Oklahoma, until 1898 and briefly at Fort Meade, South Dakota, before becoming an important member of the Edwin Glenn (see entry) 1899 exploration party to Alaska. From the base camp at Tyonek, on Cook Inlet, Lieutenant Herron and his detachment were transported to the mouth of the Susitna River. June 30 they were camped on the Kichatna River, a stream he explored for the first official time in 1899. Here Glenn "bade [them] farewell; and Godspeed to him and his men...They were bound for the mouth of the Tanana River, which we calculated they would easily reach in a comparatively short time." Herron already had explored the portage between Passage Canal and Prince William Sound, and the area around Turnagain Arm on Cook Inlet. He now proceeded up the Kichatna River, across the Alaska Range to the headwaters of the Kuskokwim River system, then to the Cosna River, the Tanana and the Yukon River. His distinguished Alaskan exploration was second only to that of Henry Allen a decade and a half earlier in significance, thoroughness and the efficiency with which it was conducted. A copy of his 77-page illustrated report with maps is held by the Library of Congress under the title: *Explorations in Alaska, 1899,* U.S. Department of War, Mil. Inf. Div., No. 31, GPO, 1901. Herron became a first lieutenant, 8th Cavalry April 23, 1899; captain, 2nd Cavalry, October 29, 1901; major, July 1, 1916; colonel, Infantry, National Army, August 5, 1917 (served in France but saw no combat); a lieutenant colonel of Cavalry January 10, 1920, and colonel of Cavalry July 1, 1920. He retired July 31, 1933, and died at Long Beach, California.

Heitman; Cullum; *Narratives of Explorations in Alaska,* 713; Orth, 15; info. from the U.S. Army Military Hist. Inst., Carlisle Barracks, Penn.

Hess, Frank Lee, geologist (1871-1955). Hess worked for the Geological Survey from 1903 until 1925, much of the time in Alaska. He was on the Seward Peninsula in 1903 and the next year made a geological reconnaissance from Eagle to Rampart on the Yukon by way of Fairbanks. In 1905 he helped make a detailed geological survey of the area adjacent to Cape Nome on the Seward Peninsula.

Orth, 15.

Hewitt, James H. (Hank), mule packer (Apr. 13, 1828-July 30, 1896). B. in New York State he was taken at 6 to Tecumseh, Michigan, where his father became the first merchant to be established. In 1849 Hewitt went overland to California and during 1850-51 was engaged in teaming and driving stagecoaches out of Sacramento. When the Rogue River Indian wars of 1851, 1856 broke out in southern Oregon, Hewitt acquired a pack mule train and commenced transporting supplies for troops engaged in the conflicts; after the wars he continued packing from Crescent City, California, to the mines, subsequently going to Walla Walla, Washington. When the Fraser River, British Columbia gold rush occurred in 1858, Hewitt went there and engaged in packing in the summer into the mining country, returning in the fall to California. With a partner named Smith he purchased another pack train and returned to Fraser River. In 1861 John (Yank) Bartlett bought the Hewitt and Smith train, Hewitt remaining with the mules as packmaster until 1862 when he bought out Bartlett's partner, establishing then the famous partnership of Hewitt and Bartlett, "known all over the Pacific slope as 'Hank and Yank,' which partnership continued intermittently until Hewitt's death." The partners were engaged for several years in packing in the northwest, and went to Arizona in 1869. Their initial major operation was in moving Army stores from Fort Goodwin to Fort Apache. In early 1872 when Crook organized his military operations in Arizona, he hired Hewitt and Bartlett as principal packers, with the 145-mule train at $1.25 per day per animal. Hank and Yank remained with the officer until the end of the initial phase of the Apache campaign in the mid-1870s. Hewitt and a dozen of his burly packers, among them no doubt Al Sieber, accompanied Crook to Camp Date Creek on his risky 1872 investigation of the Wickenburg Massacre and the search for its perpetrators. A classic melee broke out, during which big Hank Hewitt waded into the brawl to seize a huge Indian who had given the signal for the irruption and attempted assassination of Crook. Struggling to convey the Indian to the guardhouse, Hewitt became incensed and smashed his opponent into a rock, where his skull was fatally fractured. Hewitt estimated that seven Apache Mojave Indians had been killed with others wounded, adding that "many more could and probably would have been killed" but for Crook's valiant efforts to stop the fight and prevent a general outbreak. In the late 1870s Hewitt returned east to visit his elderly father and other relatives and while there contracted pneumonia, from the effects of which he never fully recovered. He resided thereafter principally at Tucson for medical reasons. When his health failed to improve and Hewitt felt himself nearing death, he went to Oro Blanco in southwestern Santa Cruz county where Bartlett resided, telling him, "Yank, I have come to pass my last days with you. We have been together so long in life, and been such true friends, let us be near each other in the grave," and his wishes were complied with. Hewitt was widely respected as "a man of noble impulses, his life without stain. He was generous to a fault, his purse ever open to the widow, orphan and deserving poor." So far as reported he never married.

Information from the Arizona Hist. Soc.; Dan L. Thrapp, *Al Sieber: Chief of Scouts,* Norman, Univ. of Okla. Press, 1964; Bourke, *On Border,* 169-70.

Hickman, William A., Mormon Danite (1815-Aug. 21, 1883). B. in Kentucky, Hickman was descended from frontiersmen and pioneers, the line having reached Virginia in 1635. When he was 3 his parents moved to Missouri and at 15, at his father's urging, he commenced the study of medicine, but preferred the law and soon transferred to that field. At 16 he married the first of his ten wives, he and his wife being Methodists initially. But Bill was attracted to Mormonism, joined the new faith and settled at Nauvoo, Illinois, a principle Mormon community. He short-

ly became an "enforcer" for Church authorities, and rapidly developed the necessary skills and ruthlessness, coming, as he later wrote, to the high regard of Brigham Young (see entry), Orson Hyde and other leaders. He reached the Salt Lake Valley where about 1858 he concluded his law studies and was licensed to practice. He became a deputy U.S. marshal under Joseph Leland Heywood, a prominent Mormon and the first U.S. marshal of Utah. Carson catalogues a long list of killings Hickman himself reported having done, by directive for the most part; although the accuracy of his autobiography is sometimes questioned, in general outlines it seems his own work. He became sheriff of Green River County, Utah, the present Uinta County, Wyoming; Fort Bridger was the county seat. Later he "went into the stock business" with Porter Rockwell (see entry), another ranking Danite chief and gunman. Hickman also became Green River County prosecuting attorney, assessor and tax collector. When a mail route was established between Salt Lake City and Independence, Missouri, Rockwell was directed to transport mail between Utah and Laramie, Wyoming, and Hickman between Laramie and Independence; later Hickman directed an express service over much of the route. Hickman was a scout against U.S. forces during the 1857 so-called "Mormon War," and with Rockwell carried out harassing missions against the advancing column. In 1857 a well-known and respected Green River trader, Richard Yates, was suspected by Young of being a spy for the United States. He was murdered in Echo Canyon while in Hickman's custody enroute from Fort Bridger to Salt Lake City, supposedly on orders of Young; Hickman wrote that he personally reported the death to Young. Nothing was done about the matter for some years. Hickman was not connected with the Mountain Meadows Massacre of September 11, 1857 (see John D. Lee entry) in southern Utah. At 42 Hickman was described as "a tough, muscular, heavily built man, full-bearded and not unhandsome." His eyes were dark blue. A man of courage, Hickman was wounded on occasion, once was given up as dying, but recovered and continued his militant ways as a "destroying Angel," as the Danites called themselves (for "Danites," see Bancroft, *Utah,* pp. 124-27). How many men he killed is unknown but, according to his memoirs the number was not inconsiderable. Bill came to have differences with Young and gradually was estranged from him, although they continued to meet on rare occasions. He made a gold-hunting trip to Montana, became friendly with Colonel Patrick E. Connor (see entry) of the 3rd California Infantry, and defended him against Mormon charges and the urging that he be removed from Utah; Hickman became associated with a son of Joseph Smith and was accused of "Josephism" (for the Josephites, see Bancroft, *Utah,* 644-46), and at length with becoming an apostate. Hickman knew what that portended, sold his property, learned that prowlers were seeking him at his camp at the mouth of Brigham Canyon, and abandoned the place. He went to California, returned to Nevada and came down with typhoid fever, from which he barely recovered. In the fall of 1870 he suffered another typhoid attack and while ill learned that a U.S. deputy marshal named Gilson wanted to meet with him. Suspicious at first, Hickman finally agreed and met the lawman in April 1871; Gilson said his mission was to clear up crimes committed in Utah Territory and questioned Hickman about the Yates murder 14 years earlier. Hickman provided a full statement of its circumstances, alleging it was done on Young's orders. By agreement, Gilson then arrested Hickman, for his own protection and to keep him in custody, during which time Hickman "gave a full statement of all the crimes committed in the Territory with which he was familiar, and with which Brigham Young and Orson Hyde were involved." January 2, 1872, Young was arrested for the murder of Yates. There being no jail he was held under house arrest for a time but apparently suffered no other inconvenience as a result of the charge; nobody was tried for the Yates offense. Hickman's book, *Brigham's Destroying Angel...* was written while he was in custody at Camp Douglas, a U.S. Army post near Salt Lake City. Hickman soon dropped from public view. He had arranged with John H. Beadle for publication of his memoirs, Beadle supplying some explanatory notes, but apparently tampering little with the manuscript. "From that time on, Bill Hickman was a marked man but, having practically written the rules, he knew how to play the game, and no other 'Destroying Angels' were ever able to get within shooting distance of him." He spent his last years at Lander, Wyoming. He died there at 68, and at peace. By the time he wrote his book, nine of his ten wives had left him, and he had fathered 24 still living children, the eldest just 18 years younger than Bill himself.

John Carson, "Use Him Up, Bill!", *True West,* Vol. 11, No. 5 (May-June 1964), 16-19, 40, 42, 44-45; Hickman, *Brigham's Destroying Angel: Being the Life, Confession, and Startling Disclosures of the Notorious Bill Hickman, the Danite Chief of Utah,* N.Y., George A. Crofutt & Co., 1872, repr. Salt Lake City, Shepard Pub. Co., 1904; Bancroft, *Utah.*

Highsmith, Benjamin Franklin, frontiersman (Sept. 11, 1817-Nov. 20, 1905). B. in the St. Charles district of Missouri, the family moved by wagon in 1823 to Texas and settled adjacent to Stephen F. Austin's colony between the Brazos and Colorado rivers. Both Highsmith's father, Ahijah M., and his mother, Deborah Turner, were descended from Indian fighters, and moved with Daniel Boone from Kentucky to Missouri. At 15 Ben fought under his friend, Captain Elliot C. Buckner (who was killed), in the June 26, 1832, Battle of Velasco, a preliminary to the Texas Revolution. He also took part in the Battle of Gonzales October 2, 1835, the first true engagement of that revolution, and was with Jim Bowie in the Battle of Concepción near San Antonio, October 28, 1835. Highsmith went with Ben Milam (see entry) in the siege of Bexar (San Antonio) and remained there under William Barret Travis (see entry), whom he regarded as his friend and for whom he had been scout on several trading trips. When Travis learned of Santa Anna's approach toward the Alamo, he sent Highsmith with a message to Colonel Fannin at Goliad to come to his aid. On his return five days later Ben observed the heavy Mexican encirclement of the Alamo, saw there was no hope for the garrison, or for him to contact it, so he raced for Gonzales, being hotly pursued by Mexican cavalry for the first few miles, and turned the dispatch over to Houston upon his arrival. Houston sent Highsmith with a second message to Fannin, but Fannin failed to relieve the Alamo garrison, only to be captured with his men and butchered in the second most famous massacre in Texas history—at Goliad. Highsmith was reputed to have been the last man out of the Alamo, and the last to bring the report from Fannin. Ben Highsmith continued with Houston's army and took part in the climactic Battle of San Jacinto April 21, 1836, where Texas's independence was won. Following that engagement he enlisted for duty along the border with Mexico. He was with a Captain Lynch on a surveying trip to Lampasas County in 1838 when the party was attacked by about 40 Indians; the only white killed was Lynch. Highsmith fought under Juan Nepomuceno Seguin along the border. July 16, 1839, he was with Colonel Edward Burleson's force that, under the false pretext that the Cherokees were inclined to join Mexican forces against Texas, unfortunately attacked the Indians, killed their co-chiefs Big Mush and Bowles (see entries) and forced the Cherokees to leave Texas—after they had done much to assure the Texas victory at San Jacinto. Highsmith was in the tough Indian fight at Brushy Creek, near the present Taylor, in 1839, the Texans losing four men killed with no report on the wounded, and the Indian loss unknown. Highsmith took part in the famed Plum Creek fight of August 11, 1840, near present Lockhart, Texas, which was an outgrowth of the equally noted Council House affair of March 19, 1840, in which a dozen Comanche chiefs were treacherously killed at San Antonio; about 40 Comanches were reported killed at Plum Creek. Soon after that engagement Houston commissioned Jack Hays to raise a company of Rangers to protect the frontier, and Ben Highsmith was one of the first to enlist. He fought in the battles of Nueces Canyon, Pinto Trail Crossing, Enchanted Rock and Bandera Pass. In each of these hard scraps the Rangers had casualties and the Indians also suffered; in the Bandera Pass fight Highsmith suffered a bad leg wound that, however, did not incapacitate him. He was in the September 18, 1842, Battle of Salado against the Mexican commander Adrian Woll, a victory for the Texans under Hays. Highsmith served under Hays in the Mexican War of 1846-48 and was in the battles of Palo Alto, Resaca de la Palma, Monterrey and Buena Vista, after which he rejoined the Rangers under Captain John S. Sutton for service on the border, but saw no more Indian fighting. He thereafter settled at Bastrop, married in 1853 and fathered 13 children. In 1882 he moved to Bandera County. In his final years he became almost blind, but retained a clear mind and sharp memory. He died at Utopia, Uvalde County.

A.J. Sowell, *Early Settlers and Indian Fighters of Southwest Texas,* N.Y., Argosy-Antiquarian Ltd., 1964, I, 1-31; Maude Wallis Traylor, "Benjamin Franklin Highsmith," *Frontier Times,* Vol. 15, No. 7 (Apr. 1938), 309-17; HT; James Kimmins Greer, *Colonel Jack Hays,* rev. ed., College Station, Texas A & M Univ. Press, 1987.

Hill, Samuel, sea captain, fur trader (Feb. 20, 1777-1825). B. at Machias, Maine, he went to sea in 1794 and after a number of voyages

became a first mate in 1800 and a captain in 1804. August 31 of that year he cleared Boston with the brig *Lydia* for the Northwest Coast and in 1805 and 1806 traded into southeastern Alaska, wintering in Revillagigedo Channel in the Alexander Archipelago. At Nootka Sound he rescued John Jewett and John Thompson, the sole survivors of the ship *Boston,* who had been captured by Indians in March 1803. In 1806 the *Lydia* ascended the Columbia River for 140 miles. Hill returned to Boston after stopping over at Canton to dispose of his fur cargo. April 1, 1809, as captain of the brig *Otter* he left Boston, arriving on the Northwest Coast in November, trading from Dixon Entrance, Alexander Archipelago. Pierce quotes a Russian report that in 1810 at the Entrance, Hill aided local Indians in driving off a rival ship, the *O'Cain,* Jonathan Winship Jr., and the *Juno,* Khristofor Benzeman, the vessels using Aleut sea otter hunters under Kuskov. In the Lynn Canal on April 2, 1811, Chilkat Indians (a minor tribe of the Tlingit) unsuccessfully attempted to capture the *Otter,* but were driven off with a white loss of two killed and six wounded. Later that summer the ship's second mate was lost by drowning. The vessel returned to Boston June 14, 1812. Hill made no more voyages to the Northwest Coast. He died at Boston.

Pierce, *Russian America: A Biographical Dictionary.*

Hindman (Heineman?), George, partisan (d. Apr. 1, 1878). Hindman came from Texas with a cattle herd in 1875, bound for Arizona. But he determined to go to work for Robert Casey on the Feliz River of New Mexico, sought to quit the herd and so nettled co-owner Bill Humphreys that a gunfight resulted, in which Humphreys was wounded slightly and Hindman's pistol was shot to pieces, some metal bits imbedding themselves in his hand. Hindman settled on a small ranch rented from Casey and in nearby mountains. One day he had a brush with a sizable grizzly bear which, although wounded several times, "chawed him up, tearing his hands and legs," while Lily Klasner reported that the bear crippled his hand and arm. She wrote that Hindman generally was "a good, quiet, inoffensive person," who rarely got into trouble, although Mullin believed he was "purportedly a professional train robber, in New Mexico on vacation." On April 1, 1878, as deputy to Sheriff William Brady, Hindman and Brady were killed from ambush at Lincoln by "five or six of the McSween men," who included Billy the Kid and other notables; Fred Waite (see entry) claimed to have killed Hindman, and there is no good reason to doubt his word. Deputies George Peppin and Billy Matthews, accompanying Brady and Hindman, were not hit.

Frederick Nolan, *The Lincoln County War: A Documentary History,* Norman, Univ. of Okla. Press, 1992; Lily Klasner, *My Girlhood Among Outlaws,* ed. by Eve Ball, Tucson, Univ. of Arizona Press, 1972; Robert N. Mullin notes.

Hinkson (Hinkston), John, frontiersman (d. 1789). B. of Irish parentage in Pennsylvania, he became a noted scout and woodsman from youth. Lord Dunmore, in a letter of December 24, 1774, to the Earl of Dartmouth, secretary of state for the colonies, spoke of a reward offered for Hinkson and a man named Cooper "for Murdering an Indian," a Delaware, in southwestern Pennsylvania. Hinkson's son told Draper that the Indian, Wipey, had a grudge against his father, and threatened to kill him, and that Hinkson's slaying of the Indian was in self-defense. Tradition has it that Hinkson commanded a company of Rangers with Dunmore's army, and probably took part in the 1774 Battle of Point Pleasant. The next year Hinkson led a company of settlers into Kentucky and erected a fort on Hinkson's (South) Fork of the Licking River not far from Paris in Bourbon County. In July 1776 they abandoned the settlement because of Indian hostility and returned east by way of Boonesborough. Hinkson brought out his family in 1780, but had just arrived at his old station, now called Ruddell's, when it surrendered to Captain Henry Bird, heading a force of Shawnees and Canadians in the British service, and Hinkson was taken prisoner. When the Indians encamped the second night thereafter they found difficulty starting fires because all the wood was wet, and it was dark before they accomplished it. In the meantime Hinkson had taken advantage of their preoccupation, slipped into the woods and concealed himself under a large log. When his escape was discovered the Indians searched but did not find him and Hinkson continued his flight, though because it was an overcast night with no stars to guide him, he lost his way and almost stumbled once again on the enemy camp. He knew that the wind came generally from the west at this time, and using that as a direction-finder he worked his way westward until weariness overcame him, when he went to sleep, finding with a heavy fog in the morning further concealment; he evaded resumed Indian searches for him and within several days reached Lexington, Kentucky, with the first news of the capture of Ruddell's Station. Hinkson became a prominent pioneer in Bourbon County. He was major of its militia in 1786, and sheriff in 1788. He took part in two Indian campaigns in 1786 and 1787, and died at New Madrid, but whether of Missouri or Kentucky is not stated; there is a Madrid in Breckinridge County, Kentucky, and a New Madrid in a county of that name in Missouri.

Documentary History of Dunmore's War 1774, ed. by Thwaites/Kellogg, Madison, Wis. Hist. Soc., 1905; *Indiana Journal,* June 29, 1833; Alexander Scott Withers, *Chronicles of Border Warfare,* ed. by Thwaites, Cincinnati, Robert Clarke Co., 1895 (1961).

Hite, Isaac, pioneer (fl. 1773-1781). A son of Joist Hite, Isaac in 1773 went down the Ohio to the Falls (near today's Louisville) with Thomas Bullitt (see entry) and followed that trip with one in 1774 led by Captain John Floyd which carried the survey into Kentucky itself. In 1775 Hite led a party to Kentucky, making one of the first settlements near Boonesborough. He thereafter took an active part in Kentucky's early events, becoming a member of the Transylvania legislature, participating in 1781 in the first Kentucky court and in other civic events. Later he removed to Jefferson County whose capital is Louisville, making his permanent home in the county. Abraham Hite Jr., who had gone out with Isaac in 1775, also settled in Jefferson County, which he represented in the state senate of 1800-1803.

Thwaites, *Dunmore.*

Hite (Heidt), Joist, pioneer (fl. 1710-1736). An immigrant from Holland, he arrived at New York in 1710, "bringing possessions and people in three ships." He settled first in Pennsylvania and in 1732 moved to the lower Shenandoah Valley of Virginia "with a numerous company, including sons and sons-in-law." He had at least four sons, among them Abraham Hite and Captain Isaac Hite. Abraham had a son, Abraham Jr., also a noted pioneer. The Hite family and the Isaac and John Van Meter families intermarried to some extent. In 1730 Isaac and John Van Meter obtained a grant of 100,000 acres; the next year they sold this to Joist Hite who became fairly prosperous, but soon discovered that the land he had purchased was also claimed by Lord Fairfax, a land speculator who in 1736 had obtained the same grant. Hite sued. His legal action dragged on for years. It ended in 1786 in favor of Hite's heirs, but Joist was "long since dead."

Harriette Simpson Arnow, *Seedtime on the Cumberland*, N.Y., The Macmillan Co., 1960; Thwaites, *Dunmore.*

Hoagland, Henry, military officer (d. c. 1782). Hoagland lived on Pigeon Creek in the Monongahela district of Virginia (West Virginia) and was prominent in actions against the Indians during border wars. He served as captain under Angus McDonald (see entry) on the Wapatomica campaign in Ohio in July and August 1774. The campaign was indecisive, although skirmishing developed. Hoagland served in Dunmore's division during the Battle of Point Pleasant, October 10, 1774, an action which effectively terminated Dunmore's War. In June 1782 he was elected captain and served as such on Crawford's ill-fated campaign against Upper Sandusky, Ohio. The expedition was broken up by Indian and British resistance, Crawford captured and executed (see entry), and Hoagland was among the missing, never to be seen again by Anglo-Americans. In his history of the Crawford campaign (1873) Butterfield said that Hoagland was "never heard of" after the action; in his *History of the Girtys* (1890) he reported that at the outset of the action Hoagland was "shot and instantly killed." In any event it is probable that he did not survive the action, at least for very long.

Thwaites/Kellogg, *Frontier Defense on the Upper Ohio, 1777-1778;* C.W. Butterfield, *An Historical Account of the Expedition against Sandusky under Col. William Crawford in 1782,* Cincinnati, Robert Clarke & Co., 1873; Butterfield, *History of the Girtys,* Cincinnati, Clarke, 1890.

Hogg, Thomas, pioneer (d. Spring 1774). According to the journal of surveyor Thomas Hanson, in April 1774 Hogg was developing a bottomland on a tributary to the Ohio River upstream from the Great Kanawha a few miles. Hogg confirmed to Hanson rumors of Indian hostility thereabouts. Soon afterward, Hogg was reported missing, presumed killed. Colonel William Fleming's orderly book was quoted by Thwaites in an entry for October 6, 1774, that his men located along the Ohio, metal and "an old fine Shirt which they judged might cost 2/ [shillings] pr. yd. and an Old Cloth Jacket, Sky blew couler, likewise an Under Jaw bone," all of

which "were Judged Toms. Hogs." Thwaites added in a footnote, "This would seem to indicate that he perished by an attack of wild beasts rather than Indians, who would surely have appropriated the metallic instruments and clothes." Thwaites' supposition is not very persuasive, however, and he gave no indication of what sort of "wild beasts" he thought possibly responsible.

Thwaites, *Dunmore.*

Holand, Hjalmar R., historical researcher, writer (Oct. 20, 1872-Aug. 8, 1963). B. at Salstroken, in Holand Parish not far from Oslo, Norway, he emigrated on April 3, 1884, from Norway to New York and settled with relatives at Chicago. Several years later he moved to Wisconsin, became an itinerant book salesman, eventually concentrating on Norwegian immigrants and farmers in Wisconsin and Minnesota. He attended the University of Wisconsin at Madison, paying his way inch by inch as he recalled, at length obtaining a master's degree, and became attracted to the Door Peninsula on the edge of Green Bay, settling at Ephraim. One of his university instructors had been Frederick Jackson Turner (see entry), and Holand spent "every summer on the [northern] frontier," gathering information for a history of Norwegian immigration and a half-dozen other books on frontier life. He was employed by Rand McNally as a traveling salesman, selling maps wholesale for advertising purposes, having exclusive rights for his company's products in five states, disposing of them by hundreds of thousands and for the first time "made good money." He built a home in the Ephraim area, and became interested as an avocation in the history of Door County. In 1908 he published *History of the Norwegian Immigration,* which went through three editions, and in 1917 published *History of Door County, Wisconsin;* other books on a variety of subjects appeared. Late in the 19th century he had heard of the discovery near Kensington, Douglas County, Minnesota, of a slab of stone with curious markings, but paid no attention to the tale until in 1907 he found himself in the vicinity, looked up the rock's discoverer, a farmer, Olof Ohman, whom he found to be "a tall, well-built man of about fifty years with a frank and rugged countenance and a quiet dignity." He was born in 1855 in Helsingland, northern Sweden, had had in all 36 weeks of grade schooling and upon Holand's request showed him the rock, lying face down as a stepping stone before the granary.

Holand instantly recognized the markings as runic, since he had often pondered runic inscriptions "in my favorite study of Norse antiquities." Ohman had grubbed out the rock while clearing land on his farm in 1898. It had been clutched by the roots of a tree estimated to be from 6 to 10 inches thick at the base. Holand offered Ohman $5 for the rock, but the farmer would take nothing since Holand said he wanted it only to study the inscriptions (there were two) on its face and edge. Holand's translation read: "Eight Goths [Swedes] and 22 Norwegians on exploration journey from Vinland westward. We had camp by [a lake with] 2 skerries one day's journey north from this stone. We were [out] and fish[ed] one day. After we came home [we] found 10 [of our] men red with blood and dead. A.V.M. [Ave Virgo Maria] save [us] from evil. [We] have 10 men [of our party] by the sea to look after our ships 14 days' journey from this island. Year 1362." Even Holand probably did not suspect that this would be the start of his principal later career: first in accurately translating the runes, then in developing theories about their provenance and spreading his theories through this country and Europe and writing half a dozen books about his basic thesis. This was that the carvings were the work of Vikings under Powell Knutsson (Paul Knutson) (see entry), sent from Norway in 1356 by King Magnus (1316-1373) of Norway and parts of Sweden in an effort to trace disappeared Christian settlers from the Western colony of Greenland, and restore them to the faith which probably had lapsed. The date of Knutsson's return to Scandinavia is not known, though Holand believed remnants of his expedition made it back in 1363 or 1364. Here is not the place to detail the long and intense controversy generated by variant views of the validity of the Kensington Stone, as it is known, and in which Holand engaged for the last 50 years of his life, during which he also supported the possible Viking origin of the Newport, Rhode Island "tower," focus of another widely rejected theory, although it does find some support, even today. Holand's volumes included *The Kensington Stone* (1932); *Westward from Vinland* (1940); *America, 1355-1364* (1946); *Explorations in America Before Columbus* (1956), and *A Pre-Columbian Crusade to America* (1962). He rounded up his experiences in his autobiography. He also wrote many shorter pieces of varying interest. Among them was, "An English Scientist in America 130 years Before Columbus," published in the Wisconsin Academy of Science and Letters *Transactions,* XLVIII (1959). It was a study of the travels of Nicholas of Lynne, a Franciscan or Carmelite friar, mathematician and astronomer of Oxford. Holand believed that Nicholas had not only reached the North Magnetic Pole, or knew of its location, but that his expedition may have been linked with that of Knutsson, perhaps with it entering Hudson Bay. Holand's theories gained some support, notably perhaps by William C. Thalbitzer, a Danish expert on runic inscriptions of the University of Copenhagen. Originally a doubter, Thalbitzer became convinced that supposed inaccuracies in the stone's inscriptions actually were common and little-known practices of the 14th century. He concluded that many of the letters were Old Swedish, with a dash of monastic script and some 14th century colloquialisms. His *Two Runic Stones, from Greenland and Minnesota,* a highly detailed and technical 71-page paper, was published in 1951 by the Smithsonian Institution as Volume 116, No. 3 of its Miscellaneous Collections. Thalbitzer, among the best authorities and most knowledgeable of all who have seriously examined the Kensington Stone's intriguing inscriptions, concluded that though earlier widespread distrust on the basis of imperfect knowledge and scant study virtually unanimously agreed it was a "crude forgery," it was now time for a fresh look and study of it. "In the development of runology and philology in the time since the stone was found...so many new facts and views have appeared that it now seems possible to maintain that this peculiar inscription—the runes as well as the contents—in spite of everything *may* be genuine," he wrote. "But false or genuine, a solution is wanted, if possible a proof." Among books that dispute Holand's views and stress belief that the stone is a forgery is Erik Wahlgren's *The Kensington Stone, a Mystery Solved* (Wahlgren was professor of Scandinavian languages at UCLA), and Theodore C. Blegen (1891-1969), *The Kensington Rune Stone: New Light on an Old Riddle;* he was dean emeritus of the University of Minnesota's graduate school, former superintendent of the Minnesota Historical Society, and was considered a careful and reliable historian. He wrote in his Introduction, however, that "I did not set out to prove the inscription either genuine or a hoax," but rather concentrated on the history of the rock and a search for a possible forger. Holand died at 90 at Sturgeon Bay, Wisconsin. He was married.

In addition to works cited above: Holand, *My First Eighty Years,* N.Y., Twayne Pub., 1957; author's correspondence with Holand; author's file on Holand and related subjects; DCB, I, 678-79, the Nicholas of Lynn entry.

Holland, Ray(mond) Prunty, editor, conservationist (Aug. 20, 1884-Feb. 20, 1973). B. at Atchison, Kansas, he completed his formal education in 1903 and worked at a variety of jobs at Atchison until 1912, during this period developing an avid interest in outdoor sports and natural history; by 9 he was hunting, fishing and camping at every opportunity. His first published article was in *Sports Afield* while he still was in school and by 1912 he was successful enough to devote himself to freelance writing and photography. In 1914 he became district inspector and game warden for the U.S. Biological Survey (later of the Fish and Wildlife Service), continuing meanwhile his writing, usually under the pen name of Bob White. In 1919 he became editor of the Bulletin of the American Game Protective Association at New York City and vice president of the organization which became the American Game Association. In 1924 he became editor-in-chief of *Field and Stream,* holding that position until 1941. Meanwhile he had become prominent in conservation and wildlife matters. While a U.S. warden Holland was charged with enforcing the Migratory Bird Protection Act of 1913 in seven states. The law, for which he had lobbied, gave the federal government authority to set seasons and bag limits to protect dwindling supplies of waterfowl. In enforcing it Holland was contested by hunters who denied he had jurisdiction over them, since they considered the law an unconstitutional infringement on state's rights. Holland had to develop an educational program in support of the law, attempting to prove to the sportsman that enforcement was in their own best interests. The issue finally went to court and the opponents were initially successful, the act being declared unconstitutional. Holland brought a case of his own in another court, but lost again. In 1916 the Canada-U.S. Migratory Bird Treaty was enacted, implemented by a Migratory Bird Treaty of 1918, giving the government the right to establish seasons, bag limits, outlaw market hunting, spring shooting and protecting songbirds. Some hunters continued to defy the restrictions, and in 1919 Holland made arrests, the state of Missouri finally testing the law in court, being defeated and the case winding

up in the U.S. Supreme Court as Missouri v. Holland. In a decision in favor of Holland, Justice Oliver Wendell Holmes Jr. ruled that the treaties of 1916 and 1918 were constitutional, the case a landmark in conservation law. Holmes stated that wild birds were not in the "possession" of anyone, that possession was the beginning of ownership, and that wild birds could not be in the possession of a state, since they may have arrived the day before and the next week might be 1,000 miles away, and beyond the state's jurisdiction. Holland regularly wrote a conservation column for the American Game Protective Association, the column being reprinted in many outdoor magazines, including *Field and Stream,* which under his editorship became among the most widely-circulated of like organs and "the recognized voice of sportsmen." It published work by noted writers and painters, and though accuracy had not been particularly prized by numerous outdoor publications of the day, *Field and Stream* under Holland insisted upon authenticity. He championed conservation of wildlife long before it was a popular cause, supported many conservation measures, opposed any type of gun control, wrote the first known statement favoring the idea of a duck stamp, a suggested 50-cent contribution to a hunting license to be amassed into an annual $1 million sum to buy and maintain duck refuges and public shooting grounds. When finally passed by Congress in 1934, the public shooting ground provision had been dropped, the price of the stamp set at $1 and by 1970 a total of $170 million had been accumulated for migratory waterfowl refuges where no shooting was permitted, although at length limited shooting was provided "to keep the birds from becoming domesticated." In the 1920s Holland sought recognition of the existence of a very large distinct species of Canada goose. He obtained little support from ornithologists until 1965, when Harold C. Hanson gave the species full scientific accreditation, and named it the Holland-Mershon goose. After his retirement from the editorship of *Field and Stream* Holland, who settled at length at Roswell, New Mexico, combined outdoor life, writing books and articles on hunting, fishing and nature. His books included *My Gun Dogs* (1929); *Nip and Tuck* (1939, 1946); *Shotgunning in the Uplands* (1944); *Shotgunning in the Lowlands* (1945); *My Dog Lemon* (1945); *Now Listen, Warden* (1946); *The Master* (1946); *Bird Dogs* (1948); *Scattergunning* (1951), and *Seven Grand Gun Dogs* (1961). He co-authored with two of his sons, *Good Shot: A Book of Rod, Gun, and Camera* (1946). Various refuges and wildlife sanctuaries were named for him. Holland was married and fathered three sons. He died at Roswell at 89, six months to the day before his 90th birthday.

NCAB, Vol. 58, 198-99; family recollections; Ted Trueblood, "Ray P. Holland: Editor/Field & Stream/1924-1941," *Field and Stream*, June 1970, 82, 195-99.

Holmes, Thomas A., wagon train entrepreneur (1804-1888). B. at Bergerstown, Pennsylvania, he was living in 1862 at Shakopee, Minnesota, and formed and led the first significant wagon train from Minnesota by the northern route to Montana, aiming for the Salmon River gold towns although the company, as such, did not make it that far. By the end of May Holmes and some of his people were encamped at Fort Abercrombie, north of present Wahpeton, North Dakota. The group, totaling some 70 men, elected Holmes "military captain" of the train because of his considerable frontier experience. He had "for nearly sixty years moved from one frontier to another, driven...by a *demon* of unrest." In the 1830s and 1840s he was a fur trader in Wisconsin when he was not involved in land promotions. He was an early settler of Milwaukee and a founder of Janesville, Wisconsin. He helped found such Minnesota towns as Shakopee, Itasca, Holmes City and Sauk Rapids; in the 1850s he roamed the Minnesota River valley, Indian trading and developing towns. Holmes knew the Red River country and visited the Fraser River of British Columbia in 1858 and was "highly respected among early Minnesotans for his intimate knowledge of Indians and frontier ways," and he once described his talents: "While I can only just about write my name, *I can skin a musk-rat quicker than an Indian.*" He led expeditions to the gold fields in 1862, 1864 and 1866. The first expedition followed initially a trail blazed two years earlier by trader Charles Larpenteur (see entry), who had traveled far north to avoid the Sioux; the trail led by way of St. Joseph (the present Walhalla), proceeded west just south of the Canadian border, then angled southerly across the Coteau du Missouri, the terminal moraine of the Wisconsin Ice Sheet of Pleistocene times, and crossed the Souris River near today's Minot. In Montana the train was guided by Blackfeet Indians along the Milk River whence the emigrants wandered on to Fort Benton and the Deer

Lodge Valley. The 1864 expedition planned to leave the middle of May; it was not too long after the Great Sioux Uprising when the hostile Indians had crossed into North Dakota where they remained, a threat to any emigrant travel. Thus the Holmes party was advised to seek a military escort and took advantage of a Colonel Minor T. Thomas (see entry) command which was intended to join Alfred Sully (see entry) in the campaign against the Sioux. The Holmes party's vanguard left Shakopee May 19. At Fort Ridgely it was organized into six divisions, each with a wagonmaster; the size of the overall train was estimated at from 113 to 175 wagons and 200 to 300 people, including 14 women. June 7 the train fell in behind Thomas's brigade. Moving across Dakota the expedition's people got on well with the troops. South of Aberdeen, South Dakota, the party crossed the James River, negotiated the Coteau du Missouri and joined Sully's command at Swan Lake Creek on the Missouri and constructed Fort Rice, south of the present Bismarck. Sully intended to march then to the mouth of the Yellowstone River and, irritated at having the emigrants tag along, told a gathering of them, "Gentlemen, I am damn sorry you are here, but so long as you are I will do the best I can to protect you," even though he thought a sizable Indian fight was imminent, and told them to stay out of the way should it take place. The column left Fort Rice July 19. The fight took place at Killdeer Mountain, the emigrants waiting it out under military protection south of the present Richardton, North Dakota. The wagon train crossed the Badlands and with the column reached the Yellowstone, losing two men by drowning in its crossing. At Fort Union it left the Sully expedition and moved out on the old emigrant trail, arriving in mid-September at Fort Benton, where the train was dissolved. The 1866 expedition was a virtual replica of the 1864 trek. Scattered parties of emigrants gathered at Fort Wadsworth (Sisseton), 25 miles west of the present Sisseton, South Dakota, where it was organized, including six companies, a full 200 men, ten women, ten children overall and 400 head of cattle. It proceeded, made a crossing of the James River south of today's Jamestown, North Dakota, and reached the Missouri south of Garrison and went on to Fort Berthold, a fur trading post. Some emigrants sold whiskey at $8 a bottle to Gros Ventre Indians camped nearby until they had all the Indians' money and a horse; this inspired a night attack on the train by drunken Gros Ventres, during which the whites shot a leader of the attackers and drove the rest off. July 19 the train left Fort Union at the mouth of the Yellowstone, traveled six days through a seemingly endless herd of buffalo, and reached Helena August 24. At 63, Holmes had now had his fill of Plains adventures and the goldfields. He settled at Shakopee for a time, then moved to Cullman, Alabama, where he farmed until his death at 84.

Helen McCann White, *Ho! For the Gold Fields: Northern Overland Wagon Trains of the 1860s,* St. Paul, Minnesota Hist. Soc., 1966.

Holt, C.G., trader, explorer (d. c. 1886). Holt was a trader at Nuchek (Port Eteches), Hinchinbrook Island, Alaska, and in the summer of 1882 as agent for the Alaska Commercial Company he ascended the Copper River, accompanied by Midnooskies, today called the Ahtena, an Athapascan people popularly known as the Copper River Indians. Holt ascended the virtually unexplored river as far as Taral, the present Chitina. He returned then to Nuchek. His objective had been to assess the possibility of establishing a trading post near the mouth of the Chitina River, a Copper tributary, "but having been crippled through some accident his purpose was defeated. He described the natives as treacherous and thievish...and illustrated the imminent dangers to which they had exposed him." A year earlier Holt had told Abercrombie that while at Taral he met a party of 10 upper Copper River natives come downstream to trade. He said they were "uncivil" to him and threatened him with their knives. Abercrombie added "but as he was entirely alone, although well armed, it would seem that had their intention been to do him harm, it could have been easily accomplished, particularly as he was lying in his tent...partially disabled as the result of a fall." Holt also said that while at Taral he had met an Indian who told him he had been to the Yukon, an overland feat no white had accomplished at that longitude. Allen reported that about a year after his 1884 or 1885 visit to Nuchek, Holt, on a subsequent trip up the river, was murdered by Copper River natives, "who seemed to cherish a violent dislike toward him."

Henry T. Allen, "Military Reconnoissance in Alaska," *Narratives of Explorations in Alaska,* 414; W.R. Abercrombie, "Supplementary Expedition into the Copper River Valley, Alaska," *Narratives,* 403, 406-407.

Hooper, Calvin Leighton, Coast Guard officer (1842-1900). Captain Hooper of the Revenue-Cutter Service "spent a number of years in Alaska during the period of early exploration and in later years was commander of the Bering Sea fleet. His annual reports to the Treasury Department contributed many geographical facts." Hooper Bay in the Yukon River delta was named for him in 1882.

Orth, 15, 429.

Hopkins, Gilbert W., mechanical engineer (c. 1830-Mar. 1, 1865). B. in New York, he was educated as a mechanical engineer and arrived in Arizona in 1859, interested in mining. He and Thomas Gardner located the Empire, or Montezuma, mine, a lead and silver property in the Santa Cruz (possibly Patagonia) Mountains midway between the famed Mowry Mine and the community of Santa Cruz, Sonora. They sold the mine to New York interests in 1860. Hopkins had served in 1861 as engineer for the Maricopa Mining Company copper mine, four miles south of the Gila on the San Pedro River. He was named by U.S. Marshal Milton B. Duffield (see entry), deputy marshal to take the 1864 census south of the Gila River, which Hopkins completed. He served in the first Territorial Assembly and as a regent for the University of Arizona, being also an incorporator of the Arizona Historical Society. He was killed by Apache Indians near Fort Buchanan on the road to Tubac. The second highest peak of the Santa Rita Mountains was named Mount Hopkins, elevation 8,572 ft. It is the site today of a major University of Arizona astronomical telescope complex and a road has been constructed to the summit of the peak. A somewhat higher mountain nearby was named for William Wrightson (see entry), another noted pioneer who also was killed by Apaches a few days earlier. Hopkins was buried at Greenwood Cemetery, New York City.

Will C. Barnes, *Arizona Place Names,* Tucson, Univ. of Arizona, 1936; Byrd H. Granger, *Will C. Barnes' Arizona Place Names,* Tucson, Univ. of Arizona Press, 1960; info. from Hayden File, Arizona Hist. Soc.

Horrell, Benedict, frontiersman (c. 1790-c. 1868). B. in Virginia, Benedict Horrell followed the frontier to Kentucky, where his son, Samuel Horrell Sr., was born, and then to Fenton, Arkansas, before moving with the clan about 1857 to Lampasas County, Texas. When the Horrells settled on a farm ten miles northeast of Lampasas, Benedict, who was 70 when the Civil

War broke out, settled on a place adjacent to Samuel Horrell and his numerous offspring. Benedict was said to have been killed in a Comanche raid on the area.

Information from Frederick W. Nolan.

Houchins, discoverer (fl. 1797-1809). A man supposedly of this name, or an approximation of it, is persistently credited by frontier myth with being the discoverer of Mammoth Cave (now a National Park), 35 miles northeast of Bowling Green, Kentucky. Even the date of the white discovery of the cave is in doubt: Houchins was said to have come across it, according to the *New York Times,* in 1797 while "pursuing (or being pursued by) a bear." The *Encyclopedia Americana* reports that "recorded evidence of the cave dates from 1798." Helen F. Randolph, writing in 1924, puts the Houchins discovery in 1809, while according to the Kentucky Historical Society it was part of a tract granted to Valentine Sim(m)ons in 1799 and "he should have known of the cave at that time," although the area is riddled with other caves in addition to Mammoth. The only census names approximating Houchins by 1810 were John Houchers and a Frances Houchen, both of Warren County, of which Bowling Green is the county seat. A 1986 publication on Mammoth Cave attributes the discovery to "Lt. Thomas Hutchins, a surveyor," but if this refers to the famed surveyor and geographer Thomas Hutchins (see entry), he cannot have been its locater since he died in 1789, at least a decade before its reputed discovery. There was another army officer named Thomas Hutchins, a man of varied accomplishments since he was a surgeon's mate, later an artillerist, and finally an engineer who left the service as a lieutenant in 1795; although further information about him is lacking, the dates of his service indicate he *could* have been the "Houchins" legend records, if he was then in Kentucky, although there seems to be no evidence that he was. In any event the true discoverer of the cave preceded the mysterious Houchins by several thousand years, for a mummified body of an Indian found within it has been estimated to have 2,000 or more years of antiquity, while discovery of Indian pottery, partially burned torches, wooden bowls and sandals are further evidence of ancient use of the cavern. The extent of the cave's many passages has still not been fully explored, but around 180 miles are known, on five levels, through the lowest of which flows the Echo River, draining into the Green River. Congress in 1926 authorized estab-

lishment of Mammoth Cave National Park, but it continued to be operated as a private tourist attraction until 1930 when the State of Kentucky acquired the property. In 1936 it was turned over to the National Park Service and became established by 1941 as a 50,696-acre reserve offering a variety of recreational opportunities, and attracting nearly one million visitors annually. It was the nation's 26th National Park.

New York Times Travel Section, Aug. 20, 1989; info. from Linda Anderson, Kentucky Hist. Soc., Apr. 9, 1992; standard ref. works.

Howard, James (Tex), desperado (d. Mar. 28, 1884). Howard was one of five gunmen who perpetrated the December 8, 1883, "Bisbee Massacre" while holding up the Joseph Goldwater -A.A. Casteñada general store at the Arizona mining camp. In the course of the robbery four non-participants were killed outright. Their names are given variously, but probably were J.C. Tapiner, Mrs. R.H. (Anna) Roberts, Deputy Sheriff Tom Smith and R.E. Duvall, with Albert Nolly being wounded mortally. Howard, with another of the five, Omer (or Comer) Sample (see entry) was seized while enjoying an outing with girlfriends at Clifton, Arizona. They were tried, condemned to hang at Tombstone, and executed with the other three gunmen: Daniel Kelly, Daniel Dowd and William Delaney (see entries). Howard and John Heath, the reported mastermind of the holdup but who took no active role in it, were rumored to have committed train robberies in the past. Heath was tried separately and sentenced to life imprisonment, but on February 22, 1884, was extracted from the Tombstone jail by a crowd from Bisbee and lynched.

Ben T. Traywick, *The Hangings in Tombstone,* Tombstone, Red Marie's Bookstore, 1991; Robert E. Ladd, *Eight Ropes to Eternity,* pub. by *Tombstone Epitaph,* 1965; A.D. LeBaron, "Bisbee's Five Black Ghosts," *True West,* Vol. 7, No. 6 (July-Aug. 1960), 12-14, 56, 57.

Howard, William Lauriston, naval officer (Jan. 10, 1860-Feb. 3, 1930). He was graduated from Annapolis in 1882 and as an ensign in 1886 explored from Fort Cosmos on the Kobuk River and Cosmos Creek near Kotzebue Sound, Alaska, to the upper Noatak River. He then crossed over to the upper Colville River and, negotiating the Brooks Range, made his way by the Chipp (Ikpaktuk) River to Dease Inlet and on to Point Barrow. He then embarked on the revenue cutter *Bear* and returned to Kotzebue Sound. It was a notable feat of exploratory travel through an unknown wilderness. Howard was promoted through grades, reaching the rank of Rear Admiral in December 1919.

Orth, 36; *Who Was Who.*

Hoyt, Henry Franklin, physician, adventurer (Jan. 30, 1854-Jan. 21, 1930). B. at St. Paul, Minnesota, he was too young to have taken part in the Sioux engagements of 1862, but his father spoke the Dakota language and the boy remembered many Indian visitors at his farm home during his childhood. At 18 he joined a surveying party for the St. Paul and Pacific Railroad Company along the Red River and in 1873 a group surveying the 49th Parallel Canadian boundary toward the Montana moutains. Hoyt entered upon the study of medicine, working with an established physician and then for a year in a hospital. He was not present at the September 7, 1876, James-Younger raid on a Northfield bank, but did inherit the skeleton of Charley Pitts (Samuel Wells), one of the bandits killed in flight; eventually it was rearticulated and much later used by another physician for study purposes in his office. Before completing a formal medical study program Hoyt ran out of money and took off for the Black Hills, reaching Deadwood in 1877. Of robust build, strong, agile and interested in individual sports, the red-haired young man throughout his adventurous life met people of importance or quite otherwise; his memory for personalities, conversations and incidents was extraordinary and usually accurate. He may have kept a diary to support his recollections. Hoyt opened a Deadwood practice, his first two customers casualties in a gunfight. After an unsuccessful mining venture he and others went by wagon to New Mexico, meeting cattleman John Chisum, then moving on to Tascosa in the Texas Panhandle, where smallpox was reported raging. He practiced medicine, although rarely found enough business to make a living. In the Panhandle the smallpox threat was real enough, but he derived more income from gunshot victims than virus casualties and when even that source of income tapered off he became a cowboy. He met Billy the Kid and the gunman's prominent associates, describing the Kid as "a handsome youth with smooth face, wavy brown hair, an athletic and symmetrical figure and clear blue eyes that could look one through and through" and, unless angry, the Kid was invariably pleasant. Hoyt obtained a fine horse from Billy (a photograph of the bill of

sale is in his book) and developed a friendship with him that continued through repeated encounters, although he gives few insights or details of their conversations. Ramon Adams concluded that Hoyt's "information on Billy the Kid is correct." Hoyt for a time became a bartender at Las Vegas, New Mexico. He was one day introduced by the Kid to a "Mr. Howard," who Hoyt understood to be Jesse James on a reconnoitering visit to New Mexico; he presents persuasive support for his belief, although proof of James's visit to New Mexico at that time is lacking. Hoyt became assistant postmaster at Las Vegas, joined the vigilantes, apparently assisted in sending assorted toughs out of this world, and eventually reopened a medical practice at Bernalillo, north of Albuquerque. As the first professionally-trained physician there he used his skills and common sense to generate a substantial and profitable practice, incidentally meeting such figures as U.S. Grant and others— on both sides of the law. Hoyt, while a court witness at Santa Fe, met Governor Lew. Wallace and through Wallace was permitted to visit a shackled Billy the Kid, then jailed at the city. It was a long and cordial conversation, Hoyt reported. He later discussed the Kid with Wallace, who also was much interested in the young outlaw. The doctor wrote that "I have both read and heard all manner of stories about what happened... between General Wallace and Billy the Kid...I knew both personally, and have discussed each of them with the other and...it is very difficult to understand what basis there ever was for the reports of serious trouble between them, threats from Billy, etc. To be frank, I cannot believe them." Having accumulated enough money, Hoyt returned to the Midwest to complete his medical training. A boxing enthusiast, he at one time passed up an invitation to spar with John L. Sullivan and having witnessed the fate of those who accepted, was glad he did. Following graduation in 1882 he became head of the St. Paul Department of Health, where he remained nine years, became chief surgeon for railways and when war with Spain broke out in 1898 was commissioned a major and chief surgeon for Volunteers. He desired appointment to the Philippines where action was underway, and through influence of Secretary of War Russell A. Alger was sent there. He served under Major General Arthur MacArthur, father of Douglas MacArthur, and participated in a score of engagements with Emilio Aguinaldo and his insurgents, being wounded and winning the Silver Star for gallantry in action. Hoyt resigned his commission in March 1902 and resumed private practice, first at El Paso, Texas, and then at Long Beach, California. After completing his reminiscences in 1928 (published in 1929) Hoyt and his wife embarked upon a pleasure trip to the Far East; he died at Yokahama and was buried at Long Beach.

Hoyt, *A Frontier Doctor,* Lakeside Press edition, ed. by Doyce B. Nunis Jr., Chicago, R.R. Donnelly & Sons, 1979).

Huggins, Eli Lundy, military officer (Aug. 1, 1842-Oct. 22, 1929). B. in Schuyler County, Illinois, he probably was raised in Minnesota for in his maturity he was fluent in the Dakota tongue and joined the military from the northern territory. He enlisted in Company E, 2nd Minnesota infantry July 5, 1861, was wounded at Chickamauga and became a corporal before his discharge July 14, 1864. He enlisted in the 1st Minnesota Artillery February 16, 1865, was commissioned a first lieutenant March 1 and mustered out September 27 of that year. He was commissioned a second lieutenant of the 2nd U.S. Artillery February 23, 1866, becoming a first lieutenant December 26. Huggins transferred to the 2nd Cavalry April 11, 1879, becoming a captain April 23. Assigned to Fort Keogh, near the mouth of the Tongue River, Montana, Huggins proved "very useful and enterprising" in weaning away from the Sioux hostiles small parties so that the surrendered Indians soon outnumbered the hostiles. Miles wrote that Huggins had "in early life, while living in Minnesota Territory, acquired a thorough knowledge of the Dakota language. Owing to his qualifications he was frequently sent north...to bring in bands of hostile Indians, and being able to speak their own language..., he impressed them favorably and accomplished excellent work." March 24, 1880, a band of Sioux raided the Fort Custer reservation, sweeping off a pony herd of the Crow scouts. Huggins was sent with troops and Cheyenne trailers, after them. He left the post March 25, and on the 26th found the trail, followed it with great difficulty and on a circuitous route through the Bad Lands and across the Rosebud, Tongue and Powder rivers, for four days covering 50 miles a day. Late April 1, the Sioux were caught up with at the head of O'Fallon Creek and a sharp fight erupted, one sergeant being killed, an Indian wounded and five captured who proved to be from Sitting Bull's camp

near the Canadian line. All 46 stolen ponies were retaken and Huggins won a Medal of Honor for his hard pursuit, its success, and Huggins' "most distinguished gallantry [and] great boldness" in the action. Through his linguistic ability, Huggins "received the surrender of Rain-in-the-Face...and 800 other Sioux" who came in to Fort Keogh in October 1880, marking the virtual termination of the Sioux War for that period, although the actual surrender of course was made to Miles. Huggins later seems to have been assigned to Alaska. On August 13, 1885, Lieutenant Henry Allen (see entry), also of the 2nd Cavalry, during his great exploration of Alaskan rivers, named a seven-mile-long island in the Koyukuk River a few miles below the present Hughes, Huggins Island after the captain who, he wrote, was "for a long time a resident of the Territory [of Alaska], and a warm friend of the expedition." It still bears the name. Huggins became a major of the 6th Cavalry January 13, 1897, lieutenant colonel of the 3rd Cavalry February 2, 1901, colonel of the 2nd Cavalry November 16, 1901, and a Brigadier General February 22, 1903, the day before he retired. He lived at San Diego, California, in his retirement and as an avocation wrote poetry, one of his books being *Winona, a Dakota Legend, and Other Poems.*

Heitman; *Who Was Who;* Nelson A. Miles, *Personal Recollections,* 310-11, Chicago, Riverside Pub. Co., 1897; Mark H. Brown, *Plainsmen of the Yellowstone,* N.Y., G.P. Putnam's Sons, 1961; *Narratives of Explorations in Alaska,* 461 and n.; Orth, 436.

Hughes, Frederick George, pioneer (Mar. 30, 1837-Sept. 16, 1911). B. at Cheltenham, Gloucestershire, England, his family when the boy was 6 moved to New York, living there and in New Jersey for a decade. At 16 Hughes ran away from home and joined two brothers in Gold Rush California. He mined initially at Hangtown (Placerville) in Eldorado County, and later on the Feather, Scott and Salmon rivers, finally settling at New York Flat near Downieville in Sierra County. On discovery of the Comstock silver lode in western Nevada he went to Washoe. In 1860 Hughes served under William Ormsby (see entry) in the Pyramid Lake War against Nevada Paiutes and took part in the disastrous May 12 battle of the 105-man contingent in which 76 of the militia were killed, including Ormsby, and most of the others were wounded. Hughes also served under John Coffee (Jack) Hays in the well-organized May-June campaign that destroyed the

Paiutes as a fighting people. August 16, 1861, at La Porte, northeast of Oroville, he enlisted in Company F, 1st California Infantry, and in 1862 joined with it and the California Column in the march to New Mexico, leaving Fort Yuma May 15, 1862, and arriving at Fort Bowie July 30, a fortnight after the celebrated, though minor, "Battle of Apache Pass." Company F reached Mesilla August 15 and Fort Craig October 4, concluding a 750-mile hike from the coast. Most of Hughes' military service was out of Fort Craig, New Mexico, with occasional scouts against Apache or Navaho Indians. During the summer of 1863 the Walker party found gold in the Prescott region; Congress already had organized the Territory of Arizona, and appointed territorial officials, a delegation of whom under Governor John H. Goodwin left Washington for their new post. Companies C and F were detailed by Carleton, the military commander, to escort the officials to the new Territory and establish there a fort. Hughes and F Company went to Los Tinos in mid-October but, the delegates not having appeared, continued on to Fort Wingate where the company waited another ten days; the delegation still not arriving "we were ordered to push on without them," Hughes said. The expedition, in cold and inclement weather, proceeded to the Little Colorado River and on to the San Francisco Mountains near the present Flagstaff, encountering only minor trouble with Indians, mainly Navaho stock thieves. Many of the wagon oxen having playing out, it was determined to cache the expedition's supplies while the main command continued to the destination, Hughes and a ten-man detail to guard the cache until relieved. "We enjoyed ourselves," he said, "for our camp was a veritable hunters' paradise...bear, elk, deer, antelope and turkey abounded in greater numbers than I have ever seen...While hunting we would see Indians almost daily," principally Tonto Apaches or Yavapais who caused no trouble. Hughes prevented one military attack on a Hualapais band, whom an officer suspected of stealing mules, but which Hughes had determined were taken rather by Navahos; an impromptu treaty was made with the natives, though later they were mistakenly attacked by another military group for which reason they went to war upon the whites in earnest. Hughes wondered, "In this instance are the [Indians] wholly at fault for sounding the tocsin of war?" The California contingent and delegation of officials first settled at Camp Clark in the Lit-

tle Chino Valley northwest of Prescott, but within months substituted for it Camp Whipple, adjacent to Prescott. Hughes was mustered out August 31, 1864, at Los Pinos, New Mexico, upon expiration of his enlistment, then re-enlisted March 6, 1865, in Company B, 1st Veteran Infantry and was mustered out finally March 6, 1866. He settled for a time at Cañada Alamosa, New Mexico, then accompanied the Mimbres Apaches in their April 1872 movement to Tularosa where he was employed as "interpreter," though from what language was not clear; he must have acquired some Apache. When O.O. Howard completed his "treaty" with Cochise October 13, 1872, the new agent, Tom Jeffords, who was a friend of Hughes, sent Zebina Streeter (see entry) to offer him the job of clerk, later to become assistant to Jeffords at the new Chiricahua Agency in southeastern Arizona. Hughes accepted, arriving at the agency November 2. He later wrote, "A few days after my arrival, Cochise made his first visit to the agency. This was the first time I met Cochise, that is, in a peaceful manner or to speak to him...He came up to me, took me by the hand with both of his, told me he had heard of me before and that from this day on he was going to be my friend. He kept his word till the day of his death," which occurred June 8, 1874. Hughes accompanied Jeffords south to Pinery Canyon where by arrangement they met about 200 of the Nedhni, or Southern Apaches from Mexico, who agreed to settle in peace on the Cochise Reserve; among them were Juh and Geronimo, a man for whom Hughes had little but contempt, believing him cowardly and with only a very small following. Eventually the question arose whether to remove the Cochise Indians to a reservation away from the Mexico border across which his young men raided persistently; Hughes believed that, if forced to remove, only about half would so do, the rest taking off for Mexico or the mountains, and events were to prove him correct. Hughes was present in Cochise's camp upon the death of that great chief. In 1876 Hughes was reported to have assisted Clum in removing those Chiricahuas who would go northward to the San Carlos Reservation. Hughes then settled at Tucson, being as interested in mining as in faro (he was a professional faro dealer, or gambler most of his life). He also entered politics in a mild way. Five times he was elected to the Territorial Council, and for three sessions was chosen president of it. Then came a personal disaster. He had become clerk for the Pima County Board of Supervisors and an officer of the prestigious Arizona Pioneers' Historical Society. The Legislature appropriated $3,000 for the Society, the sum being transferred by way of Hughes. One night the Tucson Courthouse was set afire; an investigation showed that Hughes was "far behind in his Supervisors' accounts" and it was charged that he had fired the building to wipe out records "of his peculations." Then it was discovered that most of the Historical Society's grant also "had been gambled away." Hughes fled to Randsburg, California, and then to Mexico, but eventually returned for trial, and was sentenced to Yuma Penitentiary. In December 1900 Governor Louis C. Hughes (no relation) paroled him, it having been argued that Fred Hughes was mostly "careless and not criminal," and the financial losses had been made up by two of his Supervisor friends. Hughes spent much time thereafter at the placer mines of Greaterville, south of Tucson. While sitting before his door at 5:55 p.m. he was struck by lightning and killed. "Above the eye on each temple was a tiny red mark" revealing where the bolt had struck, but his body "showed no other marks," although a pocket watch "looked as though it had been touched by a soldering iron." Hughes had been married twice, his first wife predeceasing him; he was survived by his widow, seven daughters and three sons. Burial was at Tucson. A notable pioneer for 50 years in Arizona he had accumulated, for all his faults, countless staunch friends to revere his memory

Fred G. Hughes file, Arizona Hist. Soc.; Farish, III, 40-46; James H. McClintock, *Arizona...*, Chicago, S.J. Clarke Pub. Co., 1916, II, 600-601; Edwin R. Sweeney, *Cochise: Chiricahua Apache Chief*, Norman, Univ. of Okla. Press, 1991; Jay J. Wagoner, *Arizona Territory 1863-1912: A Political History*, Tucson, Univ. of Arizona Press, 1970.

Hughes, Price, frontiersman (d. 1715). B. in Kavllygan, Montgomery County, Wales, he arrived in South Carolina around 1712 to promote Welsh colonization in that portion, or neighboring areas, of America. He became a close friend of Thomas Nairne (see entry), a noted frontiersman. Hughes was disappointed in lands secured for his settlement project near Port Royal and in 1714 received another grant of 3,184 acres in Cragen County. But already "the great West had cast its spell," and with a taste for adventure he was drawn into provincial service as a volunteer Indian agent, and traveled into the

western wilderness. A visionary, he expanded his settlement plans into an "amazing project" for a British province in the lower Mississippi Valley and his early death cut off what Crane described as "an authentic prophet of Anglo-American westward expansion." In the spring of 1713 it was suspected that the French from the Gulf coast had been tampering with the Cherokees, the powerful Indian tribe of the interior. Shortly Hughes was in their mountain country, sending intelligence by traders to the Indian commissioners of South Carolina. Hughes plotted to capture all Indian trade of the west. On the Tennessee River he met two errant *coureurs de bois* from Canada and Mobile, secured their release from their Indian captors, supplied them with trade goods and with Governor Charles Craven's approval sent them as emissaries to the Illinois and to "seven numerous nations" on the Missouri, remarking however by letter that only "God knows what the effect of so distant an embassy will be." Thus was initiated, according to Crane, "those far-reaching intrigues among the western tribes which in the next year and a half made the name of 'master You' [Mister Hughes] respected and feared throughout Louisiana." His ultimate goal was to capture the Mississippi fur trade and close the river between Canada and Louisiana to all others. An observant man, he returned to Charles Town (Charleston) from his initial inland journey enthused about the country, its resources, and the friendly natives he had met, and wrote to an acquaintance back home that "There's no land in American now left y'ts worth anything but what's on the Mesisipi," and there he planned to found a colony with many Welsh settlers who, he was convinced, awaited only his bidding to emigrate to his planned utopia. He sought aid from powerful friends in Britain and petitioned Queen Anne for aid in transporting his impoverished colonists (for he would accept no others) to his projected settlement of "Annarea," based on either Natchez or on the Yazoo River to the east. He expected French opposition, but was convinced of prior English rights based upon the South Carolina trading empire which already had advanced far inland and which he wished to take to the Mississippi himself. To further his plan an association was formed with the Chickasaw and Choctaw, they being persuaded to desert the French in favor of the British interests. In the winter of 1714-15 while proceeding down the river from Natchez to Manchac, the present

Akers between lakes Maurepas and Ponchartrain, Louisiana, Hughes was taken into custody by the French and was delivered with his interpreter and despite his loud protests, to Bienville (see entry) at Mobile. Though he was Bienville's prisoner he was treated with every consideration. For three days their earnest debate at Fort St. Louis de la Mobile continued, "a dramatic moment...in the Anglo-French duel for the heart of America," the two standing for "rival forces of empire in irreconcilable conflict." Asked why he incited the Indian to revolt, Hughes replied that the country belonged to the natives, adding that within a year 500 families from England would be settled on the great river. Bienville was sufficiently impressed to send Hughes's commission from Craven to Paris and urge that boundaries be run between Louisiana and Carolina to avoid further disputes. Hughes was then released, traveled to Pensacola where he remained briefly, then continued eastward. Near the mouth of the Alabama River he was killed by a Tohome Indian, "a tribe that had often felt the scourge of the Charles Town slave-dealers." The Tohomes were a small off-shoot of the Choctaws who shortly merged with the Mobile tribe and the joint peoples probably melded into the Choctaw tribe itself. The Tohomes were always allied with the French. Hughes's death marked the great Yamasee-Creek War against the Carolina traders which already had commenced.

Verner W. Crane, *The Southern Frontier 1670-1732,* Ann Arbor, Univ. of Michigan Press, 1929; DAB article, also by Crane; Hodge, HAI, II; Swanton, *Tribes.*

Hunt, Aurora, historical writer (Nov. 22, 1881-Nov. 8, 1965). B. at Sheldon, 15 miles southeast of Sacramento, California, she was said to have descended from "an early California family," but her father was born at Toronto and her mother in Massachusetts. She attended the University of California at Los Angeles, became interested in the history of the California military of Civil War times and at 57 attended summer sessions at the University of California at Berkeley, where she studied under Herbert E. Bolton (see entry), who encouraged her to expand her researches and helped her to organize and formalize them. The result was several outstanding books on southwestern history that remain standards in their fields: *The Army of the Pacific: Its Operations in California, Texas, Arizona, New Mexico, Utah, Nevada, Oregon, Washington, plains region,*

Mexico, etc. 1860-1866 (1951); *Major General James Henry Carleton 1814-1873: Western Frontier Dragoon* (1958); and *Kirby Benedict, Frontier Federal Judge* (1961). Late in life she was working on a biography of William Starke Rosecrans (1819-1898), a Union officer in the Civil War who at times "exhibited flashes of strategic genius," alternating with disasterous failures. His postwar history was episodic and he finally retired to his ranch near Redondo Beach, California. Miss Hunt obtained for study purposes a great quantity of family papers, but she had not completed her manuscript at the time of her death, and little has been done with her project since then. She died at Whittier, California, two weeks short of her 84th birthday. She had never married.

Information from Hunt's publications, all issued by the Arthur H. Clark Co. of Glendale, Ca.; Aurora Hunt death cert.

Huntington, Dimmick B., interpreter, missionary (May 26, 1808-Feb. 1, 1879). B. at Watertown, New York, he arrived in Utah July 28, 1847, with the Captain James Brown (1801-1863) contingent of the Mormon battalion, being drum major in a martial band and later holding high church offices. He was an Indian missionary, mainly among the Shoshonis, for forty years. Huntington was an early settler at Provo, Utah, but spent much time in the field. He served as Indian guide and interpreter for Brigham Young, who used him on many occasions. In May 1855 Young took him as interpreter on his journey to the Southern Indian Mission, and Huntington was interpreter and general assistant when Indians were summoned to Salt Lake City before the 1857 Mountain Meadows Massacre. When the Alexander Ward massacre of 18 or 19 whites of a party of about 20 and other related casualties occurred August 20, 1854, about 25 miles east of Fort Boise, Major Granville O. Haller (see entry) was assigned to punish the Indians who did it, or at any rate, some Indians. Huntington brought in a report from a man who asserted that the Ward attack had been instigated "to avenge the ravishment of one of their squaws and the stealing of their horses by a company of whites passing through their country," and the avenging troops commited about as many atrocities as the Indians were reported to have done. In early September 1855 at Salt Lake City a council was called between Ute and Shoshoni Indians, the Utes appearing armed and the Shoshonis unarmed and "it took all of the ingenuity of interpreter Dimmick B. Huntington to prevent an attack on the unarmed Shoshoni," but he accomplished it. When the U.S. Army approached Utah with a military force in 1857 the Mormons feared open conflict and Young found it necessary to quiet the excitement, particularly among the Shoshoni. He sent Huntington to East Weber on August 10 to visit Chief Little Soldier. He found the Indians "mutch excited" because of white lies about Mormon intent toward the Indians. Huntington advised the chief to be "Baptised & then he could tell when the Gentiles told him a lie." The chief retorted that he knew a man who had been baptized "& he lied all the time." Huntington then told the Indians that Young had warned that game was becoming scarce, famine was nearing, and the Indians should settle down and learn to farm "but they sat down on their buts & howled like so many Wolvs" at that idea. Huntington the next day went to Brigham City to visit a large Shoshoni camp, where he settled other problems with Chief Pocatello (see entry). Later at Farmington, Utah, he smoothed over other problems, reporting back to Young on his work. Huntington often acted as interpreter for councils between Indians and whites and on occasion was sent into Indian country to track down miscreants. In 1870 Huntington wrote a letter to the Commissioner of Indian Affairs at Washington, asserting he did so at the request of the tribesmen. He noted that "I do love them...& they observe the mosayic Law mutch more strict to day than the whites do." He sought to justify various Indian depredations because the natives, he said, had only acted according to their traditions and laws, citing such incidents over the past fifteen years. Huntington at times carried on missionary work among the Indians, particularly near Franklin, Idaho.

Brigham D. Madsen, *The Shoshoni Frontier and the Bear River Massacre,* Salt Lake City, Univ. of Utah Press, 1985; Madsen, *Pocatello, the "White Plume",* Univ. of Utah Press, 1986; Juanita Brooks, *John Doyle Lee,* Glendale, Ca., Arthur H. Clark Co., 1961; Brooks, *Journal of the Southern Indian Mission,* Logan, Utah State Univ. Press, 1972; Frank Esshom, *Pioneers and Prominent Men of Utah,* Salt Lake City, Western Epics, Inc., 1966 (photo. of Huntington, p. 71; brief biography, 950).

Hurrle, Charles, soldier, interpreter (c. 1853-Feb. 17, 1926). B. in Baden, Germany, he emigrated to the United States, became a "laborer," as he described himself, and enlisted May 5,

1876, in Company E., 6th Cavalry. He was discharged upon expiration of his term of service May 4, 1881, at Fort Apache, Arizona. Hurrle testified August 28, 1882, at the Colonel Eugene Asa Carr court of inquiry that he had "kept an Apache woman [for] about three years," although he had never married her. From her, however, Hurrle apparently learned enough of the difficult Apache language to serve as a military interpreter during the famed Cibecue incident in August 1881, when his misinterpretations may have been instrumental in igniting the action in which an officer and half a dozen enlisted men were killed, the troops' horses driven off, and Carr's column caused to withdraw to Fort Apache (see Carr, Hentig entries). Hurrle, for the last two years of his first enlistment, had been detailed as interpreter and Major Melville A. Cochrane, then commanding Fort Apache, urged that Hurrle be retained thereafter as a civilian interpreter at $75 a month, since he "speaks the Apache language probably better than any other White Man in the Country," a view which was not unanimous. However, he remained as interpreter. September 25, 1882, John Bourke, as aide to Crook, who had just completed his first inspection tour after being reassigned to Arizona, informed the commanding officer at Fort Apache that Apache women had arrived "much worried" by Hurrle's statement to them that "it was General Crook's intention to put the Indians now with him, or with whom he had been in conference, in the Guard house at San Carlos or Tucson. As such reports and all useless and senseless remarks of like character have a most mischievous effect, General Crook directs that you order your interpreter to be more exact in his statements," adding that Crook wanted no threats made, and no one put in the guardhouse or otherwise punished "without orders from himself." That same day Hurrle was released as interpreter, either by his resignation, as he asserted, or because he was fired, as Radbourne was inclined to believe. On July 1, 1883, Hurrle, citing his occupation then as "shoemaker," enlisted at Cincinnati, Ohio, in the 13th Infantry; he was discharged at Fort Wingate, New Mexico, November 4, 1885, "by way of favor upon his own application." He was described at enlistments as 5 ft., 5 in. in height, with brown hair and eyes and a ruddy complexion. He never rose above the rank of private. Late in life Hurrle drew a pension, and died at the U.S. Soldier's Home, Washington, D.C. He probably never married.

Information and documentation from Allan Radbourne, Taunton, England; for Hurrle's interpreter difficulties, see Dan L. Thrapp, *General Crook and the
Sierra Madre Adventure*, Norman, Univ. of Okla.
Press, 1972, pp. 20-23.

Huston, John, motion picture figure (Aug. 5,
1906-Aug. 28, 1987). B. at Nevada, Missouri, he
was the son of actor Walter Huston, at that date
an engineer and traveling vaudevillian. John left
a Los Angeles, California, high school without
graduating, tried professional boxing and
worked sporadically in New York theaters. He
said he had served with the Mexican cavalry; he
was a reporter, sold short stories, was a
scriptwriter and studied art at Paris. In 1938 he
became a writer for Warner Brothers, producing
scripts for such films as *Juarez, High Sierra* and
Sergeant York. In 1941 he made a highly successful directing debut with the *Maltese Falcon.*
He joined the army in 1942 and produced documentaries on World War II, including *Report
from the Aleutians,* and the memorable *Battle of
San Pietro,* perhaps the finest such film ever
made to that time; he was discharged in 1945 as a
major. After the war he tried Broadway briefly,
then returned to Hollywood, producing the outstanding *Treasure of the Sierra Madre,* for which
he also wrote the screenplay, the film receiving
ranking awards. He wrote the screenplays and
also directed such worthy films as *The Red
Badge of Courage, Moby Dick* and *The Life and
Times of Judge Roy Bean,* while films he directed
included *The African Queen, The Misfits,* and
others. Huston was famed not only for his own
taut films, but for the outstanding performances
of the actors who worked for him. For a time he
lived principally at St. Clerans Craughwell,
County Galway, Ireland, and was said to have
obtained Irish citizenship in 1964, but he
returned eventually to California and was buried
at Hollywood Cemetery.

Literature abundant; *Webster's American Biographies,* Springfield, Mass., G & C Merriam Co., 1974;
Who Was Who.

Hutchins, Thomas, geographer, military engineer (1730-Apr. 28, 1789). B. in Monmouth
City, New Jersey, he was an orphan by 16,
matured on the Pennsylvania frontier, served in
the colonial militia during the French and Indian
War and was commended for bravery. He then
joined the British army and was commissioned,
acquiring a knowledge of engineering which

enabled him to plan military works at Fort Pitt
(Pittsburgh), and at Pensacola, Florida. He kept
journals of his military travels and wrote short
papers on them which give an idea of their considerable extent: "Journal of a March from Fort
Pitt to Venango and Thence to Presqu'Isle,"
Venango being an Indian town at the confluence
of French Creek and the Allegheny River, and
Presqu'Isle located at the site of Erie, Pennsylvania; "An Historical Account of the Expedition
[Bouquet's] Against the Ohio Indians in the Year
1764"; "A Journal from Fort Pitt to the Mouth of
the Ohio, in the Year 1768," and "Remarks on
the Country of the Illinois," suggesting that he
also traveled up the Mississippi, perhaps to the
Illinois River. His more extended works included
*A Topographical Description of Virginia, Penn-
sylvania, Maryland and North Carolina* (1778)
and *An Historical Narrative and Topographical
Description of Louisiana and West-Florida*
(1784). He illustrated his journals with his own
maps. In 1762 and 1768 Hutchins visited many
northwestern tribes, including the Delawares,
Shawnees, Chippewas, Wyandots, Miamis and
Potawatomis, estimating their populations and
strengths and in 1762 under the supposed George
Groghan mission to "survey" the Great Lakes
traveling as far west as the Strait of Mackinac; he
also visited Detroit and St. Joseph, Michigan. In
the southeast he visited the Cherokees, Chickasaws and Catawbas to the same ends. It is said
that Hutchins at some time also charted at least a
portion of the courses of the Tennessee and Cumberland rivers, though how extensive these
efforts were is not clear. When the American
Revolution broke out Hutchins, a captain and
military engineer (which incorporated his training as a surveyor) was at London. He declined to
serve against his countrymen and a promotion to
major, and was imprisoned in 1779, charged with
high treason for supposedly communicating
information of military value to friends at Paris,
but was released without trial in 1780. He thereupon resigned his captain's commission, secretly
emigrated to France, presenting himself to Benjamin Franklin, then the American plenipotentiary. Possibly with Franklin's assistance
Hutchins sailed from France for Charleston,
South Carolina, where he joined the southern
army under Nathanael Greene to whose staff he
was appointed. May 4, 1781, he was named by
the Continental Congress Geographer of the
Army of the South, and July 11 the title was
altered to Geographer of the United States. He

retained this title after the war, but was allowed also to accept commissions from the various states and in that capacity he ran the western boundary between Virginia and Pennsylvania in 1783. With the seldom mentioned—in this day—Ordinance of 1785, which was in a sense the forerunner of the famed Ordinance of 1787, Hutchins was charged with the vast task of surveying and platting the public lands of what soon would become known as the Northwest Territory. He was directed personally to run the east-west line upon which the survey of the whole Northwest Territory would be based; the line ran west from the intersection of the Ohio River with the Pennsylvania border, continuing along 40°38'2" N. Lat. He led three expeditions in pursuing this work, in 1785, 1786-87, and 1788-89, taking time out in 1787 to run the boundary between New York and Massachusetts. The first expedition was aborted because of hostility of the Indians, who clearly comprehended that the survey would mean the beginning of the end of tribal lands which, one way or another, and generally without Indian consent, would come into possession of the whites. In this connection, and while waiting for the matter to be settled, Hutchins agreed with John Heckewelder (see entry), famed Moravian missionary, to survey the limits of mission lands of that sect, but the Indians warned against that, too, so the plan was abrogated. September 2, 1788, he commenced his final expedition to complete his basic work, but beyond Pittsburgh illness caused him to return to that place where, several months later, he died. Heckewelder arrived at Pittsburgh about two hours after the death and the next day conducted the funeral; although a Moravian, he led it "according to the rites of the Church of England," since Hutchins was of that faith. Major General of Militia John Gibson (see entry) had requested of Heckewelder that he handle the funeral, which the Moravian was happy to do in any case because of close friendship and respect for Hutchins.

Lit. abundant: *Webster's American Biographies,* Springfield, Mass., G & C Merriam Co., 1974; DAB; CE; Alexander Scott Withers, *Chronicles of Border Warfare,* ed. and annot. by Reuben Gold Thwaites, Cincinnati, Robert Clarke Co., 1895, pp. 43-47 and n.; Paul A.W. Wallace, ed., *Thirty Thousand Miles with John Heckewelder,* Univ. of Pittsburgh Press, 1958; Howard H. Peckham, *Pontiac and the Indian Uprising,* Univ. of Chicago Press, 1947, 1961.

Hutchinson, William Henry, historian, author (Aug. 13, 1911-Mar. 11, 1990). B. at Denver, he attended school at Oxford, Mississippi; Newark, New Jersey; Denver, and Redondo Beach, California, and earned his master's degree in 1961 at Chico State College, California, "just to show 'em I could!" as he explained. He worked in his youth at various times as horse-wrangler, cowboy, mine-mucker and during the Depression went to sea, in World War II becoming a lieutenant commander in the U.S. Maritime Service, seeing duty in the South Pacific, North Atlantic and Mediterranean. Afterward he became a freelance writer, wrote and produced several historical pageants, had his own radio and television programs, taught part-time at Chico College, where he was asked to accept a temporary appointment in 1964 and continued teaching there until his retirement in 1978 as professor emeritus of history. At some time during those years he dubbed himself "Old Hutch," and as such he was widely known thereafter. He wrote 15 books. Among them were *A Bar Cross Man,* which was a biography of Eugene Manlove Rhodes (1956); *The Rhodes Reader* (1957); *Oil, Land, and Politics,* 2 vols. (1965); *Another Verdict for Oliver Lee* (1965); *Whiskey Jim and a Kid Named Billie* (1967); *California: Two Centuries of Man, Land, and Growth* (1971), and *California Heritage: A History of Northern California Lumbering* (1974). He contributed articles to many journals, received many honors. He was visiting professor at the University of Texas in 1968, and was a lecturer at the University of California at Berkeley in 1972. He died at Chico, California, survived by his wife of 47 years, Esther Ormsby (Red) Hutchinson, who died within weeks of his death, and by two sons.

Information from Nancy Riley, History Office, Chico State Univ.

I

Ide, William Brown, frontiersman (1786-Dec. 1852). B. in Massachusetts of Pilgrim ancestry, he worked as a carpenter in Vermont and New Hampshire until 1833, and as a carpenter, farmer and occasionally a teacher in Ohio and Illinois from 1834-44. In April 1845 the Ides party, including the parents, five children and one adopted boy, and four teamsters bound for California and accompanying the group for board and transportation, left Illinois, reaching Independence, Missouri, where the 13-person group joined what became the (John) Grigsby-Ide party for Oregon. Enroute they decided for California rather than Oregon, made a swift passage of the Sierra Nevada largely through Ide's skill and energy, and on the western slopes the train split up, Ide's people "went up the valley with Peter Lassen" (see entry) to Tehama County where they stayed initially on Robert Hasty Thomes's rancho and in the spring of 1846 that of Josiah Belden, on a tract Ide later purchased. In June Ide joined the "Bear" party of insurrectionists "being apparently one of the few settlers who acted in good faith and was induced to believe the false reports that the Americans [those from the United States] were in danger" from California elements. After Captain Grigsby departed from the Bear organization Ide was chosen their commandant and held that office until the July reorganization of the forces under Fremont. This was shortly before the Bear cause was merged into that of the United States, the war with Mexico having commenced. Ide "soon came to regard himself as leader in a grand revolutionary movement, as the conqueror of California," though his men regarded him simply as temporary commandant at Sonora, California, chosen for his zeal and educational background and "they were willing to indulge him in harmless eccentricities, paying but slight attention to his grandiloquent proclamations, or to his peculiar views of himself and the republic he thought he had founded." Ide viewed Fremont's assumption of command as a grievous usurpation of his own position, and his writings on the subject "came very near to insanity." After the changeover, however, he served as a private in the California Battalion during its initial expedition to the south, but soon returned to Sonoma and the Sacramento Valley. June 7, 1847, Ide was appointed by Governor Richard B. Mason, surveyor for the northern department of California and he also performed other civil functions. In 1848-49 he "had some experience in the mines," that is, engaged in prospecting, but without positive results that were reported. His home during these years and later was at the Rancho Barranca Colorado, bought of Belden, near Red Bluff, and in 1851-52 "he seems to have held pretty nearly all the county offices in Colusa at the same time, the highest being that of county judge." The county seat was at Monroe's rancho, where he died in December. Bancroft concluded that Ide "retained to the end his fondness for long reports and for political theorizing, but with all his eccentricity he was always a most worthy and honest man, and had somewhat remarkable tact and executive ability in several directions." He was reported by some to have become a Mormon, though Bancroft found no "positive evidence" of that affiliation. Ide fathered nine children, two surviving past 1880.

Bancroft, *California,* IV-VI, *Pioneer Register.*

Igadik, Aleut sea hunter (fl. before 1740). The son of a chief on the Aleutian island of Unimak, he was blown in his kayak to the shores of a previously unknown island some 250 miles northerly of his homeland, according to an "ancient legend." He found the place thronged with fur seals, sea otters, foxes and other creatures, but without human habitation. He passed the winter hunting, then in four days paddled back to Unimak "bearing an incredible number of sea otter tails" as evidence of his discovery; he named the island Amiq. Its location was kept secret from the predatory Russians as long as possible, but Pribylov (see entry) finally heard of it through an Unalaska shaman, leading to his 1786 voyage of "discovery" to what today are called the Pribylov Islands.

Fredericka Martin, *Sea Bears: The Story of the Fur Seal,* N.Y., Chilton Co., 1960.

Ilinskii, Petr Ivanovich, Russian naval officer (fl. 1799-1842). On January 11, 1799, Ilinskii was one of ten signers of a report to Czar Paul I from the Commercial College supporting organization of the Russian American Company and providing for further strengthening of its dominance in the fur-gathering field in Alaska. In time Ilinskii became staff captain in the Pilot Corps and himself sailed to the Russian American colonies in 1817 with Captain Vasili M. Golovnin on the *Kamchatka.* At some date he surveyed a bay on the western side of Chichagof Island in the Aleutians. His sketch of the bay was published in an atlas of 1826. He died in 1842, probably at the port of Okhotsk, Siberia. Ilin Bay on the west side of Chichagof Island was named for this navigator by the Russians.

Russian Penetration of the North Pacific Ocean; Orth, 15,449.

Immell, Michael E., military officer, mountain man (d. May 31, 1823). B. at Chambersburg, Pennsylvania, his date of b. is unknown. He went to St.Louis in 1804, was commissioned an ensign of the 1st Infantry June 10, 1807, became a second lieutenant October 14, 1808, and resigned November 30 of that year. He was stationed at Belle Fontaine Barracks on the Missouri River three miles above its mouth during most of his army experience, although for a short time in 1808 he commanded a small garrison at St. Louis. In 1809 he went up the river with the Missouri Fur Company, although he was a free trapper working for Lisa in 1810 when he associated with Jean Baptiste Vallé. On April 12, 1810, he discovered the fate of James Cheek (see entry) and others who had been wiped out by a Blackfeet party near the forks of the Missouri. Later Immell joined Lisa and soon became his most trusted lieutenant. In 1812 he accompanied Lisa upriver from Fort Osage and in 1813 he was in charge of a Lisa post at the Omaha village. He "was identified with the fortunes of the Missouri Fur Company under its various names until the violent final encounter with the Blackfeet..." Immell was at Fort Osage in March 1817, when he reported discovery of some petrified mammoth bones, the information published in the *Missouri Gazette* April 12, 1817. When Lisa was ousted from control of Cabanné & Company in February 1819, Immell, who was at Fort Lisa near Council Bluffs, Iowa, was appointed to take command jointly with George Kennerly, Immell going directly on to the Sioux post to trade. He continued active in field operations of the company, was at St. Louis at least in 1821, and in 1823 was on the upper Yellowstone, together

with Robert Jones. William Gordon, a survivor, wrote of a disaster in a letter to Benjamin O'Fallon, U.S. Indian Agent at the Upper Missouri Agency, who passed the information along to William Clark at St. Louis. Gordon wrote that after reaching the Three Forks and finding the country all trapped out, Immell-Jones took 20 packs of beaver and started their return down the Yellowstone. A large party of Blackfeet Indians lay in ambush "on the side of a steep hill the base of which was washed by the River along which we had to pursue the intricate windings of a Buffaloe trace among rocks Trees &c by means of which they had secreted themselves—at this place the men were of course much scattered for a considerable distance as two horses could not pass abreast—at this unfortunate moment and under circumstances so disadvantageous they rushed upon us with the whole force pouring down from every quarter. Messrs. Immell & Jones both fell early in the engagement—a Conflict thus unequal could not be long maintained—The result was the loss of five other men killed, four wounded, the entire loss of all our horses & equipage Traps Beaver and everything—The balance of the party succeeded in escaping by making a raft and crossing the Yellow Stone." The financial loss amounted to "at least" $12,000. O'Fallon added that "Immell has been a long time on this river, first as an officer in the U.S. Army, since as a trader of some distinction. He was in some respects an extraordinary man; he was brave, uncommonly large and of great muscular strength, and, when timely apprised of danger, a host in himself." Emmell's Creek and Emmell's Prairie, Montana, were named for Immell, the creek entering the Yellowstone from the south above the Rosebud and known today as Armell's Creek, a corruption of Emmel's which is a corruption of Immell's.

Heitman; John C. Luttig, *Journal of a fur-trading Expedition on the Upper Missouri 1812-1813* ed. by Stella M. Drumm, 1920 (N.Y., Argosy-Antiquarian Ltd., 1964); Dale L. Morgan, *The West of William H. Ashley,* Denver, Old West Pub. Co., 1964; *Montana, Contributions,* II (1896), 154-55, X (1940), 286; Richard Edward Oglesby, *Manuel Lisa and the Opening of the Missouri Fur Trade,* Norman, Univ. of Okla. Press, 1963; Thomas James, *Three Years Among the Indians and Mexicans,* ed. by Milo Milton Quaife, N.Y., Citadel Press, 1966.

Ingenstrem, navigator (fl. 1830-32). The full name of this sea officer is not reported, but in the late 1820s he was sent by the Russian American Company, in whose employ he served, to the Andreanov group in the middle Aleutian chain. He spent two winters at Atka Island, correcting existing hydrographic charts of the region, concentrating on Atka and Amlia islands. In 1830-32 with Ivan Chernov, he made surveys in the Prince William Sound area and at the mouth of the Kenai River on Cook Inlet. The Ingenstrem Rocks in the western Aleutians were named for him.

Orth, 15, 455.

Ingersoll, Thomas, colonial frontiersman (Nov. 27, 1692-Oct. 9, 1748). B. at Westfield, Massachusetts, he lived near that town all the 55 years of his life. He married Sarah Dewey (1696-1778); they were parents of eight children, including a son, Daniel, who was born May 26, 1718, and died in 1754 while serving with colonial troops at the start of the French and Indian War, circumstances not reported. Thomas Ingersoll's claim to frontier fame rests with his slaying the feared Abenaki sachem and war chief, Gray Lock (see entry), "so noted for his savage cunning, his cruelty, and the great number of murders he perpetrated." He was killed on Ingersoll's estate near Westfield when the Indian "was endeavoring to surprise and scalp Mrs. Thomas Ingersoll as an act of retaliation against the esquire, who had been the means of thwarting him in some of his designs." The date of the shooting is not given, but since public notices of Gray Lock ceased in 1727 it may be inferred that his demise occurred about that time. Upon Ingersoll's death the value of his estate was inventoried at more than 9,662 pounds sterling, "a very large fortune for those days."

Lillian Drake Avery, *A Genealogy of the Ingersoll Family in America*, N.Y., F.H. Hitchcock Pub. Co., 1926, p. 132; information from Atara Clark.

Ingles, Mary Draper, captive (c. 1732-1815). On Sunday, July 8, 1755, Shawnee Indians from Ohio attacked a small settlement at Draper's Meadows (see John Draper entry) at the present Blacksburg, Virginia. Killed were Colonel James Patton, Mrs. George Draper, Casper Barrier and a child of John Draper's, while James Cull and Mrs. John Draper were wounded. Captured were Mrs. Draper despite her injury; Mary Draper (Mrs. William) Ingles and her children, George, 2, Thomas, 4, and Henry Lenard. The Indians withdrew toward Ohio; on the third night out Mrs. Ingles gave birth to a daughter whom

she was permitted to take with her. Beyond the Great Kanawha River the Indians paused to work a salt springs, making the prisoners do the labor of extracting the mineral (a century later two of Mrs. Ingles' great grandsons became salt manufacturers at the site). Many days, though an uncounted number, later the party reached an Indian town in Ohio. Here Mrs. Ingles' children, except the infant, were taken from her. Thomas was sent to the vicinity of Detroit, George to some other village and never heard from by relatives again, Mrs. Draper was sent to Chillicothe, and other prisoners scattered elsewhere. Mrs. Ingles' talent as a seamstress was put to use by her captors. At length she was sent with a Dutch or German woman of advanced years, who may have been Mrs. Henry Bingamin, and other prisoners to make salt, probably somewhere in Ohio. From this camp she and her "Dutch" acquaintance determined to escape. She decided to leave her infant in the Indian camp where presumably it would be adequately cared for by the natives. The two women, barefoot, each carrying only a blanket and a tomahawk, managed to elude search parties seeking them. They had no compass, only a vague idea where they were and the direction they wished to go, and they had no food, living for days on hickory nuts and walnuts and wild grapes. Once they found an old horse, which they rode until it became caught in quicksand and had to be abandoned. Weeks of starvation played havoc with the mind of the Dutch woman, who determined to kill Mary Ingles and consume her body. The couple engaged in a death-struggle, but Mrs. Ingles, being the stronger, managed to escape and continue on her way. Her flight in all covered at least 40 days and an estimated 800 miles. At last she staggered into a frontier clearing and was recognized by Adam Harmon, an acquaintance, who nursed her back to health and delivered her to her husband at Ingles Ferry at the present Radford, Virginia, where the Draper's Meadow survivors had resettled. Mrs. Ingles then persuaded Harmon to search for the old Dutch woman; he found her riding a horse she had picked up at an abandoned Indian camp, where she had also discovered lifesaving food. She and Mrs. Ingles forgave each other and the elderly woman was restored to her husband; if he was Bingamin they subsequently settled in Pennsylvania. Thomas Ingles came home 13 years after the Draper's Meadow raid. Mary Ingles died at 83. The Ingles had many descendants in southwestern Virginia.

John P. Hale (a great grandson of William and Mary Ingles), *Trans-Allegheny Pioneers,* Cincinnati, The Graphic Press, 1886; Thwaites, *Dunmore;* info. from the Va. Hist. Soc.; Gary Jennings, "An Indian Captivity," *American Heritage,* Vol. XIX, 5 (August 1968), 64-71, a highly fictionalized version of Mary Ingles' travail and escape.

Ingles, Thomas, frontiersman (c. 1751-post 1782). B. in Virginia, he was the son of William Ingles (see entry) and his wife, the former Mary Draper and with his mother was captured by Ohio Indians in 1755. Mary Draper Ingles (see entry) subsequently escaped and made a memorable journey home, but the boy remained with the Indians until 1768 "when he was found to be practically a young Indian in his habits and manner of living." He was sent to Dr. Thomas Walker, a noted physician and explorer, of Albemarle County, Virginia. He acquired some education during the next several years, but never became entirely accustomed to civilized life. During his winter at Point Pleasant, West Virginia, where he remained during the significant battle of October 10, 1774, which virtually terminated the Lord Dunmore War, he visited his Indian friends on the Scioto River of Ohio. In 1775 he married, presumably to a white woman, and settled at various places in southwestern Virginia. In 1782 his wife was captured and his home destroyed by Indian raiders. Later Ingles moved to Tennessee and thence to Mississippi where he died.

Thwaites, *Dunmore.*

Ingles, William, frontiersman (1729-1782). B. in Ireland he came with his father to Pennsylvania at an early age. In 1744 he made an exploring trip to southwestern Virginia. In 1748 with John Draper (see entry) he established the earliest settlement on western waters at Draper's Meadow (Blacksburg). Two years later he married Mary Draper, who in his absence from home was captured by Indians in July 1755. According to Thwaites, "she afterwards made her famous escape, and remarkable journey home, from the Ohio towns to the settlements." Ingles often was occupied with Indian wars along the frontier. In February and March 1756 he was a lieutenant on the disastrous Big Sandy expedition, commanded by Major Andrew Lewis (see entry) and doomed by the ineptitude of its guides and lack of coordination of its elements. Composed of 263 whites and 130 Cherokees, or 418 men in all, its mission was to cross the Ohio and carry war to

the Indian towns in Ohio. It reached the Sandy River, which marks the borderline of Kentucky and West Virginia of today, south from the Ohio River, but the command, already desperately short of rations, was halted a few miles from the Ohio itself. Turning homeward, the starving militiamen broke up into survival units as best they could, consuming strips of buffalo hide, moccasin strings, the belts of their hunting shirts, and the flaps of their shot pouches in an effort to remain alive until they gained the settlements, their pack horses long since butchered and consumed. From 1758-60 Ingles was roving or defending his fort at Ingles Ferry across the New River in southwestern Virginia. In 1763 he overtook a raiding party, recovered several prisoners and much booty. On the 1774 Point Pleasant campaign of Dunmore's War he served as commissary or quartermaster, with rank of major. Upon organization of Montgomery County out of Fincastle County in 1777 he became colonel of militia, but was charged with doubtful loyalty to the Patriot cause. A trial for complicity in a Loyalist plot proved inconclusive. Two years later, in 1782, he died at his home at Ingles Ferry, where his descendants became prominent citizens.

Thwaites, *Dunmore;* Alexander Scott Withers, *Chronicles of Border Warfare,* Cincinnati, Robert Clarke Co., 1895, 1970.

Insullah, Ensyla, Michael (The Little Chief), Flathead chief (c. 1784-Oct. 1860). Insullah, whose name may mean Red Feather, perhaps was half Nez Perce and half Flathead, but he came to be a major chief among the latter people. Nothing is known of his boyhood or early manhood. On July 1, 1825, a member of Peter Skene Ogden's Snake River expedition referred to Red Feather as a good looking Indian who headed 70 lodges in the absence of Flathead chief La Breche. Insullah attended the Green River rendezvous of 1835 and told Protestant missionaries Samuel Parker and Marcus Whitman that he had brought some of his people to meet "the man near to God," apparently meaning Parker, to whom he gave a horse. By that time Insullah had become a warm friend of Thomas Fitzpatrick and Robert Campbell (see entries). In 1840, learning that the Jesuit De Smet (see entry) was in the mountains, Insullah brought a band of Flatheads to meet the priest at Green River, became De Smet's first convert in that area and received the name of Michael. The Jesuit wrote of him that "The most influential among them, surnamed 'The Little Chief,' from the smallness of his stature, whether considered as a christian or a warrior, might stand a comparison with the most renowned character of ancient chivalry. On one occasion, he sustained the assaults of a whole village, which, contrary to all justice, attacked his people. On another occasion, when the Banacs [Bannocks] had been guilty of the blackest treason, he marched against them with a party of warriors not one-tenth the number of their aggressors. But, under such a leader, his little band believed themselves invincible, and invoking the protection of heaven, rushed upon the enemy...killing nine of their number. More would have been killed, had not the voice of Little Chief arrested them in the very heat of the pursuit, announcing that it was the Sabbath, and the hour of prayer. Upon this signal, they gave over the pursuit, and returned to their camp...Little Chief had received a ball through the right hand, which had entirely deprived him of its use; but seeing two of his comrades more severely wounded than himself, he with his other hand rendered them every succor in his power, remaining the whole night in attendance upon them. On several other occasions, he acted with equal courage, prudence and humanity, so that his reputation became widely spread. The Nez-perces, a nation far more numerous than the Flat-heads, came to offer him the dignity of being their Great Chief. He might have accepted it...but Little Chief...refused the offer...with this simple remark, 'By the will of the Great Master of life I was born among the Flat Heads, and if such be His will, among the Flat Heads I am determined to die.'" De Smet added that as a warrior, "still more honorable to his character are the mildness and humility manifested by him." But he could be firm. A young woman had absented herself from prayer "without a sufficient reason. He sent for her, and after reading her a lecture before all the household, enforced his motives for greater attention in the future, by a smart application of the cane." Late in life Insullah lived at times with the Flatheads and again with the Pend d'Oreilles. He was killed by Crees and Assiniboines near the Milk River of Montana.

Thwaites, EWT, Vol. 27, 289-90; Dale L. Morgan, Eleanor Towles Harris, *The Rocky Mountain Journals of William Marshall Anderson,* San Marino, Ca., Huntington Lib., 1967; Bernard DeVoto, *Across the Wide Missouri,* Boston, Houghton Mifflin Co., 1947; info. from E.F. (Ted) Mains.

Ioassaf (Ivan Ilich Bolotov), Orthodox churchman (Jan. 22, 1761-Nov. 1799). B. at Strazhkovo, near Kalinin, 100 miles northwest of Moscow, he was educated in seminaries and became a monk in 1786, by 1793 attaining the rank of archimandrite, a cleric ranking below a bishop. In that position he headed a mission to the Alaskan island of Kodiak and the trading settlement there of Shelikhov (see entry), arriving in September 1794. The mission members included Ieromonk (a monk who had been ordained a priest) Yakob Juvenal (see entry), six other priests and 10 church servitors. Ioassaf, whose mind was tainted by what he had heard in eastern Siberia of the conduct of promyshlenniki and fur traders in North America, instantly came to cross purposes with Baranov, a nominally faithful Orthodox church member but more concerned with managing and building his commercial empire. "He knew that...full control of the natives was essential to his success," and that missionaries could assist in bringing this about. To further his pragmatic aim he urged Ioassaf to send his people at once to the savage tribes, not only to get them started with their work, but to remove those undoubtedly to become his managerial antagonists beyond reach. Ioassaf pointed out that cold weather was approaching, that the missionaries must remain on Kodiak for the season and "thus Baranov was obliged to face his adversaries during the whole of a long arctic winter, and to counteract their intrigues as best he might." The Christian workers quickly became openly hostile to the manner in which business was conducted. Ioassaf was "especially bitter" in denunciations of Baranov, there being however "little doubt that many of his accusations were unfounded." Prejudices deepened and there was little cooperation. Although 12,000 natives were reported baptized it was not until July 1796 that the first church on Kodiak was completed. May 18, 1795, Ioassaf wrote to Shelikhov a long letter, part report and mostly complaints about the general manager and the abysmal conditions the missionaries labored under. Shelikhov apparently paid little attention to the wails about the miseries of life on a difficult frontier. Ioassaf also penned a routine report to his archbishop dealing with spiritual matters, the sinful practices of the Aleuts and Russians, and asking instructions on how to deal with such thorny and delicate issues. On the other hand, Baranov's letters during this period, according to Bancroft, lead to the "conviction that the part [of] the traders...was more difficult than that of the priests" and display "a marked forbearance in speaking of the missionaries and their doings." Nevertheless, in time Ioassaf came to be seen by Baranov openly as his "enemy," and it is probable that only the prelate's fate prevented an ultimate confrontation. The archimandrite was recalled to Irkutsk, Siberia, in April 1799 to be consecrated bishop of Kodiak. He sailed aboard the *Feniks (Phoenix)*, the first vessel built on the Northwest Coast and launched in August 1794. Bancroft (331-33) gives interesting details of her construction. She had made regular trips between Kodiak Island and Okhotsk, on the Siberian coast. Consecrated a bishop, Ioassaf left Irkutsk in May and found his way to the coast, where probably in October he embarked again in the *Feniks*, bound for Three Saints Harbor, Kodiak. The ship carried 90 persons including the religious entourage among whom was the Ierodiakin (priest-deacon) Stefan. He had accompanied Ioassaf to Kodiak on his original journey and in his civilian life before entering the clergy had been active in mining, smelting, surveying and architecture besides being "well versed in mathematics." The vessel never made port. Somewhere in the Gulf of Alaska, for reasons unknown, she broke up and her cargo and all on board were lost. In late 1800 Baranov wrote of "the saddest news of all, and the most disastrous to us [which was the loss] of the *Feniks*...For two months portions of the wreck have been cast on the beach in various localities, but the exact place of the disaster remains unknown." As for Ioassaf, Bancroft wrote that he had begun "his journey full of ambitious plans and with the determination to make use of his new dignity [as bishop] in overcoming all opposition, real or imaginary, on the part of his persecutors." But he embarked on the doomed ship "not to return in splendor to the scene of former misery, but to find a watery grave at some unknown point within a few days sail of his destination." At Irkutsk he had composed a geographical and ethnographical description of Kodiak and other islands of his diocese which were published posthumously; these and his letters comprised his literary legacy.

Bancroft, *Alaska;* DAB; *Russian Penetration of the North Pacific Ocean.*

Ivanov, Vasily, explorer (fl. c. 1792-1805). A veteran employee of the Lebedev-Lastochin Fur Company, he headed a party of Russian fur traders and a few Tanaina Indians which left Iliamna Lake, west of Cook Inlet, Alaska, "in the early 1790s." The group was to explore the interior of Alaska, seeking to verify rumors of rich fur regions along the Kuskokwim and Yukon rivers, though those streams were then unknown. The journey was said to have been undertaken between Christmas and Easter. Russian historians, according to James W. VanStone of the Field Museum, believe Ivanov's route from Iliamna Lake, visited Clark Lake to the north, then the upper Mulchatna River and from there by either the Holitna or Stony rivers to the Kuskokwim, of which he was the discoverer. Ivanov in his report mentioned two "large" rivers which he called the Tutna and the Balsanda. Russian geographers identify the Tutna with the Kuskokwim, and the Balsanda with the Yukon. Ivanov's party is believed to have traveled down the Kuskokwim to Oknagamut, an Eskimo village still in existence, then crossed the isthmus to the Balsanda (Yukon). "All of this is highly conjectural," conceded VanStone, and is based upon a manuscript later held by the Russian American Company. Russian historian Vasily N. Berkh interviewed Ivanov on Kodiak Island in the winter of 1804-1805, and Russian scholars today credit Ivanov with being the first Russian to explore the interior of Alaska.

James W. VanStone, *Russian Explorations in Southwest Alaska: The Travel Journals of Petr Korsakovskiy (1818) and Ivan Ya. Vasilev (1829),* Fairbanks, Univ. of Alaska Press, 1988, p. 6.

Izmailov, Gerrasim Grigoriev, Russian explorer, navigator (fl. 1770-1795). Izmailov was "considered one of the most successful navigators among Russian pioneers of Alaska," and the English explorer James Cook, who spelled his name Erasim Gregorieoff Sin Ismyloff, spoke highly of his intelligence and acuteness of observation. An imperial ukase issued at Okhotsk August 29, 1770, noting previous reports of atrocities upon native Alaskans by promyshlenniki fur traders, instructed Izmailov as a ship's master "to see that no such barbarities, plunder and ravaging of women are committed under any circumstances" during a voyage which he then apparently was contemplating. However, in Kamchatka Izmailov became innocently drawn into the notorious conspiracy of Mauritius Augustine Benijovski (see entry), and embarked with him on the *Sv Petr i Sv Pavel* from Bolsheretsk May 12, 1771, for what he supposed would be a prosperous cruise of Pacific waters. Learning of the conspiracy and true nature of the adventurer's plotting, however, Izmailov and others planned to seize the ship and return her to Bolsheretsk. Their counterplot was discovered and Izmailov and his collaborator, Fedor Paranchin and Paranchin's wife were cast ashore on the Kurile island of Ourumusir. From there they were rescued in 1772 by the merchant-trader Protodiakonov and returned to Kamchatka. In 1776 Izmailov captained a trading vessel owned or chartered by the firm of Orekhof, Lapin and Shilof. Few details are known of this voyage to Russian America though it was highly successful, Izmailov returning in 1781 with a fur cargo valued at 172,000 rubles ($86,000). During this trip, in 1778 he met with Cook at Samghanuda Bay of Unalaska Island. The English captain was particularly interested in the already semi-mythical voyage of Benijovski, although Izmailov, because of his abbreviated experience, could tell Cook very little about it. The interview was difficult because Izmailov spoke no English, Cook no Russian, and communication was largely by signs. Cook was shown Russian maps and charts of the Aleutian Islands, which were of considerable benefit to him. Before his departure October 21, Izmailov was given despatches by Cook for the British Admiralty which he promised to forward in the spring via Okhotsk and St. Petersburg. The Unalaska natives remembered Izmailov's fur-gathering role on the island, but made no specific complaints of abuses of Aleuts by him, although others were criticized harshly for cruelty. In 1783 Izmailov commanded the *Trekh Sviatiteli* on its important voyage (after wintering on Bering Island) to Kodiak Island where Shelikhov (see entry), who arrived aboard the vessel, established the first permanent Russian settlement on Alaskan soil. It was the initial phase of what later developed into the powerful Russian American Company. Izmailov henceforth worked for the Shelikhov-Golikov Company. In an official inquiry Izmailov was questioned at Kodiak July 1, 1790, about events occurring during the Shelikhov expedition seven years earlier. He could not confirm that 150 to 200 Aleuts and Russians had been killed during island hostilities, but six Russians were wounded in one action when more than 200 natives were

taken prisoner, and Shelikhov had ordered six to ten of the old men speared to death. Izmailov conceded that he had shot two native "traitors" (or patriots) by order of Shelikhov. Izmailov made repeated voyages between Okhotsk and various fur-gathering points in Alaska and in 1789 Shelikhov wrote that Izmailov might be sent with furs to Macao (near Canton) to trade, though whether this voyage was made is not reported. The *Trekh Sviatiteli*, having probably taken Shelikhov and his wife back to Okhotsk, arrived under Izmailov at Kodiak from that port once more in April 1788. It was sent to make a fresh investigation of Prince William Sound and the Alaskan bight east of it. Accompanying him was another navy master, Dmitrii I. Bocharov. The two officers were equipped with painted posts and copper plates "to mark the extent of Russia's domain" in the light of increasing visits to the region by British, Spanish and, before long, American vessels. May 10 the ship anchored at Nuchek (Hinchinbrook) Island and a wooden cross was dutifully erected proclaiming the territory Russian. May 27 the party traded at Montague Island and then proceeded to Ochek (Middleton) Island where a minor clash with natives occurred; on June 1 the ship anchored at uninhabited Kayak Island. June 11 Yakutat Bay was reached and trading commenced with the Tlingit Indians while Izmailov's Kodiak Eskimos successfully hunted in their bidarkas far out at sea. Izmailov presented Tlingit Chief Ilkhak with a portrait of Tsar Paul and a medal, while two plates were buried to assert Russian claims to the region and a slave boy of Chugach and another of Chilkoot origin were purchased, they proving valuable interpreters. Izmailov continued southeastward to Lituya Bay before returning to Kodiak to conclude his valuable cruise. He was stationed for a time at Three Saints Bay on Kodiak to look after interests of the government. In 1792 he made an unsuccessful voyage seeking further fur-gathering sites. Izmailov commanded the *Phoenix* which left May 25, 1795, on a voyage from Kodiak to Okhotsk. Further reports of his activities have not been located, but Richard A. Pierce believed he died at Okhotsk in 1796 or 1797.

Bancroft, *Alaska; Russian Penetration of the North Pacific Ocean.*

J

Jackson, Donald Dean, historian (June 10, 1919-Dec. 9, 1987). B. near Glenwood, Iowa, he was graduated in journalism from Iowa State College (now University) in 1942 and served with the Navy in the Pacific during World War II. He then took graduate work at the University of Iowa, receiving a doctorate in communications in 1948 when he joined the University of Illinois Press as editor. He remained with the Press until 1968, when he became professor of history at the University of Virginia, retiring in 1976. Meanwhile he had commenced historical editing of significant frontier material. He published *Black Hawk: An Autobiography* (1955), the best edition of this important Indian-authored memoir. He brought out a well-edited edition of *The Letters of the Lewis and Clark Expedition* (1963) which has been called "the most important contribution to Lewis and Clark literature of the twentieth century excepting the *Original Journals.*" Jackson became associated with National Historical Publications and Records Commission projects on Pike, Fremont and Washington. One of his most impressive feats was the first of these, editing the two-volume *Journals of Zebulon Montgomery Pike with Letters and Related Documents* (1966), a masterly compilation with definitive annotations. By it, Pike's complete journals were reissued for the first time since 1895, supplemented "with much that is new." His captured papers, held in Mexico for a century, were published in full and Spanish official correspondence was translated and presented for the first time. Original Pike material had been published in a confusing manner in 1810 and Jackson clarified that poor organization, bringing to it a great deal of material not available to early compilers, among them Elliott Coues, whose 1895 edition had been the best before Jackson's. Jackson's work was concerned primarily with Pike's explorations and he made no attempt to describe the officer's early life or his military career after his return from Mexico. Jackson also published *Custer's Gold* (1966) on the 1874 Black Hills Expedition. He then published the second Historical Commission project, edited with Mary Lee Spence: two volumes of *The Expeditions of John Charles Fremont*

(1970, 1973). Jackson and Dorothy Twohig, in the third such undertaking, brought out the first two volumes of *The Diaries of George Washington* and worked for eight years to advance appearance of the final four volumes, leaving upon his retirement a strong staff and 125,000 catalogued documents. Following his retirement to Colorado, he continued writing, with several books related to western history, the final one being *Among the Sleeping Giants: Occasional Pieces on Lewis and Clark* (1987). He had also published an historical novel, and *Voyage of the Steamboat Yellowstone.* Jackson died at Colorado Springs.

In addition to volumes cited; Council on America's Military Past *Heliogram* 193 (July 1988), 10.

Jackson, Sara Dunlap, archivist (c. 1920-Apr. 19, 1991). B. as Sara Dunlap at Columbia, South Carolina, she majored in sociology and was graduated from Johnson C. Smith University, Charlotte, North Carolina in 1943, worked for a year as a clerical employee at the War Department, and then joined the National Archives where she served until her retirement. She became an outstanding expert on locating documents and papers held by the military section of the Archives and was of so great assistance to a vast number of researchers it was said that she "had been thanked in more 'Acknowledgements' sections of books than any other government staff member." It is believed that relatively few researchers who plumbed the Archives for any length of time were not grateful to her for her generous assistance. This author knows from personal experience that when all else failed in the search for some elusive shred of information, Sara Jackson could and would find it for one. In addition to her work in the military archives division, she also served on Civil War projects for the Archives' National Historical Publications and Records Commission. She was a director for the Council on America's Military Past and the Friends of Fort Davis, Texas National Historic Site, and served on the executive council of the Southern Historical Association, had received honors from West Point and the Houston Civil War Round Table and was bestowed an honorary doctorate by the University of Toledo. She also did volunteer work for a library which conducted after-school tutorial programs for community youths. Her marriage to C.H. Jackson ended in divorce. Her ashes were strewn at Fort Davis.

Council on America's Military Past *Headquarters Heliogram* No. 214 (Apr.-May 1991); many years of grateful acquaintance with Sara Dunlap Jackson.

Jacobs, Captain, Delaware chief: *see,* Captain Jacobs

Jacques, Elsie Berry, researcher (Sept. 27, 1905-c. Mar. 10, 1990). B. at Bolton, about ten miles northwest of Manchester, England, she was the daughter of George Jacques, born in France, and his wife, Anne Berry, an English woman. Elsie migrated to the United States, became something of an artist, and in 1942 during World War II she joined the Women's Army Auxiliary Corps (WAAC), serving for seven months. She was spunky, contentious, kow-towed to no one and incessantly argued with her superiors, noncommissioned and even commis-sioned officers, rejecting orders if they ill-suited her and ignoring reprimands which not infre-quently floated her way. When in 1943 the Women's Army Corps succeeded the WAACs, those in the latter grouping were given the option of transferring to the new organization, or accepting an honorable discharge, which Elsie gladly embraced to the not improbable relief of the Army of the United States; she subsequently understated it: "I think my officer was glad I left." Although she remained for the latter part of her life a resident of Quincy, Massachusetts, she developed an interest in frontier history and by the early 1960s focused her attention on the life of Thomas Jonathan Jeffords (see entry), famed southwestern frontiersman and friend of Cochise, who was the ablest and most notable Apache hostile of his day. She rapidly developed into a superb researcher—diligent, innovative, tireless and devoted. She pursued every possible lead and developed some that had occurred to no one else. She accumulated a wealth of primary material on the life of Jeffords, superior to any-thing that had been done before on this intriguing man about whom no satisfactory biography had appeared. And she was ever generous with her materials. For example, she had had duplicated a considerable collection of Crook letters and other documents held by a western university; later she learned that the school's collection had

been stolen and, uninvited, had her own collec-tion copied and sent it to the university to substi-tute for what it had lost. She also freely shared photographs she had discovered with other researchers at no charge, and frequently sent books, or sets of books, to people who had aided her from time to time, or who had some use for them without the means to purchase the volumes. She had just commenced her narrative of Jef-fords' life when she died at 84 of a stroke in her Quincy apartment. The body was not discovered for an estimated ten days, and inevitably was in a deteriorating condition when found. A bumbling bureaucrat, making not the slightest effort to have Jacques's vast collection appraised or pro-fessionally evaluated, peremptorily directed that everything in the odorous apartment be carried out and burned. So perished Elsie Jacques's irre-placeable archives of documents, photographs, books, correspondence, notes and writings, to the tragic loss to historiography of an important seg-ment of the nation's record. She had never mar-ried. She was cremated, the ashes buried March 25, 1990.

Many years of correspondence with Elsie Jacques; Jacques death certificate (which mistakenly gives the date of death as February 10); information from Bever-ly Loud, secretary, Christ Church Episcopal, Quincy, Mass.

Jaeger (Iaeger), Louis John Frederick, adven-turer (Oct. 8, 1824-June 30, 1892). B. on a farm near Hamburg, Pennsylvania, he became a machinist and in 1846 went to Washington, D.C., to install machinery for ordnance work. In 1848 or 1849 an uncle offered to outfit him for the Cal-ifornia gold fields, and February 22, 1849, he left Philadelphia aboard the *Mason,* sailing around the Horn and reaching San Francisco October 6. He worked at a variety of jobs, then met George A. Johnson who had become interested in a ferry across the Colorado River at today's Yuma, where entrepreneurs had made great profits until disaster of one kind or another struck them down. Jaeger and Johnson organized a party of 11 other men, each contributing $500, and found their way to the Colorado after great hardships in crossing the desert, and overcoming fears of fresh disasters in the ferry business by those who had preceded them. They arrived at the crossing July 10, 1850, built a small stockade, constructed a rude ferry and overcame threats of violence from Indians of the vicinity. California Quarter-master General Joseph C. Morehead arrived in

October with militia to punish Indians accused of wiping out previous groups of ferrymen. When the Indians elected to fight, the Jaeger-Johnson group joined the militia in putting down the threat. The militia force then dissolved, but several months later U.S. Major Samuel P. Heintzelman (see entry) established a small military post at the crossing, naming it Camp Independence. With profits not so high as had been anticipated, most of the ferrymen sold their interests to Jaeger and William Ankrim, Johnson being among those who abandoned the business. In November Indians attacked the post and drove the military out. Jaeger, then at San Diego obtaining supplies, was on his return when he heard of the fresh disaster and hurried toward the river. He was attacked by Indians within three miles of the ferry station and severely wounded by arrows as he sped to his sanctuary, but in the pursuit and flight he shot (but did not kill) Pasqual (see entry), an important chief (who died in 1887). That night the whites quit the stockade and took Jaeger to San Diego, where he quickly recovered. In 1852 Heintzelman again was assigned to the Colorado crossing and set up a fort anew. Urged to join him, Jaeger started a small town he called Jaegerville, which prospered. In addition to the ferry business Jaeger commenced freighting. He hauled wood for his ferries from San Diego at 25 cents a pound, operated barges, started horse, cattle and sheep ranches, established a durable peace with the Indians, and in 1853 when Johnson and others returned to found the Colorado Steam Navigation Company, Jaeger became their partner. He was a stockholder in the Ajo Copper Mine in 1854 and held an interest in the profitable Venture Mine. In that year he met Charles Poston and became the first property owner in Poston's Arizona City, the present Yuma. "Years later it was said that Don Diego was the richest man in the Territory [of Arizona] and that at one time he might have been worth more than a million dollars." But he had reverses. In 1857 he lost $50,000 on an unfortunate canal scheme. During the Civil War the military, fearing a Confederate move against the lower Colorado, ordered all of Jaeger's ferries except the largest burned; in January 1862 the river overflowed its banks and washed away most of Jaegerville, but he recouped some of his losses, rebuilt his ferries with the extinction of the Confederate threat to the region, expanded his stock and mining adventures. When the Southern Pacific Railroad in 1876-77 came through Yuma

it terminated the ferry business and Jaeger then lost most of his other resources through business mismanagement. In 1877 he moved to Agua Mansa near San Bernardino, California. He tried to get the federal government to reimburse him for destruction of his ferries during the Civil War. While at Washington, D.C., in pursuit of this end he died, probably of pneumonia, broke and discouraged, but "an honest and dearly loved man of the West, a friend of everybody." He was married and fathered children.

Stephen N. Patzman, "Louis John Frederick Jaeger, Entrepreneur of the Colorado River," *Arizoniana,* Vol. IV, No. 1 (Spring 1963), 31-36; J. Ross Browne, *A Tour Through Arizona,* Tucson, Arizona Silhouettes, 1951, p. 53; Andrew Wallace, ed., *Pumpelly's Arizona,* Tucson, Palo Verde Press, 1965; HNAI, 10.

Jane, daughter of Nez Perce chief: *see,* Jane Silcott

Jarvis, David Henry, Revenue officer (b. 1852). Lieutenant Jarvis, whose first name sometimes appears as Daniel, of the Revenue-Cutter Service, conducted an extended rescue mission in the winter of 1897-98 in northern Alaska, seeking to aid whalers caught in ice floes near Point Barrow. December 16, 1897, he and three companions were landed on Nunivak Island by the cutter *Bear.* From the island the party traveled by dogsled across the delta and lake country to Andreafski, on the Yukon River, thence downstream and along the coast to St. Michael. From there one section continued along the coast of Norton Sound to Cape York, while another section crossed the base of Seward Peninsula to Kotzebue Sound. From various stations 448 reindeer were collected and driven across frozen Kotzebue Sound, and thence along the Arctic coast to Point Barrow, arriving March 29, 1898. A detailed account of the adventure was published in the 1899 report of the *Bear.* Jarvis eventually became a captain in the Revenue-Cutter Service and in 1902 was named collector of customs for Alaska. Various features are named for him in that state.

Orth, 16, 470.

Jemison, Mary, captive of Indians (1743-Sept. 19, 1833). B. at sea of Irish parentage while enroute from Belfast to Philadelphia, she became a thoroughly acculturated captive of Indians and preferred their way of life to the white existence of her day. Her parents established a farm at the confluence of Sharps Run and Conewago Creek, Pennsylvania, and here, on April 5, 1758, she, her parents, three other children and various neighbors were captured by a French and Indian war party. Most of the captives were slain, but Mary was taken to Fort Duchesne (present Pittsburgh) and was given to two Seneca women who adopted her as substitute for a brother who had been killed in battle. She was named Dehgewanus and for five years lived in the Ohio country. When she was 18, in the third year of her captivity, she married a Delaware warrior, Sheninjee, having two children by him. In 1762 she went with three Indian "brothers" to Little Beard's town on the Genesee River, near present Geneseo, New York. With the end of the French and Indian War the British offered a bounty for the return of prisoners of the Indians. A tribal chief wanted to take Mary to Fort Niagara, but her Indian family objected to giving her up, and she was content to remain with her adopted people. Her husband died and around 1766 she married an old chief, Hiadagoo (Hiakatoo), by whom she had six children. He was a kind and loving husband and father, but ferocious on the warpath. During the Revolution her home was a frequent stopping point for Joseph Brant and Walter Butler (see entries). At the close of the conflict she was offered her freedom by her Indian brother (who was responsible for her), but she preferred to stay with the Senecas. She was granted a tract of her selection along the Genesee River near the present Castile, New York, in 1797; it was where she had lived since the army of John Sullivan (see entry) had destroyed Little Beard's town in 1779. Her husband died in 1811 at a purported 103; two of her sons were killed by a third in a drunken brawl, the survivor himself killed later. In 1817 she was "naturalized" and her land title confirmed by the state legislature. "At this time she was leasing the greater part of her land to white settlers and living with a married daughter. An extensive landholder, she was noted for her kindness and generosity, having retained her English language (although with a touch of Irish brogue), although she could neither read nor write. She was a "teetotaler," neither smoked nor drank, and continued to wear Indian clothing for the rest of her life. In 1823 a physician, James Everett Seaver, interviewed and wrote of her history: *A Narrative of the Life of Mrs. Mary Jemison* (1824) which, in a century, went through 23 editions, one of the latest appearing in 1961. When the Senecas sold their Genesee lands in 1831 she moved with them to the Buffalo Creek Reservation. Late in life she accepted Christianity and was buried near the Seneca Mission Church. In 1874 her remains were moved to the present Letchworth Park, near her old home on the Genesee, where in 1910 a bronze statue was placed to her memory. She always venerated her elderly husband, was reluctant to speak of his cruelties to captives although she did concede a few of his many activities during the Revolution, including "butchering infants and beating out their brains," which was customary, or at least not infrequent in the Woodlands War.

James E. Seaver, *A Narrative of the Life of Mrs. Mary Jemison...,* ed. by Allen W. Trelease, N.Y., Corinth Books, 1961; DAB; Barbara Graymont, *The Iroquois in the American Revolution,* Syracuse Univ. Press, 1972.

Jesseaume, René, interpreter, trader: *see,* René Jusseaume

Jette, Jules (Julius), Jesuit missionary (Sept. 30, 1864-Feb. 4, 1927). B. at Montreal he became a Jesuit and volunteered for the Alaska missions, arriving at Nulato in 1898, spending almost 30 years in Alaska and becoming "the most important early scholar of the Yukon River Koyukon." He settled at Nulato among the Lower Koyukon, an Athabascan people. All of his life and work were devoted to them although "regrettably, he did not visit people living on the Middle or Upper Koyukuk," or at least work among those two of the three Koyukon divisions. Jette published papers in scientific journals devoted to ethnology and linguistic matters, but most of his writings are still in manuscript form "including a highly advanced grammar of Ten'a, the Koyukon language and a vast and superb dictionary remarkable for its sensitive ethnographic detail," frequently illustrated by the author's illuminating sketches. It is in seven volumes. In 1922 he was injured in an accident, and spent four years at Fairbanks and Seattle on a recovery program, returning to his Indian work shortly before his death. Jette's papers and hundreds of photographs he took are preserved in the Oregon Province Archives of the Society of Jesus, Gonzaga University, Spokane, Washington.

Guide to the Microfilm Edition of the Oregon Province Archives, by Robert C. Carriker, Clifford A. Carroll, S.J., W.L. Larsen, Gonzaga University, Spokane, 1976; HNAI, IV, inc. a partial bibliography.

Jocelyn, Stephen Perry, military officer (Mar. 1, 1843-Mar. 8, 1920). B. at Brownington, Vermont, he was educated at three Vermont academies until 1862. He enlisted August 22, 1862, in the 6th Vermont Infantry, was commissioned a first lieutenant August 1, 1864, in the 115th U.S. Colored Infantry from which he was mustered out February 10, 1866. On February 23, he was commissioned a second lieutenant in the 6th U.S. Infantry and a first lieutenant July 28. He was mustered out January 1, 1871, becoming a second lieutenant in the 21st Infantry March 9, 1871, and a first lieutenant April 14, 1873, ranked as such from July 28, 1866. When Colonel William B. Hazen (see entry) was named Superintendent of Indian Affairs for an area including the present Oklahoma June 30, 1869, Jocelyn was named by Hazen superintendent of Indian affairs for the "Southern Superintendency," Hazen's responsibility. Jocelyn was assigned with Captain A.F. Field, the Creek agent, to unravel the tangled matters involving claims by the Creeks for certain awards. Assessment of their petitions was completed by December 19. In May 1870 Jocelyn, Jonathan Richards and Lawrie Tatum, Indian bureau officials met with the Wichitas, who had remained loyal during the Civil War, and recommended a large reservation for them. During the Modoc War in northeastern California in 1872-73, Jocelyn was based at Fort Klamath, in southern Oregon; if he had any active role against the Modocs, it was not notable. He privately criticized Frank Wheaton (see entry) who, Jocelyn pointed out, had commanded a division in the Civil War, but now had great difficulty controlling less than a hundred "shirttail Indians." Jocelyn, commenting in a letter on those Modoc prisoners quartered at Fort Klamath, wrote that "they are a sorry, pitiful-looking set to have given so much trouble." Commanding F Company of the 21st at Fort Klamath he was disgusted by the approaching hanging of Captain Jack and three of his colleagues, which occurred at Klamath October 3, 1873. He wrote that "the officer of the day will have charge of the unpleasant duty [of the executions] but I hope to arrange it that the detail will not fall on me." The detested task fell to Captain George B. Hoge. Jocelyn became a captain May 19, 1874, remaining in the Department of the Columbia (he was in that and the Department of the Platte until 1890). He had an active role against the Nez Perce Indians in their spectacular emeute toward Canada in 1877 which was highlighted by several military actions. Jocelyn was breveted to major for "conspicuous gallantry" July 11-12 in the action at Clearwater, Idaho, in which the

troops suffered 43 casualties, 13 of them deaths, while the Nez Perce casualties were four killed and six wounded, according to McWhorter. The Battle of Clearwater was, according to ranking historian Erwin N. Thompson, "a confused affair involving a number of Army units," and not only is the part played by each of them not clearly reported, but Jocelyn's role leading to his citation is also obscure; it was not mentioned by General O.O. Howard in his book on Chief Joseph or other writings perused. Harry Lee Bailey (see entry) wrote that Captain Jocelyn had been instrumental in persuading Howard to send relief to one organizational mixup on the first day of the engagement. Jocelyn had some role in the Bannock War of 1878. He became a major of the 19th Infantry June 27, 1897; lieutenant colonel of the 25th Infantry March 31, 1899, and colonel of the 14th Infantry February 28, 1901, in that rank also serving on the General Staff of the Army. He was chief of staff of the Pacific Division from 1904-1906, and became a Brigadier General June 16, 1906. He commanded the Department of the Columbia in 1906-1907. He lived at Burlington, Vermont, in his retirement.

Heitman; Powell; Marvin E. Kroeker, *Great Plains Command: William B. Hazen in the Frontier West,* Norman, Univ. of Okla. Press, 1976; Cyrus Townsend Brady, *Northwestern Fights and Fighters,* Garden City, N.Y., Doubleday, Page & Co., 1923; Erwin N. Thompson, "Thirteen U.S. Soldiers," *Frontier Times,* Vol. 36, No. 2 (Spring, 1962), 47, 63; McWhorter, *Hear Me;* Stephen Jocelyn II, *Mostly Alkali: A Biography,* Caldwell, Idaho, Caxton Printers, 1953; *Who Was Who.*

Johnson, Albert (Johan Konrad Jonsen, "The Mad Trapper of Rat River"), desperado (July 13, 1898-Feb. 17, 1932). Almost certainly an American bank robber and outlaw, Johan Jonsen was b. of Swedish-Norwegian parentage at Bardu, 38 miles northeast of Narvik in the Lapland region of Norway. The successful search for his identity as the renowned "mad trapper" was made by Dick North, newsman-museum curator of Dawson City-Whitehorse, Yukon. His remarkable 20 year endeavor led North to investigate many false leads as divergent as the slayer of Jack Lingle, a *Chicago Tribune* reporter, as well as a disappeared Norwegian guide for Zane Grey in the Southwest. North's diligent work, outstanding for persistence and thoroughness, at last uncovered beyond reasonable doubt the true identity of the gunman. When Johan was 6 the family migrated to America, leaving Christiana

(Oslo) July 15, 1904, for New York and after a month in Minnesota reached North Dakota north of the Badlands where the Swedish father, Anders Gustaf Jonsen, homesteaded 320 barren acres he hoped to turn into wheatland; he settled there with his wife Petra, of Norwegian birth, and their children. To bolster the family's meager income young Johnny became a good trapper and also a superb rifle shot, hunting small game and at length deer and antelope. He and his older brother, Magnor, broke horses, a rough and exacting work during which they became acquainted with Bert Delker (Martinus B. Mortenson) who had followed the owl hoot trail and always packed a .44 revolver for exigencies. He had served time for horse rustling in Montana's Deer Lodge penitentiary and North suspected he had had some early connection with Cassidy's Wild Bunch. In any event, he attracted the brothers "like a magnet." Delker married a sister of Johnny's; she died in childbirth and around 1913 Johnny moved in with Delker, who honed the boy's pistol expertise to a fine edge. Delker may have inspired Johnny and Magnor to hold up the Farmers' State Bank of Medicine Lake, Montana, February 11, 1915. It was their initial attempt at outlawry, the two seizing $2,800, but in their escape rode into a posse at Dagmar, Montana. Magnor was wounded and captured, but Johnny escaped with most of the loot. He was arrested in Wyoming for horse theft, eventually was returned to Montana for the bank robbery and was sentenced to Deer Lodge, being released with Magnor in 1918; his brother joined the army and again was wounded, this time in France, earning a Purple Heart. Johnny returned to the family farm. Eventually he went to California, was tried at Susanville for grand larceny under the alias of Charles W. Johnson, was convicted, sent to San Quentin Prison and within a month was transferred to Folsom; he was paroled December 22, 1922. During his career Johnson used various aliases and no doubt committed more crimes than were charged against him. He also worked at such occupations as logging and mining. He found his way next to British Columbia where he adopted the names, successively, of Arthur Nelson and Albert Johnson, at length pursuing such wilderness activities as trapping, at which he already was accomplished. July 9, 1931, he arrived at Fort McPherson on the lower Peel River, having floating down that stream on a three-log raft. He appeared "a quiet man, not given to idle conversation" and "unsociable,"

although not reluctant to demonstrate his skill with pistols. In one instance he paced off a distance, set up two three-foot stakes and "with a pistol in each hand shot the top off of each stick, crossed hands and shot again," knocking an inch from the tops of the sticks with each fusillade. His reason for the "demonstration" was proably to "discourage prying eyes that might see he had approximately $3,400 in cash" which it may be doubted he derived from conventional labor. He would visit a trading post, pick out some item and pay for it with a large bill, pocket the change, wander around the store and select something else, paying again with a large bill and accepting change. He told a Royal Canadian Mounted Police questioner that he had been "working on the prairies last summer and winter [1930-31] and had come into the country by way of the Mackenzie River." In July and August he traversed a tough route to get to the Rat River, building a cabin some 50 miles northwest of Fort McPherson. There he tolerated no visitors, associated with no one. RCMP Constable Alfred King, in answer to a complaint that Johnson had been tampering with traplines, sought to question him, but was rebuffed. December 31, 1931, King returned with a search warrant issued by RCMP Inspector A.N. Eames and accompanied by another constable and two other men. When King knocked, Johnson shot through the door, the bullet splintering the wood and striking the officer in the chest, bowling him over and causing a serious lung wound. He was loaded on a dog sled and rushed to Aklavik, a police headquarters on the west channel of the Mackenzie delta. Inspector Eames now organized a dog team posse, but that took five days and four more to reach the Rat River cabin. Eames thought Johnson would have fled the scene but he was still there, "perhaps waiting for a snowstorm to obliterate his tracks." A call informed Johnson that King had not died and leniency for the shooting might be had, but the message was ignored. The posse fired on the cabin and Johnson countered shot for shot. After nine hours dynamite was hurled at the structure and deputy Knut Lang tried to force his way in, but failed. The standoff continued for 15 hours when Eames returned to Aklavik for more supplies. He sent Constable Edgar Millen with a detail back to the Rat River cabin, where they found that Johnson had taken advantage of a blizzard to depart. Examination of the cabin found its structure fortress-like and superbly crafted, with the floor countersunk and artifacts such as snowshoes well-constructed given the crude tools Johnson had contrived. Millen and his three companions picked up Johnson's trail on a tributary to the Rat coming down from the Richardson Mountains to the westward, across which Johnson apparently intended to seek sanctuary somewhere. After sixteen grueling days Johnson was cornered in a small canyon. In an ensuing gun battle Millen was killed and Johnson escaped over a steep cliff. Eames now wired for a plane and reinforcements, set up a base camp and appealed for civilian help. "Johnson, alone, on foot, and unable even to hunt lest rifle shots give his position away, was running circles around the Mounties with all their dog teams, Indian guides and sleds full of supplies," while the story had become news across America and Europe. A Mountie detachment west of the Richardsons joined the hunt January 21, headed by Constable Sid May. The plane was piloted by "Wop" May (no relation). Johnson was making for a high saddle in the Richardsons. The weather had turned very cold. The fugitive completed the "impossible" winter task of traversing the range in a sudden raging blizzard, enroute discarding his bedroll probably because he had grown too weak to carry it. Eames now collected his forces west of the mountains, flown there by the plane which had spotted Johnson's distinctive snowshoe tracks. A few days later, on February 17, the combined posse ran head-on into the fugitive 25 miles up the Eagle River from its junction with the Bell River. Johnson put Royal Canadian Signals Sergeant Earl Hersey out of action with a single bullet which stuck the officer in knee, elbow and chest, causing five wounds from one slug. Hersey had been kneeling and shooting at Johnson when he was hit. The posse surrounded Johnson at last on the mid-river ice. Special Constable John Moses barely peeked over a snowdrift when Johnson caught the movement, fired at him, and the fugitive fell when the crack shots of the posse put seven bullets into him; Hersey was flown to Aklavik in time to save his life. Johnson's body was estimated to weigh less than 100 pounds after his stupendous 45-day flight, afoot, with scant or virtually no food, little sleep without fires to warm him in temperatures far below zero, and his herculean efforts to escape. He bore not a shred of identification on his person, nor had he left any in his cabin. The mystery of the true identity of the man was not solved by the RCMP. It had to await the intense detective work of Dick

North who, in his book, compares 25 minute physical attributes from prison records with those of the fallen gunman to arrive at a 95 percent conviction that Albert Johnson, Johnny Johnson and Johan Konrad Jonsen had been "one and the same person."

Dick North, *Trackdown: The Search for the Mad Trapper,* Toronto, Macmillan of Canada, 1989; extended corres. of North with author; Paul St. Pierre, "Driving the Great Lonely [the Demster Highway], *New York Times,* Travel Sect., June 3, 1990, pp. 15, 38.

Johnson, James, military officer, legislator (Jan. 1, 1774-Aug. 14, 1826). B. in Orange County, Virginia, he moved with his father to Kentucky in 1779, settling at Bryant's Station where James's brother, Richard Mentor Johnson (see entry), was born. In 1782 Bryant's Station was attacked by British-supported Indians; James was then 8 years old. He became a member of the Kentucky State Senate in 1808 and joined the Kentucky militia for the War of 1812. As a lieutenant colonel he is said to have commanded the right wing of the American force at the Battle of the Thames, October 5, 1813, in which Richard Johnson led a decisive cavalry charge and personally killed Tecumseh, according to report. James Johnson as a contractor supplied troops on the western frontier in 1819-20. He was elected to Congress as a Democrat, serving from March 4, 1825, until his death at Washington, D.C. He was buried at Great Crossings, Kentucky.

BDAC; info. from E.F. (Ted) Mains.

Johnson, Noah, frontiersman (1699-Aug. 13, 1798). B. at Woburn, Massachusetts, he was a member of the famed John Lovewell expedition against the Pequawket Indians on the upper Saco River of New Hampshire and survived the savage engagement of May 8, 1725. He was one of the first settlers of Pembroke, Massachusetts, the town granted to the survivors of the expedition and the heirs of those who were killed (see Lovewell entry for narrative of the campaign). Johnson removed to Plymouth, Massachusetts, in his advanced age and died there in the 100th year of his life. He was the last survivor of the Lovewell action.

Sylvester, III, 275n.

Johnson, Peder (Pete), prospector (fl. 1885-87). B. probably in Sweden, Johnson migrated to Alaska before the famous Gold Rush and as a civilian joined the Henry T. Allen expedition of 1885. Its mission was to explore the Copper, Tanana and Koyukuk rivers, then virtually unknown. Johnson was reported to have "rendered excellent service" according to Allen's official report. Allen named a tributary of the Tanana River for Johnson; it starts at the Johnson Glacier and enters the Tanana 41 miles southeast of Delta Junction. Johnson, with John Bremner (see entry) left the Allen party on the Yukon to prospect for the rest of the summer, hoping to leave Alaska the following year and journey to the States if free transportation could be found.

Narratives of Explorations in Alaska; 411, 454; Orth, 477.

Johnson, Rachel, frontierwoman (Oct. 20, 1736-1847). A black woman slave of Yates Conwell, she was b. in Delaware colony and brought to the Ohio country by Conwell before Lord Dunmore's War of 1774. She was at Wheeling before the 1777 siege of Fort Henry and was there when the survivors of the William Foreman (see entry) party were brought in. "Her memory was very good, and she had a reputation for truthfulness," according to Thwaites/Kellogg. Her description of the Foreman disaster was graphic and detailed. During her long lifetime she remembered having seen George Washington, George Rogers Clark and "a number of prominent Western heroes." Lyman Copeland Draper interviewed her at length in 1845 and 1846; she died the next year.

Thwaites/Kellogg, *Frontier Defense on the Upper Ohio, 1777-1778.*

Johnson, Robert, colonial governor (c. 1676-May 3, 1735). B. in England, he was a son of Nathaniel Johnson who was governor of Carolina from 1702-1708. The son, a dealer in fabrics, lived at Newcastle-on-Tyne when the English Proprietors, some of whom had founded the Hudson's Bay Company in 1670, and who controlled the Carolina settlements by distant edict, in 1713 selected Robert Johnson to succeed Governor Charles Craven. He was not appointed immediately however and with others sought in vain for Crown aid for the beleaguered settlers in combatting the powerful Yamasee Indians; the royal assistance not forthcoming the colonials had to fight their war themselves. This was not an easy task, the Yamasee killing 200 to 300 of the settlers in 1715. Johnson became governor in 1717 by decision of the Proprietors, while a

rebellion against their rule was impending, supported by several other complaints. Piracy was a threat to their survival; Governor Johnson sent out an expedition under Colonel William Rhett which captured a pirate leader, Stede Bonnet, who escaped and raided Charleston harbor, was recaptured and hanged with 22 of his fellows. Johnson's first period as governor ended in 1719, at a time when colonial frustration under suffocating rulings of the Proprietors were driving them toward rebellion. The colonials requested that Johnson become governor under the Crown, if and when Carolina would become a Crown colony as distinct from a Proprietary entity. Johnson however refused, remaining loyal to the Proprietors who had named him to the position in the first place. He returned to England. In 1729 a royal government finally was established and Carolina was divided into North and South provinces; Johnson became the first governor of South Carolina in 1731. The next year he aided Oglethorpe in founding a colony of Georgia. He also directed improvements in affairs for his own people, the giving of presents to Indians to win their friendship, and the stationing of a defense force on the frontier to maintain peace. He died a fairly wealthy man, leaving three sons and two daughters, and being held in considerable esteem by his people.

Verner W. Crane, *The Southern Frontier 1670-1732,* Ann Arbor, Univ. of Mich. Press, 1956; DAB.

Jones, Ernest Lester, administrator (Apr. 14, 1876-Apr. 9, 1929). B. at East Orange, New Jersey, for reasons of health he did not receive a college education, but became a farmer near Culpeper, Virginia, until President Wilson appointed him deputy commissioner of the Bureau of Fisheries which later was incorporated in the Fish and Wildlife Service. In April 1915 he became superintendent of the Coast and Geodetic Survey, retaining the office until his death. During World War I, on furlough from his civilian position, he served as a lieutenant colonel of the Signal Corps and in France as colonel in the Division of Military Aeronautics. He then returned to the C&GS as director, and for 14 years was a member of the International Boundary Commission. With the Coast and Geodetic Survey he strongly emphasized for the safety of shipping personnel, Alaskan surveys and mapping. Jones named several geographical features of Alaska, adding to the many he had named from 1913 to 1915 while with the Bureau of Fisheries. He was author of numerous publications, including several on Alaska.

Orth, 16, 477; DAB.

Jones, John Thompson (Antelope Jack, Cheyenne Jack), adventurer (1853-June 1874). B. in England, possibly at Chester, he came to the United States and made for the frontier, earning the soubriquet of Cheyenne Jack and, later and more universally, Antelope Jack. As a buffalo hunter on the Staked Plains he and "Blue Billy," a German hunter named W. Muhler, were killed by South Plains Indians in their camp near the Canadian River "just a few days" before the noted second Battle of Adobe Walls of June 27, 1874. The bodies were reportedly mutilated by the Indians. Before burial a heavy rain washed the remains down a creek next to which they had camped. They were never recovered although English relatives sponsored an extended search for them.

T. Lindsay Baker; Billy R. Harrison, *Adobe Walls: The History and Archeology of the 1874 Trading Post,* College Station, Texas A & M Univ. Press, 1986; Chuck Parsons, *True West,* Vol. 37, No. 8 (Aug. 1990), 12; there is a file on Jones at the Panhandle-Plains Hist. Soc. Museum, Canyon, Tx.

Jusseaume, René, interpreter, trader (fl. c. 1789-1809). Of French descent and probably b. in Canada, Jusseaume became associated with the Mandan Indians, married into the tribe, became fluent in their difficult language and an interpreter of it. Many of his contemporaries asserted he was illiterate, but DeVoto shows that was unlikely to be true. David Thompson (see entry) in 1797 made a trip to the Mandan villages where he found Jusseaume who he said had been with that people for eight years, or since 1789, probably most often as a Hudson's Bay Company trader. Since Thompson joined the Northwest Company that year and Jusseaume was reported already to have switched to it, that may have brought them together, as he became Thompson's guide and interpreter; one report said he was a free trader in 1793 and with the NWC in 1794. Jusseaume had taken goods from Assiniboine House in Canada to the Mandans "probably a number of times." In 1793 he made such a trip, two of his men being killed by Sioux on the way back. In 1794 John Macdonnell sent him with a party that reached the Mandan villages in October, Jusseaume turning over half of his goods to a French trader, Ménard (whose first name is not remembered), who claimed Jusseaume had been living with the Mandans since 1778. With the rest of his goods, he built a small post midway between a Mandan village and one of the Minnetarees. The enigmatic John Thomas Evans (see entry) arrived on the upper Missouri in 1796 under instructions from James Mackay, who was in Spanish service, to do something about British traders in Spain's claimed territory; this brought expected friction between trading elements of the two nations. In March 1797 Jusseaume arrived from Canada with plenty of goods and apparent instructions from Macdonnell, whose partisan he was, to crush the opposition. DeVoto wrote that "lavish presents bought the Indians' support...Jessaume tried to buy a small massacre too but the chiefs...told Evans what was afoot and [Evans wrote] 'came to my house to guard me.' Thereupon Jessaume tried to shoot him, 'but my interpreter having perceived his design hindered the execution,'" and the Indians wanted to kill Jusseaume, but Evans would not permit it. Evans conceded victory in the rivalry to Jusseaume, however, and quitted the Mandan country on May 9, 1797, for St. Louis and home. Jusseaume settled in with the Mandans with his wife and a child or two and was there when the Lewis and Clark expedition arrived in 1804. He was hired as interpreter and adviser for the winter's stay among the Mandans, and from him, Clark wrote, "we procured some information...of the Chiefs of the Different Nations" of the region. On the expedition's return, in 1806, the leaders persuaded the Mandan chief Shahaka (see entry) to go to Washington, D.C., the Indian agreeing to the trip if Jusseaume would accompany him and the two were permitted to bring along their wives and children. This arranged, the party went down the Missouri to St. Louis. Jusseaume and Shahaka, with escort, continued on to Washington, meeting President Jefferson, who invited them to Monticello for a brief interlude. The two remained in the east for a year, visiting Philadelphia and other centers. From St. Louis they started up the Missouri for home in May 1807 with a military escort under Ensign Nathaniel Pryor, but in a clash with the Arikaras, Jusseaume was wounded, how seriously is not stated, but the injury severe enough that Shahaka believed he should not continue the journey overland three days to the Mandan villages. The party returned to St. Louis. An expedition of 150 men left in May 1809 and delivered the chief and interpreter to the home village on September 24. Alexander Henry, as quoted by Coues (III, 1178n.) scornfully described Jusseaume as "that old sneaking cheat...whose character is more despicable than the worst among the natives," and wrote that he spoke Mandan "tolerably well [and] he still retains the outward appearance of a Christian but his principles as far as I could observe are much worse than those of a Mandan; he is possessed of every superstition natural to those people, nor is he different in every mean dirty trick which they have acquired from their intercourse with a set of worthless scoundrels who are generally accustomed to visit these parts." The date and circumstances of his death are not reported.

Bernard DeVoto, *The Course of Empire,* Boston, Houghton Mifflin Co., 1952; Chittenden; A.P. Nasatir, *Before Lewis and Clark,* St. Louis Hist. Doc. Found., 1952; Hodge, HAI, II, 518-19; Elliott Coues, ed., *History of the Expedition Under the Command of Lewis and Clark,* N.Y., Dover Pubs., 1965; Clarke, *Lewis and Clark;* Nasatir, "John Thomas Evans," MM, III.

Juvenal (Iuvenalii, Yuvenaliy), Yacov Fedorovich, Orthodox churchman (d. Sept. 29, 1796). B. presumably in Russia he was a mining engineer in civilian life, also experienced in smelting, in surveying and architecture and "well versed in mathematics" before embarking upon the priesthood. He arrived at Kodiak Island, Alaska, in September 1794 with Archimandrite Ioassaf (see entry) as an Ieromonk, or monk ordained as a priest. At Shelikhov's suggestion Baranov secured Juvenal's help in opening coal pits and in smelting iron. In 1795 Juvenal began his missionary work on the mainland at Kenai Bay (Cook Inlet), and worked among the Eskimauan Chugachigmuit living from Kenai to the Copper River, thence around the Alaskan bight among the Kolosh (Tlingit) Indians, as far as Chilkat Sound and Lynn Canal near the present Skagway—little wonder that the priest came to believe that "Alaska belongs to me," so far as missionary endeavors were concerned. Juvenal and the Ieromonk Makarii circumnavigated Kodiak Island during the winter in kayaks, "oblivious to the dangers of the sea," but the full success of the exploratory missionary effort is unreported. Juvenal went to Yakutat Bay at the direction of Baranov to survey a site for a post. By June 19, 1796, he was back at Three Saints Harbor on Kodiak to open a school for boys and young men. July 12 Baranov arrived with directions from the bishop of Irkutsk, Siberia, that

Juvenal should open a station on Iliamna Lake, beyond the Aleutian Range on the mainland northwest of Kodiak. On the first leg of the round-about voyage the missionary was quartered in a dark hold crowded with bales of dried fish, the vessel's more comfortable cabins taken by Baranov, who was to visit Pavlovsk Station on Pavlof Bay near the tip of the Alaska Peninsula. The sea was choppy, so rough that Baranov demanded of the priest whether he had yet blessed the ship, which he had. Baranov growled that Juvenal was "a second Jonah," adding sourly that there were "plenty of whales around," though not offering to cast him into the sea. From Pavlovsk Station the manager sent him with a fleet of kayaks northward to St. George, at today's Kasilof, 20 miles south of the present Kenai. St. Nicholas was a post of the Lebedev-Lastochin Fur Company, bitter rivals of Baranov's firm; from there the manager warned Juvenal he would be in the care of the Lebedev traders who were "little better than robbers and murderers." Bancroft tells the subsequent tragedy of Juvenal largely in terms of the monk's "journal," as presented by Petrov (see entry) and which at least in translation Sherwood considers "almost certainly a fraud." Pierce said the journal "appears to be a fabrication, although certain of its ecclesiastical content would appear to have been beyond the competence of Petroff, so that it may have been foisted upon rather than concocted by him." The account tells that Juvenal arrived at St. Nicholas August 11, and found the personnel, contrary to Baranov's assessment, religiously faithful, courteous and helpful. He performed marriages, baptized many and conducted divine services. August 25, he set out across the Inlet by way of Kalgin Island and September 3, reached Iliamna village on the northern shore of the large lake, accompanied by Katlewah, brother of the chief, who assured the missionary he was welcome because they had "many bad men among the Iliamna people, especially his brother." At the village the priest met Shakemut, the chief, his words interpreted by a boy, Nikita, who had been a hostage of the Russians and knew their language. Shakemut, according to the "journal," invited Juvenal "to share the couch of one of his wives," of whom there were several. "I suppose such an abomination is the custom of the country...My first duty will be to preach against such wicked practices, but I could not [do this] through a boy interpreter," Juvenal allegedly confessed in his journal. His troubles mounted swiftly. The chief was nominally converted and baptized, but this itself caused dissension among the tribesmen who remained suspicious of the whole business. At length, the journal continued, the turncoat Shakemut caused Juvenal to be seduced and "a grievous sin was committed before I could extricate myself." Tensions continued to rise as all but Nikita turned against him and the priest was assassinated, Nikita escaping with the diary and other papers to a Russian settlement. Thus in outline goes the story which apparently most careful historians today reject as fictitious. Yet it is not so obvious that this is entirely true. The tale differs little in its important elements from the report of the highly respected Rezanov, who, writing November 6, 1805, on activities of Russian Orthodox missionaries in Alaska, stated: "On the Alaska Peninsula near Iliamna Lake...trade had been developed with mountain natives and offered great potential. The monk Iuvenalii (Juvenal) immediately hurried there to proselytize; he conducted forced baptisms and performed marriages, taking young women away from some [men] and giving them to others. The American natives tolerated all this madness and even put up with beatings for quite a while, but finally decided they had to get rid of this depraved person. They took counsel among themselves and solved the problem by killing the priest. There is no need to grieve over him..."

Eventually the Juvenal papers found their way to the great missionary Veniaminov (see entry), presumably on Unalaska Island, for it was there that Petrov reportedly found and translated the journal in 1878, leaving the original with the Reverend Innokentii Shashnikov there, while the English translation is at the Bancroft Library at Berkeley, California, as Father Juvenal, "A Daily Journal," (1796). Zagoskin gives the year of death as 1800, but Rezanov and Bancroft cite it as 1796, which appears to be correct. For an informed discussion of the conclusion of the Juvenal saga, one should consult Richard A. Pierce, *Russian America: A Biographical Dictionary,* 202-203, Iuvenalii entry. Pierce has done the most complete analysis of the legend, believes most published accounts of his death are imaginary and that his "journal" was indeed a fabrication of Petrov. Pierce's conclusions are not to be lightly dismissed.

Bancroft, *Alaska* (173); *Russian Penetration of the North Pacific Ocean; Russian American Colonies* (103); Morgan B. Sherwood, "Ivan Petroff and the Far Northwest," *Journal of the West,* Vol. II, No. 3 (July 1963), 305-15; Richard A. Pierce, "A Note on 'Ivan Petroff and the Far Northwest,'" *Journal of the West,* Vol. III, No. 4 (Oct. 1964), 436-39; Zagoskin; *A Guide to the Manuscript Collections of the Bancroft Library,* ed. by Dale L. Morgan, George P. Hammond, Vol. I, Pacific and Western Manuscripts (Except California), 173.

K

Kalinin, Danilo Vasilevich, sea officer (d. Jan. 9, 1813). Kalinin, b. in Russia, entered the Russian navy about 1788 and for bravery in a brief war with Sweden in 1790 was promoted to officer rank. He became an experienced navigator and served as such aboard the *Neva* on its global circumnavigation under Lisianskii. July 13, 1804, the ship reached Kodiak Island and assisted Baranov in retaking the Sitka area after the Kolosh (Tlingit) Indians had destroyed a fur trading post there. While at Kodiak Kalinin surveyed islands near Kodiak, as well as at Chiniatsk Bay. From Sitka he discovered the strait beyond Mt. Edgecumbe, and proposed naming the island to the west Kruzof Island after Admiral Aleksandr Kruse (1727-1799), which was done. Kalinin made a second voyage to Russian America, leaving Krontstadt October 20, 1806, but later left the naval service and settled in Russia until 1812 when he was persuaded to sign up for four years with the Russian American Company. His vessel was wrecked on Kruzof Island and Kalinin perished with most of the personnel aboard. Kalinin Bay and Kalinin Point on Kruzof Island were named for him.

Pierce, *Russian America: A Biographical Dictionary;* Orth, 489, 546.

Kanseah, Jasper, Chiricahua Apache (1872-1959). Through "some unexplained relationship" as Debo put it, Kanseah was a nephew of Geronimo; the boy's father died or was killed before he was born and "my mother died when they drove us like cattle from Cochise's reservation to San Carlos," Arizona. The boy, small, thin and but half grown, was turned over by Geronimo to a famous warrior, Yahnozha (1865-1954) to be trained for war, as were all Apache boys. The training must have been good, because Kanseah became "Geronimo's youngest warrior," and was a participant or observer of important events of Chiricahua life. He thought he recalled seeing Cochise but if so, it must have been as an infant. On one occasion in the Sierra Madre he was chased by a bear; Juh could not shoot the animal because the boy was in the line of fire, so he yelled at him to squeeze between two trees so close together that the bear could not

follow, and was turned away. In 1880 Kanseah was with Victorio in the last campaign of that famed chief; the boy was away with Nana when the engagement of Tres Castillos took place, Victorio was killed and his followers decimated, but the boy with Ka-ya-ten-nae and others was sent to bury the great chief and his companions after the Mexican irregulars had left, a task they performed. Kanseah, with Eugene Chihuahua, son of Chief Chihuahua, and Ace Daklugie, son of Juh, were at Cibecue Creek, Arizona, when the battle of August 31, 1881, broke out, an important action which precipitated years of operations by and against the Apaches. Kanseah, who though only about 14 was accepted as a warrior, went out with Geronimo in the 1885 emeute from San Carlos and remained with him until the September 1886 surrender to Miles. Kanseah was present and saw the fatal wounding of Emmet Crawford by Mexican irregulars in the Sierra Madre in January 1886. The young man was with Geronimo at the council with Crook in March, and broke out again with Geronimo when the war leader bolted the conference grounds for Mexico. Kanseah was on guard at the trail head when the heroic Kayitah and Martine approached bearing a white flag and seeking to pave the way for Gatewood's intrepid arrival to talk Geronimo into peace in August 1886. Geronimo reluctantly was talked out of shooting the emissaries, and the negotiations ultimately were successful. Kanseah had little use for Miles who, he maintained, "lied to us," but he conceded that Crook, though a vigorous enemy, was an honorable and worthy man. Shortly after arrival with the Apache exiles in Florida, Kanseah was sent to Carlisle (Pennsylvania) Indian Industrial School, where he remained for some time as student, and almost died of a disease which had killed many of the Apache young people there. He had entered the school November 4, 1886, was discharged November 7, 1895, and was sent to Fort Sill to rejoin his people, held there still as prisoners of war. His first wife died at Fort Sill as did their daughter. His second wife, Lucy Gon-altsis, gave birth to three children at Sill and several more at the Mescalero Reservation of New Mexico where they were sent in 1913. Lucy died in 1959 and Jasper was much depressed by her passing, asserting that now "there is nothing to keep me here." Mrs. Ball pointed out that he was in fine health and probably had years yet to live. He shook his head, and within the week he had "died in his sleep during the night."

Eve Ball, with Nora Henn, Lynda Sanchez, *Indeh,* Provo, Utah, Brigham Young Univ. Press, 1980; Griswold; Angie Debo, *Geronimo...,* Norman, Univ. of Okla. Press, 1976; corres. with Eve Ball over many years; info. from Phillip G. Nickell.

Kashevarov, Aleksandr Fillippovich, explorer (Dec. 28, 1809-Sept. 25, 1866). The son of a Kodiak Island Russian teacher and his Aleut wife was graduated from the Krondstadt (Russia) pilot's school and made two world cruises. On one of them, in the ship *Elena* he mapped previously unknown islands of the Marshall group in mid-Pacific, the vessel reaching Alaska in 1828. For many years thereafter Kashevarov commanded ships of the Russian American Company, based in Alaska. He sailed waters of the Bering and Okhotsk seas and visited the shores of California, becoming a "bold and experienced navigator." In 1838 he made his most famous journey of exploration. He was assigned to survey Alaska's Arctic coast between Point Barrow (discovered by Thomas Elson of Beechey's party in 1826) and the Return Islands (Cape Return, Return Reef), about 160 miles east of Point Barrow. They marked the westward landfall of Sir John Franklin's survey from the Mackenzie River on his 1825-27 expedition. Kashevarov as commander of the expedition was transported through Bering Strait and along the northwest coast of the continent by the brig *Poliphemus,* Ivan Chernov (see entry), captain. The vessel rounded Cape Lisburne and continued northeast until ice prevented further progress. From this point Kashevarov and 20 "of the most daring Creoles and Aleuts" continued in skin boats (kayaks and umiaks) on a 54-day further journey. They rounded Point Barrow, discovered Prokofieyev Inlet (now Dease Inlet), and Kupriyanov Bay (now Smith Bay) and may have reached Cape Halkett or Harrison Bay before native hostility forced them to turn back. The expedition, however, had almost completed the transit of the Arctic coast of the continent, leaving only a scant 100 miles to be explored. Kashevarov later worked on a compilation of maps for an atlas of the Pacific Ocean, summed up in his report of 1850. In that year he was promoted to

lieutenant captain and named commander of the Siberian port of Ayan on the Sea of Okhotsk. He later became a Major General. In 1860 the Russian American Company, as chartered power over Alaska, sought a 20-year extension of its contract to exercise that monopoly, and in 1863 a Captain Golovnin was sent to Novo Arkhangelsk to thoroughly investigate it and criticisms of its operations. His report generally was favorable although it did contain some adverse comments. The Kodiak-born Kashevarov was unhappy with that summary, however, and filed a rebuttal "exposing abuses which had hitherto been kept secret," his statements endorsed by Baron Wrangel (see entry), who headed the company's board of directors. In addition Kashevarov published articles directed against the organization's administration and guardianship of Alaska. "Are we who were born in the Russian American possessions really supposed to consider forever the best interests of the...company...and to smother within ourselves every natural striving for, and every idea about the interests of what is...our native land?" he wrote in one of them. In another he declared that Alaska did not need "the guardianship of the Company," and freedom from it would materially benefit its people and their development. The argument that the Alaskans were not yet ready for a future independent of the Company, he added, sounded to him like the "defenders of feudal serfdom," a system which Russia had suffered under in the past. Kashevarov died the year before the United States purchased Alaska from Russian, when the era of the Russian American Company came to an end.

Zagoskin; Bancroft, *Alaska.*

Kashpak (Kashmaq), interpreter (fl. 1758-1784). He was of what the Russians called the "Koniag" people of Kodiak Island, identified today as the Kaniagmiut, the largest and most powerful Eskimo tribe on the Alaskan coast; they inhabited Kodiak Island and the mainland from Iliamna Lake to Long. 159°W. Stepan Glotov, on the voyage of 1758-62 when he discovered Umnak and Unalaska of the Aleutians, was greatly assisted by his Koniag interpreter, Kashpak, who in his youth had been seized by Fox Island Aleuts and raised on Unalaska Island; he remained there when Glotov returned to Siberia. In September 1762 Ivan Korovin voyaged to Unalaska, sought out Kashpak and when the Aleuts launched heavy attacks on Russian vessels and camps, Kashpak remained loyal to the whites and at one point saved Korovin's life. Kashpak also worked for Ivan Solovev from 1764-67. He evidently returned thereafter to Kodiak Island, where he was of material assistance to Shelikhov in 1784, in one instance aiding the trader to seize a native fort on the island.

Pierce, *Russian America: A Biographical Dictionary;* Hodge, HAI.

Katleian, Tlingit chief (fl. 1799-1818). A nephew of Skautlelt, a major Tlingit chief of the Sitka, Alaska region, he and Skautlelt together led the successful Kolosh (Tlingit) attack on June 24, 1802, that carried the Russian post near Sitka, resulting in the slaying of most of the personnel and the burning of the fort. Captain Henry Barber (see entry) seized both chiefs as hostage for return of the women the natives held prisoner, and when this was accomplished, released them. October 18, 1804, when Baranov and Lisianskii attacked to regain the site, Katleian led the defense; defeated, he took his people in retreat to Chatham Strait, 150 miles to the south. In 1806 the chief was said to have prevented a second massacre at the rebuilt Sitka. In 1818, when Baranov was departing Alaska, the chief and the Russian American Company governor made peace. The Indian was "respected by Baranov for his intelligence and bravery [and] Baranov bore witness to his successor [Leontii Hagemeister) concerning this man's intelligence and ability." In the summer of 1818 the artist Mikhail Tikhanov sketched Katleian's portrait. The Indian is commemorated by Mount Katlian, 4,303 feet, northeast of Sitka, Katlian Bay and the Katlian River.

Pierce, *Russian America: A Biographical Dictionary;* Orth, 501.

Kayitah, Martin, Apache scout (1856-Feb. 15, 1934). Probably a Nedhni or southern Chiricahua as was his cousin, Charles Martine (see entry). He and Martine were the scouts with Gatewood who intrepidly entered Geronimo's hostile camp and made possible negotiations which led to the surrender and end of the Apache wars. Kayitah's father was Bish-to-yey, and his wife was Sahn-uh-shlu, a sister of Victorio, Kayitah also was a cousin of Yahnozha, a foremost warrior with Geronimo. Not much is reported of Kayitah's early life, but he was with either the party of several hundred Warm Springs Apaches who were extracted from San Carlos Reservation in April

1882 by Juh and his warriors, or was one of the Juh element who engineered the spectatcular emeute. In any event, at the subsequent battle with Lieutenant Colonel Lorenzo Garcia on Aliso Creek in Sonora, Kayitah was one of three seriously wounded, and abandoned by the fleeing Indians. All three eventually recovered and rejoined their comrades in the Sierra Madre. Kayitah and Martine were enlisted in 1886 at Fort Apache by Miles to accompany Gatewood in that officer's attempt to contact the Geronimo hostiles, then in Mexico (see Charles Martine entry for details of this endeavor). Jasper Kanseah (see entry), a nephew of Geronimo, was watching the trail to the hostile hideout with field glasses when he spied the scouts party approach. "I recognized Martine and Kayitah by their walk," Kanseah remembered later. Geronimo said that if the scouts came closer they should be shot. "They are our brothers," said Yahnozha. "Let's find out why they come. They are very brave to risk this." "When they get close enough, shoot," Geronimo repeated. "We will not shoot," said Yahnozha. "If there is any shooting done, it will be at you, not them. The first man who lifts a rifle I will kill." "I will help you...," said Fun, another leading warrior. "Let them live," grunted Geronimo, resignedly. The scouts explained their mission, and the military situation as they understood it plus Gatewood's desire to visit the camp and talk with Geronimo. The leader held Kayitah in the camp and dispatched Martine to tell Gatewood to come up the following day, the chief, Naiche, sending word that Gatewood would be safe if he came into the camp. The surrender was effected, but instead of receiving the rewards Miles reportedly had promised them, Kayitah and Martine were shipped as prisoners with the captured hostiles and the rest of the Chiricahua/Warm Springs people into 29 years of eastern exile. In Alabama Kayitah and Martine enlisted in Company I, (Indian) of the 12th Infantry, and one officer, evaluating members of the unit, considered Kayitah "a good worker." Later, at Fort Sill, the two enlisted in Company L (Indian) of the 7th Cavalry. For these enlistments, and for services in Oklahoma as scouts, the two in 1927 were belatedly granted minute pensions, though they never were adequately compensated for the stunning heroism they displayed in imperiling their lives to persuade Geronimo to talk peace with Gatewood and, later, Miles. Frank C. Lockwood visted Kayitah and Martine in the 1930s and found the former "interested in farming and [he] appreciated his home at White Tail [on the Mescalero Reservation]. He was a man of milder temper than Martine, and was pleasant to deal with. He was never a troublemaker; nor did he have much to say by way of complaint because he was sent with the hostiles into captivity." He died at Mescalero. A photograph of Kayitah and Martine together may be found in the *Arizona Historical Review*, Vol. IV, No. 1 (April 1931), facing p. 34; it also is reproduced in Debo, *Geronimo*, p. 373.

Griswold; Eve Ball, with Nora Henn and Lynda Sanchez, *Indeh*, Provo, Brigham Young Univ. Press, 1980; Dan L. Thrapp, *Conquest of Apacheria*, Norman, Univ. of Okla. Press, 1967; Angie Debo, *Geronimo...*, Norman, 1976; Frank C. Lockwood, *The Apache Indians*, N.Y., Macmillan Co., 1938.

Kell(e)y, Daniel (Yorkey, Mick), desperado (d. Mar. 28, 1884). Kelly was one of five active gunmen who perpetrated the so-called· "Bisbee Masacre" during the holdup December 8, 1883, of the Joseph Goldwater-A.A. Casteñada general store at Bisbee, Arizona. During the robbery four non-participants were killed and another wounded mortally while the bandits, including Omer W. Sample, James (Tex) Howard, Daniel Dowd and William Delaney (see entries) and Kelly escaped. Kelly later was picked up by lawman W.A. Daniels (see entry) at Deming, New Mexico, getting a barber shop shave. He told the judge at the sentencing that he had much to say but nothing probably would influence the sentencing, so he kept silent. On the scaffold he said "I am innocent of the murders...I have never yet murdered a human being." Kelly and the others were hanged from a multiple scaffold at Tombstone. John Heath (see entry), the supposed planner and ringleader of the robbery, was sentenced to life imprisonment because he had been absent from the actual crime, but Bisbee people were incensed that he had escaped execution, extracted him from the Tombstone jail and lynched him February 22, 1884. On the day of his hanging his friend "Mick" Kelly, as he signed himself, wrote an eight-stanza poem entitled "The Hanging of John Heith," the work reproduced by Traywick and Ladd.

Ben T. Traywick, *The Hangings at Tombstone*, Tombstone, Red Marie's Bookstore, 1991; Robert E. Ladd, *Eight Ropes to Eternity*, pub. by *Tombstone Epitaph*, 1965; A.D. LeBaron, "Bisbee's Five Black Ghosts," *True West*, Vol. 7, No. 6 (July-Aug. 1960), 12-14, 56-57.

Kelly, Fanny, captive (Nov. 15, 1842-Nov. 15,

1904). Although her autobiography gives her b. as in 1845, her tombstone cites the above date; it occurred at Orillia on Lake Simcoe, Ontario, and she was the daughter of James and Margaret Wiggins. In 1857 the family left for Geneva, Allen County, Kansas, to join an abolitionist colony of the Union Settlement Association, the father dying of cholera enroute. In 1863 Fanny married Josiah Shawnahan Kelly, a discharged Union veteran and farmer (c. 1827-July 28, 1867) who also was to succumb to cholera. He had unsuccessfully prospected for gold in California for three years, and five months after the wedding the Kellys joined others in a journey West. The party consisted of five wagons and 11 persons, two of them children, two black former slaves of the Cherokees, a one-eyed Methodist preacher and William J. and Sarah Luse Larimer, she a commercial photographer. The party journeyed along the Kansas River, cut northwestward to the Platte, went on to Chimney Rock and Fort Laramie, Wyoming. At dusk on July 12, 1864, on Cottonwood Creek the party was attacked by a band of Sioux under the Oglala chief, Ottawa. The minister, named Sharp, Noah Daniel Taylor, and a black, Franklin, were killed outright; Larimer and Gardner Wakefield were wounded, the latter to die eight months later from his injury, and Fanny Kelly, her niece Mary, aged 7 or 8, and Sarah Larimer with her son, Frank, 7, were captured, while Josiah escaped. Sarah and her son escaped after a single night; Fanny released her niece with instructions to find her way back to white people if possible (she perished July 13, 1864, perhaps was slain), and Fanny alone was taken by her captives on a circuitous 400-mile trip (the distance estimated) until July 25 when they reached the northern edge of the North Dakota Bad Lands, close enough for the Indians to become involved in Brigadier General Alfred Sully's engagement with the Sioux at Killdeer Mountain in August. It was during Sully's campaign that Fanny Kelly somehow made written contact with Captain James Liberty Fisk and his mammoth wagon train bound for the Montana gold fields, "but Fisk was unsuccessful in his efforts to ransom her." In all she endured five months of captivity before being freed when Major Albert A. House of the 6th Iowa Cavalry, on instructions from his superior, sent Sioux emissaries to the hostile camp directing that Fanny be released as a precondition for peace between the tribe and soldiers. She was brought in on December 9, 1864, and turned over to the garrison of Fort Sully;

scantily clad on a very cold wintry day she was placed in the post hospital for approximately two months before fully recovering. She may or may not have been sexually abused during her captivity (her own statements on the point appear confused), and her release has been tied in with rumors of an intended Sioux attack (which some believe she prevented) on the makeshift Fort Sully, on the Missouri River five miles above the mouth of the Cheyenne River. Major House, however, testified that the post was defendable and that his command was prepared for any attack on it. Congress ultimately awarded her $5,000 for her contribution in saving the fort, and later authorized $10,000 additional payment for property taken and destroyed by the Indians when the wagons were attacked, depositions testifying that they were loaded with a truly remarkable quantity of valuable merchandise, given the background of the emigrants and their estimated wealth, or lack of it, at the time. In 1867, shortly after the death of her husband, a son was born to Fanny and she named him Josiah after his father. She had commenced a manuscript of her travail when she was contacted by the Larimers who lived then at Sherman Station, Wyoming, and who invited her to join them. She did so. Unfortunately she agreed with Sarah to compose a joint narrative of their captivity, which was done, but the manuscript pirated from her much material and was published at Philadelphia without her knowledge or byline, in 1870 under the title, *The Capture and Escape: Or, Life Among the Sioux.* Fanny Kelly sued, won a judgment of $5,000, which was reversed on appeal, and eventually did win a renewed court case, but for the reduced sum of $285.50. Fanny's own narrative was published in 1871 at Cincinnati; her book has gone through 11 printings, while Sarah Larimer's book enjoyed a single one, and that abbreviated. Fanny's son was privately educated, became an Oklahoma banker, and his mother settled at Washington, D.C., where on May 6, 1880, she married William F. Gordon, a writer. She invested her money wisely, became fairly prosperous, "seemed to have acquired an affection for Indians, and entertained some of their dignitaries when they visited Washington." She died at that city and was buried in its Glenwood Cemetery.

Fanny Kelly, *Narrative of My Captivity Among the Sioux Indians,* ed. by Clark and Mary Lee Spence, Chicago, R.R. Donnelly & Sons (Lakeside Classic), 1990.

Kelly, Walter, frontiersman (d. 1774). Kelly emigrated from the Carolinas to the Greenbriar settlement of present West Virginia in 1773, and in the autumn of that year, against the warnings of his friends, established an advance settlement on the Great Kanawha River. He was killed there by Indians early in 1774, his place thereafter known as Kelly's Station, it being acquired by William Morris and becoming a noted frontier outpost, the object of repeated Indian attacks.

Thwaites/Kellogg, *Frontier Defense on the Upper Ohio, 1777-1778.*

Kelsey, Nancy, frontierswoman (Aug. 1, 1823-Aug. 10, 1896). B. in Barren County, Kentucky, as Nancy Roberts, she married Benjamin Kelsey October 14, 1838, and almost immediately commenced her lifetime of frontier wandering. She was the first white woman to cross Plains, inland desert and the towering Sierra to reach California, where she arrived with the John Bidwell-John Bartleson party in October 1841, having left Sapling Grove, Missouri, in mid-May. Nancy was the only woman with this first wagon party, and she struggled in barefooted, with her courage undiminished and a baby daughter in her arms. The company followed the Stanislaus River from the mountains into the interior valley, in November reaching Martinez, the ranch of John Marsh, going on then to the Sutter fort at New Helvetia (the present Sacramento). In the spring of 1842 Ben set up a hunter's camp and shot enough game to purchase 100 head of cattle which the Kelseys, with others, drove to Oregon for sale, harassed by Indians much of the way. Nancy watched skirmishes and saw Indians killed almost within reach. After a 600-mile trip the stock was sold at Fort Vancouver and merchandise bought for sale back in California, where they arrived in 1844, Nancy now with two daughters, while a son had died in infancy. Ben put up a log cabin in the Napa Valley near present Castoga. With stirrings against Mexican rule on the increase, he offered his services to Fremont the next year, and Nancy, with a one-month-old son in her arms, on horseback followed her husband to Sonoma although "I was so weak when I arrived...that I could not stand up." When the Bear Flag revolt broke out at Sonoma in June Nancy joined other women there in collecting material and sewing the first flag for the revolutionists, although she was not the sole "Betsy Ross" of the affair as she was credited with being. Ben, an outspoken, rough-talking man, soon quarreled with Fremont and left his service. With Mexican General Mariano G. Vallejo he was operating a profitable sawmill in 1848 when news reached them that James Marshall had discovered gold at Coloma. Ben discovered a rich diggings east of Coloma at a place still called Kelsey, just north of Placerville. He took his considerable amount of gold to Sonoma, bought sheep at a dollar a head, drove them back to the mines where he sold them for $16 each. He also exploited Indians for their labor, which proved profitable—for him. Kelsey's wanderlust continued to plague him, and in the meanderings he lost as much money as he made. He and Nancy and their growing family (10 children in all) took a thousand mile trip to Mexico and Texas to purchase cattle to drive back to California. In the course of that journey Nancy saw her 13-year-old daughter scalped by Comanches: "I loaded the guns we had and suggested that we hide ourselves. The two oldest girls ran and hid in the brush and the 16-year-old boy looked out for himself by hiding alone" as the' Indians approached, Nancy later recalled. "After they had...pillaged the camp, and started off, they found the girls. They succeeded in catching one [of them] and even now I can hear the screams as they caught her...We found her the next day, and my anguish was horrible when I discovered she had been scalped." The girl had suffered seventeen cuts from lances, but did not then die, surviving to live five more years until her death at Fresno, California. In 1870 the couple were living in the Owens Valley, east of the Sierra and were there in 1872 when a devastating earthquake struck. Three years later they lived at Lompoc. By the 1880s they were in southern California, living first at Puente, then at Los Angeles, where Ben died February 17, 1889, aged 76. At 65 Nancy homesteaded in Cottonwood Canyon in northern Santa Barbara County, 175 miles from Los Angeles. She built a cabin and scratched out a living raising chickens and selling them two days to the west at Santa Maria; occasionally she acted as midwife or even as a sort of paramedic for injured or sickened pioneers. Little more than a week after her 73rd birthday she died of cancer, her grave today marked by an informative sign erected by a Boy Scout troop. In her fragmentary reminiscences she had written: "I have enjoyed riches and suffered the pangs of poverty. I saw General Grant when he was little known. I baked bread for General Fremont and talked to Kit Carson. I have run from bear and killed all other kinds of game." Her last wish was to be buried beside Ben at Los Angeles, but due to the times and difficult traveling conditions, this request could not be met. Her grave near her homestead is almost as isolated today as the site was a century ago.

Phillip H. Ault, "Nancy Kelsey," *True West,* Vol. 36, No. 12 (Dec. 1989), 30-39.

Kemble, John Haskell, historian, naval officer (June 17, 1912-Feb. 19, 1990). B. at Marshalltown, Iowa, and raised in southern California, he was a Phi Beta Kappa graduate of Stanford University and earned his doctorate in history from the University of California at Berkeley in 1937. He taught during his professional life at Pomona College, California, headed the history department for several years, and became professor emeritus in 1977. A specialist in sea and maritime history, he also taught at the U.S. Naval War College at Newport, Rhode Island, and was a faculty member of the Munsion Institute of American Maritime History at Mystic, Connecticut. "Jack had an absolute passion for the sea," according to Doyce B. Nunis, Jr., and he served as a naval officer during World War II on the personal staff of Admiral Ernest J. King; he rose to the rank of naval captain. His publications included: *The Panama Route, 1848-1869* (1943); *San Francisco Bay: A Pictorial Maritime History* (1957); the definitive two-volume edition of *Two Years Before the Mast* by Richard Henry Dana, Jr. (1964); *To California and the South Seas: The Diary of Albert G. Osbun, 1849-51* (1966); and three volumes for the California Book Club: *Journal of a Cruise to California and the Sandwich Islands in the United States Sloop-of-War Cyane by William H. Myers, 1841-1844* (1955); *Sketches of California and Hawaii by William H. Myers, Gunner, United States Navy, Aboard the United States Sloop-of-War Cyane, 1842-1843* (1970) and *A Naval Campaign in the Californias, 1846-1849: The Journal of Lieutenant Tunis Augustus Macdonough Craven, U.S.N., United States Sloop-of-War Dale* (1973). He was a seasoned oceanic traveler, crossing the Atlantic many times, visiting South America and Australia and voyaging twice around the world. Fittingly he succumbed at sea aboard the *Canberra* on a three month around-the-world cruise; he reportedly died sitting in a deck chair while crossing the Tasman Sea, next port of call, Sydney, Australia.

Doyce B. Nunis Jr., "John Haskell Kemble: In Memoriam," Los Angeles Westerners *Branding Iron* 180 (Summer 1990), 15-16.

Kennekuk (Kenekuk), Kickapoo prophet (d. 1853). Soon after the War of 1812 a pacifist faction developed among the militant Kickapoo Indians of Illinois; it was led by Kennekuk, the "Kickapoo prophet," and sought to maintain peace with the whites rather than continuation of the historic tribal tradition of status based on scalps taken and warfare. It sought to substitute agriculture for conflict and a friendly willingness to learn white ways and customs. Kennekuk was a mystic who believed he possessed supernatural powers, including a direct line to the Great Spirit. Ostracized by his more aggressive fellows, he went into exile, establishing a religious center on the Vermillion River where he collected around 250 followers from the Illinois and Wabash river Kickapoos. By 1819 he had refined his beliefs to a system of religion, preaching fasting and meditation. His doctrines set forth a path through fire and water by which the virtuous would reach the happy hunting grounds. He taught that if his followers lived worthily, abandoned native superstitions, avoided quarrels with each other and infractions of white laws and abstained from whiskey "they would at last inherit a land of plenty, clear of enemies." Local whites appreciated his teachings and overlooked the removal requirement of the treaties of July 30 and August 30, 1819. He always promised William Clark, Indian agent at St. Louis, that he would move his people west of the Mississippi as required, but "not just yet," for one reason or another. Once a year he visited Clark and in 1833 finally led his people to the west to rejoin the Kickapoo tribe which had already transferred; the last going west in 1834. By then, of the tribe of around 2,000, Kennekuk's followers had grown to 350, the people settling near Fort Leavenworth, establishing permanent homes. The descendants still live on lands assigned by treaty in present Brown County, Kansas, near the town of Horton. By 1865 the more militant Kickapoos had moved away and only Kennekuk's people remained. The Prophet's followers received such benefits as a blacksmith to repair tools and equipment, $3,000 in farming tools, $4,000 in livestock, $3,700 to erect buildings and a sawmill, and a resident agent who was to teach them agriculture. They sold their surplus produce to Fort Leavenworth and local traders, the Commissioner of Indian Affairs noting that the Prophet's people "are approaching fast to a system of farming and government...not far inferior to white citizens." Their sawmill produced lumber for many uses.

Kennekuk began missionary work among neighboring tribes, preaching his doctrine of salvation, and was most successful among the Potawatomis, winning more than 100 converts, who upon invitation moved onto the Kickapoo Reservation. By 1844 the Potawatomis had intermarried with the Kickapoos and in 1851 articles of agreement were signed making the Kickapoos and Potawatomis of the reservation "one nation, having equal rights" and sharing in soil, resources and money. Chief Kennekuk died in 1853 and was succeeded by his son, John Kennekuk.

Arrell M. Gibson, *The Kickapoos: Lords of the Middle Border,* Norman, Univ. of Okla. Press, 1963; info. from John Sugden.

Kennicott, Robert, naturalist, explorer (Nov. 13, 1835-May 15, 1866). B. at New Orleans, he was raised at Northfield, Illinois, and early became interested in natural history; he was soon connected with the Smithsonian Institution for which he collected natural history material. At 20 he made a natural history survey of southern Illinois for the Illinois Central Railroad and a year later united with others to found the Chicago Academy of Sciences. In 1857 he commenced organizing a museum for Northwestern University at Evanston, Illinois, led a collecting expedition to the Red River of the North, and spent part of a winter at the Smithsonian studying and identifying the material he had brought back. In 1858 he made his first expedition to Arctic America, the trip sponsored by the Hudson's Bay Company. On it he visited the Mackenzie River, crossed over to the Porcupine River and followed it down to the Yukon and Fort Yukon. Kennicott spent two winters in the vicinity of the post at the confluence of the Porcupine and Yukon, compiled a vocabulary of the language of local Indians, and returned to the United States in 1862 after learning of the outbreak of the Civil War. Part of his Yukon collection was lost, but 40 boxes and bundles of ethnological and zoological specimens, weighing a ton and one-half, in 1863 reached the Smithsonian where he worked for a year classifying and studying his materials. Kennicott's journal, "replete with observations on the animal life, the inhabitants and the country in general, shows an unusual breadth of perspective and an unusual ability to interpret the first-hand facts of observation." In 1864 he became curator of the Chicago Academy of Science, and later its director. In 1865, when Western Union determined to pursue plans for an overland line from the United States, across Alaska and Bering Strait to link up with a Siberian system and eventually with Europe, Kennicott was named to head its scientific corps. He went to Alaska to survey the Yukon River as part of that grandiose program, but on May 13, 1866, near Nulato on the middle Yukon, he died suddenly of a heart condition as William H. Dall (see entry) maintained, although he was not present at the death. George Adams, however, a member of the expedition who was with Kennicott, "wrote in his diary that Kennicott had committed suicide by taking strychnine." An article by Kennicott on Russian America, published posthumously, was said to have been influential in the United States's interest in purchasing Alaska. Kennicott Glacier, River and a town by that name were named in his memory.

DAB; Pierce, *Russian America: A Biographical Dictionary;* Orth, 510.

Kephart, Horace, writer, researcher (Sept. 8, 1862-Apr. 2, 1931). B. at East Salem, Pennsylvania, he was graduated from Lebanon Valley College at Annville, Pennsylvania, in 1879 and did post-graduate work at Cornell, Boston and Yale universities. He was assistant librarian at Cornell from 1880-84, lived in Europe, principally in Italy, from 1884-86, was an assistant at Yale Library from 1886-90 and was librarian at the St. Louis Mercantile Library from 1890-1903, during which time he became an accomplished bibliographer. In addition to a consummate outdoorsman, Kephart also became a firearms expert. In 1896 he purchased a Hawken rifle that had remained in storage for many years and had never been fired, except when tested by the maker. The gun was .53 caliber and weighed 10½ pounds with a very heavy 34-inch octagon barrel. In *Shooting and Fishing* magazine of October 1, 1896, he wrote of his try-out of the firearm with various charges, revealing much of the reason why it had been a favorite weapon on the Plains and in the mountains. One of Kephart's best-known books was *Our Southern Highlanders* which appeared initially in 1913, came out in a new and revised edition in 1922, and was reprinted many times since, the latest occurring in 1949. The book revealed in-depth research among the backwoodsmen, mainly of Scot-English ancestry, of the Great Smoky Mountains and ranges of western North Carolina and eastern Tennessee. Interested among other things in the dialect of these reclusive frontiersmen, Kephart devoted

much space to dissecting and analyzing their peculiar elements of speech. "A queer term used by Carolina mountaineers, without the faintest notion of its origin, is doney...or doney-gal, meaning sweetheart," he wrote. "Its history is unique. British sailors...brought it to England from Spanish or Italian ports. Doney is simply *doña* or *donna* [and it is odd] that it would be preserved in America by none but backwoodsmen whose ancestors for two centuries never saw the tides!" Another strange word, not recorded in today's dictionaries in the mountain sense, was "feathered," as a highlander "feathered" into a victim, slaying him. Kephart's research finally found the term, dating at least from Shakespearean times and used by chronicler William Harrison (1534-93). He recorded it as a longbowman's word: "An other arrow shold haue beene fethered into his bowels," meaning to sink an arrow up to its feathers in an opponent, Kephart adding, "where else can we hear to-day a phrase that passed out of standard English when [gunpowder] supplanted the long-bow?" Among his other books, reflecting his interests and most going through many editions or printings, were *Camping and Woodcraft* (1916, 1951); *Sporting Firearms* (1918); *Camp Cookery* (1910, 1936), and *The Camper's Manual* (1923). As editor-in-chief of the "Outing Adventure Library" of the New York Outing Publishing Company, Kephart edited a series of books, all being published in 1915: George Frederick Ruxton (see entry), *Adventures in Mexico* and *In the Old West,* more complete than the Hafen-Porter edition entitled *Ruxton of the Rockies* (1950); Elisha Kent Kane's *Adrift in the Arctic Ice-Pack,* dealing with an early search for the lost Sir John Franklin expedition; *Captives Among the Indians; Castaways and Crusoes;* Powell's *First Through the Grand Canyon;* Ronalyn Gordon-Cumming's *The Lion Hunter;* Augustus Charles Hobart-Hampden's *Hobart Pasha;* Cremony's *Life Among the Apaches,* and J.D. Borthwick's *The Gold Hunter.* Kephart's *Cherokees of the Smoky Mountains* (1936) was published posthumously. Some time after his death, his house burned, and all his notes and manuscripts were consumed. He was married and fathered six children, two sons and four daughters. He made his home late in life at Bryson City, North Carolina, on the edge of today's Great Smoky Mountains National Park and almost within view of the recently-developed Appalachian Trail through the backwoods country he loved so well.

Who Was Who; NCAB 6, 322; Kephart, *Our South-*

ern Highlanders, N.Y., The Macmillan Co., 1949; Norman B. Wiltsey, "The Rifle That Opened the West," *Old West,* Vol. 1, No. 1 (Fall 1964), 32-33, 47. References to Kephart in this article were also summarized in Wiltsey's "Guns of the Old West: The Hawken," *True West,* Vol. 10, No. 2 (Nov.-Dec. 1962), 22-23, 48.

Ketchum, Frank, explorer (c. 1826-pre1898). B. at St. Johns, New Brunswick, Canada, he became a member of the scientific team headed by Robert Kennicott of the Western Union Telegraph Company's Alaskan exploration operation. When Kennicott died in May 1866 at Nulato on the Yukon River Ketchum took over as head of the science corps. With Michel (Mike) Lebarge he traveled up the Yukon by canoe to Fort Yukon in 1866; the following winter the pair duplicated that effort with dog teams on the river ice and when the spring breakup came, continued by birchbark canoe to Fort Selkirk, Canada, at the confluence of the Yukon and Pelly rivers; it was the farthest the river had been explored from the western coast. Not much more has been unearthed about Ketchum, but William H. Dall wrote in 1898: "Frank Ketchum lies under the green turf of an Unalaska [Island] hillside. May his faithful companion [Michel Lebarge] and our [Dall's] good friend survive for many happy years."

Info. from Alaska State Lby.; *Narratives of Explorations in Alaska,* pp. 19-20; William H. Dall, "A Yukon Pioneer: Mike Lebarge," *National Geographic Magazine,* Vol. IX, No. 4 (April 1898), 137-39.

Khitrov, Sofron, Russian naval officer (fl. 1740-1756). Khitrov was a ship master (a commissioned rank below a lieutenant), sailing with Bering and Alexei Chirikov in 1741 on the voyage that nominally discovered Alaska, although Michael Gwosdef (see entry) had reached it in 1732; no doubt others had as well, their names now unremembered, and there was long standing and ready commerce between the Chukchi natives of Siberia and Eskimos of the Alaskan littoral. In an early account Khitrov is listed as master of the sloop which was to accompany the expedition, but it suffered so much misfortune that he became master aboard the *Sv Petr* under Bering, his function doubtless that of a first mate; he was called "fleet master" by Chirikov, indicating a rather broad assignment. June 4 the *Sv Petr* and *Sv Pavel* left the Kamchatka port of Avatcha (see Bering, Chirikov entries), with Khitrov keeping one of the most valuable surviving jour-

nals of the expedition in addition to other duties. His journal is reportedly now held by the Leningrad archives. At noon July 16 Bering sighted Mt. St. Elias, an 18,008-foot peak of the Alaskan Panhandle (Chirikov had sighted land late on the 15th), and on the 20th came upon an island Bering named St. Elias but which today is known as Kayak Island, situated in the Alaskan bight. While a small boat was assigned to fill fresh water casks ashore, a larger boat under Khitrov was directed by Bering to make limited explorations. The important scientist Georg Steller wanted to accompany Khitrov, who endorsed the request, but for some reason Bering refused and sent Steller with the smaller boat on its limited mission. Khitrov became the only commissioned officer of the *Sv Petr* to set foot on North America. He returned, reporting he had found a land-locked harbor of some dimensions and although he encountered no natives he discovered a small wooden building the walls of which were so smooth they seemed to have been planed with sharp tools. He brought back various artifacts. Bering then impatiently raised anchor and commenced the long return, passing various islands without investigating them. A seaman named Shumagin died at an island group now named for him, and was buried ashore on one named Nagai. The *Sv Petr* laid over on August 30 while Khitrov sought to investigate a fire seen the night before. He lost his boat and nearly lost his life and those of his men before at length regaining the ship. Scurvy now struck heavily and Khitrov and a few others whose strength remained tried to navigate the ship to Kamchatka, but the company was forced to winter on Bering Island where the commander himself and many others died. Khitrov, although very ill for a time, survived and a smaller boat was constructed out of the wreckage of the *Sv Petr.* The island was quitted August 14, 1742, and on the 27th the ship came safely into Avatcha Bay. November 20, 1749, an imperial ukase bestowed a monetary reward upon survivors of the expedition. Khitrov "was made a lieutenant [as of July 15, 1744] and finally a captain of the first rank." In 1753 he became a rear admiral. He died in 1756.

F.A. Golder, *Russian Expansion on the Pacific 1641-1850,* N.Y., Paragon Book Reprint Corp., 1971; Bancroft, *Alaska; Russian Penetration of the North Pacific Ocean.*

Khlebnikov, Kyrill Timofeyevich, Russian official (Mar. 18, 1785-Apr. 14, 1838). B. at Kungur, southeast of Perm (Molotov) in the Ural region of east Russia, in 1800 he became an agent for the newly chartered Russian American Company, stationed initially at Irkutsk in eastern Siberia and in 1801 at Kamchatka. In 1813 he returned to St. Petersburg before becoming administrator of the company's headquarters at Novo Arkhangelsk (Sitka), Alaska, which he reached November 20, 1817. Captain Leontii Hagemeister was chief manager of the company succeeding Baranov, and Khlebnikov was second to Hagemeister as chief executive officer. His travels sometimes took him to California and he had visited Chile, Peru and Mexico enroute to his Alaskan post; he came to speak and read Spanish and English "and certainly he was one of the best informed persons on the Pacific coast," as his reports reflect. In his official capacity he dealt not only with Russian employees but with native Americans, hostile and friendly, "whom he understood with unusual perception and endeavored to treat fairly." He kept travel diaries, wrote illuminating reports which included notes on history, ethnology, geography, mythology, natural science and other matters of interest and sent important artifacts to what is now the Museum of Anthropology and Ethnography of the Leningrad Academy of Sciences. He departed for St. Petersburg in 1832 and became chief administrator of the Russian American Company, a member of its governing board, and was elected to the Academy of Sciences. His prolific writings included "Notes on California," "The First Settlement of Russians in America," an important biography of Baranov, and other topics. The first two parts of his notes on America were translated into English by Dmytryshyn and Crownhart-Vaughan, although they had been published in Russia in 1861; the last four parts, never published even in Russia, were to be translated and published in English. Khlebnikov died at St. Petersburg.

Colonial Russian America: Kyrill T. Khlebnikov's Reports 1817-1832, trans. by Dmytryshyn, Crownhart-Vaughan, Portland, Oreg. Hist. Soc., 1976; Bancroft, *Alaska.*

Kiasutha, Iroquois chief: *see,* Guyasuta

Kicking Bear, Oglala Sioux leader (c. 1848-post 1893). One of the leading figures in the Ghost Dance movement among the Sioux in 1890-91, Kicking Bear was a prominent Oglala, but never a chief. He had a reputation as a mighty warrior, a mystic and something of a medicine man and had

been close to Crazy Horse (see entry) in earlier years. He had stolen many horses from the Crows and other tribes, and in 1876 distinguished himself in the battles of the Rosebud, Little Bighorn, and Slim Buttes. He had become a Miniconjou through marriage to a niece of the chief, Big Foot, who also was a Miniconjou and "uncompromising hatred of the white man and all his ways, refusal to adjust to the new life [the whites brought] and rank and reputation made Kicking Bear a natural leader in the quest for the old life" that the Ghost Dance enthusiasm promised. He was brother-in-law of Short Bull, a former warrior and medicine man who would also figure largely in the Ghost Dance furor. The "Messiah craze," which had reached the Sioux the previous summer, became more prevalent. A great council was called by the Sioux of Pine Ridge, South Dakota, in the fall of 1889 to discuss the subject, and it was agreed to send a delegation to Pyramid Lake, Nevada, to meet with and learn about Wovoka (see entry), a Paiute and central figure who was reported to have important mystic powers. Kicking Bear was one of the delegation of eleven, he representing the Cheyenne River agency Sioux. The delegation returned in April 1890 as virtual missionaries, confirming the advent of a redeemer in the person of Wovoka, who would wipe out the whites, resurrect dead Indians, bring back the buffalo and restore the primacy of the Indians. Nothing much happened immediately following the report, although things seethed beneath the surface and Kicking Bear went to Wyoming to visit the Arapahoes. He returned to tell of the regeneration Wovoka's faith had worked on that tribe. Kicking Bear's report fired the Oglalas with a new faith, and evidently he taught them the steps of the new dances Wovoka had promoted. Kicking Bear's Cheyenne River agency became "the fountainhead of all lore and wisdom" about the new religion, and other branches of the Sioux tribe became infected. The devotees commenced to coalesce into groupings that white personnel on the agencies feared had militant tendencies. The fanatical Short Bull and Kicking Bear held large numbers of their people at the mouth of White Clay Creek, and others were massed on Wounded Knee Creek. The mystics' stronghold was established on a small plateau between the White and Cheyenne rivers, and there Kicking Bear, Short Bull and their followers were talked into surrendering. However, 15 miles northwest of the agency they heard of the Wounded Knee massacre, bloodied survivors met them and they went into camp on White Clay Creek. Here they were joined by Brulé and Oglala Sioux refugees from the action. But there was no real support for them, and on January 15, 1891, all the Sioux who had been out, came in and surrendered at the agency, Kicking Bear among the last. When he did so, "the Ghost Dance uprising was over." When Miles left Pine Ridge for his headquarters at Chicago on January 26, he took with him 25 Ghost Dance leaders, including Kicking Bear and Short Bull; he would confine 19 of their number at Fort Sheridan, near Highwood, Illinois. Kicking bear's "punishment" was bizarre. He and other Ghost Dance leaders were permitted to join Buffalo Bill Cody's Wild West Show for a European tour; they left Philadelphia on the steamer *Switzerland,* landed at Antwerp, and joined the show at Strasbourg. According to Russell they were with the show at least through 1893 and perhaps longer, before they were returned to their South Dakota reservation. The date of Kicking Bear's death is not reported.

Robert M. Utley, *The Last Days of the Sioux Nation,* New Haven, Yale Univ. Press, 1963; Doane Robinson, *A History of the Dakota or Sioux Indians,* Minneapolis, Minn., 1956; Don Russell, *The Lives and Legends of Buffalo Bill,* Norman, Univ. of Okla. Press, 1960.

Kikthewanund, Delaware chief: *see,* William Anderson

Killbuck, John Jr. (Gelelemend), Delaware chief (c. 1722-Jan. 1811). Wallace gives his birth year as 1737. Killbuck was said to be one of the best educated Indians of his time. He was chief of the Turtle division of the Delaware tribe as had been Netawatwees (see entry), his grandfather before him, and succeeded to that position following the 1778 death of White Eyes (see entry) who had followed Netawatwees. Already Killbuck had won a reputation in council for sagacity and discretion. Like his predecessor he strove to maintain friendship with white Americans. The Delaware war party, or that partial to the English in Revolutionary disputes, was led by Captain Pipe (Hopacan), and since his views prevailed in council Killbuck was invited by the military commander at Fort Pitt to remove with his people to an island in the Allegheny River where they would be under protection of the soldiers. But the latter could not, or would not, protect them from unruly white frontiersmen to whom virtually all

Indians were anathema. These whites had murdered nearly 100 Christian Delawares at Gnadenhutten in 1782 and, returning from that atrocity, fell upon the peaceful, and friendly, Killbuck Island people and murdered many of them. Weslager suggested that perhaps "White Eyes seniority may have been the reason the Delawares chose him to succeed Netawatwees [but] the young chief...was killed before he was able to take office." He added that "The details of what happened seem to have been covered up, although, when Brigadier General William Irvine took office at Fort Pitt, he learned something of what had happened, which he reported to George Washington in a letter dated April 20, 1782. He added that on March 24, 1782, a group of settlers attacked a party of friendly Delaware Indians then living on a small island in the river below Fort Pitt." Among those killed were two captains who had assisted the Americans on expeditions and scouts. A chief fled and swam to shore, leaving behind "the bag containing all the wampum speeches and written documents of William Penn and his successors for a number of years together, which had been so carefully preserved by them, but now had fallen into the hands of a murdering band of white people, who also at the same time killed the promising young chief above-mentioned." Butterfield believed that the attackers were not the militiamen returning from Gnadenhutten as Heckewelder held, but a separate group of Indian-haters. Killbuck also escaped by swimming the river. His services were useful in bringing about a general peace, but the Wolf division of the tribe continued to blame him for the heavy misfortunes that had befallen the Delawares. Avoiding their vengeance he remained at Pittsburgh long after peace was proclaimed. He at length joined the Moravian converts, was baptized in 1789 under the name of William Henry, declined an invitation to become head chief of the Delaware nation and lived until 1811. His direct descendant was John Henry Killbuck (1861-1922), a Moravian missionary in Alaska (see Josiah Spurr entry).

HNAI, 15; Hodge (under Gelelemende); Clinton A. Weslager, *The Delaware Indians: A History,* New Brunswick, N.J., Rutgers Univ. Press, 1972; Paul A.W. Wallace, *Thirty Thousand Miles With John Heckewelder,* Univ. of Pittsburgh Press, 1958.

Kimball, Oliver, sea captain, trader (fl. 1805-1807). A brother-in-law of Joseph O'Cain (see entry), Kimball captained the brig *Peacock* out of

Boston, leaving September 14, 1805, reaching the California coast and proceeding north to Kodiak Island, Alaska. There Baranov sought to punish Tlingit Indians who had destroyed a Russian American Company fur post at Yakutat Bay on the Alaska Panhandle in the fall of 1805, and to release any surviving Russians or Aleuts from captivity. At Baranov's request, Kimball coasted the Yakutat area and captured the Chilkat (Tlingit) chief, Asik, and two youths. Asik was released in exchange for the release of an Aleut and his wife, and the two Indian youths were taken to Kodiak where they were baptized and taken into Russian service as interpreters. Kimball secured 12 baidarkas and the Aleuts to man them to hunt along the California coast, the deal with Baranov concluded October 25, 1806. The Aleuts were commanded by the promyshlennik Timofei Tarakanov (see entry), who earlier had hunted with O'Cain. The *Peacock* anchored at Bodega Bay while the hunters ranged south as far as San Francisco Bay, where they came under Spanish cannon fire and two hunters were lost. At San Juan Capistrano four crewmen were arrested for illegal trading. August 3, 1807, Kimball returned to Kodiak with 1,231 sea otter pelts, half of which went to the RAC under his contract. The brig returned to Hawaii, then Canton, weathered a gale with some damage and was condemned and sold at Batavia in the East Indies. Kimball and the crew returned to Boston by some other vessel.

Pierce, *Russian America: A Biographical Dictionary.*

Kimbrell, George, frontiersman (Mar. 31, 1842-Mar. 24, 1925). B. at Huntsville, Arkansas, he attended the Pike's Peak gold rush of 1859 and moved down to New Mexico in 1860 for health reasons, reaching Lincoln County from Las Vegas in 1863. For a time he was a scout for the army out of Fort Stanton, New Mexico. He established a small ranch on Chaves Flats, a dozen miles east of Lincoln, marrying Paulita Romero and fathering four children. "As an Anglo married to an Hispanic, Kimbrell was the natural prey of the Horrells (see entries) but for some reason they spared his life in 1874 while killing the five Hispanics Kimbrell was traveling with," according to Nolan. Kimbrell was appointed deputy U.S. marshal in November 1878, and served as sheriff from 1879-81, but was defeated at the next election by Pat Garrett. Kimbrell served as justice of the peace for many

years and died at his home at Picacho, near Las Cruces, six days short of his 82nd birthday.

Robert N. Mullin Notes; Frederick Nolan, *The Lincoln County War: A Documentary History,* Norman, Univ. of Okla. Press, 1992.

King, James, British naval officer (1750-1784). B. at Clitheroe, Lancashire, England, he entered the Royal Navy at 12, served on the Newfoundland Station, then in the Mediterranean, and in 1771 was promoted to lieutenant and spent time at Paris and Oxford engaged in scientific studies. As a "competent astronomer" he joined Captain James Cook on the third voyage of discovery, appointed to the *Resolution* as a second lieutenant. King was ashore at the time Cook was killed in Hawaii, but he and his men returned safely to the ship. He came into command of the second Cook ship, the *Discovery* and returned to England in 1780. King assisted in preparing Cook's journals for publication and in writing the narrative of the conclusion of the voyage. His health was poor late in life and he died at Nice. King Island, a noted site in the Bering Sea, was named for him by Cook.

Pierce, *Russian America: A Biographical Dictionary;* Orth, 522.

King, Melvin A., soldier (c. 1845-Jan. 25, 1876). B. at Oswego, New York, no evidence has been found that he was a Civil War soldier, although lack of documentation does not preclude such service. King was the man whose death, probably at the hands of Bat Masterson (see entry), is his one claim to frontier fame. He enlisted October 28, 1869, in Company H, 4th Cavalry, was described as 5 ft., 5¼ in. tall with blue eyes, brown hair and a fair complexion. In 1871 he was stationed at Fort Griffin, Texas; his service record reports an occasional passing injury which might or might not have been incurred in saloon brawls; there is no evidence either way. Kiowa raiders were active into Texas from Indian Territory, and the 4th Cavalry was much in the field on patrolling or scouting duty, giving King an opportunity to become "intimately acquainted with his McClellan saddle." He apparently was a good soldier and as good a horse and mule wrangler, his company used regularly to herd remounts for Colonel Ranald Mackenzie's troops. His company joined Mackenzie in successful attacks on the Comanches, particularly in September 1874 at Palo Duro Canyon in west Texas. His enlistment expired, King was discharged October 28, 1874, still a private. He re-enlisted April 29, 1875, at Fort Richardson, Texas, in his old company, having, as Gary Roberts makes clear, no time in the interim to support Stuart Lake's allegation of King's "authenticated" raids on Kansas cow towns, since he was discharged at the end of the 1874 season for cattle driving and rejoined the army before the 1875 season commenced. He was promoted to corporal, the highest rank he attained so far as the record shows, although he is termed "Sergeant" King in most published reports of his activities and alleged activities. In May-June 1875 he and a detail took Indian ponies to Fort Sill, then was assigned as Mackenzie's orderly until October 18, 1875, when he went on detached duty at Cantonment Sweetwater, later named Fort Elliott, near present Mobeetie. Stuart Lake's fanciful description of a showdown between King and Wyatt Earp at Wichita in the summer of 1875 appears without substantiation; if such an encounter ever occurred, which is not proven, it must have involved some other 4th Cavalry soldier-deserter, for King's service during that period was in Texas. In 1874-75 Bat Masterson was a teamster hauling for the army from Camp Supply to Fort Elliott. During subsequent months he became attracted to Mollie Brennan, supposed to have been the ex-wife of an Ellsworth, Kansas, saloon-keeper, Joe Brennan; Melvin King also had taken a shine to her. On the night of January 24, 1876, King came upon them together in a saloon, apparently owned by Fleming and Thompson, where Bat regularly played poker. From that point on descriptions of what happened vary widely, but the end result was that a gunfight erupted, Mollie was shot and killed, Masterson was seriously wounded by King and then shot King, who died the following day. Thereafter the myth-makers have taken over, depicting the victim of a single shooting affray to have been a "gunfighter of frontier-wide reputation without one shred of hard evidence" to support it, but this was done by some writers to make King a formidable opponent for Earp or Masterson and help build their own legends. The best biographical work on King is by Roberts.

Gary L. Roberts, "Corporal Melvin A. King: The Gunfighting Soldier of the Great American Myth," *Real West,* Vol. 30, No. 215 (Sept. 1987), 4-7, 45-48.

King, Richard, cattleman (July 10, 1825-Apr.

14, 1885). B. in Orange County, New York, he was apprenticed to a jeweler about 1835 but didn't like the work and stowed away on the *Desdemona* to Mobile, Alabama. King worked on river boats in Alabama, rising from cabin boy to pilot, but at 16 enlisted under Captain Henry Penny's militia outfit for service in the Second Seminole War, although if he saw combat it is not recorded. But in Florida he became acquainted with Mifflin Kenedy (see entry), also a riverboat man, and during the Mexican War (1846-48) they ran riverboats on the Rio Grande, transporting men and supplies. In 1850 the two became partners in a steamboating business on the Rio Grande and two years later King bought the 75,000-acre Spanish land grant of Santa Gertrudis in Nueces County, south of Corpus Christi; he sold half of it to Kenedy in 1860. In 1861 the two contracted with the Confederate government to supply cotton to European buyers, purchasing land with the proceeds. The partnership dissolved in 1868, King retaining the Santa Gertrudis Ranch; he regularly added more acreage to it, and to other divisions he established. At one time his livestock holdings were 100,000 cattle, 20,000 sheep and 10,000 horses and at his death he owned more than 500,000 acres of land outright. After the Civil War the King interests sent Longhorn herds to Kansas rail points, although of course King himself did not accompany them. Because of outlawry he saw that the only way to protect his ranching interests was to fence, and he began with wooden fence before barbed wire came on the market. He and Kenedy were the first cattle raisers in Texas to fence large expanses of land. King also entered many peripheral businesses. In a lawsuit, King became associated with Robert J. Kleberg and later retained him as legal adviser. King had married Henrietta Chamberlain in 1854, who following King's death named Kleberg manager of the by then enormous ranch. Kleberg eventually married Alice King, youngest of King's five children; the King-Kleberg descendants remain stockholders today in the 1.25 million acre ranch. "The foundation stock of the King Ranch was the Longhorn," but early attempts were made to improve the bloodlines of its stock. Shorthorns (or Durhams) and Herefords were brought in by 1893; a distinctive breed called the Santa Gertrudis, of five-eighths Shorthorn and three-eighths Brahma, dark red in color, was developed on the ranch and established by about 1940. By then the ranch had almost 3,000 head of quarterhorses (a breed reportedly developed on the King ranch) and 80 race horses, including Assault, who became in his day the third biggest racing winner. The ranch also was an oil producer and a wild life preserve. King died of cancer at San Antonio and was buried at the site of the present Kingsville, a community named for him, in Kleberg County, Texas, although the town, as such, was not incorporated until 1904; it is today a city of some 30,000 residents.

HT; J. Marvin Hunter, *Trail Drivers of Texas,* N.Y., Argosy-Antiquarian Ltd., 1963; Robert Dyer, "Richard King—A Man for Texas," *True West,* Vol. 35, No. 3 (Mar. 1988), 28-32, 37.

Klimovskii, Afanasii Ilich, explorer (c. 1794-July 12, 1868). The son of a Russian and an Aleut girl, his career is often confused with that of his brother, Andrei Ilich Klimovskii, who was sent to St. Petersburg to study in the navigation school and who became a captain of Russian American Company vessels in Alaskan waters. In 1818 Afanasii Klimovskii participated in an expedition led by Petr Korsakovskii to Lake Iliamna and the Nushagak River, thence to Cape Newenham. The next year he explored part of the Copper River whose mouth is east of present Cordova. He may have gone 200 versts upstream to near its confluence with the Gulkana River. Pierce wrote that Klimovskii was first to describe Miles and Child's glaciers of the Chugach Mountains. In January 1825 Klimovskii became manager of a fort at the present Nuchek on Hinchinbrook Island, but his control over his employees was deemed unsatisfactory. During a smallpox epidemic in 1837 he was directed to go from Sitka to Kodiak, thence to Katmai, overland to Aleksandrovsk and St. Michael, vaccinating people as he went. He treated 636 and taught those he met to vaccinate themselves, though "unfortunately the smallpox traveled faster than Klimovskii," according to Pierce, and many died from the epidemic. Zagoskin (see entry) reported that in 1838 "the bravery of the Creole Klimovskiy saved the lives of [some of] the people of the Russian American Company's brig *Polifem*...in Kotzebue Sound." Pierce wrote that in 1840 Klimovskii was sent to quell trouble at the Aleksandrovskii redoubt on Nushagak Bay, off Bristol Bay. "He accomplished his mission, returning a year later." He then was ordered to lead an expedition to the upper Copper River, since he had already explored its lower reaches. He partially fulfilled this mission but was consid-

ered too old for such work by that time and was pensioned, living thereafter on Kodiak Island, where he died in his 75th year. He was buried on Spruce Island, north of Kodiak. He left a widow and possibly two sons.

Bancroft, *Alaska;* Zagoskin; Swanton, *Tribes,* 530; Pierce, *Russian America: A Biographical Dictionary.*

Klinkovstrem, Martin Fedorovich, sea officer (Jan. 23, 1818-Mar. 6, 1884). B. at Libau, Latvia, he probably was educated in the Russian Corps of Fleet Navigators, for he went to Alaska as an assistant navigator in 1837 and remained in Russian America for years. He made voyages to the Aleutian Islands, the Pribylovs, California and to Okhotsk, Siberia, and from 1840-45 made charts of the western Aleutians and the Commander Islands of the North Pacific. In 1845 he took the brig *Chichagov* to Atkha Island and to Copper Island of the Commanders, but was wrecked on the latter, though crew and cargo were saved. In 1862 Klinkovstrem became Russian vice consul and agent of the Russian American Company at San Francisco. He returned to Russia in 1875 and died at Wiesbaden, Germany.

Pierce, *Russian America: A Biographical Dictionary.*

Kloehr, John Joseph, citizen (June 3, 1858-Mar. 20, 1927). B. at Aschachbad, Kissingen, Bavaria, he was the eldest of six chidren of Joseph Vinzens Klohr and added an "e" to his surname after settling in the United States. The family migrated to America in 1870 and settled at Le Roy, Kansas, for two years, then removed to Coffeyville, 75 miles to the south. Here the parent established the Southern Hotel. By the time John Joseph reached maturity he was trained in the butcher business but after two years he worked for the government "handling" cattle on the Canadian River for a year, spent another prospecting in Colorado, and returned to Coffeyville to reside permanently. He traded in horses and at length entered the livery business with a brother, eventually owning the leading stable of the community with stalls for 68 head of stock and shed room for an indefinite number besides. October 5, 1892, came the Dalton (see entries) raid on banks of Coffeyville, aiming to outdo the James boys by raiding two banks in daylight at the same time. Kloehr was "reclining on a cot" at his stable when the outlaws struck. Harris Reed, a neighbor, rushed in to announce the arrival of the gang. Kloehr had no firearm handy, so crossed over to the Boswell Hardware Store, "borrowed" a Winchester and ammunition and "got into the fight without further delay." Grat Dalton, Bill Powers and Dick Broadwell were to hold up the C.M. Condon & Company Bank on Main Street, while Bob and Emmett Dalton hit the First National Bank on Union Street, the raid commencing about 9:40 a.m. A fatal delay of several minutes occurred at the Condon Bank because a cashier, Charlie Ball, protested that the safe had a time lock on it and couldn't be opened beforehand (actually, the safe, holding $40,000, was unlocked). A gunbattle between bandits and townspeople erupted. John Kloehr, wearing "a battered derby hat" and clutching his borrowed rifle, moved into the fight accompanied by City Marshal Charles Connelly and barber Carey Seaman. Kloehr killed Grat Dalton after Dalton had mortally wounded Connelly. Kloehr then mortally wounded Dick Broadwell, who also was fired on by Seaman's shotgun, although Broadwell's horse carried him a mile out of town before he slipped from the saddle and succumbed. Kloehr shot Bob Dalton through the bowels, then finished him off, after an exchange of shots, by a bullet in the chest; whether Kloehr had any part in the shooting of the four outlaws' horses that were killed was not reported. In the battle four bandits had been killed outright, or wounded mortally, four townspeople were also fatally shot, Emmett Dalton was seriously wounded and three citizens were wounded less seriously. The net loss for the two banks was $18.02—when First National counted its returned money it found $1.98 surplus; the Condon bank was short a $20 bill. John J. Kloehr won, and deserved, high praise for his coolness and bravery. Lyman J. Gage, later a U.S. Secretary of the Treasury, was instrumental in collecting $1,000 for a 2-inch gold medal with a diamond mounted on it, the medal engraved: "John Joseph Kloehr—the Emergency Arose and the Man Appeared." Among other gifts thrust upon him was a new Winchester rifle, a pair of rubber boots indicative of his "wading in" to the brawl, and a handsome hunting jacket. Kloehr was married, fathered children, and served later as alderman, school director, deputy sheriff and in other capacities. He died at Coffeyville. His grandson, John B. Kloehr, in 1935 joined the Condon National Bank (as it was then named) and served it for 56 years, rising in April 1977 from executive vice president to president

of the historic institution, a post from which he retired December 31, 1991.

Info. from John B. Kloehr, Coffeyville, Jan. 27, 1992; David Stewart Elliott, *Coffeyville Journal* ed., *Last Raid of the Daltons*, Coffeyville, Kan., 1892.

Knox, James, long hunter (d. Dec. 1822). B. in Ireland he came to America at 14, made for the frontier and became so adept a woodsman that his career as a hunter and trapper was assured. He was a leader of the 1769 Long Hunters who penetrated Kentucky and Tennessee (see Kaspar Mansker entry). Knox became a scout in Lord Dunmore's War against the Shawnees. At its close he enlisted a company for Daniel Morgan's rifle corps and "served with distinction at Saratoga and Stillwater," retiring as a major. He returned to Kentucky to settle, acquiring land and position, was member of the state legislature and married the widow of Benjamin Logan (see entry). He died at his home in Shelby County, Kentucky.

Thwaites, *Dunmore.*

Knutsson, Powell (Paul Knutson), explorer (fl. 1347-c. 1364). A probable Norwegian, Knutsson was "a distinguished man," an official in the service of the Duchess Ingeborg, and was from 1347 to 1348 "law-speaker" of Gulathing (Holand says chief justice of Gulathing district). He must have had some sea-faring experience when King Magnus (1316-1373), ruler of Norway and parts of Sweden, called upon him to lead an adventurous and possibly perilous mission. The royal command has been reprinted from a late copy, the original having disappeared. In part it read: "We desire to make known to you that you [Powell Knutson] are to take the men who shall go in the knorr [a royal merchant vessel]...from my bodyguard and also from among the retainers of other men whom you may wish to take on the voyage who are best qualified to accompany him, either as officers or men. We ask that you accept this our command with a right good will for the cause, inasmuch as we do it for the honor of God and for the sake of our soul, and for the sake of our predecessors who in Greenland established Christianity and have maintained it until this time, and we will not let it perish in our days," the document dated in October 1354. It had already been learned that the Skraelings (Eskimos) had swept down from the north and were in possession of the Western settlement of Greenland, the white inhabitants presumably having fled to some unknown or at least unreported place. The abandonment of the Western settlement had been ascertained in 1341 and a later document reported that by 1342 the people of western Greenland had become apostates and had "turned to the people of America." Knutsson and his selected party, which in Holand's view may have been linked with one headed or accompanied by Nicholas of Lynne, a Franciscan or Carmelite friar, mathematician and astronomer of Oxford, England, left Norway in 1356; it is not known whether, or when, it returned to Norway although elements may have regained the homeland in 1363 or 1364. "Powell Knutsson is not mentioned in any known document after his departure in 1356," according to Thalbitzer. Holand (see entry), a strong believer in the authenticity of the Kensington Stone, believed its inscription may provide a clue as to what happend to some of the expedition, from which inferences or conjectures might be made as to what became of others.

William C. Thalbitzer, *Two Runic Stones, from Greenland and Minnesota,* Smithsonian Misc. Coll. Vol. 116, No. 3, Wash., Smithsonian Inst., Aug. 30, 1951; Hjalmar R. Holand, *A Pre-Columbian Crusade to America,* N.Y., Twayne Pubs., 1962; DCB, I, 678-79, Nicholas of Lynne entry.

Kobelev, Ivan, Cossack explorer (1739-c.1849). B. at Anadyr, Siberia, he was a Cossack *sotnik,* or commander of 100 men of the Anadyr garrison. He thoroughly understood the Chukchi language, maintained friendly relations with that people and made a series of daring trips over the Chukotski Peninsula. He was the first Russian to visit the Diomede Islands between Siberia and Alaska, doing this in 1779, although the Cook expedition had visited them the year before. Kobelev reached the first island, named Imoglin (presently Ratmanov) July 26, 1779, where he found about 400 people living and speaking Chukchi identical with that of the Siberian mainland. July 31 he went on to Little Diomede Island, named by the Russians Krusenstern Island with about 160 people resident. "One can see the American coast from there," he reported, "and one can also see the Chukchi coast. The chief elder...is named Kaigan Momokhunin, who identifies himself as a native American, born on American soil, but not on that island." The elder reported to Kobelev that on American territory along the Yukon River there was a small island called Kymgov where people lived who

"speak Russian, read and write, worship icons, and...have big heavy beards." Kobelev asked the elder to take him there, but the native refused, probably because he feared "that Kobelev would be killed or detained...which could lead to an inquiry or trouble" with Russian authorities. But the elder agreed to take a letter from Kobelev to the mysterious Russians when he was able, and Kobelev wrote such a missive (the text printed in *Russian Penetration of the North Pacific Coast);* there is no report as to what reply, if any, was received or if it was even delivered. The elder reflected detailed knowledge of the American coast, its wildlife and people and described them well. In 1791 Kobelev himself sailed with the Chukchis to look for the bearded people, and at this time also visited King Island. That year too he guided and interpreted for Billings (see entry) on the English explorer's unfortunate traverse of the Chukotski Peninsula.

Russian Penetration of the North Pacific Coast; Zagoskin.

Kolmakov, Fedor Lavrentevich, explorer, trader (d. 1839). A resident of Tobolsk, Siberia, on the Tobol River northeast of Sverdlovsk, he was employed by Rezanov (see entry) and probably accompanied him on his first visit to Alaska in 1805. In 1806 Kolmakov petitioned to be allowed to remain in Alaska as an employee of the Russian American Company with the chief manager, Baranov, with whom he already had associated. Kolmakov became most closely linked with the expansion of the Russian fur trade into southwestern Alaska, and it has been written that his life "encapsulates the history" of that activity. Before 1818 he had traveled from Kodiak Island to Iliamna Lake, which the Russians had heard of as early as 1785 although any kind of station on that large body of water was not established until 1796. Lebedev-Lastochkin promyshlenniki however had traded and adventured there earlier. Assigned to accompany Korsakovskiy on the 1818 expedition into the western Alaskan interior, Kolmakov soon took command for obscure reasons but with Korsakovskiy's genial assent and traveled with the group from Kodiak Island to Lake Iliamna and perhaps to the mouth of the Nushagak River, all over routes he no doubt had traveled before the official "exploration" party set out. Kolmakov accompanied Korsakovskiy on a second expedition in 1819 and established Aleksandrovskiy Redoubt (Fort Alexander) in the vicinity of the present Dillingham at the mouth of the Nushagak River. It was the first Russian American Company post north of the Alaska Peninsula, with Kolmakov its manager for 20 years from its founding until his death. During this period he and Semen Lukin (see entry), his principal assistant, explored much of the Kuskokwim River; they established a satellite post at the mouth of the Holitna River, near the present Sleetmute, with Lukin in charge. Later a more advantageous site was found at the mouth of the Kvygym (Kolmakov) River east of the present Aniak where a redoubt was created, later to be known as Kolmakvovskiy (Fort Kolmakov) after Fedor. Zagoskin later wrote that Kolmakov "gained an immortal name in the interior" of Alaska, although he was illiterate, once apologizing for that failing to Baron Wrangel, then chief manager of the Russian American Company. Wrangel replied that "he would gladly send Kolmakov 10 scribblers, provided that things remained under his jurisdiction." Fedor Kolmakov's son, Petr Kolmakov also was an important explorer and fur trade figure in Alaska.

James W. VanStone, *Russian Exploration in Southwest Alaska: The Travel Journals of Petr Korsakovskiy (1818) and Ivan Ya. Vasilev (1829)*, Fairbanks, Univ. of Ak. Press, 1988; Zagoskin.

Kolmakov, Petr Fedorovich, fur trader, explorer (fl. 1829-June 12, 1843). Son of Fedor Kolmakov, Petr was probably a Creole, his mother perhaps an Aleut and he could not have been born before 1807; he was educated in Russian schools in Alaska and was literate and intelligent. He participated in the Vasilev (see entry) 1829 expedition into the interior of southwestern Alaska, by that time being an "apprentice navigator" of the naval navigator corps. He served Vasilev well and may have been also on the expedition of 1830, of which the journal has yet to be located. In 1831-32 he was on Vasilev's survey of the coast of the Alaska Peninsula. Just before this expedition, Fedor Kolmakov, for reasons unexplained, urged the chief manager of the Russian American Company to discharge Petr from naval service and assign him to the Kodiak office as a bookkeeper, but this Wrangel refused to do, noting that Vasilev had praised Petr's work during the inland explorations. When Fedor Kolmakov died in 1839, Petr succeeded him as manager of the important Aleksandrovskiy Redoubt at the mouth of the Nushagak River. That autum on a trading trip Kolmakov crossed the Takotna

River, near McGrath on the upper Kuskokwim and reached the upper Innoko River seeking a good route to the Yukon, but turned back near the confluence of the Itarod, having learned that the post at Ikogmiut (Russian Mission) had been overrun by hostile natives and the residents massacred. His journal could not be found by Zagoskin, but Petr Kolmakov's map of his journey to the Innoko was available, and the later explorer found it highly useful if not precisely accurate because Kolmakov had lacked the instruments to make it so. Petr as manager of Aleksandrovskiy Redoubt, "although an experienced fur trader and explorer [may have] lacked the administrative abilities" of his father, and in the winter of 1842 was replaced as manager. The date and circumstances of his death are not reported.

Zagoskin; James W. VanStone, ed., *Russian Exploration in Southwest Alaska: The Travel Journals of Petr Korsakovskiy (1818) and Ivan Ya. Vasilev (1829)*, Fairbanks, Univ. of Ak. Press, 1988.

Kondakov, Gerassim, creole seaman (d. 1820). Identified by Bancroft as a Kolosh (Tlingit) "creole," or of mixed Russian-American native parentage, this term may be in error and he a full-blood Kolosh (see discussion in Andrei Klimovsky entry). With two others, he was given by the Kolosh to the Russians as hostages to assure compliance with a peace arrangement. Kondakov was given his Russian name when received, and with others was sent on the *Neva*, Captain Yuriy Lisyanskiy, in 1805 to Kronstadt and there enrolled in a naval pilots school after which he was returned to Russian America. He became a mate on ships operated by the Russian American Company until his early death of unreported causes.

Bancroft, *Alaska*.

Korsakovskiy, Petr, explorer (1799-May 31, 1831). A veteran employee of the Russian American Company and well acquainted with natives of western Alaska, he was chosen by Baranov to lead explorations, among the first such Russian essays into the interior of the western mainland. He was also instructed to search for mysterious long-bearded white men reported to be descendants of the expedition of Dezhnev (see entry) of 1648-50, or even lost members of the Chirikov (see entry) 1741 exploration. In 1779 a Cossack *sotnik* (or commander of 100 Cossacks), Ivan Kobelev (see entry), interviewing Eskimos on

Imoglin Island (today's Ratmanov Island of the Diomedes), heard of these people, believed by the islanders to be truly Russians. The islanders would not take him there, but he wrote a letter to them, asking the islanders to deliver it, the results unknown. Kobelev's report was published in 1790 in *Ezhemesiachnye Sochineniia* of the Russian Academy, Part V, pp. 370-74. In 1818 or 1819 the ship *Konstantin,* captained by Dmitrii Pomatilov, visited the Kust-kukhontsy natives (possibly located near the mouth of the Kuskokwim River) and heard of people who lived "far to the north" on two large islands, these individuals of white skins and long beards who "pray in our [Russian] fashion. Certain items...obtained from them [include] a small bronze bell, a large knife...and a piece of a clock." A report from the chief administrator of the Russian American Company to Tsar Alexander I suggested that these people might be "descendants of the promyshlenniks who sailed under the leadership of Fedor Alekseev," identified by Bancroft as Fedor Alexeief, the party including Dezhnev. Four of the six boats had been lost off the Chukotski Peninsula, some of them perhaps bearing the mysterious Russians to an unknown destination on the American coast, "where our people were stranded, either because they had lost their vessels, or for some other reason." The manager had made attempts to locate them, with results unreported. Korsakovskiy has been called "the first Russian explorer of Alaska's interior," but that is not the case, since by 1796 a trading post was established on Iliamna Lake, if it had not been earlier. From it, trading and exploration parties, including that of Vasily Ivanov (see entry) in the "early 1790s" were sent as far as the Kuskokwim region and there had been penetrations of at least the fringes of the interior by promyshlenniki and others before Korsakovskiy's time. On his first expedition in 1818 he left the fur company headquarters at St. Paul, Kodiak Island, April 27, and by May 26, reached Becharof Lake, probably at the mouth of the Kejulik River. He crossed the lake, leaving by the Egelik River to Bristol Bay which was reached June 1, going up the coast to Naknek on June 2, making extensive ethnological notes on the Aglegmiut Eskimos as he progressed. June 11, he crossed Kvichak Bay and on the 14th reached Nushagak Bay. Farther along he discovered the mouth of the Togiak River and on June 26, reached Summit Island, near Hagemeister Island. Korsakovskiy had occasional difficulties

with Fedor Kolmakov, who was in charge of developing commercial relationships with the natives, but the disputes did not diminish the success of the expedition. The group threaded Hagemeister Strait and Kipalin, the Aglegmiut toyon, or leader, rounded Cape Newenham (which had been named by Cook in 1778) and penetrated Kuskokwim Bay on July 11. Korsakovskiy's and Kolmakov's success in establishing good relationships with the Eskimos of Bristol Bay was believed by the historian Berkh (see entry) the chief accomplishment of the expeditions of 1818 and 1819. Some of the natives possessed metal utensils and trade goods apparently originating in Siberia and brought across Bering Strait, filtering down to Bristol Bay through native trading channels. July 17, the expedition, upon Kolmakov's decision, headed back the way it had come. July 29, Korsakovskiy (the Kolmakov faction having separated) arrived at Lake Iliamna. August 4, it reached Eremey Rodionov's camp on Pile Bay where the explorer heard what seemed definite reports of the "kochi," the supposed descendants of the Dezhnev people. Korsakovskiy wished even at that late date to try to contact them overland, though his Aleuts lacked enthusiasm for such an endeavor. The party went to Lake Clark, north of Iliamna, thence westward to the upper Mulchatna River, principal tributary to the Nushagak. During this movement they passed through the country of the Tanaina Indians, who told Korsakovskiy how to reach the Tutna (Kuskokwim) peoples to the west. The Indians advised him, because food supplies in the interior would be sparse, to send Rodionov with five Kenian Indians, on to the Kuskokwim. The party would be small enough to find sufficient food for themselves. Rodionov set out August 18, bearing special instructions in the event he located the lost Russians. September 2, he returned after having reached the Kuskokwim at about the vicinity of Crow Village, west of Aniak and not far from the Yukon, but he had found no trace of the lost colony. September 9, Korsakovskiy regained Rodionov's summer camp on Lake Iliamna; he wished to winter there and explore further the next season, but his men objected. The expedition turned homeward September 14, and St. Paul was regained October 4. In the summer of 1819 Korsakovskiy led a second exploration westward to Kuskokwim Bay, learned of Nunivak Island but did not visit it, and established Aleksandrovskiy Redoubt, an important trading post at the mouth of the Nushagak

River. Late that season he again crossed the Alaska Peninsula and regained Kodiak Island. He died of tuberculosis.

Bancroft, *Alaska; The Russian American Colonies;* James W. VanStone, ed., *Russian Exploration in Southwest Alaska: The Travel Journals of Petr Korsakovskiy (1818) and Ivan Ya. Vasilev (1829),* Fairbanks, Univ. of Ak. Press, 1988; HNAI, 6; Zagoskin.

Kotzebue, Otto von, sea explorer (Dec. 30, 1787-Feb. 15, 1846). B. at Tallin, Estonia, the son of dramatist and author August Friedrich ·Ferdinand von Kotzebue (1761-1819), he became a Russian naval officer and served under Adam Johann von Krusenstern on the first Russian circumnavigation of the world, 1803-1806. Aboard the *Nadeshda* he with Krusenstern visited Japan, proceeding to Petropavlovsk, Kamchatka, sailing south to Canton and returning to Kronstadt August 19, 1806. In 1815 commanding the *Ryurik,* he left Kronstadt July 30, for the second global rounding; it was primarily a voyage of exploration. The *Ryurik* reached Petropavlovsk a year later, leaving almost immediately for Bering Strait in fulfillment of his mission to locate, if it existed, a strait rumored to connect the Pacific and Atlantic oceans across North America. Kotzebue touched St. Lawrence Island and on the northwest coast of Alaska on August 1, 1816, discovered a large inlet directly on the Arctic Circle which seemed to him possibly the opening of the sought-after channel. Kotzebue sailed east into the sound. By August 4, the land was closing in on both sides, the water shoaling, and exploration had to be continued in boats which determined that the waterway was landlocked to eastward. On the return what appeared to be an ice-mountain was discovered (see Eschscholtz entry) and Cape Krusenstern named for his previous commander (the important Kotzebue Sound was not named for Kotzebue until his return to Russia). August 11, the *Ryurik* sailed to St. Lawrence Island and thence to Unalaska where he ordered up supplies for a planned return to further investigate the Alaskan coast the following year; he then proceeded to San Francisco Bay without exploring the coast from Norton Sound to Bristol Bay, "one of the richest (in fur resources) portions of the territory." He conferred with Kuskov (see entry) at the Ross colony in California, then sailed for Hawaii, visiting with, and being greatly impressed by, King Kamehameha of Oahu, assuring the monarch that the intrigues of the adventurer Scheffer (see entry) did not have the approval of the tsar or Russian support. "The king seemed very much pleased by my assuring him that our sovereign never intended to conquer his islands," wrote Kotzebue. In mid-December the explorer left Hawaii to continue his explorations in Oceania, discovering on his various passages some 400 islands and island groups, making accurate astronomical locations for many of them. In the early spring of 1817 the *Ryurik* left the Caroline Islands bound once more for Unalaska, but about midway between the westernmost Hawaiian islands and the Aleutians a hurricane descended, the ship suffering "beyond description." Kotzebue himself and several seamen were injured and the vessel heavily damaged. When the great storm abated, she made her way with difficulty through heavy seas to Unalaska where she was unloaded, careened, unrigged and repaired, and within a month was again ready for sea. June 29, with Aleuts, interpreters and other assistance he had ordered up the previous year, he sailed northward once more. Beyond St. Lawrence Island, however, was now impenetrable ice and Kotzebue failed in an attempt to explore further along the continental shore for a passage eastward. In addition his injuries proved so severe the ship's surgeon warned him that to remain longer among the ice floes would endanger his life, so a withdrawal to Unalaska was ordered. The expedition stopped over briefly in Hawaii, then returned to Kronstadt, arriving July 23, 1818. Kotzebue left St. Petersburg July 28, 1823, on a third circumnavigation, his second as commander, visiting Novo Arkhangelsk from August 10, 1824, wintering in Hawaii and California, where he sided with California authorities with regard to the Ross colony as against its Russian American Company sponsors, returned to Novo Arkhangelsk February 23, 1825, and left on the homeward voyage in the autumn. English translations of his travel accounts are *A Voyage of Discovery into the South Sea and Bering Strait for the Purpose of Exploring a North-East Passage, Undertaken in the Years 1815-1818* (1821), and *A New Voyage Round the World in the Years 1823-1826* (1830). He died at Tallin.

Bancroft, *Alaska;* Zagoskin; CE; EB.

Krenitzin, Petr Kumich, Russian naval officer (d. July 4, 1770). A captain in the Russian navy, he was assigned with Lieutenant Mikhail D. Levashev (see entry) to command a secret expedition

1764-1769 to verify rumored discoveries of promyshlenniki in the Aleutians and Alaska Peninsula, and locate accurately important geographical features. The expedition, Bancroft believed, was "a praiseworthy effort, but miserably carried out." Between Okhotsk and Kamchatka in 1766 three of four vessels were wrecked. Two years later the expedition again set out in two vessels, but became separated in fog, Krenitzin wintering on Unimak Island and Levashev on Unalaska. Both parties were penned in by weather, native hostility and disease, scurvy taking a heavy toll of both companies. Neither completed even adequate maps of the island upon which it was located, and their map of the Aleutians was so inaccurate as to be of minimum utility. The venture overall had cost 112,000 rubles, and very little of value came from it. Both ships returned to Kamchatka in the summer of 1769, further hardships resulting from shortage of food over the winter, which was passed at Nishekamchatsk. By July 4, 1770, both vessels were ready for sea again, but Krenitzin, crossing the Kamchatka River in a native dugout, was spilled into the water when the craft capsized, and drowned.

Bancroft, *Alaska; Russian Penetration of the North Pacific Ocean;* Zagoskin.

Krutch, Joseph Wood, writer, conservationist (Nov. 25, 1893-May 22, 1970). B. at Knoxville, Tennessee, he was graduated in 1915 from the University of Tennessee, earned a master's from Columbia in 1916 and a doctorate, also from Columbia, in 1924. He served during World War I in the Army Psychological Corps, becoming a sergeant. He was associate professor of English at the Polytechnic Institute of Brooklyn, 1920-23; professor at Vassar College, 1924-25; and taught at Columbia's School of Journalism from 1925-31 and at the University from 1937-52. Meanwhile he was associate editor of *The Nation* from 1924-32, member of its board of editors, 1932-37, and its drama critic, 1937-52, being president of the New York Drama Critics Circle 1940-41. A respiratory problem led him to move to Tucson, Arizona, in 1952, where his writing themes turned from theater to natural history and conservation. "I didn't come West for its future, or its industry, its growth, its opportunity. I came for three reasons: to get away from New York and the crowds, to get air I could breathe, and for the natural beauty of the desert and its wildlife,"

he said. He had been regarded as a foremost drama critic, perhaps the leading one of his time, and he was widely honored for his work in that field. He wrote many books, believing his most important from that period were his *Samuel Johnson* (1944), and *Henry David Thoreau* (1948). His later works, relating to the desert and Southwest, included *The Desert Year* (1952); *The Voice of the Desert: A Naturalist's Interpretation* (1955); *Great Chain of Life* (1957): *Grand Canyon: Today and All Its Yesterdays* (1958); *The Forgotten Peninsula: A Naturalist in Baja California* (1961); an autobiography, *More Lives Than One* (1962); *If You Don't Mind My Saying So: Essays on Man and Nature* (1964); *Herbal* (1965); *Baja California and the Geography of Hope* with photographs by Eliot Porter (1967); *Birdsongs in Literature* (1967); *Most Wonderful Animals That Never Were* (1968), and *The Best Nature Writing of Joseph Wood Krutch* (1970). He also edited and contributed to many other books. He once said that "If you drive a car at seventy miles an hour, you can't reflect or think about anything...but keep[ing] the monster under control. I'm afraid this is the metaphor for our society as a whole." Again he wrote that some bright new age can only come about if "we have come to realize that wealth, power, and even knowledge are not good in themselves but only [as] the instruments of good or evil." When he made an hour-long television program about his life in the Arizona desert, he mused, "Maybe the most I can claim is that I know more about botany than any other New York critic, and more about the theater than any other botanist." He believed that to use the world and its resources for the betterment of man alone, would be to turn man into a machine and little else, adding, "and I sometimes fear that if we continue to act as though men were machines, they may actually, in the end, become sounding very much like machines." Lawrence Clark Powell wrote that "Krutch wrote books that established him as the conscience-voice of the arid lands. He became the foremost ecological spokesmen of our time." Powell believed that following his death, "Joseph Wood Krutch's books will continue to speak for him. They are...books which are the man himself, learned and visionary, earnest, decent and eloquent."

Literature abundant; *Contemporary Authors; Friends of Animals,* Fall 1970, Report, "Joseph Wood Krutch Commemorative Issue," N.Y., 3-6; Lawrence

Clark Powell, "Joseph Wood Krutch's *The Desert Year*," *Westways*, Vol. 63, No. 6 (June 1971), 14-17, 66-67.

Kukhkan, Mikhail, Tlingit chief (d. May 29, 1868). A Kolosh (Tlingit) of Alaska, he was one of three chiefs (with Skautlelt and Skaatagech) from whom Baranov acquired land for the future Sitka. Yet Kukhkan was a leader in the assault and destruction of the Sitka post in 1802 and in the flight of his people when they were driven out in 1804. However he eventually was baptized and in 1839 was given by the Russian American Company the title of principal chief of his tribe. Pierce quotes Aleksandr Markov as reporting that he was "always distinguished...by his modesty; he did not take part in disputes, traded well, collected many wares in debt, and always paid honestly and amicably." The chief was given honors, the sum of 10,000 rubles in order to build himself a house "and be able if necessary to suppress the rebellious and notify the Russians of any kind of hostile intentions of his comrades." He fulfilled his agreement but, as it was pointed out, was only one of many Tlingit chiefs and had no influence on the others. He died at Sitka.

Pierce, *Russian America: A Biographical Dictionary.*

Kupreianov, Ivan, naval officer, administrator (c. 1799-Apr. 30, 1857). He entered the naval academy at 10 in 1809. On July 4, 1819, as a midshipman in the sloop *Mirnyi* under Lieutenant M.P. Lazarev, he left on a voyage to the Antarctic with the Fabian Gottlieb von Bellingshausen expedition which circumnavigated the continent, rarely sighting the land itself except for Alexander Island of the Palmer Peninsula, which the explorers believed part of the mainland. It returned to Kronstadt in August 1821. Kupreianov visited Russian America on an 1822-25 voyage, fulfilled various naval duties and in 1828 as a Captain-Lieutenant participated in actions against the Turks in the Black Sea. August 29, 1834, as Captain, First Rank he was named chief manager for the Russian American Company of Alaska, reaching Sitka October 25, 1835. In his post, succeeding Baron Wrangel, he made extensive voyages to all parts of his suzerainty, in 1836 visiting Kodiak Island, in 1837 Atkha and Unalaska of the Aleutians, in 1838 Fort St. Dionysius, on the Stikine River, and Yakutat Bay. He promoted geographical exploration, sending Fedor Kolmakov (see entry) up the Kuskokwim River and Kashevarov (see entry) to the Alaskan north coast. In 1836 the garrison at Fort St. Michael on Norton Sound repelled a native attack. In September 1837 the English warship *Sulphur,* Captain Edward Belcher, became the first foreign naval vessel to visit Sitka, the captain being warmly welcomed and assisted by Kupreianov, Belcher writing an extensive description of Sitka and of the people there. He took "a very great liking" to Veniaminov (see entry), the outstanding Orthodox missionary and ethnologist. May 1, 1840, Kupreianov's successor, Etolin (see entry) reached Sitka, Kupreianov and his wife departing for Russia September 30, and arriving at Kronstadt June 13, 1841. In October 1852 Kupreianov became a Vice Admiral. His widow died at 82 on March 12, 1894. Kupreianov's name is perpetuated in several Alaskan geographical features.

Richard A. Pierce, *Builders of Alaska: The Russian Governors, 1818-1867,* Kingston, Ont., Limestone Press, 1986; Zagoskin; Orth 553-54.

Kurochkin, Grigoriy, interpreter (fl. 1842-1844). B. on Kodiak Island of a Russian father and Aleut mother, Kurochkin attended a school for Creole children established at Baranov's direction by Ivan Ivanovich Banner. He became markedly literate, adding to his mastery of Russian and the Eskimauan dialect spoken by the Aleuts. Upon his maturity he served six years as deacon in the Kodiak Orthodox church. By 1840 he had reached Fort St. Michael on Norton Sound, perhaps serving there from its 1833 founding by Tebenkov and may have been there in 1835 when natives almost reduced the fort. During his years at Fort St. Michael he became acquainted with the several dialects of the Kangyulit (Chnagmiut—Hodge, I, 287), or coastal Eskimos, wholly familiar with their customs and a master of wilderness travel. Upon Zagoskin's arrival at the post, Kurochkin volunteered and was promptly hired as skilled and dependable. "A literate interpreter," Zagoskin wrote, he "combined a rare gaiety of temperament with an astonishing capacity for imitation. As soon as he arrived at a native village he made himself at home, fraternized with the inhabitants, took note of their peculiarities, learned their songs and their dances, and then performed them...for an audience, of course accompanied by a variety of comments, and all in the greatest caricature. Or he rolled back his eyeballs, put one foot behind his ear, walked on his hands, and so forth," thus playing an amusing and important entertainment role in relationships between whites and primitive peoples. "Not one of the natives could equal Kurochkin in their own dances." He also was a craftsman in native skills, from building sleds to catching fish. Kurochkin, Zagoskin found, was familiar with the Yukon and may have been as far upstream as Nulato before the formal exploration of the valley. He accompanied the leader on the winter trip up the newly "discovered" Koyukuk River toward Kotzebue Sound. On the Yukon a musket, fired accidentally, broke Kurochkin's right thumb, to which was applied a birchbark splint and in two months was healed. For the first three nights, however, Koruchkin was unable to sleep; on the second, in order not to awaken his companions with his groans, he went outside for a walk, ran across a beaver and killed it with his left hand for its valuable fur. Korochkin provided an interpretation of at least one impressive Eskimo fiesta attended by members of the Zagoskin expedition (239). On Easter Sunday, March 25, 1944, by the Orthodox calendar, at the Ikogmyut (Russian Mission) trading post Kurochkin came down with a burning fever, for which Zagoskin had no reliable medicine and left to a local shaman to treat. Because, or in spite of, the doctoring he received, Kurochkin basically recovered in five days, but remained so weak that he was replaced by another interpreter for the trip to the upper Yukon and upper Kuskokwim rivers. By the June 10 arrival of the expedition from that exploration, Kurochkin was restored to health and accompanied Zagoskin to Fort St. Michael to conclude the two-year operation. Nothing further is reported of him.

Zagoskin.

Kuskov, Ivan Aleksandrovich, Russian frontiersman (1765-Oct. 1823). B. at Totma, 110 miles northeast of Volgda which is north of Moscow, he left for Siberia at 22. In 1790 he met Aleksandr Baranov, newly appointed director for the fur trading and colonization operations of Grigori Shelikhov and Ivan Golikov. Baranov was about to depart for Alaska and Kuskov joined him as clerk, later becoming assistant and sometimes alter-ego, remaining for 32 years with the eventual governor of the Russian American Company. In the spring of 1799, when Baranov determined to found a fort and trading post near

the site of Sitka, he set out from his base on Kodiak Island, coasted to Prince William Sound where Kuskov, by now his "most trusted assistant," joined him at Nuchek (Hinchinbrook) Island with 150 baidarkas (kayaks) to accompany the 200 Baranov had brought. While rounding Cape Suckling, near Kayak Island, heavy seas destroyed 30 baidarkas with their personnel. The exhausted survivors made for the coast, reached it late at night and fell asleep when they were attacked by Tlingit Indians who so reduced the force that Kuskov advised a return to Prince William Sound. But Baranov pushed stubbornly on, reaching the chosen site May 25 and a fort, strong enough when adequately guarded, was completed by summer. On his return to Kodiak, Baranov named Kuskov to command the Prince William Sound area from the new Fort Konstantin on Nuchek Island. Later he was sent to develop a base at Yakutat where, among his other duties, he directed construction of ships for the company's use. He also managed the massive otter hunting parties periodically sent out. In 1802 Tlingits destroyed Sitka and massacred many; two years later, with the help of armed vessels, Baranov retook the place and planned to rebuild the post, expanding it. In 1806 he named Kuskov to oversee all construction work at Novo Arkhangelsk as it was called (the present Sitka), and to command the fortress. Several major ships were built or purchased and based there, and Kuskov learned in 1807 that the imperial government had conferred upon him the title of commercial councillor. He was possessed of "exceptional good nature and upright character," had abundant energy and was honest, but according to Rezanov he was also hot-headed and "lacked political knowledge." Baranov, ever his strong supporter, had asked the imperial government to bestow upon Kuskov an official title and some rank "to protect him, if not from insult, at least from beatings, with which he has often been threatened." These threats against him and attempts at assassination, were made by Alaskans and later by Californians; his temper and disinclination toward conciliation may have been a factor in most of them. Under his new title he made several trips to Spanish California, trading and investigating possibilities for Russian expansion, reporting his findings to Baranov. In 1808 Kuskov was sent on the *Kadiak* to "New Albion," or central California, bringing back 2,000 otter skins and the intelligence that he had found places along the coast north of San Francisco well-adapted for agriculture and ship-building, adding that that country was devoid of any European occupation. Baranov apparently had received instructions from Rezanov to push Russian settlement southward as far as he safely could. Kuskov was sent again to California in 1810 and 1811 in furtherance of this ambition, which in 1812 resulted in the establishment of Fort "Ross," called by its owners *Rossiya,* the word for Russia, on the coast 50 miles north of San Francisco in the present Sonoma County. Built on a bluff above the sea, the fort mounted 10 guns, was surrounded by a 14-foot stockade enclosing an area of 256 by 294 feet. Buildings inside and beyond the palisade included the commandant's house, barracks for Aleut and other employees, storchouses, magazines, shops, a bathhouse, tannery and a windmill, in addition to slips for vessel construction and launching, a blacksmith shop and sheds for the baidarkas. Kuskov directed sea otter hunting, pushed agricultural and shipbuilding projects as Baranov had ordered, but the Fort Ross experiment was never much of a success. Rather than supplying foodstuffs for Russian Alaska as intended, the colony survived largely by illicit trade with the Spanish for the requirements for its own existence. Its economic contributions were minimal. In addition the settlement was a constant irritant for Spain's authorities who claimed, with no colonization in support, all of the coast north to Puget Sound. Baranov retired and left America in 1819; Kuskov in 1821 was succeded at Fort Ross by Karl Johan Schmidt, "a young man of considerable enterprise and ability," and returned to Russia by way of Okhotsk in 1822. In 1823 he died at 58 at his birthplace, Totma, where he had gone according to the Russian law of *zemlia,* which so attached a person to his commune he was required to come back there when he had completed his term of service elsewhere. Fort Ross, Kuskov's "monument," was sold for $30,000 to John A. Sutter in 1841, and dismantled.

Bancroft, *Alaska; California* II; *Pioneer Register;* Kyrill T. Khlebnikov, *Colonial Russian America,* trans. by Basil Dmytryshyn, E.A.P. Crownhart-Vaughan, Portland, Ore. Hist. Soc., 1976; DAB; Hodge II, 400.

L

Lamar, Mirabeau Buonaparte, Texas statesman (Aug. 16, 1798-Dec. 19, 1859). B. near Louisville, Georgia, he early showed intellectual capacity and interests. He attended two academies, was an "omniverous reader," became a fine horseman, a fencer, wrote poetry and took up oil painting. After a brief sally into merchandising he was for several months joint publisher of the Cahawba, Alabama, *Press* and later established the Columbus, Georgia, *Enquirer.* In 1829 he became a state senator but withdrew from re-election when his beloved wife died of tuberculosis. Lamar ran for Congress in 1832, was defeated as he was in the 1834 election, after which he sold his interest in the *Enquirer* and accompanied James W. Fannin (see entry) to Texas, where Lamar determined to settle. He declared for Texas independence, helped build a fort, wrote poetry and returned to Georgia to settle his affairs, while the Alamo fell and the Goliad massacre occurred and with it Fannin's execution. Hastening back to Texas, Lamar joined the army as a private, performed heroically at the Battle of San Jacinto, April 20, 1836, during which he was verbally commissioned a colonel commanding cavalry. Ten days after the engagement Lamar became secretary of war in President David G. Burnet's cabinet. A month later he was a Major General and named commander-in-chief of the Texas Army, but the troops refused to accept him for reasons not stated, and he retired to civilian life. Lamar was always popular with the anti-Houston element, aroused enthusiastic support from his admirers and as determined opposition from others. In September 1836 he was elected vice president, was promoted for President by anti-Houston partisans; both opposition leaders committed suicide before the balloting and Lamar was elected unopposed. Texas was in difficult straits. Only the United States had recognized her independence, Mexico threatened reconquest, the frontier Indians were bold and challenging, the treasury was virtually empty. Lamar initially opposed annexation by the United States, thought Texas should extend her empire to the Pacific, was harsh with the Indians, drove the Cherokees to Arkansas and rebuffed the Comanches, suggested creation of the city of Austin and furthered the disastrous Santa Fe Expedition. He secured the recognition of Texas independence by France, England and Holland, promoted an important education act adopted January 26, 1839, which set aside public lands for the benefit of schools and two universities, and won the title of "Father of Education" for the future state. In doing all these things Texas was brought to the verge of bankruptcy, not through Lamar's fault alone, although he was sharply criticized, if unfairly. He retired to his Richmond, Texas, plantation and after his daughter died in 1843 traveled extensively. At Washington, D.C., having come to believe that Texas's salvation lay in annexation, he reversed his former stand and lobbied for it intensively. During the Mexican War he served as a lieutenant colonel under Zachary Taylor and participated in the important Battle of Monterrey. He favored Secession, married again, was named U.S. minister to Nicaragua and Costa Rica, serving nearly two years, continued to write poetry and work on his projected history of Texas, which was not completed. Lamar died at Richmond of a heart attack. The *Handbook of Texas* entry, written by his biographer Herbert Gambrell, concluded that he had been a man "of great personal charm, impulsive generosity, and oratorical gifts. His powerful imagination caused him to project a program greater than he or Texas could actualize in three years. His friends were almost fanatically devoted to him; his enemies declared him a better poet than politician but they never seriously questioned the purity of his motives or his integrity." Lamar, in Aransas County, and Lamar County were named for him and his life and works have been the subject of several books and articles in this century.

HT; DAB; REAW; CE.

La Mothe, Guillaume, trader (c. 1744-1799). A French Canadian, he was in 1767 a trader in the Detroit area. At the outbreak of the Revolution he was in New England, returned to Quebec and found his way to Detroit again where in 1777 he became captain of a scouting, or ranger, company. In 1778 as captain of militia he accompanied

Henry Hamilton to Vincennes. He was captured there by George Rogers Clark in 1779 and sent as a prisoner to Virginia from where he was exchanged in 1781, and 1782 found him back in Detroit. He retired to St. Joseph Island in 1796, living there the rest of his life.

Thwaites/Kellogg, *Frontier Defense on the Upper Ohio, 1777-1778.*

L'Amour, Louis Dearborn, writer (Mar. 22, 1908-June 10, 1988). B. at Jamestown, North Dakota, the son of a veterinarian and part-time farm machinery salesman, he quit school at 15, roamed the west as a cowboy, logger, and followed other occupations. He went to sea out of New Orleans, visiting a number of Far Eastern ports and had a variety of experiences. He tried professional boxing for a time, but always intended to become a writer, working into the pulps at first, publishing his initial book, a volume of poems, in 1939. He served four years in the Army during World War II, two stateside and two overseas, and when released he resumed his writing. In the middle 1950s he heard that the editorial director of Bantam Books was at Los Angeles, hunting for a western writer to succeed Luke Short on their list. L'Amour phoned him and said: "This is Louis L'Amour, you've never heard of me but I want to see you right now." He came to the editor's hotel room with an envelope, said "he was going to be the next great Western writer and we'd do well to take him on." He had brought the manuscript of *Hondo,* and the editor read it while L'Amour waited. "It knocked me out," said the editor. "I signed him to a long-term contract on the spot," and it was the best, and probably the most profitable move Bantam Books ever made. *Hondo* not only was made into a John Wayne motion picture, but it was the first of an immense line of successful western books by L'Amour, more than 30 of which sold also to the movies. A New York official of Bantam books protested that L'Amour's name sounded like "a Western written in lipstick" but no one had the courage to tackle him with the thought, for fear he might get "punched out." In sum, L'Amour published more than 100 novels, all still in print at his death and which in the aggregate had sold more than 200 million copies; 80 of them were westerns, the remainder of considerable variety, ranging from a European Middle Ages tale to one set in Siberia in modern times, but his principal forte was the Old West. All were characterized by his meticulous description of

locations about which he knew personally, with all details as authentic as was possible in fiction, from guns to geology, wildlife and nature study. This all added verisimilitude to his genre, and, he believed, would promote its longevity. "I know it's literature, and I know it will be read 100 years from now," he said. In his library of 8,000 to 10,000 volumes he wrote his half dozen pages each day from 6 a.m. until noon, adding a bit perhaps in the afternoon, but he always did his exercises, kept physically fit, married but one wife and was proud of his family. He concentrated on his work so single-mindedly that he often said he could write on a traffic island in the center of a busy street and at one point demonstrated that the result was as printable as anything else he wrote. He died at 80 at his Los Angeles home, survived by his widow, a son and a daughter plus a legacy of many millions of action-laced words.

Tucson, *Arizona Daily Star* [a *New York Times* obituary], June 13, 1988; Donald Dale Jackson's "World's Fastest Literary Gun: Louis L'Amour," *Smithsonian,* Vol. 18, No. 2 (May, 1987), 154-70; *Publisher's Weekly,* Vol. 204, No. 15 (Oct. 8, 1973).

Lander, Frederick West, explorer, military officer (Dec. 17, 1821-Mar. 2, 1862). B. at Salem, Massachusetts, of adventurous forebears (his grandfather was Nathaniel West, onetime British midshipman and later a famed American privateer), he was well-educated, studying civil engineering at Vermont schools and conducting survey work on eastern railroads, where he "established a reputation for ability and thoroughness." In 1853 he served on Isaac Stevens' (see entry) staff on a northern Pacific exploration party charting a railway route from St. Paul, Minnesota, to Puget Sound. In the spring of 1854 he headed an exploration study of the feasibility of a railroad from Puget Sound to the Mississippi by way of the Columbia and Snake rivers and South Pass, Congress printing 10,000 copies of his report. During the following four years he was superintendent and chief engineer of the main overland wagon route. This involved not only arduous but occasionally hazardous duty, as in 1858 when his 70-man party was attacked by Paiute Indians, the hostiles repulsed in a "spirited engagement." In all he participated in, or led, five transcontinental surveys, earning high praise from his superiors for his work. Lander was a careful student of Indians and depredations on the overland trails, reporting on the numbers and identities of attacking Indians as best he understood them. In a report requested by the Commissioner of Indian Affairs at Washington on the conditions of Indians, Lander in 1859 wrote extensively and accurately of his visit with, among others, the reclusive yet powerful Chief Pocatello (see entry). His narrative revealed the intelligence of that Indian, whom he named "White Plume," and the Indian's ability to differentiate between rude and sometimes murderous emigrants, and a scientist such as Lander. Pocatello and Lander evidently were impressed with each other. Before the Civil War Lander advocated a railroad line from Salt Lake City to San Francisco with a branch to Puget Sound. During the Pyramid Lake War (see Ormsby entry) of 1860 Lander accompanied Jack Hays (see entry) who with 100 mounted men and 100 foot soldiers in a three-hour battle caused perhaps 25 Indians to be killed; there were eight white casualties, including three dead. The "verbose and ambitious" Lander was prominent in subsequent Indian hunting in Pyramid Lake regions where his surveying people were working. In one encounter at Mud Springs a citizen was killed while standing near Lander, whom the Indians apparently had sought to kill. Lander observed in his report that the Bannock and Shoshoni Indians were better fighters than the Paiutes and recommended that they be "thoroughly chastised." He thought that many of the depredating natives were on good terms with the Mormons and were fed by them during the "starvation season" of the year, the early spring. With the outbreak of the Civil War, Lander was given a confidential mission to Governor Sam Houston (see entry) of Texas "with full authority to order Federal troops to support Houston if thought advisable," Houston being opposed to secession and favoring Texas remaining in the Union. Nothing came of Lander's mission, however. Lander was commissioned a Brigadier General of Massachusetts Volunteers May 17, 1861. He gave distinguished service from the outset of hostilities, but died abruptly March 2, 1862. He was survived by his widow, the former Jean Margaret Davenport, a highly successful English-born actress; there were no children. "Lander was a vigorous and forceful writer and was the author of many patriotic poems of the war period."

DAB; Brigham D. Madsen, *The Shoshoni Frontier and the Bear River Massacre,* S.L.C., Univ. of Ut. Press, 1985; Madsen, *Chief Pocatello, the "White Plume,"* Univ. of Ut. Press, 1986; Madsen, *The North-*

ern Shoshoni, Caldwell, Id., Caxton Printers, 1980; Heitman.

Landes, Ruth, anthropologist (Oct. 8, 1908-Feb. 11, 1991). B. at New York City, the daughter of Joseph Schlossberg, she was graduated from New York University and earned a doctorate at Columbia. Under Columbia's auspices she did research on the Ojibway (Chippewa) Indians of the Turtle Mountain Reservation in Rolette County, North Dakota. From this work came her books, *Ojibway Sociology* (1937, 1969); *The Ojibway Woman* (1938, 1970), and *Ojibway Religion and The Midewiwin* (1968). She wrote *Santee* [Sioux] *Sociology* (1969) and *The Prairie Potawatomi: Tradition and Ritual in the Twentieth Century* (1970). She also wrote *The Latin-Americans of the Southwest* (1965). Her best known work was *The City of Women* (1947) in which she reported on life at Bahia, Brazil, where she found that women played the dominant roles in a society of descendants of African slaves. She did research in Spain, Switzerland, South Africa and Canada as well as in the United States. Throughout her career she was interested in social work in its various ramifications. She was a visiting professor or instructor at many colleges and universities and lived at Hamilton, Ontario, where she taught at McMaster University from 1965 until the end of her life. She married in 1928 and was divorced seven years later, never remarrying. She died at 82 at Hamilton.

New York Times, Feb. 24, 1991; *Who's Who in America.*

Lane, Ralph, explorer, governor (c. 1530-Oct. 1603). B. presumably at Horton, Northhamptonshire, England, he may have served in the House of Commons. In 1563 he entered Queen Elizabeth's service as an equerry, or officer of the royal household, and this led to his participation in maritime activities, although there is no evidence he ever achieved naval rank of importance. He spent two years erecting fortifications in Ireland and in 1585 joined Richard Grenville on a voyage to Virginia for Raleigh. Grenville and Lane, with 107 colonists sailed from Plymouth in seven ships April 9, at length settled on Roanoke Island of North Carolina. When Grenville returned to England, August 25, Lane was left as governor of the colony. Thwaites wrote that Lane "made an attempt in 1586" to "cross the western mountain barrier" of the Appalachians, but it is not clear that Lane's explorers traveled so far into the interior, although they did explore something of the Roanoke and Chowan rivers, both emptying into Albemarle Sound. Lane was afflicted with "the lure of precious metals," the discovery of which was "something of an obsession" with Europeans of that age. A mine was thought to be located on the Upper Roanoke (on the basis of no solid facts whatever) and that "accounts for the more complete exploration of that river in the spring of 1586." He was equally interested in exploring the shore of Chesapeake Bay to the north of Roanoke Island, and sent Harriot and White (see entries) to winter with the Chesapeake Indians, learn their language and from them extract all geographical information they possessed of the region. Lane had intended to spend at least another year in the colony when Sir Francis Drake hove into view June 9, 1586, with his flotilla following its attack on Santo Domingo and Cartegena. Drake offered either to give Lane needed shipping and some supplies or, if Lane thought best, transportation back to England. Lane accepted the offer of a ship with its escorts, but a three-day hurricane descending on June 13, drove the ship to sea where she was lost, and wrecked the escort boats, so Lane then accepted the alternate offer, to transport the colonists and himself back to England, which was done. John White's excellent maps of the Carolina coast and as far north as Chesapeake Bay, reveal no advance inland very far beyond the littoral, showing Roanoke Island, Albermarle Sound and not much penetration beyond the mouths of the Roanoke and Chowan rivers, while only the entrance of Chesapeake Bay is included. The colonists reached Portsmouth July 27. Lane concerned himself with operations against Spain thereafter, becoming inspector general of the forces sent under Drake to the coasts of Spain and Portugal in 1589. January 15, 1592, he was sent in a like capacity to Ireland, where he remained for the rest of his life, being knighted November 17, 1593. He was wounded in some affray in 1594, the injury hampering and limiting his activities for the rest of his life. He died at Dublin, where he was buried.

Richard Hakluyt, *The Principal Navigations Voyages Traffiques & Discoveries of the English Nation,* 2nd ed., 1598-1600 (1969), Vol. VIII, 319-45; Paul Hulton, *America 1585: The Complete Drawings of John White,* Chapel Hill, Univ. of N.C. Press, 1984; DAB; Alexander Scott Withers, *Chronicles of Border Warfare,* Cincinnati, Robert Clarke Co., 1895, 1970, p. 64n.

Langsdorff, Georg Heinrich von, naturalist (Apr. 18, 1774-June 29, 1852). A Russian member of the Imperial Academy of Sciences, he was a German-trained physician and took part in the Krusenstern-Lisianskii circumnavigation of the world in 1803-1807. In the course of it he accompanied Rezanov (see entry) to the Pribylof Islands and Sitka, Alaska, among other places. His two-volume *Voyages and Travels in Various Parts of the World* (London, 1814) was dismissed by Bancroft as of little value: "As a savant he was superficial; as a chronicler he was biased. In neither capacity does he add much to what was known of Russian America." On the other hand *The Russian American Colonies* lists Langsdorff's as "among the most interesting accounts" of Alaska and Russian activities there early in the 19th century. His descriptions of the Kodiak and Chugach people were noted approvingly by Wrangel. Langsdorff also described his visit to California enroute home. Upon his return he was elected an academician, in 1812 was named consul to Brazil, remaining there for seventeen years, during which he undertook explorations and natural history collecting.

Bancroft, *Alaska;* Zagoskin; *The Russian American Colonies.*

La Pérouse, Jean Francois de Galaup, comte de, French navigator (Aug. 22, 1741-c. 1788). B. at La Gua, near Albi, France, he entered the French navy at 15 and fought against the British in the Seven Years War (known in America as the French and Indian War). In 1782 he was sent to attack British forts in Hudson Bay. In August 1785 La Pérouse sailed from Brest with two frigates, *L'Astrolabe* and the *Boussole* on a scientific circumnavigation of the world, fitted out by the French government. "A full corps of scientific specialists [were aboard]; minute and carefully prepared instructions were given, accompanied by reports and charts of all that had been accomplished by the explorers of different nations; the commanders were carefully selected for their ability and experience; and in fact every possible precaution was taken to make the trip a success," wrote Bancroft. La Pérouse was to enter the Pacific by way of Cape Horn and strike the upper coast of America, search for the rumored Northwest Passage, then continue an examination of the coasts of America and Asia, as well as a study of such island groups as Hawaii and the Philippines. He sighted the Alaskan coast June 23, 1786, near latitude 60°, observing towering Mt.

St. Elias to the north. Contrary to instructions to visit the Aleutian Islands, he set his course southeastward along the rugged coast. Bering (Yakutat) Bay was passed unobserved, but July 2, La Pérouse "discovered" an inlet called Ltua (Lituya) and, thinking his sighting original, which it was not, he named it "Port des Francais," writing that it seemed to him "perhaps the most extraordinary place in the world," surrounded by magnificent scenery enclosing a bay, deep, protected and suitable for establishment of intermittent trading facilities, though he did not advocate official French presence at the site. He noted that natives already possessed knives, hatchets, iron and trade beads which he judged correctly had been gained from Russian traders, perhaps indirectly. On July 13, three boats were sent out to make final soundings for charting purposes, and since it seemed likely to be a pleasant outing seven of the ships' officers accompanied the crews of eighteen picked boatmen. On approaching the bay entrance, two of the boats were caught in a fatal riptide, capsized, and all twenty-one aboard were lost, the third craft narrowly escaping a similar fate; no bodies were ever recovered. A monument was erected on a small islet purchased of the native chief, the site named L'Isle du Cenotaphe. Clearing Lituya Bay July 30, the vessels coasted southward although weather prevented any significant sightings until August 6, when La Pérouse found he was in the area of Norfolk Sound. Bad weather made impossible a run into Dixon Entrance. "Superficial as were his observations," wrote Bancroft, La Pérouse correctly "came to the conclusion that the whole coast from Cross Sound to…the south point of Queen Charlotte Island, was one archipelago." His map of the coast from Mt. St. Elias southward to San Francisco Bay was "remarkably complete, if we consider the limited material upon which it rested. Though far superior to any map made before 1786, its value was of course much impaired [since] it was not published until 1798." La Pérouse continued southward past Nootka, which he did not visit, occasionally sighting the coast when the fog lifted, and making accurate latitudes for sites observed. September 14, the two ships reached Monterey, having made no observations of the California coast because of poor visibility. La Pérouse was piloted into Monterey Bay by Estéban José Martinez (see entry), noted navigator who had brought supplies up for the Spanish settlement from the south. Martinez questioned

La Pérouse as to what he had learned of the northwest coast, and particularly of Russian activities there, since the Spanish at this time were concerned about a supposed threat from the north to their Pacific coast empire. Pedro Fages (see entry), governor of California, supplied the French visitors with cattle, vegetables and milk in abundance, a barrel of the latter delivered daily to the ships during their stay, while the fresh food was largely responsible for a considerable improvement in the health of the explorers. La Pérouse had high praise for the civil, military and religious officials and courtesies shown his complement, the French responding with what gifts and acknowledgements they could bestow. September 24, 1786, La Pérouse raised anchor and cleared America, continuing his voyage across the Pacific, incidentally discovering Necker Island, Hawaii. The expedition also nominally discovered La Pérouse Strait (Soya Kaikyo, or Strait) between Hokkaido and Sakhalin islands, and reached Kamchatka from where journals, maps and letters were dispatched overland to Paris. In December, De Langle, captain of the *Boussole* and 11 of his men were killed by natives on Samoa, the vessels then recrossing the Pacific, arriving at Botany Bay, Australia, January 26, 1788, where La Pérouse's journal and all communications from him ceased. Decades passed with no solution to the mystery of his disappearance. Several French expeditions made fruitless searches. At Vanikoro Island of the Santa Cruz group of the New Hebrides, the hilt of his sword was recovered in 1827, and it was learned that two vessels had been driven aground during a storm. Most of the crews drowned, others died in hostilities with the islanders, and after about a year survivors departed in a vessel they had built from the wreckage. A tradition on the island of Ponape in the Carolines of Micronesia told of a boatload of whites slain around this time. In 1828 a French expedition found the wreckage of the two ships on Vanikoro Island.

Bancroft, *Alaska; Northwest Coast* I; *California* I; Warren L. Cook, *Flood Tide of Empire,* New Haven, Yale Univ. Press, 1973; EA; CE.

La Porte de Louvigny, Louis de: *see,* Louvigny, Louis de la Porte de

Larionov, Stepan Grigorevich, fur trader (d. 1805). He was an early employee of the Russian American Company, for Baranov reported him leading a hunting party in Kenai Bay in 1793. In

1796, when Novorossiisk (New Russia) was founded in Yakutat Bay in the Alaskan Panhandle, Larionov was sent with twenty-five hunters to protect the settlers. During the first winter twenty males and a number of women and children died of scurvy; by 1799 Larionov was placed in command of the post where resided some forty people. Various accounts agree that when the Tlingit Indians attacked in 1805 nearly all the residents, including Larionov, were slain; only Larionov's wife, their children and a few Aleuts were spared, though taken prisoner. In 1806 the American captain, Oliver Kimball (see entry), rescued an Aleut couple and in 1807 Baranov sent N.I. Bulygin (see entry) to Yakutat to capture Tlingits and through them to free other captives; he brought back Larionov's wife and three sons, along with the wives of two other settlers and their children. A native version of the affair said that a young warrior named Tunnux had killed Larionov.

Pierce, *Russian America: A Biographical Dictionary.*

Larkin, Thomas Oliver, consul, agent (Sept. 16, 1802-Oct. 27, 1858). B. at Charlestown, Massachusetts, he lived for years in the Carolinas and in 1831 accepted an invitation from his half-brother, John Bautista Roger Cooper, to join him at Monterey, California, where commercial opportunities were inviting. Larkin sailed from Boston and arrived at Monterey April 13, 1832. Enroute he met a fellow passenger, Mrs. Rachel (Hobson) Holmes, traveling to join her husband, though on arrival at Monterey she found she was a widow. In 1833, with a capital of $500, Larkin opened a small store, the following year starting a flour mill. He married Mrs. Holmes on board the *Volunteer* at Santa Barbara in 1833, the ceremony performed by Hawaiian Consul John Coffin Jones Jr., whom Larkin had met when his vessel stopped at Hawaii enroute to California. Jones, being a ship's master, could perform the ceremony aboard the vessel, thus avoiding entanglements with the established church in California. Mrs. Larkin was said to be the first U.S. woman in California, and their child, Thomas Larkin Jr., the first U.S. child born in that territory. Larkin Sr. rapidly expanded his commercial activities with Yankee shrewdness and "no inconvenient veneration for the revenue laws," soon trading with Mexico and Hawaii and dealing in such things as furs, horses, lumber and flour. He did not become a Mexican citizen and took no open part in California politics, although he was a quiet supporter of Juan Bautista Alvarado. Larkin remained aloof from the complicated and troublesome Isaac Graham (see entry) affair, Bancroft describing his conduct as "prudent and praiseworthy," doing what he could for the comfort of the arrested Americans while in no way backing the "loud protests and absurd threats of Graham and his gang." Although a man of scant education but of much tact and practical good sense, he was, despite his closeness with money, respected as "honorable, of sound judgment, and of conservative views." May 1, 1842, Larkin was appointed consul for the United States at Monterey, then capital of Upper California, and on April 2, 1844, formally took possession of the office and was officially recognized as consul by California officials. James A. Forbes in late 1842 had been appointed British vice-consul and was approved by California authorities in October 1843; Louis Gasquet was named French Consul pro tem, and since the regularly-appointed French consul never arrived, took over full duties of the office from 1845. Larkin was always suspicious, perhaps overly so, of the British and French agents and their sub rosa activities, as he supposed, and reported his views regularly to Washington, all of his dispatches being characterized by accuracy and fullness. A secret dispatch from Polk's secretary of state James Buchanan dated October 17, 1845, appointed Larkin also a "confidential agent," urging him to warn Californians against overseas intrigues and to look favorably toward the United States. The instructions said that the U.S. could take no part in differences between California and Mexico, unless Mexico commenced hostilities against the United States, "but should California assert and maintain her independence, we shall render her all the kind offices in our power as a Sister Republic." It added that if the Californians "desire to unite their destiny with ours, they would be received as brethren, whenever this can be done, without affording Mexico just cause of complaint." Upon receipt of this communication and extrapolating a bit from it, Larkin launched an effort in April 1846 to further separation of California from Mexico. He believed things were already progressing to this end when the Mexican War opened the way for conquest of the Territory. Larkin had no sympathy with filibusterism, apparently regarding the so-called Bear Flag Revolt of central California somewhat in that light, and he ever honored the rights and prejudices of the Californians. He felt that Fremont's "foolish" Bear Flag and other activities were nearly fatal to his plans. He went south with Robert Stockton (see entry) hoping with the help of his associate Abel Stearns (see entry) to persuade southerners to submit, for otherwise they would be left to the "mercy" of the Bears (Stearns did what he could to further Larkin's goals), but Stockton took "dishonorable steps" to prevent Larkin's success, which Stockton felt would mean loss of position for himself. Larkin's course, adjudged Bancroft, was worthy of all praise, his statesmanship "being incomparably superior to that of the opera-bouffe 'conquerors' of California." In 1845 and 1846 Larkin was correspondent of the New York *Herald* and *Sun.* In November 1846 he was captured by Californians under Manuel Castro and detained until conclusion of the war, but was kindly treated, "there being no ill-will toward him." Larkin served as consul until 1848, as confidential agent from 1846-48, as naval store-keeper in 1847-48 and as navy agent from 1847-49, but his "most important diplomatic work was in his confidential agency, the significance of which lies in the light it throws upon Polk's policy of territorial expansion." In June 1848 he was informed that with the end of the war his functions as consul and confidential agent were terminated. He thereafter turned his attention to private matters, was a member of the California Constitutional Convention, and expanded his business and real estate holdings, which were considerable. In 1850-53 he lived with his family at New York City, then returned to San Francisco as a very rich man. He died at San Francisco; his widow succumbed in 1873 at 66. They were parents of seven children, of whom five survived Larkin. He was, according to Bancroft, "a man to whom nothing like just credit has hitherto been given for his public services in 1845 and 1846."

Bancroft, *California,* III-VI, *Pioneer Register;* DAB; EA.

Larocque, Francois-Antoine, frontiersman, fur trader (1784-1869). A clerk for the North West Company, a fur trading concern, Larocque served under Charles Chaboillez (1772-1812), who was in charge of the Fort Dauphin Department on the Assiniboine and Red rivers, north of the present Canadian-United States border. In 1804 Chaboillez organized an expedition under Larocque, who was accompanied by Charles McKenzie and others, to the country of the Mandans on the Missouri River near the present Bismarck, North Dakota. Larocque was to establish trading links with the Mandans and try to reach

the Crow Indians to the westward with a similar objective. In the spring of 1805 the Crows, who had just completed their annual social-bartering visit to the Mandans and Hidatsa tribes, reluctantly permitted Larocque and another, along with several Hidatsa (linguistically related to the Crows) to accompany them to their homeland. They went by way of the Knife, Little Missouri, Powder and Tongue rivers, crossed the Wolf or Chetish Mountains, a spur of the Big Horn range, forded the Big Horn River near its lower canyon and continued northward to the Yellowstone River. A final trading session took place on an island in the river, whereafter Larocque parted from the Crows and retraced his outward path to the Mandans and ultimately to the Assiniboine fort. On this expedition Larocque may have been the first white man to explore northern Wyoming, as he was among the first to visit the interior of Montana. His trading session with the Crows had been profitable for the company, and he promised the Indians he would return to them in 1806, but this visit was not made because of a change of policy by the North West Company, inspired possibly by the success of the Lewis and Clark Expedition from the United States. Larocque kept a journal of his travels, which has been published (*Publications of the Canadian Archives,* Ottawa, 1910, No. 3, 17; also in *Original Journals,* etc., of the Northwest Company, see biblio. below). Larocque was a man of "good abilities, of great courage and energy. He was well read, studious and equally proficient in...French and English [but] decidedly preferred the latter." He soon left the fur company, since the life of an Indian trader held few attractions for him, and entered business in Montreal. In this he was "most unfortunate." He passed the last period of his life in close retirement and serious study and died, "much advanced in years, in the Grey nunnery of St. Hyacinthe," Quebec. He was married and left a son, who had progeny.

DCB V; Burton Harris, *John Colter,* N.Y., Charles Scribner's Sons, 1952; L.R. Masson, *Les Bourgeois de la Compagnie du Nord-Ouest: Original Journals Narratives Letters, etc Relating to the Northwest Company,* Vol. I, 299-313, N.Y., Antiquarian Press Ltd., 1960; info. from E.F. (Ted) Mains.

La Tules: *see,* Gertrudes Barcelo

Lea, Joseph Calloway, military officer, pioneer (Nov. 8, 1841-Feb. 4, 1904). B. at Cleveland, Tennessee, his family moved in 1849 to near Independence, Missouri, settling at a site which became known as Lea's (Lee's) Summit, named for Joseph's father. With the outbreak of the Civil War Lea enlisted in the 6th Missouri, a Confederate regiment, part of Shelby's brigade. By the third year he had become a colonel, although "he had made his reputation as a captain...and was known [as such] for the rest of his life." Lea in 1875 married Sally Wildey, the couple moving to Elizabethtown, New Mexico, in 1876 and arriving at Roswell the following year. Captain Lea became known as the "father of Roswell," a title that really belonged to Van C. Smith (see entry), and in 1893 founded there the New Mexico Military Institute. Sally Wildey Lea's two brothers, Ernest and John, followed the Leas to New Mexico, John establishing a ranch in the Tularosa Valley with headquarters at Wildey's Well, where in 1898 a famous gunfight occurred between Oliver Lee and Jim Gililland on one side, and Pat Garrett and his deputies on the other. Throughout the earlier Lincoln County War, Lea maintained a position generally of neutrality, although he had close friendships on both sides. Lea and John Chisum were credited with persuading Pat Garrett in 1880 to run for sheriff of Lincoln County on the theory that he was the proper man to quell the militant turbulence wracking the region. Lea at one point attempted to intercede with Governor Wallace on behalf of Charlie Bowdre (see entry), but Bowdre was killed before anything could come of it. At a later date Ash Upson, journalist and part-time amnuensis for Garrett, clerked in Lea's store, the most prominent commercial establishment at Roswell. Upson and Lea eventually had a falling out, however, over disappearance of a goodly stock of Hostetter's Bitters, a patent medicine laced with plenty of alcohol, which Upson sampled and found much to his taste. Lea was elected to the Lower House of the Territorial Legislature in 1889, and Lea County, created in 1917, was named for him. He died of pneumonia at Roswell. A son and daughter were born to the Leas.

William A. Keleher, *The Fabulous Frontier,* Albuquerque, Univ. of N.M. Press, 1962; Robert M. Utley, *Billy the Kid: A Short and Violent Life,* Lincoln, Univ. of Neb. Press, 1989; info. from Frederick W. Nolan.

Learnard, Henry Grant, military officer (Aug. 18, 1867-Mar. 7, 1937). B. at Wright City, Missouri, he went to West Point and was commissioned a second lieutenant in the 19th Infantry June 12, 1890, becoming a first lieutenant of the 14th Infantry March 1, 1897; He served under Captain Edwin Forbes Glenn in the 1898 exploration party in Alaska from March to November. He was instructed to take a small group and explore routes between Portage Bay on the west side of Prince William Sound and Turnagain Arm, a bay at the head of Cook Inlet. The results were inconclusive because it was the wrong season for such an investigation. May 30 Learnard was instructed to land at Resurrection Bay on the east coast of Kenai Peninsula, and explore a route from there to Sunrise City, on the south shore of Turnagain Arm. The trip was made by way of Kenai Lake and posed no great difficulties, Learnard aided at times by the many prospectors combing the region. June 20, 1898, he commanded a small expedition by paddle-wheel riverboat up the Susitna River, entering it twenty-five miles north of Ladd on the second try and succeeding, thanks to a high tide which carried the craft over bars at the mouth of the river. June 21, the boat passed Alexander's, named for "an old Indian chief," and Mt. Susitna to the west of the river "as if to guard the entrance" to the stream. June 22, the expedition arrived at the Alaska Commercial Company's store, probably at the present Susitna, twenty-three miles above the mouth of the river. With some difficulty an Indian guide was hired. Three miles above Susitna the expedition came to the mouth of the Yetna (Johnson) River, tributary to the Susitna; it had been ascended for about 200 miles by a man named Johnson, who was of the Learnard party. He reported that its headwaters were not far from headwaters of a branch of the important Kuskokwim River. Learnard here had a flat-bottomed boat built for the expedition; when completed it was found to draw only seven inches of water, empty, ten inches when loaded, was much easier to tow than the sailboat with which they had come thus far, and made upriver progress more practicable. The expedition continued upriver, most of the time moving the boat by towline. July 17, the mouth of the Talkeetna River was met, with miners clustered about waiting for an opportunity to pursue prospecting in the region. Six miles above the mouth of the Talkeetna a permanent camp was established, three men sent back to Ladd for instructions and rations. July 22, a small party was directed to map a tributary creek to the west, while on the 23rd Learnard, with Johnson, one soldier and Stephan, an Indian guide, started overland toward the east, making for the headwaters of the Talkeetna; the expedition remained out until August 27, on that date returning to their permanent camp. A side expedition under Sergeant William Yanert (see entry), 8th Cavalry, was sent to try to attain the Tanana River to the northeast. It failed to come closer than thirty-five miles from it, then returned to base, arriving after "a very hard trip." September 15, camp was struck and the party descended the Susitna and reached Tyonek. Captain Glenn arrived with the rest of the expedition September 30. The combined party reached Homer, Kenai Peninsula, October 10, and Vancouver Barracks, Washington, November 10, 1898. Learnard became captain of the 4th Infantry November 15, 1899, transferred to the 14th Infantry February 3, 1900. By April 2, 1918, he was a colonel and a Brigadier General by March 21, 1926, retiring August 31, 1931. He had served in the Philippines from 1899-1901 and was with the China Relief Expedition of 1900. He was wounded in action during the Spanish American War, won a Silver Star for "gallantry in action" at Peking August 14, 1900, and a Distinguished Service Medal for service in World War I.

Heitman; Cullums; *Narratives of Explorations in Alaska; Who Was Who.*

Lebarge, Michel (Mike), explorer, trader (1837-post 1898). B. at Chateauguay, Quebec, of French Canadian parents, he left for California in May 1865 aboard the steamer *Golden Rule* by way of Nicaragua; also aboard was Robert Kennicott, director of the scientific corps of the Western Union Telegraph Company's Alaskan endeavor. The crossing of Nicaragua involved several adventures, and Lebarge's "excellent qualities...in trying circumstances" led to Kennicott's hiring him for the company of proposed explorers of central Alaska. Kennicott died in 1866 at Nulato, but Lebarge stayed on. In that year he and Frank Ketchum (see entry), another Canadian, made the first fully-reported journey from St. Michael on Norton Sound up the Yukon River to Fort Yukon at the junction of the Yukon and Porcupine rivers. In the winter of 1866-67 the two duplicated their earlier effort, this time on the ice, and the following summer, by birchbark canoe, continued upstream into Canada, arriving eventually at Fort Selkirk at the confluence of the Yukon and Pelly rivers, the highest point to that time reached by explorers from the coast. In 1868 Lebarge engaged in the fur trade in the Yukon region with associates in the Pioneer

American Fur Company. In 1871 he joined the Alaska Commercial Company, from which he retired (with a modest competency) in 1875. He returned to Chateauguay and apparently was still living there when Dall wrote of him in 1898. Lebarge was commemorated by geographical features named for him: the Lebarge River, a northerly tributary to the Yukon below Fort Yukon, and Lake Lebarge, north of Whitehorse, which many high latitude romantics will remember from Robert W. Service's unforgettable poem, "The Cremation of Sam McGee," for it was "on the marge of Lake Lebarge" that the narrator "cremated Sam McGee."

William H. Dall, "A Yukon Pioneer, Mike Lebarge," with engraved portrait, *National Geographic Magazine,* Vol. IV, No. 4 (April 1898), 137-39; *Narratives of Explorations in Alaska,* 19-20; info. from the Alaska State Lby.; Robert W. Service, *The Spell of the Yukon,* N.Y., Barse & Hopkins, 1907.

Lebedev-Lastochin, Pavel Sergeyevich, fur trader (d. c. 1800). A merchant of Iakutsk (Yakutsk), Siberia, he vigorously entered the Alaskan fur trade late in the 18th century, financing several discoverer-adventurers, among them Gerassim Pribylov, who found the fur-seal islands named for him. Lebedev-Lastochin established a major trading company whose ambition, according to Zagoskin, extended beyond the hunt for furs. "Did the founders of the Lebedev-Lastochin Company imagine, when they founded settlements on Nuchek (Hinchinbrook) Island, on the Kenai (Cook) Inlet and on Ilyamna Lake, or sent expeditions to the upper reaches of the Kuskokwim, that they would abandon all that they had built...when the supply of fur-bearing animals should be exhausted? Certainly not. The very spaciousness of the locations they chose proves the contrary. If they had had such men [as Shelikhov or Baranov], the whole northwestern part of the American continent...would long ago have been explored, described, and settled." The company was "strong and flourishing," but its muscle did not match its vision and, in the end, it lost out. It may be that Lebedev-Lastochin himself never visited America or actually headed up operations of his firm on this continent. He depended upon factors to handle its affairs and separate posts; thus his company, which had many strengths, was weakest at the top, while the factor system led to dissension and lack of unified purpose and, ultimately, doubtless caused its downfall. In

1781 Lebedev-Lastochin with Shelikhov fitted out the *Sv Georgiy (St. George),* the vessel in which, five years later, Pribylov would make his momentous discovery. Results of the initial voyage must have been favorable, because in 1783 Lebedev-Lastochin organized a special company to increase his operations among the Aleutian Islands and on the Alaskan mainland (Bancroft, p. 186 and n., gives a breakdown on how its shares were distributed and who were its leadership figures). One of the notable officers was an experienced navigator, Potap Zaikov who, having heard of Cook's 1778 discovery of Prince William Sound,was in 1783 the first Russian of record to explore the region for its fur-gathering possibilities. Shelikhov had established the initial permanent settlement on Kodiak Island and in 1786 the *Sv Pavel,* commanded by the Lebedev-Lastochin interpreter, Petr Kolomin, anchored there with thirty-five men. They were advised, in keeping with Shelikhov's instructions to his agents, to move on and were told, as an inducement, that there were plenty of sea otters in Cook Inlet; Kolomin took the advice and established a post named St. George on the Kassilov River near the present town of Kasilov, about thirty miles below today's Kenai. It was the first permanent Russian settlement on the Alaskan mainland and became profitable, the rival Shelikhov was distressed to learn. Lebedev-Lastochin in 1791 was sponsor of an additional Kenai Peninsula post at St. Nicholas, established by the contentious Grigor Konovalov at the site of Kenai; another station was set up at Lake Iliamna north of Bristol Bay, probably around 1796, and on Nuchek Island Fort Konstantine was founded in 1793. It sought to control the rich Prince William Sound area and here the company eventually established what amounted to its Alaskan headquarters. Meanwhile there arose confusion and occasional armed clashes between the posts of Sts. George and Nicholas, with appeals by one or the other parties for referee service by Shelikhov, who had remained a somewhat silent partner of Lebedev-Lastochin (though his commercial rival), and had organized his own independent company which operated separately from the other. Predatory raids and plundering expeditions against Indians or Russians indiscriminately were conducted by the various peredovshchik, or leaders, with the booty "duly accounted for among the earnings of the company." The whole contributed to a lawless decade on Cook Inlet where "midnight raids,

ambuscades, and even open warfare," largely it would seem instigated by Konovalov, became commonplace. The basis for all the internal scuffling may have been ambition, and the possibility that a factor's esteem and financial status within the company depended upon his balance sheet; there is no other obvious way to explain the merciless internecine conflicts between elements of the same concern. "Baranov freely acknowledged...that, individually, the promyshlenniki of the Lebedev company were [proven] superior to those under his command" and had he led men of their caliber "he would have conquered the whole north-western coast of America." At length he stepped in to quiet things among the Lebedev-Lastochin free-booters, for that was what they had become. Stepan Zaikov, brother of Potap, was now in command at St. Nicholas, Kolomin held on at St. George, and Amos Balushin, a tough and ruthless operator, controlled the establishment on Nuchek Island. Baranov became convinced that Konovalov was the principle trouble-maker, sent him in irons to Okhotsk, where he was investigated, but "by a lenient committee" which agreed with the Archimandrite Ioassaf (see entry) who already had investigated and found Konovalov not so depraved as Baranov believed him to be—or, more probably, supplying satisfactory profits from his activities. Konovalov "readily managed to clear himself, and was restored to a command in Alaska." Baranov meanwhile steadily received more reinforcements than did the Lebedev-Lastochin operations and, through the Shelikhov influence at St. Petersburg, was granted imperial authority to form settlements anywhere in Alaska and the right to claim the region for 500 versts (about 300 miles) around such establishments in which no other company was permitted to set foot. Against such regulations the Lebedev-Lastochin firm could not prevail, even though it was second in power and in success of all those companies which had tried operating in Alaska. Baranov eventually found the principal Lebedev establishment at Nuchek come into dire straits; he induced most of his rival's men to join the Shelikhov company and furnished transportation to Okhotsk for the remainder. A similar fate befell other fur traders until by 1791 only two organizations remained: Shelikhov's company and the slimmed down though stubborn Lebedev-Lastochin remnants. The latter however could not endure and in 1798 were taken over by Shelikhov interests, which in the following year were granted a monopoly for trade in all Alaska under the name of the Russian American Company. Pavel Lebedev-Lastochin does not figure again in the region, although there is a report that one, "Lastochkin," who may have been this man or a relative, in 1798 made a brief and unsuccessful attempt to explore the Copper River. The place of death of Lebedev-Lastochin is not reported.

Zagoskin; Bancroft, *Alaska; Russian Penetration in the North Pacific Ocean;* Swanton, *Tribes,* 530; info. from Slavic Div., Lby. of Cong.

Le Blanc, Antonio, cattleman (fl. 1782). A Frenchman who lived on the Texas side of the Louisiana border, Le Blanc in May 1782 requested permission of Spanish authorities to drive 2,000 head of cattle, no doubt Longhorns, to Louisiana. Whether he was granted permission is not reported, but if that was done it marked one of the very first, if not the first, such drives in Texas history; the cattle probably would have been delivered to Opelousas, so the movement would represent about 200 miles, or halfway to New Orleans where James Taylor White (see entry) first drove Longhorns from Anahuac, Texas, in about 1838. There is said to have been no relationship between Le Blanc (White) and James White of Virginia origin.

Jack Jackson, *Los Mesteños: Spanish Ranching in Texas 1721-1821,* College Station, Tex. A & M Univ. Press, 1986.

Lee, Alfred Alonzo (Alfred Allee), frontiersman (fl. 1836-1865). B. in Pennsylvania rather than in North Carolina as a source mistakenly believed, he enlisted in James C. Allen's "Buckeye Rangers" June 1, 1836, the corps arriving at Galveston Island by June 15. Because of Lee's skill as a carpenter he transferred to Captain John McClure's Company F, 1st Volunteers' Regiment, engaged in the fortification of Galveston in the event of a Mexican attack. Possibly Lee returned to Ohio or Pennsylvania in 1837 and went back to Texas some time later. In December 1842 he became second lieutenant of Company A under Captain Ewen Cameron of the ill-fated Mier Expedition which embarked upon a raiding foray into Mexico by way of the Rio Grande city of Mier, upstream from Carmargo, Tamaulipas State. After some preliminary scuffling a battle with Mexican irregulars occurred and 176 surrendered Texans finally were marched into the interior for imprisonment save for the unfortu-nates who drew a black bean (as one in ten did) and were executed for a failed escape attempt. Lee was a fortunate one in that incident. He was briefly in a hospital in Mexico City for an unreported ailment, was released from imprisonment September 16, 1844, and with Mier Expedition survivors was taken by the schooner *Creole* to New Orleans and made his way back to Texas. He apparently lived in Victoria County in 1854 when he sold some of the acreage he had been given for his military role; he then moved to old Clinton (now vanished) in DeWitt County, where he died in 1865. He was married and fathered sons.

Houston Wade, "Alfred Alonzo Lee...or Alfred Allee," *Frontier Times,* Vol. 17, No. 1 (Oct. 1939), 32-35.

Lee, Fitzhugh, military officer (Nov. 19, 1835-Apr. 28, 1905). B. in Fairfax County, Virginia, he was a nephew of Robert E. Lee, who almost expelled him from West Point for misbehavior, but he was graduated 45th in his class. He was commissioned a brevet second lieutenant in the 2nd Cavalry July 1, 1856, and became a second lieutenant January 1, 1858, meanwhile having been assigned to Texas where he saw much action against Indians. Lee was in Earl Van Dorn's hard fight at a Comanche and Kiowa village fifteen miles south of Old Fort Atkinson in present Ford County, Kansas, on May 12, 1859. Lee was seriously, almost fatally, wounded in the action. He led a charge on a flank of the Indian position and was confronted by an armed Indian; Lee fired his pistol at the instant the Comanche loosed an arrow: the Indian was killed instantly, and simultaneously his arrow struck Lee in the right side, penetrated the rib cage and the officer's right lung, and he bled freely through the mouth. But surgeons were able to staunch the flow of blood and he was transported 200 miles back to Camp Radziminski on Otter Creek in Indian Territory on a litter between two mules. His recovery was painful, and slow. In addition to Lee, three other officers and twelve men were wounded, two enlisted men killed and the Indians lost 49 warriors killed and 36 captured, including women and children. January 14, 1860, Comanches stole twenty-four horses and mules from near Camp Colorado, near Austin, Texas, and Lee volunteered to lead a pursuit through bitter cold and sifting snow; the stock was recovered and Lee set out after one of the Comanches, pursuing him for seven miles and catching up in a rocky ravine where after a desperate hand-to-hand fight in which Lee narrowly missed another arrow wound, he managed to kill his opponent, although only the officer's thick winter clothing kept him from knife and other wounds. Lee became a first lieutenant March 31, 1861, but resigned May 21, and joined the Confederate army. His outstanding cavalry career in that conflict commenced under Major General J.E.B. Stuart, Lee becoming a Brigadier General at 27 on July 24, 1862, and a Major General August 3, 1863. He was severely wounded, recovered, became Robert E. Lee's chief of cavalry corps and surrendered shortly after Appomatox. He farmed in Virginia, was governor of the state from 1885-89 and was consul-general at Havana, Cuba, from 1896-98. In the Spanish American War he became a Major General of Volunteers and by special act of Congress, a Brigadier General of the U.S. Army February 11, 1901, retiring March 2, 1901, one of the few Confederate General Officers to be reinstated in the United States Army in so high a rank. He died at Washington, D.C.

Heitman; Harold B. Simpson, *Cry Comanche: The 2nd U.S. Cavalry in Texas 1855-1861*, Hillsboro, Tex., Hill Jr. Coll. Press, 1979; Patricia L. Faust, ed., *Historical Times Encyclopedia of the Civil War*, N.Y., Harper & Row, 1986; DAB.

Leffingwell, Ernest deKoven, polar explorer (1875-Jan. 27, 1971). B. at Knoxville, Illinois, he studied geology, physics and mathematics at Trinity College, Hartford, Connecticut, and at the University of Chicago. Hearing a Fritjof Nansen lecture, Leffingwell became enthused about Arctic exploration. He applied to join the Evelyn Briggs Baldwin-William Ziegler expedition which embarked for Franz Josef Land north of Novaya Zemlya early in the 20th century and was appointed head of the expedition's scientific staff. "During the troubles of this markedly unsuccessful expedition, which...failed in its attempt to reach the North Pole," Leffingwell became a close friend of Ejnar Mikkelsen (see entry), a young Danish sea captain also interested in polar exploration. In May 1906 the two explorers and their Anglo-American Expedition, co-sponsored by Harvard and Toronto universities, left Vancouver Island for the Alaskan Arctic coast. They found their way blocked by ice and established a good base camp on Flaxman Island, 130 miles northwest of the point where the Alaskan-Canadian border touches the Arctic

Ocean. Here they wintered. With spring Leffingwell, Mikkelsen and Storker T. Storkerson, first officer on the expedition ship, *Duchess of Bedford,* spent a month sledging north from their base over sea ice in search of land rumored to exist somewhere in the Beaufort Sea. They located and established the edge of the continental shelf, but found no land, the non-existence of such finally demonstrated by Stefansson and Storkerson at later dates. Mikkelson returned south in 1907 but Leffingwell remained on the island to continue his scientific survey of the region. In 1908 he went south for more equipment and a new vessel and returned in the summer of 1909 for three more years of research and exploration. He mapped accurately about 150 miles of coast and pursued his geological investigations along with other studies. In 1912 he again went south and returned in the summer of 1913 for a final year of Arctic work. In 1914 the Geological Survey provided him desk space at Washington, D.C., to write up his report, *The Canning River Region, Northern Alaska,* a comprehensive description of the geography and geology of the Alaska he had studied at his own expense and largely alone for six years. He retired to a ranch in southern California where he lived for twenty years, then moved to Carmel, California, for the rest of his life. When he died at Carmel at 96 he was probably the oldest of Arctic explorers. The small number (though distinctly valuable) of his publications "denied him the place he deserves in the history of Arctic exploration. His account of the Canning River [Flaxman Island] region was the first detailed geological description of any part of the North American Arctic...His and Mikkelsen's employment of Vilhjalmur Stefansson as anthropologist in 1906 brought to the Arctic one of the keenest intelligences of their time. And, as testimony to the mutual understanding and affection between Leffingwell and the Eskimos with whom he lived and worked, his last name became and remains a common first name among them."

Info. from John Schwoerke, Spec. Coll., Dartmouth Coll. Lby.; Orth, 17, 570.

Leith, John, frontiersman, trader (c. 1743-c. 1832). B. at Leith, Scotland, his father emigrated when John was young to the Pedee River, South Carolina where he soon afterward died. The boy, whose year of birth is conjecture, journeyed northward, spending some time at Little York, Pennsylvania. At 15 he was at Fort Pitt, so named in 1758 when the English fort was constructed on the ruins of the French Fort Duquesne. Leith hired out to an Indian trader and with him started for the Ohio wilderness. Hostilities were underway between white Americans and Indians. A chief, having taken a liking to Leith, adopted him into his tribe, possibly Shawnee. The Indians moved farther west to the Miami River, and here Leith matured. At 23 he married a white woman, Sally Lowry, who had been captured by Indians when twenty months old at Big Cove, above Pittsburgh, and had grown up in the Indian village; she was 18 at her marriage. Leith had two children and was living with his family at Salem, one of the Moravian towns on the Muskingum (Tuscarawas) River in 1781; he removed to the Upper Sandusky region after the 1782 massacre at Gnadenhutten. He was employed as Indian agent and trader at the town of Half King (see entry), a Wyandot leader, later in 1782 when Crawford's army approached. It was defeated by the Indians. Leith and his family continued to reside in Indian country for the eight succeeding years, but in 1790 they moved to Pittsburgh, arriving November 2. From there they went to Bud's Ferry, where some of his wife's relatives gave them a cordial welcome. After farming in the vicinity for some years, Leith moved to Ohio where he lived the rest of his life. In 1873 a grandson, George W. Leith, was living at Nevada, Ohio.

Consul W. Butterfield, *An Historical Account of the Expedition Against Sandusky Under Col. William Crawford in 1782*, Cincinnati, Robert Clarke Co., 1873; Paul A.W. Wallace, *Thirty Thousand Miles with John Heckewelder*, Univ. of Pitts. Press, 1958.

Lemmon, George Edward (Ed), cattleman (May 23, 1857-Aug. 25, 1945). B. at Bountiful, Utah, he was brought to Nebraska in 1866 by his parents and at 13 began working with cattle, commencing "nearly 75 years of activity on the cattle ranges of the western great plains from the Canadian border to Texas [and entering] many business enterprises." He created and successfully operated "far-flung ranch empires" during his long and colorful career. On January 5, 1958, he and James (Scotty) Philip (see entry) were the first South Dakota men elected to the National Cowboy Hall of Fame. Late in the 1870s he went to the Black Hills, and established spreads in the northwestern part of South Dakota. His stock interests steadily expanded, his headquarters in 1902 established as the L-7 Ranch near the present site of Lemmon, a community just south of the North Dakota line. "During that time land was plentiful and settlers and cattlemen few and far between...The L-7 leased 865,000 acres on the Standing Rock Reservation and enclosed it with a three-wire fence, making it the largest fenced pasture in the world. The town of Lemmon eventually was founded at the site of his headquarters. A newspaper obituary said that "'Dad' Lemmon was one of the few remaining Texas trail drivers [at his death] who made the delivery of herds from Texas to northern maturing ranges, these herds laying the foundation of the cattle industry in western South Dakota. His range life covers experiences in Wyoming, Nebraska, the Dakotas, Montana and Texas." As a mere boy he had met James Butler Hickok, and lived through the 1864 Indian raids in Nebraska. After entering the cattle business he once bossed "the single biggest roundup in history," claimed he roped and branded 900 cattle in a day, and over time handled more than a million head of cattle, which may be a one-man record. His acquaintanceships were wide and covered much of the west in a career which spanned activities from cowboy through range manager to ranch owner, and during those years he of course had contacts, fleeting or otherwise, with solid stockmen like himself and plenty of people outside the law or quite heedless of it. He wrote his recollections piecemeal and in no particular order, just "whatever came to mind," the manuscript being edited and arranged in an orderly way by Nellie Snyder Yost. Lemmon died at the community named for him; he was survived by two sons, James H. Lemmon, a businessman, and Roy Edward Lemmon, associated with Universal Pictures of Hollywood. Ed Lemmon was 88 at his death.

Boss Cowman: The Recollections of Ed Lemmon, ed. by Nellie Snyder Yost, Lincoln, Univ. of Neb. Press, 1969; *The Lemmon Tribune*, Aug. 30, 1945; info. from the S.D. State Hist. Soc.; Wayne C. Lee, *Scotty Philip: The Man Who Saved the Buffalo,* Caldwell, Id., Caxton Printers, Ltd., 1975.

Levashev, Mikhail Dmitriyevich, Russian naval officer (d.c. 1775). A Navy lieutenant, he was promoted to captain-lieutenant when selected by Krenitzin (see entry) to be second in command of a secret Russian expedition of 1764 -1769 to the Aleutian Islands to verify reports of promyshlenniki discoveries, construct accurate charts of the chain and investigate Russian abuses of Aleut natives. The expedition was miserably handled from the start, lost many men and several ships, and the only true value accruing from it was ethnological information collected by Levashev on Unalaska Island, where he was forced to winter (see Krenitzin entry for details of the expedition). The two vessels in 1769 returned to Nishekamchatsk, Levashev's ship arriving August 24. After a difficult winter Krenitzin was drowned July 4, 1770, when trying to cross the Kamchatka River and Levashev assumed command, arriving at Okhotsk August 3, 1770, and returning to St. Petersburg October 22, 1771, seven years and four months from his departure on the important, but not-well conducted expedition. Zagoskin wrote that Levashev died "about 1775," no cause of death given.

Bancroft, *Alaska;* Zagoskin; *Russian Penetration of the North Pacific Ocean.*.

Lewis, Charles, frontiersman (1733ːOct. 10, 1774). The youngest son of John Lewis of Augusta, unlike his brothers was born after the family reached Virginia. He became "especially noted" as a "gallant Indian fighter and frontiersman." He was captain of a company under his brother, Andrew Lewis (see entry) and George Washington which advanced for the defense of the frontier after Braddock's defeat in 1755. As a spinoff of the Pontiac War of 1763, Charles Lewis raised 150 volunteers in a single night, pursued raiding Indians and October 3, 1763, collided with them on the south fork of the Potomac River, killing twenty-one with no white losses in the most notable of several skirmishes that year on the Virginia frontier. In 1764 he accompanied Bouquet's (see entry) expedition against the Ohio Indians. Ten years later, by then a colonel and county lieutenant for Augusta County, Lewis had a prominent role in Lord Dunmore's War, leading a contingent of Augusta men at the Point Pleasant battle of October 10, 1774. He was mortally wounded early in the engagement. "Charles Lewis was popular, and beloved by all the Western army; his loss was a general affliction." He was married and left five small children. Lewis County, West Virginia, was named for him.

Thwaites, *Dunmore;* Alexander Scott Withers, *Chronicles of Border Warfare,* Cincinnati, Robert Clarke Co., 1895, 1970.

Lewis, John, frontiersman (1678-Feb. 1, 1762). Of either Welsh or French Huguenot origin, he was b. in County Donegal, Ireland, married a

Scot woman, Margaret Lynn, in 1716 and in 1729 killed a man of high station and fled to Portugal. In 1731 "after strange adventures" he emigrated to America, and was joined there by his family, including sons Andrew and Thomas (see entries). He established himself near Staunton, Virginia, on the frontier, built a fortress-like stone house which in 1754 successfully withstood an Indian siege. He was colonel of the Augusta County militia from 1743, became a presiding justice in 1745 and high sheriff in 1748. At 73 in 1751 he assisted Andrew, then agent for a land company, to explore and survey a grant on the Greenbrier River, so named because "the old man became entangled in the thicket of greenbriers." He died at his fortress-home at 84. His son, Andrew, commanded the victorious forces at the Battle of Point Pleasant concluding Lord Dunmore's War of 1774.

Alexander Scott Withers, *Chronicles of Border Warfare,* Cincinnati, Robert Clarke Co., 1895, 1970.

Lewis, Oscar, historical writer (May 5, 1893-July 11, 1992). B. at San Francisco, Lewis lived there virtually all of his life. From 1917-19 he served with the overseas Ambulance Service of the American Expeditionary Force, after which he resettled at San Francisco, engaging in freelance writing and publishing many books, most with historical and some of frontier interest. He considered most important among his works: *The Big Four: The Story of* [Collis P.] *Huntington,* [Leland] *Stanford,* [Mark] *Hopkins* [1813-78], and [Charles] *Crocker* (1938); *Silver Kings* (1947), and *High Sierra Country* (1955). Others of historical or frontier interest included: *Lola Montez: The Mid-Victorian Bad Girl in California* (1938); *Sea Routes to the Gold Fields* (1947); *California Heritage* (1949); *Sagebrush Casinos* (1953); *The Town That Died Laughing,* about Austin, Nevada (1955), and *Sutter's Fort* (1966). He wrote a number of brief publications for historical societies, along with a scattering of juveniles. Lewis died at 99 years of age at San Francisco. He was married.

Contemporary Authors; Council on America's Military Past *Headquarters Heliogram,* 224, July 1992, p. 6.

Lewis, Thomas, frontiersman (1718-Jan. 31, 1790). B. in Ireland and an older brother of Andrew and Charles Lewis, he emigrated with the family to Virginia about 1731, joining their father, John Lewis (see entry), who had adventurously preceded them. Thomas was too near-sighted for military service, though he may have taken part in the Braddock campaign in 1755. Of culture and refinement, he became prominent in public affairs, collected one of the largest libraries of his time, and was an accomplished mathematician. He served in the Virginia House of Burgesses and in 1775 was a delegate to the Virginia convention. In 1778 with his brother Andrew he was an Indian commissioner; in that capacity the two brothers negotiated and signed the first Indian Treaty ever drawn up between the United States and an Indian tribe. This pact, with the Delawares, was completed at Fort Pitt September 17, 1778, with Thomas and Andrew signing for the nation, and Captain Pipe, Captain White Eyes and Captain John Killbuck Jr., for the three divisions of the Indian tribe. Thomas Lewis voted for the U.S. Constitution in the ratifying convention of 1788. He died at his home in Rockingham County, Virginia.

Thwaites, *Dunmore;* Alexander Scott Withers, *Chronicles of Border Warfare,* Cincinnati, Robert Clarke Co., 1895, 1970; Charles J. Kappler, *Indian Treaties 1778-1883,* N.Y., Interland Pub., Inc., 1972.

Liebigstag, Ahtena chief (fl. 1885). Allen, on his ascent of the Copper River, Alaska, contacted this toyon, leading man or chief four days above Taral (Chitina), finding him "nearly equal in rank to Nicolai (see entry), though not nearly such a diplomat." Allen wrote that "never have I known lines of caste to be so rigidly drawn" as in this Athabascan camp. "I was considered the chief, and in ascending the bluff natives had come down to escort us up and carry my bed... I...entered the spruce-bough tepee. There I found all allotted places according to rank: Liebigstag and blood relatives on the right side, 'retainers to camp' on the left. Places on his left and right respectively were reserved for Nicolai and myself. [Private Fredrick] Fickett [the expedition meteorologist] was assigned a place with the *'oi polloi. '*" He concluded that "These tyones barely condescended to consider me their equal, and on no occasion would they consider my men as such. They were reluctant to believe that any one who would pull on the rope of a boat, carry a pack, or take equal foot with his men could be a tyone." Liebigstag rendered the explorers considerable service by guiding them upstream from his camp for several days.

Henry T. Allen, "Military Reconnaissance in Alaska," *Narratives of Explorations in Alaska,* 435.

Lillard, Richard Gordon, writer, conservation-

ist (June 3, 1909-Mar. 19, 1990). B. at Los Angeles, California, he graduated from Stanford University in 1930, earned a master's degree at the University of Montana in 1931 and his doctorate from the University of Iowa in 1943, having also studied at Harvard. His professional career was spent teaching at a variety of colleges and universities and he was a professor of English and American studies at California State University of Los Angeles from 1965 until shortly before his death. He told *Contemporary Authors* that he was "an amateur gardener, a semi-professional ecologist, and a professional conservationist," and his writings supported that description. His works of frontier interest included *Desert Challenge: An Interpretation of Nevada* (1942); *The Green Forest* (1947); *Eden in Jeopardy: Man's Prodigal Meddling with His Environment—the Southern California Experience* (1966); with Edna Bakker, *The Great Southwest* (1972); with Mary V. Hood, *Hank Monk and Horace Greeley* (1973), and *My Urban Wilderness in the Hollywood Hills* (1983). In addition he wrote a column, "About Nature," for *Westways* magazine, was an editorial assistant for the *Mississippi Valley Historical Review* in 1942-43, and at his death was working on a book on the natural history of the Santa Monica Mountains of California. Thomas R. Cox, in the *Western Historical Quarterly* wrote that "He belonged to the progressive school of historiography" who was "an unreconstructed Jacksonian who saw good in everyone," and won the respect and friendship of even those who disagreed with his most strongly held positions on conservation and other matters. He was married twice and fathered two daughters.

Contemporary Authors; Western Historical Quarterly, Vol. XXI, No. 3 (Aug. 1990), 407-408.

Lincoln, Able L., physician (c. 1820-Apr. 23, 1850). A native of St. Louis, Lincoln served as a contract physician during the Mexican War. He reached the Yuma Crossing of the Colorado River in 1849, saw profitable possibilities of a ferry service there and returned in 1850 with the financial backing of J.P. Brodie, a Hermosillo, Sonora, businessman. Lincoln established his ferry business at the base of Pilot Peak, constructing two boats from wagon boxes, and hired some Anglos to work them. Rates were $1 a person and $2 a head for livestock for the crossing. John J. Glanton (see entry), former scalp-hunter and now head of a rough party of desperadoes, informed Lincoln he should buy protection from

Indians and, by invitation or otherwise, became Lincoln's partner in the lucrative operation, promptly raising the fees. When another white established a competing ferry, Glanton destroyed that boat, had the ferryman killed and re-established the Lincoln ferry-monopoly. In mid-April Lincoln wrote a letter home saying that business was good, his ferry had crossed 20,000 passengers and taken in $60,000, but added that "this is an unsafe place to live." Glanton returned from San Diego with a mule load of whiskey. He and his associates got drunk and the much abused Yuma Indians, taking advantage of the fact, slew Glanton, Lincoln and three others, then killed six men operating the ferry, and burned the bodies.

David P. Robrock, "Scalp Hunters Come to Yuma Crossing," *True West,* Vol. 37, No. 2 (Feb. 1990), 16-21.

Linn, Benjamin, military officer (1738-Dec. 23, 1814). B. in New Jersey, he was a younger brother of Colonel William Linn (see entry), and lived in early life in Maryland. In 1769 he and his brother removed to the Monongahela River where Benjamin devoted considerable time to hunting and lived much with the Indians. Early in 1776 he went to Kentucky, joined the Harrodsburg garrison and distinguished himself for bravery in the attack of March 7, 1777. When militia was organized for Kentucky County in early 1777 he was made a lieutenant. In April, with one other companion, he was sent by George Rogers Clark to scout the situation at Kaskaskia in the Illinois country, narrowly escaped detection as a "spy," and "retired in haste." This had not been his first visit to Kaskaskia. He returned to Harrodsburg, married Hannah Sovereigns July 9, 1777, and for this or some other reason did not join Clark for his Kaskaskia or Vincennes expeditions, but joined him at the latter place in July 1779. In 1782 he founded the first church in the Green River country and the second Baptist church in Kentucky. He died at the residence of his daughter in Huntsville, Alabama.

Thwaites/Kellogg, *Frontier Defense on the Upper Ohio 1777-1778.*

Linn, William, military officer (1734-Mar. 5, 1781). B. in Warren County, New Jersey, he moved in his youth to western Maryland and took part in John Forbes' campaign of 1757-58 which was designed to oust the French from Fort Duquesne at the forks of the Ohio River. One element was repulsed by the French before reaching

the site of the post, but it had been burned and abandoned and Forbes occupied it without opposition on November 25, 1758. The replacement was named Fort Pitt. In June 1774 Linn was on Angus McDonald's campaign from Wheeling, West Virginia, across the Ohio River to Wapatomica, an Indian town on the Muskingum River about sixteen miles below Coshocton, Ohio. Six miles from the town McDonald's force ran into an ambush by about 50 Indians; two whites were killed and others wounded, including Linn. The deserted town was then burned. When George Gibson raised his rifle company at Fort Pitt in 1775, Linn joined as a first lieutenant, and accompanied Gibson on a venturesome expedition to New Orleans, bringing gunpowder up the Mississippi and Ohio rivers to Fort Pitt. In 1777 he with nine men joined William Foreman's (see entry) scout from Fort Henry at Wheeling to the Ohio River; Linn was the ranking officer, but Foreman commanded the largest element and so ignored Linn's sound advice on how to operate in Indian country. As a result, Foreman ran into an ambush laid by the Wyandot chief Half King and 40 warriors in a narrow defile and was killed along with about 20 men, others being severely wounded. Linn, who had cautioned against following the trail down the depths of the defile and instead urged paralleling that route on high ground, escaped unscathed with his men. The story persists that when Linn heard the ambush firing, he and his handful of men dashed down the slope toward the scene, firing their weapons and shouting so that the Indians, no doubt fearing reinforcements had arrived, fled and prevented the carnage from being complete. Thwaites commented that "the story of Linn's gallant attack...is without foundation," but whether he meant that it was without eye-witness support or was wholly false is not clear. Linn's party helped a seriously wounded man who had escaped to hide himself, and then "put off in hot haste" to bring news of the disaster to Wheeling's Fort Henry. The next year, with George Rogers Clark he took part in the Kaskaskia, Illinois, campaign and subsequently settled near present Louisville, Kentucky. In 1780 he was colonel of militia on an Indian campaign, but the next year was wounded mortally by an Indian near his home.

Thwaites/Kellogg, *The Revolution on the Upper Ohio, 1775-1777,* Madison, Wis. Hist. Soc., 1908; Alexander Scott Withers, *Chronicles of Border Warfare,* ed. by Thwaites, Cincinnati, Robert Clarke Co.,

1895, 1970; Wills De Hass, *History of the Early Settlement and Indian Wars of Western Virginia,* Wheeling, H. Hoblitzell, Pub., 1851, 230-34.

Lister, Robert Hill, anthropologist, archeologist (Aug. 7, 1915-May 17, 1990). B. at Las Vegas, New Mexico, he was graduated in 1937 from the University of New Mexico, earned a master's degree there in 1938 and after serving from 1941-45 with General George Patton's 3rd Army in Europe earned a doctorate from Harvard in 1950. He had joined the University of Colorado in 1947, remaining on its faculty until 1971. In 1970-71 he was president of the Society for American Archeology and while heading the National Park Service Chaco Project in 1972-73 he also was the NPS chief archeologist at Washington, D.C. Following retirement, Lister and his wife, the former Florence Ellen Cline, also a scientist-writer, were associated with the Arizona State Museum at Tucson, then returned to Colorado where they were involved with the Crow Canyon Archeological Center at Cortez, while living at Mancos. The Listers "participated in numerous archeological expeditions in places such as Egypt, the Sudan, Spain, Morocco, Mexico and Central America." Lister wrote, often with his wife, nearly a dozen books, among the most popular of which was *Chihuahua: Storehouse of Storms* (1966), published by the University of New Mexico Press. They also combined in publication of *Earl Morris & Southwestern Archeology* (1968). Their volume, *Those Who Came Before* (1983) dealt with archeology of the southwest. His other titles included: *Excavations at Cojumatlan, Michoacan, Mexico* (1949); *Excavations at Hells Midden, Dinosaur National Monument* (1951); *Present Status of Archeology of Western Mexico* (1955); *Archeological Investigations on Uncompaghre Plateau, West Central Colorado* (1956); *Archeological Investigations in the Northern Sierra Madre Occidental..., Mexico* (1958), and *Contributions to Mesa Verde Archeology* (1965). Lister died following a heart attack while leading a tour to sites near Blanding, Utah. He was survived by his widow and two sons.

Bernard Klein, Daniel Icolari, *Reference Encyclopedia of the American Indian,* N.Y., B. Klein and Co., 1967; info. from Karl H. Schwerin, Dept. of Anthropology, Univ. of N.M.; *Who's Who in America; Albuquerque* (New Mexico) *Journal,* May 19, 1990.

Lisyanskiy (Lisianski), Yuriy Fedorovich,
naval officer (Apr. 2, 1773-Feb. 22, 1837). B. at Nadin, Russia, of noble parentage, he was educated at the Kronstadt naval academy and at 15 became a midshipman, serving during a minor conflict with Sweden and being present at the battle of Reval (Tallinn) in 1790. Later he served in the English navy where he met Adam Johann von Krusenstern and after visiting the United States returned to Russia in 1800, appointed to captain a frigate and made a knight of St. George, 4th class. Lisyanskiy was second in command of Krusenstern's global circumnavigation of 1803-1806, captaining the *Neva,* one of two vessels purchased in England for the endeavor. The expedition left Kronstadt August 7, 1803, the sloop *Nadeshda* (Hope) carrying Krusenstern and Rezanov (see entry) who was named minister plenipotentiary to Japan in the vain effort to open that country to Russian commerce. The ships parted company in the Pacific, the *Nadeshda* continuing on her Nipponese mission while Lisyanskiy and the *Neva* made directly for Alaska's Kodiak Island where the Russian American Company was headquartered. July 13, 1804, St. Paul's Harbor (Pavlovsk) was sighted and Lisyanskiy greeted by Ivan Banner, the company manager in the absence of Baranov. The ship's commander learned of the Kolosh (Tlingit) destruction of company fortifications at the present Sitka, Alaska, and that Baranov had asked for assistance in dealing with the uprising and rebuilding the post. The *Neva* left Kodiak August 15, reaching Sitka Sound on the 20th, joining two other Russian ships there, Lisyanskiy becoming in effect flotilla commander. Baranov, who had been at Yakutat on a fur-gathering effort, arrived September 19. Preliminary negotiations with the hostiles were unsatisfactory and October 1, the *Neva* and other vessels opened fire on enemy positions ashore. An ill-advised landing party under Baranov attempted to carry the Kolosh fort but was beaten back with ten killed and 26 wounded, including Baranov himself, shot through the arm. Had the withdrawal of the landing party not been effectively covered by naval guns Baranov's party might have been wiped out. To Lisyanskiy therefore was due credit for saving the manager and his detachment, the ultimate defeat of the Kolosh and preservation of the Russian American Company interests at this important site, and of its future prosperity. These successes were not overlooked by Baranov—nor would they go unrecognized at St. Petersburg. The day after his rescue Baranov asked Lisyan-

skiy to take formal charge of the operations. The officer at once opened a brisk fire on the hostile fort, doing enough damage that the Kolosh sued for peace. Lisyanskiy demanded that the fort be evacuated. The Kolosh agreed, but failed to do so until the officer moved some guns by raft nearer the shore, when they at last quit their fort, leaving it strewn with the bodies of their children, slaughtered lest their cries reveal their hiding places to the enemy, and about 30 warriors, slain. The Kolosh it appears had exhausted their musketry ammunition. Lisyanskiy believed they fled fearing vengeance for "their late cruelty and perfidy, but that if ammunition had not failed them, they would have defended themselves to the last extremity." He also was confident that if Baranov had adopted the officer's original suggestion to harass the enemy from the ships, cut off their water supply and communication with the sea, the fort might have been captured without loss of a single Russian. Two of the *Neva's* men had been killed in Baranov's essay and fourteen of the ship's company wounded. The enemy fort was destroyed, and on the site a strongly defended and expansive settlement called Novo Arkhangelsk constructed, eventually to be renamed Sitka. Lisyanskiy left for Kodiak where he wintered. He investigated conditions on the island, estimating the native population at some 4,000, about half of the total before decimation by European-brought diseases and heavy losses due to perilous forced hunting of furs demanded by the invaders. Lisyanskiy studied natives of Ugak (Igak) Bay, Kiliuda (Killuda) Bay and Sitkalidak Island, all on the east coast of Kodiak, being handicapped by having to work through an interpreter. His manner, though condescending, was tempered by gifts of food "and other trifles" to the semi-starved natives. June 14, 1805, he left Kodiak for Novo Arkhangelsk, arriving on the 22nd. While waiting for the Kolosh to come in, Lisyanskiy caused an exact survey to be made of Norfolk Sound, particularly the island on which Mt. Edgecumbe is situated, and to while away the time, made the first recorded ascent of that dormant volcano. It resembles Japan's Mt. Fujiyama in shape and snow-cap, dominating the skyline from Sitka, and although only 3,274 feet high, is an interesting climb. A peace treaty was arranged with the Kolosh who had finally recontacted the Russians and September 1, he sailed for Canton, the *Neva's* fur cargo valued at 450,000 rubles; it included 3,000 sea otter skins and 150,000 other furs. Arriving at Macao in

December he joined Krusenstern who had wintered in Kamchatka. The *Neva* reached Kronstadt August 4, 1806, being well received by personages of high rank, including the tsar himself, who complimented the captain on the appearance of the ship and on his important work in Russian America. The two commanders received the order of St. Vladimir, third class, and a pension of 3,000 rubles a year for life. Lisyanskiy was promoted to commander of the Imperial Navy. He wrote *A Voyage Round the World, 1803-6*, the English translation appearing in London in 1814. Bancroft believed that Lisyanskiy's account of the defeat of the Kolosh was "probably the most reliable [as he] was an eye-witness of all that transpired, took a leading part...and writes without bias...though perhaps taking a little too much credit for his own share in the achievement." A small island in the western extension of the Hawaiian chain is named Lisianski, possibly for this officer.

Bancroft, *Alaska;* Zagoskin; *The Russian American Colonies.*

Little Priest, Winnebago chief (d.c. 1865). Not much is known of the origins of Little Priest, but by 1862 he was a sub-chief or chief with a following of Winnebagos in Minnesota. On August 18, he and eleven of his people happened to be visiting the Mdewakanton Sioux Chief Little Crow (see entry), the day that the Sioux, largely under leadership of Little Crow, launched the Great Sioux Uprising in the Minnesota River Valley. Whether, and to what extent Little Priest and his Winnebagos took part in that massive assault on frontier whites is unknown with surety. Roddis explained: "The belief that Winnebago and Chippewa were taking part was felt and expressed on every hand [although] the Winnebago were relatively few in number...the Indian agent there, [St. A.D.] Balcombe, a man of ability and judgment, was certain of the loyalty of their chief, Little Priest, and his people. Nevertheless there were so many charges that a number of Winnebago under Little Priest himself had taken part in the attack on Fort Ridgely that General [John] Pope ordered the arrest of the Chief and eleven of his men who were tried before the Military Commission. They were completely exonerated..." Nevertheless Little Priest and most of the Winnebagos were exiled from Minnesota and eventually given a portion of the Omaha Reservation in Thurston County, Nebraska, the Omahas and Winnebagos being linguistically akin and friendly toward each other. During the Patrick E. Connor (see entry) expeditions on the Northern Plains in 1865, about 90 Pawnee scouts were augmented by about 100 "Omaha" scouts, who turned out to be Winnebagos under Little Priest, "all veteran Indian fighters, and well-equipped," according to Finn Burnett (see entry). On one occasion during the construction of Fort Connor (Fort Reno), Wyoming, the Winnebagos were attacked by a large party of hostiles and "Little Priest, their chief,...became separated from his warriors and was found surrounded by a number of the enemy. He was on foot, his horse having been killed, he was fighting hand to hand with the bunch and giving good account of his prowess, when his warriors charged in and relieved him. He succeeded in getting away with two scalps of which he was very proud." Captain E.W. Nash of Decatur, Nebraska, was the officer commanding the Winnebago scouts with Little Priest in actual control, for "he was a very brave Indian and a great fighter, and these Indian soldiers gave very little heed to any orders unless given them by Little Priest," according to Albert M. Holman. Between the Tongue and Big Horn rivers of present Wyoming-Montana one command encountered a large band of Indians whom the Winnebagos supposed were hostile Sioux and raced to attack in a "helter skelter manner." But the oncoming 400 Indians frantically waved white cloths, indicating they were peacefully inclined. Captain Albert Brown ordered Little Priest to halt the excited charge of his scouts "as he was the only person who had any control of them," but the chief said he could not call off the pursuit because "they would not listen to him for they had come out to fight Indians and this was an opportunity" they did not want to miss. The captain spurred up alongside Little Priest, drew his revolver and threatened to shoot the chief, and Little Priest had second thoughts. He pulled up his pony and with "a wave of his hand his followers each came to a stand still," and Brown had his peaceful parley, the matter ended. Little Priest was severely wounded in November 1865, according to Dunlay, "in an encounter in which he held off a number of the enemy single-handedly with his Henry repeating rifle; his wounds eventually proved mortal."

William Watts Folwell, *History of Minnesota,* II, St. Paul, Minn. Hist. Soc., 1961; Louis H. Roddis, *The Indian Wars of Minnesota,* Cedar Rapids, Ia., Torch Press, 1956; Ed Shannon, "The Wandering Winneba-

gos," *Frontier Times,* Vol. 45, No. 5 (Aug.-Sept. 1971), 30-31, 68-69; LeRoy R., Ann W. Hafen, *Powder River Campaigns and Sawyers Expedition of 1865: A Documentary Account...,* Glendale, Ca., Arthur H. Clark Co., 1961; Thomas W. Dunlay, *Wolves for the Blue Soldiers,* Lincoln, Univ. of Neb. Press, 1982, p. 37.

Lochry (Laughrey, Lockery, Loughrey), Archibald, military officer (1733-Aug. 24, 1781). Of Scot-Irish parentage, Lochry was b. in northern Ireland. He emigrated to America, became a justice of peace for Bedford County, Pennsylvania, and when Westmoreland County was organized in 1773 was made county lieutenant. As colonel, he commanded a body of volunteers plus a company of Rangers in a descent of the Ohio River from Pittsburgh in support of George Rogers Clark, who had gone ahead. About eleven miles below the mouth of the Great Miami River, in the present state of Indiana, the Lochry element was ambushed by Iroquois under Joseph Brant (see entry) and George Girty (see entry), supported by 100 of Butler's Rangers commanded by Captain Andrew Thompson. Every man of the 101 under command of Lochry, as the colonel himself, were either killed or captured; the dead included, in addition to the 48-year-old Lochry, six officers and 30 privates. The prisoners were taken to Canada.

Consul W. Butterfield, *History of the Girtys,* Cincinnati, Robert Clarke Co., 1890, 1950; Thwaites/Kellogg, *Frontier Defense on the Upper Ohio, 1777-1778,* Madison, Wis. Hist. Soc., 1912, 1977; info. from the Hist. Soc. of Western Penn.

Lockhart, Jacob, frontiersman (fl. c. 1770-1785). An early settler of the Greenbrier region of present West Virginia, he accompanied Matthew Arbuckle on an expedition to the Ohio Indian towns to recover horses "some time before Lord Dunmore's War." During that conflict he served as scout. He was killed by Indians "shortly after the Revolution."

Thwaites/Kellogg, *The Revolution on the Upper Ohio 1775-1777,* Madison, Wis. Hist. Soc., 1908.

Logan, Benjamin, frontiersman (1743-Dec. 11, 1802). B. of Scot-Irish parentage in Augusta County, Virginia, his father died in 1757, whereafter Benjamin at 14 took care of the support of his mother and five younger siblings. Under the Virginia law of primogeniture he was heir of the estate, of sizable proportions. In 1764 he was sergeant on Henry Bouquet's (see entry) expedition against the Ohio Indians, on which the first general peace since the Pontiac War was concluded. About 1771 he and his brother, John, moved to the Holston River region of Virginia-Tennessee where he raised hemp, on which there was a royal bounty. In the Point Pleasant campaign of Lord Dunmore's War of 1774, Logan served as a lieutenant of Virginia militia. In 1775 he moved to Kentucky, building Logan's Station ten miles from Boonesborough; it became one of the more famous of early Kentucky frontier posts. Logan called it St. Asaph's, and it is today's Stanford, south of Lexington. His family was brought out in 1776, and in the autumn the fort was besieged by a large body of Indians who eventually were beaten off. May 30, 1777, a war party estimated at 57 Indians attacked the post again by surprise. One of the defenders was severely wounded outside the fort as the assault commenced. "The magnanimous and intrepid Logan resolved on making an effort to save him." He could obtain no volunteers to go out with him, except one man who faltered when he saw the stiffness of the assault, leaving Logan alone in the face of the enemy. He "rushed quickly through the gate, caught the unhappy victim in his arms, and bore him triumphantly into the fort, amid a shower of bullets aimed at him; and some of which buried themselves in the pallisades close by his head." Realizing that the siege might be a long one, and that more ammunition was essential if the place be saved, Logan slipped out of the fort at night, traveled afoot almost without sleeping to the Holston settlements and returned in ten days—a most notable feat of frontier hardihood and endurance in the face of Indian hostility. Logan had many other opportunities to demonstrate his determination and heroism. In 1779 he was second in command of the John Bowman (see entry) expedition against the Ohio Indians who had been responsible for almost incessant attacks on the Kentucky frontier. In May (some reports erroneously put the expedition in July) the operation under Colonel Bowman and Captain Logan advanced upon the villages of Chillicothe; they had crossed the Ohio River at the mouth of the Licking River and approached the target settlement unobserved. The command was then split, half under Bowman, the remainder under Logan who was to circle the village for a dawn attack from either side. "Logan followed the plan and directed his men to conceal themselves...until they received the sig-

nal for the attack" which was to come from Bowman's element. No order was received. A dog barked. A warrior cautiously approached Logan's concealment and someone fired a gun; Logan's men initiated an assault and moved into the village, preparing for a final assault, when an order was received from Bowman ordering a withdrawal which "became difficult and dangerous, for the men were exposed to Indian fire. Several men were killed." Bowman had received a report, which he thought valid, of the approach of 100 reinforcing warriors under Simon Girty. The rumor was false, but the attack was nullified by the uncertainty it caused. Nine whites had been killed, others wounded, while the Indian loss was unknown. Logan had an important role in George Rogers Clark's Piqua campaign of 1780, which involved a march northward from the Ohio River to the Shawnee village at Piqua. The command numbered nearly 1,000 men and resulted in a heavy assault on the village, using artillery when feasible, on August 8, when Joseph Rogers, Clark's nephew, was among those slain. The total white loss was seventeen killed and "a number wounded," for an estimated Indian loss of six killed and three wounded. Logan missed the famous Battle of Blue Licks, Kentucky, on August 19, 1782, but he rushed up with a relief column which though too late for the action probably hastened the departure of the British-led Indians. As a representative from Kentucky, he was for three terms a member of the General Assembly of Virginia, of which Kentucky then was a part. He attended the 1792 convention which drafted Kentucky's first state constitution; he eventually was named Brigadier General of militia. He continued to be politically active during the rest of his life. He fathered eight children, one of whom, William Logan, became a U.S. Senator briefly, resigning to run for governor; he lost. Benjamin Logan was a tall, spare man with a powerful frame and was "a typical Westerner, with the faults and virtues of his race."

Thwaites, *Dunmore;* Indianapolis, *Indiana Journal,* June 29, 1833; Alexander Scott Withers, *Chronicles of Border Warfare,* Cincinnati, Robert Clarke Co., 1895, 1970; DAB.

Long, Jack, scout (b.c. 1855). A Coyotero Apache, Long was b. near the White Mountains, Arizona, and enlisted as a scout at least as early as 1875, re-enlisting thereafter for six-month terms through 1880; by 1879 he was a sergeant.

He was described on enlistment rolls as 5 ft., 4 in. in height, with black eyes, black hair and copper complexion. One of Gatewood's "favorite scouts," Long was wounded in a very hard fight with hostiles north of Janos, Mexico, October 27-28, 1879, "but killed two Chiricahuas to make up for it." This engagement was between Morrow-led troops and Victorio-Juh Apaches. Long was in fights against Victorio's hostiles on the upper Cuchillo River, New Mexico, and May 23, 1880, he had a key role in Chief of Scouts Henry K. Parker's signal victory over Victorio on the upper Palomas River, the only unqualified triumph recorded against that chief within the United States.

Dan L. Thrapp, *Victorio and the Mimbres Apaches*, Norman, Univ. of Okla. Press, 1974; Allan Radbourne to author, Oct. 12, 1972.

Long Hair (E-she-huns-ka), Crow chief (d. c. 1852). A rival of Arrapooash, or Rotten Belly, famed chief of the River Crows, Long Hair was considered by Bradley the greater of the two. After their rising jealousy led to a split in the tribe, Long Hair became chief of the larger faction, the Mountain Crows. His principal claim to notice was the extraordinary length of his hair, his principle vanity, with estimates ranging from 9 feet, 11 inches to 36 feet in extent; the painter, George Catlin, reported that the traders Sublette and Campbell assured him that "they had measured his hair by correct means, and found it to be ten feet and seven inches in length; closely inspecting every part of it at the same time, and satisfying themselves that it was the natural growth." Long Hair came into public view when at the Mandan villages on August 4, 1825, he signed the first Crow treaty with the United States, Benjamin O'Fallon and Colonel Henry Atkinson being the commissioners and Long Hair foremost of sixteen Crow chiefs and leading men to touch pen to the paper. It was principally a friendship pact, with no land cessions involved. As a young man Long Hair dreamed that he would become great in proportion to the growth of his hair, so he tied weights to it, which he assumed aided its growth and every few months separated the locks and stuck the strands together with pine gum so that "none of his hair could become lost [and] if any fell out the gum prevented it from dropping." By the age of 50 it attained its maximum length. "This cumbersome bunch of hair he rolled up into two large balls [about three feet in length each] and carried them in front of his saddle when riding. When on foot, the rolls were attached to his girdle. On great festivals he mounted on horseback, unrolled his hair, and rode slowly around the camp with his scalplocks trailing behind him on the ground." Whether his astounding hair growth truly brought him to notice is unknown, although it made his mark of fame as a chief. It was pointed out that "he also is spoken of as a brave man. He...was well liked, and died a few years" before 1856. Zenas Leonard, who wrote his manuscript no later than 1837, wrote of Long Hair that he was "quite a worthy and venerable looking old man of seventy-five or eighty years of age. He uses every possible precaution to preserve his hair, which is perfectly white, and has never had it cut since his infancy. He worships it as the director or guide of his fate through life..." Leonard's estimate of the chief's age at that early date obviously was too great, and his statement that the hair of the chief was then "perfectly white" is not supported elsewhere in any account that has come to notice. The date and circumstances of his death are not reported.

Montana, Contributions, IX, 134-35, 312-23; Edwin Thompson Denig, *Five Indian Tribes of the Upper MIssouri*, Norman, Univ. of Okla. Press, 1973, 193-94; *Adventures of Zenas Leonard: Fur Trader*, ed. by John C. Ewers, Norman, 1959; info. from E.F. (Ted) Mains.

Lord, Hugh, military officer (d. June 2, 1829). B. presumably in England, he was commissioned captain in 1762 and in 1770 was assigned to the 18th Royal Irish Regiment, then in America. He went to Illinois, probably with Lieutenant Colonel John Wilkins, whom he succeeded in command of that region in 1771. Wilkins had been very unpopular with the inhabitants, whereas Lord was much liked by them. In 1772 he directed the abandonment of Fort Chartres, near Kaskaskia in present Randolph County, because of flood damage. The garrison was removed to Kaskaskia where a house formerly belonging to Jesuit missionaries was stockaded and the redoubt named Fort Gage. Lord's withdrawal from Illinois early in May 1776 was caused no doubt by failure of the John Connolly (see entry) plot to divide the colonies. Philippe Rastel de Rocheblave (1727-1802) was left in command of Kaskaskia, although without a garrison. Lord remained at Detroit until 1777. In 1778 he became a major and was assigned to the 75th Regiment, which took no part in the American

Revolution operations. In the Napoleonic wars Lord was a major of the 7th Royal Irish Regiment, and commandant of the island of Jersey.

Thwaites/Kellogg, *The Revolution on the Upper Ohio, 1775-1777,* Madison, Wis. Hist. Soc., 1908.

Lorimier, Pierre Louis, trader (Mar. 1748-June 26, 1812). B. at Lachine, Canada, he with his father in 1769 established a trading post on the west bank of the Great Miami River, at a place named Pickawillany, in the present Shelby County, Ohio. Lorime's Creek was named for him. He became an agent and prominent interpreter for the British during the Revolution and later Indian wars. He also was active in the field with the Indians, and in 1778 was with the party that captured Daniel Boone. Raids by Shawnee and Delaware Indians under Lorimier were so effective that George Rogers Clark in 1782 rifled his post and he narrowly escaped capture, fleeing to Wapakoneta, Auglaize County, Ohio, though all his stores were lost. Thwaites said he remained in British service until 1793, but the *Dictionary of American Biography* said in 1787 he moved with a large band of Shawnees across the Mississippi River, settling near the present St. Mary, Missouri, resuming his Indian trading. Lorimier's Indians were welcomed by the Spanish, then in control of Missouri, who saw them as buffers against the Osage. Lorimier was appointed agent of Indian affairs. He settled at the site of today's Cape Girardeau and in 1808 laid out the town on his own land grants; he was appointed captain of militia and commandant for the district. After the Louisiana Purchase of 1803 Lorimier was named by the United States one of the judges of the court of common pleas. He served as interpreter for those tribes with whose language he was familiar, and while unlettered he was highly intelligent and "a man of great natural ability." He also was a "firm, brave, and successful commander, feared and respected by the Indians. His reputation for justice, both as an official and as a man, became firmly established." He was married twice, each time to a half-breed Shawnee woman; by the first he had several children. One son, who went by the name of Louis Loramier, went to West Point, was commissioned an ensign in the 1st Infantry November 14, 1806, a second lieutenant January 20, 1808, and resigned December 31, 1809, dying October 3, 1831.

Thwaites/Kellogg, *Revolution on the Upper Ohio, 1775-1777,* Madison, Wis. Hist. Soc., 1908; DAB; Heitman.

Louvigny, Louis de la Porte de (La Porte de Louvigne, Louis de), military officer (c. 1662-Aug. 27, 1725). After service for six years in the Navarre Regiment of France, Louvigny arrived in New France in 1683 and soon distinguished himself in expeditions against the Iroquois in present New York state. In 1689 Frontenac (see entry), who had been returned to Canada to stiffen its frontier defenses, sent Louvigny to Michilikmackinac with 170 men to reinforce that post and relieve the commandant, Olivier Morel de la Durantaye (see entry), ostensibly to prevent the Ottawas from cooperating with the Iroquois or, as some suspected, to expand fur trading operations at that distant post. It also was charged that Louvigny had won the assignment because of bribery of Frontenac's secretary. Nevertheless, "Louvigny turned out to be an able commandant." He was relieved in 1694 to return to France to attend to personal business, but November 7, 1699, by now a captain, he was named to command Fort Frontenac at the site of today's Kingston, Ontario, at the source of the St. Lawrence River from Lake Ontario. There he and his garrison spent the winter pursuing the fur trade, for which he was arrested for violating an edict against such pursuits at western military posts and narrowly escaped a court-martial. He was returned to France to let the King decide his fate, but his punishment was slight and before long he was named town major of Quebec. He was influential among the Iroquois, no doubt because of his trading experience with them, and when Ottawas in 1705 attacked a Seneca hunting party, carrying off prisoners to Michilimackinac, Louvigny was ordered to go to that post, free the prisoners, and bring the Ottawas back to Montreal to meet with the Senecas. His mission was successful, he was honored and chosen to command once again at Michilimackinac which was reestablished in 1712 after having been closed down for several years. In 1716 Louvigny commanded an expedition to subdue the Fox Indians of Wisconsin. The Fox stronghold at Green Bay was taken, the enemy sued for peace, and Louvigny was financially rewarded for fine work. He had become an important and influential man in New France and in 1720 the position of commander-in-chief of the upper country was created for him. In 1724 he returned to France, was named governor of Three Rivers, but the vessel upon which he was returning to Canada struck a reef off Cape Breton and sank with all on board lost. He left his widow and four surviving children.

DCB, II; Parkman, *Count Frontenac and New France, A Half Century of Conflict,* I.

Lovewell, John, frontiersman (Oct. 14, 1691-May 8, 1725). B. in a part of Dunstable, Massachusetts, that is today Nashua, New Hampshire, his father of the same name had fought under Benjamin Church (see entry) in the climactic Great Swamp Fight of King Philip's War, December 19, 1675. Lovewell Jr. acquired a 200-acre farm, a wife and two children. The town was attacked by hostile Indians c. 1724. A pursuit company was ambushed and only a few men escaped, among them Josiah Farwell, Lovewell's brother-in-law. Lovewell and others petitioned the Massachusetts government for a commission "to kill and destroy their enemy Indians." The General Court granted them two and one-half shillings a day payment plus a bounty for male Indian scalps. In the first excursion Lovewell led thirty men north of Winnepisawkee Lake where on December 10, 1724, they came upon a lone wigwam in which were a man and a boy; they killed and scalped the man and brought the boy to Boston, for what fate was not reported. Taking 70 men, Lovewell again visited the wigwam where the body of the slain Indian still lay. Because of lack of provisions Lovewell sent 30 men home and with the remaining 40 pushed on through snow until on February 20, 1725, they struck a fresh trail and following up, discerned just at sunset Indian campfire smoke. They crept to the encampment after midnight on February 21, surrounded the ten sleeping Pequawket Indians they found and killed nine outright, wounding the tenth, who was caught up with by a dog while trying to escape and was also dispatched. The war party, apparently coming down from Canada, had been equipped with new guns, plenty of ammunition and other supplies, all of which was seized as war booty. By February 24, Lovewell and his men reached Dover with "ten scalps stretched on hoops and elevated on poles," after which they went to Boston where they were paid 1,000 pounds sterling in bounties while the muskets, of fine quality, brought 7 pounds each. On April 16, 1725, Lovewell left Dunstable with 46 men on his final adventure. In the party were Farwell as lieutenant, Benjamin

Hassell (see entry), a cousin of Lovewell's and, as sergeant, Noah Johnson. The expedition made for the community of the Pequawkets on the headwaters of the Saco River at the site of today's Fryeburg, Maine. At Lake Ossipee he constructed a simple fort and garrisoned it lightly. With a reduced party of 34 men on May 8 he crossed the Saco just above Lovewell's Pond where they saw a motionless Indian watching them. Suspecting an ambush, Lovewell asked his men whether they wanted to advance or to call it a day; they urged him on. They mortally wounded the Indian "who notwithstanding returned the fire, and wounded Capt. Lovewell in the belly. Upon which Mr. [Ensign Seth] Wyman fired and killed him." Two bands of Pequawkets meanwhile had come upon the white trail, followed it and seized the packs the colonial party had left before going into action. When after slaying the Indian they started back; they found their packs missing, and here the Pequawkets assailed them. Lovewell was killed, Farwell and Jonathan Robbins were wounded as were eight more whites, while Hassell in a panic fled back to safety and into ignominy for his overwhelming prudence. All others remained to fight. The struggle continued through the afternoon, with both sides suffering heavily. The Indian sachem, Paugus, whom many of Lovewell's party knew well, was among those killed, shot it was said by either Wyman or John Chamberlain. Of the 34 whites, nine were unwounded or only slightly hurt, 11 badly wounded, the remainder killed outright or mortally shot. Chaplain Jonathan Frye, Robbins and Farwell, all wounded, were left to "perish of wounds, exposure, and starvation somewhere in the Saco woods." The bodies of Lovewell, Robbins and the others who could be found were buried, where they were discovered by a relief expedition sent out from Dunstable. The battle itself became famed in border annals; ballads were written about it and about Lovewell, and the memory endures to this day. Fryeburg, Maine, incidentally, was named not for the chaplain, but for his father's cousin, General Joseph Frye, original grantee of the land on which it is situated.

Sylvester, III; Samuel Penhallow, *History of the Indian Wars,* 1726 (Williamstown, Mass., Corner House Pubs., 1973); Hodge, HAI (under Pequawket); DAB; Parkman *Half Century of Conflict,* I; info. from E.F. (Ted) Mains.

Lowe, Percival Greene, soldier (Sept. 29, 1828-

Mar. 5, 1908). B. at Randolph, New Hampshire, he became a sailor in coastal shipping for two years, then went into the daguerreotype (early photography) business and in 1849 shipped on a whaler for a brief deep sea experience in the middle Atlantic and Caribbean. October 17, 1849, he enlisted for five years in the 1st U.S. Dragoons, being mustered out in the summer 1854 as first sergeant. During his service he met nearly sixty officers who became Generals in either the Union or Confederate service during the Civil War or later. Lowe wrote that he "kept an accurate journal of some of the campaigns" in which he took part, and this is reflected in his *Five Years a Dragoon...And Other Adventures on the Great Plains.* It was considered by Don Russell, its editor in a later appearance, as unusual "because it was written by an enlisted man of the Regular Army during a time of peace—disturbed only by those police actions we call Indian wars," and describes a period between the Mexican and Civil wars which "marked the beginning of more than half a century of almost continuous Indian warfare." During Lowe's enlistment his regiment (though not necessarily his company) became involved in sixteen Indian fights. He participated in long, frequently tedious marches during which he "saw the Santa Fe Trail and the Oregon Trail in their days of heaviest wagon traffic," while the posts he knew included Forts Leavenworth, Riley, Laramie, Union and Kearny, each acquiring lasting fame and some longevity. During his army and civilian career Lowe met such noted white frontiersmen as Jim Bridger, Tom Fitzpatrick, Andrew Drips, William Bent, Lucien Maxwell, Kit Carson, Francis X. Aubrey, John M. Hockaday and Frank Grouard, among others, and the noted Indians Spotted Tail, Man-Afraid-of-His-Horses, Satanta or perhaps Satank of the Kiowas, and Fall Leaf, a Delaware Indian and onetime guide for Fremont and the scout some consider the discoverer of Pike's Peak gold. Following his enlistment he served as civilian with the Quartermaster department for five years. In 1855 he was master of transportation of an expedition sent to construct Fort Riley, Kansas, and "there he survived one of the worst cholera epidemics ever to strike an army post." The following year he was in charge of transporting supplies for troops assigned to quell Kansas disorders; in 1857 he was in charge of transportation for Colonel Edwin Vose Sumner's Cheyenne campaign and in 1858 was in charge of wagon trains

for the Utah Expedition. He joined the Pike's Peak gold rush in 1859 and settled then at Denver where he engaged in business from 1860. He turned down a commission as a lieutenant colonel of Colorado Volunteers during the Civil War, because he didn't think the conflict would last long, although he continued contracting to freight supplies for the armed services. He moved after the war to Leavenworth, where he held civic offices, was police commissioner, then sheriff, and served as a state senator. He died at San Antonio, Texas, and was buried in the military cemetery at Leavenworth. One of his three brothers was Thaddeus Sobieski Constantine Lowe, who became a balloonist and headed the army's initial air reconnaissance element during the Civil War, after which he built an electric railway from his home at Pasadena, California, to the summit of nearly Mount Lowe, 5,593 feet, three miles west of Mount Wilson. A son, Percival Greene Lowe Jr. (see entry), served well in exploration work under Abercrombie in Alaska.

Lowe, *Five Years a Dragoon,* Norman, Univ. of Okla. Press, 1965 (first ed. pub. in 1906); *Narratives of Explorations in Alaska.*

Lowe, Percival Greene Jr., military officer (Nov. 18, 1863-May 9, 1910). The younger son of Percival Greene Lowe (1828-1908), author of *Five Years a Dragoon,* he was b. at Fort Leavenworth, Kansas, and educated at Pennsylvania Military College as a civil engineer. He enlisted in B Company, 18th Infantry September 29, 1885, becoming a sergeant before being commissioned a second lieutenant in the same regiment February 11, 1889. He became a first lieutenant of the 4th Infantry April 22, 1896, and transferred back to the 18th May 24, 1897. In 1898 he was a member of the Alaska exploratory party of Captain William R. Abercrombie (see entry). After many adversities, there remained by June 30 only two officers with the expedition, wrote Abercrombie, Lowe and himself, "but as Lieutenant Lowe is a man to be killed but not conquered, no alarm was felt." The purpose of the expedition was to explore thoroughly and chart routes for possible military roads from Valdez, Alaska, at the head of Prince William Sound, into the rugged Copper River country which Abercrombie first explored in 1884. From the river it was hoped that a route could be developed, or at least laid out, entirely on American (as distinct from Canadian) soil from the Copper River to Eagle on the Yukon northwest of Dawson, the route traversed today by the Copper River-Taylor highways. With eleven pack ponies, three mules and some extra horses, Lowe and his small detachment crossed the perilous Valdez glacier in early July and arrived at Klutina Lake, then followed its outlet, the Klutina River, downstream to Twelve Mile, being that distance below the lake; the party reached Copper Center July 31. August 6, the Sanford River, "one of the worst streams of the Copper River country," was attained and on August 21, Lowe arrived at the Slahna (Slana) River, going on to Mentasta Creek. August 26, the summit of Meiklejohn (Mentasta) Pass was crossed, opening to full view "the great Tanana Valley." Following down the Tetlin River, Lowe reached the Tanana itself. "Our objective now was the Yukon," he reported. "We entered a country that, up to that time, had not been mapped from actual observation. All the information obtained in relation to it was gotten from Indians." On September 5, Dennisons Fork of Forty-Mile River was reached with the mountains around them getting higher, and by September 11, Lowe believed he had arrived at Walkers Fork, but couldn't be sure. September 12, "I determined to make a break for Forty Mile [River] and after several days reached Millers Creek," following that until September 19. Most of the later progress was over Canadian territory. Lowe re-entered United States territory briefly at Moose Creek, and "I rigged a small pole and hoisted the American flag for the first time." The mouth of Moose Creek on Forty-Mile River was 26 miles from the Yukon River. He left his worn out horses with a member of the expedition to care for over the winter, on September 21, purchased a boat and the expedition "went down the [Forty-Mile] river, the first 3 miles being on American soil. We lined down one rapid, shot another, and landed at [the community of] Forty Mile six hours after starting." Lowe had not quite reached his objective, Eagle on the Yukon, but he had come within forty miles of it and had proven that the way for an "All-American" road from Valdez and the Copper River by way of the Tanana to Eagle was feasible. The route would be ultimately followed by paved highways. Lowe found that "Forty Mile is a large cabin village, with a trading store and warehouse, and is on the right bank of [Forty-Mile] river where it empties into the Yukon." It was too late to catch the last steamer for Fort Michael, so the expedition had to work up the great river, attempting to reach the Alaskan Panhandle to the south. The party took commercial boats to Dawson, arriving September 26, passed Fort Selkirk October 1, and by way of Whitehorse reached Bennett Lake and White Pass on October 18, proceeding by a 20-mile hike and the railway to Skagway. Ordered to the Philippines from Alaska, Lowe organized the first Philippine Scouts (which became known as Lowe's Scouts). Once when returning from Manila to San Fernando on a train laden with provisions and ammunition, the train was wrecked by natives believing it was a pay train. Lowe "by quick and courageous work saved the train after a hard fight," though four passengers were killed and others wounded. Lowe became a captain of the 25th Infantry June 8, 1899. He was retired for disability in line of duty September 23, 1903. He died at Colgate, Oklahoma, from meningitis and was buried at Fort Leavenworth. He was not married.

Lowe, "From Valdez Inlet to Belle Isle, on the Yukon," *Narratives of Explorations in Alaska;* Heitman; *Army and Navy Journal,* May 21, 1910; info. from the U.S. Army Military Hist. Inst., Carlisle Barracks, Penn.

Lowie, Robert Harry, ethnologist (June 12, 1883-Sept. 21, 1957). B. at Vienna, Austria, he was brought to the United States at 10 and graduated Phi Beta Kappa from the College of the City of New York in 1901, receiving his doctorate from Columbia in 1908, having come under the influence of anthropologist Franz Boas (see entry). From 1908 until 1921 he was associated with the American Museum of Natural History of New York City in its department of anthropology. He was associate curator from 1913 to 1921, following which he spent thirty years on the faculty of the University of California at Berkeley. He was a full professor from 1925 to 1950. Lowie undertook field expeditions: to the northern Plains tribes, from 1906-14, 1916 and 1931; to Lake Athabaska in 1908; to the plateau tribes, 1914-15, and to the Hopi of the southwest in 1915 and 1916. He belonged to many professional organizations and was president of the American Ethnological Society in 1920-21. Lowie is probably best known in a frontier sense for his *The Crow Indians* (1935, 1956), but he was a very prolific writer, his bibliography including nearly 500 books, monographs, articles and reviews. His monographs included *The Assiniboines* (1909); *Social Life of the Crow Indians* (1912); *Societies of the Crow, Hidatsa and Man-*

dan Indians (1913); *The Sun Dance of the Crow Indians* (1915); *The Age-Societies of the Plains Indians* (1916); *Myths and Traditions of the Crow Indians* (1918); *Notes on Shoshonean Ethnography* (1924) and *Shoshonean Tales* (1924). Among his books were *Culture and Ethnology* (1917); *Primitive Society* (1920); *Primitive Religion* (1924); *The Origin of the State* (1927); *Are We Civilized?* (1929); *Introduction to Cultural Anthropology* (1934); *The History of Ethnological Theory* (1937), and *Indians of the Plains* (1954). He lived at Berkeley in his retirement and was buried there. Lowie was married to Luella W. Cole in 1933.

*Who Was Who; * Paul Radin, "Robert H. Lowie, 1883-1957," *American Anthropologist,* Vol. 60, No. 2 (1958).

Lukin, Ivan Semenovich (Ivan Simonsen Lukeen), explorer (1823-post 1868). A son of Semen Lukin (see entry), Ivan was three-quarters native. He was a well-traveled explorer and trader in the interior of Alaska and Zagoskin in 1842-44 made good use of him. As an employee of the Russian American Company, he is believed to have made the first journey from St. Michael on Norton Sound, Alaska, up the Yukon River to Fort Yukon at the confluence of the Yukon and Porcupine rivers. He did this in the summer of 1863, but the information was not made public. The editor of Zagoskin said that in 1868 he made what apparently was a second journey, this time to Dawson, or Fort Dawson in Yukon Territory of Canada. He may have been the Ioann (Ivan) Lukin who died on the Yukon March 22, 1886.

Narratives of Explorations in Alaska, 19; Zagoskin; Pierce, *Russian America: A Biographical Dictionary.*

Lukin, Semen Ivanovich, trader, explorer (c. 1800-May 11, 1855). A Creole, son of a Russian and a native American mother, his father was killed in 1805 at Yakutat Bay, Alaska, by the Tlingit Indians and Semen was brought to Kodiak Island and raised in the family of Baranov, chief manager of the Russian American Company. A literate man, versed in several Alaskan languages, he accompanied Vasilev in 1819 when Aleksandrovskiy Redoubt was built at the mouth of the Nushagak River, the most important of Russian western trading stations in Alaska to that time. Lukin served primarily as interpreter at the post, as he had been with Vasilev. In 1832 with the veteran frontiersman Fedor Kolmakov he

established a trading post on the middle Kuskokwim River, relocated in 1832 to the confluence of the Kuskokwim and Kolmakov rivers east of Aniak where the post was named the Kolmakov Redoubt, Lukin becoming the manager. "During his extensive trading expeditions, Lukin explored much of interior southwestern Alaska." He was of considerable assistance to the important explorer Zagoskin during the latter's expedition to interior Alaska and the Yukon valley in 1842-44, and Zagoskin came to admire and depend upon Lukin. Of him Zagoskin wrote: "We have often seen a dozen natives in his little room who will wait silently for days at a time until he returns from his work in the woods or at the fish-trap. If guests arrive at mealtime, the piece of *yukola* [dried fish, usually salmon] and the teapot...are divided among those present. As he knows their customs well, he never asks who a visitor is or for what purpose he has come...Lukin is as available by night as by day; the visitor taps at the window and then enters freely." The natives about Fort Kolmakov called him *tyatya,* which Zagoskin wrote was the Russian for "daddy," in return for his "shining the light of Christianity upon them, for ending quarrels between them," and for other kindly services to them. Was such a man, Zagoskin added, "not worthy of our greatest respect?" Lukin was not always a mild character, however. On one occasion when obstreperous natives threatened his establishment he threw the ringleader out of the window, whereupon the others fled. Lukin, a devout Christian, spent each Sunday, a day of rest, in reading the Scriptures, but he was not a sedentary man. He spent much time exploring all the tributaries of the Kuskokwim and other streams within reach, although he was careful not to venture into regions controlled by hostile or untrustworthy natives if he could avoid it. He was married to a native woman and had at least two children. The circumstances of his death are not reported.

Zagoskin; James W. VanStone, ed., *Russian Exploration in Southwest Alaska: The Travel Journals of Petr Korsakovskiy (1818) and Ivan Ya. Vasilev (1829),* Fairbanks, Univ. of Ak. Press, 1988; Bancroft, *Alaska.*

Lutke, Feodor Petrovich, Russian naval officer (1797-1882). Lutke circumnavigated the world aboard the sloop *Kamchatka* from 1817 to 1819 and in the fall of 1818 put in at New Arkhangel (Sitka), Alaska, and then visited the California coast, stopping first by the Russian Ross colony north of San Francisco. Here he met Ivan A. Kuskov (see entry) and while Lutke could not come ashore, was supplied with fresh foodstuffs by Kuskov and wrote in his diary, "It is unnecessary to add that they took no payment" for the provisions. Lutke made some general geographical observations about Ross as well as the site, with which he was not favorably impressed. The *Kamchatka* then sailed for Monterey, a Spanish base south of San Francisco. Lutke's ship joined the *Kutuzov*, under Hagemeister (see entry), and together they put in to Monterey Bay September 8. Lutke again had interesting notes on the Spanish officialdom and port and environs of Monterey. He and others went on horseback to San Carlos Mission at Carmel, where Father Juan Amoros "received us very cordially," their interpreter being an Irish deserter from an American ship who had acquired some status at the mission. Lutke had much to write of the mission—its construction, treatment of the Indians, the daily lives of missionaries and subjects, and appears to have been an objective witness. He also described the presidio of Monterey, which he considered ineffective at best. "Sitka is a Gibraltar compared to Monterey," he wrote. The Spanish would not permit Russians to enter the fort, but that made little difference, Lutke wrote, "since the entire fort could easily be seen from the ship." He noted that California officially carred on no trade with anyone but Spanish vessels, or "at least it is not supposed to," although such trade was too beneficial for both the Spanish ashore and the carriers at sea to be completely ignored. The *Kamchatka* returned to Bodega Bay and contacted Kuskov again at the Ross settlement. While in the vicinity Lutke jotted down observations on the local Indians. His comments are interesting, though they would have been more so had he had an able interpreter. Lutke's comments on the geographical situation of the Ross settlement and its harbor, "Little Bodega Bay," called Rumiantsev by the Russians, are useful. He also digresses on Kuskov and Russian-Spanish relations in the time of which he wrote and earlier. September 28, the *Kamchatka* set sail and quitted the California coast. In 1826 Lutke, commanding the corvette *Seniavine* left Kronstadt in company with the sloop *Moller,* Captain M.N. Staniukovich, on another round-the-world voyage which lasted until 1829. He reached Sitka June 24, 1827. July 31, he left for Unalaska Island, arriving August 22, and remaining eight days. He went then to the Pribylov Islands and proceeded to Kamchatka enroute back to Russia. In 1835 an account of this voyage was published at St. Petersburg; it includes an atlas and a separate volume called "Nautical Part." "This work contains hydrographic and geographic information...and is considered to be an important reference in the evolution of our geographic knowledge in Alaska," wrote Orth. Lutke named many features on the north side of the Alaska Peninsula. Cape Lutke on the south coast of Unimak Island commemorates him.

The Russian American Colonies; Orth, 19, 605.

Lyon, King, stage driver (b. c.1836) B. in New York State, Lyon was listed as 24 years old in the 1860 U.S. Census of Arizona, by then having become a stagecoach driver indicating considerable frontier experience, for that was not an occupation for a novice. He was employed on the Tucson-Mesilla leg of the Butterfield Overland Stage line. Driving a coach from Dragoon Springs to Apache Pass on February 6, 1861, the vehicle had just entered the latter defile when it was ambushed by Chiricahua Apaches, possibly under Cochise, and Lyon was wounded, his leg, by some reports, broken by the bullet. He toppled to the ground but line superintendent William Buckley leaped to his assistance, wrestling him into the vehicle, Lyon being taken on to the Apache Pass stage station. From that point his story becomes exceedingly misty. On February 8, a detachment of soldiers and civilians herded mules to Apache Springs for watering. The party was attacked by an estimated 70 Indians who succeeded in driving off virtually all of the stock, and the *Mesilla* (New Mexico) *Times* reported that "Moses Lyon, one of the party and in the employ of the Overland Mail Company..., was shot dead and a soldier wounded..." in the affair. No other reference to a "Moses" Lyon has surfaced, and if the victim was a mistaken identification for "King" Lyon his original wound must have been less serious than earlier believed. One knowledgeable source suggested that Moses Lyon may have been King Lyon's brother, but documentation is lacking to support that view. It may be significant however that nothing further on King Lyon is found anywhere in the literature of this well-publicized affair. A man named Lyons who was reportedly captured with one, Jordan, by Cochise from a wagon train earlier was not only of different surname, but obviously was another individual. The timing and manner of demise of King Lyon have not been definitely established.

U.S. Census for Arizona, 1860, p. 43; Edwin R. Sweeney, *Cochise: Chiricahua Apache Chief,* Norman, Univ. of Okla. Press, 1991; info. from Sweeney; Robert M. Utley, "The Bascom Affair: A Reconstruction," *Arizona and the West,* Vol. 3, No. 1 (Spring 1961), 59-68; Benjamin H. Sacks, "New Evidence on the Bascom Affair,." *AW,* Vol. 4, No. 3 (Autumn 1962) 261-76; Office of Indian Affairs, Microcopy 234, Letters Received, Roll 550, N.M. Superintendency, C984, Tully to Collins, Feb. 17, 1861.

Lyon, Nathaniel, military officer (July 14, 1818-Aug. 10, 1861). B. at Ashford, Connecticut, he went to West Point from which he graduated 11th in his class of 52 and was commissioned a second lieutenant of the 2nd Infantry July 1, 1841. He served in Florida during the Second Seminole War (1835-42). Lyon was a very able officer, of quick intelligence and quick temper, though characterized as "contentious, tyrannical," by Utley. During the Mexican War he distinguished himself at the battles of Veracruz, Cerro Gordo, Contreras and Churubusco and became a first lieutenant February 16, 1847. In September 1849 Pit River Indians in California killed Captain William Warner (see entry) and in the spring and summer of 1850 General Persifor Smith (see entry) sent Lyon with a force of dragoons and infantry against tribesmen believed to be hostile, or bordering on that status. Lyon led his expedition first to Clear Lake, 50 miles north of San Francisco; some 400 Indians took refuge on an island and, crossing to it with his force by boat, Lyon drove the Indians into a tule swamp and slaughtered between 60 and 100, though how many were males was not reported. Lyon then crossed a divide to the Russian River and located another 400 natives on another island which the troops made "a perfect slaughter pen," slaying between 75 and 150; white losses, if any, were not stated. In July, Lyon led one more expedition, this time against the Pit River Indians themselves, the results inconclusive. He became a captain June 11, 1851. He was stationed at Fort Riley, Kansas, "in the middle of the murderous political climate of 'bleeding Kansas,'" where the pro-slavery excesses he witnessed turned him into a "furious" opponent of that institution. In 1861 he was transferred to St. Louis where on May 17, he became a Brigadier General of U.S. Volunteers; here he defied pro-Confederate Governor Clai-

borne F. Jackson, thwarting his supposed intent to seize the important St. Louis Arsenal. Lyon captured the official's militia and paraded the prisoners through turbulent St. Louis. His action may have been ill-timed, and assuredly was hotheaded, but it saved the arsenal and probably Missouri for the Union, although it precipitated civil hostilities within that state. At the initial important battle, at Wilson's Creek, Lyon was killed, "impetuously trying to lead a last charge" against his Confederate opponents. He was granted posthumously the thanks of Congress for his actions at Wilson's Creek.

Heitman; *Who Was Who;* DAB; Robert M. Utley, *Frontiersmen in Blue,* N.Y., The Macmillan Co., 1967; Patricia L. Faust, ed., *Historical Times Encyclopedia of the Civil War,* N.Y., Harper & Row, 1986.

Lytle, John T., cattleman (Oct. 8, 1844-Jan. 10, 1907). B. at McSherrystown, Pennsylvania, he went to Texas in 1860 with his father's family and settled at San Antonio. Then 16, he worked on the ranch of his uncle, William Lytle, 15 miles southeast of town. In 1863 he enlisted in Company H, 32nd Texas Cavalry and served in the trans-Mississippi department until the end of the Civil War. He returned to work two years on his uncle's ranch, then decided to go into business for himself and ranched in Frio County until 1873. For about fifteen years he "directed the movement" of about 450,000 Longhorns in customary trail herds rarely numbering more than 3,000 head in each, they being delivered to Kansas, Colorado, Montana and elsewhere. Of course he did not accompany trail herds himself, but acted as broker between Texas cattlemen and stock purchasers in the north, and during this time "he directed investments in livestock aggregating $9 million, a record never before equalled." He spent the fall and winter traveling over Texas, lining up prospective sales, then in the spring rode north to arrange for cattle transfers, then rode south to meet the herds moving northward to finalize arrangements. In 1875 he sold his Frio ranch holdings and leased pastures in Frio and Maverick counties, raising stock himself in addition to his trail operations. In this business he had as partners at various times John W. Light, T.M. McDaniel and Charles Schreiner. With others at one time he invested in 500,000 acres in Coahuila, Mexico. In 1879 Lytle moved to a ranch in Medina County, 25 miles south of San Antonio and in 1904 moved to Fort Worth. He died at San Antonio. The town of Lytle in

Atascosa County was named either for him, according to the *Trail Drivers of Texas,* or for his uncle, William Lytle, as reported by the *Handbook of Texas.*

Hunter TDT; HT, Supplement; REAW; info. from E.F. (Ted) Mains.

Mc

McAfee brothers, frontiersmen (fl. 1773-1814). The five brothers who lived with their families on Sinking Creek, Botetourt County, Virginia, were James, Robert, George, William and Samuel. James, Robert and George, together with James McConn Jr., and Samuel Adams, then 18, explored Kentucky in 1773 with Bullitt and Hancock Taylor (see entries). At one time they nearly perished of starvation and suffered numerous other hardships, returning home by way of Powell's Valley and the Clinch River The trio, together with William and Samuel McAfee and others, returned to Kentucky in 1775. Two of them, unnamed, joined Henderson's Transylvania party but with the failure of that endeavor returned to Virginia. In 1779 the final emigration of the McAfee families and the two brothers who had returned east was made, the five establishing McAfee's Station on Salt River, Mercer County, six miles below Harrodsburg. In 1781 it sustained a sharp Indian attack, the enemy driven off. William McAfee had been killed in George Rogers Clark's Piqua, Ohio, campaign of August 1780; Robert went to New Orleans with produce in 1795 and there was slain by a Spaniard who tried to rob him; Samuel died in 1801, George died on his Salt River farm in 1803, and James lived until 1814.

Thwaites, *Dunmore.*

McBeath, George, fur trader (c. 1740-Dec. 3, 1812). B. in Scotland, he reached Canada shortly after 1763 and in 1765 entered the fur trade, going on his initial trading expedition that year and in subsequent years annually fitting out canoes which he took to Lake Superior and adjoining regions. From 1772 he worked out of Michilimackinac and joined a company sending annual trade canoes to Grand Portage, Minnesota, and Lake Winnipeg. In 1776 he went into partnership with Simon McTavish (see entry) and in 1779 entered the North West Company, a growing fur trade monopoly which became the strongest rival of the Hudson's Bay Company. McBeath continued his association with it, but also engaged in independent fur dealings that proved profitable enough so that he pushed them

vigorously. At length however his fortunes commenced to falter and in 1792 he disposed of the last of his shares in the NWC and retired from the fur trade altogether, thereafter holding political and civil offices in Canada. He was "quite an important figure in the fur trade," but never aspired to control any segment of it. As a founder of the North West Company, his operations had been concentrated largely in Wisconsin. In 1783 he accompanied Charles de Langlade to Prairie du Chien, Wisconsin, to hold a conference with the northern Indians and announce to them the Peace of Paris which terminated the American Revolutionary War and the hostilities between the United States and England in which they had been involved. McBeath died at Montreal.

Thwaites/Kellogg, *The Revolution on the Upper Ohio, 1775-1777,* Madison, Wis. Hist. Soc., 1908; DCB V.

McClure, Robert John Le Mesurier, British naval officer (Jan. 28, 1807-Oct. 17, 1873). B. at Wexford, Ireland, he was educated at Eton and Sandhurst and entered the navy in 1824. He made his initial voyage to the eastern Arctic in 1836, served on the Great Lakes and in the West Indies until 1846 and in 1848-49 under Ross participated in the first search for John Franklin as a first lieutenant on the *Enterprise.* On the second Franklin search, this time from the Pacific, McClure commanded the *Investigator* sailing in company with Captain Richard Collinson and the *Enterprise.* McClure rounded Point Barrow, Alaska, northernmost land of the North American continent, continued eastward through Prince of Wales Strait and into Melville Sound, where ice blocked him. In September 1851 his ship was caught in the pack off Banks Island. McClure climbed to the island's highest point from where he could see Melville Island across what is today's McClure's Strait; beyond lay Melville Sound, and McClure thus had seen, although not navigated, the Northwest Passage sought for so long, the search bringing tragedy to so many. The following year the crew abandoned the *Investigator* as lost, and sledged across the ice to join the *Resolute* at Dealy Island, just south of Melville Island. He reached England in 1854, was knighted, won gold medals, was promoted to captain and eventually to Vice Admiral. He died at London.

Pierce, *Russian America: A Biographical Dictionary.*

McColloch, Samuel, frontiersman (1750-July 30, 1782). McColloch was described by Thwaites as "a noted borderer," who about 1770 came from the south branch of the Potomac to Short Creek, West Virginia. In the fall of 1777, while moving to the relief of Fort Henry (Wheeling), West Virginia, then being besieged, he was set upon by Indians and escaped by jumping his horse down a precipice said to be 200 feet high. In 1779 although a representative from Ohio County, West Virginia, to the Virginia legislature, he was on the Daniel Brodhead campaign up the Allegheny River. McColloch was in charge of Van Meter's Fort on Short Creek in Brooke County, West Virginia, where he was wounded mortally by Indians near that place.

Thwaites/Kellogg, *The Revolution on the Upper Ohio*, 1775-1777, Madison, Wis. Hist. Soc., 1908.

McCormick, Alexander, trader (d. 1803). An Irishman, he had been a trader at Fort Pitt and in the Indian country for "some time" before the Revolution. In 1777 he had a trading house at Half King's village near Upper Sandusky, Ohio. He became friendly with the Moravian missionaries, "on several occasions protecting them from insult and injury." In 1780 McCormick took part in the expedition of Henry Bird (see entry) to Kentucky. About 1785 he married Elizabeth Turner, an Indian captive; they settled below the rapids of the Maumee River on the ground where Anthony Wayne's battle of Fallen Timbers was fought. "Possessed of a humane temperament [McCormick] rescued many captives from the Indians," and his place on the Maumee became a well-known trading site. Following the Fallen Timbers engagement, McCormick moved to western Ontario, dying eventually at Colchester. He fathered children, Lyman Draper interviewing a son in 1863.

Louise Phelps Kellogg, *Frontier Advance on the Upper Ohio, 1778-1779*, Madison, Wis. Hist. Soc., 1916.

McCracken, Harold, explorer, writer (Aug. 31, 1894-Mar. 16. 1983). B. at Colorado Springs, he was educated at Drake University, Des Moines,

Iowa, and Ohio State University until 1915, and was awarded several honorary doctorates. He was an ornithological collector for Iowa State University in 1912, and leader of an Ohio State expedition to Alaska in 1915-17. He served as an enlisted man in the photographic section of the Signal Corps and on special duty with the intelligence and avaiation research divisions at Columbia University during World War I. McCracken mined in Alaska from 1919-20 and led an Ohio State Museum's photo-scientific expedition for study of the Alaskan brown bear and other big game from 1922-23, winnning recognition as an authority on the brown bear. In 1928 he was co-leader of an American Museum of Natural History expedition for archeological research in the Aleutian Islands; mummified bodies of Stone Age natives were discovered and an Arctic walrus group collected for the museum's Hall of Ocean Life. From 1958-74 McCracken was director of the Buffalo Bill Historical Center and the Whitney Gallery of Western Art at Cody, Wyoming, becoming director emeritus in 1974. He was survived by his widow, a son and a daughter. McCracken wrote 31 books, including nonfiction and fiction and a number of them juvenile-oriented. His adult nonfiction included: *God's Frozen Children* (1930); *Alaska Bear Trails* (1931); with Harry Van Cleve, *Trapping: The Craft and Science of Catching Fur-Bearing Animals* (1947); *Frederic Remington, Artist of the Old West* (1947); *Toughy, Bulldog in the Arctic* (1948); *Portrait of the Old West* (1952); *The Beast That Walks Like Man: The Story of the Grizzly Bear* (1955); *The Charles M. Russell Book: The Life and Work of the Cowboy Artist* (1957); *Hunters of the Stormy Sea* (1957); *George Catlin and the Old Frontier* (1959); *The Frederic Remington Book: A Pictorial History of the West* (1966); *Roughnecks and Gentlemen,* an autobiography (1968); *The American Cowboy* (1973); *The Frank Tenney Johnson Book: A Master Painter of the Old West* (1974), and *The Mummy Cave Project in Northwestern Wyoming* (1978). McCracken died at Cody and was buried at Columbus, Ohio.

CA; *Who Was Who;* info. from Peter H. Hassrick, Buffalo Bill Hist. Center; McCracken death cert.

McCrea, Joel, actor (Nov. 5, 1905-Oct. 20, 1990). B. in South Pasadena, California, he was grandson on his father's side of a stagecoach driver and on his mother's side of a participant in the California Gold Rush. He was educated at

Pomona College, turned to acting at 23 and became a featured player at 24 in *The Silver Horde*. He appeared in 80 movies, many of them westerns such as *Wells Fargo* (1937), *Union Pacific* (1939), *The Virginian* (1946) and *Ride the High Country* (1962), but he was versatile enough to perform in a wide range of motion pictures. With his first paycheck he commenced buying ranch land and eventually owned large working spreads near Camarillo and Shandon, both north of Los Angeles; he became a millionaire through such activities and listed his profession as "ranching," and acting as his "hobby." He was a devoted fan of William S. Hart, early cowboy actor, and a friend of Will Rogers and William Randolph Hearst. He died at Woodland Hills, California at 84, leaving his widow, Frances Dee, to whom he had been married for 57 years, and three sons.

New York Times, Oct. 21, 1990.

McCulloch, Henry Eustace, Ranger, military officer (Dec. 6, 1816-Mar. 12, 1895). B. in Rutherford County, Tennessee, he was a brother of Ben McCulloch (see entry), accompanying Ben to Texas in 1835 but returning shortly to Tennessee. He went back to Texas, now independent, in 1838. The next year he joined a company under Captain Mathew Caldwell for Indian operations and in the Plum Creek Fight of August 12, 1840, near the present Lockhart, Henry McCulloch "showed exceptional bravery" against a large band of Comanche Indians. He later served as first lieutenant in Jack Hays's (see entry) Texas Rangers and took part in the engagement at Salado near San Antonio September 18, against Mexican General Adrian Woll (see entry), which resulted in a reverse for the Mexicans who suffered about 60 killed, for 36 dead and about 15 captured in Texas losses. In 1843 McCulloch was elected sheriff at Gonzales, later settling at Seguin. During the Mexican War he operated against Indians and in 1850 became captain of a Ranger company to protect San Antonio from Indian attacks from the west. He served as state representative and later as state senator and in 1859 became U.S. marshal for eastern Texas. He was commissioned colonel in the Confederate Army in 1861 and became Brigadier General the following year, most of his Civil War service in north Texas. He died at Seguin. McCulloch was married.

HT; John Henry Brown, "Gen. Ben McCulloch— His Indian Fighting Days," *Frontier Times,* Vol. 52, No. 6 (Oct.-Nov. 1978), 23, 44-46.

McDonald, Angus, frontiersman (c. 1727-1779). A Scot Highlander of Clan Glengarry, he was educated at Glasgow, participated in an unfortunate revolution in 1745 and fled to America. About 1754 he settled at the frontier town of Winchester, Virginia. He fought against Indians during the earlier wars and retired in 1763 as a captain, entitling him to 2,000 acres of Virginia land. In 1769 he was appointed militia major for Frederick County, and with William Crawford established a fort at Point Pleasant in the present West Virginia, overlooking the Ohio River. In June 1774 he commanded a 400-man expedition into Ohio attacking Shawnee towns of Wapatomica on the Muskingum River near the present Dresden; McDonald was promoted to lieutenant colonel in December 1774. He was a staunch Whig, but declined to serve in the Revolution, unwilling to serve under a colonel who had no military experience. McDonald was "a man of commanding figure and strong personality, and a rigid disciplinarian."

Thwaites/Kellogg, *Dunmore;* Alexander Scott Withers, *Chronicles of Border Warfare,* Cincinnati, Robert Clarke Co., 1895, 1970.

McDonald, William Jesse, Texas Ranger (Sept. 28, 1852-Jan. 15, 1918). B. in Kemper County, Mississippi, the family moved in 1866 to Rusk County, Texas. Two years later, at 16, McDonald was tried for treason following a conflict with Union authorities, but was acquitted. In 1872 he was graduated from a commercial college at New Orleans, went into the grocery business until he became a deputy sheriff of Wood County, Texas, establishing "a reputation for fearless law enforcement, expert marksmanship, and lightning quick disarming of his opponent," according to his *Handbook of Texas* biographer, Rie Jarratt. In 1883 in Wichita County, he managed cattle, then entered the lumber business and moved to Hardeman County where he became deputy sheriff, special ranger and U.S. deputy marshal, during which his hard-bitten police activities "made him a Texas legend." In January 1891 Texas Governor James Stephen Hogg made McDonald captain of Company B, Frontier Battalion of Texas Rangers. One of his men, who joined August 22, 1898, was Special Texas Ranger James Brown Miller (see entry), a noted gunman who did not remain on the force long. Stationed at Amarillo with eight men, McDonald strongly supported law and order in the Panhandle in a number of difficult and perilous cases. In

April 1905 he served as bodyguard for President Theodore Roosevelt who later entertained McDonald at the White House. At Brownsville, Texas, in August 1906 his handling of a difficult troop situation reportedly gave him the reputation of a "man who would charge hell with a bucket of water." Governor Thomas M. Campbell made him state revenue agent in January 1907. In 1912 he acted as bodyguard for Woodrow Wilson , who later as President appointed McDonald the U.S. marshal of the northern district of Texas. McDonald died of pneumonia at Wichita Falls and was buried at Quanah, in Hardeman County.

HT; Bill C. James, *Jim Miller: The Untold Story of a Texas Badman,* ed. by Robert W. Stephens, Wolfe City, Tex., Henington Pub. Co., 1989.

McDowell, John, military officer (d. Dec. 14, 1742). McDowell was of Scot descent and was b. in Ulster, Ireland. He came to America in early manhood, settling first in Pennsylvania, then in the Shenandoah Valley, becoming a surveyor and spending five years on land surveys. He joined the Augusta, Rockbridge County, militia and as a captain was ordered to intercept a party of Northern (probably Iroquois) Indians who, on the warpath against the South Carolina Catawbas, had plundered settlers in Virginia; John Peter Salling (see entry) was a member of this company which overtook the Indians on the north branch of the James River, fifteen miles from McDowell's place. In the resulting engagement McDowell and seven other whites were killed, the Indians suffering small losses. This was the initial battle between whites and Indians in the Shenandoah Valley of Virginia.

Alexander Scott Withers, *Chronicles of Border Warfare,* Cincinnati, Robert Clarke Co., 1895, 1970.

McDowell, Samuel, pioneer (1735-1817). B. in Pennsylvania, he was taken to Augusta County, Virginia, in 1737 and five years later his father, John McDowell, was killed by Indians. Samuel McDowell served with Braddock in 1755 and in 1774 commmanded a company in Lord Dunmore's War. He represented Augusta County in the Virginia state convention of 1776, and commanded a regiment that fought under Nathaniel Greene and took part in the campaign against Cornwallis. In 1783 he moved to Kentucky, becoming one of the most prominent citizens of that commonwealth, a judge, a member of seven conventions working toward statehood, and a

member of its constitutional convention of 1792. He died near Danville.

Thwaites, *Dunmore.*

McGuire, Francis, frontiersman (c. 1754-Sept. 20, 1820). McGuire was the son of an Irish immigrant, Thomas McGuire, who settled first on the South Branch of the Potomac River and in 1772 removed to Washington County, Pennsylvania, where he settled on upper Buffalo Creek. Francis McGuire became a militia major and noted in border history; he established a fort, probably on Buffalo Creek some miles above its mouth. He died at 66 and was buried near Independence, Pennsylvania. His widow, Barbara, died December 29, 1835 at 81.

Joseph Doddridge, *Notes on the Settlement and Indian Wars,* p.p., 1912, 1960; Thwaites/Kellogg, *Frontier Defense on the Upper Ohio 1777-1778.*

McIntire, James, lawman, desperado (b. 1846). B. in Brown County, Ohio, he went to Texas while young and hired out to James C. Loving (1836-1902) of Weatherford, becoming a cowboy on Loving's Jack County ranch. March 17, 1869, he was involved in an Indian fight with few casualties on either side; his later brushes with Comanches were probably more serious. About 1870 McIntire quit ranch work to become a buffalo hunter, reporting he had "the finest time on earth" at it and "quit way ahead of the game," again after narrow escapes from hostile Indians. He sold his hunting outfit at Fort Griffin, returned to the Loving ranch, but soon joined the Texas Rangers under a "Captain Hamilton" who is not otherwise identified. He was with Major John B. Jones (see entry) who headed 28 Rangers and Sheriff Tom Wilson of Palo Pinto County who on July 12, 1874, attacked 100 Indians believed to be Kiowas, Comanches and Apaches in what was known as the Lost Valley fight near Jacksboro. The Rangers lost two killed and two wounded, while Indian losses were thought to be three dead and several wounded. The Ranger company "prowled the buffalo grounds" with warrants, bringing in 102 suspects and other adventurers. The Rangers took a hand in the Fort Griffin difficulties between Regulators and Moderators, rescuing Marshal William C. Gilson and sending him to Austin with information leading to the arrest of principals in the Fort Griffin turmoil. Hamilton soon quit, as did some of the Rangers, the company disintegrated and Captain June Peak (see entry) enlisted those hanging on.

McIntire and N.F. Locke went into the saloon business at Fort Belknap; eventually they moved operations to Mobeetie. Here McIntire became acquainted with Wyatt Earp, Doc Holliday and Mysterious Dave Mather, who were peddling fake gold bricks. McIntire advised friends against buying the spurious articles and ordered "the brick dealers out of town." He said in 1902 that this nearly caused him serious trouble since the dealers had "bad reputations all over the West." McIntire, John W. Poe and Tom Riley became deputies to Sheriff Henry Fleming, the law in a dozen Panhandle counties. In June 1879 at his Canadian River camp McIntire was approached by hard cases including alleged representatives of John Selman (see entry) and Long John Longhurst, another buffalo hunter turned outlaw, seeking McIntire's cooperation with what DeArment called the "Great Outlaw Confederacy," a loose aggregation of about 175 desperadoes. McIntire listened to the proposition from men unaware that he was a deputy sheriff, and his reply was noncommittal. Later he confided his information to Moses Wiley, a Wheeler County attorney, and made out an affidavit of his knowledge which was sent to Major Jones with Wiley's endorsement. Nothing came of it, probably because Longhurst was killed by a "man named Trujillo," according to Pat Garrett, Selman nearly died of smallpox and the so-called confederacy, left leaderless, quickly disintegrated. McIntire and Poe pursued horse thieves by way of Dodge City to Las Vegas, New Mexico, arriving January 26, 1880, four days after the men they held warrants for had come to a sad ending in a saloon fight with Mather, Chief of Police Joe Carson (see entries), and others. McIntire became city marshal of Las Vegas at $12 a day, plus what he could make fining arrestees what they could pay, giving them back $2 "for a fresh start," turning $1 over to the county and splitting the remainder with the justice of the peace. McIntire became city marshal at Lake Valley, north of Deming, and held an appointment as deputy U.S. marshal when he became involved in the posse murder of two ranchers in 1883. With Timothy Isaiah, Jim Courtright and W.C. Moore he fled the territory with a price on his head of either $500 or $1,000 according to various versions. He was captured by Texas Rangers, broke jail, was recaptured in Louisiana and taken to New Mexico for trial, but was acquitted and returned to the Panhandle late in the 1880s. In Oklahoma in 1901 he contracted smallpox, at one point was declared dead and believed he had died, was taken to view heaven and hell before he was "restored" to life. He was so unnerved that he wrote a book, *Early Days in Texas. A Trip to Hell and Heaven,* privately published in 1902. Nothing further is reported of him.

T.C. Richardson, "Tough Hombres and Their Uses", *Frontier Times,* Vol. 53, No. 1 (Jan. 1979), 6-7, 38-39; Ed Bartholomew, *Wyatt Earp: The Untold Story,* Toyahvale, Tex., Frontier Book Co., 1963; Leon Claire Metz, *John Selman: Texas Gunfighter,* N.Y., Hastings House, 1966; R.K. DeArment, "The Great Outlaw Confederacy," *True West,* Vol. 37, No. 9 (Sept. 1990), 14-19.

[The following is a replacement for the entry which appears in Vol. II, p. 910]

McIntosh, Lachlan, military officer (Mar. 17, 1725-Feb. 20, 1806). B. near Raids, in Badenoch, Scotland, he was brought at 11 by his parents to Georgia. In wars with the Spaniards McIntosh's father was captured, sent as a prisoner to Spain and returned with his health broken to Georgia, where he soon died. In 1745 Lachlan and a brother attempted to return to Scotland to assist the military campaign of the Young Pretender (Bonnie Prince Charlie), but were prevented by Oglethorpe from doing so. At Charleston, South Carolina, McIntosh became a protegé of Henry Laurens "who had a warm friendship for him." Educated well, he became a surveyor. When the Revolution broke out, McIntosh was named to head Georgia troops as colonel. The first engagement, with British men-of-war at Savannah, was so successful that McIntosh in September 1776 was named Brigadier General in the Continental Army, to command in Georgia. An unfortunate "political and personal dispute" with Button Gwinnett, a signer of the Declaration of Independence, led to a duel May 16, 1777, in which McIntosh killed Gwinnett. Laurens then urged Washington to call McIntosh to the main army and he spent the winter at Valley Forge. Washington admired McIntosh's military ability and his knowledge of Indian character and in May 1778 named him to relieve Edward Hand in command at Fort Pitt, Pennsylvania. McIntosh took over in August, quickly organizing an expedition to move into the Indian country and in October built Fort McIntosh at the mouth of Beaver Creek, 29 miles from Pittsburgh. In the autumn Fort Laurens, named for McIntosh's friend, was constructed near the

Delaware towns on the Tuscarawa River, about a mile from the present site of Bolivar, Ohio, southwest of Canton. McIntosh led a three-day expedition to Laurens in 1779 to relieve the post under British siege since February (see John Gibson entry), but the investment had been lifted before he arrived. McIntosh was recalled from Fort Pitt at his own request in 1779; he returned to Georgia, was wounded in the siege of Savannah and was captured at Charleston when that city surrendered. Following the Revolution McIntosh returned to Georgia to find his property in ruins. He was elected a delegate to the Continental Congress in 1784, serving one term. His latter years were spent in obscurity and he died at Savannah.

BDAC; Thwaites/Kellogg, *Frontier Defense on the Upper Ohio, 1777-1778;* Louise Phelps Kellogg, *Frontier Advance on the Upper Ohio 1778-1779,* Madison, Wis. Hist. Soc., 1916.

McJunkin, George, discoverer, cowboy (Jan. 9, 1851-Jan. 21, 1922). B. a slave probably near Rogers Prairie, or Store (near the present Normangee), Texas, on the Old San Antonio Road which is followed today by Texas State Highway 21, McJunkin by his outstanding talents and innovative work became "a most uncommon" man. At the close of the Civil War he learned that blacks had won freedom. He was 14 and continued for a time helping his blacksmith father shoe horses and do what iron work employer John Sanders McJunkin and others required. Longhorn herds passing by occasionally inspired George to become a trail rider. Meanwhile he learned Spanish from neighboring vaqueros who also taught him their superb lariat skills and how to ride rough horses; he always got on well with Mexicans. Early in 1867 he left home. West of Comanche he became a horse wrangler on a drive to Abilene, the only railhead city receiving cattle at the time. In 1868 he associated with Gideon Roberds, who was driving horses west, and hired George to gentle some of the animals for sale. It was Roberds who bestowed upon the young black the name of George McJunkin, since he had to call him something and the youth knew only that his first name was George, and he had worked for McJunkin. The outfit paused in Palo Duro Canyon, then Comanche country, where a brother of Gideon's was killed by Indians. The party then continued northwest to the Cimarron country below Johnson Mesa in northeastern New Mexico. Roberds later established a horse ranch east of Trinidad, Colorado, on the

Purgatoire (Picketwire) River. Here McJunkin worked, and taught Roberds' sons to ride in exchange for reading lessons and the use of their textbooks. "No reading, no riding," he told them. He had purchased a violin and became a favorite fiddler for country dances; he learned to write as well as read; he produced the best-trained cutting horses in the vicinity and other ranchers got him to educate stock; he had learned the proper way to geld horses and was so proficient that other stockmen hired him to treat their young horses. McJunkin also became interested in rocks and fossils, although he had no instructor, and collected some he admired and wondered about. He was hired by Dr. Thomas E. Owen to work on his sizeable ranch in the Cimarron Valley back in New Mexico, and McJunkin settled in there, becoming at length ranch foreman over white cowboys who respected him for his skills and personality and never resented taking orders from a black man, even though most of them were southerners. One of the neighbors had given him a Bible, which he now could read, and permitted him to use a family encyclopedia. He acquired a transit telescope and learned to run lines to pipe water and build fences with the newly invented barbed wire. He also used the scope at night to study the stars, learning the names of many of them; eventually he saved an army officer from a roughing up by three would-be payroll robbers and was presented a superior telescope for having done so. He found it useful in many ways. George's talents seemed endless. Once during a savage many-day "northern," or blizzard, he saved a party of fourteen men through his intimate knowledge of the country and where to find shelter and help. When Dr. Owen died, his sons, now matured, took over the ranch and McJunkin accepted an invitation from William H. Jack to manage the 8,000-acre Crowfoot Ranch adjacent to Owen's place. August 27, 1908, a furious rainstorm, the worst in memory, virtually flooded that corner of New Mexico, causing many casualties and great property damage, washing away homes, structures and deeply eroding what had been small arroyos. After the storm, McJunkin noted one ravine, deepened from two or three feet to more than ten. There he found bones where flood waters had gouged out a fresh wall ten feet below the surface. He thought one looked like a buffalo bone, of which he had seen many after the hide hunters littered the plains with bison carcasses, "but it's the biggest buffalo bone I ever saw," he said. He collected several and saved them in his house, but he couldn't interest others to inspect the site, which he named the Bone Pit. His curiosity grew, however. After several years he met Carl Schwachheim at Raton, which launched "a series of events that would put the names of George McJunkin and Carl Schwachheim into many an important scientific book." He described his bone finds to Carl, who also was a collector, and told him where the Bone Pit was, giving precise directions. But Schwachheim had no transportation and couldn't find a way to get the forty miles to the Pit for several more years; neither did anyone else before McJunkin died in 1922, perhaps as popular as any man in the valley. On July 1, 1922, Schwachheim and Fred Howarth of a Raton bank who also was an amateur collector, decided finally to visit the Bone Pit, with Carl the guide and Howarth furnishing transportation; with them went the Reverend Roger Aull, a Catholic priest, and two other men. They collected a gunny sack full of bones, but for four more years could find no one to identify them. Then in 1926 on a business trip to Denver, Howarth and Schwachheim took bones to the Colorado Museum of Natural History and showed them to the director, Jesse D. Figgins, who instantly recognized them as an important find. Figgins employed Schwachheim to commence excavation at the Pit. August 2, 1927, Carl located a curiously shaped spearpoint between two bison ribs which subsequent dating placed at 9,000 to 10,000 years of age. The bones represented an extinct form of buffalo, *Bison antiquus occidentalis,* which was a bridge-species, or subspecies, between the widespread earlier *Bison antiquus antiquus* and the modern buffalo and probably had existed for a relatively short time: from about 11,000 years to around 5,000 years ago, by which time the modern bison had evolved. It was a relatively giant species and George McJunkin's interest in it was thoroughly justified. Had he not noticed the exposed fossils in the first place and kept interest in the deposit alive among his friends and acquaintances until the great discovery was made, the existence of the newly named *Folsom Culture* (titled after a nearby community) which revolutionized scientific thinking about the antiquity of man in the western hemisphere, might not have occurred, at least on the basis of that particular discovery; there have been many subsequent finds confirming the early date as a minimum for man's presence in America. McJunkin never married.

Franklin Folsom, *Black Cowboy: The Life and Legend of George McJunkin,* Niwot, CO., Roberts Rine-

hart, pubs., 1992; Jerry N. McDonald, *North American Bison: Their Classification and Evolution,* Berkeley, Univ. of Cal. Press, 1981; HT.

McKay, William Cameron, physician, scouts commander (Mar. 18, 1824-Jan. 2, 1893). B. at Astoria, Oregon, his mother was a daughter of Chief Comcomly of the Chinooks and his father was Thomas McKay, the son of Alexander McKay of Astor's Pacific Fur Company, who was killed aboard the *Tonquin* by Northwest Coast Indians. Thomas later married a Cayuse woman and fathered Donald McKay (see entry), who thus was half-brother of William. William early became associated with Dr. John McLoughlin, Hudson's Bay Company factor of Fort Vancouver and became interested in a medical career. His father planned to send him to Edinburgh for his education, but Protestant missionary Marcus Whitman persuaded him to send the boy instead to Fairfield, New York, and with his brothers, John and Alexander, William accompanied Methodist missionary Jason Lee east in 1838. He completed his medical studies at Geneva, New York, and Willoughby, Ohio, graduating at 19 with a license to practice medicine. He returned to Oregon in 1843 by way of Montreal and the Hudson's Bay Company's annual express. At Vancouver he was variously clerk, doctor, trader, miner, soldier, coroner and eventually concentrated on medicine exclusively and gradually separated from the HBC, establishing a trading post on McKay Creek (named for him) south of Pendleton, eastern Oregon. During the Indian War of 1855 he was burned out, with a property loss of about $20,000. "William McKay was blessed with a healthy constitution, a lively sense of humor from both sides of his heritage, and a fondness for Scotch whisky. He was an energetic and outgoing individual with a keen eye for detail and [an excellent] memory...Dr. McKay was short and stocky with eyes, hair, and skin of the Indian [and when possible] was well dressed in a silk hat and Prince Albert coat. Thru gold rimmed spectacles his dark eyes beamed with kindliness [and] he was intensely interested in his profession." His first wife died young and in 1856 he married Margaret Campbell, daughter of a North West Fur Company factor, and also half Indian. McKay was interpreter and a council secretary to Governor Isaac Stevens and Joel Palmer, superintendents for Indian affairs in Washington and Oregon respectively, treating with many tribes. In 1861 President Lincoln appointed him resident physician at the Warm Springs Indian Agency between Bend and The Dalles, Oregon. McKay and John Darragh (see entry) were chosen to command Indian scouts during a war with Paiute hostiles in 1866-67. Major General H.W. Halleck, commanding the Division of the Pacific, relayed to Major General Frederick Steele, commanding the Department of the Columbia, a Secretary of War view that "the law does not authorize the appointment of special officers to command Indian Scouts but you can select hired interpreters for that purpose. Limit the pay to that of a second lieutenant of cavalry." Thus McKay and Darragh were actually commissioned October 26, 1866, "interpreters," but with the rank of lieutenants to command scouts over a lengthy period; ultimately they were promoted to "captain" for their work. They were "sent into the field," noted Bancroft, "with the humane orders to kill and destroy without regard to age, sex, or condition," and this of course aroused controversy. The directive apparently originated with Oregon Governor George L. Woods who, rebuffed in his bloodthirsty suggestions by Steele and Halleck, had gone over their heads to Secretary of War Edwin Stanton, who instructed the officers to "conform to the governor's wishes," which was reluctantly done. Questions subsequently raised about the morality of tactics which caused the deaths of native women and children were not generally raised at the time, except by officials in supervisory control over the Indians and by the Indians themselves, who argued that if they fulfilled such savage directives, it would only mean retaliation in kind by the Paiute Indians when opportunity arose. These arguments, too, were ignored. The campaign, according to McKay's journal, commenced November 1, 1866, and terminated November 13, 1867, after Paiute "submission to white superiority in numbers and technology." Despite the vicious instructions a few prisoners were taken, mainly of noncombatants. In 1868 McKay was appointed interpreter to surrendered Paiute bands, and also served as agency physician at the Klamath, Oregon, Reservation and in 1870 at the Warm Springs Agency. In 1872-73 he became agency physician at the Umatilla Reservation near Pendleton. Following the Modoc War in which Donald McKay served as chief of scouts after William declined such an appointment, the brothers took a group of Indian veterans on a grand tour of the eastern states; it was a financial disaster, saved by President Grant, who arranged

for enough funds to return the Indians to their reservations. William McKay served intermittently as physician at various agencies while also undertaking a private practice, but holding to the Indian work as a remunerative mainstay for the rest of his life. He supplied much information to the Bancroft history writers for the two-volume history of Oregon, reflecting in "amazing detail" his knowledge of events passed. He died leaving an estate of only $523.50 for his wife and children.

Keith, Donna Clark, "William McKay's Journal, 1866-67: Indian Scouts," I, II, *Oregon Hist. Qtly.,* Vol. LXXIX, Nos. 2, 3 (Summer/Fall 1978) 120-71, 268-333; Bancroft, *Oregon,* II.

McKee, Alexander, fur trader, partisan (c. 1735-Jan. 14, 1799). B. in western Pennsylvania, the son of Irish trader Thomas McKee, and a Shawnee woman, he was a lieutenant in Pennsylvania forces during the French and Indian War and entered the Indian department in 1760 as assistant to George Croghan. In 1711 he was justice of the peace for Bedford, later for Westmoreland County. In 1772 he became deputy agent under William Johnson. In the early 1770s he married a Shawnee woman and for a time lived in an Indian village in Ohio. With the Revolution, McKee was inclined toward the British side, and was privately commissioned by Lord Dunmore a lieutenant colonel in a battalion to be raised near Fort Pitt, but this plan did not work out. Suspected of Loyalist sympathies, he was kept under close surveillance, though under parole he was allowed his liberty until August 1777, when he was briefly confined. He "adroitly evaded" an effort to remove him to an Eastern post, and March 28, 1778, accompanied by Matthew Elliott and Simon Girty, slipped out of the Fort Pitt region and went to Detroit where English authorities made him captain in the Indian department and, later, deputy agent. He was fluent in Shawnee and probably conversant with other Indian languages, as well as English and possibly some French. For the remainder of the Revolution he helped direct Indian operations against the American frontier to the point where he was considered by white Americans a "renegade," or worse. He received large pay and considerable honor and authority, and personally led expeditions against the frontier. After the conflict ceased McKee's talents were still used to encourage Indian resistance to American settlement in the Northwest Territories, and McKee established a trading post and home on the Maumee River in northwest Ohio. He held various civil positions until the early 1790s when American-Indian hostilities again became intense. McKee had worked to develop an Indian buffer state between British and American regions in Ohio, but this failed to materialize. With others he assisted the Indians opposing American expansion with military supplies, advisers and in other ways. He was accused of "continuing to incite the Indians against the borderers." He played a role in organizing native Americans in opposition to Anthony Wayne's operations and "the battle of Fallen Timbers was fought within sight of his house and store on the Maumee," but Wayne's triumph was decisive and his great victory terminated massive Indian threats to the Border. After the British evacuated Detroit in 1796, McKee moved to Malden, Ontario. He had been during many difficult years "the most important official organizing Indian resistance to the American advance" into Ohio. He never was a "renegade," as Americans charged, any more than were other Loyalists who fought for the cause in which they believed. McKee died of lockjaw at this Ontario home.

Thwaites/Kellogg, *The Revolution on the Upper Ohio, 1775-1777*, Madison, Wis. Hist. Soc., 1908; DCB IV.

McKee, Thomas, military officer, frontiersman (c. 1770-Oct. 20, 1814). A son of Alexander McKee and an Indian woman who probably was Shawnee, he was b. in a Shawnee village on the Scioto River of Ohio and with his father's help became an ensign in the 60th British Infantry March 29, 1791, becoming a lieutenant February 5, 1795, and a captain February 20, 1796. According to the *Dictionary of Canadian Biography* he was active in Indian affairs, participating in an unsuccessful attack on Wayne's Fort Recovery in Mercer County, Ohio, took part in various Indian councils and became superintendent of Indian affairs for the Northwestern District in 1796, the next year assuming as well the superintendency of Indian affairs in the Amherstburg District. He suffered increasingly from an alcohol problem, but his fluency in Indian tongues, particularly Shawnee, enabled him to retain influential posts in which he dealt with Indians. He also held political office. After the 60th Infantry had been withdrawn from Canada, McKee served in the militia, attaining the rank of militia major, but drinking was a constant prob-

lem. He fathered three children by an unknown mother, and then married a white woman by whom he had a son, leaving his widow and son virtually destitute when he died enroute to Montreal. His principal value to the British cause was his influence over and respect among Indians.

DCB, V.

McKee, William, frontiersman (1732-1816). Of Scot-Irish descent he probably was b. in Ireland but while young emigrated to the Shenandoah Valley of Virginia and became active in Indian wars. He said he had been with Braddock on the day of his famous defeat, July 9, 1755. He had been ranked as captain of militia, but served as lieutenant in Captain John Murray's company in Lord Dunmore's War of 1774 and after the Point Pleasant battle of October 10, in which Murray was killed, was appointed to succeed in command of the company. He afterward served in the Virginia legislature and around 1790 moved to Kentucky, settling in Lincoln County where he lived the rest of his life.

Thwaites, *Dunmore.*

McKinney, Thomas Christopher (Kip), lawman (Mar. 19, 1856-Sept. 21, 1915). The son of Thalis (John) McKinney and a nephew of Collin McKinney, signer of the Texas Declaration of Independence, Kip also was related to 22-year-old Robert McKinney, who died at the Alamo March 6, 1836. Kip was b. at Birdville, near Fort Worth. He and his father drove a herd from Palo Pinto County, Texas, to New Mexico in the late 1870s. They reached the Seven Rivers country in time to become involved in partisan scuffling involving the "Seven Rivers Warriors," according to Keleher, and Kip later became a deputy to Sheriff Pat Garrett and was based for a time at Roswell. May 8, 1881, Deputy McKinney killed Bob Edwards, "a notorious horse thief from southwest Texas," although the fact that Edwards apparently was a Tunstall-McSween partisan in the Lincoln County War may have somewhat tainted the characterization. In a shootout at Hank Harrison's ranch on the Black River near Rattlesnake Springs, Kip reported that Edwards opened fire on him with a Winchester at close range and McKinney in return put a bullet through his head. Mullin reported that this fight occurred May 17, but that was the date an account of it may have appeared in the *Las Vegas Gazette.* Two months later McKinney, as deputy, accompanied Garrett and John W. Poe (see entry) to Fort Sumner, New Mexico, where Poe had heard Billy the Kid was hiding out and had persuaded Garrett to check on the rumor. McKinney and Poe waited outside while Garrett entered Pete Maxwell's bedroom on the night of July 14; they saw an under-sized man approaching, but neither knew nor recognized the Kid, who was wary but entered Maxwell's room to check on them and was killed by Garrett. McKinney who had no other role in the shooting, had remained outside and as the stranger approached, caught his spur in a loose board of the porch and nearly fell, but recovered. Not much is reported of McKinney thereafter. He died at Carlsbad, New Mexico, and is buried there, as is his wife Theresa Letitia (July 13, 1867-Oct. 30, 1940).

William A. Keleher, *Violence in Lincoln County 1869-1881*, Albuquerque, Univ. of New Mex. Press, 1957, p. 349; Robert N. Mullin notes; info. from Chuck Parsons and Ed Bartholomew; Leon C. Metz, *Pat Garrett: The Story of a Western Lawman*, Norman, Univ. of Okla. Press, 1974; Mullin ed., *Maurice G. Fulton's History of the Lincoln County War*, Tucson, Univ. of Ariz. Press, 1968; Eve Ball, *Ma'am Jones of the Pecos*, Tucson, Univ. of Ariz. Press, 1969.

McLoughlin, John Jr., fur trader (Aug. 18, 1812-Apr. 20, 1841). B. at Fort Vancouver on the Columbia he was the second son of John McLoughlin Sr., and his half-Indian wife. John Jr. was educated at Montreal briefly, went to Paris to study medicine, an unsuccessful venture, returned to Montreal in 1834, got into debt and was imprisoned in 1836. After an initial refusal he was accepted by the Hudson's Bay Company through the influence of George Simpson, head of the HBC in America and was sent to Fort Vancouver for a short period. He was assigned to Fort Stikine (the present Wrangell), Alaska, where he was placed in charge, but alcohol got the better of him and in a dispute shots were fired, one of which killed McLoughlin.

Pierce, *Russian America: A Biographical Dictionary*.

McManus, George Henry, military officer (Dec. 23, 1867-Aug. 27, 1954). B. in Iowa, he went to West Point and was commissioned a second lieutenant of the 3rd Artillery June 30, 1893, becoming a first lieutenant March 2, 1899. In that year, stationed in Alaska he left Circle City on the Yukon River April 3, assigned to explore the region between that section of the Yukon and the Tanana River. He was accompanied by H.R.

Redmyer, a reindeer specialist who had charge of a government herd of the animals, and a Tanana Indian guide. The trip to Miller Creek was made quickly and without incident, but from there progress was limited by flooding and glare ice on which the unshod reindeer could establish no footing. McManus's efforts to purchase a dog team at an Indian camp proved fruitless, so on April 21, he returned to Circle City. His expedition had reached only 145 miles southwest of base, and came within 55 miles by trail of the Tanana. His reindeer had been stampeded away with a band of caribou (a closely-related species) and were lost. While his mission was unsuccessful in reaching the Tanana, McManus learned of a trail from Circle City to that stream and he was able to sketch a map of the region from Indian reports. McManus served at Circle City until June 17, 1899, and at Fort Egbert, Eagle City, to August 4, 1899, when he terminated his Alaska service. He was on the China Relief expedition in 1900, then served in the Philippines and returned to the United States December 30, 1902. He became a major in the Coast Artillery July 1, 1910; a lieutenant colonel July 1, 1916, a temporary colonel August 5, 1917, and a temporary Brigadier General October 1, 1918. He earned a Distinguished Service Medal for his work in moving troops and supplies to Europe, and a Navy Cross December 1, 1929, for his cooperation with the Navy in troop movements and organizing the quick turn-around of transports at Hoboken, New Jersey. McManus retired a Brigadier General December 31, 1931, and died at the Presidio of San Francisco.

Heitman; Cullum; *Narratives of Explorations in Alaska;* info. from the U.S. Army Mil. Hist. Inst., Carlisle Barracks, Penn.

McNab, Frank, stock detective (c. 1851-Apr. 19 or 29, 1878). Of Scottish descent, he was employed by Hunter & Evans cattle interests as a stock detective to protect H&E, or Chisum cattle from rustlers. Upon Dick Brewer's slaying by Andrew L. Roberts, McNab on April 4, became captain of the so-called Regulators in Lincoln County New Mexico, although he did not hold the position long. On April 19 or 29, 1878, he was bushwacked at the Fritz Ojo Ranch; nearly 25 Dolan adherents were indicted for the slaying, but none was convicted. According to Nolan he had previously been involved in asserted gunplay and incidents in Kansas, the upper Texas Panhandle, and Colorado.

Robert N. Mullin notes; Frederick Nolan, *The Lincoln County War: A Documentary History,* Norman, Univ. of Okla. Press., 1992.

McTavish, Simon, fur trader (c. 1750-July 6, 1804). B. at Strath Errick, Scotland, he reached New York in 1764 and Detroit in 1772 where he entered the fur trade in a minor way, gradually expanding his interests which focused on the region above the Great Lakes. His attention centered on Michilimackinac and Grand Portage, Minnesota, in 1776 taking George McBeath (see entry) as partner. As his business interests developed he became a founder of the North West Company, a major fur concern that became a rival to the Hudson's Bay Company in many areas; Benjamin Frobisher was "the brains of the company" initially, but he died in April 1787 and McTavish the same year became the virtual administrator and most powerful member of its directorship. Eventually the NWC became a trade monopoly which McTavish directed from his Montreal headquarters. Although fiercely opposed by McTavish, a merger with the Hudson's Bay Company came about shortly after his death. At that time his estate amounted to more than 125,000 pounds sterling. He was "certainly the colony's most important businessman in the second half of the 18th century. Like his friends, the Frobishers, he was shrewd and far-sighted, but he possessed an even greater sense of organization and management." He died at Montreal.

Thwaites/Kellogg, *The Revolution on the Upper Ohio, 1775-1777,* Madison, Wis. Hist. Soc., 1908; Paul Chrisler Phillips, *The Fur Trade,* II, Norman, Univ. of Okla. Press, 1961; DCB, V.

M

Mackenzie, Alexander, explorer, fur man (1764-Mar. 12, 1820. B. at Stornoway, Lewis Island, most northerly of the Outer Hebrides, Scotland, his father took him to New York in 1774. When the Revolution broke out the aunts caring for him went with Alexander to an estate in the Mohawk Valley of Iroquois country, believed a safe haven for Loyalists. But in 1778, shortly before Sullivan's operation, he was sent to Montreal for his brief schooling. In 1779 Mackenzie joined a fur trading firm of James Finlay and John Gregory; the company, later constituted as Gregory, MacLeod, eventually became an integral part of the North West Company, a strong competitor of the Hudson's Bay Company. In 1784 Mackenzie commenced trading for his firm at Detroit and after a few months of apparent success he became a partner in Gregory, MacLeod. In return he was asked to go to Grand Portage, at the northeasternmost tip of Minnesota, and soon was assigned to a department in Saskatchewan headquarters. He was much interested in a map the redoubtable Peter Pond (see entry) had drawn from what he had learned himself, and from Indians familiar with the northern country. It showed a river from Lake Athabasca to Great Slave Lake, from which a second large river flowed northwest. Having heard from a narrative of the third voyage of Captain James Cook (see entry) of an inlet on the Alaskan coast that Cook assumed was the estuary of a large river, Pond at once concluded that this was the mouth of the river from Great Slave Lake, and so sketched it on his map. Mackenzie, who had little training in the use of navigational instruments, became interested in tracing the course of this hitherto unexplored stream. Pond returned to his Athabasca post in 1787 and Mackenzie went with him as understudy and coadjutor. They arrived in late 1787 and when Pond left in the spring of 1788, Mackenzie took over. Fully believing in Pond's theory that the "great river" had its course across Alaska, Mackenzie set out from the new Fort Chipewyan on Lake Athabasca June 3, 1789, with four French Canadian voyageurs and other personnel. After leaving Great Slave Lake their progress down the river was swift, about 75 miles a day,

and its length of 1,075 miles was covered in two weeks. It had become apparent that this river would not lead to the Pacific, and Mackenzie realized it must debouch into the Arctic Ocean, which it did. The party spent four days on Garry Island, initially named Whale Island because numerous white whales were observed hard by, then returned the way it had come, regaining Fort Chipewyan September 12. Mackenzie had been the first white to explore the great river eventually named for him. The legend that he had called it the River Disappointment, because it had not opened the way to the Pacific, was doubted by W. Kaye Lamb, who noted that in most surviving transcripts of the letter in which Mackenzie is alleged to have so-named the stream he refers to it only as the Grand River. Mackenzie already had a second expedition in mind, this time to actually find a route to the Pacific, preferably one by water. To improve his woefully inadequate knowledge of navigation equipment and techniques he paid a private visit to London in 1791-92. October 10, 1792, he again left Fort Chipewyan and started up the Peace River; near its junction with the Smoky River he constructed Fort Fork, or Fork Fort, leaving there May 9, 1793, in a 25-foot birchbark canoe, into which were loaded 3,000 pounds of baggage and the 10 members of the expedition. Alexander MacKay was second in command. Shortly after departure the virtually impassable Peace River Canyon presented difficulties so great as to nearly nullify the operation by desertion, but Mackenzie stilled the clamor and pushed on by a herculean portage around the great defile. The party reached the confluence of the Parsnip and Finlay rivers which unite to form the Peace, and on the advice of an Indian ascended the Parsnip. By June 18, the Fraser River was reached. He went down the Fraser four days before learning that it was a mistaken course, and returned to the Blackwater River. Here he cached the canoe and, packing what necessities he had, journeyed overland, following Indian trails for the most part. He crossed the 6,000-ft. Mackenzie Pass and July 17, descended to the Bella Coola River, two days later coming to its discharge into "a narrow arm of the sea." In this manner, it is often written, he concluded the first journey across North America north of Mexico, but of course that is less than accurate. The initial exploration across America from Atlantic tidewater to Pacific tidewater was completed by De Soto and Coronado (whose expeditions were tenuously linked: see pp. 1617-1618) in 1540-43, or 250 years, a quarter of a millenium, before Mackenzie gained the narrow arm of the Pacific in 1793. But he completed his exploration more than a decade before Lewis and Clark accomplished theirs, and deserves full honors for a bold and noteworthy feat. Mackenzie regained Fort Chipewyan August 24, 1793, bringing all of his party back in good health. He made no more extended explorations, nor did he remain long on the frontier. He soon returned to Montreal and engaged in the management end of the fur trade he had pushed to its farthermost limits. In 1801 he published the journals of his two expeditions, and thereby became a celebrity. King George III knighted him in 1802. From 1805 onward he lived mostly in Scotland. He was married in 1812 to Geddes Mackenzie; they had three children. He died at Mulinearn, near Dunkeld, Scotland, at the age of 56.

Literature abundant; the best brief account of his life is by W. Kaye Lamb, former Dominion archivist and national librarian of Canada, in DCB, V; Morton M. Hunt, "First by Land," *American Heritage*, Vol. VIII, No. 6 (Oct. 1957), 42-47, 94-95, includes a small-scale but very useful map by John Teppich of Mackenzie's explorations; Arthur P. Woollacott, *Mackenzie and His Voyageurs: By Canoe to the Arctic and the Pacific 1789-93*, London, J.M. Dent & Sons, 1927.

Mad Trapper of the Yukon: *see,* Albert Johnson

Madden, Dan(iel), military officer (Feb. 2, 1833-Jan. 25, 1907). B. at Liverpool he came to America at 14, enlisted December 9, 1850, in Company E of the 2nd Dragoons and served with it and Company H of the 1st Dragoons until December 9, 1855. He was stationed in New Mexico from 1852-55 and was engaged in expeditions against Navaho and White Mountain Apache Indians until the end of his enlistment. He re-enlisted in Company B, 2nd Dragoons, rising to first sergeant by 1861. Madden was stationed at Fort Riley, Kansas, and was on the Utah Expedition of 1857 during his second enlistment. He was commissioned a second lieutenant of the 6th Cavalry November 1, 1861, was wounded and ended the Civil War as a first lieutenant with

two brevets, one for operations against Confederates under Lee. Madden became a captain May 10, 1867. Following the Civil War he was stationed initially at Fort Richardson, near Jacksboro, Texas. Madden and his Company C arrived at Camp Grant October 11, 1875, and went to Fort Bowie in October 1878, scouting occasionally on the border of New Mexico, particularly when the Apache, Victorio, was out. In September 1880 Indians wrecked a stagecoach west of Fort Cummings, New Mexico, killing Emery S. Madden, 19, a son of Captain Madden, with two others. During the Geronimo breakout in 1885 Madden and two troops of the 6th were active in scouting operations in southern New Mexico, although whether he had any contact with hostiles is not reported. He became a major, 7th Cavalry, May 21, 1886, and was stationed at Fort Bayard, New Mexico, until his retirement October 5, 1887, after more than 30 years of military service. Madden, whose wife and two other sons predeceased him, died at Dorchester, Massachusetts.

Heitman; Powell; Constance Wynn Altshuler, *Cavalry Yellow & Infantry Blue,* Tucson, Ariz. Hist. Soc., 1991; Dan L. Thrapp, *Conquest of Apacheria,* Norman, Univ. of Okla. Press, 1967.

Madockawando, Tarrateen (Abenaki), chief (c. 1630-c. Sept. 1698). A chief of the Penobscot segment of the Abenaki Indians of Maine, he was an adopted son of Assiminasqua, noted chief of the Kennebecs, another Abenaki people. Madockawando was often inclined toward peace with the whites, including the English colonists, until they made themselves enemies by persistent depredations upon Indian lands. As a probable off-shoot of King Philip's War, the Abenakis engaged in hostilities with the English, their war enduring until November 6, 1676, when a treaty was signed at Boston by Mog(g) or Mugg (see entry), later being ratified on the Penobscot River by Madockawando. The peace thus established did not last long, however. Madockawando's followers united with the French to wage war against English settlements and although the chief led many raids against the frontier, his treatment of prisoners was humane. One of his daughters married Abbadie de St. Castin (see entry), and some said she became his "principal" wife. St. Castin was a French Baron who became an Abenaki chief and whose status with the French to the north did Madockawando no harm. His counsel was often sought by the chief, and his advice usually followed. During King William's War of 1688-99 (also called St. Castin's War) Madockawando's record was varied, but when he was hostile he could be very effective. In 1691 he attacked York, Maine, killed 77 colonists and laid the place in ashes. He died shortly before the conflict ended. Major James Converse and Captain John Alden arrived at Penobscot October 14, 1698, and were "informed that Madockawando, the noted Sagamore [or chief, was] lately Dead," with no details given as to the circumstances of his demise, although apparently it was peaceful.

Hodge, HAI; Sylvester, II; *Narratives of the Indian Wars 1675-1699*, ed. by Charles H. Lincoln, N.Y., Barnes & Noble, 1913, 1959.

Magoffin, Susan Shelby, diarist (July 30, 1827-Oct. 26, 1855). The daughter of Isaac Shelby Jr., a wealthy Kentuckian, Susan was b. near Danville; she was a descendant of Evan Shelby and her grandfather was Isaac Shelby (see entries), both prominent pioneers. On November 25, 1845, she married Samuel Magoffin (1801-1888), a brother of the famous James Magoffin (see entry), Samuel too being a veteran Santa Fe trader. He was 27 years Susan's senior, but she was "hopelessly in love with the tall, big-boned Kentuckian, and intrigued by his seemingly romantic and hazardous career as a frontier merchant." She was only 18 at the outset of her journey down the Santa Fe Trail and into Chihuahua with her trader-husband, and her observant, accurate and lively narrative not only is a pleasure in itself, but "quite aside from its worth as a trail journal, a Mexican War account and an insight into the political [and] economic role of the American borderlands merchant [her diary] has a final merit as social history." She had a sense of humor and a goodly fund of nerve to go with it: on a trailside stroll in Kansas she "steped almost onto a large snake; it moved and frightened me very much. Of course I screamed and ran off, and like a ninny came back when the snake...had gone and I can't tell where. I came back to look for it." Accompanying the large wagon train was the noted painter, John Mix Stanley (see entry), a few of whose works of this period survive, although most were destroyed by fire. Susan's description of Bent's Fort in eastern Colorado is animated and brings the place to life as vividly as does almost any other contemporary description. She suffered a miscarriage there, but faithfully reported that concurrently an Indian

woman had a baby and in half an hour was at the nearby Arkansas River bathing "herself and it," and afterward going about her affairs. Susan commented that "It is truly astonishing to see what customs will do. No doubt many ladies in civilized life are ruined by too careful treatments during child-birth, for this custom of the hethen is not known to be disadvantageous..." Her word-pictures of Las Vegas and Santa Fe, New Mexico, are generous. She quickly set about learning Spanish to communicate better with the strange people she met; they reacted warmly to her, and she returned the affection. She was as interested in the peons and their problems as with the upper social and political levels. Susan also was tolerant of their religious faith. Though raised a Protestant and faithful in her belief, on February 21, 1847, a Sunday, she confided to her journal that "This morning I have been to mass—not led by idle curiosity, not by a blind faith, a belief in the creed there practiced, but because tis the house of God, and whether Christian or pagan, I can worship there within myself, as well as in a protestant church, or my own private chamber..." Her descriptions of Stephen Watts Kearny and Zachary Taylor give interesting sidelights on these ranking officers and glimpses of them in the field. Susan is as generous in her portraits of Spanish officials, military officers and social leaders. She reported what she observed of war developments during the occupation of Chihuahua. Her journal depicts the hopes and dreads, the rumors, optimistic and pessimistic, and the behind-the-scenes civilian roles brought about by the conflict. Unfortunately the diary ends with the entry for September 8, 1847, before she suffered a siege of yellow fever at Matamoras. During her illness she gave birth to a son, either stillborn or who shortly died. She returned to New Orleans by sea, lived for a time at Lexington, Kentucky, and in 1852 she and her husband settled near Kirkwood, Missouri. Her third child was born in 1851 and she died shortly after another daughter was born, being buried at St. Louis. Afterward Samuel Magoffin married one of her cousins who also was named Susan Shelby.

Susan Shelby Magoffin, *Down the Santa Fe Trail and Into Chihuahua*, ed. by Stella M. Drumm, Lincoln, Univ. of Nebr. Press, 1982; info. from E.F. (Ted) Mains; info. from the Missouri Hist. Soc.

Maguire, Rochfort, British naval officer (fl. 1852-54). Commanding the British naval vessel

Plover, Maguire wintered in Moore Harbor, Elson Lagoon just east of Point Barrow, Alaska, in 1852, 1853 and 1854 and "made several trips yielding geographical information which was incorporated in the charts made by Master Thomas Hull. Maguire and his ship's surgeon, John Simpson, are credited with naming and reporting Eskimo names for a number of Arctic features. Simpson recorded considerable information about the Eskimo of northern Alaska and was responsible for drawing a map of the north coast between Point Barrow and Humphrey Point," northwest of where the Alaska-Canada border reaches the Arctic coast. Captain Maguire was engaged in the search for the lost Sir John Franklin at the time of his Arctic voyage.

Orth, 13-14, 615; *Narratives of Explorations in Alaska,* 367.

Mahko, Bedonkohe, Apache chief (c. 1770-c. 1830). Although Geronimo's autobiography reported in a note by the editor (p. 35n.) that Mahko was "chief of the Nedhni Apaches," he was in fact the chief of the Bedonkohe Apaches, whom some ethnologists believe were identical with the Mogollon Apaches from the New Mexico mountain range of that name. Griswold said that the homeland of Mahko and his people was in the area of the present Clifton, Arizona. Geronimo, who never saw the chief, said that his own father, Taklishim (The Gray One) was a son of Mahko and thus Geronimo was a grandson. "My father often told me of the great size, strength, and sagacity" of Mahko, he reported, adding that the old chief died while Taklishim was "a young warrior," and was succeeded as chief for many of his people by Mangas Coloradas, who more properly was chief of the Mimbres Apaches. Mahko was said by Jason Betzinez, his great great grandson, to have been peace-loving as well as powerful, generous, raising much corn and many horses which he traded with the Mexicans, who greatly respected and trusted him; the chief was wise enough to store quantities of corn, dried beef and venison in caves to be shared with the needy of his tribe and in the event of famine. Mahko, though a lover of peace, had the reputation for being a great warrior, fighting only when attacked, although there was one story of an epic battle with another Apache tribe. The Mahko people used bowstrings of yucca fibre; the opponents bowstrings of sinew, basically a superior product. As the battle approached, Ussen (the Great Spirit) sent a rain which caused the yucca strings to tighten and the sinew strings to stretch and become useless, so Mahko "won the battle." Betzinez wrote that the Mexicans admired Mahko's business ability, adding that "No emergency ever arose during Mahko's time which caused the Bedonkohes to fight the Mexicans." Historians of today might dispute that conclusion. Mahko became the patriarch of his people, his fame enhanced by the renowned activities of his descendants. He had two wives and six children who grew to maturity; three of his sons and two daughters were by his first wife, and a daughter by the second. Besides Taklishim, who fathered Geronimo, there was a daughter, Na-dos-te, who married Nana, a venerable war leader of the Mimbres Apaches. Another son was grandfather of a wife of Chief Naiche of the Chiricahuas. The third son was related by marriage to Mangas Coloradas. Mahko also was related to such famous Apaches as Fun, Tsisnah and Perico, Geronimo's "best" warriors. The daughter of Mahko by his second wife was mother of Ish-keh (Ishton), wife of the noted Nedhni chief Juh, a great warrior leader. Lacking a strong Bedonkohe leader to succeed him, the tribe fragmented, much of it eventually coming under leadership of Cochise of the Chiricahuas. Mahko died at peace, before Anglo Americans in any numbers had penetrated the country of his people.

Griswold, 90-91; *Geronimo's Story of His Life,* ed. by S.M. Barrett, N.Y., Duffield & Co., 1906, p. 35; Jason Betzinez, W.S. Nye, *I Fought With Geronimo,* Harrisburg, Pa., Stackpole Co., 1959; Angie Debo, *Geronimo: The Man, His Time, His Place,* Norman, Univ. of Okla. Press, 1976; Eve Ball, with Nora Henn, Lynda Sanchez, *Indeh: An Apache Odyssey,* Provo, Ut., Brigham Young Univ. Press, 1980.

Main Poc (Wenebeset, the Crafty One), Potawatomi war chief (d. 1816). An important leader of the Kankakee River, Illinois, Potawatomis, Main Poc's principal name meant "Withered Hand," because of his crippled left hand from which the digits were missing from birth; of religious inclination, he claimed the deformity was a special gift from the spirits with whom, as a shaman, he believed himself in constant communication. He was eloquent, his medicine was strong, his reputation as a war leader redoubtable. By 1807 he was a convert of the Prophet, the Shawnee Tenskwatawa, brother of Tecumseh. The Prophet was "delighted" with his new follower whom he considered the most influential Indian in Illinois. Main Poc scorned the important Treaty of Greenville of August 3, 1795, which less belligerent leaders of his tribe did sign, and he and Turkey Foot of the Tippecanoe region remained hostile to the United States and to Indians in Spanish territory across the Mississippi. From 1796 Main Poc's fighting men attacked wandering bands of Wea, Piankasha, Cherokee and Chickasaw, some of whom were enroute to Fort Massac, Illinois, on the Ohio River. When the United States efforts to quell the hostility proved ineffectual a peace convention was called in October 1805 at St. Louis, but only two minor chiefs of the Potawatomi attended, and Main Poc again shunned the meeting. Shortly afterward he led a large war party across the Mississippi and struck an Osage village, killing 34 women and children and taking back to Illinois about 60 prisoners, Main Poc's village holding some of them until 1807. Late that year the Prophet invited him to visit the Shawnee village on the Auglaize River of Ohio, the Potawatomi remaining there for two months and urging the Prophet to remove his village to Indiana. Enroute to their Illinois country, Main Poc passed through Fort Wayne, where he met William Wells (see entry), who invited the Potawatomis to winter there, which they did. Wells believed, a bit optimistically, that he had undermined the Prophet's influence with Main Poc and secured the chief's loyalty. In April, however, the chief told Wells he intended to renew hostilities with the Osages, and he evidently remained inimical to United States' interests. Wells believed that a visit to Washington, D.C., might convince the chief of the futility of belligerence toward white Americans and in the autumn of 1808 accompanied Main Poc and other Potawatomi to the capital where the chief met President Jefferson and listened to his arguments for peace between his people and the Osages, and acceptance of a settled and agricultural way of life. This suggestion was of no interest to Main Poc. In September 1810 he led a large war party of Potawatomis, Sauks and Kickapoos against the Osages again, killing several but being wounded himself, distressing his followers, who had believed him protected by his power from war injuries. Recovered, the chief established a village at Crow Prairie, north of Lake Peoria, Illinois, from where his young men raided through southern Illinois, causing minor depredations but raising an uproar among the settlers. Governor Ninian Edwards called out the militia to still the turbu-

lence. The chief visited the Sauk and Kickapoo villages seeking support for the Prophet's planned uprising and in June 1811 went to Amherstburg, Ontario, spending the winter there trying to lure bands of Ottawas and Chippewas from any United States leanings. Main Poc missed the Battle of Tippecanoe November 7, 1811, where Harrison and the Prophet's followers fought inconclusively, but for the Potawatomis "the War of 1812 had already started," with Main Poc more openly pro-British. He remained for a time on the Raisin River near Detroit, but sent Wabameme, another chief, to visit Potawatomi villages in Indiana and Illinois, urging them to prepare for war. In early 1812 Tecumseh began to collect young warriors. In June he traveled to Malden, Ontario, to secure gunpowder from the British and to meet with Main Poc. News that war had finally been declared reached the Potawatomis in July, but most tribesmen awaited the return of Main Poc and Tecumseh from Canada with powder and ammunition. Main Poc was not in the great Potawatomi triumph at Chicago when Wells was among the fallen. Eastern Michigan tribesmen crossed into Canada to join those under Main Poc and Tecumseh and to assist the British against Detroit. Main Poc was wounded July 19 in a skirmish with an American patrol near Fort Maldan on the Canard River; he survived the painful wound. August 9 he directed an ambush against American forces and, to avenge his earlier wound, split the skull of an American prisoner with his tomahawk. After the American victory in the Battle of the Thames, Ontario, October 5, 1813, and the death there of Tecumseh, most of the Indian allies of the British wanted to make peace; Main Poc and other leaders signed an armistice providing that they should go home and remain quiet, although the chief had no such intention. Since the British had withdrawn, Main Poc needed supplies from the Americans during the winter and it was feared he would renew hostilities in the spring. Western Potawatomis continued hostilities until the war was seen to be wholly lost, but Main Poc, still a hard-core pro-British chief, remained loyal in principal, although his situation prevented warlike activities of any consequence. News of the Treaty of Ghent filtered into the Indian camps and although Main Poc tried once more to raise warriors for renewed hostilities the effort was unsuccessful. With the war lost, most of the Potawatomi leaders, including Topinbee,

Noungeesai or Five Medals, Mitteeay and others signed the treaty September 8, 1815; Main Poc refused to attend the conference and returned to his camp on the Yellow River of Indiana. In failing health, unable to adjust to peace, he drank heavily and "died while hunting in Michigan during the spring of 1816."

R. David Edmunds, *The Potawatomis: Keepers of the Fire,* Norman, Univ. of Okla. Press, 1978; Charles J. Kappler, *Indian Treaties 1778-1883,* N.Y., Interland Pub. Inc., 1972.

Makarii, Orthodox missionary (fl. 1794-1799). Ieromonk Makarii, that is, a monk ordained as a priest, arrived at Kodiak Island in September 1794 in the entourage of Archimandrite Iossaf with others destined to open mission fields in Alaska. He and Juvenal (see entry) completed a missionary-exploration circumnavigation of Kodiak, Makarii then assigned to Unalaska Island with a spiritual mission covering virtually all of the Aleutians. He had shown special interest in teaching and entered eagerly upon his duties, meeting opposition of occasional severity from the few remaining promyshlenniki there (the sea otters, whose luxuriant fur was the primary attraction for Russians in Alaska, had all but been wiped out around many of the islands). "It is impossible to ascertain whether Makarii was really an eloquent preacher...or whether his success was solely due to circumstances; but success he certainly had." Within a few years virtually all of the Aleuts were baptized and reportedly Christian, though no attempt was made to translate Scripture or ritual for them and Veniaminov (see entry) twenty years later found them Christian largely in name only. Makarii wrote a detailed report dated October 5, 1797, in which he accused Shelikhov fur interests of cruelly mistreating Aleuts on the islands. The company, he wrote, "treats the native islanders in the most barbaric manner. They have no humane instincts. They take the wives and young daughters [of the natives] as their sexual partners. They kill any who refuse to hunt sea otters, and early in the spring they send out the healthy and sick alike, against their will...Because they are so severely beaten, many of them commit suicide. Any of the Aleuts who bring in too few foxes are stretched out on the ground and beaten with heavy sticks mercilessly...I did try as much as possible to encourage the natives to have hope in Imperial great mercy, but [such does not come]...Although the administration sends writ-ten instructions...that the islanders are not to be abused and robbed...the Russians do not heed these instructions, but do as they please. On the islands they simply say, 'the sovereign is far away, so do whatever you wish...As long as there are sea otters there will be no problem.'" Bringing what he described as "important government secrets" which should reach Imperial officials though not intended to leave the islands, Makarii left his post June 25, 1796, wintered on the Kuril Islands, leaving June 30, 1797, and reaching Okhotsk on the Siberian coast July 28 and Iakutsk September 12. Apparently the fur trading interests were more closely attuned to the tsar's interests than the missionaries, for an imperial rescript later read: "The monk Makar, who has exceeded the bounds of his duties and meddled with affairs that did not concern him, is hereby informed that though we pardon him this time for absenting himself wilfully from his appointed post of duty, he must not repeat the offence, and must allow complaints made by the Aleutians to go through their proper channels." Father Makarii joined bishop-designate Iosaf aboard the *Phoenix,* which went down with all hands sometime in May 1799.

Bancroft, *Alaska; Russian Penetration of the North Pacific Ocean.*

Makhov, Jakob, seaman (fl. 1838-1844). A sailor with the 15th Russian Navy Fleet, he accompanied Zagoskin as orderly when on December 30, 1838, that officer left St. Petersburg for Novo Arkhangelsk (Sitka, Alaska) and service with the Russian American Company. When Zagoskin in 1842 launched his two-year expedition into interior Alaska, Makhov volunteered so insistently that Zagoskin took him along. He was taken ill at Fort St. Michael on Norton Sound, however, and was abed from September until December unable to use his legs, the nature of his illness unreported. Zagoskin was forced to leave him there when he set out on his eventful journey.

Zagoskin.

Maksutov, Prince Dmitrii Petrovich, Russian administrator (May 10, 1832-Mar. 21, 1889). Of Tatar descent, his title of prince, according to Pierce, can be traced back to the 16th century, and the family remained Moslem until the 18th century. He entered the naval academy at 8 and June 1, 1849, was assigned to the Black Sea fleet as a midshipman. March 28, 1851, he became a lieutenant and soon was assigned to the east coast of Siberia. In August 1854 he and his brother gallantly assisted in the defense of Petropavlovsk, Kamchatka, against an Anglo-French squadron, although the brother was mortally wounded. Dmitrii was given the honor of bearing news of the successful defense to St. Petersburg and Tsar Nicholas I decorated and promoted him to Captain-Lieutenant. After further sea duty the prince became assistant chief manager of the Russian American Company at 25. A month after his marriage to Adelaide Ivanovna Bushman, daughter of a naval academy English teacher, Maksutov and his bride set out across Siberia, reaching Sitka, Alaska, September 14, 1859. The Maksutovs became close friends of the Furuhjelms, he the Finnish-born chief manager. Maksutov's wife died December 19, 1862, after birth of the third child, and the next year the prince was summoned to St. Petersburg, leaving Sitka May 19, 1863, and arriving in September. A growing Russian faction favored selling Russian America to the United States because of the colony's increasing unprofitability. Maksutov opposed the sale, urging instead expansion of its settlements and more exploration. December 2 the Tsar appointed him acting chief manager of the Russian American Company. He married again, left St. Petersburg February 7, 1864, and May 26, arrived at Sitka. Little is known of his activities during subsequent years, but in the late spring of 1867 news arrived that despite his opposition, on March 30, 1867, at Washington, D.C., Russia and the United States had signed a treaty for sale of Alaska for $7.2 million; Russia ratified the treaty May 14, and the United States May 28, and Maksutov made ready for the transfer. In September United States navy vessels reached Sitka and on October 10, Brigadier General Jefferson Davis arrived with two companies of troops, followed on October 18, by Brigadier General Lovell Rousseau (see entry) and Captains A.A. Peshechurow and F.F. Koskul, representatives of Russia and the Russian American Company, respectively. The actual transfer of the huge territory from Russia to the United States was formalized that afternoon. Maksutov, after winding up company affairs and turning over the various properties to the Americans, left Sitka for the last time January 6, 1869, and by April 30, was back at the family estate at Tula, south of Moscow. The prince eventually came into financial difficulties, his second wife died June 18, 1881, at 36 and there were rumors she had taken her own life.

Upon his own death Maksutov was buried at St. Petersburg. Most of the family papers were destroyed during the October Revolution in 1917, but there is a family tradition that Maksutov had received a Sitka land grant from U.S. President Grant. Pierce found Maksutov "a man of courage and integrity, to whom personal reputation and honor were above material considerations. He was devoted to Alaska [and] the turn of affairs in 1867 was disappointing and the hasty and wasteful retreat which he was compelled to execute brought disillusionment which deepened after his return to Russia."

Richard A. Pierce, *The Builders of Alaska: The Russian Governors 1818-1867,* Kingston, Limestone Press, 1986; Archie W. Shiels, *The Purchase of Alaska,* College, Univ. of Alaska Press, 1967; Bancroft, *Alaska.*

Malakhov, Petr Vasilevich, explorer, fur trader (c. 1800-post 1844). A son of Vasilii Ivanovich Malakhov and an Aleut woman, Malakhov has been credited with being the first European to sight Mt. McKinley, tallest peak in North America, although the attribution is questionable. In February 1816 he apparently was an apprentice navigator on a Lieutenant I.W. Podushkin voyage to Hawaii. He was to be taught navigation enroute, according to Baranov, who noted that the youth already was literate and knew arithmetic. Malakhov in 1818 reportedly led an expedition out of Fort St. Nicholas to explore the country north of Cook Inlet. In his report to Russian American Company governor Yanovsky (see entry) he said he had traveled the region east of the Kuskokwim River, crossed a chain of mountains and discovered a large river flowing northward, upon whose banks were many native settlements or lodgings. The stream, not otherwise identified, may have been a northward flowing tributary of the Kuskokwim or other waterway. Malakhov neither identifies nor describes the mountains, although if he went very far north of Cook Inlet he would have observed McKinley. Farquhar reports, without identifying a source, that "in 1834 a Russian party under Malakoff ascended the Susitna River and must have seen the Alaska Range." That expedition is not elsewhere mentioned and may be a confusion with the 1818 or the 1844 endeavor. In November 1818 he was sent from Sitka to St. Petersburg aboard the *Kutuzov* for training, arriving at Kronstadt September 6, 1819. August 6, 1820, the RAC head office in

Russia reported to Sitka that he had "completed nautical studies" and directed his employment in Alaska. In 1830, as mate of the sloop *Urup,* he made a voyage from Sitka to Okhotsk, Siberia, and in 1831 he was a mate on the *Chichagov* during a Bering Sea cruise. In the spring of 1837 he arrived at Fort St. Michael on Norton Sound where he was to succeed Andrei Glazunov as manager, and to continue efforts to establish a fur station on the Yukon River. He left St. Michael February 8, 1838, on the 11th arrived at Unalakleet and on the 26th at the Yukon. By March 10 he with four men reached the village of Nulagito at the mouth of the Nulato River. Malakhov found the place suitable for a fur post, but went 50 miles farther up the Yukon to discover the Koyukuk River, which he named. On May 3, when the ice went out, Malakhov and his party brought inland beaver fur down the Yukon, the first group to descend the river from Nulato to the coast. Malakhov accompanied Aleksandr Kashevarov's (see entry) 1838 expedition along the Arctic coast to Point Barrow and, by skin boats, somewhat beyond. Discovered were Prokofiiyev Inlet (now Dease Inlet) and Kupriyanov Bay (now Smith Bay). In the winter of 1838-39 he was instructed to establish a trading post at Nulato. He left St. Michael November 19, and reached Nulato March 28, finding a smallpox epidemic there at its height. Late in 1839 he made another trip to Nulato but found the people had been wiped out by disease and his party returned to the mouth of the Unalakleet River; the region was upset by the smallpox epidemic, which as blamed upon the Russians. The situation was tense. Malakhov feared that one of his men, the creole, Lavrentii Ovchinnikov, was plotting mutiny and shot him dead. At Sitka Governor Etolen (see entry) appointed a commission to investigate and although the explorer was exonerated, the district court at Okhotsk was dissatisfied with the result and told the RAC to send Malakhov to Okhotsk for further interrogation. He appears to again have been cleared, for shortly he was back at Sitka. Etolen in 1843 sought to precisely locate the rumored Lake Plaveshnoe (Tazlina) north of the Chugach Mountains with a view to establishing a fur post there. He directed Malakhov to ascend the Susitna River and find a way easterly to the lake. Malakhov set out in the summer of 1844, but reached only Lat. 62°50', Long. 148°46', and demonstrated that the route to the lake from St. Nicholas was impractical. No further word on Malakhov has been located.

Russian Penetration of the North Pacific Ocean; Bancroft, *Alaska;* Francis P. Farquhar, "The Exploration and First Ascents of Mount McKinley," *Sierra Club Bulletin,* Vol. 34, No. 6 (June 1949), 95-109; Zagoskin; Pierce, *Russian America: A Biographical Dictionary.*

Malakhov, Vasilii Ivanovich, fur trader (fl. 1786-1807). B. probably in European Russia, he was at Shelikhov's initial post on Kodiak Island, Alaska, and, according to Pierce, was one of Baranov's "old voyagers." March 27, 1786, Shelikhov sent him with Konstantin Samoilov to punish the chiefs of Shuyak and Afognak islands, north of Kodiak, who had slain a party of Russian traders. The leaders were put to death and a village wiped out. After Shelikhov left in May, Delarov made Malakhov baidarschik, or foreman, over the Kenai Bay working personnel, remaining there for a number of years. Baranov mentioned him in 1792 when he was seeking to counter incursions of the Lebedev-Lastochkin (see entry) company. The trouble in 1797 mounted to guerilla warfare between the Lebedev-Lastochkin company and the natives, who destroyed outposts at Iliamna and Tuniunak, killed 20 Russians and about 100 of their native supporters. Baranov sent Malakhov and an armed party to the aid of the Lebedev-Lastochkin people and when the rival company pulled out of Kenai Bay (Cook Inlet) in 1798 Malakhov was placed in charge of Fort Nikolaevsk there. Russian-native turmoil continued for years along the western Alaskan coasts. April 23, 1807, Baranov indicated that Malakhov was then storekeeper at Pavlovskia harbor, Kodiak. No further word of this individual has been recovered. He was the father of Petr Vasilevich Malakhov, an explorer and sea officer for the Russian American Company.

Russian Penetration of the North Pacific Ocean; Pierce, *Russian America: A Biographical Dictionary.*

Maledon, George, hangman (d. May 6, 1911). His parents were German immigrants with a French name and settled at Detroit, Michigan, where George was schooled and in young manhood moved to Fort Smith, Arkansas, soon joining the city police force. During the Civil War he served in the Union army, then returned to Fort Smith, becoming a deputy sheriff. When headquarters of the federal district court of western Arkansas was established Maledon became a U.S. deputy marshal. An executioner being required, he took the job, although it was always a part-time activity for him, and he retained the deputy marshal position for years, assigned as a prison guard. When Isaac C. Parker (see entry) became presiding judge of the district there was plenty of occupation for a good executioner, and Maledon willingly accepted the job, being paid $100 for each hanging, minus the small burial charges which he had to pay out of his own pocket. Maledon considered the hangings "honorable and respectable work and I mean to do it well." In all it is believed he hanged 60 men, and shot an additional five who tried to escape from the Fort Smith jail while he was on duty. He was married and fathered a daughter who died at 18 from a bullet in the spine, after an unfortunate romance with a married man, Frank Carver, who beat the gallows with the help of attorney J. Warren Reed. After the death of Judge Parker, Maledon met S.W. Harman who came to Fort Smith publicizing a book he said he had written, *Hell on the Border,* about the Fort Smith court. Maledon joined him in a tour of the lecture circuit, displaying his ropes, telling which ones were used to hang various outlaws, and giving a talk about the court. After a year of this activity, Maledon purchased a small farm, but he was not able physically to operate it, being a small man of uncertain health. He entered a soldier's home at Johnson City, Tennessee, remaining there until his death. He had haunted eyes and a spade beard which whitened as he aged.

Bruce Goolsby, "The Hangman," *Frontier Times,* Vol. 37, No. 2 (Feb.-Mar. 1963), 47; James D. Horan, Paul Sann, *Pictorial History of the Wild West,* N.Y., Crown Pubs., 1954; info. from E.F. (Ted) Mains.

Malott, Catharine (Mrs. Simon Girty Jr.), frontierwoman (b.c. 1766). B. in Maryland, she was the eldest child of Peter and Sarah Malott who with their family were in a flotilla of three flatboats coasting down the Ohio River toward Kentucky in late March 1780. A few miles below Cantina Creek, which empties into the river from Ohio, twenty-one miles below Wheeling, West Virginia, the emigrants were attacked by Delaware Munsees (the Wolf division of the Delaware tribe), the leader of the hostiles probably Washnash, a well-known warrior. Two boats escaped and went on to Kentucky; the third was taken with three men killed and twenty-one men, women and children captured. Peter Malott was in one of the crafts which escaped, but his wife, Sarah, and their daughter, Catharine, then 14,

were among those taken eventually to a Delaware or Munsee town on the Scioto River of Ohio. Simon Girty was not involved in the attack, although it has been variously reported that he was so engaged. Catharine was adopted into a Delaware family, and there she matured. Girty at some point became aware of her presence, her acknowledged attractiveness, and determined to marry her. She assented to the arrangement, perhaps in order to return to civilization. Her mother was said to be at Detroit at the time, trying to assemble her scattered family. The Indians were loath to give the girl up, but Girty reportedly assured them he would only take her to visit her mother and then return her to the Munsees, which he had no intention of doing. She accompanied him to Detroit. In August 1784, Simon Girty and Catharine Malott were married and settled two miles below present Amherstburg, Essex County, Ontario; he was 43 and she was 18. The site was across the river and about eighteen miles below Detroit where Girty was frequently employed as an interpreter and in Indian work generally. The couple had at least two sons and a daughter, some of their descendants rising to local prominence. Catharine left him for a time because of his persistent drunkenness and brutality when under the influence, but in 1816, when he was around 75, blind, crippled and virtually helpless, she returned to nurse him through his final months (he died February 18, 1818). Little is reported of Catharine Malott Girty thereafter except that she was religiously inclined, and retained her attractiveness for, in the words of one writer, in her old age "her comeliness did not forsake her."

C.W. Butterfield, *History of the Girtys,* Cincinnati, Robert Clarke & Co., 1850, 1950; Thwaites/Kellogg, *Fronter Defense on the Upper Ohio, 1777-1778.*

Mankato (Ma-Kaw-to, or Blue Earth), Mdewakanton chief (d. Sept. 23, 1862). There were at least two chieftains of this name among the Mdewakanton branch of the Santee Sioux, the present community of Mankato, Minnesota, being named for the earlier individual. The younger chief was a son of Good Road, a group leader who in 1838 had been involved in troubles with the Chippewa on the river named for them, but had survived. Young Mankato was a member of a delegation which on June 19, 1858, at Washington signed a treaty providing for definition of reservation limits, funds to be paid to chiefs and head men, and peaceful relationships for the future. Mankato also was referred to in an Indian Affairs report for 1860, representing his band which came under control of the lower Sioux Agency on the Minnesota River. He, however, took a very active part in the Great Sioux Uprising of 1862-63. He was a leader of the second attack on Fort Ridgely August 20-22, 1862, in which an estimated 800 hostiles were involved, an engagement in which Little Crow, the principal leader, was wounded slightly by a cannon ball. On September 3, in the celebrated Battle of Birch Coulee, Mankato was a principal leader, and three weeks later he was killed by a cannon ball at the Battle of Wood Lake, which effectively terminated major hostilities in Minnesota, the action then moving into Dakota Territory.

Hodge, HAI; William Watts Folwell, *A History of Minnesota*, 4 vols., St. Paul, Minn. Hist. Soc., 1956, II; Charles J. Kappler, *Indian Treaties 1778-1883*, N.Y., Interland Pub., 1972; info. from John Sugden.

Mansfield, Henry Buckingham, naval officer (Mar. 5, 1846-July 17, 1918). B. at Brooklyn, he was graduated from the Naval Academy in 1867, became an ensign in 1868, master in 1870 and lieutenant in 1871. Mansfield was a member of an expedition to Siberia to study an eclipse of the sun in 1869, and later commanded a launch from the *Mohican* which cut out and burned the piratical steamer *Forward* in the Tecupan River, Mexico. He was engaged in coast survey and hydrographic work and commanding Coast Survey steamers from 1871-93. As a lieutenant commander he took the Coast and Geodetic Survey steamer *Patterson* from 1889 on extended surveys in the Alexander Archipelago of the Alaskan Panhandle until 1891; an account of his work was published in the Survey's annual reports for 1890. He is commemorated by Mansfield Peninsula on the northern part of Admiralty Island, and other features. Mansfield became commander in 1897, captain in 1902 and Rear Admiral at his retirement June 15, 1905, whereafter he resided at Brooklyn until his death. He was married.

Orth, 19, 620; *Who Was Who.*

Marchand, Etienne, French sea captain (Jan. 13, 1755-May 15, 1793). B. on Grenada in the West Indies, he was a sea captain with much experience when he tried to open a French trade with the Northwest Coast, though his experience was a financial debacle. His Alaska ambitions may have been inspired by reports of La Perouse (see entry) and other accounts. In 1790 a Marseille commercial house invited him to lead a trading expedition to the upper Pacific coast, and December 14, Marchand sailed with the *La Solide* and a 50-man crew. August 7, 1791, he arrived at Sitka Sound, but found the Indians sufficiently supplied with Russian and other goods and hard traders. Marchand, however, acquired 100 sea otter pelts and took them to China, where he ran into trouble because China and Russia were at odds and the Chinese refused "Russian" furs. Marchand took them to Europe, arriving April 1, 1792, at Toulon, the furs being sold but for not nearly enough to pay for the voyage. "Thus, though a success technically, the voyage was a commercial failure," concluded Pierce.

Pierce, *Russian America: A Biographical Dictionary.*

Marin de la Malgue, Paul, French colonial officer (Mar. 1692-Oct. 29, 1753). Baptized at Montreal, he was, according to Duquesne, born with a tomahawk in his hand and was destined for a notable career on the frontier. By 1720 he was serving in the west, commissioned an ensign in 1722 and assigned to command Chagouamigon (near Ashland, Wisconsin), where he used the post's monopoly in the fur trade to defray expenses and sought to retain Indian loyalty to French interests. He became a lieutenant in 1741. During King George's War (1745-48) he campaigned on the New York frontier, in 1746 leading a war party that destroyed Saratoga (Schulyerville); by 1748 he was a captain. He then commanded Green Bay, Wisconsin, where fur trade profits were lucrative, but the King's expenses in maintaining the strategically important post were equally high. Marin was chosen by Governor Duquesne to establish defenses from Lake Erie to the Ohio Valley to assure French control of the area in the face of England-inclined frontier expansionists. In 1753 Marin established Fort Presque'isle (Erie) on the south shore of Lake Erie and with his 2,000 men was directed to construct a road south to the Allegheny River and establish and garrison a line of posts to the Ohio River. Marin ruthlessly set out on his mission, warned protesting Iroquois off, showed no mercy toward his own flagging laborers and troops, ironed colonial traders caught in the area and sent them to Montreal, and ultimately caused the death of some 400 of his command through over-work and rations so poor that scurvy appeared among them. Marin pushed himself as relentlessly as he drove others, and in the end drove himself to death. He died at Fort de la Riviere au Boeuf, the present Waterford, Pennsylvania. The following year the difficult assignment was completed with construction of Fort Duquesne at the forks of the Ohio. The endeavor had achieved its objective, and the French hold on this portion of the frontier seemed, for the moment, secure.

W.J. Eccles, *The Canadian Frontier 1543-1760,* N.Y., Holt, Rinehart and Winston, 1969; DCB III.

Marsh, John, pioneer (June 5, 1799-Sept. 24, 1856). B. at South Danvers, Massachusetts, he was graduated from Harvard in 1823, in October becoming tutor to officers' children at Fort St. Anthony, now St. Paul, and later at Fort Snelling, Minnesota. He remained two years, studying medicine under the post surgeon, Dr. Edward Purcell. In 1824 and 1825 he was sub-agent to the Sioux at the St. Peter's Sioux Agency at the confluence of the Mississippi and Minnesota (then called St. Peter's) rivers. There he became attracted to Marguerite Decouteaux of French-Sioux parentage; they married and lived together until her death seven years later, raising an only son, Charles; Marsh compiled a Sioux dictionary and grammar. When he was discharged, Lewis Cass (see entry) arranged for him to be named sub-agent at Prairie du Chien, Wisconsin. Marsh, however, retained his close attachment to the Sioux. In 1830 he informed them that a party of Fox Indians was expected at his agency, and by some he was held responsible for an attack made upon the Foxes, the incident perhaps contributory to the Black Hawk War. Agent Joseph Montfort Street (see entry) had been pressing for Marsh's removal because he was overly partial to the Sioux and also for his private trading ventures. Marsh was discharged later in 1830; he sent his wife and son to New Salem, Illinois, for their protection while he remained on the (Red) Cedar River, which flows south from Minnesota across central Iowa. Marsh volunteered to bring a party of Sioux warriors for service in the 1832 Black Hawk War, but they saw little if any combat. Marguerite died and Marsh was formally charged with illegal sale of arms to Indians. He "fled" down the Mississippi to St. Louis, moved over to Independence on the Missouri, for two years engaging in merchandising until, suffering a financial reverse, he went to Santa Fe, arriving in 1835, and by January 1836 he was at Los Angeles. The next month he was granted a license to practice medicine. In early 1837 he was in the Monterey district, having sold his Los Angeles practice, and was now searching for a cattle range, purchasing one in the northern San Joaquin Valley at the foot of Mt. Diablo near today's Antioch. He resumed the practice of medicine, accepting the heavy payments he demanded in cattle and becoming wealthy in livestock, since for many years he was the only physician in the upper valley. He saw the possibility of California becoming another Texas, and encouraged immigration, writing letters published in Missouri and at New Orleans, extolling the advantages of California, and cordially greeting immigrants as they arrived. In 1844-45 he joined Sutter's force against the native Californians, but took little part in subsequent political troubles; he wished to see California taken over by the United States, although he did not favor filibustering. The discovery of gold drew him to the mines for a time, adding to his rapidly growing fortune. He married again in 1851, his second wife dying within a few years, leaving him a daughter who, with her half-brother, inherited his large estate. "In person he was tall, heavy, athletic, and commanding. He was fond of books and a linguist of no mean ability. As a businessman he was adroit, exacting, and not overscrupulous," concluded the *Dictionary of American Biography,* while the *Reader's Encyclopedia of the American West* contended that "to Mexicans and Anglos alike he was disliked as a hard, miserly, embittered man." He seems, however, to have had admirers and a few warm friends, and Bancroft believed that Marsh was "a man of great intelligence, varied accomplishments, and of singular experiences of life. Vallejo and other Californians speak of him in terms of warm praise, as a man of more than ordinary ability." He was murdered by three of his vaqueros, disgruntled over poor wages and perhaps other matters. One of his slayers was sentenced to life about 1866 and Bancroft wrote that in 1886 he was still in prison.

Black Hawk War, Vol. II, Part I, 130-31n., Vol. II, Part III, 1474; Bancroft, *California,* III-VI; *Pioneer Register;* DAB; REAW.

Marsh, S.J., prospector (fl. 1901-1903). With another prospector, F.G. Carter, Marsh in September, 1901, arrived at Collinson Point in Camden Bay, about 80 miles west of the Alaskan-Canadian border at the Arctic Ocean. They wintered on the beach, explored some of the inland streams and reported three large rivers between the Canning and Colville rivers. In April 1902 Marsh moved inland to Cache Creek for further explorations. He met Carter and H.T. (Ned) Arey (see entry) and the trio wintered in the mountains. In February 1903 Carter crossed the divide into the Yukon drainage, Marsh joining him in April, waiting until the Chandalar River was navigable and following it to the Yukon, into which it flows downstream from Fort Yukon.

Orth, 19.

Martin, Joseph, frontiersman 1740-Dec. 18, 1808). B. in Albemarle County, Virginia, he was a rebellious boy of great energy and ran away to join the army in 1756. He afterwards became a hunter and trapper and in the course of explorations visited Powell's Valley, most westerly of several long narrow valleys in southwestern Virginia and northeastern Tennessee, created by the sources of the Tennessee River. It was named for Ambrose Powell by its discoverer, Thomas Walker (see entry) in 1750; the first cabin was erected in it by Joseph Martin in 1768. The next year he took up a large tract in the valley, and planted corn. After Lord Dunmore's War of 1774, during which Martin participated in defense of a frontier fort and as a leader of scouts, he became the Powell's Valley agent for the Transylvania Company and established a colony 50 miles west of the settlements. He was ever active in Indian warfare, commanded a company against the Cherokee in 1776 and in 1777 was appointed by the new government an Indian agent, "a postition of responsibility and power." He resided for many years at Long Island on the Holston River and was frequently a commissioner drawing up treaties. His influence was felt in counteracting British intrigues. He resigned as Indian agent in 1789. He served in the legislature and in 1800 he ran the boundary line between Virginia and Tennessee. Martin died at his home in Henry County. "He was a man of much mental, physical vigor, a born leader, brave to a fault," according to Thwaites.

Thwaites, *Dunmore.*

Martine, Charles, Apache scout (1858-July 31, 1937). A Nedhni of the southern Chiricahuas, Martine had been captured as a boy and sold to a Mexican family near Casas Grandes "and he knew the ways of the Mexicans." This knowledge proved of assistance to Juh, the Nedhni

chief, in some operations south of the border. He was closely associated with Martin Kayitah throughout his life and Kayitah was his cousin, as was Yahnozha, a foremost warrior who accompanied Geronimo. Martine may have taken part in the turbulence surrounding Geronimo and Juh prior to the last bolt of Geronimo in 1885 from the San Carlos Reservation in Arizona, but if so details are lacking. At any rate he was not with Geronimo when he fled south after his March 1886 peace conference with Crook, and remained on the Fort Apache Reservation where in the summer, Miles enlisted Martine and Kayitah to accompany Lieutenant Charles B. Gatewood into Mexico in an effort to contact Geronimo and persuade him to talk peace. According to George Martine, Charles's son, Miles promised the two Apaches that "If you come back alive and Geronimo surrenders I will have the government give you a good home at Turkey Creek [on the Fort Apache Reservation] and...everything you need will be furnished you. And the government will give you seventy thousand dollars if you are successful; you will get the money as soon as Geronimo surrenders and you get back." George Martine added that "neither Martine nor Kayitah had any idea of what seventy thousand dollars might be—just that it was a big sum. They had no use for money but they wanted a home at Turkey Creek...They had not asked for money; but because Miles promised it, they looked for it until they died. Of course they did not get it." Another report says they were promised ten ponies apiece and still another pledge was given of $100 apiece. They got nothing. Charles Martine related how the tiny peace mission progressed, deep into Mexico until word came that Geronimo had been talking peace near Fronteras, to the north, so Gatewood and his two scouts and associates went to Fronteras, picked up the trail and found where Geronimo was based on a mountain near the Bavispe River. Bearing a white flag they approached the hostile camp, having been seen and closely watched by Jasper Kanseah (see entry) and Yahnozha. Geronimo wanted the two shot as they approached but Yahnozha objected, asserting he would shoot the first Apache, including Geronimo, who sought to interfere with the two scouts. Geronimo relented and the two boldly entered the hostile camp, still at risk of their lives. Geronimo agreed to talk with Gatewood and held Kayitah in his camp while Martine was released to inform the officer. Gatewood persuaded the hostiles to surrender, which was done at a conference with Miles north of the border. Then, in the ultimate act of white betrayal, Martine and Kayitah not only received no part of the reward promised them by Miles, but were shipped into eastern exile as prisoners with the hostiles. During their captivity at Mt. Vernon Barracks, Alabama, both Martine and Kayitah enlisted in Company I (Indian) of the 12th Infantry. On August 29, 1894, Second Lieutenant Allyn K. Capron briefly evaluated the Indians under his command in that organization. Martine, he judged, was a "worthless character," but elsewhere in his report he stated that "all the men of this company are excellent soldiers," so he may have written his individual assessment on a different day. Later Martine and Kayitah apparently enlisted in Company L (Indian), 7th Cavalry, for they were on its muster roll in May 1897. Kayitah at Fort Sill headed a village named for him; when Martine succeeded Kayitah as head of the community it became known to many as Martine's village. In 1913 both scouts joined those Apaches electing to move to the Mescalero Reservation in New Mexico, having been freed of their nominal captivity. At one point at Mescalero Martine remarked that he no longer "believed in the old [Apache] ways. I am a member of the Reformed Church and have been for many years." Martine had married Cah-gah-ahshy, his earliest wife who is remembered. She died and was buried at Mescalero. In about 1927 Martine and Kayitah were finally given small pensions, not for their heroism in being instrumental in ending the Geronimo outbreak, but for their enlistments in the armed forces in Alabama and at Fort Sill. Frank C. Lockwood interviewed Martine in the 1930s, finding him then at about 80 "very feeble in both body and mind," and being cared for at the agency hospital. He died on the reservation, the cause listed on his death certificate as "senility." A photograph of Martine and Kayitah together, taken about 1905 appears in the *Arizona Historical Review*, Volume IV, No. 1 (April 1931), facing p. 34, and is also reproduced in Debo, *Geronimo*, p. 373.

Griswold; Eve Ball, with Nora Henn and Lynda Sanchez, *Indeh*, Provo, Brigham Young Univ. Press, 1980; Dan L. Thrapp, *Conquest of Apacheria*, Norman, Univ. of Okla. Press, 1967; Angie Debo, *Geronimo...*, Norman, 1976; Capron's Report to Marion P. Maus, author's collection; Frank C. Lockwood, *The Apache Indians*, N.Y., The Macmillan Co., 1938; info. from Lynda Sanchez.

Martinez y Santiestevan, Antonio José, Catholic priest, enigma (Jan. 17, 1793-July 27, 1867). Described as "the most enigmatic figure in nineteenth century New Mexico [he] was an uncompromising individualist, and a man of intellect in an intellectual wasteland." He was b. in Abiquiu, in northwest New Mexico, into an aristocratic and wealthy family which moved in 1804 to Taos. In his younger days Martinez married and fathered a daughter, but was robbed by death of both wife and child. He then commenced studies for the priesthood at Durango, Mexico, and was ordained a presbyter in 1822. He served various New Mexico parishes and in 1830 became curate of Taos, where he made his base thereafter. He remained intellectually restless, and became as much interested in politics as religion. Upon the death of his noted father, Martinez inherited a sizable estate, which he expanded through business acumen, becoming "one of the most influential men in the northern country." He was generous with his wealth, contributing to charities, to promising candidates for the priesthood, and even to political causes. He acquired a printing press and published various journals along with religious material, all of which added to his influence. In 1835 Santa Anna sent Colonel Albino Pérez as governor to New Mexico. He was "an excellent man," but he was not by birth a New Mexican. This generated dissatisfaction. Opposition grew through tangled financial matters, political jealousies, and Pérez's own conduct in his office, and about August 1, 1837, a revolt broke out among the northern Pueblo Indians, who were backed in part by the disaffected Mexican population. Pérez moved a slight force against the rebel headquarters north of Santa Fe, but this was repulsed, and Pérez fled, was taken and killed. Martinez was regarded by many as one of the principals in the revolution, although his precise role was never defined and remains speculative. His opposition to American occupiers of Santa Fe and New Mexico in 1846 and 1847 was marked. Twitchell wrote that "He realized that the coming of the Americans was a death blow to his power and prestige...and he is said to have done everything he possibly could to create a sentiment of suspicion and distrust" against the invaders. No one except the principals of the 1847 Taos Uprising knew precisely what part he had in the insurrection. "He was a very crafty man and the American authorities could never affirmatively fix upon him any active participation" although numerous natives in later years agreed that they had been guided by his counsel and advice. He hated Charles Bent (see entry), the American governor who once said the priest "will spare no means to injure me." Bent was assassinated in the revolt. The priest possessed open imperfections. "He maintained a harem and fathered several children, one of whom later became a Presbyterian minister." In his political life he was increasingly active, being elected to two legislative assemblies, a matter which brought to him the displeasure of Jean Baptiste Lamy, first bishop of the territory, who arrived in 1853 and with whom Martinez quickly came to cross-purposes. The bishop believed the clergy should take no part in politics, and as a result of this and other criticisms, Martinez, pleading old age and infirmity, resigned as priest of the Taos parish, quickly coming to odds with his successor, a Spanish priest named to the post by Lamy. Eventually Martinez set up an independent church. Lamy, unable to solve this problem gently, suspended Martinez from the exercising of priestly functions. This strengthened rather than weakened the opinionated priest, and he collected a considerable following. Matters became so tense that Lamy excommunicated him. Martinez died at Taos and was buried in the cemetery there.

Twitchell, *Leading Facts,* II; Martinez, "Apologia of Presbyter Antonio J. Martinez,...1838," *New Mexico Historical Review,* Vol. III, No. 4 (Oct. 1928), 325-46; E.K. Francis, "Padre Martinez: A New Mexico Myth," NMHR, Vol. XXXI, No. 4 (Oct. 1956), 265-89; REAW; info. from E.F. (Ted) Mains.

Mason, Barney, gunman (1848-Apr. 11, 1916). B. at Richmond, Virginia, of Irish parentage he early went to Texas, later moving on to New Mexico, where he became a deputy for Sheriff Pat Garrett and was closely associated with him during the Lincoln County War. December 29, 1879, he killed John Farris at Fort Sumner; Farris had taken part in the Mason County War of central Texas, and his slaying "may have been the feud's final act." January 14, 1880, Mason married 17-year-old Juanita Madril at Anton Chico. Garrett, at the same time, with the same witnesses and in the same church, wed Apolinaria Gutiérrez; Juanita and Apolinaria may have been sisters, or half-sisters, for Eve Ball reported that thereafter Garrett and Mason were "brothers-in-law." Mason was with Garrett at the December 19, 1880, killing of Tom O'Foliard at Fort Sumn-

er, and two days later at the Stinking Springs killing of Charles Bowdre. At the latter affair Billy the Kid was captured and Mason was prevented by Jim East and Lee Hall from killing him. Mason upbraided Garrett for failure to share rewards for bounties collected, but apparently never gained anything from them. He was occasionally indicted for rustling, was sentenced May 1, 1887, to 18 months for that failing, but was pardoned November 16 of the same year by Governor Edmund G. Ross. Mason promptly got into another legal entanglement, dallied briefly with an outlaw grouping, then commenced farming near Tucumcari, New Mexico. He settled his family in a dugout home; heavy rains one day caused the roof to collapse, killing his wife and children. Mason died of a cerebral hemorrhage and was buried in the Union Cemetery at Bakersfield, California. He was described by Utley as being, during the Lincoln County War, short, stocky, red-faced, red-haired, and hot tempered.

Chuck Parsons, *True West,* Vol. 37, No. 8 (Aug. 1990), 13-14; Robert N. Mullin notes; Robert M. Utley, *Billy the Kid,* Lincoln, Univ. of Nebr. Press, 1989; Eve Ball to author, May 27, 1973.

Mason, Samuel, military officer, desperado (c. 1750-July 1803). B. in Virginia, he was believed to be of the distinguished Mason family. He became a militia officer and as captain commanded a company at Fort Henry at Wheeling, West Virginia, in the summer of 1777. General Edward Hand (see entry), warned of an intended attack on Wheeling and ordered the mustering of all militia between the Ohio and Monongahela rivers to its defense. By the end of August eleven companies had assembled there and Fort Henry was considered "Indian proof." The non-appearance of the enemy for some time, however, caused authorities to permit nine companies to go home, leaving only the companies of Mason and Captain Joseph Ogle at Fort Henry. The hostiles arrived August 31, on the morning of the 1st fired on several men who were rounding up horses and Mason, hearing the shots, with fourteen men went to the rescue, according to De Hass. The main body of the enemy lay in ambush, slaying all but Mason, who was twice wounded, narrowly averting death by shooting an attacker, then concealing himself behind a log. Captain Ogle now advanced to the rescue, finding his way through a heavy fog with difficulty and bringing with him a dozen scouts, Martin Wetzel (see entry) among them, De Hass reported. The same fate that had met Mason's party greeted Ogle's and of the 26 men who had sallied from the fort, only three survived, two of them badly wounded. There remained within the fort a small garrison, but it was quickly reinforced and successfully withstood the attack of an estimated 380 Indians. Thwaites reviews the incident and concluded that the whites actually lost fifteen killed and had five wounded, while the enemy loss was one killed and nine wounded. Some of the deeds reported for this first siege in 1777, according to Thwaites, were enacted in the second siege, that of September 11, 1782, adding, "but most of them are purely mythical." Mason, recovered, commanded Fort Henry again in 1778. He lived subsequently on Buffalo Creek, later on Wheeling Creek outside of town where he kept a tavern. After the Revolution he moved with his family to Washington County, Tennessee, but was soon forced out for "petty" thieving. He next appeared in Russellville, then in Henderson, Kentucky, where outlawry again forced him out. In 1797 he dwelt at Cave-in-the Rock, south of Shawneetown, Illinois, with his sons and others practicing river piracy upon passing boatmen. Mason was next heard of along the lower Mississippi, he with his band reportedly guilty of robberies along the Natchez Trace, and continuing piracy along the river, his spreading notoriety spurring many efforts to apprehend him and break up his band. Spanish authorities arrested him in January 1803 near New Madrid, Missouri; taken into custody also were his four sons, and a man known as Setton, or Taylor, or Wells, but who in reality was the notorious Wiley (Little) Harpe, and others. The Spanish determined that none of Mason's crimes had been committed on the Spanish side of the river and the desperadoes were ordered turned over to American authorities at Natchez. Enroute, Mason on March 26, killed the commander of the boat, and with his outlaw party made his escape. Rewards had been offered for him and in July he was killed by Harpe and James May, who brought in Mason's head, hoping for a reward. Both men were recognized, however, as themselves members of Mason's vicious band, and were hanged February 8, 1804, at Old Greenville, Mississippi. Mason was described as a large man of an agreeable nature who was not ordinarily interested in murder, except in cases of what he deemed necessity.

Thwaites/Kellogg, *The Revolution on the Upper Ohio, 1775-1777,* Madison, Wis. Hist. Soc., 1908; Wills De Hass, *History of the Early Settlement and Indian Wars of Western Virginia,* Wheeling, H. Hoblitzell, Pub., 1851, 1960; Alexander Scott Withers, *Chronicles of Border Warfare,* Cincinnati, Robert Clarke Co., 1895, 1970; DAB.

Matchikiwis (Madjeckewiss, etc.), Chippewa (Ojibway) chief (c. 1735-c. 1805). B. in northern Michigan he belonged to a fraction of his people who inhabited central and northern Michigan. He grew to be tall and powerful and by his midtwenties was a recognized war chief. When Pontiac's warriors besieged Detroit and threatened British holdings in the upper Midwest, Matchikiwis welcomed the opportunity for conflict and planned the capture of Fort Michilimackinac, near the present Mackinaw City, on the strategic Strait of Mackinac. Charles de Langlade (see entry), a trader with vast Indian experience, cautioned the commandant, Captain George Etherington, of the danger of an Indian attempt against the post, but the officer dismissed the warning. On June 2, 1763, Matchikiwis and his followers were engaged in a game of lacrosse outside the fort pickets. The chief threw the ball over the defenses and the warriors rushed in, apparently to recover the ball, when waiting women handed them firearms they had concealed beneath their blankets. Within minutes the garrison was destroyed and the Indians controlled the post, shortly leaving its ruins to join Pontiac in his siege of Detroit. When that blockade was lifted and Michilimackinac recaptured by the British, Matchikiwis was returned from his Quebec confinement with high honors paid to flatter him and obtain his loyalty to the English. During the Revolution he was a staunch ally of the British. He claimed to have been with Burgoyne in New York, then returned to the Northwest. He became friends with the Michilimackinac officers, went to Detroit to strengthen the resolve of Indians there when an attack by George Rogers Clark was feared, took part in the council at Cross Village, Michigan, on July 4, 1779, and accompanied an English officer to secure the support of the Potawatomis, then was sent to the Illinois country to harass the white Americans. He was named to command Indian allies in the expedition of British Captain Emmanuel Hesse to attack the Spanish village of St. Louis, Missouri. When the assault failed Matchikiwis harassed the region of Prairie du Chien, Wisconsin. In September 1783 he accompanied Jean-Baptiste Cadot, a relative through marriage, to Chequamegon Bay, Wisconsin, to settle a conflict between the Ojibway/Chippewas and the Foxes and Sioux. Matchikiwis came into dispute with the British over the paucity of their support for the Indians when the Revolution wound down. He joined the confederacy which was defeated by Anthony Wayne at the Battle of Fallen Timbers in 1794 when the British apparently gave little or no assistance to the Indians. Under the name of Mashipinashiwish (Red Bird), he signed the significant Greenville Treaty of August 3, 1795, which gave to the Americans most of the northern Ohio Valley and land around Niagara, Detroit and Michilimackinac. The exact date of his death is unestablished.

Info. from John Sugden; Lyman C. Draper, "Notice of Match-e-ke-wis," *Wisconsin Historical Collections,* Vol. 7 (1876), 188-94; DCB, V, 567-68.

Mathews, George, military officer, governor (Aug. 30, 1739-Aug. 30, 1812). Of Irish descent, he was b. in Augusta County, Virginia. At 18 he commanded a volunteer company against Indians, and at 22 pursued a party of raiders, killing nine of them. He took part in the important Battle of Point Pleasant, West Virginia, October 10, 1774. As colonel of the 9th Virginia Regiment he fought at Brandywine and Germantown, where he was captured and confined on a prison ship in New York Harbor until 1781, when he was exchanged. He promptly joined Nathaniel Greene's force as colonel of the 3rd Virginia. After the Revolution he moved to Georgia and engaged in farming until he was elected governor in 1787; while in that office he was elected to the First Congress in 1789, serving until 1791, and was again elected governor, serving from 1793-96. In his initial term as governor he supported John Sevier and the Franklin government; in his second he signed the notorious Yazoo Acts, which involved fraudulent land matters along the Yazoo River. After falling into disfavor for his support of the Yazoo actions, Mathews returned to prominence around 1810. In 1811 he was appointed commissioner to settle Florida troubles and when that effort failed he was appointed a Brigadier General. He incited a rebellion in 1812 against Spanish authority, a move that Washington finally "suppressed and repudiated," an action at which Mathews was greatly incensed. He started toward Washington, D.C., to take issue with the federal government, but contracted a fever and died at Augusta, Georgia,

on his 73rd birthday. He was, judged Thwaites, "a unique and pronounced character."

BDAC; DAB; Thwaites, *Dunmore.*

Matthews, Sampson, frontiersman (fl. 1755-1781). A brother of Archer and George Matthews, Sampson was keeper of a tavern at Staunton, Virginia, and a prominent citizen of Augusta County. He had served as a quartermaster in the French and Indian War and also had been a deputy sheriff and justice of the peace. Sampson was officially styled a "master driver of cattle" while with Charles Lewis's Augusta regiment in the Point Pleasant, West Virginia, campaign which terminated in the October 10, 1774, battle against Shawnees that effectively ended Lord Dunmore's War. In 1777 Captain John Bowyer wrote to Colonel William Fleming that on information from Sampson Matthews the garrison at the Greenbrier River post was virtually out of rations and facing starvation. In March 1778 Matthews and Samuel McDowell were named commissioners to deal with Ohio Indians as requested by the Delaware peace chief White Eyes (see entry). The commissioners invited White Eyes to send or bring noted men to Pittsburgh for the treaty-making procedure. In 1781 Matthews was colonel of a regiment raised to repel General Benedict Arnold's marauding invasion of Virginia.

Thwaites, *Dunmore;* Reuben Gold Thwaites, *Frontier Defense on the Upper Ohio 1777-1778,* Madison, Wis. Hist. Soc., 1912, 1977.

Maxwell, Thomas, scout (d. 1787). A brother of the competent Captain James Maxwell, Thomas settled on Blue Stone, Tazewell County, Virginia, in 1772. Captain Daniel Smith (see entry) was very disappointed in Thomas Maxwell's performance as a scout, a position to which he had appointed him upon James Maxwell's recommendation; yet Dan Smith appeared to get over his displeasure, for he continued to use Thomas in that capacity. Thomas Maxwell was in Captain Isaac Shelby's company at the 1780 Battle of King's Mountain. He was killed by Indians on a later occasion.

Thwaites, *Dunmore.*

Mazahsha, Sisseton Sioux chief: *see,* Red Iron

Mazzanovich, Anton (Tony Dalton), historical writer (Apr. 30, 1860-July 31, 1934). B. at

Lesina, Dalmatia, Austria, he was brought at 8 to America by his parents, landing at New York in October 1868 and reaching San Francisco December 24. Anton enlisted in the army January 29, 1870, at not quite 10 years of age which, he later said, was "the youngest soldier, probably, that ever enlisted in the Regular Army"; he was assigned to the band of the 21st Infantry, but was honorably discharged August 11, 1873, at Fort Vancouver, Washington, at the request of his father, Lorenz Mazzanovich, on the basis of his tender age (and to help support the family). At 20 he again enlisted February 10, 1881, at San Francisco in Troop M, 6th Cavalry, was transferred to the band on March 1, and to Troop F August 21, 1881; he was honorably discharged July 10, 1882, at Fort Grant because of disability; he was a private throughout his military service. His Company F was not present at the noted Cibecue battle and aftermath, August 30-31, 1881, but was involved in the pursuit of Juh and Geronimo when they plunged south from San Carlos Reservation to Mexico. Mazzanovich may well have been in the hard fight at Cedar Springs (Graham Mountain), October 2, and at South Pass of the Dragoon Mountains on October 4. In his book, Mazzanovich describes at length related operations in which he was not personally engaged, as in the spring 1882 emeute of hundreds of Apaches from San Carlos toward Mexico, the incident evidently engineered by Juh. Mazzanovich's personal Indian-fighting experience with the army was very limited as a soldier but more extensive as a civilian packer afterward. He worked at a general store-saloon for a few months following his discharge, then became cook for a pack train and shortly was promoted to packer. He had nothing to do with Crook's great Sierra Madre adventure of 1883 although it is difficult to discern that fact from his book; he did, however, pack supplies to the border for Crook's use on his return. Mazzanovich subsequently joined what he called "the New Mexico National Guard, or Rangers," a kind of informal militia group in which he served under the name of George E. Bolton. The outfit to which he nominally belonged, operated in 1885 in the San Simon Valley and along the east front of the Chiricahua Mountains, but made no contact with Geronimo's hostiles. An indication of how impetuously foolish Mazzanovich occasionally was came shortly when he and his friend, Horace Ambler, a lieutenant of the

"Rangers," sighted seven Apaches wearing the red headbands of the enlisted scouts and determed to "make seven good Indians," adding that "neither of us had any use for these Apache scouts, as they were treacherous and could not be depended upon in an emergency." But the remainder of the scout command under a Lieutenant Bailey (perhaps Albert Sidney Bailey, who commanded a scout company, although the dates do not jibe) appeared and, wrote Mazzanovich, "that settled our making any 'good' Indians," fortunately for him and for the conduct of operations against the Apaches. To have assassinated scouts enlisted in the U.S. service, for no rational reason, might have ignited a catastrophe, the ramifications of which could have been serious. The rest of Mazzanovich's book is interesting, but very little is based upon his own experiences. He wrote many papers on Arizona and southwestern historical subjects, but is best known for his book, *Trailing Geronimo,* which went through three printings, the best being the third. He worked as a brakeman for the Southern Pacific Railroad near Clifton, Arizona, ran a dance hall on the side, and his talents as actor and singer came to the fore. He took the stage name of Tony Dalton, joined the Howard Dramatic Company, a traveling theater group, and "barnstormed" through the West. He became night foreman at Universal City in Los Angeles and producer Dustin Farnum gave him the role of a Mexican commandante in "The Light of the Western Stars" for $75 a week, after which he acted in other movies. He also worked on Broadway, New York, with various stage productions, although apparently not as an actor. He settled in retirement at Los Angeles.

Anton Mazzanovich, *Trailing Geronimo,* Los Angeles, p.p., 1926, 1931; info. from the Ariz. Hist. Soc.

Meade, Richard Worsam, naval officer (Oct. 9, 1837-May 4, 1897). B. at New York City, he graduated form the Naval Academy fifth in his class in 1856. January 23, 1858, he became a lieutenant and a lieutenant commander on July 14, 1862. He commanded the naval battalion that put down the July 13, 1863, draft riots in New York. After distinguished Civil War service he was promoted to commander September 20, 1868, and in that rank reconnoitered portions of the Alexander Archipelago in the Alaskan Panhandle with the *Saginaw* in 1868-69, roughly surveying various places enroute. Meade Glacier near the Lynn Canal and Meade Point of Kuiu Island were named for him, his maps incorporated in official hydrographic charts. In 1871-73 he commanded the *Narragansett* on a 60,000-mile Pacific assignment, mostly under sail, protecting American interests in many places and concluding the first United States treaty with Samoa. Meade continued to rise in his profession and retired in 1895 as a Rear Admiral. He died at Washington, D.C. Meade was married and fathered a son and four daughters.

DAB; Orth, 22, 631.

Medvedev, Denis, explorer, fur trader (d. 1763). In 1762 he cleared Petropavlovsk, Kamchatka, for the Aleutians, wintered on Bering Island with Ivan Korovin who captained another shipload of adventurers, the two vessels proceeding in 1763 to the eastern Aleutians, where Medvedev decided to winter on Umnak and Korovin on Unalaska islands. Much abused natives revolted against the Europeans in December, attacked Korovin and were beaten off only with heavy white losses. Korovin and his men re-embarked and in April were wrecked on Umnak Island, being subjected there to fresh attacks. July 21 they found the charred remains of Medvedev's ship, the *Zakhariia I Elizaveta,* and, in a hut, 20 bodies including that of Medvedev. Pierce reports that in 1970 archeological excavations led by anthropologist W.S. Laughlin found a mass grave containing remains of 13 Russians and one Aleut, with coat buttons and a signet ring, possibly identifying one skeleton as that of Medvedev.

Pierce, *Russian America: A Biographical Dictionary.*

Medvednikov, Vasilii Georgevich, fur trader (d. June 24, 1802). An employee of the Russian American Company in Alaska, Medvednikov in 1792 left Unalaska by baidara, coasted the north shore of the Alaska Peninsula to the Kvichak River at the head of Kvichak Bay and traveled upstream to Iliamna Lake, continuing along its northwestern shore to the Newhalen River "where he erected a cross." He then made his way to Kodiak Island and the RAC headquarters. In 1796 Medvednikov headed the expedition which founded the Russian settlement at Yakutat Bay, an imortant harbor at the head of the Alaskan Panhandle; 30 families and a number of promyshlenniki left Kodiak aboard the *Tri Svi-*

atitelia, commanded by Gerasim Pribylov (for whom the Pribylov Islands were named) and arrived at the bay June 25. Construction began under I.A. Polomoshnoi. Medvednikov returned to Kodiak aboard the ship. Baranov directed him to further reconnoiter Lake Iliamna, which was accomplished in part. In 1799 Medvednikov was appointed foreman for the RAC station near the present Sitka. He was instructed to find a suitable site for the establishment, selected one which did not please Baranov who, with Medvednikov, tramped all over the region hunting a better one, could not locate any and settled for the site Medvednikov had already chosen. Baranov left for Kodiak with Medvednikov in charge of construction for the fort "already well along toward completion." He also was charged with defense of the site, but on a holiday, June 24, 1802, a large force of Kolosh (Tlingit) Indians stormed the place and Medvednikov was among the first to fall. About 20 Russians and 130 Aleuts were slain, the buildings plundered, collected furs seized and the structures burned.

Pierce, *Russian America: A Biographical Dictionary.*

Melnikov, Afanasii, cossack (fl. 1725-1730). In 1725 he was sent from Iakutsk, Siberia, to the Chukotski Peninsula and on his return reported that in April 1730 there appeared "from an island in the sea two men who had walrus teeth fastened to their own." They told Melnikov that it required "a day to go from the Chukchi Cape to their island and another day from there to another island...which island is called the great land. On this great land are to be found all kinds of animals—sables, beavers, land otters, and wild deer. All kinds of green trees grow there." Melnikov, conceding that "such reports cannot be trusted," yet urged that a voyage be made seeking to confirm this report. The great land, of course, was Alaska.

Pierce, *Russian America: A Biographical Dictionary.*

Melville, George Wallace, naval officer, explorer (Jan. 10, 1841-Mar. 17, 1912). B. at New York City, he studied at the Brooklyn Collegiate and Polytechnic Institute and then worked for an engineering firm until July 29, 1861, when he entered the Navy's Engineer Corps as third assistant engineer. He served on various vessels throughout the Civil War and by

1865 was first assistant engineer. His naval service was varied, on many seas and offered countless opportunities for Melville to exhibit his innovative services and "for the successful performance of the routine duties of his profession he was often commended by his superior officers." It was said that he revealed an "amount of mechanical ability, energy, and engineering skill rarely found." In 1873 he served aboard the *Tigress* in the search for the *Polaris,* the Arctic ship of Captain Charles F. Hall, being commended for "great fertility of resource, combined with thorough practical knowledge." Deeply interested in polar exploration, he volunteered as chief engineer of the *Jeanette* under George W. De Long (see entry) for an extended expedition, during which the vessel was held fast by ice for nearly two years, drifting northwestward from Bering Strait by Arctic Ocean currents. Melville took possession of Henrietta Island of the De Long group northwest of Wrangel Island for the United States in what the commander described as a "brave and meritorious action." After the *Jeanette* was crushed by ice and sank, Melville, De Long and the party traveled over the pack until they came to open water, then embarked in three ship's boats for the Siberian coast to the south. One boat was lost in a gale and the other two separated, De Long reaching a western mouth of the Lena River, an uninhabited area, and Melville's boat attaining an eastern river mouth, to be succored by natives. Within weeks, although still weak from his ordeal, Melville led a search party to the west, but could not find the De Long group. Months later he headed a renewed effort and found their bodies, journals and impedimenta. In 1881 Melville became a chief engineer and in 1884 as such he accompanied the *Thetis* in the Greely Relief Expedition, being among the first to reach the remnants of the party at Cape Sabine of Ellesmere Island to bring them off. He had no further polar experience. He became chief of engineers of the Navy in 1887 and played an important part in modernization of the service, credited with introduction of the triple screw, of vertical engines and other innovations. He received many honors from governments, scientific and other societies and from universities. He retired as a rear admiral in 1903. The *Dictionary of American Biography* described him as while "sometimes gruff and irascible, he possessed a dauntless and masterful spirit, which suited his massive frame, leonine

head, and great dome-like forehead." He died at Philadelphia, survived by his second wife. He had written *In the Lena Delta* (1885), which described some of his Arctic adventures.

CE; DAB; *Who Was Who.*

Mendenhall, Walter Curran, geologist (Feb. 20, 1871-June 2, 1957). B. at Marlboro, Ohio, he was graduated from Ohio Normal University in 1895, studied at Harvard and Heidelberg universities and joined the Geological Survey in 1894, remaining with it until his death, being director from 1930 until 1943. He was attached to the Edwin Glenn (see entry) 1898 Alaskan expedition and was with the party exploring the Matanuska River Valley and across the Alaska Range to the Tanana River. In 1900 he worked with topographer William Johns Peters on the eastern part of the Seward Peninsula. In 1901 with topographer Dewitt Lee Reaburn he made a topographic and geologic reconnaissance from Fort Hamlin, 40 miles northeast of Rampart on the Yukon, by way of Dall, Kanuti, Alatna and Kobuk rivers to Kotzebue Sound. In 1902 he was geologist for a party headed by Thomas Golding Gerdine (see entry) in the Copper River Valley. Mendenhall was a member of the American Association for the Advancement of Science, president of the Geological Society of America in 1936, a member of the National Academy of Sciences and belonged to other prestigious organizations. He lived in retirement at Chevy Chase, Maryland, and was buried at Marlboro, Ohio. He was married.

Orth, 22; *Who Was Who.*

Mercado, California missionary: *see,* Vásquez del Mercado, Jesús María

Mercer, Hugh, physician, military officer (c. 1725-Jan. 12, 1777). B. in Aberdeenshire, Scotland, he was educated as a physician at the University of Aberdeen, joined the army of Charles Edward (Bonnie Prince Charlie), the Young Pretender, and was at the disastrous Battle of Culloden, whereafter he promptly emigrated to America, settling at Mercersburg, Pennsylvania He practiced medicine for a decade, but when the French and Indian War broke out became an officer in the provincial corps as a captain, eventually becoming colonel of the Third Battalion. He took part in Braddock's 1755 expedition and was wounded at the July 9 action, which saw the command all but destroyed. Mercer took part under John Armstrong (see entry) in the successful attack on Kitanning, a Delaware town on the upper Allegheny River, September 8, 1756. He accompanied the 1758 expedition of John Forbes (see entry) to occupy the ruins of the abandoned French Fort Duquesne; he was appointed commandant of Fort Pitt, built on the ruins of Duquesne, and in 1759 conducted negotiations with leaders of the Six Nations and other tribes. He had become acquainted with George Washington, who suggested that he settle at Fredericksburg, Virginia, where he again took up the profession of medicine. He belonged to the same Masonic Lodge as Washington and sometimes was a guest at Mount Vernon. He married at Fredericksburg and fathered four sons and a daughter. With the American Revolution he again entered the military, becoming colonel of the 3rd Virginia Infantry and on June 5, 1776, was commissioned a Brigadier General. His service in the early part of the Revolution was worthy. He was at the Battle of Trenton, New Jersey. On January 3, 1777, at Princeton, his horse was shot from under him, he was bayoneted in seven places and from these wounds he died. Washington characterized him in a letter to the president of the Continental Congress as "the brave and worthy Gen'l Mercer."

Thwaites, *Dunmore;* DAB.

Merriam, C(linton) Hart, naturalist (Dec. 5, 1855-Mar. 19, 1942). B. at New York City he went to Yale from 1874-77 and earned an M.D. from the College of Physicians and Surgeons at Columbia in 1879; he had a medical practice from 1879 until 1885 when he became chief of the U.S. Biological Survey, retaining that position until 1910. From 1910-39 he conducted biological and ethnological investigations under a special trust fund established by Mrs. E.H. Harriman. With respect to Merriam's field experiences, he had been naturalist for the Hayden Survey of 1872, visited the Arctic seal fishery from Newfoundland as surgeon aboard the ill-fated *Proteus* in 1883 and Alaska in 1891, investigating the fur seal condition on the Pribylov Islands. Merriam conducted numerous biological explorations in the west and held positions with a variety of organizations. He was the author of a great many works, including about 400 papers on zoological, botanical, ethnological and historical subjects. Among his publications, some booklength and others more brief, were:

The Birds of Connecticut (1877); *Mammals of the Adirondacks* (1882-84); *Trees, Shrubs, Cactuses and Yuccas of Death Valley* (1898); *Laws of Temperature Control of Geographic Distribution of Terrestrial Animals and Plants* (1894); *Synopsis of the Weasels of North America* (1896); *Life Zones and Crop Zones of the United States* (1898); *The Indian Population of California* (a paper published in the *American Anthropology* which Kroeber identified as "the only serious attempt to approach this subject critically," Vol. VII, 594-606, 1905); *The Dawn of the World: Myths and Weird Tales Told by the Mewan Indians of California* (1910); *Review of the Grizzly and Big Brown Bears of America* (1917); *Earliest Crossing of the Deserts of Utah and Nevada to Southern California—Route of Jedediah Smith in 1826* (1923); *First Crossing of the Sierra Nevada—Jedediah Smith's Trip from California to Salt Lake in 1827* (1923); *The Buffalo in Northeastern California* (1926), and *The Classification and Distribution of the Pit River Tribes of California* (1926). Merriam's wife predeceased him, and he was survived by two daughters. He made his home in retirement at Berkeley, California.

Who Was Who; CE; various bibliographies referring to Merriam's papers on his selected subjects.

Michler, Nathaniel, military officer (Sept. 13, 1827-July 17, 1881). B. at Easton, Pennsylvania, he went to West Point and graduated 7th in a class of 38, being commissioned a brevet second lieutenant of the Topographical Engineers July 1, 1848, and a second lieutenant April 7, 1854. In his professional capacity he made surveys and reconnaissances in Texas and New Mexico from 1848 to 1851. In January 1849 Michler, together with Second Lieutenant Francis T. Bryan, explored the country near Aransas Pass and Corpus Christi, Texas, for an army depot, and laid out a road to San Antonio. In the early summer Michler ran a road from Port Lavaca on the Gulf to San Antonio. In June and July he surveyed a route from Corpus Christi to Fort Inge on the Leona River, and reconnoitred the Frio and Nueces rivers. His "most impressive" service, however, was a road survey from Fort Washita, Oklahoma, to Horsehead Crossing on the Pecos River in furtherance of a plan to connect the Red River posts with the Rio Grande settlements overland. He left Fort Washita November 9, 1849, charting a route through the Cross Timbers, along the Red River and thence to the main fork of the Brazos and although he met many Indian parties, all were peaceful. Michler's final road-surveying assignment in Texas was to trace a route from San Antonio to Ringgold Barracks, "the most important military depot on the lower Rio Grande." This was done in September 1850 in company with Second Lieutenant Martin Luther Smith (later a Confederate Major General). In 1851 Michler joined the Mexican Boundary Survey and was connected with it until 1857, after its field work was completed. Under Michler's direction the western half of the survey, from the Rio Grande to San Diego, California, was completed October 14, 1855, the remainder of his time devoted largely to compiling his excellent and informative report. Michler, as principal assistant to First Lieutenant William Hemsley Emory (see entry), sailed from New York September 20, 1854, reaching San Diego by way of Panama and San Francisco and arriving at Fort Yuma on the lower Colorado River December 9. The survey work was routine, but Michler's report enlivened the technical details by perceptive descriptions and comments on such side issues as the Indians he encountered. He gave "perhaps the most complete description of Quechan [a Yuman tribe] appearance," according to Forbes. Michler wrote that "these Indians are of a dark brown color; during the cold weather, of dull and dirty appearance, but in summer bright and glossy from bathing in the river." The men were of "medium height, well formed and slender; not muscular the deltoid muscles alone being largely developed arising from the peculiar mode of throwing the arms while swimming; active and clean-limbed; their features not disagreeable, although they have large noses, thick lips, and high cheekbones; their chests are well-developed and figures manly, indicating activity but not strength." The women, he noted, had figures "fine and plump, the bust is well developed, the mamma firm; the arms finely moulded; the hands small and pretty; the legs beautifully formed and well-rounded, and nicely turned ankles...altogether they possess a very voluptuous appearance. Their deportment is modest, and their carriage and bearing erect and graceful." He also found the Quechans "good-natured, laughing and talking all the time." Michler became a first lieutenant May 19, 1856, and a captain September 9, 1861. His Civil War service was excellent; he was promoted to Major of Engineers (the Engineer Corps having absorbed the Topographical Corps March 3,

1863), and became a lieutenant colonel October 16, 1877, by which time he also was a brevet Brigadier General. His further service, while creditable, had little frontier interest. Michler died at Saratoga Springs, New York, and was buried at Easton. His first wife pre-deceased him, and the second survived him.

Cullum; Heitman; DAB; "Report of Lt. N. Michler," *Report of the United States and Mexican Boundary Survey,* 34 Cong., 1 Sess., HED 135; William H. Goetzmann, *Army Exploration in the American West 1803-1863,* New Haven, Yale Univ. Press, 1959; Jack D. Forbes, *Warriors of the Colorado: The Yumas of the Quechan Nation and Their Neighbors,* Norman, Univ. of Okla. Press, 1965; Odie B. Faulk, *Too Far North...Too Far South,* Los Angeles, Westernlore Press, 1967.

Middleton, John, partisan (c. 1854-1885). B. in Tennessee, he was described by Utley as "a beefy drifter off the Texas cattle trails," though little else is known of his early life. Webb mentions a Texas Ranger, "Sergeant Middleton," serving under McNelly in 1874, but gives no first name and there is no evidence except the cognomen that it is the same man, although the John Middleton of the Lincoln County War, who "feared nothing and nobody" and was an expert with firearms, would have been useful to any Ranger outfit. He was dark complexioned, with black hair, black eyes and "a huge black mustache," stood 5 ft., 10 in., in height and weighed 180 pounds. Despite his appearance, which John Tunstall described as "about the most desperate looking man I ever set eyes on," he was "reserved and soft spoken," though what he said was listened to with respect. Middleton was sent by the cattle firm of [Robert D., probably] Hunter and Jesse Evans (not the Lincoln County partisan, but a Kansas stockman) to New Mexico in 1876 to obtain cattle from John Chisum, but for some reason the mission fell through. In Lincoln County Middleton was hired October 20, 1877, by Tunstall, being "recognized for his marksmanship with pistol and rifle." In late October he was one of six men under special constable Dick Brewer pursuing a much larger force driving cattle stolen from the Tunstall Feliz River Ranch and other layouts. Brewer dropped out but Middleton took over and caught up with the rustlers within ten miles of the Texas border. He threw down on the thieves, forced peaceful release of the cattle with no shooting, and brought them back. It was a bold, impressive feat. At the Tunstall place Middleton worked not only with Brewer but also with Billy the Kid. February 18, 1878, Middleton, Brewer, the Kid and Robert Widenmann, with Tunstall left the ranch at 9 a.m., driving horses to Lincoln. At about 5:30 p.m. Tunstall was assassinated in the initial significant killing of the Lincoln County War. Middleton had urged his employer to escape to the timber, but Tunstall, misunderstanding his danger or the plea, failed to do so. From that time onward Middleton was active in the war on the side of the Tunstall-McSween faction as opposed to Dolan elements. Sheriff William Brady and George Hindman were shot down at Lincoln April 1, 1878, and subsequently indictments were returned against Middleton, the Kid and Henry Newton Brown for the Brady killing, but Middleton and Brown escaped prosecution. April 4, Middeton was involved in the famed battle at Blazer's Mill in which Brewer was killed, Andrew L. (Buckshot) Roberts wounded mortally, Middleton suffered a heavy chest wound which was expected to be fatal, although it was not immediately so, and others were wounded less seriously. Possibly because of his injury, Middleton apparently took no part in the Five Days Battle at Lincoln, and appeared next at Fort Sumner from where he, with Fred Waite (see entry), and the Kid in September 1878 drove stolen horses to Tascosa in the Texas Panhandle. From there the Kid returned to New Mexico, Waite went on to Indian Territory, and Middleton to Kansas, never being prosecuted for his role in any of the Lincoln County War episodes. In Kansas he "reformed" and was staked to $300 by Evans with which he opened a grocery at Sun City on the Medicine Lodge River in Barber County south of Pratt. In January 1880 Evans demanded return of the money, Middleton complying though it broke him to do so. He then lived at Painted Post, Barber County, as a Hunter and Evans cowboy for $25 a month and in 1881 was working in Comanche County, west of Barber. He wrote several letters to England to John Partridge Tunstall, the father of Henry, apparently soliciting funds, but without result, the elder Tunstall dying June 10, 1882. Middleton eventually married an "heiress," but died from the effects of the Blazer's Mill wound which had damaged a lung. His death reportedly occurred in the Texas Panhandle. He was not the John Middleton wanted in San Saba County, Texas, in 1886 for cattle theft, nor he who was reportedly a lover of Belle Starr, who were another man or men of the same name.

Frederick W. Nolan, *The Life and Death of John Henry Tunstall,* Albuquerque, Univ. of N.M. Press, 1865; Robert M. Utley, *Billy the Kid: A Short and Violent Life,* Lincoln, Univ. of Nebr. Press, 1989; William A. Keleher, *Violence in Lincoln County,* Albuquerque, 1957; Robert N. Mullin notes; Mullin, ed., *Maurice G. Fulton's History of the Lincoln County War,* Tucson, Univ. of Ariz. Press, 1968; Donald R. Lavash, *Sheriff William Brady: Tragic Hero of the Lincoln County War,* Santa Fe, Sunstone Press, 1986; info. from Frederick W. Nolan.

Mikkelsen, Ejnar, polar explorer (Dec. 23, 1880-May 1, 1971). B. in northern Denmark, he lived at Copenhagen until at 14 he went to sea, following that pursuit in sailing ships for five years, during which he voyaged on all the world's oceans. Before he was 20 he had a master's license and had determined to become an Arctic explorer. In 1900 he accompanied G.C. Amdrup's expedition to survey the Greenland east coast between Scoresby Sund (Sound) and a new Eskimo settlement at Angmagssalik, 600 miles to the south. Shortly afterward he joined the Evelyn Briggs Baldwin-William Ziegler Polar Expedition which established a base on Franz Josef Land north of Novaya Zemlya in an effort to attain the North Pole, although the expedition never got much farther north than its base. On this adventure Mikkelsen became firm friends with the head of the scientific element of the expedition, Ernest deKoven Leffingwell (see entry), a geologist and naturalist. Mikkelsen and Leffingwell in 1906 determined to explore into the Beaufort Sea north of Alaska in search of a rumored but yet undiscovered land. May 20, 1906, under sponsorship of Harvard and Toronto universities, their schooner, *Duchess of Bedford,* left Victoria, British Columbia, with their expedition which also was to include a young anthropologist, Vilhjalmur Stefansson (see entry). Bad ice conditions forced them to put in at Flaxman Island, 130 miles northwest of the point where the Alaskan-Canadian border touches the Arctic Ocean. They made sledge trips over the ice and disproved the existence of the rumored new land. Leffingwell decided to remain on the island in the hut they had built, and Mikkelsen returned to civilization. In 1909 he offered to lead an expedition to east Greenland to search for remains of three men from the *Danmark* expedition of 1906-1908. He sailed in June aboard the *Alabama.* They were forced to winter on the east coast, the following season locating remains of one of the missing men. Mikkelsen and Iver Iversen searched at Danmark Fjord in northeastern Greenland for records of the lost party, found some of them, but returned to base too late. The rest of their party had abandoned the wrecked *Alabama* and been taken off by a passing Norwegian ship. It was the summer of 1912 before another Norwegian ship took Mikkelsen and his partner back to civilization. In 1922 Mikkelsen suggested colonizing Scoresby Sund with Eskimos from Angmagssalik; his idea was controversial but by 1924 he had secured sufficient support, built a base on the sound and the next year Eskimo pioneers arrived to occupy it. There were difficulties and hardships, but the colony caught on, population increased and because of excellent hunting conditions, "the people of Scoresby Sund are now better off than their compatriots at Angmagssalik." Mikkelsen was appointed Inspector for East Greenland, a position he held from 1930 until his retirement in 1950. He wrote many papers in scientific journals and such books as *Conquering the Arctic Ice* (1909); *Lost in the Arctic: The Story of the Alabama Expedition* (1913) and five volumes of autobiography. He died at 91.

Info. from John Schwoerke of Spec. Coll., Dartmouth College Lby.; Orth, 17, 1078.

Miller, James Brown (Jim), assassin (Oct. 25, 1861-Apr. 19, 1909). B. at Van Buren, Arkansas, he was one of nine children of Jacob and Cynthia Miller and as an infant was taken to Robertson County, Texas. For some undisclosed reason he was living with his grandparents in Coryell County as a child (Jacob may have died while the boy was young, but his mother lived at least until 1884). When he was 8 both grandparents were murdered at their Evant, Texas, home. Shirley reported that Miller was arrested for the killings, but was not prosecuted; James wrote there was "no evidence to substantiate" his role in the killings, but there was none to refute it, either. The murderer was never otherwise identified. During Miller's life-span of 47 years he had many occupations. "He was a deputy sheriff, city marshal, Texas Ranger, gambler, livery stable owner, stockman, swindler, real estate agent and...hired gunman." Jim's initial recorded involvement with the law was when his sister Georgia's husband, John Coop was slain by shotgun July 30, 1884. Miller was convicted, sentenced to life, but appealed and the conviction was overturned; Georgia died July 18, 1885. In 1887 Miller was hired by Emanuel (Mannen) Clements (see entry), a McCullock County

rancher, Jim meeting his future wife, Sarah Francis (Sally) Clements, Mannen's daughter, during that employment. Mannen was killed March 29, 1887, by City Marshal John Townsend over a political dispute, and Townsend was shot one night by Miller but survived the wound, although he may have lost an arm because of it. Jim and Sally were married February 15, 1888. Miller early became a gunman for hire. Former Texas Ranger James B. Gillett reported that at Alpine, Texas, Jim was heard to volunteer to kill for $200 a judge somebody wanted out of the way. He eventually would kill anyone for a fee, which might range from $50 to $2,000, depending upon what the traffic would bear. Those who paid often backed him with expert legal counsel; he was hard to convict, and even harder to be ultimately punished for any misdeed. September 14, 1896, Miller killed George A. (Bud) Frazer in a Toyah, Texas, saloon. He was indicted, obtained a change of venue, and was acquitted. On January 16, 1898, William Janes was murdered on Old Elm Creek, McLennan County, and Miller was suspected of being connected with the crime, though the facts were unclear. August 22, 1898, he became briefly a Special Texas Ranger of Company B, commanded by Captain William J. McDonald (1852-1918), a "Texas legend." Miller's application stated he was 6 ft., 1 in. tall, had black hair, dark grey eyes and a dark complexion. He was indicted in connection with the Janes murder November 11, 1899, with two others, but the charge later was dismissed, although Jim was convicted October 3, 1901, of perjury and given five years; the verdict was reversed on appeal. Joe Earp, believed to have been a principal in the Janes slaying, somehow aroused Miller's ire and was killed, his murderer never identified. J.M. Standlee, the district attorney who had prosecuted Miller, died mysteriously, apparently of arsenic poisoning, a demise Miller was suspected of engineering, but no charges were filed. He lived at Fort Worth from 1901 to 1904 as a "real estate agent," and although he made extended trips occasionally for "business" purposes, he escaped prosecution for any illegal activities. March 10, 1904, T.D. (Frank) Fore was shot, dying the 13th. Miller was indicted for murder but acquitted on a plea of self defense. February 29, 1908, the noted Pat Garrett (see entry) was killed near Las Cruces, New Mexico, and many students of the affair think Jim Miller killed the erstwhile lawman; very few seem to believe that Wayne Brazel, who confessed to the shooting, actually did it. February 27, 1909, at

Ada, Oklahoma, Miller with a shotgun, his favored weapon although he used others, killed (Allen Augustus) Gus Bobbitt, apparently an honorable and well-thought-of man who left a widow and four children. Bobbitt had been in dispute with Jesse West and Joe C. Allen over livestock and other matters; and two apparently paid Miller $2,000 plus $3,000 in the event he was arrested, to kill Bobbitt. The three along with Berry B. Burrell, a livestock speculator who once had been involved in a forgery scheme with Miller, were extracted by a 40-man mob from the Ada jail, taken to a nearby barn and lynched. Miller supposedly remarked, "Boys, you were a long time hanging the right man!" Members of the mob were said to have tried to get Miller to "confess his crimes" before his execution. He retorted, "Just let the record show that I've killed 51 men." He asked that his diamond ring be sent to his wife at Fort Worth, and that a diamond stickpin be presented to the jailer for his kindness. The lynchers were never publicly identified, but there was no general recrimination for their night's work, the executions, with Miller going last, being conducted at 2 a.m. on a Sunday morning. Jim Miller was a complex man. He never smoked, swore or drank liquor except possibly on extremely rare occasions. He was a faithful Methodist churchman although he belonged to no known congregation. He was true to his wife who later married Roy J. Redwin and after he died moved to East Texas where she succumbed October 7, 1938, her body returned to Fort Worth to be buried beside her first husband. Miller's youngest son died February 3, 1957, and in June 1979 his older son and daughter died on the same day. O'Neal could locate evidence that Miller killed only 12 men; Shirley believed he killed at least 18, seven of them alleged and "unproven," and James fewer than that. But Miller, being a skilled and often secretive assassin, was practiced in covering his tracks or he would not have survived as long as he did. The fact that there is little or no existing evidence for many of his killings proves nothing. There would seem to be little reason to dispute his figure of 51 killed during his long career. After all, he was the primary authority.

Bill C. James, *Jim Miller: The Untold Story of a Texas Badman,* ed. by Robert W. Stephens, Wolfe City, Tex., Henington Pub. Co., 1983, 1989; Glenn Shirley, *Shotgun for Hire: The Story of "Deacon" Jim Miller, Killer of Pat Garrett,* Norman, Univ. of Okla. Press, 1970; O'Neal, *Gunfighters.*

Miller, James Knox Polk, traveler, diarist (Apr. 26, 1845-Jan. 13, 1891). B. at Port Jackson, New York, he was early orphaned and went into business with an uncle at Clyde, on the barge route between Syracuse and Rochester, New York. Miller apparently could not get along with his relative, "appropriated" part of the firm's assets, left behind a considerable debt and at 19 ran away to the West, adopting the alias of J. Sidney Osborn. Unlike countless other western-bound youngsters he kept a highly literate, interesting and occasionally copious diary from its start at Chicago August 10, 1864, until April 8, 1868, by which time he was at Paris; the work is considered by its editor, "one of the best of all western diaries." Miller went by the Overland Trail to Salt Lake City where he wintered. He was interested in the Mormon establishment, writing of Brigham Young, Heber C. Kimball and, in his youthful naiveté, of William A. Hickman (see entry), a Danite "destroying angel" of the faith. Hickman, a comparatively well-educated attorney as well as a practiced executioner, managed to convince Miller that he was a "law-and-order" man, mainly interested in accosting horse rustlers. Miller's diaries, according to his editor, revealed the "passion, verve, and even vulgarity" of Heber Kimball's "style of frontier preaching" as no one else had done. "It is remarkable that a lad Miller's age possessed patience enough to record in detail the speeches" of such church officials, and his writings show "what Mormonism meant to a 'Gentile.'" From the Mormon capital Miller went to Virginia City, Montana, where the Alder Gulch gold frenzy was cresting, although he apparently concentrated on the more civil aspects of its post-vigilante existence, joining a literary society, attending theatrical performances, continuing his omniverous reading, while not neglecting to record the seamier side of the boom town. He accumulated around $7,000 in gold dust and in the middle of 1867 decided to go east, intending to travel on to Europe. He took a steamboat from Fort Benton, Montana, to Omaha, where he missed the vessel's departure and had to race overland to St. Louis where he arrived an hour before the *Waverly* docked— with his gold. He sailed from New York for Europe in 1867, visiting Paris, Rome, Alexandria, Cairo and Jerusalem. He returned to Helena, Montana, a year after he had left and opened a business at Deer Lodge for a time. In a printed circular letter from Brooklyn, of May 31, 1875, (or in a letter to a New York newspaper, as Rolle reports), Miller explained that after eleven years of living under his alias, he was resuming his rightful name. He opened a business at Deadwood, South Dakota, around 1876, became a real estate entrepreneur, president of the Deadwood Central Railroad and was successful in various enterprises. He contracted tuberculosis and died at 46 at Santa Barbara, California. He was married twice, his first wife predeceasing him.

Andrew F. Rolle, *The Road to Virginia City: The Diary of James Knox Polk Miller,* Norman, Univ. of Okla. Press, 1960; info. from the Bancroft Lby., Berkeley, Cal., which holds the Miller diaries.

Miller, Nyle H., historical society executive (Nov. 16, 1907-Aug. 6, 1988). B. at Anthony, southwest of Wichita, Kansas, he was graduated from William and Mary College, Williamsburg, Virginia, majoring in history and journalism. He worked as a linotype operator at Wichita and in 1931 joined the Kansas State Historical Society as head of its newspaper division, building its collection to one of the finest in the country. In 1951 he became secretary, which evolved into executive director of the society, a post from which he retired in 1976 when he was succeeded by Joseph W. Snell. Miller was a member of the council of the American Association for State and Local History from 1956 to 1964, vice president of the organization from 1964 to 1968, and its secretary from 1969 to 1972. He also served on the council of the Western History Association. He wrote or contributed to various books, the most important of which was *Why the West Was Wild* (1963), which he compiled with Snell and which Ramon Adams considered "one of the most important books" on the Kansas cowtowns and their law officers. It was published in only 1,500 copies, was out of print within weeks, but an abridged edition, entitled *Great Gunfighters of the Kansas Cowtowns,* was quickly brought out by the University of Nebraska Press. Miller also published *Kansas Frontier Peace Officers Before TV* (1958) and, with Edgar Langsdorf and Robert W. Richmond, *Kansas, a Pictorial History* (1961). Rosa wrote that Miller was "one of those remarkable individuals who devoted themselves to their chosen profession with an energy and zeal that was awe-inspiring. He was also one of those rare people who had no enemies, only friends."

Joseph G. Rosa, "Nyle H. Miller," English Westerners' Soc. *Tally Sheet,* Vol. 35, No. 2 (Spring, 1989), 30-31; Western Hist. Assoc. *Newsletter,* Fall, 1988, 4;

Council on America's Military Past, *Headquarters Heliogram,* 196, Nov. 1988.

Miller, Samuel, military officer (d. July 7, 1778). Miller lived on Big Sewickley Creek, near Greensburg, Westmoreland County, Pennsylvania, and became a captain in 1776, leaving to join the southern army. He was reported to command a company called in the summer of 1777 to Fort Henry, near Wheeling, to thwart an anticipated Indian attack, but it withdrew before the attack was made. He was at Valley Forge in January 1778, but in March was ordered west to Fort Pitt. On July 7, while taking a detachment of nine soldiers of the 8th Pennsylvania Regiment as a reinforcement to Fort Hand, near Kittanning northeast of Pittsburgh, he was ambushed by Indians and killed, as were seven men of his detachment.

Thwaites/Kellogg, *Frontier Defense on the Upper Ohio, 1777-1778.*

Miller, Samuel Carson, pioneer (Nov. 4, 1840-Oct. 6, 1909). B. at Peoria, Illinois, he and his brother Jacob (Jake) went with their parents to California, Sam, 15, and Jake, 25. After mining with little profit in Calaveras County, the Miller boys recrossed the Sierra Nevada to the Comstock silver boom in Nevada, but soon found freighting more rewarding than silver mining. Early in 1861 the Millers returned to California, met Joseph Reddeford Walker (see entry) and joined his prospecting party which worked through the southwest, visited Colorado and ended up at Prescott, Arizona. At 21 Sam was said to be the youngest member of the group. He had experiences with hostile Indians, on one occasion killing a presumed enemy and at another time being wounded in the leg. Sam made the first significant gold strike on Lynx Creek, near Prescott, but eventually returned to freighting, with mule teams bringing loads from Colorado River ports to army posts, mainly under government contracts. Among the Hualapais (Walapais) Indians of northwestern Arizona in 1866 were three important chiefs, or headmen, the foremost of whom was Wauba Yuma (or Yuba). He was leader of the Hualapais Yavapai Fighters subtribe, a body composed of four bands: the Hualapais Mountaineers, the Lower Big Sandy River group, the Mahone (Mohon) Mountaineers and the Juniper Mountaineers. From the founding of Fort Mojave on the Colorado April 29, 1859, there had been cooperation between the

Yavapais Fighters and Anglo elements, and Wauba Yuma (see entry), a man important enough to have four wives, sought to keep it that way. Merchant William H. Hardy of Hardyville, north of Fort Mojave, had made a peace with the Indian to promote his own considerable freighting interests. He gave Wauba Yuma a "treaty" he might exhibit to other whites to avoid trouble with them. Wauba Yuma tried to show it to Sam Miller whose party was camped at Beale Springs near present Kingman, the whites already uneasy by reports that Hualapais had recently killed a prospector named Edward Clower at the Willows, farther east. Miller's story was that Wauba Yuma had ridden into camp, wanting to negotiate for flour, horses and mules. After a brief argument, Miller swept up his Hawken rifle and "sent a bullet crashing through the lungs of the Indian, tearing a hole in his body as big as his hand." A varying account said that Miller and other freighters consulted, decided the Indian meant mischief, "and was at once shot." In either event it was murder, and a senseless one at that. The Prescott *Miner* growled that "the conclusion that the tribe wished to wage war with the whites is premature, and that the killing of Wauba-Yuba will prove an unprofitable step...to have taken [him] was a harsh and, we fear, a most unfortunate measure," as indeed it proved. The incident ignited a two-year conflict, the so-called "Walapais War," that cost many red and white lives, all to little purpose. Miller was arrested at Fort Whipple, delivered to the U.S. marshal, examined by a federal commissioner, and held for a grand jury, which discharged him with a "unanimous vote of thanks," in keeping with white sentiment in the territory. But as its legacy "The road from Hardyville to Prescott is lined with graves...and the early miners of Mojave County were waylaid while prospecting, and killed at their cabins, shafts and tunnels, until for a long time the mines were practically abandoned." Shortly before the railroad arrived in Arizona, in the mid-1870s, the Millers disposed of their animal-freighting interests and engaged in ranching a few miles northeast of Prescott. Jake Miller died April 7, 1899, at the Miller ranch. Sam suffered several strokes and died nearly a year after his wife had succumbed. Farish gives the date of Sam Miller's demise as October 12. He was survived by four sons and a daughter.

Farish, II; Dan L. Thrapp, *Conquest of Apacheria,* Norman, Univ. of Okla. Press, 1967; Henry F. Dobyns, Robert C. Euler, *Wauba Yuma's People: The Compar-*

ative Socio-Political Structure of the Pai Indians of Arizona, Prescott, Ariz., Prescott College Studies in Anthropology No. 3, Prescott College Press, 1970; Mary G. Stano, "The Path to Misfortune," *True West,* Vol. 38, No. 1 (Jan. 1991), 35-37; info. from E.F. (Ted) Mains.

Miner, Ezra Allen (Bill), desperado (Dec. 27, 1846-Sept. 2, 1913). B. at Onondaga, south of Lansing, Michigan, he went west as a youth, tried cowboy life and at 17 in 1863 performed his first known illegal act—horse stealing, this in California. The report that Miner was hired by Brigadier General George Wright, commander of the Department of the Pacific, to carry a message to an officer on the Gila River in Arizona in 1863 appears to be fiction, originating with Miner himself since it appears in an autobiographical manuscript he is said to have dictated to a prison guard in his advanced age. All published details of the incident can easily be disproven. Rickards finds "no record of his first stage robbery," but San Quentin, California, Penitentiary archives show that Miner became inmate number 3248 on April 5, 1866, for robbery (he was then 19), and there is no reason to assume that it was his initial like offense. He was released July 13, 1870, and after holding up a Sonora, California, stage re-entered San Quentin less than a year later as number 4902. Out for a retrial on February 9, 1872, he was returned as prisoner 5206 March 30, and served out his term, being released July 14, 1880. November 6, he held up the Sonora stage again and took $3,700 in gold dust, returning then to Onondaga, Michigan, his home town, where he remained until his money was gone. He went to Colorado in March 1881 where with Stanton T. Jones he robbed a Del Norte stage for slight gain, was chased down by a posse, escaped after a brief shooting affair and Miner joined up with Billy Leroy, a hardened stage robber. They held up coaches. With Leroy's brother joining them they attempted to stop a stage between South Fork and Wagon Wheel Gap, but the vehicle's horses bolted, shooting erupted, the driver was killed and a passenger wounded. Miner escaped but the Leroys were captured, returned to Del Norte, and lynched. According to Miner's fanciful manuscript he then embarked on a "world tour," replete with all sorts of adventures that almost certainly never took place, for on November 7, 1881, he and another robbed a stage, again in Tuolumne County, California, took $3,700 and were themselves captured. Miner soon was back in San Quentin, this time as prisoner 10191. He was now 38 and his sentence was for 25 years. After four years he escaped, was recaptured and ultimately served more than 19 years before being released June 17, 1902, free from jail but in no sense reformed. He was now 59. He found his time-worn targets, the stagecoaches, all but things of the past, so with Charles Hoehn and a man known as Williams in September 1903 held up an eastbound express of the Oregon Railroad and Navigation Company out of Portland. The attempt was bungled through inexperience, however, and Bill Miner fled to British Columbia, where he lived as George Edwards on a small farm near Princeton. Being a congenial man with a pleasant personality, he was popular with the neighbors. After a time he became associated with William (Shorty) Dunn, an individual of career tastes similar to Miner's and in September 1904 the pair staged the first train holdup in Canadian history. It was of a Canadian Pacific transcontinental express and the event transpired west of Mission Junction around 9:30 p.m. September 10, 1904. The loot reportedly included $1,000 in currency, gold dust worth about $6,000, plus $50,000 in United States bonds. Miner and his companion returned to Princeton, resumed their pastoral life until November 1905, when they held up a train near Seattle, making off with $30,000. May 8, 1906, at a town called Ducks, east of Kamloops, the Canadian Pacific again was struck, but the loot was negligible. Miner and two accomplices were arrested May 14, tried at Kamloops, convicted June 1 and sentenced to life imprisonment. Miner, probably with outside help, escaped from New Westminster Penitentiary August 8, 1907. He may have traveled abroad during subsequent years, though there is no proof, and he was working for a time in Pennsylvania, then in Virginia and February 18, 1911, he led a small group that perpetrated Georgia's first train robbery; he was hunted down, tried at Gainesville and on March 11, 1911, sentenced to twenty years. October 21, he escaped once more; he was now 65. He eluded bloodhounds, and with a fellow escapee, Tom Moore, remained for two and a half weeks until cornered at St. Clair, Georgia, where in a gunfight Moore was killed and Miner surrendered. Back in confinement at the State Prison Farm at Milledgeville, northeast of Macon, Bill on June 29, 1912, sawed off his ball and chain, cut through his bars and with two companions

escaped into the night. One prisoner was drowned in a boating mishap, Miner and his remaining companion separated and before long Miner again was picked up by a sheriff's posse, muttering, "I'm getting a bit old for this sort of thing." He was 66. Taken to the prison hospital he lasted for more than a year before he died from what was described as a gastric ulcer. He was buried in the Milledgeville Cemetery and 50 years later a suitable stone was placed over his grave at the expense of a Georgia historian who dimly remembered Bill Miner and his escapades, or some of them. It had his true name, the date of his birth and the date of his death, all wrong, but Miner would not have objected. In his lifetime the facts were always pretty well scrambled by himself, anyway.

Chuck Parsons, *True West,* Vol. 37, No. 5 (May 1990), 13; Vol. 37, No. 6 (June 1990), 12; Colin Rickards, "Bill Miner—50 Years a Hold-up Man," English Westerners' *Brand Book,* Vol. 8, No. 2 (January 1966), 9-12; Vol. 8, No. 3 (April 1966), 1-5; Ed Kirby, "Bill Miner—The Grey Fox: He Was an Outlaw for Nearly Fifty Years!," *Quarterly of the National Association and Center for Outlaw and Lawman History,* Vol. X, No. 1 (Summer, 1985), 3-6, 16-17; Bruce Wishart, "Bill Miner: The Canadian Years," *True West,* Vol. 37, No. 1 (January, 1990), 28-37; O'Neal, *Gunfighters;* info. from E.F. (Ted) Mains.

Mitchell, William Lendrum (Billy), military officer (Dec. 29, 1879-Feb. 17, 1936). B. at Nice, France, while his parents were temporarily abroad, he was raised at Milwaukee. He studied at George Washington (then Columbian) University, Washington, D.C., but when the Spanish American War broke out enlisted at 18 in the 1st Wisconsin Infantry; the influence of his father, U.S. Senator John Lendrum Mitchell persuaded Brigadier General Adolphus Greely (see entry), chief of the Signal Corps, to recommend him for a commission and he became the army's youngest second lieutenant, assigned to a Signal company. He superintended the stringing of 136 miles of telegraph wire in Cuba, was posted to the Philippines and at 20 was acting chief Signal officer on the staff of General Arthur MacArthur, establishing miles of telegraph lines and, incidentally, meeting Frederick Funston (see entry) and listened avidly to his tales of Alaska. Greely, countering Mitchell's plans to resign after his Philippine service, suggested he go to Alaska where establishment of a telegraph line connecting far-flung army posts was going slowly.

Mitchell made an investigatory trip in 1901 and recommended improvements in construction practices which appealed to Greely, who sent him back to carry them out. Colonel George M. Randall (see entry) was commander of the Department of Alaska. Mitchell, now the youngest first lieutenant in the army, was charged with building that portion of the system between Fort Liscum, at Valdez, a southern port, and Fort Egbert at Eagle City on the upper Yukon; he described this work around 1935 in his *The Opening of Alaska.* "In new countries the first effort is to get means of communication," Mitchell wrote. "In Alaska the telegraph system was the wedge which cleft open the country to communications." He added that "to a young lieutenant…it seemed as great an undertaking as the Lewis and Clark Expedition, Fremont's trip to California, or the opening of the routes…to the Pacific coast." By 1901, with the Gold Rush already peaking, Alaska had become far more settled than it had been during Henry T. Allen's exploration work a decade and a half earlier. Mitchell's party took the railroad from Skagway to Whitehorse, a riverboat to Dawson and another to Fort Egbert and Eagle City, Alaska. It was planned for the telegraph line to run from Eagle City to Valdez, and another line to follow the Yukon River to Fort St. Michael on Norton Sound, from where eventually there would be wireless (radio) contact made with Nome. Mitchell, always intellectually alert, describes interestingly everything he observed or heard about in the sub-Arctic during a fascinating period, from Canadian police detective work, to sled dogs of various kinds, Indians, saloon girls, and big game. He was interested in the history of Russian Alaska and reported what he had learned with fair accuracy during the trip down the Yukon to St. Michael. Colonel Randall and Major Wilds P. Richardson (see entry) were in charge at the headquarters of the American Army in the North at that point. Mitchell went by boat to Nome and from there to Seattle. His reconnaissance over, Mitchell was ordered by Greely to commence construction of the projected lines and took ship once again from Seattle. At Eagle City he prepared to begin construction and bought good sled dogs for winter preparations. The first line was south to Valdez. Narrowly avoiding occasional catastrophes, Mitchell laid out caches during the winter along the prospective lines so that work could proceed uninterruptedly during the warm summer and and thus speed

construction. By the summer of 1903 the line was connected from Eagle City to Valdez where a new cable to the United States could take over; the line down the Yukon to St. Michael also was working. Mitchell was ordered to Washington to report fully on the network and what should be done for its maintenance in the future. In three years he had covered much of frontier Alaska and in recognition he was promoted to captain, the youngest of his rank in the army. His further career was spectacular, but with little frontier interest. He was graduated from the Army Staff College in 1909, served again in the Philippines until 1911, reconnoitered Japanese activity in the neighboring islands and in a subsequent report in 1912 indicated his belief that "war with Japan was inevitable and that the Philippines were in great danger." From 1913-16 he was the youngest officer to serve on the Army General Staff, spoke five languages and had some understanding of two more dialects; he was too old at 36 for army flight training, but took pilot instruction on his own and became a major in the Aviation Section of the Signal Corps. In World War I he was commander of air forces as a Brigadier General of the American Expeditionary Force, advanced the cause of Eddie Rickenbacker to become a pursuit pilot, and was the first American officer to fly over German lines. Following that war he became assistant chief of the Air Service, urged that it become a separate air arm, demonstrated the power of the bomber with effective strikes upon three obsolete warship targets in July and three more in September 1921, and further advanced the cause of the air service, becoming the public's darling and the hero of the Air Corps. Following a trip to the Far East Mitchell warned in a lengthy report of Japan's growing air strength and again of his belief that war with that country was inevitable. For his attacks on the War and Navy departments in connection with destruction of the dirigible *Shenandoah,* he was court-martialed and suspended from the service for five years. He resigned in 1926. In 1935 before Congressonal hearings "he spoke at length and with great forcefulness on the theme which was to give him immortality—the importance and value of air power in war," and with remarkable foresight he stressed the strategic significance of Alaska in the coming era of air power. In January 1936 he fell ill of influenza, complicated by heart trouble, and died at New York City. Mt. Billy Mitchell, a few miles north of Valdez, Alaska, was named in his honor. He had written: *Our Air Force* (1921); *Winged Defense* (1925), and *Skyways* (1930), and numerous articles.

Literature abundant; Mitchell, *The Opening of Alaska,* Anchorage, Cook Inlet Hist. Soc., 1982; CE; DAB.

Moale, Edward, military officer (Jan. 29, 1840-Sept. 27, 1913). B. in Maryland he was commissioned a first lieutenant in the 19th U.S. Infantry May 14, 1861, and came out of the Civil War a captain with brevets to colonel of Volunteers. He transferred to the 37th Infantry September 21, 1866, and to the 3rd Infantry August 11, 1869. Moale served in Georgia, Arkansas and at Fort Leavenworth to March 1867 when he became commander of the headquarters guard of Hancock's Indian expedition in March and April of that year. He continued on frontier duty until 1890. In December 1872, while commanding the post at Fort Dodge, Kansas, Moale turned back a vigilante attempt to lynch an Arapaho chief, Spotted Wolf, for no other reason than that he was an Indian. The chief had been brought to Dodge City for medical attention after being injured in a wagon accident. Moale, given word of the gathering storm, dispatched Captain Tullius Tupper (see entry) with a dozen troopers, to escort the Indian out of harm's way, which was done. Spotted Wolf was returned to Camp Supply, Indian Territory, by W.D. Lee, who had business interests there. Moale became a major February 1, 1887, a lieutenant colonel December 4, 1891, and a colonel February 4, 1897, retiring January 31, 1902, and being promoted to Brigadier General April 23, 1904.

Heitman; Powell; *Who Was Who;* Gary L. Roberts, "Spotted Wolf and the Dodge City Toughs," *True West,* Vol. 24, No. 3 (Jan.-Feb. 1977), 10-11, 32, 36.

Moffatt, George, military officer (1735-1811). Moffatt was but a youth in 1749 when his father disappeared on a journey from Virginia to South Carolina, believed to have been killed by Indians. In 1763 George was captain of a Virginian ranging company which was ambushed by Indians they were pursuing, and fifteen whites were killed. The following year he pursued an Indian band that had killed his step-father, John Trimble, and captured Moffatt's sister and half-brother. In a sharp action he rescued the prisoners. Moffatt served as a captain under Colonel Andrew Lewis in the 1774 campaign of Lord Dunmore's War, which was virtually terminated with the successful engagement at Point Pleasant, West Virginia, on October 10. Several of the noted officers in that campaign were his relatives, including William Christian, an uncle, and Captain Samuel McDowell, his brother-in-law. During the Revolution he operated in the south commanding a regiment at Guilford Court House; he was county lieutenant of Augusta County, Virginia, from 1781 to 1783. He died at his Augusta County home about eight miles northwest of Stanton.

Thwaites, *Dunmore.*

Mog(g) (Mugg), Abenaki chiefs (d. May 16, 1677; c. 1663-Aug. 23, 1724). There were two chiefs of this name, the earliest the father of the second. The older was a sagamore, or chief, of the Penobscot branch of the Abenakis and comes into prominence during hostilities associated with King Philip's War, although the Abenakis were not directly involved in that sanguinary conflict. He was later called Mogg Hegone. Mog went to Boston on behalf of Madockawando (see entry) to sign a peace November 6, 1676, and offered to remain as hostage until captives were exchanged. Mog was taken on vessels sent to the Penobscot River to have the treaty ratified by Madockawando, and was sent inland to bring out more captives, but "he did not return." An escaped captive reported that Mog had joined the Indians on the Kennebec "who were the real leaders in the war in those parts," and "boasted greatly of the trick he had played upon the English, and threatened great things to be done against them in the spring" of 1677. October 12, 1676, about a hundred hostile Indians appeared before Blackpoint (the present Scarboro, Maine), the most heavily garrisoned English fort in that region; the Indians were loathe to assault the place, appreciating its strength, but asked for a parley with the commandant, Henry Jocelyn and during their long discussion the entire garrison and dependents evacuated the post for Wells, Portsmouth and other safe towns. Jocelyn appears to have been as much surprised as the Indians by this withdrawal; he was taken prisoner with his family, but was kindly treated and shortly restored to "his friends," afterward residing at Plymouth, Massachusetts, for the remainder of his life. The regional commandant, Captain Joshua Scottow, who had thought the post "absolutely secure," was amazed at its desertion and after the peace treaty was signed in November reoccupied it, leaving Sergeant

Bartholomew Tippen, a more effective commander than Jocelyn, in charge. May 13, 1677, a large body of hostiles, confident of an easy victory, made a resolute attack on Blackpoint, but this time found it resolutely defended; in three days the garrison lost only three men killed and on the 16th Tippen himself made a fine shot, killing Mog and causing the attackers to withdraw. Mog, Jr., was 14 at the time of his father's death and upon maturity he became a chief of the Norridgewock branch of the Abenakis, his headquarters on the Kennebec River south of present Madison, Maine, where he came under the influence of the Jesuit, Sébastian Rale (see entry) and accepted Christianity. Mog led, or took part in, numerous raids on the frontier during King William's War (1688-99) and Queen Anne's War (1702-13) and "carried captives and scalps to Quebec." Following termination of Queen Anne's War, Mog and other chiefs July 11-13, 1713, signed a treaty, ratified by a gathering of about 400 Abenakis July 18 at Casco Bay, the Indians surprised to learn that the French had given up all Abenaki lands to the English without consulting them. The English rapdily advanced along the coast of Maine and the lower Kennebec River. Mog and others agreed that the English might settle lands they had occupied before hostilities, but the whites were not content with that and Mog and Mowurna, another chief, went to Quebec in 1716 seeking arms and troops to retaliate, but left only partially satisfied. Matters degenerated further with factions holding disparate views of what should be done and with whom to ally themselves. Massachusetts in July 1722 declared war on the Abenakis, although there was opposition to this step on the part of many English colonists and of Connecticut alike, the latter holding that "the War [is] not just on the English side." The governor at Quebec, Vaudreuil (see entry) secretly supported the Indians with arms and ammunition. In September 1722 the Norridgewocks, with other Indians making up about 400 fighting men in all, destroyed English settlements on the lower Kennebec and "scores of skirmishes kept the frontier aflame from eastern Maine to the Connecticut Valley." August 23, 1724, Norridgewock was attacked by the English; Mog, Rale and about 24 Abenakis were killed, their scalps taken to Boston where they "brought £505 in bounties."

Hodge, HAI; Sylvester, II; George M. Bodge, *Soldiers in King Philip's War,* Leominster, Mass., p.p., 1896; DCB, II.

Mokohoko (Jumping Fish), Sauk chief (d. 1878). Of the ruling Sturgeon clan of the Sauk tribe which strongly supported Black Hawk (see entry) in his resistance to white pressure, he was a bitter enemy of Keokuk (see entry), who was cooperative with the whites, and later of Keokuk's son, Moses Keokuk. It is not known whether Mokohoko took any part in the Black Hawk War of 1832, but if he did do so it was as a very young man who had not yet come into the hereditary chieftainship eventually his. The Sauk became a fragmented people after the Black Hawk affair and the Sturgeon clan was the most conservative element of it. Of the dozen treaties signed by portions of the tribe between the pact at the conclusion of the war, intitialed at Fort Armstrong, Illinois, September 21, 1832, through the agreement signed at Washington February 18, 1867, Mokohoko signed only that of May 18, 1854, also at Washington. In 1837 the Sauk and Foxes relinquished most of their Iowa lands and accepted a reservation across the Missouri River in Kansas, and here Mokohoko was determined to remained. Many of the Foxes later returned to Iowa to live on lands of those who had purchased them, but the Sauk remained in Kansas until the government insisted upon their removal to Indian Territory. In 1867 four of the five leading chiefs signed a treaty providing for the transfer, only Mokohoko abstaining. He and his band refused to relocate, saying they were not a part of the treaty. In December 1874 Mokohoko visited President Grant and was told his people would have to remove; they did so, but promptly returned to Kansas and stubbornly refused to go back to Oklahoma until 1886, eight years after Mokohoko's death. His band had also become "the backbone of the conservatives' opposition to acculturation," initially opposing education, health measures introduced by the whites, Christianity and all other "civilizing" initiatives, later adjusting to some of them, if reluctantly.

Hodge, HAI; HNAI, 15, p. 654; William T. Hagan, *The Sac and Fox Indians,* Norman, Univ. of Okla. Press, 1958; Charles J. Kappler, *Indian Treaties 1778-1883,* N.Y., Interland Pub. Inc., 1972, 631-33.

Montgomery, John, frontiersman (c. 1748-1794). B. in Botetourt County, Virginia, he early came to prominence in civil and military capacities. He was supposed to go out with William Christian's regiment for the Point Pleasant, West Virginia, action of October 10, 1774, which virtually ended Lord Dunmore's War, but a letter he wrote to Colonel William Preston (see entry) on October 2 indicates that he did not go, perhaps because of the danger of Indian hostilities in his own vicinity. In the 1776 Cherokee campaign he served under Christian and was stationed at Long Island on the Holston River at its close. In 1778 he was ordered out with George Rogers Clark to Kentucky, becoming one of Clark's four captains on the historic Illinois campaign. When Kaskaskia was taken, Montgomery was sent to Virginia with dispatches and ordered to enroll a regiment for Clark's reinforcement, he to be lieutenant colonel of it. Instead he joined Evan Shelby's 1779 campaign against the Tennessee Chickamaugas (Cherokees), and he did not reach Illinois again until May, but then continued on that operation until the close of the war. He settled in southwest Kentucky, later removed to the Cumberland Valley and eventually founded Clarksville, Tennessee, which he named for his former commander. In 1793-94 he accepted a commission from the French diplomat, Edmond Charles Edouard Genét, to strike at Spanish Florida (Clark to be Major General and commander of the unlikely scheme), but President Washington caused the whole plan to be abandoned. Montgomery went out on the Nickojack campaign in middle Tennessee in 1794, by which a white expedition sallied against the Cherokees and lost a few men killed but considered the trip successful. In the early 1790s Montgomery slew one of the last buffaloes in Tennessee. In 1794 he was killed by an Indian while on a hunting excursion, near the mouth of the Cumberland River.

Thwaites, *Dunmore;* Harriette Simpson Arnow, *Seedtime on the Cumberland,* N.Y., The Macmillan Co., 1960.

Mooney, James, frontiersman (d. Oct. 10,1774). A neighbor of Daniel Boone on the Yadkin River of North Carolina, Mooney accompanied Boone and Findley on the memorable trip to Kentucky, setting out May 1, 1769. In December Boone and John Stuart were captured by Indians, but escaped early in January 1770. Findley, Mooney and others now elected to return home. Findley went by way of West Virginia to Pennsylvania, and the others through Cumberland Gap to North Carolina; Stuart not long afterward was killed by Indians. Mooney became a scout and as such served in William Russell's company in preparation for the Battle of Point Pleasant, West Virginia, October 10, 1774, which virtually terminated Lord Dunmore's War. In anticipation

of that action by a few hours, Mooney and Joseph Hughey were hunting and were accosted by a war party led by Cornstalk, the noted Shawnee chief (see entry). Hughey was killed by Tavenor Ross, a white who had been captured by Indians as a child, grown up among them and now was considered a "renegade." He later returned to the settlements and presumably lived in civilization thereafter. Mooney brought in the news of the shooting; in the Point Pleasant action later in the day, he, too, was killed.

Thwaites, *Dunmore;* Reuben Gold Thwaites, ed., Alexander Scott Withers, *Chronicles of Border Warfare,* Cincinnati, Robert Clarke Co., 1895, 1970.

Moraga, Gabriel, military officer (c. 1768-c. June 13, 1823). A son of José Joaquín Moraga (see entry), he was b. in northwestern Mexico "some years before his parents came to California" in 1775-76. He enlisted in the army in 1784 and was wed July 16, at San Francisco to Ana Maria Bernal with Francisco Palou (see entry) officiating. In 1788 Moraga became corporal in the Monterey company and for a dozen years commanded various escoltas or guards, becoming an accomplished Indian fighter. By 1820 he had taken part in 46 expeditions against Indians and ten battles with them. From 1800 to 1806 he was sergeant in the Monterey company, then being transferred to San Francisco as alférez, or ensign, a commissioned rank, although he was considered by some to be unlettered. By 1810 the Indians had become more troublesome than ever and Moraga, by then considered the pre-eminent Indian fighter of the time, was kept very busy at his specialty. In May he was sent to Carquinez Strait, near Suisun. On the 22nd the Spanish crossed the strait by boat and after a hard fight with 120 Indians captured eighteen who were released "as they were almost sure to die of their wounds." The survivors withdrew to their huts, from which they wounded two corporals and two soldiers. Occupants of two of the three shelters were killed, but those of a third chose to perish in flames. The report of this "brilliant affair" was sent by the viceroy to Spain, where the king's regency approved the "glorious action" and Moraga was given a brevet lieutenancy. That year Moraga completed two expeditions to the San Joaquin Valley, on the first of which he named the San Joaquin River, although not the discoverer of it. His second expedition was to Bodega Bay. In November he quelled some undefined disorders at San Gabriel near Los Angeles. In

1818 he became a lieutenant of the Santa Barbara company and the next year led an expedition toward the Colorado River. He suffered persistently from rheumatism and sought repeatedly to retire, but his application, although endorsed by many California officials, was never acted upon. The date of his death is not recorded, but he was buried June 15, 1823, in the cemetery of Santa Barbara Mission. Bancroft wrote that he was an "honest, moral, kind-hearted, popular, and a very energetic and successful officer," and another describes him as a "tall, well built man of dark complexion, brave, gentlemanly, and the best California soldier of his time."

Bancroft, *California,* II.

Moraga, José Joaquin, Spanish military officer (c. 1735-July 13, 1785). B. at Fronteras, Sonora, he was son of a soldier who died in battle, presumably with Apaches. He enlisted in the army about 1756 and by 1774 was an 'alférez, or ensign, accompanying Juan Bautista de Anza on his second expedition to California. The command left Tubac, Arizona, October 23, 1775, a column of 235 military and civilian personnel and 825 head of livestock; advance elements arrived at San Francisco March 27, 1776, by which time Moraga was a lieutenant, appointed to that rank upon recommendation of Anza "because of his ability to write," and commanding one of three divisions of the Anza expedition. After exploring the peninsula of San Francisco, the Anza command withdrew to Monterey from which Moraga and others, once resupplied by ship, moved north again, arriving at the site of the future San Francisco June 27. The presidio of San Francisco was founded September 17, and Moraga assumed command of the post, entertaining the company "with all the splendor circumstances would allow." Mission de los Dolores was established October 8 or 9, Moraga attending the founding ceremony upon his return from further explorations of peninsula, bay and environs. Moraga subsequently founded Mission Santa Clara and the pueblo of San Jose. His record as an officer was "an honorable and stainless one." He became quite deaf in his later years as a result of "exposure," as was supposed. He also took part in various punitive forays against Indians who had committed what the Spanish considered hostile acts, although he was mainly noted for his administrative abilities. His most famous son was Gabriel Moraga (see entry).

Ronald L. Ives, *José Velásquez: Saga of a Border-*

land Soldier, Tucson, Az., Southwestern Mission Res. Ctr., 1984; Bancroft, *California,* I.

Morehead, Joseph C., adventurer (d. pre-1882). B. in Kentucky he became a lawyer and served as a lieutenant in Company D, 1st New York Volunteers, arriving in California in 1847. He represented San Joaquin in the first California legislature of 1849-50. When the California Militia was organized c. 1850, Morehead became quartermaster-general. News reaching California of the slaying of erstwhile scalp hunter John C. Glanton (see entry) and a dozen others by Yuma Indians, Morehead, under gubernatorial appointment, organized a punitive force which became known as the Gila Expedition. It numbered more than 60 loosely-organized and ill-trained men who marched to the Yuma Crossing of the lower Colorado River in September 1850. Finding the Indians quiet, there was little fighting to be done. Morehead heard that the Yumas had seized a reported $80,000 that Glanton and his ruffian colleagues had collected in ferry fees (which may have been a prime cause for the Gila Expedition in the first place). He demanded that the Indians return the money while his men commenced destroying Indian crops by way of punishment. In retaliation the Yumas attacked the Californians, forcing them to fort up in a stockade from which Morehead's "expedition" decamped in a temporary absence of an attacking force. "The cost of Morehead's fiasco in supplies and other requisitions added $120,000 to the new state's debt," it was reported. Filibustering now attracted Morehead, and receiving an invitation which "rebel leaders in Mexico were not backward in extending," he organized an expedition southward: one small portion headed for Sonora out of Los Angeles; another showed up at La Paz, in Lower California, and Morehead sailed in May 1851 with a company for Mazatlan. "On reaching Mexico the broken bands found the aspect so changed or unpromising that they were glad to slink away under the guise of disappointed miners." Bancroft said Morehead died "before" 1882, but gave neither the date nor circumstances of his demise.

David P. Robrock, "Scalp Hunters Come to Yuma Crossing," *True West,* Vol. 37, No. 2 (Feb. 1990), 16-21; Bancroft, *Pioneer Register; California,* V. VI, VII.

Morés, Marquis de, Antoine Amédée Marie Vincent Amat Manca de Vallombrosa, entrepreneur, adventurer (1858-1896). A trained French army officer, "who had already lost a small fortune on the Paris security markets," married in 1882 the well-financed Medora von Hoffman whose interests, in addition to her husband, ranged from painting to hunting. The Marquis was employed by his banker father-in-law at New York City, but in 1883, wearied of so staid a business, went to bleak western North Dakota, founding in April a town named for his wife, Medora (population in 1970 about 133). Heavily engaged in his various businesses, mainly visionary, the marquis also built an elaborate chateau where he and his wife spent some $700 a month (at the 1880s dollar) on household expenses, including servants to change the table linen after each course of a meal; sterling silver hair brushes laid out so that two servants could together brush out Medora's hair; a special smoke-device in the bedroom to eliminate bedbugs, and similar innovations, improbable in frontier North Dakota; little wonder that the marquis became unpopular locally. He founded the Northern Pacific Refrigerator Car Company and a packing plant which was to ship refrigerated dressed beef to New York City where it was to be retailed, hopefully undercutting all opposition, but major packing houses undercut the entrepreneur instead, and the plant failed. He established a freight route between Medora and Deadwood, this too was unsuccessful. He attempted to ship Pacific coast salmon to New York, but profits eluded him. His apparent sole victory during his three years in Dakota was at a trial for the murder of William Riley Luffsey, one of three men who had ambushed him following a land dispute. The court case, according to Tweton, was "colorful," with the marquis acquitted. Leaving Dakota he went to India for a tiger hunt. In 1888 he devised a scheme for a railroad through French Indo-China into China proper, but failed to get a concession for it. He returned to France, entered politics for several stormy years, developed an anti-Semitic bias, worked for socialism and promoted the idea of credit for workers, as well as public housing. In 1896 he was assassinated in Morocco by anticolonialists. His most permanent fame came from his failed complex of entrepreneurial schemes in the North Dakota badlands.

D. Jerome Tweton, *The Marquis de Morés: Dakota Capitalist, French Nationalist,* Fargo, N.D. Inst. for Regional Studies, 1972; REAW; article on Marquis de Morés, also by Tweton, *New York Times,* July 30, 1989.

Morfi, Juan Agustín, Franciscan (d. Oct. 20, 1783). The date of his b. is not known but it occurred in Galicia, Spain. He came to America in 1755 or 1756 and was ordained a Franciscan May 3, 1761, at Mexico City, suggesting that he was probably b. around 1736, although this is conjecture. He was intellectually-inclined and a noted orator. He taught theology at the Old College of Santa Cruz de Tlaltelolco and was a lecturer on sacred theology, possibly at Querétaro, one of the principal Franciscan centers of Mexico. In December 1776 Teodoro de Croix, newly appointed commandant general of the Provincias Internas, the northern provinces of Mexico including Texas and New Mexico, organized an inspection tour of his new charge and Morfi became his chaplain. The extended journey commenced August 4, 1777, and extended as far as San Bautista de Rio Grande and San Antonio de Bexar before returning to Mexico in early 1778. Morfi thereafter busied himself collecting documents on Texas and writing his *Memorias para la Historia de Texas,* which Bancroft cited as "the standard authority for Texas history down to this date," or 1884. It has since been translated and published in English (see bibliography). Included in the *Memorias* are passages which "particularly concern the various [tribes of] Indians of the Province of Texas; their tribal divisions, characteristics, customs, traditions, superstitions," and other matters. These excerpts were translated and printed privately at San Antonio, Texas, in 1932 by Frederick C. Chabot. Morfi at times spoke out against oppression of Indians in northern Mexico. The Franciscan's *Diario* of his journey with Croix has also been published, and Bancroft found considerable value in the friar's *Colección de Documentos,* which refer not only to Texas but also to New Mexico. Thomas translates and publishes (pp. 87-114) for the first time Morfi's "Geographical Description of New Mexico" of 1782, believing Morfi must have written this earlier than 1782 but after 1778. Thomas's notes (pp. 371-73) are also enlightening. Morfi never personally visited New Mexico, and his "description" was not original with him, he taking it verbatim from a former missionary at Zuñi, Damian Martinez; this fact was unknown to Thomas when he worked on the document. In 1782 Morfi was elected guardian of the Convento Grande de San Francisco in Mexico; he died the following year.

Juan Agustín Morfi, *History of Texas, 1672-1779,* 2 vols., trans., etc., by Carlos Eduardo Castañeda,

Albuquerque, The Quivira Soc., 1935; Alfred Barnaby Thomas, *Forgotten Frontiers: A Study of the Spanish Indian Policy of Don Juan Bautista de Anza...,* Norman, Univ. of Okla. Press, 1932, 1969; *New Mexico Historical Review,* Vol. VIII, No. 1 (Jan. 1933), 57-58; NMHR, Vol. X, No. 1 (Jan. 1935) 56; HT; Porrua; Bancroft, *North Mexican States and Texas,* 2 vols. I, 631 (mistakenly cited in the Index as p. 664); info. from Bernard L. Fontana.

Morgan, George, Indian trader (1742-1810). B. at Philadelphia he early joined the well-known Indian trading firm of Baynton, Wharton and Company, and in 1764 married a Baynton daughter. The firm suffered heavy losses by reason of the Pontiac War and associated interruptions, but was recompensed at the 1768 Fort Stanwix, New York, treaty; a grant was obtained which laid the foundation for the Indiana Company, of which Morgan for many years was secretary and agent. He early visited Indian country and made himself popular with the tribesmen. During this period he made a trip down the Illinois and Mississippi rivers as early as 1766. He was living on the Illinois River in 1768, but left before the outbreak of the Revolution in 1776. In April of that year he was appointed Indian agent for the Middle Department by Congress, remaining in Pittsburgh in that capacity until he resigned in 1779. He then joined the eastern army, achieving rank of colonel by the end of the war. Following the Revolution he settled at Princeton, New Jersey, becoming its college trustee. In 1788-89 he developed a plan and founded the colony of New Madrid on the Spanish side of the Mississippi, but he failed to secure proper authorization from Spanish authority and abandoned the settlement. In 1796 Morgan built an estate called "Morganza" in Washington County, Pennsylvania; there the Aaron Burr plot was first detected and reported. He died at his home.

Thwaites/Kellogg, *The Revolution on the Upper Ohio, 1775-1777,* Madison, Wis. Hist. Soc., 1908.

Morgan, Lewis Henry, anthropologist, ethnologist (Nov. 21, 1818-Dec. 17, 1881). B. near Aurora, New York, he was descended from early 17th century immigrants to America and was graduated in 1840 from Union College, at Schenectady, New York. He then read law for four years, was admitted to the bar, settled at Rochester, and became legal adviser to a railroad being constructed from Marquette, Michigan, to the Minnesota iron mining region, acquiring thereby some wealth. He early became deeply interested in Iroquois history, political, social and ethnological manifestations, and this enthusiasm endured throughout his life. By chance he met Ely Parker (see entry), a descendant of Seneca chiefs and himself eventually a sachem, Parker being as interested in the customs and ethnology of his people as Morgan had come to be. Morgan's first important book, *League of the Ho-de-no-sau-nee, or Iroquois* (1851) was dedicated to his friend and collaborator, Ely Parker. It was acknowledged as "the fruit of our joint researches," and has been accepted as virtually the first scientific account in any detail of an Indian tribe to be published. It laid the basis for most subsequent studies of that important people and remains useful—and in print—today. Morgan became known as the "Father of American Anthropology," but his interests and influence spread far beyond the borders of the Northeast. He eagerly joined a secret society, the Gordian Knot, which was patterned after the Iroquois Confederacy, or as much of it as could be reconstructed. Ely Parker and Morgan became its leading spirits and its principal thrusts were to study and perpetuate Indian lore, to educate Indians and to help them become integrated into what the whites considered a civilized society. In Morgan's case his interest developed into a studious investigation of Iroquois institutions, legends and customs and from these into further researches among other tribes, and then into world anthropology. He was sent to Washington, D.C., by the Gordian Society to use his legal talents and training to defeat ratification of what the Senecas believed to be a fraudulent treaty in favor of a private land company which would have acquired Seneca lands despite their opposition. Morgan succeeded, became so popular with the Indians as a result that October 1, 1847, they adopted him into the Hawk Clan of the tribe and gave him the name of Tayadawahkugh and made it possible for him to further pursue his studies with eager native assistance. His work became increasingly known in white circles as well, and his several important papers added not only to knowledge of the Iroquois culture but also to his own renown. In 1858 he published a well-received pamphlet, *Laws of Consanguinity and Descent of the Iroquois,* which discussed the clan system and kinship understandings of the tribe. On a trip to Michigan in his railroad interests he discovered that the Ojibway kinship system closely paralleled the Iroquois practice. This broadened his perspective and he subsequently visited Indians of the upper Plains and as far north as the Hudson Bay region, ultimately collecting kinship material on 70 tribes. His further inquiries extended to the primitive world generally. His work and the theories developed therefrom were eventually published in a 600-page volume by the Smithsonian Institution. What he considered his magnum opus was his *Ancient Society or Researches in the Lines of Human Progress,* which developed from his consanguinity studies. Much of his work on these lines, and his theories evolved therefrom, are unacceptable today, but the influence of his concepts "has been acknowledged by many even to the present day." The *Ancient Society* work sought to classify the cultures of the world into such progressive stages as savagery, barbarism and civilization, and this attracted the attention of Friedrich Engels, who sought to apply its teachings as support for the materialistic theories that formed the genesis of what later became Marxist Communism. Morgan was widely honored for his work. In 1875 he helped organize an anthropology section for the American Association for the Advancement of Science, was its first chairman, and became president of the AAAS in 1879. He also was elected a member of the National Academy of Sciences. He was married.

Literature abundant: Lewis Henry Morgan *League of the Iroquois* (1851), N.Y., Corinth Books, 1962 with intr. by William N. Fenton; DAB; CE; REAW; HNAI, 15.

Morley, William Raymond (Ray), railroad locater (Sept. 15, 1846-Jan. 3, 1883). B. in Hampton County, Massachusetts, he was mustered into Company F of the 9th Iowa Infantry March 18, 1864, and became associated with restoring the Chattanooga and Atlanta railroad line for Sherman, thus learning something about railway construction from the ground up. Following the Civil War he became manager for the 2 million-acre Maxwell land grant in New Mexico, and in 1876 was briefly editor of the Cimarron, New Mexico, *News and Press,* until the plant was sacked by a mob. It threw the press into the Cimarron River because the paper had criticized the so-called Santa Fe Ring; the noted Clay Allison (see entry) was reported to have had something to do with the violence, though whether he personally took part was not reported. Morley then joined the fledgling Atchison, Topeka and Santa Fe Railroad, working as line locater

under chief engineer Albert Alonzo Robinson (1844-1918). Morley was described as having "the reputation of being a good friend—and a good hater; an out-of-doors man whose written reports often looked like hentracks; a man who could locate a line through wild country better than most rail pioneers." The American Society of Civil Engineers said Morley "possessed remarkable powers of observation and memory, and in the discernment of the best line for a railway his knowledge and judgment were extraordinary." While others selected routes by laborious study and calculation, Morley "perceived them by intuition...and his preliminary lines traced on horseback with hand level, pocket compass and aneroid barometer, came to be considered almost as authoritative...In mountain work, he had no superior, and perhaps no equal." In southeastern Colorado in 1878 Morley was a significant factor in the Santa Fe's seizure of a route over Raton Pass into New Mexico, and later he was spectacularly successful in the railroad's out-thinking and out-maneuvering the Denver and Rio Grande line for the Royal Gorge route along the upper Arkansas River near the present Canon City. It was he who found that the AT&SF intention to pass its main line through Santa Fe, its namesake city, was impractical; the New Mexico capital was served by a branch line, instead. For his work in locating the Raton Pass and Royal Gorge routes, William Barstow Strong (1837-1914), general manager and later president of the line, presented Morley with a gold-mounted Winchester rifle. In the early 1880s Morley and Strong became interested in the Mexican Central and other possible lines south of the border, including one to Guaymas on the Gulf of California. Morley was reconnoitering such a route when at Santa Rosalia, 200 miles from Chihuahua City, he was accidently shot and killed when drawing his gift-Winchester by the muzzle from a wagon bed. It is curious that an experienced outdoorsman such as Morley would attempt to draw a loaded rifle, muzzle first, from its storage place, but there was no hint of foul play.

Norman Cleaveland, *The Morleys—Young Upstarts on the Southwest Frontier,* Albuquerque, Calvin Horn, pub., 1971; info. from Phillip G. Nickell; James Marshall, *Santa Fe: The Railroad that Built an Empire,* N.Y., Random House, 1945.

Morris, William, frontiersman (fl. 1774-1780). Of the Greenbriar River settlement, West Virginia, Morris took part in the October 10, 1774, Battle of Point Pleasant which effectively ended Lord Dunmore's War, being wounded as a member of Captain Matthew Arbuckle's company. Recovered, he purchased the settlement created by Walter Kelly, who had been killed by Indians earlier in the year; the place thereafter was known as Kelly's Station, and Morris built a fort there which withstood several Indian skirmishes. Morris was one of the notable men of Kanawha Valley history. He became a member of the Virginia Assembly from Kanawha County. He had many descendants, some achieving note.

Thwaites/Kellogg, *Frontier Defense on the Upper Ohio, 1777-1778.*

Morse, Henry Nicholson (Harry), lawman (Feb. 22, 1835-Jan. 11, 1912). B. at New York City, he went to sea at 10 but refused to go as a cabin-boy, signing on as an ordinary seaman. He spent four years sailing between New York and Liverpool. On February 4, 1849, he shipped on an old East India packet, *Panama,* for San Francisco, arriving August 8. He worked at odd jobs, went to the mines and accumulated enough to commence harbor shipping with a fleet of small craft, operated a hotel at Redwood City and finally settled at Oakland. He conducted a series of businesses and in 1862 was named deputy provost marshal for Alameda County, the next year being elected sheriff, meanwhile commissioned a captain of a home guards militia organization for ten years, subsequently becoming a lieutenant colonel. Morse held the position of sheriff for seven consecutive terms, fourteen years. "He...made it a rule, whenever a crime of magnitude was committed in his county, to never let the culprit escape ultimately, and no great crime was ever committed within his jurisdiction, whose perpetrator escaped final detection and capture." Morse was 27 when first elected. By courage and good police work he cleaned up much of the outlawry in his and neighboring counties. "Threats against his life became numerous, and repeated efforts were made to waylay and assassinate" him. In 1865 he had a gunfight with Narciso Bojorques, a noted outlaw, being saved only when the desperado's pistol misfired, then wounding him in the side whereafter Bojorques escaped, only to be slain five months later by another. "Although Morse was in many desperate fights, he probably was never nearer losing his life than in his encounter with Bojorques." In a second gunfight that year

Morse and a Chilean horse thief and murderer, Noratto Ponce, had a duel in the blackness of night, firing only at the gun flashes of the opponent. Morse shot down the other's horse, but the outlaw got away; six weeks later Morse learned where he was being nursed back to health and accosted him. When Ponce aimed his revolver at him, Morse shot him dead with a Henry rifle; Ponce's body showed three pistol wounds and thirteen buckshot wounds from the night duel earlier. On an 1868 pursuit of Joe Newell, Morse pursued him for 41 days "across the most unsettled part of the state," following vague clues for 1,200 miles and twice crossing the Sierra Nevada range. Newell finally was picked up at a railroad camp, brought back to Oakland and tried, sentenced to a mere five years. When he got out he one day shot at Morse, who chased him into a gambling hall and beat him up but, having no outstanding warrant against him, let him go only to be shot and killed in a private fight months later. Morse was as much detective as law enforcer. He "continued to keep track of every member of the various bandit organizations [although] it is impossible to determine how many desperadoes he secured or drove from the district." Perhaps his outstanding gunfight was in 1871 against Juan Soto, a noted outlaw and gunman, who with two companions rifled a store of Thomas Scott on January 10 and killed a clerk, Otto Ludovici. Morse tracked Soto down in the Panoche Mountains 50 miles from Gilroy. The sheriff burst into an adobe house where he found Soto among a dozen of his friends and a scuffle ensued, Morse fighting off his assailants. "A magnificent pistol duel took place between the two men in the open ground around the house and corral." One of Morse's bullets rendered Soto's pistol useless. Soto dashed into the house and got three more firearms, ran out toward a horse which bolted and Morse shot the opponent through the shoulder with his rifle. Soto then rushed him, and Morse was obliged to shoot him through the head. The Soto band was broken up and all those specifically wanted were arrested. Morse was of considerable assistance in running down the noted outlaw Tiburcio Velasquez, although he was not in on the conclusion of that pursuit. After leaving the sheriff's office, he set up his own detective agency, handling successfully a variety of prominent cases, though most of them were of little frontier interest. He did have a role, however, in unraveling the Black Bart (Charles E. Bolton) series of stagecoach holdups. Morse enlisted a detective force of 60 carefully selected men, finding that the San Francisco area offered plenty of opportunity for his kind of business. From 1882 Morse became interested in mining and by 1907 had considerable mining property in California, Nevada and Oregon. In 1903 he retired from his detective agency, though maintaining a controlling interest in it. He had always been meticulously honest in all his dealings, in his profession and out. His wife died in 1907 and of his seven children five predeceased him. He became ill in 1911 and died early in 1912; his estate came to $500,000, "ample evidence of his business acumen."

Charles Howard Shinn, *Graphic Description of Pacific Coast Outlaws: Thrilling Exploits of Their Arch-Enemy Sheriff Harry N. Morse,* ed. by J.E. Reynolds, Los Angeles, Westernlore Press, 1958.

Mortar Chief, Creek leader (d. 1774). A perceptive and even visionary Creek leader, he was never able to enlist numbers great enough to enforce his view that the greatest enemy of the Creeks (he was of the Upper Towns) were the English, and to that insight he throughout his career sought to strengthen Creek trade and other ties to the French and Spanish as counter-balances to the British. Yet he was not so much anti-English as he was pro-Indian, and sought to build alliances to balance one European faction against another for the benefit of his people. He was well-connected. A sister married the Gun Merchant, long a leading Creek. A brother married a Cherokee, which gave him some influence among that nation. In pursuit of his purpose to neutralize the European factions, he sided from 1720 for many years with the French at Fort Toulouse, near the confluence of the Coosa and Tallapoosa rivers north of present Montgomery, Alabama. He opposed a Creek war with the Cherokees when he saw cooperation between them against the English as more beneficial for the Indians, although he did not necessarily favor war by the Creeks and Cherokees with the English—only resistance to inroads and to the English appetite for Indian lands. He opposed an alliance of Creeks, Cherokees and English against the Choctaws, who were supported by the French. He saw the necessity for the Creeks to obtain trade goods in growing quantities, and that the French would be unable to supply these in any regular manner, but did not wish to see any trading country become too powerful at the expense of its customers. In 1756 he repudiated his brother-in-law Gun Merchant's agreement with the English to allow them to establish a fort in Creek country, and in 1756-57 he conspired to form an alliance of Creeks, Cherokees, Shawnees, Chickasaws and Catawbas against or in resistance to, the English. He sometimes appeared to be inconsistent, although it is doubtful if in his own mind he saw it that way. When outrages in Virginia fanned Cherokee resentment of the British in 1758, he urged his Creeks to join the Cherokees in retaliations against the English. When the Choctaws at one point appeared to be swinging behind the English, the Mortar attempted to provoke a Creek-Choctaw war to drive the Choctaws back toward the French in order to maintain the balance he believed necessary on the southern frontier. His bellicose views may have contributed to the Cherokee War of 1760, in which he participated, though he was unable to bring the Creeks into the conflict alongside the Cherokees, and afterward was forced to attempt a reconciliation, somewhat stiffly, with the English. He continued most of his life to agitate against British expansionism, however, and as late as 1769-71, when the Shawnees were building a confederacy against the Virginians, he was trying to cement a peace between Creeks and Choctaws so that they could better aid the Shawnees. In 1772 the Mortar was planning an alliance of all the southern tribes, and hoped to encourage the French (who in fact had lost out in America as a result of the French and Indian War) and Spanish to establish a strong trade in the south to counterbalance the British. To this end he set out for New Orleans, and enroute was killed in a fracas with Choctaws in the autumn of 1774. A persistent intriguer, he was not an aimless one. A strong theme runs through his life: to counter excessive English interference with the Creeks and the diminution of Indian lands, but he for many reasons was unable to persuade more than a minority of his nation to support his views.

Info. from John Sugden; David H. Corkran, *The Creek Frontier, 1540-1783,* Norman, Univ. of Okla. Press, 1967; Corkran, *The Cherokee Frontier: Conflict and Survival, 1740-62,* Norman, 1962.

Moser, Jefferson Franklin, naval officer (May 3, 1848-Oct. 11, 1934). B. at Allentown, Pennsylvania, he was graduated from the Naval Academy in 1868. He was a member of repeated expeditions from 1869 to 1875, exploring and surveying routes for a possible ship canal across

Nicaragua and Panama, and was on Coast and Geodetic Survey duty from 1875 to 1896. Moser commanded the steamer *Albatross* of the Bureau of Fisheries in Alaskan waters during 1897 and 1898, his hydrographic notes and sketches published by the C&GS in 1899. In 1900-1901, the *Albatross* visited most of the important salmon streams from Dixon Entrance to the Nushagak River. He made sketch maps of the streams and reconnaissance charts of Alitak Bay, parts of the Kodiak Island coast and Afognak Bay and completed a reconnaissance of the coast between the Alsek River delta and Yakutat Bay. He became a Rear Admiral and retired September 29, 1904. Moser was general superintendent and vice president of the Alaska Packers Association of San Francisco from 1904 to 1918, but returned to naval duty from August 6, 1917, to June 15, 1919. He was author of *Alaska Salmon and Salmon Fisheries* (1899) and *Alaska Salmon Investigations* (1902). His west coast home was at Alameda, California. He named many Alaskan geographical features and some of them have been named for him.

Orth, 22, 659; *Who Was Who.*

Mosholatubbee, Choctaw chief (d. Sept. 30, 1838). A great chief of the Choctaws during the emigration period and earlier, he was born in the last half of the 18th century. He joined Jackson in 1812 with warriors who assisted in the war against the Creeks, with whom the Choctaws were usually hostile, anyway. In December 1824, as one of the Choctaw delegation to Washington, D.C., he met Lafayette. Mosholatubbee, as leading chief, signed a series of treaties that resulted in migration of the Choctaws from Mississippi to Indian Territory. These included the Treaty of Choctaw Trading House, Mississippi, October 24, 1816; that of Treaty Ground, Mississippi, October 18, 1820; that of Washington, D.C., January 20, 1825, and the Treaty of Dancing Rabbit Creek, Mississippi, September 27, 1830. Debo gives the most detailed and best discussions of these various treaties, and Mosholatubbee's gradual disillusionment with the United States, its promises and its lack of performance to fulfill them. Catlin painted the Choctaw's portrait, reproduced in Swanton. Mosholatubbee died of smallpox at the agency in Arkansas and his name was later applied to a district in Indian Territory.

Hodge, HAI; Swanton, *Indians of Southeastern United Statese;* Angie Debo, *The Rise and Fall of the*

Choctaw Republic, Norman, Univ. of Okla. Press, 1967.

Mountain Lamb (Umentucken Tukutsey Undewatsey), Shoshone woman (d. June 1837). Reported by Joe Meek to have been first the wife of Milton Sublette and then the wife of Meek, historian Doyce Nunis considered her simply "a figment of Joe Meek's imagination," although Dale Morgan seems to have accepted the story at face value; he added that "Milton's marital affairs may require untangling." By the account given Frances Fuller Victor, perhaps by Meek himself, Sublette had taken her for his woman, possibly after a previous wife had died or left him, he having fathered at least one of her two children by 1832. When Sublette was forced to leave the Rockies to seek eastern medical attention and sent word in 1835 that he could not then return, Meek took Mountain Lamb as his wife. He was quoted as asserting that "she was the most beautiful Indian woman I ever saw," and he outfitted her to match her spectacular comeliness. During the summer of 1835, he reported, she escaped a band of Blackfeet by swimming the Yellowstone River. She once faced down, pistol in hand, a mountain man bully named O'Fallen. On one occasion, probably also in 1835, a party of a dozen Crows captured Mountain Lamb, and she was rescued by Meek alone, who shot one of her captors. When Bannocks raided an 1837 Green River rendezvous, one casualty was reported to be Mountain Lamb, struck in the heart by a Bannock arrow.

Frances Fuller Victor, *The River of the West,* p.p., Hartford, Ct., 1870, repr. Columbus, Ohio, Long's College Book Co., 1950, pp. 175ff., 197-98; Doyce B. Nunis Jr., "Milton Sublette," MM, IV; Harvey E. Tobie, "Joseph L. Meek," MM, I; Dale L. Morgan, Eleanor Towles Harris, *The Rocky Mountain Journals of William Marshall Anderson,* San Marino, Ca., Huntington Lbry., 1967; Stanley Vestal, *Joe Meek: The Merry Mountain Man,* Lincoln, Univ. of Nebr. Press, n.d., 161-66, 204-205, 209-210; info. from E.F. (Ted) Mains.

Mounts, Providence, military officer (d. 1784). B. in Maryland, he was reported to have served with Washington at Fort Necessity, Pennsylvania, at the start of the French and Indian War. In 1768 he removed to the Youghiogheny River in Fayette County, erecting a mill on a creek there emptying into the river, the site now occupied by Connellsville. During the Revolution he was colonel of the 2nd battalion of Westmoreland militia and took part in Edward Hand's 1777-78 expedition against Ohio Indians. Mounts also served in the pursuit of Indians who had sacked Hannahstown in 1782. He died in 1784.

Thwaites/Kellogg, *Frontier Defense on the Upper Ohio, 1777-1778.*

Mukhin, Nikolai, colony administrator (d.c. 1805). Apparently from Kursk, Russia, he arrived at Kodiak Island, Alaska, around 1800 and was sent to succeed I.G. Polomoshnoi as head of the new Russian American Company settlement at Yakutat Bay, on the Alaska Panhandle. His activities and competence pleased I.A. Kuskov (see entry), who told Mukhin "to take extra precautions" against being surprised by the Tlingit Indians in the vicinity who bordered on hostile. Shortly the settlers, grown fearful, wanted to abandon the site but were told there was not enough transportation. Mukhin, apparently becoming incapable of quelling the growing unrest, was succeeded as leader by Stepan Larionov (see entry), but seems to have remained in the colony, which was destroyed by the Tlingits in 1805. "Mukhin was probably slain in the attack, as his name does not reappear."

Pierce, *Russian America: A Biographical Dictionary.*

Muldrow, Robert, topographer (1864-1946). A topographer with the Geological Survey from 1887 to 1928, Muldrow joined George Eldridge (see entry) in an 1898 reconnaissance of the Susitna River valley from its mouth on Cook Inlet northward to about the northern boundary of the present Mount McKinley National Park. He is commemorated by Muldrow Glacier, northeast of the peak and a favored route for early climbers of the mountain. Alfred Brooks named the glacier for Muldrow in 1902.

Orth, 12, 664.

Muller, Gerhard-Friedrich, historian (Oct. 18, 1705-Oct. 11, 1783). B. at Herford, Westphalia, he attended the University of Lepizig and in 1725 moved to St. Petersburg, Russia. He became associated with the Russian Academy of Sciences, in 1831 becoming a professor, having taught Latin, history and geography. By 1732 he began to publish articles on Russian history and by 1765 these had been collected in nine volumes. In 1733 Muller joined the Second Kamchatka Expedition of Bering (see entry). During

the following decade he traveled to many principal points of Siberia, "discovering a mass of archival material on the history, archeology, ethnography and current state of the region." He returned to St. Petersburg, in 1748 took Russian citizenship and was appointed historiographer, but a speech the following year on the origins of the Russian people was alleged by prominent chauvinists to be anti-Russian in that it did not sufficiently glorify the Russian people, and stressed the Scandinavian origin of the Russian state. "In 1750 these quarrels caused Muller to be demoted," and his salary to be cut by two-thirds. The first volume of his major work, *Description of the Siberian Realm,* was published in 1750; it was followed shortly by part of the second volume. Pierce noted that in 1936 and 1941 about half of the published chapters were reprinted in the Soviet Union "along with a mass of previously unpublished supporting documents," as *History of Siberia,* but World War II interfered with appearance of the rest of it, which has yet to be brought out. The third of the nine volumes of his collected articles is devoted in part to information about Alaska. Muller's 1758 volume on *Voyages from Asia to America* was translated and published at London in 1761 and "provided researchers with a fairly accurate picture of the geography of the region." Muller was stricken by paralysis in 1772 but continued to work until his death. "He left a massive collection of documents in 258 portfolios...which are still a mine of information [on] the history, ethnography, statistics and economy of Russia, particularly Siberia, with information on early voyages to the Aleutian Islands."

Pierce, *Russian America: A Biographical Dictionary.*

Muravyev, Matvei Ivanovich, administrator (1780s-1833). Muravyev entered the Russian naval academy February 13, 1793, became a midshipman in 1802 and fought against the Swedes in 1808 and the French in 1813. He served with distinction as a lieutenant under Golovnin on a global circumnavigation on which hydrological investigations were made in the Aleutians. Kodiak Island was reached July 9, 1818, and Sitka July 28, the expedition visiting California enroute home. October 12, 1819, Muravyev became a Captain-Lieutenant and December 20, was appointed chief manager of the Russian American Company in Alaska; he reached Sitka September 11, 1820, succeeding

Yanovskii on September 15. He was an active official, revising those policies of his precedessors he deemed unwise. Baranov, after suffering a debacle at Sitka at the hands of the Tlingit Indians, ordered them kept at a distance from the post, but Muravyev apparently decided it was better to keep an eye on the potential enemy than to live in fear of a sudden attack, and reversed Baranov's decision. While he permitted the Indians to come under the shadow of the post, he greatly strengthened its palisades, established rules that they could not visit the fortress at night or without a written pass, strengthened patrols and guards and made the post so secure that succeeding administrators followed his precepts. Leaving the office manager, Khlebnikov, in charge, Muravyev on May 27, 1821, embarked on an inspection tour of the company's possessions, then divided Alaska into districts in order to improve administration. Russia brought the threat of starvation to the struggling Alaskan colonies by imposing a ban on foreign shipping into its provinces while not itself supplying them with necessary foodstuffs. Muravyev met the very real crisis by scrounging what supplies could be obtained in California and Hawaii and by legerdemain of every sort managed to keep his region afloat until the unwise law was modified. In this he revealed his intelligent and innovative nature and the flexibility of his administration. During his managerial period he also encouraged exploration of the distant, still-largely unknown Alaskan reaches. Voyages under Vasiliy Stepanovich Khromchenko, Adolf Karlovich Etolin and Mihhail Nikolayevich Vasilev in 1822-23 conducted surveys of the coast from Bristol Bay to the Kuskokwim River, Nunivak Island was visited, Norton Sound explored and other segments of the coast charted. He made an agreement with the authorities in California for joint sea otter operations. Muravyev's health deteriorated while he served in Alaska and he was relieved July 29, 1825, by Lieutenant Petr Egorovich Chistiakov, and reached Kronstadt September 1, 1826. Muravyev then served two years in the headquarters office of the Russian American Company at St. Petersburg and held various government posts until his death. It is believed that he was married to a Creole girl who under his request had followed him to Russia, coming overland across Siberia, but the date of the marriage, if it occurred, is not reported.

Richard A. Pierce, *Builders of Alaska: The Russian*

Governors 1818-1867, Kingston, Ont., Limestone Press, 1986; Bancroft, *Alaska;* Zagoskin; *The Russian American Colonies; Colonial Russian America: Kyrill T. Khlebnikov's Reports, 1817-1832,* Portland, Ore. Hist. Soc., 1976.

Murray, Alexander Hunter, fur trader (1818-Apr. 20, 1874). B. at Kilmun, Argyllshire, Scotland, he was well educated and became "a skilled observor," emigrating to the United States. For some years he was employed by the American Fur Company, in 1842 managing Fort Van Buren, on the Yellowstone at the mouth of the Rosebud River, and later took charge of Fort Alexander, named by Larpenteur for Alexander Culbertson, across the Yellowstone from Van Buren, which was burned. Murray left the AFC in 1845, crossed into Manitoba to Fort Garry where he joined the Hudson's Bay Company. The HBC sent him to Fort McPherson in the Mackenzie River district on the Peel River near its confluence with the Mackenzie. Murray became a senior clerk with the firm, although one problem was that "his men will not stay any length of time with him," perhaps because of his "undiplomatic," or short-fused manner. But he was determined, strong-willed and an able man. For these and other reasons George Simpson, commanding the HBC's Northern Department, personally selected him to establish Fort Yukon, in the present Alaska. He left Manitoba for Fort Simpson, at the junction of the Liard and Mackenzie rivers. Fellow travellers included Colin Campbell, commander of the Athabasca District, and his two daughters, one of whom was Anne, 17. She was interested in sketching and Murray, then 27, by comparison something of an artist, soon became her tutor and then her close companion. Before they reached Fort Chipewyan they were engaged, and at Fort Simpson they were married, in the absence of clergy in such a primitive region by signing a contract before Murdock McPherson, commander of the post, who pronounced them man and wife. It was a lasting marriage, and productive, for over time they became parents of three sons and five daughters. Murray's Fort McPherson instructions were to follow up on John Bell's 1844 journey to the Yukon River and establish there a trading post. Bell already had created an outpost, Lapierre House, on the upper Procupine River at its confluence with the Bell River. Murray reached that place, in the region of the Kutcha-Kutchin tribe, an Athabascan people of "greater energy and more warlike character" than neighboring Athabascans. They offered no opposition to the HBC personnel, but perhaps recalling the belligerence of Plains Indians, Murray remained wary of them. June 18, 1847, he and his men left Lapierre House for the Yukon, weighted down with arms and ammunition and taking along plentiful supplies for the new post where Murray felt he might encounter not only Indian hostility but possible trouble from Russians, although in fact the rivals never explored that far up the great river. Down the Porcupine a week's travel he reached the Yukon and wrote in his journal that "I never saw an uglier river, every where low banks, evidently lately overflowed, with lakes and swamps behind, the trees too small for building, the water abominably dirty and the current furious." Mosquitoes were a constant torment. On June 26, he located a suitable site near the junction of the Porcupine and Yukon. A fort was commenced June 27, and Murray at once began trading with Indians for inland furs of good quality. He insisted upon strong fortifications, noting that "When all this is finished, the Russians may advance when they d---d please." Most HBC forts were merely sprawling collections of structures used solely to serve trading purposes, but Murray made of Fort Yukon an exception, a fortress bastion impregnable for any attack the Indians or small parties of whites might level. He and his wife remained four years, leaving in the summer of 1851 with three daughters, said to have been the first white children born in Arctic America. (See Charles W. Raymond entry for an account of the United States takeover of the post in 1869, after purchase of Alaska). Murray returned to Fort Garry in 1852 and was stationed at various Canadian posts thereafter, becoming a chief trader in 1856. He retired in 1867 and lived for seven years on a small farm on the Red River until his death at 56; Anne survived him for 33 years, until 1907.

Theodore J. Karamanski, *Fur Trade and Exploration: Opening the Far Northwest 1821-1852,* Norman, Univ. of Okla. Press, 1983; Melody Webb, *The Last Frontier: A History of the Yukon Basin,* Albuquerque, Univ. of N. Mex. Press, 1985; Charles Larpenteur, *Forty Years a Fur Trader on the Upper Missouri,* Lincoln, Univ. of Nebr. Press, 1989; Pierce, *Russian America: A Biographical Dictionary.*

Murrell, John A., desperado (c. 1804-c. 1845). The date of his birth is not universally agreed upon. One source gives 1794, another c. 1800, but most believe 1804 was the probable year, the birth occurring at a roadside tavern near Columbia, Tennessee, about 40 miles south of Nashville. His father was an itinerant preacher and his mother an itinerant whore. "My mother...learnt me and all her children how to steal as soon as we could walk. At ten years old I was not a bad hand." Murrell quickly graduated into horse theft, Negro stealing and murder. Court records show that he was fined for "riot" near Nashville in 1823. In 1825 he was arrested for gambling. Twice in 1826 he was tried for horse stealing, the second time getting a year in prison, during which he was branded "H.T." on both thumbs for horse thief. In the early 1830s young Virgil Stewart became associated with Murrell, reportedly trying surreptitiously to gather evidence against him for black-stealing and in the course of this undertaking, becoming something of an amanuensis for Murrell, keeping a written account of what he said and claimed to have done. By his own admissions, as Stewart recorded them, Murrell was a killer as well as robber, using the ancient method of disposing of the bodies by filling their abdominal cavities with stones and sinking the corpses in streams. He had apparent organizing ability as well as murderous inclinations. His slave stealing began in a modest way. He would promise a slave to lead him to freedom if the black would let him sell him once or twice on the way. When the slave had been thus stolen, sold and stolen again, often enough to become notorious, Murrell would kill him and dispose of the body. "Once he dealt with a whole Negro family that way—father, mother and children all." He moved ahead, organizing with other rogues into a clan he called the Mystic Confederacy, but his master plan, according to Stewart, was a great Negro rebellion. Stewart collected evidence that Murrell planned to incite a revolt in the Delta country that he predicted would sweep away the whites and eventually even capture New Orleans. It was to commence on July 4, 1835, a holiday when the slaves might gather unnoticed and the insurrection break out. There is much uncertainty and controversy about this erratic scheme and whether it ever existed, but it came to very little if it did. Stewart notified authorities of the intended revolt and in July 1834 Murrell was tried in circuit court, Jackson, Tennessee, on the relatively minor Negro-stealing charge. He was defended by Milton Brown (1804-1883), who subsequently became a U.S. Representative (1841-1847) and afterwards a railroad president and prominent businessman. In this instance Brown lost his case and Murrell received ten years in the state prison at Nashville. During his term he contracted tuberculosis and died at Pikesville, Tennessee. Stewart's narrative was rewritten and embroidered by the *Police Gazette* and even more so by later writers "until some weary editor topped it finally with *The Pictorial Life of the Great Western Land Pirate*." Mississippi historian John Francis Hamtramck Claiborne believed Stewart was "a notorious scamp," and that "the whole story was a fabrication." Writing in 1860 he said that "Murrell was simply a thief and counterfeiter, and Stewart was his subordinate, who, having quarreled with him, devised this plan to avenge and enrich himself. The whole 'plot' [of the insurrection] may now be regarded as one of the most extraordinary and lamentable hallucinations of our times." Yet men were hanged for "participation" in it, shots were fired and panic flared in many areas, if briefly.

Jonathan Daniels, *The Devil's Backbone: The Story of the Natchez Trace*, N.Y., McGraw-Hill Book Co., American Trails Series, 1962; Paul I. Wellman, *Spawn of Evil*, Garden City, N.Y., Doubleday & Co., 1964; James D. Horan, Paul Sann, *Pictorial History of the Wild West*, N.Y., Crown Pubs., 1954; DAB; BDAC; info. from E.F. (Ted) Mains.

Mushalatubbee: *see,* Mosholatubbee

Mylnikov, Nikolai Prokofevich, fur trader (d.c. 1802). Although he never visited Alaska or saw the North American coast, Mylnikov was not without influence on development of the northwest fur trade. He was a guild merchant of Irkutsk, Siberia, and in 1779 joined Grigorii Shelikhov (see entry) in a fur trading venture which got no farther than the Komandorskie Islands; in 1780 he, Shelikhov and others organized a second venture, this time to the Aleutians, but the vessel was wrecked upon its return in 1786 with great losses to the combine. In 1792 Mylnikov established a rival company and after Shelikhov's death in 1795 he and his sons, Dmitrii, Iakov and Mikhail, "became bitter rivals of the Shelikhov interests" with which they had earlier cooperated. Mylnikov was rebuffed when he approached I.L. Gilikov, Shelikhov's onetime partner, for a merger since he himself lacked funds to develop his interests. So his firm turned to Natalia Shelikhov, widow of the pioneer fur merchant, to form a united company. This was accomplished July 20, 1797, but there was so much conniving and chicanery involved by the Mylnikov faction that an Imperial order was issued July 8, 1799, creating the Russian American Company, to consist of Shelikhov's interests and those of the Mylnikov company. This, however, did not settle matters between them and lawsuits by the Mylnikov people "swamped the courts" with charges against their partners. The Shelikhov heirs finally succeeded in transferring headquarters of the firm from Irkutsk to St. Petersburg where higher officials could assist in controlling the "obstreperous Irkutsk merchants," and the situation at last became manageable, although Mylnikov remained head of the Irkutsk office until his death. Pierce has worked out details of this sordid business affair.

Pierce, *Russian America: A Biographical Dictionary.*

Myres, Sandra Lynn, historian (May 17, 1933-Oct. 16, 1991). B. at Columbus, Ohio, she was graduated in 1957 from Texas Tech College of Lubbock, earned a master's degree there three years later and a doctorate from Texas Christian University in 1967. From 1963 she taught at the University of Texas at Arlington, where she became a full professor. Her books included *S.D. Myers: Saddlemaker* (1961); *Force Without Fanfare: The Autobiography of K.M. Van Zandt* (1968); *The Ranch in Spanish Texas* (1969); *Cavalry Wife: The Diary of Eveline M. Alexander* (1976); *Ho for California! Women's Overland Diaries from the Huntington Library* (1980), and *Westering Women and the Frontier Experience* (1982). At her death she was working on two books, *Plainswoman: The Canadian and United States Experience,* and *Victoria's Daughters: Nineteenth Century Frontiers-women in Australia, New Zealand, Canada and the United States West.* She contributed papers and other writings to more than 200 serial publications, was president of the Western History Association in 1987-88, served on various national historical committees and the Washington, D.C., National Endowment for the Humanities, among other organizations. She died at Arlington, Texas, following a lengthy illness.

American Military on the Frontier: Proceedings of the 7th Military History Symposium, U.S. Air Force Academy, 1976, pub. at Washington, D.C., 1978, p. 184; Council on America's Military Past, *Headquarters Heliogram,* 218, November 1991, p. 4; biographical sketch, WHA, July 11, 1986.

N

Nagaief (Nagaev), Leontiy, Russian explorer, fur trader (fl. c. 1780-1787). The discoverer and explorer of Alaska's Copper River, Nagaief's relationship, if any, to a noted Russian hydrographer, Admiral Nagaief is unknown, but both were acquainted with the Aleutian Islands and Alaskan waters. Leontiy Nagaief had reached Unalaska Island at least by 1780 as a *baidarshchik* or leader of fur gatherers and traders. An investigation in 1790 by government inspectors into charges of cruelties and abuses by Russian traders against the Aleuts heard testimony that Nagaief had remained on the island after Delarov (see entry) had left for Kodiak Island. One witness said that "the companies of [Stepan Iakovlev] Cherepanov and Nagaief do not inflict such cruel abuse and murder [upon the natives as did other Russians] but they send us out to hunt against our will and force us to provide food and do domestic work without pay," adding that Nagaief paid so little for sea otter pelts, provided no clothing for the Aleuts who served him and sent them out naked to hunt and fish to the point where many fled his company for that of Cherepanov where they were treated better. Hodge reported that Nagaief discovered the mouth of the Copper River, east of the present Cordova, Alaska, in 1781, and this may be true although it was on August 18, 1783, that he met other Russians on Nuchek Island, bringing in many sea otter skins which had been made into garments and reporting he had been the first European to ascend the Copper River for any considerable distance. He had met a large number of natives and traded with them advantageously, although they refused him a guide to a large and safe harbor they had reported and that they indicated would be suitable for Russian ships. On Nuchek Island Nagaief met 28 men of the ship, *Sv Alexei,* fourteen of whom had been wounded in an attack by the Chugach Eskimos. This was part of a larger attempt by the Russians to occupy for trading purposes Prince William Sound. Bancroft wrote that "the only subordinate commander of this expedition who seems to have actually explored and intelligently described these unknown regions, was Nagaief," nearly all the valuable information collected from the endeavor coming from this man. He told Zaikov, overall leader, that the Chugaches had informed him that they met in war and trade with five neighboring tribes, the description of the tribes and their locations "doubtless correct at the time," although with the white invasion and expansion of fur trading most of the tribes shortly became dislocated. Nagaief also reported that the Yullits (Ahtena), or Copper River basin natives, an Athabascan Indian people, lived only on the upper river, but traded copper and land furs with the coast Eskimos for seal skins, dried fish and oil. In 1787 Nagaief acknowledged receipt of an imperial ukase, stating that he had read it.

Russian Penetration of the North Pacific Ocean; Hodge; Bancroft, *Alaska.*

Nahilzay (Ny-les-shizie, Ny-ith-shizeh), Chiricahua Apache war leader (c. 1837-c.1882). Considered by informed persons to be Cochise's war chief, Nahilzay was close to Taza, Cochise's son, and with him led many raids into the Sonoita Valley of southern Arizona in the early 1870s and perhaps before; he also was active in Mexico. He became one of the dozen war captains of Cochise's band, and was one of three believed possible successors to Cochise following his 1874 death, but Taza, the son, won out and Nahilzay loyally supported him; after Taza's death in 1876, Nahilzay became a member of the band of Naiche, Cochise's second son. In 1879 he participated in negotiations to bring Juh and Geronimo from Mexico to the San Carlos Reservation in Arizona, then accompanied them on their 1881 bolt for Mexico again. He was a leading man in a fight near Casas Grandes in 1882 where he was captured by Mexicans, sent to a Chihuahua City jail and was never heard from again. He was married to E-nah-dez-lee and fathered a son, Fred Do-as-ka-da, who died at Fort Sill.

Edwin R. Sweeney, *Cochise: Chiricahua Apache Chief,* Norman, Univ. of Okla. Press, 1991; Griswold, 116.

Nairne, Thomas, frontiersman (d. Apr. 1715). B. in "North Britain," or Scotland or, possibly of Scottish descent on a Carolina plantation, he first appeared in Carolina records in 1698 as a landowner on St. Helena Island, between Port Royal and St. Helena sounds, South Carolina. He became, in Crane's words, "a veteran of the warpath and the council house, the ablest frontiersman of his day in the South," particularly during Queen Anne's War (1701-13). He was captain of a company under Governor James Moore (see entry) in a campaign against Spanish St. Augustine, but the adventure "had its true setting in the international contest for the region of the Gulf [of Mexico] and the Mississippi," and "the affair and its sequel, the Apalache campaign, were not untouched by scandal." At any rate, it was unsuccessful (see Moore entry for details of the operation). Nairne also conducted partisan activities in later raids into Florida. He wrote in 1705, "We have these two past years been intirely kniving [raiding] all the Indian Towns in Florida which were subject to the Spaniards..." and an official map bore the legend across this region: "Wholly laid waste being destroyed by the Carolinians, 1706." Nairne may have been the pamphleteer who in 1710 wrote that "there remains not now, so much as one Village with ten Houses in it, in all Florida, that is subject to the Spaniards" except those under protection of the guns of St. Augustine, it alone remaining in their hands and even it "is continually infested by the perpetual Incursions of the Indians, subject to this Province." An Assembly act July 5, 1707, named Nairne to appoint "two watches southward" to guard against Spanish incursions or those perhaps of hostile Indians. In the autumn of 1707 Nairne, by now provincial Indian agent, and Chickasaw Indian trader Thomas Welch drafted an elaborate western campaign plan, adopted by the assembly. Nairne had been the obvious choice as Indian agent, the first appointed in Carolina, for he had long experience with the neighboring Yamasee tribe and as a partisan. Nairne and Welch, while conceding the importance of reducing Mobile in the struggle against the French to the west, cautioned that first priority should be to wean the powerful Choctaw and the Yazoo tribes from the French to the English side. Nairne's plan was to raise volunteers among the Indian traders, and to assemble a much larger force of Indians. His design, he later wrote, "was to fall down [from the north] against the French with a fleet of Eighty canoes man'd with 500 Indians and 1000 [others] by land [with] 15 English on the one part and 36 on the other. With these forces I pretended Either to

destroy or remove into our Territory all the Salvages from Mobile to the Mississippi, and up the river to 36 Degrees of Latitude." Something apparently of a visionary, he also was a man of action and in 1708 achieved at great personal risk a peace with the Choctaws, while Welch concluded a peace with the Yazoo and other river tribes. Only a rumor from Jamaica that the Spanish and French were raising a massive attempt against Charles Town (Charleston) halted development of a major English assault on Mobile, after the Indians the French might count on as allies had been neutralized. Another obstacle to pursuing the Mobile and western adventure was the imprisonment of Nairne June 23, 1708, for five months on the ludicrous charge that he had been involved in a plot to dethrone Queen Anne and replace her with the Pretender Prince of Wales. The case never reached trial, the charge having its apparent origin in a smouldering feud between Nairne and Sir Nathaniel Johnson, the then governor of Carolina. In 1710 Nairne went to England to clear his name, which was done, "but meanwhile he had lost his Indian agency, and his great Louisiana [military project had come to nought." While in Jail he had penned "one of the most remarkable documents in the history of Anglo-American frontier imperialism," urging English "continental dominion." Only South Carolina, he wrote, could effectively extend English hegemony against French aggrandizement and Spanish expansionism from New Mexico. He urged extensive and purposeful colonization directed toward furthering this grand goal, and in this "grandiose scheme Nairne's imagination carried him beyond the vision of his generation," though elements of it endured long after his time. In November 1712 Nairne was restored as the principal Indian agent, and was praised by Indian commissioners for his "capacity and diligence" in negotiations with western tribes. Nairne, who apparently desired safe commercial relations with the powerful Yamasee Indians, had appealed to England for a missionary to work among them, and the Society for the Propagation of the Gospel sent the Reverend Samuel Thomas who immediately found that it was "not safe to venture among" so wild a tribe and preferred to work among comparatively docile black slaves. Although Thomas had become a protege of the governor, Nairne was among those who excoriated him for "abandoning" his charge. The important Yamasee War of 1715-16, "a far-reaching revolt against the Carolinian trading regime" and individual traders for their excesses and tyrannies, as the Indians viewed them, "takes rank with the more famous Indian conspiracies of colonial times." In all, 200 to 300 settlers were killed before the hostiles were pushed down into Florida. The war opened April 15, 1715, Good Friday, at Pocotaligo Town, an important Yamasee settlement near the border between today's Beaufort and Jasper counties of South Carolina. Nairne and several traders and others were at the town and instantly captured and Nairne, it was reported, was burned at the stake by slow fire, "a refinement of torture which was protracted for several days," as the conflict spread through the southeast. In the 1690s Nairne had married Elizabeth Quintine, by whom he fathered a son.

Verner W. Crane, *The Southern Frontier: 1670-1732*, Ann Arbor, Univ. of Mich. Press, 1929/1956; DAB, the Nairne article also written by Crane from material in his book; Hodge, HAI; Swanton, *Tribes*.

Nakvasin, Prokhor, fur man (d. 1802). He was on Kodiak Island in 1795 and from 1799 a clerk at Sitka, a literate, useful employee. He was at Sitka when the Kolosh (Tlingit) Indians stormed the post in 1802, and was among the slain. Various sites along the Alaskan coast were apparently named for him.

Pierce, *Russian America: A Biographical Dictionary;* Orth, 671.

Nasatir, Abraham Phineas, historian (Nov. 24, 1904-Jan. 18, 1991). B. at Santa Ana, California, the loss of his left hand at 9 forced him to abandon hope of becoming a physician or concert violinist, and he became a historian almost by accident. A devout Orthodox Jew, he was graduated from high school at 14, entered the University of California at Berkeley late in the semester and was forced to take a history course under Herbert Bolton because that was the only opening; he found the subject fascinating, became a noted Boltonian scholar himself, was graduated from college at 16, earned his master's degree in 1921 and a doctorate from Berkeley in 1926, when he was 22. He was an instructor at the University of Iowa in 1926-27, joined what ultimately became California State University at San Diego in 1928 when its enrollment was 350, became a full professor in 1934 and was retired in 1974 when the school had 32,000 students. Nasatir became research professor emeritus, permitting him to work and lecture there until

his death at 86. He was Fulbright lecturer at the University of Chile in 1959-60, vice consul to Paraguay from 1936-41, and to Ecuador from 1941-43, while retaining his faculty position at San Diego. His historical specialty was Spanish regimes in the Mississippi Valley, and some of his best-known and most valuable writings were in this field. He took on the history of the French in California as a hobby, became a leading historian in that area, publishing standard works relative to it. His principal teaching field was Latin American history, though at one point he was asked to teach a course in English history, for which he felt scarcely qualified "because I never had had a course on the history of England." But he took the task on, teaching a course for eighteen years on the subject and bringing it to wide recognition and respect. He was widely honored and greatly appreciated and his profound knowledge of Spanish and other languages was reflected in his historical researches. He edited collections of documents and accumulated from 300,000 to 500,000 pages of manuscripts, most requiring translation. Among his 20 books were: *Inside History of the Gold Rush* (1935); *French Activities in California* (1945); *Before Lewis and Clark: Documents Illustrating the History of the Missouri 1785-1804,* two vols. (1952); *French Journalists in the Gold Rush* (1965); with Noel M. Loomis (Nasatir providing the research and factual material, Loomis the narrative) *Pedro Vial and the Roads to Santa Fe* (1967); *Spanish War Vessels on the Mississippi* (1968); with H.M. Bailey, *Latin America: Development of Civilization,* 3rd ed. (1973), while his final volume was *Borderland in Retreat: From Spanish Louisiana to the Far Southwest* (1976). He was survived by his widow, Ida Hirsch Nasatir.

Eugene K. Chamberlin obituary in *Western Historical Quarterly,* Vol. XXII, No. 2 (May 1991), 258-59; *Who's Who in America; San Diego Union,* June 13, 1976; Herb Brin, *Heritage,* Los Angeles, Calif., Feb. 20, 1969.

Natches (Natchez), Paiute chief (fl. 1860-1882). A prominent son of Old Winnemucca and a brother of Sarah and Numaga Winnemucca (see entries), Natches apparently participated in the Pyramid Lake War of 1860 in western Nevada, but soon made peace with the whites and took no more hostile actions. February 26, 1875, he was reported to have recaptured Patsey Marley, "the notorious stage robber," who had escaped from Sheriff Andy Fife of Nevada's Lincoln County earlier "by jumping from a flying train." Natches turned him over to law officers. In January 1880 he, Sarah, her cousin Captain Jim, and her father, Old Winnemucca journeyed to Washington, D.C., with Special Agent of the Bureau of Indian Affairs J.M. Hayworth. They conferred with Secretary of the Interior Carl Schurz and later met President Rutherford B. Hayes. The Indians were promised much, but received little. Later that year Natches was engaged in farming in the Lovelock area east of Pyramid Lake with others of the Winnemucca Paiutes. Sarah established her progressive settlement on the Lovelock farm of Natches for a short time. Natches became chief of the Winnemucca Paiutes when Old Winnemucca died October 21, 1882. He was photographed together with his father, Sarah, brother Numaga and cousin, Captain Jim, at Washington in 1880; it is reproduced in HNAI 11, p. 458; there also are pictures of the Paiute leaders in *Nevada Indians Speak,* following p. 148.

Ferol Egan, *Sand in a Whirlwind: The Paiute Indian War of 1860,* Reno, Univ. of Nevada Press, 1985; HNAI, 11, *Great Basin;* Jack D. Forbes, *Nevada Indians Speak,* Reno, 1967; *Panamint* (Calif.) *News,* Mar. 4, 1875, p. 2.

Natiotish, White Mountain Apache (d. July 17, 1882). Natiotish, a leading man of the White Mountain Apaches of eastern Arizona, apparently participated in the engagement at Cibecue August 30, 1881, and perhaps in the attack on Fort Apache the following day. Afterward he headed about 40 recalcitrant Indians who remained in hiding for almost a year on the San Carlos-Fort Apache Reservation. He was reported killed in November 1881, but that rumor was premature. In April 1882 the redoubtable Juh, on his stunning raid on San Carlos to "liberate" several hundred Mimbres Apaches, conferred with Natiotish on Eagle Creek, but if he tried to persuade him to join in the operation against San Carlos, he failed, and Natiotish remained in the wilderness recesses of San Carlos. In July 1882 the Apaches, probably under Natiotish, opened fresh hostilities by slaying four San Carlos policemen, stripped 400 feet of telegraph wire from the poles and cast it down an arroyo, wounded a man at McMillen, a small mining camp, and swept into the Tonto Basin, depredating and collecting adherents as they raced ahead. They laid an ambush at what was known was Big Dry Wash above the Mogollon Rim, intending to surprise pursuing army units. But the ambush

was detected by Al Sieber and his scouts and in a subsequent battle, one of the celebrated actions of the Apache wars, Natiotish and some sixteen of his followers were slain, while the troops lost a soldier and a scout killed, and several wounded, including two officers.

Dan L. Thrapp, *Al Sieber: Chief of Scouts,* Norman, Univ. of Okla. Press, 1964; Thrapp, *Juh: An Incredible Indian,* El Paso, Texas West. Press, 1973, 1992.

Neill, Hyman G. (Hoodoo Brown), confidence man (fl. 1872-1881). Reportedly born "of good family" at St. Louis, he was "wanted by the law at Pueblo," Colorado, as early as 1872. There were charges against him at Wichita, Kansas, in 1873, and the next year he was fined for vagrancy, refused to pay and was forced to work it out. Hoodoo "was certainly in Kansas earlier, and was in and out of Dodge City." By 1879 he had reached Las Vegas, New Mexico, where he "assembled, by accident or design, a group of notorious confidence men, gamblers and killers," organized the police force "consisting principally of former Dodge City gunfighters, and collected money for their salaries from the local merchants, who not only wanted but needed plenty of protection." His "crime syndrome" included Wyatt Earp, Doc Holliday, Dave Mather and many others. Hoodoo set himself up at "New Town," the railroad section of Las Vegas, as "unofficial mayor, peace justice and acting coroner," and the sector became "a haven for the sporting and criminal element." A flurry of stagecoach robberies followed. After the murder of Michael Keliher by J.J. Webb March 2, 1880, Neill was charged with larceny and conspiracy by the established legal machinery of Las Vegas and fled town, perhaps to Texas, his conspiratorial web broken up. He was reported, apparently falsely, as having been killed at Caddo, Indian Territory, but later to have re-established himself at Casa Colorado, New Mexico, along the Rio Grande north of El Paso. He may have operated briefly at Deming, New Mexico, around 1881, when the railroad was building in that vicinity. He then disappears, perhaps under another name, and his ending is undefined. Neill was not the same man as the Hoodoo Brown who ran a road ranch near Meade, Kansas. This was George W. Brown (see entry), whose biography is well established.

Ed Bartholomew, *Wyatt Earp: The Untold Story, Wyatt Earp: The Man & The Myth,* Toyahvale, Tex., Frontier Book Co., 1963, 1964; C. Robert Haywood,

*Trails South: The Wagon-Road Economy in the Dodge
City-Panhandle Region,* Norman, Univ. of Okla. Press,
1986.

Neill, Thomas Newson (Beau Neill), military
officer (Apr. 9, 1826-Mar. 12, 1885). B. at
Philadelphia, he went to West Point and was
commissioned a brevet second lieutenant of the
4th Infantry July 1, 1847, a second lieutenant of
the 5th Infantry September 8, 1847, and a captain
April 1, 1857. He took part in the Utah expedition of 1857-58 and later served in New Mexico.
February 17, 1862, Neill was commissioned
colonel of the 23rd Pennsylvania Volunteers,
ending the Civil War as a Brigadier General and
brevet Major General of Volunteers. He became
a major of the 20th Infantry September 21, 1866,
a lieutenant colonel of the 1st Infantry February
22, 1869, and was assigned to the 6th Cavalry
December 15, 1870. By the start of 1875 the so-
called Red River War was all but over and numbers of Cheyennes reached their agency near Fort
Sill and surrendered. Trouble broke out April 6,
1875, at the Cheyenne Agency when young
Black Horse was killed trying to avoid being
shackled with others of his people. More than
100 hostiles fled to a sand dune south of the
North Fork of the Canadian River where they
recovered cached weapons. Neill ordered Captain William A. Rafferty (see entry) with M
Company of the 6th to dislodge the Indians, later
directing Captain S.T. Norvell, Company M, and
Captain A.S.B. Keyes of D Company, both of the
10th Cavalry, to assist Rafferty. Eleven
Cheyennes were killed and nineteen troopers
wounded, but the Indians escaped during the
night. Neill, upon Rafferty's report, sharply criticized the conduct of the 10th Cavalry soldiers,
although they had suffered most of the casualties.
Neill never retracted his criticism, although
Keyes and Norvell requested an official inquiry,
which never transpired, either. Neill became
commandant of West Point later in 1875, remaining in that position until he became colonel of the
8th Cavalry April 2, 1879. He retired April 2,
1883, and died at Philadelphia.

Heitman; Cullum; William H. Leckie, *The Buffalo
Soldiers,* Norman, Univ. of Okla. Press, 1967; Leckie
and Shirley A. Leckie, *Unlikely Warriors: General
Benjamin Grierson and His Family,* Norman, 1984;
DAB.

Nelson, Edward William, naturalist (May 8,
1855-May 9, 1934). B. at Amoskeag, near Man-

chester, New Hampshire, he was raised on a
farm; when his father was killed in the Civil War,
the mother took her sons to Chicago, although
the home was lost in the 1871 great Chicago fire.
Nelson briefly attended Northwestern University
at Evanston, Illinois, tried teaching and 1872
joined an Edward Cope (see entry) fossil hunting
expedition to Wyoming, Utah and Nevada. In
1876 he entered Johns Hopkins University to
study biology, but in 1877 left college for good
and accepted an opportunity to do field work in
Alaska. He conducted meterological observations at St. Michael on Norton Sound for the
Army Signal Corps until 1881, and devoted
much of his time to studying local populations
and collecting for the Smithsonian Institution.
He made sledge journeys, one of which, from
December 1878 to March 1879, was of about
1,200 miles through the Yukon delta region. In
1881 he joined John Muir aboard the revenue
cutter *Corwin* on a cruise to the Bering Sea and
Arctic Ocean. Nelson Island in the Yukon delta
was one of several geographic features named
for him. He wrote reports that "became classics
in their respective fields, dealing with the birds in
one case, and Eskimos in another" he had
observed and studied. Upon his return to Washington, D.C., he contracted tuberculosis and was
sent to Arizona, where he recovered his health
and again made valuable collections in the southwest. The Department of Agriculture sent him to
Mexico in 1892; he devoted fourteen years to
studying and writing of every biological aspect
of the natural life of that country, and "the results
of these expeditions were his greatest achievement in the field." He was author of many papers
on aspects of his studies, though his general and
summary reports were never published. From
1916 until 1927 Nelson was chief of the Bureau
of Biological Survey of the Agriculture Department (the bureau becoming part of today's Fish
and Wildlife Service). Nelson retired in 1927. He
served as president of such societies as the American Society of Mammalogists, the Biological
Society of Washington, and the American
Ornithologists Union. More than 100 animals
and plants were named for him.

Orth, 25, 681; DAB; *Who Was Who.*

Neolin: *see,* Delaware Prophet

Netsvetov, Iakov Egorovich, Orthodox churchman (1804-July 26, 1867). B. probably on St.
George Island of the Pribilof group, the son of

Egor Vasilevich Netsvetov, a teamster from Tobolsk, Siberia, and Marila, an Aleut from Atkha Island of the Aleutians, he became the first Orthodox native American priest. He also was the first priest to serve in the central and western Aleutian Islands, which he did from 1829-44, and the first Christian missionary to the Yukon region where he was stationed from 1844-63. Raised on St. George, Iakov worked for the Russian American Company until 1823 and studied at the Irkutsk, Siberia, Techological Seminary from October 1, 1825, graduating the next year with certificates in theology and church history. March 4, 1828, he was consecrated parish priest of the Atkha District where he went accompanied by his Russian wife, Anna. He encountered many difficulties generated by district head Ivan Sizykh, but overcame them, Wrangel removing Sizykh in 1831. In addition to his priestly duties he was active in intellectual pursuits, becoming a co-worker with the great missionary Veniaminov (see entry) in developing an Aleut script to accommodate all dialects of the native language, joined Veniaminov in a translation program and contributed to Veniaminov's ethnographical works. Netsvetov's wife died at 28 and other tragedies spotted his life to the point where he wished to enter a monastery in Siberia, but for several reasons was unable to do so. At last he accepted an opportunity to become a missionary on the Yukon. There he learned new languages, devised another script, built a new church and Orthodox community, and resumed activities that had marked his earlier life. Failing in health he finally was relieved in 1863 and brought to Sitka where he died at 59 and was buried July 29, 1867, at the entrance to the Tlingit Church of Sitka, which no longer exists. Pierce has many additional details of his life and the whereabouts of his surviving writings and records of his accomplishments.

Pierce, *Russian America: A Biographical Dictionary;* Melody Webb, *The Last Frontier: A History of the Yukon Basin,* Albuquerque, Univ. of New Mex. Press, 1985.

Nevodchikof, Mikhail, explorer (fl. 1741-1750). B. at Oustioug, Russia, he went to Tobolsk, the administrative and commercial center of western Siberia, as a "peasant" but Bancroft stresses that does not mean he was only an agricultural laborer since many of this class were engaged in trade or commerce. Nevodchikof was a silversmith. He had little success in Tobolsk

and went on to Kamchatka where he entered government service. He joined Bering's 1741 expedition which led to the discovery of Alaska and on it learned enough to be navigator for a group of promyshlenniki, who built a *shitika* (a plank boat whose strakes were sewn together, rather than riveted) and named it *Yevdokia.* The vessel left the Kamchatka River September 19, 1745, and in six days sighted the first of the Blishni (near) group of the Aleutians. Passing Attu, the initial major island, Nevodchikof anchored near the second, Agattu, where the explorer promptly ran into difficulty with the Aleuts and wounded one, the first native to be shot in Russia's bloody conquest and domination over Alaska and its aboriginal people. The adventurers determined to winter on Attu and returned to that island where Nevodchikof and others purchased a umiak or open skin boat and in another skirmish killed fifteen of the islanders. "These and like outrages of the promyshlenniki were not known in Russia until after several years, and if they had been it would have made little difference," observed Bancroft. The company wintered on Attu and spent the next season hunting sea otters and other valuable fur-bearers. September 14, 1746, the *Yevdokia* finally departed homeward, the craft battered by six weeks of gales. October 30, she was wrecked on an island short of the Kamchatka mainland; after some fighting with the islanders, the castaways built two bidars by the following spring, departed June 27, 1747, and finally arrived at a Kamchatka port July 21, bearing only 320 sea otter pelts of all the furs they had taken from the Aleutians, the rest being lost in the shipwreck. Upon receiving word of the adventurers' return Tsarina Elizabeth issued a ukase appointing Nevodchikof a master in the imperial navy "in which rank he was retained in the government service at Okhotsk," an administrative center on the Siberian coast. Nevodchikof is usually considered the discoverer of the Aleutian Island chain, although Attu and other islands were raised by Chirikov and Bering on their return from Alaskan discovery; at any rate the peasant-explorer was the first to occupy, winter upon and hunt among the Aleutians, so he probably was the effective discoverer of them. An islander, Temnak, was brought away with the *Yevdokia* and in 1750, after being baptized, was sent to Okhotsk where he was named Pavel Nevodchikof, the pilot, having acted as his godfather, adopting him.

Bancroft, *Alaska;* Swanton, *Tribes,* 532.

Newell, Samuel, military officer (1754-1841). Of English parentage, he was b. aboard ship while his parents were emigrating to America where they settled first in Frederick County, Virginia, then removed to the Holston River Valley where Samuel grew up. He and his brother James both fought in the October 10, 1774, battle of Point Pleasant, West Virginia, the climactic action of the Lord Dunmore War. And both accompanied the subsequent march of the victors toward the Ohio Indian towns. The operation was aborted when Dunmore called the column back as it verged on another action against the Shawnees. Samuel Newell was active in the Indian wars and border engagements during the Revolution. He was a lieutenant in the King's Mountain action of 1780, being severely wounded. The next year, as a captain of militia and settled on French Broad River, he was active in the unsuccessful effort to create the state of Franklin. In 1797 he moved to Somerset, Kentucky, where he was a judge for many years. Late in life he retired to Montgomery, Indiana, where he resided until his death.

Thwaites, *Dunmore.*

Nichols, Henry Ezra, naval officer (1843-1899). As a lieutenant commander Nichols commanded the Coast and Geodetic Survey steamer *Hassler* from 1881 to 1883. He made surveys in the Kaigani and Wrangell Straits in the Alexander Archipelago of the Alaskan Panhandle; in 1882 he worked in the Revillagigedo Channel and north to Wrangell, and in 1883 surveyed coves and harbors north of Dixon Entrance. From 1888-90 he was assigned to revise the Coast Pilot, the revision published in 1891 and sometimes referred to as the "Nichols Coast Pilot." In the Alexander Archipelago, a bay, a group of islands, a mountain and a passage have been given his name.

Orth, 25, 686.

Nicholson, Thomas, scout (fl. 1774-1783). A well-known scout and interpreter, Nicholson with Thady Kelley and Jonathan Zane guided Major Angus McDonald's 1774 expedition to Wapatomica Indian village, sixteen miles below the present Coshocton, Ohio. A slight skirmish short of the town aborted the operation. They later served under Lord Dunmore in his 1774 war with the Shawnees and other Indians. At one point, Butterfield reported, Thomas and his brother, Joseph, "who...had lived among the

Indians, desired them to get up for [Dunmore's] diversion, an Indian dance; which they did, greatly to the admiration and astonishment of the governor. They interspersed the performance with Indian songs and yells that made the welkin ring." Thomas Nicholson on occasion was entrusted with significant work. In October 1775 he was sent with a Delaware Indian to hurry up chiefs and noted men desired to attend an important meeting, presumably at Fort Pitt, with the Commissioner for Indian Affairs. November 2, 1777, General Hand informed Colonel George Morgan that "Tom Nichols [Nicholson] and party are returned; they were out 6 weeks and a day; he has been to Muncy and Musquaghty towns, Le Boeuf and to the head of French Creek, but could not discover any appearance of a regular enemy." "Musquaghty" referred to a village of Foxes which may have been on the upper Allegheny River. December 10 John Gibson informed Hand that a Nicholson mission to the Delawares in Ohio had returned from Beaver Creek "where they were kindly received by the Indians," but the chief told Nicholson it would not be safe for him to come in any closer to Fort Pitt "as they might fall in with Enemy Indians..." With his brother, Joseph, Thomas Nicholson was guide for the ill-fated William Crawford expedition of 1782 to Upper Sandusky, Ohio. At the close of the Revolutionary War Nicholson retired to Pittsburgh, where he drops from view.

Thwaites/Kellogg, *Dunmore; The Revolution on the Upper Ohio, 1775-1777,* Madison, Wis. Hist. Soc., 1908; *Frontier Defense on the Upper Ohio, 1777-1778,* Madison, 1912; Consul W. Butterfield, *History of the Girtys,* Cincinnati, Robert Clarke Co., 1890, 1950; Alexander Scott Withers, *Chronicles of Border Warfare,* Cincinnati, Clarke, 1895, 1970; Joseph Doddridge, *Notes on the Settlement and Indian Wars,* Pittsburgh, 1912, 1960.

Nickell, Kels Powers, stockman (1855-1929). B. in Morgan County, Kentucky, his father, John D. Nickell, was murdered by John Jackson Nickell, a second cousin February 7, 1863; the killer was executed on Johnson's Island in Lake Erie September 2, 1864, on a court martial order signed by Abraham Lincoln. Kels Nickell at 18 married Ann Brown and a son named John D. Nickell II was b. in 1874. Kels enlisted in K Company, 5th Cavalry September 2, 1875. He was one of two troopers sent to confirm reports of the Custer fight, reaching the battleground June 27, 1876, before the victims had been buried. He and his wife agreed on an amicable divorce September 8, 1877, although Kels did not return to Kentucky for it. His enlistment expired in 1880 and he opened a blacksmith and farm machinery repair shop at Cheyenne, Wyoming. Kels on December 27, 1881, married Irish-born Mary Mahoney, 16, and the two homesteaded 160 acres and purchased 480 more acres on the Chugwater River north of Iron Mountain station, Wyoming. The Nickell family gradually increased to nine children, the eldest of whom was William, or Willie (May 4, 1887-July 18, 1901). The red-haired Kels was a good rancher and by 1898 ran 1,000 head of cattle and was considered well-to-do, but he was quarrelsome, stubborn and convinced that sheep would prove more profitable than cattle. He inadvisably sold his stock, bought 1,000 head of sheep, moved them onto his range and apparently thereby earned the ire of his cattle-raising neighbors. Threats mounted and tension grew for three years until the July morning in 1901 when Willie Nickell, apparently mistaken for his father, was murdered from ambush within a mile of his home, with Tom Horn (see entry) accused as slayer. August 4, Kels was shot from ambush in a field half a mile from his ranch house; his arm was shattered and he also was wounded in his hip and side, though he recovered in a Cheyenne hospital. There he learned that several hundred of his sheep had been killed by club or rifle. Kels and Mary gave up their Iron Mountain home in the autumn of 1901 and moved to Cheyenne. Nickell requested permission to observe the hanging of Horn, an event for which he fervently wished, though his attendance was denied. When newsman John C. Thompson, who had witnessed the execution, rushed past to wire in his story, Nickell demanded: "Is the son of a bitch dead?" Assured that he was, Nickell seemed content. He lived at Cheyenne for the rest of his life; Kels and Mary (1865-1936) are buried in the Lakeview Cemetery, Cheyenne, beside their murdered son, Willie.

Phillip G. Nickell (no confirmed relation), "The Family Horn Destroyed," *Real West,* Vol. 29, No. 211 (Dec. 1986), 23-25; addtl. info. from Phillip G. Nickell.

Nikitin, Grigoriy, hunter (fl. 1829-1844). Nikitin was of the Tungus, a reindeer-using people who, also familiar with birchbark water craft, lived along the Lena and nearby rivers of eastern Siberia. He was a hunter for the P.T. Kozmin exploration party of 1829-1831 which surveyed

the Shantar Archipelago in the southern Okhotsk Sea west of upper Sakhalin Island. Nikitin was at Fort Michael on Norton Sound when Zagoskin arrived in 1842 to commence his two-year exploration of interior Alaska, and volunteered, a fortunate choice for the group. Each of the expedition members, Zagoskin wrote, "was master enough of his knife to be able to make himself a sled, or a pair of snowshoes...but for the article to turn out perfectly straight, light, and handy, it took a person like the native-born hunter Nikitin...The Tungus was the best shot of the expedition, a boat builder, carpenter, locksmith, blacksmith, tailor and finally, something of a cook, particularly in the preparation of pemmican." Besides, he added, "there was not a native on the Yukon who could overtake Nikitin in a footrace." Even before joining Zagoskin, Nikitin was familiar with parts of the Yukon, spoke some native dialects and was occasionally sent to collect frozen fish for dog food for winter trips. He accompanied Zagoskin on the expedition from Nulato up the frozen Koyukuk River toward Kotzebue Sound, although that feature was not reached. Nikitin often brought in fresh meat from game he had shot and Zagoskin wrote that he was "particularly grateful, as Providence had seen fit to provide me with some experienced and resourceful men [such as Nikitin, and] it is a pleasure to acknowledge...the labor and intelligence of [such] men." He wrote how his agile "little hunter Nikitin" surpassed the Eskimos and other natives at their own athletic games, enjoying such sports as he did so. On the upper Kuskokwim River on one occasion "we watched for half an hour the humorous and, at the same time, cautious way in which a bear was stalking a crane." The crane, moulting at the time, could not fly, but tried to keep out of the bear's way until Nikitin "interrupted their maneuvers by shooting at the bear, who ran off wounded into the woods; there was no time to follow him." Nikitin probably was paid off when Zagoskin reached Fort Michael again in 1844. There is no further word of him.

Zagoskin.

Nikolai, Ahtena chief (fl. 1885-1898). Described by Henry Allen as "one of the most intelligent of the Midnooskies" (Copper River Indians of the Athapascan linguistic family), Nikolai conceded in 1885 that "there had been three massacres of Russians" on the Copper, the one highest up the stream probably that of Serebrennikov and his assistants in 1848 (see entry), which Nikolai said was done by Upper Copper River Indians, another near the mouth of the Copper by coast peoples, or Eskimos, and the third just below Taral (Chitina) by his own people. Nikolai justified the latter action, citing wrongs inflicted upon them by the Russians. He reported, wrote Allen, that "Three Russians and as many sleds drawn by natives were enroute to Taral with merchandise. The natives were not allowed to sleep, and were compelled to haul the Russians who slept on the sleds. At a preconceived sign the head of each was crushed with an ax." Nikolai professed to know nothing of the other incidents, "and if he did he would not talk about them." Nikolai traveled with Allen's expedition as far north as the Tazlina River, proving of great value as guide and wilderness travel expert. From the Tazlina he was sent back to Nuchek with letters and a carefully-packed box of those photographic plates thus far exposed. Enroute, however, the curiousity of the Indians caused them to open the box, thus permitting the sunlight to ruin all the plates. In 1898 J.J. Rafferty (see entry), on an exploratory mission up the Copper, also visited with Nikolai and, informing him that he was acquainted with Allen and had been sent by "the same chief that had sent Lieutenant Allen," thus immediately winning the chief's favor. An engraving of Nikolai and his wives faces p. 432 of *Narratives.*

Narratives of Explorations in Alaska, 414, 431-35, 619.

Nimwha (Munseeka), Shawnee chief (d. 1780). A brother of Cornstalk (see entry), Nimwha succeeded that Indian as chief of the Shawnee tribe following Cornstalk's murder in 1777. Nimwha had taken part in Pontiac's War. He was present at Bouquet's 1764 treaty at Fort Pitt, and later treaties there in 1768 and 1775. In 1778 he led the detachment that captured Daniel Boone in Kentucky. The following year he led the besiegers of Fort Laurens, near the present Bolivar, Ohio, on the Tuscarawas River. His death from unreported causes occurred early in 1780.

Thwaites/Kellogg, *The Revolution on the Upper Ohio, 1775-1777,* Madison, Wis. Hist. Soc., 1908.

Noch-ay-del-klinne, Apache medicine man (c. 1845-Aug. 30, 1881). A White Mountain Apache, he was b. in the east Arizona highlands. According to Lockwood, he was an ascetic, slender, light-skinned man weighing about 125 lbs. and standing about 5 ft., 6 in. tall, who "naturally became a medicine man." At 26 in 1871 he was a

delegate to Washington, D.C., to meet President Grant and, with other delegates, was presented a large silver medal bearing on one side a portrait of Grant and the legend: "United States of America: Liberty, Justice and Equality," and on the reverse the date, 1871, and legend: "On Earth Peace Goodwill Toward Men." Noch-ay-del-klinne was wearing this medal when he was killed. In the late 1870s and early 1880s the Ghost Dance unrest had begun to ripple through certain tribes and had even reached the Apaches of Arizona. In June 1881 Noch-ay-del-klinne began a series of religious dances not far from Fort Apache that continued for weeks, increasing in fervor and alerting white authorities to what they perceived to be potential hostilities. Late in the summer at Cibicu, 45 miles west of Fort Apache, the dances appeared to be reaching a climax. Noch-ay-del-klinne had as a young man gone to school for a time at Santa Fe where he came under the influence of certain Christian doctrines, being particularly impressed by the Resurrection. He was now reportedly talking of raising some of the dead, including the great chiefs Mangas Coloradas, Cochise and Victorio, and this had a powerful effect upon his followers. The unrest grew so intense and the situation so grave, as it appeared to San Carlos Indian Agent Joseph Tiffany, that he requested Colonel Eugene Asa Carr to visit Cibicu where he wanted the medicine man "captured, or killed, or both." Carr organized a column, arrived August 30 at the Indian camp at Cibicu and interviewed Noch-ay-del klinne for the purpose of taking him hostage, though his explanation to the Apaches of what he was about may have been faultily translated by the interpreter (see Charles Hurrle entry). At any rate, the medicine man was arrested and taken a short distance down Cibicu Creek to where the military planned to camp overnight. Probably because of a misunderstanding of the soldiers' intent, a gathered throng of excited Indians moved into the camp and firing broke out, some of the Army scouts mutinying and joining the attackers in order to "rescue" Noch-ay-del klinne. Carr had directed that if such an attempt be made the Indian was to be killed. He was shot by Sergeant John F. McDonald and Trumpeter William O. Benitas and, not yet being dead, was axed by Sergeant John A. Smith, who stripped the medal from the dead medicine man's throat for a souvenir (Mazzanovich presents photographs of the front and reverse of the medal on p. 92 of *Trailing Geronimo*). The Battle of

Cibecue, in which an officer and half a dozen enlisted men died, as did Noch-ay-del-klinne and possibly other Apaches (including three scouts, executed later for alleged mutiny), sparked a long series of hostilities on the southwestern frontier, culminating in Crook's 1883 expedition into the Sierra Madre of Mexico in order to persude potentially hostile bands to return to the Arizona reservation.

Frank C. Lockwood, *The Apache indians,* N.Y., The Macmillan Co., 1938; Dan L. Thrapp, *General Crook and the Sierra Madre Adventure,* Norman, Univ. of Okla. Press, 1972; Eve Ball, "Cibicu, An Apache Interpretation," *Troopers West,* ed. by Ray Brandes, San Diego, Calif., Frontier Heritage Press, 1970, 121-33; Anton Mazzanovich, *Trailing Geronimo,* Los Angeles, p.p., 1931.

Noche, George, Apache scout (d. April 20, 1914). Noche, described by Debo as "a dependable scout," was of the ten-man delegation headed by Chatto (see entry) sent to Washington, D.C., by Miles in 1886 to negotiate removal of the Chiricahua Apaches from Arizona into eastern exile. At Washington, however, they unanimously opposed removal, and since some had never been at war with the whites, they saw no reason for transfer outside the Southwest. Noche had been first sergeant under Captains Wirt Davis and Emmet Crawford through the 1885-86 final campaign against Geronimo. It was Noche who advised Miles to send Martine and Kayitah—who were cousins—to seek out and persuade Geronimo to surrender since, he said, only these two could approach the enemy and live. Despite his loyal service, he was sent east with the hostiles and others who had remained peaceful, being stationed successively in Florida, Alabama and Fort Sill, Oklahoma. At the latter place he headed an Apache village named for him. In 1911 Noche, Kayitah and Martine were enlisted in a scout company, with pay and no obligations. Eventually Noche became a Christian and took the first name of George. At one point he became ill and was treated at Fort Bayard near Silver City, New Mexico. In 1913 when those Apaches wishing to go to New Mexico were allowed to do so, Noche and his family were among those who accepted, although Noche died the following year. He was buried on the Mescalero Reservation.

Angie Debo, *Geronimo: The Man, His Time, His Place,* Norman, Univ. of Okla. Press, 1976; info. from Phillip G. Nickell; Griswold.

North, Robert, renegade (d. Oct. 1869). His date and place of birth are unreported. North claimed to have lived among the Arapahoes of the Northern Plains from childhood. As a young man he took an Arapaho wife and then took another wife, the daughter of Many Bears, head chief of the prairie Gros Ventres. Grinnell quotes from "The Renegade Chief," by Joseph H. Taylor's *Sketches of Frontier and Indian Life on the Upper Missouri and Great Plains* (Bismarck, North Dakota, 1897) to the effect that: "North was accused of assisting in the destruction of ten miners on the Yellowstone near the mouth of Powder River in 1863, and was leader of the Arapaho contingent of hostiles who assisted at the massacre of the eighty soldiers near Fort Phil Kearny [the Fetterman Massacre, December 21] in 1866. North, with his Arapaho wife, was hanged in Kansas in October, 1869, by vigilantes or robbers, while heading for the camp of the Southern Arapahoes." Grinnell adds: "Some of these statements are certainly untrue," but does not specify which he disbelieves. The account of North having contributed to "the destruction of ten miners," doubtless refers to the night attack May 13-14, 1863, by unidentified Indians on the James Stuart (see entry) prospecting expedition out of Bannack, Montana, the only such party of "miners" in the specified region at the time and date, although the action occurred on the Big Horn River and not the Powder, and Stuart lost four men killed in that and related incidents, and several wounded, some seriously. North's version is the first solid clue as to the tribe which launched the attack. Whether North took part in the Fetterman attack will be discussed below. November 10, 1863, North submitted to Governor John Evans of Colorado a statement (probably oral since he could neither read nor write) that the Comanches, Plains Apaches, Kiowas, the Northern Arapahoes, Cheyennes and Sioux had all pledged to go to war with the whites as soon as they could obtain ammunition, in the spring of 1864. This "Evans seems to have accepted without investigation, and it apparently made him lose his head." He sent North's statement to Washington, declaring his belief that the Indians contemplated war. Evans, wrote Grinnell, "was quite ignorant of Indians, and it is perhaps not strange that he was imposed on by North." Although Evans wrote Indian Commissioner William P. Dole that "I am fully satisfied with the truthfulness of [North's] statements," the reliable George Bent flatly disclaimed the report of "this miserable white man who had been loafing around Arapaho camps and living off the Indians for years," and called the North report "a lie from beginning to end." While there is an obvious linkage between North's dire warning to Evans and the November 29, 1864, Sand Creek Massacre, the Indian "war" of 1864 did not spring from any fancied confederated Indian attacks, but a conflict with the Cheyennes alone that began over two simple cases of cattle theft and subsequent troop retaliation. North's report to Evans was entirely illusory. There is a report that North received from Evans a commission as captain in the Colorado Volunteers, but if so he took no reported military role in forthcoming events. He was present when the Arapahoes drew rations at Fort Laramie in the spring of 1865, was arrested, confined in the post guardhouse, and either won freedom or escaped, appearing in 1866 with the Arapahoes, who joined the Sioux in hostilities along the Bozeman Trail and its military posts. September 21 Second Lieutenant Winfield Scott Matson, with 40 men, was attacked by an estimated 300 Sioux and Arapahoes five miles from Fort Kearny, and during the "fluid action of the Indians' withdrawal," Matson suddenly was confronted by a horseman, a white man dressed like an Indian who identified himself as Captain Bob North. On September 23, in a rainstorm Indians struck a civilian cattle herd near the fort, driving off 100 head, and Captain Frederick H. Brown led a pursuit of ten miles before overtaking the raiders. The hostiles repeatedly charged the pursuing party, the soldiers startled to see a white man leading them and swearing liberally in English. On the last Indian charge the white leader was shot off his horse, but was carried from the field by an Indian. In his official report Colonel Carrington wrote: "Brown and a few men charged the Indians with revolvers, killing five Indians and one white man, I think Bob North, who led them in every case, and wounding sixteen." North, however, was not killed nor was he wounded seriously, for he appears to have been active with his Indian friends shortly afterward. Although Taylor's report, as reprinted by Grinnell, asserts that North took part in the Fetterman disaster, and other writers have followed that lead, proof that he did so would be impossible to obtain, although it is not improbable. Arapahoes were in the fight and North, although erratic, seems to have been an important man among them. He was in the vicinity. He was a man of considerable courage,

and he never seems to have shunned a fight. But there remains no definite link between North and the Fetterman incident and none of the major chroniclers of the engagement: Vaughn, Brininstool and Hebard, Dee Brown and others seem to have advanced the rumor—which is not to assert that it is invalid. North and his Arapaho wife were lynched in Kansas while enroute to the Southern Arapahoes, apparently for no reason save that they were recognized and disposed of on general principles. North was considered by certain of his contemporaries to be crazed, which he may have been. His statement that he had lived among Indians since his early childhood obviously is not true, since he spoke English fluently.

George B. Grinnell, *The Fighting Cheyennes,* Norman, Univ. of Okla. Press, 1956, p. 134n.; Margaret Coel, *Chief Left Hand: Southern Arapaho,* Norman, 1981; Wayne R. Austerman, "North the Renegade," *True West,* Vol. 33, No. 12 (Dec. 1986), 14-18; Dan L. Thrapp, *Vengeance: The Saga of Poor Tom Cover,* El Segundo, Calif., Upton & Sons, 1989, 97-100; Stan Hoig, *The Sand Creek Massacre,* Norman, 1974; Dee Brown, *Fort Phil Kearny: An American Saga,* N.Y., G.P. Putnam's Sons, 1962.

Nosov, Nikhailo Ivanovich, frontiersman, fur hunter (fl. c. 1822-1834). B. at Kargopol, Russia, he worked for the Russian American Company in Alaska from around 1822, trading with the Tlingit Indians, becoming fluent in their language and thoroughly versed in their customs and ways. RAC Governor Chistiakov in October 1825 wrote that Nosov kept his accounts "with scrupulous honesty" and "He had traded with the Kolosh [Tlingits], and for three years has headed fur hunting parties. He got along well with the savages." Veniaminov (see entry) wrote in an 1840 book that Nosov, during trouble with the Tlingit at Sitka, "knowing their language, strode fearlessly alone, into the native settlement and restored order." There were times, however, when he appeared not to have catered to native wishes so well and in 1834 his wife complained of "his cruelty to her and the children." Nosov provided the Kolosh vocabulary used by Wrangel for a book on Russian America.

Pierce, *Russian America: A Biographical Dictionary.*

Numaga (Young Winnemucca), Northern Paiute war chief (d. 1871). Although Sarah Winnemucca and some other Paiutes denied it,

Numaga was considered a son of Winnemucca by Richard O. Clemmer and Omer C. Stewart in HNAI 11, 536-37. He apparently was of the Pyramid Lake, Nevada, band of Paiutes. He had worked in California's Santa Clara valley, acquired some English and for most of his life was a determined friend of the whites. It was reported, however, that he led the Paiutes in the 1860 war with the whites and in the battle south of Pyramid Lake in which Ormsby (see entry) and 75 other whites were killed and most of the remaining 29 members of the militia party were wounded. Afterward Numaga retired with his people to the Pyramid Lake "reservation," established in 1859, which was not a federal reserve because the Northern Paiutes at that time had no treaty with the United States. Egan described him in a fictionalized work on the 1860 war, as "no ordinary man. He was at least six feet tall, had broad shoulders, a thick chest, and made an imposing figure"; a photograph in HNAI, 11, 458 tends to partially verify the description. Numaga remained friendly with the whites following the war and reportedly "died of tuberculosis at the Big Bend of the Truckee River." He was often referred to simply as Winnemucca, or Young Winnemucca, leading in references referring to him to considerable confusion with his father, the old chief Winnemucca.

HNAI, 11; Ferol Egan, *Sand in a Whirlwind: The Paiute Indian War of 1860,* Reno, Univ. of Nev. Press, 1985; Bancroft, *Nevada, Colorado & Wyoming,* 208; Jack D. Forbes, *Nevada Indians Speak,* Reno, 1967, with photos. between 148-49.

Nute, Grace Lee, historian (Oct. 13, 1895-May 4, 1990). B. at North Conway, New Hampshire, she became a noted historian of the fur trade and the exploration of Minnesota and neighboring areas. She was graduated in 1917 from Smith College, Northampton, Massachusetts, earned a master's degree in history at Radcliffe College, Cambridge, in 1918 and a doctorate in American history at Harvard in 1921. Her Harvard professor and advisor was Frederick Jackson Turner, who recommended her to become curator of manuscripts at the Minnesota Historical Society, St. Paul. She remained on the society's staff for 36 years. She organized and catalogued a mass of manuscripts that had been accumulating since the society's founding in 1849. Two of her pamphlets, *Copying Manuscripts* (1935) and *Care and Cataloguing of Manuscripts* (1936) are widely used guideposts in their field. Among her major writings are *The Voyageur* (1931); *The Voyageur's Highway* (1941); *Caesars of the Wilderness: Médard Chouart, Sieur des Groseilliers and Pierre Espirit Radisson 1618-1710* (1943); *Lake Superior* (1944), and *Rainy River Country: A Brief History of the Region Bordering Minnesota and Ontario* (1950). She also was professor of history at Hamline University, St. Paul, 1927-1960, and visiting professor of history at Macalester College, St. Paul, 1956-1959. Following her retirement from the society in 1957 she coordinated cataloging, preservation and storage of the papers of James J. Hill, founder of the Great Northern Railroad, and of his son, Louis W. Hill, the papers located in the James J. Hill Reference Library, St. Paul. She was a member of Phi Beta Kappa and a number of professional organizations. She traveled widely in this country and abroad, and took many research trips, traveling the routes of the voyageurs by canoe and snowshoe; when she was 80 she undertook a wintertime snowshoe trip into Yellowstone Park. Dr. Nute's major interest aside from history was nature, which led her into gardening which she still pursued at 92, bird watching and, after her vision failed, identification of birds by their songs. She died at Menlo Park, California, after having resided at Walnut Creek nearby for a decade. She never married.

Info. from Jeri Richtman, of the Minn. Hist. Soc.

O

Oacpicagigua, Luis, Pima leader (fl. 1751-1752). An ambitious, though not overly-loved Pima leader, Oacpicagigua had been made captain general of his people by the Sonoran governor, Colonel Diego Ortiz Parrilla, whose regime dated from 1749. The appointment of Don Luis was in recognition for his services leading some 400 Pimas in a punitive action against the militant Seris. But despite the favors shown him, he led a Pima revolt beginning in November 1751 at his home town of Saric, 25 miles southwest of present Nogales on the U.S.-Mexico border. On November 20 or 21, Oacpicagigua had entertained a party of Spanish acquaintances at his home and surprised and killed all eighteen of them by means of a large force he had readied for the occasion. Oacpicagigua's forces killed about 121 Spaniards in all, but the rebellion, which never had much popular support, quickly wilted; Don Luis charged that it had originated in harsh and oppressive treatment of his people by the Jesuits who, in their turn, accused him of being vain and anxious for personal power, with the notion of becoming chief of all the Pimas. Tubutama, 45 miles southwest of Nogales, Caborca, Sonoita and other places were attacked, and unrest spread as far north as Bac, where the noted mission San Xavier del Bac south of Tucson now stands. One result of the uprising was that a new presidio was built at Tubac, first permanent settlement in Arizona by the Spanish. In 1752, in the face of rising Spanish military presence, Oacpicagigua and the Spaniards made a peace.

Info. from John Sugden; Edward H. Spicer, *Cycles of Conquest,* Tucson, Univ. of Ariz. Press, 1962; Bancroft, *North Mexican States and Texas,* I, 543-45.

O'Cain (Ocane), Joseph, sea captain (d.c. 1809). Of pivotal importance in originating and developing the important Northwest Coast sea otter fur trade, O'Cain was born probably around 1775 (conjecture) in Ireland, possibly of English parentage. He was brought to Boston at an early age and when old enough shipped aboard the English *Phoenix,* Captain Thomas Moore, for Bengal, India. From there the ship reached Santa Barbara, California, in 1795 where O'Cain was left at his own request to "become a Christian," a commonly stated goal of those wishing to remain in Spanish Catholic possessions. O'Cain at the time was listed as a pilot (navigator) and carpenter. In 1796 he was sent by Spanish authority aboard the *Aranzacu,* Captain Juan B. Matute, to San Blas on the west coast of Mexico, from where in some manner he returned to Boston. There he was married March 14, 1799, in a Baptist church to Abigail (Nabby) Kimball (1781-Oct. 11, 1817). O'Cain shipped as supercargo aboard the brigantine *Betsy,* Charles Winship, master; the ship left Boston August 3, 1799, was seized off Chile and released at Valparaiso in April 1800, reaching California. Winship and O'Cain were stranded at San Blas when the ship's crew, fearing seizure of their valuable cargo of furs, hastily quitted the port, leaving the two men ashore. Winship (see entry) died at San Blas and O'Cain regained the east coast as mate or supercargo aboard the *Enterprise,* Captain Ezekiel Hubble, which touched at San Blas in December 1800, conducted fur operations on the Northwest Coast and reached New York in 1802 after calling at Canton. January 23, 1803, O'Cain in the 280-ton, 18-gun ship *O'Cain,* named for him and owned by Abiel and Jonathan Winship Jr., Benjamin P. Homer and others, left Boston and reached Kodiak Island, Alaska, in the early autumn. In October O'Cain met with Aleksandr Baranov, Russian governor of Alaska and outlined a new and hopefully profitable scheme he had conceived. All sea otter, beaver and seal skins heretofore obtained by Yankee traders on the coast had been acquired by bartering with natives who were indifferent hunters at best; only the Aleuts, a divergent branch of the Eskimauan linguistic stock, had reduced sea otter hunting to a successful science, and the Aleuts were subject to Russian control. O'Cain proposed that he be granted the right to "borrow" Aleut hunters, make his seasonal operation southward along the coast well into Spanish territory, and return the natives to Kodiak in the autumn, giving half of the profitable take to Baranov's Russian American Company. For many reasons, detailed by Ogden, Baranov liked the idea, accepted it, and O'Cain shipped 40 Aleuts and 20 baidarkas, or kayaks with which they traditionally hunted, the natives under command of a Russian, Afanasii Shvetsov (see entry), whom Bancroft calls "a shrewd official, sent along to make observations," adding that he was a "tried servant of the company." The experiment was a success. Some 1,800 otters were taken on this initial hunt, the Aleuts returned to Kodiak, half of the furs turned over to the Russians and O'Cain left the Northwest Coast September 8, 1804, reaching Canton January 2, 1805, and Boston July 1. O'Cain's experiment opened the door for Boston interests and seafarers to acquire fabulous wealth trading in sea otter and other pelts and, incidentally, to bring the otters to within a hair's breadth of extinction, a threat from which they only now, more than a century later, are recovering. Jonathan Winship (see entry), who had been with O'Cain on this pioneering voyage, took the *O'Cain* out on her second trip to the Pacific, while Joseph O'Cain took the 343-ton, 18-gun *Eclipse* to the west coast, leaving Boston January 26, 1806, and reaching Novo Arkhangelsk (Sitka) in August. He now proposed to Baranov trade possibilities at Nagasaki, Canton and perhaps ports in eastern India, which he knew from his initial voyage. Baranov sent a considerable number of pelts with him, which O'Cain exchanged in Canton "at almost no profit," according to Khlebnikov. He took on a Chinese cargo, put in at a Kamchatka port where he disposed of much of it for 200,000 rubles, proceeded toward Kodiak, but in September the *Eclipse* was wrecked in the Aleutians. O'Cain, Khlebnikov reported, was killed in the disaster, but Archibald Campbell (see entry), a survivor, told it somewhat differently. After the *Eclipse* ran aground part of the crew set out to find help. The remainder, under the resourceful O'Cain, built a 70-ton brig out of the wreckage. The mate and boatswain then separated from O'Cain "in consequence of a difference," and O'Cain put to sea with a mixed crew of Americans, Aleuts and some Russians. "It was reported that she had foundered at sea, and all on board perished," including O'Cain. Still another version was sent to Tsar Alexander I by the Russian American Company administration September 22, 1810, saying in part: "When he [O'Cain] set out from [Kamchatka] en route to Baranov on Sitka, he had a shipwreck near the island of Unalaska. He built a small vessel from the wreckage of the *Eclipse,* set out in it in 1809, but was again wrecked between the islands of Umnak and Sanak. Although the ship was lost he managed to survive the night by using ice floes to reach shore;

however, both he and a young Sandwich Island [Hawaii] woman eventually succumbed. The rest of the crew survived." Baranov believed he had been duped by O'Cain, but since the captain was dead "the matter was now concluded." It was probably a Captain Brown reaching Boston with the *Derby* August 10, 1811, who brought word of the captain's death. November 25, 1812, O'Cain's widow married Captain Reuben Newcomb, a prominent shipbuilder and shipmaster of Hampden, Maine, who became a successful hotel man. Peter Newcomb, son of Nabby and Reuben Newcomb, in early manhood left for Australia, writing home occasionally, then went "deep into the interior" of the continent, penetrating what was described as "a very wild and dangerous territory," and was never heard from again. Abigail's other son by Newcomb died in infancy.

Info. from Edwin G. Sanford, Coord. of Social Sciences, Boston Pub. Lby.; Adele Ogden, *The California Sea Otter Trade 1784-1848;* Berkeley, Univ. of Calif. Press, 1941; Samuel Eliot Morison, *The Maritime History of Massachusetts, 1783-1860,* Boston, Houghton Mifflin Co., 1941; *Colonial Russian America: Kyrill Khlebnikov's Reports, 1817-1832,* trans. by Basil Dmytryshyn, E.A.P. Crownhart-Vaughan, Portland, Ore. Hist. Soc., 1976; Archibald Campbell, *A Voyage Around the World, from 1806 to 1812,* Edinburgh, 1816 (Honolulu, Univ. of Hawaii Press, 1967); *The Russian American Colonies;* Bethuel Merritt Newcomb, *Andrew Newcomb 1618-1686 And His Descendants,* rev. ed., New Haven, Conn., Tuttle Morehouse & Taylor Co., 1923, pp. 326-27; Bancroft, *California* I, II; *Pioneer Register.*

Ogle, Joseph, military officer (d. Feb. 24, 1821). The precise relationship between Joseph and Jacob Ogle, who was killed in the William Foreman (see entry) disaster in West Virginia, is not given but that there was a relationship was probable, and Jacob was a sergeant in Joseph Ogle's company. The Ogles were among the earliest settlers of Ohio County, West Virginia. Captain Joseph Ogle took part with his 38-man company in the defense of Fort Henry, at Wheeling August 31-September 1, 1777. Jacob Ogle was killed September 27. In 1781 Joseph commanded a company on Daniel Brodhead's expedition against Coshocton, on the Muskingum River of Ohio. Later that year he emigrated to Illinois "where for the remainder of the Indian wars he maintained his reputation as an Indian fighter." He died in St. Clair County, Illinois.

Thwaites/Kellogg, *Frontier Defense on the Upper*

Ohio, 1777-1778; Wills De Hass, *History of the Indian Wars of Western Virginia,* Wheeling, E. Hoblitzell, 1851, 1960, p. 278.

Oldham, John, trader (c. 1600-July 1636). A contentious man, probably from Lancaster, England, his death at the hands of Indians was a precipitating factor in the bloody Pequod War of 1637 in New England. He arrived at Plymouth in July 1623 aboard the *Anne,* not intending to become a colonist for he was of the Anglican faith, "a man of parts, but high-spirited and extremely passionate." He and other "Strangers" were forbidden to trade with the Indians at first, although later this ban was lifted. Oldham could not initially get along with the "Saints," and periodically was ousted from the territory they controlled, settling first at Nantasket (the present Hull), Massachusetts, and later at Cape Ann, northeast of Gloucester. As a merchant he entered commercial relations between Massachusetts and Virginia, and eventually traded extensively with Indians. In 1628 Oldham returned briefly to England, taking along the ousted Thomas Morton (see entry) of Merry Mount, tried unsuccessfully to advance a commercial scheme for the Massachusetts Bay Company, returned to New England and settled at Watertown, west of Boston, where he became "a substantial citizen." Making his peace with the Saints, he occupied posts of some significance, expanding his trading activities, but in July 1636, while on an expedition to Block Island he was murdered for having treated Indians harshly, by Pequods as was supposed, with the connivance of some Narragansetts. His death was one of the "chief episodes," or excuses, for the Pequod War which resulted in the virtual extinguishment of the tribe. He was married.

George F. Willison, *Saints and Strangers,* N.Y., Reynal & Hitchcock, 1945; DAB; Swanton, *Tribes,* 31-33; Hodge, HAI, II, 226-31.

Old Tassel (Onitositah, Kaiyatahee), Cherokee chief (d. June 1788). A brother of Doublehead (see entry), and head chief of the conservative faction of the Cherokees, he was respected for his honesty and strict adherence to the truth. He succeeded Attakullaculla (see entry) in 1777 as principal chief of the tribe, although he had little control over Dragging Canoe's militant Chickamaugas, or Lower Cherokees of Tennessee. Old Tassel was a fine orator, was opposed to war with the whites, but in his search for continued peace

and amicable relations with Anglo Americans he was traveling an impossible road. He was present at the duplicitous council of Sycamore Shoals March 17, 1775, by which Richard Henderson (see entry) and others acquired a vast expanse of the heart of Cherokee country. Old Tassel denounced Henderson as a "rogue and a liar" and repudiated the boundaries there established, but it did no good. The terms of the treaty of July 20, 1777, at the Great Island of the Holston River dismayed Old Tassel, for by it and an earlier pact on May 20, the Cherokees turned over more than five million acres of their lands for an inconsequential return. He managed to secure some revision of the harsh terms by those pacts. Old Tassel sent a letter to Joseph Martin, Virginia commissioner to the Overhill Cherokees, requesting him to send it on to the governor of North Carolina. The communication said: "We are a poor distressed people, that is in great trouble... Your people from [the] Nolichucky [River settlements] are daily pushing us out of our lands. We have no place to hunt on. Your people have built houses within one day's walk of our towns. We don't want to quarrel with our elder brother; we therefore hope our elder brother will not take our lands from us, that the Great Man above gave us. He made you and he made us; we are all his children... We are the first people that ever lived on this land; it is ours." No action appears to have been taken in response to the letter. Old Tassel, the head chief, and Hanging Maw, the war chief, continued doing their utmost to get along with the whites who by 1784, following the Revolution, settled in ever greater numbers on Cherokee lands. Neither the governor of Virginia nor the governor of North Carolina seemed able to prevent bloodshed by moving the whites off of Cherokee lands. Old Tassel had protested a treaty supposedly signed by several of his people and delegates from the abortive "state" of Franklin in the spring of 1785. He was invited to meet Franklin's governor John Sevier's representatives at Dumplin Creek to enter into "a treaty of amity and friendship." Old Tassel sent Anco in his place, and Anco was inexperienced in treatymaking, did not understand the full meaning of the document, and signed it on May 31. November 18 Old Tassel brought the treaty and other difficulties of the Cherokees to Hopewell where the Indians were to negotiate their first treaty with the United States, Old Tassel once commenting that the "truth is, if we had no lands, we should have fewer enemies." Upon arriving at

Hopewell with 36 chiefs and 918 of his people, Old Tassel was asked to state any grievances the Cherokees had, and did so, but past treaties showed that, rightly or wrongly, the Cherokees had agreed to reductions in their lands by the papers they had signed. Old Tassel and the other Cherokee elders signed the November 28 Hopewell treaty. Dragging Canoe's disapproving Chickamaugan militants at last broke into hostilities with the "citizens" of Franklin, each revenge attack inciting a fresh assault from the other side. The Chickamaugas killed Colonel William Christian. Sevier called out the Franklin militia and August 3, 1788, they formally charged Old Tassel and Hanging Maw with the Christian slaying and those of others, but by then the Cherokees were dead. Old Tassel, still attempting to remain neutral with his people, learned that the Franklinites were having none of it. In June, while under a flag of truce, Old Tassel, Hanging Maw and two others were assassinated by the Franklinites.

Info. from John Sugden; Grace Steele Woodward, *The Cherokees,* Norman, Univ. of Okla. Press, 1963.

Olinger, (John) Wallace, partisan (June 3, 1849-Feb. 25, 1940). B. at Delphi, Indiana, he was a brother of Robert Meridith Olinger (see entry) and early became a buffalo hunter on the South Plains. Later he went into ranching with William H. Johnson, first in Texas, then at the JA6 place near Seven Rivers, New Mexico. The out-of-the-way ranch was described as a "refuge for strayed cattle." Olinger became involved in the Lincoln County War from the start, being a member of the "posse" which assassinated John H. Tunstall February 18, 1878, later making a useful legal statement of the affair. He took part in the skirmish at Lincoln April 30. During the Five Days Battle of July 1878 Olinger fired the shot that killed McSween (see entry), as he later told his family. Johnson, involved in a family dispute with his father-in-law, Hugh Beckwith, was killed by him who was wounded by Olinger, Beckwith recovering in the Fort Stanton hospital while Olinger was briefly incarcerated in the fort's jail. In 1883 Olinger married Johnson's widow, the former Camelia Beckwith; they lived in Kansas and elsewhere until 1913 when they separated. Olinger went to California, settling at Santa Monica where he worked as a gardener until 1935. He died at the Valley View Sanitarium, Los Angeles. He was described as having eyes so pale blue that they were "almost white."

Robert N. Mullin notes; William A. Keleher, *Violence in Lincoln County,* Albuquerque, Univ. of New Mex. Press, 1957; Robert M. Utley, *Billy the Kid: A Short and Violent Life,* Lincoln, Univ. of Nebr. Press, 1989; Frederick W. Nolan, *Life and Death of John Henry Tunstall,* Albuquerque, 1965; info. from Nolan.

Olinger, Robert Meridith, partisan (Apr. 1, 1850-Apr. 28, 1881). B. at Delphi, Indiana, he was a brother of John Wallace Olinger. The report that he was part Cherokee is undoubtedly false. He was 6 ft., 3 in., in height, weighed around 240 pounds, had a pocked face and wore his hair long, his idol being Wild Bill Hickok. Olinger probably served in the Civil War, once claiming he had been a bush-whacker in it, though Eve Ball maintained that his reputation as of that profession dated *after* the conflict, not during it. He first appears on New Mexico records November 4, 1878, when he registered to vote at Lincoln, as did his brother. Olinger became a partner of John Beckwith in a Seven Rivers ranch, but already had acquired a minor reputation as a gunman. He killed Juan Chavez, his "friend," and shot in the back a John Hill in a little-remembered incident. On August 29, 1879, he killed John A. Jones at the Milo Pierce ranch, Jones three days previous having killed Olinger's partner, John Beckwith. He was formally charged with murder for this action and when he was killed two years later the document was on his person, apparently having been served on him, though there the matter seems to have ended. Despite his association with Seven Rivers undesirables and his gunplays, Olinger was appointed deputy U.S. marshal for Lincoln in April 1880 and on April 15, 1881, was named deputy by Sheriff James W. Fourtine of Mesilla, Dona Ana County, his initial mission being to bring Billy the Kid from Santa Fe to Mesilla, and then to take him to Lincoln for trial for the murder of William Brady. Olinger seemed to enjoy tormenting the slight Kid when in his company, to the point of engendering his antipathy, if not hatred. When the Kid was lodged in a room next to the sheriff's office on the second floor of the Lincoln County courthouse, Olinger and Deputy James W. Bell were assigned to guard him, shackled as he was with leg irons and handcuffs. In contrast to Olinger, Bell was kind to Billy and considerate of him. Bell and Olinger also were responsible for five other prisoners held at the courthouse. At 6 p.m. April 28, Olinger took the five across the street to the Wortley Hotel for dinner. While the party was gone, the Kid slipped free of a cuff, overwhelmed Bell and when the deputy tried to escape, killed him with Bell's revolver, then swept up Olinger's heavily loaded twin-barreled shotgun. He waited at a window overlooking the street between the courthouse and hotel until Olinger emerged, having heard the shots fired at Bell. "Bob, the Kid has killed Bell!" reported Gottlieb (Godfrey) Gauss, an acquaintance. Olinger glanced up at the window into the barrels of the Kid's weapon. "Yes, and he's killed me, too!" he replied. As Billy recalled the incident: "I stuck the gun through the window and said, 'Look up, old boy, and see what you get.' Bob looked up, and I let him have both barrels right in the face and breast." Later, passing the corpse in the street, the Kid touched it with his boot toe, muttering, "You are not going to round me up again." Olinger, a relatively minor character in the Lincoln County War, died with his one claim to enduring fame the manner and cause of his demise.

Robert N. Mullins notes; Don Cline, "Robert Olinger, Outlaw and Lawman Killer," *Quarterly of the National Association and Center for Outlaw and Lawman History,* Vol. IX, No. 4 (Spring, 1985), 11-13; Philip J. Rasch, Lee Myers, "The Tragedy of the Beckwiths," English Westerners' Society *Brand Book,* Vol. 5, No. 4 (July, 1963), 1-6; Robert M. Utley, *Billy the Kid: A Short and Violent Life,* Lincoln, Univ. of Nebr. Press, 1989; William A. Keleher, *Violence in Lincoln County,* Albuquerque, Univ. of New Mex. Press, 1957; info. from Nolan.

Olivares, Antonio de San Buenaventura, Franciscan (fl. 1699-1718). Not much appears to be known of the life of this missionary/administrator who is credited with having been the actual founder of San Antonio, Texas. In 1699 he left the Franciscan station at Querétaro, where he had been positioned, and went to northern Mexico with another Franciscan, Marcos de Gruena, to administer the mission of San Juan Bautista de Rio Grande in Coahuila. By 1708 he had become guardian of the college of Querétaro. April 5, 1709, he led an expedition into Texas with the Franciscan Isidro Felix de Espinosa (1679-1755) and Captain Pedro de Aguirre, commander of the Presidio of Rio Grande del Norte with 14 soldiers. They crossed the Rio Grande from San Juan Bautista mission and later negotiated the Nueces River, reaching the present site of San Antonio April 8. They proceeded to the Colorado River, arriving April 19, but, unable to contact

the Tejas Indians as they had hoped, returned to the Rio Grande. Father Olivares had become interested in developing Texas missions; he had his companions draw up detailed accounts of their expedition and late in 1709 he took these narratives to Spain to present them to the Spanish King, seeking his support. He went to Mexico City in late 1716 to advance his dream of a permanent mission at the source of the San Antonio River where the city is now located. He remembered from the 1709 expedition the ideal location and even more "the character of the Indians of the region, seemingly more tractable than others whom the explorers had encountered." He presented his project at a propitious moment: authorities were discussing the need for a supporting station for the East Texas stations, and before the end of the year the Viceroy, the Marqués de Valero named Martín de Alarcon, the new governor of Coahuila, to direct the project with Oliveres commissioned to found the mission, having ten soldiers for its protection. By May 1717 Olivares was enroute; by May 1, 1718, he had laid the foundation for the Misión San Antonio de Valero (the Alamo); the presidio was established five days later, and thus Olivares became the true founder of San Antonio. Alarcon formally placed the mission under supervision of Father Olivares.

HT; John Francis Bannon, *The Spanish Borderlands Frontier 1513-1821,* N.Y., Holt, Rinehart and Winston, 1970; Bancroft, *North Mexican States & Texas,* I, 614.

O'Meara, Walter Andrew, writer (Jan. 29, 1897-Sept. 29, 1989). B. at Minneapolis, he attended the University of Minnesota and was graduated from the University of Wisconsin in 1920 after service to sergeant in the Army during World War I. He was a reporter for the Duluth, Minnesota, *News-Tribune* in 1918, but spent most of his professional life with advertising agencies; he was publicity director for Adlai Stevenson in his presidential campaigns against Eisenhower. He wrote at least sixteen books, most of them novels or youth books, but his adult nonfiction works included: *The Savage Country* (1960); *The Last Portage* (1962); *Guns at the Forks* (1965); *Daughters of the Country: The Women of the Fur Traders and Mountain Men* (1968), and *We Made It Through the Winter* (1974). The last book, subtitled, "A Memoir of Northern Minnesota Boyhood," was autobiographical. During World War II he worked at

Washington for the Office of Strategic Services. He died at Cohasset, Massachusetts.

CA; Tucson, *Arizona Daily Star,* Oct. 1, 1989.

Opechancanough [Note: this is an addition to this Indian's entry. See Vol. II, pp. 1085-86.] Historian Carl Bridenbaugh, who holds a doctorate from Harvard and has specialized in Atlantic seaboard colonial history, with others makes a somewhat persuasive case that Don Luis de Velasco (see entry, 1477) and Opechancanough (see entry) were one and the same. Luis was the son of a chief and brother of another chief, tribe not identified, but the Powhatan is a likely nominee. He was b. about 1545, was taken by the Spanish in 1561 when he would have been 16 years of age, and shipped to Spain and later Mexico, where he assumed the name of Luis de Velasco, for the Viceroy, Luis de Velasco, probably at his baptism. Opechancanough, the older brother of Powhatan (by about two years), would have been 77 at the time of the 1622 uprising, and 99 at that of 1644, when he was so old and feeble that he had to be carried to the field of combat on a litter. The theory "cannot be proved," Bridenbaugh concedes, but it is "a reasonable, workable, and plausible hypothesis into which the known facts fit...[It] explains nearly all of the matters that have hitherto been obscure, preventing our understanding of many events in the early history of Virginia." The hypothesis originally was developed by historians Clifford Lewis and Albert Loomie.

National Geographic, Vol. 173, No. 3 (Mar. 1988), 356-60; Hodge, HAI, I, 121, "Axacan" entry; II, 880, Luis de Velasco entry.

Ortega, José Francisco, soldier, discoverer, military officer (c. 1734-Feb. 3, 1798). B. at Celaya (Zelaya), Guanajuato, Mexico, he was a warehouse clerk who enlisted in the Spanish army October 1, 1755, became a corporal in 1756 and a sergeant in 1757. He shortly resigned, being interested in mining, and for a time was "alcalde" for all mining camps of Baja California. When Gaspar de Portolá became governor, Ortega, since he was literate and an able soldier, was allowed to re-enlist as sergeant, assigned initially to tend the royal warehouse accounts. He accompanied Portolá's expedition that helped establish San Diego, Upper California, in July 1769, distinguishing himself on the march by enterprising scouting activities. From San Diego he joined an expedition, again under Portolá,

with Captain Fernando Rivera y Moncado as military commander, assigned to relocate Monterey Bay. It left July 14, 1769. Ortega came down with scurvy near Morro Bay north of the present Santa Barbara, but it did not incapacitate him. Monterey was reached but not recognized as the bay glowingly described by Vizcaino (see entry) in December 1602 (although it had been cursorily discovered in 1542 by Cabrillo). Because identification was uncertain it was determined to proceed north and this was done, with Rivera's soldiers under Ortega guiding the advance much of the time. Their work was so effective that an official diarist (Miguel Costansó) considered them "the best troopers in the world." Nearing the northern limit of the march the Farallon Islands and Point Reyes were sighted, though of course not visited. The expedition halted short of San Francisco Bay, which was discovered by Ortega on an exploration northward November 1-3; a party of soldiers on a hunting foray returned with an almost identical report about the same time, but Ortega is considered the official discoverer of this most important coastal feature. A subsequent exploration by Ortega November 7, 1769, probably reconnoitered the site of San Francisco, revealed the configuration and extent of the bay and as a result of this the waterway was shown "in recognizable form" on Costansó's map of 1771. November 11, the expedition commenced its return journey, exploring the vicinity of Monterey Bay more carefully from November 28, until December 10, erecting a large cross and leaving claim of discovery, and regaining San Diego January 24, 1770, Ortega for a time being commander of the guard. He returned to Loreto, Baja California, from where he was kept busy with explorations, military work in Sinaloa and journeys to San Diego. He became a great favorite of the Franciscan missionaries, particularly Junipero Serra, who in 1773 urged Ortega's appointment as commandant in California, succeeding Pedro Fages. He was commissioned lieutenant that year and as such commanded at San Diego for more than eight years. In 1781 he founded Santa Barbara, where numerous descendants still live. He planned its buildings, fortifications and irrigation works, for which he received great credit, serving at the community until 1784. He was in command at Monterey from September 1787 until March 1791. Ortega was retired as a brevet captain at Loreto in 1795. Like most officers of similar commands he was "in some trouble with his accounts...and was oppressed by debt in the last years of his life," the deficit being $2,597; his sons paid it off. Ortega died suddenly at the Casil Rancheria near Santa Barbara, and was buried at the Santa Barbara mission cemetery, being survived by his widow and many children.

Ronald L. Ives, *Jose Velasquez; Saga of a Borderland Soldier,* Tucson, Ariz., Southwestern Mission Research Ctr., 1984; Bancroft, *California,* I.

Osgood, Ernest Staples, historian (Oct. 29, 1888-June 22, 1983). B. at Lynn, Massachusetts, he was graduated from Dartmouth College in 1908, taught history briefly in Ohio and later at Helena, Montana, where he became interested in western themes. Osgood enrolled for graduate work in the University of Wisconsin in 1924 and in 1927 received his doctorate after working with Frederic Logan Paxson and having become acquainted with Frederick Jackson Turner. His first and most notable book was *The Day of the Cattleman* (1929), based upon his doctoral dissertation, "The Northern Cattle Range, 1865-1890," a definitive work on the beef industry of the second half of the 19th century. Osgood became an instructor at the University of Minnesota in 1927, his students in time included Robert G. Athearn (see entry), Clark C. Spence, a student of western mining, and Charles L. Mowatt, who came from England to study under Osgood after reading a review of his cattleman work. Osgood remained for 30 years at the university, taking occasional western pack trips in connection with research for other writing endeavors, one of which was intended to be a history of Montana. When important field notes of William Clark were discovered in 1953 in a St. Paul, Minnesota, attic, Osgood at once became interested, authenticated them within two months and pored over them for a decade, in 1964 publishing them under the Yale University imprint as *The Field Notes of Captain William Clark, 1803-1805,* a work done as was his custom, with "meticulous care." Osgood had retired from the University of Minnesota in 1957, then lectured on frontier history for ten more years at the College of Wooster, Ohio, which bestowed upon him an honorary doctorate in 1980. He married twice, his first wife succumbing in 1957. He died at Wooster at 94. He wrote an autobiographical essay, "I Discover Western History," published in the *Western HistoricalQuarterly,* Volume III, No. 3 (July 1972), 241-51. Although he published sparingly, his was a wide reputation

"based on quality rather than on quantity." The work that did appear seems destined to endure.

Clark C. Spence, "Ernest Staples Osgood: 1888-1983," *Arizona and the West,* Vol. 27, No. 2 (Summer, 1985), 95-98, with portrait; *REAW.*

Osgood, Wilfrid Hudson, naturalist (Dec. 8, 1875-June 20, 1947). B. at Rochester, New Hampshire, he was graduated from Stanford University in 1898 (and earned a doctorate at the University of Chicago in 1918). He became a biologist in the Department of Agriculture, where he worked from 1897 to 1909, being in charge of biological investigations in Alaska from 1899 to 1909. He made a biological reconnaissance in 1899 from Skagway to the headwaters of the Yukon River and down its course across Alaska to the delta, the results published by the Department of Agriculture in 1900. Osgood studied the Cook Inlet region in 1900, and in 1902 made an overland expedition across the upper Alaska Peninsula, then by way of the Chulitna and Nushagak rivers to Bristol Bay and return. A report, with map, was published by the Agriculture Department in 1904. Osgood made biological studies in 1903 between Eagle and Rampart on the Yukon and in the area of Glacier Mountain, 21 miles west of Eagle. He also did extensive research and fieldwork on the fur seals (and other life) of the Pribilof Islands, the results published by the U.S. Fish Commission as *Fur Seals of the Pribilof Islands* (1915). When he left government service he became assistant curator of mammalogy and ornithology at the Field Museum of Natural History of Chicago from 1909 to 1921, and was curator of zoology from 1921 to 1940 when he retired. During his active career he conducted biological explorations, besides those in Alaska, in Canada, many parts of the United States, in several countries of Latin America, in Ethiopia, Indo-China, led expeditions to various places, was a fellow of the American Association for the Advancement of Science and numerous scientific and professional organizations. He wrote prolifically in scientific and popular publications. He was unmarried and lived at Chicago until his death.

Orth, 25; *Who Was Who..*

Owen, Abraham, military officer (1769-Nov. 7, 1811). B. in Prince Edward County, Virginia, he accompanied his father, Brackett Owen, to Shelby County, Kentucky, in 1785. Some descendants of Owen insisted that his first name was

Abram, but documentation originating with him reveal that he considered Abraham his true first name. He first appears in military annals accompanying Lieutenant Colonel James Wilkinson in the summer of 1791 in a campaign on the White and Wabash rivers of Indiana, the results inconclusive. He was a lieutenant in Captain Lemon's Company under Arthur St. Clair in the disastrous defeat November 4, 1791, in which the whites suffered 918 casualties including 647 dead; Owen came out of the debacle with two wounds, one in the chin and the other in an arm. He recovered in time to take part in the expedition of John Hardin (see entry) on the upper Wabash and White rivers; good results were had. It is not known whether Owen took part in Anthony Wayne's expedition which culminated in the Battle of Fallen Timbers, Ohio, of August 20, 1794. Owen became surveyor of Shelby County in 1799, and afterwards a magistrate. He commanded the first militia company raised in the county with Singleton Wilson his lieutenant; they had been associates in the Wilkinson campaign. Owen soon was promoted to major, and then colonel of a regiment, and Wilson was promoted to captain, having served with distinction as a scout in the Wayne operation. Owen was elected to the legislature "by the largest vote ever polled in the county" and with Benjamin Logan became a member of the convention which framed the second constitution for Kentucky, which had entered the Union in 1792; he later became a member of the senate. In 1811 he was the first to join William Henry Harrison (see entry) for the operation which terminated in the Battle of Tippecanoe between the Harrison forces and those of Tecumseh under the Indian leader's brother, the prophet Tenskwatawa. The action occurred on Tippecanoe River in the Wabash country of Indiana, just north of present Lafayette. Owen was named by Harrison as aide-de-camp. In the dawn battle, when the Indians attacked Harrison's camp, there came the mystery of the switched horses. Harrison's was a light-gray animal, conspicuous in the early light, while Owen's was a bay, not so easily perceived. Tucker wrote that the gray "had wandered from the stake to which he had hitched it," and Harrison jumped on the bay and rode to the firing, while Owen found the gray, "mounted it and was shot instantly by the Indians in ambush," they no doubt believing their target was Harrison. Dr. J.D. Eggleston, however, in a footnote to a document held by the Kentucky Historical Society, wrote that "Col. Owen, just before the battle, knowing that Harrison rode a spirited horse and would be singled out by the Indians, suggested that he and the general exchange horses. This was done, Harrison not realizing the purpose Owen had in view. The latter rode out and deliberately drew the fire of the Indians, who thought they were shooting Gen. Harrison. Thus ended in a great climax the life of a distinguished soldier and patriot, whose sacrifice gave to the United States one of its presidents." In 1819-20 Owen County, Kentucky, was named in the colonel's honor. Owen was married and fathered a sizable family; his son, or grandson, Clark Owen (see entry) became "a distinguished citizen of Texas, having won a high rank in her civil and military annals."

Info. from the Kentucky Hist. Soc.; Reed Beard, *The Battle of Tippecanoe*, Lafayette, Ind., p.p., 1889, 4th ed., Hammond Press, Chicago, 1911; Glenn Tucker, *Tecumseh: Vision of Glory*, N.Y. Bobbs-Merrill Co., 1956.

Owen, Clark L., frontiersman (1808-Apr. 6, 1862). B. in Shelby County, Kentucky, he was the son, or perhaps the grandson, of Abraham Owen (see entry), killed in the Battle of Tippecanoe November 7, 1811. Clark Owen established a mercantile business at New Castle, Kentucky, but left to take part in the Texas Revolution, reaching Texas in March 1836. He enlisted in a company of Kentucky Volunteers July 18, and was mustered out a lieutenant on November 17; he then joined the Texas army as a captain in May 1837. He took part in the celebrated Plum Creek fight against Comanches August 11, 1840, near the present Lockhart. Owen was commander of Texas forces around Corpus Christi in 1841 and took part in the ill-fated Mier Expedition of 1842, but survived it. Houston offered him the position of secretary of the treasury, which Owen declined, but accepted that of commander of troops in the southwest, and became a senator in the Sixth Texas Congress in 1841-42. He married, engaged in stock raising and, although opposed to secession, volunteered for the Confederate army, raised Company I, 2nd Texas Infantry, and was killed at Shiloh.

Info. from the Kentucky Hist. Soc.; HT.

Owen, William O., claimant (Aug. 22, 1859-Aug. 3, 1947). A scrappy little pioneer surveyor of Wyoming, Owen became obsessed with a desire to become known as the first climber to scale 13,766-ft. Grand Teton Peak, even though Nathaniel Pitt Langford and James Stevenson asserted they had reached the top of the mountain 26 years earlier (see Langford and Stevenson entries). Owen knew of still another successful climb five years before his own. He made his initial attempt in 1891, reached what was later called the "Upper Saddle" below the peak itself, but could not find a way to the top. Each summer thereafter he tried again, in 1897 attempting to scale the peak by five different routes—and failed. August 11, 1898, Owen with another climber, Franklin Spencer Spalding, who was an Episcopal priest, and ranchers Frank I. Peterson and John Shive, finally scaled the Grand, Spalding finding the route and hauling Owen up by rope, then permitting the claimant to go the short distance remaining to be first at the top for whatever credit there was in that. "A seething Uncle Billy [Owen]...would spend the next thirty years denouncing Stevenson and Langford, and lobbying for his climbing party—but mostly himself— to be acclaimed the first to have scaled the mountain," one of America's most spectacular peaks, wrote Moss. Owen twisted many arms to get official credit for the "first climb" and in 1927 the second highest peak in the range was named Mount Owen. In 1929 when the range became part of Grand Teton National Park, a bronze plaque commemorating Owen's supposed feat was placed atop the mountain, though it was removed, perhaps by vandals, in 1977, which was just as well. Historian Hiram Chittenden examined all the evidence then available and concluded it was "overwhelmingly in favor of the claim of N.P. Langford and James Stevenson to have climbed the mountain in 1872," while believing that Owen and his supporters had failed to supply believable evidence to the contrary. It should be noted that both Langford and Stevenson were highly accomplished and honorable men who were never known to have falsely claimed any of numerous achievements. Many years later it was learned that Sidford Hamp, 19, in 1872 had kept a diary; he and a companion had accompanied Langford and Stevenson as far as the Upper Saddle, where they remained "whilst the other two [Langford and Stevenson] got to the top." Among Owen's papers after his death was discovered "a bombshell casting a shadow every bit as dark on Uncle Billy as he had cast upon the 1872 efforts of Langford and Stevenson," wrote Moss. "A letter dated April 31, 1899 from Dr. Charles Kieffer [who] wanted Owen to know that [Kieffer] had reached the top of the Grand on September 10, 1893, six years before" Owen had done so. Kieffer's letter included a map he had sketched of the route followed and "interestingly, marked an ice field at the same location Langford had noted in 1872." The letter, Moss concluded, "was devastating to Owen's credibility [and] he withheld the information his entire life." Moss added that "the truth is, the difficulty and danger of climbing the Grand Teton is overstated. Each year thousands of people ranging from juniors to geriatrics make the climb on any one of a hundred different routes and variations [and] in winter the face of the peak has been descended by skiers." There is no doubt that Owen made an early climb of the Grand Teton, but his efforts to establish himself as first to do so were as discreditable as he repeatedly charged Langford and Stevenson had been, and in denial of those claims Owen had ruthlessly impugned the integrity of two highly worthy notables of the frontier. Owen died at Los Angeles.

Wayne F. Moss, "The Grand Question," *True West*, Vol. 35, No. 9 (Sept. 1988), 14-19; Moss to author, Nov. 30, 1991.

P

Pakhomov, Luka, frontiersman (fl. 1803-1844). Reportedly a Creole, he worked closely with Baranov (see entry) and by 1843 was at Fort St. Michael on Norton Sound, Alaska; he may have been there since its founding in 1833. He volunteered to serve with Zagoskin, who referred to him as "a hale old man" and was glad to obtain his services for the important expedition into the Alaskan interior. Pakhomov accompanied Zagoskin in his winter exploration of the Koyukuk River toward Kotzebue Sound, although the party did not reach that place. Nothing further is reported of him.

    Zagoskin.

Panov (Panof), Grigorii, fur merchant (fl. 1758-1793). He and his brother, Petr, were merchants originally from Totma, east of Kharovsk, Russia. They were among the "few ambitious merchants of Eastern Siberia who conceived the idea" of establishing permanent Russian colonies on the North American continent—Alaska and environs—and inspired government assistance to that end. The Panov brothers are listed among the owners of the fur-gathering ship *Iulian* which left the mouth of the Kamchatka River September 2, 1758, carried on a successful hunt for several years on Unimak and Unalaska islands in the Aleutians, and returned with a profitable cargo August 31, 1762. In addition to the profits, Panov received a gold medal from Catherine II for his part in opening the fur trade for Russia in the Aleutians. A Captain Panov was associated with the adventurer Benyovski (see entry) in 1770 on Kamchatka as a member of the secret society of exiles, but this may not be the noted merchant, although Bancroft wrote that "in 1778 the two Panov brothers associated themselves with Arsenius Kuznetzof, also one of the former companions of Benyovski," so the matter is not clear cut. In 1777 the brothers associated with Shelikhov (see entry), fitting out the *Barfolomei i Varnabas* which put out from Nishekamchatsk, returning four years later with a cargo valued at 58,000 rubles. In 1778, as noted above, they together with Kuznetzof built the *Sv. Nikolai* which left Petropavlovsk on a seven-year voyage, returning with a rich cargo of furs, many indicating that they had been collected on the Alaskan mainland. In 1780 they sent out the aged vessel, *Sv Yevpl,* which was wrecked on her return to Kamchatka, but the cargo, valued at 70,000 rubles, was saved. In 1779, too, the brothers' sloop, *Kliment,* was working around Kodiak Island. It may have been this vessel that planned to winter on the southern tip of Kodiak in 1780, but "difficulties" with the natives cost them so many men that "they finally had to beat a hasty retreat." The navigator Afanasii Ocheredin commanded this ship. In 1783 in a harbor on Nuchek (Hinchinbrook) Island 28 men from the Panov ship *Alexei* were encountered by Nagaief (see entry), who learned that 14 of them had been wounded by the Chugach natives during a night attack, one of a series of desperate encounters with Eskimos or Indians who deeply resented the Russian presence and the ruthlessness with which they treated the indigenes. There is little evidence that the Panov men conducted themselves so barbarously, however. When Unalaska natives were invited to list their complaints of ill treatment before government inspectors in 1789-90, they said specifically that "We suffer greatly when our young girls, wives, daughters and sisters are taken, which all companies do except for Panov's which is more orderly than others who were here before and after his company." How Panov disciplined his men to behave themselves better than those of other firms was not reported. In 1790 Aleuts under Panov direction, and probably originating from Unalaska Island, were hunting among the Sannakh and Shumagin islands; the company's operations, with several ships out much of the time, were very wide ranging. In 1793 or earlier, the Panov fur collectors lost an interchange with Baranov (see entry) at Prince William Sound and were forced to give up collected furs to him. There is no further report of operations by the Panov brothers, but before the decade of the 1790s ended, all firms save Shelikhov's would be forced to conclude their oeprations in favor of the newly chartered Russian American Company, which had obtained a royal monopoly for the fur trade in Alaska.

    Bancroft, *Alaska; Russian Penetration of the North Pacific Ocean; The Russian American Colonies.*

Papequah, Kickapoo chief (fl. 1842-1870s). A leader of the militant faction of the southern Kickapoos, Papequah's 500 people in 1842 established a series of villages on White Horse Creek, a tributary of the Washita River, Indian Territory. Without an agent they roamed freely, depredated widely and occasionally skirmished with military units for several years. They raided south into Texas, slipping past dragoon patrols, "plundering and burning farms and ranches, killing cattle, and collecting their most valuable loot—horses." Eventually the Texans came to believe it would be better for them to have the Kickapoos remove to Texas where they would be under watchful eyes and control, than to have them reside in Indian Territory, from where they raided unrestrained by any adequate police force. As a result of their invitations the southern Kickapoos became fragmented into three bands: Papequah's 500, who remained on the Washita; about 300 (later to grow to 700) under Pecan, settled on the Canadian, and another 300 under Chief Mothakuck, who accepted the Texas invitation and settled on the Brazos River. The bands visited back and forth, joined for festivals, and remained in close contact until the Civil War, when the tribe collected on White Horse Creek under Papequah perhaps for the eventual race to southern Kansas, avoiding the white conflict; from Kansas they would emigrate to Mexico. Papequah's band became noted as agriculturists and traders, including trading in human beings; the brave, intelligent Kickapoo traders providing "the only channel of communication between the eastern [white] settlements and the [dreaded] Comanches," of whom they were in no way in awe. They were regularly called upon by General Zachary Taylor for such special assignments as the return of white captives of the Comanches and other Plains tribes. Meanwhile the famous Seminole leader Coacoochee (or Wildcat: see entry) planned to establish a colony of his people south of the Rio Grande and by early 1850 his Seminoles and a Kickapoo contingent led by Papequah crossed the Rio Grande and settled temporarily at Piedras Negras in northern Mexico, welcomed by the Mexicans as a buffer element against raids by Kiowas, Comanches and Plains Apaches. The Kickapoos and Seminoles performed their function well for a year or more, but visiting chiefs persuaded the Kickapoo faction to return to their people remaining on White Horse Creek. They remained there for awhile, then moved westward to join Mothakuck's followers on Big Beaver Creek. With remoteness from military surveillance, Kickapoo raids on Texas greatly increased in scope and returns, this causing a more massive retaliatory series of campaigns by ranger units against them. Old Chief Pecan died in 1860, to be succeeded by a younger man of the same name; Mothakuck was succeeded by an active warrior named Machemanet, but Papequah, still in full vigor and daring enough to command the loyalty of his warriors, remained of the "old guard." Confederate Brigadier General Albert Pike sought to persuade the Kickapoos, among other peoples, to sign a paper aligning themselves with the Confederacy, but the Kickapoos would not do this, professing that they would "join any side but that on which the Texans fight." This ostracized them from most of the Indian Territory Indians. Partly as a result, on October 23, 1862, Papequah led his warriors in a surprise attack on Fort Cobb at the junction of Pond Creek and the Washita, killed three white traders, left Indian Agent Matthew M. Leeper Sr. (see entry) for dead, looted agency stores and the next day cornered the hated Tonkawas near the Wichita Agency and killed and scalped more than 100 of the enemy. Driving a huge stolen horse herd before them, they raced back to their camps on Walnut Creek in Kansas. Pecan and Papequah held numerous discussions during 1863 and later anent Mexican invitations to remove to northern Mexico, joining the Kickapoos and others already there, including Machemanet's large band which had settled there. During the summer of 1864 Papequah's people were joined by more than 100 northern Kickapoos from Fort Leavenworth headed by Chief Nokowhat and in September the combined party of 700 or more traveled west, then south through the Texas Panhandle, by New Year's Day 1865 reaching the South Concho River, deciding to camp for a few days on Dove Creek. The weather was bitterly cold. A troop of 20 Confederate scouts under Captain N.W. Gillentine of the 2nd Military District, had struck their trail. Captain S.S. Totten and Captain Henry Fossett, commanding a combined force of 400 militiamen, joined Gillentine and January 8 they struck the Kickapoo camp by surprise. The Indians recovered quickly and by their superior marksmanship and better weapons took a fearful toll among the attackers, the Texans losing 26 including 4 officers killed outright and 60 others wounded, 10 mortally, while the Kickapoos lost 15; it was the worst defeat the Texans had ever suffered from

Indians in living memory. A lengthy investigation by Brigadier General J.D. McAdoo reported later that the Kickapoos had been doing their utmost to avoid contact with Texans, they had committed no depredations, their destination was Mexico, they "were not in the pay of Union agents" as Totten and Fossett maintained, and that Totten and Fossett "without any council of war, without any distribution of orders, without any formation of line of battle, without any preparation, without any inspection of camp, without any communication with the Indians...without any knowledge of their strength and position," had pitched into them, and in addition had committed clearcut atrocities during the action. Trooper Scrutchfield's diary entry for January 8 put it clearly: "made an attack. Got whipped." The Kickapoos gained Mexico, joined their comrades there and "considering the attack at Dove Creek to be a declaration of war by the Texans...were able to rationalize their merciless campaign along the Rio Grande until the 1880's." No report of the date or circumstances of the death of Papequah has been found, but he was active at least into the 1870s and remained in Mexico.

Info. from John Sugden; Arrell M. Gibson, *The Kickapoos: Lords of the Middle Border*, Norman, Univ. of Okla. Press, 1963; *War of the Rebellion Records*, Series I, Vol. 48, Part I, pp. 26-29.

Pareja, Francisco de, Franciscan missionary (d. Jan. 25, 1628). B. at Auñon, in the diocese of Toledo, Spain, the date of his birth is not known, but if he came to Florida shortly after his ordination, which would probably have come at approximately the age of 25, he would have been born about 1570, although this is conjecture only. He joined the Franciscan Order in the Province of Castile and reached Florida with Fray Juan de Silva and companions in 1595. He labored most of his 21 years in missionary work at San Juan del Puerto, in the vicinity of today's Jacksonville. Those years were spent almost entirely among the now-vanished Timucuan Indians whom he served "with sanctity and incredible zeal," learning their language (which had a very complex grammar) to a point of fluency, converting it into written form, and teaching the natives to read and write in it. His mission reports were of value and he made frequent journeys into the interior of then little known Florida, although the Spanish had commenced to conquer its Indians in 1565 "while the Franciscans mis-

sionized them." The Timucuan proper were centered around the present St. Augustine, but cognate tribes, with mutually intelligible tongues, occupied most of north Florida. The principal center of missionary activity was St. Augustine itself. Pareja's labors were backed by the woman chief of the province whom the Spaniards called Doña María, and supporting her were the chiefs of other Timucuan towns. In 1612 two catechisms by Pareja in the Timucuan language were printed at Mexico City; a Confessions was published in 1612-13, his important Timucuan grammar appeared in 1614, and another catechism in 1627. Besides these, he is said to have written treatises on Purgatory, the Pains of Hell, the Joys of Heaven, one on the Rosary of the Blessed Virgin and a book of prayers (three of his rare works are held by the New York Historical Society). In 1616 he was elected provincial of the Province of Santa Elena, which included Cuba, Florida and Georgia. Shea presents a facsimile of Pareja's signature on p. 156, and HNAI 4, p. 484 reproduces an illustrated page from the 1627 catechism printed in Timucuan. Francisco de Pareja died at Mexico City.

Info. from Bernard L. Fontana; info. from the Acad. of Amer. Franciscan Hist. ; Hodge, HAI, II, 753; John Gilmary Shea, *The Catholic Church in Colonial Days,* N.Y., John G. Shea, 1886; Maynard Geiger, O.F.M., *Biographical Dictionary of the Franciscans in Spanish Florida and Cuba (1528-1841)*, Franciscan Studies, Vol. XXI, Paterson, N.J., St. Anthony Guild Press, 1940, p. 85; *New Catholic Encyclopedia,* Vol. 10, Washington, D.C., Catholic Univ., 1967, p. 1000.

Parker, Charles, desperado (fl. 1887-1907). A brother of George LeRoy Parker (Butch Cassidy), he worked as a cowboy on several Wyoming ranches and according to Bill Walker "he knew the cow game. Also, he was a pretty good two-gun man, and was always practicing target shooting." In March 1887 an Army paymaster, Daniel N. Bash, stopped with his escort at Antelope Springs, Wyoming, for lunch. Bash carelessly left his valise containing $7,500 in the vehicle. Parker dashed up, grabbed the valise and galloped away; he was not caught. Walker said Parker bought a Kansas farm, married and hid out for two years until his wife cashed a marked $20 bill and Charlie was picked up. He drew ten years.

D.F. Baber, as told by Bill Walker, *The Longest Rope...,* Caldwell, Id., Caxton Printers, 1940, 40-43; Oliver Knight, *Life and Manners in the Frontier Army,*

Norman, Univ. of Okla. Press, 1978; *Army-Navy Journal*, Mar. 26, 1887, p. 692.

Parker, Cynthia Ann, captive (1827-late 1870). B. in Clark County, Illinois, her parents, Silas and Lucy Parker, took the family in 1832 to Texas, locating in today's Limestone County and building Fort Parker on the headwaters of the Navasota River, east of the Brazos. It was solidly constructed and "if properly defended...could have held off a large enemy force." However, no Indian raids occurred for many months and the residents became careless, even leaving the bullet-proof gates ajar for long periods of time. May 19, 1836, an Indian party estimated to number several hundred and including Comanches, Kiowas and Kichais (Caddos) attacked and killed five, including John Parker, his sons Benjamin F. and Silas M., and Samuel M. Parker and his son, Robert. Captured was Cynthia Ann, daughter of Silas, and four others; other fugitives fled. Cynthia, then 9, and the four other prisoners traveled with their captors six days before reaching Grand Prairie, where they were distributed among four Comanche bands and one to the Kichais. Cynthia was taken by a Quahadi (Kwahadi) Comanche party, beginning 25 years of captivity and becoming more Indian than white, a fully acculturated Comanche woman. White Texans first learned something of her continued existence in 1840 when Colonel Leonard Williams, a trader, and an Indian guide, Jack Henry, met with Comanches on the Canadian River. Here Williams saw a white girl who, he learned, was Cynthia Ann. He tried to purchase her release but failed, although Chief Pahauka (Pah-hah-yo-ko) permitted him to speak with her. She merely stared at the ground and refused to reply to his questions, this probably because, in Hacker's view, she so rapidly assumed Comanche ways that she did not wish to leave. In 1845 Commissioner of Indian Affairs William Medill was told that federal agents had sighted Cynthia Ann among the Comanches on the Washita River, Oklahoma. He instructed P.M. Butler and M.G. Lewis, on a fact-gathering expedition among Texas and southwestern Indians, to attempt to confirm current rumors. They found a 17-year-old girl and two other white children among the Yamparika Comanches on the Washita, the Indians referring to them as the "Parker children." Butler and Lewis reported that a warrior claimed the girl as his wife. They revealed that "from the influence of her alleged

husband, or from her own inclination, she is unwilling to leave" the Indians, and "she would run off and hide herself to avoid those who went to ransom her." It was impossible to learn whether she was indeed Cynthia Ann Parker, but the age and circumstances indicate that it was she. Other Indian agents heard rumors of her whereabouts, but all efforts to ransom her proved futile, although the bands concerned were willing, if she assented. The Indians reported she had fully adapted to Comanche life, was treated like any other woman of that people, and apparently was content. During the 1840s she married Peta Nocona (see entry), a warrior who had led the Fort Parker attack and "many other victorious raids." The marriage seemed a happy one; her husband treated her well, and she returned the affection. The marriage produced two sons—the celebrated Quanah Parker (see entry), Pecos, and a daugher, Topsannah. A story that her brother John visited her several years after she was married, but found that she "refused" to be rescued, may be apocryphal. A story in a Houston newspaper in 1847 reported that she had "married an Indian chief and is so wedded to the Indian mode of life, that she is unwilling to return to her white kindred." Even if she were restored to her relatives she no doubt would take the first opportunity to "escape" back to the Indians, the article added. A year later agent Robert Neighbors (see entry) reported he had tried without success to win her "freedom," and in 1851 Victor Rose, a trader, while visiting a Comanche village reported he had seen Cynthia Ann and failed to get her to agree to return to her relatives, saying she was "happily married; I love my husband, who is good and kind," and that she could not forsake her children. This story, too, has been questioned. Hostilities between the races continued, and Peta Nocona reportedly led several successful raids against the Texans. On December 18, 1860, a Ranger force under Sul Ross (see entry) attacked a Comanche village and in a fight described by a number of conflicting reports, the Rangers captured Cynthia Ann with her daughter and reportedly mortally wounded her husband; Hacker has full details of this engagement, pp. 24-27. There were numerous reports that Peta Nocona had not been killed there or was not even in the engagement. Raids and hostilities continued, or even increased as one atrocity piled upon another and, Hacker concluded, "In retrospect the frontier society of Texas that accepted Cynthia Ann's return was no more 'civilized' than that of the Comanches." Cynthia Ann was taken to Camp Cooper, in present Throckmorton County on the Clear Fork of the Brazos where her uncle, Colonel Isaac Parker, in late January contacted her and learned that it was indeed his niece. Horace R. Jones (see entry), a reliable and dependable interpreter (who had personally witnessed her capture by Texans while with Sul Ross) handled communications between the woman and her uncle. Cynthia Ann was then 34. "With her capture [she] was torn from the Indian life to which she had become accustomed..., stripped of her husband, her sons, her friends, and ultimately her Indian identity. Her suffering as a result of these losses was apparent in the few remaining years of her life." Her reunion with white relatives and friends was unhappy. She was taken first to Birdville to Isaac Parker's farm. She often tried to run away, apparently in order to return to the Indians. She frequently wept. She feared the whites would kill her. Her white acquaintances were unable to comprehend the reasons for her grief and longing for her past life. She was very lonely. She was taken to live with her younger brother, Silas, who also had been captured with her but early ransomed. He lived on a farm north of Tyler. She was unhappy there and moved to live with her sister, Orlena, on Slater's Creek. Although she is not known to have learned of it, her son, Pecos, died of smallpox about 1863. Her beloved daughter died of influenza and pneumonia December 13, 1863. Cynthia Ann moved again to a location owned by Ruff O'Quinn, her brother-in-law on the line between Henderson and Anderson counties and lived there for the rest of her life. Between June and December 1870, weakened by self-imposed starvation, she died of influenza. Buried initially near her home, she was reinterred through the efforts of her son, Quanah, on December 4, 1910, at the Post Oak Mission cemetery, five miles from Quanah's Cache, Oklahoma, home. According to Hacker, Quanah himself learned from Horace Jones that his father, Peta Nocona, had not been killed in the Peace River "massacre," if that is what it was, but lived and fought for years afterward, apparently dying in the middle 1870s of unknown causes. Jones said he and Peta Nocona met at Fort Sill in the early 1870s and had a long talk, and Jones was a very knowledgable man, fluent in Comanche, well known to most leaders of the tribe, and he was scrupulously honest. Charles Goodnight said that the Indian killed was a chief named No-bah, "but Nocona

died long afterward while hunting plums on the Canadian." There is much evidence that he was not killed in the Peace River affair and the case for his survival is persuasive. He probably was absent from the camp struck by the Rangers, which contained mostly women and children, the warriors away for various reasons. Cynthia Ann must have learned early on that he had not been slain and lived and raided as he had before. Thus it appears that her persistent attempts to "escape" from the whites lay less with an amorphous wish to resume Indian life than with a normal determination to rejoin her husband and sons. Her affection for them, which was apparently returned by Peta Nocoma (who never remarried), seems to have been the compelling motivation.

Margaret Schmidt Hacker, *Cynthia Ann Parker: The Life and Legend,* El Paso, Texas Western Press, Southwestern Studies 92, 1990; HT.

Pasqual, Quechan (Yuma) chief (c. 1800-1887). Pasqual, said to have been born around 1800, was raised at Alamo Mucho on New River, which parallels the lower Colorado River, lying to the west of it. He grew to great size for one of his robust people, Lieutenant Nathaniel Michler, an engineers officer writing in 1854 that Pasqual was "an immense man, near six feet four inches in height." Earlier Lieutenant Thomas Sweeney wrote that "he is tall and stately; and his countenance of the mildest expression; and yet he is the most remarkable character in this country for his indomitable love of adventure. His body is covered with wounds he has received in various encounters." Almost all of such injuries were received in inter-tribal conflicts, of which Pasqual was often a participant, but one may have been received by a pistol shot from Louis Jaeger (see entry) late in 1850. By then Pasqual already was known as a chief by the whites, and to his people as a *kwanami* (war leader) and by 1854 as a *kwoxot*, or tribal chief, following Macedón who had been killed by the Cocopas. "Pasqual served as principal leader of the Quechans from 1854 until his death in 1887," wrote Forbes. By then his settlement lay just north of the Gila River and east of the Colorado. Pasqual appears to have been the last of the kwoxots of the Quechans, and despite his adventurous life, his death was peaceful. A photograph of Pasqual and a white man who may be Jaeger is included on p. 94 of *Handbook of North American Indians,* Vol. 10.

Jack D. Forbes, *Warriors of the Colorado: The*

Yumas of the Quechan Nation and Their Neighbors, Norman, Univ. of Okla. Press, 1965; HNAI 10; Stephen N. Patzman, "Louis John Frederick Jaeger...," *Arizoniana,* Vol. IV, No. 1 (Spring, 1963), 31-36.

Patterson, Robert, frontiersman (fl. 1775-1788). Patterson arrived in Kentucky in 1775 and in 1776 commanded a party of seven bringing dispatches up the Ohio River for the commandant of Fort Henry at Wheeling. The group passed Point Pleasant and during the night of October 11 or 12, near the mouth of the Hockhocking River were fired upon by Indians. James Wermock and Joseph McNutt were killed and Patterson wounded severely, lying in the woods eight days before rescue. Patterson recovered and April 1, 1779, commenced a block house, thus founding the Kentucky city of Lexington, which shortly became the center of thriving stations and communities. Patterson took part in the notable battle of Blue Licks, Kentucky, August 19, 1782, and was heavily wounded once more. Seeing him unhorsed and badly hurt, Aaron Reynolds sprang from his own saddle, pushed Patterson into it and enabled him to escape, although himself captured by Indians; he shortly escaped. Matthias Denman, with Patterson and John Filson, who had authored the first history of Kentucky, founded Cincinnati, Ohio, in 1788, the place first being given the name of Losantiville by Filson, a former school teacher and the name, according to Thwaites, "a pedagogical hash of Greek, Latin, and French: *L,* for Licking [it was established opposite the mouth of the Licking River]; *os,* Greek for mouth; *anti,* Latin for opposite; *ville,* French for city." Filson was killed and scalped by Indians the following October. The remainder of Patterson's career is not reported.

Thwaites/Kellogg, *The Revolution on the Upper Ohio, 1775-1777,* Madison, Wis. Hist. Soc., 1908; Alexander Scott Withers, *Chronicles of Border Warfare,* Cincinnati, Robert Clarke Co., 1895, 1970.

Patton, James, frontiersman (1692-July 8, 1755). B. in County Londonderry, Ireland, he became a ship's captain and crossed the Atlantic 25 times with indentured emigrants bound for Virginia. He also served in the Royal Navy in the wars with the Netherlands. He secured a grant of 120,000 acres adjacent to the Blue Ridge and himself settled in the colony in 1735. In 1745 he became the initial resident of Draper's Meadow, where Blacksburg is now situated. He was the

uncle of William Preston (see entry) and to his settlement also came John Draper, William Ingles (see entries) and others. Thwaites described him as "a man of wealth, enterprise and influence" who was a justice, a sheriff, an Indian treaty commissioner and at length the county lieutenant of Augusta County. On Sunday, July 8, 1755, the day before the Braddock debacle in Pennsylvania, Shawnee Indians from Ohio attacked the Drapers Meadow outpost. Preston was away at the time of the attack. Patton, according to Hale, was writing at a log table in one of the cabins, his broadsword within an arm's reach. As the Indians stormed up, Patton clutched his sword and rushed to meet them, cutting down two before he was shot and killed (see Mary Draper Ingles for further details on the raid).

Alexander Scott Withers, *Chronicles of Border Warfare,* ed. by Reuben Gold Thwaites, Cincinnati, Robert Clarke Co., 1895, 1970; John P. Hale, *Trans-Allegheny Pioneers,* Cincinnati, The Graphic Press, 1886.

Paul, Rodman Wilson, historian (Nov. 6, 1912-May 15, 1987). B. at Villanova, Pennsylvania, he taught history at Harvard (from where he was graduated in 1936 and earned a doctorate in 1943) and Yale before going in 1947 to the California Institute of Technology at Pasadena, remaining there for 40 years. His books principally concerned mining, but they also extended into the West generally. Among them were: *California Gold, 1848-73; The Beginning of Mining in the Far West, 1848-1880; The Far West and the Great Plains in Transition, 1859-1900; Roughing It; Mining Camps,* and *California Gold Discovery.* He was past chairman of the National Archives Advisory Council, a former president of the Western History Association, and held other honorary positions. He died at Pasadena.

Council on America's Military Past *Headquarters Heliogram* 185 (June 1987); *Contemporary Authors;* REAW.

Paul Wilhelm: *see,* Wurttemberg, (Frederick) Paul Wilhelm

Paxson, Edgar Samuel, artist (Apr. 25, 1852-Nov. 9, 1919). B. at East Hamburg (now called Orchard Park), south of Buffalo, New York, he was educated in a log schoolhouse and for one year in a Quaker's Institute at East Hamburg. He worked as a logger in Wisconsin, a hunting guide in Minnesota, was a teamster in a freight wagon train for Wyoming Territory in 1876 and arrived the next year in Montana, where he was briefly a driver for the Overland Stage Company. He took part in some capacity in the 1877 Nez Perce campaign, served for ten years, private to second lieutenant in the 1st Regiment of the Montana National Guard and was a first lieutenant in the 1st Montana Infantry during the Spanish-American War, serving eight months in the Philippines when ill health caused his retirement from military service. Meanwhile he had developed his artistic talent, becoming noted for pictures of frontier characters and incidents, some in watercolors, others in oils. One of his pictures was the graphic illustration of the noted encounter of John Bozeman, for whom the Bozeman Trail was named, and Tom Cover, famed frontiersman, with Blackfeet Indians in which Bozeman was killed and Cover wounded. Prominent among his major undertakings was a picture of Custer's Last Stand, an enormous work measuring more than ten feet long, six feet tall, weighing half a ton and based upon twenty years of research and taking eight years to complete. It includes more than 200 figures, the majority depicted so accurately from photographic or other likenesses that they can be easily recognized by any Custer enthusiast, pro or con. Indian leaders Gall, Two Moon, Crow King, Hump and White Bull were among those who posed for the artist, who knew Indian sign language and something of native languages. The Little Big Horn painting was completed in 1899 and although displayed from time to time at Washington, D.C., at several world's fairs and expositions around the country, always drawing high praise, it remained generally in Montana for 63 years, never finding a place suitable for its permanent display. Finally, on February 19, 1963, it was moved to the Vanderbilt Whitney Gallery of Western Art at Cody, where it is permanently displayed under suitable conditions. Another Paxson work, "The Last Gleam," also is shown there. Among his other well-known accomplishments are six murals in the lobby of the House of Representatives at Helena, Montana, and his Lewis and Clark murals in the Missoula County Courthouse. Paxson, in addition to his major paintings, also did illustrations for publications. He is represented in collections in this country, at London, Paris and other cities, and was honored widely. He made his home late in life at Missoula. He was married and fathered a son.

Who Was Who; William Edgar Paxson, Custer's Last Stand," *True West,* Vol. 11, No. 1 (Sept.-Oct., 1963), 14-16, 52-53 (Paxson was a grandson of the artist; this issue of *True West* has a color reproduction of a portion of the Last Stand painting for its cover); REAW.

Pearce, E.D., pioneer: *see,* Elias Davidson Pierce

Peeples, Abraham Harlow, frontiersman (June 11, 1822-Jan. 29, 1892). B. in Guilford County, North Carolina, he enrolled June 25, 1846, at Point Isabel, Texas, in Company C, 2nd Texas Mounted Volunteers for Mexican War service. He participated in the Battle of Monterrey September 21-24 and as a private was honorably discharged at Monterrey on October 2, 1846. Peeples went to California in 1849, engaged in mining and related activities and it is probable that at Downieville he became acquainted with Dr. David Gould Webber (see entry), a local physician. In the spring of 1863 Peeples, with Webber and Joseph Green, left for Arizona to seek a rumored, fabulously wealthy, lost silver mine. At Yuma they were joined by Pauline Weaver, a noted mountain man and Indian scout of whom Peeples had requested guiding services. Also joining the party were Henry Wickenburg (see entry), a black, Ben McLendon (see entry), and "three other Americans." The party left Yuma in early April, traveled up the Colorado River to the gold camp of La Paz north of the present Ehrenburg, then cut inland, crossed the Plamosa Mountains and at a point about sixteen miles north of present Wickenburg made for a flat-topped mountain 6,391 feet tall, in the outskirts of which Peeples killed three or four antelope, therefor naming the uplift Antelope Peak. The party camped on a stream under the mountain, finding with gold pans good colors; the next day four Mexicans who had accompanied them, while hunting strayed horses came upon a shallow basin atop a ridge in the vicinity, the depression about 800 by 1,000 feet. There they found the surface strewn with gold in nuggets and chunks, handfuls of which they showed to Peeples privately. Early the next morning the whole party clambered up the hill and found the Mexican report true; it is said that the group recovered $250,000 in gold in a short time, packing it to Tucson to be shared equally, they also naming the site Rich Hill, the most famous such find in Arizona history. "For many years following the discovery, following the summer rains, nuggets in quantity were secured," and it was estimated that the site produced about $500,000 overall; the only reason it was not mined professionally was lack of water. Peeples engaged in ranching and mining in Peeples Valley, just north of Rich Hill. In November 1863 Indians, probably Yavapais, broke down his corral and swept off 29 head of horses and mules Peeples valued at about $2,500. King Woolsey (see entry), another noted pioneer, organized in January 1864 his famous pursuit expedition, crossed the Verde River, finally coming upon Indians—who may or may not have been the guilty ones—at what became Bloody Tanks, on Fish Creek near the Salt River, killing about 25 of them. Peeples became a prominent pioneer, serving as a Yavapai County supervisor and holding other public positions at various times, keeping saloons, the first at Weaver, near Rich Hill. He was an organizer of a major irrigation works on the Salt River near Phoenix, was a justice of the peace at Wickenburg, and at the age of 69 died at Phoenix, where he was buried.

Hayden Collection, Ariz. Hist. Soc., Tucson.

Penn, William, Quaker, statesman (Oct. 14, 1644-July 30, 1718). B. at London into an Anglican family, his father was Admiral Sir William Penn and his mother either Anglo-Irish or Dutch. Young Penn early was influenced by Puritan understandings and after two years at Oxford was expelled "on account of his non-conformist...activities." His angered father sent him to the continent to get over his religious waywardness, but Penn attended a Huguenot academy which only furthered his liberal spiritual inclinations. He studied law for a year at London, went to Ireland in 1666 to take charge of some of his father's estates, listened eagerly to Quaker preaching and after a stretch in prison for his religious convictions (he was not unacquainted with imprisonment for indebtedness or other minor infractions) soon became an avowed and active Friend, as the Quakers were properly called. A gifted writer, he published tracts on religious subjects, including his noted *No Cross, No Crown,* and also wrote on political subjects. He preached in England, the Netherlands and Germany, supported freedom of conscience (not an overly popular cause in his day), and determined to create a haven in America for members of the often beleaguered Society of Friends. His father died in 1670 and in 1672 Penn married. He con-

tinued his manifold activities in religion and politics and commenced his connection with America in New Jersey, part of which came into possession of the Quakers, Penn becoming a trustee in its management. In 1677 about 200 settlers arrived by way of the Delaware River to found Burlington, New Jersey, bringing with them a document on Concessions and Agreements for their government, no doubt drafted by Penn and considered a "great charter of liberties," and Penn's "gift to American government." Among other basic liberties, many foreign to English legal thought of the day, it "provided friendly methods for the purchase of Indian lands," and even in trials in which Indians were concerned, that the jury was to be made up of six Indians and six whites. It is in Penn's relationships with Indians that the frontier aspect of his activities rests, and this entry will be forced by space limitations to say little about the non-frontier impact, however worthy, of this gifted man. Suffice it to say that the Concessions and Agreements document has been defined as "the broadest, sanest, and most equitable charter draughted for any body of colonists up to [his] time." William Penn's principal effort and impact was in Pennsylvania, the huge tract named for its extensive forests and not for William Penn but for his father, the Admiral and close friend of Charles II (1630-1685). William had inherited from the Admiral a large fortune, and also a huge claim for funds loaned by his father to Charles; upon William's petition the King in 1681 granted him a huge tract including the bulk of today's Pennsylvania; in 1682 Penn also secured from the Duke of York, who became James II (1633-1701), the region of Delaware, which ultimately was established as a separate province. In Pennsylvania, where he laid out the city of Philadelphia, Penn's advanced ideas or ideals for democratic government were stressed, but "the brightest page in [his] political record is the story of his dealing with the American Indians...a worthy testimonial to William Penn." He took measures to protect the Indians from the rum and rapacity of white traders, and tried by every means to satisfy them in negotiations for lands, by these means earning their loyalty and respect. "Not until his descendants, who forsook his faith and his just policy, had betrayed and defrauded the natives, did the frontiers of Pennsylvania know the terrors of savage warfare." The Indians for their part adhered to promises incorporated in the various treaties Penn made with them and stating that "the Indians and the English must live and Love as long as the Sun gave Light." Penn's first stay in America lasted less than two years. In England King James was deposed in 1688 and Penn's friendship for him led to a charge of treason, the crown taking and holding his American colony from 1692-94; it was restored after he was vindicated of all treasonable activities. In 1694 his wife died and he married again a year later, both marriages proving happy and successful. Penn continued his writings throughout his life, and through them and his preaching he became an influence on Peter the Great of Russia and others. In 1697 he presented to the Board of Trade the first perfected plan for a union of all American colonies with a central congress to assist in their government. Because of difficulties in Pennsylvania he returned to his colony briefly from 1699-1701, showing continued interest in the Indians by meetings with them, arranging fresh agreements and renewing former covenants of friendship. He did what he could to counter the evils of slavery and by will provided for eventual manumission of his own slaves. He attempted to suppress piracy, granted a charter to Philadelphia and the noted Charter of 1701 to Pennsylvania, which guaranteed religious liberty and reformed some aspects of the government of the colony. The War of Spanish Succession (1701-14) was accompanied by a Parliamentary effort to annex proprietary colonies to the Crown, and Penn was forced to return to England, where he succeeded in retaining control, although again he suffered humiliations, debtor's imprisonment for a time, and seemingly endless troubles. In 1712 he suffered an apoplectic attack which limited his activities until his death at 74. His enduring fame rests upon his own outstanding qualities and his work in religion, in colonization, and in promoting the ideals and causes by which he lived and demonstrated with his life and works.

Literature abundant: CE, DAB.

Perrin, Edward, frontiersman (c. 1729-Oct. 15, 1779). From Antietam, Maryland, Perrin moved west and settled about seven miles east of Wellersburg, Pennsylvania, probably near Buffalo Creek. While hunting with two companions he was shot and killed by Indians on a stream fourteen miles above the mouth of Short Creek, known since as Perrin's Creek. He was about 50 when killed and left a widow and several children.

Thwaites/Kellogg, *Frontier Defense on the Upper Ohio, 1777-1778.*

Peshewah: *see,* Jean Baptiste Richardville

Peters, William John, explorer (Feb. 5, 1863-July 10, 1942). B. at Oakland, California, he did not attend college but engaged in various government surveys from 1885-87 and in 1898 led a reconnaissance party with Alfred Brooks as geologist to the White and Tanana rivers of eastern Alaska. In 1899 the same party continued explorations from the head of Lynn Canal, in the panhandle, to Eagle on the Yukon River. In 1900 Peters investigated the southeastern portion of the Seward Peninsula above Norton Sound and reconnoitered northern Alaska in 1901 with Frank Charles Schrader as geologist. The expedition crossed the Brooks Range at Anaktuvuk Pass to the Arctic coast, then followed it westward to Cape Lisburne. In 1902 Peters made a topographic map of the Juneau area. His name is preserved by Lake Peters in northern Alaska and Peters Glacier on Mount McKinley (Denali). He accompanied a polar expedition to Franz Josef Land from 1903-1905, the expedition named in honor of William Ziegler, a businessman who largely financed it. Peters was in command of Magnetic Survey ships *Galilee* and *Carnegie* from 1907-13, and he accompanied a Hudson Bay expedition in 1914. He lived in his later life at Chevy Chase, Maryland, and was associated with the Department of Terrestrial Magnetism of Washington, D.C.

Orth, 25-26, 751; *Who Was Who.*

Petrov (Petroff), Ivan, historical writer, enigma (c. 1830 or 1842-post 1892). Petrov was translator and important assistant to Hubert Howe Bancroft in the compilation of *History of Alaska* and also wrote the substantial (226 oversize pages) "Population, Resources, Etc. of Alaska" for the *Tenth Census* of 1880, described by famed geologist Alfred Hulse Brooks (see entry) as a "most notable contribution to the knowledge of Alaska's geography and resources." Petrov was a significant—and controversial—figure in assembling the history of Russian America, and in its published presentations. His origins are as obscure as the conclusion of his life, and his own summary of his beginnings, as it appears in Bancroft's *Literary Industries* leads to as many questions as answers. According to Bancroft, Petrov was born at St. Petersburg in 1842. A San Francisco magazine, *The Wave,* reported by an unidentified columnist on November 19, 1892, that Petrov was "now past sixty years of age," as learned through close acquaintanceship. If that figure is accurate it would make his date of birth around 1830. It is possible that the date of 1842 reported by Bancroft may be a transposition of the figure 1824, though that is only speculation. Bancroft wrote that Petrov early displayed a "wonderful faculty" for linguistics and was employed in the Department of Oriental Languages of the St. Petersburg Academy of Sciences. He came to the attention of academy member M. Brosset, a student of Armenian antiquities and literature, who took him on a two-year expedition to Georgia and Armenia. Brosset made that journey in 1847-48 when Petrov, according to the Bancroft birth date, would have been only 5 or 6; by the columnist's statement he would have been perhaps 17 or 18 or possibly older, and by the transposition theory, 23 or 24. Petrov reported that he sailed for New York in 1861, enlisted in the 7th New Hampshire Company and served under New Hampshire-born Benjamin Franklin Butler, was wounded twice and before his 1865 discharge was commissioned a lieutenant of Volunteers. He had acquired a facility in English and at New York contracted to serve five years at Sitka, Alaska, for the Russian American Company as an English and German translator. He reported that he was delayed at San Francisco and used the available time to make a horseback journey through Idaho, Washington and Oregon, during which he ran afoul of hostile Shoshones; his horse was killed and he wounded but escaped. He then embarked for Sitka where he found his promised post already filled, so he became a chief trader on Cook Inlet, holding the position until the 1867 sale of Alaska by Russia to the United States, when he returned to San Francisco and entered the service of Bancroft, whose "history factory" was then flourishing. Sherwood's investigation showed, however, that at least part of his story was fabricated. Records reveal that he had enlisted in Battery F, 2nd U.S. Artillery in July 1867 at Fort Colville, Washington, deserted, was imprisoned at Fort Vancouver and sent to join his battery in Alaska, where his services were desired as a "valuable" interpreter. In July 1870 he was discharged at Fort Kenai, on Cook Inlet. In January 1871 he enlisted again, this time at Sacramento, deserted for the second time and wrote for the San Francisco *Bulletin* and the *Chronicle* until

1874, when he joined Bancroft. His military record was finally cleared April 4, 1883, when he was officially discharged by Special Order 45 of the AGO upon application to the Secretary of War by Hayward M. Hutchinson of the Alaska Commercial Company. By then he was deeply involved with Bancroft on *Alaska,* published in 1886. The results of his efforts are sometimes disputed today. A highly regarded recent work, *Russian Penetration of the North Pacific Ocean,* concluded that Bancroft was hampered by his reliance upon Petrov "who was inexperienced in historical research and made certain highly inaccurate translations; indeed at times he produced wholly fictitious accounts" (lxvi), though citing no examples; *Russian American Colonies,* by the same authors repeated the charge: "Unfortunately Bancroft...relied on a Russian-born assistant to make translations for him; Ivan Petrov not only translated but indeed invented documents. Although Petrov's fraud was eventually exposed, for years scholars accepted the work as authentic" (lxxvi). Again the "fraud" was not specified, but see the Juvenal entry as a possibility, although that case is not clear-cut. On the other hand, Petrov's major labors for Bancroft were of recognized merit. "Petroff must have been largely responsible" for *Alaska,* "the single most important history of the northland," believed Sherwood. "He wrote a good part of it, he translated the major Russian sources..., researched Russian records in Alaska and Washington, and collected statements on Alaska...It is safe to assume that Petroff's work was the foundation if not all of the superstructure." Petrov's elaborate paper for the Tenth Census, which has been republished in *Narratives of Explorations in Alaska,* was his second great contribution to Alaskan understanding and history. He was perhaps "the most competent person in all respects who could have been selected for the work," according to then Governor Alfred P. Swineford, who added that the report was "fully as complete and reliable as could have been expected." For it Petrov examined Alaska by six major districts, covering each in turn, his overall knowledge of the sub-continent perhaps matched by very few, although his work had been preceded by William H. Dall's *Resources of Alaska,* published in 1870 and with which Petrov of course was thoroughly familiar. Brooks said that Petrov was the first to exhibit any "clear conception of the distribution of [the] mountain ranges in Alaska," and Sherwood concluded that the Russian reported on the territory's resources "with measured reserve," assessing each in a balanced, accurate way. An excellent writer, he has been accused of reflecting more journalism in his report than scientific awareness, but the labor called for the expertise of the journalist rather than of the specialist, and Petrov was a master of the craft when he chose to be. This is not to concede that the finished report lacked substance, for it did not. Petrov's presentation, for example, of the 1880 awareness of the invaluable sea otter, its history, range of distribution, the techniques for its pursuit and collecting its precious fur, and the outlook for its future had never been approached in scope until he wrote, and his assessment of that animal remains useful today. His evaluation of the region's timber resources, mainly based upon personal reconnaissance, is still sound. His presentation of such census concerns as population counts, collected as necessary from missionaries, traders and others whose reliability was uneven, were probably as accurate as could be assembled at that time. Gold had been discovered in Alaska by then only in limited amounts, and his awareness of the territory's mineral resources must be intuitive, rather than evidential. The report's ethnological matter was largely an adaptation of material from William Healey Dall, then generally recognized as an Alaska expert in numerous fields, although history apparently was not one of them. In all, the Petrov Report was something of a master work. His several trips to Alaska during this period are not clearly defined, however. In 1890 he was hired once more to direct the Eleventh Census of Alaska, on this occasion claimed to have journeyed about 12,000 miles, a scarcely credible figure. Upon conclusion of this work he was engaged by the State Department to translate Russian documents for use in settlement of a growing controversy with Britain over pelagic hunting in the Bering Sea. Now, however, for whatever reasons, "in his translations, Petrov interpolated whatever might be of assistance to the American case, and he forged other statements not in the original documents." Discovery of such "grave inaccuracies" forced him to confess, when he was dropped from government service. His superior wrote that "confronted with his fraud, Petroff quietly acknowledged his guilt but gave no explanation or any excuse." Secretary of State John W. Foster added that, "It is supposed that he made the interpolations in order that I might be better pleased with his work." Petrov's name was expunged from the Eleventh Census

publication because of his aberrations in the State Department case, and Petrov thereafter fades into obscurity, *The Wave* columnist reporting that he continued linguistic work, laboring on Chinese and Japanese and "Malayan on the side." The date and place of his death are unreported. In 1871 Petrov's military service record shows him to have been 5 ft., 11 in., in height, with black hair, grey eyes and a fair complexion, and at that time he apparently was married and had become a father. Sherwood summarizes his essay on Petrov: "He is a likable character for all his delinquencies. As an authority on Alaska, only…Dall could claim wider experience in the field, in the library, and in print. The influence of Petroff's Tenth Census report and Bancroft's *History of Alaska* on subsequent investigations is incalculable…Petrov's writing is balanced and calm, if occasionally flippant and inconsistent. It is usually reliable, by nineteenth century standards. [These two works] are his monuments."

Info. from the Alaska State Library and Archives; *Narratives of Explorations in Alaska;* Bancroft, *Alaska; Literary Industries; Russian Penetration of the North Pacific Ocean; The Russian American Colonies;* Morgan B. Sherwood, "Ivan Petroff and the Far Northwest," *Journal of the West,* Vol. II, No. 3 (July 1963), 305-15; Richard A. Pierce, "A Note on 'Ivan Petroff and the Far Northwest,'" *Journal of the West,* Vol. III, No. 4 (Oct. 1964), 436-39; Sherwood, "A Note on the Petroff Note, *Ibid,* 440.

Philip, James Scotty, cattleman, buffalo conservor (Apr. 30, 1858-July 23, 1911). B. in Morayshire, Scotland, he emigrated to the United States in 1874, locating initially at Victoria, Kansas. He soon became a ranch hand near Cheyenne, Wyoming, and began a lifelong friendship with Hiram B. (Hi) Kelly (see entry). When rumors of gold in the Black Hills flourished in 1875, Scotty with other prospectors filtered into the Indian region. Because they were there illegally, the army hustled them to Fort Robinson, Nebraska; Scotty returned to Cheyenne, made an abortive second trip to the Black Hills and again was ousted by the army. At Cheyenne he once more found means to finance a trip to the Hills, this time heading for Deadwood Gulch. His stay there was unprofitable and in 1877 he became a civilian teamster for the army out of Fort Laramie, Wyoming. That employment didn't last long, and Philip returned to South Dakota, sold hay to the army and established a ranch eight miles north of the Red Cloud

Agency, engaging in freighting also and expanding his holdings whenever feasible. In January 1878 he became a scout and courier for the army and saw some slight service against the Dull Knife people who had fled their exile in Oklahoma and engaged in a virtually miraculous hegira northward toward their old country. Once the band had split, with the Little Wolf faction going into Montana to be quartered with the Northern Cheyennes and the Dull Knife grouping being incarcerated at Fort Robinson, Philip's days as scout were over. In 1879 he married Sarah (Sally), the half-Sioux daughter of Joseph Larabee, and by her fathered nine children, four of whom predeceased him (Sarah's sister, Helen [Nellie] had married Crazy Horse, the great Oglala chief and war leader). Philip now settled into freighting in earnest between Sidney, Nebraska, Deadwood, South Dakota, and Fort Pierre, on the Missouri River. He expanded his ranch and his herds steadily grew. His wife, as an Indian woman, was due a land allotment along the Bad River in western South Dakota, and Philip settled there where there was good grass and an abundance of room. A town named Philip was eventually established at his ranch headquarters, and still exists with a population of around 1,000. About 1891 Scotty launched another brand, the 73 which although he soon sold out his interest, became a famous establishment. In 1900 Scotty attended a cattlemen's convention at Fort Worth, Texas. When he got back to Fort Pierre he heard that Pete Dupree on the Cheyenne River Reservation had died and remembered that Pete had raised a few buffalo he had roped on the Grand River twenty years before. Philip purchased the herd, including a number of cattalo, or crossed buffalo and cattle, the mixture in his opinion neither one nor the other and "not worth a damn," but he wanted the buffalo and had to accept also the mixed breed, which he promptly sold off. He prepared a 2,000-acre pasture fenced as strongly as possible to hold the buffalo away from his own cattle. Scotty's livestock peaked at 40,000 head on his several ranges, after which the number declined to 15,000-23,000 head at any one time. His buffalo at his death numbered about 400 head. Philip thus became one of the saviors of the buffalo, although not the only one, since Charles Goodnight, Charles P. Allard, Samuel Walking Coyote and others were important in this endeavor. Yet Philip's herd supplied animals for zoos and smaller preservation efforts and the strains he

nurtured and developed are reflected in many of the 90,000 buffalo alive today all over the country. Philip from time to time entered in a minor way various businesses including banking and trading, but his principal interest was always cattle—and buffalo. He was a South Dakota state senator briefly, had warm friendships over the west and "for a quarter of a century he was known from the Black Hills to the Mexican border." He died at 53 following a cerebral hemorrhage, which may have resulted from herculean efforts to free his new-fangled automobile which was stuck in the mud near his home. His widow, Sarah, died in 1938 when she was well into her eighties. In 1925 the buffalo herd was liquidated; 200 head were killed in a filmed grand hunt, and the remainder distributed to parks and reserves. Scotty and his longtime friend, Ed Lemmon, were the first two South Dakota men elected into the National Cowboy Hall of Fame at Oklahoma City, this on January 5, 1958.

Wayne C. Lee, *Scotty Philip: The Man Who Saved the Buffalo,* Caldwell, Id., Caxton Printers, Ltd., 1975; REAW; Nellie Snyder Yost, ed., *Boss Cowman: The Recollections of Ed Lemmon,* Lincoln, Univ. of Nebr. Press, 1969; David A. Dary, *The Buffalo Book,* Chicago, Swallow Press, 1974; Fort Pierre, *Stock Grower News,* July 27, 1911; info. from the South Dak. Hist. Soc.; Ike Blasingame, *Dakota Cowboy: My Life in the Old Days,* Lincoln, 1948; info. from E.F. (Ted) Mains.

Phips, William, colonial governor (Feb. 2, 1650/51-Feb. 18, 1694/95). B. of modest parentage on the frontier of Maine, he was a ship's carpenter and commanded at least one sailing vessel, perhaps others. He listened to the tales of sea rovers referring to supposed fabulous wealth on sunken Spanish ships and searched for a sponsor for an expedition to recover such wealth, at last interesting Charles II, King of England, in his design. He was given command of H.M.S. *Rose,* and set out for the Bahamas in September 1683. His first venture was fruitless, but a second, financed by the Duke of Albemarle, located a sunken treasure ship off Hispaniola (today's Haiti) and recovered about 300,000 pounds sterling, Phips gaining therefrom also a knighthood, a coat of arms and much colonial prestige. According to Samuel Sewall he was sworn in as High Sheriff or Provost Marshal-General at Boston July 6, 1688; he felt he was "ill-received" in his new post of high authority, and went to England to complain at court; while at London he became acquainted with Increase Mather, noted

Congregational minister and political power in Massachusetts, and brother of Cotton Mather. Phips became a parishioner of the Mathers following the overthrow of Governor Edmund Andros and won their support for his political career. He commanded a Massachusetts 1690 King William War (1688-97) expedition against Port Royal, Nova Scotia, captured it from the French, the feat adding to his growing prestige, even though his subsequent attempt to capture Quebec failed. Enroute toward that goal he descended upon the establishment of the famed explorer, Louis Jolliet, on Anticosti Island in the Gulf of St. Lawrence (Jolliet himself was away), burned his buildings and captured Jolliet's wife and mother-in-law. Phips commanded a second expedition against the French, but failed to take Montreal. He returned to England to seek royal support for a third expedition but King William, deep in the problem of whether to establish a dominion or charter form of government for Massachusetts, temporized; the monarch finally decided on a mixed political organization which required appointment by the king of a royal governor. Increase Mather was granted the right to nominate someone, and named his friend Phips, who thus became the initial royal governor of Massachusetts. Phips arrived at Boston in May 1692 and found himself faced with vexing political and spiritual problems, one of the latter being "the witchcraft mania" sweeping the colony. He first appointed a commission to try those accused of witchcraft, and then abruptly brought the persecution to an end. He became a center for contention and factional dispute. Phips supported universal taxation for support of the Congregational Church, but was bitterly opposed by those of other faiths; he obstructed customs collectors and "connived at piracy," but failed to protect the frontiers against raids by French and Indians or to aid colonies in their own defense as the wilderness guerilla warfare persisted. Instead of conciliating the differences between those who still supported charter government and the strong faction desiring dominion government, he was ruthless in crushing opposition to his own views. Sir William liked to fraternize with his former tradesmen friends and others of low station, which alienated aristocratic elements. He was a man of short temper and prone to furious physical violence, once publicly caning a royal navy captain who refused to obey him and, again, bullied a collector of customs for attempting to seize a vessel suspected of illegal trading. The opposi-

tion and charges against him led to his eventual recall to London to face mounting accusations, but he died before the hearings began, a fortunate thing for him because, as the *Dictionary of American Biography* put it, his death "was the only thing which prevented his recall, for the evidence of maladministration was very strong against him."

DAB; *The Diary of Samuel Sewall*, 2 vols., ed. by M. Halsey Thomas, N.Y., Farrar, Straus and Giroux, 1973; Parkman, *France and England in North America*, Library of America, I, 772-73n.

Pico, Andrés, military officer (1810-1876). B. at San Diego, he was a brother of Pio Pico and in 1836-38 was in charge of the Jamul rancho east of San Diego in addition to holding one or two public positions. During that period he took an active part on behalf of the south in the sectional strife against the central government at Monterey, "being half a dozen times a prisoner in that play at warfare and diplomacy." From 1839-42 he was an ensign in the San Diego company, obtaining lands at Santa Margarita, San Juan Capistrano and Temécula, all in southern California. He was sent to Mexico in 1844 by Governor Manuel Micheltorena to obtain funds for California defense and upon his return devoted himself as a captain to perfecting the defenses and organization of militia at Los Angeles. In 1845 he joined the revolutionists and was in military command at Monterey and later at Los Angeles. In the turbulent California political scene he became chief in command upon the flight of José Castro, surrendered and was paroled, but broke his parole to serve under José Maria Flores at Los Angeles. Andrés Pico commanded the Californians at the victory against Kearny forces at San Pasqual, the outstanding achievement of his life and the most important military event during the American conquest of California. Pico also took part in the fights of January 1847 and, being left by Flores in chief command, concluded with Fremont the Treaty of Cahuenga, closing the California war. In 1848-49 he headed a group of miners in the gold fields on the Mokelumne River. He lived at San Jose in 1849-50 and thereafter at Los Angeles, establishing claims to several ranchos, holding public offices and became, in 1858, a Brigadier General of militia and in 1860-61 was a state senator. He died, possibly on his San Fernando estate. Bancroft wrote that Pico was "a brave, reckless, coarse-grained, jovial, kind-hearted, popular man; abler in several respects than his brother Don Pio [Pico}, but not overburdened with principle." He never married.

Bancroft, *California*, III-V; *Pioneer Register.*

Pico, Pio, activist, governor (May 5, 1801-Sept. 11, 1894). B. at San Gabriel Mission, California, where his father commanded a cavalry detachment, the boy was raised at San Diego. He at length opened a small shop, as he grew entered in some fashion into public life and in 1829 secured title to the Jamul rancho, east of San Diego. In 1831 he was a leader of the southern opposition to Governor Manuel Victoria and in 1832, according to plan should have been governor pro tem, but Bancroft states that he was unable to secure the place, though he is often said to have been governor that year. He held various positions, some of them politically important and from 1837-39 was an active partisan against the government of Juan Bautista Alvarado, "being more than once a prisoner, though like others never in a fight, and playing a not very creditable part in the sectional strife." Pico was from time to time a member of the governing juntas, holding positions of varying responsibility; in 1842 he was suspected of plotting with representatives of England for control of California, but that is unproven. In 1844-45 he was once more a member of the junta, captain of defenders against American involvement and was appointed a commandant of a squadron, probably of cavalry. He operated against Micheltorena and upon his downfall in 1845, Pico, as president of the junta, became acting governor from February 22. His office was confirmed in Mexico and April 18, 1846, he took the oath as the last governor of California before the United States takeover. As the Ango forces approached, Pico left for Mexico, supposedly to get assistance to resist the invaders. Aid was unavailable to him and in 1848 he returned to California, residing until 1864 at Santa Margarita, near San Luis Obispo, and from that year in the Los Angeles area. He had been a claimant of several ranchos, but one by one they slipped away until the last, of 60,000 acres, was lost to a swindler named Bernard Cohn, Cohn's crooked interpreter, "Pancho" Johnson, and through a transparently dishonest court decision, leaving Pico a pauper. As a governor he had done nothing to distinguish his brief administration in any way, and in his career had done little more, but Bancroft judged him to have been a man "abused far beyond his just deserts; a man of ordinary intelligence and limited education; of generous, jovial disposition, reckless and indolent; with a weakness for cards and women; disposed to be fair and honorable in his transactions, but [unable to] avoid being made the tool of knaves; patriotic without being able to do much for his country." He was married, but there is no record of any children, except for a daughter in whose Los Angeles home he died at 93. In 1877 he had dictated the story of his life and career to Thomas Savage for the Bancroft collection; it has been translated into English and published.

Don Pio Pico's Historical Narrative, trans. by Arthur P. Botello, ed. by Martin Cole and Henry Welcome, Glendale, Calif., Arthur H. Clark Co., 1973; Bancroft, *California,* II-V; *Pioneer Register.*

Pidge: *see,* T.C. Robinson

Pierce (Pearce), Elias Davidson, pioneer (1824-1897). B. in northern Ireland he arrived in Virginia in 1839 and five years later moved to Indiana. He read law and practiced until the Mexican War, from which he emerged possibly as a captain of Volunteers. In 1849 he joined the California Gold Rush, became a prospector and itinerant trader and served in the California legislature in 1852. Late that year he journeyed to the Nez Perce region of Idaho, was impressed with its possibilities, but came back to settle at Yreka in the northwest corner of California. Forty-two miles southeast rose the 14,162-foot Mount Shasta, "one of the most striking physical features of northern California," which had been discovered February 14, 1827, by Peter Skene Ogden, famous Hudson's Bay Company brigade leader. In September 1854 Pierce alone made the first recorded ascent of the peak, although whether he was actually the first to scale it is unknown; the initial ascent by scientists was made in September 1862 when Josiah Dwight Whitney of the state Geological Survey scaled it to find the summit littered with "a mixture of tin cans and broken bottles, a newspaper, a Methodist hymn book, a pack of cards...and other evidences of a bygone civilization," according to William H. Brewer, Whitney's assistant. There must have been considerable traffic up there since Pierce's feat. Pierce returned to the Northwest some time later, although the record is confused and the precise year unknown. At some point (perhaps on his earlier trip) he had led an eight-week expedition from Walla Walla, Washington, or thereabouts through the country west of the Snake River, "taking in the Malheur, Burnt, Powder, and

Grande Ronde rivers. He reported finding an extensive gold-field on these streams, with room for thousands of miners, who could make from three to fifteen dollars a day each." Pierce "stampeded to rich diggings in the Fraser River district of British Columbia in 1856" and while there he "undoubtedly" had learned of scattered gold finds to the south. At some time in the late 1850s he heard of possible gold in the Nez Perce country. From Walla Walla he gathered a score of followers and started in that direction, although there were difficulties. The military sought to prevent the party from invading Indian country; at Alpowa, the Snake River town of the important chief, Timothy (see entry), Pierce was warned away by Indians "who threatened his life if he continued his invasion" of their country. His attempts to push inland anyway were thwarted by armed and determined Nez Perce warriors. He did secure permission of Timothy to winter near Alpowa, and during that season of 1859-60 he met 18-year-old Jane (see entry), daughter of Chief Timothy and, despite the Indian's opposition, persuaded Jane to guide his party (by a route defined by Bailey) and September 30, discovered gold in the vicinity of present-day Orofino. Before pulling back to Walla Walla, Pierce City, about a dozen miles east of Orofino, was founded December 3, and named for Elias Pierce. He also is credited with making the first commercial gold discovery in Idaho. With the following spring the prospector surge into the gold country burgeoned; the Nez Perce had lost out, and the flood of whites had come to stay. Pierce may have profited little from his discovery, however. In 1865-66 he joined in a stage line venture from Sacramento to southwestern Idaho, but Indian hostility ended that endeavor. "Then in 1869 Pierce heard that his girlfriend back in Indiana (to whom he had been engaged for twenty years but whom he had not seen during that time) was getting restless; he hurried back, got married," wrote Idaho historical writer Merle W. Wells, and took his bride to Oakland, where they settled. Pierce engaged in mining until 1884 when he went back to Indiana in retirement.

REAW; Robert G. Bailey, *River of No Return: Historical Stories of Idaho*, Lewiston, Id., R.G. Bailey Printing Co., 1947; Bancroft, *Oregon* II; *California: A Guide to the Golden State*, N.Y., Hastings House, 1947; Gloria Griffen Cline, *Peter Skene Ogden and the Hudson's Bay Company*, Norman, Univ. of Okla. Press, 1974; info. from E.F. (Ted) Mains.

Pike, James, adventurerr (d. Oct. 14, 1867). B. in Ohio, he enlisted in the 4th Ohio Cavalry November 20, 1861, and served as a corporal throughout the Civil War. On October 27, 1863, he arrived at Major General William T. Sherman's headquarters in western Tennessee as "a dirty, black-haired individual with mixed dress and strange demeanor" bearing a message from Grant at Chattanooga, come by way of George Crook's headquarters in northern Alabama. Pike told Sherman "in his peculiar way, that General Crook had sent him in a canoe; that he had pulled down the Tennessee River, over Muscle Shoals, was fired at all the way by guerillas, but on reaching Tuscumbia he had providentially found it in possession of our troops," and eventually had reached Sherman. The General found Pike "a singular character," and just the sort of man to successfully complete such a dangerous mission. Sherman "got him a horse," sent him back to Crook, but told Pike that "if I could ever do him a personal service, he might apply to me." In early 1864 when Sherman was preparing his Atlanta campaign, Pike again appeared, reminded him of his offer and when Sherman asked what he wanted, Pike replied that "he wanted to do something *bold,* something that would make him a hero." Sherman told him of the forthcoming movement against Atlanta and that he wanted the bridge across the Savannah River at Augusta, Georgia, burned about July 4, when he intended to be in the vicinity of Atlanta. He warned Pike the chances were three to one that he would be caught and hanged, but the danger increased his determination to tackle the mission to throw the Confederate rear into confusion. However, "the bridge was not burnt, and I supposed that Pike had been caught and hanged," Sherman wrote. But in February 1865, near Columbia, South Carolina, Pike showed up again, this time as a released prisoner of war, and "gave me a graphic narrative of his adventures, which would have filled a volume." He had twice tried to burn the bridge and had failed, was captured, escaped, was captured by Northern forces "because of his [disreputable] looks," and got out of that scrape, as well. Sherman arranged to get him cleaned up, properly dressed and used him as a messenger. On March 31, 1866, Pike was commissioned a second lieutenant of the 1st Cavalry and was posted to Oregon where on September 27, 1867, he became a first lieutenant. Shortly afterward he wrote Sherman reporting that he was "tired of the monotony of garrison life, and wanted to turn Indian, join the Cheyennes on the Plains, who were then giving us great trouble, and after he had gained their confidence, he would betray them into our hands." Sherman quickly wrote him that "he must try and settle down and become a gentleman as well as an officer...and forget the wild desires of his nature." Pike was killed by the "accidental discharge of a pistol" which, Sherman concluded, "probably saved him from a slower but harder fate."

Memoirs of General W.T. Sherman, N.Y., Library of America, 1990, 383-85.

Pionsenay (Peñon), Chiricahua leader (d.c. Dec. 1877). A brother or half-brother of Eskinya (see entry) and of parentage unremembered, Pionsenay was to whites an incorrigible, a renegade, an outlaw, while to the Apaches he was intrepid, daring, a hero and probably something of a patriot, all of which was normal classification for frontier times. He probably was b. in the 1820s and in time came into leadership of a small grouping or band of followers as intractable as himself. He was a "captain," or group leader associated with Cochise and in 1872 was with that chief at Janos, Chihuahua, according to report. He earned a reputation as a successful raider and a militant averse to settling upon a reservation permanently. In 1876 Pionsenay, Eskinya and their followers were on the Chiricahua Reservation in southeastern Arizona. Rations being lean, they and Cochise's son, Taza, were permitted to supplement their rations by hunting and gathering. Following a dispute Taza returned to the Chiricahua Mountains. Near the Dragoons was a stagecoach station on the Mesilla-to-Tucson line operated by Nicholos M. Rogers and his assistant, A.O. Spence, who padded their income by bootlegging whiskey to Apaches in return for Mexican loot. April 7, Pionsenay traded with Rogers for liquor, got drunk, wanted more whiskey which Rogers would not sell him, and Pionsenay killed both Rogers and Spence. The next day the Apaches, still drunk, killed another white man and stole some horses. With Jeffords as guide, troops cornered the militants in the rocky Dragoons but could not dislodge them, and withdrew. May 3, Agent Clum (see entry) was ordered to suspend Jeffords, who had been agent on the Chiricahua reserve, and "if practicable remove Chiricahua Indians to San Carlos." Taza had become chief of the Chiricahuas following the death of Cochise, and he assented to the transfer. But June 4, Eskinya and Pionsenay slipped into the rancheria, tried to persuade him to go on the warpath instead; when he

refused, fighting erupted, Eskinya was killed and Pionsenay shot in the shoulder, believing for a time his wound was mortal. He agreed to surrender to Clum and twenty scouts under Tauelclyee brought him in, Clum placing him under arrest. Enroute to San Carlos, however, the party was met by Pima County Sheriff Charles Shibell (see entry) and his deputy, Ad(am) Linn, armed with a warrant, who demanded and received the prisoner on June 13, at 2 p.m. At 9 p.m. Pionsenay escaped, wounded as he was, and headed for Mexico. By the spring of 1877, fully recovered, he headed a band of ten fighting men, as did his colleague, Nolgee, and had resumed raiding in Sonora and occasionally, in Arizona. In April Clum removed the Mimbres under Victorio to San Carlos from their Ojo Caliente Reservation and Pionsenay, hovering in the distance, followed the exodus to Camp Goodwin, it going on then to San Carlos. Pionsenay lurked about the southern rim of the reservation, keeping some sort of contact with Victorio and his people and was believed to have urged them to flee their confinement. August 28, Pionsenay, Nolgee and their followers, now reduced to eighteen, came within four miles of the subagency where Ezra Hoag was in charge. The outcasts sent word they wanted to surrender, but Hoag replied that he had no authority to negotiate with them, so the Pionsenay people stole five horses and filtered away. Into September Pionsenay kept in close contact with the Mimbres and "no doubt it was this wild Indian who helped crystallize Victorio's strengthening intent to bolt." Hoag reported that "Pionsenay wields a great influence over all of them, and they fear him worse than the devil." In early September Victorio and his followers finally did escape the reservation and Pionsenay, his work concluded satisfactorily, faded south into Old Mexico. According to Sweeney, he was killed at or near Janos in either late 1877 or early 1878, circumstances unreported.

Edwin R. Sweeney, *Cochise: Chiricahua Apache Chief,* Norman, Univ. of Okla. Press, 1991; Dan L. Thrapp, *Victorio and the Mimbres Apaches,* Norman, 1974; Thrapp, *Conquest of Apacheria,* Norman, 1967; Woodworth Clum, *Apache Agent: The Story of John P. Clum,* Boston, N.Y., Houghton Mifflin Co., 1936, 180-84.

Pipe, Captain, Delaware chief: *see,* Captain Pipe

Piper, Edmund (Edward) A., cattleman (c.

1819-Aug. 8, 1896). B. in Ohio, probably near Circleville, 25 miles south of Columbus, he completed in 1846 what the Federal government termed the earliest "authenticated" drive of Texas cattle to the upper United States. Longhorn drives commenced modestly, possibly with Antonio Le Blanc (see entry), who in 1782 may have driven 2,000 head from East Texas, for 200 miles into Louisiana. They continued with James Taylor White (see entry) who about 1838 drove a herd from Anahuac County, Texas, to New Orleans, possibly the first to have completed such an operation. The Department of the Interior *Report on the Productions of Agriculture* (10th Census) declared, on p. 965, that "there is a report of a drive to Missouri in 1842, but the earliest perfectly authenticated record of a business venture of that kind found was for 1846 when Edward [sic] Piper...drove 1,000 head of Texas cattle to Ohio, where he fed and sold them." It may be that Tom Candy Ponting (see entry), who was at Columbus in 1847, heard of this incident and it inspired him to make his well-known drive years later. Drives increased from 1846 to 1861, and from 1850 there were occasional stock movements to California, while others later were destined for Arizona and New Mexico. The first drive to Chicago was completed in 1856, and maiden aunts of the author, who were born shortly before the Civil War and raised at Tallula, Illinois, remembered from their childhood seeing Texas cattle passing through enroute to Chicago. Piper was listed in the Department of the Interior report as among the "prominent stockmen of Texas" along with Jesse Chisholm and Charles Goodnight (p. 974), but this comment apparently referred to people who opened new market trails rather than to ranchers as such. At least by 1853 Piper had settled at Decatur, Macon County, Illinois. April 4, 1854, he married Sarah Jane Querry (d. Dec. 19, 1868) and July 8, he joined Masonic Lodge 8, remaining affiliated with it for the rest of his life. Piper may have established, or renewed, an acquaintance with Ponting who had settled with his livestock interests in neighboring Christian County and who in 1853 journeyed to Fannin County, Texas, where he purchased Longhorns to be driven back to his Christian County property; Ponting's autobiographical book was published at Decatur in 1907. The 1860 Census reported Piper's occupation as a grain dealer, and a Decatur City Directory for 1871-72 listed him as a stock agent, no doubt a livestock agent, which he had been all the time anyway.

The *Decatur Republican* for January 30, 1868, reported that Piper had applied for the superintendency of that segment of the T.W. & W. Railway, noting that Piper's supporters of his application were "among the heaviest stock shippers on the line," a fact it said that "will doubtless have due weight" with the railroad, and which also indicated his long-standing career as a livestock agent. Following a December 24, 1868, lengthy first-page obituary for Sarah Piper, the *Republican* added: "Circleville, O., papers, please copy"; since Sarah Querry Piper had never lived in Ohio, the notice can only suggest that Edmund Piper was from that community originally. Piper fathered six children, never remarried, and died at Decatur.

Dept. of the Interior, *Report on the Productions of Agriculture as Returned by the Tenth Census,* Wash., G.P.O., 1883, sec. on "Meat Production, Texas, Historical," 965-78, which includes statistical and other material on development of the Texas cattle industry, trail driving, etc.; info. from Rosella Vohs, Decatur Genealogical Research Committee; Illinois State Hist. Lby.; Walter L. Emmons, Macon County (Ill.) Hist. Soc.; Piper death cert.; Ramon F. Adams, *The Rampaging Herd,* Norman, Univ. of Okla. Press, 1959, p. 291, No. 1815.

Piper, John, militia officer (1730-1816). B. in Ireland his family brought him at the age of 2 to America, the father dying shortly after landing at Wilmington, Delaware. The widow and her sons moved to Shippensburg, Cumberland County, Pennsylvania. In 1764 Piper joined Bouquet for the Ohio campaign against hostile Indians. In 1772 he settled on Yellow Creek, Bedford County, Pennsylvania, where he built an imposing place on Piper's Run; his large stone house was still standing in 1860, in possession of his descendants. In 1776 he raised a company and served a year in the Continental Army, then was assigned to frontier defense as colonel of the Bedford County militia. He later served in the state legislature and from 1790 as an associate justice of his county. He died at his home.

Thwaites/Kellogg, *Frontier Defense on the Upper Ohio, 1777-1778.*

Pisago Cabezon, Bedonkohe (Chiricahua) Apache chief (c. 1770-c. 1846). Probably the father of the noted Cochise and his brothers, or half-brothers, Coyuntura and Juan, Pisago Cabezon succeeded his father, also named Pisago (or Visago), after the elder was killed in 1793 by Sonoran troops in the Enmedio Mountains, just below the Chihuahua border. Pisago Cabezon, who was something of a moderate Apache leader, came into Janos, Chihuahua, and remained near that presidio intermittently until the end of Spanish control. He had several wives and fathered perhaps as many as thirteen children. Many of the noted Chokonen leaders of the 1840s and 1850s were related to him by blood or marriage. From time to time Pisago Cabezon turned hostile toward the Mexicans and led raids or attacks on various centers; he was an able war leader, when he chose to become such. March 30-April 2, 1838, Pisago and his men captured a Mexican supply train of ten wagons bound for the important Santa Rita copper mines of southern New Mexico; the Mexicans surrendered the wagons and made their way back to Chihuahua City with only twenty-two horses, all they had left. In November 1839 the chief was falsely reported killed near the Mimbres River of New Mexico. A few years later George W. Kendall (see entry), a reliable Texas writer, reported meeting Pisago, who "came down and with two Indians together greeted and embraced me." He described Pisago as of "middle height, strong and well built, some sixty-five or seventy years of age, and with hair as white as snow." In the spring of 1840 the notorious James Kirker (see entry) surprised Pisago's camp, reportedly killing ten men and capturing twenty-two other people. In August 1842 Pisago Cabezon agreed to a fresh truce at Janos, but the Mexican murder of several Apaches near Fronteras sent them once more on the warpath; eventually his followers withdrew to southern New Mexico, living with Mangas Coloradas for a time and probably joining in raids on Sonora. Seven such raids were carried out in early 1844. Sweeney reported that Pisago Cabezon "passed from the scene in 1845 or 1846, possibly a victim of Kirker's massacre" of scores of Apaches at Galeana July 6, 1846, although if this Apache did die there it would seem improbable that a chief so famed would not have been mentioned among the casualties.

James Griffen, *Apaches At War & Peace,* Albuquerque, Univ. of New Mex. Press, 1989; Edwin R. Sweeney, *Cochise: Chiricahua Apache Chief,* Norman, Univ. of Okla. Press, 1991.

Plenisner, Fedor Khristian Novich, explorer, administrator (d. 1778). B. in Kurland, Latvia, he entered Russian service in 1730 and was sent to Okhotsk, Siberia, where he became a member of Bering's second expedition as "artist" and a clerk to Bering himself. The 1741 expedition resulted in the discovery of northwest America, but on the return the commandant's ship, the *Sv. Petr* was wrecked on what is now named Bering Island. The party wintered there and Bering and many others perished of scurvy, starvation and other ailments. Plenisner, with Steller (see entry) and three other Germans were among the survivors. The men still alive built a craft from the wreckage of the *Sv. Petr* and returned to Kamchatka in 1742. During the following winter Plenisner lived with Steller, apparently working on sketches for Steller's reports. Plenisner remained in Siberia; in 1759 he was named commandant at Okhotsk and in 1791 as a lieutenant colonel, of the Anadyr region. From then on he was principally concerned with the Chukotski Peninsula, Bering Strait and, by sending out parties, exploration of the North American coast in the Strait region, although he did not accompany the expeditions. Late in life he came upon hard times, was tried for various offenses and was acquitted, moved to St. Petersburg and died there. He was married and left a family.

Pierce, *Russian America: A Biographical Dictionary.*

Pluggy, Mohawk leader (d. Dec. 29, 1776). As a leader among the Mohawks, Pluggy took a band of unorganized, undisciplined followers westward and settled at Pluggy's Town, at the present site of Delaware, Ohio, 25 miles north of Columbus. Pluggy took part in the French and Indian War, and he counseled with Lord Dunmore at Fort Pitt in September 1774, just before the climactic battle at Point Pleasant, West Virginia, which concluded Dunmore's War. Hodge reported that Pluggy's followers were, or seemed to be, "chiefly Mingo," but this lacks support elsewhere. Pluggy's people were inveterate raiders. In October 1776 it was reported that Pluggy and his band "is gon for Centuck." This party attacked near the lower Blue Licks on Christmas Day, some whites bringing sorely needed gunpowder to Boonesborough, Harrodsburg and McCleland's Station, the only three sites not evacuated by settlers who had fled Kentucky because of persistent Indian raiding. Two whites were killed, including John Gabriel Jones, the leader and with George Rogers Clark a delegate from Kentucky to the Virginia legislature; two others were captured. Four days later the raiders struck McClellan's Station, the present Georgetown north of Lexington. Pluggy was killed and the attack thereupon faded away.

Thwaites/Kellogg, *The Revolution on the Upper Ohio, 1775-1777*, Madison, Wis. Hist. Soc., 1908; Hodge, HAI.

Pocatello, (White Plume), Shoshoni chief (c. 1815-Oct. 1884). B. in the Grouse Creek area of northwestern Utah, he became known in maturity as a Bannock Creek Shoshoni of southern Idaho. In time he developed into the most powerful chief of the Northwestern Shoshoni. The first written mention of Pocatello was an August 11, 1857, journal entry by Mormon Indian agent Dimmick B. Huntington (see entry), calling him Koctallo; two years later Frederick W. Lander (see entry) wrote of him as Pocataro. Of all Pocatello's observers, probably Lander came closest to understanding the proud young chief and called him the "White Plume" in recognition of "his supremacy over his followers." The chief always referred to himself as Tonaioza. When he was a youth the horse was introduced into his country, altering in many ways the Indian lifestyle. In about 1847 Pocatello became headman of Kuiya, a small village near Lynn and Yost in the Grouse Creek Valley. Within a few years his influence extended as far east as the present Kelton, north of Salt Lake. By 1857 when he first appears in written records he controlled the region of Bannock Creek, the bend of the Portneuf River and the area around the present Pocatello, Idaho. "It was a remarkable rise to power by one so young...his leadership qualities and his willingness to challenge the Mormon settlers and the emigrant trains" becoming evident. Brigham Young met so far as possible the Indian fear of white aggresion by supplying Pocatello's people with partial rations, but unrest continued to rise, not only because of Mormon population expansion but also due to friction generated by emigrants thronging the overland trails. Depredations on both sides became more commonplace. Young had been named superintendent of Indian affairs and by the time he concluded this duty in 1857 Pocatello had evolved into "prominence as the aggressive and dangerous leader of the Northwestern Shoshoni band who controlled the California and Salt Lake trails..." Although Pocatello was cleared of involvement in certain depredations against emigrants, he undoubtedly was implicated in incidents near Massacre Rocks, southwest of American Falls, and the City of Rocks, farther southwest. A number of whites were killed or wounded in these actions, and much property and livestock lost. "Pocatello's well-organized and unremitting attacks at City of Rocks and Massacre Rocks in August 1862 were a forceful sign of the Indian leader's anger and frustration over the mounting emigrant intrusion into his homeland...But it was a last-gasp effort to stem the tide of white incursion." The chief and his people avoided Connor's Bear River massacre January 29, 1863, of Chief Bear Hunter (see entry) and hundreds of his followers, but Connor announced plans to seek Pocatello out along with other Shoshonis who had eluded his operation. The officer set out May 6, 1863, but he could not find the chief, who had moved with his followers to the upper Green River, Wyoming, and Connor returned to Salt Lake City May 30. Upon Pocatello's initiative Connor signed the Treaty of Box Elder July 30, 1863, the Chief X-ing the document first for the Indians; it was signed by Utah Governor James Duane Doty (see entry) and Connor for the whites. The treaty finally established peace along the trails and provided compensation to the Indians for emigrants' destruction of game in their country, and other Shoshoni needs. Doty and Connor recognized Pocatello as the most important of northwestern Shoshoni chiefs by designating the precise boundaries of his homeland. Patrick Connor had Pocatello arrested in October 1863 on an allegation of theft and other misdeeds leveled by stagecoach impressario Ben Holladay, but the latter quickly withdrew his complaint; Potatello was turned over to Utah Indian Superindentent O.H. Irish who immediately released him, having learned that the Shoshonis understood Connor planned to hang their chief and had fled to the mountains to prepare for war, an eventuality Irish was determined to avoid. The chief gradually became friendly with the whites in his area and neighboring regions. June 14, 1867, the Fort Hall, Idaho, reservation was established and Pocatello and about 200 of his followers soon arrived there, although the chief continued his "wanderings through the Mormon settlements of Northern Utah," and any untoward incident that occurred when he was in, or suspected to be in, the vicinity was attributed to him, often without justification. Aging and weary, the chief returned permanently to the Fort Hall Reservation in 1876. He took no known part in the Nez Perce campaign of 1877, or the subsequent Bannock and Sheepeater conflicts. Judge Walter Taylor Oliver from Virginia, now settled ten miles above American Falls, left an account of the death and burial of Pocatello. The decease occurred on Bannock Creek and interment was in the waters of the Snake River. The city of Pocatello, Idaho (population c. 50,000), is named for the chief.

Brigham D. Madsen, *Chief Pocatello the "White Plume,"* Salt Lake City, Univ. of Utah Press, 1986; HNAI, 11; Charles J. Kappler, *Indian Treaties 1778-1883,* N.Y., Interland Pub. Co., 1972.

Polutov, Dmitry, Russian fur collector (fl. 1772-1783). Polutov, captain of the *Arkhangel Sv Mikhail,* was a prominent fur man in the early development of Alaska, although he was notably cruel toward the natives. His ship, the property of Feodor Kholodilof, sailed from Bolsheretsk in southwestern Kamchatka September 8, 1772, with a crew of 63. The vessel reached Unalaska Island in the Aleutian chain, where Polutov remained two years, adding constantly to his reputation for brutality and ruthlessness. The Aleuts complained bitterly of the treatment they received from him to government inspectors investigating reports of such excesses on June 7, 1789, some years after Polutov was killed. Polutov proceeded to Kodiak Island, anchoring probably in Ugak Bay. The natives, however, would have nothing to do with him and he finally wintered on Atka Island, midway in the Aleutian chain, the following year returning to Nizhne Kamchatsk, on the east coast of Kamchatka. He had brought a very rich cargo, including 3,720 sea otter skins and numerous pelts of other species. Polutov visited Kodiak Island again in 1776. In 1783 he, along with Potap Zaikov and Eustrate Delarov (see entries) attempted to expand Russian trading to the mainland, reaching Prince William Sound July 27, anchoring first at Kayak Island, then extending exploratory cruises into the Sound itself and shortly coming into hostile contact with the Chugach (Chugachigmiut) Eskimos who proved fiercer and more determined fighters than the Aleuts, showing little fear of Russian guns and whipped the invaders in several small engagements. Nevertheless, the predatory Russians persisted, stole women from any unprotected villages they came across and committed barbarities, as was not infrequently their custom. Only Zaikov showed restraint, but Polutov was a notorious raider. In 1790 a woman who had once been forcibly detained by Polutov (although she praised Zaikov as a just man) related to Martin Sauer,

Billings's secretary, how the natives won their revenge. A wood-cutting party had been sent ashore from each ship and pitched their tents close to one another. In the darkness natives crawled up, dispatched the lone sentry and then, stealing into Polutov's tent, massacred him and his companions without molesting Zaikov's tent or his people. The woman spoke of numerous complaints against Polutov, who had stolen their furs without paying for them and forcibly carried off many women.

Bancroft, *Alaska; Russian Penetration of the North Pacific Ocean.*

Ponce, Chihennes Apache chiefs (fl. 19th century). There were two chiefs of record of this name, father and son. Two individuals named Ponce are listed in the 1876 census of the Ojo Caliente Reservation of New Mexico: Ponce Grande and Ponce Chiquito, but "Ponce Grande" may well be the son of the original Chief Ponce, and "Ponce Chiquito" could be a son of Ponce Grande and thus a grandson of the original. Nothing further is reported of Ponce Chiquito. The second prominent Ponce was believed by Sweeney to have been born around 1840. The elder Ponce in 1850 was one of three major chiefs of the Gila (Mimbres) Apaches, his peers being Mangas Coloradas and Delgadito, as reported by Bartlett. This Ponce's chieftainship covered that territory from the Burro Mountains east to the Rio Grande and northward to the Santa Barbara Valley, 100 miles above El Paso. Ponce and Delgadito, Bartlett reported, were "men of more than ordinary character, intellect and influence and seem reasonable and practicable in their views and expectations." Howard reported in 1872 that the younger Ponce's "father had been in his [own] lifetime Cochise's friend," which may explain Thomas Jefford's remark that as a result young Ponce was "a favorite friend of the old man," or Cochise. Howard's description of the elder Ponce would seem to imply that he was a near-contemporary of Cochise and perhaps of about the same age, Cochise having been born around 1810. The place of the birth of either Ponce must have been in southwestern New Mexico. Cremony, writing of c. 1851, told of nearly shooting for an antelope a boy hunter disguised as such, the youngster turning out to be "the son of Ponce, a chief," who at the time was an important counselor to Mangas Coloradas. This Chief Ponce and Cremony came into dispute over whether Cremony should be sole interpreter at Apache discussions with Bartlett, which suggests Ponce's lack of confidence in Cremony's ability as a linguist. According to Cremony's record of the meeting, however, Ponce displayed by his remarks his logic, forcefulness of address, and outspoken views toward white intrusion into Apache country. Ponce the elder signed with his "X" the Provisional Compact of 1853, negotiated at Fort Webster on the Mimbres River by William Carr Lane, governor and superintendent of Indian Affairs for New Mexico and, for the Apaches, by Ponce, Victorio, Cuchillo Negro, Delgadito and others. Cremony suggested Ponce was killed by California troops during the Civil War, but Sweeney suggests that the elder Ponce was killed in the early 1850s. The younger Ponce becomes prominent during the period of General Howard's negotiations with Cochise in 1872. Howard described this Ponce as "a thick-set, pleasant-visaged young Indian" who also was "intelligent, speaking Spanish with readiness—a big-hearted, lazy fellow in camp, but quick enough on a scout or a hunt." Sweeney wrote that Ponce had "a tendency to stutter," and spent much time in northern Mexico. His physical build and speech impediment may have caused some to confuse him with the famous Nedhni chief, Juh, but his lack of even a wisp of military genius, which Juh possessed abundantly, should readily clear up that misapprehension. Eve Ball reported that Ace Daklugie, son of Juh, said that his father had often spoken of young Ponce as a "trusted warrior." Because of his strong friendship with Cochise, and the chief's confidence in his integrity, Ponce proved invaluable as a guide for Howard to the Cochise camp in the Dragoon Mountains of Arizona where Howard's mission proved successful (see Howard, Cochise entries). In 1877 Ponce, by now associated with Geronimo, was arrested with that war leader at Ojo Caliente and was taken with the rest of the Mimbres Apaches to Arizona's San Carlos Reservation, a place they hated and bolted as quickly as they could. No report has been uncovered defining when, where and under what circumstances Ponce met his death, but Sweeney believed it occurred shortly after the 1877 emeute from San Carlos.

LR, OIA, 1824-81, microfilm roll 546, NM Superintendency B81, John R. Bartlett to Alex H.A. Stuart, Feb. 19, 1852; John C. Cremony, *My Life Among the Apaches*, Glorieta, New Mex., Rio Grande Press, 1969; O.O. Howard, *My Life and Experiences Among Our Hostile Indians*, Hartford, Conn., A.D. Worthington &

Co., 1907; Howard, *Famous Indian Chiefs I Have Known*, N.Y. Century Co., 1908; Edwin R. Sweeney, *Cochise: Chiricahua Apache Chief*, Norman, Univ. of Okla. Press, 1991; Eve Ball to author, April 15, 1972.

Ponting, Tom Candy, cattleman (Aug. 26, 1824-Oct. 11, 1916). B. near Radstock, Somerset, England, his father was a "cattle grazer," so Tom came by his profession early. Three of the nine Ponting children migrated to America, and Tom, at 23, went in 1847 to Columbus, Ohio. In 1846 Edmund Piper (see entry), with the first herd of Texas Longhorns brought to the upper United States, took them to a range, probably a few miles south of Columbus. Whether Ponting met Piper or not, he could not have failed to have heard of this novel livestock experiment. He may well have visited the place where Piper in 1847 was fattening his stock, and he would take earnest and lasting note of the affair. In 1848 Ponting went to Milwaukee, where he sold cattle for a local firm, then entered business for himself. His capital amounted to $125 brought from England and $45 he had saved thus far in America, and he spent the latter for a mare, trading her for nine heifers which he sold for $90, thus doubling his initial investment. He then engaged in buying stock, camping out as he moved from place to place in the fenceless and lightly-settled Middle West. In 1849 he reached the future Champaign, Illinois, then an open plain with no inhabitants. He sold calves and lean cows to emigrants, and fat cows to butchers, and in 1850 settled in Christian County, southwest of Decatur and Macon County. There were no banks, and he carried his finances in large silver dollars in his saddlebags. By this time he had found a partner, Washington Malone, and they acquired a wagon, two yoke of oxen, and got on well with what settlers they came across. During his peregrinations he probably met Piper, perhaps for the second time, who, by 1853, was living in the Decatur area where he had become a livestock agent. Piper may have refreshed Ponting's awareness of the earlier exploit, and that same year he and Malone went south through Missouri, Arkansas and Indian Territory to north Texas. In Fannin County Ponting and Malone obtained 350 steers (Gard wrote "about 700 head") and 45 horses and started them north. Ponting's later narrative was praised by Dobie, who noted that accounts of Texas cattle drives before 1870 are few, and Ponting's was one of the first. The herd was driven to Illinois and wintered on the 1,100-acre farm Ponting had established. "This was the first experiment in Texas cattle, none having been previously seen" in that portion of Illinois. In June 1854 about 150 head were "started for New York. An old ox with a bell was led ahead, and the strangers from Texas followed behind. At the Wabash [River] the ox was...ferried over, and the [cattle] swam across in good order behind. At Muncietown, Indiana, they were shipped on board [railroad] cars. They created a great sensation on their arrival at New York. Their long horns fixed attention...When it was discovered that they were from Texas, people were astonished. Solon Robinson interviewed Mr. Ponting, and published a long account...in the New York *Tribune*," on July 4. The story said that it cost $2 a head to trail the cattle from Texas to Illinois, and $17 a head to bring them on to New York where they sold for up to $80 a head. The newspaper added that the stock were 5 to 7 years old, "long-legged with long taper horns and something of a wild look," and they did not appeal much to New York epicurean tastes, although that might improve had they been fattened longer in the Midwest. Another newspaper said that they were "barely able to cast a shadow," and they probably "would not weigh anything were it not for their horns." But the drive was profitable and until the Civil War others followed, although not by Ponting. The 1857 financial crash swept away all Ponting's means and "left him $20,000 worse off then nothing," but within a few years he had paid all his debts. He continued to handle Texas cattle bought at Abilene, Kansas, then switched his attention to stock from Colorado, Oregon and Montana, finally taking up the breeding of Shorthorns. He had been raised in a part of England where Herefords were common and retained his admiration for that stock. In 1879 he introduced the breed to his section of Illinois, believing them superior to Shorthorns as "making more pounds of beef to a less quantity of corn." Ponting had married the former Margaret Snyder in 1856 and they had three sons, his widow and sons surviving him. He died at 92 years of age at a Decatur hospital and was buried at Moweaqua, fifteen miles south of Decatur.

Ponting death cert.; info. from Decatur Geneal. Soc. Rsrch. Comm.; Ponting, *Life of Tom Candy Ponting* (1907), Evanston, Ill., Branding Iron Press, 1952; Wayne Gard, *The Chisholm Trail* (1954), Norman, Univ. of Okla. Press, 1976.

Pope, Saxton Temple, surgeon, archery enthu-

siast (Sept. 4, 1875-Aug. 8, 1926). He was b. in Texas, probably at Fort Stockton where his father, Benjamin Franklin Pope (1843-1902), was stationed as army assistant surgeon. Benjamin Pope ultimately attained the rank of colonel and following Civil War service was posted to a variety of frontier establishments from Dakota to Arizona; Saxton, who may have been named for brevet Brigadier General Rufus Saxton (1824-1908), thus grew up well acquainted with frontier life. He went to California around 1894 and by 1911 was instructor of surgery and research at the medical school of the University of California, San Francisco, from where he may earlier have graduated. That year Ishi (see entry), last Stone-Age Indian in the contiguous United States, was brought to live at the Museum of Anthropology adjacent to the Medical School, and Pope became Ishi's physician and closest friend, learning from him something of the Yahi language, and carefully mastering from the remarkable Indian such wilderness skills as the making of bows and stone arrowheads, fire by sticks, and all manner of customs, myths, knowledge and lore of this last of the Yahi (Yana) Indians. Pope began to practice with the bow under Ishi's guidance in 1912 and six years later published a detailed monograph on Yahi archery [Saxton Pope, *Yahi Archery,* Univ. of Calif. Pubs. in American Archaeology and Ethnology, Vol. 13, No. 3, 103-52, 1918]. Pope developed a "tremendous love and enthusiasm" for archery. He, writer Stewart Edward White and others became experts in using the bow and arrow in the pursuit of game, large and small, all under Ishi's direction. "In any attempt to understand the pursuits of war and the chase among prehistoric or aboriginal peoples, it is essential that we know how the [bow and arrow] works and what can be done with it. Pope's [writings] give us more of this information than any other source," wrote anthropologist Robert F. Heizer. "The best aboriginal flight arrows that Pope ever found...were those made by Ishi," and he also learned from the Indian of the superiority, in some respects, of obsidian arrow points over steel. Pope's and Ishi's doctor-patient relationship might have continued as such, but Pope "one day [saw] Ishi absorbedly fashioning a bow. He joined Ishi outside where he could observe him closely, and got Ishi to show him his shooting stance, his hold, and method of release...That same afternoon found the two of them practicing...and so began Pope's mastery of the art of the bow [which] was the passion of Pope's later years. Theirs…was a congenial and fruitful conjunction of temperaments and interests. It would be difficult…to say which of the two meant the most to the other." Ishi considered Popey, as he called him, "the brightest, the least predictable, and the most fascinating person in the world. He liked him very, very much," and was delighted to learn that Pope was an adept amateur magician, to Ishi, thereby, "a powerful shaman." Pope and Ishi "spent hours together, week after week, month after month. Together they spoke a pidgin Yana [Yahi] English all their own." They experimented with various types of bows in the museum collection and "lived in a happy communion in the Robin Hood world" of archery as a way of life. Ishi became fascinated with Pope's surgical skill, and often watched, through glass doors, intricate operations. Eventually Pope gave Ishi a white coat and spectator's mask and "took him into the operating room where, from the visitor's stand, he could see everything that happened." Kroeber continued that "Ishi watched Pope operate many, many times." Following Ishi's death from untreatable tuberculosis, Pope published *The Medical History of Ishi* [UC-PAA, Vol. 13, No. 5, 175-214, 1920]. Pope was ever-absorbed by the practical application of archery—in the hunt, for small or large game, and late in his life he and White undertook a hunting expedition to Tanganyika where they tested their skills and equipment against African big game. Pope wrote two books: *Hunting With the Bow and Arrow,* and *Bows and Arrows,* which was originally published as *A Study of Bows and Arrows* (1923) but has since been reprinted under the shorter title. Pope died at San Francisco of pneumonia less than a month before his 51st birthday. He was married and had fathered children.

Pope, *Hunting With the Bow & Arrow,* N.Y., G.P. Putnam's Sons (1923), 1925 with added chapter by Stewart Edward White; Pope, *Bows and Arrows,* Berkeley, Univ. of Calif. Press, 1962; Theodora Kroeber, *Ishi in Two Worlds,* Berkeley, 1961 (with Pope portrait between pp. 100-101), see esp. pp. 152-53; Robert P. Elmer, *Target Archery,* N.Y., Alfred A. Knopf, 1946, pp. 428-30; Heitman, Powell, for detail on Pope's father, Saxton Pope's death cert. (which errs by citing Benjamin Franklin Pope as B.H. Pope).

Porcupine Bear, Cheyenne chief, outlaw (fl. 1837-post 1900). A chief of the Cheyenne Dog Soldiers, Porcupine Bear was said by one historian to have been a son of Big Head, but this is unlikely to have been the famous Big Head; perhaps it was an earlier individual so named. Forty-two young warriors of the Bowstring Society in 1837 were overrun by mounted Kiowas and all were killed. When word reached the Cheyenne main encampment the problem was turned over to the Dog Soldiers, of which Porcupine Bear was first chief. He took up the war pipe and visited all the camps of the Cheyennes and Arapahoes (who were closely associated with the Cheyennes). Last of all he visited the camp of the Omissis (the Northern Cheyennes) on the South Platte. While he was there American Fur Company traders arrived with much liquor, and everyone proceeded to get drunk. Two of Porcupine Bear's cousins commenced fighting; the one getting the worst of it called repeatedly to Porcupine Bear to come to his assistance. The chief was singing war songs to himself, and was very drunk himself. When one of the young men tried to stab the other, Porcupine Bear in a rage seized the knife and stabbed the aggressor two or three times, then gave the weapon to the other and demanded that he finish off the wounded man, which he did. "For this deed Porcupine Bear and all his relations were outlawed by the tribe, and the Dog Soldier Society…was also disgraced." As the Cheyennes later moved south to find and engage the Kiowas in a revenge attack, Porcupine Bear, as an outlaw, gathered a camp of his own, made up mainly of his relations, and people treated as outcasts and not permitted to camp or move with the rest of the tribe, and went south apart. A large village of the Kiowas and Plains Apaches (or Kiowa Apaches) was located. Porcupine Bear and his outlaws were first to strike the enemy. Porcupine Bear with his lance knocked a Kiowa off of his mule, then rushed after others. He counted 20 coups in this battle and killed 12 Kiowas. The tribe did not recognize his magnificent deeds, since he was an outlaw, but everyone knew what he and his young men had done. Porcupine, the son of Porcupine Bear, was killed after doing great things and killing several of the enemy in this engagement. Porcupine Bear and his followers broke through ancient custom and changed themselves from a society of warriors (the Dog Soldiers) to a camp, or separate division of the tribe, and this arrangement apparently became permanent. In a later fight, around 1845, Porcupine Bear received the name of "Lame Shawnee," because a Delaware with whom the Cheyennes were fighting shot him through the thigh. He outlived the Plains wars and resided in his advanced years on a reservation, presumably in Oklahoma, where he became, according to George Bent, "our oldest man." Bent wrote to Hyde that Porcupine Bear had "recently died," but the date of the letter is not known, although the correspondence between Bent and Hyde commenced in 1905 and continued to around 1918 when George Bent died. Possibly it was in one of the early letters that Bent reported the death of Porcupine Bear.

George E. Hyde, *Life of George Bent,* Norman, Univ. of Okla. Press, 1968; George Bird Grinnell, *The Fighting Cheyennes,* Norman, 1956; Donald J. Berthrong, *The Southern Cheyennes,* Norman, 1963; info. from E.F. (Ted) Mains.

Porter, Eliot Furness, photographer, conservationist (Dec. 6, 1901-Nov. 2, 1990). B. at Winnetka, Illinois, he was graduated from Harvard in 1924 and earned an M.D. there in 1929, teaching biochemistry and bacteriology at Harvard and Radcliffe College from 1929 to 1939 and being associated with the Masschusetts Institute of Technology in 1943-44. He early became interested in natural history and photography, devoting himself full time to those pursuits from 1939. He became a pre-eminent color photographer of his day. His work was exhibited in some of the nation's foremost art galleries and photography salons, and appeared in many books. He received numerous honors. His books included: about Henry David Thoreau, *In Wildness is the Preservation of the World* (1962); *The Place No One Knew: Glen Canyon on the Colorado* (1963, 1966); *Forever Wild—The Adirondacks* (1966); *Summer Island: Penobscot Country* (1966); *Baja California—The Geography of Hope* (1967); *Galapagos...The Flow of Wildness* (1968); *Appalachian Wilderness* (1970); *Birds of North America—A Personal Selection* (1972), and *Antarctica.* He also co-authored *Down the Colorado* (1969), and *The Tree Where Man Was Born—An African Experience* (1972). He was divorced from his first wife, having fathered two sons, and had three sons by his second wife, who survived him. He had made his home at Tesuque, New Mexico, just north of Santa Fe, since the mid-1940s and died at Santa Fe from complications from amyotrophic lateral sclerosis, or "Lou Gehrig's disease."

Contemporary Authors; *Who's Who in America.*

Posey, Thomas, military officer, politican (July 9, 1750-Mar. 19, 1818). B. in Fairfax County, Virginia, he moved at 19 to Augusta County and served in the French and Indian War. At the outbreak of the Revolution he was commissioned a captain and served under Washington, Morgan and Gates. Afterward he moved to Spotsylvania County, Virginia, where he served as county lieutenant from 1786 to 1793. He was a Brigadier General under Anthony Wayne in preparing his expedition against the Middle Western Indians. Afterward he removed to Kentucky where he was in the state senate, was acting lieutenant governor and was Major General of militia after 1809. He moved to Attakapas, Louisiana, and was appointed to fill a vacancy in the United States Senate, serving from October 8, 1812, to February 4, 1813. He then was appointed governor of Indiana Territory from 1813-16, when he became Indian agent. He died at Shawneetown, Illinois.

BDAC; DAB; Thwaites, *Dunmore.*

Potochkin, explorer (fl. 1798-1799). An early explorer of the Copper River of Alaska, he set out September 12, 1798, from Nuchek to travel up the stream, accompanied by natives in their baidarkas. They reached the mouth of the river September 23, and went upstream as far as ice permitted. They continued by land because even above the ice the swiftness of the river made baidarkas progress impossible. By October they had reached native villages where a chief, Nakulasta, lived and took a census of that and other populated sites. They continued past the confluence of the Copper and Bremner rivers. They spent the early part of the winter at a village, learned that eight days farther there were copper deposits, and four days upstream they reached the village of Kalakhis, a local chief. After listing the people there they returned, leaving January 10, 1799, for the homeward journey. No further word has been located of this adventure.

Pierce, *Russian America: A Biographical Dictionary.*

Powell, Donald M., historian (May 25, 1914-Oct. 29, 1987). B. at Yonkers, New York, he was graduated from Swarthmore College, received a master's degree from Duke University in 1938, and earned a library science degree in 1942 from the University of Michigan. He served to master sergeant in the army from 1942-45, arrived in Arizona in 1946 and joined the University of Arizona's library department, where he worked for 32 years. He headed the library's reference department for 18 years and directed its Special Collections Department from 1973 until his retirement in 1977. In 1957 he served six months with the College of Agriculture at Abu Ghrabe, Iraq, as a library consultant. His writings included: *The Peralta Grant: James Addison Reavis and the Barony of Arizona* (1960); *An Arizona Gathering* (1960); *Arizona Fifty* (1961); edited John Marion's *Notes of Travel Through the Territory of Arizona* (1965); *New Mexico and Arizona in the Serial Set, 1846-1861* (1970); *Arizona Gathering II* (1973), and edited John Ross Browne's *Adventures in the Apache Country* (1974). He died at Tucson.

Tucson, *Arizona Daily Star,* Nov. 1, 1987; *Contemporary Authors.*

Power, Thomas Jefferson, frontiersman (d. Feb. 10, 1918). Power, from Texas, was the father of Thomas Jefferson Power Jr. (1893-1970), and John Grant Power (1891-1976), who was b. in Grant County, New Mexico. The three Power men went to the Klondyke, Arizona, region in 1909. Seven years later they took over a poorly-paying gold mine in Kielberg Canyon, in the Galiuro Mountains south of Klondyke and a good day's horseback ride from the small community. "This was still the frontier," wrote Cowgill. "The Apache Kid was more of a threat...than the German Kaiser," and the Power young men were alleged by some to have been draft dodgers, unenthusiastic about a war in Europe. Perhaps because of this their wilderness cabin was besieged on February 10, 1918, by Graham County Sheriff Robert McBride, deputies Martin Kempton and Kane Wootan and U.S. Deputy Marshal Frank Hayes. Inside the cabin, besides the three Powers, was Tom Sisson, described as "an old Army scout." A shootout erupted. Tom Jefferson Sr. was killed, as were Sheriff McBride and the two deputies. Tom Power Jr., John Power and Sisson escaped to Mexico, then returned to face trial at Safford, Arizona, and all three were sentenced to life in prison. Sisson died in confinement at Florence, Arizona, in 1957. Tom and John Power were pardoned by Governor Paul Fannin after 42 years incarceration on April 27, 1960. Tom died in 1970 and John in 1976, both as free men. The whole affair was highly controversial, for the Powers had many friends—and many enemies—in the region. Supporters believed they were victims of vengeful law enforcement; detractors tended to think the men were "little more than

mean-spirited murderers." The Powers "had a reputation for shooting first and asking questions later," according to Cowgill. "From the law enforcement viewpoint the shootout was a failure since three of the four officers were killed. And three of the four suspects escaped custody." Their log cabin suffered vast neglect in the 70 years following the famous affair, but was restored through the efforts of E.D. (Bud) McBryde, a Pinal County superior court judge who recruited acquaintances, made a horseback trip to the site and decided "it was a shame that the cabin was going to pot. [It] was in the wilderness but we wanted to see if we could preserve it. There's an awful lot of history there..." They packed in supplies and with help from 19 people an estimated 654 hours were spent on reconstruction. It now stands in about the shape it was in on that February morning in 1918.

Pete Cowgill, *Arizona Daily Star,* May 18, 1990 (with photographs and map); Tom Power, *Shootout at Dawn,* Phoenix, Phoenix Books, 1980; Darvil B. McBride, *The Evaders,* Pasadena, Calif. Pacific Book and Printing Co., 1984; info. from E.F. (Ted) Mains.

Prat, Pedro (Pierre), surgeon (d.c. 1771). Of French origin, he was a royal army surgeon in 1769 and sailed from San Blas to La Paz, Baja California, aboard the *San Carlos,* leaving January 9, 1769, for Upper California and arriving at San Diego Bay April 29, with all the ship's company, including Dr. Prat, suffering from scurvy. The surgeon remained at San Diego doing medical work while the Portolá expedition went north to Monterey. He treated Juan Vizcaino's hand, wounded in an Indian attack in August 1769 and cared for others suffering from scurvy and various ailments. April 16, 1770, Prat sailed for Monterey aboard the *San Antonio* with Junípero Serra and others. The ship arrived May 31, and the mission and presidio of San Carlos Borromeo de Monterey were founded June 3. Bancroft said that Prat died in California sometime in 1772-73, but Ives wrote that shortly after reaching Monterey he "lost his reason and was sent back to the mainland of Mexico where he died apparently in 1771,"

Bancroft, *California,* I; Ronald L. Ives, *José Velásquéz: Saga of a Borderland Soldier,* Tucson, Ariz., Southwestern Mission Research Ctr., 1984.

Pratt, John Francis, Coast and Geodetic Survey officer (1848-1929). Pratt commanded the steamer *Patterson* in Alaskan waters and in

1898-99 had general supervision of all Coast and Geodetic Survey parties in the Bering Sea. He directed surveys of the lower Yukon River and St. Michael Harbor on Norton Sound. In 1902 he took soundings in the Bering Sea adjacent to St. Lawrence Island and in 1903 took Pacific Ocean soundings from the entrance of Juan de Fuca Strait to Cape St. Elias preparatory to laying a deep-sea cable. In 1904 Pratt was in charge of a survey of the Kiska Island region in the western Aleutians.

Orth, 26, 776.

Pratt, Richard Henry, military officer, educator (Dec. 6, 1840-Mar. 15, 1924). B. at Rushford, New York, his parents took him as a child to Logansport, Indiana, where he received some education before he had to work because his father had been robbed and murdered returning from the California gold fields. Richard Pratt became an apprentice tinsmith. He enlisted as a corporal in the 9th Indiana Infantry April 20, 1861, serving until July 29; he became a sergeant in the 2nd Indiana Cavalry September 18, was commissioned a first lieutenant of the 11th Indiana Cavalry April 20, 1864, becoming a captain September 1. He was commissioned a second lieutenant of the 10th U.S. Cavalry March 7, 1867, and a first lieutenant July 31 that year. He participated in winter campaigns against the Cheyennes, Comanches and Kiowas in 1868-69, and again on the southern Plains in 1874-75, a minor "war," in which only eight servicemen lost their lives, but many Indian prisoners were taken. Pratt, who was becoming interested in Indians while performing military duties, was placed in charged of Indians seized and escorted 72 ironed captives from Fort Sill April 28, 1875, to the East coast. Eventually they arrived at Fort Marion, near St. Augustine, Florida. Here, as months passed, Pratt cared for his charges, found work for them to do, and discovered a willingness on the part of younger Indians to learn. Thus he commenced his program of education for them in English and in white man's ways. Government assistance was almost completely absent, but Pratt bombarded with letters legislators at Washington, government officials and all others able to help. At last he was authorized to begin to educate Indians with 22 pupils to start, their place of learning a previously all-black school. Through assistance from private sources and individual benefactors, Pratt eventually obtained use of facilities at Carlisle Barracks, Pennsylvania, for

an "all-Indian school" and by the Army Appropriation Bill of 1878 was detailed permanently to Indian education pursuits. The system he put into place emphasized such handicrafts as wagon making, upholstery, tinsmithing, shoe repairing, tailoring and blacksmithing for the boys, and housekeeping, cooking and nursing for the girls; enrollment at length reached 1,000. However, the Indian students seemed to suffer inordinately from such white diseases as tuberculosis and other disorders, and Indian parents were often reluctant to permit their children to attend the boarding school where the death toll remained high. Yet Carlisle School became famed for, among other things, its athletic programs and the prowess of such students as Jim Thorpe, since acclaimed as America's finest athlete of the first 50 years of this century. Congress established more Indian schools, copying the teaching system used by Pratt at Carlisle Barracks. The officer meanwhile had been promoted regularly: to captain, February 17, 1883; to major of the 1st Cavalry July 1, 1898; lieutenant colonel of the 14th Cavalry February 2, 1901, and to colonel of the 13th Cavalry January 24, 1903. He was retired February 17, 1903, and promoted to Brigadier General April 23, 1904. On July 1, 1904, he was relieved of the superintendency of the Carlisle School, where in 25 years he had seen 5,000 Indian boys and girls from 70 tribes pass through the educational system he devised. Pratt "believed that the solution of the Indian problem did not lie [in preserving or developing] Indian culture but was rather in teaching the individual Indian to make a place for himself in the white man's world." His philosophy thus was completely at odds with that of the later John Collier, who saw in recovery and retention of Indian culture the means to restore and reinvigorate Indian pride in background and history and thus give them the self-respect to leverage them into creating a worthwhile lifestyle for themselves. But Pratt preceded Collier by two generations, and in his time found a warm reception among many whites for his philosophy of guiding the Indian into an alien culture. Following his retirement Pratt continued to advocate citizenship for Indians and to discuss Indian policy. He died at the army hospital in San Francisco. He was married and fathered four children. He was well over 6 ft. tall and weighed some 200 pounds.

Heitman; DAB; Angie Irons, "Richard Henry Pratt: 'That Indian-loving Pest,'" *True West,* Vol. 35, No. 12 (Dec. 1988), 28-32, 37.

Preston, Guy Henry, military officer (May 29, 1864-Dec. 12, 1952). B. in Masschusetts he went to West Point and became a second lieutenant of the 9th Cavalry July 16, 1888, a first lieutenant of the 4th Cavalry February 25, 1896, and transferred back to the 9th March 14. In 1898 he was a member of the expedition of W.R. Abercrombie (see entry) to Alaska, where his principal activity was an attempt to explore a route across Valdez Glacier, near Port Valdez on the south coast. He spent about a month trying to get supplies and men over the glacier, but found it very difficult in May to do this, particularly without pack animals. When Abercrombie left for the States to purchase pack stock, Preston took over command of the expedition. July 8 he was ordered relieved from duty in Alaska and rejoined his regiment in the States. He was promoted to captain February 2, 1901, major of the 4th Cavalry February 29, 1912, lieutenant colonel of the 6th Cavalry July 1, 1916, and colonel May 15, 1917. He became a Brigadier General April 16, 1918, and saw brief service in France during World War I.

Heitman; Cullum; *Who Was Who; Narratives of Explorations in Alaska.*

Preuss, Charles, topographer (1803-Sept. 1, 1854). B. in Germany he became a surveyor and draftsman for the Prussian government, emigrating to the United States in 1834 and joining the U.S. Coast Survey. He met John Charles Fremont (see entry) in 1841 through the survey director Ferdinand R. Hassler. Fremont described Preuss as "a strange figure—a shock of light curly hair standing up thick about his head, and a face so red that we attributed it to a wrong cause instead of to the cold and the nervousness and anxiety which turned his speech into stammering." Fremont "sat him down by the fire," upon the initial meeting, on a chilly pre-Christmas evening. He added that "This was the beginning of our long friendly comradeship [and his] years of faithful and valuable service as topographer on my journeys, during which his even temper and patient endurance of hardship earned my warm regard." He found that Preuss also had a "cheerful philosophy of his own which often brightened dark situations," although at least one recent Fremont scholar found Preuss a rather "grumpy," if gifted, cartographer. Preuss accompanied Fremont on the explorer's first two expeditions; he did numerous sketches and a fine map for the report of the second one, Carl Wheat, a

ranking specialist on trans-Mississippi maps and mapping, calling it "a monument of western cartography." It was widely depended upon for years. On one occasion, accompanying Fremont from the crest of the Sierra Nevada toward Sutter's Fort on the Sacramento River, Preuss became lost for three days and was "reduced to eating raw frogs to sustain himself," which perhaps was when he turned grumpy. Upon his return to Washington, Preuss had the means to acquire "a comfortable home of his own" and converted its large front room into a study where he could work on sketches or maps as he wished; it was there he completed the extraordinary map. He turned down an invitation to join Fremont's third expedition, largely because of his wife's objections, since she had "worried enough about her husband [on the first two operations] and wanted no more of it." However, he was persuaded by Fremont to join the latter's disastrous fourth expedition (1848-49) in which an attempt was made to cross the southern Colorado Rockies in winter, an effort that cost the lives of eleven men, including that of the famous guide, Old Bill Williams (see entry). Preuss blamed Williams for the disaster, although unfairly, since Williams had warned Fremont against attempting to cross the mountains in that season, and was making a heroic attempt to bring assistance to the marooned expedition when he was killed. Once the bitter season was past, the expedition reached California, Preuss with it. He performed surveying projects in California and returned to Washington about 1850. He refused in 1853 to accompany Fremont on a fifth expedition and instead joined one of the Pacific Railroad surveys. On his return to Washington he became ill and "in desperation hanged himself from a tree," the suicide perhaps related to a "morose and melancholy strain in his personality," as Erwin Gudde, a translator of his diaries from German to English, suspected.

REAW; Fremont, *Narratives of Exploration and Adventure,* ed. by Allan Nevins, N.Y., Longmans, Green & Co., 1956; Robert V. Hine [who wrote the REAW sketch], *Edward Kern and American Expansion,* New Haven, Yale Univ. Press, 1962; info. from Andrew Rolle.

Pribylov, Gerassim Loginovich, discoverer (d. 1796). Among the noteworthy promyshlenniki seafarers of the 18th century, Pribylov and Gavriil (Gavrilo) Pribylov, who may have been his brother, were active in the Bering Sea, among the Aleutian Islands and in southern Alaska. Nothing is certainly reported of their early lives and careers, although one legend is that Gerassim was a peasant's son, another that his father had served under Bering on one of his expeditions. He became a master in the Russian navy, connected with the Siberian port of Okhotsk, but in 1778 entered the employ of the fur company of Lebedev-Lastochin and for several years before 1786 hunted and traded through the Aleutian Islands with little profit, even though a skilled navigator. In 1786 he became the European discoverer of record of the first of four seal islands that now bear his name (see Igadik entry) and are among the economically most valuable sites in the sub-Arctic. The voyage of the sloop *Sv Georgiy* had been fitted out by the company and presumably was to search for islands by repute already known to the Aleuts as rich in fur bearers. Pribylov left Illiuliuk harbor on Unalaska in early summer and June 25, raised an island, naming it St. George after his vessel's patron saint. On June 29, 1787, the party first saw another major island of the group 30 miles to the north of St. George and rarely visible from it; it, too, was rich in fur animals and was named St. Paul. These Russians' repute as its discoverers was thrown into doubt by discovery on St. Paul of the brass hilt and trimming of a sword, a clay pipe, and remains of a fire; obviously some adventurer had been there before Pribylov. He found the entire archipelago so thickly populated with fur bearers that he left 20 Russians and 20 Aleuts to hunt. In two years they secured more than 2,000 sea otter pelts, 40,000 fur seals, 6,000 blue foxes, 36,000 pounds of walrus tusks and 18,000 pounds of walrus whiskers, the total worth 253,018 rubles ($126,504), one of the richest of recorded fur cargoes. The United States has possessed the islands since the 1867 purchase of Alaska and manages the controlled annual take of seals, the proceeds divided among this country, Canada, Japan and the Soviet Union. Pribylov served on the Joseph Billings (see entry) expedition aboard the *Slava Rossie* of Gavriil Sarychev and with others of the vessel's company was "doomed to pass a wretched winter" in Illiuliuk Bay in 1791-92, scurvy proving a disastrous challenge. The ship reached Avatcha Bay, Kamchatka, June 16, 1792. Baranov had decided upon Pribylov to head an expedition from Kodiak to found Novo Arkhangelsk (now Sitka) in the summer of 1796, but Pribylov died shortly before the undertaking commenced.

Fredericka Martin, *Sea Bears: The Story of the Fur Seal,* N.Y., Chilton Co., 1960; Bancroft, *Alaska,* 191-93; Zagoskin; *Russian Penetration of the North Pacific Ocean;* CE.

Price, Stan, Alaska bear man (Nov. 4, 1900-Dec. 5, 1989). B. in Missouri, he spent his young manhood traveling about the West repairing generating equipment for the Westinghouse Electric Corporation. He then decided "to try his luck" in Alaska and in 1927, having built a 40-foot sailboat at Seattle, made his way to Windham Bay, on the east coast of Admiralty Island, at present a national monument. For 17 years he drilled 32 tunnels and "mined considerable gold," before moving on to Pack Creek, just north of the bay. His first wife died at the Sitka Pioneers' Home and in 1975 Price married again, this wife remaining seven years before departing for the mainland. After the site became a national monument and Tlingit Indians abandoned the area around 1953, the great Alaskan brown bears returned, primarily for the salmon fishing they followed in season. Stan and his first wife, Edna, raised a bear cub they had found, but after a couple of years it moved off into the wilderness; the Prices raised another cub and by 1971 she brought her two cubs to Pack Creek. The mother showed a slight remembrance of Stan's voice, but no other sign of recognition. Other females brought their cubs to the area "evidently because they feel safe there," and the bear population steadily increased. Price, in 60 years in Alaska, never felt the need to carry a gun. Only twice was he threatened by the bears: on one occasion he struck a threatening bear on the nose with his shovel, and on the second swatted a bear on the nose with his walking stick. In both instances the animal then lumbered off. When the salmon began their run in summer there often were as many as 25 brown bears at once in sight. The bears usually ignored human visitors (in the decade of the 1980s some 4,000 visitors overall came to observe the animals, with no person being injured, although Price always urged caution since the creatures have a deserved repute of being potentially very dangerous). Stan Price's garden supplied berries for himself—and also for the bears, which tended to ignore his three-strand electric fence until he scolded them into leaving either through the hole in the fence by which they entered or they "made a new one" to get out. In the early 1980s several media outlets featured Stan Price and his bears, and visitors increased until 1,000 came in a single season. Not all of them were quite welcome, however, especially not those who burdened themselves with weaponry or who "sometimes do very stupid things, such as throwing rocks at sleeping bears, yelling, splashing—anything to make the bears 'do something.'" Price well knew which of "his" bears were tolerant of visitors and which were not. As the grizzlies became accustomed to people they on occasion became nuisances, and wildlife managers sometimes sprayed a pesky one with a pepper mixture to discourage too much intimacy. The Forest Service and Alaska Department of Fish and Game in 1987 began restricting visitation at the Pack Creek Co-operative Management Area, as it now is named, and modest restrictions were placed on viewing the animals. At 90, Stan Price died at Juneau of cancer.

Aubrey Stephen (Steve) Johnson, "The Bear Man of Pack Creek," *Defenders,* Vol. 64, No. 6 (Nov./Dec. 1989), 22-28; *Defenders,* Vol. 65, No. 2 (Mar./Apr. 1990), 42; info. from Steve Johnson.

Prindle, Louis Marcus, geologist (1865-1956). A geologist for the Geological Survey from 1902 until 1935, he worked in Alaska as assistant to Alfred Brooks from 1902 until 1911 in exploration of the Mount McKinley area. Prindle spent each season in the Yukon-Tanana region and in parts of the Alaska Range. Mount Prindle in the White Mountains and Prindle Volcano near the head of Fortymile River were named for him.

Orth, 26, 778.

Puget, Peter, British naval officer (c. 1762-Oct. 31, 1822). Puget entered the Royal Navy as a midshipman August 1, 1778, and in 1786 went to the West Indies on the *Europa,* of which George Vancouver (see entry) was a lieutenant. In 1791 when Vancouver set out to explore the west coast of North America, Puget sailed with him as a second lieutenant of the *Discovery.* He later commanded the *Chatham* of the expedition. Puget was first to explore thoroughly the immense waterway now called Puget Sound, Washington, in April-May, 1791; Vancouver originally named only the head of the sound above Dana's Passage, Puget Sound. But popular use eventually extended the title to include the whole inlet as far as Bellingham Bay. Bancroft grumbled that "it is not correct to call these waters, in some places well nigh fathomless, by the name of sound, which implies shallowness, but there is no

withstanding custom and convenience." Puget also did "much of the detailed exploring and preliminary map-making in both British Columbia and Alaska," and Orth lists several geographical features named for the officer. Puget was promoted to captain after the ship's return to England in 1795, and commanded warships, at times in combat. He was knighted in 1815, became a rear admiral in 1821, and died at his home at London.

Pierce, *Russian America: A Biographical Dictionary;* Bancroft, *Washington, Idaho & Montana;* Orth, 781.

Pullen, R.J., British naval officer (fl. 1849). Pullen and Royal Navy lieutenant W.H. Hooper took a party of 25 men and four boats from the *Plover,* Commander T.E.L. Moore, on a voyage along the Arctic coast from Wainwright Inlet, Alaska, to Fort Simpson on the Mackenzie River. The operation continued from June 25 to October 3, 1849, and was the first such effort in the search for the lost Sir John Franklin expedition which ultimately was found to have come to grief in the archipelago north of Canada. Accounts by both Pullen and Hooper were published.

Orth, 13.

Purtov, Egor, fur hunter (fl. 1792-1795). A citizen of Irkutsk, Siberia, he became associated with Shelikhov by 1792 as one of the earliest Russian fur hunters in Alaska, and with other Russians and 170 baidarkas of Aleuts hunted in and near Chugach Bay, on the south coast of the Kenai Peninsula. The next season he hunted near Yakutat Bay where he had difficulty with stormy weather and from the Kolosh (Tlingit) Indians. Baranov wrote that "I feel indebted to Purtov and to his obedience. Thanks to him, we made this experiment in hunting beyond Cape [St.] Elias to the glory of the Empire, for Kinai [Kenai] Bay is almost hunted out." Cape St. Elias is at the southwestern end of Kayak Island, southeast of present Cordova. In May 1794 Purtov and others led 500 baidarkas, with two or three men to the boat, for Icy and Yakutat bays to hunt sea otters. The party returned by August and Purtov reported he had trouble with representatives of the Lebedev-Lastochkin Company (see entry) from Nuchek Island, but had killed about 500 otters. At Yakutat Bay they had encountered the British ship *Chatham* (Peter Puget, captain) and established cordial relations, the British adding their strength toward encouraging amicable relations with the

Indians of the coast. Archimandrite Ioasaf, in a letter to Shelikhov, gave a negative view of Purtov, as he did of practically everyone else he met, his opinion included in a letteer of May 18, 1795, the last reference to Purtov that Pierce has discovered.

Pierce, *Russian America: A Biographical Dictionary.*

Pushkarev, Gavriil, frontiersman (fl. 1741-1762). Listed occasionally as a Navy quartermaster or sometimes a sergeant of Cossacks, Pushkarev sailed with Bering in 1741 and weathered the "terrible winter" on Bering Island, being based thereafter at Okhotsk, Siberia. He believed that there must be undiscovered land to the south of Bering Island, since sea otters and fur seals from that place invariably disappeared to the south and it was believed that they never strayed far from land. This theory, however, came to nothing. He was assigned to accompany an Ivan Bechevin expedition which in 1760 left Bolsheretsk, southwestern Kamchatka, with Pushkarev aboard the *Gavril,* bound for the Aleutians. In January 1762 he and Nikofor Golodov landed on an unnamed island that may have been Unalaska and a series of bloody encounters with natives ensued, in one of which Golodov was killed, the affrays precipitated no doubt by Russian excesses. These included the kidnapping of 25 young women "under the pretext they were to be employed in picking berries and gathering roots for the ship's company." When Kamchatka was sighted a boat was sent ashore with six men and 14 of the girls. Two of them ran away and another was killed (Pushkarev himself was said to have accompanied the boat). In "a fit of despair" the other girls "threw themselves into the sea and were drowned. In order to rid himself of troublesome witnesses to this outrage, Pushkarev had all the remaining islanders thrown overboard" except for one boy and an interpreter. Reports of these atrocities reached the Okhotsk chancellery which issued an imperial ukase, acknowledging the "indescribable outrages and abuses on the inhabitants, and even...murder" and warned future expeditions "to see that no such barbarities, plunder and ravaging of women are committed under any circumstances," though such admonitions rarely proved weighty in controlling promyshlenniki activities in distant Alaska.

Bancroft, *Alaska; Russian Penetration of the North Pacific Ocean.*

Q

Queho, Southern Paiute Indian (d. pre-1940). Queho was characterized by Don Ashbaugh as "Nevada's No. 1 public enemy" who won his reputation by a series of depredations spread over nearly three decades. Queho first was suspected in the death of another Paiute during a tribal fight on a small reservation near Las Vegas. Shortly afterward he attacked one, Hi Bohn, at Las Vegas, breaking both his arms with a club before escaping "southward into the mountains." In November 1910 Queho killed two men in the El Dorado mining district along the Colorado River twenty miles south of present Hoover (Boulder) Dam; a posse found his tracks easy to identify since he had one leg shorter than the other, giving him a distinctive limp. The posse traced Queho to the Gold Bug Mill on the Arizona side of the river where he had slain a watchman, then disappeared once more. The Paiute's closest colleague, Long-haired Tom, told a posse that Queho was dead, but the report was in error. Nothing more was definitely heard of him until early January 1919 when his footprints were found near the bodies of two murdered miners in the Moapa Valley, northeast of Las Vegas. January 21, Mrs. Maude Douglas was shot and killed at the Techatticup Mine by a "mysterious assassin," whose tracks again implicated Queho. Rewards of $2,500 failed to secure the desperado, although it was learned that he occasionally holed up in a cave in the Black Canyon of the Colorado. November 27, 1927, a newspaper reported that Long-haired Tom's body had been found near the Colorado River and Deputy Sheriff I.W. Allcock thought he had died of snakebite. In 1940 two explorers found the mummified remains of an Indian in a Black Canyon cave, and Deputy Sheriff Frank Wait, who had trailed the Paiute as early as 1919, identified them as those of Queho because of the difference in the length of his legs. A legal battle ended with possession of the mummy by the Las Vegas Elks Lodge, where it was displayed for years.

Don Ashbaugh, *Nevada's Turbulent Yesterday,* Los Angeles, Westernlore Press, 1963.

R

Radin, Paul, anthropologist (Apr. 2, 1881-Feb. 21, 1959). B. at Lodz, Poland, the son of a rabbi, he was brought as an infant with his parents to Elmira, New York. He early acquired Latin, Greek and Hebrew, entered the City College of New York at 14 and was graduated in 1902 when he enrolled at Columbia to study zoology, later switched to history, and at Munich and Berlin studied anthropology. Back at Columbia he came under the influence of Franz Boas (see entry), earned his doctorate in 1911 and had come to know such famed scientists as A.L. Kroeber, Clark Wissler, Edward Sapir and Robert Lowie (see entries). He worked for two years at the Bureau of American Ethnology, then joined Sapir at the Geological Survey of Canada, where he studied the Ojibwa (Chippewa), and from 1908-13 worked among the Winnebago, the results of which included two of his early works of prominence: *Autobiography of a Winnebago Indian* (1920) and *The Winnebago Tribe* (1923, 1970), the manuscript of which was completed in 1916. Another of his best-known works was *Primitive Man as a Philosopher* (1927). At the University of California, Berkeley, Radin worked again with Kroeber and Lowie, cementing his friendship and relationship with them. From 1931 he became interested in the Penutian family of California, the five tribes covering about half of the state, centered on San Francisco Bay and the interior valleys. Radin, however, always linguistically-inclined, also developed interests in the immigrant Italians, the Spanish and Mexicans, and other minorities of the San Francisco region. He published regularly, including *The Story of the American Indian* (1927, 1934); *Social Anthropology* (1932); *Method and Theory of Ethnology* (1933) and *Primitive Religion* (1937). He published *Indians of South America* (1942), rounding out a work he had commenced with *The Story of the American Indian,* and in 1953 published *The World of Primitive Man,* similarly completing the work commenced in *Primitive Religion.* In 1941 he left Berkeley to join the faculty of Black Mountain College, east of Asheville, North Carolina, whose "experimental and unstructured nature appealed to him." He taught at various colleges and from 1949-57 lived and worked in Europe before returning to head the Department of Anthropology at Brandeis University at Waltham, Massachusetts. He died at New York City.

DAB; *Who Was Who.*

Rafferty, J.J., guide (fl. 1885-1898). An experienced and resolute frontiersman who led a small party of men at the direction of Captain William Abercrombie (see entry) into the Copper River country in late spring of 1898, he also had become acquainted with First Lieutenant Henry Allen (see entry) on Allen's famous exploration of parts of Alaska in 1885. On his 1898 trip great hardships were met with, Rafferty conquering them all to fulfill his difficult mission. "My instructions were to explore practicable routes or trails into the interior," he wrote in his report. "My starting point was Port Valdez [Alaska], which I left May 3," his party including W.E. Goodman Jr., Peter Harrington, John Curran and a soldier, C.H. Kuhlman, all Alaskan veterans. Equipped with three man-hauled "Yukon sleds," heavily laden, they were to cross Bates Glacier and Pass northeast of Valdez, then run down the Tasnuna River, crossing Copper River on the ice which should still be solid, then go up the Bremner River to its source, cross over to the headwaters of the Chettyna (Chitina) and work down that to the Copper again. Weather conditions made travel all but impossible at the start, but Rafferty got his party past swarms of prospectors to the summit of Bates Pass by May 6, where it was learned the snow was gone from the reverse slope so the sleds quickly became useless. Rafferty wrote that "it is my judgment that, if one goes properly prepared for the trip, many of the hardships could be avoided." The trail over the Pass was poorly laid out, the pitch sometimes so steep that a block and tackle had to be used to hoist loads and sleds up the grades. Ordinary clothing he found was superior to furs for wearing and comfort, while "waterproof" leather was useless and rubber shoes with leather uppers were preferable. Beyond the pass boats had to be built to carry the mission forward, despite a lack of proper tools for the work and little saw timber available. Klutina Lake was navigated despite heavy ice blocks and June 1 the party started down the Klutina River, the outlet for the lake, but many difficulties remained before the Copper River was reached June 9. The expedition remained at Copper Center for three days, finding the place thronged with prospectors, many discouraged enough to strike for home. Yet Rafferty concluded that "if it be the object of the Government to find a practicable route to the interior from the coast, it is hardly possible that a better one will be found than that starting from Port Valdez. The greatest obstacle is the Bates Glacier; but in my opinion if taken in the proper manner and at the right time, the heaviest mining machinery could be transported over it, and after the summit, 4,860 feet...there is found a grade to the Copper over which a man can haul 500 pounds to the sled during the winter months. In the summer there is a water route over which an experienced boatman, accustomed to rapid water, can take a year's provisions in one trip." A pack train could also work handily in that country, Rafferty believed, and feed could be found for the stock with hay for winter being cut during the short, intense summer season. June 13, "the expedition started down the Copper, after having heard hair-raising tales of the dangers ahead" because of violent rapids and strong current. "Of four parties of prospectors who had gone down, three had been wrecked..." Indians along the shores, awaiting the salmon run due to commence, were hospitable and friendly and downstream travel was swift, the river ranging from a mile in width to "a few hundred feet" in the narrows. They were warned by a white man of rapids below where it was advisable to line the boat, but there was no place to land so they had to shoot them and found the rapids "the worst so far encountered." The Chitina was reached June 14 and two days later the party "paid a formal visit" to Chief Nikolai (see entry) at "his summer house at Taral" (the present Chitina), whom they found amiable, humorous and helpful so far as he was able. "It had been my intention...to leave the boat and go up over Nikolai's trail to the summit back of Taral, thence to the head waters of the White River, prospecting for a feasible route to the Yukon country," wrote Rafferty, adding, however that because of high water "it was folly [with his heavy boat] to attempt the voyage upstream," so he sought to obtain the guidance of Nikolai or one of his Indians to attempt the journey by trail. Nikolai "invited us to his house,

where we ate salmon off china dishes, drank tea from cups and saucers, and used knives and forks that would have passed muster in civilization." Learning that Rafferty was acquainted with Lieutenant Allen who on his 1885 expedition had become a close friend of Nikolai's, the Indian proved even more cordial, said it would require fifteen days for a man with a pack to reach the head of the Chitina River but that he could not provide Rafferty with a guide because the salmon now were running and he needed every available man to lay in the winter's supply of fish. While awaiting instructions from Abercrombie Rafferty prospected the region around Taral, finding "a few colors of gold," and much indication of copper. The area was thoroughly explored. Learning that the Spanish American War had commenced, Rafferty sent the soldier, Kuhlman, back to try for fresh orders from Abercrombie or in his absence from another officer; Curran and Harrington decided to strike for the Klondike and its rumored gold riches, and only Goodman remained with Rafferty. The two decided to run the perilous rapids through Wood Canyon, a blind defile of grim history in the parties who had drowned in it, but Rafferty found it negotiable at high water. June 30, camp was made at the mouth of the Bremner River, 50 miles below Taral; progress downstream continued, the boat alternately serving as conveyance and being lined empty down rapids that heavily damaged it, requiring extensive repairs. Alagnik at the mouth of the Copper was gained at length and Port Valdez July 7, the hazardous trip concluded.

Rafferty, "From Port Valdez to Copper River, down that River, Thence to Prince William Sound," *Narratives of Explorations in Alaska,* 612-21.

Ramsey, Alexander, frontier governor (Sept. 8, 1815-Apr. 22, 1903). B. near Harrisburg, Pennsylvania, he was orphaned at 10, commenced the study of law at 22 and was admitted to the bar in 1839. He practiced at Harrisburg and became interested in Whig (and later, Republican) politics. He served as U.S. Congressman from 1843-47, worked hard for the election of Zachary Taylor who as president appointed Ramsey governor of the newly established territory of Minnesota. He arrived at his post May 27, 1849, initially a guest of Henry Hastings Sibley (see entry), a prominent Democrat; although Ramsey and Sibley became political rivals, their close personal friendship endured for more than 30 years. In 1850 Ramsey, who was also *de facto* superintendent of Indian affairs, called a council of mutually hostile Sioux and Chippewa chiefs in an effort to bring peace between them. The meeting succeeded somewhat, but neither side would depart the council until hostages were exchanged to assure a safe return of the delegates. The first major task to engage Ramsey was to clear Sioux title to southern Minnesota and make room for expected white immigration onto the former Indian lands. An abortive Sioux meeting called for Mendota in October 1849 was followed by a better prepared council in July 1851 at Traverse des Sioux, when a treaty was signed by 35 chiefs. By it the Sisseton and Wahpeton Sioux sold to the United States all their lands in Iowa and those in southern Minnesota for $1,665,000, most of the sum to be paid within half a century. The treaty was finalized with no more than customary chicanery, Ramsey credited with bringing about this huge boom to the bright white future of the territory. August 5, the commissioners obtained assent to a second treaty, this time at Mendota with the Wahpekute and Mdewakanton bands of Sioux. Around 35 million acres of most desirable land had been obtained for white use by the two treaties. Ramsey was later charged with fraud in the negotiations, but the U.S. Senate of course exonerated him. His territorial governorship ended with the appointment of a Democrat by President Franklin Pierce. Ramsey became mayor of St. Paul in 1855. Two years later he was very narrowly defeated by Sibley in the first election of a Minnesota governor, it having become a state May 11, 1858. Sibley did not run in 1859 and Ramsey won over another Democrat. It was during his term that the Great Sioux Uprising broke out when Sibley, Ramsey's "political foe and personal friend" was appointed by the governor colonel (later becoming Brigadier General) and commander of the forces which would crush the outbreak; no better choice could have been made. August 22, 1862, Ramsey issued a proclamation summoning militia of the affected counties and by the following day they were "pouring in a living stream up the Minnesota Valley" toward the troubled area, within three days totaling about 1,400 men , including 300 "very irregular cavalry." Ramsey also commissioned State Supreme Court Justice Charles E. Flandrau, another political rival and friend, a colonel to command troops in the Blue Earth region, a key area of hostilities (see Flandrau entry). Between them, Sibley and Flandrau with Ramsey's strong support shattered the uprising in a matter of weeks, although some hostilities lingered on farther west for a year or more. In a letter to President Lincoln October 22, 1862, Ramsey reported that the Indian war was "virtually over," and so was his impact specifically on the frontier, although his public life was only in mid-career. Ramsey retired as governor in July 1863 to take a seat as U.S. Senator, a position to which he had already been elected. He was re-elected in 1869, serving until March 3, 1875. Ramsey was Secretary of War in President Rutherford B. Hayes' cabinet from 1879-81, chaired the commission to carry out provisions of the George F. Edmunds Bill to suppress polygamy in Utah, and then retired to private life in Minnesota. He headed the Minnesota Historical Society from 1891 to 1903. He was married and fathered three children, one of whom attained maturity. Ramsey's political career was marked by "industry and practical ability." The *Dictionary of American Biography* concluded that he was "clear-headed, cautious, and judicious...a shrewd politician and an excellent judge of human nature, with a gift for making friends." He died at St. Paul, in the county named for him, and was buried in Oakland Cemetery.

Literature abundant; William Watts Folwell, *A History of Minnesota*, 4 vols., St. Paul, Minnesota Hist. Soc., 1926 (1956-69); Isaac V.D. Heard, *History of the Sioux War*, N.Y., Harper & Bros., 1864 (1975); BDAC; DAB.

Ramsey, Josiah, frontiersman (fl. 1764-1781). The son of Thomas Ramsey, a famous hunter of western Virginia, Josiah was captured by Indians of unidentified tribe as a child and was returned to the settlements only after Henry Bouquet's 1764 treaty with the Ohio Indians, who probably were the kidnappers. He was at the October 10, 1774, Battle of Point Pleasant, West Virginia, and suffered from a lack of provisions enroute home. Josiah Ramsey was a scout on the Cherokee expedition of 1776. In 1780 he moved to Kentucky and in 1781 settled at Cumberland where he became major of militia and "frequently served against the Indians." He died "at an advanced age," at his son's home in Missouri.

Thwaites, *Dunmore*.

Randlett, James Franklin, military officer (Dec. 8, 1832-Dec. 12, 1915). B. at Newmarket, New Hampshire, he enlisted in Company F, 3rd New Hampshire Infantry August 15, 1861, and eight days later was commissioned captain, emerging from the Civil War a lieutenant colonel and being mustered out July 20, 1865. He was commissioned captain of the 39th Infantry June 6, 1867, joined the 8th Cavalry December 15, 1870, and was assigned to eastern New Mexico to control comanchero activities in support of hostile Indians. May 28, 1871, he captured a pack train of 23 burros loaded with powder, lead, cloth and trinkets on the Staked Plains, supposedly enroute to Comanche country. The next day he intercepted 510 head of cattle coming from Comanche country in charge of traders. The burros were killed, the goods destroyed and traders arrested were jailed at Fort Bascom, north of present Tucumcari, New Mexico. Later, apparently stationed at Fort Stanton, Randlett became inadvertently involved in what seemed normal Lincoln County turbulence, this time centering on a location for the Mescalero Apache Reservation headquarters and assorted trading matters. May 18, 1873, Indian Agent Samuel Bushnell invited Randlett to join him and John H. Riley (see entry) in seeking a site for the new agency. This evolved into a dispute with Randlett on one side and the Dolan and Murphy interests on the other. The origin of the fracas is unclear, although Randlett had no use for the Murphy faction. At its height Dolan tried to kill Randlett, who held him off until a sergeant of the guard could take the hot-tempered Dolan to the Fort Stanton guardhouse where Murphy, too, was briefly lodged. Nolan concedes that the dispute was hard to unravel, but in any event Randlett emerged unscathed, although Dolan apparently had sought to shoot him and did fire a pistol. The incident passed except for the usual legal residue, which proved inconclusive. Randlett became major of the 9th Cavalry July 5, 1886, and lieutenant colonel October 4, 1896. He was active in the later Oklahoma, where for part of the time he was agent to the Kiowa Indians, with whom he was very popular, and he may have served as agent of the Uintah and Ouray Utes in Utah, perhaps in 1891-93. While at the Kiowa Agency he selected a site for the seat of Caddo County, his choice becoming the present city of Anadarko, Oklahoma. A few miles south of Utah's Fort Du Chesne, which Randlett commanded, was the small town of Leland, which in 1905 was renamed Randlett in his honor; there also is the small town of Randlett, south of Lawton, Oklahoma, which may have been named for him. Randlett retired December 8, 1896, and was promoted to colonel

on the retired list April 23, 1904. He died at La Mesa, California, near San Diego, survived by two children, his wife having predeceased him.

Frederick Nolan, *The Lincoln County War: A Documentary History,* Norman, Univ. of Okla. Press, 1992; William A. Keleher, *Violence in Lincoln County,* Albuquerque, Univ. of New Mex. Press, 1957; Heitman.

Rastel, Phillippe Francois, Sieur de Rocheblave, military officer (1727-1802). B. in France, he early joined the army, came to New France c. 1750, entered the colonial army as a cadet and served at Fort Duquesne (Pittsburgh), and on the Illinois frontier. At the close of the French and Indian War he went to Kaskaskia, Illinois, married in 1763 and later crossed the Mississippi into the Spanish possessions and for a time was connected with the Spanish government at Ste. Genevieve, Missouri. In 1776 the last British officer who quitted Kaskaskia left Rastel in command, but with neither garrison nor support. On July 4, 1778, he was captured by George Rogers Clark, sent a prisoner to Virginia, evaded parole and joined the British at New York. He finally retired to lower Canada and died at Varennes.

Thwaites/Kellogg, *Frontier Defense on the Upper Ohio, 1777-1778.*

Ratmanov, Makar Ivanovich, Russian naval officer (July 17, 1772-Dec. 21, 1833). B. at Toropets, Russia, he became a naval midshipman in 1789 and joined the first Russian around-the-world voyage, 1803-1806, under Krusenstern, Ratmanov being senior officer on the sloop *Nadezhda.* By 1805 the vessels were in the North Pacific where one of the Diomedes Islands, between the United States and Russia, was known for a time as Ratmanov Island, named for him. In 1819 Ratmanov because of illness could not accept command of an Antarctic expedition, which therefore was led by Bellingshausen and resulted in discovery of the Antarctic continent. Ratmanov died a vice admiral of the Russian navy.

Pierce, *Russian America: A Biographical Dictionary.*

Ravenscroft, Thomas, military officer (c. 1750-post 1823). Ravenscroft was raised in the family of William Crawford (see entry), and his initial military service was in the 1774 army of Lord Dunmore, participating in the Battle of Point Pleasant, West Virginia. In 1775 he enlisted in

Captain John Stephenson's company and later joined the 13th Virginia Regiment under Colonel William Russell, being discharged late in 1777 or early 1778, when he went into Ohio with Hand's "Squaw Campaign." In 1781 he was a lieutenant with George Rogers Clark for the abortive expedition against Detroit and when that was cancelled joined Colonel John Floyd in September, was captured and taken prisoner to Detroit, sent on to Montreal, escaped June 20, 1782, was shortly recaptured, exchanged at the close of the Revolution and returned to Kentucky. There he married either the widow or daughter of John Hinkson, or Hingston. He was living in Harrison County, Kentucky, in 1823.

Thwaites/Kellogg, *Frontier Defense on the Upper Ohio, 1777-1778.*

Ray, Patrick Henry, military officer (May 8, 1842-Oct. 30, 1911). B. in Waukesha County, Wisconsin, he enlisted in the 2nd Wisconsin Infantry May 7, 1861, served in A and K Companies and rose to first sergeant of the 1st Wisconsin Artillery by July 13, 1863, when he was commissioned a second lieutenant, being mustered out a captain April 2, 1866. He served as a second lieutenant in the 33rd Infantry from March 7, 1867, and in the 8th Infantry from May 3, 1869. He accompanied David Stanley's expeditions to the Yellowstone River in 1872 and 1873. A year later he was on Colonel John Eugene Smith's 1,000-man expedition from Fort Laramie northeast to the White River, Dakota, seeking to terminate a Sioux crisis at the Red Cloud Agency. Ray was then assigned to Arizona, serving until 1877 at Forts Yuma, Lowell and Apache, for five months commanding A Company of Indian Scouts, and in 1881 ws stationed at Fort Halleck, Nevada. As acting signal officer he was assigned in 1881 to command an International Polar Expedition to Point Barrow, Alaska. The expedition left San Francisco July 18, 1881, aboard the schooner *Golden Fleece,* landed at Plover Bay, Siberia, August 21, and reached Point Barrow September 8. An observatory was erected while the *Golden Fleece* sailed for her wintering port, leaving the land party at their isolated station, the mission to conduct observations in meteorology, magnetism and such other subjects as possible, the station to be occupied until August 22, 1883. In March 1882 Ray made an exploratory journey into the Alaskan interior. In June 1882 a steam whaler, the *North Star,* out of New Bedford (Captain

Owen) hove into view, Ray visiting her and finding she was assailed by increasingly restless pack movements; July 8, she was crushed by the ice about two and one-half miles offshore, but Ray's boats brought the crew safely off to the station and during succeeding weeks all were taken aboard other whalers operating in the area. Observations continued to be taken regularly, although all contact with the outside world again ceased in September. March 28, 1883, Ray left the station for the interior by dog sled and with Eskimo guides. March 29, he crossed the Inaru River, discovered the Meade River and shortly after the Usuktuk tributary of the Meade. On April 2, Ray made his farthest south, from an elevation near which he observed about 50 miles beyond a low uplift he named the "Meade Mountains," believing them holding the source of the Meade River; they are probably today's Lookout Ridge, or the parallel range of foothills to the north. Because his Eskimo guide did not wish to go further south, having never been so far into the interior, Ray was forced to turn back and arrived at the Point Barrow station April 7, suffering from severe snowblindness. On his two exploratory journeys he had covered about 1,000 miles. Ray had intended exploring the coast by whaleboat to the east of Barrow as far as the boundary with Canada, but late ice prevented this. Ice also made it difficult for Ray to get off with his party, which he did eventually in the topsail schooner *Leo* August 29, 1883, after closing down the station and giving cooperative Eskimo neighbors a farewell banquet of hard bread and molasses, for which they were grateful. The *Leo* reached St. Michael September 8; here Ray found "very much to our surprise" Lieutenant Schwatka (see entry) who had reached St. Michael after tracing the course of the Yukon by raft throughout most of its length. Taking aboard this second party, the overcrowded schooner left St. Michael September 11, put in at Unalaska Island the 17th for repairs, which were quickly effected, departed the 22nd and reached San Francisco October 7. The expedition in 27 months had sailed 7,500 miles, "established and maintained itself at the northern extremity of the continent and successfully carried out the instructions received from the Chief Signal Officer, and brought back the record of an unbroken series of hourly observations in meteorology, magnetism, tides, and earth temperatures, besides a large collection in natural history and ethnology, and penetrated into the interior to a point never before visited by civilized man." Ray prepared his report at Washington, D.C., and was a delegate to the International Polar Congress at Vienna from March to July 1884. Stationed at Fort Gaston, east of Trinidad, California; he was acting Indian agent at the Hoopa Valley Reservation in August-September 1885. In 1886-87 he served at Arizona and Nebraska posts. He became a captain of the 8th Infantry in 1889. August 4, 1897, Ray again was ordered to Alaska, the Klondike gold rush having lured many prospectors and miners to that territory. His instructions were to make a complete report and recommendations as to necessary measures to assure the establishment of law and order, the advisibility of stationing troops at the gold fields, and whether food supplies were sufficient to sustain the surging population during the winter. Ray was urged to observe "carefully and accurately" and to make his report reasoned, comprehensive and thoroughly reliable. Ray's initial impression at St. Michael on Norton Sound, where he had arrived from the States on August 18, was that the situation would prove very difficult and he called for army officers to manage it, since "we are not dealing with sane men, but a crowd of gold lunatics." He took the riverboat *John J. Healy* up the Yukon, intending to reach Dawson and then return downstream via the last boat out before winter to Fort Yukon, but the *Healy* was prevented by low water from proceeding above Fort Yukon and Ray and Lieutenant Wilds Richardson were forced to remain there as winter set in. September 13, Ray penned a lengthy report on the state of affairs in the Yukon Valley, the population, character and prospects of the region, and his proposals for the development, protection of civilian rights and also of transportation and other matters. He found conditions not so severe as had been feared, food supplies plentiful, largely because of Canada's insistence that all entering the Northwest Territory bring 1,000 pounds of provisions. Ray was not impressed with mineral possibilities in Alaska as known to that point, but thought transportation, particularly roads, should be rapidly developed. He recommended that "not less than" two companies of troops be stationed at the mouth of the Tanana River, with one at St. Michael and others elsewhere. Ray left Fort Yukon February 22, 1898, traveling by dog team up the frozen river more than 1,100 miles and by way of Chilkoot Pass, arriving at Dyea near Skagway April 7. He became major in the 8th Infantry March 2, 1899,

lieutenant colonel December 8, 1901, and colonel of the 4th Infantry August 12, 1903. After service in Cuba he was assigned to command the District of North Alaska (the region above Latitude 60°) and established the first American military posts at Nome, at Fort Gibbon at the mouth of the Tanana River and Fort Egbert at Eagle City on the Yukon near the Canadian Line. Ray served thereafter in the Philippines. He became a Brigadier General and was retired May 8, 1906, making his home at Youngstown, New York, until his death at Fort Niagara. He was married.

Narratives of Explorations in Alaska; Who Was Who; Heitman; Powell; *Army and Navy Journal,* Nov. 4, 1911; info. from the U.S. Army Military Hist. Inst., Carlisle Barracks, Penn.

Raymond, Charles Walker, military officer (Jan. 14, 1842-May 3, 1913). B. at Hartford, Connecticut, he went to West Point, was graduated first in his class and commissioned June 23, 1865, a first lieutenant of Army Engineers. He became a captain March 21, 1867. After being assigned to west coast defenses for engineering work, particularly at Alcatraz Island and Fort Stevens, Oregon, he was named in 1869 to head an exploration party to the Yukon Valley of Alaska, the territory recently acquired by purchase from Russia. April 6, he left San Francisco aboard the brig *Commodore* for Sitka, the ship carrying upon her deck a 50-foot sternweel steamer, the *Yukon,* designed to be the first such vessel to attempt the ascent of the great river for which she as named. Raymond reached Sitka April 24, left May 9, and arrived at Unalaska Island the 21st. The *Commodore* left Unalaska June 8, and after a very difficult passage reached St. Michael in Norton Sound June 29. The little steamboat passed her trials well and July 4, the expedition, towing two large open boats, left for the mouth of the Yukon, entering it the following day; party members included Michael Lebarge, a trader familiar with the upper Yukon, and other knowledgeable frontiersmen. The steamer first terrified, then delighted unsophisticated natives along the stream. July 12, it reached Anvik, a native village at the mouth of the Anvik River, Nulato July 19, and Fort Adams, near the present Tanana at the mouth of the Tanana River, on the 22nd. "On the 31st of July, at 4 p.m. we arrived at Fort Yukon, thus successfully terminating the first journey by steam ever made on the Yukon River. The time of actual travel, including stoppages for wood, was 23 days, and the distance passed over about 1,040 statute miles," Raymond reported. One of his primary missions was to establish the longitude of Fort Yukon to determine whether it was in American or British territory; a good observation of the solar eclipse August 7, enabled Raymond to compute an approximate longitude, "sufficiently accurate to set at rest the question," he learning that Fort Yukon was definitely in United States territory. He had been cordially received by John Wilson, Hudson's Bay Company factor and now had the unenviable duty of informing him that the territory belonged to the U.S.A., and that the introduction of trading goods and British trade with the natives from this point were illegal, must cease and that the company must vacate its establishment. "I then took possession of the buildings and raised the flag of the United States over the fort," the captain reported. The steamer started her return journey August 10, but the officer remained at Fort Yukon, taking confirmatory observations. The season rapidly closed down, and Raymond determined to return to the coast. He wished to do so in bark boats, of whose versatility and dependability he had heard much, but none was available. A small skiff was rapidly built, named the *Eclipse,* and August 28, Raymond, with Private Michael Foley, 9th Infantry, John J. Major and two Nulato natives embarked. After an adventurous descent of the Yukon wherein the boat received such a battering that it became virtually a wreck, the party September 13, reached the Anvik native settlement, unable to proceed farther in that craft. Because of the lateness of the season, natives were afraid to attempt to descend the Yukon to its mouth, but Raymond finally persuaded trader John Clark to assemble six birchbark canoes and Indians to man them in an endeavor to ascend the Anvik River to that point closest to St. Michael. Persevering through almost incredible difficulties, the tiny party arrived at St. Michael, boarded the *Commodore,* the captain sailing September 27, for San Francisco and arriving November 6, seven months after departure for Alaska. Raymond's complete report, including much ecological, geographical, ethnological and exploratory matters of interest, is included in *Narratives of Explorations.* Most of Raymond's subsequent army service was with the Engineers in one capacity or another. While teaching at West Point he designed buildings and a water supply system. He was a member of an expedition to Tasmania in 1874-75 to study a

transit of Venus. He became a major February 20, 1883, worked on east coast river and harbor improvements and at his special interest, terrestrial magnetism. Raymond was involved in the design and construction of the Hudson River tunnel for New York City and was an important consultant for George Washington Goethals in planning and construction of the Panama Canal. Raymond became a lieutenant colonel May 18, 1898, colonel in January 1904 and Brigadier General in June 1904, when he was retired. He was married twice, his first wife dying in 1901 and the second surviving him; two of his sons became army officers.

Heitman; Powell; Cullum;*Narratives of Explorations in Alaska;* DAB.

Reaburn, Dewitt Lee, topographer (b. 1871). Reaburn commenced work in Alaska in 1900 and the following year with Mendenhall (see entry) made a topographic survey from Fort Hamlin on the Yukon by way of the Dall, Kanuti, Alatna and Kobuk rivers to Kotzebue Sound. In 1901 with Alfred Brooks he made a continuous survey over 800 miles from Cook Inlet to the Yukon along the west flank of the Alaska Range. From 1903 he participated in work on the Alaska-Canadian boundary.

Orth, 28.

Red Iron (Mazahsha), Sisseton Siouix chief (b. c. 1812). Called by some a principal chief of the Sissetons (one of seven main divisions of the Dakota Nation), Red Iron headed his own village and was an influential and highly intelligent man of apparent integrity. By 1852 he had come to cross-purposes with Minnesota Governor Alexander Ramsey (see entry) over white acquisition of Indian lands and was under arrest for his opposition to what has been described as a "monstrous conspiracy" by the whites against the Indians. He had been forced to sign the July 23, 1851, Traverse des Sioux Treaty, although opposed to it on principle and in 1852 was still under arrest. Red Iron was brought into the December 1842 council with Ramsey under military guard, and was described by an eye-witness as "about forty years old, tall and athletic; about six feet high in his moccasins, with a large, well-developed head, aquiline nose, thin, compressed lips, and physiognomy beaming with intelligence and resolution." Ramsey tried to bully him, and failed. In Heard's transcript of the council interchange between Red Iron and Ramsey it is plain where integrity lay, and it was not with Ramsey. As a result of the chief's refusal to accept extortionist measures against the Indians he was broken as chief by Ramsey, who was acting superintendent of Indian affairs for Minnesota by reason of holding the title of governor. The Ramsey-generated rape of Indian lands and swindling the Indians even of the annuities that were their due was, according to Meyer "a thoroughly sordid affair, equal in infamy to anything else in the long history of injustice perpetrated upon the Indians by the authorized representatives of the United States government in the name of that government." The subsequent investigation of Ramsey's role in the affair, in which he was whitewashed by the Senate, seemed equally nefarious. "When the whirlwind was reaped a decade later [in the Great Sioux Uprising of 1862] the immediate victims were the comparatively innocent white settlers near the reservation, not the men ultimately responsible. In the end, of course, the ones who suffered most were, as always, the Indians." In 1858 Red Iron led a delegation of nine Upper Sioux chiefs to Washington, D.C., the results unreported. Despite his treatment in previous years, Red Iron was among the principal chiefs opposed to the uprising when it came, and "either took no part or joined very reluctantly in a few battles, meanwhile giving all the aid they safely could to white victims." Little is reported of Red Iron following the great conflict.

Isaac V.D. Heard, *History of the Sioux War...of 1862 and 1863,* N.Y., Harper & Bros., 1864, 1975 (has engraving of Red Iron, p. 155); William Watts Folwell, *A History of Minneseota,* II, St. Paul, Minnesota Hist. Soc., 1961; Roy W. Meyer, *History of the Santee Sioux: United States Indian Policy on Trial,* Lincoln, Univ. of Nebr. Press, 1967 (the Sissetons were part of the Santee division).

Red Pole (Reed Pool, Musquaconocah), Shawnee civil chief (d. Jan. 28, 1797). Probably a younger brother of Blue Jacket, war chief of the Shawnees, Red Pole may have belonged to the Pekowi division of the tribe and first appears in the records when he signed the Treaty of Fort Finney, Ohio, January 31, 1786. He was remembered by the Americans for dignified deportment, urbanity, and oratorial ability—and also for his propensity for heavy drinking, in keeping with his brother's like inclination. Red Pole assisted Captain Johnny, Captain Snake, Blue Jacket (see entries) and other Shawnee chiefs to construct a vast inter-tribal confederacy between 1789 and 1795 He appears most vividly as the principal western spokesman at the great intertribal congress at the Glaize (the junction of the Maumee and Auglaize rivers, Ohio) in the fall of 1793. He assailed the Iroquois for tardy support of the Indian confederacy, and he persuaded the council to accept the fact that the confederacy would make peace with the United States only with a boundary along the Ohio River; this accorded with an earlier treaty of Fort Stanwix, New York. He advocated a widening of the confederacy, and British help in future negotiations with the United States. Red Pole did not take part in negotiations of 1793, however. Instead he took an embassy to the Cherokees and Creeks in the south. He returned north early in 1795 and assisted Blue Jacket in mustering support for the Treaty of Greenville, Ohio, which both signed August 3, 1795. His presence apparently pleased the United States for on September 28, Timothy Pickering, secretary of war, wrote President Washington that while "the chiefs who signed the treaty are not numerous," he noted among them "Blue Jacket, the great warrior of the Shawanoes [and] Misquacoonacaw, their great speaker..." Red Pole accompanied Blue Jacket to Philadelphia in the winter of 1796-97, meeting Washington, but fell ill on the return trip. In spite of the attentions of three doctors he died in Pittsburgh "to the inexpressible grief of the other Indians, and indeed of all others that had any knowledge of him," it was reported. He was buried in Trinity Church Yard, Pittsburgh, his stone inscribed, "Misquacoonacaw, or Red Pole, Principal Village Chief of the Shawanee ...lamented by the United States." This, according to John Sugden, "raised the possibility that when the Ohio Shawnees divided in 1795 and the greater part remaining with Captain Johnny, the principal chief, Red Pole was raised to the position of head civil chief of the more pacific, if smaller, group influenced by Blue Jacket."

Info. from John Sugden.

Red Shirt, medicine man (fl. 1851-1885). Red Shirt, a Koyukon Athapascan medicine man of considerable local fame, was "implicated" in the slaying in 1851 of the English naval officer John James Barnard (see entry), according to Henry T. Allen, who did not elaborate on the charge, but who met Red Shirt on Allen's imporant 1885 exploration of the Koyukon and other Alaskan rivers. *Narratives of Explorations in Alaska* has a striking engraving from a photograph of Red Shirt, taken no doubt by Allen. Allen visited Red Shirt's important village, 156 miles up the Koyukuk River from Nulato and just above Colwell Bend, almost due north of the confluence of the Yukon and Koyukuk rivers. The date and circumstances of Red Shirt's decease are unreported.

Narratives of Explorations in Alaska, facing p. 416 (map); facing p. 452 (photo); 462; 469 (placement of village).

Relles, Apache chief: *see,* Reyes

Reno brothers, desperadoes (fl. 1861-1868). B. and raised near Seymour, southern Indiana, the brothers included John (the oldest), Frank (the leader), Clinton (nicknamed "honest Clint" because so far as the record shows he took no part in outlawry), Sim[e]on (Sim), and William (Wilk), and their sister, Laura Ellen Reno, all the offspring of a Pennsylvania Dutch mother and Swiss father, and all considered by one biographer, "handsome." The boys commenced their desperado careers immediately following the Civil War during which they had participated largely as "expert bounty jumpers," being paid for war enlistments first on one side, then the other, and deserting as quickly as they got the money. Once the war was over they settled on farms near Seymour , where they shortly assembled "a desperate, skilful cohort of safe-burglars, counterfeiters, and highwaymen" and pursued a reign of lawlessness that took them into three states before their brief careers were terminated. After minor criminal activities they acquired lasting fame by organizing and carrying out the first major train robbery in the history of the United States, seizing some $10,000 from an Ohio and Mississippi Railroad express at Seymour on October 6, 1866. William Reno, it is said, labored for an hour trying to open the train's safe for additional loot, but gave up and emptied his pistol at it in rage. The following spring the gang robbed the Daviess County treasury at Gallatin, Missouri, of $22,065 in tax collections. This brought the Pinkerton agency into action, and by a ruse Allan Pinkerton and some associates caught John Reno at the Seymour railroad depot and spirited him away, although Frank Reno tried to head off the fleeing train, but missed it at Quincy, Illinois. John was taken to Missouri where he was sentenced to two, twenty-five or forty years, depending upon which

"authority" one reads (Johnson reported he was pardoned by a Missouri governor in 1876, opened a saloon and around 1886 was arrested for passing counterfeit money and went back to prison). In 1868 the band robbed the Harrison County Bank at Magnolia, Iowa, of $14,000. Pinkerton managed to capture the desperadoes at Council Bluffs, Iowa, where they were jailed, but on April 1, 1868, they escaped, painting on the wall, "April Fool!" before departing. The Renos' most lucrative escapade occurred on May 22, 1868, when they held up a Jefferson, Missouri and Indianapolis Railroad flyer outside Marshfield, Indiana, taking $96,000 in gold and government bonds. In a later abortive train holdup near Seymour, Pinkerton outguessed the bandits and in a shootout several men were wounded and the Renos with their followers fled with detectives in close pursuit. Some gang members were quickly taken, but the three Renos got away again; five of the captured men were lynched by vigilantes, two at one time and three at another. Simon and William Reno were at length arrested and housed in the Floyd County jail at New Albany, Indiana. Frank escaped to Canada, was taken at Windsor, Ontario, and after a lengthy extradition battle was returned to the States to join his two brothers and Charles Anderson, another of the imprisoned gang. On December 11, 1868, vigilantes stormed the jail and, following honest resistance by Sheriff Fullenlove, they took the three Renos out of their cells and hanged them. Frank and William died instantly, but Simon failed to get a good drop. After the vigilantes had left he recovered consciousness and for half an hour sought to pull himself up to loosen the strangling rope, this before the eyes of other jailed prisoners watching the performance. At last his strength failed and he choked to death. During their brief, violent career, the Renos had robbed or tried to rob other trains and places and several people were reported killed during various of their rascalities, but the foregoing are the best documented. Laura Ellen Reno, whose photograph is published by Horan and Sann, was an "evil influence...acknowledged by all," according to one writer, but she was never tried or even charged with any crime. He wrote that "years later—in 1900—an elderly woman living near Seymour, the wife of a respectable farmer, admitted to a newspaper correspondent that her maiden name had been Laura Reno."

Richard W. Rowan, *The Pinkertons,* Boston, Little, Brown and Co., 1931 (Ch. 14, "A Family of Outlaws," repr. by the Public Lby. of Fort Wayne and Allen County, Ind., 1955); James D. Horan and Paul Sann, *Pictorial History of the Wild West,* N.Y., Crown Pubs., 1954; Jay Robert Nash, abridged edition, *Bloodletters and Badmen,* Book I, N.Y., Warner Paperback Lby., 1975, pp. 324-28; Dorothy M. Johnson, *Western Badmen,* N.Y., Ballantine Books, 1970; info. from E.F. (Ted) Mains.

Reyes (Relles), Chokonen (Chiricahua) chief (d. July 6, 1846). A noted, moderate chief of the Chokonen, or Chiricahua Apaches, Sweeney considered him to possibly have been the father of Cochise; the other principal condidate, and he whom Sweeney prefers being Pisago Cabezon (see entry). In the mid-1830s Reyes apparently lived in the rancheria of El Sarampion in the lower Peloncillo Mountains of southwestern New Mexico. He was a member of a large Apache force which included Pisago Cabezon and raided Fronteras, Sonora, January 8, 1834, running off about 50 horses. Reyes was generally considered by the Mexicans to be an intelligent Indian leader whom they thought to be among the most reasonable and reputable of those Apaches taking part in truce agreements in August 1836 in Sonora and in 1842 at Janos, Chihuahua. Hostilities later resumed and in 1844 he joined in raids on Sonora, yet Reyes nevertheless was the prime mover in a truce in May 1846 at (San) Buenaventura, Chihuahua, southeast of Galeana. In May Reyes settled at Galeana himself. The notorious scalp hunter James Kirker (see entry) arrived at Galeana July 6, while peaceful Apaches were drawing rations, and murdered about 130 of both sexes and all ages, including Reyes, before moving on to San Buenaventura to kill 18 more.

William B. Griffen, *Apaches at War & Peace,* Albuquerque, Univ. of New Mex. Press, 1989; Edwin R. Sweeney, *Cochise: Chiricahua Apache Chief,* Norman, Univ. of Okla. Press, 1991.

Rezanov, Nikolai Petrovich, Russian expansionist (Apr. 8, 1764-Mar. 13, 1807). B. at St. Petersburg, he served in the army, then entered civil service, becoming an able administrator. He was a "man of parts and ambition, of noble birth but scant patrimony," and became an eager protege of Grigorii Ivanovich Shelikhov, whose daughter he wed in 1795 and with whom he lived happily until her death eight years later. Shelikhov had done much to open Alaska to Russian interests, being a fur trader himself, and founder of the first Russian colony on Kodiak Island in 1784. Two years later he returned to Russia bearing the germ of an idea for a monopoly to be granted by the tsar to him and his interests for trading and development in Alaska. This idea he transmitted to his son-in-law whose brilliant mind and boundless ambition eagerly seized upon it. He worked to gain for Shelikhov and himself rights parallel to those granted the English East India Company [for an analysis and critique of the Russian American Company, and a denial that it was simply a Russian version of the East India Company, see *The Russian American Colonies,* XXXIV-XLIII]. Because of his royal connections the plans were brought to the attention of Catherine II and she was "on the point of granting a charter" at her death in 1796. Shelikhov had died at Irkutsk in 1795 and his widow, Natalia, who herself had been to Kodiak Island and was active in her husband's business, now turned to Rezanov as her chief adviser and the person to carry on Shelikhov's commercial aspirations. Free traders had descended upon Alaska, bestowing all manner of abuses and disorders in their avid pursuit of wealth. This situation bolstered the imperial government's determination to bring a measure of order to that distant realm, both for the profit involved and to strengthen Russian control. Rezanov, who had been a favorite of Catherine, now pursued his connections with her successor, the weak-minded Paul and August 11, 1799, the Russian American Company was formed as the monopoly organization for the trade and colonization of Alaska; Rezanov had been more influential than anyone else in its creation. August 7, 1803, having been appointed minister plenipotentiary to Japan in the imperial hope of opening commercial relations with that tightly locked country (an endeavor which failed) he left Kronstadt with Adam Johann von Krusenstern's famed around-the-world expedition. One of its endeavors was to open sea communications with the Alaskan outpost, a more efficient means of servicing that frontier than by land routes across Siberia by which each contact frequently took two or three years to complete. Rezanov with his significant connections with Russian royalty apparently had been influential in winning the tsar's authorization for the Krusenstern operation itself. After failure of his Japan mission, Rezanov left the expedition on the coast of Siberia and June 24, 1805, shipped on the brig *Maria* for Alaska. The vessel lay over at St. Paul Island of the Pribylof group where Rezanov was appalled at the waste he found of pelts of fur seals scattered everywhere and rotting through neglect. He concluded that "unless an end were put to this wanton destruction, a few years more would witness the extirpation of the fur-seal," as it very nearly did. Rezanov next stopped at Beaver Inlet on Unalaska Island and from a station near there wrote a letter directly to the emperor, as he was authorized to do. In it he said that the Pribylofs, with their incredible numbers of fur seals "would be an inexhaustible source of wealth were it not for the Bostonians, who undermine our trade with China for furs...As over a million [fur seals] had already been killed, I gave orders to stop the slaughter at once, in order to prevent their total extermination..." He also urged stronger measures against the New England traders, development of American sources of food staples other than meat, negotiations with the Spanish for trade with their territories, military action against Japan to force that country to open her ports, and recommended stronger measures against lawless Russians and others who frequently oppressed the native Alaskans, although he also urged exile to Alaska of prison labor from Russia and Siberia to help the vast colony quickly obtain a hard working and useful population. July 25, the *Maria* sailed for St. Paul, the port on Kodiak Island, and around the end of August for Novo Arkhangelsk (Sitka) where he met with and admired the work of Baranov, learned about Tlingit hostility which occasionally flared up, passed out reprimands, advice, medals and instructions with equal facility, copied off an Indian dictionary which others had prepared, sent to Russia voluminous reports, and endured an unusually harsh winter before leaving in the spring of 1806 for San Francisco, where he arrived in April. He managed to trade goods he had brought from Alaska, was frequently guest in the home of José Darío Arguello, presidio commander, and became affianced to Arguello's daughter, Concepción, "for reasons of state," as he put it. Rezanov took the abundant foodstuffs he had bartered for (671 fanegas [a fanega was 2.58 bushels] of wheat, 117 of oats, 140 of peas and beans, and abundant flour, tallow, salt and other supplies) to Novo Arkhangelsk. In August he sailed back to Okhotsk and set out for Russia. Winter, however, befell him on the long and arduous journey and at 43 he died at Krasnoyarsk, on the Yenisei River in central Siberia.

Bancroft, *Alaska;* Kyrill T. Khlebnikov, *Colonial Russian America,* trans. by Basil Dmytryshyn, E.A.P. Crownhart-Vaughan, Portland, Oregon Hist. Soc., 1976; CE; DAB.

Richardson, Rupert Norval, historian (Apr. 28, 1891-Apr. 14, 1988). B. near Caddo, Texas, he was graduated in 1912 from Hardin-Simmons University at Abilene, Texas, and in 1928 received a doctorate from the University of Texas. After a few years as a high school principal he became professor of history at Hardin-Simmons in 1917 and eventually its president by 1945, ending his professional career in 1953 when he was named president emeritus. He also taught at the University of Texas for several summers. Richardson was a second lieutenant in the Army in 1918 and held scholarly positions with various organizations. He wrote *The Comanche Barrier to South Plains Settlement* (1933); with C.C. Rister, *The Greater Southwest* (1934); *Texas; the Lone Star State* (1943); *The Frontier of Northwest Texas* (1963); *Along the Texas Old Forts Trail* (1972) and other works of non-frontier interest. He edited the West Texas Historical Association Yearbook from 1929. He died at Abilene, a fortnight short of his 97th birthday. He was married and was survived by a son.

Info. from Hardin-Simmons Univ. Alumni Assn.

Richardson, Wilds Preston, military officer (Mar. 20, 1861-May 20, 1929). B. in Texas he went to West Point and was commissioned a second lieutenant of the 8th Infantry June 15, 1884. He served with H Company at Angel Island, California, until December 29, 1885, when the company was assigned to Arizona for the 1885-86 Geronimo campaign. Richardson served at the community of Bowie and Fort Bowie, in the field from June 27 until September 10, 1886, and then at Fort Lowell, near Tucson. In November he was assigned to Fort Niobrara, Nebraska. He had experience as a quartermaster officer, an engineer officer and as adjutant, and became a first lieutenant December 16, 1889; he was aide to Kautz, who commanded the Department of the Columbia from 1891-92. Richardson then taught tactics at West Point until 1897, when he was assigned to accompany Captain P. Henry Ray (see entry) to Alaska to investigate rumors of lawlessness in the interior and alleged destitution facing prospectors and other pioneers of that territory. On August 4, 1897, Ray and Richardson were ordered to Alaska on their mission. They arrived by steamer August 18, at St. Michael on

Norton Sound, and left aboard the river steamer *John J. Healy* August 29, but the boat so late in the season could not proceed beyond Fort Yukon. Ray had planned to remain aboard to Dawson while Richardson would debark at Circle City, 90 miles above Fort Yukon. Ray would then return to Fort Yukon by the last boat leaving Dawson before ice shut off steamboat navigation. As it happened, however, the *Healy* was prevented by low water from advancing, having reached Fort Yukon September 12, and both Richardson and Ray seemed forced to remain there as winter closed in. They had one serious confrontation with lawless elements seeking to control, for their own profit, food supplies at Fort Yukon and vicinity, but through steadiness, flexibility and courage the officers, who were without additional military support at the post, faced out and won over the unruly elements and from then on remained in acknowledged control. Ray managed to leave Fort Yukon February 23, 1898, by dogsled for Juneau, leaving Richardson in charge. Richardson praised the Canadian Mounted Police at Dawson, whose population was under 15,000, yet because of police efficiency "with all its motley population and vicious elements [Dawson remained] a most orderly and law-abiding town," whereas on the American side of the border there was a situation "without any semblance of law, civil or military" from St. Michael to the Canadian line. Richardson spent the winter "providing for the destitute people" who wintered near the post, including the sick and resourceless Indians. On January 16, the thermometer sank to 62° below zero, and from February 16 to 22 it averaged more than 50° below. Within 30 miles of the post, wood parties from two commercial firms cut and stored more than 6,000 cords of firewood for the summer steamers. The ice broke May 13, "the earliest opening of the river in many years." The first steamer arrived June 5. Richardson took passage June 6, on the *Portus B. Weare* for Dawson, where it remained thirteen days then put about and went down the length of the Yukon to Fort Michael, arriving July 5. Richardson was promoted to captain April 26, 1898, while he still was in Alaska, where he remained through 1899. In that year he wrote a summary report which is informative and interesting, discussing the Yukon River in detail: its currents, widths, depths and appearance, also the type and number of steamboats then operating on it, the luxury or lack of it provided by them, the use of dogs, amounts of game found in the Yukon Valley, the

kinds of minerals and the mining camps, and other aspects of value or interest to the War Department and those interested in the subjects. Richardson became adjutant of the Department of Alaska in 1900, in charge of constructing Fort William H. Seward from 1902-1904, and was named a member of the board of road commissioners for Alaska from 1905. He became major of the 9th Infantry April 7, 1904, transferring to the 13th Infantry in 1908, becoming a lieutenant colonel March 11, 1911, colonel April 28, 1914, and a brigadier general of the National Army, August 5, 1917.

Heitman; Cullum; *Who Was Who; Narratives of Explorations in Alaska.*

Richardville, Jean Baptiste (Peshewah, The Lynx), Miami chief (c. 1761-Aug. 13, 1841). B. on St. Marys River near Fort Wayne, Indiana, his father was Antoine Joseph Drouet de Richerville, a trader, and his mother, Tacumwah, sister of Pacanne, who was an uncle of Little Turtle (see entry). Richardville was educated in part at Three Rivers, Quebec, and became fluent in Miami, French and English. After the death of the Miami chief, Pacanne, in 1814, the chieftainship fell to his nephew, Peshewah. The chief may have "fought in raids and battles as a young man," but in his maturity he became rather an eloquent, gifted political leader and businessman. "As principal chief he was the guardian and spokesman for the tribe," and managed to buttress his position by cooperation with and, at times, in the interests of the federal government. By 1818, however, he "abandoned white dress and became all Miami Indian," whether through loyalty to his tribe or expediency in leading his people was never clear. Eventually he ceased the use of English or French speech, but retained his business acumen and became regarded as the wealthiest Indian in America and richest man in Indiana, with property valued at upwards of $1 million—in pre-inflation currency. He was a master "at meeting the land cession and emigration demands of the federal government," and to the end of his life was an important and influential man in representing the Miamis in dealings with the whites. His children and other descendants received fine educations and "came to be considered important members of white communities." A portrait of him is reproduced in Anson's *Miami Indians,* facing p. 110. He died at about 80. The town of Russiaville, southwest of Kokomo was, in variant form, named for him.

Hodge, HAI; Bert Anson, *The Miami Indians,* Norman, Univ. of Okla. Press, 1970; info. from John Sugden; Harvey Lewis Carter, *The Life and Times of Little Turtle,* Chicago, Univ. of Illinois Press, 1987.

Ringgold, Cadwalader, naval officer (Aug. 20, 1802-Apr. 19, 1867). B. in Washington County, Maryland, he became a navy midshipman May 4, 1819, a lieutenant in 1828 and a commander in 1849. He had commanded the schooner *Weasel* against West Indies pirates and the *Porpoise* on the Wilkes exploring expedition from 1838-42, during which the vessels not only visited the West Coast, but also the Antarctic, confirming the existence there of a great and hitherto virtually unknown continent. In 1849-50 Ringgold again visited the California coast, thereafter commanding a North Pacific surveying and exploration expedition. This operation resulted in explorations and surveys in the North Pacific, the Aleutian Islands, the Bering Sea and along the Siberian coast; among the discoveries was Ringgold Island, adjacent to Adak Island, and associated features. Ringgold reached China in 1854 and suffered a severe attack of intermittent fever "which greatly weakened him physically and mentally." This caused Commodore Matthew Calbraith Perry, who had recently "opened" Japan to foreign trade and relations, to summon a medical survey of Ringgold, and upon its finding that he had become insane ordered command of the expedition taken over by Commander John Rodgers and Ringgold to be sent back to the United States. Ringgold had recuperated from his illness meanwhile, a medical survey upon his return declared him fully recovered and in 1857 he was promoted to captain and put on the active list. His Civil War record was outstanding and he retired for reasons of age August 20, 1864, two years later becoming a Rear Admiral on the retired list. He was unmarried. He died at New York City of apoplexy.

Orth, 25, 806; DAB.

Ritter, Homer Peter, surveyor (fl. 1898-1904). With the Coast and Geodetic Survey, he was in charge of a party that from 1898 to 1903 mapped the Copper River delta in Alaska and the eastern part of Prince William Sound. In 1904, in command of the steamer *McArthur* he with John Francis Pratt (see entry) surveyed Kiska harbor in the western Aleutians.

Orth, 18, 807.

Rivera Villalón, Pedro de, military officer (c. 1664-Nov. 24, 1744). B. at Antequera, northwest of Málaga, Spain, he joined the army while young, served in the Netherlands War of 1672-78, then in Extremadura and later as an officer in the naval armadas. By 1683 he was stationed at Veracruz and may have worked with a German engineer, Jaime Franck, who designed defenses for Florida, but it is uncerain whether the Pedro de Rivera who did so was Pedro de Rivera Villalón who also was an accomplished line officer. He was promoted eventually to colonel of infantry, commanding the San Juan de Ulúa fortress at Veracruz; by 1710 he had become *maestre de campo* when he became provisional governor of Tlaxcala, an interior state. When the commanding general of the Armada de Barlovento died July 10, 1712, Rivera was named lieutenant general of the Armada, embarking January 19, 1713, on the *Santísima Trinidad,* a 52-gun frigate, to escort silver ships to Spain. He took part in quelling a civil turbulence in Spain, leaving for Mexico again in the summer of 1715. Upon his arrival at Veracruz he was given command of land forces, putting down piracy and unruly elements in the Caribbean, later serving as governor of Yucatan where not only English buccaneers were active, but there also was Indian unrest. When Juan de Acuña, the Marqués de Casafuerte, became Viceroy in 1722, an initial concern was the line of 23 presidios on the northern frontier of New Spain. The posts, the Viceroy reported to King Felipe V, were "costly, inefficient, undermanned, exploited by their officers, and unwieldy," and suggested Rivera for the task of assessing the problems and recommending corrections, but to do so he should be appointed Brigadier in order to outrank frontier officers and provincial governors. Approval granted, Rivera was informed of his new mission, rank, and given outlines of what it was hoped to be accomplished in the north. His small expedition, including skilled assistants, left Mexico City November 21, 1724, remaining in Zacatecas over the holidays, inspected garrisons of Nayarit, Durango and Nueva Vizcaya (Chihuahua). By March 1726 he had entered New Mexico, passing through El Paso and Albuquerque to Santa Fe, solving difficult issues enroute and making inspections as thorough as possible. Once more at El Paso (the present Juarez) Rivera turned west to Sonora, uncovering matters principally at Fronteras, circling down through the state, coming back by way of Janos and resting during the spring of 1727 to enable his cartographic team to complete maps of the routes through Sonora and Chihuahua. The following six months involved lengthy trips across Texas as far as Adays (Adais), where in October a presidio named Nuestra Señora del Pilar de los Adaes had been located adjacent to the mission of San Miguel de los Adaes (near the present San Augustine, Texas) on the extreme eastern frontier. Inspection of the presidio at Bahía del Espíritu Santo (in Calhoun County) was the longest stop in Texas, made during November. The return journey passed through San Antonio, crossed the Rio Grande, and arrived at Mexico City in 1728, concluding a 7,000 mile trip of the most exacting nature and the resulting reports the most comprehensive of any until that time. Rivera spent three and one-half years on his inspection, during which his wife had died at the capital, she having borne him eight children, four of them sons. Within six weeks after his return Rivera was commissioned to draft a formal report which he entitled a *Proyecto,* and when that was completed he was assigned to write a draft of regulations to guide military activity in northern New Spain; this was entitled the *Reglamento.* It was completed by March 1729, was signed into law in April, pending approval of the King. Since it projected a saving of 178,000 pesos a year, that was a formality. Rivera remained at Mexico City for about two years handling derivative matters. He was promoted to Mariscal de Campo (field marshal) without the salary of that rank, but the King altruistically awarded him an additional 12 pesos a day for the time he spent on his long inspection trip, for a total of 15,636 pesos, so "he was now a mariscal with the pay of a Brigadier and the bonus of a frontier explorer!" He returned as governor to Veracruz but within six months was made governor of Guatemala. His administration was a succesful one; he was succeeded October 16, 1742, by a Peruvian official. Rivera died at Mexico City and was buried in the chapel of the community's cathedral.

Pedro de Rivera and the Military Regulations for Northern New Spain 1724-1729, compiled, ed., by Thomas H. Naylor, Charles W. Polzer, S.J., Tucson, Univ. of Ariz. Press, 1988.

Robbins, Jonathan: *see,* John Lovewell entry

Roberts, Andrew L. (Buckshot; Bill Williams; Al), gunman (d. April 5, 1878). A nervy, durable gunman, his origins and background are as clouded as those of any frontier figure could be. Nolan has him, under the pseudonym Bill Williams, involved in the Horrell War in New Mexico in the

1870s. Mullin reported that Roberts at one time had worked for Buffalo Bill Cody, supplying game to feed railroad construction crews on the Plains. One account said he had served in the regular army in the Civil War and against Indians, rising to first sergeant and that later, while serving with the Texas Rangers, had received the charge of buckshot. This gave him his nickname and crippled his right shoulder, preventing him from raising his arm when standing and forcing him to shoot from the hip unless firing prone or seated. He was said to have been 5 ft., 4 in. in height and although some considered him "stocky," he weighed only 120 pounds, at least in his young manhood. He preferred a mule to a horse, considered by some to attest to his good judgment. Mullin reported that Roberts had deserted from the regular army at Fort Stanton, New Mexico around October 1877, and no attempt was made to apprehend him "as he was considered undesirable and the officers did not want him back," although one wonders why he was permitted to enlist in the first place in view of his buckshot-induced physical handicap. In February 1878 he operated a Murphy Company store at South Fork, near the Mescalero Agency in New Mexico. Maurice Fulton said that Roberts was "virtually of the band of cattle thieves and murderers serving the Murphy-Dolan outfit," and he seems to have been a member of the "posse" which killed Tunstall, although it was not charged that he had any role in the shooting itself. Nevertheless he thus became one of the partisans the Tunstall avengers most wanted to take. They had their opportunity in the celebrated battle of Blazer's Mill, the establishment owned and operated by Joseph Hoy Blazer (see entry). Roberts refused to surrender on Dick Brewer's warrant for his arrest because he felt he would be murdered if he did so, as had happened to others. A gunfight broke out, Charlie Bowdre inflicting a mortal gut shot on Roberts at the outset, but this precipitated a general melee rather than terminating the fight. Still on his feet, Roberts staggered into Dr. Blazer's office, dragged a mattress to the doorway and found a .45-60 hunting rifle and plenty of cartridges to replace his emptied weapons, lay on the mattress and fired tellingly at his opponents. He shot John Middleton through the lung, a serious wound; knocked Bowdre out of the fight with a bullet that struck his cartridge buckle, cutting the belt in two and effectively neutralizing Bowdre; shot the thumb from George Coe's hand; grazed Billy the Kid, and finally, killed Brewer with a shot in the head. Brewer was buried and Roberts, who died about noon the next day, was buried beside him and "it is one of history's little ironies that no one any longer knows which grave is which."

Paul A. Blazer, "The Fight at Blazer's Mill: A Chapter in the Lincoln County War," *Arizona and the West,* Vol. 6, No. 3 (Autumn, 1964), 203-10; Frederick W. Nolan, *The Lincoln County War: A Documentary History,* Norman, Univ. of Okla. Press, 1992; Robert N. Mullin notes; Mullin, ed., *Maurice G. Fulton's History of the Lincoln County War,* Tucson, Univ. of Ariz. Press, 1968; Robert M. Utley, *Billy the Kid: A Short and Violent Life,* Lincoln, Univ. of Nebr. Press, 1989.

Roberts, John, pioneer (d. Sept. 24, 1774). Living with his family on Reedy Creek, a tributary of the north fork of the Holston River in the present Sullivan County, Tennessee, Roberts believed the quiet area too remote from Indian hostility to warrant withdrawing to any neighboring fort, despite rumors of warfare in the north. September 24, an Indian war party led by Logan, it later was reported, descended upon the homestead; Roberts, his wife and several children were killed. James, 10, was captured. One of the children, tomahawked and scalped, survived for "some days." Major Arthur Campbell (see entry), in a fragment of a letter quoted by Thwaites, gives this account of the wounded child: "upon whose first appearance, my little hero ran off, his Uncle called, he knew his voice and turned and ran to him rejoiced; his Uncle questioned him, and he returned sensible Answers. Shewed his murdered Parents and sisters his Brother [James] is not found, and I supposed captivated. He received but one Blow with a Tomhake on the back of the Head, which cut thro his scull, but it is generally believed his Brains is safe, as he continues to talk sensibly, and being an active wise Boy, what he relates is Credited. For my part I don't know as I ever had tenderer feelings of compasion, for any of the human Species. I have sent for him, and employed an Old Man that has some Skill to attend him. I wish I could get Doctr. Lloyd to him. If he cannot come, please try if the Doctor could not send me up some Medicines with directions...." Logan, probably a Cayuga chief (see entry) arrived back at his village October 21, with the Roberts boy, James, whom he had seized, along with two black prisoners. The ultimate fate of James and when he was recovered, if he was, is not reported.

Thwaites, *Dunmore.*

Roberts, Robert B., historical writer (Mar. 5, 1911-Nov. 1, 1986). B. at New York City, he intended to become a Columbia University history major when the 1929 Depression wiped out that possibility, and his advanced education was forced to depend upon the New York Public Library; he spent much time in its American History Room. He compiled a collection of biographies of noted American orators with selections of their speeches, but could not find a publisher for it. He worked for 28 years for IBM while pursuing as an avocation the collecting of information about United States and Canadian forts. He gathered ephemeral pamphlets, photographs, rare line drawings and diagrams of trader posts and both militia and federal military installations. His collection became extensive and of unique quality, and his correspondence with libraries, historical agencies and historians supportive of it. He retired to Lehigh Acres, Florida. Roberts published *New York's Forts in the Revolution* (1980) and in 1984 received an acceptance from the Macmillan Company for his magisterial *Encyclopedia of Historic Forts: The Military, Pioneer, and Trading Posts of the United States* (1987) which lists more than 3,000 forts, camps, cantonments, barracks, posts, redoubts, blockhouses and batteries, the most detailed listing of United States fortifications published to that time. His wife was killed in an automobile accident in which Roberts was injured seriously, and he found he had lung cancer the year before publication of his major work. He donated his collection of fort material to the U.S. Military Academy Library at West Point; the collection also includes the manuscript for a Canadian fort encyclopedia.

Alan C. Aimone obituary article, Council on America's Military Past *Heliogram* 184 (Apr. 1987), 11; correspondence with Aimone.

Robertson, Cady, soldier, explorer (c. 1850-post 1900). As a sergeant of Troop E, 2nd Cavalry, Robertson joined Lieutenant Henry T. Allen in early 1885 for an extended exploration of the little known interior of Alaska (see Allen entry for details). Robertson was first of the party to reveal traces of scurvy, his body early in June being "covered with black spots, which developed later into...scurvy," Allen reported. It was due to the paucity of proper food and vitamin-rich rations which could have prevented it. Subsequently Allen and Fred W. Fickett, meteorologist of the party, also contracted the disease. July 26, the party reached the confluence of the Tanana and Yukon rivers and here Allen wrote that he found Robertson "in a critical condition from scurvy." Allen directed Robertson to take the riverboat *Yukon* to St. Michael on Norton Sound, probably because he was in no physical condition to continue the exploration. Robertson River, a tributary to the Tanana River, was named for the sergeant by Allen, and Robertson Glacier on Mount Kimball, the source of the river, may have derived its name from that of the stream. Robertson, in 1898 testimony supporting Fickett's claim for pension benefits because of the long-lasting effects of illness contracted in Alaska, noted that from March until September 1885 "we were compelled to live upon what we found in the country—which was simply meat and fish without salt or vegetables, being frequently reduced to the extremity of eating carron [carrion] and refuse matter of all [kinds] picked up by the way side. The lack of nourishment, connected with the extreme exposure of the party, engendered scurvy upon all of us, it first appearing on me in June, next on Lieut. Allen, and lastly upon Fickett." By the time he wrote this statement, Robertson was ordnance sergeant, stationed at Fort Snelling, Minnesota. He last was reported there in 1900, at the age of 50.

Henry T. Allen report, *Narratives of Explorations in Alaska;* Fred W. Fickett, pension file, Vets. Admin., Phoenix, Ariz.

Robinson, Levi H., military officer (d. Feb. 9, 1874). B. in Vermont, he became sergeant of F Company, 10th Vermont Infantry July 16, 1862, and was commissioned a second lieutenant in the 119th U.S. Colored Infantry regiment February 18, 1865. He was commissioned second lieutenant in the 14th Infantry April 19, 1866, and first lieutenant August 11 of that year, John Eugene Smith becoming regimental colonel in 1870. February 9, 1874, Robinson and Corporal James Coleman having separated themselves from a Fort Laramie wood train, were ambushed by a large party of probable Sioux Indians and were slain. The incident occurred on Cottonwood Creek, twelve miles east of Laramie Peak. Smith, his commanding officer, later that year founded famed Camp (later Fort) Robinson, Nebraska, naming it for the young officer.

James C. Olson, *Red Cloud and the Sioux Problem,* Lincoln, Univ. of Nebr. Press, 1965; *Chronological List;* EHI; Heitman.

Robinson, T.C. (Pidge, T. Chanders), Texas

Ranger (Nov. 27, 1847-Apr. 4, 1876). B. probably near Rustburg, Campbell County, Virginia, he may have acquired the nickname Pidge there. In the early 1870s, perhaps in 1873, he became involved in some sort of difficulty with Justice James Walton, and about that time arrived at a feuding relationship with a neighbor, Jesse E. Mitchell; it may have been over a sister of his opponent, Pidgie E. Mitchell. "It is evident that T.C. Robinson and Pidgie E. Mitchell were in love, but brother Jesse E. Mitchell for some reason prohibited that love to flourish," and Robinson felt it necessary to leave Virginia. At Austin, Texas, he worked briefly for the *Daily Democratic Statesman,* and later, not very successfully, as a cowboy and, finally, according to the muster roll of July 25, 1874, he joined the Leander H. McNelly (see entry) Special Force of Texas Rangers, "sort of an adjunct to the Frontier Battalion." Under the name of T. Chanders, Robinson initially was first sergeant but soon was named lieutenant of the force which was assigned to quell, if possible, the famed Sutton-Taylor feud in DeWitt County. Later it operated against Mexican cattle rustlers along the Rio Grande. During this period a memorable series of humorous and vivid descriptions of Robinson's adventures with the Rangers, and poems about his activities and thoughts began to appear in Austin newspapers, all identified by the sole name of "Pidge." Some of the letters intrigued C.L. Sonnichsen, then researching Texas feuds, and Sonnichsen's interest in them was picked up by Chuck Parsons, gunman researcher, who at length determined Pidge's true identity and the events of his short life. Having served some time with the Rangers, Pidge determined to take care of unfinished business back home. He took a leave from the force, as well as one of its Navy Colts, and returned to Campbell County with the apparent intent to kill Jesse Mitchell. He arrived home April 1, 1876. A newspaper story said that on Sunday, April 3, Robinson and Mitchell met "at New Providence Church, near Rustburg...to settle an old feud with pistols. Robinson was shot in the abdomen, and the other received one shot in the hand, which glancing went through his cheek and lodged in the back of his head. Another shot took effect in the breast. The latest report states that Robinson is dead and Mitchell could not survive." Pidge actually died April 4, and Mitchell recovered.

Chuck Parsons, "In Search of 'Pidge,'" Chicago, *Westerners Brand Book,* Vol. XXXXI, No. 2 (Summer, 1986), 23-26, 36-38.

Robinson, William, captive (fl. July 12-Sept. 24, 1774). Robinson was captured on the Monongahela River July 12, 1774. He was taken to the Indian towns, and saved from burning at the stake by the famous Cayuga chief, John Logan (see entry), and then was adopted into an Indian family. Logan dictated to Robinson, who was literate, the following letter, dated July 21: "To Captain [Michael] Cresap—What did you kill my people on Yellow Creek for. The white People killed my kin at Conestoga a great while ago, & I though[t nothing of that.] But you killed my kin again on Yellow Creek, and took m[y cousin prisoner] then I thought I must kill too; and I have been three time[s to war since but] the Indians is not Angry only myself

CAPTAIN JOH[N LOGAN]"

The Yellow Creek incident occurred April 30, 1774, Yellow Creek being an affluent of the Ohio River, coming in from the north about 50 miles below Pittsburgh. There the Daniel Greathouse party of whites was met by an Indian group of five men, one woman and an infant child. The whites gave the Indians rum, three of them becoming drunk. The sober Indians were challenged to shoot at a mark, and once their guns were emptied in that fashion, the whites shot both down; the three inebriated Indians were tomahawked, the woman mortally wounded, before she died pleading for the life of her baby who, she said, was "kin to themselves," since it was supposed to have been fathered by John Gibson, a trader. The Conestoga incident was the massacre of 20 inoffensive Conestoga (Susquehanna) Indians by the Paxton boys at Lancaster, Pennsylvania, in December 1763. Logan had been understandably incensed by these mindless killings of his people, and so had conducted a raid into Tennessee, on which he retaliated in the only way he could. The letter was left September 24 in the partially destroyed cabin of John Roberts who, with his wife and several children, was slain, one boy, James, being saved and carried back to the Indian towns by Logan (see Roberts entry).

Thwaites, *Dunmore.*

Rodgers, John, naval officer (Aug. 8, 1812-May 5, 1882). B. near Havre de Grace, Maryland, he was appointed a naval midshipman April 18, 1828, and served aboard the *Constellation* in the Mediterranean. On his return he studied at the Norfolk, Virginia, naval school and for a year at the University of Virginia, then rejoined the active navy and served with the Brazil Squadron for three years. He then engaged in surveying the Florida coast and in cooperating with the Army during the Second Seminole War, as commander of the *Wave* and later the *Jefferson.* On October 12, 1852, as a lieutenant he was ordered to the North Pacific Exploring and Surveying Expedition, which continued intermittently until the Civil War. He succeeded the ill Cadwalader Ringgold (see entry) in command of the expedition in 1854. It already had engaged in explorations of the Aleutian Islands, the Bering Sea and the Siberian coast and now Rodgers "sailed into the Arctic Ocean where he explored unknown regions and obtained information that corrected the Admiralty charts." His Civil War record was distinguished and he emerged a commodore, and on December 31, 1869, became a Rear Admiral. His subsequent service was varied and outstanding, but with little frontier interst. Rodgers was married and fathered three children.

Orth, 25, 812; DAB.

Rodionov, Eremey, trader, explorer (fl. 1796-1818). Rodionov was a veteran trader and Russian fur man in Alaska. In 1796 he brought tidings from Yakutat Bay to Kodiak Island of the suffering for want of food at that distant Russian colony. In 1800 he was a Baranov agent at Nuchek (Hinchingbrook) Island, Baranov writing him an extended letter reporting in detail the construction of a trading redoubt at Three Saints Bay on Kodiak. Rodionov by 1818 had established a fur trading camp on Pile Bay of Lake Iliamna and here Korsakovskiy (see entry) came during his explorations to the west, learning from natives around the camp what he considered definite reports of the existence of a lost Russian colony to the west or north. Because of the lateness of the season, Tanaina Indians advised Korsakovskiy not to try to travel westward himself, but to send Rodionov (who was reported to be already trading with the Tutna, or Kuskokwim people) with five Kenians in his stead. The trader agreed to undertake the mission. He left August 18, and returned September 2, having reached the Kuskokwim River about at Crow Village, west of Aniak, but found no trace of the lost Russians; whether Korsakovskiy employed Rodionov again on his 1819 exploration is unreported, for his journal of that endeavor has not been located.

James W. VanStone, *Russian Exploration in Southwest Alaska: The Travel Journals of Petr Korsakovskiy (1818) and Ivan Ya. Vasilev (1829),* Fairbanks, Univ. of Alaska Press, 1988; Bancroft, *Alaska;* Zagoskin.

Ro(d)gers, David, military officer (d. Oct. 4, 1779) B. in Ireland, he early emigrated to this country, settling as a merchant in Oldtown, Maryland. In 1775 he established a settlement five miles above Wheeling, West Virginia, on the Ohio River. In 1776 he represented the West Augusta district in the Virginia legislature and that year was appointed a captain in the continental service, but for some reason failed to qualify and instead became county lieutenant for the new Ohio County. Indian unrest on the border brought him back to the frontier where he settled for a time at Mt. Braddock, in the present Fayette County, Pennsylvania. Later he married the widow of Michael Cresap (see entry) and located on the Potomac in Hampshire County, present West Virginia. January 14, 1778, he was sent as a special envoy to New Orleans to bring back supplies for the western states. He left Pittsburgh in June, reached New Orleans in September after considerable delays and found that the goods had already been sent to St. Louis, where they awaited him. He secured them there and in the fall of 1779 started up the Ohio. From George Rogers Clark at the Falls of the Ohio (Louisville) he secured reinforcements and resumed his upriver movement, now commanding a force of 70 men. About three miles below the mouth of the Little Miami River, on October 4, he discovered an Indian party of Senecas (Mingos), Wyandots (Hurons), Delawares and Shawnees under direction of Matthew Elliott, Simon Girty and George Girty (see entries). The Indians killed 42 of Rogers' men, and Simon Girty later boasted that he himself had killed Rogers; five of the men, including John Campbell (see entry), were taken prisoner. The Indian loss was two killed and three wounded; they obtained much loot, including considerable specie and many firearms.

Thwaites/Kellogg, *The Revolution on the Upper Ohio, 1775-1777,* Madison, Wis. Hist. Soc., 1908; Consul W. Butterfield, *History of the Girtys,* Cincinnati, Robert Clarke Co., 1890, 1950.

Rogers, Harrison G., mountain man (d. July 14, 1828). B. in Virginia, Rogers, who Dale Morgan wrote "managed to live his [early] life in perfect privacy" before joining Jedediah Smith in 1826, was living in 1819 in the Boonslick country of Missouri, across the river from Franklin and near present Boonesville. September 14, he signed a petition to the President by "inhabitants of the Howard Lake District," much of which became the later Howard County, Missouri. Otherwise nothing is reported of his age or birth. He shared with Smith a Protestant faith, was "educated, intelligent, sharply observing" and an able and diligent subordinate. He was selected as clerk, later to become second-in-command of Smith's important explorations into the southwest. Rogers first comes into full view with his keeping of a journal and daybook commencing in August 1826 (see Smith entry for exploration details). Rogers' writings are sources on the expeditions second only to the records of the commander himself. The two journals today are held by the Missouri Historical Society. Entries relating to the Smith explorations begin on August 5; day book entries and diary entries are intertwined in them. Though devoutly Protestant, Rogers paid tribute to "Old Father Sanchus," [the Franciscan, José Bernardo Sanchez (1778-1833)], in charge at San Gabriel Mission, near present Los Angeles. Sanchez, wrote Rogers, "has been the greatest friend that I ever met with in all my travels, he is worthy of being called a christian, as he possesses charity in the highest degree, and [is] a friend to the poor and distressed. I ever shall hold him as a man of God, taking us when in distress, feeding, and clothing us, and may God prosper him and all such men." Rogers was favorably impressed by the mission staff as well: "They all appear friendly and treat us well,...allow us the liberty of conscience, and treat us as they do their own countrymen, or brethren," he wrote. Rogers accompanied Smith, leaving southern California as directed by Spanish officials, although as soon as the settlements were past they turned north and established a secure camp on the Stanislaus River, west of today's Yosemite National Park. Here Smith left Rogers in command of an eleven-man detail as with two companions he returned across the Great Basin to the trappers' rendezvous of 1827. While camped on the Stanislaus, Rogers was met by Sergeant Francisco Soto, who brought an angry letter from Captain Luis Antonio Argüello, commandant of the San Francisco Presidio. It accused the party of behaving in a "very bad manner," committing hostile acts against Mexican interests, illegally exploring Mexican territory and violating international law. Rogers persuaded Soto that the Smith people had done no harm and asked him to deliver mollifying letters to Argüello and Governor José María Echeandía. They rebutted all charges of illegal activity, Rogers offered to come in and explain in person the intent and status of the explorers if the Mexican officials so desired, and sought to convince them that the trapper party only wished peaceably to leave for the Columbia River. Apparently the letters were successful, for no significant reply was forthcoming. Smith returned in mid-September 1827, uniting with the Stanislaus element. Following a winter of efforts to obtain necessary supplies and livestock from Mexican sources, along with official permission to leave the country, the Smith group left in January 1828. Rogers was ever an active hunter. Smith at one point noted his ability in pursuit of antelope and in southern California Rogers once wounded a bear and killed a wolf. Now on the Feather River in early March he killed one grizzly and wounded another, which he followed into a "verry bad thicket" where the animal charged him. Rogers "fired a moment before the bear caught him. After biting him in several places he went off," but, returning, "caught Mr. Rodgers and gave him several additional wounds." Rogers was "verry badly wounded being severely cut in...10 or 12 places." Smith treated the gashes with soap and sugar plasters but the injuries were so incapacitating that the company was obliged to lie by for nearly a week and even then Rogers could travel only a short distance every two or three days. It was a narrow escape. He did not fully recover until the end of March. The company crossed the Klamath River May 25, reached the sea June 8, on July 9 was at Coos Bay and the 11th arrived at the mouth of the Umpqua River, camping on a small island July 13, at the confluence of the Defeat River (the present Smith River). Here on July 14, Smith and two others left the camp in charge of Rogers while they conducted a brief reconnaissance of the surroundings. Rogers was told under no circumstances to permit Indians to enter the camp, but for some reason ignored the directive; about 100 Umpqua Indians (identified by Morgan as Kelawatsets) entered the camp and in an unguarded moment fell upon the whites, killing fifteen while a single man, Arthur Black (see entry), escaped. Rogers was among those slain.

Dale Morgan, *Jedediah Smith and the Opening of the West*, N.Y., Bobbs-Merrill Co., 1953; George R. Brooks, ed., *The Southwest Expedition of Jedediah S. Smith*, Glendale, Calif., Arthur H. Clark Co., 1977; David J. Weber, *The Californios versus Jedediah*

Smith 1826-1827, Spokane, Wash., Arthur H. Clark Co., 1990; Maynard Geiger, O.F.M., *Franciscan Missionaries in Hispanic California 1769-1848*, San Marino, Calif., The Huntington Lby., 1969; Robert Glass Cleland, *This Reckless Breed of Men*, N.Y., Alfred A. Knopf, 1950.

Rohn, Oscar, mining engineer, geologist (June 27, 1870-Sept. 19, 1923). B. at West Bend, Wisconsin, he became an accomplished geologist and respected mining engineer before entering government work in Alaska in 1898. Rohn authored three papers in *Narratives,* published in 1900, and descriptive of his Alaskan work. The first of these, "Trails and Routes," summarized his findings on detailed reconnaissances of the virtually roadless region east of the Copper River and south of the Wrangell Mountains. Rohn described nearly every existing trail and reasonable alternative that might be laid out, leading to important geographical or mining areas, present or in prospect. The second paper, "An Expedition into the Mount Wrangell Region," discussed at length his 1899 exploration of this jumbled, mountainous region, topographically, and with a view toward its eventual mineral-extracting possibilities. It discussed in a cursory way the geology of the region, for Rohn was a trained geologist, and the feasability of railroad and road construction, since he was also a specialist in those matters. He discussed the Chitina River valley's geographical nature, and that of its tributary, the Nizina, which "rises in a tremendous glacier in the range to the north separating the Chitina from the Tanana" river valley. He described the Wrangell Mountain group and its drainages, and bestowed names on some features, such as Mount Abercrombie (Mount Frederika) after the army officer in charge of the 1898-99 explorations, and Meiklejohn Pass in the Mentasta Mountains (the pass apparently not named by Lowe, as stated in Orth). Rohn also showed clearly that the "Mount Tillman" as named by Allen (see entry), did not exist, at least in the site Allen indicated, and explained how the error had probably been made. Rohn also discussed the occurrences of copper and viable placer deposits in the region he reconnoitered. He explained that the exploration and geographical definition of the country studied were necessary "to the development" of the region. The "Narrative and Itinerary" section of his paper revealed in a detailed way his arduous work and accomplishments. His third paper,"Geology of the Wrangell Mountains," details his geological examination of that important uplift, based upon observation, study of the specimens and fossils he collected, and conjectures based upon his field examinations. Sample: "At the head of the Kots(i)na River are found a series of very regular, nearly horizontally banded rocks, indicating in every respect bedded rock of sedimentary origin. The absence of any sign of sedimentary rocks in the bed of the river led me to climb the mountains to examine these rocks, and, to my surprise, I found them to be amygdaloidal, volcanic diabeses much resembling the old diabases of the Keweenawan area of Lake Superior." Similarly knowledgeable and detailed analyses follow virtually every observation made by Rohn during his valuable reconnaissance. He also discussed glaciers and glaciation in the Wrangell region. In 1900 Rohn was in charge of a large iron mining company in the Mesabi Range of northeastern Minnesota. In 1906 he went to Butte, Montana, to take charge of the ailing East Butte Copper Mining Company, then reported to be $600,000 in debt; under Rohn's management it became a major producer of copper and financially profitable. Later he worked in Nevada "where he enjoyed high standing as a geologist and mining engineer." Rohn had become consulting engineer for a Butte mining concern owning the Pittsburg and Montana Company. From his office at Denver he became general manager of the Pittsmont operation, as it was subsequently called, of the East Butte Company. At the age of 53 he suffered a freak accident at the shaft where he was caught by a new skip-dump being installed, and half of his head sheared away, Rohn being instantly killed. He was married and was survived by his widow, two sons and three brothers.

Narratives of Explorations in Alaska; Orth, 354, 813; info. from Alaska State Lby., Juneau; *Anchorage Daily Times,* Sept. 20, 1923; *Butte Daily Miner,* Sept. 20, 1923; Rohn death cert.

Roquefeuil, Camille de, French naval officer (Jan. 28, 1781-1831). B. in France, at 20 he entered the French navy as an aspirant on *La Chiffonne;* when the British sank his frigate he transferred to *La Fleche,* which also was sunk. Eventually he became an ensign and then a lieutenant, winning the Legion of Honor in 1812. In 1816 a Bordeaux merchant employed him to lead a trading expedition to the Northwest Coast of America and to China, to somewhat restore

French international trade following the Revolution and Napoleonic wars which had all but destroyed it. Roquefeuil cleared Bordeaux October 19, 1816, with *Le Bordelais,* and August 5, 1817, arrived at San Francisco. After a South Seas cruise the ship on April 5, 1818, reached Sitka, Alaska. The new Russian American Company governor, Hagemeister (see entry), agreed to supply Roquefeuil with 30 baidarkas for Kodiak sea otter hunters and Roqufeuil commenced hunting in the Alaskan Panhandle. His Aleut hunters were attacked by Indians and of 47 then on shore, 20 were killed, 12 wounded and the rest escaped with two missing and one additional hunter dying of wounds. His Aleuts refused to hunt any longer. Roquefeuil returned to Sitka and after a bit more unsuccessful cruising among the Alaskan islands, the French officer returned to California, then back to Sitka and finally cleared the Alaskan coast December 13, for Canton, regaining Bordeaux November 21, 1819, concluding an unprofitable voyage, although he did complete a circumnavigation of the world. His journal was published in 1823. Roquefeuil was disappointed in not immediately receiving a Navy promotion, left the service for the merchant marine and, although the delayed naval promotion did finally reach him, he died while on the Indian Ocean and was buried at St. Paul on the Isle de Bourbon (now La Reunion, one of the Mascarene Islands, 400 miles east of Madagascar). Pierce reported that no trace of his grave remains.

Pierce, *Russian America: A Biographical Dictionary.*

Rosenberg, Nikolai Iakovlevich, naval officer, administrator (d. Nov. 29, 1857). B. of a Baltic noble family of German origin in Lithuania, he entered naval school December 28, 1819, and in 1826 as a midshipman commenced service on several Baltic Sea vessels. December 24, 1829, he joined the Russian American Company and from 1831-39 commanded several of its ships in Alaskan service. He left Sitka in 1839, returned to St. Petersburg, fulfilled civilian occupations until Novemer 13, 1847, when he re-entered the navy as a lieutenant and again joined the Russian American Company. He became a Captain-Lieutenant December 6, 1849, and January 25, 1850, was appointed Captain, Second Rank and chief manager of the company, assuming office October 14, 1850. During his brief governorship the company greatly expanded its commercial activities with the 596-ton *Imperator Nikola I,* built in New York, the 650-ton *Tsesarevich,* bought in Hamburg, the 500-ton *Kadiak,* bought in Lubeck, Germany, the pride of the fleet, the 1,200-ton *Sitka* ordered from Hamburg, and the 900-ton *Kamchatka.* The company also took up whaling since the sea otter trade had greatly diminished due to over-hunting of the animals. The ice trade with California proved lucrative, and Alaska had an inexhaustible supply, bringing $20 to $25 a ton at San Francisco. October 22, 1850, the British sloop-of-war *Enterprise* reached Sitka. She was commanded by Richard Collinson and was in search of survivors of the lost John Franklin Arctic expedition; one of Collinson's officers was the ill-fated Lieutenant John Barnard (see entry). In 1852 Rosenberg asked to be relieved because of ill health and for unspecified "family reasons," and in November the company authorized him to return to Russia, leaving affairs in the hands of Aleksandr Ilich Rudakov, Captain, Second Rank. Rosenberg left for Siberia June 2, 1853, crossed overland to St. Petersburg. He became Captain, First Rank August 30, 1855, two years before his death.

Richard A. Pierce, *Builders of Alaska: The Russian Governors 1818-1867,* Kingston, Ont., Limestone Press, 1986; Bancroft, *Alaska.*

Rotten Belly, River Crow chief (c. 1789-1834). Denig described Rotten Belly as a foremost Crow chief who might have ranked with Tecumseh and Pontiac with equal opportunities, but as it was his activities "were confined to petty attacks on the hostile nations" surrounding his people. As a very young man he achieved local note by leading small parties of horse thieves against Cheyennes, Arapahoes, Bannocks, Sioux and Blackfeet and so remarkable was his success, and so few the casualties among his followers, that at 30 he had become "chief of the Crow Nation." He had many things in his favor: he had "large and rich connections," was a prophet or medicine man capable of mustering supernatural aid for his activities, though in his general conduct he was "not an agreeable man, but rather of a quiet, surly disposition. He spoke little, but that in a tone of command. His great superiority over others consisted in decision, action, and an utter disregard for the safety of his own person." As chief he enacted many good laws and rules for the preservation of his people, led the camp with good judgment, caused his followers to trade for more guns and ammunition, established regular

camp sentinels night and day and saw to it that no hostile neighbors could make headway against his people or stock. "Whoever approached the camp was killed. Warriors were on the alert and well prepared." As chief he planned and led great battles against enemies. In the first of these, against 80 lodges of Blackfeet on the Musselshell River, more than 100 Blackfeet were killed, 230 women and children taken prisoner and more than 500 head of horses seized while the Crows lost only 22 men, though others were wounded. At one time the Cheyennes ambushed a sizable body of Crows and decimated them. Rotten Belly was called upon to avenge the losses and he mustered a great force including nearly 600 warriors, led them for ten days southward until a principal Cheyenne camp was located in the valley of the Arkansas River, and in a successful and well-planned attack more than 200 enemies were killed, 270 women and children captured, upwards of 1,000 horses taken and much loot seized, all at a cost of only 5 Crows killed and 10 or 15 wounded. This was close to the year 1833 when a terrible smallpox plague occurred, decimating the nation, although Rotten Belly himself escaped the infection. He did what he could to recoup Crow losses and reorganize the camps following the scourge. He had long wished to attack the American Fur Company's fort at the mouth of the Maria River on the upper Missouri, for this post supplied the Blackfeet with arms, ammunition and other items in trade. Rotten Belly sent a strong party under Little White Bear, his relative, to scout the installation and bring back a report, but on their return the Little White Bear element was ambushed and destroyed by a Blackfeet war party headed by Spotted Elk, an experienced warrior. Little White Bear himself was killed. The Crows went on to lay siege to the fort, but it failed to have the desired result and a huge Blackfeet assemblage arrived to break it up, 800 lodges of them. The Crows drew away, but Rotten Belly shortly halted them. A small Blackfeet war party of some 20 men was encountered, they seeking to join their people around the fort. The Crows attacked and killed two while the rest fled to a rude breastwork "made by war parties, everywhere to be met with in the Blackfeet district." The Crows should then have left them alone and gone away to fight some other time, but Rotten Belly's pride was injured, his standing as a chief in jeopardy, and besides, he was already garbed in "his gay and costly war suit." Shouting, "One last stroke for the Crow

Nation; two Blackfeet cannot pay for the loss of The Little White Bear!" he rode alone into the stockade, among his enemies, "but received a dozen arrows in his body and fell to rise no more." His followers then rushed into the stockade and wiped out the remaining Blackfeet with no further loss to themselves. Rotten Belly's body was wrapped in its warrior shroud and deposited on a tree in the country of the Blackfeet, to be, as he said, "a terror to them even after death."

Edwin Thompson Denig, *Five Indian Tribes of the Upper Missouri,* Norman, Univ. of Okla. Press, 1973; *Montana, Contributions,* IX (1923), 299-307.

Rotten Belly (Tack-en-su-a-tis), Nez Perce chief (fl. 1832-1871). This Indian leader was involved in the Blackfeet fight with mountain men at Pierre's Hole July 18, 1832, and was wounded in the stomach; the injury festered and from this his best-known name originated. It later healed completely. Rotten Belly was described as a "tall, commanding-looking fellow" who became a major chief of his people and, in the early years, a warm friend of Protestant missionaries. His ardor for the new faith cooled considerably, and then, in his advanced age, reignited. He was one of the Nez Perce and Flathead chiefs who counseled with Samuel Parker and Marcus Whitman (see entries) at the Green River Rendezvous in 1835, both missionaries considering him the "first chief" of his tribe, but it is not clear that he actually was such. Parker reported that Rotten Belly said at council that "He had heard from white men a little about God, which had only gone into his ears; he wished to know enough to have it go down into his heart...and to teach his people." The next year Rotten Belly met Whitman and his wife, Narcissa, and Henry H. Spalding and his wife, Eliza, at the Rendezvous of 1836, also on the Green River, and escorted them to Fort Walla Walla; later in the summer he helped Spalding select the site of the famous Lapwai Mission, just east of present-day Lewiston, Idaho. Spalding was generous in his praise of Rotten Belly in the early years, writing at one time that "He is very strict in his observance of morning and evening prayers, and in the observance of the Sabbath. I do believe that if there is one in the darkness of heathenism that wishes to do right it is this chief." Rotten Belly must soon have wearied of missionary strictures for on April 22, 1839, Spalding confessed in his diary that the Indian had left the mission (after a

quarrel with Spalding, who was not the easiest person to get along with). Spalding wrote of his disillusionment: "Really I fear they will all prove to be a selfish, deceptive race of beings." In a letter of February 6, 1840, to his Boston headquarters, missionary Asa Bowen Smith reported of Rotten Belly that "people at home may think...that he is a christian, but he is far from it. Instead of being settled with Mr. S. [Spalding] he has become his enemy & proves to be a very wicked man & now spends much of his time in the buffalo country. It is now very evident [that] when his selfish expectations were not gratified, he showed out his wickedness. These Indians are often very shrewd & managed well with strangers to take advantage of them..." The Lapwai mission was broken up in 1847; it had had no great success. In 1842 a French-Canadian Catholic priest, Modeste Demers, baptized Rotten Belly in that faith, but it too failed to hold his affection for very long. Little more is heard of Rotten Belly until 1871 when Spalding returned to lead a great revival among the Nez Perce. On November 12, there was a baptismal service for this Protestant faith and heading the list of those receiving the sacrament were Tack-en-su-a-tis, or Rotten Belly, and the famed chief Lawyer, along with 19 other men and 23 women. Spalding bestowed upon Rotten Belly the biblical name of Samuel. No record has been located of when and where the old chief died, although one of his sons and two daughters were still living in 1935 near Stite, Idaho. Rotten Belly, the Nez Perce should not be confused with Rotten Belly, the Crow chief, who was killed in 1834 (see entry).

Clifford Merrill Drury, *The Diaries and Letters of Henry H. Spalding and Asa Bowen Smith Relating to the Nez Perce Mission 1838-1842,* Glendale, Calif., Arthur H. Clark Co., 1958; Drury, *Marcus and Narcissa Whitman and the Opening of Old Oregon,* 2 vols., Glendale, Clark, 1973; Alvin M. Josephy Jr., *The Nez Perce Indians and the Opening of the Northwest,* New Haven, Yale Univ. Press, 1965; Dale L. Morgan, Eleanor Towles Harris, eds., *The Rocky Mountain Journals of William Marshall Anderson,* San Marino, Calif., Huntington Lby., 1967.

Roundhead (Stayeghtha, Stiahta), Huron (Wyandot) chief (d.c. Oct. 1813). A Wyandot (Huron) chief, he was b. in the mid-18th century, possibly near the Detroit River, between Lake St. Clair and Lake Erie. He probably fought in the wars of the 1790s against the Americans, for he was the seventh Wyandot signatory to the 1795

Treaty of Greenville. Reginald Horsman, in the *Dictionary of Canadian Biography,* said that Roundhead arrived at the Greenville Council which preceded the treaty signing at the end of July from the vicinity of Detroit with a party of Wyandots, Shawnees, Six Nations, and Delawares, this when the "proceedings were almost over." By this agreement Indians surrendered most of Ohio and some of Indiana, and five years later Roundhead agreed to an English treaty surrendering 2,500 acres of Canada to the whites. Yet Roundhead continued to be bitterly opposed to the white American interests. He was close to Tenskwatawa, the Shawnee prophet, and to his brother, Tecumseh, in the movement to counter white expansionism and aggression by means of a pan-Indian movement. In 1807 he, Tecumseh, Blue Jacket and the Panther, probably a Shawnee chief, were sent to the Ohio governor to inform him the Prophet intended only peace with the whites. When Tecumseh ordered the death of Leatherlips (see entry) in 1810, he assigned the execution to Roundhead since both he and the victim were Huron chiefs. When the War of 1812 erupted, Roundhead was living in Ontario as chief of about 60 of his people near Windsor. "He became one of the most active Indian leaders in the fighting in the Detroit frontier region," apparently convinced that the best hopes of stemming the American advance lay with the British. In August 1812 he led Indians in a battle at the present Wyandotte, Michigan, and had an important role in the capture of Detroit. September 27-28 he participated with Major Adam C. Muir of Henry Procter's command in an attack on Fort Miami (the present Fort Wayne), Indiana. Roundhead urged Muir to hold his position and continue the fight against the defenders, but Muir decided upon a withdrawal. In January 1813 Roundhead was a leader in a British-Indian victory over the United States forces at the present Monroe, Michigan, and in the spring led 1,200 Indians in the siege of Fort Meigs, Ohio. Roundhead's brother, John Battise, a man of "great size and personal strength," was killed fighting for the British at Meigs. October 23, 1813, General Procter wrote that "The Indian Cause and ours experienced a serious Loss in the death of Roundhead." He gave no details. Roundhead was spoken of as a fine-looking man and a celebrated chief. A village in Hardin County, Ohio, southeast of Lima, is named for him.

Hodge, HAI; Reginald Horseman article, DCB, V, 774-75; info. from John Sugden.

Rousseau, Lovell Harrison, military officer, legislator (Aug. 4, 1818-Jan. 7, 1869). B. near Stanford, Kentucky, he was sparsely educated but read law at Louisville and was admitted to the Indiana bar in 1841. He served as a Whig in the Indiana Legislature, was a captain in the Mexican War, and then became a criminal lawyer at Louisville. He served in the Kentucky Senate but when the Civil War broke out, being an ardent opponent of Seccession, served in the Union Army, becoming a Major General of Volunteers with a distinguished record until his resignation as a Volunteers officer November 30, 1865. On March 28, 1867, he became a Brigadier General in the Army, following a tempestuous period as a Representative in the U.S. Congress, where his hot temper occasionally generated difficulties. Rousseau's only frontier experience was in 1867 when he was assigned to Sitka, Alaska, in his rank as brevet Major General to meet with representatives of the Czar and formally receive possession of Alaska following its purchase, as well as neighboring islands and stations. These included Fort Kenai, Kodiak, Fort Wrangell, St. Michael on Norton Sound, the Pribylov Islands and other elements of what then was considered by many a huge and valueless wilderness save for its fur trade and fisheries. The treaty for sale of the 586,400 square miles for $7.2 million had been signed March 30, 1867, at Washington by Secretary of State William H. Seward for the United States, and Baron Edward de Stoeckl, Russian ambassador. Ratification followed and the purchase was formally proclaimed by President Andrew Johnson on June 30. The transfer ceremony took place October 18, 1867, at Sitka with Rousseau and Prince Dmitry Maksutov, the Russian governor, the principals. His single visit to Alaska was abundantly sufficient for Rousseau who, upon his return to Washington, earnestly urged that he not be assigned there again. He was given command of the Department of Louisiana and died at New Orleans, burial at Arlington.

Heitman; Archie W. Shiels, *The Purchase of Alaska,* College, Univ. of Alaska Press, 1967; BDAC; DAB; Bancroft, *Alaska.*

Rucker, Daniel Henry, military officer (Apr. 28, 1812-Jan. 6, 1910). B. at Belleville, New Jersey, he was commissioned a second lieutenant from Michigan in the 1st Dragoons October 13, 1837, and was assigned to Fort Gibson, Cherokee Nation, where he served in 1838-39 when he was posted to Fort Wayne (at the present Watts, Oklahoma) until April 1840. He was then assigned to Fort Leavenworth until October 1844 when he was stationed at Fort Towson, Indian Territory, for a year. In the Mexican War of 1846-48 he won a brevet to major in the Battle of Buena Vista, and was promoted to captain February 7, 1847. In August 1848 he commanded Company E, 1st Dragoons in an overland expedition under Lawrence Pike Graham (see entry) from Coahuila, Mexico, to Los Angeles, California, an episodic adventure best reported by Cave Couts (see entry) whose colorful diary has been published. The 500-man expedition included four dragoon companies totaling about 275 men, 205 teamsters and others. The adventure "was attended by much toil and hardship...much dissension on the march and later," according to Bancroft, and it arrived at its destination "so late that [the dragoons] had no opportunity even to desert for the mines." The overland rush to California in 1848-50 by ill-supplied and worse-informed emigrants resulted in ghastly suffering, as "many started with scanty supplies and poorer animals," numbers of which perished in the Nevada and eastern California wastelands to the point that "the effluvia revived the cholera, and sent it to ravage the enfeebled crowds...not alone with this and other scourges, but with famine and cold...until California was filled with pity, and the government combined with the miners and other self-sacrificing men in efforts for the relief of the sufferers." Rucker directed troops sent eastward with supplies for which, as well as other efforts, $160,000 was appropriated from civil funds and countless lives were saved, much hardship ameliorated. Rucker remained in the mountains until "the last of the migration" had crossed into the California central valley. He was stationed at San Luis Rey in May 1850 but that post was quickly abandoned "on account of the wholesale desertion of the soldiery...by the attractions of gold-getting in the mines." He then served at Forts Union, Conrad (south of Socorro) and Albuquerque in New Mexico until November 1860, when he returned to Washington, D.C., to become Depot Quartermaster, at which he was occupied throughout the Civil War. He was promoted to colonel and Acting Quartermaster General of the army in January 1867, Chief Quartermaster of the Department of the East at Philadelphia from 1868 to 1882, becoming Quartermaster General at Washington February 13, 1882, and retiring ten days later as Brigadier

General and brevet Major General. He lived at Washington for the remainder of his life, dying at the age of 97.

Heitman; Powell; Ezra J. Warner, *Generals in Blue,* Baton Rouge, Louisiana State University Press, 1964; Bancroft, *California,* V, VI, VII.

Rudakov, Aleksandr Ilich, naval officer, administrator (1817-Oct. 16, 1875). After attending naval school from 1829-33 he served briefly in the Baltic and was assigned to the Black Sea as a midshipman December 19, 1834. April 14, 1840, he became a lieutenant and two years later was assigned to the Baltic Fleet once more. November 1, 1844, he joined the Russian American Company, reaching Sitka, Alaska, in 1845. He spent several years commanding ships on company business to California, Hawaii, Kamchatka and the Aleutians. April 19, 1850, he left Sitka for Anian, Siberia, and went overland to St. Petersburg where May 9, 1851, he became Captain-Lieutenant and July 11 was appointed assistant chief manager of the Russian American holdings as Captain, Second Rank. He arrived at Sitka May 7, 1852, and when Rosenberg (see entry) left in 1853, took over managing the company and colony until the arrival of Voevodskii (see entry) April 17, 1854. Rudakov remained in Alaska until 1857 when, as Captain, First Rank he returned to St. Petersburg, left the company and resumed navy duty. He became a Rear Admiral in 1865 and Vice Admiral in 1870, when he retired.

Richard A. Pierce, *Builders of Alaska: The Russian Governors 1818-1867,* Kingston, Ontario, Limestone Press, 1986.

Russell, Israel Cook, geologist (Dec. 10, 1852-1906). B. at Garrattsville, New York, he was graduated from the University of the City of New York in 1872 with a degree in civil engineering. He took graduate work at the School of Mines of Columbia College and eventually received his doctorate from New York University. Russell was a member of the transit of Venus expedition to New Zealand in 1874-75, taught at the Columbia School of Mines from 1875 to 1877 and joined the Geological Survey in 1880. In 1889 he traveled to the Yukon River, helping establish a portion of Alaska's eastern boundary with Canada. In 1890-91 he explored the Malaspina Glacier, 38 miles northwest of Yakutat, as well as the Yakutat Bay and the Mount St. Elias regions, the party mapping more than 1,000 square miles.

Russell Fjord off Yakutat Bay was named for him, as he was its discoverer. In 1892 he became professor of geology at the University of Michigan. At his death he was president of the Geological Society of America. Russell was author of *Lake Lahontan* (1885); *Lakes of North America* (1895); *Glaciers of North America* (1897); *Volcanoes of North America* and *Rivers of North America,* among other works.

Orth, 28, 821; *Who Was Who.*

Rutherford, Griffith, military officer (c. 1731-c. 1800). B. in Ireland, he emigrated to America and settled near Salisbury, North Carolina, from where he served in the provincial congress and was commissioned in 1776 a Brigadier General of militia. On July 14 he wrote the North Carolina Council of Safety that "I am Under the Nessety of sending you by Express, the Allerming Condition, this Country is in, the Indians is making Grate Prograce, in distroying & Murdering, in the frunteers of this County, 37 I am informed was killed last Wednesdauy & Thursday, on the Cuttaba [Catawba] River...three off oure Captans is kild & one Wounded. This Day I set out with what men I can Raise for the Relefe of the Distrest." In September he led 2,400 men to put down hostilities by the Cherokee Indians who had attacked some frontier settlements, aided as was supposed by Loyalist elements. Supporting his movement was a column of 1,800 men from South Carolina, under Colonel Andrew Williamson and Virginians under William Christian. Rutherford moved ahead of the main body with 500 men, crossed the Blue Ridge and, receiving reinforcements struck rapidly into Cherokee country. Williamson's men meanwhile "made short work of the [Cherokee] Lower Towns," Rutherford's column laid waste the Middle Towns, and Christian "took the Overhill Towns without a struggle." In October Rutherford returned to his North Carolina base. It was reported that 36 Indian villages had been destroyed and the Cherokees whipped to the point that Dragging Canoe took his still inveterately hostile followers westward to Chickamauga Creek (near present Chattanooga), Tennessee, beyond reach of the colonials. The majority of Cherokees in the spring of 1777 agreed to a peace of sorts with the Americans, which was Rutherford's final goal. August 16, 1780, he was taken prisoner by the British while commanding a brigade in the battle of Camden, South Carolina, but was exchanged in 1781. Following the Revolution he served at times in the North Carolina legislature until 1786 when he moved to Tennessee. In September 1794 he became president of the Tennessee legislative council. He died in Tennessee.

Robert McHenry, ed., *Webster's American Military Biographies,* Springfield, Mass., G.&C. Merriam Co., 1978; Douglas L. Rights, *The American Indian in North Carolina,* Winston-Salem, N.C., John F. Blair, 1957; Grace Steele Woodward, *The Cherokees,* Norman, Univ. of Okla. Press, 1963; James H. O'Donnell, III, *Southern Indians in the American Revolution,* Knoxville, Univ. of Tenn. Press, 1973; info. from E.F. (Ted) Mains.

Rynning, Thomas Harbo, soldier, lawman (1866-June 18, 1941). B. at Christiania (Oslo), Norway, he was brought to Beloit, Wisconsin, at age two. His father died when Rynning was ten. In 1878 his mother and an uncle undertook to raise him but Tom ran away. He became a Texas bullwhacker, then a cowboy and said he took part in cattle drives to Dodge City, Kansas. In 1885 he enlisted in the 8th Cavalry's D Troop under Captain James Franklin Randlett. That summer Cheyennes and other Indians strongly objected to cattlemen leasing reservation lands for grazing purposes, and it was feared an outbreak was possible. General Sheridan, commander in chief of the Army was directed to Indian Territory to settle the dispute (Hutton, *Sheridan,* 360-63). Rynning, as an enlisted man, was involved only peripherally; he described the incident as more hairy than it was, but it was his initial experience with volatile Indians. Transferred as a packer to Troop C he served under First Lieutenant Samuel Fountain in New Mexico. Near Alma, December 19, 1885, he was in a fight with Apaches led by Josanie (Ulzana) in which five whites were killed, two wounded, while again Rynning's recollections magnified it to 16 whites killed and "quite a few wounded," among them Lieutenant Farrand Sayre, though it was Lieutenant De Rosey C. Cabell who was wounded, and he not seriously. Returning to D Troop Rynning accompanied several Sierra Madre Apache scouts, but his autobiography gives no clues as to which ones, except that he was with the Lawton-Wood command at Geronimo's surrender. From Fort Davis, Texas, in 1888 he accompanied Lieutenant Colonel John Kemp Mizner and the 8th in what he reported was one of the longest marches of cavalry history to Fort Meade, South Dakota. Rynning spent several years soldiering in Sioux country, was mustered out a sergeant in 1890, went to California and thence to Tucson, Arizona. He enlisted in Roosevelt's Rough Riders during the Spanish American War, emerging as a second lieutenant. In 1902 Governor Alexander O. Brodie, a Rough Riders lieutenant colonel, named Rynning captain of the Arizona Rangers, succeeding Mossman (see entry). Wagoner described him as a "careful, executive-type of officer who personally made few arrests," although he was efficient, fearless and handled such monumental tasks as illegal (for the day) miners' strikes and like problems effectively. Rynning established Ranger headquarters at Douglas, a tough border town in which he reported Lorenzo (Lon) Bass, "brother" to Sam Bass, was a saloon owner with "a long record of killings." Lon Bass was killed by Ranger William W. Webb (Rynning, 207-209). Adams however believed that Sam "had no brother in that country. I think the author simply made an assumption..." Heading a force of "volunteers," Rynning cooperated with Emilio Kosterlitzky (see entry) in quelling 1906 disorders coincident to a huge strike at William C. Greene's Cananea mine in Sonora. The "volunteers," wrote Sonnichsen "never fired a shot" and there were no casualties, the historian adding that as described in the autobiography either "Rynning's memory was bad, or his editors embroidered his text." March 1, 1907, Rynning was appointed by Governor Joseph E. Kibbey warden of the Yuma Territorial Prison and being an experienced contractor also was directed to build a new penitentiary at Florence to replace the Yuma establishment. When statehood came in 1912 Rynning lost his position through politics, but was renamed to it in 1921 when the administration changed. One prisoner called Downing was really, Rynning became convinced, Frank Jackson (see entry), onetime righthand man of Sam Bass (Rynning, 326-30). Upon parole Downing/Jackson got into a drunken fight at Willcox, Arizona, and was killed. Rynning eventually settled at San Diego, California, where he became an undersheriff and deputy U.S. marshal, and where he died at 75. His autobiography, while colorful, is unreliable on details as Adams makes clear and a close reading supports; this may be the fault of his writers rather than of Rynning who was a reliable man of fine record.

Thomas H. Rynning, *Gun Notches,* as told to Al Cohn, Joe Chisholm, N.Y., Frederick A. Stokes, 1931; Joseph Miller, ed., *The Arizona Rangers,* N.Y., Hastings House, 1972; Paul A. Hutton, *Phil Sheridan and His Army,* Lincoln, Univ. of Neb. Press, 1985; Lee Myers, "Soldier's Hill, New Mexico," *English Westerners' Brand Book,* Vol. 24, no. 1 (Winter, 1986), 1-12; Ramon Adams, *Burs Under the Saddle,* Norman, Univ. of Okla. Press, 1964; Jay J. Wagoner, *Arizona Territory: 1863-1912,* Tucson, Univ. of Arizona Press, 1970; C.L. Sonnichsen, *Colonel Greene and the Cooper Skyrocket,* Tucson, Univ. of Arizona Press, 1974.

S

Salling, John Peter (or Peter Adam Salling), explorer (fl. 1724-1747). Of German birth or descent, he with a brother, Henry, early settled in the forks of the James River in southern Rockbridge County, Virginia. "The details of his early explorations in the West are involved in doubt, but that he had such adventures there seems no good reason to doubt." Some place them as starting about 1724, but Thwaites believed the probable time was 1738-40. Family tradition believed that the Virginia governor hired Salling and a son to explore to the southwest. But early legends, as recounted by Withers, give Salling's experiences a much wider, and probably more fanciful, scope; they say that Salling, a Williamsburg weaver, and Thomas Morlin, a peddler, being adventurously inclined, passed up the Shenandoah to the Roanoke where Salling was captured by Cherokees while Morlin escaped and made his way home. Salling was taken to Tennessee "where he remained for some years." On a hunting expedition to the Kentucky salt licks, and when seeking buffalo with Cherokees a party of Illinois Indians captured Salling, taking him to Kaskaskia, Illinois, where he was adopted by a woman whose son had been killed in a local war. Salling frequently went on hunting expeditions with his new captors, sometimes far to the south. On one occasion he went to the mouth of the Arkansas and once to the Gulf of Mexico. Spaniards who needed an interpreter purchased him from his Illinois Indians; they took him to the post of Crevecoeur, on Lake Peoria, Illinois, and thence he went to Frontenac, Canada, was "redeemed" by the governor of Canada who sent him to the Dutch settlements of New York from where after six years' absence he found his way home again. Family tradition, however, according to Thwaites, believes that after capture near the present Salem, Roanoke County, Virginia, Salling and son were taken to the Ohio River; they escaped and descended the Mississippi until taken by Spaniards. The son died, the father was sent by sea to Spain to be tried for being a British spy, but the Spanish vessel was captured by an English ship and Salling was landed at Charleston whence he journeyed home after a three-year absence, arriving in 1740. Salling kept a journal which was extant in 1745, for a diary by Captain John Buchanan in the Wisconsin Historical Society library said he spent two days that year copying a part of it. Du Pratz, in his *History of Louisiana,* said Salling (whom he spells Sallee) made the trip in 1742, but in that year Salling was named in the muster roll of Captain John McDowell's militia company, and he probably was in an Indian fight December 14 that year, in which McDowell was killed. In 1746 Salling himself was a militia captain in the Rockbridge district of Augusta County, and in September 1747 he was cited in connection with a court-martial. There is no further word of him. Descendants, named Sallee, "now live in Kentucky and Tennessee," Thwaites noted in 1895.

Alexander Scott Withers, *Chronicles of Border Warfare,* ed. by Reuben Gold Thwaites, Cincinnati, Robert Clarke Co., 1895, 1970; Antoine Simon Le Page du Pratz, *History of Louisiana,* ed. by Joseph G. Tregle Jr., 1774, Baton Rouge, Louisiana State Univ. Press, 1975.

Sample, Omer (Comer) W. (Red), desperado (d. Mar. 28, 1884). Sample, termed by Barnes a "rustler," was one of five desperadoes who perpetrated the December 8, 1883, "Bisbee Massacre" while holding up the Joseph Goldwater-A.A. Casteñada general store at the Arizona mining town. The gunmen sought the $7,000 payroll of the Copper Queen Mine, but they were too early; it had not yet arrived. Between $900 and $3,000 (reports differ) was taken along with expensive watches and rings, while four people were killed outright, their identities given variously but probably were: Deputy Sheriff Tom Smith, John C. Tapiner, Mrs. R.H. (Anna) Roberts and R.E. Duvall. Albert Nolly was shot in the abdomen and later died and Sample was reported wounded slightly. Dave Rousseau, who lived in a canyonside home 80 feet above the street, by report, apparently heard the shooting below and rushed to his porch to see what was up; he either caught a stray bullet or leaned too far over the railing and tumbled to his death. Red-haired Sample and James (Tex) Howard were seized at Clifton, Arizona, because of Sample's largesse with the stolen jewelry.

Sample was seriously wounded in a scuffle with the law, but recovered before his execution. Asked at the sentencing if he had anything to say, Red replied: "No, sir. Nothing [that] would influence you." He and the other four—Howard, Daniel Kelly, Daniel Dowd and William Delaney (see entries)—were hanged from a multiple scaffold at Tombstone, Arizona. For some unclear reason a Cochise County community was named for Sample, although it was as short-lived as the original; a post office was established for it July 26, 1886.

Ben T. Traywick, *The Hangings at Tombstone,* Tombstone, Red Marie's Bookstore, 1991; Robert E. Ladd, *Eight Ropes to Eternity,* pub. by *Tombstone Epitaph,* 1965; A.D. LeBaron, "Bisbee's Five Black Ghosts," *True West,* Vol. 7, No. 6 (July-Aug. 1960), 12-14, 56-57; Will C. Barnes, *Arizona Place Names,* Tucson, Univ. of Ariz. Gen. Bul. 2, Jan. 1, 1935; info. from John Gilchriese.

Sánchez de la Barrera y Gallardo, Tomás, Laredo founder (1709-Jan. 1796). B. near Monterrey, Nuevo Leon, Mexico, he served in the Spanish army and later managed a ranch in Coahuila Province. Spanish control moved north to the Rio Grande, and Sánchez also ventured in that direction. José Vasquéz Borrego, a major cattle owner, on August 22, 1750, received a grant to maintain a ferry service across the river, and founded Nuestra Señora de Dolores, the first hacienda in that region north of the Rio Grande. Tomás Sánchez located a cattle ranch on the south side of the river, within sight of Dolores. In 1754 he petitioned Colonel José de Escandón, governor and captain general of Nuevo Santander, for permission to establish a settlement on the north bank; the governor wanted instead to have a town founded on the Nueces River. Sánchez, after investigating that possibility, thought his idea preferable, and the governor granted him permission to establish one near Paso de Jacinto, or the "old Indian crossing," as it was called. Thus Sánchez became the founder of Laredo, one of the most important cities on the Rio Grande and port of entry into Mexico. It was located about 30 miles upstream from today's San Ygnacio; only the ruins of some colonial structures remain of the hacienda. Laredo was founded May 15, 1755, Tomás Sánchez holding the offices of chief justice and alcalde, almost uninterruptedly for the rest of his life. A man of fair complexion and blue eyes, Sánchez was married twice, fathering children by each of his wives. He died at 87 following a brief illness; his burial place was "lost in the march of time," but a red granite monument to him was dedicated October 16, 1938, by representatives of the Texas Centennial Celebrations commission.

Seb S. Wilcox, Laredo historian, "Don Tomás Sánchez, Founder of Laredo," *Frontier Times,* Vol. 16, No. 3 (Dec. 1938), 12-25; HT.

Sands, George Henry, military officer (Mar. 29, 1856-Nov. 10, 1920). B. in the District of Columbia, he went to West Point and was commissioned a second lieutenant of the 6th Cavalry June 12, 1880. Posted to Camp Thomas, Arizona, he commanded B Company. When the Juh-led emeute of Loco from San Carlos Reservation occurred in April 1882 Sands, "with a few men...overtook the rear guard before they were well clear of the reservation and exchanged a few shots." The regimental return stated that one Indian was wounded. Sands had no further reported hostile contact, although like virtually all soldiers during those years, he must have been constantly active in scouting. He became a first lieutenant October 19, 1887, a captain in 1897 and was engineer major of Volunteers during the Spanish American War. He became a major, 10th Cavalry, October 20, 1905. He was a colonel with the 4th Cavalry on Pershing's punitive action into Mexico in 1916, retired in August of that year but was recalled in 1917 for active duty with the War Plans Division of the Army War College. He died at Washington, D.C., leaving his widow, a daughter and a son.

Heitman; Cullum; W.H. Carter, *From Yorktown to Santiago: With the Sixth Cavalry,* Baltimore, Lord Baltimore Press, 1900; *Chronological List;* Constance Wynn Altshuler, *Cavalry Yellow & Infantry Blue,* Tucson, Ariz. Hist. Soc., 1991.

Sarychev, Gavriil (Gavrilo) Andreyevich, Russian naval officer (1763-1831). The Russian-born Sarychev became an outstanding hydrographer and as a naval lieutenant was second in command of the Joseph Billings (see entry) 1785-93 expedition to the North Pacific. He frequently operated independently and was regarded by those acquainted with his services as an able, conscientious and dedicated officer, cartographer and geodecist. In September 1785 Sarychev was sent to the Siberian port of Okhotsk with an advance party of shipbuilders to construct the two vessels deemed necessary for the expedition, the plans having been drafted by

Lamb Yeames, an English ship architect. August 3, 1786, Sarychev and Billings set out for the Kolyma River delta, assigned to locate the exact position of Nizhne Kolima and to chart the Arctic coast from there eastward toward East Cape of the Chukotski Peninsula. The party wintered under trying conditions, but managed to construct two vessels, the *Pallas* and *Yasatchnoi,* with which they set out May 25, 1787. By July 25, they had reached a point about where Mys (Cape) Billings was located and here the leader decided to return, although Sarychev and other officers were convinced the sea route was open around East Cape and into the Pacific. Sarychev even offered to complete the journey in an open umiak with six men, camping on the beach at night, but Billings rejected the notion. After some delays the expedition assembled at Okhotsk September 1788. The *Slava Rossie,* larger of the two projected vessels, was launched in July 1789 (the smaller vessel was wrecked trying to leave the harbor) and October 1, reached Petropavlovsk on the east coast of Kamchatka. May 1, 1790, the expedition in the *Slava Rossie* embarked, sighted Amchitka Island in the Aleutian chain May 22, and Unalaska on June 1. The ship reached Kodiak Island June 29, and anchored off Montague Island July 19. Sarychev took a ship's boat with crew on a three-day reconnaissance of Prince William Sound, narrowly—and unwittingly—escaping an ambush, learning of it only much later from an Aleut interpreter at the port of Okhotsk. A very old native one day came aboard the ship and told them when he was a boy, a vessel approached his homeland on Kaye (Kayak) Island and a ship's boat put ashore some men whose actions Sarychev identified with the landing of Khitrov (see entry) from Bering's party in 1741, substantiating that this was Bering's landfall in that historic visit. The *Slava Rossie* reached Petropavlovsk October 14, and the party wintered in Kamchatka, while Lieutenant Robert Hall supervised construction of a new escort vessel at Okhotsk. Hall was instructed to meet the *Slava Rossie* at Bering Island, or if that proved impossible, at Unalaska Island. Sarychev with Billings embarked in the larger ship May 19, reached Bering Island on the 28th, but bad weather prevented their awaiting Hall at that point and the ship went on to Unalaska, arriving June 25. Hall's vessel had not arrived; his whereabouts were unknown and Billings decided to leave some provisions, give up his plan to study and

chart Cook Inlet, and proceed at once to St. Lawrence Bay [Zaliv Lavrentiya] on the Chukotski Peninsula of East Cape. Sarychev was deeply disappointed by the decision, but could do nothing about it. Instructions were left for Hall to follow the *Slava Rossie* to the bay, the ship clearing Unalaska July 8, and August 3, reached St. Lawrence Bay. Billings determined to proceed overland to the Kolyma River, completing his survey of the peninsula, while Sarychev would take the *Slava Rossie* back to Unalaska Island. The day after Billings left, Sarychev proceeded toward Unalaska, although the ship badly needed supplies available only at Petropavlovsk. The vessel anchored at Unalaska August 28, finding that Hall and his ship, the *Chernui Orel* (Black Eagle), had arrived there shortly after Billings had left and, pursuant to instructions, had followed the *Slava Rossie* toward St. Lawrence Bay; however, he returned about September 1. The expedition passed a long, cold and cruel winter, seventeen men dying of scurvy. The ships left for Kamchatka May 16, 1792, lost sight of each other June 7, and on June 16, the *Slava Rossie* arrived at Avatcha Bay. The expedition ultimately was disbanded. Bancroft believed a significant aspect of it was "the preliminary experience gained by Sarychev, who subsequently published the most complete and reliable charts of the Aleutian Islands [whose] reliability stands acknowledged to the present day [1886]." The expedition accomplished only some of its objectives, but the result was "not due to Billings' ineptitude, as some Russian and Soviet writers have suggested, nor was its success due to Sarychev's abilities," concluded the *Russian Penetration of the North Pacific Ocean.* The expedition did "prepare a series of quite accurate maps of the North Pacific, and it also gathered valuable ethnographic and linguistic materials" on the native peoples encountered. Sarychev published a description of his travels in northeastern Siberia and northwestern North America. He also authored a book on marine geodesy, an atlas of the Pacific Ocean and other works. He eventually became an admiral and member of the Admiralty and directed the Russian Ministry of Marine. He was, according to Zagoskin, "one of the most educated naval men of his time."

Bancroft, *Alaska;* Zagoskin; *Russian Penetration of the North Pacific Ocean.*

Sauer, Martin, English seafarer (fl. 1785-1807). Probably b. in England he may have been of German descent, but not much is known of the beginning or end of his life. In 1785 at St. Petersburg, he was invited to join the Joseph Billings (see entry) voyage of exploration to the North Pacific, his function to be private secretary and interpreter for Billings. Sauer agreed on condition that he be allowed to publish an account of the voyage upon his return. He left with the expedition October 25, and returned to St. Petersburg March 10, 1794. He reported that he was "so much afflicted with rheumatism" and with other ailments as to be virtually incapacitated, but financial assistance from British merchants of the city helped him through and he recovered, in part because of his travels through southern Russia's warmer climate. Pierce quotes M.I. Belov, who wrote on the basis of archival materials that Sauer was "a former officer of the British trade office," and knew Russian, English, German and French languages. On his return from the expedition, the Belov version went on, Sauer fled with important documentation of the expedition, and reached England where "the materials appeared in his book," published in 1802 in Russia; an English translation appeared in 1807. The volume, entitled *An Account of a Geographical and Astronomical Expedition...Performed, by Command of...Catherine the Second...in the Years 1785 to 1794,* describes two voyages from Kamchatka. The first visited Unalaska, Kodiak, Montague Island, and Prince William Sound, Alaska. The second went north to St. Lawrence Island and landed on the Alaska coast at Cape Rodney, near the present Nome. It was the first account of the Sarychev expedition and "contains an abundance of detail, corroborating and complimenting the works of Sarychev and Merck." Sarychev said that Sauer in 1807 was then a broker on the St. Petersburg stock exchange. The date and circumstances of his death are not reported.

Pierce, *Russian America: A Biographical Dictionary;* Richard H. Aleson book catalog, *Voyages and Travels,* Winter, 1992-93, p. 42.

Sawyers, John, military officer (1745-1831). B. in Virginia he early went west. In 1774 he was in Evan Shelby's company at the important Battle of Point Pleasant, West Virginia, against the Shawnees. Sawyers also was on the 1776 Cherokee expedition and the 1779 operation against the Chickamaugas, a Tennessee branch of the Cherokees. He also commanded a company under Shelby at the significant King's Mountain battle of 1780. He served as major, then as colonel of militia, and represented his district in the state assembly.

Thwaites, *Dunmore.*

Saxton, Rufus, military officer (Oct. 19, 1824-Feb. 23, 1908). B. at Greenfield, Massachusetts, he went to West Point and became a brevet second lieutenant of the 3rd Artillery July 1, 1849, and a second lieutenant of the 4th Artillery September 12, 1850. He had taken part in the Seminole troubles in Florida in 1849-50 and served in Texas in 1850-52. He was assigned to the Isaac Stevens (see entry) party charting a railroad route from St. Paul to Puget Sound in 1853-54 and on the return trip led an expedition from the mouth of the Columbia River, northward of the Lewis and Clark route, to Fort Benton, Montana, by a way Saxton believed had never been "traversed by white men," although this is improbable. Stevens, in his Order No. 18, congratulated Saxton "for indomitable energy, sound judgment, and the most crowning accomplishment [on behalf of] all men who seek to advance the honor and renown of their country." Saxton was promoted to first lieutenant March 2, 1855, and shortly joined the Quartermaster Corps where he served with such distinction during the Civil War that he was twice denied the opportunity to accept appointment of colonel of Volunteers because, according to Quartermaster General Montgomery C. Meigs (1816-1892), Sherman had protested that "no man can take your place" in quartermaster work and Meigs' belief that his department had "no more intelligent or zealous officer," although rank suitable to his abilities was not available in that organization (Saxton did later become Brigadier General and brevet Major General of Volunteers, however). He was made a captain May 13, 1861, a major July 29, 1866, and was chief quartermaster on the Northern frontier in 1866, of the Department of the Columbia in 1869-73, of the Department of the Missouri, 1875-79, of the Military Division of the Pacific and Department of California 1879-82, and at various eastern departments at other times. Saxton retired October 19, 1888.

Heitman; Cullum; Powell.

Scarouady (Half King), Oneida chief (d. June 1757). This individual, sometimes confused with Half King Scruniyatha (see entry), a Seneca chief, was an Oneida who earned the title of "Half King," which meant a principal spokesman for his people. His residence initially was on the

Ohio River in western Pennsylvania, where he came to occupy the kind of leadership over western tribes as did Shikellamy (see entry), another Oneida chief, earlier over the tribes of central Pennsylvania. Scarouady became a close associate of the Seneca Half King Scruniyatha (Tanacharison), and was mentioned in colonial documents as early as 1747. In his younger life he had been pro-French, but later became anti-French and pro-English and "his special importance lies in the role he played in events leading to the outbreak of Anglo-French hostility in 1754." His specialty was in managing relations between the Iroquois and Shawnees. A demand by Scruniyatha that the French withdraw from the western region was rejected, and Scarouady took a delegation of Iroquois, Shawnees, Delawares, Hurons and Miamis to Carlisle, Pennsylvania, by way of Winchester, Virginia, seeking support for the Indian position; at Carlisle both Scarouady and Scruniyatha insisted they spoke not for the Iroquois alone, but for other Indians on the Ohio River as well. January 7, 1854, Scarouady was at Philadelphia enroute to the Six Nations (Iroquois) with a message from Robert Dinwiddie, lieutenant governor of Virginia, and to discuss various matters. Scruniyatha died of pneumonia October 4, 1754, at the home of John Harris at the present Harrisburg, and Scarouady succeeded him, moving his base from Logstown, below Pittsburgh, to Aughwick (Fort Shirley), the present Shirleysburg on Aughwick Creek south of Mount Union, Pennsylvania. He thus became Half King, or spokesman for the Indians of central as well as western Pennsylvania. In May 1755 he urged Indians at Fort Cumberland, on Wills Creek on the upper Potomac, to join the Braddock expedition, and he was with Braddock at the disastrous defeat by French and Indians July 13, 1755. The next year he attended several conferences and, an orator of ability, made a number of speeches, sometimes being joined by Andrew Montour (see entry). One of his speeches was made July 1, 1756, at a conference of the Iroquois with Sir William Johnson on behalf of the Delawares and Shawnees. Scarouady remained "a firm friend of the English colonists, and as strong an enemy of the French" to the end of his life. He died at Lancaster, Pennsylvania.

Hodge, HAI; DCB, III; info. from John Sugden.

Schaefer, Jack, writer (Nov. 19, 1907-Jan. 24, 1991). B. at Cleveland, Ohio, he was graduated in 1929 from Oberlin College, studied for a year at Columbia and became a newspaperman with United Press, later working for the *Virginia-Pilot* of Norfolk, Virginia, the *Baltimore Sun,* and the New Haven, Connecticut *Journal-Courier.* He was best known for his first novel, *Shane* (1949), about a gunfighter, which in 1953 was made into a popular motion picture. His other books included *First Blood* (1953), *The Canyon* (1953), *Company of Cowards* (1957); *Heroes Without Glory: Some Goodmen of the Old West* (1965), and his last work, *The American Bestiary: Notes of an Amateur Naturalist* (1975). In his later life he turned to writing nature material. He lived for the last twenty years of his life at Santa Fe, where he died at 83. He was married and was survived by his widow, a daughter and three sons.

New York Times, Jan. 27, 1991.

Scheffer, Georg Anton, adventurer (Jan. 27, 1779-c. 1836). B. at Munnerstadt, Bavaria, he passed his surgeon's examination in 1805 at Wurzburg and began to practice medicine. Invited to Russia in 1808, he became a surgeon with the Moscow police and in 1812 was constructing balloons "to watch the movements of Napoleon's invading army." October 8, 1813, Schaeffer left Kronstadt aboard the *Suvarof* with Captain Aleksey Petrovich Lazarev (1788-1851), and reached Novo Arkhangelsk (Sitka), Alaska, in November 1814. Lazarev, "in common with all naval officers," was prejudiced against Baranov, governor of Alaska, and of the Russian American Company, and quickly aroused his ire. Scheffer, too, had quarreled with the captain, remained at odds with him, thus winning Baranov's lasting indulgence. At the earliest opportunity Scheffer abandoned the *Suvarof* and remained for a time at Novo Arkhangelsk currying Baranov's ego and, being something of a linguist and "a plasible adventurer," convinced the governor that he, Scheffer, was "the man to carry out his schemes for colonization in the Hawaiian Islands." Aboard the *Isabella,* an American fur trading ship, Scheffer left Novo Arkhangelsk October 17, 1815, and on Christmas Eve reached Hawaii. He went first to the island of Hawaii and then to Oahu, where he was granted extensive lands suitable for cultivation (at this time he passed as a botanist, interested in Hawaiian verdure rather than political intrigue, his real concern) and he had been promised by Baranov strong naval support to further his island plotting. With arrival of two of the three

Russian ships Baranov had promised, Scheffer built a fort at Honolulu and raised the Russian flag. This affront could not go unchallenged and John Young, governor of Oahu and adviser to King Kamehameha, ordered Scheffer and his Russian supporters off the island; they withdrew to Kauai. Here Scheffer quickly gained the goodwill of King Kaumualii (Tomari), persuaded him to sign agreements by which Kauai and another island came under protection of Russia and the Russian American Company, and promised support in a war of conquest against Kamehameha. Scheffer constructed blockhouses and by 1817 seemed virtual ruler of Kauai, but his position remained "far from secure." Kamehameha, learning of the nature of Scheffer's negotiations, or machinations, complained to Kotzebue (see entry) of the doctor's conduct and was assured that his activities were not sanctioned by the tsar. Kamehameha persuaded Kaumualii to expel Scheffer to Oahu, from which he quickly found it politic to withdraw, sailing to Canton and on to St. Petersburg where he found that the tsar, unwilling to risk a naval war with Britain over distant Hawaii, had disapproved of the agreements with Kaumualii; even the Russian American Company directors could not agree on whether to support the manipulative doctor. Scheffer left Russia in something like disgrace. He wound up in Brazil, where he ingratiated himself with Dom Pedro I (1798-1834), the Portuguese-born emperor. The monarch conferred upon him the resounding title of Count von Frankenthal and gave him a commission to recruit men in Germany for his imperial bodyguard. He helped bring about Brazil's independence from Portugal. In 1836 he went on an expedition into the interior, and never returned.

Bancroft, *Alaska;* Zagoskin; Harold Whitman Bradly, *The American Frontier in Hawaii: The Pioneers 1789-1843,* Stanford Univ. Press, 1942, repr. by Peter Smith, Gloucester, Mass., 1968; Pierce, *Russian America: A Biographical Dictionary.*

Scherum (Serum), Hualapais (Walapais), chief: *see* Cherum

Schmalsle, William F., scout (fl. 1874). Called by Nye "a brave little German," Schmalsle may have been b. in Germany. From his photograph, p. 130 of *Hostiles and Horse Soldiers,* and the engraving on p. 173 (different portraits) of Miles's *Personal Recollections,* he was probably about 25 years of age in 1874, thus having been

b. around 1850, although this is conjecture. He was reported to have been a buffalo hunter when the Red River Campaign was organized and several of his occupation were hurriedly hired as "scouts" for the military, whether they had any Indian experience or not. Schmalsle accompanied Captain Wyllys Lyman, 5th Infantry, having scouted for First Lieutenant Frank Baldwin, who joined Lyman's wagon train earlier. When Baldwin continued his independent mission, Schmalsle remained with Lyman and his 36 wagons driven by civilian teamsters, and more than 100 soldiers, including Company I, 5th Infantry and a detachment of the 6th Cavalry. September 9, 1874, the train was besieged by a large force of Kiowa and Comanche warriors and perhaps a few Cheyennes. The siege continued through September 10, when Schmalsle volunteered to take a message to Camp Supply, 88 miles distant in Indian Territory. In the evening Schmalsle raced his horse in "a feat of daring" past the startled besiegers and though heavily pursued, remained ahead of the enemy until he stampeded a buffalo herd. His trail was lost among the countless footprints. His horse stumbled over a prairie dog hole, but recovered, although Schmalsle lost his rifle in the incident. The horse gave out after a long run and the scout continued afoot, reaching Camp Supply at 8:30 a.m. September 12, and delivering his message for aid to Lieutenant Colonel William H. Lewis, 19th Infantry. He quickly collected 45 cavalrymen, seven scouts and the post surgeon and this force, under Lieutenant Henry Kingsbury and with Schmalsle as guide, rapidly returned to the beleaguered train, which was reached at 2 a.m. September 14, after the attacking Indians had withdrawn. On November 4, Schmalsle scouted for a detachment under Baldwin consisting of 23 empty wagons, Troop D, 6th Cavalry and Company D, 5th Infantry, the command heading for the Washita for supplies. Baldwin was instructed to watch for hostile sign, and if opportunity arose to attack any party found. November 8, on the north branch of McClellan Creek, Schmalsle, scouting in advance, located at daylight a large hostile camp he believed was of the Cheyenne Grey Beard's band, because he had sighted the chief's distinctive tepee in the camp. Baldwin sent Schmalsle on to inform Miles of the discovery and launched his famous "wagon charge" which resulted in capture of the camp, though not of the Indians, and recovery of two of the four German girl captives (see German entry). No further report on Schmalsle's activities has been located.

Lonnie J. White, *Hostiles & Horse Soldiers,* Boulder, Colo., Pruett Pub. Co., 1972; William H. Leckie, *Military Conquest of the Southern Plains,* Norman, Univ. of Okla. Press, 1963; Nelson A. Miles, *Personal Recollections,* Chicago, Riverside Pub. Co., 1897, 172-73; W.S. Nye, *Carbine & Lance: The Story of Old Fort Sill,* 11th printing, Norman, 1983; James L. Haley, *The Buffalo War,* Garden City, N.Y., Doubleday & Co., 1976.

Schofield, George Wheeler, military officer (Sept. 20, 1833-Dec. 17, 1882). B. at Gerry, Chautauquah County, New York, he was a brother of Major General John M. Schofield, of Charles Brewster Schofield, a West Pointer who died a lieutenant colonel in 1901, and of the Reverend J.V. Schofield of St. Louis. George Schofield on October 5, 1861, became a first lieutenant of the 1st Missouri Artillery and was promoted to captain September 1, 1862. During the war years he served as aide to his brother, General John Schofield, as lieutenant colonel of the 2nd Missouri Artillery, being mustered out November 20, 1865, a brevet Brigadier General of Volunteers for services in southeastern campaigns. He was commissioned major of the 41st U.S. Infantry July 28, 1866. In the army reduction of 1869 Schofield was left unassigned until December 15, 1870, when he joined the 10th Cavalry. He became acting Inspector General of the Department of the Missouri, then went to Fort Sill where his wife, Alma, 24, died March 27, 1879. Later that year his horse fell with him and he injured his knee, remaining on sick leave for about a year. On December 30, 1881, he became lieutenant colonel of the 6th Cavalry and went to Arizona early in 1882, commanding initially at Fort Thomas. He led a force including Companies L and B of the 6th, with Apaches and Dan Ming as chief of scouts April 1882 in pursuit of the Juh-Loco party of several hundred Indians fleeing the San Carlos Reservation. They struck the hostile trail eighteen miles east of Fort Thomas, pursued and scattered the Apaches, finding it impossible to trail them further. At Eagle Creek they had come upon the bodies of three slain prospectors, still warm, but the troops had no rations, their pack train could not keep up, and the officer ordered it to return to Fort Thomas, the troops soon following. Schofield came under press criticism for abandoning the pursuit when the condition of the victims indicat-

ed he was close upon the hostiles. Shortly after this he was relieved from command at Fort Thomas and given command of Fort Apache, a more imposing installation but in a quieter sector. On December 17, 1882, a striker was building a fire in the fireplace while Schofield combed his hair at a nearby washstand. The officer requested the striker to leave the room and "he had barely closed the door when a shot was fired. [Schofield had] placed the pistol to his right eye, and the ball passed through his head, blowing half his head off." The suicide was attributed officially to the officer's poor health, and some sort of investigation possibly underway, perhaps of the Loco pursuit, was dropped. Smith & Wesson, firearms makers, had commenced developing their No. 3 model revolver late in the Civil War and eventually a "second model" of No. 3 was sold beginning late in 1871. Schofield was the first American army officer to obtain one, while he was stationed at Fort Leavenworth as a major of the 10th Cavalry. He was much interested in the .44 caliber weapon for military use. With an inventive turn of mind, having already developed certain artifacts with military applications, on June 20, 1871, he patented a barrel latch pivoted on the frame for the No. 3, instead of on the barrel, suggesting also changes for more easily removing the cylinder from the frame for cleaning. The extractor improvements were patented April 22, 1873. The revolver became known as the Schofield Model, and saw considerable military and civilian use. Schofield eventually received modest royalties on weapons sold. He was buried at the City Cemetery at Freeport, Illinois.

Heitman; *Army and Navy Journal,* Dec. 23, 1882, p. 461; Roger D. Hunt, Jack R. Brown, *Brevet Brigadier Generals in Blue,* Gaithersburg, Maryland, Olde Soldier Books, 1990, p. 538; info. from the U.S. Military Hist. Inst., Carlisle Barracks, Penn., Apr. 16, 1992; John E. Parsons, *Smith & Wesson Revolvers,* N.Y., William Morrow & Co., 1957; author's file on Schofield.

Schrader, Frank Charles, geologist (Oct. 6, 1860-Feb. 1944). B. at Sterling, Illinois, he studied at the University of Kansas and at Harvard where he secured a master's degree in 1894. He taught geology at Harvard from 1895-96 and was a geologist for the Geological Survey from 1896 until 1932, when he retired because of age (at 72), thereafter contributing five more years of service without pay. Schrader specialized in mining geology, and traveled to "nearly all parts of Alaska" as well as in the lower United States. He spent six successive seasons in Alaska, commencing in 1896 with a reconnaissance from the head of Lynn Canal in the Panhandle, over Chilkoot Pass and down the Yukon River to St. Michael on Norton Sound. In 1898 he worked with Abercrombie (see entry) from Port Valdez and along the Copper River. The next year he was in charge of parties exploring the Chandalar and Koyukuk rivers, both northerly tributaries of the Yukon. In 1900 and 1902 he worked in the Copper River Valley and in 1901 was geologist on a reconnaissance in northern Alaska. He belonged to many professional societies, including the American Association for the Advancement of Science, and wrote numerous articles for the Geological Survey and geographical magazines. Many geographical features in Alaska were named for him. He was married.

Orth, 32, 844; *Who Was Who.*

Scott, Molly, pioneer woman (fl. 1782). It was Molly Scott, according to eye-witness Lydia Boggs Cruger, who ran the gunpowder from the Ebenezer Zane house to Fort Henry during an Indian siege in West Virginia September 11, 1782, the powder enabling the defenders to hold off 200 or more Indians and a British officer and soldier rangers. It was not Elizabeth (Betty) Zane, according to Mrs. Cruger, whose reliability and good memory were attested by Thwaites/Kellogg. Not too much is reported of her personal life; in various accounts of the siege of Fort Henry, an Andrew Scott and a Robert Scott have been mentioned as present; Robert, being c. 18 at the time, may have been a brother of Molly Scott, or perhaps a brother-in-law if she was married at the time. Mrs. Cruger stated that she admired both Betty Zane and Molly Scott and was a friend of both. McWhorter believed the Molly Scott legend the "more plausible" of the two. No report of the later life of Molly Scott has been located by the writer; The DAB Patriot Index for Virginia/West Virginia does not list her name or give any biographical details.

Wills De Hass, *History of the Early Settlement and Indian Wars of Western Virginia,* Philadelphia, H. Hoblitzell, 1851, 1960, pp. 269-71, 280-81; Lucullus V. McWhorter, *The Border Settlers of Northwestern Virginia from 1768 to 1795,* Hamilton, Ohio, Republican Pub. Co., 1915, 153-56.

Serebrennikov, Rufus, explorer (d. June 25,

1848). Bancroft reports other Serebrennikov-named Russians who explored and traded for furs in 18th century Alaska, and Rufus, identified as a Creole by Allen, may have descended from any one of them. Rufus Serebrennikov was a graduate of a commercial school of navigation at St. Petersburg, Russia, and as an ensign was ordered in 1847 by Mikhail Tebenkov, chief manager of the Russian American Company, to conduct an exploration of the Copper River and to reach some tributary of the Yukon if he could. Native hostility and difficult geography had defeated earlier attempts to explore the important stream. August 14, 1847, Serebrennikov and eleven assistants, most of them Aleuts, arrived at Alaganik, on the westerly channel of the Copper delta, east of the present Cordova. They started upriver, but due to the current were forced for a time to cordelle boats with towlines. September 1, the leader's craft struck a submerged rock and valuable articles were lost, including his watch, without which calculations of longitude were impossible. By September 4, the expedition had reached the confluence with the Chitina River, where it wintered, a low temperature of 40° below zero being recorded at one time. May 16, 1848, Serebrennikov again started upstream with his party supplied with 100 fish, 150 pounds of bread, 4 butchered wild sheep and tea and sugar. He passed small native villages, most of their men away hunting or in other pursuits. By May 22, the sheep carcasses had been consumed and the men were rationed one fish each per day; on the 24th the ration was reduced to half a fish per day. The Tazlina tributary, coming from the west, was explored as far as Lake Plaveznie (Tazlina). By June 3, a baidara or umiak was constructed and two days were spent exploring the lake. On June 5, the party descended the Tazlina to the Copper and resumed progress up that river. Serebrennikov and three of his men were murdered by Ahtena Indians led by Chief Messala somewhere above Chistochina, either because they had mistreated natives or were unfeeling about Indian problems. Serebrennikov's partial journal and other papers were turned over to Tebenkov by a native who had brought them in. He said the slayings were done by upper Copper River natives.

Henry T. Allen, "Military Reconnoissance in Alaska," *Narratives of Explorations in Alaska,* 414, 434; Richard A. Pierce, *Builders of Alaska: The Russian Governors, 1818-1867,* Kingston, Ont., Limestone Press, 1986, 30; Bancroft, *Alaska.*

Seroweh, Cherokee war chief (fl. 1756-1761). A war chief or "Mankiller" of the Lower Cherokee town of Estatoe, he led a contingent under Richard Pearis, a Virginia packhorse man and agent for Robert Dinwiddie, lieutenant governor of Virginia, to fight against the French on the Monongahela River in 1756. Seroweh served with the redoubtable Andrew Lewis (see entry) with one of the only two Cherokee parties to operate on the Virginia-Pennsylvania frontier during the French and Indian War. After his service, he returned to Estatoe. Here in the winter of 1758-59 he came under the influence of a captured French ensign, Francois-Louis Pícote de Belestre, son of the famous Francois-Marie Pícote de Belestre (1719-1793), the ensign, one report says, eventually becoming in his own right a Cherokee chief. Pícote de Belestre had been captured in Pennsylvania in the same action in which Swallow Warrior, an uncle of Seroweh, had fallen. Now the Frenchman assumed the task of turning Cherokee loyalties from supporting British against the French to favoring the French against the British. Having the ear of Seroweh, who had succeeded Swallow Warrior as war chief of Estatoe, he made great progress. He was assisted in his design by excesses of English colonists of Carolina against the Cherokees, and by Cherokee uneasiness over the losses in the north fighting for the seemingly ungrateful English. In June 1759 Seroweh authorized a leading warrior, Yachtanno, to take English scalps, he taking three of them in early July. An English embargo on ammunition sold to the Cherokees in response to threats of Cherokee hostility, exacerbated the situation, and Seroweh and others commenced talking with the Creeks about joint war against the British. An abortive attack by the Creeks, suported by Seroweh and others, upon Indian Superintendent Edmund Atkin miscarried and although that might have been the spark to ignite a Creek and Cherokee war against the English, it failed to produce one. A Lower Towns negotiating mission to Charleston attempting to smooth out differences with English Governor William Henry Lyttleton failed to accomplish anything due largely to Lyttleton's lack of initiative. The governor decided to hold the negotiators as hostages for peace on the Carolina frontier. The Cherokees were "in no position to bargain," since Lyttleton's hostages included 28 headmen and he "had an army behind him." On December 21, 1759, Seroweh and one other were released, but the main issue dividing the parties,

a 1730 treaty provision requiring the Cherokees to hand over for execution individuals who had killed Englishmen, was not resolved. When in January a smallpox epidemic and other calamities threatened, Lyttleton withdrew with what progress he thought had been made, but "he left behind him a Cherokee nation inflamed against the English." And he left what hostages remained, about 22, in Fort Prince George, near the present Walhalla, South Carolina. Seroweh determined to free them. January 19, 1760, the Mankiller and blanketed warriors demanded admission to the fort, ostensibly to exchange the killers the English wanted, for hostages the Cherokees wished to free. A Lieutenant Coytmore, the commandant, agreed to admit three or four and when the gates were opened a dozen warriors squeezed in, parleyed for a time with the officer while the three "killers" the English intended to execute, escaped, then withdrew. Meanwhile the long-expected conflict between the Cherokees and the English had commenced. Seroweh sent rumors through the nation to announce the war and hundreds of Cherokees besieged Fort Prince George while traders were slain wherever found. Coytmore was assassinated, the soldiers in Fort Prince George turned on the 22 hostages and killed them all. The bloody war raged on with numerous killings, sometimes in sizable numbers. During a brief truce Ensign Milne, who had succeeded the slain Coytmore in command of Fort Prince George, succeeded in capturing Seroweh by ruse. February 24, 1760, Lord Jeffrey Amherst, British commander-in-chief in America, sent Colonel Archibald Montgomerie with 1,300 men to campaign against the Cherokees, hoping to extinguish the war. June 1-2 the command burned and destroyed Estatoe and four other villages, killed 60 to 80 Cherokees and took 40 prisoners before pulling back to Fort Prince George. Hoping to win Cherokee goodwill, Montgomerie released four of the hostages Milne now held, including Seroweh. Seroweh, rather than grateful for his release, remained bitter at Milne's treachery in seizing and holding him, and warned his fellows that Montgomerie's overture for peace talks was merely a feint to draw them together and put them to death. Montgomerie now determined upon a march into the mountains to punish the enemy, but Seroweh and others laid an ambush for him by 600 warriors from the Lower and Middle Towns. The British regulars lost 17 killed and 66 wounded, and the provincials and rangers with them lost others.

The British withdrew under cover of night and at last reached their ships, the campaign ended. In the fall fresh peace talks were spoken of, but events decreed otherwise and a new siege of Fort Prince George failed due to the lack of Cherokee organization. With promises of French and perhaps Creek assistance, Seroweh determined to continue the war, although he respected a truce Oconostota (see entry) had arranged at Fort Prince George itself, and avoided the place. By the spring of 1761, however, Seroweh once more was talking peace, but now Charleston was in no mood for it. A powerful new English force under Lieutenant Colonel James Grant had been ordered to Carolina to terminate the Cherokee War. The Little Carpenter, or Attakullaculla (see entry) tried to head off the column's approach, but Grant would not be deterred, although he sympathized with the enemy, realizing that the Indians "have been the worst used" and would accept peace if they knew how to bring it about. Grant thoroughly ravaged the Middle Cherokee country, and after 33 days arrived back at Fort Prince George, having burned 15 towns, ruined 1,500 acres of corn and "destroyed the Cherokee appetite for war," while exhausting his own command. "But," commented an historian, "it was an unnecessary campaign. The same Peace which eventuated could have been without it." Little is heard of Seroweh thereafter, although he presumably remained an important man.

Info. from John Sugden; David H. Corkran, *The Cherokee Frontier: Conflict and Survival, 1740-62*, Norman, Univ. of Okla. Press, 1962; DCB, IV, p. 634.

Serven, James E., weapons specialist (Dec. 20, 1899-Sept. 2, 1985). B. at Pearl River, New York, he was graduated from Brown University, Providence, Rhode Island, and by 1933 was editor of a trade magazine at New York City which wanted to transfer him to Chicago. He declined, and bought a ranch at Sonoita, Arizona, where he remained eight years. He moved to a ranch near San Juan Capistrano, California, and began writing about the West and guns, returned to Tucson in 1960 and wrote several books, including a history of Pima County. Among his works were *Colt Firearms, 1836-1954* (1954); "The Hawken Rifle," *American Rifleman* (April 1951); "Hawken Rifle," *American Rifleman* (December 1963); *Paterson Pistols* (1946) and *Conquering the Frontier* (1972). He died at Tucson, survived by his widow and two sons, and was buried at Nyack, New York.

Tucson, *Arizona Daily Star*, Sept. 5, 1985.

Settle, William Anderson Jr., historian (Aug. 20, 1915-Mar. 1, 1988). B. at Greenville, Missouri, he was graduated from Southeast Missouri State College (now University) in 1938 and earned his master's and a doctorate at the University of Missouri, the latter in 1945. After five years instructing at the Greenville High School, he taught history at the University of Missouri until 1945, then joined the history faculty at the University of Tulsa, becoming professor in 1954. He headed the departments of history and political science from 1946-68, in 1968 directed the history department alone, and became the J.P. Walker Professor of History in 1971. In 1966 he culminated 25 years of interest in and study of the career of Jesse James with publication of *Jesse James Was His Name...or...Fact and Fiction Concerning the Careers of the Notorious James Brothers of Missouri*. When published it was, and perhaps still remains, the finest work in print on the outlaw careers of Jesse and Frank James and their impact upon their society and region. Settle was married and fathered a son and a daughter. He died at Tulsa.

Who's Who in America, 1974-75; Settle's *Jesse James Was His Name...*, Columbia, Univ. of Missouri Press, 1966; info. from William E. Goodwin, Dir. of Personnel and Bus. Svcs., Univ. of Tulsa, Dec. 20, 1991.

Sevier, Valentine, military officer (1747-1800). The younger brother of John Sevier of Tennessee, Valentine was b. in Rockingham County, Virginia and moved to the neighborhood of the Shelbys in Frederick County in 1773, becoming sergeant in Evan Shelby's militia company. Sevier served in the 1776 Cherokee campaign, was captain in that against the Chickamaugas (the Tennessee Cherokees) in 1779 and led a company against the British in North Carolina in 1780 which culminated in the battle of King's Mountain. Eventually he rose to become militia colonel and retired to Clarksville, Tennessee, which had been named for George Rogers Clark. According to Arnow he paid for his temerity in settling so far out on the frontier by the 1794 loss of most of his family to an Indian massacre and the destruction of his station, or fortified place of residence. Sevier, in addition to several rifles, owned a big brass blunderbuss, and during the siege of his place he loaded it with metal spoons, scrap iron, bullets and anything else that came to hand. It fired with the roar of a cannon which, in miniature, it was, and the powerful kick of the weapon knocked out two of his teeth while its effect on the Indians who were killing his children was not reported. He died at Clarksville.

Thwaites, *Dunmore;* Harriette Simpson Arnow, *Seedtime on the Cumberland,* N.Y., The Macmillan Co., 1960.

Shahaka (Sheheke), Mandan chief (c. 1765-post 1811). Also known as Le Gros Blanc, or Big White, his name in translation means "coyote." He was principal chief of Metutahanke, the Mandan Lower Village on the Missouri, below the mouth of the Knife River. He was described by Brackenridge (see entry) on one occasion as fat, of gentle disposition, undistinguished as a warrior and "extremely talkative, a fault much despised amongst the Indians." But later the traveler considered him "a fine looking Indian, and very intelligent—his complexion is fair, very little different from that of a white man much exposed to the sun," adding that the chief was "rather inclining to corpulency." Shahaka, through his favorite interpreter, René Jusseaume (see entry), was of considerable help to Lewis and Clark, who bestowed upon him a medal, and upon their return in 1806 from the Pacific, they persuaded the chief to accompany them to St. Louis and to Washington, where he and Jusseaume met President Jefferson. Shahaka and Jusseaume remained in the east for a year. Probably at Philadelphia artist/engraver Charles Saint-Mémin made a portrait of the Indian by means of a physionotrace (reproduced by Hodge, II, 518), the original held by the American Philosophical Society of Philadelphia. Accompanied by Jusseaume, Shahaka left St. Louis for the Mandans in May 1807, their military escort commanded by Ensign Nathaniel Pryor (see entry), who as a sergeant had accompanied Lewis and Clark. With the group going upriver were 24 Sioux provided with a separate escort, and two trading parties under Pierre Chouteau. In a clash with the Arikara, then at war with the Mandans, the party suffered casualties, Jusseaume among those wounded. Shahaka rejected Pryor's suggestion that the journey be completed overland because of his interpreter's wound and the encumbrance of women and children. The company withdrew to St. Louis from where another expedition departed in May 1809 and delivered Shahaka, laden with presents, to his village on September 24. He fell into disrepute among his people, however, who considered the tales of his travels exaggerated and largely untrue. He was killed in a fight with the Sioux at some later date. His medal, bearing the date 1797, was preserved by his descendants, as were the legends of his many exploits.

Hodge, HAI, II, 518-19; Clarke, *Lewis and Clark;* Thwaites, EWT, V, 151 VI, 137.

Shakes (Kah Shakes, Sheksh), Tlingit chief (fl. 1818-1835). A chief of the Stikine (Tlingit) Indians, living at Shakes Village on Etolin Island, southwest of Wrangell, Alaska, he once received a gold medal from Baranov (see entry) as an important toion the Russians desired to placate, but its effectiveness was not exactly evident. By 1833 he had lost it, and in the following year was to get a replacement. Friction arose over Shakes' demand for more rum than he had been receiving, and Wrangel, then governor of the Russian American Company, directed that the chief be told to settle down or "we will send as many ships with cannon as there are Shekhs. Let him think it over, that the Russians are not the English." George Simpson, who headed the Northern Department of the Hudson's Bay Company, visited Fort Stikine (now Wrangell), a post leased from the Russians, and wrote that Shakes "had been spoiled by the Russians with too much indulgence, was rather difficult to be managed; and he was, in fact, at the bottom of every plot that was hatched against the whites." Simpson added that "Shakes was said to be very cruel to his slaves, whom he frequently sacrificed in pure wantonness in order to show how great a man he was." Once the chief struck a white man while drunk and received a pair of black eyes in return. He "ordered a slave to be shot at once by way of satisfying his wounded honor and of apologizing to the person whom he had assaulted." A number of geographical features were named for the Indian as Kah Shakes.

Pierce, *Russian America: A Biographical Dictionary;* Orth, 485; Swanton, *Tribes,* 542; Hodge, HAI, II, 521.

Shannon, Samuel, military officer (d. 1781). Shannon in 1773 took up land at Ligonier, Westmoreland County, Pennsylvania. He headed a company of rangers from 1777-81. In the latter year he accompanied the ill-fated company of Archibald Lochry (see entry), as an officer. He was sent ahead down the Ohio River by Lochry with a message to George Rogers Clark but was captured by the Indian party under Joseph Brant and George Girty lying in wait for the Lochry expedition. He was persuaded to advise the Lochry force to surrender, which it did not do until after a disastrous engagement. Shannon was sent a captive to the Lower Sandusky. He managed to escape and had reached a hill opposite Wheeling when he was recaptured by an Indian raider returning from the West Virginia settlements, and was tomahawked.

Thwaites/Kellogg, *Frontier Defense on the Upper Ohio, 1777-1778.*

Shearer, Robert, militia officer (d. 1780). Shearer was a prominent citizen of the later Washington County, southwestern Pennsylvania. In the fall of 1777 he may have acted with the Bedford County militia and was stationed at Beech Bottom Fort, a dozen miles north of Wheeling, West Virginia, on the Ohio River. It is not known how long he remained there. Shearer was killed by Indians while cultivating corn at his homestead. His relationship to William Shearer, who accompanied the 1782 Crawford expedition to the Sandusky region of Ohio, is not stated.

Thwaites/Kellogg, *Frontier Defense on the Upper Ohio, 1777-1778.*

Sheffer, Dr. G.A.: *see* George Anton Scheffer

Sheheke, Mandan chief: *see,* Shahaka

Sheksh, Tlingit chief: *see,* Shakes (Kah Shakes)

Shelby, Evan, frontiersman, military officer (1719-Dec. 4, 1794). B. in Cardiganshire, Wales, he was brought by his family to this country about 1734, settling first in Pennsylvania, then in Maryland, where he acquired major land holdings and became interested in the Indian fur trade, his operations extending as far as Michilimackinac and Green Bay, Wisconsin. He served as a scout with the Braddock campaign in 1755, according to Thwaites, was a lieutenant in Captain Alexander Beal's company in 1757-58, a captain of rangers in both Maryland and Pennsylvania and led the advance for the John Forbes column which occupied Fort Duquesne (Fort Pitt) in 1758. Following the French and Indian War he re-entered the Indian trade and in 1771 removed to Holston on the border of Tennessee and Virginia, where he settled, having suffered heavy commercial losses in the Pontiac War of 1763-64. Residing in Fincastle County of Virginia, he commanded the Fincastle Company in Lord Dunmore's War, taking an active part in the October 10, 1774, Battle of Point Pleasant, present West Virginia, where he succeeded to over-

all command late in the engagement because of the death or disability of his superior officers. In 1776 he was named by Governor Patrick Henry a major in the Colonel William Christian command on a Cherokee expedition to the Overhill towns below the Tennessee River, Christian taking them without opposition with his 1,800-man force. On January 8, 1779, Governor Henry directed Shelby to "raise three hundred men" to proceed to the towns of the Chickamaugas, an errant branch of the Tennessee Cherokees near present Chattanooga, and "totally destroy that and every settlement near it which the offending Indians occupy." In April Shelby, with 600 Virginia and North Carolina volunteers, invaded the Chickamaugan towns, burned 11 of them and carried off much loot; this operation cost "little effort since the warriors were...fighting in behalf of the British on South Carolina and Georgia borders." It was learned by extension of the Virginia-North Carolina boundary that his home was in the latter state and in 1786 North Carolina made him a Brigadier General of militia. In August 1787 he was elected governor of the short-lived state of Franklin, but declined the honor and withdrew from public life. He was buried at Bristol, on the Virginia-Tennessee border. Shelby was described as of stocky build, muscular, straightforward to the point of being blunt and aggressive in civil or military matters. His best known descendant was Isaac Shelby, a governor of Kentucky.

Thwaites, *Dunmore;* Grace Steel Woodward, *The Cherokees,* Norman, Univ. of Okla. Press, 1963; Alexander Scott Withers, *Chronicles of Border Warfare,* Cincinnati, Robert Clarke Co., 1895, 1970; DAB.

Shelby, Isaac, military officer, governor (Dec. 11, 1750-July 18, 1826). B. in the present Washington County, Maryland, he was the son of Evan Shelby (see entry), received a good education, served as deputy sheriff, and moved in 1773 with the family to the present east Tennessee. He served as a lieutenant in his father's Fincastle Company in Lord Dunmore's War of 1774, taking a responsible part in the October 10 battle at Point Pleasant, today's West Virginia, which virtually terminated the military operations. His letter describing the action, reprinted in *Dunmore's War,* 269-77, is perhaps the best report by a participant of the Point Pleasant campaign. Isaac Shelby remained as second in command at Fort Blair on the site of the battle until July 1775, when he withdrew from military service and surveyed lands in Kentucky for the Transylvania Company and for himself for about two years. Virginia Governor Patrick Henry in 1777 appointed him commissary of supplies for militiamen assigned to frontier posts and on July 20 of that year he attended a treaty signing meeting with Cherokee Indians at Fort Henry (Wheeling). Shelby was instrumental in arranging supplies for a projected expedition against the Ohio Indians and Detroit, and for George Rogers Clark's Illinois campaign, and for an operation attended by his father, against the Chickamauga Cherokees of Tennessee. His Revolutionary War contribution was distinguished, he having a major role in the victory at King's Mountain October 7, 1780, and again at Cowpens, January 17, 1781. In 1783 he moved to Boonesborough, Kentucky, and was married there April 19, to Susannah Hart, daughter of Captain Nathaniel Hart; they became parents of eleven children. Shelby was a major figure in the political organization of Kentucky and, when it became a state, served as its first governor, 1792-1796, during which term he gave strong support to Wayne's operations against Ohio/Indiana Indians. In 1812 he again was elected governor of Kentucky and had a role in the victory over the British October 5, 1813, in the Battle of the Thames. In March 1817 he declined, because of his age, President Monroe's offer of the post of Secretary of War. With Andrew Jackson he concluded a treaty with the Chickasaw Indians in 1818, providing for white purchase of Indian lands west of the Tennessee River. Shelby was interested in educational matters, political, military and civil affairs all of his life and during his first administration in Kentucky he had a major role in thwarting assorted schemes to swing Kentucky toward the British interest (see John Connolly entry) and involve in efforts to open the Mississippi through Spanish-held New Orleans. He was an intelligent, forthright, affable man of ability and integrity.

Thwaites, *Dunmore;* Alexander Scott Withers, *Chronicles of Border Warfare,* Cincinnati, Robert Clarke Co., 1895, 1970; Harriette Simpson Arnow, *Seedtime on the Cumberland,* N.Y., Macmillan Co., 1960; DAB.

Shelikhov, Grigorii Ivanovich, frontier entrepreneur (1747-July 31, 1795). The founder of the first permanent Russian colony in North America was b. at Rylsk, province of Kursk, Russia, and after the death of his parents was by 1775 in eastern Siberia. He soon engaged in shipping

activities in the Aleutian Islands and the Kuriles, north of Japan. He formed a partnership with Pavel S. Lebedev-Lastochin (later his principal rival) and occasionally with other merchant-adventurers in promoting fur collecting endeavors from 1776 to 1783. "Between 1777 and 1795 Shelikhov had an interest in fourteen of the thirty-six Russian ships venturing in the North Pacific." In 1781 he married a wealthy widow also interested in commerce, Natalia Alekseevna (her last name at that time is unreported); she was a person of great energy, intelligence and ambition, and was of assistance to Shelikhov in his operations. By 1783 he had become wealthy enough to finance his own endeavors and in partnership with Ivan Larinovich Golikov (who may never himself have visited Alaska) sailed from Okhotsk August 27, with a three-ship expedition, bound for the Aleutians. Natalia went along as the first white woman known to have reached Alaskan waters. The expedition wintered on Bering Island and on August 3, 1784, reached Kodiak Island whose northeastern harbor was named Three Saints after Shelikhov's flagship, the *Trekh Sviatiteli.* Relations with natives initially were good, helped by a solar eclipse on August 5, which the islanders interpreted as signalling the importance of the visitors, but hostility soon was engendered. On August 9, an exploring party ran into large numbers of islanders and became involved in the first of a series of engagements in which the natives suffered more than the Russians; the latter seized women and children as hostages and in the end they prevailed. In many parts of Alaska the Russian occupation was accompanied by "great violence," and Kodiak was no exception. Shelikhov was a very determined man, and he could be ruthless. It was reported that up to 200 natives and Russians were killed in the occupation of the island, hundreds were taken prisoner and Shelikhov was reported to have ordered that "six to ten of the old men be taken out...and speared to death," presumably as an example to others. Gerasim Grigoriev Izmailov (see entry), a navigator, testified that "he himself shot two native traitors [or patriots] by order of Shelikhov," and there undoubtedly were other like instances accompanying the establishment of the settlement, and making it secure. Shelikhov was not by nature cruel as were, for example, Illarion Belaev, Gavriil Pushkarev and Ivan Solovev (see entries), whose infamies were legendary. Russian authority at St. Petersburg, including the Tsarina, Catherine the Great herself (in her ukase of August 13, 1787) ordered that the natives not be mistreated in any way, and the worst reported excesses were sometimes investigated "but in the end [officials] punished no one." Despite sporadic fighting, fortifications and houses were built, schools opened for Aleut children with instruction in Russian, arithmetic and the Orthodox Christian faith. Shelikhov heavily promoted missionary work, perhaps from religious conviction, surely for business purposes. Russians were in Alaska for gain, and at this time gain could come only from fur. The Aleuts were masters of hunting, their cooperation and services must be had, and cooperation of a docile, tractable, converted people was considered necessary. Gradually islands and nearby portions of the continent were explored, promyshlenniki discovered Iliamna Lake (at first called Shelikhov Lake) beyond Cook Inlet and stations were built on the inlet coasts and Afognak Island north of Kodiak. Shelikhov's interests in exploration and expanding his company continued throughout his life and in 1794, in an effort to extend Russian territory "to the limits of the Icy Sea" or Arctic Ocean, he sent a 90-man expedition from Kodiak "to open up the mainland of America to the north and northeast [and seek] a passage to Baffin Bay, even if it should be overland." Another party of 30 men set out across the tundra the following year. The results of these two expeditions are not known. In 1795 the company established Slavorossia in Yakutat Bay. Domination of the Aleuts was considered a prerequisite for control of the territory, but prosperity also depended heavily upon Aleut services, for only they had the expertise to successfully hunt the prized sea otter whose pelt was the most valuable commodity of the region. Shelikhov made every effort to gain and manage the assistance of the Aleuts. Largely by his own efforts he became "the leading entrepreneur in Russia's expansion across the North Pacific to North America." He sought and acquired from Catherine the right to use penal labor to build his empire. This meant that he could obtain skilled though unfortunate European workmen who had come afoul of law or regulations for minimal wages or none at all. Such labor made good business sense, to him. He ardently desired the right of monopoly over all commercial development in Alaska, and pushed this project strongly through friends in court, but Catherine, though she honored and respected him, would consent only to a monopoly in the

areas where his interests already dominated, denying him the overall monopoly during his lifetime. It would come eventually in the form of the Russian American Company granted by Tsar Paul I in 1799 to the residual Shelikhov interests merged with those of the Nikolai Myalnikov (Muilnikof) firm as the most fortunate survivors of some 40 companies which entered the Alaskan field between 1743 and 1799 [For a careful analysis and assessment of the Russian American Company, restrictions upon it, its duties and its rights, see *The Russian American Colonies*, XXXIV-XLIII]. One of Shelikhov's most astute moves in development of his company was appointment in 1790 of Aleksandr Baranov (see entry) to head it and eventually to become, in effect, governor of Alaska. After the solid establishment of his North American interests Shelikhov spent his time in Siberia or St. Petersburg. He wrote a two-volume work, published at the capital in 1792-93 and at once translated into English under the title: *Grigor Shelikov's Journeys from 1783 to 1787...*, later extended to 1790; various elements in these autobiographical books and some of their facts questioned by others. After Shelikhov died at his Irkutsk headquarters, his widow, granted by Paul rank of nobility, ably took over direction of the firm with the strong assistance of her son-in-law Rezanov (see entry). She continued to head it "for many years," and died March 25, 1810, at Moscow. The viability and strength of the Russian American Company, whose creative genius obviously was Shelikhov, were significant for the fledgling United States, for Britain also was interested in the region and "had Alaska fallen under British dominion the opportunity for its acquisition by the United States would probably never have come." Shelikhov Strait, the important waterway between Kodiak Island and the Alaska Peninsula, is named for the entrepreneur, as were other geographical features.

Literature abundant; Bancroft, *Alaska; Russian Penetration of the North Pacific Ocean;* Zagoskin; CE; *The Russian American Colonies.*

Shepherd, David, frontiersman (d. 1795). B. in Berkeley County, Virginia, in 1770 he removed to the west, settling at the forks of Wheeling Creek in the present Ohio County, West Virginia. Shepherd became county lieutenant for Ohio County when it was created, and acted in that capacity until his death. He commanded Fort Henry (Wheeling) during its siege in 1777, and led a regiment on Daniel Brodhead's Coshocton expedition of 1781. He served in the Virginia legislature from 1783 to 1785 and "during the Indian wars was efficient in guarding the frontier."

Thwaites/Kellogg, *The Revolution on the Upper Ohio, 1775-1777*, Madison, Wis. Hist. Soc., 1908.

Sherman, James D., gunman: *see,* Jim Talbot(t)

Shields, James George, British naval officer (d. 1799). B. in England and a shipwright, he went to Russia probably in the late 1780s and served for a time as second lieutenant in the Ekaterinburg (Sverdlovsk) Regiment. He learned to speak and write Russian and around 1790 by agreement with Shelikhov was sent to Okhotsk, Siberia, where he was to construct ships, with four other Britons. One was built, and Shields sailed another, the *Orel,* to Kodiak Island, Alaska, where he was to create still another vessel, but found there was neither material nor expertise there for that program. Shields transferred his operations to Chugach Bay on the southern tip of Kenai Peninsula where suitable timber was to be found, and there constructed the *Phoenix.* His problems were compounded by ill-feeling between himself and the powerful Baranov, governor of the Russian American Company, although the difficulties at last were ironed out. The *Phoenix* was ship-rigged and "a triumph of hard work and improvisation," for there was little iron available, nor tar nor other requirements for ship construction and substitutes must be created for most necessities. The vessel was completed in September 1794. Shields then built the *Delfin* and the *Olga,* two small craft, on an island near Kodiak. He was sent to survey the coasts between Lituya Bay and the Queen Charlotte Islands in southeastern Alaska and off British Columbia, arriving back at Kodiak September 15, 1795. He now desired to build still another small craft and survey the Alaskan coast from Bristol Bay to Bering Strait, enroute attempting to solve the problem of the possible existence of a "lost" Russian colony rumored to be descendants of the Gwozdef expedition (see entry). Nothing came of this endeavor. In 1796 the Englishman surveyed Chilkat Bay and the harbor on Sitka Island where Baranov wished to establish a colony, and in 1798 he took the *Phoenix* to Okhotsk. The next year, remaining in command, the *Phoenix* commenced her return to Kodiak, but was lost at sea with all hands, the details of her fate never ascertained.

Pierce, *Russian America: A Biographical Dictionary.*

Shingas (Shingiss), Delaware war chief (d. c. 1763). Probably a nephew of Sassoon (Olumapies), who died in 1747, Shingas became "King," or spokesman for the Turkey faction of the Delawares living at Logtown, eighteen miles down the Ohio from Fort Duquesne. In 1752 he succeeded the deceased leader as war chief of his people. Because of the ferocity of his eventual raids upon the whites he became known as "Shingas the Terrible" along the Pennsylvanian frontier, although there is dissent about the depravity of his character. George Washington in 1753 visited Shingas, who he called "King of the Delawares," at the chief's home, two miles below the French fort, then accompanied Shingas to Logtown during his mission to French posts above the Ohio River. Shingas, nominally at peace with the English at the time, in company with five Ohio chiefs representing Delawares, Shawnees and Mingos, met with Braddock in 1755 to offer their assistance in his operation against Duquesne, but found him little interested. Asked what he intended to do with the Ohio land after removing the French, Braddock replied that the English should "Inhabit and Inherit" it. When Shingas then asked if those Indians who had assisted the General might be allowed to live and hunt upon the land, Braddock "haughtily replied 'that no Savage Should Inherit the Land.'" The chiefs then replied "That if they might not have liberty to Live on the Land they woud not Fight for it To wch Genl Braddock answered that he did not need their Help and had no Doubt of driving the French and their Indians away." Shingas and the others returned to their peoples following the rebuff, and awaited Braddock's collision with the French and their Indians. When it came "they made it their Business to draw nigh the place where the Engagement Happened that they might see what passed at it," still hoping for an English victory. It did not come. They not only observed the Braddock debacle, but also witnessed the French victory celebration at Duquesne "where naked British prisoner soldiers were tortured and burned at the stake." The Delawares now suffered from loss of their crops due to inclement weather and the people became restless under the resulting hardship. They were increasingly convinced that the British could not win their war against the French, Braddock's rebuff still rankled, and Shingas "made a fateful decision" and allied the Delawares of the Ohio River with the French, as did the neighboring Shawnees. October 16, 1755, Shingas's warriors attacked a white settlement near the present Selinsgrove, Pennsylvania, killing and scalping 13 men and women, capturing 11 others. Meanwhile he sent an emissary to the Susquehanna Delawares (another major faction of the tribe) urging them to help him rid the land of the English. Shingas, his brother Pisquetomen, Killbuck and other war leaders obtained abundant ammunition and supplies from the Fort Duquesne French, and increasingly terrorized settlers in Pennsylvania, Virginia and Maryland. French officers sometimes accompanied them, as did Ensign Dagneau Douville, who was killed by Virginians 25 miles east of Fort Cumberland. Shortly afterward another party of French and Indians attacked a Virginia detachment, killing 17 and losing nine, while Shingas himself was wounded, although not seriously. "Before the end of November 1755 the Pennsylvania frontier from the Maryland border to the Delaware water gap was aflame." The hostile successes had impressed the Susquehannas enough so that a sizable fraction of that people now joined the raiders. When Shingas and his war captains launched their attacks "it was with malice in their hearts and an obsession to destroy white people. This hatred caused them to inflict terrible atrocities on settlers of all nationalities and of all ages. No white family was safe." The hostiles "waged a commando war which was an orgy of bloodletting that marked the Delawares as brutal and ruthless warriors who showed no mercy," wrote Weslager, adding that "there can be little question that the English brought this disaster upon themselves," though there was no single cause. It sprang from long periods of abuse of the Indians, or fancied abuse: broken promises; unscrupulous traders who cheated and debauched their customers, and who spread smallpox, contagious fevers, venereal diseases, and other evils. April 14, 1756, Governor Robert Hunter Morris of Pennsylvania finally declared formal war upon the Delaware Nation. He offered cash bounties for Indian prisoners and generous awards for scalps of men and women. September 8, 1756, Colonel John Armstrong destroyed the enemy village of Kittanning, killing Captain Jacobs (Jachebus?), a brother of Shingas. While this alone did not cause Shingas or his captains to seek peace, the war spirit at last had begun to cool, in large part because the French fount of munitions and supplies had waned to the point

that the Indians could not maintain their earlier pressure upon the English. Many Delawares could see that the tide was turning against them, for all their earlier victories. Shingas's own people were tiring of war. Finally his brother Pisquetomen himself carried a message signed by fifteen Delaware chiefs and important men, including Beaver, still another brother of Shingas, to the English, seeking a good peace. This had the predictable result of a change in the leadership of the Logtown Delawares. The English, in reaction to the peace initiative, decreed that Shingas's brother Beaver (Tamaqua) should now be "King," or the Turkey faction spokesman, and in such matters their word prevailed, for they alone could decide with whom they would speak. Besides, Shingas's scalp continued to generate attractive awards: the Pennsylvanians offered a reward of 350 pieces of eight, or dollars, and Virginia offered 50 pistoles (at $4 each) for his head. He saw enough of the likely future to be willing for Beaver to take over the scepter, and the Delaware councilors believed it would be easier to come to terms with the English if Beaver, rather than Shingas the Terrible, was their spokesman. November 25, 1758, Brigadier General John Forbes had seized the abandoned ruins of Fort Duquesne, finally terminating French assistance to the Delawares, and July 9, 1759, Beaver and his associates signed a peace at the newly-named Fort Pitt with George Croghan, deputy for Sir William Johnson, British Indian agent. They promised to deliver several hundred prisoners they had taken, and an imperfect and uneasy peace at last was agreed upon. Beaver formally became chief of the Turkey Delawares in 1761. In the winter of 1763-64 Shingas died, probably on the Muskingum River, Ohio. Although he had fiercely won the title of the most dreaded of all the hostiles (and retained it for generations after his demise), the Moravian missionary John Heckewelder, who knew the Indian well, had a much more open opinion of his character. "Whether in peace or in war [King Shingas] was a man of distinction: active and resolute in battle, but at the same time magnanimous, sensitive to a point of honor, and kind to those dependent on him." In hostility he was "a bloody warrior, cruel in his treatment, relentless in his fury. His person was small, but in point of courage, activity and savage prowess he was said to have never been exceeded by anyone." Yet another Moravian, Christian Post, reported that "however implacable in battle, [he] never treated a prisoner with cruelty [and] in his own community was considerate, generous and capable of the warmest personal attachments." Shingas's beloved wife died of fever in the summer of 1762 and Heckewelder upon invitation attended the impressive six-hour funeral rites for her, writing of it at length, and of the deep emotion Shingas obviously felt at the loss of his spouse.

Clinton A. Weslager, *The Delaware Indians: a History,* New Brunswick, N.J., Rutgers Univ. Press, 1972; Paul A. Wallace, *Thirty Thousand Miles With John Heckewelder,* Univ. of Pittsburgh Press, 1958; Alexander Scott Withers, *Chronicles of Border Warfare,* Cincinnati, Robert Clarke Co., 1895, 1970; HNAI, 15, p. 223.

Shmakov, Nikolay, hunter (fl. 1842-1844). A Creole, half native American, half Russian, he joined Zagoskin at Fort St. Michael on Norton Sound in 1842 as a hunter. On January 11, 1843, it was reported he had frozen his big toes on the winter journey to Nulato on the middle Yukon; Zagoskin had to leave him at ʼKhogoltlinde, an Eskimo settlement opposite the present Kaltag, for a few days to thaw and heal them, but in February he still was not ready to travel, seriously weakening Zagoskin's party. Later he rejoined the expedition and April 28, 1844, killed a deer to feed the then hard-pressed band. Nothing further is reported of him.

Zagoskin.

Shoshone Mike (Tosaponaga, Ondongarte), Shoshoni Indian (d. Feb. 26, 1911). The victim of the last Indian massacre in the United States, Shoshone Mike was considered by some a Bannock and not a Shoshoni, but Bergon, who has done the most minute investigation of his origins, discovered Fort Hall records showing that he was a Hukendeka (Hohandika) Shoshoni, and traced his lineage back for five generations. His Shoshone name, Tosaponaga, meant Split White, and Ondongarte meant Sitting Light. By some whites he was known as Mike Daggett. The Hukendeka Shoshoni traditionally inhabited the region west of Great Salt Lake and in 1862 they suffered severely from California Volunteers. Bergon, who was born at Ely, Nevada, is of Basque descent and researched the Shoshone Mike story over many years. He found that Mike tired of life on the Fort Hall Reservation of Idaho and for twenty years "pursued a traditional way of life in the Nevada borderlands." In 1910 one of Mike's sons was killed by a white horse thief, who was killed in his turn by the Indians. This caused them to withdraw farther into the Nevada

deserts and mountains. "Here they survived a terrible winter by stealing cattle for food." On being discovered they killed three Basque sheepmen and a cattleman, bringing upon them an intensive search by posses from Nevada and California. The pursuit covered between 200 and 300 miles. The fleeing family was caught up with on February 26, 1911, in a dry wash named Rabbit Creek in northwestern Nevada. In the fight that followed four Indian men, including Mike, two women and two children were killed by the posse, and one white among the attackers also died (although this was the last "massacre" of Indians, Mike was not the last "hostile" Indian in the United States [see William Posey entry]). Four children were taken alive, placed in a Reno jail since there was no other place to put them. Eventually the federal government directed the Fort Hall superintendent, Evan W. Estep (he was in charge of the reservation from October 1, 1910, to the spring of 1914), to take care of the children and they were moved to Fort Hall by train in November 1911. Three of the children died within a year; the fourth survived tuberculosis and was adopted by Estep and his wife, Rita, and christened Mary Jo. She moved with her adoptive parents to reservations in Montana, New Mexico and eventually to Yakima, Washington. She was just 18 months old at the time of the massacre, was told of it, but never asked for details. Treated as a white girl, most of her friends were non-Indians. She was graduated from Central Washington University at Ellensburg with a degree in music and taught for forty years before retiring in 1974. She had assumed that the other three children who survived the killings were her siblings until Hyde's book revealed that they were her uncle and two aunts. Mary Jo died December 19, 1992, at a Yakima nursing home, apparently following ingestion of a mistaken medicine.

Frank Bergon, "Shaping the Past: The Search for Shoshone Mike," *Vassar Quarterly,* Vol. LXXXIV, No. 1 (Winter, 1987), 16-19; Bergon, *Shoshone Mike* (novel), N.Y., Viking, 1987; *Ventura* (California) *Star-Free Press,* Sept. 5, 1988, story reprinted in English Westerners' *Tally Sheet,* Vol. 35, No. 3 (Summer, 1989); Dayton O. Hyde, *The Last Free Man,* N.Y., Dial Press, 1973; *Arizona Daily Star,* March 17, 1993; info. from E.F. (Ted) Mains.

Shvetsov (Shoetzof, Shutzof), Afanasii, Russian frontiersman (fl. 1795-1810). A Russian *starovoiazhnyi promyshlennik,* or "old voyaging fur trapper and trader," Shvetsov had reached the

Alaskan region at least by 1795, already an experienced man and perhaps married to an Aleut woman, since he was fluent in that Eskimauan tongue. When Joseph O'Cain made his 1803 deal with Baranov for the temporary employment of Aleut sea otter hunters, Shvetsov and Timoteo Tarkanov were assigned by the governor to go along and "command" the Aleuts. But Shvetsov was to do more than that. Baranov "wanted to get acquainted with the inhabitants of California …and, above all, he wished to discover how far the influence of the Americans extended over the Californians and the savages on other portions of the Northwest Coast." Bancroft, who refers to Shvetsov as "a tried servant of the Russian American Company," wrote that the agent was "ordered to observe closely all parts of the coast…to mark the number and character of the inhabitants, and to procure information of all hunting-grounds which might in the future be utilized by the company without the assistance of foreigners." He was to scan seaports Americans used for trading purposes and to ascertain prices and products of the countries visited. Shvetsov thus was much more than merely a foreman of otter hunters. The ship *O'Cain* left Kodiak Island with Shvetsov and forty Aleut hunters October 26, 1803, worked down the coast to Lower California so efficiently that Spanish officials complained there "was not an otter left" in their wake, and returned to Kodiak in June 1804 with 1,800 otter skins (700 of which O'Cain had gathered by illegal trading with Spanish missionaries and soldiers). Shvetsov was the *baidarshchik,* or overseer of open boat hunting parties for the Karluk trading post of western Kodiak Island in 1805. June 26, 1808, he was commander of otter hunters for George Washington Eayrs of the ship *Mercury* which hunted along the coast as far as Lower California and finally returned to Sitka in June 1909. It too was a successful hunt. March 10, 1810, Shvetsov took an otter hunting party to the Bay of Islands east of Cape Edgecumbe, but contaminated water made most of his Aleuts so ill he had to abort the operation. Nothing further was reported of Shvetsov except that in 1819 his "widow" petitioned the company for a pension because her husband had "opened to the Russian American Company and to the Russian empire, the valuable trade of California," which he at least had a strong role in doing.

Bancroft, *Alaska;* Adele Ogden, *The California Sea Otter Trade 1784-1848,* Berkeley, Univ. of Calif. Press, 1941; info. from E.A.P. Crownhart-Vaughan,

exec. dir. of North Pacific Studies Ctr., Oregon Hist. Soc.

Silcott, Jane, Nez Perce woman (1842-Jan. 17, 1895). The daughter of the famed Nez Perce chief Timothy (see entry), she was warned by her father against guiding white prospectors into Idaho, but reportedly because of a love affair with one of them did so anyway in 1860. This led to discovery of recoverable amounts of gold at a place called Orofino, east of present Lewiston; this ignited a rush by prospectors, who overran Nez Perce lands and brought with them all the evils Timothy had feared. Jane married a half-breed Nez Perce, fathered a son who drowned and after her husband died she married John Silcott, a white, a successful contractor and businessman. On or near her 53rd birthday her clothing caught fire near an open fireplace and she died from the effects. Jane was buried on an eminence overlooking her husband's ferry across the Clearwater River near its confluence with the Snake, her husband, upon his death, being buried beside her.

Robert G. Bailey, *River of No Return: Historical Stories of Idaho,* Lewiston, R.G. Bailey Printg. Co., 1947.

Simpson, George Gaylord, paleontologist, evolution theorist (June 16, 1902-Oct. 6, 1984). B. at Chicago, he was raised in Colorado where his father's career was in land development and mining. He studied at the University of Colorado in 1918 and 1919 and completed his undergraduate work at Yale, where he earned a doctorate in 1923 (also receiving over the years a dozen honorary degres from universities in this country and abroad). A thorough-going genius in several directions, Simpson was still "a bundle of contradictions," according to Harvard's Stephen Jay Gould: "He defined the science of paleontology in our times…Simpson unified paleontology with modern evolutionary theory by arguing for the consistency between principles of evolutionary change in modern populations and the sweep and pageant of the fossil record. He became [an architect of] the modern synthesis of evolution…He was also a great empirical paleontologist, who established the modern classification of mammals and wrote hundreds of papers on fossil bones, fauna and environments [and] the finest biology textbooks of his generation [while his] *The Meaning of Evolution* is still the best popular book about the basis and implications of his science." Simpson also was a great field paleontologist. He did research for Yale's Peabody Museum in 1924-26 on Mesozoic mammals, became associated with the American Museum of Natural History of New York in 1924, remaining with it until 1959, by which time he had become Curator of Fossil Mammals and chairman of its department of geology and paleontology. He then became associated with the Museum of Comparative Zoology at Harvard and in 1967 joined the University of Arizona as professor of geosciences; he died as professor emeritus. He led expeditions to collect fossil mammals in northern Texas, Montana, New Mexico, Florida and southeastern states, Argentina, Venezuela and Brazil; he also professionally visited Mongolia (where, ever interested in linguistics, he also briefly studied that language); Antarctica, as a result of which he wrote *Penguins: Past and Present* (1976); Indonesia, about which he wrote a paper on its zoogeography and, among many places, in 1961 to East Africa. This trip, made largely for his own information and education, had also an ulterior motive. Ever since 1935, and perhaps earlier, the noted British paleontologist, L.S.B. Leakey, who was making a dazzling array of spectacular fossil hominoid finds in East Africa, had come under some suspicion from conservative colleagues in England, at one time even being rebuked by the estimable scientific publication, *Nature*. One of Simpson's goals was to attempt to determine whether Leakey's reports "tallied well with the field evidence and, in some detail, whether his collecting was tied in with precise and trustworthy field data." Simpson found to his complete satisfaction that Leakey's field operations "met the highest professional standards at that time" and that while one might differ with his expressed judgments, "his statements of fact were indeed factual." Although associated with various universities at times, Simpson "disliked teaching and had almost no students," although his books invariably were of instructional value (many are texts), were usually very readable, good-humored, thoroughly researched, innovative and possessed permanency to a high degree. They included (this list is not complete): *Attending Marvels; A Patagonian Journal* (1934); *Horses* (1951); *The Meaning of Evolution* (1949; rev. ed., 1967); *Life of the Past: An Introduction to Paleontology, The Major Features of Evolution*, and *Evolution and Geography* (all in 1953); *This View of Life: The World of an Evolutionist* (1964); *Life* (1957, 1965); *The*

Geography of Evolution (1965); *Biology and Man* (1969), and *Concession to the Improbable: An Unconventional Autobiography* (1978). His scientific papers, many of them book-length, numbered around 800; an excellent sample illustrating the profundity and thoroughness of his research and completeness in handling a subject, is his "Holarctic Mammalian Faunas and Continental Relationships During the Cenozoic," *Bulletin of the Geological Society of America*, Vol. 58, No. 7 (July 1947), 613-88. This deals in admirable comprehensiveness with faunal migrations from Asia to America and from America to Asia via the Bering land bridge during the recent geological era, whenever the landbridge emerged above sea level. Gould wrote that while "a few friends considered him generous and outgoing [to] most colleagues he seemed at best distant, at worst petty or even cruel," although that judgment would seem overly harsh. He wrote the splendid biographical sketches of Henry Fairfield Osborne (1857-1935) and Walter Granger (see entry) for the *Dictionary of American Biography* and each, while characteristically thorough, honest and overlooking no major flaws of the subjects, are warmly positive even though each may have held positions with which Simpson in private would disagree. During World War II Simpson served to major in Army intelligence in North Africa, but won only a single battle: he defeated General George Patton, who had insisted he shave off his characteristic Van Dyke beard, and remained happily hirsute. On a first reading of the immensely popular, *The Meaning of Evolution*, some no doubt gathered an impression that Simpson was an atheist, but he flatly denied that in a letter to this author in 1969: "Although most Christians and some others think I am an atheist," he wrote, "I am not. I do not believe that an invisible anthropomorph ever impregnated an espoused Jewish virgin, so it's true I am not a Christian...However no rational person can fail to feel awe for this mysterious universe and its first cause. The god really is ineffable...There is no name for this religion, but it is a religion." Simpson married twice, the first marriage ending in divorce after the birth of four daughters, a second wife, the former Anne Roe, a Harvard University professor emeritus, survived him after 46 years of a happy union. He died at Tucson, Arizona.

Who's Who in America; Stephen Jay Gould, review, *New York Times Book Review,* Feb. 14, 1988;

Donald E. Savage, review, *New York Times,* Nov. 25, 1984; Leigh M. Van Allen, review, *American Scientist,* Vol. 76 (Sept.-Oct. 1988), 505-506; S. David Webb, review, *Science,* Vol. 240 (May 20, 1988), 1067; Tucson, *Arizona Daily Star,* Oct. 8, 1984; personal acquaintance with author.

Simpson, Thomas, explorer, trader (July 2, 1808-June 6, 1840). A cousin of Sir George Simpson, he was b. in Scotland and in 1829 was sent to Canada by the Hudson's Bay Company. He was credited with discovery of Victoria Island in the Canadian archipelago and with Peter Warren Dease (see entry) conducted an important exploration of the Arctic coast. June 1, 1837, they led a party of fourteen men descending the Mackenzie River from Fort Good Hope, just below the Arctic Circle, to the coast, then followed the shore westerly. They reached Demarcation Point July 15, and Franklin's Point Beechey July 24. Their boat was stopped by ice July 31, near Point Return, the most westerly longitude reached by Franklin in 1826. Simpson, accompanied by five men then continued on foot, by means of canvas canoe and in umiaks borrowed from the Eskimos, to Point Barrow, reached August 3, thus completing the charting of the northern coast of the American continent which Beechey and Elson had already pushed from Bering Strait to Point Barrow. Simpson returned to rejoin Dease August 6. Dease Inlet was named by Simpson for his colleague, and Simpson Lagoon was named for Thomas Simpson by the explorer Ernest de Koven Leffingwell at a later date. Simpson was killed in 1840, by natives, by his own men, or by his own hand.

Zagoskin; *Narratives of the Explorations in Alaska,* 367; Orth, 32, 867; CE.

Sindt (Synd, Syndo), Ivan (Joann), naval explorer (d. 1779). A Baltic German in the Russian navy, he had served as a marine on the Bering-Chirikov expedition of 1741 whereafter he remained in Siberia and was promoted to naval lieutenant. He was appointed to command a 1764-67 North Pacific expedition, directed to closely monitor the private seaborne fur trade from America, survey with precision the islands between Kamchatka and America, and determine their resources, although "Sindt did not have the necessary leadership qualifications for such an assignment." In a ship named the *Sv Pavel* he sailed from Okhotsk, Siberia, in 1764, failed to clear Kamchatka the first season, trans-

fered to the *Sv Ekaterina* in June 1765, wintered on Kamchatka again and the following year reached Bering Strait, "jotting down on his chart as he moved along a multitude of imaginary islands extending up to latitude 64° 59', and reported a mountainous coast" near the Chukotski Peninsula. September 2, 1767, he began his return voyage and finally reached Okhotsk in 1768. He submitted to the Admiralty a report and a map of Bering Sea islands, his chart "so filled with errors and exaggerations [it] took years to correct." Possibly because of the uselessness of his map, Sindt's report never was published. He died at Okhotsk of unreported causes. His was the second government-sponsored expedition to the North Pacific after Bering's, the third being that of Krenitzin and Levashev (see entries).

Russian Penetration of the North Pacific Ocean; William Coxe, *Account of the Russian Discoveries Between Asia and America,* London, T. Cadell, 3rd ed., 1787 (N.Y., 1966); Bancroft, *Alaska.*

Skaatagech, Tlingit chief (fl. 1799-1800). One of three principal chiefs (the other two being Skautlelt and Koukhkan) of a Kolosh (Tlingit) tribe at the present site of Sitka, Alaska. In July 1799 they ceded for payment to Baranov the site on which he built the first Russian fur trading post and redoubt. It was destroyed by the Tlingit in an attack in 1802.

Pierce, *Russian America: A Biographical Dictionary.*

Skautlelt, Tlingit chief (fl. 1799-1802). He was one of three Tlingit (Kolosh) chiefs, the other two being Skaatagech and Koukhkan, of a region on the Alaskan coast, who ceded for payment to Baranov the site for the future Sitka, Alaska. He also was known to the Russians as Mikhail, evidently having been baptized. He was lavishly treated with gifts by Baranov and pledged loyalty to Russia. During the fatal Tlingit attack on Sitka in 1802, Skautlelt was observed standing on a hill opposite the commandant's house, shouting orders to his followers, who destroyed the settlement and killed most of the whites and Aleuts present.

Pierce, *Russian America: A Biographical Dictionary.*

Skillern, George, pioneer (fl. 1758-1793). An Augusta County, Virginia, pioneer, he worked for the army in a civilian capacity as early as 1758. In 1764 he became a justice, continuing as such when Botetourt County was formed in 1770. Six years later he became lieutenant colonel of county militia and in 1777 was at Fort Randolph, Point Pleasant, West Virginia, engaged in Indian operations, although it is not clear whether he saw combat. He was, however, at Randolph when the noted Shawnee chief Cornstalk was murdered November 10, 1777, although he had nothing to do with it, nor were his troops involved. Skillern did take a deposition on the affair, seeking facts about it, and General Hand reported that Skillern was one of the officers aware of "the most active of the party" of slayers. In December 1777 he was ordered to return to Botetourt County with his command and probably undertook no further frontier service. In 1780 he succeeded Colonel William Fleming (see entry) as county lieutenant and "the following year was active in the defense of the state during the invasions," probably of the British. He still was county lieutenant in 1793. In 1788 he was an incorporator of Pattonsburg, building a home two miles from the community. Skillern apparently left no male descendants.

Thwaites/Kellogg, *Frontier Defense on the Upper Ohio, 1777-1778.*

Skinya, Apache militant: *see,* Eskinya

Slaughter, George, military officer (d. June 17, 1818). As a colonel George Slaughter served under Dunmore in the Point Pleasant campaign which terminated in the October 10, 1774, engagement which virtually ended the Lord Dunmore War against primarily Shawnee Indians. Slaughter was in Andrew Lewis's (see entry) division which bore the brunt of the fighting. He was among those remaining at Point Pleasant while Lewis took the bulk of his command on a subsequent expedition against the Ohio Indians. Colonel Slaughter raised a Virginia company in 1776 and joined the 8th Virginia Regiment for the Revolutionary battles of Brandywine and Germantown. Upon his return to western Virginia he joined Shelby in the 1779 expedition against the Chickamauga (Cherokee) towns in Tennessee. Later that year he started with reinforcements for George Rogers Clark in Illinois. His company was forced to winter in the mountains, and arrived at Louisville with 150 Virginia soldiers in June 1780, taking command of the place. After aiding Clark in the Piqua, Ohio, campaign in August 1780, Slaughter served in the Virginia House of Delegates in

1784, then settled briefly in Jefferson County, Kentucky and afterward at Charlestown, Indiana, where he died.

Thwaites, *Dunmore;* Alexander Scott Withers, *Chronicles of Border Warfare,* Cincinnati, Robert Clarke Co., 1895, 1970.

Slaughter, William Alloway, military officer (d. Dec. 4, 1855). B. in Kentucky, he went to West Point from Indiana, was commissioned a brevet second lieutenant of the 2nd Infantry July 1, 1848, and a second lieutenant of the 4th Infantry November 6 of that year. Grant met him while enroute to California, the ship lying at anchor in Panama Bay. He wrote that Slaughter "was very liable to sea-sickness. It almost made him sick to see the wave of a table-cloth when the servants were spreading it. Soon after his graduation [from West Point], Slaughter was ordered to California and took passage by a sailing vessel going around Cape Horn. The vessel was seven months making the voyage, and Slaughter was sick every moment of the time, never more so than while lying at anchor after reaching his place of destination. On landing in California he found orders which had come by way of the Isthmus, notifying him of a mistake in his assignment; he should have been ordered to the northern lakes. He started back by the Isthmus route and was sick all the way. But when he arrived at the East he was again ordered to California, this time definitely, and at this date was making his third trip. He was as sick as ever, and had been so for more than a month while lying at anchor in the bay. I remember him well, seated with his elbows on the table...his chin between his hands, and looking the picture of despair. At last he broke out, 'I wish I had taken my father's advice; he wanted me to go into the navy; if I had done so, I should not have had to go to sea so much.'" But it was his last voyage. He was promoted to first lieutenant June 22, 1854, and assigned to the Northwest. He was actively engaged in the Indian war of 1855 in Washington Territory. November 3, commanding 50 regulars, he pursued hostiles to the crossing of the White River, where the Indians fought them off. In a six hour exchange of fire across the stream, Slaughter claimed 30 or more of the enemy slain for a loss of one soldier killed and another slightly wounded. Yet the Indians seemed to be getting the best of it with the whole country between the Cowlitz River and Olympia to the north deserted of settlers, who fled to Puget Sound settlements for protection. Slaughter was directed to proceed with his company to the White and Green rivers, southeast of Seattle. He was attacked at night at Bidding's Prairie, a mile from Puyallup, on November 24 and had 40 horses stolen from him during a heavy fog. The Indians involved were Klikitats, Nisquallies and Niscopes, who continually harrassed the troops. Reinforced by men of the 4th Artillery from Fort Steilacoom, he set out again to engage the elusive enemy, and camped at the forks of the White and Green on Brannan's Prairie, taking possession of a small log house. While in conference with other officers, his men lighted fires to dry clothing soaked by incessant rains, and at 7 p.m., by the light of the blazes, the hostiles sent a bullet through his heart and Slaughter "died without uttering a word." The firing continued for three hours, causing other casualties, but "nothing that had occurred during the war cast a greater gloom...than the death of the gallant Slaughter," according to Bancroft. Slaughter's remains were taken down White River to Seattle, and sent to Steilacoom "where was his family."

Heitman; U.S. Grant, *Memoirs,* N.Y., Library of Amer., 1990, I, 133; Bancroft, *Washington, Idaho, and Montana,* 120-23.

Smith, Bill, desperado (c. 1865-1902). Smith was described as six feet in height, slender and "straight as an arrow," with black eyes and black hair, and a cowboy by trade. He was well and favorably known in southwestern New Mexico and northeastern Arizona until about 1898 when he was jailed for some offense, broke out, imprisoning the jailor in his own cell, and fled. He gathered a band of seven as reckless as himself, including three of his brothers. With the gang he reportedly held up a Union Pacific train in northern Utah, then returned to Arizona, in the early fall of 1901, being seen driving a bunch of stolen horses near Springerville, Arizona. Crimes occurred regularly, "post offices were robbed...and several persons were killed...small stores were raided," holdups became common, and "so frequent did these depredations become and the murders so numerous that even in that sparsely settled country the people became aroused and began the formation of vigilance committees." The gang's headquarters were on the Black River in northern Graham County. October 7, 1901, Arizona Rangers Charles Tafolla (Tafoya) and Will Maxwell had a fight with the Smith gang and were killed. Bill Smith fled to Mexico, but occasionally returned to Dou-

glas, Arizona, for a bit of night life; in so doing he came into a fight with Ranger Dayton Graham and a policeman, Tom Vaughn, both of whom were wounded seriously. Upon recovery Graham persistently hunted for Smith and in 1902 killed him at a monte table; steel hacksaw blades were found sewn into Smith's coat. He obviously was prepared for any eventuality save death.

O'Neal, *Gunfighters;* Joseph Miller, ed., *The Arizona Rangers,* N.Y., Hastings House, 1972; info. from E.F. (Ted) Mains.

Smith, James, frontierman (1737-1812). B. in Franklin County, Pennsylvania, he was captured at 18 by Indians in the spring of 1755 and was at Fort Duquesne (Pittsburgh) at the time of the Braddock Battle of July 1755. He observed the council at which the Indians decided when and where to attack Braddock, confident that "we'll shoot them down all as one piegeon." The ambush force, he said, consisted of about 400 Indians with very few Frenchmen (see Braddock entry), but history tells it slightly differently. Following the abandonment of Duquesne by the French, Smith was taken to Montreal from where he escaped in 1759, reaching his Pennsylvania home in 1760. He served as an ensign in 1763 during the Pontiac turmoil, and was a lieutenant in 1764 in Bouquet's campaign against the Ohio Indians. In 1766 he joined company with Joshua Horton, Uriah Stone, William Baker and another James Smith and by way of the Holston River explored south of Kentucky at a time when the area was entirely uninhabited by whites, and also visited the region between the Cumberland and Tennessee rivers; Stone's River, a branch of the Cumberland, was named by them as its "discoverers." Smith was a leader for some years of the Pennsylvania "Black Boys," so named for painting their faces like Indians. They sought to dissuade traders from supplying arms and ammunition to the natives. At one point Smith was falsely accused, tried for murder and acquitted. As troubles with England mounted, he was selected for frontier service. He was a captain in the Pennsylvania armed forces, in 1777 was a major under Washington, and in 1778 (or in 1779) as a colonel of militia led an expedition against an Indian town on French Creek, not far from today's Meadville, Pennsylvania. In 1781 or 1788 (accounts differ) he moved to Kentucky, was active in politics and as a Presbyterian minister performed missionary work and preached among the Indians. He wrote a "valuable account," according to Draper, of his Indian captivity, a treatise on Indian warfare and "two controversial pamphlets against the Shakers," a religious sect. He died in Washington County, Kentucky, at 75. He was married.

Alexander Scott Withers, *Chronicles of Border Warfare*, Cincinnati, Robert Clarke Co., 1895, 1970; Harriette Simpson Arnow, *Seedtime on the Cumberland*, N.Y., The Macmillan Co., 1960; Thwaites/Kellogg, *Frontier Defense on the Upper Ohio, 1777-1778*.

Smith, John A., soldier (c. 1855-Oct. 1925). During his enlisted service Smith served to sergeant with D Company of the 6th Cavalry against Indians of Texas, the Indian Territory, under Miles in the so-called Red River War of 1874-75, and in Kansas, New Mexico, Arizona and Old Mexico from 1875-84. In 1881 he was stationed at Fort Apache, Arizona. He served on Colonel Eugene Carr's (see entry) Cibecue operation which was directed to "capture or kill" a medicine man, Noch-ay-del-klinne, who was believed stirring unrest among Apache Indians on the reservation. The Indian was taken prisoner, but as the command pulled away an irruption caused some of the scouts to mutiny, and Noch-ay-del-klinne allegedly sought to escape. Sergeant John F. McDonald shot him and Trumpeter William O. Benitas also fired a bullet into him, but he was not killed, and Smith then took an axe and "dispatched the wounded Apache." As he knelt beside the body to make sure the medicine man was dead, he saw a large medal around the neck of the victim, "which he appropriated" (Mazzanovich presents photographs of both sides of the medal on p. 92 of his book); the medal had been presented to the Indian by President Grant on a visit to Washington by a Native American delegation, and bore the legend, "On Earth Peace Good Will Toward Men" with the date, 1871. When Smith learned Mazzanovich was writing a book mentioning the incident he begged him not to write the way "he had to send the medicine man to the 'Happy Hunting Grounds,' [commenting that] it was rather an unpleasant method of bumping the medicine man over the long trail, but it was the only way under existing conditions." After leaving the army Smith settled at Burnett, Washington, where he died.

Anton Mazzanovich, *Trailing Geronimo*, 3rd. ed., Los Angeles, p.p., 1931.

Smith, John Eugene, military officer (Aug. 3, 1816-Jan. 29, 1897). B. in the canton of Berne, Switzerland, he was brought by his parents to America at 1, raised in Philadelphia, received some education and became a jeweler, following that profession at St. Louis, then at Galena, Illinois. He organized the 45th Illinois Infantry in 1861 and was commissioned colonel of it July 23. He served with distinction during the Civil War, became Brigadier General of volunteers November 29, 1862, and ably commanded a division under Grant at Vicksburg and under Sherman at Savannah, ending the Civil War a brevet Major General and being mustered out April 30, 1866. He became colonel of the 27th U.S. Infantry July 28 1866; in July 1867 he assumed command of Fort Phil Kearny, Wyoming; this was half a year after the Fetterman disaster near that post, which was in hostile Sioux territory. Although the fort was comparatively lightly-manned, Smith had brought new breech-loading Springfield rifles and metallic cartridges to replace the old muzzle-loaders the Fetterman troops had carried, so that in combat effectiveness the strength of the garrison was maintained. After briefly commanding the 15th Infantry in 1870 Smith was assigned to the 14th Infantry December 20 of that year. In the winter of 1873-74 turbulent Sioux descended upon the Red Cloud and Spotted Tail agencies of Dakota and "made of them nightmares of anarchy," the agents terrified and no nearby troops to pacify the area. In early March 1874, on Sherman's authority, Smith "led a formidable expedition of nearly 1,000 cavalry and infantry from Fort Laramie in a punishing winter march to White River," Dakota. The troublemakers stampeded off and the crisis passed. Smith, in northern Nebraska not far from the Red Cloud Agency, established a permanent post he named in honor of First Lieutenant Levi H. Robinson, whose slaying by Sioux near Mount Laramie, Wyoming, had sparked the trouble at the agencies leading to Smith's winter march. Fort Robinson became a key military base in the Sioux War of 1876. In the summer of 1877 and into 1878 trouble among the Bannocks of Idaho brought Smith and three companies of the 14th Infantry from Fort Douglas, Utah, to Fort Hall Agency in December. In January 1878 a Bannock who had drunkenly shot several whites was arrested, and this "created such an alarm" that Smith seized 53 Bannock warriors, confiscating their horses and arms, "adding still more to their resentment." This led to the so-called Bannock War of 1878, in which Smith had no recorded role. Having reached the age of 62, he retired May 19, 1881, and settled at Chicago, where he died; he was buried at Galena. Smith was survived by three sons.

Heitman; Powell; Robert M. Utley, *Frontier Regulars*, N.Y., Macmillan Co., 1973; DAB.

Smith, Matthew, Indian killer (fl. 1763-1764). Smith was a leader of the "Paxton (Paxtang) Boys" who perpetrated the savage murder of twenty Conestoga Indians, the last of the Susquehannas (as some have it), that being an Iroquois-speaking, powerful people of some 5,000 or more in the early 17th century. The remnant was settled in the Manor of Conestoga, a region northwest of the present community of Conestoga, Pennsylvania. White neighbors considered them for the most part as harmless vagabonds, who survived by "beggary and the sale of brooms, baskets, and wooden ladles" made by the women, while the men hunted or otherwise occupied themselves. In the northwestern corner of the present Lancaster County was a region known as Donegal, today comprising five townships and two boroughs. Adjacent to it along the Susquehanna River to the northwest was a region known as Paxton, or Paxtang, centered approximately in the Harrisburg region of today. The Paxton area had been all but destroyed by Delaware raiders under Shingas (see entry) in 1755 and the town of Paxton burned out. Although the raid had never been repeated, the hatred it engendered was deep and long-lasting, and remained a motivator to arouse the passions of the Paxton "gang [who] were known for their disrespect of the law, and [for] rough living." They came, under one pretext or another, to suspect the peaceful Conestogas of "secretly abetting the enemy, acting as spies, giving shelter to scalping parties, and even aiding them in their depredations," although if any were so inclined it could not have been more than one or two, their guilt supported by only the most flimsy evidence. The Paxton men had formed a body of rangers, "noted for their zeal and efficiency in defending the borders," and Matthew Smith became a principal leader. He had some education, was popular and of great influence among the rangers, with whom he shared general hatred of all Indians and suspicion against the Conestogas. In mid-December 1763 he learned that a suspected Indian had been traced to the Conestoga Manor. With five companions he reached the native settlement at night; reconnoitering, he claimed he saw "a number of armed warriors" in the village and withdrew, determined to annihilate the Con-

estogas. He mustered about fifty men of Paxton and Donegal and reached the Conestoga settlement at dawn of December 14, and killed all six Indians found at the place, then withdrew, their hatred only partially appeased. The sheriff of Lancaster County, being apprised of the affair, collected the remaining fourteen Indians and placed them for their greater security in the Lancaster jail, a strong stone building believed stout enough to thwart any attempt against it. An express was sent to Philadelphia, reporting the outrage; the governor issued a proclamation denouncing the act and offering a reward for arrest of the perpetrators. But the Paxton Boys were determined to complete the work they had begun. The band was reassembled, their leader now Lazarus Stewart (see entry) whose principal aim, as was later testified, was to gain custody of a suspected murderer, have him tried and, if found guilty, executed. He was alone in his restraint, if that is what it was. The mob, in which Matthew Smith again took a prominent role, on December 27 reached the Lancaster jail at 3 p.m., burst open the doors, rushed in and "the work was soon finished. The bodies of men, women, and children, mangled with outrageous brutality, lay scattered about the yard; and the murderers were gone." Most of the people of Lancaster were in church at the time for a delayed Christmas service, and there was no one to stop the massacre which required less than a quarter of an hour. Even this atrocity did not slake the Indian-hatred of Smith and his followers, and late in January 1764 he led a force variously estimated at 500 to 1,500 men toward Philadelphia to assassinate the Moravian converts being retained for their security in that city. After an abortive attempt to move the Indians to New York had failed, they were returned to Philadelphia where preparations were made to repel the raiders, and so complete was their readiness that the Paxton Boys halted at nearby Germantown, where Matthew became their spokesman with Philadelphia arbitrators Benjamin Franklin and three others. "The rioters received them with marks of respect; and, after a long conference, the leaders of the mob [gave] over their hostile designs, the futility of which was now sufficiently apparent," because of Philadelphians' preparations for resistance. The Paxton crowd was assured of a hearing, Smith and James Gibson were approved as the spokesmen before city authorities and the touchy matter at length was resolved without further bloodshed. Smith and Gibson laid before the

Assembly a "Remonstrance," with a "Declaration" added to it, giving their side of the issue (the texts printed by Parkman). No action was ever taken on the memorials by the Assembly "and the memorable Paxton riots had no other definite result than that of exposing the weakness and distraction of the provincial government, and demonstrating the folly and absurdity of all principles of non-resistance," for it was in violation of such Quaker principles that the city had been forced to arm itself and thus thwart the Paxton Boys' ruffianly plans. Little more has been uncovered on the life of Matthew Smith.

Parkman, *The Conspiracy of Pontiac*, II, 128-67, Appendix E, 375-404; info. from Randall Rankin Snyder, curator, Lancaster (Penn.) County Hist. Soc.

Smith, Persifor Frazer, military officer (Nov. 16, 1798-May 17, 1858). B. at Philadelphia, he was graduated from the College of New Jersey (which became Princeton University) in 1815, studied law and in 1819 moved to New Orleans where he held public office and commanded militia units, becoming adjutant general of Louisiana with rank of colonel. In 1836 he raised a 600-man regiment with Thomas Lawson (who would become surgeon-general of the Army) as second in command, the unit to see service in the Second Seminole War in Florida under Brigadier General Edmund Gaines (see entry). It arrived at Fort Brooke at the head of Tampa Bay February 10, 1836, and on the 13th took the field. The regiment's initial assignment was along the Carlosahatchee (Sanybel) River, whose mouth is at Fort Myers, and its head near Lake Okeechobee, though "his operations covered the whole country from that river south to Cape Sable [at the southern tip of Florida]. The results were one or two skirmishes, in which he lost a few men, probably killed some of the enemy, and took 243 prisoners," according to John T. Sprague. Following Smith's return from Florida he became judge of Lafayette, and later of Jefferson Parish, Louisiana. At the outbreak of the Mexican War he was commissioned colonel of Mounted Rifles May 27, 1846, and Brigadier General December 30, ending the conflict as a brevet Major General for his services at Monterrey, Contreras and Churubusco and being for a time military governor of Mexico City. Following the war Smith was assigned November 15, 1848, in his brevet rank to command the Pacific Division; from 1850-56 to command the Department of Texas, and from 1856 the Western Department with headquarters

at St. Louis. In each of these stations he pushed for aggressive activity against hostile Indians, while his rank and positions precluded taking the field in person, although "the absence of civil authority in California, Indian uprisings [on the South Plains], and border warfare in Kansas made each of these posts in turn difficult." Smith arrived in California February 26, 1849, as military governor aboard the first steamship to arrive at San Francisco, bringing also the first "installment of gold-seekers from the United States." At the outset Smith probably blundered in formally considering all non-U.S. citizens in California for the gold fields "trespassers" and thus not eligible to benefit from their labors; this, Bancroft reported, gave an opening to the "Hounds," a loose aggregation of "Australian criminals and deserting English sailors," giving them an excuse to rob "every Mexican or Californian" they came across upon the ground they were "foreigners," as were, of course, the Hounds themselves. Smith selected, or approved selection of, Benecia, near the mouth of the Sacramento River, for his military headquarters, and Mare Island, at the head of San Francisco Bay, for a naval yard. He determined to punish Pit River Indians accused of killing Topographical Engineer William Warner (see entry) in the Sierra, and other natives near Clear Lake fifty miles north of San Francisco who were alleged to have committed sporadic depredations. He dispatched a military expedition of dragoons and infantry under "contentious, tyrannical" Captain Nathaniel Lyon (see entry) initially to Clear Lake where some 400 Indians had taken refuge on an island, Lyon's force killing between 60 and 100, then advancing across a divide to the Russian River where another 400 Indians were surrounded, the troops making the refuge "a perfect slaughter pen," with some 75 to 150 natives killed. A second expedition in July penetrated the Pit River country, seeking the slayers of Warner, the results less sanguinary than the earlier affairs. When Major General George M. Brooke died March 9, 1851, he was succeeded by Smith as commander of the Department of Texas, with instructions to lay out a new system of frontier forts, defend the Texans, carry the war to the Indian homeland, and reduce expenses. His plan was to establish an outer line of forts beyond the frontier settlements, and an inner line of posts from which the cavalry would operate against hostile intrusion while the infantry at the outer line would endeavor to cut off escape. His program was sound enough on paper, but for a number of reasons, including Indian resourcefulness, it did not work out. Campaigns he ordered against such persistent raiders as the Mescalero Apaches, had little effect. Smith was relieved from his Texas command by Albert Sidney Johnston and, in failing health, moved to St. Louis to take over the Western Department, in the course of which he directed Edwin Vose Sumner the elder (see entry) in 1857 to undertake an operation against the Cheyennes, during which, on July 29, Sumner conducted his fabled "saber charge" against the Indians; it did little to enhance the reputation of that weapon. Smith was promoted to Brigadier General December 30, 1856. In April 1858 he was assigned to command the Department of Utah, but died at Fort Leavenworth while preparing to take over his new command. He was buried at Philadelphia. His first wife died in 1852 and his second, the widow of Major Francis W. Armstrong, was mother of Frank C. Armstrong, who became a Confederate Brigadier General. Smith fathered a son who became a New Orleans physician.

Heitman; DAB; John T. Sprague, *The Origin, Progress and Conclusion of the Florida War,* 1848, repr. Gainesville, Univ. of Florida Press, 1965; John K. Mahon, *History of the Second Seminole War,* Gainesville, 1967; Bancroft, *California,* V, VI; Robert M. Utley, *Frontiersmen in Blue,* N.Y., Macmillan Co., 1967.

Smith, Philip Sidney, geologist (July 28, 1877-May 10, 1949). B. at Medford, Massachusetts, he was graduated from Harvard University in 1899 (and earned a doctorate from that school in 1904), instructing in geology and physiography there from 1900 to 1906 when he joined the Geological Survey, remaining with that organization until 1946, when he retired. Smith was chief Alaskan Geologist from 1924 to 1946. He began his work in the territory on Seward Peninsula in 1906. In 1910 he made a survey from the Koyukuk River Valley to the upper Kobuk River and traced its course. The next year he worked the Alatna River and then the Noatak River. He also in later years worked in the Lake Clark, Iditarod and Fairbanks areas. The Philip Smith Mountains of the Brooks Range were named for him in 1950. Smith, who at one time was acting director of the Geological Survey, belonged to numerous professional and other organizations, including the American Association for the Advancement of Science, the American Polar Society and the Arctic Institute of North America, and he wrote many reports and other papers for the Survey and technical publications. Upon retirement his home was alternately Washington, D.C., and Wolfeboro, New Hampshire, where he was buried.

Orth, 32, 753; *Who Was Who.*

Smith, Redbird, Cherokee chief (1850-1918). B. near Fort Smith, he was a full-blood Cherokee, the son of a blacksmith-farmer, and was prominent among latter-day Indians who opposed and resisted the "Americanization" of the tribe. When the Dawes Act of 1887 threatened to split up communal land holdings in favor of severalty, Smith restored the decaying Keetowah Society which had been formed for the protection of Cherokee rights following the Civil War. At one point he told a Senatorial committee that before the Dawes Commission "I stood up for my rights. I stood for the treaties and agreements that were made by my fathers with the Government of the United States." He was jailed briefly, then released and forced to sign against his will the document the Dawes people desired. He said, "I say that I never will change" his opposition to severalty. He said "I can't stand and live and breathe if I take this allotment [in severalty]. Under the allotment rules I would see all around me—I see now all around me and all the Indians—people who are ready to grab from under us my living and my home. If I would accept such a plan I would be going in starvation. To take and put the Indians on the land in severalty would be just the same as burying them, for they could not live." Redbird Smith also formed, or assisted in forming, the Four Mothers Society, drawing its large membership from the "five civilized tribes," those who also opposed the Dawes policy. His groups raised money to hire lawyers and lobby in Washington. Smith encouraged Indians to refuse to be counted in the U.S. Census of 1900; he was arrested and himself forced to enroll in 1902. The Cherokees were compelled finally against their will to sign the allotment agreement in 1905. Redbird Smith became the principal chief of the Cherokees in 1908 and withdrew to the hills to live a life free of white interference.

Info. from John Sugden; R.K. Thomas, "The Redbird Smith Movement," BAE Bulletin 180, Part 16, Wash., Govt. Printg. Ofc., 1961; Angie Debo, *And Still the Waters Run: The Betrayal of the Five Civilized Tribes,* Princeton Univ. Press, 1940, 1972.

Smith, William Bailey, pioneer (1738-Oct. 19, 1818). B. in Prince William County, Virginia, he early migrated to North Carolina where he was associated with Richard Henderson (see entry) and others, and in 1775 was at the Treaty of Sycamore Shoals by which the Cherokees sold a vast extent of present Kentucky and Tennessee (to much of which they had no legitimate claim), and went to Boonesborough during that summer. He was there when the Boone and Callaway girls, daughters of Colonel Richard Callaway, were captured (in 1776) by Shawnees, and aided in their rescue. In the summer of 1777 he returned to the Yadkin and brought out a relief party to the battered settlements. George Rogers Clark had known Smith in Kentucky and commissioned him a major, assigning him to collect recruits in the Holston River settlements for his expedition to the Illinois country; the errand was only partially successful. Smith arrived at Boonesborough in June or July, taking part in the principal siege there, his final military service. Back in North Carolina he was commissioned to run the boundary line between that state and Virginia, today being the line which separates Kentucky and Tennessee. This occupation of 1779-80 won him a tract of land on Green River. He moved there in 1794, settling at Smith's Ferry, where he lived the rest of his life.

Thwaites/Kellogg, *Frontier Defense on the Upper Ohio, 1777-1778.*

Snake, Shawnee chiefs (fl. 1780-mid-1830s). According to John Sugden, a specialist on the Shawnee Indians, there were at least two, and possibly several, prominent Shawnee chiefs of this name or a variation of it, and it is difficult to separate them out. He believes that the most likely solution is that a person known as Black Snake, or Captain Snake, was a famed war leader in the 18th century and lived at least until 1809, and a second individual also known by his Shawnee name of Shemenetoo, "probably the youngest of the famous Snakes," was most active between 1806 and the middle 1830s, when he died west of the Mississippi River. And there may have been a third individual by that name, or even others, Captain Snake, the first known of that name, was also referred to as Blacksnake or Pataso. He was a fearsome war chief. He twice solicited more British support for the warriors during the Revolutionary times, particularly from 1781 into 1782. It was his arrival, with 140 warriors, that broke the stalemate in the Battle of

Sandusky July 5, 1782, and enabled Indians and British to totally defeat the American force under Colonel William Crawford (see entry). In 1788 and 1790 he led highly successful forays against Ohio River boats, capturing many prisoners and much plunder. He also acted as a diplomat, visiting the Iroquois in New York in late 1789, attempting to persuade them to support a new Indian confederacy, which they apparently were reluctant to do. In August 1790 he attended an inter-tribal council at the Huron settlement on the Detroit River. He at that time had a town at the head of the Maumee River of Ohio, but in 1792 moved down that stream to establish a village at the Glaize, the junction of the Auglaize and Maumee rivers at present Defiance, Ohio. There Olive Spencer, a prisoner, found him "a plain, grave chief of sage appearance." He did not sign the Treaty of Greenville, Ohio, August 3, 1795, and British agent Matthew Elliott reported he had died before then, which doubtless was in error, for a chief, who seems to have been the same man, appeared in negotiations between Shawnees and whites in Ohio. In 1806 and 1807 he tried to resolve difficulties between Tecumseh's people and Ohio settlements, at a Springfield meeting in June 1807 and in 1809 he was referred to as "Old Snake," after which he disappears. It was reported he had died at the Shawnee town of Wapakoneta on the Auglaize River. Shemenetoo, a younger Snake, is more definitely traced. John Johnson, a longtime Indian agent with the Shawnees, remembered a man, probably this Snake, as "a mischievous, bloodthirsty character always opposed to peace," and who was not much of an orator. He first comes into view in 1806 and 1807, arbitrating difficulties between Shawnees and whites in Ohio. He is probably the Snake who signed Shawnee addresses to the Quakers and the U.S. President under the name of "Young Snake" in April 1809, in both cases requesting missionaries and complaining about annuities. As Big Snake he signed the Treaty of Greenville, Ohio, July 22, 1814, as Shammonetho; the Treaty of Spring Wells, near Detroit, September 8, 1815, as Shemenetoo, or Big Snake, and the Treaty at the "foot of the Rapids of the Miami" on September 29, 1817, as Shemenetu. Eventually he migrated west of the Mississippi where he died at an advanced age, possibly in Kansas, in the 1830s. A daughter, Nenexse, married Black Hoof (see entry), a leading Shawnee. From letters signed by *both* Snakes in 1806, 1807 and 1809, it is clear that the foregoing two were separate individuals. That there were still other men named Snake and active in Shawnee affairs seems clear from evidence John Sugden has gathered, and he added that "it is unlikely if the biographies of these chiefs will ever be completely disentangled."

Information from John Sugden.

Snelling, William Joseph, writer (Dec. 26, 1804-Dec. 24, 1848). B. at Boston, he was the son of Josiah Snelling (see entry), was raised by relatives after his mother died, entered West Point in 1818 but left after two years and went west to be with his father at a frontier post. He lived for a time among the Sioux Indians, tried trapping near Fort Snelling, married a French girl of Prairie du Chien though she soon died, and shared in the unrest associated with the 1827 Chippewa-Sioux trouble (see Josiah Snelling entry). Following the death of his father, Snelling returned to Boston and became a writer, at times showing flashes "perhaps of genius," but circumstances prevented his ever developing such a quality. He is best known, in a frontier sense, for his *Tales of the Northwest; or, Sketches of Indian Life and Character* (1830). "He was sincere, fiery, and uncompromising, ever a champion of the oppressed," but failed to concentrate his talents. He became editor of the *Boston Herald* in 1847, but died a year later.

DAB.

Solomon, Isadore Lekan, pioneer (1844-Dec. 4, 1930). B. in Germany, he migrated to New York City about 1860, going on to Bradford County, Pennsylvania, where he worked for a relative for several years, then moved to Towanda where he engaged in livery stable management, staging and other occupations until 1876. He went to New Mexico intending to settle there, but hearing of better prospects in Arizona he selected a site at the present Solomon, initially called Solomonville in eastern Arizona, opening a general store. Governor Fremont named him Graham County treasurer, a position he held through subsequent elections for four years, while he was postmaster of Solomon for sixteen years from 1880. He also engaged in sheep raising on a large scale, and probably was affiliated with George H. Stevens (see entry) since he had some ownership in a large flock decimated by Juh-led raiders in the April 1882 campaign which resulted in the exodus of several hundred Apaches from the San Carlos Reservation to

Mexico. It was said that "a number of sheep herders in [Solomon's] employ were murdered by Indians, one man having been tied to a tree and stoned to death, the remaining ones shot, and about five hundred sheep killed," a noted incident of that Apache operation. On several occasions Solomon, when traveling, was attacked by Indians and road agents, but always escaped uninjured. He expanded his interest into irrigation projects, various commercial endeavors and banking. He had been married in Germany in 1872 and his son became a prominent banker at Tucson; he predeceased his father by one year. Solomon retired to Los Angeles about 1920, where he died and was buried. He was survived by his widow and five daughters, all of whom lived in California.

Info. from the Ariz. Hist. Soc.; *Arizona Historical Review,* Vol. 3, No. 4 (Jan. 1931); info. from E.F. (Ted) Mains.

Solovev, Ivan (Feodor), assassin of Aleuts (d.c. 1770). By reputation the most murderous of the frequently lawless and unruly promyshlenniki or Russian trader-adventurers, he made "many fortunate voyages [which] brought him great profits" in furs from the Aleutian Islands, but he was a "shiftless man and rather dissipated" and accumulated little wealth. His first recorded role in the fur trade was in 1748 when he was a partner of an Irkutsk merchant, Emilian Ugof, engaged in Aleutian trading. In 1765 his ship was anchored in an Unalaska bay, having left Kamchatka August 24, 1764. He learned of the sad fate of the Zakar Medvedev fur gathering expedition, slaughtered piecemeal by Aleuts after giving the natives intense provocations, and Solovev determined to avenge these deaths. In an initial affray 100 Aleuts were slain. Reinforced by promyshlenniki under Ivan Korovin, a man named Kokodin and others, Solovev organized a punitive expedition, with the result that "the bloodshed perpetrated by this band of avengers was appalling." Aleuts were slaughtered all over Unalaska and on other islands. Solovev heard that 300 natives had assembled in a fortified village and laid siege to it. He placed bladders filled with powder under the log structure and blew it up. Inmates who survived the explosion were butchered by musket and sabre. Lieutenant Gavrill Davydov (see entry) wrote that during this campaign Solovev put to death 3,000 Aleuts, although another authority, Vassili Berg, put the figure at "only" 200, many perishing as the result of great cruelty. Veniaminov (see entry), the universally respected missionary-ethnologist who became the foremost authority on the Aleuts, their language and their history, accused Berg of making Solovev's bloody career appear less criminal and repulsive than it was. He wrote that "nearly a century has elapsed since that period of terror, and there is no reason for concealing what was done...or for palliating or glorifying their cruel outrages upon the Aleuts." In one instance he stated "upon good authority" that Solovev experimented with the penetrative power of musketry by tying twelve Aleuts in file and discharging his firearm at the front individual at short range, the bullet lodging finally in the ninth man. This incident was confirmed by Aleut accounts. In 1789-90 Russian government inspectors interrogated Aleuts about treatment of them by Russian seamen and promyshlenniki. The testimony included: "We...suffer greatly when our young girls, wives, daughters and sisters are taken, which all companies do... Although we see our women forced to become sexual partners and treated cruelly, and although we know the terrible tempers of the hunters, we cannot fight back and we cannot even speak out against this. We have to endure because we are afraid of what may happen. When the peredovshchik (leader) Solovev came he plundered the islands of Unalaska, Sannak, Akun, Akutan, Asutan and Igilga and shot all the men on them. And as final outrage he lined up men one behind the other to see how many could be killed by one shot from his firearm. All the companies know their promyshlenniks treat us cruelly." Although it had been promised that such atrocities would be stopped, "nothing has happened." During February 1766 one young Aleut voluntarily came into the Russian camp and asked to be baptized, Bancroft sardonically commenting that if the promyshlenniki claimed this request a "miracle" he would acquiesce, for "nothing but the mighty power of God could have sanctified the heart of this benighted one under these bright examples of Christianity." Solovev raised anchor and left the blood-soaked islands June 1, 1770, reaching Kamchatka July 5, with his ill-gotten booty. Upon his arrival Solovev and another were taken on to Okhotsk and dispatched to St. Petersburg, presumably for investigation, but both died of consumption on their journey through Siberia.

Bancroft, *Alaska; Russian Penetration of the North Pacific Ocean.*

Sommereisen, Valentine, Catholic missionary-priest (May 28, 1829-Jan. 23, 1897). B. at Rufach on the French-German border, he studied for the priesthood at Paris where he met the Reverend Augustine Ravoux, one-time missionary among the Dakota (Sioux) Indians. He urged Sommereisen to complete his studies on the American frontier; thus it was that Bishop Joseph Cretin, Minnesota's first Catholic bishop, concluded Sommereisen's instructions, ordained him March 8, 1856, and assigned him to Mankato with responsibility for 36 other mission stations within a 50-mile radius. The priest spent fourteen years at that work, incidentally learning the Dakota language and becoming influential among that people and among the Winnebagos, a Siouan-speaking tribe resident since 1856 on the Blue Earth River, south of Mankato. Following the Great Sioux Uprising of 1862 a military commission sentenced 306 of the Indians to death, although President Lincoln commuted all but 38, their execution set for December 26. Father Ravoux came to Mankato and he and Sommereisen with two Protestant ministers were present when the death sentences were read. Twenty-four of the condemned asked Ravoux and Sommereisen to help them prepare for death, three who already had been baptized asked to receive their first Communion and the other twenty-one, along with nine others, requested baptism. On Christmas Day this was done, Sommereisen recording their Dakota and Christian names in the parish baptismal records. Nine years later Sommereisen was stationed at Yankton, South Dakota, where he no doubt renewed his acquaintance with the Sioux, some of whom had been moved to that region from Minnesota. He made various trips to military posts along the Missouri River and occasionally went into Montana, where he met Custer. A newspaper reporter called Sommereisen "an old Indian missionary...known to nearly all the Indians of this region." Along the Yellowstone River on August 4, 1873, Dr. John Honsinger, the 7th Cavalry's regimental surgeon, and a sutler, John Baliran, were killed by Sioux; the next day Sommereisen officiated at their burial. First Lieutenant James Calhoun, Custer's brother-in-law, wrote: "The Catholic Father who read the services at the grave was a man of more than common faith in his religion, and thought he could travel entirely alone in any part of the country with impunity...Desiring to accompany the Expedition, but not arriving at Fort Rice in time...he commenced the journey alone, riding in a little, old-fashioned buggy, from the top of which projected a large black cross. A little yellow pony drew the vehicle, and although he saw Indians once during his trip, he overtook the command in safety at the Yellowstone River...He carried no arms, and depended solely upon spiritual aid for assistance in case of an emergency. Having passed many years of his life among the Indians, he felt perfectly at home with them, and said he would never be molested by any tribe..." After his frontier work in Minnesota, South Dakota and Kansas, Sommereisen retired from the active ministry at 50 in 1879 and spent the remaining nineteen years of his life near Hays City, Kansas, "attending to his vineyard, orchard, and gardens," which were profitable. He died at Hays City and was buried in St. Joseph's cemetery there.

The Rev. Blaine Burkey, "Santee Godfather," Chicago Westerners *Brand Book,* Vol. XL, No. 1 (Mar., Apr. 1983-85, 1-3, 8).

Sonnichsen, (Charles) Leland, writer (Sept. 20, 1901-June 29, 1991). B. at Fonda, west of Fort Dodge, Iowa, he was raised on a Minnesota farm and was graduated from the University of Minnesota in 1924, then studied at Harvard where he received his master's degree in 1927 and his doctorate in 1931. After teaching briefly in the Midwest, he joined the Texas College of Mines in 1931; it is now the University of Texas at El Paso. Although he had intended to join the faculty of "some Ivy League school," he remained at El Paso until his retirement 41 years later. As a member and later the head of the English department he taught every course offered in that branch of learning. During his first year he was directed to teach "the Life and Literature of the Southwest," a course designed by J. Frank Dobie; Sonnichsen objected to the assignment, but had to accept it and soon fell in love with the course, teaching it until his retirement. His interest in the Southwest aroused, he gradually raised his horizon to include not only west Texas, but neighboring states, and took in such frontier phenomena as Indians, gunmen, feuds, the study of cities and oral history, Sonnichsen becoming, in his own words, "a grassroots historian" as well as a prolific writer. He said that in all he had written 26 books, but those were only the volumes that bore his name; he also wrote, or rewrote, others for or in the name of someone else, so that his total output probably was somewhat higher. His own production was of wide variety. His first book was *Billy King's Tombstone* (1942), and his first considerable success, *Roy Bean: Law West of the Pecos* (1943). Others of his authorship having some relevance to the frontier included: *Cowboys and Cattle Kings* (1950); *I'll Die Before I'll Run,* dealing with Texas feuds (1951); with William Morrison, *Alias Billy the Kid* (1955); *Ten Texas Feuds* (1957); *The Mescalero Apaches* (1958); *Tularosa: Last of the Frontier West* (1960); *The El Paso Salt War* (1961); *Outlaw: Billy Mitchell alias Baldy Russell, His Life and Times* (1965); *Pass of the North* (1968), second volume (1980); *Morris Parker's White Oaks* (1971); *Colonel Greene and the Copper Skyrocket* (1974); *Tucson: The Life and Times of an American City* (1982), and as editor, *Geronimo and the End of the Apache Wars.* Sonnichsen retired from the Texas faculty in 1972 and moved to Tucson to become editor of the *Journal of Arizona History,* retiring after five years to become senior editor, and then editor emeritus. He married twice and was survived by his widow, Carol, a son, two daughters and a stepson. Sonnichsen's output was always highly readable, laced with humor but never weakened by it. His history instincts were very sound, and his factual material solidly based upon reliable sources so that, while he was somewhat fascinated by western fiction, none of it appeared in his product unless to illustrate a point. His geniality was phenomenal and the informal "Doc Sonnichsen fan club," as English writer Frederick Nolan put it, had numerous "members." He died at 89 while working in his yard; memorial services were held for him at Tucson and El Paso.

John Bret-Harte obituary, *Arizona Daily Star,* June 30, 1991; acquaintanceship and correspondence with the author.

Soto, Juan, desperado (fl. 1871). Soto was a central California outlaw and gunman, the details of whose life are unreported save for his death, and the crime which caused it. On January 10, 1871, he with two others entered a store of Thomas Scott at Sunol, near Fremont in Alameda County. They killed a clerk, Otto Ludovici, fired a volley into the Scott living quarters at the back of the store, and rode off. Sheriff Harry Morse (see entry) arrived next morning, concluded that Soto had been one of the bandits involved, and spent months seeking his whereabouts. He finally located them in the Panoche Mountains, about fifty miles southeast of Gilroy in the present San

Benito County. His posse approached the adobe house. Morse left his Henry rifle in a saddle scabbard, but carried a revolver into the house with him; his deputy had a double-barreled shotgun. Morse found Soto surrounded by a dozen henchmen, covered him with his pistol and told the deputy to put the cuffs on the fugitive, but the deputy lost his nerve and fled. A muscular Mexican woman clutched Morse from behind, while a powerful Soto ally grabbed his wrist. Morse threw off his assailants and fired at Soto, the bullet puncturing his hat. Soto lunged at the sheriff, and Morse backed out of the door when "a magnificent duel took place between the two men in the open ground." Morse dropped to the ground thus evading four successive bullets from Soto's weapon. One of Morse's bullets wrecked Soto's pistol and Soto dashed back into the house while Morse leaped to retrieve his rifle from the saddle. Soto grabbed three pistols in the adobe, rushed out of the house trying to mount a horse already saddled and bridled, but the animal bolted and Soto ran up a hillside. Morse shot him through the shoulder at a distance of about 150 yards. The outlaw turned and raced toward Morse. The lawman calmly sent a bullet through his head.

Charles Howard Shinn, *Graphic Description of Pacific Coast Outlaws*, Los Angeles, Westernlore Press, 1958.

Southack, Cyprian, cartographer (Mar. 25, 1662-Mar. 27, 1745). B. at London, his father was a naval lieutenant and the boy, at 10, saw naval action in an engagement at Southwold Bay, East Suffolk, England, May 28, 1672. The action was between Dutch ships under Michiel Adriaanszoon de Ruyter, and the English under the Duke of York (later King James II), aided by the French; the Dutch won. In 1685 Southack went to Boston with a navy commission, guarding the New England coast against pirates and privateers, commanding a number of warships in succession and, from 1697 to 1714, the Massachusetts Province Galley. Rowing vessels were important in colonial times; nearly all small sailing men-of-war were fitted to row. New England traders built a number of "runners" or "gallies," which were ships or brigantines built for speed under sail and to row well. Of such apparently was the Massachusetts Province Galley. Southack had been on Sir William Phips expedition which captured Fort Royal, Nova Scotia, in 1690, and in 1698 he commanded the Galley when it transported Colonel John Phillips and

Major James Converse from Boston to arrange peace with Indians near Casco Bay, or the site of the present Portland, Maine. In 1704 he commanded the Galley in Benjamin Church's (see entry) operation against Indians and French in Maine and Nova Scotia. He continued his naval work, although with little frontier relevance. During his numerous cruises along the New England coast he drafted several important charts, apparently using only his log and compass. Among these works were: *Draught of New England, Newfoundland, Nova Scotia and the River of Canada* (1694); *A Draught of Boston Harbor* (1694); a chart of the St. Lawrence River (1710); a chart of English plantations from the mouth of the Mississippi to the St. Lawrence River (1717); *The Harbour of Casco Bay and Islands Adjacent* and *Map of Casco Harbour* (1720, revised in 1734 and 1775, and also issued as a map), and compiled a chart of the British Empire in North America and a map of the coast of New England. Southack died at Boston; he was married.

DAB.

Sowell, Andrew Jackson, frontiersman, historical writer (Aug. 2, 1848-July 4, 1921). B. at Seguin, Texas, the family moved when the boy was six to a place on the Blanco River in Hays County, northeast of San Antonio. At seven he narrowly missed capture by an Indian and again sat out an Indian fight in which two defenders were killed. At 22 he joined the Texas Rangers and took part in a Wichita campaign along the Red River in north Texas. Sowell left the Rangers in 1871, but his unbounded admiration for that organization continued all his life. Sowell also had great respect for the pioneers of southwest Texas and interviewed scores of them for newspaper columns and for his most impressive book, *Early Settlers and Indian Fighters of Southwest Texas* (1900, 1964). His other published books included: *Rangers and Pioneers of Texas* (1884); *Life of Bigfoot Wallace* (1899); *History of Fort Bend County* (1904); *Captain John F. Tom: A Biography* (c. 1906); *Incidents Connected with the Early History of Guadalupe County, Texas* (n.d.). Sowell had a sense of humor that appeared here and there in his writings. For example, in writing of Wallace, a notable Texas character of fabulous adventures, Sowell digressed: "As near as he ever came to kissing a woman..., was while he was a prisoner in Mexico, with his hands tied behind him. He bit an old Mexican woman on the back of the neck for making faces at him." He also told how a Lipan Apache woman fed Bigfoot peculiar-tasting meat which Wallace discovered was Comanche flesh and which Wallace was determined that "now...he had got him down [he] would try to keep him down." Sowell admired manliness in friend or foe. He told of an Indian who had been shot a dozen times, but somehow remained erect, facing his foes, arms folded across his breast, singing his death song until he breathed no more. To Sowell it was a gesture "majestic and impressive and noble." Sowell died in Bexar County.

HT; Joe B. Frantz intr. to 1964 edn. of *Early Settlers and Indian Fighters;* info. from Michael R. Green, Tex. State Archives.

Spanberg, Martin Peter, Danish-born naval officer (1720-1761). B. at Jerne, near Esbjerg, Jutland, he entered the Russian naval service and in 1720 was a lieutenant 4th class. He was said to have spoken Russian poorly, was without culture, coarse, cruel and greedy, but a good practical seaman. In 1725-30 he took part in Bering's (see entry) first Kamchatka Expedition and in 1728 sailed as an important officer with Bering on the *Sv. Gabriil* through Bering Strait to the Chukotsk Sea, being forthright in his recommendations to Bering on what course then to follow, although his advice was not accepted. In 1730 he returned to St. Petersburg and was promoted to captain, 3rd rank. In 1731-44 he participated in the Second Kamchatka Expedition, but was concerned largely in exploration and charting of the Kurile Islands, attempts to open to Russian shipping Japanese ports and following Bering's demise on the island named for him, took over command of the expedition. In 1745 he was sentenced to death for returning to St. Petersburg without permission, in 1747 was pardoned, though demoted to lieutenant. In 1749 he was tried for the wreck of a ship which he commanded, but again was pardoned. In 1751 he became a captain 1st rank, and died a decade later.

Pierce, *Russian America: A Biographical Dictionary.*

Spears, Robert, soldier (d. Nov. 27, 1846). November 26, a command of Doniphan's column found that Navaho Indians had run off 873 sheep from near their camp near Fray Cristobal, south of Socorro, New Mexico, the animals having been assembled to supply mutton for the troops enroute to Mexico. Spears and James

Stewart, another Lafayette County, Missouri, volunteer, were sent to trail the animals, through the "incredible carelessness" of their commanding officer leaving with no arms of any kind. Their bodies were discovered the next day, one with thirteen arrows penetrating it, the other with six or seven. Their heads had been smashed with rocks and "their bodies treated in a shocking manner." Apparently the animals were not recovered.

Susan Shelby Magoffin, *Down the Santa Fe Trail and Into Chihuahua,* Lincoln, Univ. of Neb. Press, 1982; Frank McNitt, *Navajo Wars,* Albuquerque, Univ. of New Mex. Press, 1972; Twitchell, *Leading Facts,* II, 218-19n.

Spotswood, Alexander, colonial official (1676-June 7, 1740). B. in Tangier where his father was physician to an English garrison, Alexander served in the War of Spanish Succession, was wounded, captured and exchanged and June 23, 1710, became lieutenant governor of Virginia under George Hamilton, Earl of Orkney, the nominal governor. Spotswood, a man of vigor and vision, "sought to regulate and stabilize the fur trade and...to finance an enlightened Indian policy." He accomplished many reforms in the colony's governing policies, sometimes working at cross purposes with such powerful figures as William Byrd and with the governor's council, but eventually pressure from England smoothed things out, occasionally to Spotswood's advantage. From his arrival, Spotswood was interested in the problems of the frontier, and in 1714 he himself passed over the Blue Ridge into country drained by streams feeding the great rivers of the Mississippi Valley. Thwaites explained that at this time "the English colonists...wanted the over-mountain country watered by the Ohio, but were too weak at first to hold on for agricultural settlement lands so far from home, in the face of a savage foe. The French wanted the valley solely for the fur trade, but Iroquois opposition long kept them from entering," and the resulting rivalry and desires eventually culminated in the French and Indian War, though this was long after Spotswood's time. Spotswood instituted the Order of the Golden Horseshoe to interest Virginians in the West, and in 1716 may have made a second journey beyond the limits of the settlements. He sought to negotiate pacts with friendly Indians to counter Iroquois raids against the Virginia colonies; at length he negotiated a treaty with the powerful Iroquois by which they were to remain north of the Potomac and west of the Blue Ridge, and "he watched with apprehension" the troubles of the Iroquois-related Tuscaroras of North Carolina in 1712 and of the Yamasees of South Carolina in 1715, providing assistance to the Carolinas in their conflicts with those tribes (the Tuscaroras beginning in 1713, commenced with their migration north to join the Iroquois, a movement not entirely completed until 1802). Backing the Indians, Spotswood believed, were the Spanish and French, and he urged upon English officials the seizure of Florida and occupation of the Appalachians before the French did so. Spotswood sought to encourage settlement of the frontier, and beyond it, by exempting pioneers from taxes and bestowing other financial benefits upon them. Removed from office in 1722 he retired to Spotsylvania County where he had an enormous land grant. In 1724 he went to England to settle land title questions, and married there, fathering four children. Six years later he returned to Virginia. When war with Spain broke out in 1739 he was assigned the raising of a regiment of which he was colonel and was appointed Major General and second in command of an expedition under Lord Cathcart to Cartagena on the north coast of South America, but he died at Annapolis before the operation got under way.

Alexander Scott Withers, *Chronicles of Border Warfare*, Cincinnati, Robert Clarke Co., 1895, 1970; DAB; Louis Knott Koontz, *Robert Dinwiddie: His Career in American Colonial Government and Westward Expansion*, Glendale, Calif., Arthur H. Clark Co., 1941.

Spotted Wolf, Cheyenne chief (1820-c. 1896). A chief of the Northern Cheyennes, he married Wind Woman (d. 1915), a sister of Black Kettle and Gentle Horse, and is not to be confused with Spotted Wolf, an Arapaho chief of the same era. Spotted Wolf was the son of another Cheyenne named Spotted Wolf, who was born about 1800 and later was called Whistling Elk. About August 1, 1867, he engineered the first, and probably the only, wreck of a railroad train by Indians, although another Cheyenne leader, Turkey Leg, is sometimes credited with the feat. About four miles east of the railroad station of Plum Creek (the present Lexington, Nebraska), the Cheyennes by "interfering with the rails," and not because they "took out a culvert" as is sometimes reported, caused the overturning of a handcar and subsequently ditching a westbound

freight train. When the engine was derailed at night the Cheyennes killed as many of the train crew as they could find, including also a party of men repairing the telegraph line near the station. One of the linemen was scalped but not killed; his name was William Thompson and after the Indians left he found his scalp. He was three days getting to Omaha where a Dr. Moore attended him and he recovered. Thompson had the scalp framed and took it with him to his native England; about 25 years later he sent it back to Moore, who gave it to the Omaha Public Library, where it was exhibited for many years. Having done away with the whites, the Spotted Wolf raiders broke open the freight cars. "When daylight came the goods were strewn over the ground: bolts of silk and calico, sacks of flour, sugar, coffee &c.; boxes of shoes, barrels of whisky and all kinds of stuff. The Indians...got very drunk. Taking hold of the end of a bolt of calico or silk, a young man would mount his pony and gallop wildly across the prairie, the bolt of cloth bounding and leaping behind while unrolling in great billowy waves...Some took hot coals from the engine and scattered them in the empty boxcars, setting the train into a blaze." Pawnee scouts later hunted for and attacked a party of Cheyennes who had hoped to share in the spoils, killing fifteen of them, but they were not Spotted Wolf's people. Spotted Wolf was in the Battle of Beecher Island in September 1868 south of the present Wray, Colorado. He and others crept up through tall grass and rescued wounded who were close to the white positions; it was a perilous and heroic action. The Spotted Wolf who conferred November 20, 1868, with William B. Hazen, superintendent of Indian Affairs for Indian Territory (shortly before Custer's Washita action) was the Arapaho of that name, and not the Cheyenne. Gary L. Roberts's article on a Spotted Wolf who was nearly lynched at Dodge City in 1872 refers as well to the Arapaho. In 1873 the Northern Cheyenne Spotted Wolf was of a party of chiefs who visited Washington, D.C., and met with President Grant, but the meeting was not a success in that they did not get the President to agree with their understanding that they would not have to move from their homeland in the present Montana to Indian Territory. In 1874 Spotted Wolf apparently took some part, how major is not known, in operations against white soldiers in the so-called Buffalo War of the South Plains. Spotted Wolf was in the vicinity of the fight at Sappa Creek, Kansas,

April 23, 1875, but whether actually involved in that engagement in uncertain. In it the army officer, Austin Henely (see entry), claimed 19 Cheyennes and 8 women and children were killed; the Cheyennes reported 7 Cheyenne men and 20 women and children slain. The killed Indian whom Henely believed was Whirlwind, actually was White Bear.

George E. Hyde, *Life of George Bent,* Norman, Univ. of Okla. Press, 1968; George Bird Grinnell, *The Fighting Cheyennes,* Norman, 1956; Grinnell, *Two Great Scouts and Their Pawnee Battalion...,* Lincoln, Univ. of Nebr. Press, 1973; Stan Hoig, *The Peace Chiefs of the Cheyennes,* Norman, 1980, pp. 128-30, 175n15; Gary L. Roberts, "Spotted Wolf and the Dodge City Toughs," *True West,* Vol. 24, No. 3 (Jan.-Feb. 1977), 10-11, 32, 36; info. from E.F. (Ted) Mains.

Spring, Agnes Wright, historian (Jan. 5, 1894-Mar. 20, 1988). B. at Delta, Colorado, she was taken by the family in 1903 to a ranch on the Little Laramie River, 23 miles west of Laramie, Wyoming, where she matured. She was graduated from the University of Wyoming at 19, became assistant librarian for the State Supreme Court at Cheyenne, and then, in 1916-17 studied journalism at Columbia University. Following a brief career as newspaperwoman she returned to Wyoming where she became State Librarian and State Historian, as well as "superintendent of weights and measures." February 14, 1921, she married Archer T. Spring, a geologist; it was a happy union. Mrs. Spring was appointed editor and chief writer for the Works Progress Administration's *Wyoming Guide* (1941), still considered a standard for that genre. In the late 1940s she joined the staff of the Colorado Historical Society, becoming editor of *Colorado Magazine,* and Colorado State Historian from 1954, retiring from that position in 1963. She published about 20 books and 600 shorter pieces, largely on historical and biographical subjects. Her first book was *Caspar Collins:...Indian Fighter of the Sixties* (1927). Her *Seventy Years Cow County: A History of the Wyoming Stock Growers Association* (1942), was a "much acclaimed" work. Her best-known book was *Cheyenne and Black Hills Stage and Express Routes* (1949, 1964). Others of her frontier-oriented works included *A Bloomer Girl on Pikes Peak* (1949); *When Grass Was King: Contributions to the Western Range Cattle Industry Study,* with W. Turrentine Jackson and Maurice Frink (1956); *A Pioneer in the Black Hills: The Story of Richard B. Hughes*

(1957); Floyd Barth's *Horse Wrangler,* written by Spring (1960); *Dude Wrangler, Government Hunter, Line Rider* (1964); E.L. Bennett's *Boom Town Boy: A Story of Creede, Colorado,* ed. by Spring; and *Colorado Charley, Wild Bill's Pard* (1968), reprinted as *Good Little Bad Man: The Life of Colorado Charley Utter* (1987). Spring was inducted into the National Cowboy Hall of Fame and National Cowgirl Hall of Fame, and received other honors. She died at 94 at Fort Collins, Colorado.

Joseph G. Rosa, "Agnes Wright Spring," English Westerners' Society *Tally Sheet,* Vol. 34, No. 3 (Summer, 1988), 54-55; Western Hist. Assn. Newsltr., (Summer, 1988), 4; *True West,* Vol. 35, No. 7 (July 1988), 5; Colorado Heritage *News,* April 1982, p. 2.

Spurr, Josiah Edward, geologist (1870-1950). In 1896 he accompanied Frank C. Schrader (see entry) on a geological reconnaissance from Lynn Canal in the Alaskan Panhandle, over Chilkoot Pass to the Yukon and down the length of that river to St. Michael on Norton Sound. In the summer of 1898, accompanied by topographer William Schuyler Post he made a reconnaissance of southwestern Alaska, starting at Cook Inlet, crossing the Alaska Range and descending the Kuskokwim River. From its mouth they returned to Nushagak River and then crossed the Alaska Peninsula. On the lower Kuskokwim the two obtained Eskimo names for various features from Moravian missionaries, Dr. Joseph Herman Romig (b. 1872) and John Henry Kilbuck (1861-1922). Kilbuck was a lineal descendant of John Killbuck Jr. (Gelelmend), noted 18th century Delaware chief who had been converted by the Moravians and given the name of William Henry. An account of the expedition was published in the 20th Annual Report of the Geological Survey. Mt. Spurr in the Alaska Range, the Post River in the Kuskokwim system and Kilbuck Mountains and Mt. Romig in that range commemorate the foregoing men.

Orth, 33, 518, 774, 814, 910; *Who Was Who.*

Stagg, Mrs. Joseph (Mrs. Jacob Drennon), pioneer (c. 1755-1845). The daughter of Edward Mills and sister of John Mills, she early married Captain Jacob Drennon (see entry) and was at Fort Henry in 1777 during the first siege of that place. When the alarm came she fled to the fort with an infant child, leaving an adopted boy in the cabin in her haste to depart. Remembering this she dashed back through the gates of the fort, which were closing, wrapped the boy in a feather matting and raced back to the fort, unharmed, although several bullets from Indian guns lodged in the matting. The Drennons later moved to Kentucky, settling in Mason County until Jacob was killed on the Ohio River in 1787, after which she married Joseph Stagg. For many years they lived in Fleming County. She died at the age of 90 in her son-in-law's home in Harrison County, Kentucky.

Thwaites/Kellogg, *Frontier Defense on the Upper Ohio, 1777-1778.*

Stalnaker, Samuel, pioneer (fl. 1748-1781). Dr. Thomas Walker had met "the old German" Stalnaker around 1748 and on his exploration of 1750 stopped by Stalnaker's remote frontier place on the middle fork of the Holston River long enough to help the pioneer raise his cabin, hoping by this kindness to persuade him to guide the Walker party toward the still-to-be-discovered Cumberland Gap. Stalnaker would not go, however, but gave directions for finding the place, apparently having visited the Gap before the "explorers" got there. Stalnaker was a well-known trader to the Cherokees. June 18, 1755, Indians raided his place, killed his wife and son and took Samuel prisoner. He soon escaped and was at a council of war in 1756. Arnow said that 26 years later he was "still there...and still telling people how to get to Kentucky."

Thwaites, *Dunmore;* Harriette Simpson Arnow, *Seedtime on the Cumberland,* N.Y., The Macmillan Co., 1960.

Staniukovich, Mikhail Nicholaevich, Russian naval officer (d. Dec. 29, 1869). He entered Russian naval cadet corps May 12, 1797, served in European waters and as a captain-lieutenant cleared Kronstadt August 20, 1826, commanding the sloop *Moller* on an expedition around the world, visiting Kamchatka and Russian America (Alaska), reaching Unalaska Island August 13, 1827. Adverse winds prevented him from surveying the coast of Unimak Island as he intended, and he wintered in Hawaii. In April 1828 he visited several Aleutian islands, again reaching Unalaska the 27th and June 3 commenced a survey of the north shore of the Alaska Peninsula, starting at Isanotskii Strait between Unimak Island and the Alaska Peninsula and ending at the mouth of the Naknek River at the northeastern corner of Bristol Bay. The survey charted Moller Island, named for the sloop, and Khudobin

Island, named for the assistant navigator aboard, Andrei Khudobin. Bad weather prevented further survey work; he returned to Unalaska Island July 26, and August 3 left for Petropavlovsk, Kamchatka, arriving back at Kronstadt in 1829. His remaining service was distinguished, but in European waters and he died an Admiral. He was married and fathered a son who followed him into the navy.

Pierce, *Russian America: A Biographical Dictionary.*

Stanley, Henry Morton (John Rowlands), newsman, explorer (1841-May 10, 1904). B. at Denbigh, Wales (Packenham writes flatly that Stanley was "the illegitimate son of feckless Welsh-speaking parents, Elizabeth Parry and John Rollant," anglicized to Rowlands), his farmer father died shortly after the boy's birth and he was reared from infancy to six years by his maternal grandfather, who himself succumbed in 1847 and with that death vanished the "last vestige of humane treatment the child was to know." The cruel abandonment of the boy by his mother, and the equally heartless rejection by virtually all of his other relatives prefaced an adolescence of Dickensian horror from which his eventual development into a strong and sensitive man of integrity and world-renown seems little short of miraculous. For his surmounting all the evil influences upon his early life he gave credit to his Bible and to God, his strong faith continuing throughout his life. In 1859 he shipped as a cabin boy for Louisiana; he found work there with a merchant, Henry Morton Stanley, who became interested in the boy, informally adopted and bestowed upon him his own name, although the elder Stanley died in Cuba in 1861. Young Stanley enlisted that year in the Dixie Grays, was captured at Shiloh and held at Camp Douglas, Chicago. He enrolled in the Federal artillery, but his persistent ill health caused his discharge; after a brief, unhappy return to England he came back to America, enlisted in the U.S. Navy, was present in the operation against Fort Fisher, North Carolina, in 1864-65 and with conclusion of the Civil War turned to journalism. Despite the haphazard nature of his maturation he had become well-read, and a vigorous, insightful student of events. He crossed the nation to Salt Lake City, Denver and other places, sending to various newspapers letters describing what he saw, and his meditations. Editors liked what he wrote and readily accepted his offerings. In 1867 the *Week-*

ly Missouri Democrat of St. Louis assigned him to accompany Major General Winfield Scott Hancock (see entry), who commanded the Department of Missouri, on his rather disorganized Indian campaign on the central Plains. Hancock, without interviewing a single Indian, and on the basis of no verifiable information, had come to believe as factual, rumors that the Cheyennes and other Indians were plotting a massive uprising, which he was determined to abort. Since no such event was in process, Hancock's mission became one of confusion and aimless posturing. He narrowly missed assassination by the Cheyenne warrior Roman Nose (see entry), a near-disaster Hancock never learned about. Stanley became an admirer of Hancock. The newsman's reports were accurate, readable and helped establish his reputation as a competent and trustworthy reporter. He continued his Plains coverage with an assortment of other journalists attending the significant Medicine Lodge Treaty Council in October of 1867, which concluded with agreements with Cheyennes, Comanches, Kiowas, Arapahoes and Kiowa-Apaches. The council was held in the present Barber County, Kansas. Stanley became one of the most prominent of those covering it, he formally signing two of the three resulting pacts as "attesting" to them. In discussing the work of the correspondents, Douglas C. Jones wrote that Stanley and one other were "apparently more closely involved with [Peace] Commission discussions than anyone else in the press group." Stanley wrote his dispatches as letters to his editors, "but there was something more personal in his material than there was in many of the stories that came from Medicine Lodge." Jones wrote that "Stanley's style made easy, enjoyable reading, but often his humor fell rather heavily," although some of his stories were "done with taste and wit." He continued that "his stories always bounced along with gaiety and charm," adding that "reporting the social life and the jokes and antics of the other newsmen seemed to give Stanley great pleasure." As a special correspondent for the *Democrat* Stanley received $15 a week and expenses, but he also contributed to the *New York Herald, Times* and *Tribune,* the *Chicago Republican,* the *Cincinnati Commercial,* "and others," in all bringing his average weekly income to around $90, and he managed to save about $3,000. With conclusion of the Medicine Lodge story, Stanley's relevance to the American frontier terminated, although his spectacular career and adventures abroad were yet to

commence. He went to New York and at the *Herald* office, "by a spasm of courage," asked to see James Gordon Bennett Jr., the managing editor, who complimented him on his free-lance work and permitted Stanley to talk him into a deal: Stanley would pay his own way to Abyssinia, where he would accompany a British expedition against the Emperor Theodore in 1868; if his stories were important enough, exclusive and of sufficient interest, he would be placed on the *Herald's* permanent staff. So it was arranged. His military coverage provided important exclusives, he next was directed to "find" the missing Africa missionary, Dr. David Livingstone, and the rest is history. His many years of subsequent work were of immense importance and "his geographical discoveries alone place Stanley's name first among African explorers." It was Stanley who labeled Africa the "Dark Continent," and he was not without his own dark side, as many would affirm. "A Welsh writer had said of his countrymen that they are 'narrow, but dangerously deep,' and Stanley was Welsh." To the end of his life he was bewildered by the gratuitous cruelties that marred his childhood. At 49 he married an English woman, and died at his London house in Whitehall. Services were held for him in Westminster Abbey, although the Anglican dean, for reasons best known to himself, refused him burial there among many of lesser character, faith and accomplishment, and he was interred at Pirbright, near Wimbledon, leaving his widow and an adopted son.

Literature abundant: *The Autobiography of Sir Henry Morton Stanley,* ed. by his wife, Dorothy Stanley (1909), Boston, Houghton Mifflin Co., 1937; Douglas C. Jones, *The Treaty of Medicine Lodge,* Norman, Univ. of Okla. Press, 1966; DAB; Donald J. Berthrong, *The Southern Cheyennes,* Norman, 1963; Thomas Packenham, *The Scramble for Africa: The White Man's Conquest of the Dark Continent from 1876 to 1912,* N.Y., Random House, 1991.

Stanley-Brown, Joseph, geologist (1858-1941). A Geological Survey scientist, Brown in April 1891 was detailed a special agent for the U.S. Treasury Department to study the seals of the Pribilof Islands. He made contour maps of St. Paul and St. George islands of the group, and also detailed maps of the various seal rookeries, all published in the *Proceedings of the Fur Seal Arbitration Tribunal* of 1893. He then became superintendent of the North America Commercial Company, doing business in Alaska.

Orth, 33.

Stanton, Robert Brewster, engineer, explorer (Aug. 5, 1846-Feb. 23, 1922). B. at Woodville, Mississippi, he was graduated from Miami University, Ohio (of which his Presbyterian minister father was president) in 1871 and earned a master's degree there in 1878. He was resident engineer of the Cincinnati Southern Railroad from 1874-80, division engineer for the Union Pacific from 1880-84 and in 1882-83 built the famed "Georgetown Loop," or Devil's Gate Viaduct, between Georgetown and Silver Plume, Colorado, a notable engineering achievement. He left the Union Pacific in 1884 and went into private practice as a consulting and civil and mining engineer, being general manager of the Idaho Territory Mine for two years. His major frontier experience was as chief engineer for the projected Denver, Colorado Canyon and Pacific Railroad and head of its survey of the Grand Canyon of the Colorado River to investigate the feasability of a railroad down the length within the canyon of that great river from Colorado to the present Yuma, from where it might proceed to the California coast. John Wesley Powell had explored the river twenty years earlier, but "this survey was in a very real sense an exploration venture itself." It commenced March 28, 1889, at Grand Junction, Colorado. Frank M. Brown, as president of the company, was the leader of the exploration/survey party, but Frank C. Kendrick supervised the work of one section down the Colorado to its confluence with the Green River in Utah. The principal group under Brown and with Stanton as chief engineer, traveled by rail to Green River, Utah, and embarked in six boats May 25, traveling down the Green to the Colorado, where it took over the principal task from the Kendrick survey and continued down the main stream. In Marble Canyon below Lees Ferry, Brown's boat overturned in a rapids on July 10, and the leader was drowned; his body was never found. Two other men lost their lives in a subsequent accident. Later on the "accident-plagued" expedition cached supplies, the party scrambling out of the canyon to return to Denver. The company reorganized, Stanton assumed its leadership in order to complete the survey. It reached the river at the head of Glen Canyon in December 1889 with a twelve-man party. The photographer broke his leg and had to be evacuated, another man left the group in the Grand Canyon, a boat was smashed in a rapid and "it was necessary to reduce the party by three more men." Stanton, with six men and "a new cook," completed the survey April 26, 1890, reaching tidewater on the Gulf of California, Stanton later making field examinations of a possible route for a Yuma to San Diego line. In a subsequently-written narrative of the expedition, Stanton concluded that: "The line as proposed is neither impossible, or impracticable, and as compared with some other transcontinental railroads, could be built for a reasonable cost. From an operating standpoint, it would have many advantages in grades, distance, and permanency of its roadbed, and, through the driest section of the western country, have an unlimited supply of water, and it would be possible to operate 1,000 miles of its line, yes, the whole of it, by electricity generated by the power of the river tumbling down beside its tracks." He answered the question sometimes heard of the expense of bridging numerous side canyons with the reasonable rebuttal that "they would be crossed almost always at an elevation of from 50 to 100 feet above their beds, where, at their mouths, they cut through solid rock; so that side canyons, which are from three to six miles wide on top in many instances, would be crossed with a single span bridge of 100 feet in length." He believed there was a "fairly good showing" that the route, if built, would be commercially successful, but of course it never was constructed. Stanton was an engineer at various mines in this country, Canada, Mexico, the West and East Indies and explored for gold in Sumatra in 1904. He wrote, *The Cañons of the Colorado River of the West for Railway Purposes* (1892), and *The Great Land-Slides on the Canadian Pacific Railway in British Columbia* (1898). Two years before his death he had completed his final revision of a 1,038-page manuscript entitled "The River and the Canyon: The Colorado River of the West, and the Exploration, Navigation, and Survey of its Canyons, From the Standpoint of an Engineer," which was never published. Smith has excerpted material from that work for his account of the Stanton adventure. Stanton died at New York City.

Who Was Who; Dwight L. Smith, ed., *Robert Brewster Stanton: Down the Colorado,* Norman, Univ. of Okla. Press, 1965.

Stayeghtha (Stiahta): *see,* Roundhead

Steen, Alexander Early, military officer (d. December 7, 1862). The only son on Enoch Steen (see entry), Alexander was b. probably c. 1827 (conjecture) in Missouri. He was commissioned a second lieutenant, Infantry, on March 6, 1847, and assigned to the 12th Infantry April 9, being breveted to first lieutenant for services in the battles of Contreras and Churubusco, Mexico; he was mustered out July 25, 1848. He was commissioned a second lieutenant of the 3rd U.S. Infantry June 30, 1852. Most of his service was in the Southwest. Late in 1856 Steen was sent to investigate the disappearance of two Mimbres Apaches, one of whom was Costales, a Mexican captive who had been raised among the Apaches and was now a sub-chief. They had been pursuing Mexican stock thieves. Steen reported that he arrived at the San Diego crossing of the Rio Grande at 9 p.m. December 31, and at daylight "I commenced an examination which resulting in finding in the sleeping room of the ferry house a quantity of blood on the floor...," and the body of Costales was fished out of the river. "He had evidently been killed while asleep, his head was split open with a blow from an axe, his throat was cut and the entire scalp taken off." The body of Ratón, Costales's companion, was never found. Steen participated in the Bonneville expedition against the Gila Apaches, serving under Captain Richard Stoddert Ewell in the operation's only sizable engagement against the Indians, which occurred June 27, 1857. Steen was wounded in the corner of the right eye by an arrow, but apparently was not blinded by it. He became a first lieutenant September 18, 1857. Although his father remained loyal to the Union and retained his military rank, young Steen resigned May 10, 1861, and returned to Missouri to join Secession forces. Heitman reports that he became a Brigadier General in the Confederate army, but this is in error. He was commissioned a captain and briefly became a Brigadier General in the Missouri State Guard, but within weeks relinquished that rank to become colonel of the 10th Missouri Infantry. Heitman wrote that he was killed in the "battle" of Kane (Cane) Hill, Arkansas, November 27, 1862, but that skirmish occurred November 25, and other sources assert that Steen was shot in the head in the Battle of Prairie Grove, near Fayetteville, Arkansas, on December 7, 1862, which is more probable. He left his widow, Georgia, daughter of Colonel Pitcairn Morrison (see entry).

Heitman; SED 11, Vol. II, 35th Congress, I Session, Serial Set 920, 135-41; info. from the Missouri Hist. Soc.; Natl. Archives Trust Fund Board.

Steller, Georg Wilhelm, naturalist (Mar. 10, 1709-Nov. 12, 1746). B. at Winsheim, Franconia, northeastern Bavaria, Germany, he studied theology and natural science in the universities of Wittenberg, Leipsig and Jena and settled in Halle, Saxony, where he continued researches in botany, anatomy and medicine. Steller became a brilliant scientist though a difficult man to work with since he was ebulliently eager to offer advice and suggestions, often on subjects he knew little about, and some considered him officious. In 1734 he joined the Russian army as a staff surgeon before Danzig and in December was sent to St. Petersburg with a shipload of wounded soldiers. He became surgeon to the Bishop of Novgorod, Theophanos Prokopovich, favorite of Peter the Great, remaining with the churchman, except for work in Siberia and beyond, for the rest of his life. Steller at length was assigned to study the natural history of Kamchatka. He reached there in 1738 and for two years sent to the museum at St. Petersburg frequent and valuable shipments of specimens. He at length was persuaded by Bering to accompany him on his 1741 expedition which would result in the discovery of Alaska, Steller to head up the natural science work, and also to be chief surgeon and chaplain. He joined Bering at Petropavlovsk, the captain's newly-built base at Avatcha Bay on the east coast of Kamchatka. From here Bering and Steller sailed aboard the *St. Peter* June 4, 1741 (see Bering, Chirikov entries for accounts of the expedition), entering the Gulf of Alaska. Steller reported that he sighted the first land on July 15, though no one believed him. The next day, however, high snow-capped mountains (one of them probably Mt. St. Elias) were observed and the coast, broken with bays and islands, was in plain view; this was in Latitude 58° 28', probably below Yakutat Bay in the Alaska panhandle. Steller for days had been deeply engaged identifying growing indications of land, the seaweeds and kelps, sea birds and such marine animals as the sea otter, and now the virgin land and its wilderness opened before his excited gaze. When it came time to lower the boats, Steller wished to go ashore in the larger one, destined for further exploration, but Bering, although his good friend, forbade this, and the naturalist had to settle for a briefer trip in the lesser craft. Golder explained that "Steller was not the most agreeable person...He was too willing to instruct and give advice on all matters, even navigation, and had the faculty of believing himself always in the right. The result...was unfortunate...It came to the point that whatever Steller suggested, even when in his own province, was almost sure to be disapproved. [Yet] in many cases his advice was sound, and had it been taken, much suffering and hardship would have been avoided." As soon as he stepped from the boat he began to search for traces of humans. The amount of work he did on that single day "is remarkable and shows him to have been a man of great ability." He came across ashes and bones showing what animal life existed there, small shellheaps and dried fish from which he deduced the customs of the people of the region; he located a habitation with artifacts which suggested that the natives were closely related to those of Siberia. He dispatched specimens to the ship and urged that assistants be sent so even more work could be done in the limited time at his disposal, meanwhile studying botanical and zoological specimens he discovered. His enthusiasm grew. He was investigating terrain, objects and people that no other scientist had yet observed and was nonplused when word came from Bering that since the ship's water casks were now replenished, Steller must return immediately or he would be left behind. The captain's insistence led Steller to comment wryly in his journal that this long and expensive expedition seemed planned only to fetch American water to Asia, and that a decade of preparation for this truly enormous discovery was valued at a mere ten hours of exploration! Bering, already suffering from scurvy, could scarcely wait to get away from this coast he had sought so long; he felt he must regain Kamchatka before winter. Discovery was enough for him; scientific exploration meant little. The *St. Peter* much later put in at the Shumagin Islands of the Aleutians, named for a man who was buried there, and Steller was sent ashore with a boat to load fresh water. Seamen filled the casks with brackish water despite his surgeon's warning that it might have harmful effects on those drinking it, while fresh water was available to them; he was not listened to. Steller gathered berries and grasses to be used for anti-scorbutic purposes, but he had not sufficient time to collect nearly enough. In all, 30 of the ship's company died of scurvy or related ailments, and most of the remainder became too ill to perform serious work. Steller himself seems to have escaped the worst ravages of the disease, perhaps because of his sensible—and novel—treatment by devouring fruits and grasses with their, at that time, unknown vitamins that would control scurvy. The *St. Peter* at last grounded on what became known as Bering Island, a short distance from

Kamchatka. Here the Danish commander died and those who survived underwent a harsh and terrible winter, a period Steller put to the best scientific use: studying marine life and making detailed entries of his findings in his journal, which is the best published account of the entire voyage. He was first to scientifically describe the North Pacific sea lion, the fur seal, and wrote the only documented study ever made of the Steller sea cow which in a mere 27 years was brought to extinction by Russian hunters. "Usually entire families [of the sea cows] keep together, the male with the female, one grown offspring and a little, tender one. To me they appear to be monogamous. They bring forth their young at all seasons, generally however in the autumn, judging from the many new-born seen at that time...I observed them to mate preferably in the early spring [and] I conclude that the fetus remains in the uterus more than a year...These gluttonous animals eat incessantly..." The huge, dugong-like creature, largest of recent Sirenians, measured sometimes twenty feet in length, weighed up to four tons and was wholly inoffensive, easily and hence wantonly destroyed for meat and the tough hide which was used in constructing boats. Fresh meat helped cure the castaways of scurvy and, having built a new vessel out of the wreckage of the *St. Peter,* the survivors regained Atacha Bay August 27, 1742. Steller by 1744 completed his natural history survey of Kamchatka, also attempting, with little success, to develop profitable agricultural processes there. He was enroute to Russia across Siberia when he was falsely accused of some unrecorded offense and dragged into jail. Soon after being freed he died at 37 between Tobolsk and Catherinesburg (Yekaterinburg or Ekaterinburg, since 1942: Sverdlovsk, 300 miles southwest of Tobolsk). He was "generally mourned" by the scientific community of Europe.

Bancroft, *Alaska;* F.A. Golder, *Russian Expansion on the Pacific 1641-1850,* N.Y., Paragon Book Reprint Corp., 1971; Ernest P. Walker, *Mammals of the World,* 2nd ed., Baltimore, Johns Hopkins Press, 1968, II, 1334-35.

Stephen, Adam, military officer (d. 1791). B. probably in Scotland and educated as a physician, he went to Virginia at an early age and settled in the lower Shenendoah Valley. In 1754 he was the senior captain in Colonel Joshua Fry's colonial regiment, and when George Washington assumed command Stephen became a major. He was with Washington at Great Meadows, Pennsylvania, in 1754 and the following year was severely wounded at the Braddock defeat, but recovered. He was on John Forbes' expedition to occupy the burned and abandoned French fort of Duchesne at the present Pittsburgh, and commanded the Virginia regiment raised in the 1763 Pontiac War. He occupied civilian positions until the Lord Dunmore War when he was second in command to the governor, but apparently saw no combat. An ardent Whig, he was in communication with the Virginia leaders of the Revolution and in 1776 became a Brigadier General, early in 1777 becoming Major General, having served with honor at Brandywine. But he was charged with drunkenness at the Battle of Germantown, was cashiered and retired to his home at Martinsburg, Virginia. He took an active political role in Virginia and in 1791 died at his home "at an advanced age." Thwaites wrote that "he was a man of great stature and powerful strength, much feared by the Indians, although beloved by his friends." One of his daughters became wife of Alexander Spottswood Dandridge (see entry).

Thwaites, *Dunmore.*

Stephenson, John, military officer (c. 1737-post 1790). A half-brother of William Crawford (see entry), Stephenson was born in Virginia, served in the French and Indian War and about 1768 moved to Fayette County, present West Virginia, settling on Jacob's Creek. In 1770 he was visited there by George Washington, returning from his journey into the western lands. In 1774 Stephenson commanded a company under Dunmore and was active on the Virginia side during a dispute with Pennsylvania over the boundary question. He served with the southern forces during the Revolution but became ill in mid-1777 and returned home. He was a volunteer on Hand's "Squaw Campaign" of 1778 (see Edward Hand entry), and that of Lachlan McIntosh's 1778-79 operation and about 1790 removed to Kentucky, living the rest of his life on the South Fork of the Licking River. He left no descendants. He was described by Thwaites/Kellogg as "a large, active man, brave, kind, and popular."

Thwaites/Kellogg, *Frontier Defense on the Upper Ohio, 1777-1778.*

Sterling, James, trader (fl. 1759-1783). B. in Ireland, he served in Pennsylvania forces early in the French and Indian War, was a commissary in the British attack on Fort Niagara in 1759 and in Amherst's expedition against Montreal in 1760.

He then became a representative of a Schenectady, New York, trading firm and in July 1761 went to Detroit, becoming western agent for his firm. He acquired a knowledge of French and possibly of some Indian languages and traded as far west as Michilimackinac. He became romantically involved with Angélique Guillerier and it is reported that she told him of Pontiac's 1763 plans for a surprise attack in May on the Detroit garrison; Sterling informed Commandant Henry Gladwin (see entry) in time to foil the plot. "The identity of Gladwin's informant has not been established, but Angélique was in a position to know what was occurring. Shortly after their marriage Sterling wrote that she was "used to trade from her infancy, and is generally [said] to be the best interpreter of the various Indian languages at this place; her family is in great esteem amongst the Indians, so much so that her father was suspected to have been chosen by the Indians to command here in case they had succeeded." During Pontiac's siege Sterling commanded the local militia. Because of his differences with Hamilton (see entry) and others he was sent to Quebec in 1777, released and returned to Detroit but in 1778 he went to England. He continued business relations with American associates, however, and is thought to have located in Pennsylvania following the Revolutionary War. The date and place of his death are not reported.

Thwaites/Kellogg, *The Revolution on the Upper Ohio, 1775-1777,* Madison, Wis. Hist. Soc., 1908; DCB IV.

Stevenson, Matilda Coxe Evans, ethnologist, Zuñi specialist (c. 1850-June 24, 1915). B. at San Augustine, Texas, she was raised and educated at Washington, D.C., and Philadelphia. April 18, 1872, she married James Stevenson (1840-1888: see entry), an ethnologist and explorer of the Geological Survey and from 1879 with the Bureau of Ethnology; Matilda at once became interested in that science, accompanied her husband on various expeditions and was fascinated with the Zuñi of the New Mexico and Hopi of the Arizona pueblos. She found them "more accessible, less modified and more amenable to study" than most of the pueblo tribes. She commenced her studies in learning the ways of Zuñi women by "conducting a one-woman campaign to introduce the pueblo to the use of soap," making good use of a male transvestite to further that cause. Her first important paper on the people was "The Religious Life of the Zuñi Child," in the fifth annual report of the Bureau in 1887. The following year she published "Zuñi Religions" in *Science.* She then began working among the Sia people of the Rio Grande pueblos, publishing "The Sia" in the 11th annual report of the Bureau of Ethnology in 1894. Her culminating study of the Zuñis was encompassed in her "encyclopaedic" work, "The Zuñi Indians: Their Mythology, Esoteric Fraternities, and Ceremonies," in the 23rd annual report of the Bureau, in 1904. The *Dictionary of American Biography* noted that "her fortitude in carrying out the work necessary for this study is almost unexampled among ethnologists, and her success in winning the confidence of the Indians was a triumph of character." Her last major work was the "Ethnobotany of the Zuñi Indians," in the 30th annual report in 1915. She also worked among the Tewa and Taos Indians, publishing the results of her studies. Her published work and collections assured her "a secure position in ethnological science." Her works on the Sia and the Zuñis "will stand forever as enlightened descriptions of western cultural scenes now gone" forever.

DAB; Bernard L. Fontana article in REAW.

Steward, Julian Haynes, anthropologist (Jan. 31, 1902-Feb. 6, 1972). B. at Washington, D.C., he was graduated from Cornell University in 1925 and earned a doctorate from the University of California at Berkeley in 1929. He did ethnographic research among the Shoshoni Indians of the northwest and on the basis of that study published *Basin-Plateau Aboriginal Sociopolitical Groups,* Washington, D.C., Bureau of American Ethnology Bulletin 120, 1938 (1985). After being affiliated with several universities, Steward joined the Bureau of Ethnology in 1935; he became senior anthropologist in 1938 and director of the Institute of Social Anthropology from 1943 to 1946. He was editor of the massive *Handbook of South American Indians,* 7 volumes, appearing from 1944 to 1957, a survey of peoples, their history and cultures published by the Bureau of Ethnology in cooperation with the Department of State. He taught at Columbia University from 1946 to 1952, then joined the University of Illinois, where he achieved professor emeritus status in 1967. In his professional life he became a leading neo-evolutionist and the founder of the theory of cultural ecology, and was an early proponent of area studies. His theoretical work drew on such disciplines as anthropology, archeology, history, ecology and ethnography. His core thesis of social evolution was described in his *Theory of Culture Change:*

The Methodology of Multilinear Evolution (1955) which suggested that social systems arise out of labor patterns which are determined by a people's adaptation to the natural environment upon which their culture depends. The requirements of differing physical and historical settings, he believed, produce distinct social manifestations resulting in what he called "multilinear evolution." He expressed the view in his *Irrigation Civilizations* (1955) that the collective labor and some measure of centralized authority required for successful irrigation of arid lands resulted in social stratification, however rudimentary, and finally in the development of a state. He died at Urbana, the home of the University of Illinois.

EB; EA; *Who Was Who.*

Stewart, George Rippey, writer (May 31, 1895-Aug. 22, 1980). B. in Sewickley, Pennsylvania, he graduated from Princeton in 1917, earned a master's degree from the University of California in 1920 and his doctorate from Columbia in 1922. He served in the army 1917-19, was an instructor at the University of Michigan 1922-23, and taught to professor at the University of California, Berkeley, for 40 years, from 1923 to his retirement in 1962, when he became professor emeritus. He was a prolific writer, producing novels as well as thoroughly-researched nonfiction, some of them historical works. The best known of them was probably his still-reliable history of the Donner party, *Ordeal By Hunger* (1936, 1960), to the later edition of which was added an important Supplement, including Stewart's analysis of other writings on the ill-fated wagon party of 1846, three additional primary narratives of importance, and other material. He also wrote the valuable *The California Trail* (1963). His other nonfiction works included *Bret Harte* (1931); *Names on the Land* (1944); *Year of the Oath* (1950); *Pickett's Charge* (1960) and *Committee of Vigilance: Revolution in San Francisco* (1964). He wrote a juvenile work, *To California by Covered Wagon* (1954). Stewart was married and fathered a daughter and a son. In 1952-53 he was a Fulbright professor of American literature and civilization at the University of Athens, and in addition to Greece he and his family had lived in France and Mexico at one time or another. He received various awards and honors for his literary products.

Contemporary Authors.

Stewart, Lazarus, Indian killer (fl. 1763-1771).

A resident of the region of Donegal in the northwestern corner of present Lancaster County, Pennsylvania, he with accompanying men joined Matthew Smith in the massacre of inoffensive Conestoga (Susquehanna) Indians in December 1763 (see Smith entry for details of the affair and its aftermath). Stewart was in command at the December 27, assault upon the Lancaster Jail and murder of the fourteen remaining Conestogas who had been held there for security. The Reverend John Elder, a respected Presbyterian minister of Paxton, a point of origin for the miscreants, stoutly defended the accused: "The characters of Stewart and his friends were well established. Ruffians nor brutal they were not; humane, liberal and moral, nay, religious." He defended Stewart against attempts to put him on trial at Philadelphia for the murders, rather than nearer home. "It is evidently not the wish of the [prosecutors] to give Stewart a fair hearing. All he desires is to be put on trial at Lancaster, near the scenes of the horrible butcheries, committed by the Indians [in past years], when he can have the testimony of the Scouts or Rangers, men whose services can never be sufficiently rewarded." Stewart himself, in a formal Declaration much later, defended his actions and added, "If a white man kill an Indian, it is a murder far exceeding any crime upon record; he must not be tried in the country where he lives, or where the offence was committed, but in Philadelphia, that he may be tried, convicted, sentenced and hung without delay. If an Indian kill a white man, it was the act of an ignorant Heathen, perhaps in liquor; alas, poor innocent! he is sent to the *friendly Indians* that he be made a *Christian.*" So intense grew the controversy over trying any of the perpetrators of the Lancaster massacre, that no arrests were attempted for a long time. Eight years afterward, in 1771, however, Stewart was charged with murdering the Conestogas. Learning that his trial was to take place in Philadelphia "and thence judging that his condemnation was certain, he broke jail and escaped." He wrote his Declaration, gathered his followers about him, set the provincial government of Pennsylvania at defiance, and withdrew to Wyoming, between Scranton and Wilkes-Barre, where unwelcome settlers from the Connecticut Valley had intruded to the disapproval of the Pennsylvania authorities. Here, under the settlers' protection, he felt safe from prosecution. Little more has been uncovered about him.

Parkman, *The Conspiracy of Pontiac,* II, 126-39;

info. from Randall Rankin Snyder, curator, Lancaster County Hist. Soc.

Stirling, Matthew Williams, anthropologist (Aug. 28, 1896-Jan. 23, 1975). B. at Salinas, California, he was graduated from the University of California in 1920, earned a master's degree from George Washington University in 1922 and received an honorary doctorate in 1943 from Tampa University. He taught anthropology at the University of California for two years, was assistant curator, division of ethnology for the National Museum at Washington, D.C., from 1921-24, was chief of the Bureau of American Ethnology at the Smithsonian Institution from 1928-47 and its director from 1947-58, being archeologist emeritus thereafter and also collaborator in archeology for the National Park Service from 1958. He belonged to a number of scientific societies. He headed archeological expeditions to southern Mexico, Panama, Costa Rica, Ecuador and also did field work in Europe and the East Indies, leading a Netherlands-American expedition from 1925-27 to central New Guinea. His published works included *Origin Myth of Acoma* (1942); *Stone Monuments of Southern Mexico* (1943), and *Indians of the Americas* (1955). He lived in retirement at Washington, D.C., and was buried at Gettysburg National Military Park. He was married.

Who Was Who; Bernard Klein, Daniel Icolari, *Reference Encyclopedia of the American Indian,* N.Y., B. Klein and Co., 1967.

Stockton, Charles Herbert, naval officer (Oct. 13, 1845-May 31, 1924). B. at Philadephia he went to the Naval Academy, then at Newport, Rhode Island, saw some active duty as a midshipman toward the end of the Civil War, became an ensign in 1866, master in 1868 and lieutenant in 1869. His principal frontier service was in 1889-91 when he commanded the *Thetis* and was assigned the duty of examining the whaling interests of the United States in Alaskan waters. The *Thetis* ran the coast of Alaska from Dixon Entrance, threading the Aleutians near Unalaska Island, passed through Bering Strait and continued along the northern coast of Alaska from Point Barrow to the Mackenzie River. The Stockton Islands were named for him by Ernest deKoven Leffingwell (see entry) in recognition of his contribution to knowledge of the geography of the Arctic coast. His further service was creditable, though it bore little frontier interest.

He became a specialist in international law and wrote learnedly on that subject, including his standard work, *Outlines of International Law* (1914). He was married twice, fathering children by each marriage. January 7, 1906, he became a Rear Admiral, and retired form the Navy October 13, 1907.

Orth, 33, 909; DAB.

Stockton, Robert Field, naval officer (Aug. 20, 1795-Oct. 7, 1866). B. at Princeton, New Jersey, he graduated from the College of New Jersey (Princeton), and entered the navy as a midshipman September 1, 1811, serving through the War of 1812. He was transferred to the Mediterranean and was active in the "war" against Algiers under Commodore John Rodgers and in other actions there from 1816-20; his further duty required operations against slave traders and pirates. In 1821 he negotiated for the American Colonization Society a territorial concession on the African west coast that became Liberia. Going on furlough then Stockton and his father-in-law were instrumental in construction of the Delaware and Raritan Canal. He became interested in naval architecture and assisted in construction of the steamship, *Princeton,* "of which he was commander when one of [her] guns exploded and killed several cabinet members." He was promoted to captain in 1838 and returned to active service with the navy. War with Mexico seemed imminent and he was ordered to proceed in the U.S.S. *Congress* to the Pacific and reinforce the squadron there. He arrived at Monterey, California, in July 1846 after the war had begun, relieving Commodore John D. Sloat on July 23, as commander of American naval forces on that coast. His actions in the conquest of California are controversial. He collected a land military force which included Fremont (see entry) and his contingent, occupied Los Angeles in August, issued a proclamation on July 29, declaring California a territory of the United States and organized a civil and military government with himself as governor and commander-in-chief. Unfortunately for the success of his plans, the Mexicans promptly recaptured Los Angeles. Stockton's subsequent moves, according to DeVoto, were based upon his efforts to convince Washington, D.C., that there was an active military opposition to American control, that the "enemy" were scoundrels but that Stockton had beaten them at their game, and that he had made the conquest of the huge territory a fact, with Fre-

mont now as governor and American control secure. However, Kearny soon arrived with his land army and solid authority and Stockton's visionary satrapy crumbled while the General took over and organized the occupation. On January 17, 1847, Stockton sailed homeward and May 28, 1850, he resigned from the navy. Always interested in politics, he was elected as a Democrat to the United States Senate and served from March 4, 1851, until his resignation on January 10, 1853. During his incumbency he introduced a bill to ban flogging in the navy. He was a member of a peace commission held at Washington in February 1861 to avert the impending Civil War; it failed. Stockton then retired from public life. He became president of the Delaware and Raritan Canal Company and, being a racing enthusiast, imported fine blooded horses from England to improve his stock. He died at Princeton.

BDAC; Susan Shelby Magoffin, *Down the Santa Fe Trail and into Chihuahua,* Lincoln, Univ. of Neb. Press, 1982, pp. 154-55, note by Stella M. Drumm; REAW; DAB; Bernard DeVoto, *The Year of Decision 1846,* Boston, Little, Brown and Co., 1943.

Stoner (Holsteiner), Michael, frontiersman (fl. 1767-1801) B. possibly in Germany but more probably in Buck County, Pennsylvania, near Daniel Boone's birthplace, he migrated to the Shenandoah Valley of Virginia and early became a long hunter and probed deep into the wilderness, often alone, for he "never was less alone than when alone in the woods." He became a superb marksman, better than Daniel Boone, "indifferent at target practice, but against Indians or game held to be the best shot in Kentucky" or anywhere else. He was a large man, speaking with a strong German accent and other frontiersmen sometimes poked good-humored fun at him, asserting that sometimes he would "prod a bear's den with his rifle muzzle and demand, 'Who keeps da house?'" One of Stoner's earliest and most famous trips was in 1767 when he and Samuel Harrod went down the Ohio River from Pittsburgh, visited Kentucky and proceeded to the Illinois country. From there they went as far south as the site of the future Nashville, Tennessee. June 20, 1774, Colonel William Preston (see entry), having charge of defenses of Fincastle County, Virginia, authorized Captain William Russell to employ two faithful woodsmen to go to Kentucky and inform the several surveying parties at work there of the danger of Indian hostility. June 26, Russell reported he had engaged, to start immediately, "two of the best hands I could think of—Daniel Boone and Michael Stoner," and hoped the surveyors would be warned in time. Stoner and Boone journeyed overland to Harrodsburg where James Harrod (brother of Samuel) and thirty men were laying out a town; at Fontaine Blue, three miles below, they found other surveyors, whom they warned, and on the Kentucky River contacted Captain John Floyd's crew of eight men. Stoner and Boone descended to the mouth of the Kentucky and thence to the Falls of the Ohio (Louisville) and found more surveyors at Mann's Lick, four miles southeast. "Indians were making bloody forays through the district, and the scouts had frequent thrilling adventures." Finally, after an absence of 61 days and traveling 800 miles, they regained the Clinch River and Russell's place in safety. The next year Stoner again accompanied Boone, as did about 25 others, into Kentucky, to blaze a trail to the Boonesborough they hoped to create; two years later Stoner was wounded in the defense of that settlement. Stoner spent much of his long life in the Cumberland Valley, establishing a station at a place known as Stoner's Lick on Stone's River in Tennessee. Thwaites wrote that he finally developed a station called by his own name on a branch of the Licking River, in the later Bourbon County, Kentucky, northeast of Lexington. In 1801 he completed a deposition concerning the people and places he had known in the neighborhood of present Mill Springs, between Burnside and Monticello, as they existed in 1775. It is informative.

Thwaites, *Dunmore;* Harriette Simpson Arnow, *Seedtime on the Cumberland,* N.Y., The Macmillan Co., 1960; Alexander Scott Withers, *Chronicles of Border Warfare,* Cincinnati, Robert Clarke Co., 1895, 1970; info. Jan. 22, 1991, from Thomas D. Clark.

Stoney, George Morse, naval officer (1852-1905). In 1883 Lieutenant Stoney was sent to St. Lawrence Bay, Siberia, with gifts for natives who had been kind to the crew of the *Rodgers* which had burned while searching for the lost polar ship *Jeanette.* Stoney had been on the *Rodgers* and voyaged to St. Lawrence Island aboard the revenue cutter *Corwin* which then proceeded to Kotzebue Sound, Alaska, where Stoney borrowed a boat and explored Hotham Inlet and the lower course of the Kobuk River. He returned in 1884 and explored some 300 miles up the Kobuk only to find he had been pre-

ceded by a few days by Cantwell (see entry). Stoney returned in 1885, proceeding up the Kobuk once more, and again finding Cantwell just ahead of him. An abbreviated report of his explorations was published in 1900 and some of his maps are in the National Archives.

Orth, 33-36, 920.

Storkerson, Storker T., polar explorer (June 26, 1883-Mar. 22, 1940). B. at Trondenes (or Tromso), Norway, he went to sea at 15 and sailed over all the world, then attended a navigation school at San Francisco. He joined the Ernest Leffingwell-Ejnar Mikkelsen (see entries) Arctic expedition in 1906 in British Columbia, signing on as seaman aboard the party's ship, the *Duchess of Bedford,* and when the mate fell ill at Port Clarence, Alaska, became its first officer. On this expedition Storkerson first met its anthropologist, Vilhjalmur Stefansson, with whom he would become closely affiliated in later years. Storkerson Point, eleven miles west of Beechey Point on the Alaskan coast, was named by Leffingwell in 1907. The ship was dismantled at Flaxman Island off the Arctic coast and after the expedition dissolved Storkerson married the half-Eskimo daughter of Danish trader Charles Klinkenberg (Klengenberg) and remained in the north. On Stefansson's 53-month expedition from 1908-12 he and Storkerson renewed their collaboration, exploring the archipelago north of the continent. Stefansson wrote in *The Friendly Arctic* (1921) that "Storkerson and I had spent five years with the Eskimos of northern Canada and Alaska [during the earlier period], dressing as they did and making camp after their fashion." At the beginning of his significant 1913-18 Arctic expedition Stefansson, rather by chance met Storkerson once more, this time at a deserted Eskimo house two days east of Herschel Island, which lies near the Canada-Alaska border. The Norwegian was alone, his family residing inland along the Mackenzie River and he returning to Fort McPherson from "a hard trip" on which he had lost some of his dogs to disease and harnessed himself with the remaining dogs to move his heavily-laden sledge. "From the first it had been my intention to try to engage Storkerson, who was about the best 'all around' man it was possible for the expedition to get," wrote Stefansson. Storkerson happily joined up for "there was enough of the poet about [him] so he could see...the romantic side of the search for undiscovered lands, and of...forays into the unknown," and besides, his trapping was an activity which was laborious and poorly remunerative. He was energetic, cooperative, and an excellent ice man. On the initial northerly exploration in 1914 only Storkerson and Ole Andreasen accompanied Stefansson. Banks Island was reached and Storkerson Bay on the west coast named. In 1915 the islands of Borden and Brock, north of Mackenzie Island were discovered, while in the autumn Storkerson commenced the survey of northeastern Victoria Island. In June 1916 Lougheed and Meighen islands were found, adjacent to the Sverdrup group. Storkerson Peninsula, the northerly thumb of Victoria Island, was named after more survey work and Stefansson Island, immediately beyond, was named. In 1918 Stefansson had planned to sledge north 200 or 300 miles from Alaska into the Polar Basin, then drift with the ice which is in constant, though slow, movement. The explorer fell seriously ill, however, and Storkerson undertook to fulfill this mission, which he did from March to November. Instead of drifting northwest, as was hoped, the floe they rode zigzagged with the wind and evidently found little or no current. The party finally returned to the coast after 238 days, or eight months, on the ice. They had taken but three months' food with them—and returned with 55 days' rations left—thus demonstrating the possiblity of living on the polar sea by game and fish, as Eskimos did on coastal ice floes. Storkerson summed up the scientific results of his Arctic drift: "We discovered that no permanent current exists in the Beaufort Sea" in the latitudes visited and that the ice drifts are "governed by the wind exclusively." He added that "We have definitely proved that [the reported] 'Keenan Land' does not exist. The drift of our ice floe was right through the territory where Keenan Land" was supposed to lie, and "instead of finding land we found a depth of more than 1,600 fathoms without reaching bottom." The expedition also confirmed "that the Arctic Sea is not so inhospitable as people think. My party of five men were able to live safely and comfortably on it and never went without a meal...So far as we could judge we could have lived on the ice eight years as easily as eight months." Return of the party to the Alaskan coast from Latitude 73.9° in the winter darkness of the polar ocean, and through awful weather, was itself a tribute to Storkerson's intrepidity, as Stefansson remarked: "This has always been considered, and rightly, the most difficult

and dangerous season of the whole year to travel...There are nearly continuous snowstorms and fogs. The thin ice lies treacherous under a blanket of snow that gives the same appearance to stretches that would support an elephant [or] would engulf a child at play. The only safety lies in jabbing your ice spear through the snow ahead continually to discover if the ice beneath is firm or mushy. Storkerson's official report of this journey [glosses over one] which would have been (but for the skill and judgment of the men who made it) the most difficult and dangerous ever attempted in the Arctic...This journey had every terror of darkness and ice and storm that has taxed alike the strength, courage and descriptive powers of the explorers of the past." In 1920 Storkerson was appointed Resident Manager at Baffin Island of the Hudson's Bay Reindeer Company; Stefansson, too, was affiliated with this enterprise. Storkerson, however, after completing arrangements for purchasing the deer in Norway (or Lapland) resigned in 1921 before the animals arrived. He returned eventually to Trondheim where later he spent several years in the Reitgjerdet Asylum, his condition diagnosed as schizophrenic. He ended his life in the Hammerfest Nursing Home, at Trondheim. He had fathered three children.

Info. from John Schwoerke, Special Collections, Dartmouth College Lby.; Vilhjalmur Stefansson, *The Friendly Arctic,* N.Y., Macmillan Co., 1921, 1944; Orth, 921.

Street, Joseph Montfort, journalist, military officer, Indian agent (Dec. 18, 1782-May 5, 1840). B. in Lunenburg County, Virginia, he met at Richmond a controversial newspaperman, John Wood, and with Wood on July 7, 1806, began to publish the *Western World* at Frankfort, Kentucky. It was a feisty, federalist sheet which seems to have specialized in a form of investigative reporting with some successes: it caused the retirement of U.S. Senator John Brown (1757-1837) to private life; forced Aaron Burr to appear before a Kentucky Grand Jury twice; generated libel suits and made Street "everywhere the object of vituperation and revenge." He was challenged to a series of duels, demonstrated by them both his courage and his skill and refused to fight any more such combats. Wood became estranged from him, left the paper, which Street continued to publish until he lost control of it as he also lost a libel suit in which he was assessed damages far beyond his ability to pay. He therefore took his wife and son, the first of fourteen children, to the frontier. In 1812 he built a log cabin at Shawneetown, Gallatin County, Illinois, where he held many public posts and, an obviously capable man, became a Brigadier General of Illinois militia. In 1827 he was named Indian agent to the Winnebago at Prairie du Chien, Wisconsin, upon the recommendations of Secretary of State Henry Clay and Illinois Governor Ninian Edwards. Upon his arrival at his new post he tried unsuccessfully to remove whites from the lead mines, located on the reservation and which the Indians properly owned. In the 1832 Black Hawk War, Street used his influence to keep the Winnebago quiet and out of harm's way, and it was to Street that they brought Black Hawk, the Prophet and other captives, convinced he would treat them fairly. In 1838 Street tried, again without success, to end fraudulent practices accompanying Indian disbursements, and in so doing implicated Simon Cameron (1799-1889), then a commissioner engaged in settling certain Winnebago claims; Street never quailed before taking on anyone he suspected of wrong-doing. He was transferred to the Rock Island Winnebago Agency of Illinois, which was removed in 1839 to Iowa. Street died at Agency City, near Ottumwa, Iowa; his wife, Eliza Maria, was daughter of famed Brigadier General Thomas Posey (see entry) of Dunmore's War and the Revolution and who had been Indian agent at Shawneetown from 1816 until his death two years later.

Black Hawk War, II, 10nl; DAB; BDAC for John Brown material.

Stroud, Adam, pioneer (d. 1772). A German emigrant to West Virginia, Stroud settled in the Elk River area a short distance below Bulltown where the Delaware chief Captain Bull lived on the Little Kanawha River in the present Braxton County. In June 1772 a war party of Shawnees killed Stroud, his wife and their seven children, their house was plundered and their cattle driven off. Because the trail led in the direction of the friendly Bulltown Delawares, frontiersmen assumed that Bull's people were to blame, and viciously (and erroneously) retaliated on them (see Captain Bull entry).

Alexander Scott Withers, *Chronicles of Border Warfare,* Cincinnati, Robert Clarke Co., 1895, 1970; Thwaites, *Dunmore.*

Stuart (Stewart), John, frontiersman (1749-

1823). B. in Scotland, he came to this country and in 1769 established a first settlement on Greenbrier River, West Virginia, where the community of Frankford is now. He constructed a palisaded place named Fort Spring on his estate. In addition to holding civilian offices, Stuart commanded a company under Charles Lewis in the October 10, 1774, Point Pleasant battle against Shawnees, an action which effectively concluded Lord Dunmore's War. In 1820, at the age of 70, he wrote a narrative of that affair, the account being published in *Virginia Historical Collections,* i, 37-68. He died at his Greenbrier home.

Thwaites, *Dunmore.*

Sullivan, Daniel, adventurer (d. 1790). Apparently born in Virginia, Sullivan told British Governor Henry Hamilton of Detroit c. 1777 that he had been captured by the Delaware Indians "when young," around the year 1763. After living with them nine years, or in 1772 or 1773, "I went to live with my Relations in Virginia," but with the onset of the Revolution and having no way to live but by hunting, he returned "to my Delaware relations and determined to live with them until I could do better." In a deposition to Colonel John Cannon from Fort Pitt, March 20, 1778, he reported that "agreeable to my Contract with you in behalf of the State of Virginia, I proceeded to the Indian Country in February 1777," returning in March with what intelligence he could gather. He wrote that he had found the Delawares "perfectly disposed for Peace with the United States," but although he met at Cuyahoga, Ohio, with representatives of half a dozen other tribes he could learn little of consequence about their intentions. Sullivan then was hired by James Howel, a trader, "agreeable to Col. [George] Morgan's directions" to go as a batteau man to Detroit with furs and bring away goods, and no doubt learn what he could. It took eight days to reach Detroit, when Sullivan was taken to Hamilton, who demanded to know who he was and what was his business. Hamilton accepted his explanations and released him. Sullivan stayed at the home of William Tucker (see entry), an interpreter for the governor of the Ottawa and Chippewa tongues; Tucker's wife had been born in Hampshire County, Virginia, was acquainted with Sullivan's sister and had much to tell Sullivan of Hamilton's use of Indians in frontier warfare against the Americans. The next day Pluggy's son (see Pluggy entry) saw Sullivan walking about Detroit, went to Hamilton and with John Montour's support informed the governor of Sullivan's activities, so the intelligence agent was arrested, "loaded with Irons, Hand and Feet, and in seventeen days was sent to Niagara and from thence to Montreal and Quebec." He was dispatched to New York, paroled in early 1778 and at Pittsburgh wrote the deposition to Cannon. In 1780 he was at Louisville and founded a station (or homestead) in Jefferson County. In 1782 he was wounded at the siege of Wheeling. In 1785 he was at Vincennes and in some way connected with George Rogers Clark's expedition of 1786 against the Wabash tribes. In 1790 Sullivan was killed by Indians near Vincennes. He was decribed as "very stout [strong?] and very brave and every inch a soldier."

Thwaites/Kellogg, *Frontier Defense on the Upper Ohio 1777-1778.*

Sullivan, James, military officer (fl. 1769-1805). In 1769 or earlier, Sullivan settled on the west side of the Monongahela River, Virginia. In 1774 he served in Dunmore's Division in Lord Dunmore's War though the division was too late to take part in the October 10 Battle of Point Pleasant. Upon enlistment of the West Augusta, or 13th Virginia Regiment in 1776, Sullivan became one of its captains; in 1779 he served at Fort McIntosh at the mouth of Beaver Creek, 29 miles from Pittsburgh. In 1780 he removed to Kentucky, settling a station not far from Louisville. In George Rogers Clark's campaign that year against the Indian villages of Piqua, Ohio, Sullivan acted as master of horse; he was a captain in Clark's second operation against Piqua in 1782. Sullivan became quite wealthy as a land-owner at Louisville, and prominent in the community. He was a large, powerful man and very active. He died "early in the nineteenth century" near St. Louis at the home of his son, John C. Sullivan; another of his sons was named George Rogers Clark Sullivan.

Thwaites/Kellogg, *Frontier Defense on the Upper Ohio, 1777-1778.*

Surphlitt (Surplus), Robert (Robin), Indian man (fl. 1778-1803). A cousin of Alexander McKee, he fled Pittsburgh in company with McKee, Simon Girty and Matthew Elliott in March 1778, making for Detroit and the British side of the Revolutionary War. He was placed on the payroll of the Indian Department and used as a messenger to the Ohio tribesmen. Reduced to

half-pay after the conflict, he was pensioned in 1796 for services as "late lieutenant of the Western Indians." In 1803 he petitioned for a land grant, living at the time, he said, not far from the Niagara frontier.

Thwaites/Kellogg, *Frontier Defense on the Upper Ohio, 1777-1778.*

Swan, John, pioneer (fl. 1767-1770). B. in Loudoun County, Virginia, he settled with his family on the Potomac River and moved c. 1769 to the Monongahela River in Greene County, building a blockhouse there in 1770. Lieutenant John Swan, who served in William Harrod's company on George Rogers Clark's expedition, was probably his son. He served on the 1778 operation to Kaskaskia and may have gone out as captain on the 1780 campaign against the Shawnees. He may have been that son of John Swam who, taking his family to Kentucky, was shot and killed enroute down the Ohio River; otherwise nothing is reported on the later life of John Swan Jr.

Thwaites/Kellogg, *Frontier Defense on the Upper Ohio, 1777-1778.*

Sweeney, Martin A., frontiersman (c. 1845-June 23, 1878). B. in Massachusetts, he became a professional prizefighter and at 21, in 1865 enlisted in Company F, 14th U.S. Infantry, quickly becoming first sergeant. He may have seen Civil War service in a Masschusetts regiment, although evidence is lacking. Discharged from the army in 1868, he became a blacksmith on the Gila River reserve. In August 1874 he became clerk and major domo at an annual salary of $1,200 under Agent John P. Clum of the San Carlos, Arizona, Apache Reservation. Clum later wrote that Sweeney was of great help, terming him "honest, industrious, good-natured, fearless, he carried out my instructions almost before I issued them. His military training, plus his sympathetic understanding of Apache character, enabled him to teach military tactics to the Indians so that they not only learned how to drill, but enjoyed it, and became excellent soldiers." Clum's description is at variance with that of Henry Lyman Hart, a subsequent agent, who reported that Sweeney was "notoriously a drunkard, gambler, and a hard case generally," which may have been composed as a rationale for firing him, which he did. In 1877 when Clum brought the Warm Springs Apaches, including Geronimo and Victorio, from Ojo Caliente, New Mexico, to

San Carlos, Sweeney was placed in charge of the movement of the 453 Indians, which he did efficiently, the column arriving May 20. In July Clum, in a huff with superiors, resigned as agent, leaving Sweeney in temporary charge of the important reservation and recommending his appointment as agent; Sweeney, upon consideration however, turned down the job. From September 1872 he had had mining interests in the Tombstone, Arizona, vicinity. In 1878, either near Babocomari Creek northwest of Tombstone or at the Grand Central Mine at Tombstone, as Sheriff Charles Shibell believed, he was killed by Oliver Boyer, then going under the alias of Jack Friday (Boyer had an interest in the Grand Central Mine), who thereupon took off for Mexico. Banta said that he was retained by Shibell to go after Boyer, secured extradition papers from Governor Anson Safford, conducted a long and eventful search for him, caught up at length in Sonora and brought him back for trial. "He got twenty-five years; there were extenuating circumstances; Sweeney was known to be a tough character, although I knew he never used a shooting iron," Banta wrote. Sweeney was reported to be 5 ft., 8½ in. in height, stocky in build, with red or sandy hair and a ruddy complexion. He was not married.

Dan L. Thrapp, *Conquest of Apacheria,* Norman, Univ. of Okla. Press, 1967; *Victorio and the Mimbres Apaches,* Norman, 1974; Ralph Frederick Ogle, *Federal Control of the Western Apaches 1848-1886,* Albuquerque, Hist. Soc. of New Mex., 1940; *Albert Franklin Banta: Arizona Pioneer,* ed. by Frank D. Reeve, Albuquerque, HSNM, Vol. XIV, Sept. 1953, 70-71, 78-98.

Symonds, Frederick Martin, naval officer (May 16, 1846-Mar. 14, 1926). B. at Watertown, New York, he graduated from the Naval Academy in 1867, became an ensign December 18, 1868, a master March 21, 1870, and a lieutenant March 21, 1871. Symonds was an officer aboard the *Jamestown,* Captain Lester A. Beardslee (see entry) commanding, sent to Sitka, Alaska, in 1879 because of a threatened Indian uprising which, however, did not materialize. Symonds and Lieutenant Gustavus Hanus (see entry), both having worked for the Coast and Geodetic Survey, were described by Beardslee as "enthusiastic surveyors," and both had geographic features named for them because of their work on the expedition. Symonds, who had no other reported frontier experience of consequence, rose steadily to the rank of Rear Admiral December 1, 1902. He was married. He made his home after retirement at Galesville, Wisconsin.

Orth, 8, 938; *Who Was Who.*

T

Takmakov, fur trader (fl. 1797). A fur trading foreman for the Lebedev-Lastochin Company in Alaska, he was put in charge of a station including a fortification on Lake Iliamna at the northern end of the Alaska Peninsula. In 1797 it consisted of a palisade, surrounding earthen barracks and ancillary structures, staffed by about fifteen Russians and Kamchadals, with their families. "All of them were killed two or three years later," presumably by native Americans, according to Filipp Kashevarov who with Vasilii Medvednikov stopped there in 1797. Zagoskin saw some ruins there c. 1843, but the exact site of the place is not known today.

Pierce, *Russian America: A Biographical Dictionary.*

Talbot, Theodore, explorer, military officer (1825-Apr. 22, 1862). B. at Washington, D.C., according to Heitman, or in Kentucky as Bancroft believed, Talbot joined Fremont's second expedition west in 1843, keeping a careful journal of his travels and the events he witnessed. Bancroft reported Talbot was "a young man of good education." Thomas Fitzpatrick was guide for the first part of this expedition, with Kit Carson taking over for the western segments. The party went first to Oregon, then to Pyramid Lake on the east side of the Sierra Nevada, which was crossed into California and returned east, reaching St. Louis August 7, 1844. Talbot also took part in the third Fremont expedition, that of 1845-47 in which he went again to California. He was a trusted and responsible officer and, Bancroft reported, "in California acted as Fremont's confidential agent," sometimes commanding secondary parties whose missions were of some consequence. After leaving Bent's Fort, Fremont with 60 men explored the upper reaches of the Arkansas River and Great Salt Lake. Near the headwaters of the Humboldt River in Nevada the party was divided: Fremont with the smaller segment reached Walker Lake on Novemer 23, where the leader was joined by the other portion of his expedition, which Talbot led. Late in the month the expedition again split, with Fremont commanding a smaller segment and Talbot leading the larger element, guided by famed mountain man Joseph Reddeford Walker (see entry), "who had been met somewhere on the way as he was likely to be at any time or place in the great basin." This group, accompanied by Edward Meyer Kern (see entry) as topographer, left Walker Lake December 8, moving north to the west of Walker's 1843 route until on December 16, they reached the head of Owens River, named for Richard Owens of the Fremont party. They continued southward to the original Walker Pass, discovered by Joe in 1834, threaded it and reached the south branch of the Kern River, named for Edward Kern. They camped at the forks of that stream to await Fremont—who was waiting for them on the Kings' River, which he had mistaken for the Kern. The meeting finally came about at San Jose. When the insurrection against the Mexican rulers of California erupted, Talbot enlisted as sergeant major of Fremont's California Battalion July 23, 1846, becoming first lieutenant and adjutant August 8. In the fall of 1846 he with a detachment of nine men was stationed at Santa Barbara, and when Mexican forces demanded a surrender on parole, all ten escaped. They were experienced mountaineers and lurked in the range within sight of Santa Barbara for a week, hoping a man-of-war might appear and recapture the town. They then crossed into the interior valley and pushed on to Monterey, but only after severe hardships, Talbot reporting that "I suffered more from downright starvation, cold, nakedness, and every sort of privation than in any other trip I have yet made, and I have made some rough ones." The group arrived at Monterey November 8, and joined Fremont who had landed there from the *Sterling* an American ship. Talbot was honorably discharged from his California military service February 6, 1847. Commodore W(illiam) Bransford Shubrick (1790-1874), an officer of great experience, arrived to command naval forces on the Pacific coast early in 1847, succeeding Stockton, who had gone east. Shubrick sided with Kearny in the latter's conflict with Fremont over authority in California. February 13, he sent dispatches to Washington with Talbot, who reached the capital June 3, 1847. He did not return to California, but testified in Fremont's defense at the officer's court-martial of April 7, 1848, on charges of mutiny, disobedience of lawful command of his superior officer, and conduct to the prejudice of good order and military discipline, the specifications to the charges listed in Bancroft (*California* V, 456n.). Fremont was found guilty on all charges. Talbot was commissioned a second lieutenant of the 22nd Artillery to date from May 22, 1847, and became a first lieutenant September 22, 1848, remaining in that rank until April 27, 1861. On March 16, he had become brevet captain, assistant adjutant general, on July 3, brevet major and August 3, major assistant adjutant general. He died at Washington, D.C.

Heitman; Bancroft, *California,* IV, V, *Pioneer Register;* Robert V. Hine, *Edward Kern and American Expansion,* New Haven, Yale Univ. Press, 1962; info. from E.F. (Ted) Mains.

Talbot(t), Jim (James D. Sherman, James Daniels), gunman (d. Aug. 1896). B. in DeKalb County, Missouri, Talbot, or Sherman (or James Sherman Talbot, which may have been his true name), was once described in a wanted circular as well-built, light complexioned, blond hair and whiskers, pale blue eyes, a note adding that he "generally gambles and carouses around saloons. He is wanted in several places for horse stealing and shooting men. Is a bad outlaw." He was reported to be related through his mother to William Tecumseh Sherman, although confirmation is wanting. Bat Masterson wrote that Talbot was "courageous as a lion," but although a fine pistol shot, once emptied his gun at a St. Louis dentist "without as much as puncturing his clothes [because he] forgot that there were a set of sights on his pistol." He had believed the dentist had insulted his wife. Talbot was wanted at Albany, Texas, for killing a man (one lawman said he heard Talbot had murdered a man and woman elsewhere in Texas) and in 1881 was working for the "toughest cow outfit in Texas," a ranch owned by brothers Alonzo (Lon), Eugene (Cap) and Hyrum (Hie, or Hy) Millett on the Brazos River in Baylor County. Lawmen caught up with him and others there and in a shootout Talbot was slightly wounded, Shackelford County Deputy Sheriff Henry Herron was shot through the hip by a Winchester bullet and his horse killed; Sheriff Green Simpson was shot through both arms, and a deputy sheriff named Perry was shot "five times in various parts of his body, none being fatal." One other man was slightly wounded. Talbot threatened to finish off Herron, but

was dissuaded. In the fall of 1881 the Milletts sold their ranch to W.E. Hughes and John N. Simpson and made up their final trail herd for Kansas, a drive on which Talbot had a role, along with Tom Love (see entry), John Cook as foreman (his real name was Crusaw Baird), and five others. The cattle arrived at Caldwell in November, Talbot intending to settle there, and obtaining a house for his wife and two children. In December a Caldwell banker, J.S. Danford, abandoned bank and the town in a great hurry, and disgruntled depositors offered a reward to anyone bringing him back. Talbot returned Danford at gunpoint and when "one mourner said he would give $25 to anyone that would shoot him," Talbot cocked his pistol. The prize offer was hastily withdrawn and even when Jim offered to do the banker in for only $20 it was not renewed. On the night of December 16, Talbot and rambunctious friends attended a play and "became so loud and obscene as to disturb the whole house," the next day continuing with the aid of George Spears, a local sport, to tree the town. City Marshal John Wilson with the aid of several citizens, including former mayor and erstwhile lawman Mike Meagher (see entry) attempted to quiet the uproar. Skirmishes culminated in a gun battle in which Meagher was killed by Talbot and Spears also was slain. Talbot was credited by one of his opponents with great bravery during this fight and as "a bold and fearless man and a desperado who recognized cowardice as a crime." Those followers of Talbot who could get mounted fled, making for Indian Territory, closely pursued by posses which could not catch them. January 12, 1882, the gunmen presented their side of the story in a letter to the Kansas City *Times,* asserting they had been "basely misrepresented [as] cutthroats" in screaming stories in much of the Kansas press; the cowboys blamed John Wilson for initiating the imbroglio, stating he was on "a protracted drunk" when he did so. The letter was signed by Talbot and four of his associates. Outlawed now in Kansas as well as Texas, Talbot went to California, where he cowboyed under the name of James D. Sherman and by 1889 was foreman of the Marks and Newfield ranch in Mendocino County, north of San Francisco. In a drunken debate over the "fast draw" Talbot that year killed a man at Ukiah, the county seat. He was cleared by a coroner's jury on self-defense, but was formally tried later and sentenced to San Quentin prison; the California Supreme Court gave him a new trial, but Kansas authorities extradited him for the earlier Meagher slaying. A trial in April 1895 ended in a hung jury and a later trial acquitted him. He returned to California to find his wife had run off with Bryce Vallele; Talbot hunted the two up, brought his wife back, but in August 1896 was shot and killed from ambush. Vallele was suspected, but Talbot had plenty of other enemies and his slayer was never apprehended.

R.K. DeArment, "Toughest Cow Outfit in Texas," Part II, *True West*, Vol. 38, No. 5 (May 1991), 22-26; Nyle H. Miller, Joseph W. Snell, *Why the West Was Wild*, Topeka, Kansas State Hist. Soc., 1963.

Taliaferro, Laurence, military officer, Indian agent (Feb. 28, 1794-Jan. 22, 1871) The spelling of his first name is given with a "u" by Heitman and army records, but with a "w" by the *Dictionary of American Biography*. He was b. in King George County, Virginia, of a distinguished family, was well educated and enlisted at 18, August 5, 1812, in a light infantry volunteers company. He became an ensign in the 1st U.S. Infantry July 2, 1813, a second lieutenant August 14, 1813, first lieutenant June 30, 1814, and transferred to the 3rd Infantry May 17, 1815. With that regiment he served at various frontier posts. When Fort Snelling, as it came to be called, was established in Minnesota at the confluence of the Mississippi and St. Peter's (Minnesota) rivers for protection of the fur trade, to prevent British encroachment, encourage settlement and safeguard the interests and welfare of Sioux and Chippewa Indians, it was necessary to add to the staff of the post a civilian Indian agent. President James Monroe "personally selected Lawrence Taliaferro and commissioned him Indian agent" March 27, 1820, in preparation for which duty he resigned from the Army April 1, 1819, although retaining his rank. For seven years his jurisdiction embraced both the Sioux and Chippewa, but in 1827 the latter came under the Sault Sainte Marie agency while the Sioux remained under Taliaferro's supervision. For twenty years "Taliaferro was the most important and influential civil official on the upper Mississippi." Folwell wrote that the agent had "two qualifications for dealing with red men: one, absolute truthfulness; the other, a tolerance of Indian fondness for gaudy apparel, ceremonial, and oratory." He added that "it is to his credit that he was cordially hated by all who could neither bribe nor frighten him to connive at lawbreaking to the harm of Indians. In spite of complaints and machinations

of traders and politicians he held his place until 1839, when he voluntarily resigned after a sixth appointment—a fact as creditable to four presidents, their cabinets, and the Indian Office as to the incorruptible and high-toned Virginian." In keeping perhaps with his state's tradition, he brought to Minnesota a number of black slaves. He gave his servant girl, Harriet Robinson, in marriage to Dred Scott, plaintiff in the celebrated U.S. Supreme Court case, and Taliaferro himself performed the nuptial ceremony. "Later he emancipated all his servants, at a time when, as he estimated, their money value would have been twenty-five or thirty thousand dollars." There were frequent clashes between Sioux and Chippewas during his tenure, with casualties on both sides, this making "his position anything but a sinecure [and] his endeavors to keep peace …were earnest and often successful, for the Indians came to believe that [he] was their friend and protector." In one clash the Sioux, who were the aggressors, had small loss but the Chippewas suffered 21 killed and 29 wounded. The reasons for his eventual resignation are not clear, perhaps not even to Taliaferro, but they are given by Folwell as: firstly, the Indian Office had "failed to enable him to fulfill treaty stipulations, thereby discrediting him with the Indians." Secondly, "he had been kept in the dark as to the views and intentions of that office, when the American Fur Company [always his most bitter enemy] or individuals connected with it, had been well informed in advance," in the third place, "he had not been so well provided as other agents," even to having to himself supply presents for the Indians, and "finally, 'from the fault' of the Indian Office, he had been threatened with assassination," although details of that interesting suggestion are not given. In the summer of 1839 he resigned and left the Indian country, as well as a quarter-breed daughter, born August 17, 1828, who was educated at his expense at a local mission school; she married a former soldier and lived for a time at West St. Paul. In the Great Sioux Uprising of 1862 she was captured by hostiles and not retaken for six weeks. In the summer of 1828 Taliaferro married Eliza Dillon, daughter of a Bedford, Pennsylvania, hotel keeper; she accompanied him to St. Peter's Agency. They had no children. Most of Taliaferro's time after 1840 was spent at Bedford. March 14, 1857, he re-entered the army as a military store-keeper of the Quartermaster Department and served at San Antonio, Fort Leavenworth, Pittsburgh and Bedford. Virginia-born and former slave-holder (although he voluntarily freed his slaves), he was an ardent Union man during the Civil War. He retired August 27, 1863, and died at Bedford, survived by his widow. A great quantity—although not all, some having been lost—of his journals and other papers are held by the Minnesota Historical Society of St. Paul.

William Watts Folwell, *A History of Minnesota,* Vol. I, St. Paul, Minn. Hist. Soc., 1956; Heitman; DAB.

Talizhnik, Nikifor, interpreter (fl. 1843-44). A Creole b. in California, he acquired certain skills of the Californians and some mastery of a native tongue from his mother, who may have been an Aleut. He was a member of the staff at Fort St. Michael on Norton Sound when on June 4, 1843, he became interpreter for Zagoskin, whose principal interpreter, Kurochkin, was disabled. Talizhnik, Zagoskin wrote, "knew the [Eskimo] language of the coast and was quick at understanding all native dialects." He was somewhat less than perfect, however. Zagoskin in his journal wrote that "I shall not here include the interpreter's account of how shamans heal with spells and witchcraft, because whenever the interpreter does not understand he interprets on his own, consequently often wrongly." But Talizhnik occasionally was of help. Zagoskin considered it "my duty" to explain how he elicited information on Athabascan Indians in the upper Innoko River: "Every answer to my questions was given to Vtornik [who had been hired as a guide to interior Alaska], who told it to [Talizhnik], who told it to me. Thus even a perfectly accurate piece of information could be distorted through the oral transfer between interpreters who barely understood each other." On one occasion on the upper Yukon, a coastal-type dog approached camp, its face and mouth full of porcupine quills. It was too fearful to come up of its own volition, but "Talizhnik, skilled Californian *vaquero* that he is, lassoed it," the quills were extracted and the dog recovered. His owner later was found "and he was exremely grateful to us" for having saved the valuable animal. Zagoskin makes no further entry on Talizhnik, and Kurochkin soon rejoined the expedition.

Zagoskin.

Tarakanov, Timofei Osipovich, foreman of sea otter hunters (fl. 1802-1820). Described by Pierce as "a man of unusual talent," he may have survived the Tlingit attack on Sitka in 1802 when all the Russians the Indians could catch were slain. In 1803 when Boston sea captain Joseph O'Cain (see entry) arranged a deal with Baranov to "borrow" Aleut sea-otter hunters for an expedition down the Pacific coast, Tarakanov and Afanasii Shvetsov (see entry) were assigned to lead the hunting crews with their twenty baidarkas. The ship left Kodiak Island October 26, took 1,100 otters off California and O'Cain purchased about 700 additional pelts from missionaries and Spanish authorities, the crew returning in June 1804. On October 25, 1806, Tarakanov left with Captain Oliver Kimball in the *Peacock* and twelve baidarkas, the party returning to Sitka August 3, 1807, after a successful hunt. September 29, 1808, Baranov sent Tarakanov with hunters on the schooner *Nikolai,* Captain Nikolai Bulygin (see entry) in an attempt to trade with Indians at the mouth of the Columbia River; the *Nikolai* was wrecked on Destruction Island off the Washington coast and Tarakanov was enslaved by neighboring Indians with other survivors. Many, including Bulygin and his wife, died at the hands of the Indians, but Tarakanov, "a man of initiative and ingenuity," gained the confidence of his captors and May 10, 1810, a Captain Brown rescued him and others still alive and returned them to Sitka June 9. Tarakanov was sent out again that month, with his Aleuts was hunting off San Francisco Bay and reached Sitka again sometime in 1812. Pierce believes that the Bancroft account of Tarakanov in California and Hawaii thereafter is an Ivan Petrov fraud, but thinks that for the next several years "he must have been resident at Fort Ross [above San Francisco] or at Sitka." February 9, 1818, Tarakanov was named supercargo on the *Otkrytie,* a Russian American Company vessel sent to Hawaii to unravel the tangle that had resulted from the efforts of Scheffer (see entry) to obtain Russian control of the islands, but nothing much was accomplished. In April 1820 Tarakanov was sent from Sitka to Okhotsk, Siberia, and thence overland to St. Petersburg to report to the main RAC office about the Hawaiian affair, and he may never have returned to Alaska. Nothing definite has been learned about his life in later years or anything of the date and circumstances of his death.

Pierce, *Russian America: A Biographical Dictionary.*

Taylor, Charles, sea-captain (fl. 1829-1832). A ship's captain out of Boston, Taylor with the *Vol-*

unteer left Honolulu February 13, 1829, reached Sitka March 11, then traded down the Alaskan Panhandle as far as the Queen Charlotte Islands, eventually reaching Kaigani on the south end of Dall Island. There the Haida Indians (a division of the Tlingits) attacked the *Volunteer* for reasons not specified, several of the crew were wounded and "a number" of the attackers killed. Taylor took five Indians hostage and August 31, turned them over to the Russians at Sitka, their disposition unknown, although Pierce believed "they may have been returned to Kaigani." Taylor from 1830 captained the brig *Griffon* on the Pacific coast, she having varying fortune in sea otter hunting and Taylor returning with her to Hawaii in September 1832. Nothing further is reported of Taylor.

Pierce, *Russian America: A Biographical Dictionary;* Ogden.

Taylor, Hancock, frontiersman (d. c. 1774). An uncle of President Zachary Taylor, Hancock Taylor in 1769 was with a party of explorers to the Falls of the Ohio River (Louisville, Kentucky). From there the group floated down the Mississippi River to New Orleans and returned to the Atlantic colonies by sea. In 1773 Taylor was surveying in Kentucky, accompanying James, Robert and George McAfee and Captain Thomas Bullitt. Taylor was leader of a surveying party sent out in the spring of 1774 by William Preston, but was shot by Indians and died on Taylor's Fork of Silver Creek in Madison County, Kentucky.

Thwaites, *Dunmore.*

Taylor, Thomas Ulvan, engineer, historical writer (Jan. 2, 1858-May 28, 1941). B. in Parker County, Texas, he attended Carlton College at Bonham and was graduated from Sam Houston State College (now University) at Huntsville, then received civil engineering degrees from the University of Virginia in 1883 and from Cornell University, Ithaca, New York, in 1895. He began teaching at the University of Texas in 1888, persuaded it to open a School of Engineering and became its dean in 1896, remaining such until 1930. He retired in 1937 but continued to teach some classes thereafter. Most of his professional life was spent teaching engineering subjects and most of his writing was on technical engineering matters, but he also became intensely interested in Texas history and produced numerous articles and several books in that field. Among them

were: *Bill Longley and His Wild Career* (n.d.), which Adams considered "a fairly accurate account which the author culled from contemporary newspapers, state records, and interviews with personal friends of the outlaw," adding that it was "scarce." Taylor also wrote *The Chisholm Trail and Other Routes* (1936), and *Jesse Chisholm* (c. 1939). Among his shorter pieces was one on the Lee-Peacock feud, which appeared in *Frontier Times,* Volume 3, No. 8 (May 1926), 19-28, and Volume 5, No. 6 (March 1928), 252-53; later it was reprinted as an 18-page pamphlet by *Frontier Times;* Adams also lists it as scarce. Taylor wrote a book of reminiscences, or a partial autobiography, *Fifty Years on Forty Acres* (1938). Taylor died at Austin, Texas, survived by his widow and a daughter; a son had predeceased him.

Frontier Times, Vol. 18, No. 10 (July 1941), 431-32; HT.

Tebenkov, Mikhail Dmitrievich, naval officer, administrator (1802-Apr. 3, 1872). B. in Russia, he entered the navy and became a midshipman in 1821. In January 1825 he joined the Russian American Company and went to Sitka, Alaska, being promoted to lieutenant, commanded various ships and from 1829 to 1831 surveyed Norton Sound and the Alexander Archipelago. Tebenkov Bay of Norton Sound was named for him, as was Fort St. Michael, established by another in 1833. Returning to St Petersburg, Tebenkov served in the Russian American Company's headquarters until 1835, then took the company ship *Elena* to Sitka, arriving April 16, 1836, remaining overseas until 1840 when, with the rank of Captain-Lieutenant, he returned to St. Petersburg, left the company and navy and worked at civilian pursuits until January 26, 1844, when he rejoined the navy. April 24, he was promoted to Captain, Second Rank and was named chief manager of the Russian American Company, taking over from Etolin on July 6, reaching Sitka September 1. In 1848, hearing of the gold discovery in California, Tebenkov had the company warehouses ransacked for old goods and sent a cargo to San Francisco along with a mining engineer. The cargo sold quickly and in about three months the Russian party washed out eleven pounds of gold form the Yuba River and with the proceeds the Russians bought a good Bremen ship. In 1849 Tebenkov sent a second cargo which also sold well, but a third cargo in 1850 found the California outlets well stocked and sold only partially. The cargo included three prefabricated houses, built at Sitka. Tebenkov found increasing supply difficulties for the Russian colonies, with west coast interests focused on California gold, but the company's commercial transactions proved profitable in Hawaii for the first time. Tebenkov's relationships with Tlingit and other natives were good, but a measles epidemic in 1848 inflicted casualties among many of them, although the Tlingits suffered less than others. Tebenkov pushed explorations of the interior of Alaska as much as he could. In 1846 he sent an expedition up the Yukon from Nulato, and in 1847 sent a party under Ensign Rufus Serebrennikov (see entry), a Creole, up the Copper River with instructions to reach the Yukon, if he could. The party started with three baidarkas from the mouth of the Copper August 14, 1847, wintered at the mouth of the Chitina River, in the spring worked farther up the Copper, but June 25, Indians killed Serebrennikov and three of his party, although an Indian brought Serebrennikov's journal and notebooks to Tebenkov that the valuable geographical information gained would not be lost. Tebenkov was very active, improving shipping and the various mills near Sitka and directing construction of churches and community buildings. He also supervised preparation of an atlas of the Pacific coast, the plates engraved at Sitka and taken to St. Petersburg for publication, it proving one of the most valuable works of its kind and useful for many years. October 14, 1850, Tebenkov concluded his five-year term as chief manager and relinquished the position to his successor, Nikolai Iakovlevish Rosenberg. He returned to Russia March 18, 1851, and resumed naval duties, rising at length to Vice Admiral, twelve years before his death.

Richard A. Pierce, *Builders of Alaska: The Russian Governors, 1818-1867,* Kingston, Ont., Limestone Press, 1986; Bancroft, *Alaska;* Zagoskin.

Teedyuscung, Delaware chief (c. 1705-Apr. 19, 1763). B. near Trenton, New Jersey, Teedyuscung, whose name translates as "he who makes the earth tremble," was the son of Captain Harris, a noted Delaware, and in early manhood moved from the Trenton area to the Forks (the confluence of the Delaware and Lehigh rivers near Easton), Pennsylvania. The Indians settled at the Forks considered themselves a separate entity from other Delawares and their chief was Nutimus, although he was not as tractable as

another Delaware named Sassonan, who soon was supported successfully by whites as head chief of that people. Sassonan died in 1747. Teedyuscung gradually emerged as a leading man among these eastern Delawares and "being shrewd and cunning played a game of diplomacy between the Iroquois, the Ohio Indians, and the authorities of Pennsylvania." The Iroquois, or Six Nations, had militarily dominated the fractured Delawares to the point of virtual suzerainty over them; the Ohio Delawares were a large segment of the tribe whose principle center was Logtown, eighteen miles below the forks of the Ohio River where Fort Duquesne was located, and the Pennsylvania officials by now had little interest in maintaining the fairness and good relations established by William Penn (1644-1718) and were much less scrupulous in their dealings with Indians. The famed "Walking Purchase" agreement was a case in point. By this deed, signed August 25, 1737, implementing a 1686 royal document, the Delawares were brazenly cheated out of a large segment of territory along the Delaware River from Wrightstown, above Philadelphia, northward to the Forks, and inland to the vicinity of present Reading. By the mid-1770s Moravian missionaries had established a center, Gnadenhutten (their first village of that name) near the present Lehighton, where their work with the eastern Delawares was concentrated. Teedyuscung was converted and he and his family baptized by the missionary Christian Post (see entry) in 1750; the Indian spoke English well, the first name of Gideon was bestowed upon him and he acquired the nickname of "Honest John." Because of his developing diplomatic skills his influence and fame spread, although on April 24, 1754, he and 65 others left the mission, re-establishing themselves at Wyoming, on the Susquehanna River between the present Scranton and Wilkes-Barre. In 1755 during the French and Indian War and following the Braddock debacle he was cajoled by Shingas (see entry) of the Ohio Delawares, a famed and implacable raider, to come over to the French side and join in ravaging the Pennsylvania frontier. For some time Teedyuscung and his Moravian Indians remained neutral, but the temptation to war proved great, particularly in view of the successes of Shingas. Eventually Teedyuscung half-heartedly seceded from the "neutralists" and joined the faction of the Susquehannas now raiding in concert with Shingas and for French interests. He gathered followers, called himself a war captain, in the winter of 1755 organized a raiding party of thirty men which "included three of his sons, three half-brothers and a nephew," fell upon a white settlement and returned to Wyoming January 3, 1756, with prisoners, scalps and loot. Finding the town deserted and fearing English reprisal, Teedyuscung led his people and their prisoners north to Tunkannock, then to Tioga to the northwest, and still later to a tributary of the Chemung River. He headed no more raids and turned his attention to negotiations and diplomacy which were, in any event, his long suit. After the English success at Kittanning, northeast of Fort Pitt, on September 8, 1756, Teedyuscung "of his own volition and completely independent of the Six Nations... entered into peace negotiations with [Pennsylvania Governor] Robert Hunter Morris, and with William Denny who succeeded Morris...in August of 1756." A truce was concluded at Easton and the chief and 300 of his people were enteretained at a "sumptuous dinner at which an armistice was proclaimed with the Susquehanna Delawares." He brought leadership, which had been lacking, to the eastern Delawares. He brought councilors and his own interpreter to conferences, even though he himself could speak English. He was unique in demanding his own clerk to record minutes of the meetings. At a peace conference he claimed to speak not only for the Delawares, but also for ten other tribes, including members of the Six Nations to whom he was supposed to be subservient. He proclaimed himself "the kind of Delaware king [spokesman] that a succession of English governors had long sought. He maintained that the Delawares were now independent of the Six Nations," observing that "formerly we were Accounted women [by the Iroquois] but now they have made men of us." Teedyuscung personally had no birthright claim to chieftainship; in his younger days he had supported himself as a broom- and basket-maker, but now he believed he had soared to new heights, insisting that he spoke not only for the ten tribes he previously had listed, but for eight additional, including even the distant Ottawas and Chippewas, which naturally strained credulity. He had some slight weaknesses, as his addiction to alcohol, claiming to be able to down a gallon of rum in a single day and even if that were exaggeration, he could come close to it. He loved finery. When attending conferences with the governor he was "resplendent in a gold-laced coat, riding boots

with silver shoe buckles, checkered cloth breeches, and stockings with scarlet gartering." He had won the moral and financial support of influential Philadelphia Quakers and that added to his prestige. He became the pawn of Pennsylvania political factions, was used by one element against another for ends far removed from Indian welfare, and probably was ignorant of the uses to which he was manipulated. The motives of all sides were clouded in any case, and complicated by such factors as the unwelcome migration into Pennsylvania of Connecticut Valley settlers. Teedyuscung had long since moved back to Wyoming, where he sought unavailingly to secure valid legal land titles to the properties on which his people had settled. The Philadelphia government felt it could not award such documents since the land was claimed by the Six Nations, with whom friendly relations were vital. Then on an April evening in 1763 Teedyuscung was murdered as he lay asleep (in a drunken stupor from liquor given him by his assailants, as was charged) and his house was burned over him; surrounding buildings also were lost to flames and Wyoming quickly reduced to ashes. Thwaites wrote, "The Iroquois, who were the guilty party, threw the obloquy upon the Connecticut settlement whereupon Teedyuscung's followers murdered all the band," but he does not say whether he meant the band of Iroquois or that of the Connecticut settlers.

Clinton A. Weslager, *The Delaware Indians: A History,* New Brunswick, N.J., Rutgers Univ. Press, 1972; Paul A.W. Wallace, ed., *Thirty Thousand Miles With John Heckewelder,* Univ. of Pittsburgh Press, 1958; Thwaites, EWT, I, 186-87n.

Terrell, John Upton, historical writer (Dec. 9, 1900-Dec. 1, 1988). B. at Chicago he became a newspaper reporter, a Washington and a war correspondent, before turning to the writing of books, initially fiction and later nonfiction dealing largely with frontier subjects. He also wrote more than a dozen juvenile books, most concerned with branches of the government and their workings. Among his adult nonfiction books dealing with American history were: *Journey Into Darkness* (1962); *Furs By Astor* (1963); *Black Robe: The Life of Pierre-Jean De Smet* (1964); *War for the Colorado River,* 2 vols. (1965); with George Walton, *Faint the Trumpet Sounds: The Life and Trial of Major Reno* (1966); *Traders of the Western Morning: Aboriginal Commerce in Pre-Columbian North*

America (1967); *The Six Turnings: Major Changes in the American West, 1806-1834* (1968); *Zebulon Pike* (1968); *Estevánico the Black* (1968); *LaSalle* (1968); *The Man Who Rediscovered America: John Wesley Powell* (1969; *Navajos* (1970); *Land Grab: The Truth About the "Winning of the West"* (1972); *Pueblos, Gods and Spaniards* (1973), and *The Plains Apache* (1975). Terrell was married (his wife predeceased him) and died at Upland, California. He was buried at Pomona, California.

Contemporary Authors; Terrell death certificate.

Tetherow, Solomon, frontiersman (1800-Feb. 1879). B. in East Tennessee, he lived for a time in Alabama and Missouri and at 21 married Ibba Baker. He accompanied Ashley (see entry) in 1822 up the Missouri and Yellowstone rivers. Subsequently Tetherow operated a keelboat on the Missouri to Council Bluffs, Iowa, which then was a trading post of the American Fur Company. He was a pilot on the first steamboat on the upper Mississippi. Tetherow afterward migrated to Texas, but finding that a "sickly country," returned to Missouri. During the large migration to Oregon in 1845 Tetherow was elected at Independence captain of a 66-wagon train of about 300 persons. According to Bancroft nothing unusual occurred between the Missouri and the Snake rivers, while at Fort Hall efforts were made, in part by British interests seeking to stem the tide of immigration to Oregon, to turn parties from the Northwest to California, but Tetherow and the bulk of his people persevered on the original course. Tetherow settled on the Creole River where Dallas later was founded. In 1847 Governor George Abernethy of Oregon attempted to get Joseph Meek to carry an important dispatch to the military governor of California, Richard B. Mason, but it being mid-winter and Meek being all too familiar with the deep snows in the mountains between Oregon and California, turned down the request; the governor then named Jesse Applegate (see entry) to carry the dispatch. Applegate enlisted sixteen men, among them Solomon Tetherow, and set out about February 1, but the attempt was futile, either on horseback or with improvised snowshoes. The company was forced to return, Applegate referring to Tetherow as his "faithful and valued friend and helper" on the expedition. Tetherow became a well-known Oregon pioneer, settling at length at Luckiamute, in Polk County, where he died at about 79, survived by his children.

Bancroft, *Oregon, I,* 509-10, 679n.; Keith Clark, Lowell Tiller, *Terrible Trail: The Meek Cutoff, 1845,* Caldwell, Idaho, Caxton Printers, 1966.

Tikhanov, Mikhail, artist (c. 1789-Oct. 6, 1852). He was b. a serf of Prince Golitsyn, but his artistic talent was discovered at an early age and at 17 he won a scholarship at the Academy of Art at St. Petersburg, Russia, where he studied particularly historical painting. He soon was relieved from his serf status and in May 1817 was recommended for Golovnin's round-the-world voyage, being assigned to the sloop *Kamchatka.* Forty-three of his paintings are preserved in an album in the Academy of Arts Museum at Leningrad, nineteen of them made in Alaska and five in California. Tikhanov's Alaskan pictures include portraits of aborigines of the Aleutians, Kodiak, Sitka and elsewhere, and "careful portrayal of clothing, ornamentation and weapons make these watercolors an indispensable ethnographic source." One was of "Toion [Chief] Nankok of Kodiak," a leader who helped retake Sitka in 1804. At Sitka Tikhanov also painted "Katlean [Katleian], a Kolosh toion from Sitkha Island," the only portrait of the famed leader of the attack of 1802 which wiped out the Russian colony there. Tikhanov in addition sketched the celebrated Baranov, a picture which is the basis for other famed portraitures of the man responsible for the early successes of the Russian American Company in Alaska. In September 1819 the expedition returned to Kronstadt, but Tikhanov's health had so deteriorated that he "never was capable of creative work again." He died at 74.

Pierce, *Russian America: A Biographical Dictionary.*

Tikhmenev, Petr Aleksandrovich, Russian naval officer, historian (d. Sept. 7, 1888). B. in Russia he joined the Imperial Navy, was commissioned and in the early 1850s sailed with the frigate *Pallada* from Kronstadt to the Far East. From 1857 he served with the Russian American Company as naval officers were permitted to do. Although not an academically-trained scholar he became "the first great student of the [Alaskan] region and of the Russian American Company in particular." When he determined to write a history of the firm, company officials gave him every assistance, and he completed his two-volume work in five years. It was translated into English and published in 1978 as *A History of the Russian-American Company.* While he did not treat in depth with political or personnel problems or foreign policy matters, the publication "remains a monumental pioneering work which must be consulted by every scholar interested in Russia's American colonies."

Zagoskin; *The Russian American Colonies.*

Timberlake, Henry, military officer, ethnologist (1730-Sept. 30, 1765). B. in Hanover County, north of Richmond, Virginia, he joined a militia regiment commanded by George Washington in 1756. Two years later he served in the expedition of John Forbes (see entry) against Fort Duquesne (Pittsburgh) in the Colonel William Byrd III regiment, having been appointed to a cornetcy of horse (a commissioned rank of cornet; this was the fifth grade of commissioned officer, just below an ensign, in a British cavalry troop, a cornet being the individual who carried the standard). Brigadier General John Stanwix who over the ruins of Fort Duchesne had built the sturdier Fort Pitt in 1759, named Timberlake to command Fort Necessity in Fayette County, Pennsylvania. In early 1761 Timberlake was ordered to rejoin Byrd's regiment to operate against Cherokee Indians then besieging British Fort Loudon on the Little Tennessee River. Peace was made with the Cherokees November 19, 1761, the Indians requesting that an officer visit their towns in their own country. Timberlake, now an ensign, volunteered and left on a 22-day journey to the Cherokee towns, enroute, while traveling by skiff down the Holston and up the Little Tennessee, making notes on the courses of these rivers and later executing an excellent map showing the streams, Indian towns, naming the chief or "governor" of each and "what Number of Fighting Men they send to War" (the map is reproduced by Randolph between pp. 144-45). Timberlake spent three months with the Indians, then returned to Virginia with a large party of them. In May, Timberlake, two other whites and three Cherokees including the chief, Outacite or Mankiller (Wootassite, Wrosetasatow, etc.), Ostenaco, and Uschesees, went to England, Timberlake probably financing the trip himself. At London large crowds gathered to see the Cherokees and Timberlake was criticized for charging the public to observe the Indians, though he may have felt he had to recoup his expenses in some way. He was commissioned a lieutenant for his work with the Cherokees and married an English woman. The Indians shortly returned to America and Timberlake followed at a later date, rejoining his regiment but was soon retired on half-pay, the Virginia Council refusing to reimburse him for his expenses in the Cherokee country. In 1764 he took a second party of Indians to London and then attempted to make good his losses by writing his *Memoirs,* heavily dependent upon his observations and knowledge of Cherokee culture. His narrative describes the difficult journey to Chota, leading town of the Overhill Cherokees, and the enthusiastic welcome everywhere extended to him. He described in detail the personal adornment of men and women. He was particularly interested in warfare practices, mentioning that cruelty of the women toward prisoners was worse than the fighting. He witnessed ceremonies and many dances, including the pantomime enactment of a bear hunt. He revealed details of some of the dances he observed and understood, no doubt with the help of an unnamed interpreter who traveled with him. "As to religion," Timberlake wrote, "every one is at liberty to think for himself...but the major part do not give themselves that trouble. They generally concur, however, in the belief of one superior Being, who made them, and governs all things..." He discussed their crafts, including the making of canoes, houses and Town Houses, or community structures, and discussed food preparation and supplies which were of considerable variety. He described hunting and fishing methods, the organization of their society and alluded to the women occasionally taking part in war expeditions, thereby gaining unusual respect. He considered the Cherokees a "hardy" people, many of whom lived to a great age, and although he was not impressed with the durability of many marriages, some did last for a lifetime and Cherokee women married to white soldiers were loyal to their men, even in time of war. Timberlake may have died before his book was published and in any event did not profit from its great popularity, but "he left to posterity one of the best accounts of the southeastern Indians to be written during the colonial period of American history." The book is considered by ethnologists as "dependable source material," because of Timberlake's diligence and also the deep knowledge and considerable skill of his interpreter(s). The work was quickly translated into German and French and has been reprinted in this country as late as 1948.

J. Ralph Raymond, *British Travelers Among the Southern Indians, 1660-1763,* Norman, Univ. of Okla. Press, 1973; DAB.

Timothy (Tamootsin, Timosa, Tammutsa), Nez Perce chief (c. 1808-post 1874). A Nez Perce village chief whose center was at Alpowa, meaning "the place where the Sabbath is observed." It was on the Snake River below the confluence of the Clearwater, in western Idaho. Timothy was "one of [the Protestant missionary Henry H.] Spalding's first converts, and was without a doubt the most faithful and sincere of native Christians." He and Spalding met at the 1836 Green River trapper rendezvous and Timothy became impressed with the missionary, invited him to stay at Alpowa while looking for a site for the first mission station among the Nez Perces. Timothy guided him to Lapwai, which Spalding selected as the place for the mission to be established. The missionary organized there the First Presbyterian Church of Oregon Territory and on November 17, 1839, "Timothy Timosa, a native of considerable influence, some 31 years of age," was baptized and commenced farming a small acreage in the Lapwai Valley. Timothy's wife, Tamar, also joined the church later. Timothy proved a faithful convert and a lifelong friend of Spalding, counseling him about the Indian mind and affairs, helping him at every turn, eventually becoming an elder of the church, and greatly assisting Spalding in learning the Nez Perce language to the point where he preached fluently in it. When another prominent missionary, Marcus Whitman, his wife, Narcissa, and others were felled in the notorious Whitman massacre at Waiilatpu Mission in Washington Territory on November 29, 1847, Timothy engaged in the pursuit of the ringleader of the Cayuse perpetrators, Tiloukaikt, although the effort was unsuccessful and the Cayuse, taken by other means, was hanged with four others of the assaulting party. Timothy for a time operated a ferry across the Snake River not far from Alpowa; he was of material assistance to Major Edward Steptoe in his 1858 Palouse expedition into the present Washington state, transporting the expedition across the river and, with a score of followers, serving as guide and scout for the military operation into country imperfectly known to whites and poorly mapped. Timothy was in no way responsible for the disaster which befell Steptoe's command near the present town of Rosalia, but succeeded in guiding the defeated command out of danger in their withdrawal. Steptoe gave the Nez Perces much credit for their help. Timothy's daughter, Jane (1842-1895), who had fallen in love with a white man, John

Silcott (and later married him), against the wishes of Timothy had in 1860 guided white prospectors to Orofino, Idaho, where the first important gold discovery in Idaho was made. It ignited a stampede which brought the evils Timothy and others of the Nez Perce had dreaded. In 1868 Timothy, with the noted chiefs, Lawyer and Jason, were taken to Washington, D.C., where on August 13, they signed a treaty modifying one of 1863. The new pact provided certain advantages for the United States, although it was not a major document. The final reference to Timothy uncovered thus far was in May 1874 when he rode horseback to see Spalding, who was on his death bed; the chief did this out of affection for the missionary whose teachings he had fully accepted and whose friendship he treasured.

Clifford M. Drury, *The Diaries and Letters of Henry H. Spalding and Asa Bowen Smith Relating to the Nez Perce Mission 1838-1842,* Glendale, Calif., Arthur H. Clark Co., 1958; Drury, *Marcus and Narcissa Whitman and the Opening of Old Oregon,* 2 vols., Glendale, Clark, 1973; Robert G. Bailey, *River of No Return: Historical Stories of Idaho,* rev. ed., Lewiston, Idaho, R.G. Bailey Printg. Co., 1947; Francis Haines, *The Nez Perces,* Norman, Univ. of Okla. Press, 1955; info. from E.F. (Ted) Mains.

Todd, John, frontiersman (1750-Aug. 19, 1782). B. in Pennsylvania, he was early orphaned but was educated at the classical academy of his uncle, John Todd, of Louisa County, Virginia. He studied law, practiced for a time at Fincastle, Virginia, and participated with John Lewis's company in the Battle of Point Pleasant, Lord Dunmore's War, October 10, 1774, in West Virginia. In 1775 he removed to Kentucky, was a member of the Transylvania Legislature, and a delegate from Kentucky to the Virginia assembly. He may have participated in George Rogers Clark's Kaskaskia campaign, but was not at Vincennes as has been claimed. In 1777 he was a captain of Kentucky militia and the next year county lieutenant of newly-created Illinois County and for a year its commandant. In 1780 he was again delegate to the Virginia assembly, was married and returned to Kentucky, where he erected the first fort at Lexington and was county lieutenant of Fayette County. He was killed by Indians at the famous Battle of Blue Licks, northeast of Lexington.

Thwaites, *Dunmore;* Alexander Scott Withers, *Chronicles of Border Warfare,* Cincinnati, Robert Clarke Co., 1895, 1970.

Todd, Levi, military officer (1756-1807). B. in Pennsylvania, he was educated in Virginia and went to Kentucky with John Floyd in 1776. In 1778 he was a lieutenant in George Rogers Clark's Kaskaskia expedition. Following seizure of that place he was sent on a secret mission to the Spanish across the Mississippi, then escorted Clark's prisoners to Virginia. In 1779 as a captain he commanded a company on John Bowman's expedition against the Sandusky villages of Ohio. Late that year he laid out a station ten miles above Lexington, Kentucky, but soon removed to the community, where he became one of its first settlers. In 1782 as a major of militia he raised a force to relieve Bryant's Station, under Indian attack, and then took part in the Battle of Blue Licks, northeast of Lexington, where his brother, John Todd, was killed. Levi Todd eventually became a Brigadier General of militia, then a Major General. He was active in the political life of Kentucky, holding several responsible positions. He was married, left a large family, and a grand-daughter became the wife of Abraham Lincoln.

Thwaites/Kellogg, *The Revolution on the Upper Ohio, 1775-1777,* Madison, Wis. Hist. Soc., 1908.

Tolstykh, Andreyan, trader, explorer (d. Oct. 2, 1765). A merchant from Selenginsk, on the Selenga River south of Lake Baikal, he entered the North Pacific fur trade in the middle eighteenth century and between 1746 and 1765 discovered a number of Aleutian islands, the group now named in his memory the Andreanofs. This chain extends from Amukta Pass to Amchitka Pass, or from about 172° to 179° W. Longitude. In 1746 Tolstykh was navigator and captain of the *Sv. Ioann (St. John),* a trading ship of Feodor Kholodilof, leaving the Kamchatka River August 20, with 46 promyshlenniki and six Cossacks. They wintered on Bering Island, had a moderately profitable hunt the following summer and reached Kamchatka again August 14, 1747. Tolstykh fitted out another vessel and sailed August 19, 1749, wintered on Bering Island and the following May reached the Aleutians. He reported he had come to an island the inhabitants of which had not previously paid tribute (demanded by Russians of all primitive peoples). The natives were related to the Chukchi of Siberia, he thought, for they decorated themselves in the same manner. The island, however, is difficult to identify. Tolstykh returned to Kamchatka with a rich cargo: 1,772 sea otters, 750

blue foxes and 840 fur seals. In 1750 he, not only a man of courage but also of imagination, captured a family of foxes on the Komandorskie Islands, of which Bering is one, and loosed them on the fox-less Aleutian island of Attu; they swiftly increased to 1,000 and by 1760 promyshlenniki regularly hunted them. In 1756 Tolstykh, by then considered "the most famous navigator" of the day, was hired to command the *Andreian i Natalia,* named for him and his wife, who accompanied him. The ship left Kamchatka River in September and again wintered on Bering Island where, just fifteen years after discovery not a single sea otter was to be found; already they had been exterminated. In June 1757 he set sail and in eleven days reached Attu where with the elaborate gifts of a copper kettle and a suit of Russian clothes he made fast friends with Tunulgasan, the island's most influential chief. After a year as the chief's guest Tolstykh left with a very rich cargo of 5,360 sea otters and 1,190 blue foxes, reaching Kamchatka in late 1758. The commander now purchased the *Andreian i Natalia* and under a special imperial ukase left September 27, 1760, wintered on Bering Island, embarked in June and reached Attu August 5. He found that Tunulgasan had died and "too many Russians" already were there, sailed on and on August 28, reached Adak Island of the Andreanof group. He reported discovering Kanaga, Tagalak, and other islands he named Tchechina, Atchu, Amlag and Atach. More importantly from the Russian viewpoint, he found "multitudes" of sea otters. Some hunting parties were based on Adak, others working as far east as Adak and Amlia islands. After a most successful three years the commander started homeward June 14, 1764, stopping at Attu to land his interpreters and repair his badly leaking ship and taking aboard Russians who had survived a shipwreck. Attu was left August 27, and on September 4, the Kamchatka coast was sighted, but in trying to weather Cape Kamchatka the *Andreian i Natalia* was lost, though Tolstykh saved both crew and cargo, valued at 120,000 rubles ($60,000). The next year, in command of the *Sv Petr,* he left Bolsheretsk, Kamchatka, in August, made a fruitless search for new lands and after two months attempted to make the Kamchatka port of Petropavlovsk for the winter. On October 2, 1765, the vessel broke up on the rocks off Cape Shipunski and only three of the 63-man crew were saved. It is not stated whether Tolstykh was a survivor, but he is not mentioned again among the living. On March 2, 1766, the Tsarina Catherine II commended Tolstykh for his discovery of six Aleutian islands and bestowed upon him economic and financial privileges, but her gesture came too late.

Bancroft, *Alaska; Russian Penetration of the North Pacific Ocean;* Zagoskin.

Tom, John Files, frontiersman (Apr. 22, 1818-1906). B. in Maury County, Tennessee, he went with his family to Texas in 1835, settling at Washington-on-Brazos; his father, William Tom, had served under Jackson at the Battle of Horseshoe Bend against the Creeks March 27, 1814, and the Battle of New Orleans against the British January 8, 1815. In Texas both William and John joined Austin's army and went on to San Antonio to fight the Mexicans in the Battle of Concepción, October 28, 1835, and in the Grass Fight November 26, an incident in the siege of San Antonio (Bexar) against General Martin Perfecto de Cós. John Tom at 17 was gunner boy with Colonel James C. Neill's artillery during the successful siege of San Antonio, but left the community February 11, 1836, to join Houston's force on the Colorado River. He served in Captain William Warner Hill's company which, because of Hill's illness, was commanded at the Battle of San Jacinto, April 21, 1836, by Captain Robert Stevenson, also a native of Tennessee. "John Tom at this time was...boyish in appearance, and wore a pair of girl's stockings and buckskin moccasins." He accompanied the charge which opened the engagement but in the course of it his left knee was smashed by a musket ball and he was left for dead on the field. When the action was over and the triumph with the Texans, two of Tom's youthful friends, John Milton (Milt) Swisher and Lewis Chapman Clemons, remembering where he had fallen, found him alive and carried him to the camp. Tom "suffered great pain for many days and was carried home as soon as possible," where he was cared for until recovered, although he was left with a permanent limp. He was married in 1840, becoming father of four daughters and in 1846 moved to Guadalupe County before it was organized after which he became sheriff, holding the office for the limit of four years. In 1862 he moved to Atascosa County, south of San Antonio, then just being settled and on the frontier. "The Indians were very hostile and made many raids through this county and in 1863 Mr. Tom received a commission to raise a company of

rangers for frontier protection." He led his rangers in a fight on San Miguel Creek in which there were losses, possibly on both the Comanche and the Texan side. He was elected in 1873 to the House of Representatives in the Texas Legislature; his wife died that year and in 1875 he married again, becoming parent of seven children by his second spouse. Tom moved to Frio Town, southwest of San Antonio, and in 1893 broke anew the left leg which had been wounded at San Jacinto, this occurring during a riding accident and leaving him on crutches. Following his death he was buried at Leakey, in Edwards County.

HT; A.J. Sowell, *Early Settlers and Indian Fighters of Southwest Texas,* I, 32-37, N.Y., Argosy-Antiquarian Ltd., 1964.

Tomlinson, Samuel, militia officer (d. Sept. 1, 1777). A brother of Joseph Tomlinson, Lieutenant Samuel Tomlinson arrived at the Grave Creek, West Virginia, neighborhood about 1771. He served as an officer in the company of Captain Samuel Mason (see entry) and was killed in the attack on Fort Henry, or Wheeling, by Indians and British.

Thwaites/Kellogg, *Frontier Defense on the Upper Ohio, 1777-1778.*

Tovey, Mike, shotgun messenger (d. June 15, 1893). Tovey for 28 years was a shotgun messenger for Wells Fargo. Little is reported of his origins, but it was said he had been in "many tight corners," and was considered one of the best in his line. September 5, 1880, at the East Walker River Bridge, Nevada, bandits Bill Jones (whose real name was Frank Dow) and Milton Sharp robbed a southbound Carson City-Bodie stage of $3,000, then lay in wait for the northbound stage on which Tovey was messenger. That stage halted while Tovey went forward afoot to investigate the looted strongbox of the first vehicle; the hidden outlaws fired at him, missing Tovey but killing the near leader of the six-horse team. Tovey saw Jones emerging from a thicket and killed him with his shotgun. Sharp then fired, wounding Tovey in the right arm, incapacitating him. Sharp escaped but later was sentenced to twenty years in the Nevada State Prison, from which he escaped August 15, 1889. A year later, still a fugitive, the popular Sharp was pardoned by Governor R.K. Colcord, a generally acceptable action. June 15, 1893, in Amador County, California, Tovey was riding shotgun for the

Ione-Jackson stage. A holdup was attempted and in an exchange of gunfire Tovey was killed.

Harry Sinclair Drago, *Road Agents and Train Robbers,* N.Y., Dodd, Mead & Co., 1973; O'Neal, *Gunfighters;* info. from E.F. (Ted) Mains.

Trapeznikov, Nikifor, merchant (fl. 1743-1764). Typical of the promoters who entered the fabulously rich Alaskan fur trade in the 18th century, Trapeznikov, a businessman of Irkutsk, Siberia, dispatched eighteen voyages between 1743 and 1764. Some of his vessels remained out for years and returned with cargos of great value; others were shipwrecked or otherwise lost. Although he probably never visited the Alaskan islands himself, the efforts he promoted typified the entrepreneurship which characterized exploitation of Alaska's fur resources during this period. In 1749, for instance, he ordered a sloop, the *Boris i Gelb,* built and sent to the Aleutians where it passed four winters, returning with a cargo valued at 105,736 rubles (more than $50,000). On the next voyage the ship was wrecked near Bering Island; another was built of the remains of the first, but it, too, was lost. Trapeznikov meanwhile had had still another vessel constructed, the *Sv. Nikolai,* with the Cossack, Radion Durnev, as commander; it discovered new lands, passed two winters in the hunt and returned to Kamchatka with a cargo valued at 187,268 rubles, including 3,027 sea otters, the most valuable furs of all. One of Trapeznikov's vessels returned in 1757 with a cargo worth 254,900 rubles, among the richest hauls of record. Vassili Berg wrote that "it would be of interest to know how much wealth Trapeznikov realized out of all these enterprises [but] through losses sustained in some of his undertakings, and through bankruptcy of some of his debtors, Trapeznikov suddenly found himself reduced from wealth to poverty," and he died a pauper, leaving barely enough to cover his burial costs.

Bancroft, *Alaska; Russian Penetration of the North Pacific Ocean; The Russian American Colonies.*

Trent, William, military officer (c. 1715-1778). B. in Lancaster County, Pennsylvania, he was in the service of that colony during King George's War (1745-48) and as early as 1749 was employed as a confidential Indian agent. In 1752 he formed a fur-trading partnership with George Croghan (see entry) and in 1754 was a Virginia commissioner at the Treaty of Logstown, Pennsylvania, below the present Pittsburgh. That year he also was commissioned to raise a company and take possession of the forks of the Ohio. He was driven out by the French. Trent accompanied John Forbes' expedition in 1758 to reoccupy the ruins of Fort Duquesne and in 1759 was in the Indian service under Sir William Johnson. He lost heavily during the Pontiac War of 1763, but was reimbursed at the Treaty of Fort Stanwix (at Rome, New York) in 1768. He was commissioned a major in the Revolutionary Army. He died in Cumberland County, Pennsylvania.

Thwaites/Kellogg, *The Revolution on the Upper Ohio, 1775-1777,* Madison, Wis. Hist. Soc., 1908.

Trigg, Stephen, frontiersman (d. Aug. 19, 1782). A prominent resident of Fincastle County, Virginia, he was active politically and helped guard the border in Revolutionary War times. In 1779 he went to Kentucky as land commissioner, erected a station in Lincoln County and represented Kentucky County in 1780. He directed Lincoln County defenses against Indians as a militia officer. He took part in the noted action at Blue Licks, northeast of Lexington, in August 1782, with 181 other Kentuckians, including Daniel Boone. The Indians located, Boone recommended that the whites await reinforcements before attacking them, but hot-headed Major Hugh McGary brushed aside such advice and commenced the action. Trigg, who had sided with Boone, had no recourse but to follow, and fell "fighting gallantly to the last," as did 60 others, while eight were captured.

Thwaites, *Dunmore;* Reuben Gold Thwaites, *Daniel Boone,* N.Y., D. Appleton & Co., 1902.

Trueman, Alexander, military officer (d. c. Apr. 20, 1792). B. in Maryland he became an ensign in the 3rd Maryland Battalion of the Flying Camp from June to December 1776 and a captain in the 6th Maryland Regiment from December 10. He transferred to the 2nd Maryland January 1, 1781, and retired January 1, 1783. Trueman was commissioned a captain of the 1st U.S. Infantry June 3, 1790, and a major of infantry April 11, 1792. He was a peace commissioner with Colonel John Hardin (see entry) and a Mr. Freeman to the Indian villages on the Miami River of Ohio, in the hope of arriving at a treaty which might have made unnecessary St. Clair's expedition and battle of November 4, 1791, and Anthony Wayne's 1794 operation which ended with the Battle of Fallen Timbers on August 20 of that year. In June 1791, under a directive from General Wilkinson (see entry), the three left Fort Washington (Cincinnati) and, Roosevelt wrote, "soon fell in with some Indians, who on being shown the white flag, and informed of the object of their visit, received them with every appearance of good will...A few hours later the treacherous savages suddenly fell upon and slew the messengers of peace. It was never learned whether the deed was the mere wanton outrage of some blood-thirsty young braves, or the result of orders given by one of the Indian councils." Heckewelder noted that they were "certainly...murdered," but his editor, based upon an account in the *Pennsylvania Magazine*, Vol. 12, p. 40, in a footnote to Heckewelder's book said that "they were released from captivity after the defeat of the Indians by General Wayne at Fallen Timbers." However, Heitman conclud- ed that Trueman had been "wounded in action with Inds on the Miami Ohio 4 Nov 1791; found dead about 20 Apr 1792 having been killed scalped and stripped by Inds in Ohio," adding: "see *American State Papers Indian Affairs* vol I, p 243," and his is probably the most authoritative version of the outcome of the mission.

Heitman; Theodore Roosevelt, *The Winning of the West*, 6 vols., N.Y., G.P. Putnam's Sons, 1900, Vol. V, pp. 176-77; Paul A.W. Wallace, *Thirty Thousand Miles With John Heckewelder*, Univ. of Pittsburgh Press, 1958; Heckewelder, *History, Manners and Customs of the Indian Nations Who Once Inhabited Pennsylvania and the Neighboring States*, N.Y., Arno Press, Inc., 1971, 182-84.

Tucker, Tom, partisan (d. 1929?). The begin- nings and end of this gunfighter are uncertain. He may have come from Texas and he possibly was in his middle twenties when he first appears as an Aztec Land and Cattle Company (the Hash Knife outfit) cowboy. He was tall, weighed about 220 pounds, was described in Arizona as "a big, good-natured chap, not hunting for trouble of any kind," but later in New Mexico was suspected of involvement in assorted killings and very dan- gerous when drunk. The Hash Knife had been organized about 1883 with headquarters on the Little Colorado River just west of Holbrook, Ari- zona, its 60,000 head of cattle ranging as far south as the Tonto Basin. Its riders were often fine cowmen, but not a few had reputations of records for violence in other places, they seeking the Hash Knife as a refuge from the law. Tucker was involved in the opening phase of the famed Pleasant Valley War; other riders who figured in the feud, generally on the side of the Tewksburys (see entries) included Tom Pickett, John Paine and Roxy and Peck, all described by Forrest as gunfighters. Some, like Pickett, had been involved in the Lincoln County War of New Mexico, although Tucker had no known connec- tion with that one. After Old Man (Mart) Blevins (see entry) disappeared in Pleasant Valley or its environs, Tucker, Paine and Robert M. Glasspie started in early August 1887 with other riders to either hunt him up or "start a little war of our own." Hampton Blevins rode with them. About noon they reached the old Middleton (Newton) Ranch where members of the Tewksbury faction were holed up, and asked for something to eat, which was denied them. As they turned away shooting erupted from the house, with the result that Blevins and Paine were killed, Tucker grave- ly wounded with a bullet through his right lung and a nick in his ear, and two others of the Blevins-Graham faction wounded slightly, for no losses to the Tewksbury side, from which Jim Tewksbury is reported to have done the most shooting damage. That Tucker survived was regarded as something of a miracle, and healing took a long time. As soon as he could ride he left Pleasant Valley; he had had enough of the feud he had helped to ignite. Tucker was said at one time to have killed an Anglo at Silver City, New Mexico, along with several Chinese, but was cleared on a plea of self-defense. While a deputy sheriff in Santa Fe County he had killed Hipolito Vigil in 1892, claimed that Vigil had resisted arrest, fired on the officer and had been dis- patched, and again was cleared. Tucker became associated with Oliver Lee in the Lee-Good feud east of the Rio Grande and west of the Sacramen- to Mountains, and was suspected of involvement in several killings, including that of Walter Good, son of John Good; nothing was proven against Tucker, however. He appeared as a wit- ness for Lee in the 1899 trial for the deaths of Albert J. Fountain and his son, a celebrated inci- dent of the Lee-Fountain troubles. In 1905 Tuck- er was a cattle inspector at Socorro, New Mexico. Sonnichsen wrote that "at some later date he disappeared in the Sacramento Moun- tains, possibly as an aftermath of the Lee-Foun- tain trouble. He is said by some to have returned to Texas, where he died in 1929." The reported date of his death was supplied by Forrest, who also reported that Tucker in the "latter 1890's" was serving as undersheriff to a Sheriff Cunning- ham of Santa Fe, who had sought "a fearless deputy to help exterminate numerous bad men" in his section of New Mexico.

Earle R. Forrest, *Arizona's Dark and Bloody Ground,* Caldwell, Idaho, Caxton Printers, 1964; Clara T. Woody, Milton L. Schwartz, *Globe, Arizona,* Tucson, Ariz. Hist. Soc., 1977; C.L. Sonnichsen, *Tularosa: Last of the Frontier West,* Old Greenwich, Conn., Devin-Adair Co., 1972; William A. Keleher, *The Fabulous Frontier,* Albuquerque, Univ. of New Mexico Press, 1962; A.M. Gibson, *The Life and Death of Colonel Albert Jennings Fountain,* Norman, Univ. of Okla. Press, 1975.

Tucker, William, frontiersman (c. 1743-1805). B. in New Jersey he was taken by his parents at an early age to the Virginia frontier. In 1754 Tucker's father was killed by Indians while harvesting grain and two sons, including William, aged 11, were captured by the Chippewa Indians. He was a prisoner for seven years. He entered the Indian trade at Detroit, and was present there during the Pontiac siege of 1763. He may have supplied Gladwin with information of the coming attack, his report perhaps saving the garrison. Ten years later he revisited Virginia, married and returned to Detroit with his bride and several slaves. During the Revolutionary War he was an interpreter of Chippewa and Ottawa and a captain in the British Indian Department. At the close of the war he settled on a farm near St. Clemens, Michigan, a northern suburb of Detroit, where he lived the rest of his life. His sons served with the American forces in the War of 1812, and many descendants in 1908 still lived in Michigan.

Thwaites/Kellogg, *The Revolution on the Upper Ohio, 1775-1777,* Madison, Wis. Hist. Soc., 1908.

Turner, Henry Smith, military officer, businessman (Apr. 1, 1811-Dec. 16, 1881). A first cousin once removed of Robert E. Lee, Turner was b. in King George County, Virginia, went to West Point upon the recommendation of President Jackson and became a brevet second lieutenant of the 1st Dragoons July 1, 1834. He was commissioned a second lieutenant August 15, 1835, the regiment commanded by Stephen Watts Kearny. Turner became a first lieutenant March 3, 1837, and an aide to brevet Brigadier General Henry Atkinson. In 1839-40 he studied at the French Military School at Saumur, his report of findings there being "highly approved" by his military superiors and heavily influencing later cavalry instruction in the United States. His

service included stations at Fort Des Moines, Iowa; Fort Gibson, Indian Territory; Jefferson Barracks, Missouri, and Fort Leavenworth. As assistant adjutant general of the Third Military Department, he participated in Kearny's march to South Pass in 1845, keeping a journal of the operation. April 21, 1846, he was promoted to captain, becoming AAG of the newly-formed Army of the West and in that capacity accompanying Kearny to California. In the hard engagement with Mexican lancers at San Pasqual he commanded American forces for a few hours when Kearny was incapacitated, Turner himself suffering a slight, though painful lance wound; he concealed his injury from his comrades until after the action. He was of the small group that drove Andrés Pico's lancers from Mule Hill, where Kearny's force was besieged. In January 1847 he commanded a mixed grouping of Americans at the slight engagements of the San Gabriel River and the plains of Mesa, California, being breveted to major for his work in the three operations. At Monterey he struck up a friendship with William Tecumseh Sherman, the latter writing that "from that day to this [1875], Turner and I have been close friends." Turner strongly sided with Kearny in his memorable dispute with Fremont and testified November 25, 1847, at Washington at Fremont's court-martial. He resigned from the army July 1, 1848. Turner's subsequent career, in banking and other business pursuits, was worthy, but has little frontier interest. He had married, and farmed briefly at Normandy, a St. Louis suburb and in 1850 became assistant treasurer of the United States at St. Louis, awakening an interest in finance. He was associated with Sherman in operating a bank at San Francisco and thereafter divided his time between St. Louis, New York, and the west coast. During the Civil War, Turner, although a loyal Virginian, was shown by Clarke to have strongly favored holding the Union together and in opposition to what he considered "the heresy of Secession." He took no active military role in the Civil War. He died at his home at St. Louis, survived by his widow, Julia Mary Hunt Turner, and several of their seventeen children.

Dwight L. Clarke, *The Original Journals of Henry Smith Turner with Stephen Watts Kearny to New Mexico and California 1846-1847,* Norman, Univ. of Okla. Press, 1966; info. from E.F. (Ted) Mains.

Turner, Marion F., partisan (c. 1831-July 11, 1908). He entered New Mexico from Texas in

1872 and commenced cattle raising in a small way on the lower Pecos River. April 15, 1875, he killed Juan Montoya at Blazer's Mill for no apparent reason. He was friendly with John Chisum initially, Chisum encouraging Turner to file a desert land claim, but around 1878 the two had a falling out. Turner became a deputy to Sheriff George Peppin of Lincoln County in 1878-79. He was discharged from a formal charge of the murder of McSween May 7, 1879, pleading "Governor's Pardon" as pledged by Governor Lew. Wallace. In September 1879

Turner married the 16-year-old niece of Frederick Charles Godfroy, Mescalero Indian agent; the family violently disapproved of the union , kidnapping the young wife and sending her to a seminary at Godfroy's home town of Monroe, Michigan, a divorce later being arranged. After the Lincoln County War, Turner settled in California and became a leading merchant at Artesia. He died at the age of 77.

Robert N. Mullin notes; Frederick Nolan, *The Lincoln County War: A Documentary History,* Norman, Univ. of Okla. Press, 1992.

U

Underhill, Ruth Murray, anthropologist (Aug. 22, 1884-Aug. 15, 1984). B. at Ossining, New York, she was educated at Vassar College, studied also at the London School of Economics and the University of Munich, and earned a doctorate from Columbia University in 1937. A Quaker, she did social work with New York agencies, was a researcher and instructor at Columbia from 1930-35 and was with the Bureau of Indian Affairs as an anthropologist from 1936-47, when she became a professor of anthropology at the University of Denver, remaining there as professor and professor emeritus thereafter, frequently lecturing on her preferred subject at other colleges during her active years. She was a member of the American Association for the Advancement of Science and several professional organizations, and was honored for her writing and other activities. She wrote 19 books, several of them about the Papago Indians whose language was among the five she spoke. She enjoyed mountain climbing and other outdoor activities. Among her books were *The Autobiography of a Papago Woman* (1936, 1979); *Singing for Power: The Song Magic of the Papago Indians of Southern Arizona* (1938, 1976); *First Penthouse Dwellers of America* (1938, 1976); *Indians of Southern California* (1938, 1980); *Social Organization of Papago Indians* (1939, 1969); *The Papago Indians and Their Relatives, the Pima* (1940, 1977); *Pueblo Crafts* (1944, 1977); *The Northern Paiute Indian* (1945, 1980); *Papago Indian Religion* (1946, 1969); *Red Man's America* (1953, 1971); *The Navajos* (1956); *Red Man's Religion* (1965), and *So Many Kinds of Navajos* (1971). She died at Denver.

Contemporary Authors.

Ustiugov, Andrei, Aleut seafarer (d. Aug. 28, 1825). In 1818 he was assigned to a northern land expedition commanded by Petr Korsakovskii and Dmitrii Pomatilov of the sloop *Konstantin.* By that time Ustiugov had learned something of navigation, was literate, and could complete geographical description. Andrei accompanied the expedition to the mouth of the Kuskokwim River, and compiled the first map of the Alaskan coast from Bristol Bay to Good News Bay. In the next year he took over command of the *Konstantin.* The great missionary, Veniaminov, in 1841 wrote that "Ustiugov, an Aleut, was a very experienced sailor. His maps of Nushagak and several other districts are deemed correct to this day."

Pierce, *Russian America: A Biographical Dictionary.*

Utuktak, Feofan, Eskimo interpreter (fl. 1838-1843). A Maleigmiut, or Eskimo from Norton Sound, he was an interpreter for the 1838 expedition of Kashevarov (see entry) by baidara along the Arctic coast of Alaska to a point east of Point Barrow. Kashevarov praised his "constant readiness for work and exemplary patience" during the exploration and urged that he be officially honored for his "invaluable service." Apparently Utuktak had gone to Point Barrow before Kashevarov and had prepared a map useful to the expedition commander. In July 1842 Zagoskin tried to hire Utuktak as an interpreter, but the Eskimo declined, saying he had formerly been a bachelor "but that he now had two beautiful wives, and because of them his wants were fulfilled."

Pierce, *Russian America: A Biographical Dictionary.*

V

Vallejo, Mariano Guadalupe, military officer (July 7, 1808-Jan. 18, 1890). B. at Monterey, then capital of Spanish California, he was attached at 15 to the Monterey garrison as a cadet and by 1827 was an ensign at the presidio of San Francisco. He commanded several scouts against Indians, one to the Sierra Nevada from San Miguel, and a second to the Tulares in the interior valley in which an action occurred. Vallejo had a man killed and 15 wounded. In a later expedition into the Tulares with a company of 35 men he killed 48 Indians and suffered no casualties. May 19, 1829, he led a scout from Monterey, joining one from San Francisco and with Vallejo in overall command. The 107-man expedition crossed the San Joaquin River on rafts and arrived at the scene of his earlier Tulares fight, meeting abruptly with "a cloud of arrows." The enemy was protected in a heavy wood which Vallejo torched to flush the hostiles out, though many escaped; a number were wounded judging from evidence found when the Spaniards withdrew the following day. Vallejo pursued one party of escaping Indians, surrounded them and when they chose to fight rather than surrender, attacked. He had eight men wounded and perhaps other casualties, and the Indians suffered heavily before Vallejo was forced to withdraw by lack of ammunition. He returned to San Jose June 4, and Monterey June 13. The persistent report that he had hanged or otherwise executed women and men captives on this expedition was officially investigated, with indecisive results. In 1830 he was elected a deputy to the territorial congress. In 1832 he supported the rebellion of the Californians against the Mexican governor, Manuel Victoria, and the new governor, José Figueroa, was his close friend, which did no harm to his career, although Figueroa died in 1835. Vallejo was dispatched in 1833 to the northern frontier to investigate reports that the Russians of Fort Ross plotted mischief, but he found them peacefully carrying on their fur collecting and no threat to Mexican California. His report did cite warlike activities of northern Indians and an increasing possibility of eventual American immigration from the east. Figueroa decided upon establishment of a military post in the northern region, and assigned

Vallejo to found and command one. Pending that development Vallejo was promoted to lieutenant. In 1835 he established the authorized post and community of Sonoma north of San Francisco Bay and was named military commander and director of colonization on the northern frontier while also assigned to engage in Indian pacification. From this time Vallejo was "indefatigable in his efforts to promote the settlement and development of the north, efforts that were none the less praiseworthy because they tended to advance his own personal interests. From 1835 he was the most independent and in some respects the most powerful man in California." In 1836 he took part in the revolution of his nephew, Juan Bautista Alvarado, and with its success was made comandante general of California, and thereafter was courteously referred to as "General." He took office November 29, 1836, being promoted to colonel by California authorities, although he and Alvarado soon became estranged following a "petty quarrel." He took no personal part in sectional scuffling of 1837-39. He continued to give close attention to development of his northern frontier, and also to reorganization of the presidial companies in anticipation of an inevitable foreign invasion, though precisely from which source of several possibilities was uncertain. With his estrangement from Alvarado, Vallejo retired to his post at Sonoma where with his troops and Indian allies "he made himself a semi-independent chieftain, a *cacique* on the Spanish-American pattern, and the most powerful figure in the north." Here for the most part he was left to himself until the end of the Mexican regime. He had encouraged American settlement since, he said, he was "powerless" to prevent it. Fremont proved his nemesis and with the Bear Flag Revolt Vallejo and his brother were imprisoned, their cattle stolen, and were kept incarcerated for two months by "the unaccountable Fremont." Vallejo was described as "a powerful agent in securing the submission of California to the United States," and he indulged to some degree in an involvement in politics once that had been accomplished. He was elected to the constitutional convention of 1849 and was a state senator, but spent the latter part of his life clearing titles to his considerable land holdings. He succeeded in some part, although he died at Sonoma "in comparative poverty," that is, "poverty" compared with his previous lavish lifestyle. Bancroft wrote that "I have found none among the Californians whose public record in respect of honorable conduct, patriotic zeal, executive ability, and freedom from petty prejudices of race, religion, or sectional politics is more evenly favorable than his." He was married and fathered at least thirteen children by his wife while, Bancroft conceded, he was "by no means strict in his relations with women."

Bancroft, *California*, II-VII, *Pioneer Register;* DAB.

Van Bibber, John, Peter, frontiersmen (d. 1796, 1821). Of Holland ancestry, they probably were born in Pennsylvania and moved to Maryland, settling around 1771 in the present Greenbrier County, West Virginia. John Van Bibber made an early exploration into Kentucky, then passed down the Ohio and Mississippi rivers to New Orleans. In 1773 he was of a small party of surveyors who explored the Great Kanawha River of West Virginia, inscribing his name on a cliff below the falls, still known as "Van Bibber's Rock." Both Van Bibbers, with a third brother, Isaac, took part in Lord Dunmore's War of 1774, and the climactic Battle of Point Pleasant, West Virginia, on October 10. In the action Isaac was killed. Afterward both surviving brothers were captains of militia. Peter had a blockhouse on Wolf Creek, an important frontier outpost. About 1781 the two moved to the Kanawha Valley. Peter died at Point Pleasant in 1796; John lived until 1821. Peter's sons, Matthias and Jacob, were noted in later border warfare; his daughter married a son of Daniel Boone.

Thwaites/Kellogg, *The Revolution on the Upper Ohio, 1775-1777,* Madison, Wis. Hist. Soc., 1908.

Vancouver, George, discoverer (June 22, 1757-May 12, 1798). B. at King's Lynn, England, he enlisted as an able-bodied seaman in 1771 in the Royal Navy, came to the attention of James Cook (see entry) and was appointed to the *Resolution* as a midshipman in training on Cook's second voyage of discovery. In 1776 Cook appointed Vancouver a midshipman on the *Discovery,* the companion ship to the *Resolution* on his third expedition, to seek out, if it existed, the Northwest Passage from the Pacific side of the American continent. On this voyage Vancouver came to no particular note except that one reference work states it was he who named Prince William Sound in the Alaskan bight; because of his low rank, on a supporting vessel at that, the report seems unlikely, however. February 13, 1779, on the island of Hawaii Vancouver narrowly missed assassination by a native; the following day Captain Cook was killed in a similar incident. Upon the 1780 return of the expedition Vancouver passed his examination for lieutenant. "His eight years' service with Cook had given him an incomparable opportunity to receive training in seamanship and hydrographic surveying under the greatest navigator of the age," and he had made the most of it. After nine years in fighting ships, mainly in the Caribbean, Vancouver in 1791 was named to command another vessel named *Discovery* which with the tender, *Chatham,* was to enter the Pacific, visit Hawaii, but principally to examine the coast between 30° and 60° N. Latitude (from Baja California to Prince William Sound), studying it intensively for any navigable waterway that might qualify as a Northwest Passage, albeit Cook already had demonstrated convincingly that nothing of the sort existed. The vessels sailed from Falmouth April 1, 1791, touching the American coast about 110 miles above San Francisco April 17, 1792. Vancouver reached Juan de Fuca Strait April 29, although he was by no means discoverer of it, for Juan de Fuca himself probably sighted the feature named for him in 1592 and others since had visited some portions of it. But Vancouver was first to thoroughly explore and survey it, scattering names as he progressed. He sent exploring parties in small craft to inspect various parts of the inlet, while *Discovery* and *Chatham* on April 30, anchored hard by the sandy point Vancouver named Dungeness. In the afternoon Joseph Baker, the third lieutenant, from his small boat sighted the 10,750-ft. peak named Mount Baker after him. Port Townsend was named "in honor of the noble marquis"; Mount Rainier "after my dear friend Rear-Admiral [Peter] Rainier," Hood Canal named for Lord Hood, Point Wilson "after my esteemed friend Captain George Wilson," and so on almost ad infinitum, Bancroft wryly commenting, "Indeed, it were well for one coveting easy immortality to be a friend of Captain Vancouver's about this time, the aboriginal owners and occupants being, like earlier Spanish navigators, wholly ignored." [Bancroft, *British Columbia,* 20). The southern part only of the inlet was named Puget Sound for Peter Puget, who first explored it; custom has since extended this title to the entire complex, although it is far deeper than a "sound" by rights should be. Vancouver worked northwards to Nootka Sound, then returned down the coast to San Francisco and Monterey, California and wintered in Hawaii, returning in 1793. In July he reached Portland Inlet, southernmost Alaska, closely examining its branches; in the ships' boats he continued northward through Behm Canal. On returning down its southwestern arm along Revillagigedo Island Vancouver had a narrow escape from musket-armed natives. He returned by way of Duke of Clarence Strait to his ships, having demonstrated that the mythical Northwest Passage reportedly traversed in 1640 by the equally-mythical Bartholomew de Fonte was indeed a fiction. By September 8, Vancouver was at Port Protection on the northern tip of Prince of Wales Island; other nearby islands were investigated and the mouth of the Stikine River observed. Vancouver had now conclusively demonstrated that the unbroken continent extended from San Francisco and Monterey to above Prince of Wales Island. It was late in the season, and his two ships bore south to San Diego and down the Baja California coast to 30° Latitude, fulfilling that part of his instructions, before wintering once more in Hawaii. He decided to commence his 1794 work at Cook Inlet and work east and south along the Alaska coast. March 15, he left Hawaii and April 12, entered the inlet, continuing up it to its head, finding, as the Russians already knew, that it was not the mouth of a great river, as Cook had supposed, and so changed its name on his charts from Cook River to Cook Inlet. Vancouver mentioned that from the inlet he could see "distant stupendous mountains covered with snow, and apparently detached from each other," suggesting that he may have been the first European other than Russians to view Mt. McKinley, highest peak in North America. It is about 125 airline miles north of the upper end of Cook Inlet and the line of sight is virtually unobstructed. He rounded Kenai Peninsula to enter Prince William Sound, resurveying it in its various ramifications. Vancouver had contacted Russian establishments in Cook Inlet and also did so in the sound region. The *Discovery* left the sound June 20, to rejoin the *Chatham,* which had continued the survey as far east as Yakutat Bay. Cross Sound was entered July 7, and anchor was cast near Port Althorp on the northern extremity of Chichagof Island. From here a boat explored Lynn Canal toward the present Skagway. August 1, the ships anchored at Cape Ommaney at the southern end of Baranof Island, thus meeting with the northernmost survey point of the preceding season. "Vancouver had achieved a veritable triumph," being able to "remove every doubt, and set aside every opinion of a north-west passage...existing [connecting] the north Pacific and the interior of the American continent." August 24, 1794, the expedition left by way of California and Cape Horn for England, where it arrived in September 1795. His survey expedition, covering four and one-half years, was the longest ever made for that purpose. The distance sailed was some 65,000 miles, while small boat excursions added 10,000 to that. Vancouver lost but one man to disease, another of mussel poisoning, and four were drowned. He now weathered apparently spurious charges of brutality toward one or two of his men, settled at half-pay at Petersham, near Richmond Park, worked hard preparing his 500,000-word narrative for publication, and died at 40 when the manuscript was within 100 pages of completion. His marine survey has proven astoundingly accurate even by modern standards, most of the names he bestowed upon geographic points of prominence were retained, and on the whole his work placed him "in the class of his commander," Captain James Cook; there could be no higher praise.

Bancroft, *Alaska; British Columbia; Washington, Idaho and Montana; Northwest Coast;* DCB; CE; Francis P. Farquhar, "The Exploration and First Ascents of Mount McKinley,I," *Sierra Club Bulletin,* Vol. 34, No. 6 (June 1949), 95.

Van Meter, John, pioneer (c. 1738-c. 1803). An early settler west of the Allegheny Mountains, Captain Van Meter in 1771 resided at the present town of Waynesburg, Greene County, Pennsylvania. Early in the Revolution he commanded a company of rangers from Westmoreland County. During the Indian wars his home was raided, his wife and daughter killed and a son, John, made captive. The son never returned to civilization but became in habits and orientation an Indian. After the Revolution John Sr. married Mrs. Jemima Bukey, mother of the "famous spy," or scout, Hezekiah Bukey, and settled in Brooke County, Virginia, where he lived the rest of his life.

Thwaites/Kellogg, *Frontier Defense on the Upper Ohio 1777-1778.*

Vasilev, Ivan Filippovich, sea officer, cartographer (1776-July 15, 1812). B. in Russia of a seafaring family, he began his own career at 12 on galleys in the Baltic Sea, entered navigation school in 1789, in 1797 became a navigator. After varied service in European waters he requested service with the Russian American Company, around the turn of the century was accepted. October 20, 1806, he sailed as navigator on the sloop *Neva* under Lieutenant Hagemeister (see entry), arriving at Sitka, Alaska, September 13, 1807. From then until 1809 he made maps of Sitka, of Sitka Island and of the harbor and other parts of Kodiak Island and "his maps were used extensively by later cartographers." Vasilev was not universally loved, however, and was one slated for death by mutineers at Sitka. Their plot was uncovered and the mutineers arrested. In 1811 Vasilev and his family went to Petropavlovsk, Kamchatka, where he was given command of the *Novaia Finliandiia.* He left the port October 12, 1811, for Atkha Island in the Aleutians. He wintered there and in 1812 arrived back at Okhotsk, Siberia, where he was drowned in the harbor when his three-place baidarka overturned in choppy waters.

Pierce, *Russian America: A Biographical Dictionary.*

Vasilev, Ivan Iakovlevich, explorer (1797-post July 7, 1838). In 1814 he entered the Kronstadt navigator's school, in 1819 became a noncommissioned navigator's mate and until 1820 served on the Baltic Sea. In 1821 he entered the service of the Russian American Company , arriving at Sitka, Alaska, in November 1822 and between 1823 and 1828 visited on company business Kodiak, Unalaska Island, California, the Commander Islands and Okhotsk, Siberia. In 1827 he became an ensign in the Corps of Fleet Navigators. Vasilev was instructed by company chief manager Petr Egorovich Chistiakov in 1829 to attain the source of the Nushagak River and then cross over to explore the Yukon and Kuskokwim rivers if possible. He was directed to start from Alexandrovskiy Redoubt, built a decade earlier at the mouth of the Nushagak, there to pick up the veteran fur man Semen Lukin (see entry), assess the quantities of beaver in the interior and contact and return accurate information on peoples of the region who must supply Russian trading posts with furs. His instructions were minute, detailed and extensive. Vasilev set out from Kodiak March 31, 1829, left Katmai

April 18, and reached Naknek Lake the 25th, crossed Nushagak Bay April 30, and reached Aleksandrovskiy Redoubt May 1. Here he made up his expedition for the interior with himself in command, Petr Kolmakov as second in command, Lukin, Aleksey Baturin and Ivan Andreev, Russians and about ten natives; the expedition was equipped with one-hatch and three-hatch baidarkas, or kayaks. It explored up the Aleknagik River to the west of the redoubt, then commenced the trip by boat up the Nushagak, their primary mission, on May 31. On June 11, they passed the mouth of the Mulchatna River, principal tributary of the Nushagak, and on the 12th explored the Nuyakuk River, principal western tributary of the Nushagak, which Vasilev believed to be the main stream. He then returned and went up the true Nushagak, which he called the Ilgayak River, as far as the Chichitnok River, about the place where the following summer he would pass over to the Kuskokwim drainage. By June 16, Vasilev had returned to the Nuyakuk River, believing it the Nushagak, and ascended it toward the west to the Tikchik Lakes, arriving the 20th. After failing to obtain guides to the Kuskokwim he proceeded to Nuyakuk Lake, explored Chauekuktuli Lake and others of the Wood River lakes. He also explored the Wood and Togiak rivers but, unable to reach the Kuskokwim so late in the season, returned to Kodiak. April 6, 1830, he was promoted to second lieutenant. Despite Vasilev's failure to reach the Kuskokwim, let alone the Yukon, Chistiakov was pleased with the results of the expedition, which included a rather accurate map of the expedition's travels, and directed the explorer to resume his work in 1830. He departed from Aleksandrovskiy Redoubt June 19, attained the source of the Holitna River and explored down it to the Kuskokwim, returning down that river despite some native hostility, rounded Cape Newenham and Cape Constantine to reach once more Aleksandrovskiy Redoubt July 29. His journal and map arrived at Sitka in April 1831 and eventually reached St. Petersburg, where Zagoskin (see entry) may have consulted it. Vasilev was plagued by ill health from his return from the second expedition. In 1831-32 he explored the eastern coast of the Alaska Peninsula and in 1833 he was at Sitka in charge of an expedition mapping islands and straits in Sitka Bay, but his health continued to deteriorate and he returned to St. Petersburg in 1834. Although seriously ill he was promoted to first lieutenant of fleet navigators and for three years served in the Baltic Sea. The last information concerning this service was on July 7, 1838; the date of his death is unreported. He was much honored for his geographic work in Alaska, and received financial benefits and the Order of St. Vladimir, 4th Degree, presented to him by Baron Wrangel himself.

James W. VanStone, *Russian Exploration in Southwest Alaska: The Travel Journals of Petr Korsakovskiy (1818) and Ivan Ya. Vasilev (1829),* Fairbanks, Univ. of Alaska Press, 1988; Zagoskin; Bancroft, *Alaska.*

Vasilev, Mikhail Nikolaevich, Russian naval officer (c. 1770-June 23, 1847). B. either in 1770 or on November 4, 1777, he was educated in the naval cadet corps and until 1819 served in European waters. In 1819, commanding the sloop *Otkrytie,* he made an around-the-world voyage, stopping off at Russian America. His mission there was to discover a water route in northern latitudes to the Atlantic Ocean. He followed the Arctic coast of North America, explored Bering Strait and Norton Sound and in 1820 sailed from the Bering Sea to the Chukotsk Sea, reaching Lat. 71°6'N., Long. 116±8'W., or 165 kilometers north of Icy Cape, 45 kilometers farther north than Cook had attained. In sailing from Bristol Bay to Bering Strait he discovered Nunivak Island about 60°N., naming it Otkrytie Island, after his ship. The expedition returned to Kronstadt in 1822. Vasilev eventually became a rear admiral and Intendant-General of the Fleet.

Pierce, *Russian America: A Biographical Dictionary.*

Vásquez del Mercado, Jesús María, missionary (b.c. 1808). A controversial Franciscan missionary whom Bancroft described as "a quarrelsome and vicious padre who did much harm, though of good abilities and education," had a full name almost as long as the troubles he caused in Upper California: Jesús María y José Guadalupe de la Trinidad Vásquez del Mercado. He studied at the College of Guadalupe in Zacatecas, being ordained a priest December 4, 1831, and was assigned as a missionary to California April 7, 1832. He reached Monterey January 15, 1833, with Governor José Figueroa and others and during his stay in Upper California served at Missions San Rafael (1833-34), San Antonio (December 9, 1834-39), Santa Clara (1839-44), and at Soledad as well (1834-39).

Shortly after his arrival at San Rafael he informed Figueroa that the Russians at Fort Ross were luring neophytes from the mission, purchasing stolen cattle and threatening Mexican rights in other ways; Figueroa sent the reliable Mariano Vallejo (see entry) to investigate the Russian activities, Vallejo finding that there was no truth to the reports, and the matter subsided. In 1834 Mercado bitterly accused Angel Ramirez, a Mexican commander, for his mistreatment of Indians; the dispute raged for a short time, but Ramirez and Mercado eventually patched the matter up and became, if not friends, at least companionable with each other, enjoying cock fights, gambling and other diversions. February 24, 1844, Antonio María Pico, the alcalde, charged Mercado with illicit use of mission property, insubordination and calumny and directed that he appear before Pico, which he refused to do, with the end result that he was shipped back to Mexico He became disaffiliated with the College of Zacatecas July 10, 1846, affiliated with San Fernando College at Mexico City, and nothing further is reported of him. Mercado, in conversation with William Heath Davis Jr., who arrived in California aboard the *Volunteer* and eventually wrote the noted *Sixty Years in California,* met the missionary at Santa Clara, found him "a brilliant conversationalist," who informed Davis of the existence of gold in the Sacramento Valley, but when Davis suggested that the fact ought to be publicized widely to bring in the inevitable prospectors, Mercado demurred, saying immigration would be dangerous because "they would pour in...overrun the country [and the] work of the missions would be interfered with." This was the first time Davis had heard of gold in northern California and it was at least half a decade before its discovery at Sutter's Mill in 1848. Mercado and another Zacatecas Franciscan, Miguel Muro (1790-1848) implied they had learned of the gold from Indians. Bancroft wrote of Mercado: "Though a man of good abilities and education, of fine presence and engaging manners, he was an intriguer, arbitrary in his acts, and always ready to quarrel with any one who would not accept his views. Especially did he deem it his mission to quarrel with secular authorities, and on the few occasions when there was no real cause of complaint he had no scruples about inventing pretexts...He is represented as a hard drinker, a gambler, and a libertine—the father of many half-breed children at each of the missions where he served; and all that can be said in mitigation of this bad reputation is that much of the testimony, though not all, comes from men who were not friendly to the padre, being directly, or indirectly parties to some of the many controversies."

Bancroft, *California,* IV, 682n., *Pioneer Register;* Maynard Geiger, O.F.M., *Franciscan Missionaries in Hispanic California 1769-1848,* San Marino, Calif., Huntington Lby., 1969.

Velásquéz, José, Spanish soldier (c. 1717-Nov. 2, 1785). B. at San Ildefonso de Ostímuri, a mining and pastoral community in southeastern Sonora, he received some education and enlisted at 34 on January 1, 1751, at Loreto, Baja California, in the Spanish army as a cavalry *soldado de cuera,* or leather-armored frontier soldier. After sixteen years on May 1, 1768, he became a corporal. Two years later he became sergeant, by which time the 54-year-old soldier had accumulated twenty years of arduous service. He was involved in much exploration, courier and administrative duty on the scantily populated peninsula. Velásquéz was a member of the first land expedition from Velicatá, Baja California, to what became San Diego in Upper California in the spring and early summer of 1769. This party was under Captain Fernando Javier de Rivera y Moncada (see entry) and was joined at San Diego by two sea parties and another land expedition. Velásquéz served with the Portolá (see entry) expedition which left San Diego July 14, 1769, to relocate Monterey Bay and found a settlement there; because of uncertainty as to the site the expedition explored its way northward until near San Francisco Bay which was discovered by Ortega on a reconnaissance of which Velásquéz probably was a member. He volunteered as courier to bear written notice of the successful founding of Monterey, leaving that place June 14, 1770, carrying the documents to San Diego, thence to Loreto and on to Todos Santos Bay. The trail distance was about 1,440 miles, covered in 49 days in the heat of mid-summer; a discussion of this journey is in Ives (96-98). From Todos Santos Velásquéz carried his dispatches to Mexico City, delivering them to the Viceroy's office before returning to Loreto to resume military duties. April 2, 1771, he was made sergeant, becoming "the soldier most in the governor's confidence." February 2, 1773, he was promoted to the commissioned rank of alférez, or ensign, and shortly became commander at San Fernando de Velicatá, northernmost mission in Baja Cali-

fornia and an important supply point for Upper California endeavors. He explored sites for new missions between Velicatá and San Diego, and reconnoitered the upper coastline of the Gulf of California seeking a viable harbor for sea-going ships, but there was none. He made at least two other explorations in the interior of Lower California. September 20, 1780, he was transferred to San Diego as second in command to José Ortega (see entry) and later to Lieutenant Joseph de Zuñiga. Velásquéz was peripherally involved in the founding of Los Angeles (1781) and, following the Yuma massacre of Rivera and others, was sent in February 1782 toward the Colorado in coordinated military actions against the Yumas, but this punitive operations was aborted. Velásquéz reached San Sebastian but may not have arrived at the Colorado River. In May 1783 he was directed to explore the country east of San Diego for a new and better route to the river; the reconnaissance was carried out efficiently, but a usable route was not discovered. Velásquéz's diary and his sketch map are included in Ives (169-75). At 68 and with 35 years in uniform he had become "one of the most experienced soldiers in the Californias." In October 1785 he suffered a hand injury from an unreported cause but nevertheless led soldiers northward in pursuit of a deserter. At San Gabriel Mission, near Los Angeles, he died on All Soul's Day, apparently from blood poisoning. He was a widower though no information has been found on his wife, who probably died before his entry into military service.

Ronald L. Ives, *José Velásquéz: Saga of a Borderland Soldier,* Tucson, Ariz., Southwestern Mission Research Ctr., 1984.

Veniaminov (Innokentii), Ivan Evseevich, prelate, ethnographer, linguist (Aug. 26, 1797-Mar. 31, 1879 [Russian calendar dates]). B. at Anginskoe near Irkutsk, Siberia, with the name of Ivan Evseevich Popov, he began to read at 4 and at 7 became the first of the age on record permitted to read Scripture in an Orthodox church. In 1806 at 9 he entered a theological seminary at Irkutsk, his last name changed to Anginskii. In 1814 the Bishop of Irkutsk died and it was decided to give his last name to the most promising student in seminary, so Ivan was named Veniaminov in the bishop's honor. Ever interested in things mechanical, he studied clock-making on the side, built a water clock for a church at Irkutsk, pocket watches for his classmates and, later in life, clocks and other devices for Alaskan churches and missions. In 1817 while still at the seminary he married Ekaterina Sharina and became a deacon, in 1821 was ordained a priest. In 1823 he volunteered for mission work in Alaska and reached Unalaska, his station, June 24, 1824. Although the Russian American Company had a commercial monopoly over Alaska and controlled marketing of all furs obtained in that vast territory, Father Veniaminov was granted a solitary exception to the general prohibition on private dealing in pelts and was allowed to receive furs his parishioners and others wished to donate by way of recompense for his mission efforts. But he flatly rejected the offer, asserting that it would become a barrier between him and other Russians, and also basically disturb his Aleut people. He wrote the company that in his opinion "a simple, sincere, and without any remuneration, teaching of the Faith would impress people more effectively than the same teaching remunerated by donations." In order to build accommodations for himself, family, and the church he envisioned, he taught the Aleuts carpentry, cabinetmaking, blacksmithing, brickmaking and laying and July 29, 1826, the first Unalaska church was consecrated. In order to preach and teach more effectively he earnestly undertook to learn the Aleutian-Fox language, while methodically studying the ethnography of the natives, the flora and fauna of the islands, carefully recorded daily temperatures, winds, tides and barometer readings and opened schools, writing the textbooks himself. He left Unalaska in 1834, having spread Christianity all over the islands, and leaving the Aleuts with a novel "belief in human kindness, cooperation and the value of knowledge." He had composed the first Aleutian grammar, compiled the first Aleutian-Fox vocabulary, translated the catechism and Book of Matthew, wrote a 658-page book, *Notes on the Islands of the Unalaska District* (1840, English edition, 1984), consisting of two parts on the Aleutian Islands and a third, written in Sitka, on the Tlingit Indians, the whole considered still a cornerstone for any study of the islands or the natives whose ethnography is covered by it. He also wrote numerous shorter works of unvarying merit. From Unalaska he was transferred to Sitka (Novo Arkhangelsk), where his work was among Russians and, largely, the Tlingits, whose language and ethnography again absorbed his attention. The Tlingits were a suspicious and militant people, and only Veniaminov

was able to persuade them to accept inoculation to halt a smallpox epidemic. The Russian priest learned that the Franciscan missionaries of California lacked musical instruments, so he made barrel organs for them, delivering the first to California in person. He wrote "Notes on Kolosh [Tlingit] languages and other Russian-American languages." In 1839 his wife died and Veniaminov was free to become a monk. In 1838 he had left America for St. Petersburg, in 1840 became a monk, adopting the name of Innokentii and was appointed Bishop of Kamchatka, the Kurile Islands, and the Aleutian diocese, retaining the position for 27 years and traveling widely from his see at Yakutsk, building churches and schools and expanding the work of the faith. In 1850 he became archbishop. In 1868 he became Metropolitan of Moscow and Kolomensk, the most elevated hierarchical rank in the Russian church. He was totally blind by the time of his death, on the Saturday before Easter, 1879, but had continued his labors until the end. Vivid legends of "our good Father" continue in many parts of Alaska and elsewhere. His papers are in the Alaska Historical Society and Museum, Juneau.

Literature abundant; Helen A. Shenitz, "Our Good Father," *Russian Orthodox Journal,* Vol. 30, No. 10 (Feb. 1957), 6-10; Bancroft, *Alaska;* HNAI, Vol. 4, 692-93; DAB, under Innokentii; info. from the Alaska Hist. Lby., Juneau.

Virgin, Thomas, mountain man (d. July 14, 1828). From Hamilton County, Ohio, he was married and had fathered six children, it appears, although it is not certain that all his heirs were of his issue. He was first reported in the Rocky Mountains around 1824, and he probably was a friend of Isaac Gilbreth (see entry), both being members of Jedediah Smith's second expedition to California. Virgin was badly wounded in the head by a Mohave war club, but recovered in the attack at the Colorado River crossing c. August 18, 1827, which saw ten of Smith's men slain. Virgin had nearly recovered by the time Smith reached the Mexican settlements, but Smith was forced to leave him for further recuperation in the San Bernardino Valley. Gilbreth decided to remain with his friend. Virgin, once recovered and sufficiently interrogated to satisfy Mexican officials, was allowed to rejoin Smith December 13, 1827, at Mission San José. Smith wrote: "He had been imprisoned for some time and frequently without anything to eat and strictly forbidden to speak to any one, and abused in almost every

way. On the 5th (of December) [Governor Eche-
andia] released him and instructed the [mission]
fathers to forward him on to St. Joseph [San
José]. He was much rejoiced to see us and I am
sure I was quite glad to see the old man again."
Virgin accompanied Smith north and was killed
in the Umpqua massacre in Oregon along with
fourteen others of Smith's men. His Missouri
estate was probated at St. Louis, the $650 owed
him by Smith, Jackson and Sublette being his
sole asset. Morgan noted that the Virgin River of
southern Utah was sometimes believed to have
been named for Thomas Virgin, but the name
actually was of Spanish origin, referring to the
Virgin Mary.

   Dale Morgan, *Jedediah Smith and the Opening of
the West,* N.Y., Bobbs-Merrill Co., 1953; Morgan, *The
West of William H. Ashley,* Denver, Old West Pub. Co.,
1954.

Voevodskii, Stepan Vasilevich, naval officer,
administrator (1805-Sept. 17, 1884). Entering
the Russian naval cadet corps March 22, 1818,
Voevodskii as midshipman and lieutenant served
in European waters and in 1827 took part in the
Battle of Navarino against the Turks. In 1834 he
joined the Russian American Company, arriving
at Sitka, Alaska, in 1835 and for four years commanded company ships on voyages as far south
as California. In 1837 he became a Captain-Lieutenant. September 30, 1840, he took a company
ship to Kronstadt. In 1853 as Captain, First Rank
he was named manager for the company, arriving
at Sitka April 17, 1854. Events coincident to the
Crimean War cost the Russian American Company some vessels in capture or impoundment
but the firm, with permission of the Russian government, in February 1854 proposed to the Hudson's Bay Company that the territories of both
organizations be declared neutral. The British
concern, feeling as insecure adjacent to the Russian company as the latter did in opposition to the
British organization, agreed, and pointless hostilities were avoided. Despite the conflict
Voevodskii by purchasing new vessels, augmented the company's shipping capacity. Some
minor difficulties with the Tlingit Indians in
1855 led to a clash in which the natives sought to
breach the Sitka palisade but were driven off,
with a loss to the defenders of 2 killed and 19
wounded, and to the hostiles of a reported more
than 70 killed. One hundred men of the Siberian
line battalion were brought to Sitka in 1854, the
first Russian soldiery to be stationed in Alaska,

and the force was augmented by an additional
100 men brought in 1856; with them came workmen bringing typhoid fever, which endured for
two years. A mining engineer from Finland (then
part of Russia), Enoch Hjalmar Furuhjelm, was
brought in to develop coal mining, but the effort
was not profitable and he returned to Finland in
1862. June 22, 1859, Voevodskii was relieved as
chief manager by Johan Hampus Furuhjelm,
brother of the mining engineer. In 1860 Voevodskii was named governor of Astrakhan, in 1877
became a Rear Admiral, and two years later,
Admiral.

   Richard A. Pierce, *Builders of Alaska: The Russian
Governors 1818-1867,* Kingston, Ont., Limestone
Press, 1986.

Voznesenskii, Ilia Gavrilovich, naturalist (June
19, 1816-May 17, 1871). B. at St. Petersburg, he
early became attracted to natural history and at
13 accompanied a natural history expedition to
the Caucasus as an associate of the Academy of
Sciences Zoological Museum. Since the Academy wished to build up its collections from Russian America, Voznesenskii was sent to Sitka,
Alaska, for three years, ultimately extended to
ten for collecting purposes. He reached Sitka
May 1, 1840. Every facility was granted him and
he made the most of his opportunities. He taught
Zagoskin (see entry) how to prepare specimens,
visited and collected at the Ross Colony, California, and elsewhere in that area including Sutter's
Fort on the Sacramento River. He spent months
collecting on Kodiak Island and the Alaska
Peninsula, at Unalaska Island and the Pribylov
group and even at Attu Island and the Alexander
Archipelago in the Alaskan Panhandle. He also
collected in Kamchatka and finally returned to
Kronstadt June 21, 1849. "The ten year expedition had been an enormous success. Voznesenskii had collected and mounted 3,687 specimens
of mammals, birds, and fish, and a great number
of amphibians, shells, annelida, mollusks,
zoophytes and other creatures...There were
bones and a skull of a sea cow [now extinct] discovered on Bering Island, mammoth tusks and
teeth...and skulls of various peoples." He also
collected 10,000 insects, 2,000 specimens of
dried plants, and soil samples and rock specimens, a large collection of ethnological artifacts
from weapons to adornments and made more
than 150 drawings "and a great amount of journals, notes and memoranda." Voznesenskii was
honored for his work, rose to high position, but

never had time to put his collections in order, although they were preserved. "His place in the history of science is secure because of his talent for gathering and dispatching...such a vast number of specimens pertinent to various fields. His harvest...is still of enormous benefit to science, and is only now being examined."

Pierce, *Russian America: A Biographical Dictionary.*

Wabokeshiek: *see,* White Cloud

Waddell, Hugh, military officer (c. 1734-Apr. 9, 1773). B. at Lisburn, County Down, Ireland, he was taken by his father to Boston, later emigrating to North Carolina and in 1754 as a lieutenant accompanied the regiment of James Innes in an attempt to drive the French from the Ohio River Valley, becoming in the course of the unsuccessful operation a captain. He was clerk of the council of Governor Arthur Dobbs, who had been a friend of his father, and in 1755 the governor directed him to protect the frontier from Cherokee and Catawba Indians. To do so he built Fort Dobbs five miles north of Statesville and "near the South Yadkin." The fort was completed in 1756, of good size and substantial construction, and "it containes three floors, and there can be discharged from each floor at one and the same time about one hundred muskets." Captain Waddell, its commandant, met with Cherokee and Catawba representatives and concluded a treaty with them. February 27, 1757, the fort was attacked by Cherokees. In his report Waddell said that "Dogs making an uncommon noise" alerted the small garrison, and he with a Captain Bailie and eight men went out to reconnoitre. About 300 yards from the fort they were attacked by 60 to 70 Indians. He ordered his men not to shoot until he gave the word, and after the enemy had fired (and emptied their weapons) and the space between them had closed to "not further than 12 steps" he gave the order and a heavy fire resulted, he was sure, in their being "a good deal confused," when he and his party regained the post which had come under attack from another body of hostiles. The combined defense force then "repulsed [them] with I am sure a considerable loss [that] cou'd not have been less than 10 or 12 killed and wounded," although they fled with the Fort's horse herd. The defenders had two men wounded, "one of whom I am afraid will die as he is scalped," and one boy killed near the fort. A post named Fort Waddell subsequently was built near the forks of the Yadkin, garrisoned by a company of Rangers. Waddell commanded at Fort Dobbs until late in 1757. Governor Dobbs then sent him as major com-

manding three companies to join the expedition of John Forbes, who in 1758 occupied the ruins of the French post of Fort Duquesne at the present site of Pittsburgh. Waddell accomplished much scouting work and "dressed and acted like an Indian" in doing so. He was considered "the foremost soldier" of North Carolina before the Revolution. He also acquired much land, had mercantile interests, was frequently a member of the colony's assembly, became wealthy and politically influential. He visited Ireland and England in 1768. He was close to the new governor, William Tryon, although occasionally at odds with him over one matter or another, and commanded the military escort for him on visits to the Cherokees in 1767 and 1771. Waddell was militantly opposed to the back country Regulators who struggled against excessive taxes, and was somewhat effective as General and commander-in-chief under Tryon. He died from an illness of some duration. He was married.

DAB; Douglas L. Rights, *The American Indian in North Carolina,* Chapel Hill, Winston-Salem, John F. Blair, pub., 1957; info. from E.F. (Ted) Mains.

Wade, Albert or John (Kid), rustler (c. 1860-Feb. 8, 1884). The Kid, as he was called, may have been associated at one time with Pony Diehl, but he became best known as a colleague of Doc Middleton and after Middleton went to the penitentiary appears to have inherited leadership of what remained of the Pony boy's horse rustling group. During 1877-78 the Middleton band specialized in stealing horses from the Sioux Reservation of Dakota, although they appeared to have broader interests as well. Through a comic exchange of holdups, as recounted by Carson, the Kid and Doc came to admire each other, and soon associated. In July 1879, when Middleton was taken following a Nebraska shootout with law officers, Wade escaped. Still a rustler and desperado, he was lynched by vigilantes after an extended months-long search and endeavor to corral him; his father had been lynched several months earlier. Kid Wade had been arrested finally at Le Mars, northwestern Iowa, by Sheriff John Ennis and his deputy, Kirk Elder, the Kid having in his possession a stolen horse from Nebraska's Broken Bow, Custer County. The detailed narrative of the extended pursuit and final execution of Wade is told in *Pioneer History of Custer County,* by Butcher (see entry), 221-32. It has been written in some quarters that Wade was lynched because vigilantes feared if left alive he might implicate some of the "better citizens" of the region; this has never been authenticated.

John Carson, *Doc Middleton: The Unwickedest Outlaw,* Santa Fe, Press of the Territorian, 1966; Solomon D. Butcher, *Pioneer History of Custer County,* Denver, Sage Books, 1965.

Waite, Frederick T., partisan (Sept. 23, 1853-Sept. 24, 1895). B. at Fort Arbuckle, Pauls (not Paul's) Valley, Indian Territory, he was the son of Thomas Waite, a major rancher, and Catherine McClure Waite, daughter of a Chickasaw, Ellen Paul, for whom Pauls Valley was named. She came to Indian Territory with the Chickasaw Removal of 1830-40 and died October 24, 1895. Fred was well educated, having attended schools and colleges at Bentonville, Arkansas, St. Louis and Champaign, Illinois. After working for a time in a business house he went to New Mexico in 1877 and soon became involved with Billy the Kid in the Lincoln County turmoil. Frank Coe called him an "OK lad," and "Billy liked Fred immensely, and the two soon became inseparable companions," according to Utley. They planned a joint ranching operation, which never materialized. Both became deeply involved in trouble coinciding with the Lincoln County War, and both were present, perhaps taking significant roles, in the assassination of Sheriff Brady (see entry) April 1, 1878, at Lincoln when George Hindman also was killed, the fatal bullet being fired "almost certainly...by Fred Waite." He was indicted April 22, for that killing, although never prosecuted. Waite was present at the San Patricio skirmish June 27, 1878, between an 11-man McSween faction and one headed by Sheriff Peppin's 20-man posse and a 35-man Fort Stanton military detachment. His whereabouts during the Five Day Battle at Lincoln are unknown; he might not even have been present, although it would be odd if he were not. After that engagement he continued to befriend Sue McSween, widowed by the affair. Following it the "regulators" of the Tunstall-McSween faction disintegrated. In September 1878 the Kid, Waite and a few others drove stolen horses to the Texas Panhandle for sale and a frolic and by late October

Waite had decided to return to Indian Territory. By 1879 he was back there, served for a time with the Indian police, and later was appointed Permit Collector for the Chickasaw Indian Territory. In 1889 he was elected to the Territorial legislature and became Speaker of the House. He died at Pauls Valley. His second wife survived him by forty years or more.

Robert N. Mullin notes; Robert M. Utley, *Billy the Kid,* Lincoln, Univ. of Nebraska Press, 1898; info. from Frederick W. Nolan.

Waldo, David, frontiersman (Apr. 30, 1802-May 1878). B. at Clarksburg, Harrison County, Virginia, he emigrated to Missouri in 1820, settling in Gasconade County, where he logged enough pine timber to sell for $500, using the proceeds to study medicine at Transylvania University, Lexington, Kentucky. In 1821 he became sheriff of Gasconade County, held other offices and by 1827 was a practicing physician. In 1831 he moved to western Missouri, went into partnership with David E. Jackson (see entry) and entered the Santa Fe trade; his participation in this business as merchant, freighter, and mail contractor extended for thirty years, making him one of the wealthiest men in western Missouri. During the Mexican War he captained a company from Jackson County, and attached to Doniphan's command. "Being a fine Spanish scholar he translated the laws of the United States into Spanish, and what was called the 'Kearny Code.'" He also translated Mexican documents into English. He was married in 1849 to Eliza Jane Norris. Waldo died at Independence, Missouri, where he had lived about fifty years.

Susan Shelby Magoffin, *Down the Santa Fe Trail and Into Chihuahua,* Lincoln, Univ. of Neb. Press, 1982, pp. 64-65, note by Stella M. Drumm; Carl D.W. Hays, "David E. Jackson," MM, IX.

Walker, Alexander, taxidermist, naturalist (Aug. 11, 1890-Aug. 13, 1975). B. in western Nebraska but "raised mostly in Iowa," he early became interested in natural history, took a mail order course from the Northwestern School of Taxidermy of Omaha, Nebraska, and during his life of self-taught skills created a natural history museum now viewed by an estimated 60,000 visitors a year. The Omaha school, he confided, conveyed competence in "just rough work, you know, the essentials," and using that as a basis he studied every book on the subject he could find, learning from each such important things as how to make snow for habitat groups. Walker went to Oregon in 1912, the next year taking a two-month wagon tour of eastern Oregon with his father, ostensibly looking for land to purchase, but the young man was more interested in studying birds and wild animals along the way. The Walkers eventually settled at Tillamook near the coast west of Portland. Walker worked for the Fish and Game Department for two years as a collector, then took an examination for wildlife refuge manager and passed it, but meanwhile received an offer from the Cleveland Natural History Museum to collect birds for study purposes. He sent in 8,000 specimens during a three-year period of work in Oregon, California and Arizona, many items of his collection winding up at the Smithsonian Institution of Washington, D.C. "I found 18 or 20 new species of birds," he said, "and I once had a flea named for me!" Walker also became an expert photographer. He was one of very few cameramen ever to photograph the pine mouse, a tiny, reddish creature living in the northwestern evergreens, which almost never comes to earth and obtains the water it needs from the dew and mist settling on the trees. Walker assembled a collection of more than 60 hummingbird species from this country, Central and South America. He made private excursions to Montana, Alaska, Canada and Africa in pursuit of his interests. In 1951 Tillamook County received a $4,520 grant from a lumberman's widow to start a natural history and historical museum, and decided to allot a spare courtroom to it, offering the natural history curatorship to Walker. "I had never made a habitat group in my life to that time," he said, "and I learned as I went along." He came to know many of the famed zoologists and naturalists of his time, including the animal painter, R. Bruce Horsfall, George B. Grinnell, mammologist Victor H. Cahane and William Beebe of the New York Zoological Society, and he could call on their help when he needed it. What he put together was probably one of the finest natural history exhibits in the Northwest, although he was limited in funds, often had to make do with what specimens were sent in, and had not the means for major expeditions. Yet he got around. At 84 he took a trek to Alaska's famed Pribylov Islands, explaining that "I better do my chasing while I'm still young. Some day I'll get old and won't be able to do it." His self-taught habitat groups are sometimes striking, one showing a quarrel over a jackrabbit by a bobcat

and a red-tailed hawk; another is of an Oregon Marsh Group, collected in Lake County of eastern Oregon and including a sandhill crane, snow egret, avocet and other typical marsh birds, while a Tillamook Seabird Group contains about 60 birds in one setting. Walker conceded that, like most taxidermists, he had help with background painting. Among his interesting assemblages were skull collections: of the canines, including coyote to wolf and various stages between, arranged so a viewer can detect the progressive differences between species; the cat skull collection includes the cougar, leopard, African lion and others, with the distinctions readily apparent. Walker's organized and classified collection of 4,000 mammal specimens was donated at his death to the Oregon State University zoological research department. Walker was a small man, thin, quick in movement. He admitted he "didn't even have a television set," and was content with his books, photographs, and plans for the future. His wife predeceased him and he left two sons. He died at Tillamook two days after his 85th birthday.

Extended interview, Sept. 14, 1971; info. from M. Wayne Jensen Jr., Dir., Tillamook County Pioneer Museum; Walker death cert.

Wallace, Richard, frontiersman (d. c. 1785). Wallace had a mill and blockhouse on McGee's Run, a branch of the Conemaugh River, Pennsylvania, as early as 1774. It was a center for parties of rangers protecting the frontier, and was often attacked by hostiles. Richard Wallace joined the Archibald Lochry (see entry) expedition down the Ohio in 1781; it was destroyed by an Iroquois party led by Joseph Brant and others, and Wallace was captured, taken to Montreal and eventually returned to his home. Around 1785 he joined Alexander Barr for another trip down the Ohio, this time to locate lands. Both Wallace and Barr were killed by Indians on this endeavor.

Thwaites/Kellogg, *Frontier Defense on the Upper Ohio, 1777-1778.*

Ward, Edward, military officer (fl. 1754-1787). Ward was closely associated with William Trent and George Croghan (see entries) and was a half brother of Croghan. In 1754, while an ensign, he surrendered the forks of the Ohio to the French, they building Fort Duquesne there. In 1756-57 Ward was a lieutenant and from 1757-59 a captain of the 1st Pennsylvania battalion. He took part in John Forbes' 1758 expedition to occupy the ruins of Fort Duquesne after the French had burned and abandoned it. Following the French and Indian War Ward became an Indian agent stationed at Pittsburgh, holding the position for several years. In later life he held civilian positions and was living at Pittsburgh as late as 1787.

Thwaites/Kellogg, *The Revolution on the Upper Ohio, 1775-1777,* Madison, Wis. Hist. Soc., 1908.

Ward, James Sr., frontiersman (c. 1727-Oct. 10, 1774). B. in Ireland, he was brought to America in infancy and raised in Augusta County, Virginia. In about 1749 he married the daughter of Patrick Lockhart and they became parents of seven children, including at least three sons of frontier note. Ward was a lieutenant in the French and Indian War, serving with John Forbes in 1758 in the expedition to occupy the former French Fort Duquesne at the present site of Pittsburgh, and in the 1764 operation of Henry Bouquet against the Ohio Indians. In 1769 he moved to Greenbriar County in present West Virginia. Ward was killed while serving as a captain in the Battle of Point Pleasant, West Virginia. Two of his sons, James Jr. and Charles, became pioneer Kentuckians, and a third, John Ward, was captured at 3 by Ohio Indians, raised among them, and was killed in a skirmish with whites (see entry).

Thwaites, *Dunmore;* Thwaites/Kellogg, *Frontier Defense on the Upper Ohio, 1777-1778.*

Ward, James Jr., frontiersman (Sept. 19, 1763-Feb. 27, 1846). B. in Staunton, Virginia, his family took him at 6 to Greenbriar County, present West Virginia. His father (see entry) was killed in the October 10, 1774, battle at Point Pleasant, West Virginia, which virtually terminated Lord Dunmore's War. In 1780 James Jr., with William and Charles Ward, made an exploring visit to Kentucky and in 1785 moved there permanently. James Ward settled near Washington, in Mason County. As a captain he went on Benjamin Logan's expedition against the Ohio Indians in 1786, accompanied Colonel John Edwards' expedition in 1791, again into Ohio, and was on Simon Kenton's expedition of 1793 to Paint Creek, in southern Ohio. On this expedition the only "hostile" killed was James's brother, John Ward, who had been captured by the Shawnees at 3 and raised among them, perhaps being active in their hostilities. In 1794 James Ward accompanied Anthony Wayne's decisive campaign against the Ohio and Indiana Indians, which ter-

minated in the victory of Fallen Timbers on August 20. Ward was a Presbyterian, becoming an elder in the Washington church of that denomination. He was interviewed at length in 1845 by Lyman C. Draper, the results held by the Wisconsin Historical Society.

Thwaites, *Dunmore;* Thwaites/Kellogg, *Frontier Defense on the Upper Ohio, 1777-1778.*

Ward, John, captive (d. 1793). The son of James Ward Sr., he was captured at 3 by Ohio Indians and raised among them, marrying an Indian woman, perhaps a Shawnee. Simon Kenton, a prominent frontiersman, had met John Ward and his daughter, Sutaw-nee while a prisoner of the Shawnees and John had indicated he preferred to live with the natives to a point where he was considered a "white Indian" by the borderers. In April 1793 Kenton led an expedition into the Ohio Indian country, one of his followers being either James Ward, as reported by Thwaites, or William Ward, as Jahns has it; both were sons of James Ward Sr., and thus brothers of John. The white party moved up Paint Creek, in southern Ohio, and located a camp of about 30 Indians; an indecisive engagement took place at night and with dawn the Indians had fled, leaving behind one fatality—John Ward; the white party withdrew to the Ohio River, 50 miles south, the expedition at an end.

Thwaites, *Dumore;* Thwaites/Kellogg, *Frontier Defense on the Upper Ohio, 1777-1778;* Patricia Jahns, *The Violent Years: Simon Kenton and the Ohio-Kentucky Frontier,* N.Y., Hastings House, 1962, pp. 238-39.

Ward, William, pioneer (d. 1822). The eldest son of James Ward Sr., he was b. in Virginia, probably at Staunton, and may have served as a sergeant in Robert Doack's militia company in Lord Dunmore's War; his father (see entry) was killed in the Battle of Point Pleasant October 10, 1774, which effectively terminated that conflict. On November 10, 1777, Ward, with Captain John Anderson and Richard Thomas, signed a deposition on the murder of Cornstalk, noted Shawnee chief, by white ruffians, an incident which he witnessed although protesting against it. He was a nephew of Captain Matthew Arbuckle (see entry), a famous frontiersman. Ward emigrated to Mason County, Kentucky, and served in the state legislature (1792-95). He moved to Ohio about 1800 and in 1804 laid out the town of Urbana, in Champaign County, where he died.

He was grandfather of the well-known sculptor, John Quincy Adams Ward (1830-1910).

Thwaites/Kellogg, *Revolution on the Upper Ohio, 1775-1777; Frontier Defense on the Upper Ohio, 1777-1778;* Thwaites; *Dunmore.*

Warner, Matt (Willard Erastus Christiansen), desperado, justice of peace (1864-Dec. 21, 1938). B. at Ephraim, Utah, into a devout Mormon family, he was raised on a farm near Levan, south of Nephi and early became a range rider, breaking horses and learning cowboy skills. At 13 he got into a fight with Andrew Hendrickson, hit him in the head with a rock, believed he had killed him (he had not) and took off for Brown's Hole in northwestern Colorado and adjacent portions of Utah and Wyoming. It was a haven for rustlers and outlaws. He assumed the alias, Matt Warner. He went to work for Jim Warren, a rustler, and turned to that occupation himself. He initially joined Elza Lay and Lew McCarty (son of noted outlaw Tom McCarty, Matt's brother-in-law) in a masked holdup of a peddler, taking his money and goods, the victim not reporting the incident because "all officers were in partnership with the outlaws." Eventually, at Telluride, Colorado, Warner met George LeRoy Parker (Butch Cassidy, see entry) and at length joined the Wild Bunch desperados. Even before his chance meeting with Parker/Cassidy, Warner had matured into a full-blown desperado, operating as far south as Mexico, most frequently in concert with Tom McCarty, who had married Matt's sister. Not all of his escapades are known in detail, but there was a steady progression downward. March 30, 1889, Warner and McCarty were believed to have held up the First National Bank of Denver, taking $21,000; McCarty denied he was the robber, but there is evidence to the contrary. June 24, 1889, Cassidy, Warner and McCarty robbed the Telluride bank of $10,500. After a round-about escape they finally settled for the winter in Star Valley, south of Jackson Hole where Matt became enamored of Rosa Rumel, 14 (he was then 25), and married her at Montpelier, Idaho, September 4, 1889. After many minor holdups and some major ones in Oregon and the Northwest, Matt on September 24, 1892, with Tom McCarty and Tom's brother, George, held up the bank at Roselyn, Washington, taking $20,000, of which Matt got away with half. He later was arrested, was cheated of his accumulated savings of $41,000 by a crooked lawyer, was abandoned by his wife and baby

daughter and returned to Brown's Hole to again meet Cassidy and Lay. Later he was reconciled with Rosa. Some miles from Vernal, Utah, in 1896, Warner became involved in a complicated prospecting matter in which he was hired to provide protection for E.B. Coleman, a 52-year-old prospector from Davenport, Iowa, then living at Salt Lake City. Coleman claimed he had discovered the Homestake lode of the Black Hills, had arrived at Alder Gulch, Montana, shortly after discovery of a rich placer gold field there, and now was in pursuit of a reputed copper discovery. He was being annoyed by David Milton, Adoniram W. (Dick) Staunton and brother Isaac Staunton. Coleman hired Warner and William Wall to "frighten" the trio away from his camp. May 7, 1896, a gun battle broke out, with Warner and Wall firing into the trio's tent, from where their opponents were shooting back. Milton was fatally hit, as was Dick Staunton, while Ike Staunton was badly wounded. Warner, Wall and Coleman were jailed at Vernal, where there was serious threat of lynching since the victims were highly regarded locally. Cassidy visited Matt in jail and offered to provide legal assistance as soon as he had "raised" enough cash to do it. The case against Warner and Wall was transferred under change of venue to Ogden, Utah, where Samuel A. King, a prosecuting attorney, became fully aware of the nature of the complex matter. He reported that "There was no question but that Warner and Wall were innocent of the charge [of first degree murder]. They acted purely in self-defense," since the opposing trio had fired on them first. Coleman was freed by the court while the other two were convicted of manslaughter and sentenced to five years in Utah Penitentiary; they were released for good behavior after three years and four months. While in prison "many of the cases against [Warner] became barred by the statute of limitations." He settled in Price, Carbon County, Utah, remarried (his first wife having died) and fathered three more children. He was elected justice of peace, served occasionally as deputy sheriff, detective and night policeman. In 1912 he ran for sheriff but under his true name of Willard Christiansen, which few remembered, and "had he run under the name of Matt Warner" he would no doubt have been elected by a landslide. While justice of peace his court drew large crowds and his judgments "were the talk of the town." Totally ignoring the law, legal practices and lawyers, he frequently took the cases over himself, deciding "on the facts he drew out and upon his own primitive idea of justice and humanity." The people believed "his decisions were just," vocally supported them, and "the attorneys were afraid of him." When Kelly's Cassidy book was privately published in 1938, Warner read it and was infuriated by Kelly's references to his sometimes abusive treatment of his first wife. He insisted that he and his wife had an amicable relationship throughout and wondered where Kelly had obtained information to the contrary. "I got it from the Salt Lake *Tribune,*" explained Kelly. "She told the story herself." That appeared to mollify Warner, somewhat. His doctors previously had informed him that he had a kidney problem and to quit drinking whisky, and he had abstained for two years. After he read Kelly's book, however, "he was so mad he bought a quart of whiskey and drank it on the way home to Price. When he got there he...kept on drinking heavily for ten days. Then he died...His family says I killed him," Kelly wrote.

Matt Warner, as told to Murray E. King, *The Last of the Bandit Riders,* N.Y., Bonanza Books, 1940; Charles Kelly, *The Outlaw Trail: The Story of Butch Cassidy and the "Wild Bunch,"* N.Y., Devin-Adair Co., 1959, enlarged edition; John Rolfe Burroughs, *Where the Old West Stayed Young,* N.Y., William Morrow and Co., 1962.

Warner, William Horace, military officer (1812-Sept. 26, 1849). B. in New York, he went to West Point and July 1, 1836, was commissioned a second lieutenant of the 1st Artillery. July 7, 1838, he became a second lieutenant of the Topographical Engineers and was promoted to first lieutenant September 1, 1841. As a member of the staff of Stephen Watts Kearny he went to California in 1846, was wounded at the action of San Pasqual near Warner's Ranch December 6 and 7 and won a brevet to captain for his performance. Warner, a skilled surveyor, made the first survey of the proposed city of Sacramento, California, laying out the streets for the city, including Front Street along the Sacramento River. In 1847 Warner visited Monterey and obtained a lot in San Francisco, in 1848 engaging in trade with William Tecumseh Sherman at Coloma. In 1849 he led an army expedition of 80 men (of whom 34 deserted within a month for the mines) to examine routes from the Humboldt Valley to the Sacramento River. He was ambushed and killed by Pit River Indians near Goose Lake on the upper Feather River. His body, with nine arrows

piercing it, was recovered the following spring. The Warner Mountains were named for him.

Heitman; Bancroft, *California,* V, VI, VII, *Pioneer Register;* Susan Shelby Magoffin, *Down the Santa Fe Trail and Into Chihuahua,* Lincoln, Univ. of Neb. Press, 1982, p. 87 note by Stella M. Drumm.

Wasson, Chippewa chief (c. 1730-post 1776). B. probably in the Saginaw Valley of Michigan, he achieved greatest fame for his role in the Pontiac War of 1763 to which he brought 250 men to further Pontiac's cause. The siege of Detroit was already a month old when Wasson appeared May 31; Wasson and Pontiac together, it was reported, decided at that point to cease direct attacks on the fort and concentrate on starving the defenders out. In July Wasson's nephew was killed by the British. Wasson went to Pontiac and asked him to hand over captured Captain Donald Campbell for revenge. "My brother, I am fond of this carrion flesh which you guard. I wish some in my turn," he was said in the *Navarre Journal* to have demanded. "Give it to me." Pontiac handed Campbell over and the prisoner was taken by Wasson to his camp, where the young men stripped the officer of his clothes, when Wasson tomahawked him and cast his body into the river where it floated downstream to be recovered and buried by the whites. A more bizarre description reports that Wasson had cut Campbell's heart from his body, "eating it reeking hot." Campbell had been a hostage in the Ottawa camp, and the Ottawas in recompense for the loss of their prisoner sought to execute John Rutherford, a prisoner of the Chippewas, but Wasson took Rutherford into his own lodge until the turmoil had passed. The next month Wasson dictated a letter to Gladwin, commandant of the fort, demanding its surrender, but received no reply. The siege of Fort Detroit dwindled away in the fall. The next summer Wasson again visited the fort, which now was at peace, and asked pardon for his part in the siege. He was a speaker at John Bradstreet's peace conference of September 7, 1764. Wasson attended other peace conferences in the summers of 1765, 1776 (at Fort Pitt) and possibly attended a council at Detroit May 19, 1790, although this may have been another of the same name. Wasson's name was long honored by the Saginaw Chippewas as having been a "great chief."

Thwaites/Kellogg, *The Revolution on the Upper Ohio, 1775-1777,* Madison, Wis. Hist. Soc., 1908;

Howard H. Peckham, *Pontiac and the Indian Uprising,* Chicago, Univ. of Chicago Press, 1961; *Journal of Pontiac's Conspiracy 1763* (Navarre Journal), ed. by Clarence Monroe Burton, trans. by R. Clyde Ford, Detroit, Mich. Soc. of the Colonial Wars, 1912; DCB IV.

Waterman, Thomas Talbot, anthropologist (Apr. 23, 1885-Jan. 6, 1936). B. at Hamilton, Missouri, the youngest of ten children of an Episcopal clergyman, Waterman was graduated in 1907 from the University of California at Berkeley with a major in Hebrew, since he intended to study for the ministry. But he went on a field trip as an assistant to Pliny Earle Goddard (1869-1928), an ethnologist specializing in Athapascan dialects, their mission to record some of these in northern California, and "this experience was decisive in diverting [Waterman] from divinity to anthropology." He obtained a doctorate under Franz Boas in 1913 from Columbia University. Meanwhile, at the University of California he was Museum Assistant from 1907-1909 and instructor and assistant curator from 1910 to 1914. It was while so occupied that he became the first scientist to attempt to interview Ishi (see entry), the last Stone-Age Indian in the contiguous United States, who had been recovered, emaciated and starving, near an Oroville, California, slaughterhouse on August 29, 1911. Waterman collected what partial vocabularies existed of northern Indian dialects, most of the tribes now vanished, and hastened to Oroville where he met Ishi, held in the county jail for safe-keeping from curious throngs who wanted to see the wild "savage." Waterman gradually gained his confidence. He tried several vocabularies without recognition on the Indian's part until he commenced to pronounce some Yana words, which Ishi understood in part, establishing at length that he was a Yahi Indian, of the southernmost portion of the Yana tribe. Confidence gained, Ishi commenced to eat food brought to him, and September 4, accompanied Waterman to the university museum at San Francisco, where he was welcomed by Alfred Louis Kroeber (see entry) and others of the Department of Anthropology staff. The rest is history. Waterman became "Ishi's first friend." The two men liked and understood one another," Ishi seeming to Waterman an "old man," and Waterman to Ishi as "a brash but lovable young man." With Waterman Ishi took his first train trip (to San Francisco from Oroville), had his first view of San Francisco, and "Waterman's was the first private home to which Ishi went as a dinner guest to sit at a white man's table with [the white's] wife and children." At a later time, when the linguist Edward Sapir worked regularly with him, Ishi lived for three months with the Watermans, the Indian's amiability and neatness making him a desirable model for his host to follow, according to an amused Mrs. Waterman. By 1921 Waterman was associate professor of anthropology at Berkeley, and had served as such also at the University of Washington, after which he became affiliated with the Heye Foundation's Museum of the American Indian of New York City. He was with the Bureau of American Ethnology, Washington, in 1922 and later the Muséo Nacional of Guatemala City. He taught at Fresno (California) State College from 1924-27, "mainly teaching geography, as there was then little demand for anthropology" at smaller institutions. He spent a year at the University of Arizona and then went to Honolulu where he taught at the Territorial Normal College and the University of Hawaii, and was appointed Territorial Archivist a few months before his death. Kroeber wrote that "Waterman was first of all a brilliant, incisive, colorful teacher, rarely systematic and sometimes erratic, but extraordinarily stimulating," and to his thousands of students he "made anthropology mean something real to them." His interests were wide, touching such subjects as folklore, Aztec antiquities, Yana history, Makah whaling, Paiute phonetics, Yurok linguistic affixes (or additions to words), Pueblo pottery, and human races. He also wrote widely, principally for serials but also such volumes as *Source Book in Anthropology* (with Kroeber), and *Sidelights on the American Indian,* which remains in manuscript. His wide variety of serial publications appeared in the *American Anthropologist, Journal of American Folk-Lore, University of California Publications in American Archaeology and Ethnology,* which carried his monograph on "The Yana Indians" in Volume 13, of 1918, and in other outlets. By his first wife he fathered a son and a daughter; he was divorced in 1926 and the following year married again; both wives and his progeny survived him.

A.L. Kroeber, "Thomas Talbot Waterman," which includes biblio., *American Anthropologist,* Vol. 39 (1937), 527-29; info. from the Dept. of Anthropology, Berkeley, July 22, 1992; Theodora Kroeber, *Ishi in*

Two Worlds, Berkeley, Univ. Of Calif. Press, 1961, esp. pp. 148-49.

Watts, John (Kunnesseei), Cherokee war leader (c. 1750-c. 1808). B. of a white trader and a sister of Old Tassel (see entry), he thus was a nephew of Old Tassel and of a brother, Doublehead. He became an able war leader, but he lacked the ability to control "the more determined spirits among the Chickamauga," or the most militant element of the Cherokees. After the death of Old Tassel in 1788, he joined the Chickamaugas and participated in a fight on Lookout Mountain in 1788 and stormed Gillespie's Station that same year; a "station," in frontier parlance, meant a fortified homestead, sometimes a retreat for neighborhood use, but which offered some protection against Indian attacks. In 1792 Watts succeeded Dragging Canoe, the leading spirit of the Chickamaugas, as head war leader of the faction. July 2, 1791, he signed a treaty between the federal government and the Cherokees at the treaty ground on the Holston River, as Kunoskeskie, pledging perpetual peace, but the very next year he launched a Chickamauga campaign against Tennessee settlements. He was defeated at Buchanan's Station, south of the Cumberland, September 30, 1792; he captured Cavett's Station the following year but his, that is the Chickamauga, towns were destroyed by militia in 1794 and Watts concluded a peace at Tellico Blockhouse in October or November. Apparently it held. Watts visited Philadelphia in 1796 and died at Willstown, Tennessee.

Info. from John Sugden; Grace Steele Woodward, *The Cherokees,* Norman, Univ. of Oklahoma Press, 1963.

Wauba Yuma (Wavio'ma), Hualapais leader (d. Apr. 3, 1866). The Hualapais (Walapais) Indians of northwestern Arizona were grouped into three subtribes, the largest of which, called the Yavapais Fighters, had as chief in the 1860s Wauba Yuma (or Yuba), a leader prominent enough to have four wives. The area of this grouping included Juniper Mountain, Mahone (Mohon) Mountain, Lower Sandy River, and Hualapais Mountain bands. Kwasula (Quasula), a son of Wauba Yuma and later himself a chief of the Yavapais Fighters, said that his father was "a peace chief of Fort Rock," adding that his influence extended far south, for he had friends among the Pimas and Maricopas, living in south-

ern Arizona. Long before forming such ties, however, he had been recognized as a chief by the Hualapais. Wauba Yuma not only was a peace and a war chief, but also political leader of his subtribe and as such in 1865 placed his "X" on a "treaty" with merchant William Hardy who sought protection for his toll road between Hardyville, which he had founded on the Colorado River, and Prescott. The paper would also, Hardy assured the chief, signal to whites his peaceful intentions and thus protect him and his people from white aggression. March 30, 1866, the cabin of Edward Clower was burned, Clower perishing in the blaze, his death and destruction of the building assumed by the whites to be the work of Hualapais Indians. Samuel C. Miller (see entry) and his freighting organization camped April 3, 1866, at Beale Spring near the present Kingman. Wauba Yuma approached the teamsters, the Indian shortly murdered by a shot from Miller's Hawken rifle which tore "a hole in his body as big as his hand." Miller's story was that Wauba Yuma and he had argued over flour and livestock the chief desired to obtain (neither Miller nor Wauba Yuma being proficient in the other's language), and that Miller decided that for the safety of his party he must eliminate the chief, for he believed that "once a chief falls the 'jig is up,'" and Indian hostility would be dismantled. A varying account said that the freighters determined that the Indians "meant to wage war...[so] they determined to kill Wauba Yuma, and he was at once shot." Responsible whites disapproved of the summary execution, predicting it would open the hostilities it was meant to prevent, which it did, the two-year Walapais War resulting directly from it. Nothing was done to Miller for his precipitate action. Wauba Yuma was succeeded as leader of the Yavapais Fighters by two of his sons, one following the other. Kwasula said that his father's death had been accidental, that "unknown to him the whites had ambushed a spring [Beale's Spring], awaiting some marauding Indians, and instead Wauba Yuma had fallen victim," which was probably the explanation the Indian was forced to accept.

Farish, II; Henry F. Dobyns, Robert C. Euler, *Wauba Yuma's People: The Comparative Socio-Political Structure of the Pai Indians of Arizona,* Prescott College Press, 1970; Amer. Anthro. Soc. *Memoirs 42: Walapais Ethnography,* ed. by A.L. Kroeber, 156.

Waxell, Sven, Swedish sea captain (1701-Feb.

14, 1762). B. at Stockholm, he served in the English fleet in the Baltic, in 1725 entered Russian service as a navigator and Febuary 2, 1733, as a lieutenant volunteered for Bering's second North Pacific expedition. He became first officer of Bering's *Sv. Petr.* After the leader's death on Bering Island, Waxell commanded survivors until their return to the mainland in 1742. His account was the first published information to appear in western Europe on Bering's expedition. His manuscript had an episodic history, was lost, but finally turned up in a Leningrad bookstore in 1938, was translated and published and "stands beside Steller's as a vivid first-hand personal narrative of the expedition." Upon his return to St. Petersburg, Waxell was assigned to check and compare journals of ships and officers of the expedition, and draft a chart, on which he drew the first picture of an Alaskan Aleut in a baidarka, and the only known contemporary picture of the sea cow, a species which rapidly became extinct. Waxell eventually became captain first rank in the Russian navy, in which he served until 1761. He was married and fathered three sons, all granted patents of nobility in tribute to their late father's achievements.

Pierce, *Russian America: A Biographical Dictionary.*

Weadock, Jack F., newspaperman (Mar. 17, 1899-Aug. 18, 1870). B. at St. Marys, Ohio, he was raised in the livestock and farming business. World War I interrupted his plans for college and he served overseas in the 146th infantry of the 37th Division as an intelligence scout, his regiment involved in seven major engagements from the Ardennes Forest to surrender of the German forces. Seeking an army appointment to West Point, he enlisted in the 7th Cavalry and was stationed at Fort Bliss, Texas, but a gunshot wound suffered in line of duty prevented the appointment; he remained in the cavalry for the three years of his enlistment. He had been a reporter for the Lima (Ohio) *Republican Gazette* and upon leaving the army worked for the El Paso *Post* before settling at Tucson where he joined the *Arizona Daily Star,* remaining with it for 46 years as sports writer, sports editor, news editor, city editor, managing editor and executive editor. He became widely known for his "Arizona Yesterday" column, the name later changed to "Desert Notebook." It was oriented largely to the spectacular history of Arizona and during his years of writing it Weadock became familiar

with many surviving pioneers and adventurers, such as the lawman Jeff Milton (see entry), who was his confidant and friend. *Dust of the Desert,* a collection of Weadock's columns, was published in 1936 and reprinted in 1963. *This Is the West* (1958) was another collection of his columns. Weadock died at Tucson, leaving his widow, a daughter and a son, and plentiful memories of his generosity toward others pursuing historical research into Arizona's past, and his wide range of specialized interests.

Arizona Daily Star, Aug. 19, 1970; *Tucson Daily Citizen,* Aug. 18, 1970; personal acquaintance with Jack Weadock.

Webber, David Gould, physician, intellectual, prospector (Sept. 12, 1809-June 8, 1883). B. in Livingston County, New York, this remarkable man of universal interests and capacities went to work at 16 on New York canals in the summers, attended school in winters and after two years, became a pharmacy clerk and studied under a Dr. Woodworth of Springfield, Pennsylvania. Three years later he bought the physician out, continuing the practice for twelve years. He married Margaret Bradish in 1833, fathering a son born in 1835. Mrs. Webber died in 1842, after which Webber practiced briefly, taking his son and two orphan girls along. He moved to Chicago in 1843, bought an interest in a flour mill, became a contractor on the Illinois Canal for four years, and in 1849 left for California by way of the Isthmus of Panama. In April 1850 he settled at Downieville in Sierra County. He established a practice in a tent hospital he had built, treating all comers, indigent or prosperous alike, while retaining and furthering his interests in mining, assaying, horse-breeding and lumbering, as well as in rocks, plants and birds; he had an "extreme fondness for animals, but his distinguished trait was charity toward all." Webber also superintended building of the first wagon road to Downieville, the initial bridge across the Yuba River; the town's courthouse and county jail, was superintendent of county schools for two years, and meanwhile found time to locate all the land around what then was called Little Truckee Lake, though it soon became known as Webber Lake, dominated by Webber Peak, an 8,100-ft. mountain. Because of a falls at the outlet there were no fish in it until Webber stocked it with trout. Trees were also his hobby. He heard of some remarkable firs in the distance, hired a guide to take him there and came upon a stand of *Abies amabilis,* or silver fir, so named for its smooth, silver-tinted trunk. It grows only in a few alpine regions of California (although is more common from Oregon to Alaska), and is said to be the "most exquisite evergreen in the world." Seeds of this tree before long were being sold at London and in Germany "at their weight in gold." In 1860 he built the Webber Lake Hotel, which he operated in the summers, having as guests such noted Californians as the artist, Charles Nahl, and Lola Montez (see entries), though she couldn't stand the altitude, thin mattresses and lack of wine and quickly departed. The painter and amateur botanist, Thomas Hill, was another prominent guest. During his active life in the Sierra Nevada Webber became acquainted with Abraham Harlow Peeples and Charles Baldwin Genung (see entries) and in early 1863 he joined Peeples in an expedition to Arizona in pursuit of doubtless chimerical rumors of a lost silver mine of "fabulous" richness. The party of eight left Yuma in April guided by Pauline Weaver, a onetime mountain man of intimate knowledge of the Arizona wilderness (see Peeples entry for details). They found no silver mine but about sixteen miles north of present Wickenburg (whose founder, Henry Wickenburg, was a member of the Peeples-Webber group), they made the stunning discovery of Rich Hill: a find of scattered gold nuggets and "chunks" littering a basin atop a mountain near Antelope Peak. The discoverers were reported to have scraped up with their fingers and such rudimentary implements as pocket knives, $250,000 on their brief initial visit. They transported their wealth to Tucson, divided it equally, and Dr. Webber took his $40,000 back to California, although the journey was a rough test for his nerves since the men he traveled with appeared to him a lawless band to whom he was careful not to divulge what he was carrying on his pack mule. At a spring near the San Jacinto Mountains (near present Palm Springs, California) the Webber group came upon Genung, who immediately recognized Webber "who I met several years before at Webber Lake." The doctor took Genung aside, told him what his mule was carrying, "he being one of the eight original locaters" of Rich Hill, adding that "he was afraid of his companions as they were a bad lot," Genung later wrote. Webber apparently returned to the lake with his riches intact. With these proceeds he built an open-air hospital and a solarium, retaining his custom of treating without payment persons short of resources, along with

those able to afford his services (the hotel and solarium still stand in sturdy defiance of the elements). Dr. Webber transferred his basic medical practice to Sierraville, and later to Loyalton, fifteen miles north of the lake. Webber's son had died in 1856 at Sacramento, but the doctor continued throughout his life to collect and raise orphan children, taking in at least thirteen of them, paying for their board and schooling, some at academies in San Francisco and one for two years of study in Europe. All of his wards flourished in chosen professions: two became physicians, another a merchant, one a lawyer and another an accountant. Dr. Webber died at 73 at Loyalton, and is buried in the Old Cemetery there.

Info. from the Calif. State Lby., Sacramento; *Illustrated History of Plumas, Lassen & Sierra Counties,* San Francisco, Fariss & Smith, 1882; Idwal Jones, "Doctor Webber's Lake," *Westways,* Vol. 56, No. 11 (Nov. 1964), 32; Charles Baldwin Genung, "Yavapai Country Memories, 1863-1894," ed. by Kenneth M. Calhoun, Tucson Corral of Westerners *Smoke Signal,* Vol. 43-44 (Spring and Fall, 1982), 36; info. from City of Loyalton.

Wells, Dennis Jay, historical researcher (Sept. 24, 1938-Mar. 2, 1990). B. at Lima, Ohio, he earned an engineering degree from the University of Arizona in 1956, and followed engineering professionally during his life. But his principal avocation was history, particularly the history of the southwest desert. He carefully researched the course of the 1870s military telegraph along the Gila Trail through Arizona Territory. More markedly, he discovered, carefully recorded, and interpreted inscriptions carved by Anglo travelers on the malpais cliffs overlooking the Gila River, not far from Agua Caliente. He called his discovery, which was along the earlier wagon route to California, slightly different from today's principal highway, "Arizona's Independence Rock." He, and his wife, Reba, and some friends located the world's tallest known saguaro cactus, now recorded in the *Guiness Book of World Records.* Wells died at Phoenix, survived by his widow.

Council on America's Military Past *Heliogram* 208 (June-July 1990); info. from Don Bufkin, Reba Wells.

Wells, E. Hazard, newspaperman, explorer (fl. 1889-1898). Wells first entered Alaska in the summer of 1889 "as the representative of a league of newspapers," and journeyed from Dyea, near Skagway, down the Yukon from its Canadian upper waters to St. Michael on Norton Sound. He found "a few gold miners...at work at that time upon the Forty-Mile Creek," but it was before the Gold Rush proper had commenced. In 1890 he again entered Alaska, this time by Chilkoot Pass (which had first been threaded by Whites in 1878), Wells having made a joint arrangement with an illustrated weekly (Leslie's) and the U.S. Coast and Geodetic Survey "to write descriptive articles and do some geographical work." He was accompanied by Jack Dalton and three other men and conceived the idea of building the road which ultimately was named the Dalton Trail. "We followed the Indian trail to the head waters of the Talkeetna, discovering and mapping Lakes Maude and Arkell, and later mapping the Talkeetna River down to its junction with the Yukon." Later, with three men, including an Indian, he struck up the Forty-Mile River from the Yukon, went across country to the Tanana River and "proceeded about 120 miles toward the head waters of the Copper and Susitna rivers, mapping Forty-Mile Creek, Lake Mansfield, Razonback Divide, the Tok River, and other points on the way." He returned then to the Tanana, and descended it 600 miles to the Yukon. In 1897 he entered the Yukon country for the third time, by way of White Pass, and reached Dawson September 20, this time writing articles for the Scripps-McRea newspapers "in Cincinnati, St. Louis, and other cities." He became convinced of gold-bearing possibilities of Alaska "rivaling those of the British Northwest Territory," citing evidences of gold he himself had found along the Tanana and its tributaries. Wells noted favorably Canadian restrictions on anyone, prospector or otherwise, entering the north country with less than 1,000 pounds of provisions (a year's supply), to cut down on the numbers of destitute and improvident individuals attracted by reports of gold. He described the geography of the country and traveling conditions within it. Wells differed with Lieutenant Henry Allen (see entry) on the possibility of boat navigation of the upper Tanana River, believing that Allen had visited the stream when the water was at its lowest, concluding therefore that rapids would make upriver movement impossible for any considerable distance. To the contrary, Wells visited the river at high water when, he believed, its navigation for virtually its whole length was practicable, at least in

certain seasons. He devoted considerable space to recounting the development of trails and roads through the sub-Arctic, to the presence of various diseases and to dog transport and other means of travel, his conclusions generally judicious and probably sound. In December 1897, Army Captain P.H. Ray (see entry), winter-bound at Fort Yukon, desired to get dispatches out to superiors in the States. He hired Frederick Gasch to go by dog team to Dawson and deliver them to John J. Healy (see entry), an important transportation figure, asking that Healy somehow transit them to "outside." Healy hired Wells, "a most reliable messenger," to take them out over the winter trails by way of Skagway to Seattle for transmittal to Washington, D.C. Healy's company would advance Wells $1,000 for expenses, recompense to come from the government along with a suitable emolument for Wells's services; the correspondent figured the total should come to about $2,500. He left Dawson December 20, and despite temperatures as low as 40° below zero reached Skagway January 24, the next day sailing for Seattle. Arriving January 30, he was instructed by the War Department to turn the dispatches over to Brigadier General Henry Merriam, commanding the Department of the Columbia at Vancouver, Washington. He did so and then, as might be expected, had great difficulty recovering expenses or anything else, since no one believed himself authorized to make payment. How the matter was resolved does not appear in the records scanned.

Wells's contributions, *Narratives of Explorations in Alaska*, 511-16; 539; 556-57.

Wells, Henry, expressman (Dec. 12, 1805-Dec. 10, 1878). B. at Thetford, Vermont, he was apprenticed to a tanner and shoemaker firm and around 1841 became agent at Albany for Harnden's Express, between New York and Albany. He rapidly expanded into all sorts of express business as far west as the Great Lakes and St. Louis and in 1850 formed by merger what became the American Express Company, of which he was president for eighteen years. His association with William G. Fargo began in 1844. Two years later he organized Wells, Fargo and Company to expand his business to California and in this firm lies his significance for frontier history. In 1857 the business of the east and the California interests were linked by establishment of the Butterfield Overland Mail Company, Butterfield representing the Wells, Fargo interest which also was somewhat involved indirectly and through Russell in the Pony Express, a briefly spectacular although financially unrewarding service to the west coast. Wells, Fargo never had an operating involvement in the Pony Express, however, By 1860 Wells, Fargo had become dominant in the express business and had a virtual monopoly of it in California. Whether the firm ever operated stage coaches in California under its own name is disputed, this although it did accumulate various subsidiary stage lines. Building of the railroad to California and business mergers and re-alignments saw the Wells interests continuing its leading role until 1873 when he retired as president of the American Express Company, although not from business matters entirely nor from his social involvements. He founded Wells Seminary for women, now Wells College at Aurora, New York, and, being afflicted with a speech impediment, established several schools for people similarly handicapped. Wells died at Glasgow, Scotland, and was buried at Aurora, New York. He married twice, his first wife predeceasing him.

Literature abundant: REAW; DAB; Waddell F. Smith, *Pony Express versus Wells Fargo Express,* San Rafael, Calif., Pony Express History and Art Gallery, 1966; W. Turrentine Jackson, "Wells Fargo: Staging over the Sierra," *California Historical Society Quarterly,* Vol. LIX, No. 2 (June 1970), 99-133; info. from E.F. (Ted) Mains.

Wenemouet (Awenemwet, Nimimitt, etc.), Penobscot, Abenaki chief (d. Mar. 1730). With thirteen other Abenaki he signed a peace with the English January 7, 1698, at the present Merespoint, Maine. He visited Quebec in late 1702 with other Penobscots and in company of the Jesuit, Pierre de La Chasse (see entry). The Abenaki were not interested in fighting Quebec's wars with the English unless it was to assure continued French support for them when they faced difficulties with Massachusetts. Queen Anne's War ended in 1713 and the next year Wenemouet and other Abenaki chiefs signed a peace with the English at Portsmouth, July 28, 1714. The Penobscots joined other Abenakis in 1722 against the English, and in 1724 or 1725 Wenemouet became head chief of the Penobscots, but because of weak French support he welcomed English peace suggestions when they came. Massachusetts Lieutenant Governor William Dummer and Wenemouet agreed to a cease fire

east of the Kennebec River and July 31, 1725, Dummer ordered hostilities to cease against the Penobscots. A peace treaty was concluded August 5, 1726. From that point forward, Wenemouet endeavored to secure and expand a true peace with French and English. A satisfactory pact with all branches of the Abenakis was concluded July 27, 1727. Near the end of his life he was described as looking "more like a frenchman than an Indian." He had been an important influence freeing the Penobscots from their ties to the French in Canada, and eventually arranging a peace with the English and "he enabled his people to avoid defeat and to retain at least part of their ancient territory into modern times."

Info. from John Sugden; DCB, II, 664-66; Parkman, *A Half Century of Conflict;* Sylvester, III.

Westdahl, Ferdinand, surveyor (fl. 1865-1902). In command of the Coast and Geodetic Survey steamer *McArthur,* he surveyed the coast of Alaska from Unimak Island and the Samnak Islands eastward to Prince William Sound, his studies published in the Survey's annual reports for 1901 through 1903. Earlier he had been employed by the Western Union Telegraph Expedition in Alaska of 1865-67, and by the Alaska Commercial Company in 1880, "but little information pertinent to his earlier work has been found."

Orth, 42.

Whistler, John, military officer (d. Sept. 3, 1829). B. in England, he came to America with John Burgoyne and with his commander, was captured at Saratoga October 17, 1777. With other British prisoners he was held at Boston until the end of the Revolution. Following peace he married an American girl and settled at Hagerstown, Maryland, where his son William (c. 1784-Dec. 4, 1863) was born; he, too, became a prominent military officer. John Whistler enlisted in the American army, becoming lieutenant adjutant for levies (enlistments) in 1791; he became an ensign in the 1st Infantry April 11, 1792, transferred to the 1st Sublegion September 4, and became a lieutenant November 27 of that year. He took part in the Northwestern Indian Wars, serving under Arthur St. Clair (see entry), escaping the great disaster that befell that force November 4, 1791, and served under Anthony Wayne (see entry) in the Battle of Fallen Timbers August 20, 1794, which won the Ohio-Indiana country for the white forces. He joined the 1st

Infantry November 1, 1796, and the following July 1, became a captain. In 1803 Captain Whistler and a company of soldiers were sent to the present site of Chicago with instructions to build Fort Dearborn, which was done, its establishment marking the true beginning of the city. The post was burned after the Fort Dearborn (Chicago) Massacre of 1812 (see William Wells entry), and Whistler in 1815 rebuilt it on the identical site; the area had been granted by Indians as one of the concessions of the Treaty of Greenville of 1795. John Whistler was honorably discharged June 15, 1815, and two years later moved to St. Charles, Missouri, and in 1818 he was a military storekeeper at St. Louis. He died at Bellefontaine, Missouri. No portrait of Whistler is known to exist.

Heitman; Joseph Kirkland, *The Story of Chicago,* I, Chicago, Dibble Pub. Co., 1892, 50-51.

White, Georgie, Colorado River rafter: *see,* Georgie Helen Clark

White, James M., merchant (d. October 25, 1849). White, whose headquarters were at Santa Fe, in 1848 opened commission and forwarding houses at that city and at El Paso, and seemed to prosper. October 18, 1848, he left Santa Fe, reached the Missouri border in mid-November and St. Louis November 23, bringing $58,000 in gold and silver coins, and bullion. It had been a rough trip because of bad weather most of the way. White apparently intended to make Santa Fe his home and, accompanied by his wife, Ann Dunn White, her daughter, 8, an employee, William Callaway, a black servant, Ben Bushman, two or three Germans and a Mexican, along with a black woman servant for Mrs. White, left Independence September 15, 1849. Their thirteen wagons, laden with goods, joined a large wagon train including ten vehicles owned by St. Vrain & McCarty and others with merchandise for Francois X. Aubry, captain of the combined column. By October 23, the train, following a snowstorm, had reached the vicinity of Point of Rocks, New Mexico, when White determined to let his wagons lumber on to Santa Fe while he, with his people would push ahead in two light carriages, able to arrive at the destination sooner. October 25, the White party was attacked by about 100 Jicarilla Apaches, all of the men slain and Mrs. White, her daughter and maid servant captured. News of the massacre reached Santa Fe October 29, and Aubry arrived the next day.

There followed much futile activity as scouts, Indians, traders and the army, spurred by sizeable rewards, tried to find Mrs. White and her two companions. On November 3, a 40-man military element under Captain William Nicholson Grier, with Kit Carson, Robert Fisher and Antoine Leroux as guides, picked up the trail of the Indians from the massacre site, followed it for ten or twelve days according to Carson who reported that it was "the most difficult trail I ever followed." In every campsite they passed they found some of Mrs. White's clothing, perhaps left by her as a guide to the pursuit. When they came in sight of the hostile camp, Carson wanted to attack at once, but Leroux wished to parley and Grier sided with Leroux; this gave the enemy time to decamp, after firing an arrow through Mrs. White's heart as she sought to escape. Her body was still warm when the troopers came upon it. She was shoeless, in tattered clothing and "literally worn to the bone." There was no sign of the child or the maidservant. In 1851 some Shawnee hunters said they saw a girl of the child's description among the Comanches who possibly had bought her from the Apaches, but she was never located by whites again.

Donald Chaput, *Francois X. Aubry: Trader, Trailmaker and Voyageur in the Southwest, 1846-1854,* Glendale, Arthur H. Clark Co., 1975; Barry, *Beginning of the West; Official Correspondence of James S. Calhoun...,* ed. by Annie Heloise Abel, Wash., G.P.O., 1915, 63-74; Veronica E. Velarde Tiller, *The Jicarilla Apache Tribe: A History, 1846-1970,* Lincoln, Univ. of Neb. Press, 1983; Susan Shelby Magoffin, *Down the Santa Fe Trail and Into Mexico,* ed. by Stella M. Drumm, Lincoln, 1982.

White, James Taylor, cattleman (1789-1852). B. in Louisiana he was of "a numerous clan which relocated to Opelousas [Louisiana] from Virginia around 1782." Some accounts have him in Texas in 1819 although he said he brought his family to Texas in 1828; both dates may be correct. Although some have believed members of the clan were driving herds of Longhorns to Opelousas as early as 1790, others believe that unlikely. Some hold that he established the Longhorn cattle industry in southeastern Texas; his herds roamed from east of the Trinity River to far west of that stream and to the Gulf of Mexico on the south. His JTW brand was probably recorded about 1830, and in the 1840s his cattle numbered upwards of 8,000 head. It is said that he drove a Longhorn herd from Anahuac, Cham-

bers County, to New Orleans about 1838, being
the first known to have completed such a drive.
He sold the cattle for cash which he deposited in
New Orleans banks. By his death he had become
known as the "Cattle King of Southeast Texas."
A man "not tall, but broad and strong," he drove
successive herds of cattle to New Orleans and
accumulated in the banks there some $150,000,
making him by one report, the richest man in
Texas. He was married and had many descendants. Jackson stated that his name was not anglicized from the French, Le Blanc, men of that
name also being among the earliest cattlemen
and drovers of Texas.

"The First Cattle Ranch in Texas," *Frontier Times,*
Vol. 13, No. 6 (Mar. 1936), 304-308; Tom Martin,"The
Livestock Cavalcade of Texas," *Frontier Times,* Vol.
17, No. 3 (Dec. 1939), 95; Jack Jackson, *Los Mesteños:
Spanish Ranching in Texas 1721-1821,* College Sta-
tion, Tex. A&M Univ. Press, 1986; HT.

White, Jim, prospector (c. 1837-post 1907). A
veteran prospector, White with George Strole
and a Captain Baker in 1867 was working the
San Juan River country in southeastern Utah
when attacked by Utes or Paiutes, and Baker was
killed. The other two, according to White,
reached the Colorado River by night, fashioned a
raft of three cottonwood logs lashed together and
hastily shoved off downstream. White reported
that on the fourth day Strole was washed off and
drowned. Weeks later, on September 8, White
and the raft reached the little Mormon town of
Callville, Nevada, below the mouth of the Virgin
River, the site now submerged by Lake Mead.
The sixteen-day trip left White "a pitiable object,
emaciated and haggard from abstinence, his bare
feet literally flayed by constant exposure to
drenching water, aggravated by occasional
scorchings of a vertical sun; his mental faculties,
though still sound, liable to wander and verging
close on the brink of insanity." Three weeks
later, when he had recovered somewhat, he wrote
a letter to his brother describing his harrowing
experience: "...i Went over folls from 10 to 15
feet hie, my raft wold tip over three and fore
times a day...fore seven days i had noth[ing] to
eat to [except] rawhide knife cover. The 8 days I
got some musquit beans...the 16 days i arrive at
Callville Whare i Was tak Care of by James
Ferry...i see the hardes times that eny man ever
did in the World but thank god that I got thrught
saft..." By his account he had floated through the
entire Grand Canyon with its numerous, often

perilous rapids, all this two years before John
Wesley Powell (see entry) made the "first" successful transit of that stretch of wild Colorado
River. The event naturally stirred up an intense
controversy, ramifications of which are heard to
this day. Among the noted voices in opposition
were those of Frederick S. Dellenbaugh (see
entry), who accompanied Powell's second journey down the great river, and Robert Brewster
Stanton (1846-1922) who led a memorable, dis-
aster-plagued expedition down the river in 1889-
90. Those who believe White's tale is true
include Richard E. Lingenfelter, a meticulous,
thoroughly-informed southwestern historian;
former Senator Barry Goldwater, who has rafted
the Colorado, and the noted Georgie White
Clark, who has traversed the Colorado in pneu-
matic craft for nearly forty years, taking thousands of people downriver. She is quoted: "I
positively think White made the trip. Dellenbaugh and Stanton of course don't want that in
history. It would be very possible, even in *high*
water, to make the trip." White, for a time,
worked as a blacksmith, and finally settled at
Trinidad, Colorado, where he worked as an
expressman. He was considered simple, honest
and straightforward, and was interviewed in
1907 by Stanton, who found him a man of 70
who gave Stanton an account identical with that
he had told at Callville in 1867. Stanton believed
that although he had floated down the river some
distance, it was probably from no more than sixty
miles above Callville. This seems at variance
with White's physical condition when brought
ashore.

Frank Waters, *The Colorado,* N.Y., Rinehart &
Co., 1946; Robert Brewster Stanton, *Down the Col-
orado,* ed. by Dwight L. Smith, Norman, Univ. of Okla.
Press, 1965; Stanton, *Colorado River Controversies,*
commentaries by Otis R. Marston, Martin J. Anderson,
Boulder City, Nev., Westwater Books, 1982.

White, Jim (Jim Wilson), boss hunter (1828-
Fall 1880). B. in Illinois to English immigrant
parents, he left home in his teens, and from Westport, Missouri, worked as a bullwhacker on the
Santa Fe and Chihuahua trails for several years.
During the Civil War he served with Federal
forces according to DeArment, or with Confederate elements as Edgar has it, as a grain buyer
and wagon boss. After the war he became a
freighter for the army out of Fort Leavenworth,
hauling supplies to western posts. He was at Fort
Phil Kearny, Wyoming, in December 1866, and

his wagons assisted in bringing in the 82 bodies of men lost in the Fetterman massacre. The following summer, according to DeArment he participated in the celebrated Wagonbox fight north of Kearny. In the winter of 1867-68, working out of Fort Union, New Mexico, he helped move the Navahos from Fort Sumner to Fort Wingate as they were returned to their ancestral homeland. In 1868 at Mora, New Mexico, a Mexican was killed in a fight and Wilson shot two officers who had accused him of participating in the slaying, which he had not. With another he fled south toward Las Vegas; a posse trailed them closely and the two dropped three members of it, dispersing the law group, but subsequent "wanted" posters persuaded Wilson to change his name to Jim White. The foregoing is more probable than Edgar's yarn which reportedly originated with White himself as to events that led him to adopt a new name. DeArment said White assisted in two small cattle drives from Texas to Kansas railheads, then joined J. Wright Mooar (see entry) in hunting buffalo, at first for the market, and when a hide outlet opened White developed into an expert and innovative hide hunter. He became "the Boss Hunter" to many and to some, "the greatest buffalo hunter that ever lived," although others no doubt would claim to share that title. White worked with a number of famed frontiersmen, including Thomas C. Nixon and the numerous renowned frontiersmen Nixon hired. After a couple of years hunting buffalo out of Dodge City, White went to Texas and continued his work, for a time with Frank Collinson as partner. He had continued success in obtaining hides though coming into shooting scrapes with Mexican *ciboleros,* Kiowas and Comanches. "White had the reputation of being a tough character. He operated best alone or with his own men" Edgar reported. By the spring of 1878 he had sold 10,000 buffalo hides, but the herds were gone from the southern plains and he headed north again, by fall reaching the Big Horn Mountains of Wyoming. Here he met Oliver Hanna, reportedly an erstwhile Indian scout for the army, and threw in with him. Hanna wrote later that he "could see by his outfit that he was a real hunter and a good one. He had three 16-pound Sharps rifles, 700 pounds of lead and five kegs of powder and other paraphernalia." White, about 50 at the time, was 6 ft., 2 in., tall, rawboned and weighed about 200 pounds. After market hunting for the winter, White located a good buffalo country in the Yellowstone area in 1879, and

Hanna joined him during the following winter. White soon kept six skinners busy; he secured 2,000 hides in one season, according to a Miles City newspaper, and 2,800 in the next. In the fall of 1880 White and Hanna established a camp on Shell Creek in the Big Horn Basin against the west slope of the Big Horn Mountains. But that country was "a rendezvous for all kinds of outlaws," wrote Hanna. One day three men camped not far distant; Hanna went down and visited with them, but he found them unfriendly and he was not comfortable with them. "That night something seemed to tell me to go back over to my cabin on the east side of the mountains and check on things." When he returned in about a week, White, wagons, mules and everything else were gone, but Hanna found fresh dirt under some pine trees. He discovered Jim White buried there, shot in the back of his head. Subsequent examination showed that he had been killed by a .50 caliber bullet, "possibly from the same gun that killed his own victims." His tally book which, upon earlier questioning, he had read to Hanna one evening showed he had killed 16,000 buffalo in Texas, in Kansas, and in the northern country. On May 5, 1979, he was reburied "with dignity and honor" at the Old Trail Town cemetery near Cody, Wyoming, after 99 years of resting in what had become a hayfield of the Irvy Davis ranch at the mouth of Shell Canyon.

R.K. DeArment, "Boss Hunter," *True West,* Vol. 36, No. 4 (Apr. 1989), 20-27 (inc. photograph of Jim White); Bob Edgar, "The Reburial of Jim White, Buffalo Hunter," Chicago Westerners *Brand Book,* Vol. XXXVI, No. 5 (Nov. 1979), 33-35, 39.

White Cloud (Wabokeshiek, Winnebago Prophet), medicine man (c. 1794-c. 1841). Half Winnebago and half Sauk, he was known as The Prophet and was largely responsible for Black Hawk's War in that he encouraged that chief to conduct his 1832 hostile operations in Illinois and Wisconsin. He presided over the Prophet's Village on the Rock River, Illinois, the site of the present Prophetstown. According to Hodge he was "noted for his cruelty and his hostility toward [white] Americans." Black Hawk around 1830 hoped for outside aid for his planned military adventure and sent emissaries to the Creeks, Cherokees, Osages and other tribes of the south seeking it. The young chief Neapope (see entry), Black Hawk's right-hand man, made a trip to Malden, Ontario, and returned saying he had promises of British assistance, that he had stopped at The Prophet's Village and the Winnebago had pledged that Potawatomis, Chippewas and Ottawas would aid the Sauks and Foxes, while the British had agreed to furnish weapons and other supplies and, if defeated, the Indians could retreat to the Red River region of Canada for refuge. Black Hawk was elated at all this, but the more realistic Keokuk (see entry) openly disbelieved the reports. Black Hawk moved on to war and disaster (see Black Hawk entry), climaxed by the reverse at Bad Axe, Wisconsin, in July-August 1832 and a few days later he was captured with The Prophet by Winnebagos Chaetar and One-Eyed Dekaury in an attempt to reach Prairie La Crosse, where they expected to cross the Mississippi to safety. The hostiles were delivered to Illinois militia Brigadier General Joseph Montfort Street (1782-1840), Indian agent at Prairie du Chien, on August 27, 1832. Sent to Jefferson Barracks near St. Louis they were ironed and fitted with ball-and-chain "to their extreme mortification," and in April 1833 were taken to Washington, D.C., where they met President Jackson, who greeted them cordially. White Cloud appealed to him for their freedom, but they were sent instead to Fortress Monroe and held there until June 4. Major John Garland was instructed to escort them back to the Midwest by way of Norfolk, Baltimore, Philadelphia, New York, Albany and the Great Lakes, a tour which the Indians enormously enjoyed and were impressed by the might and wonder-working of the white people, including a balloonist's ascent and a fireworks display. The Prophet was released to the Winnebagos at Prairie du Chien. In his early forties he was said to be six feet tall, inclined to obesity but strongly built, with long, matted hair, a low forehead, large, deeply sunken eyes, fleshy nose, thick lips and a "savage expression," a description obviously not made by an admirer. On her deathbed one of his wives accused him of murdering her, and the Prophet was described as "a dangerously vicious individual," not the sort Black Hawk should have chosen for his chief adviser. Hagan concluded that "among the Indians, perhaps only the Prophet deserved the opprobrium heaped upon him." Having lost prestige as a prophet, White Cloud, or Wabokeshiek lived in obscurity among the Sauks in Iowa until their removal to Kansas, and died eventually among the Winnebago. At Jefferson Barracks his portrait had been painted by Catlin and is now in the National Museum; another portrait, by R.M. Sully, was made while

The Prophet was a prisoner at Fortress Monroe, and is reproduced by Hodge, II, 886.

Info. from John Sugden; Hodge, HAI, II, 885-86; William T. Hagan, *The Sac and Fox Indians,* Norman, Univ. of Okla. Press, 1958.

White Mingo (Kayashuta), Seneca chief (d. 1790?). White Mingo lived on the Allegheny River above Pittsburgh and his mark, or signature, appeared on Henry Bouquet's treaty of 1764. He is mentioned in a document of December 10, 1777, sent by John Gibson to General Edward Hand from Fort Pitt. Blacksnake (see entry) reported that he had no knowledge of White Mingo having any role in the Revolution, but Blacksnake was more familiar with operations against the New York frontier than against that in Pennsylvania where White Mingo operated. The date of death of White Mingo is uncertain. In *Revolution on the Upper Ohio,* Thwaites reported that he died "before 1777," but that seems incorrect in view of the Gibson letter to Hand. One of his name was reported to have died on the site of Fort Wayne, Indiana, in 1790.

Thwaites/Kellogg, *Frontier Defense on the Upper Ohio, 1777-1778.*

White Plume: *see,* Pocatello

White Shield (A-che-kan-koo-ani), Cheyenne chief (d. May 1, 1918). The son of Wind Woman and Spotted Wolf (see entry), White Shield, whose name originally was Young Black Bird, in his own right became a chief and noted warrior of his tribe. A Cheyenne chief whose name is identical with White Shield but is translated as Little Shield, signed the May 10, 1868, Treaty at Fort Laramie between General Sherman and others, and leaders of the Northern Cheyenne and Northern Arapaho, the two Indian peoples being closely associated. In the early 1870s White Shield and his small band, possibly at the urging of George Bent, came onto the reservation at Darlington, since moved to Concho, Oklahoma, where John D. Miles was agent. But they could not have stayed long. Nye reported that White Shield was active in the second Battle of Adobe Walls, June 27, 1874; White Shield however took no part in the so-called Buffalo War of 1874 on the South Plains. He soon was in the north, having a major role in the famed Battle of the Rosebud, June 17, 1876. He rescued Two Moon under heavy fire. At one point "two brave men, White Shield and a Sioux, charged on the troops, and all the Indians followed them." White Shield killed a man and "ran over and counted coup on him." Once a bugler could not control and mount his horse and White Shield "rode between him and his horse, to knock the reins out of his hands and free the horse. He did not get the horse, but counted coup on the man..." Before this great battle, which ended in at least a draw and, as some believe, an outright defeat for George Crook and the soldiers, White Shield received minute instructions and medicine from his father, Spotted Wolf, who told him, "if you yourself get in a bad place, do not get excited, but try to shoot and defend yourself. That is the way to become great. If you should be killed, the enemy when they go back will say that they fought a man who was very brave; that they had a hard time to kill him." Throughout the battle turmoil, White Shield was very prominent, and his feats were several. He also was in the June 25, fight against Custer. He was fishing in the Little Big Horn when the soldiers approached, and instantly dressed and mounted his war horse and rode toward the action. He saw Tom Custer killed and stripped, reporting that "he died with his pistol in his hand." After the Custer command was wiped out White Shield joined those who returned to the Reno siege and took part in that. White Shield was at Dull Knife's village on the Red Fork of the Powder River in the foothills of the Big Horn Mountains, when it was struck November 25-26 by Ranald Mackenzie, and just missed being with the Cheyenne party which was most directly attacked and overrun. In the general fight "many men did brave things. White Shield and Medicine Bear and Long Jaw and Big Crow showed much bravery." Hoig, in *The Peace Chiefs of the Cheyennes* presents a portrait photograph of White Shield taken "before 1877." The chief probably died on the Cheyenne-Arapaho Reservation in Oklahoma.

George Bird Grinnell, *The Fighting Cheyennes*, Norman, Univ. of Okla. Press, 1956; Grinnell, *The Cheyenne Indians*, 2 vols., Lincoln, Univ. of Neb. Press, 1972; George E. Hyde, *Life of George Bent*, Norman, 1968; W.S. Nye, *Carbine and Lance*, Norman, 1983; Stan Hoig, *The Peace Chiefs of the Cheyennes*, Norman, 1980; info. from E.F. (Ted) Mains.

Whymper, Frederick, artist (July 28, 1838-post 1882). B. at London, he was the son of an artist and brother of mountaineer Edward Whymper (1840-1911) and of Charles H. Whymper (1853-1941), also an artist. Frederick left England in June 1862 for Victoria, British Columbia, where he spent three years, visited San Francisco frequently and sketched and painted along the Pacific coast. In 1864 he met Charles S. Bulkley (see entry), leader of the noted Western Union Telegraph expedition seeking to install a line to hook up the United States with Siberia and Russia. Whymper volunteered to accompany the party as artist. He left Victoria July 30, 1865, going first to Sitka, Alaska, then to St. Michael on Norton Sound, visited Petropavlovsk, Kamchatka, and spent time on the Siberian coast. He stopped off at Unalakleet and Nulato on the lower Yukon and in the summer of 1867 went upstream to Fort Yukon at the confluence of the Yukon and Porcupine rivers, where it was learned that a successful Atlantic cable obviated any need for a trans-Asian telegraph line. Many of Whymper's art works picturing places he visited were published in the *Illustrated London News*. He reached San Francisco in October 1867 and the next year his book, *Travel and Adventure in the Territory of Alaska,* was published at London. It contained many of his works. Pierce reported that Whymper was said to have painted in California until about 1882, but the date and circumstances of his death are not known.

Pierce, *Russian America: A Biographical Dictionary.*

Wieghorst, Olaf, artist (Apr. 30, 1899-Apr. 27, 1988). B. at Viborg, Jutland, Denmark, He arrived at New York December 31, 1918, speaking no English and with a capitalization of $1.25. He already was into drawing and painting and was enthusiastic about the American West he had never seen except, as he later said, "in the movies." He saw a newsreel in New York of Pershing pursuing Pancho Villa into Mexico, and enlisted in the 5th U.S. Cavalry, served a three-year hitch in the Southwest. Then, his English having developed satisfactorily, he worked around the West as a cowboy for two years before returning to New York, already an accomplished youthful artist, specializing in horses and scenes he had come to know. At New York he married, joined the Mounted Division of the New York Police Force and remained with it until retirement, twenty years later. "I used to break and train horses for them," he said. "I was on their show team, did a lot of trick riding." On the side he worked hard at his art—he had sold a first picture earlier for forty cents, enough to convince him that art was to be his true profession. "I used to go around to museums to learn composition and things like that," he said, never having had formal art training. While he was a policeman he got a friend to peddle his pictures at Madison Square Garden when a rodeo was scheduled. By then he was charging as much as $35 for a painting, and once received $300 for one. After his retirement from the Police Force he and his wife moved to El Cajon, California, which he made his headquarters, though traveling throughout the west, particularly to Arizona and New Mexico, on research trips. At first he sold pictures from the back of his station wagon, his prices rising to $400 to $800 each, and his reputation rising steadily as an extraordinary artist of western subjects: horses, cattle, cowboys, Indians, scouts, Army figures—all things he well knew from his own experience. The turning point in his career came, he believed, when he had a one-man show at the Grand Central Gallery in New York. "After that," an admirer said, "they stood in line to buy his stuff." The prices for his work kept pace with his meteoric rise in national awareness as the logical successor to Remington and Russell, and probably the last of frontier painters of much personal experience on the frontier, even though it was swiftly fading by the time he came to it. But the honesty, the simple forcefulness of his art, made his paintings, drawings and bronzes unique and steadily enhanced their value. In 1982 he sold one painting for $140,000; by that time he was "recognized by many to be the foremost American western painter." Two of his oils, "Navajo Madonnah" and "Navajo Man," sold that year for $450,000 and were resold within three years for $1 million, at that time said to be the highest price ever paid for the work of a living American artist. His pictures hung in the White House during the presidencies of Dwight Eisenhower, Gerald Ford and Ronald Reagan, and collectors of his art included John Wayne, Roy Rogers and Gene Autry, as well as Barry Goldwater and Clint Murchison. Although his work appeared in varied media, he believed that "oils are what I do best," and some of his finest works are of that genre. Wieghorst died at La Mesa, California, three days short of his ninetieth birthday, and he was survived by his widow, Mabel and a son. He asked that there be no religious services in his memory and that his ashes be scattered over the wild Mogollon Rim of central Arizona.

William Reed, *Olaf Wieghorst,* Flagstaff, Ariz., Northland Press, 1969; Ed Ainsworth, *The Cowboy in*

Art, N.Y., World Pub. Co., 1988; Tucson, *Arizona Daily Star,* Oct. 18, 1981, Apr. 29, 1988.

Williams, Jarret, Indian trader (fl. 1773-1778). Before 1773 Williams had dwelt in the Watauga settlement near the North Carolina-Tennessee border. In 1774 during Lord Dunmore's War he enlisted in the company of Captain Evan Shelby (see entry), probably fought at the Battle of Point Pleasant, West Virginia, and afterward resumed trading with the Cherokees. He had a "yard" at Chota, the favored town or "capital" of the Cherokees as did traders Isaac Thomas and William Fawling. On the night of July 8, 1776, the "beloved woman" of the Cherokees, Nancy Ward (see entry) informed the three traders of the intent of Dragging Canoe and other militants to strike the white settlements along the Holston and perhaps the Tennessee rivers on July 20, and urged them to escape and warn the pioneers. She desired to avert bloodshed and save the lives of both her people and the settlers. Jarret Williams successfully fled Chota and brought word of the Cherokee plans, permitting the settlers to prepare for the attack. Williams was reimbursed by the North Carolina legislature for his losses in the Cherokee war, to the amount of 100 pounds sterling. He joined George Rogers Clark's Illinois expedition in 1778 as a lieutenant, and received an Illinois grant for his role. He then settled on Floyd's Fork of the Salt River, in Bullitt County, Kentucky, where he lived the remainder of his life.

Thwaites/Kellogg, *The Revolution on the Upper Ohio, 1775-1777,* Madison, Wis. Hist. Soc., 1908; Grace Steele Woodward, *The Cherokees,* Norman, Univ. of Okla. Press, 1963.

Williams, Leonard H., frontiersman (d. 1846). In the spring of 1827 Williams was residing at Nacogdoches, east Texas. Although unlettered, he was involved in business affairs and other activities. July 15-16, 1839, he took part in the Battle of Neches, west of Tyler, when about 500 Texans fought an estimated 700 Cherokees under Chief Bowles (see entry) who was killed "wearing a handsome sword and sash which had been given him by President Sam Houston," and who had been peripherally significant in the Texas victory at San Jacinto earlier. By the engagement, the Cherokees were unworthily forced from their Texas lands. In the spring of 1840 Williams, by then a trader to the Comanches, met Indians on the Canadian River. As

Williams talked with Chief Pahauka he observed a white girl in the Comanche camp and learned that she was the celebrated captive, Cynthia Ann Parker (see entry). He tried to arranged her release, offering a ransom. The chief was willing but the Indian council decided otherwise even when Williams raised the price he would pay to a dozen mules and several hundred dollars in trade goods. The council directed that Williams leave the camp, but the chief permitted him to talk first with Cynthia Ann who sat under a tree, eyes downcast, and refused to speak to him, either having forgotten her English or because the Comanches had warned her to remain silent. Williams reluctantly returned to the settlements, relaying information about the captive to the Parker family. In 1842 Houston named Williams one of four commissioners to deal with Indians and in that year he discovered two white children who had been captured near Austin by Comanches. In September 1843 Williams helped arrange an Indian treaty council with Texas and in April 1844 was a commissioner at a Comanche council at Tehuacana Creek near Torrey's Trading Post in McLennan County. Williams was a McLennan County freighter for several years, working principally for John F. Torrey's Indian frontier trading houses. John S. Ford (see entry), editor of the Austin *Texas Democrat,* wrote Houston May 19, 1846, that it was reported that Comanches had killed Williams, no date given.

HT; Margaret Schmidt Hacker, *Cynthia Ann Parker,* Texas Western Press, Southwestern Studies 92, 1990.

Williams, Richard Gott, frontiersman (b. June 23, 1812). B. in Culpeper County, Virginia, Williams in 1826, very early in the trade, reportedly outfitted twelve freight wagons and embarked on a commercial venture to the Spanish southwest, the caravan pushing beyond Santa Fe to El Paso and Chihuahua City. Verification for this adventure is difficult to obtain; Barry reports that late in May 1826 a caravan of 80 to 100 persons left Missouri for New Mexico, including "waggons and carriages of almost every description," while the "amount of merchandise taken...[was] very considerable," but does not give a date for completion of the trip to Santa Fe or elsewhere. Oscar Williams said that his grandfather's party was accompanied by the youthful Kit Carson, both Carson and R.G. Williams being from the same region of Kentucky. Barry said the party Carson accompanied

left Fort Osage, Missouri, in August and reached Santa Fe in November 1826, including James Collins, a later Indian superintendent, William Wolfskill and other well-known Plains figures, but does not mention Williams, adding that the size of this party was unknown. Oscar Williams reported that his grandfather lost about $100,000 on the return trip in horses and other goods run off by Arapaho Indians [more probably Pawnees]. Little further has been found on Richard Gott Williams.

Oscar Williams; Barry, *The Beginning of the West; Williams Family Genealogy* (as mentioned by Oscar Willams), II, 1935.

Williams, Roger, clergyman, free thinker, Indian friend (c. 1603-early 1682/83). B. at London of middle class parentage he was intellectually-inclined and was graduated from Cambridge in 1627, becoming an ordained Anglican minister about 1629. He made many friends among the Puritans and in 1631 came to Boston where he became a teacher and after two years at Plymouth the minister of Salem church. He found himself equally opposed to theocratic states and to civil authorities having the right to "enforce the Ten Commandments," or interfere in the religious beliefs of the citizenry. Authorities also found deeply objectionable Williams's conscientious protests against imperialistic expropriation of American territories. He attacked English royal charter claims as a violation of the rights of Indians, and he objected to other things as well, his views anathema to the established order. October 9, 1635, the General Court ordered him banished and the magistrates, learning of his intention to found a "radical" community to the south on Narragansett Bay, sought to apprehend him but, forewarned, he escaped in mid-winter. He joined friendly Indians at Pokanoket, principal settlement of the Wampanoags and residence of Massasoit and King Philip on the east side of Narragansett Bay (the place known to the English as Sowams). Williams suffered privations but had gathered sufficient followers by 1636 to found Providence, the earliest Rhode Island settlement. During the Pequod War of 1637 Williams, fluent in Indian languages, interceded in a council at which Pequods and Narragansetts sought to reconcile their differences and form a united front against the whites, by offering the Narragansetts, on the part of his own persecutors in Massachusetts and elsewhere, an alliance against their old enemies, the Pequods. "The

Narragansetts succumbed to the suggestion, thus playing into the hands of the English and leading not only to the Pequots' destruction but also eventually to their own," in the subsequent King Philip's War of 1675-76, although this sequence was not Roger Williams' intent by any means. He may have sought only to prevent an alliance between the two powerful tribes in order to prevent a more drastic war than at length transpired, though his action left the Pequots to fight alone against overwhelming white forces. Williams was a realist. Although he spoke harshly of Indians on occasion, his comments even so were mild compared with those of other English settlers, and throughout his lifetime, by strict honesty and forbearance in his dealings with the tribes, and his honorable arrangements with them, retained their trust and even affection. To Providence came those whites seeking refuge from religious persecution in Britain as well as in Massachusetts. Williams went to England and through influence of powerful friends secured in 1644 a patent uniting Providence with other Rhode Island towns; the patent was annulled in 1651, but Williams had it restored, and its guarantee of absolute freedom of conscience was later confirmed by a royal charter in 1663. In 1654 Williams was elected president of the Colony, and served three terms. During this period Jews first came to Rhode Island and later the Quakers as well, persecuted throughout New England; Williams welcomed them as a matter of principle, although he strongly disagreed with their views. In 1643 he had written his important *Key into the Language of America,* which has gone through half a dozen printings, the latest in 1973; it is considered "undoubtedly the best description of the Indians of New England," and "the most important source on seventeenth-century Narragansett culture." Through his later years he remained a steadfast friend of Indians, protesting to Puritan colonies against unfair treatment and seeking peaceful relations between the parties. "Curiously, although he enjoyed the full confidence of the Narragansetts and preached to them, he gave over the attempt at religious conversion." He had become skeptical of divine claims of the churches and after a few months as a Baptist in 1639 he had become a Seeker, accepting no creed while remaining a Christian. Despite his influence with the Narragansetts he found himself tragically unable to avert the sanguinary King Philip's War, in which he served as captain of militia and tried to at least prevent the burning

of Providence by the hostiles. March 29, 1676, they swarmed against the town and "although the aged Roger Williams [he was then in his seventies], the life-long friend of the southern tribes, went forth to meet them, unarmed, and leaning upon his staff, he was met by their old men, and warned by them that it would not be safe, even for him, to venture amongst them; and they said also, that there were many 'stranger indians' mixed with their tribes. He was thus forced to retire to the garrison-house with the rest of the inhabitants, while the Indians...burned some thirty houses of the town." Those torched included the home of Williams himself. The government of Massachusetts, "much to its credit," at this point rescinded its years-old ban on Williams and offered him sanctuary in one of the Bay towns, although he did not accept the offer. Indian prisoners, in Rhode Island as in other colonies, were customarily sold into service, Williams "an active participant in the venture." This was not technically slavery, however, for the captives were "sold for specified periods of service, and many if not all of them remained within the colony." The action apparently was interpreted as punishment of a sort, rather than riddance of the offenders. Williams died between January 16, and March 15, 1682/83. He was regarded by many as rash and of hasty judgment, but his integrity was never doubted and even those ardently opposed to him granted that he was true to his beliefs. In his own generation he was "a provocative and significant figure," and left his mark on American thinking by his belief in separation of church and state, on freedom of religious thought and non-governmental interference in that faith, and his commitment to honesty in dealings with Indians and the under-privileged; these have had a profound and lasting impact on American thinking. "Colonial thinker, religious liberal, and earliest of the fathers of American democracy, he owes his enduring fame to his humanity and breadth of view, his untiring devotion to the cause of democracy and free opportunity, and his long record of opposition to the privileged and self-seeking."

Literature abundant: CE; DAB; Douglas Edward Leach, *Flintlock and Tomahawk: New England in King Philip's War,* N.Y., Macmillan Co., 1958; George M. Bodge, *Soldiers in King Philip's War...,* Leomister, Mass., p.p., 1896, p. 382; HNAI, 15.

Williams, William Franklyn, frontiersman

(1870-Nov. 10, 1940. Williams, his father, Jonathan Paul Williams (b. c. 1849), Benjamin Williams (d. c. 1943) were among the 19th century visitors to famed Rainbow Bridge in southern Utah. They saw it, as did many others, a quarter century or more before the official "discoverers" reached it in 1909 (see Byron Cummings, Jim Mike entries). Richardson wrote that "scores of [white] men saw the bridge long before 1909," the Williams trio among them. Many left names and dates inscribed at the foot of the bridge or in its immediate vicinity. Among those Richardson noted were C.M. Cade, 1869 or 1889; Ed Randolph, 1880; Jim Black, 1881; W.D. Young, 1882; George Emmerson, 1882; W. Brockway, 1883; the Williamses in 1883 and 1884; John Hadley, 1885 and G.E. Choistilan, 1888, along with others of later date; for several Richardson adds biographical details. All names and dates were obliterated early in the 1920s, possibly because "those inscriptions disproved the claim that no white man had seen Rainbow Natural Bridge prior to its 'official' discovery," Richardson concluded. Jonathan Williams had erected his first trading post in Blue Canyon in 1882, and the other Williamses also were Navaho traders. Jonathan, the first white child born in Marysville, California, had brought his family by wagon to northern Arizona in 1878 (he was later killed in Mexico). The Williams boys, Bill and Ben, first saw the bridge around November 20, 1884, but "they never said much except that they didn't think anything of it." They, too, found names chiseled into the soft sandstone or written with charcoal, some identical with those Richardson recorded. When he heard about the Cummings-Douglass claim to have "discovered" the bridge, Bill laughed. "Why I saw that bridge twenty-five years ago with Dad and Ben," he said, according to his daughter, Mrs. Ernest Joseph Yost, a longtime newspaperwoman of Flagstaff, Arizona. William Williams and his wife were killed in a head-on auto crash while enroute from Flagstaff to their home at Winslow, Arizona.

Weldon F. Heald, "Who Discovered Rainbow Bridge?" *Sierra Club Bulletin,* Vol. 40, No. 8 (Oct. 1955), with photos, 24-28; Gladwell Richardson, *Navajo Trader,* Tucson, Univ. of Ariz. Press, 1986, pp. 61-62.

Willing, James, naval officer (Feb. 9, 1751-Oct. 13, 1801). B. at Philadelphia of a family prominent in colonial affairs, his oldest brother, Thomas, was a noted financial figure, a partner of Robert Morris and aided in financing the new nation. In 1774, James moved to Natchez, where he "dissipated his patrimony," returned in 1777 to Philadelphia and secured from Congress a commission as a Navy captain, with permission to proceed to the Mississippi and secure the neutrality of residents along its banks, and to bring back to the states what provisions he could secure. He enlisted a company and in an armed boat christened *Ratttletrap* left Pittsburgh January 10, 1778. At Natchez he succeeded in obtaining a pledge of neutrality from prominent citizens, but was accused of pillaging and inflicting damages upon property there. Willing went on to New Orleans, captured a small British vessel at Manchac, a small post below Baton Rouge, and used this craft for further depredations upon the property of presumed British sympathizers. The next year he sent his troops upriver under charge of Lieutenant Robert George, who placed them at command of George Rogers Clark. Willing himself proceeded to Mobile, Alabama, where he was captured and nearly hanged, but was finally shipped as prisoner to New York City and kept on Long Island under parole with other American officers. Because of a dispute with a British officer, Willing was loaded with irons and incarcerated at New York City for three months before one of his sisters, married to a British officer, interceded for him with Sir Henry Clinton, who at length permitted him to return to Philadelphia under parole until he was exchanged (he was said to have been exchanged for Henry Hamilton, governor of Detroit). Willing never married and died at Philadelphia.

Thwaites/Kellogg, *Frontier Defense on the Upper Ohio, 1777-1778.*

Willison, George Findlay, writer (July 24, 1896-July 30, 1972). B. at Denver, he studied at the University of Colorado, was a Rhodes Scholar at Oxford and studied at the Sorbonne of the University of Paris; he had been in the army machinegun corps in 1918 before continuing with higher education. Willison was a newspaperman at Denver and New York, a writer for, and eventual national editor-in-chief of, the Federal Writers Project at Washington, D.C., from 1936-41, and worked as a writer, public relations expert and in like capacities for many political, national and international organizations. He wrote several books, best known of which was *Saints and Strangers: Being the Lives of the Pilgrim Fathers and Their Families...* (1945); he also wrote *Behold Virginia: The Fifth Crown...* (1951). His other books included *Here They Dug Gold* (1931); *Our Pilgrim Fathers* (1965), and *Patrick Henry and His World* (1969), and edited *The Pilgrim Reader: The Story of the Pilgrims as Told by Themselves and Their Contemporaries...* (1953). He was working on a biography of Tom Paine late in life. Willison married and fathered a son.

Contemporary Authors.

Williston, Samuel Wendell, paleontologist (July 10, 1852-Aug. 30, 1918). B. at Roxbury, Massachusetts, his parents took him at 5 to Manhattan, Kansas, where he was graduated in 1872 from the Kansas State Agricultural College. In 1873-74 he was a collector of dinosaur and other fossils for Othniel C. Marsh (see entry). In 1876 Marsh took him to Yale at New Haven, Connecticut, Williston, remaining with Marsh until 1885, taking part in collection expeditions to Montana and Colorado during that period. He studied medicine and received his M.D. from Yale Medical School in 1880, and a Ph.D. in 1885, teaching at Yale until 1890 while conducting a private medical practice. In 1890 he went to the University of Kansas at Lawrence, teaching historical geology, physiology and becoming dean of the school of medicine, holding state medical positions before renewing his interests in paleontology, as a result of which he wrote important papers upon Cretaceous period reptiles and a "classic work" on Mosasaurs, the typical genus of Pythonomorpha of the upper Cretaceous, a group of marine reptiles (related to present day Monitor lizards) with a long, snakelike body, scaly skin and lizard-shaped heads. Williston also wrote widely on the Diptera (flies), publishing in 1908 the *Manual of North American Diptera,* containing more than 800 figures he had sketched. In 1902 he headed the department of vertebrate paleontology at the University of Chicago, becoming particularly interested in Permian age fossils. He authored *American Permian Vertebrates* (1911), *Water Reptiles of the Past and Present* (1914), and, published posthumously, *The Osteology of the Reptiles* (1925), which was edited from Williston's basic work by William King Gregory. Williston was survived by his widow, three daughters and a son.

DAB; *Who's Who in America;* CE.

Wilson, John, trapper (c. 1797-post 1841). B. in

Scotland he came to America as a weaver, then became a trapper and in 1826 joined Jedediah S. Smith's exploration party from a Rocky Mountain rendezvous to southern California (see Smith entry for details). Wilson was troublesome and contentious and Smith discharged him at Tulare Lake in the San Joaquin Valley on January 17, 1827, "in consequence of his cursing my self and every thing else," and hired an Indian to take him to the nearest mission "and should be glad to see him no more." Wilson, at the demand of Governor Echeandía, was interrogated at Monterey May 19, 1827, by Juan José Rocha. The trapper said he had had a falling out with Smith over the course of their journey to California, at Tulare Lake his horse had fallen on him, crushing his chest, he bleeding from the mouth and with an Indian made his way to San Miguel Mission where he recovered, went on to Monterey and San Francisco where he was arrested, probably for being in the country illegally. Smith, in a separate interview, claimed he had reprimanded Wilson for beating his horse and the Scotsman became so angry and foulmouthed Smith believed him "crazy and malicious," and thus directed him to leave his party. Upon being denied permission to settle in California, Wilson applied to rejoin Smith's band, was allowed to accompany it without pay, but shortly was again discharged, imprisoned briefly by the Mexicans, then allowed to settle in California. In 1841 he was permitted to marry Maria F. Mendoza of San Carlos; there is no further report of him.

George R. Brooks, *The Southwest Expedition of Jedediah S. Smith,* Glendale, Calif., Arthur H. Clark Co., 1977; David J. Weber, *The Californios versus Jedediah Smith 1826-1827,* Spokane, Wash., Clark, 1990; Bancroft, *Pioneer Register.*

Wilson, William, Indian trader (d. 1796). Wilson, "a well-known Indian trader," was a resident of Pittsburgh, frequently acting as interpreter of those Indian languages with which he was familiar. He had a trading post near Beaver River, northwest of Pittsburgh. In 1793 he supplied information that led to the arrest and trial of the popular Samuel Brady (see entry) who, in the end, was acquitted of Indian murders. In 1793 Wilson was at Detroit, later moved on to Cincinnati and eventually to Greenville in western Ohio, where he lived the rest of his life.

Thwaites/Kellogg, *The Revolution on the Upper Ohio, 1775-1777,* Madison, Wis. Hist. Soc., 1908.

Winnebago Prophet: *see,* White Cloud

Winship, Abiel, ship owner (July 23, 1769-Apr. 10, 1824). The oldest son of Jonathan Winship Sr., he was b. at Boston, became a land holder and through association with Benjamin P. Homer and others a major ship owner, a number of vessels in which he had an interest trading around the world. He belongs here because he was important in developing the sea otter fur trade of the Northwest Coast and dealings with Russians in Alaska, Spanish in Middle America, King Kamehameha in Hawaii and the disposal of Pacific coast furs at Canton, China. With his brothers Jonathan Jr., and Nathan Winship he projected the first settlement on the Columbia River between the Russian north and Spanish south; the undertaking, which was launched the year before Astoria was founded, failed. But it was "significant not only because it was the first effort to build an American post in the Pacific Northwest, but because enterprising merchants saw the Columbia River as a vital link" in Pacific commerce and exploration. Abiel Winship lived virtually all of his life at Boston.

Charles Winship biblio; Dorothy O. Johansen, Charles M. Gates, *Empire of the Columbia: A History of the Pacific Northwest,* N.Y., Harper & Row, 1957.

Winship, Charles, sea captain (Jan. 4, 1776-Dec. 4, 1800). The son of Jonathan Winship (Jan. 18, 1747-Oct. 13, 1814), he was b. in Massachusetts and August 3, 1799, became captain of the brigantine *Betsy,* owned by the Boston firm of Benjamin P. Homer and Abiel Winship, Charles's brother. The ship, with Joseph O'Cain, supercargo and Nathan Winship also aboard, was said to be the first American vessel to reach the California coast, being also first to enter San Diego Bay, where she lay from August 25 to September 4, 1800. Bancroft wrote that "it is not unlikely that...the *Betsy* [was] the pioneer of the two [Upper and Lower] Californias, in addition to legitimate trade farther north; or at least Captain Winship may have engaged in exploring the new field, in which his brothers subsequently reaped so rich a harvest." Charles Winship received assistance at San Diego (although the coast was nominally closed to any but Spanish shipping), and was warned to touch no other Spanish port. Later, however, he put in at San Blas, Nayarit, Mexico, with an elaborate tale of renewed distress. A Spanish warship entered the port and Winship's crew, fearing seizure of the ship's contraband furs, put to sea under command of the mate named Brown in such haste as to leave Winship and O'Cain ashore. Charles Winship died at 24, cause of death not stated. He was reported by Bancroft to have succumbed in Chile, but the historian confused him with his nephew, Charles S. Winship who, after an unprofitable sealing voyage in southern waters, put in at Valparaiso and died of sunstroke January 27, 1823. The *Betsy* returned from Canton to Boston in October 1801.

John Perkins Cushing Winship, *Historical Brighton,* I, Boston (1899), 126-27;Bancroft *Northwest Coast,* I, 308-309; info. from Col. E.W. Giesecke, Midlothian, Virginia; Ogden.

Winship, Jonathan Jr., sea captain (July 11, 1780-Aug. 6, 1846). B. near Boston, he left home as supercargo around 1800 aboard a ship owned by his brother Abiel and Benjamin P. Homer, eventually becoming master. January 23, 1803, he departed Boston aboard the *O'Cain,* a 280-ton ship whose captain was Joseph O'Cain, who had accompanied Charles Winship (see entry) to the west coast on a trading and fur gathering mission in 1799-1801. The vessel reached Kodiak Island in October 1803 and shipped 20 Aleut hunters and 20 baidarkas, or kayaks, hunting sea otters down the coast to Spanish America, collecting 1,800 pelts and other furs as well. The Aleuts were returned to Kodiak in September 1804. The ship left for Canton to dispose of her cargo and reached Boston July 1, 1805. Jonathan Winship as captain and his brother Nathan as mate left Boston with the *O'Cain* in October 1805, reaching Sitka April 1, 1806, where 100 Kodiak hunters and 12 women were shipped, the natives commanded by Sysoi Slobodchikov in accordance with an agreement with Baranov. The hunt proceeded down the Pacific coast. In its course the *O'Cain* touched at Trinidad Head, discovered in 1775 by the Spaniards Hezeta (Heceta) and Bodega y Quadra. Below Trinidad Jonathan Winship became the discoverer of record of Humboldt Bay, a landlocked inlet south of the present Eureka, California. The *O'Cain* itself did not enter the bay, which was explored by Winship and Slobodchikov in baidarkas, its extent and nature learned. The hunt continued southward to Lower California, Kodiak being regained November 9. January 16, 1807, a fresh hunt commenced, duplicating the earlier trip, an overall total of 4,819 otter skins being taken. They were disposed of at Canton early in 1808 and June 15, the *O'Cain* arrived back at Boston. Winship left Boston in May 1809, arriving at Sitka in December and remaining in the Pacific for six years. For a time during the War of 1812 Jonathan's *O'Cain*, Nathan Winship's *Albatross* and another vessel were blockaded at Honululu by the British frigate *Cherub*. Jonathan eventually slipped away and made a run for Canton, being pursued by a Britisher and escaping capture only by "the timely intervention of a fog." Soon after reaching Canton news of the settlement of the war was received. A banquet for British and American seamen was held to celebrate peace, the event attended by many Chinese guests. As the British concluded a rousing rendition of their national air the American turn came and Jonathan Winship, having imbibed a good deal of Chinese wine, leaped upon the long dining table and danced an energetic Yankee jig its length, kicking procelain, bottles, glasses and food in all directions, outdoing the British and sending the Chinese into "ecstasies," according to a scarcely impartial reporter who added that "the Bulls were completely thrown in the shade—the Americans [made] objects of reverential admiration." Winship returned to Honolulu and July 15, 1815, left Hawaii aboard another ship for Boston, the *O'Cain* continuing her Pacific adventures under Captain Robert McNeil. During his Pacific years Jonathan had advised his brother, Nathan, also a sea captain (see entry) on establishment of the first white American post on the Columbia River, in Oregon. He now retired from the sea, having acquired a considerable fortune, and settled at Brighton (annexed by Boston in 1873). Interested in horticulture, he established the "Winship Nurseries" devoted to flowers and other botanical cultivation; it became famous and he prospered. January 20, 1825, he married Miriam Arms Lyman, who died November 15, 1836; Jonathan married Mary Knight Prince, March 8, 1838, who died August 21, 1843. He fathered children by both of his wives.

See Charles Winship biblio.; J.P.C. Winship, *Historical Brighton*, I, Boston, George A. Warren, pub., 1899, 123-44; Warren Heckrotte, "The Discovery of Humboldt Bay: A New Look at an Old Story," *Terrae Incognitae*, Vol. V (1973), 27-41; info. from E.W. Giesecke, Midlothian, Virginia; Ogden.

Winship, Nathan, sea captain (May 25, 1778-July 8, 1820). A brother of Abiel, Jonathan Jr. and Charles Winship, Nathan was prominent in Northwest Coast sea otter gathering and also a pioneer of the Oregon country. He was aboard the *Betsy*, a 104-ton, 10-gun brigantine captained by Charles Winship on the 1799-1801 initial recorded voyage of an east coast trading vessel to the California coast. Because of feared Spanish efforts to seize her cargo Charles Winship (see entry) and Joseph O'Cain were stranded at San Blas, Nayarit, Mexico, and a mate named Brown, with Nathan Winship and the crew escaped with the vessel and made Canton, returning to Boston in October 1801. Nathan was mate under Jonathan as captain aboard the *O'Cain*, a 280-ton ship which left Boston in October 1805 and reached Sitka April 1, 1806. The party hunted down the Pacific coast to Lower California, returning to Sitka and Kodiak Island by way of Hawaii in November 1807. On this hunt Jonathan Winship discovered Humboldt Bay, below present Eureka, California. After a second hunt the *O'Cain* left Sitka in October for Canton and June 15, 1808, reached Boston again. As part owner and captain of the 165-ton *Albatross*, Nathan Winship left Boston July 6, 1809, with an important additional mission: to found the first white settlement on the Northwest Coast between the Russian establishments of Alaska and the Spanish of the Californias. While signing up 25 Kanakas (Hawaiians) during a fortnight layover in Hawaii Nathan received a letter from Jonathan, then aboard the *O'Cain*, urging him to proceed with all dispatch to the Columbia River to head off any movement by the Russians in that direction; the letter also gave Nathan explicit instructions and advice as to establishment of the post and subsequent operations from it. Necessary articles, including livestock for the settlement, were brought from Boston by the *Albatross* and Jonathan recommended as the best site one about forty miles up the Columbia on the south side of the river opposite present Oak Point, Washington. The *Albatross* entered the Columbia May 26, 1810, and June 4, the ship anchored at the selected position. Felling and hewing for the structure commenced and a space cleared for planting, the initial breaking of soil by a white man in Oregon. June 8, there was a heavy rain and the river rose, covering the planted land and building site. The next day the embryo structure was dismantled and another, presumably safer position, was selected. But the Indians became troublesome. Consultation with the chiefs revealed that it was their practice to obtain skins from tribes upriver and transport them to the

Columbia's mouth for bartering with occasional trading vessels. For economic reasons, therefore, they would strongly oppose any such settlement as Winship planned. The captain realized it would be unsafe as had been intended, to leave the proposed establishment unprotected by the ship's cannon and concluded that the land belonged to the Indians after all. June 12, he gave up the project and reembarked his men. It was a year before the founding of Astoria by the John Jacob Astor interests near the mouth of the river. The *Albatross* made a hunt down the coast as far as Cedros Island and returned to Sitka by October 22. Winship had left parties of sealers on the Farallons and Cedros islands, but he had no luck trying for otters because they were in the thick kelp beds about Santa Barbara Island and he had no Aleuts with baidarkas to hunt them out. In Alaska he enlisted fifty Kodiak Aleuts under a Russian commander named Lasseff and his otter hunting became more successful. Nathan remained in the Pacific, hunting and trading as far south as the Marquesas Islands and north to Alaska until 1816 when in October the *Albatross* was sold to Kamehameha I, the great king of Hawaii, who always had been cordial to American traders. Nathan Winship may have returned to Boston on the *O'Cain,* which reached Hawaii in July 1816, left Canton January 7, 1817, arriving at Cowes, England, June 8, and Boston October 15, thus having circumnavigated the world.

See Charles, Jonathan Winship biblios.

Winthrop, Theodore, traveler, writer (Sept. 28, 1828-June 10, 1861). B. at New Haven, Connecticut, he was graduated from Yale and in 1848 traveled to Europe and elsewhere. In 1853 he visited San Francisco, Oregon and Washington, returning to the States by horseback across the Plains. While paddling about Puget Sound in a dugout canoe with Clallam Indian companions, Winthrop glimpsed the majestic peak that Vancouver had named Mt. Rainier after a British rear admiral, Peter Rainier (c. 1741-1808); Rainier's only recorded experience with Americans was when he was severely wounded while capturing a privateer July 8, 1778, he then commanding the sloop *Ostrich.* Winthrop now learned from his Indians that their name for the peak was Tacoma, which he thought much more apt than Rainier for the spectacular, snow-capped mountain. Winthrop adopted the native name and published it in his *The Canoe and the Saddle* (1863), which appeared posthumously. The name he preferred

has been promoted steadily by the community of Tacoma, Washington, but the U.S. Board on Geographical Names in 1890 chose to retain Rainier, even though board chairman C. Hart Merriam confirmed in a statement May 11, 1917, that the Indian title took chronological precedence. Winthrop's *Life in the Open Air* also appeared in 1863. He was a literary figure of prominence in his own time and after, but his further career had little frontier relationship. He was killed in the battle of Big Bethel, Virginia, while serving as "military secretary" to Brigadier General Benjamin Butler.

Francis E. Smith, *Achievements and Experiences of Captain Robert Gray 1788 to 1792,* Barrett-Redfield Press, Tacoma, Wash., 1923, p. 16; DAB.

Wislizenus, Frederick Adolph, physician, author (May 21, 1810-Sept. 22, 1889). B. at Koenigsee, Schwarzburg-Rudolstadt, Germany, he was orphaned at a young age, raised by an uncle and his wife, and studied natural history at the University of Jena, at Gottingen and at Tubingen. He became involved in an abortive student uprising and fled to Switzerland, continuing studies at Zurich and as a physician practiced at Paris hospitals. In 1835 he landed at New York, practiced medicine at Mascoutah, St. Clair County, Illinois. He became interested in seeing the Rocky Mountain west, and in 1839 at Westport, Missouri, joined a fur-trading party to the Green River trappers' rendezvous. He went on to Fort Hall, gave up his earlier design to visit the Pacific coast and returned by way of the Arkansas River and the Santa Fe Trail to St. Louis. In 1840 he published a travel journal which was later translated from the German by his son as *A Journey to the Rocky Mountains in the Year 1839.* He settled down at St. Louis to practice medicine for several years. In early 1846 he joined the trading caravan of Albert Speyer for Santa Fe and Chihuahua City, the wagon train rumored to be carrying arms for the Mexican government. From Santa Fe it moved southward; Wislizenus, aided by the scientific materials he had brought along, made notes of the natural features encountered and collected specimens. In Chihuahua state he was encountered by an anti-American mob (the Mexican War having broken out in the meantime) and was captured. Doniphan's Regiment, arriving in 1847 won his release and Wislizenus joined the military as a surgeon, returning to St. Louis by way of the Rio Grande, the Gulf of Mexico and the Mississippi

River. His narrative of his journey was submitted by Senator Thomas Hart Benton to the Senate and published in 1848 as a *Memoir of a Tour to Northern Mexico,* appearing in *Senate Miscellaneous Document 26,* 38th Congress., 1st Session. His initial publication "remains a classic of the late trapper period" and the later one was praised by Alexander von Humboldt, since it gives for most of the region its earliest scientific description and study. Wislizenus "did heroic duty" during the 1848-49 cholera epidemic. In 1850 at Constantinople during a tour abroad he married Lucy Crane, sister of the U.S. minister to Turkey. Upon his return he traveled to California, hoping to settle there, but did not elect to do so and returned to St. Louis in 1852. He was a founder of the Missouri Historical Society and of the Academy of Science of St. Louis. Some years before his death he was afflicted with total blindness. He died at St. Louis, being survived by his widow and their son.

DAB; Thwaites, EWT; El Paso, Texas, *Password,* El Paso County Hist. Soc., 1973, 1974; info. from E.F. (Ted) Mains.

Withers, Alexander Scott, historian (Oct. 12, 1792-Jan. 23, 1865). B. near Warrenton, Fauquier County, Virginia, he was graduated from Washington College, studied law at William and Mary and was admitted to the bar at Warrenton, but abandoned his practice in 1813 because he found it not to his taste. For some time he managed his widowed mother's plantation but about 1827 moved to West Virginia, settling at Clarksburg where he commenced collecting materials for his principal life's work, *Chronicles of Border Warfare,* a study of the frontier of northwestern Virginia and related areas. Because of the financial failure of his publisher, however, he profited not at all from his great work, published in 1831. Withers settled at length at Weston, West Virginia, engaging in agricultural pursuits and serving for several years as a magistrate. He died at Parkersburg, West Virginia. He was about six feet tall, of a studious nature, fathered two sons and three daughters and during the Civil War strongly favored the Union, one son, Henry W. Withers, serving in that army with the 12th Virginia Infantry.

Lyman Copeland Draper memoir for the 1895 edition of Withers' work, for which Reuben Gold Thwaites was editor and annotator.

Wolf Chief, Cheyenne leader (fl. 1826-1905).

The dates given suggest that there were two Wolf Chiefs among the Cheyennes. The first was leader in 1826 during a move of the tribe south of the Platte; the second was a "young" chief of the Hevataniu, or Hairy Clan, in 1864 and was still living according to George Bent in a letter of March 6, 1905. The Hairy Clan included the tribe's most able horse thieves and its members also were "the best at running down wild horses," most common on the South Plains. The later chief became an expert in Cheyenne ceremonialism and dogma. On one occasion he violated a tabu against eating the heart of a buffalo, which was done unwittingly; to absolve him it was believed he must then eat the heart of an enemy. The Cheyennes killed a Crow Indian, the heart was removed and Wolf Chief made himself eat it, although declaring that "he never tasted anything so disagreeable...He could hardly swallow it." But it freed him from the tabu. On May 16, 1864, a white command under Lieutenant George S. Eayre of Colorado troops encountered Cheyenne Indians on the Smoky Hill River about fifty miles northwest of Fort Larned, Kansas. Wolf Chief, Lean Bear, who was another noted chief, and others went to treat with Eayre. Wolf Chief told Bent that "We rode up on a hill and saw the soldiers coming in four groups with cannon drawn by horses. When we saw the soldiers all formed in line, we did not want to fight. Lean Bear, the chief, told us to stay behind him while he went forward to show his papers from Washington which would tell the soldiers that we were friendly...Lean Bear had a medal on his breast given him at the time the Cheyenne chiefs visited Washington in 1862." When within twenty or thirty feet of the officer commanding "he called out an order and the soldiers all fired together. Lean Bear and Star were shot, and fell from their ponies. As they lay on the ground, the soldiers rode forward and shot them again." The troops now opened fire from cannons loaded with grape. A number of troops and Indians were killed, and they fought for some little time, until Black Kettle (see entry) rode up and stopped the fight. "He told us we must not fight with the white people, so we stopped," said Wolf Chief. He added that some of the Indians were so angry that they would not listen to Black Kettle, but pursued the troops several miles. This may be the basis for reports that the Indians "chased Eayre's outfit into Fort Larned." Eayre's report to Chivington stated that the Indians had attacked his command and after a 7½-hour fight he had "succeeded in driving them from the field. They lost 3 chiefs and 25 warriors killed; ...My own loss is 4 men killed and 3 wounded..." John W. Smith and Alfred Gay, both married to Cheyenne women, in June questioned the Cheyennes about the fight and were told that only two chiefs and one warrior had been killed; Smith and Gay were considered reliable. After the November 1864 Sand Creek massacre, which Wolf Chief apparently missed, he took part in the great raids of retaliation in 1865. He and George Bent reconnoitred the Platte Bridge situation and recommended that "this would be a good place to make the big raid the chiefs were planning," which took place in July. In the spring of 1868 Wolf Chief, on a buffalo hunt, narrowly escaped disaster when a bull he had wounded gave persistent chase to the chief's horse and pugnaciously would not quit for some time. Subsequent to the Battle of the Washita on November 27, 1868, Custer visited the South Plains and at a Cheyenne village secured release of two white captives, an encounter which Wolf Chief witnessed. In 1873 Wolf Chief killed a white buffalo, a rare and impressive event. The chief was a principal informant for Grinnell and because he was knowledgeable on Cheyenne customs and culture, his testimony became important in Grinnell's two-volume work, *The Cheyenne Indians*.

George E. Hyde, *Life of George Bent*, Norman, Univ. of Okla. Press, 1968; George Bird Grinnell, *The Fighting Cheyennes*, Norman, 1956; Grinnell, *The Cheyenne Indians*, 2 vols., Lincoln, Univ. of Neb. Press, 1972; Stan Hoig, *The Sand Creek Massacre*, Norman, 1961; Donald J. Berthrong, *The Southern Cheyennes*, Norman, 1963; J.W. Vaughn, *The Battle of Platte Bridge*, Norman, 1963.

Wood, James, military officer (1750-1813). A son of a colonel of the same name who had fought in the French and Indian War and founded Winchester, Virginia, James Wood the younger served as captain under Major Angus McDonald (see entry) in the 1774 summer campaign against the Wapatomica towns on the Muskingum River of Ohio. The 400-man column on July 26 crossed the Ohio River 24 miles below Wheeling, West Virginia, taking seven days' rations and marching northerly for about 85 miles until it was ambushed six miles short of its objective. A slight skirmish resulted in killing four Indians at a cost of two killed and four wounded, the army reaching the Muskingum August 2. After another brief clash the next day the villages were found

deserted; they were burned and 70 acres of standing corn destroyed, whereupon the command returned to Wheeling. "The results of the expedition were slight, ravages upon the frontiers thereafter increasing rather than diminishing." Wood was in Dunmore's Division of the army which fought at Point Pleasant October 10, 1774, in the climactic engagement of the Lord Dunmore War. The following year he made a "hazardous journey" to the Indian towns again, to summon the tribesmen to a treaty council at Pittsburgh. Excerpts from the extended journal of this undertaking are printed textually in Thwaites and Kellogg pp. 34-67. In 1776 Wood became colonel of the 8th Virginia Regiment, served throughout the war and retired as a Brigadier General. From 1796-99 he was governor of Virginia, noted for his anti-slavery principles. He died at his Winchester home.

Thwaites/Kellogg, *The Revolution on the Upper Ohio, 1775-1777*, Madison, Wis. Hist. Soc., 1908; Thwaites, *Dunmore*.

Wrangel, Baron Ferdinand Petrovich von, Russian naval officer, administrator (Jan. 9, 1797-June 5, 1870). B. at Pskov, Russia, near the Estonian border, he was graduated from the Russian naval academy in 1815 and under V.N. Golovnin sailed around the world in 1817-19 in the sloop *Kamchatka*. From 1820-23 he commanded a Russian naval expedition which completed mapping Siberia's northeastern coast; although he searched for what later became known as Wrangel Island, 100 miles north of eastern Siberia, he did not find it. From 1825-27 he led a second world-girdling expedition in the sloop *Krotky*, and in 1829 he was named to succeed Petr Togorovich Chistyakov as governor of the Russian American Company, arriving at Sitka, Alaska, in 1830. He at once implemented his interest in explorations and the development of a virtually unknown territory. From reports of earlier expeditions Wrangel was convinced overland communication was possible between Bering Bay (the present Yakutat Bay at the head of the Alaskan Panhandle) and Norton Sound, and he ordered Lieutenant Mikhail Tebenkov to the sound by sea; Tebenkov in 1833 founded Mikhaielovsk (the present St. Michael) on its southern shore in anticipation of such overland contact, which however could not be established at that time. Other expeditions Wrangel sent out explored much territory but for the most part failed to achieve their primary objectives. He desired to chart the entire coastline of Alaska but was distracted by several matters. One was a dispute with the Hudson's Bay Company over fur trade territories, the English firm employing a clause in an 1825 Russian-Anglo treaty, providing free access across Russian territory to their inland posts, using this as an excuse to establish trading establishments along such waterways, particularly the Stikine River, flowing out of British Columbia to the sea near the present port of Wrangell. Upon Wrangel's request the Russian government nullified that treaty clause and to enforce the new restriction the governor had Fort Dionysi constructed at the present site of Wrangell; after one brief confrontation with the English the matter was resolved (though temporarily only). Another issue requiring Wrangel's attention was negotiation with Mexican authorities in California. Governor José Figueroa demanded abandonment of the Ross settlement north of San Francisco, although he died September 19, 1835. Wrangel, shortly to be succeeded by Ivan Antonovich Kupriyanov in his Russian American Company post, went south, stopping off at the Ross establishment, then meeting Kupriyanov at San Blas, Mexico. He attempted to negotiate the Ross colony matter with authorities at Mexico City, but these talks failed and the Ross endeavor was doomed. It was sold to John A. Sutter in 1841. In Russia Wrangel served as a director of the Russian American Company from 1840-49, in the latter year becomng a vice admiral. He was naval minister from 1855-57 and retired in 1864. He opposed the sale of Alaska to the United States in 1867, but failed to prevent it. Wrangel was a founder in 1845 of the Russian Geographical Society. He died at Tartu, Estonia, then part of the Russian empire. The Wrangel Island he did not find north of Siberia, and Wrangell Island and a port city in the Alaskan Panhandle were named for him, as were the Wrangell Mountains and other Alaskan geographical features.

Bancroft, *Alaska;* CE; EB; F.A. Golder, *Russian Expansion on the Pacific 1641-1850,* N.Y., Paragon Book Reprint Corp., 1971; David P. Henige, *Colonial Governors from the Fifteenth Century to the Present,* Madison, Univ. of Wis. Press, 1970, p. 276; Zagoskin.

Wright, William, journalist: *see,* Dan DeQuille

Wrightson, William, pioneer (Mar. 17, 1827-Feb. 17, 1865). B. at Albany, New York, of English parentage he studied for the Episcopal

ministry and also civil engineering, and became "a great linguist—spoke French, Italian, Spanish, German, Latin, Greek and Hebrew." He taught at an Albany preparatory school, then in 1852 joined his younger brother, John, at Cincinnati operating a printing shop which published the *Railroad Record,* an ardent exponent of railroads to connect the Mississippi Valley and the Pacific coast. Reports of mineral riches caused Wrightson to abandon his editorial work and form a company for Arizona to work mines near the Mexican Border. Wrightson's party reached Tubac in the winter of 1858 and spent several hundred thousand dollars to open and establish reduction works at the Santa Rita mines; incidentally, his party had transported to Arizona its initial printing press which produced at Tubac the first newspaper of the region, the *Arizonian.* Wrightson made several trips to Washington, D.C., and "exercised great influence in getting the Territorial organization of 1863 through Congress and approved by the President." On February 17, 1865, about a fortnight before Gilbert Hopkins (see entry) would be killed by Indians, Wrightson was slain by Apaches in almost the identical place, midway between Fort Buchanan and Tubac. His body was recovered, taken overland to the Pacific coast, sent by sailing ship around Cape Horn to New York City and interred in the family lot at Albany. John Wrightson, also employed at the Santa Rita silver mine, had been killed in 1859 by a Mexican national and his body also was returned to Albany for burial. Because of William Wrightson's significance in the early history of Arizona there were attempts to name the highest peak (elevation 9,432 ft.) of the Santa Ritas for him, but local people persisted in calling it Old Baldy, that being the nickname of Richard Stoddert Ewell who served as a Dragoon captain at Fort Buchanan before the Civil War and became a famed Lieutenant General in Confederate forces during that conflict. However, Wrightson supporters continued their efforts and January 8, 1930, the Board of Geographical Names, Department of the Interior, formally adopted the permanent name for it of Mount Wrightson, which it bears today.

Charles D. Poston obituary article, *Arizona Weekly Star,* Mar. 11, 1880; info. from the Hayden Collection, Ariz. Hist. Soc.; Will C. Barnes, *Arizona Place Names,* Univ. of Ariz. Bulletin 5, Tucson, 1935; Byrd H. Granger, *Will C. Barnes' Arizona Place Names,* Tucson, Univ. of Ariz. Press, 1960; Estelle Lutrell, *News-*

papers and Periodicals of Arizona 1859-1911, Univ. of Ariz. Gen. Bulletin 15, Tucson, 1949, p. 102.

Wurttemberg, (Frederick) Paul Wilhelm, Prince of, traveler (1797-1860). B. near Stuttgart in southwestern Germany, he was the nephew of King Friedrich I of Wurttemberg. The Prince (later the Duke of Wurttemberg) became interested in natural history, traveled widely, and made several trips to the United States during the first half of the 19th century. Knowledge is incomplete on all but the first of these, since his diaries and notes have been but partially translated, and some were lost in World War II bombardments. Paul's initial journey is narrated in his *First Journey to North America in...1822 to 1824,* published in German and later translated into English. This adventure began with a voyage on a three-master from Hamburg to New Orleans, arriving December 20. Two weeks later he sailed for Havana, where he studied the geological, physical, social and political aspects in Cuba for a month, then returned to New Orleans, on the passage narrowly missing capture by an Argentine privateer. He took a riverboat to St. Louis where he arrived in the spring, requesting of William Clark, Superintendent of Indian Affairs for the West, a passport into the interior, which Washington had already instructed Clark to grant. Clark reported to Secretary of War John C. Calhoun that he had issued the document for botanical study purposes, adding that Paul seemed inoffensive enough and had set out for Council Bluffs. Clark suspected that he would "neither have inclination nor perseverance to go much further. He is fond of killing birds and collecting plants which appears to be the source of greatest pleasure to him. As to political, or any other talents which he may possess I can say but little, as they appear to be very limited." Paul traveled by keelboat to Franklin where he left the craft, traveled overland to the mouth of the Kansas River, reached Liberty, Missouri, June 16, 1823, staying briefly with Louis Bertholet, attempted by pirogue to explore the Kansas River but was roundly defeated by swarms of mosquitoes. He met "a youth of sixteen years of age whose mother [Sacajawea] had accompanied the Messrs. Lewis and Clark...to the Pacific Ocean..." The prince was attracted to the intelligent and active boy and on his return, with the consent of Clark, took Baptiste Charbonneau to Europe for several years' exposure to European education and culture, based at his ancestral cas-

tle at Mergentheim, thirty miles northeast of Stuttgart. Meanwhile the Prince had resumed his keelboat passage up the river. In August he visited the Oto Indians and traveled overland to a Missouri Fur Company post at the mouth of the White River in present South Dakota, his host being the veteran trader Joshua Pilcher (see entry). By September 9, Wurttemberg had returned to Council Bluffs. September 17, he left its Fort Atkinson, accompanied by Captain Bennet Riley (see entry) and traveled overland to the Pawnee villages, remaining three days among the Grand Pawnees and Loup Pawnees (on Loup Fork of the Platte River), then returned to the Missouri. He resumed the downstream journey October 2, picked up Baptiste at the mouth of the Kansas, and reached St. Louis October 24. November 3, Wurttemberg and Baptiste took passage on a riverboat for New Orleans. At length they boarded the brig, *Smyrna,* and following a weather-delayed voyage reached Havre February 14, 1824. For six years, Prince Paul later wrote, Baptiste was "my companion...on all my travels over Europe and northern Africa until 1829, when he returned with me to America..." The second journey to the New World lasted three years. The Prince left St. Louis December 29, and traveled horseback to the present Kansas City, reached January 5, 1830. He went upriver to Fort Leavenworth where he found his "old friend" Bennet Riley in command, and by February was at Council Bluffs. With spring he boarded an American Fur Company boat to Fort Tecumseh (Fort Pierre), across the Missouri from today's Pierre, South Dakota. August 20, he left the post in a pirogue accompanied by James Andrews, a Canadian trapper, reached Leavenworth September 24, went on to St. Louis and by riverboat to New Orleans. At some point he made a study trip to the northern and central states of Mexico, studying its flora and fauna. In the summer of 1831 he journeyed to Lake Itasca, Minnesota, the source of the Mississippi River, arriving there three years before its "discoverer," Henry Rowe Schoolcraft, reached the lake, in 1834. Subsequently Paul visited Texas, Colorado, western Kansas and Nebraska before returning to Europe, where he spent seven years arranging, classifying and studying his geological, botanical, zoological and ethnological specimens and constructing a museum to house them near the palace. He was invited then by the Khedive of Egypt, Mehmed Ali, to join an expedition to the upper Nile, where he sketch-mapped an area of 500,000 square miles peopled by 25 million hitherto unknown (to the Europeans) native peoples, whom he attempted to ethnologically describe. In 1849 Paul set out on his longest expedition to the Americas. He first visited west Texas from San Antonio to the Rio Grande, traveled across Mexico and sailed in 1850 from Acapulco to San Pedro and up the coast to Sacramento, spending a month with John Augustus Sutter (see entry) and visiting the gold fields before returning by way of Panama to New Orleans, which he reached early in 1851. He again went up the Mississippi with various side trips and describing the swiftly growing cities (St. Louis had burgeoned from 5,600 when he first visited it to 80,000). He went westward from St. Louis to South Pass, down the Green River to Utah where he visited the Mormon settlements in the Salt Lake Valley, and returned by way of the Platte River. Accompanied by artist-adventurer Heinrich B. Moellhausen, 26, on the night of November 14, the two were overtaken by a savage Plains blizzard, while still 120 miles from a white establishment to the east. After struggling forward bit by bit and being snowbound for days on end, a mail stage from Laramie came along; the Prince and Moellhausen flipped a coin to see which would be squeezed into the overladen vehicle; royalty won. The Prince said that the succeeding ten days "were as hard as any through which I had passed." He reached Independence December 4, in "critical" condition, but was well cared for at that "lovable, hospitable" community. At length he traveled by post wagon to Boonville, recuperated further, and reached St. Louis in late December. In 1852 he left New Orleans to visit every state east of the Mississippi, studying the singular expansion of white civilization in the newly-settled country. In 1853 he traveled to South America, exploring the upper Orinoco, Amazon, Magdalena and La Plata rivers, explored Patagonia and the Tierra del Fuego Archipelago, then sailed up the west coast of South America and returned to New Orleans by way of the Isthmus of Panama. Paul spent the following two years journeying about eastern United States and returned to Germany in 1856. In early 1857 he once more returned to the United States and the following year went to Australia, where he studied the mining camps, the Murray River country, and the aborigines of the interior; at some point he also visited Tasmania and New Zealand. He returned to Europe by way of Ceylon (Sri Lanka), the Red Sea and the Mediterranean. Wurttemberg was "a fine sketch artist," and illustrated his voluminous diaries with all manner of pictures. An 1844 photograph of the Prince in hunting garb, made with a camera he constructed himself, is reproduced by Barry, p. 199, and by Butscher, facing p. 181. He planned to devote himself to the study, classification and arrangement of his countless specimens from all quarters of the world, and in preparing his written notes for publication, but died abruptly four months after return from the last adventure; most of his writings were believed lost until 1928 when quite by accident they were found in a trunk by an archivist, but many have since been lost irretrievably.

Louis C. Butscher, "A Brief Biography of Prince Paul Wilhelm of Wurttemberg," *New Mexico Historical Review,* Vol. XVII, Nos. 3, 4 (July, October 1942), 181, 225, 294-354; Barry, *Beginning of the West; Chardon's Journal at Fort Clark 1834-1839,* ed., notes by Annie Heloise Abel, Pierre, Dept. of State of South Dak. Hist., 1932; MM I, 209-11, 221, II, 296; *Travellers on the Western Frontier,* ed. by John Francis McDermott, Urbana, Univ. of Illinois Press, 1970; info. from E.F. (Ted) Mains.

Wyman, Seth, frontiersman (d. c. 1725). From Woburn, Massachusetts, he was among the most effective Indian fighters of his day. Wyman signed on as ensign for the Lovewell expedition which left Dunstable (present Nashua), New Hampshire, April 15, 1725, and located Pequawket Indians near the present Fryeburg, Maine, on May 8. An engagement opened with a single Indian who fired on and mortally wounded Lovewell just as the native was killed by Wyman. The white party was attacked about 10 a.m. by a numerically-superior band of Indians, of whom Wyman killed five or six from his position behind a fallen tree. Wyman appears to have been unwounded in the fight during which a dozen of the whites were killed and others wounded mortally while most of the rest were hit, eleven dangerously so. Wyman assumed command with the death of Lovewell and incapacitation of Lieutenants Josiah Farwell and Jonathan Robbins, both wounded mortally. "It was probably under [Wyman's] direction" that what remained of the party was salvaged, and it was "the keen and fearless Seth Wyman [who] crept up among the bushes, shot the chief conjurer," the enemy sachem, Paugas, and thus caused the Indians to break off the fight (another source says John Chamberlain killed Paugas). Wyman, "now the only commissioned officer left alive, and who had borne himself throughout with the utmost intrepidity, decision and good sense," regained Dunstable May 15. He was immediately commissioned a captain, presented with a silver-hilted sword, and given a monetary reward. Under fresh inducements for Indian hunting, Wyman with a command set out, presumably the same summer, but "the extremity of the Heat prevented their Marching far. Many of them sickned of the Bloody Flux, and some dyed after their return," including Wyman, whose death was "very much lamented."

Samuel Penhallow, *History of the Indian Wars,*, 1726 (Williamstown, Mass., Corner House Pubs., 1973); Parkman, *Half Century of Conflict,* I.

Y

Yanert, William, soldier, pioneer (1864-1952). As a sergeant of Troop K, 8th Cavalry, Yanert took a responsible part in the 1898 Alaskan expedition of Edwin Glenn (see entry), under instructions of Lieutenant Henry Learnard (see entry). He was directed to leave from the Chulitna River, a tributary of the Susitna River, and proceed to the Tanana River, making a topographical map and detailed report of the country traversed. He left August 12, 1898, and by September 3, he had reached a stream which his guide, Bate, a "Skittig" (Haida) Indian, told him was a tributary of the Tanana; Yanert took it to be the Cantwell (Nenana) River. Since the guide refused to go farther, being wary of the Tanana Indians, Yanert was forced to return to Learnard's camp. His narrative was lucid, detailed and complete enough to impress Learnard, who wrote in his own report that "Sergeant Yanert...has proven himself a worthy man and thorough soldier, well meriting promotion to the grade of second lieutenant, and he is recommended...for favorable consideration...Attention is respectfully invited to his map and report and to the manner in which he performed all the duty intrusted to him. If work in Alaska is to be continued no better commissioned officer for such work could be secured...than he would prove to be." Yanert was not, however, promoted to commissioned rank. In 1899 he was assigned his second independent mission in Alaska. He left the middle fork of the Susitna River July 14; on July 18, he was within sight of Mount McKinley, July 30, he reached Lake Talkeetna. August 12, he gained the Talkeetna River and August 22, returned to his starting point again after a 277-mile reconnaissance. Yanert left the army soon thereafter and by 1900 was at St. Michael on Norton Sound. He accompanied Lieutenant Hjalmar Erickson in 1900 and 1901 searching out a route for a military road between Rampart and Eagle on the middle Yukon River. He settled in 1903 with his brother, Herman Yanert, in the Yukon Flats at a place he humorously named Purgatory, twenty miles southwest of Beaver. Yanert in 1916 made a compass survey map of the Yukon Flats, an area 180 miles long and 70 wide, encompassing the confluence of the Yukon and Porcupine rivers. Yanert Fork (stream), a tributary to the Nenana River, and Yanert Glacier, the source of the stream, were named for William Yanert.

Narratives of Explorations in Alaska; Orth, 43, 783, 1064.

Yanovskii, Semyon Ivanovich, administrator (Apr. 15, 1789-Jan. 6, 1876). B. at Glukhov, in the Chernigov region of Russia, he entered the naval academy at 15 and saw service in European waters until 1815 when he entered the Russian American Company and sailed for Alaska. He arrived at Sitka July 25, 1817, met Irina, daughter of the company's chief manager, Baranov (see entry) and married her January 7, 1818. Four days later Hagemeister (see entry) succeeded Baranov as chief manager, but on October 24, poor health caused him to quit Alaska for Europe, and he appointed Yanovskii as acting chief manager in his stead. Yanovskii, on the same day Hagemeister sailed, wrote the head office of the company at St. Petersburg that his family situation required his return to Russia within two years "and I would like to go even earlier." July 30, 1819, leaving Khlebnikov in charge at Sitka, the manager left for an inspection tour to Kodiak, the Fox Islands and the Pribylov Islands. While he was gone a contagious fever struck Sitka, was carried to Kodiak, and about 100 people died, the lack of a physician in Russian America being responsible for the heavy casualties. Yanovskii applied to the head office for a physician and for the first time one was at length assigned to Alaska. Yanovskii also became acquainted with the Monk Herman, member of the 1794 religious mission to Kodiak. Father Herman, no intellectual giant, yet deeply spiritual, persistently visited and cared for the sick and his devotion and spiritual understandings made a lasting influence on Yanovskii. The monk at one time had complained of a virulent letter he had received for some reason from Baranov, who never was overly influenced by religion but gave it perfunctory support for political reasons. Herman was the last member of the eighteen churchmen who accompanied Iossaf (see entry) to Alaska in 1794. He died at 81 in 1837 on Spruce Island and after his death was sanctified by the Russian Orthodox Church. September 11, 1820, a ship arrived at Sitka from Okhotsk on the Siberian coast, bringing navy Captain Matvei Muravyev, Yanovskii's successor as governor and chief manager and May 4, 1821, the replaced official embarked with his family for Okhotsk. They reached St. Petersburg early in 1822. His governorship of the Russian American Company had been almost without incident and with no outstanding accomplishments, except for an interesting census he had ordered. Irina soon died, leaving him with a son, Alexander, 5, and a daughter, Maria, 2; he had four children by a second marriage. Alexander entered a monastery, Maria died at an early age, and a son, Ivan, by the second marriage was fatally wounded at Sevastopol in the Crimean War. In fulfillment of an ambition sparked by his association with Monk Herman forty years earlier, Yanovskii on October 1, 1864, entered a monastery at Kaluga, Russia, becoming the monk, Sergius. His second wife died at 73 and Sergius at 86.

Richard A. Pierce, *Builders of Alaska: The Russian Governors 1818-1867*, Kingston, Ontario, Limestone Press, 1986; *Russian Penetration of the North Pacific Ocean; The Russian American Colonies;* Bancroft, *Alaska.*

Yarberry, Milt(on), desperado (c. 1848-c. 1881). B. at Walnut Ridge, Randolph County, Arkansas, he turned desperado at some point and around 1871 was in the Fort Smith area where he met Dave Rudabaugh, Mysterious Dave Mather, and perhaps Wyatt Earp. Rudabaugh and Yarberry were in "the robbery and holdup business" at the time. Yarberry shot and killed a drover who refused to be robbed, and fled to Texas. He became known around Dodge City and was at Canon City, Colorado, during the "railroad wars." He operated a variety show, "got into debt to everyone he could take," and finally fled town. In 1879 he was at Las Vegas, New Mexico, where, with an Hispanic or possibly Indian woman nicknamed Steamboat, he ran a dance hall and may have associated with Doc Holliday. This business failed or closed, and Milt followed the tie cutters south toward Albuquerque. A freighter was robbed and killed twenty miles south of Las Vegas and Yarberry was suspected, but was not prosecuted for "lack of evidence." He became a police officer at Albuquerque; his gun got in the way of his police duties, however—he killed two men and was hanged. One of those killed was Harry Brown, an employee of the Adams Express Company, who was shot down March 27, 1881. Brown had been born in Tennessee in 1857 and was said to have been the youngest son of Neil Smith Brown and nephew of John Calvin Brown, both onetime governors of the state. Young Brown went west at 19 in 1876, was the express messenger during the January 27, 1878, train robbery at Kinsley, Kansas, and saw to it that nothing was lost to the robbers. Brown later associated with Dave Rudabaugh and was killed by Yarberry, Rudabaugh's "colleague," in a dispute over a woman.

Ed Bartholomew, *Wyatt Earp: The Untold Story; Wyatt Earp: The Man & The Myth,* Toyahvale, Texas, Frontier Book Co., 1963, 1964.

Yong, Thomas, sea captain, explorer (b. 1579). B. at London of a merchant family, he apparently attained some measure of prosperity and in 1633 at the age of 54 he petitioned Charles I for authority to lead, at his own expense, an expedition to America for the discovery, occupation, and exploitation of "uninhabited" lands. He was supported by an influential group of Catholics, although there is no evidence that he himself was Catholic or sought to promote Catholic settlements in America. Yong was accompanied by his nephew, Robert Evelyn Jr. (b. 1606) and sailed from England with two vessels in May 1634. He reached Virginia in July, built a shallop, and set sail up the coast July 20. He "discovered" the Delaware River (although it had long been known to the Dutch) and named it the Charles River. Up it, he had been informed by natives, a few days from the bay, the river issued from a large lake and "mediterranean sea" which he believed doubtless was a water route to the Orient. However, he was never able to navigate above a falls, and soon abandoned the Delaware for northern New England. Samuel Maverick (c. 1602-c. 1676), in a description of New England written about 1660, said: "One Captaine Young (sic) and 3 men with him in the Yeare 1636 went up the River [Kennebec] upon discovery and only by Carying their Canoes [portaging] some few times, and [in addition] not farr by Land came into Canada [St. Lawrence] River very neare Kebeck [Quebec] Fort w[h]ere by the French Captain Young was taken, and carried for ffrance but his Company returned safe." Nothing further is reported of Thomas Yong.

Narratives of Early Pennsylvania, West New Jersey and Delaware 1630-1707, ed. by Albert Cook

Myers, N.Y., Charles Scribner's Sons, 1912, pp. 33-49; C.A. Weslager, *Dutch Explorers, Traders and Settlers in the Delaware Valley 1609-1664*, Philadelphia, Univ. of Penn. Press, 1965; Weslager, *The English on the Delaware 1610-1682*, New Brunswick, N.J., Rutgers Univ. Press, 1969.

Yost, Nellie Snyder, writer (June 20, 1905-Jan. 16, 1992). B. in a sod house near North Platte, Nebraska, she was a 1923 graduate of a high school at Maxwell (1960 population, 347) but the education there commenced continued all her life. She held many state, regional and western organization positions and received a number of awards for her writings. Yost spent most of her life on ranches in Lincoln County, an historically-rich area of the Great Plains where Buffalo Bill's most famous ranch was located and with the remains of Fort McPherson vying for tourist attention. Her first book was the well-received *Pinnacle Jake* (1951), a biography of her father; her third, *No Time on My Hands* (1963), a biography of her mother. She also wrote, with John Leakey, *The West That Was: From Texas to Montana* (1958); *Call of the Range: Story of the Nebraska Stock Growers Association* (1966); ed., *Boss Cowman: The Recollections of Ed Lemmon, 1857-1946* (1969); *Medicine Lodge: The Story of a Kansas Frontier Town* (1970); ed., Clark Fuller, *Pioneer Paths* (1974); ed., Bartlett Richards, *Defender of the Grasslands* (1977); *Buffalo Bill in North Platte* (1977); *Before Today* (1977); *A Man as Big as the West: The Ralph Hubbard Story* (1979); *Buffalo Bill: His Family, Friends, Fame, Failures, and Fortunes* (1979), ed., Paul E. Young, *Back Trail of an Old Cowboy* (1983) and, privately printed, *Keep On Keeping On* (1964). She was married twice, her first husband pre-deceasing her, and she was the parent of a son. She died at North Platte, Nebraska.
Contemporary Authors; True West, Vol. 39, No. 5 (May 1992), p. 5.

Young, William H. (Apache Bill), captive (Jan. 17, 1844-Oct. 3, 1921). B. at Philadelphia, he was the son of John Horne Young and the former Bridges Burton. He left for the west in 1852, visited an uncle, Silas Young, at Fort Worth, then joined an emigrant party for California. In Arizona the company threaded Nugent Pass (see John Nugent entry), coming down Tres Alamos Wash to the San Pedro River, camping at the Vinaterilla Ranch about nine miles north of present Benson. Apaches raided the camp before

sundown and 8-year-old Bill was run down by a rider: "I saw a horse almost over me...someone grabbed me by the back of the shirt and swung me up and sat me astride right in front of him," he said. "After several days...we came to what appeared to be a permanent camp in the Chiricahua Mountains. There they turned me over to the squaws [for] whom I helped pack wood and water and helped with their tanning of hides...I fell into their customs, and was always a willing worker and the squaws named me 'Nalapi Enchos,'" which Young interpreted as "good friend." The men began to teach him to use the bow, ride a horse and shortly "to take me out on their marauding trips. I would hold their horses while they would plunder the immigrant trains," sometimes killing the whites, stealing or destroying the wagonloads of provisions. "I made a number of trips in southern Arizona, New Mexico and northern Mexico." The Indians at that time had few firearms except what they could seize from defeated emigrants. He said that "these Indians made their headquarters in the Chiricahua Mountains at what is called the Horse Shoe Bend. Raton and Miguel Tuerto [blind in one eye] were the leaders of these outlaws..." In the fall of 1858 Young was a member of a marauding expedition into Mexico; it made camp a dozen miles east of Fronteras, near the Pesqueira Ranch; in a surprise attack by Mexicans the Indians were driven off and Young was captured after nearly being shot for an Indian. "They noticed I was white and had light hair...They spoke to me in Spanish. I could not understand them," but they took him to Fronteras and turned him over to "a Mexican by the name of Elías," who treated him kindly, got him cleaned up and into pants instead of a G-string, and found that although he could not speak Spanish, he also had forgotten English, so had to communicate through an Apache interpreter. "I was now close to 15 years of age and quite husky," said Young. After about three weeks at Fronteras, Manuel Gallegos, a noted frontiersman, and four other Mexicans took the boy to Fort Buchanan in southern Arizona, where he was turned over to its commander, Captain Richard Stoddert Ewell (see entry), 1st Dragoons. Through an interpreter Ewell questioned the boy, who had forgotten his first name but knew the family name was Young. "Ewell instantly knew that I was the missing son of John Young who had served under General Scott in Mexico and who had sent notice to all detachment commanders on duty in Arizona and New Mexico to be on the lookout for me as no trace had been found of my death. He wrote my father who was in Philadelphia...In the meantime the troopers had taken interest in me and were teaching me to speak English, and it all came back to me like a dream." During the following months the boy was permitted to accompany soldiers on scouts. He eventually was taken to San Francisco, put on a sailing ship around Cape Horn for New York City and was reunited with his parents. In 1862 he enlisted in the 95th Pennsylvania Infantry but, not yet of age, was discharged, only to re-enlist February 23, 1863, in K Company, 3rd Pennsylvania Heavy Artillery under the name of W.H. Burton, his mother's maiden name. In March 1864 he transferred to the 188th Pennsylvania Infantry, serving until the end of the Civil War. Knowing the Apache language he was hired as scout and interpreter and attached to Company C, 1st U.S. Cavalry, First Lieutenant Charles Henry Veil, and with that outfit he arrived once more in Arizona. He was assigned to the Tonto Basin where a skirmish with the Indians was had, and then moved to Camp Grant, from where he was in on the relief of the Apache-beleaguered Estevan Ochoa-Pinckney Tully wagon train, a celebrated incident. Young met virtually all of the famed frontiersmen and characters of southern Arizona, and drifted between Tucson, Tubac, Fort Crittenden (which had succeeded Fort Buchanan) and "most of the next two and one-half years we put in scouting...and running down these outlawed Indians that would break from their main tribe." In February 1869 he was ordered to Fort Whipple at Prescott, then to Fort Wingate, New Mexico, and finally to Fort Stanton to interpret for a peace council between Jicarilla Apaches and the military. "I left the service in the spring of 1870," he said, went to Tularosa and spent the following five years on the lower Rio Grande and at Silver City, New Mexico. Young interpreted for a time for Mormon settlers of northern Mexico, then became involved in the Victorio unrest. Although Young asserted he had taken part in the annihilation of Victorio's band at Tres Castillos in October 1880, his account of the action is somewhat confused, though it contains enough details to bear out Young's claim of participation. He also confuses Nana's Raid with the Juh-led Loco emeute from San Carlos, but he may have been in on the 1882 Colonel Lorenzo Garcia fight with a portion of the Apache migration. He became a deputy sheriff under Harvey Whitehill at Silver City, and was active later as a ranger in and out of Mexico running down assorted outlaws. Eventually he retired and moved into the Old Soldiers' Home at Los Angeles, where he died at 77.

"An Early Chapter in the Life of Apache Bill," by David L. Hughes, manuscript in Hayden File, Ariz. Hist. Soc.; it was copied March 31, 1929, by Charles Morgan Wood; Young death cert.

Z

Zagoskin, Lavrentiy Alekseyevich, explorer, ethnographer (May 21, 1808-Jan. 22, 1890). B. at Nikolayevka, near Penza, some 350 miles southeast of Moscow, he entered the Naval Cadet Corps at Kronstadt in 1822 and entered the Navy as a midshipman in 1826. He volunteered for difficult duty on the Caspian Sea, remaining there for eight years, became a lieutenant in 1832 and for three years after 1835 served aboard combat ships on the Baltic Sea. On this often boring duty he read assiduously and wrote essays which sometimes reflected his ethnographic interests. December 8, 1838, Zagoskin received permission to transfer services to the Russian American Company, then controlling the commercial and colonization enterprises in Alaska. He left St. Petersburg on December 30, spent a few days at Penza and went on to the Pacific coast, writing descriptive travel articles as he progressed. July 9, 1839, he assumed command of the brig *Okhotsk,* and with her reached Novo Arkhangelsk (Sitka), headquarters of the company, on October 6. He spent two years on trading cruises, including one to California, being accompanied on the return by a noted scientist, Ilya Gavrilovich Voznesenskiy, from whom he learned much about collecting and describing scientific specimens. In the spring of 1842 Alaskan Governor Etolin (see entry) suggested that he undertake a lengthy trip to the little known Alaskan interior, the invitation following an 1840 letter Zagoskin had written to former Governor Wrangel (see entry), now director-in-chief of the Russian American Company at St. Petersburg, offering a plan for such an expedition. His orders were to discover by what routes furs were exported from Alaska to Siberia (beyond company control and profit), to establish his base at Fort St. Michael on Norton Sound and to trace the Yukon and Kuskokwim rivers to their sources if possible, to chart portages, describe as fully as possible the country drained by those two great waterways, eventually to traverse overland the region from Kotzebue Sound to Cook Inlet, meanwhile making such thorough scientific studies as were feasible, including ethnographic work, all of which he was to fully report in his dispatches and journal. May 4, 1842,

the *Okhotsk* left Sitka bearing Zagoskin and his five Creole companions: Nikolay Shmakov, Tomorey Glazunov, Prokopiy Vertopakhov, Pavel Akylyayuk and Jacob Makhov; others added later were Grigoriy Kurochkin, interpreter; Luka Pakhomov; Grigoriy Nikitkin and a man named Bazhenov. Zagoskin made a two-week reconnaissance from St. Michael to Unalakleet on the east coast of Norton Sound, then spent four months at the fort, preparing for a winter expedition up the Yukon. He used this time also to study the history of the post, the life of Russian settlers, customs of surrounding tribes, and measured the tides, collected botanical and geological specimens, recorded statistics on important fishes of the region and of bird life, recording also meteorological data and the depth of permafrost in the soil. He collected Eskimo ethnological material and attended their ceremonies, his Creoles being fluent in Eskimauan dialects. Very little escaped Zagoskin's enthusiastic and inquiring attention. Descriptions of Eskimo fishing and hunting techniques paralleled natural history observations in his writings, often in great and interesting detail. December 4, 1842, his expedition left Fort Michael, traveled to Unalakleet, penetrated the interior and came out on the frozen Yukon, temperatures recorded as low as 30° Fahrenheit below zero and enough colder at times to freeze the thermometer. The party arrived at Nulato on January 15, making that their headquarters for months. He explored the pass to Kotzebue Sound, but did not reach the coast. Yukon ice broke May 5, and Zagoskin continued by watercraft up the stream. He contacted Athabascan Indians, interviewing them with some difficulty for lack of suitable interpreters, noted all nature's signs of spring, explored little known or completely unknown river systems until June 30, when upstream progress was halted by impassable rapids and he was forced to turn back. He regained Nulato July 7, and August 14, reached Anvik where Andrei Glazunov (see entry) had first arrived in 1835. August 23, Zagoskin reached Ikogmyut (Russian Mission) after his journey, on which the Yukon had now been described and explored for 420 miles upstream. During the coming winter he meticulously charted portages between Ikogmyut and the Kuskokwim River and Fort Kolmakov, near the present Amiak. A winter month was occupied tracing the course of the lower Innoka River. He left Fort Kolmakov May 19, for the upper Kuskokwim, by June 12 reaching Takotna before returning to the post, and thence to Ikogmyut again. He departed June 13, gained the coast June 17, and on the 21st, 1844, reached Fort Michael, having been gone one year, six months and sixteen days on his various missions. He had traveled during that time "on foot and by skin boat (kayak) about 5,000 versts," or 3,300 miles. He had come to love the country and its native peoples, for whom he had developed empathy and invariably treated with warmth and understanding. Loving the mighty rivers and abundant wildlife, he had become the consummate wilderness traveler and explorer, with rarely a harsh word about anything he had encountered, whether freezing temperatures, semi-starvation, boat accidents, gigantic bears or minute mosquitos. Zagoskin reached Sitka September 26, spent the winter putting his journals, diary and notes in order and preparing reports and proposals. May 16, he left for Okhotsk, on the Siberian coast, and thence crossed the enormous land to St. Petersburg, where he arrived late in 1845. Wrangel, the organizer of the Russian Geographical Society, took immense interest in Zagoskin's work and helped see his writings to publication. They were well received; he won high honors and his work remains today a scrupulously accurate contribution on matters he investigated and of usefulness to students and researchers until this time. Zagoskin retired from the Navy January 14, 1848. He served as a militia commander, though without seeing combat service, during the Crimean War and settled afterward at Abakumovo between Ryazan and Pronsk, his wife having inherited some property there. He was ever liberal in a political sense, was drawn to the Decembrists, opposed serfdom, retained his interests in science, took up horticulture and was deeply offended when Russia sold Alaska to the United States in 1867 "at the whim of the tsar." He died at 81.

Lieutenant Zagoskin's Travels in Russian America 1842-1844: The First Ethnographic and Geographic Investigations in the Yukon and Kuskokwim Valleys of Alaska, ed. by Henry N. Michael, pub. for the Arctic Inst. of North America, Univ. of Toronto Press, 1967.

Zaikov, Potap Kuzmich, explorer, cartographer

(fl. 1772-1791). A navy "master," perhaps a captain, in 1772 he commanded the *Sv Vladimir,* owned by the company of Orekhof (Oregkhov), Ivan Lapin and Shilof, and assigned to an exploratory fur-gathering mission in the North Pacific, an operation that covered seven years. Zaikov was a skilled navigator, a determined, thorough man who made the most of every opportunity for knowledge that came his way. The ship cleared Okhotsk, on the Siberian coast, September 22, 1772, reached Kamchatka October 1, after buffeting by autumn seas. Zaikov decided to winter there and did so at the mouth of the Voroskaia River, 110 miles north of Bolsheretsk. The ship left June 12, 1773, rounded the Kamchatka Peninsula by the Kuril Strait, searched futilely for islands to the south and southeast and by July 26, reached Copper (Mednyi) Island, southeast of Bering Island; Zaikov sought to substantiate rumors that the island was rich in copper ore, but although some pieces of that mineral were found along the shore and he sighted a "cliff that looks as if it contains copper ore," his studies were inconclusive. His party collected furs from various species of marine animals. Sea otters were taken during September and October when their fur was prime, the meat dried for use on future voyages. July 30, 1774, the ship with its 69-man complement reached Attu, westernmost Aleutian island and by that time completely Russianized, inhabitants speaking that language and accustomed to trading for Russian products. Zaikov made extended notes on the wildlife, herbiage, people and ethnography, geography and the precise location of the lands he encountered. Leaving ten men there and on Agattu Island to hunt, Zaikov on July 4, 1775, sailed eastward along the northern shores of the Aleutian chain, on July 19, reaching Unimak Island at the tip of the Alaskan Peninsula, encountering there a ship belonging to the Vologda merchant Fedor Burenin and his company, with whom Zaikov joined forces. He discovered Isanok Strait between Unimak and the peninsula, hunting as far south as the Sanak Islands and perhaps the Shumagin Islands as well. Zaikov learned much of the geography and ethnology of the Alaskan mainland along the peninsula and also of Kodiak Island during the three years his men hunted and traded for furs, most of his fascinating information coming from careful interrogation of Aleut and other informants. The *Sv Vladmir* left Unimak for the return voyage May 27, 1778, wintered on Umnak

Island where the ship was repaired and refitted and May 19, 1779, left for Attu to pick up the promyshlenniki left there to hunt, en route charting or correcting the maps for such islands as Adak, Tanaga, Kamaga, Amchitka, Buldir and others. He reached Okhotsk September 6, 1779, in seven years having lost only 12 men while his cargo of furs was very rich: 4,372 sea otters, 3,949 foxes, 92 land otters, 1 wolverine, 3 wolves (the first brought from America), 18 mink, 1,725 fur seals and 350 pounds of walrus ivory, the whole valued at 300,416 rubles ($150,208), although at the prices the Russian American Company soon set for furs, it would have amounted to 1,603,588 rubles ($801,794). Probably in 1779 Zaiko obtained at a Kamchatka port tracings of charts made by Cook of his navigations in American waters, these in return for favors Zaikov had extended to the English discoverer; they were of much use to the Russian in his own future investigations of the new land. In August 1781 Zaikov put to sea in a galiot owned by Orekhof, the Tula merchant, with a complement of seventy men; they wintered on Bering Island, then reached Unalaska Island of the Aleutians, where he joined forces with the veteran fur trader Feodor Kholodilov for a moderately profitable season. In the spring Zaikov was elected commander of an expedition of three ships, he in the *Alexandr Nevski,* the *Sv Alexei* commanded by Evstrat Delarov, and the *Sv Mikhail,* commanded by Dmitri Polutov. The flotilla sailed eastward to continue earlier explorations and reached Chugach Bay (Prince William Sound) and Sukli (Montague) Island where the Chugach (an Eskimo people) were frequently hostile, having already had experience of the Russians, although Zaikov's was the first visit to the sound of any Russian sea-going vessels. Eight whites were killed, another eight died of illness of his own party, but trade was profitable for his ship, although the other two were not so fortunate. A native woman told Martin Sauer, secretary to Joseph Billings in 1790, that she had been kidnapped by Polutov and subsequently became acquainted with Zaikov. She praised the latter as "a just man," but her people in 1784 massacred Polutov and his party for ill-treatment, while refraining from molesting Zaikov or any of his people. Other incidents occurred against Russian elements who abused the natives, although Zaikov's men were usually spared. Leontiy Nagaiev, an expedition subordinate commander, discovered the Copper River, the mouth of which

is east of Cordova, and was the only man who "actually explored and intelligently described" unknown regions among the 300-man expedition, though Zaikov's journal-description of the country, its resources and its people was "both minute and correct," according to Bancroft, who examined it. Zaikov's later movements are unclear from existing historical records, but he may have remained at Unalaska as his headquarters for several years. There is a vague suggestion that he may have been contacted there by the Spanish expedition of Estéban José Martinez and Gonzalez Lopez de Haro in the summer of 1788, a meeting which concluded amicably. He apparently returned to Siberia for good in 1791. Potap Zaikov was a brother of Stepan Kosmovich Zaikov, who was affiliated with the Lebedev-Lastochin Company.

Russian Penetration of the North Pacific Ocean; Bancroft, *Alaska;* Zagoskin.

Zaikov, Stepan Kosmovich, fur trader (fl. 1793-94). A brother of Potap Zaikov and a fur trader of experience and ability, he was placed in command of the Lebedev-Lastochin post at St. Nicholas (Kenai) in 1793, succeeding Grigorii Konovalov, who had been taken to Okhotsk to face charges of causing dissension among traders and trading posts. Stepan at the time was also accused of wrongdoing, the outcome unreported. He was considered "a man of ability and knowledge," some of which he might have gained if he had accompanied his brother on any of Potap Zaikov's important explorations. In 1794 Stepan was host to the English explorer George Vancouver at St. Nicholas. Nothing further is reported of him.

Bancroft, *Alaska.*

Zane, Andrew, frontiersman (c. 1750-c. 1785?). Andrew was one of five noted frontiersman sons of William Zane, all of whom participated in the founding of Wheeling, present West Virginia. His approximate date of b. is conjecture, he being born between 1747 and 1754. Andrew Zane took part in the defense of Fort Henry at Wheeling during an Indian attack from August 31, to September 1, 1777. With a small party he left the fort to get some horses a mile distant; they were attacked by several Indians who did not fire upon them, not wishing to signal their presence, but tried to kill or capture them as quietly as possible. Zane made his escape by leaping off of a cliff one report said was some seventy feet in height.

"Zane was much bruised in the fall, and his gun was broken to pieces, but in the course of the day he reached Col[onel] Shepherds fort," at the forks of Wheeling Creek where Little Wheeling comes in about six miles above Fort Henry, which is at Wheeling; the attackers were beaten off. Andrew was reported killed by Indians, not during this or a subsequent siege, but while scouting at a later date. De Hass wrote he was "killed by Indians, while crossing the Scioto" River in Ohio; this appears to be a confusion with the reported death of Andrew's brother, Silas (see entry) on the Scioto but, in any event, authorities agree that Andrew at some date was killed by Indians.

Thwaites/Kellogg, *Frontier Defense on the Upper Ohio, 1777-1778;* Wills De Hass, *History of the...Indian Wars of Western Virginia,* Wheeling, H. Hoblitzell, 1851, 1960, p. 337.

Zane, Elizabeth (Betty), pioneer woman (1766-1826). Betty Zane was the sister of Ebenezer and the other Zane young men (see entries) and was the youngest child of William Zane. In 1782 at 16 she was said to be at the Ebenezer Zane home near Fort Henry (Wheeling), present West Virginia, when a large body of Indians with a British officer and forty soldier-rangers in support, attacked the place. According to the Zane descendants' belief (which is disputed by some other authorities), at a crucial moment in the siege Betty Zane heroically ran from the fort to the Zane house where gunpowder was stored, gathered up a quantity in a tablecloth and with it raced back to the fort, where it was sorely needed for the defense. The run was made through a hail of bullets from the besiegers, but she was unharmed and her heroism was instrumental in saving the garrison, the fort, and the community. Others believe the heroine was Molly Scott (see entry) and not Betty Zane, who was said by a responsible authority to be away at the time, at the residence of her father near Washington, Pennsylvania. The Zane version of the incident, highly fictionalized, was vividly presented in Zane Grey's first novel, *Betty Zane* (1903). Grey was a great grandson of Ebenezer Zane. Betty Zane married Ephraim McLaughlin; when he died she married Jacob Clark and lived in Ohio, presumably for the rest of her life.

Wills De Hass, *History of the Early Settlement and Indian Wars of Western Virginia,* Philadelphia, H. Hoblitzell, 1851, 1960, pp. 269-71, 280-81; Lucullus V. McWhorter, *The Border Settlers of Northwestern*

Virginia from 1768 to 1795..., Hamilton, Ohio, Republican Pub. Co., 1915, 353-56; Zane Grey, *Betty Zane,* N.Y., Triangle Books, 1903, 1941; info. from the West Virginia Dept. of Educ. and the Arts, Div. of Culture and Hist., and from the *DAR Patriot Index,* Washington, D.C., 1966.

Zane, Isaac, captive (c. 1753-1816). B. on the south branch of the Potomac River, he was youngest of several brothers who afterward became the first settlers of Wheeling, West Virginia (see Ebenezer Zane entry). When 9 Isaac was captured by Wyandot (Huron) Indians and taken to their village on the Mad River of Ohio. There the boy grew up, married a Wyandot woman by whom he fathered eight children, and became influential among the tribe, by one report a chief, although this is not confirmed. He never was known to have waged war on whites, often warned border settlers of planned raids, and frequently acted as a guide or interpreter. In 1793 Ensign Levi Morgan, commanding a company of Rangers, came upon a hunting camp of Isaac Zane and through incompetence slightly wounded Zane's daughter. Zane, rather than seizing an opportunity for revenge, courteously assisted the assailant in reaching the settlements. About 1795 Zane bought an 1,800-acre tract in the present Logan County, Ohio, and settled near Zanesville, where he died.

Thwaites/Kellogg, *The Revolution on the Upper Ohio, 1775-1777,* Madison, Wis. Hist. Soc., 1908; Alexander Scott Withers, *Chronicles of Border Warfare,* Cincinnati, Robert Clarke Co., 1795, 1970.

Zane, Jonathan, frontiersman (1749-1824). B. in Berkeley County, present West Virginia, Jonathan became a highly skilled woodsman. De Hass wrote that he was "perhaps the most experienced hunter of his day in the west. He was a man of great energy of character, resolution, and restless activity. He rendered efficient service to the settlements about Wheeling [West Virginia], in the capacity of spy [scout]. He was remarkable for an earnestness of purpose, an energy and inflexibility of will which often manifested itself in a way truly astonishing." The Zane brothers were "ready at all times, to resist and punish the aggression of Indians [but] were scrupulously careful not to provoke them by acts of wanton outrage, such as were then, too frequently committed along the frontier." Jonathan was with Ebenezer Zane when he founded Wheeling in 1769, and made it his home when he was not beyond the frontier. With his brother, Silas, Jonathan in 1771 explored through summer and fall the Ohio River country, being among the first to do so. In June 1774 Jonathan, with Thomas Nicholson and Thady Kelley (Tady Kelly) were guides for Angus McDonald's (see entry) campaign to the Wapatomica villages of Ohio, Thwaites reporting of Jonathan that "a better woodsman...perhaps never lived." Zane prided himself on his marksmanship. Once, near Wheeling he saw five Indians jump into a river and make for an island in midstream. He killed four before they crossed the river. The fifth concealed himself behind a log. After several attempts to dislodge him, Zane was about to abandon the effort when he observed a small portion of the Indian's body below the log. He drew a fine sight, fired, and the fifth Indian tumbled into the stream. Zane guided many expeditions against Indians. In the one under Daniel Brodhead up the Allegheny River in 1779 against the Indian town of Buchaloons he was severely wounded. Jonathan Zane and John Slover were guides for Crawford's ill-fated expedition against Sandusky in Ohio in 1782. On June 4, when close to the Indian towns Zane strongly recommended that the operation be aborted lest it meet an overwhelming force of Indians led by British partisans. Crawford placed "great weight" upon the recommendation since he "knew Zane to be exceedingly well versed in Indian strategy." Zane argued that the Indians must be concentrating at some nearby place "for a determined resistance. The views of Crawford coincided with those of Zane." But a council of officers determined that the advance should continue that afternoon, "but no longer." The Indians shortly attacked and disaster resulted, Crawford himself being captured and burned at the stake in a celebrated frontier incident (see Crawford entry). Zane escaped the bloody affair with many others, he returning to Wheeling. In 1796 Congress gave permission to Jonathan and Ebenezer Zane and John McIntire (McIntyre) to lay out a road from Wheeling to Limestone (Maysville), Kentucky, following an ancient Indian path. This became the noted Zane's Trace which was widely used, cutting off the great elbow of the Ohio River between those communities and making travel between them easier, shorter and faster. In 1799 Jonathan Zane laid out Zanesville, Ohio, with McIntire, who was his brother-in-law and Ebenezer's son-in-law. In 1800 Jonathan laid out Lancaster, Ohio, as New Lancaster, the "New"

later dropped. As payment for laying out the road, Jonathan had received three parcels of Ohio land of 640 acres each: on one he founded Zanesville, on the second, Lancaster, and the third was rich bottomland on the Scioto opposite Chilicothe. From these lands he profited greatly. He or Ebenezer founded across the Ohio from Wheeling a short-lived town named Canton (though not the thriving city of Canton existing today). As Thwaites remarked, Zane's Canton "quickly perished." It was laid out about 1808. Jonathan Zane married Ann Mills and fathered at least nine children who survived, one of whom, Asa Zane, in 1846 lived in Indiana. Where Jonathan Zane died is not reported, although he left "large landed possessions."

Wills De Hass, *History...and Indian Wars of Western Virginia,* Wheeling, H. Hoblitzell, 1851, 1960; C.W. Butterfield, *An Historical Account of the Expedition Against Sandusky under Col. William Crawford in 1782,* Cincinnati, Robert Clarke & Co., 1873; Alexander Scott Withers, *Chronicles of Border Warfare,* Cincinnati, Clarke, 1895, 1970; Thwaites/Kellogg, *Frontier Defense on the Upper Ohio, 1777-1778;* Thwaites, EWT, IV, 125, 222, 226, 233, XI, 176; info. from the West Virginia Dept. of Educ. and the Arts, Div. of Culture and Hist., and from the *DAR Patriot Index,* Washington, D.C., 1966.

Zane, Silas, frontiersman (1751-1785). One of five noted sons of William Zane, Silas accompanied his older brother, Ebenezer (see entry) to the region of the present Wheeling, West Virginia, which was founded and first settled by the Zanes in 1769. In the spring of 1771, with his brother Jonathan, Silas explored down the Ohio River, remaining out until fall. He was an active partisan in border wars against the Indians, and also active in the Revolution. He was commissioned a first lieutenant of the 13th Virginia Regiment December 28, 1776, and was promoted to captain February 9, 1777, serving in that rank for a year. McWhorter wrote that Zane took part in the defense of Fort Henry at Wheeling when it was invested by Indians August 31-September 1, 1777, but Thwaites denied this was so, reporting he was in service in the eastern states at the time. Silas, however, was active in defense of Fort Henry when it was besieged by Indians and British in September 1782, being joined by Jonathan and Andrew Zane. There is a faint suggestion that he commanded briefly at Fort Pitt, but proof is lacking. Thwaites/Kellogg report that at the close of the Revolution, Silas Zane went with George Green to the Indian country, with goods for a Maryland trader. On their return, about 1785, "the two traders were waylaid and murdered on the Scioto [River, of Ohio]. Silas Zane left an infant son of the same name." The foregoing *might* be a confusion with Andrew Zane, who was reported in one version to have been slain by Indians on the Scioto at an unspecified date. Silas was married to Mrs. Katherine Ryan.

Lucullus V. McWhorter, *The Border Settlers of Northwestern Virginia,* Hamilton, Ohio, Republican Pub. Co., 1915, pp. 450, 487; Wills De Hass, *History of the...Indian Wars of Western Virginia,* Wheeling, H. Hoblitzell, 1851, 1960, pp. 281, 337; Alexander Scott Withers, *Chronicles of Border Warfare,* Cincinnati, Robert Clarke Co., 1895, 1970; Thwaites/Kellogg, *Frontier Defense on the Upper Ohio, 1777-1778.*

Zane, William, patriarch (1712-post 1777). A grandson of Robert Zane, who emigrated from Denmark to America in 1673 and settled at Newton, New Jersey, William was part Indian since Robert's first wife was of that race, although the tribe is not specified. William broke with the Quaker sect of his family and removed to the south branch of the Potomac River in present Berkeley County, West Virginia, where his son, Isaac (see entry) was captured by Wyandot (Huron) Indians and raised by them in Ohio. The other sons, Ebenezer, Silas, Jonathan and Andrew (see entries) were largely explorers, hunters and wilderness travelers, were early on the Ohio River, and all settled near Wheeling, which Ebenezer founded. William Zane wrote General Hand at Fort Pitt on June 22, 1777, that "being more than sixty years old, with a constitution much shattered by five years' captivity in Braddock's war, the loss of his negro carried off by the Indians deprives him of means of support. He requests...return of this man [the black] if the Indians make peace." William was then 65 years old. No report of the date of his death, or the age at which he died, has been located.

Thwaites/Kellogg, *Frontier Defense on the Upper Ohio 1777-1778.*

Zarembo, Dionysius Fedorovich, Russian naval officer (fl. 1834-39). A lieutenant captain in the Imperial Navy, he commanded the brig *Chichagof* in 1834 to survey Wrangell Harbor in the Alaskan Panhandle. That year he also founded the community of Wrangell, surrounding it with a stockade. In 1838 he surveyed and named

Woewodski Harbor on Admiralty Island in the Alexander Archipelago.

Orth, 44.

Ziegler, William, businessman, polar enthusiast (Sept. 1, 1843-May 24, 1905). B. in Beaver County, Pennsylvania, he was raised in Iowa, worked variously as a printer and pharmacist, entered business for himself in 1868 and enjoyed enormous success with the manufacture of Royal Baking Powder, "long the most popular brand in America." Through this and other enterprises he amassed a fortune estimated at his death to have reached $30 million. Around the turn of the century he became deeply interested in polar exploration, and used his wealth to further this interest. In 1901 he financed an Evelyn Briggs Baldwin attempt to reach the North Pole; it failed. Ziegler then financed another expedition, this time under Anthony Fiala, who had been photographer on the first attempt. The second expedition established a base in 1903 on Franz Josef Land, north of Novaya Zemlya, but it got little farther north than its base of operations. One of the party was William John Peters (see entry); others included two men later prominent in polar exploration, Ernest deKoven Leffingwell and Ejnar Mikkelsen (see entries). The expedition was unheard from for two years. Just before his death Ziegler sent out two relief ships which eventually reached the explorers' base and rescued the men in August 1905. Ziegler was married, fathered no children but adopted two.

DAB; Orth, 25-26, 751; info. from the Dartmouth College Lby., Stefansson Collection.

Ziolkowski, Korczak, sculptor (Sept. 6, 1908-Oct. 20, 1982). B. of Polish descent at Boston, he was orphaned at 1, "grew up abused and overworked, and though he never had a lesson, took to sculpting in an almost magical way." Through his award-winning depiction of Polish pianist-statesman Ignace Jan Paderewski, statues of Noah Webster (at West Hartford, Connecticut), Wild Bill Hickok (at Deadwood, South Dakota), and Sitting Bull (at Mobridge, South Dakota) and many others he became widely known. One summer he was assistant to Gutzon Borglum (1867-1941) in the work of carving from Mount Rushmore in the Black Hills the busts of Washington, Lincoln, Jefferson and Theodore Roosevelt. Sioux Chief Henry Standing Bear then wrote Ziolkowski asking him to carve an Indian memorial, saying "My fellow chiefs and I would like the white man to know the red man had great heroes, too." Ziolkowski decided to carve the greatest (in dimensions, at any rate) statue ever created, this one to depict the chief Crazy Horse (see entry) on Thunderhead Mountain, five miles north of Custer in the southern Black Hills. The finished memorial will reveal Crazy Horse, long hair blowing in the wind, an outstretched arm raised over the head of his plunging horse, the whole to be 641 feet long and 563 feet high, taller than the Washington Monument, while the four Mount Rushmore heads would fit easily into that of Crazy Horse. The "carving would be done in the round, a three-dimensional" work visible from all directions. Although he started with only $174 of his own, he twice turned down federal grants of millions of dollars, believing the project should be paid for by private donations, his own funds, and from earnings from visitors to the site (there is a modest fee per car or per person to view the work). He commenced it in 1947, conceding that "Everybody says I'm nuts. Hell, you've got to be nuts to do a thing like this." Ziolkowski was married twice; his first wife divorced him in 1949 after fourteen years of marriage. Later he wed Ruth Ross. She and six of his ten children continue to labor on the enormous monument, which they vow will be completed, even if by a future generation of Ziolkowskis. His last words to his family before his death were, "You must work on the mountain, but you must do it slowly—so you do it right." Ziolkowski, often said that, "if the mountain isn't finished my whole life will have been wasted." By 1991 a rough outline of the horse and rider was visible. Most recently work has been done to detail Crazy Horse's 90-foot-tall head and face. The forehead, 32 feet high, has been finished, and labor continues on the facial features, under the overall guidance and direction of Ruth Ziolkowski. The sculptor's earlier work is well represented in permanent collections at the San Francisco Art Museum, at Symphony Hall, Boston, at Vassar College and at other places. Ziolkowski lived at Crazy Horse, South Dakota, and died at a Sturgis hospital. Funeral services were conducted at the monument site.

Phoenix, *Arizona Republic,* Oct. 22, 1982; Michael Pearce, "Indian in the Mountain," *Wall Street Journal,* July 1, 1988; *New York Times,* May 5, 1991; *Who Was Who.*

Supplemental Index

Since formal entries in this encyclopedia are arranged alphabetically, they are rarely listed in the Supplemental Index. Rather, this calls attention to names and subjects appearing incidentally, to supplement the biographies. The Index also includes names of numerous individuals not given formal attention in the body of the work, while the subject listings may assist the rounding out of information about significant or interesting incidents, themes or activities.